SIDDUR
סדור נר תמיד
NER TAMID

TRANSLITERATED SEPHARDIC SIDDUR

WEEKDAY

עץ אחד
EITZ ECHAD

Editing, format design and layout, artwork were all made in-house by Eitz Echad in the United States of America.

WWW.EITZECHAD.COM

Foreword: The World of Jewish Prayer

The Hebrew Bible is the foundation of the Jewish faith. The closing of the biblical canon in the Second Temple era did not end the vibrant spirituality of the Jewish people. The rabbis responded to the changing conditions of their time by invigorating Jewish life with the ability to survive the catastrophic destruction of the Second Temple in Jerusalem. Consequently, Jewish prayer utilizes the idioms and expressions of the Tanakh, i.e., the Hebrew Bible and the Sages of Israel.

While honoring personal prayer, Judaism is a liturgical religion. Many essential prayers, e.g., the Baruch She'amar, Amidah, Alenu, Kiddush, Havdalah, etc., are ascribed to the Anshei Knesset HaGedolah, the Men of the Great Assembly. According to rabbinic lore, the this Assembly included many biblical prophets of Israel, i.e., Haggai, Zechariah, Ezra, etc. The Assembly stretched over many years into the Maccabean period. The Men of the Great Assembly established many of the Jewish practices that are known to us today. While the rabbis did not invent prayer, they did engineer Jewish rituals with a consciousness of God's presence in a world devoid of the Holy Temple.

Traditional Jewish prayer expresses the fundamental values and beliefs of Judaism. Jewish prayer recollects the historical experiences of the Jewish people affirms the present, and it looks forward to final redemption. While personal prayer is undoubtedly encouraged, Jewish prayer is generally collective. The individual prays "for us" and on behalf of all of the People of Israel. We pray for peace "upon us and all Israel" because each Jew is responsible for one another.

This is not simply an exercise in reminding the individual to notice the needs and sufferings of others. It is intended to make the individual aware that they are part of an extended family. This aspect is a crucial difference between Judaism and other religious traditions. The Jewish people are an ethnoreligious group. Judaism encompasses not only a religious faith in God but includes a unique history, a historic homeland, a language, and a family kinship. When Jews speak of the Patriarchs, Abraham, Isaac, and Jacob, or the Matriarchs, Sarah, Rebekah, Rachel, and Leah, they are not simply invoking their spiritual memory. They also remember their forebears.

Judaism is a well-regulated religious tradition. There are specific laws for observing the commandments of the Torah. This leads to a fundamental question. Is prayer a commandment? If so, how can such a spiritual and personal endeavor be regulated? Why should prayer be structured? Is this not counterintuitive to the spiritual nature of prayer?

To this, the rabbis answer that all fulfillment is derived from a structure. Art is a discipline. Music is a discipline. Notes and instructions are followed to create something beautiful. Yet rules can kill spontaneity. One of the greatest Jewish sages of the medieval period, the Spanish Rabbi Moses ben Maimon (known as the

Rambam or Maimonides), asserted that prayer was a daily obligation prescribed by the written Torah. Deuteronomy 11:13 states:

"And it shall come to pass, if ye shall hearken diligently unto My commandments which I command you this day, to love the L-RD your G-d, and to serve Him with all your heart and with all your soul...."

He interpreted the service of the heart mentioned in the previous passage as referring to prayer.[1] In contrast, another great rabbi of the medieval period from Spain, Rabbi Moses ben Nachman (known as the Ramban or Nachmanides), believed that daily prayer was a rabbinic decree. The Torah only prescribed the obligation to pray in times of emergency.[2]

Rabbi Joseph Dov Soloveitchik reconciled these two positions by noting the sensitivity of the human condition. As humans, we are always in crisis, and hence, we are in desperate need of prayer every day. Both the Rambam and the Ramban experienced severe religious persecution during their lifetimes, and I believe they both would have agreed with Rabbi Soloveitchik's assertion.

This prayerbook provides a unique contribution to the world of Jewish prayer. It provides an accessible tool for individuals from varied Sephardic backgrounds with insights from the Shulchan Arukh and other halakhic sources. It gives the eager student a resource that will allow them to "grow" with the siddur as their Hebrew skills mature. This siddur is particularly noteworthy because it also incorporates elements from historic Spanish-Portuguese communities, historically formed from former Conversos or B'nei Anusim, who returned to Judaism centuries ago and whose spirit and courage continue to draw many Anusim to return to the faith of their fathers.

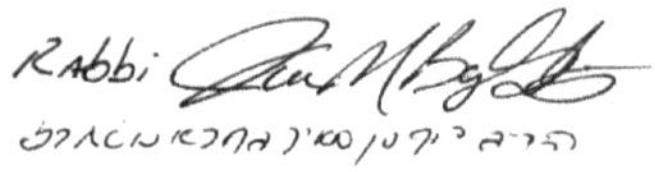

Rabbi Dr. Juan Marcos Bejarano Gutierrez
Yeshivat Meor Enaim
B'nei Anusim Center for Education

1. *[The Talmud in Taanit 2a also relates that the service of the heart is accomplished by prayer. See Maimonides' Mishneh Torah, Hilchot Tefilah 1:1.] However, Rabbi Moses ben Maimon asserted that the actual content of prayer and the number of daily prayers was rabbinic. [Hilchot Tefilah 1:1. Hayim Halevy Donin, To Pray as a Jew (New York: Basic Books, 1980), 10. Also see Charles Wengrov, trans., The Chafetz Chayim, The Concise Book of Mitzvoth (New York: Feldheim, 1990), 19-20.]*

2. *[Commenting on Sefer Ha-mitzvot (mitzvat asei 5), the Ramban states refers to prayer as being mandated only in times of crisis when the Torah (Numbers 10:9) writes, "And when ye go to war in your land against the adversary that oppresseth you, then ye shall sound an alarm with the trumpets; and ye shall be remembered before the LORD your God, and ye shall be saved from your enemies." For the Ramban it is a mitzvah to respond to every crisis by calling out to God in prayer.]*

Introduction: About the Siddur

This siddur is the fruit of about two years of much labor, but truly a labor of love. The intention of creating this came about as a congregational need for helping those with Converso or B'nei Anusim backgrounds (Spanish and Portuguese Jews who accepted Christianity in order to avoid death) to be able to join in with Jewish practice as well as be able to have a great resource to learn and grow with minimal hinderance. While in exile, the Sephardic B'nei Anusim have faced a difficult task of re-entering the world of Judaism and becoming members of often reluctant and even suspicious Jewish communities. Citing Yosef Karo, author of the Shulchan Arukh, in a letter to a community in Kandiyah, Greece:

"...We have heard that Jews who had lived in Spain and were forced to convert have now come to your kehillah in order to live freely as Jews and keep all the mizvot openly. Instead, you remind them of the sins they committed in Spain and, when a disagreement arises between them and the people of your kehillah, you claim these blessed baalei teshuvah are meshumadim (converts to Christianity). This is a terrible sin, because you are slamming the door in the faces of baalei teshuvah. The Mordechai (a Rishon from Ashkenaz) recorded in his sefer that Rabbenu Gershom decreed that any Jew who does not openly accept ba'alei teshuvah should himself be considered menuddeh (not part of the Jewish people). Therefore, from today and henceforth, may every person be exceptionally careful in his dealings with these ba'alei teshuvah, and never again refer to them as meshumadim. And if, has veshalom (may Hashem forbid), the word escapes someone's lips, be he young or old, let him sit completely alone for an entire day and with his own mouth confess his ugly sin. And further, he must undertake never to do so again...Written this 15th of Tammuz, here in Sefat, in the year 5328, (1568), David ben Zimra, Yosef Caro, Moshe miTrani and Yisrael de Kuriel."

- quoted from The Story of Maran Bet Yosef: R Yosef Caro, Author of the Shulhan Aruch (The Sephardic Heritage Series), Artscroll, 1986.

We therefore feel it is our duty and a great mitzvah to bring these souls, as well as anyone closer to the light of Torah and Judaism. This siddur combines a traditional HaMizrach text which generally follows *Tefillat Yesharim*. We've seen with various common scenarios today, that those with B'nei Anusim backgrounds tend to be very zealous and studious when coming to Judaism. Many are not satisfied with the other various nusachim or rites. If attending a Sephardic congregation, more than likely a HaMizrach nusach is utilized. We kept to a format that incorporates customs of different communities, it will generally say "some say:" before a prayer or section that includes the custom of a different community . We kept the kabbalistic prayers, but generally do not translate or transliterate them, except for the "L'shem Yichud" prayer before Sefirat Omer, in the view of Chacham Ovadia Yosef, zt'll. We then provided the transliteration. We utilized a more modern, universal phonetic system, as it seems easier to understand for everyone who is new to hebrew. The translation was compiled predominantly from a combination of *Book of Prayers* by Moses Gaster (Spanish-Portugese), altered, as well as original translation. We put the time into making the translation unique, modern and not just simply using Old-English so that the import can be clear for anyone. We maintained transliterated Hebrew names and words to help in understanding as well as communicating in community. We then provided translation of certain laws from the Shulchan Arukh, as well as a few other sources, for a basic understanding of Sephardic Judaism.

May we continue to feel the importance of כל ישראל ערבים זה לזה / "All Yisrael are responsible for one another", caring for one another within the community, outside of the community, within Eretz Yisrael, and all over the world, a responsibility to all of עם ישראל / the people of Yisrael.

Kelil
President of Eitz Echad

SHACHARIT / MORNING PRAYER

Hashkamat HaBoker / Rising in the Morning

One should be as strong as a lion to rise in the morning for the service of the Creator. At any rate, one should not delay his prayers until after the congregation has prayed. Better are few supplications with kavanah (intention) than many without kavanah. (SA, OC 1:1,4)

Modeh Ani

When awaking from sleep, one should say:

women: (Modah)	**האשה:** (מוֹדָה)
Modeh Ani Lefaneicha Melech	מוֹדֶה אֲנִי לְפָנֶיךָ מֶלֶךְ
Chai Vekayam Shehechezarta Bi	חַי וְקַיָּם שֶׁהֶחֱזַרְתָּ בִּי
Nishmati Vechemlah. Rabah	נִשְׁמָתִי בְּחֶמְלָה. רַבָּה
Emunatecha.	אֱמוּנָתֶךָ:

I offer thanks to You, everlasting King, Who has mercifully restored my soul within me; Your faithfulness is great.

LAWS OF NETILAT YADAYIM / WASHING OF HANDS

One should first pour water on his right hand and then his left. The water must be poured three times on each hand up to the wrist. Dipping the hands into a vessel filled with water constitutes valid washing for prayers. He who is awake all night should wash his hands without saying the blessing; and the same law applies to a case where one washed his hands before dawn had arisen. If one has no water, he may clean his hands with gravel or earth, and say the blessing: "Al Netilat Yadayim". He who sleeps during the daytime should wash his hands without saying the blessing. The minimum amount of water is a revi'it (approx. 3oz), you should add more water though, as Rav Chisda said "I washed a full hand of water and I was given a full hand of good. It is customary to wash out one's mouth as well. (SA, OC 4,158:10) Some have the practice to wait to make the blessing "Al Netilat Yadayim" until coming to the assembly, and arrange them with the rest of the blessings. The children of Sephardim do not do so. (SA, OC 6:2) Bless before washing, because every mitzvah you should bless before you do the mitzvah. But the custom is to bless after washing, because sometimes your hands aren't clean, so you bless after you clean your hands and before you do the second washing. (SA, OC 158:11) Only wash your hands with a vessel. All vessels are kosher for this, even galalim vessels (stone vessels, earthenware vessels, etc.) The vessel must be able to hold a revi'it of liquid. (SA, OC 158:11, 159:1)

Netilat Yadayim / Washing of Hands

Baruch Attah Adonai Eloheinu	בָּרוּךְ אַתָּה יְהֹוָה אֱלֹהֵינוּ
Melech Ha'olam Asher	מֶלֶךְ הָעוֹלָם. אֲשֶׁר
Kideshanu Bemitzvotav	קִדְּשָׁנוּ בְּמִצְוֹתָיו
Vetzivanu Al Netilat Yadayim.	וְצִוָּנוּ עַל נְטִילַת יָדָיִם:

Blessed are You, Hashem our God, King of the universe, Who has sanctified us with His commandments, and commanded us concerning the washing of hands.

Asher Yatzar

Every day when using the restroom, bless "Asher Yatzar" and not "Al Netilat Yadayim" [every time] even if one wants to learn or pray right away. (SA, OC 7:1)

Baruch Attah Adonai Eloheinu	בָּרוּךְ אַתָּה יְהֹוָה אֱלֹהֵינוּ.
Melech Ha'olam Asher Yatzar Et	מֶלֶךְ הָעוֹלָם. אֲשֶׁר יָצַר אֶת
Ha'Adam Bechochmah. Uvara	הָאָדָם בְּחָכְמָה. וּבָרָא
Vo Nekavim Nekavim. Chalulim	בוֹ נְקָבִים נְקָבִים. חֲלוּלִים
Chalulim. Galui Veyadua Lifnei	חֲלוּלִים. גָּלוּי וְיָדוּעַ לִפְנֵי
Chisei Chevodecha. She'im	כִסֵּא כְבוֹדֶךָ. שֶׁאִם
Yisatem Echad Mehem. O Im	יִסָּתֵם אֶחָד מֵהֶם. אוֹ אִם
Yipate'ach Echad Mehem. Ei	יִפָּתֵחַ אֶחָד מֵהֶם. אִי
Efshar Lehitkayem Afilu Sha'ah	אֶפְשַׁר לְהִתְקַיֵּם אֲפִלּוּ שָׁעָה
Echat. Baruch Attah Adonai	אֶחָת. בָּרוּךְ אַתָּה יְהֹוָה
Rofei Chol-Basar Umafli	רוֹפֵא כָל־בָּשָׂר וּמַפְלִיא
La'asot.	לַעֲשׂוֹת:

Blessed are You, Hashem, our God, King of the universe, Who has formed man in wisdom, and created in him many openings and cavities. It is revealed and known before Your glorious Throne, that if one of them were closed or one of them opened, it would be impossible to survive, even for a short while. Blessed are You, Hashem, Who heals all flesh and works wonders.

Elohai Neshamah

Elohai Neshamah Shenatata Bi	אֱלֹהַי נְשָׁמָה שֶׁנָּתַתָּ בִּי
Tehorah. Attah Veratah. Attah	טְהוֹרָה. אַתָּה בְרָאתָהּ. אַתָּה
Yetzartah. Attah Nefachtah Bi.	יְצַרְתָּהּ. אַתָּה נְפַחְתָּהּ בִּי.
Ve'attah Meshamerah Bekirbi.	וְאַתָּה מְשַׁמְּרָהּ בְּקִרְבִּי.
Ve'attah Atid Litelah Mimeni.	וְאַתָּה עָתִיד לִטְּלָהּ מִמֶּנִּי.
Ulehachazirah Bi Le'atid Lavo.	וּלְהַחֲזִירָהּ בִּי לֶעָתִיד לָבוֹא.
Kol-Zeman Shehaneshamah	כָּל־זְמַן שֶׁהַנְּשָׁמָה
Vekirbi. Modeh	בְקִרְבִּי. מוֹדֶה
Women: (Modah) Ani Lefaneicha	**האשה:** (מוֹדָה) אֲנִי לְפָנֶיךָ
Adonai Elohai Velohei Avotai.	יְהֹוָה אֱלֹהַי וֵאלֹהֵי אֲבוֹתַי.
Ribon Kol-Hama'asim Adon	רִבּוֹן כָּל־הַמַּעֲשִׂים אֲדוֹן
Kol-Haneshamot. Baruch Attah	כָּל־הַנְּשָׁמוֹת. בָּרוּךְ אַתָּה
Adonai Hamachazir Neshamot	יְהֹוָה הַמַּחֲזִיר נְשָׁמוֹת
Lifgarim Meitim.	לִפְגָרִים מֵתִים:

My God, the soul which You have endowed me with is pure. You have created it. You have formed it. You have breathed it into me. You preserve it within me, and You will after reclaim it and restore it to me in the life to come. So long as there is soul within me, I confess before You, Hashem my God and God of my fathers, that You are the Sovereign of all creation, the Ruler of all living, the Lord of all souls. Blessed are You, Hashem, Restorer of the souls to the dead.

Birkhot HaShachar / Blessings of the Morning

When making blessings, one should concentrate on the meaning of the words. When mentioning the name "Hashem", concentrate on the meaning of the proclamation is lordship, that He is the Master of all, and concentrate on the writing of Y-d H-ei that was, is, and will be. And when one mentions "Elohim", concentrate on that He is Powerful, Master over everything and Master of the powers of everything. (SA, OC 5)

Baruch Attah Adonai Eloheinu	בָּרוּךְ אַתָּה יְהֹוָה אֱלֹהֵינוּ
Melech Ha'olam Hanotein	מֶלֶךְ הָעוֹלָם. הַנּוֹתֵן
Lasechvi Vinah. Lehavchin Bein	לַשֶּׂכְוִי בִינָה. לְהַבְחִין בֵּין
Yom Uvein Lailah.	יוֹם וּבֵין לָיְלָה:

Blessed are You, Hashem our God, King of the universe, Who gives even to the rooster understanding to make us recognize day from night.

Baruch Attah Adonai Eloheinu	בָּרוּךְ אַתָּה יְהֹוָה אֱלֹהֵינוּ
Melech Ha'olam Pokei'ach	מֶלֶךְ הָעוֹלָם. פּוֹקֵחַ
Ivrim.	עִוְרִים:

Blessed are You, Hashem our God, King of the universe, Who opens the eyes of the blind.

Baruch Attah Adonai Eloheinu	בָּרוּךְ אַתָּה יְהֹוָה אֱלֹהֵינוּ
Melech Ha'olam Matir Asurim.	מֶלֶךְ הָעוֹלָם. מַתִּיר אֲסוּרִים:

Blessed are You, Hashem our God, King of the universe, Who releases the bound.

Baruch Attah Adonai Eloheinu	בָּרוּךְ אַתָּה יְהֹוָה אֱלֹהֵינוּ
Melech Ha'olam Zokeif	מֶלֶךְ הָעוֹלָם. זוֹקֵף
Kefufim.	כְּפוּפִים:

Blessed are You, Hashem our God, King of the universe, Who raises up those who are bowed.

Baruch Attah Adonai Eloheinu	בָּרוּךְ אַתָּה יְהֹוָה אֱלֹהֵינוּ
Melech Ha'olam Malbish	מֶלֶךְ הָעוֹלָם. מַלְבִּישׁ
Arumim.	עֲרֻמִּים:

Blessed are You, Hashem our God, King of the universe, Who clothes the naked.

Baruch Attah Adonai Eloheinu	בָּרוּךְ אַתָּה יְהֹוָה אֱלֹהֵינוּ
Melech Ha'olam Hanotein	מֶלֶךְ הָעוֹלָם. הַנּוֹתֵן
Laya'ef Koach.	לַיָּעֵף כֹּחַ:

Blessed are You, Hashem our God, King of the universe, Who gives strength to the weary.

Baruch Attah Adonai Eloheinu	בָּרוּךְ אַתָּה יְהֹוָה אֱלֹהֵינוּ
Melech Ha'olam Roka Ha'aretz	מֶלֶךְ הָעוֹלָם. רוֹקַע הָאָרֶץ.
Al Hamayim.	עַל הַמָּיִם:

Blessed are You, Hashem our God, King of the universe, Who stretches out the earth over the waters.

Baruch Attah Adonai Eloheinu	בָּרוּךְ אַתָּה יְהֹוָה אֱלֹהֵינוּ
Melech Ha'olam Ha'meichin	מֶלֶךְ הָעוֹלָם. הַמֵּכִין
Mitz'adei Gaver.	מִצְעֲדֵי גָבֶר:

Blessed are You, Hashem our God, King of the universe, Who guides the steps of man.

Baruch Attah Adonai Eloheinu	בָּרוּךְ אַתָּה יְהֹוָה אֱלֹהֵינוּ
Melech Ha'olam She'asah Li	מֶלֶךְ הָעוֹלָם. שֶׁעָשָׂה לִי
Kol-Tzarki.	כָּל־צָרְכִּי:

Blessed are You, Hashem our God, King of the universe, Who has provided for all my needs.

בָּרוּךְ אַתָּה יְהֹוָה אֱלֹהֵינוּ מֶלֶךְ הָעוֹלָם. אוֹזֵר יִשְׂרָאֵל בִּגְבוּרָה:

Baruch Attah Adonai Eloheinu Melech Ha'olam Ozeir Yisra'el Bigvurah.

Blessed are You, Hashem our God, King of the universe, Who girds Yisrael with might.

בָּרוּךְ אַתָּה יְהֹוָה אֱלֹהֵינוּ מֶלֶךְ הָעוֹלָם. עוֹטֵר יִשְׂרָאֵל בְּתִפְאָרָה:

Baruch Attah Adonai Eloheinu Melech Ha'olam Oteir Yisra'el Betif'arah.

Blessed are You, Hashem our God, King of the universe, Who crowns Yisrael with glory.

בָּרוּךְ אַתָּה יְהֹוָה אֱלֹהֵינוּ. מֶלֶךְ הָעוֹלָם. שֶׁלֹּא עָשַׂנִי גּוֹי:

האשה אומרת: (גּוֹיָה)

Baruch Attah Adonai Eloheinu Melech Ha'olam Shelo Asani Goy.

women say: (Goyah)

Blessed are You, Hashem our God, King of the universe, Who has not made me an idolater.

בָּרוּךְ אַתָּה יְהֹוָה אֱלֹהֵינוּ מֶלֶךְ הָעוֹלָם. שֶׁלֹּא עָשַׂנִי עָבֶד:

האשה אומרת: (שִׁפְחָה)

Baruch Attah Adonai Eloheinu Melech Ha'olam Shelo Asani Aved.

women say: (Shifchah)

Blessed are You, Hashem our God, King of the universe, Who has not made me a slave. **women say:** (a maid-servant)

A man blesses:

Baruch Attah Adonai Eloheinu	בָּרוּךְ אַתָּה יְהֹוָה אֱלֹהֵינוּ
Melech Ha'olam Shelo Asani	מֶלֶךְ הָעוֹלָם. שֶׁלֹּא עָשַׂנִי
Ishah.	אִשָּׁה:

Blessed are You, Hashem our God, King of the universe, Who has set upon me the obligations of a man.

A woman blesses without pronouncing Hashem's name and Kingship:

Baruch She'asani Kirtzono.	בָּרוּךְ שֶׁעָשַׂנִי כִּרְצוֹנוֹ:

Blessed is He Who made me according to His Will.

Baruch Attah Adonai Eloheinu	בָּרוּךְ אַתָּה יְהֹוָה אֱלֹהֵינוּ
Melech Ha'olam Hama'avir	מֶלֶךְ הָעוֹלָם. הַמַּעֲבִיר
Chevlei Sheinah Me'einai	חֶבְלֵי שֵׁנָה מֵעֵינָי.
Utenumah Mei'af'appai. Vihi	וּתְנוּמָה מֵעַפְעַפָּי. וִיהִי
Ratzon Milfaneicha Adonai.	רָצוֹן מִלְּפָנֶיךָ יְהֹוָה.
Elohai Velohei Avotai.	אֱלֹהַי וֵאלֹהֵי אֲבוֹתַי.
Shetargileini Betoratecha.	שֶׁתַּרְגִּילֵנִי בְּתוֹרָתֶךָ.
Vetadbikeini Bemitzvoteicha.	וְתַדְבִּיקֵנִי בְּמִצְוֹתֶיךָ.
Ve'al Tevi'eni Lidei Chet. Velo	וְאַל תְּבִיאֵנִי לִידֵי חֵטְא. וְלֹא
Lidei Avon. Velo Lidei Nisayon.	לִידֵי עָוֹן. וְלֹא לִידֵי נִסָּיוֹן.
Velo Lidei Vizayon. Vetarchikeni	וְלֹא לִידֵי בִזָּיוֹן. וְתַרְחִיקֵנִי
Miyetzer Hara'. Vetadbikeini	מִיֵּצֶר הָרָע. וְתַדְבִּיקֵנִי
Beyetzer Hatov. Vechof Et-Yitzri	בְּיֵצֶר הַטּוֹב. וְכוֹף אֶת־יִצְרִי
Lehishta'bed Lach. Uteneni	לְהִשְׁתַּעְבֶּד לָךְ. וּתְנֵנִי
Hayom Uvechol-Yom Lechein	הַיּוֹם וּבְכָל־יוֹם לְחֵן

Ulchesed Ulerachamim	וּלְחֶסֶד וּלְרַחֲמִים
Be'eineicha Uve'einei Chol-	בְּעֵינֶיךָ וּבְעֵינֵי כָל־
Ro'ai. Vegameleini Chasadim	רוֹאַי. וְגָמְלֵנִי חֲסָדִים
Tovim. Baruch Attah Adonai	טוֹבִים. בָּרוּךְ אַתָּה יְהֹוָה
Gomel Chasadim Tovim	גּוֹמֵל חֲסָדִים טוֹבִים
Le'ammo Yisra'el.	לְעַמּוֹ יִשְׂרָאֵל:

Blessed are You, Hashem our God, King of the universe, Who removes sleep from my eyes and slumber from my eyelids. And may it be Your will, Hashem, my God and God of my fathers, to make us familiar with Your Torah and to cause us to adhere to your commandments. And do not bring us into sin, or to iniquity, or to be tested, or to be dishonored. And distance me from the evil inclination and adhere me to the good inclination. And force my inclination to submit to You. And grant me today, and everyday, grace, loving-kindness, and mercy in Your eyes and in the eyes of all who see me, and bestow loving-kindnesses upon me. Blessed are You, Hashem, Who bestows loving-kindnesses to His nation, Yisrael.

Yehi Ratzon Milfaneicha Adonai.	יְהִי רָצוֹן מִלְּפָנֶיךָ יְהֹוָה.
Elohai Velohei Avotai.	אֱלֹהַי וֵאלֹהֵי אֲבוֹתַי.
Shetatzileini Hayom Uvechol	שֶׁתַּצִּילֵנִי הַיּוֹם וּבְכָל
Yom Vayom. Me'azei Fanim.	יוֹם וָיוֹם. מֵעַזֵּי פָנִים.
Ume'azut Panim. Me'adam Ra'.	וּמֵעַזּוּת פָּנִים. מֵאָדָם רָע.
[Me'ishah Ra'ah.] Miyetzer Ra'.	[מֵאִשָּׁה רָעָה.] מִיֵּצֶר רָע.
Mechaver Ra'. Mishachein Ra'.	מֵחָבֵר רָע. מִשָּׁכֵן רָע.
Mipega Ra'. Me'ayin Hara'.	מִפֶּגַע רָע. מֵעַיִן הָרָע.
Umillashon Hara'. [Mimalshinut.	וּמִלָּשׁוֹן הָרָע. [מִמַּלְשִׁינוּת.

Mei'edut Sheker. Misinat	מֵעֵדוּת שֶׁקֶר. מִשִּׂנְאַת
Habriyot. Mei'alilah. Mimitah	הַבְּרִיּוֹת. מֵעֲלִילָה. מִמִּיתָה
Meshunah. Mei'chalayim Ra'im.	מְשֻׁנָּה. מֵחֳלָאִים רָעִים.
Mimikrim Ra'im.] Midin Kasheh.	מִמִּקְרִים רָעִים.] מִדִּין קָשֶׁה.
Umiba'al Din Kasheh. Bein	וּמִבַּעַל דִּין קָשֶׁה. בֵּין
Shehu Ven-Berit. Uvein She'eino	שֶׁהוּא בֶן־בְּרִית. וּבֵין שֶׁאֵינוֹ
Ven-Berit. [Umidinah Shel	בֶן־בְּרִית. [וּמִדִּינָהּ שֶׁל
Gehinam.]	גֵּיהִנָּם]:

May it be Your will, Hashem, my God and God of my fathers, to deliver us this day and every day from the shameless and from insolence, from the wicked, from an evil man, [from an evil woman,] from the evil inclination, from an evil friend, from an evil companion, from a bad mishap, from an evil eye, from evil speech, [from informers, from false witness, from the hatred of others, from libel, from an un-natural death, from severe illnesses, from harmful occurences,] from a harsh judgment, and from an harsh litigant, whether he is a son of the covenant or whether he is not a son of the covenant [and from the judgment of Gehinnom].

Blessings of the Torah

Baruch Attah Adonai Eloheinu	בָּרוּךְ אַתָּה יְהֹוָה אֱלֹהֵינוּ
Melech Ha'olam Asher	מֶלֶךְ הָעוֹלָם. אֲשֶׁר
Kideshanu Bemitzvotav	קִדְּשָׁנוּ בְּמִצְוֹתָיו
Vetzivanu Al Divrei Torah.	וְצִוָּנוּ עַל דִּבְרֵי תוֹרָה:

Blessed are You, Hashem our God, King of the universe, Who has sanctified us with His commandments, and commanded us concerning the words of Torah.

Veha'arev Na. Adonai Eloheinu.	וְהַעֲרֶב נָא. יְהֹוָה אֱלֹהֵינוּ.
Et-Divrei Toratecha Befinu	אֶת־דִּבְרֵי תוֹרָתְךָ בְּפִינוּ
Uvefifiyot Ammecha Beit	וּבְפִיפִיּוֹת עַמְּךָ בֵּית
Yisra'el. Venihyeh Anachnu	יִשְׂרָאֵל. וְנִהְיֶה אֲנַחְנוּ
Vetze'etza'einu. Vetze'etza'ei	וְצֶאֱצָאֵינוּ. וְצֶאֱצָאֵי
Tze'etza'einu. [Vetze'etza'ei	צֶאֱצָאֵינוּ. [וְצֶאֱצָאֵי
Ammecha Beit Yisrael.] Kulanu	עַמְּךָ בֵּית יִשְׂרָאֵל.] כֻּלָּנוּ
Yodei Shemecha. Velomedei	יוֹדְעֵי שְׁמֶךָ. וְלוֹמְדֵי
Toratecha Lishmah. Baruch	תוֹרָתְךָ לִשְׁמָהּ. בָּרוּךְ
Attah Adonai Hamlamed Torah	אַתָּה יְהֹוָה הַמְלַמֵּד תּוֹרָה
Le'ammo Yisra'el.	לְעַמּוֹ יִשְׂרָאֵל:

Hashem our God, make these teachings of Your Torah pleasant in our mouth and in the mouth of all Your people the household of Yisrael, that we, our children and children's children, [and the children of Your nation, the House of Israel,] may all know You and learn Your Torah for the love of it. Blessed are You, Hashem, Teacher of the Torah to Yisrael Your people.

Baruch Attah Adonai Eloheinu	בָּרוּךְ אַתָּה יְהֹוָה אֱלֹהֵינוּ
Melech Ha'olam Asher Bachar	מֶלֶךְ הָעוֹלָם. אֲשֶׁר בָּחַר
Banu Mikol-Ha'ammim Venatan	בָּנוּ מִכָּל־הָעַמִּים וְנָתַן
Lanu Et-Torato. Baruch Attah	לָנוּ אֶת־תּוֹרָתוֹ. בָּרוּךְ אַתָּה
Adonai Noten Hatorah.	יְהֹוָה נוֹתֵן הַתּוֹרָה:

Blessed are You, Hashem our God, King of the universe, Who has chosen us from all the nations and gave us His Torah. Blessed are You, Hashem, Giver of the Torah.

Priestly Blessing (Numbers 6:22-27)

Vaydaber Adonai El-Mosheh	וַיְדַבֵּר יְהֹוָה אֶל־מֹשֶׁה
Lemor. Daber El-'Aharon Ve'el-	לֵּאמֹר: דַּבֵּר אֶל־אַהֲרֹן וְאֶל־
Banav Lemor. Koh Tevarechu Et-	בָּנָיו לֵאמֹר כֹּה תְבָרְכוּ אֶת־
Benei Yisra'el; Amor Lahem.	בְּנֵי יִשְׂרָאֵל אָמוֹר לָהֶם:
Yevarechecha Adonai	יְבָרֶכְךָ יְהֹוָה
Veyishmerecha. Ya'er Adonai	וְיִשְׁמְרֶךָ: יָאֵר יְהֹוָה ׀
Panav Eleicha Vichuneka. Yissa	פָּנָיו אֵלֶיךָ וִיחֻנֶּךָּ: יִשָּׂא
Adonai Panav Eleicha. Veyasem	יְהֹוָה ׀ פָּנָיו אֵלֶיךָ וְיָשֵׂם
Lecha Shalom.	לְךָ שָׁלוֹם:
Vesamu Et-Shemi Al-Benei	וְשָׂמוּ אֶת־שְׁמִי עַל־בְּנֵי
Yisra'el; Va'ani Avarechem.	יִשְׂרָאֵל וַאֲנִי אֲבָרְכֵם:

And Hashem spoke to Moshe, saying: Speak to Aharon and his sons, saying: So will you bless the children of Yisrael. Say to them:

"Hashem bless you and keep you. Hashem make His countenance shine upon you, and be gracious to you. Hashem lift up His countenance upon you and give you peace."

And they will set My name upon the Children of Yisrael, and I will bless them.

Tikkun Chatzot / Midnight Rectification

The Shulchan Arukh says, it is fitting for every person who has fear of Heaven to be anguished and concerned regarding the destruction of the Temple. (OC, 1:3) "Rejoice with Yerushalayim, And be glad with her, all of you that love her; Rejoice for joy with her, All of you that mourn for her; Rejoice with Yerushalayim, And be glad with her, all that love her; Rejoice for joy with her, All that mourn for her." (Is. 66:10) From here our Sages of blessed memory said "Anyone who mourns over Yerushalyim will merit to see her rejoicing; and who does not mourn over Yerushalayim will not see her rejoicing." (BT, Taanit 30b) Tikkun Chatzot was adapted by the Arizal for this purpose. It consists of two parts, Tikkun Rachel and Tikkun Leah. The ideal time is from Chatzot (halfway between sunset and sunrise) until one hour before sunrise. (Kaf HaChayim 551:222) If one wakes before Both are not recited on Friday night, Yom Tov, Chol HaMoed Pesach, Rosh Hashanah and Yom Kippur. Days that Tikkun Leah is only said are: days when there is Tachanun not said, Chol HaMoed Sukkot, the 10 days of repentance (Rosh Hashanah to Yom Kippur), a year of Shemittah in Yisrael, a day after the New Moon before Rosh Chodesh, and days of Counting the Omer. (Kaf HaChayim 1:11-13). On the days between the straights (The Three Weeks, 17th of Tammuz to 9th day of Av, but not on the day of the 9th), say only Tikkun Rachel. (Kaf HaChayim 551:223)

Tikkun Rachel

Some say before:

לְשֵׁם יִחוּד קוּדְשָׁא בְּרִיךְ הוּא וּשְׁכִינְתֵּיהּ. בִּדְחִילוּ וּרְחִימוּ. וּרְחִימוּ וּדְחִילוּ. לְיַחֲדָא שֵׁם יו"ד קֵ"י בְּוָא"ו קֵ"י בְּיִחוּדָא שְׁלִים (יהוה) בְּשֵׁם כָּל יִשְׂרָאֵל. הריני מוכן לומר תיקון רחל ותיקון לאה כמו שסדרו לנו רבותינו זכרונם לברכה לתקן את שורשה במקום עליון לעשות נחת רוח ליוצרנו ולעשות רצון בוראנו. וִיהִי נֹעַם אֲדֹנָי אֱלֹהֵינוּ עָלֵינוּ וּמַעֲשֵׂה יָדֵינוּ כּוֹנְנָה עָלֵינוּ וּמַעֲשֵׂה יָדֵינוּ כּוֹנְנֵהוּ:

Vidui / Confession

Ana Adonai Eloheinu Velohei	אָנָּא יְהֹוָה אֱלֹהֵינוּ וֵאלֹהֵי
Avoteinu. Tavo Lefaneicha	אֲבוֹתֵינוּ. תָּבֹא לְפָנֶיךָ
Tefillateinu. Ve'al Tit'alam	תְּפִלָּתֵנוּ. וְאַל תִּתְעַלַּם
Malkeinu Mitechinateinu.	מַלְכֵּנוּ מִתְּחִנָּתֵנוּ.
She'ein Anachnu Azei Fanim	שֶׁאֵין אֲנַחְנוּ עַזֵּי פָנִים
Ukeshei Oref Lomar Lefaneicha	וּקְשֵׁי עֹרֶף לוֹמַר לְפָנֶיךָ
Adonai Eloheinu Velohei	יְהֹוָה אֱלֹהֵינוּ וֵאלֹהֵי

Avoteinu Tzaddikim Anachnu	אֲבוֹתֵינוּ צַדִּיקִים אֲנַחְנוּ
Velo-Chatanu. Aval Chatanu.	וְלֹא־חָטָאנוּ. אֲבָל חָטָאנוּ.
Avinu. Pasha'nu. Anachnu	עָוִינוּ. פָּשַׁעְנוּ. אֲנַחְנוּ
Va'avoteinu Ve'anshei Veiteinu.	וַאֲבוֹתֵינוּ וְאַנְשֵׁי בֵיתֵנוּ:

Our God and God of our fathers, may our prayer reach you; do not ignore our plea. For we are neither insolent or obstinate to say to you: “Hashem our God and God of our fathers, we are just and have not sinned.” Indeed, we and our fathers have sinned and our household.

Ashamnu. Bagadnu. Gazalnu.	אָשַׁמְנוּ. בָּגַדְנוּ. גָּזַלְנוּ.
Dibarnu Dofi Velashon Hara.	דִּבַּרְנוּ דֹפִי וְלָשׁוֹן הָרָע.
He'evinu. Vehirsha'nu. Zadnu.	הֶעֱוִינוּ. וְהִרְשַׁעְנוּ. זַדְנוּ.
Chamasnu. Tafalnu Sheker	חָמַסְנוּ. טָפַלְנוּ שֶׁקֶר
Umirmah. Ya'atznu Etzot Ra'ot.	וּמִרְמָה. יָעַצְנוּ עֵצוֹת רָעוֹת.
Kizavnu. Ka'asnu. Latznu.	כִּזַּבְנוּ. כָּעַסְנוּ. לַצְנוּ.
Maradnu. Marinu Devareicha.	מָרַדְנוּ. מָרִינוּ דְבָרֶיךָ.
Ni'atznu. Ni'afnu. Sararnu.	נִאַצְנוּ. נִאַפְנוּ. סָרַרְנוּ.
Avinu. Pasha'nu. Pagamnu.	עָוִינוּ. פָּשַׁעְנוּ. פָּגַמְנוּ.
Tzararnu. Tzi'arnu Av Va'em.	צָרַרְנוּ. צִעַרְנוּ אָב וָאֵם.
Kishinu Oref. Rasha'nu.	קִשִּׁינוּ עֹרֶף. רָשַׁעְנוּ.
Shichatnu. Ti'avnu. Ta'inu	שִׁחַתְנוּ. תִּעַבְנוּ. תָּעִינוּ
Veti'ata'nu. Vesarnu	וְתִעְתַּעְנוּ. וְסַרְנוּ
Mimitzvoteicha	מִמִּצְוֹתֶיךָ
Umimishpateicha Hatovim Velo	וּמִמִּשְׁפָּטֶיךָ הַטּוֹבִים וְלֹא
Shavah Lanu. Ve'attah Tzaddik	שָׁוָה לָנוּ. וְאַתָּה צַדִּיק
Al Kol Haba Aleinu. Ki Emet	עַל כָּל הַבָּא עָלֵינוּ. כִּי אֱמֶת
Asita. Va'anachnu Hirsha'enu.	עָשִׂיתָ. וַאֲנַחְנוּ הִרְשָׁעְנוּ:

We have trespassed, we have dealt treacherously, we have robbed, we have spoken slander and evil speech, we have committed iniquity, and have done wickedly; we have acted presumptuously, we have committed violence, we have forged falsehood and deceived, we have counseled evil, we have uttered lies, we were angry, we have scoffed, we have rebelled and violated Your words, we have blasphemed, we have committed adultery, we have revolted, we have acted perversely, we have transgressed, we have broken faith, we have been hard and we have distressed father and mother. we have been stiff-necked, we have acted wickedly, we have corrupted, we have done abominably; we have gone astray ourselves, and have caused others to stray; we have also turned aside from Your good precepts and commandments, and it has not profited us; "But You are just concerning all that is come upon us; for You have dealt most truly, but we have done wickedly." **(Nehemiah 9:33)**

Mah-Nomar Lefaneicha Yoshev	מַה־נֹּאמַר לְפָנֶיךָ יוֹשֵׁב
Marom. Umah-Nesapeir	מָרוֹם. וּמַה־נְּסַפֵּר
Lefaneicha Shochein Shechakim.	לְפָנֶיךָ שׁוֹכֵן שְׁחָקִים.
Halo Kol-Hanistarot Vehaniglot	הֲלֹא כָּל־הַנִּסְתָּרוֹת וְהַנִּגְלוֹת
Attah Yodea'. Attah Yodea Razei	אַתָּה יוֹדֵעַ. אַתָּה יוֹדֵעַ רָזֵי
Olam. Veta'alumot Sitrei Kol-	עוֹלָם. וְתַעֲלוּמוֹת סִתְרֵי כָּל־
Chai. Attah Chofes Kol-Chadrei	חָי. אַתָּה חוֹפֵשׂ כָּל־חַדְרֵי
Vaten. Ro'eh Chelayot Velev. Ein	בָטֶן. רוֹאֶה כְלָיוֹת וָלֵב. אֵין
Davar Ne'lam Mimeka. Ve'ein	דָּבָר נֶעְלָם מִמָּךְ. וְאֵין
Nistar Mineged Eineicha. Yehi	נִסְתָּר מִנֶּגֶד עֵינֶיךָ: יְהִי
Ratzon Milfaneicha Adonai	רָצוֹן מִלְּפָנֶיךָ. יְהֹוָה
Eloheinu Velohei Avoteinu.	אֱלֹהֵינוּ וֵאלֹהֵי אֲבוֹתֵינוּ.

שֶׁתִּמְחוֹ לָנוּ אֶת־כָּל־
חַטְּאוֹתֵינוּ. וּתְכַפֵּר לָנוּ אֶת־
כָּל־עֲוֹנוֹתֵינוּ. וְתִמְחוֹל
וְתִסְלַח לְכָל־פְּשָׁעֵינוּ:

Shetimchol Lanu Et-Kol-
Chat'oteinu. Utechapeir Lanu Et-
Kol-'Avonoteinu. Vetimchol
Vetislach Lechol-Pesha'einu.

Before You, All-Exalted, what can we say? Before You Throned-Supernal what can we tell? For You know what is hidden, And that which is revealed. You know the mysteries of the universe, And the inner secrets of all living. You search into all man's inner chambers, And see into his mind and heart. There is nothing that is hidden from You, Nothing concealed from Your eyes. May it be Your will, Hashem our God, God of our fathers, to deal mercifully with us. Pardon us all our sins, forgive us all our iniquities, absolve us from all our transgressions, "and pardon our iniquity and our sin, and take us for Your heritage." **(Exodus 34:9)**

Psalms 137

עַל נַהֲרוֹת | בָּבֶל שָׁם יָשַׁבְנוּ גַּם־בָּכִינוּ בְּזָכְרֵנוּ אֶת־צִיּוֹן: עַל־עֲרָבִים
בְּתוֹכָהּ תָּלִינוּ כִּנֹּרוֹתֵינוּ: כִּי שָׁם שְׁאֵלוּנוּ שׁוֹבֵינוּ דִּבְרֵי־שִׁיר
וְתוֹלָלֵינוּ שִׂמְחָה שִׁירוּ לָנוּ מִשִּׁיר צִיּוֹן: אֵיךְ נָשִׁיר אֶת־שִׁיר־יְהֹוָה
עַל אַדְמַת נֵכָר: אִם־אֶשְׁכָּחֵךְ יְרוּשָׁלָ͏ִם תִּשְׁכַּח יְמִינִי: תִּדְבַּק־לְשׁוֹנִי |
לְחִכִּי אִם־לֹא אֶזְכְּרֵכִי אִם־לֹא אַעֲלֶה אֶת־יְרוּשָׁלַ͏ִם עַל רֹאשׁ
שִׂמְחָתִי: זְכֹר יְהֹוָה | לִבְנֵי אֱדוֹם אֵת יוֹם יְרוּשָׁלָ͏ִם הָאֹמְרִים עָרוּ |
עָרוּ עַד הַיְסוֹד בָּהּ: בַּת־בָּבֶל הַשְּׁדוּדָה אַשְׁרֵי שֶׁיְשַׁלֶּם־לָךְ
אֶת־גְּמוּלֵךְ שֶׁגָּמַלְתְּ לָנוּ: אַשְׁרֵי | שֶׁיֹּאחֵז וְנִפֵּץ אֶת־עֹלָלַיִךְ
אֶל־הַסָּלַע:

Al Naharot Bavel. Sham Yashavnu Gam-Bachinu; Bezochrenu. Et-Tziyon. Al-'Aravim Betochah; Talinu. Kinoroteinu. Ki Sham She'elunu Shoveinu Divrei-Shir Vetolaleinu Simchah; Shiru Lanu Mishir Tziyon. Eich. Nashir Et-Shir-Adonai Al Admat Nechar.

Im-'Eshkachech Yerushalayim Tishkach Yemini. Tidbak-Leshoni Lechikki Im-Lo Ezkerechi Im-Lo A'aleh Et-Yerushalayim Al Rosh Simchati. Zechor Adonai Livnei Edom. Et Yom Yerushalayim Ha'omerim Aru Aru; Ad Haysod Bah. Bat-Bavel. Hashedudah Ashrei Sheyshalem-Lach; Et-Gemulech. Shegamalt Lanu. Ashrei Sheyochez Venipetz Et-'Olalayich. El-Hassala.

By the rivers of Babylon, there we sat down, we wept, when we remembered Tziyon. Upon the willows in the midst there we hung up our harps. For there they that led us captive asked of us words of song, and our tormentors asked of us joy: 'Sing us one of the songs of Tziyon.' How can we sing Hashem's song in a foreign land? If I forget you, Oh Yerushalayim, let my right hand forget her cunning. Let my tongue cleave to the roof of my mouth, if I don't remember you; if I don't set Yerushalayim above my most chief joy. Remember, Hashem, against the children of Edom the day of Yerushalayim; who said: 'Destroy it, destroy it, even to the foundation of it.' Oh daughter of Bavel, that are to be destroyed; happy will he be, that repays you as you have served us. Happy will he be, that takes and dashes your little ones against the rock.

Psalms 79

מִזְמוֹר לְאָסָף אֱלֹהִים בָּאוּ גוֹיִם | בְּנַחֲלָתֶךָ טִמְּאוּ אֶת־הֵיכַל קָדְשֶׁךָ
שָׂמוּ אֶת־יְרוּשָׁלַםִ לְעִיִּים: נָתְנוּ אֶת־נִבְלַת עֲבָדֶיךָ מַאֲכָל לְעוֹף
הַשָּׁמָיִם בְּשַׂר חֲסִידֶיךָ לְחַיְתוֹ־אָרֶץ: שָׁפְכוּ דָמָם | כַּמַּיִם סְבִיבוֹת
יְרוּשָׁלָםִ וְאֵין קוֹבֵר: הָיִינוּ חֶרְפָּה לִשְׁכֵנֵינוּ לַעַג וָקֶלֶס לִסְבִיבוֹתֵינוּ:
עַד־מָה יְהֹוָה תֶּאֱנַף לָנֶצַח תִּבְעַר כְּמוֹ־אֵשׁ קִנְאָתֶךָ: שְׁפֹךְ חֲמָתְךָ
אֶל־הַגּוֹיִם אֲשֶׁר לֹא־יְדָעוּךָ וְעַל מַמְלָכוֹת אֲשֶׁר בְּשִׁמְךָ לֹא קָרָאוּ:
כִּי אָכַל אֶת־יַעֲקֹב וְאֶת־נָוֵהוּ הֵשַׁמּוּ: אַל־תִּזְכָּר־לָנוּ עֲוֹנֹת רִאשֹׁנִים
מַהֵר יְקַדְּמוּנוּ רַחֲמֶיךָ כִּי דַלּוֹנוּ מְאֹד: עָזְרֵנוּ | אֱלֹהֵי יִשְׁעֵנוּ עַל־דְּבַר
כְּבוֹד־שְׁמֶךָ וְהַצִּילֵנוּ וְכַפֵּר עַל־חַטֹּאתֵינוּ לְמַעַן שְׁמֶךָ: לָמָּה | יֹאמְרוּ

הַגּוֹיִם אַיֵּה אֱלֹהֵיהֶם יִוָּדַע בַּגּוֹיִם לְעֵינֵינוּ נִקְמַת דַּם־עֲבָדֶיךָ הַשָּׁפוּךְ׃
תָּבוֹא לְפָנֶיךָ אֶנְקַת אָסִיר כְּגֹדֶל זְרוֹעֲךָ הוֹתֵר בְּנֵי תְמוּתָה׃ וְהָשֵׁב
לִשְׁכֵנֵינוּ שִׁבְעָתַיִם אֶל־חֵיקָם חֶרְפָּתָם אֲשֶׁר חֵרְפוּךָ אֲדֹנָי׃ וַאֲנַחְנוּ
עַמְּךָ | וְצֹאן מַרְעִיתֶךָ נוֹדֶה לְּךָ לְעוֹלָם לְדוֹר וָדֹר נְסַפֵּר תְּהִלָּתֶךָ׃

Mizmor. Le'asaf Elohim Ba'u Goyim Benachalatecha, Timme'u Et-Heichal Kodshecha; Samu Et-Yerushalayim Le'iyim. Natenu Et-Nivlat Avadeicha. Ma'achol Le'of Hashamayim; Besar Chasideicha. Lechayto-'Aretz. Shafechu Damam Kammayim. Sevivot Yerushalayim Ve'ein Kover. Hayinu Cherpah Lishcheineinu; La'ag Vakeles. Lisvivoteinu. Ad-Mah Adonai Te'enaf Lanetzach; Tiv'ar Kemo-'Esh Kin'atecha. Shefoch Chamatecha. El-Hagoyim Asher Lo-Yeda'ucha Ve'al Mamlachot; Asher Beshimcha. Lo Kara'u. Ki Achal Et-Ya'akov; Ve'et-Navehu Heshamu. Al-Tizkor-Lanu Avonot Rishonim Maher Yekademunu Rachameicha; Ki Dallonu Me'od. Ozrenu Elohei Yish'enu. Al-Devar Kevod-Shemecha; Vehatzileinu Vechapeir Al-Chatoteinu. Lema'an Shemecha. Lamah Yomeru Hagoyim Ayeh Eloheihem Yivada Bagoyim Le'eineinu; Nikmat. Dam-'Avadeicha Hashafuch. Tavo Lefaneicha Enkat Asir Kegodel Zero'acha; Hoter. Benei Temutah. Vehasheiv Lishcheineinu Shiv'atayim El-Cheikam; Cherpatam Asher Cherefucha Adonai. Va'anachnu Ammecha Vetzon Mar'itecha Nodeh Lecha. Le'olam Ledor Vador; Nesapeir. Tehilatecha.

A Psalm of Asaph. God, the nations have come into Your inheritance; they have defiled Your holy Temple; they have made Yerushalayim into heaps. They have given the dead bodies of Your servants to be food to the fowls of the heaven, the flesh of Your saints to the beasts of the earth. They have shed their blood like water all around Yerushalayim, with no one to bury them. We have become a taunt to our neighbors, a scorn and derision to them that are all around us. How long, Hashem, will You be angry forever? How long will Your jealousy burn like fire? Pour out Your wrath upon the nations that don't know You, and upon the kingdoms that don't call upon Your name. For they have devoured Yaakov, and laid waste his habitation. Do not remember against us the iniquities of our forefathers; let Your compassions speedily come to meet us; for we are brought very low. Help us, Oh God of our salvation, for the sake of the glory of Your name; and deliver us, and forgive our sins, for Your name's sake. Why should the nations say: 'Where is their God?' Let the avenging of Your servants' blood that is shed be made known among the nations in our sight. Let the groaning of the prisoner come before You; according to the greatness of Your power set free those that are appointed to death; And give to our neighbors sevenfold of their reproach, which they have reproached You, Hashem. So we that are Your people and the flock of Your pasture will give You thanks forever; we will tell of Your praise to all generations.

Lamentations 5:1-21

זְכֹר יְהוָה מֶה־הָיָה לָנוּ הבית (הֲבִּיטָה) וּרְאֵה אֶת־חֶרְפָּתֵנוּ: נַחֲלָתֵנוּ
נֶהֶפְכָה לְזָרִים בָּתֵּינוּ לְנָכְרִים: יְתוֹמִים הָיִינוּ אין (וְאֵין) אָב אִמֹּתֵינוּ
כְּאַלְמָנוֹת: מֵימֵינוּ בְּכֶסֶף שָׁתִינוּ עֵצֵינוּ בִּמְחִיר יָבֹאוּ: עַל צַוָּארֵנוּ
נִרְדָּפְנוּ יָגַעְנוּ לא (וְלֹא) הוּנַח־לָנוּ: מִצְרַיִם נָתַנּוּ יָד אַשּׁוּר לִשְׂבֹּעַ
לָחֶם: אֲבֹתֵינוּ חָטְאוּ אינם (וְאֵינָם) אנחנו (וַאֲנַחְנוּ) עֲוֹנֹתֵיהֶם
סָבָלְנוּ: עֲבָדִים מָשְׁלוּ בָנוּ פֹּרֵק אֵין מִיָּדָם: בְּנַפְשֵׁנוּ נָבִיא לַחְמֵנוּ
מִפְּנֵי חֶרֶב הַמִּדְבָּר: עוֹרֵנוּ כְּתַנּוּר נִכְמָרוּ מִפְּנֵי זַלְעֲפוֹת רָעָב: נָשִׁים
בְּצִיּוֹן עִנּוּ בְּתֻלֹת בְּעָרֵי יְהוּדָה: שָׂרִים בְּיָדָם נִתְלוּ פְּנֵי זְקֵנִים לֹא
נֶהְדָּרוּ: בַּחוּרִים טְחוֹן נָשָׂאוּ וּנְעָרִים בָּעֵץ כָּשָׁלוּ: זְקֵנִים מִשַּׁעַר
שָׁבָתוּ בַּחוּרִים מִנְּגִינָתָם: שָׁבַת מְשׂוֹשׂ לִבֵּנוּ נֶהְפַּךְ לְאֵבֶל מְחֹלֵנוּ:
נָפְלָה עֲטֶרֶת רֹאשֵׁנוּ אוֹי־נָא לָנוּ כִּי חָטָאנוּ: עַל־זֶה הָיָה דָוֶה לִבֵּנוּ
עַל־אֵלֶּה חָשְׁכוּ עֵינֵינוּ: עַל הַר־צִיּוֹן שֶׁשָּׁמֵם שׁוּעָלִים הִלְּכוּ־בוֹ:
אַתָּה יְהוָה לְעוֹלָם תֵּשֵׁב כִּסְאֲךָ לְדוֹר וָדוֹר: לָמָּה לָנֶצַח תִּשְׁכָּחֵנוּ
תַּעַזְבֵנוּ לְאֹרֶךְ יָמִים: הֲשִׁיבֵנוּ יְהוָה | אֵלֶיךָ ונשוב (וְנָשׁוּבָה) חַדֵּשׁ
יָמֵינוּ כְּקֶדֶם: כִּי אִם־מָאֹס מְאַסְתָּנוּ קָצַפְתָּ עָלֵינוּ עַד־מְאֹד: הֲשִׁיבֵנוּ
יְהוָה | אֵלֶיךָ ונשוב (וְנָשׁוּבָה) חַדֵּשׁ יָמֵינוּ כְּקֶדֶם:

Zechor Adonai Meh-Hayah Lanu. Habitah Ure'eh Et-Cherpateinu. Nachalateinu Nehefchah Lezarim. Batteinu Lenochrim. Yetomim Hayinu Ve'ein Av. Immoteinu Ke'almanot. Meimeinu Bechesef Shatinu. Etzeinu Bimchir Yavo'u. Al Tzavarenu Nirdafenu. Yaga'nu Velo Hunach-Lanu. Mitzrayim Natanu Yad. Ashur Lisboa Lachem. Avoteinu Chate'u Ve'einam. Va'anachnu Avonoteihem Savalenu. Avadim Mashelu Vanu. Porek Ein Miyadam. Benafshenu Navi Lachmenu. Mipenei Cherev Hamidbar. Orenu Ketanur Nichmaru. Mipenei Zal'afot Ra'av. Nashim Betziyon Inu. Betulot Be'arei Yehudah. Sarim Beyadam Nitlu. Penei Zekenim Lo Nehdaru. Bachurim Techon Nasa'u. Une'arim Ba'etz Kashalu. Zekenim Misha'ar Shavatu. Bachurim Mineginatam. Shavat Mesos Libenu. Nehpach Le'evel Mecholenu. Nafelah Ateret Roshenu. Oy-Na Lanu Ki Chatanu. Al-Zeh. Hayah Daveh Libenu. Al-'Eleh Chashechu Eineinu. Al Har-Tziyon Sheshamem. Shu'alim Hillechu-Vo. Attah Adonai Le'olam Teshev. Kis'acha Ledor Vador. Lamah Lanetzach Tishkacheinu. Ta'azvenu Le'orech Yamim. Hashiveinu Adonai 'Eleicha Venashuvah. Chadesh Yameinu Kekedem. Ki Im-Ma'os Me'astanu. Katzafta Aleinu Ad-Me'od. Hashiveinu Adonai Eleicha Venashuvah. Chadesh Yameinu Kekedem.

Remember, Hashem, what has come upon us; behold, and see our reproach. Our inheritance is given to strangers, our houses to aliens. We have become orphans and fatherless, our mothers are as widows. We have drunk our water for money; our wood comes to us for price. To our very necks we are pursued; we labor, and have no rest. We have given the hand to Mitzrayim, and to Assyria, to have enough bread; Our fathers have sinned, and are nothing; and we have borne their iniquities. Servants rule over us; there is none to deliver us out of their hand. We get our bread with the peril of our lives because of the sword of the wilderness. Our skin is hot like an oven because of the burning heat of famine. They have ravished the women in Tziyon, the maidens in the cities of Yehudah. Princes are hung up by their hand; the faces of elders are not honored. The young men have borne the mill, and the children have stumbled under the wood. The elders have ceased from the gate, the young men from their music. The joy of our heart has ceased; our dance has turned into mourning. The crown is fallen from our head; woe to us for we have sinned. For this our heart is faint, for these things our eyes are dim; For the mountain of Tziyon, which is desolate, the foxes walk upon it. You, Hashem, are enthroned forever, Your Throne is from generation to generation. Why do You forget us forever, and forsake us for so long a time? Turn us to You, Hashem, and we will return; renew our days as of old.

Isaiah 63:16-18, 64:7-11

הַבֵּט מִשָּׁמַיִם וּרְאֵה מִזְּבֻל קָדְשְׁךָ וְתִפְאַרְתֶּךָ אַיֵּה קִנְאָתְךָ וּגְבוּרֹתֶךָ הֲמוֹן מֵעֶיךָ וְרַחֲמֶיךָ אֵלַי הִתְאַפָּקוּ׃ כִּי־אַתָּה אָבִינוּ כִּי אַבְרָהָם לֹא יְדָעָנוּ וְיִשְׂרָאֵל לֹא יַכִּירָנוּ אַתָּה יְהוָה אָבִינוּ גֹּאֲלֵנוּ מֵעוֹלָם שְׁמֶךָ׃ לָמָּה תַתְעֵנוּ יְהוָה מִדְּרָכֶיךָ תַּקְשִׁיחַ לִבֵּנוּ מִיִּרְאָתֶךָ שׁוּב לְמַעַן עֲבָדֶיךָ שִׁבְטֵי נַחֲלָתֶךָ׃ לַמִּצְעָר יָרְשׁוּ עַם־קָדְשֶׁךָ צָרֵינוּ בּוֹסְסוּ מִקְדָּשֶׁךָ׃

וְעַתָּה יְהוָה אָבִינוּ אָתָּה אֲנַחְנוּ הַחֹמֶר וְאַתָּה יֹצְרֵנוּ וּמַעֲשֵׂה יָדְךָ כֻּלָּנוּ׃ אַל־תִּקְצֹף יְהוָה עַד־מְאֹד וְאַל־לָעַד תִּזְכֹּר עָוֺן הֵן הַבֶּט־נָא עַמְּךָ כֻלָּנוּ׃ עָרֵי קָדְשְׁךָ הָיוּ מִדְבָּר צִיּוֹן מִדְבָּר הָיָתָה יְרוּשָׁלַםִ שְׁמָמָה׃ בֵּית קָדְשֵׁנוּ וְתִפְאַרְתֵּנוּ אֲשֶׁר הִלְלוּךָ אֲבֹתֵינוּ הָיָה לִשְׂרֵפַת אֵשׁ וְכָל־מַחֲמַדֵּינוּ הָיָה לְחָרְבָּה׃ הַעַל־אֵלֶּה תִתְאַפַּק יְהוָה תֶּחֱשֶׁה וּתְעַנֵּנוּ עַד־מְאֹד׃

Habeit Mishamayim Ure'eh. Mizevul Kodshecha Vetif'artecha; Ayeh Kin'atecha Ugevurotecha, Hamon Me'eicha Verachameicha Elai Hit'apaku: Ki-'Attah Avinu. Ki Avraham Lo Yeda'anu. Veyisra'el Lo Yakiranu; Attah Adonai Avinu. Go'alenu Me'olam Shemecha. Lamah Tat'enu Adonai Midderacheicha. Takshiach Libenu Miyir'atecha; Shuv Lema'an Avadeicha. Shivtei Nachalatecha. Lammitz'ar Yareshu Am-Kodshecha; Tzareinu Bosesu Mikdashecha.

Ve'attah Adonai Avinu Attah; Anachnu Hachomer Ve'attah Yotzreinu. Uma'aseh Yadecha Kulanu. Al-Tiktzof Adonai Ad-Me'od. Ve'al-La'ad Tizkor Avon; Hen Habet-Na Ammecha Chulanu. Arei

Kodshecha Hayu Midbar; Tziyon Midbar Hayatah. Yerushalayim Shemamah. Beit Kodshenu Vetif'arteinu. Asher Hilelucha Avoteinu. Hayah Lisrefat Esh; Vechol-Machamaddeinu Hayah Lechorbah. Ha'al-'Eleh Tit'apak Adonai Techesheh Ute'anenu Ad-Me'od

Look down from heaven, and see, even from Your holy and glorious Habitation; Where is Your zeal and Your mighty acts, The yearning of Your heart and Your compassions, that are now restrained toward me? For You are our Father; for Avraham does not know us, and Yisrael does not acknowledge us; You, Hashem, are our Father, our Redeemer from everlasting is Your name. Hashem, why do You make us error from Your ways, and harden our heart from Your fear? Return, for Your servants' sake, the tribes of Your inheritance. Your holy people, they have nearly driven out; Our adversaries have trampled down Your Sanctuary.

But now, Hashem, You are our Father; we are the clay, and You are our Potter, and we all are the work of Your hand. Do not be overly angry, Hashem, neither remember iniquity forever; behold, look, we beg You, we are all Your people. Your holy cities have become a wilderness, Tziyon is become a wilderness, Yerushalayim a desolation. Our holy and our beautiful House, where our fathers praised You, is burned with fire; and all our pleasant things are laid waste. Will You refrain Yourself from these things, Hashem? Will You hold Your peace, and afflict us greatly?

Isaiah 62: 6-9

עַל־חוֹמֹתַיִךְ יְרוּשָׁלִַם הִפְקַדְתִּי שֹׁמְרִים כָּל־הַיּוֹם וְכָל־הַלַּיְלָה תָּמִיד
לֹא יֶחֱשׁוּ הַמַּזְכִּרִים אֶת־יְהֹוָה אַל־דֳּמִי לָכֶם׃ וְאַל־תִּתְּנוּ דֳמִי לוֹ
עַד־יְכוֹנֵן וְעַד־יָשִׂים אֶת־יְרוּשָׁלִַם תְּהִלָּה בָּאָרֶץ׃ נִשְׁבַּע יְהֹוָה בִּימִינוֹ
וּבִזְרוֹעַ עֻזּוֹ אִם־אֶתֵּן אֶת־דְּגָנֵךְ עוֹד מַאֲכָל לְאֹיְבַיִךְ וְאִם־יִשְׁתּוּ
בְנֵי־נֵכָר תִּירוֹשֵׁךְ אֲשֶׁר יָגַעַתְּ בּוֹ׃ כִּי מְאַסְפָיו יֹאכְלֻהוּ וְהִלְלוּ
אֶת־יְהֹוָה וּמְקַבְּצָיו יִשְׁתֻּהוּ בְּחַצְרוֹת קָדְשִׁי׃

Al-Chomotayich Yerushalayim Hifkadti Shomerim. Chol-Hayom Vechol-Hallaylah Tamid Lo Yecheshu; Hamazkirim Et-Adonai Al-Domi Lachem. Ve'al-Titenu Domi Lo; Ad-Yechonen Ve'ad-Yasim Et-Yerushalayim Tehilah Ba'aretz. Nishba Adonai Bimino Uvizroa Uzo; Im-'Etten Et-Deganech Od Ma'achal Le'oyevayich. Ve'im-Yishtu Venei-Nechar Tiroshech. Asher Yaga'at Bo. Ki Me'asfav Yocheluhu. Vehilelu Et-Adonai Umekabetzav Yishtuhu Bechatzrot Kodshi.

I have set watchmen upon Your walls, Yerushalayim, they will never hold their peace day or night: 'You that are Hashem's remembrancers, take no rest, And give Him no rest, until He establish, and until He makes Yerushalayim a praise in the earth.' Hashem has sworn by His right hand, and by the arm of His strength: Surely I will no more give your corn to be food for your enemies; and strangers will not drink your wine, for which you have labored; But they that have garnered it will eat it, and praise Hashem, and they that have gathered it will drink it in the courts of My holy Sanctuary.

Psalms 102:14-15; 147:2

אַתָּה תָקוּם תְּרַחֵם צִיּוֹן כִּי־עֵת לְחֶנְנָהּ כִּי־בָא מוֹעֵד: כִּי־רָצוּ עֲבָדֶיךָ אֶת־אֲבָנֶיהָ וְאֶת־עֲפָרָהּ יְחֹנֵנוּ: בּוֹנֵה יְרוּשָׁלַםִ יְהֹוָה נִדְחֵי יִשְׂרָאֵל יְכַנֵּס:

Attah Takum Terachem Tziyon; Ki-'Et Lechenenah. Ki-Va Mo'ed. Ki-Ratzu Avadeicha Et-'Avaneiha; Ve'et-'Afarah Yechonenu. Boneh Yerushalayim Adonai Nidchei Yisra'el Yechanes.

You will arise, and have compassion upon Tziyon; for it is time to be gracious to her, for the appointed time has come. For Your servants take pleasure in her stones, and love her dust. Hashem builds up Yerushalayim, He gathers together the dispersed of Yisrael.

Tikkun Leah

Psalms 42

לַמְנַצֵּחַ מַשְׂכִּיל לִבְנֵי־קֹרַח׃ כְּאַיָּל תַּעֲרֹג עַל־אֲפִיקֵי־מָיִם כֵּן נַפְשִׁי
תַעֲרֹג אֵלֶיךָ אֱלֹהִים׃ צָמְאָה נַפְשִׁי | לֵאלֹהִים לְאֵל חָי מָתַי אָבוֹא
וְאֵרָאֶה פְּנֵי אֱלֹהִים׃ הָיְתָה־לִּי דִמְעָתִי לֶחֶם יוֹמָם וָלָיְלָה בֶּאֱמֹר אֵלַי
כָּל־הַיּוֹם אַיֵּה אֱלֹהֶיךָ׃ אֵלֶּה אֶזְכְּרָה | וְאֶשְׁפְּכָה עָלַי | נַפְשִׁי כִּי
אֶעֱבֹר | בַּסָּךְ אֶדַּדֵּם עַד־בֵּית אֱלֹהִים בְּקוֹל־רִנָּה וְתוֹדָה הָמוֹן חוֹגֵג׃
מַה־תִּשְׁתּוֹחֲחִי | נַפְשִׁי וַתֶּהֱמִי עָלָי הוֹחִלִי לֵאלֹהִים כִּי־עוֹד אוֹדֶנּוּ
יְשׁוּעוֹת פָּנָיו׃ אֱלֹהַי עָלַי נַפְשִׁי תִשְׁתּוֹחָח עַל־כֵּן אֶזְכָּרְךָ מֵאֶרֶץ יַרְדֵּן
וְחֶרְמוֹנִים מֵהַר מִצְעָר׃ תְּהוֹם־אֶל־תְּהוֹם קוֹרֵא לְקוֹל צִנּוֹרֶיךָ
כָּל־מִשְׁבָּרֶיךָ וְגַלֶּיךָ עָלַי עָבָרוּ׃ יוֹמָם | יְצַוֶּה יְהֹוָה | חַסְדּוֹ וּבַלַּיְלָה
שִׁירֹה עִמִּי תְּפִלָּה לְאֵל חַיָּי׃ אוֹמְרָה | לְאֵל סַלְעִי לָמָה שְׁכַחְתָּנִי
לָמָּה־קֹדֵר אֵלֵךְ בְּלַחַץ אוֹיֵב׃ בְּרֶצַח | בְּעַצְמוֹתַי חֵרְפוּנִי צוֹרְרָי
בְּאָמְרָם אֵלַי כָּל־הַיּוֹם אַיֵּה אֱלֹהֶיךָ׃ מַה־תִּשְׁתּוֹחֲחִי | נַפְשִׁי
וּמַה־תֶּהֱמִי עָלָי הוֹחִילִי לֵאלֹהִים כִּי־עוֹד אוֹדֶנּוּ יְשׁוּעֹת פָּנַי וֵאלֹהָי׃

Lamnatzeach. Maskil Livnei-Korach. Ke'ayal. Ta'arog Al-'Afikei-Mayim; Ken Nafshi Ta'arog Eleicha Elohim. Tzame'ah Nafshi Lelohim Le'el Chai Matai Avo; Ve'era'eh. Penei Elohim. Hayetah-Li Dim'ati Lechem Yomam Valailah; Be'emor Elai Chol-Hayom. Ayeh Eloheicha. Eleh Ezkerah Ve'eshpechah Alai Nafshi. Ki E'evor Bassoch Edadem. Ad-Beit Elohim Bekol-Rinah Vetodah. Hamon Chogeg. Mah-Tishtochachi Nafshi Vatehemi Alai Hochili Lelohim Ki-'Od Odenu. Yeshu'ot Panav. Elohai. Alai Nafshi Tishtochach Al-Ken. Ezkorcha Me'eretz Yarden; Vechermonim. Mehar Mitz'ar. Tehom-'El-Tehom Korei Lekol Tzinoreicha; Chol-Mishbareicha Vegaleicha. Alai Avaru. Yomam Yetzaveh Adonai Chasdo. Uvallaylah Shiroh Immi; Tefillah. Le'el Chayai. Omerah Le'el Sal'i Lamah Shechachtani Lamah-Koder Elech. Belachatz Oyev. Beretzach Be'atzmotai. Cherefuni Tzorerai; Be'omram Elai Chol-Hayom. Ayeh Eloheicha. Mah-Tishtochachi Nafshi Umah-Tehemi Alai Hochili Lelohim Ki-'Od Odenu; Yeshu'ot Panai. Velohai.

For the Leader; Maskil of the sons of Korach. the heart pants after the water brooks, So my soul pants after You, Oh God. My soul thirsts for God, for the living God: 'When will I come and appear before God?' My tears have been my food day and night, While they say to me all day: 'Where is your God?' These things I remember, and pour out my soul within me, How I passed on with the crowd, and led them to the House of God, With the voice of joy and praise, a multitude keeping a festival. Why are you downcast, my soul? And why do you moan within me? Hope in God; for I will yet praise Him. For the salvation of His countenance. Oh my God, my soul is cast down within me; Therefore do I remember You from the land of Yarden, And the Hermonim, from the Mount Mitzar. Deep calls to deep at the voice of Your waterfalls; All Your waves and Your billows have gone over me. By day Hashem will command His lovingkindness, And in the night His song will be with me, Even a prayer to the God of my life. I will say to God my Rock: 'Why have You forgotten me? Why do I go mourning under the oppression of the enemy?' Like a crushing in my bones, my adversaries taunt me; While they say to me all the day: 'Where is Your God?' Why are you cast down, Oh my soul? And why do you moan within me? Hope in God; for I will yet praise Him, The salvation of my countenance, and my God.

Psalms 43

שָׁפְטֵנִי אֱלֹהִים | וְרִיבָה רִיבִי מִגּוֹי לֹא־חָסִיד מֵאִישׁ מִרְמָה וְעַוְלָה
תְפַלְּטֵנִי׃ כִּי־אַתָּה | אֱלֹהֵי מָעוּזִּי לָמָה זְנַחְתָּנִי לָמָּה־קֹדֵר אֶתְהַלֵּךְ
בְּלַחַץ אוֹיֵב׃ שְׁלַח־אוֹרְךָ וַאֲמִתְּךָ הֵמָּה יַנְחוּנִי יְבִיאוּנִי
אֶל־הַר־קָדְשְׁךָ וְאֶל־מִשְׁכְּנוֹתֶיךָ׃ וְאָבוֹאָה | אֶל־מִזְבַּח אֱלֹהִים אֶל־אֵל
שִׂמְחַת גִּילִי וְאוֹדְךָ בְכִנּוֹר אֱלֹהִים אֱלֹהָי׃ מַה־תִּשְׁתּוֹחֲחִי | נַפְשִׁי
וּמַה־תֶּהֱמִי עָלָי הוֹחִילִי לֵאלֹהִים כִּי־עוֹד אוֹדֶנּוּ יְשׁוּעֹת פָּנַי וֵאלֹהָי׃

Shofteni Elohim Verivah Rivi. Migoy Lo-Chasid; Me'ish Mirmah Ve'avlah Tefalleteni. Ki-'Attah Elohei Ma'uzi Lamah Zenachtani Lamah-Koder Et'hallech. Belachatz Oyev. Shelach-'Orecha Va'amitecha Hemah Yanchuni; Yevi'uni El-Har-Kodshecha. Ve'el-Mishkenoteicha. Ve'avo'ah El-Mizbach Elohim. El-'El Simchat Gili Ve'odecha Vechinor. Elohim Elohai. Mah-Tishtochachi Nafshi Umah-Tehemi Alai Hochili Lelohim Ki-'Od Odenu; Yeshu'ot Panai. Velohai.

Be my judge, Oh God, and plead my cause against an ungodly nation; Deliver me from the deceitful and unjust man. For You are the God of my strength; why have You cast me off? Why do I go mourning under the oppression of the enemy? Send out Your light and Your truth; let them lead me; Let them bring me to Your holy mountain, and to Your dwelling-places. Then will I go to the altar of God, to God, my exceeding joy; that I can praise You upon the harp, Oh God, my God. Why are you cast down, Oh my soul? And why do you moan within me? Hope in God; for I will yet praise Him, The salvation of my countenance, and my God.

On days when Tachanun is not recited, this psalm is not recited.

Psalms 20

לַמְנַצֵּחַ מִזְמוֹר לְדָוִד: יַעַנְךָ יְהֹוָה בְּיוֹם צָרָה יְשַׂגֶּבְךָ שֵׁם | אֱלֹהֵי יַעֲקֹב: יִשְׁלַח־עֶזְרְךָ מִקֹּדֶשׁ וּמִצִּיּוֹן יִסְעָדֶךָּ: יִזְכֹּר כָּל־מִנְחֹתֶךָ וְעוֹלָתְךָ יְדַשְּׁנֶה סֶלָה: יִתֶּן־לְךָ כִלְבָבֶךָ וְכָל־עֲצָתְךָ יְמַלֵּא: נְרַנְּנָה | בִּישׁוּעָתֶךָ וּבְשֵׁם־אֱלֹהֵינוּ נִדְגֹּל יְמַלֵּא יְהֹוָה כָּל־מִשְׁאֲלוֹתֶיךָ: עַתָּה יָדַעְתִּי כִּי הוֹשִׁיעַ | יְהֹוָה מְשִׁיחוֹ יַעֲנֵהוּ מִשְּׁמֵי קָדְשׁוֹ בִּגְבֻרוֹת יֵשַׁע יְמִינוֹ: אֵלֶּה בָרֶכֶב וְאֵלֶּה בַסּוּסִים וַאֲנַחְנוּ | בְּשֵׁם־יְהֹוָה אֱלֹהֵינוּ נַזְכִּיר: הֵמָּה כָּרְעוּ וְנָפָלוּ וַאֲנַחְנוּ קַּמְנוּ וַנִּתְעוֹדָד: יְהֹוָה הוֹשִׁיעָה הַמֶּלֶךְ יַעֲנֵנוּ בְיוֹם־קָרְאֵנוּ:

Lamnatzeach. Mizmor Ledavid. Ya'ancha Adonai Beyom Tzarah; Yesagevcha. Shem Elohei Ya'akov. Yishlach-'Ezrecha Mikodesh; Umitziyon. Yis'adeka. Yizkor Chol-Minchotecha; Ve'olatecha Yedasheneh Selah. Yiten-Lecha Chilvavecha; Vechol-'Atzatecha

Yemalle. Neranenah Bishu'atecha. Uveshem-'Eloheinu Nidgol; Yemalei Adonai Chol-Mish'aloteicha. Attah Yada'ti. Ki Hoshia' Adonai Meshicho Ya'anehu Mishemei Kodsho; Bigvurot. Yesha Yemino. Eleh Varechev Ve'eleh Vassusim; Va'anachnu Beshem-Adonai Eloheinu Nazkir. Hemah Kare'u Venafalu; Va'anachnu Kamnu. Vanit'odad. Adonai Hoshi'ah; Hamelech. Ya'aneinu Veyom-Kor'enu.

For the Leader. A Psalm of David. May Hashem answer you in the day of trouble; The name of the God of Yaakov set you up on high; May He send out help from the Sanctuary, And support you out of Tziyon; May He receive the memorial of all your meal-offerings, And accept the fat of your burnt-sacrifice; Selah. May He grant you according to your own heart, And fulfill all your counsel. We will shout for joy in your victory, And in the name of our God we will set up our standards; May Hashem fulfill all of your petitions. Now I know that Hashem saves His anointed; He will answer him from His holy heaven. With the mighty acts of His saving right hand. Some trust in chariots, and some in horses; But we will make mention of the name of Hashem our God. They are bowed down and fallen; But we have risen, and stand upright. Save, Hashem; May the King answer us on the day that we call.

Psalms 24

לְדָוִד מִזְמוֹר לַיהֹוָה הָאָרֶץ וּמְלוֹאָהּ תֵּבֵל וְיֹשְׁבֵי בָהּ: כִּי־הוּא עַל־יַמִּים יְסָדָהּ וְעַל־נְהָרוֹת יְכוֹנְנֶהָ: מִי־יַעֲלֶה בְהַר־יְהֹוָה וּמִי־יָקוּם בִּמְקוֹם קָדְשׁוֹ: נְקִי כַפַּיִם וּבַר־לֵבָב אֲשֶׁר | לֹא־נָשָׂא לַשָּׁוְא נַפְשִׁי וְלֹא נִשְׁבַּע לְמִרְמָה: יִשָּׂא בְרָכָה מֵאֵת יְהֹוָה וּצְדָקָה מֵאֱלֹהֵי יִשְׁעוֹ: זֶה דּוֹר דֹּרְשָׁו מְבַקְשֵׁי פָנֶיךָ יַעֲקֹב סֶלָה: שְׂאוּ שְׁעָרִים | רָאשֵׁיכֶם וְהִנָּשְׂאוּ פִּתְחֵי עוֹלָם וְיָבוֹא מֶלֶךְ הַכָּבוֹד: מִי זֶה מֶלֶךְ הַכָּבוֹד יְהֹוָה עִזּוּז וְגִבּוֹר יְהֹוָה גִּבּוֹר מִלְחָמָה: שְׂאוּ שְׁעָרִים | רָאשֵׁיכֶם וּשְׂאוּ

פִּתְחֵי עוֹלָם וְיָבֹא מֶלֶךְ הַכָּבוֹד׃ מִי הוּא זֶה מֶלֶךְ הַכָּבוֹד יְהֹוָה צְבָאוֹת הוּא מֶלֶךְ הַכָּבוֹד סֶלָה׃

Ledavid. Mizmor L'Adonai Ha'aretz Umelo'ah; Tevel. Veyoshevei Vah. Ki-Hu Al-Yamim Yesadah; Ve'al-Neharot. Yechoneneha. Mi-Ya'aleh Vehar-Adonai Umi-Yakum Bimkom Kodsho. Neki Chapayim. Uvar-Levav Asher Lo-Nasa Lashav Nafshi; Velo Nishba Lemirmah. Yissa Verachah Me'et Adonai Utzedakah. Me'elohei Yish'o. Zeh Dor Doreshav; Mevakshei Faneicha Ya'akov Selah. Se'u She'arim Rasheichem. Vehinase'u Pitchei Olam; Veyavo. Melech Hakavod. Mi Zeh Melech Hakavod Adonai Izuz Vegibor; Adonai Gibor Milchamah. Se'u She'arim Rasheichem. Use'u Pitchei Olam; Veyavo. Melech Hakavod. Mi Hu Zeh Melech Hakavod Adonai Tzeva'ot; Hu Melech Hakavod Selah.

A Psalm of David. The earth is Hashem's, and the fullness of it; The world, and all that dwell there. For He has founded it upon the seas, And established it upon the floods. Who will ascend into the mountain of Hashem? And who will stand in His holy place? He that has clean hands, and a pure heart; Who has not taken My name in vain, And has not sworn deceitfully. He will receive a blessing from Hashem, And righteousness from the God of his salvation. Such is the generation of them that seek after Him, That seek Your face, even Yaakov. Selah. Lift up your heads, you gates, And be lifted up, you everlasting doors; That the King of glory may come in. 'Who is the King of glory?' 'Hashem strong and mighty, Hashem mighty in battle.' Lift up your heads, you gates, yes, lift them up, you everlasting doors; That the King of glory may come in. 'Who then is the King of glory?' 'Hashem of hosts; He is the King of glory.' selah.

Psalms 67

לַמְנַצֵּחַ בִּנְגִינֹת מִזְמוֹר שִׁיר׃ אֱלֹהִים יְחָנֵּנוּ וִיבָרְכֵנוּ יָאֵר פָּנָיו אִתָּנוּ סֶלָה׃ לָדַעַת בָּאָרֶץ דַּרְכֶּךָ בְּכָל־גּוֹיִם יְשׁוּעָתֶךָ׃ יוֹדוּךָ עַמִּים | אֱלֹהִים יוֹדוּךָ עַמִּים כֻּלָּם׃ יִשְׂמְחוּ וִירַנְּנוּ לְאֻמִּים כִּי־תִשְׁפֹּט עַמִּים מִישֹׁר

וּלְאֻמִּים | בָּאָרֶץ תַּנְחֵם סֶלָה: יוֹדוּךָ עַמִּים | אֱלֹהִים יוֹדוּךָ עַמִּים
כֻּלָּם: אֶרֶץ נָתְנָה יְבוּלָהּ יְבָרְכֵנוּ אֱלֹהִים אֱלֹהֵינוּ: יְבָרְכֵנוּ אֱלֹהִים
וְיִירְאוּ אוֹתוֹ כָּל־אַפְסֵי־אָרֶץ:

Lamnatzeach Binginot. Mizmor Shir. Elohim. Yechonenu Vivarecheinu; Ya'er Panav Itanu Selah. Lada'at Ba'aretz Darkecha; Bechol-Goyim. Yeshu'atecha. Yoducha Ammim Elohim; Yoducha. Ammim Kulam. Yismechu Viranenu. Le'ummim Ki-Tishpot Ammim Mishor; Ule'ummim Ba'aretz Tanchem Selah. Yoducha Ammim Elohim; Yoducha. Ammim Kulam. Eretz Natenah Yevulah; Yevarecheinu. Elohim Eloheinu. Yevarecheinu Elohim; Veyire'u Oto. Chol-'Afsei-'Aretz.

For the Leader; with string-music. A Psalm, a Song. May God be gracious to us, and bless us; May He cause His face to shine toward us; Selah. That Your way may be known upon earth, Your salvation among all nations. Let the people give thanks to You, Oh God; Let the peoples give thanks to You, all of them. Let the nations be glad and sing for joy; For You will judge the people with equity, And lead the nations on earth. Selah. Let the people give thanks to You, Oh God; Let the peoples give thanks to You, all of them. The earth has yielded her increase; May God, our own God, bless us. May God bless us; And let all the ends of the earth fear Him.

Psalms 111

הַלְלוּיָהּ | אוֹדֶה יְהֹוָה בְּכָל־לֵבָב בְּסוֹד יְשָׁרִים וְעֵדָה: גְּדֹלִים מַעֲשֵׂי יְהֹוָה
דְּרוּשִׁים לְכָל־חֶפְצֵיהֶם: הוֹד־וְהָדָר פָּעֳלוֹ וְצִדְקָתוֹ עֹמֶדֶת לָעַד: זֵכֶר עָשָׂה
לְנִפְלְאוֹתָיו חַנּוּן וְרַחוּם יְהֹוָה: טֶרֶף נָתַן לִירֵאָיו יִזְכֹּר לְעוֹלָם בְּרִיתוֹ: כֹּחַ
מַעֲשָׂיו הִגִּיד לְעַמּוֹ לָתֵת לָהֶם נַחֲלַת גּוֹיִם: מַעֲשֵׂי יָדָיו אֱמֶת וּמִשְׁפָּט
נֶאֱמָנִים כָּל־פִּקּוּדָיו: סְמוּכִים לָעַד לְעוֹלָם עֲשׂוּיִם בֶּאֱמֶת וְיָשָׁר: פְּדוּת |
שָׁלַח לְעַמּוֹ צִוָּה־לְעוֹלָם בְּרִיתוֹ קָדוֹשׁ וְנוֹרָא שְׁמוֹ: רֵאשִׁית חָכְמָה |
יִרְאַת יְהֹוָה שֵׂכֶל טוֹב לְכָל־עֹשֵׂיהֶם תְּהִלָּתוֹ עֹמֶדֶת לָעַד:

Halleluyah Odeh Adonai Bechol-Levav; Besod Yesharim Ve'edah. Gedolim Ma'asei Adonai Derushim. Lechol-Cheftzeihem. Hod-

Vehadar Po'olo; Vetzidkato. Omedet La'ad. Zecher Asah
Lenifle'otav; Chanun Verachum Adonai Teref Natan Lire'av; Yizkor
Le'olam Berito. Koach Ma'asav Higid Le'ammo; Latet Lahem.
Nachalat Goyim. Ma'asei Yadav Emet Umishpat; Ne'emanim. Chol-
Pikudav. Semuchim La'ad Le'olam; Asuyim. Be'emet Veyashar.
Pedut Shalach Le'ammo. Tzivah-Le'olam Berito; Kadosh Venora
Shemo. Reshit Chochmah Yir'at Adonai Sechel Tov
Lechol-'Oseihem; Tehilato. Omedet La'ad.

Halleluyah. א I will give thanks to Hashem with my whole heart, ב In the council of the upright, and in the congregation. ג The works of Hashem are great, ד Searched out by all of them that have delight in them. ה His work is glory and majesty; ו And His righteousness endures forever. ז He has made a memorial for His wonderful works; ח Hashem is gracious and full of compassion. ט He has given food to them that fear Him; י He will ever be mindful of His covenant. כ He has declared to His people the power of His works, ל In giving them the heritage of the nations. מ The works of His hands are truth and justice; נ All His precepts are sure. ס They are established forever and ever, ע They are done in truth and uprightness. פ He has sent redemption to His people; צ He has commanded His covenant forever; ק Holy and awesome is His name. ר The fear of Hashem is the beginning of wisdom; ש All those that practice it gain good understanding; ת His praise endures forever.

Psalms 51

לַמְנַצֵּ֗חַ מִזְמ֥וֹר לְדָוִֽד׃ בְּֽבוֹא־אֵ֭לָיו נָתָ֣ן הַנָּבִ֑יא כַּאֲשֶׁר־בָּ֝֗א
אֶל־בַּת־שָֽׁבַע׃ חָנֵּ֣נִי אֱלֹהִ֣ים כְּחַסְדֶּ֑ךָ כְּרֹ֥ב רַ֝חֲמֶ֗יךָ מְחֵ֣ה פְשָׁעָֽי׃
הרבה (הֶ֭רֶב) כַּבְּסֵ֣נִי מֵעֲוֺנִ֑י וּֽמֵחַטָּאתִ֥י טַהֲרֵֽנִי׃ כִּֽי־פְ֭שָׁעַי אֲנִ֣י אֵדָ֑ע
וְחַטָּאתִ֖י נֶגְדִּ֣י תָמִֽיד׃ לְךָ֤ לְבַדְּךָ֨ ׀ חָטָאתִי֮ וְהָרַ֥ע בְּעֵינֶ֗יךָ עָ֫שִׂ֥יתִי לְ֭מַעַן
תִּצְדַּ֥ק בְּדָבְרֶ֑ךָ תִּזְכֶּ֥ה בְשָׁפְטֶֽךָ׃ הֵן־בְּעָו֥וֹן חוֹלָ֑לְתִּי וּ֝בְחֵ֗טְא יֶחֱמַ֥תְנִי
אִמִּֽי׃ הֵן־אֱ֭מֶת חָפַ֣צְתָּ בַטֻּח֑וֹת וּ֝בְסָתֻ֗ם חָכְמָ֥ה תוֹדִיעֵֽנִי׃ תְּחַטְּאֵ֣נִי

בְּאֵזוֹב וְאֶטְהָר תְּכַבְּסֵנִי וּמִשֶּׁלֶג אַלְבִּין: תַּשְׁמִיעֵנִי שָׂשׂוֹן וְשִׂמְחָה תָּגֵלְנָה עֲצָמוֹת דִּכִּיתָ: הַסְתֵּר פָּנֶיךָ מֵחֲטָאָי וְכָל־עֲוֹנֹתַי מְחֵה: לֵב טָהוֹר בְּרָא־לִי אֱלֹהִים וְרוּחַ נָכוֹן חַדֵּשׁ בְּקִרְבִּי: אַל־תַּשְׁלִיכֵנִי מִלְּפָנֶיךָ וְרוּחַ קָדְשְׁךָ אַל־תִּקַּח מִמֶּנִּי: הָשִׁיבָה לִּי שְׂשׂוֹן יִשְׁעֶךָ וְרוּחַ נְדִיבָה תִסְמְכֵנִי: אֲלַמְּדָה פֹשְׁעִים דְּרָכֶיךָ וְחַטָּאִים אֵלֶיךָ יָשׁוּבוּ: הַצִּילֵנִי מִדָּמִים | אֱלֹהִים אֱלֹהֵי תְּשׁוּעָתִי תְּרַנֵּן לְשׁוֹנִי צִדְקָתֶךָ: אֲדֹנָי שְׂפָתַי תִּפְתָּח וּפִי יַגִּיד תְּהִלָּתֶךָ: כִּי | לֹא־תַחְפֹּץ זֶבַח וְאֶתֵּנָה עוֹלָה לֹא תִרְצֶה: זִבְחֵי אֱלֹהִים רוּחַ נִשְׁבָּרָה לֵב־נִשְׁבָּר וְנִדְכֶּה אֱלֹהִים לֹא תִבְזֶה: הֵיטִיבָה בִרְצוֹנְךָ אֶת־צִיּוֹן תִּבְנֶה חוֹמוֹת יְרוּשָׁלָםִ: אָז תַּחְפֹּץ זִבְחֵי־צֶדֶק עוֹלָה וְכָלִיל אָז יַעֲלוּ עַל־מִזְבַּחֲךָ פָרִים:

Lamnatzeach. Mizmor Ledavid. Bevo-'Elav Natan Hanavi; Ka'asher-Ba El-Bat-Shava. Choneni Elohim Kechasdecha; Kerov Rachameicha. Mecheh Fesha'ai. Herev Kabeseni Me'avni; Umechatati Tahareni. Ki-Fesha'ai Ani Eda'; Vechatati Negdi Tamid. Lecha Levadecha Chatati Vehara Be'eineicha. Asiti Lema'an Titzdak Bedovrecha. Tizkeh Veshoftecha. Hen-Be'avon Cholaleti; Uvechet. Yechematni Immi. Hen-'Emet Chafatzta Vatuchot; Uvesatum. Chochmah Todi'eni. Techate'eni Ve'ezov Ve'et'har; Techabeseni. Umisheleg Albin. Tashmi'eni Sason Vesimchah; Tagelenah. Atzamot Dikkita. Haster Paneicha Mechata'ai; Vechol-Avonotai Mecheh. Lev Tahor Bera-Li Elohim; Veruach Nachon. Chadesh Bekirbi. Al-Tashlicheini Milfaneicha; Veruach Kodshecha. Al-Tikach Mimeni. Hashivah Li Seson Yish'echa; Veruach Nedivah Tismecheini. Alamedah Foshe'im Deracheicha; Vechata'im. Eleicha Yashuvu. Hatzileini Middamim Elohim. Elohei Teshu'ati; Teranen Leshoni. Tzidkatecha. Adonai Sefatai Tiftach; Ufi. Yagid Tehilatecha. Ki Lo-Tachpotz Zevach Ve'ettenah; Olah. Lo Tirtzeh. Zivchei Elohim Ruach Nishbarah Lev-Nishbar Venidkeh; Elohim. Lo Tivzeh. Heitivah Virtzonecha Et-Tziyon; Tivneh. Chomot Yerushalayim. Az Tachpotz Zivchei-Tzedek Olah Vechalil; Az Ya'alu Al-Mizbachacha Farim.

For the Leader. A Psalm of David; when Natan the prophet came to him, after he had gone in to Batshava. Be gracious to me, Oh God, according to Your mercy; According to the multitude of Your compassions blot out my transgressions. Wash me thoroughly from my iniquity, And cleanse me from my sin. For I know my transgressions; And my sin is ever before me. Against You, You only, have I sinned, And done that which is evil in Your sight; That You may be justified when You speak, And be in the right when You judge. Behold, I was born in iniquity, And in sin did my mother conceive me. Behold, You desire truth in the inward parts; Make me then, to know wisdom in my inmost heart. Purge me with hyssop, and I will be clean; Wash me, and I will be whiter than snow. Make me to hear joy and gladness; That the bones which You have crushed may rejoice. Hide Your face from my sins, And blot out all of my iniquities. Create me a clean heart, Oh God; And renew a steadfast spirit within me. Do not cast me away from Your presence; And do not take Your holy spirit from me. Restore to me the joy of Your salvation; And let a willing spirit uphold me. Then I will teach transgressors Your ways; And sinners will return to You. Deliver me from bloodguilt, Oh God, God of my salvation; So my tongue will sing loudly of Your righteousness. Hashem, open my lips; And my mouth will declare Your praise. For You don't delight in sacrifice, or else I would give it; You have no pleasure in burnt-offering. The sacrifices of God are a broken spirit; A broken and a contrite heart, God, You will not despise. Do good in Your favor to Tziyon; Build the walls of Yerushalayim. Then You will delight in the sacrifices of righteousness, in burnt-offering and whole offering; Then they will offer bulls on Your Altar.

On a day that Tachanun is recited, one should say:

Ad Anah Bichyah Betziyon	עַד אָנָה בִּכְיָה בְּצִיּוֹן
Umisped Birushalayim. Takum	וּמִסְפֵּד בִּירוּשָׁלָיִם: תָקוּם
Terachem Tziyon. Tivneh Chomot	תְּרַחֵם צִיּוֹן. תִּבְנֶה חוֹמוֹת
Yerushalayim.	יְרוּשָׁלָיִם:

Until Anna wept in Zion and mourned in Yerushalayim. Arise, and have compassion upon Tziyon, build the walls of Yerushalayim. **(Ps. 102:14, 51:20)**

אֱלֹהֵינוּ וֵאלֹהֵי אֲבוֹתֵינוּ. מֶלֶךְ רַחֲמָן רַחֵם עָלֵינוּ. טוֹב וּמֵטִיב הִדָּרֶשׁ לָנוּ. שׁוּבָה עָלֵינוּ בַּהֲמוֹן רַחֲמֶיךָ. בִּגְלַל אָבוֹת שֶׁעָשׂוּ רְצוֹנֶךָ. בְּנֵה בֵיתְךָ כְּבַתְּחִלָּה. כּוֹנֵן בֵּית מִקְדָּשְׁךָ עַל מְכוֹנוֹ. הַרְאֵנוּ בְּבִנְיָנוֹ. שַׂמְּחֵנוּ בְּתִקּוּנוֹ. וְהָשֵׁב שְׁכִינָתְךָ לְתוֹכוֹ. וְהָשֵׁב כֹּהֲנִים לַעֲבוֹדָתָם. וּלְוִיִּים לְדוּכָנָם. לְשִׁירָם וּלְזִמְרָם. וְהָשֵׁב יִשְׂרָאֵל לִנְוֵיהֶם. וְשָׁם נַעֲלֶה וְנֵרָאֶה וְנִשְׁתַּחֲוֶה לְפָנֶיךָ: יְהִי רָצוֹן מִלְּפָנֶיךָ יְהֹוָה אֱלֹהֵינוּ וֵאלֹהֵי אֲבֹתֵינוּ. שֶׁתַּעֲלֵנוּ בְשִׂמְחָה לְאַרְצֵנוּ. וְתִטָּעֵנוּ בִּגְבוּלֵנוּ. וְשָׁם נַעֲשֶׂה לְפָנֶיךָ אֶת קָרְבְּנוֹת חוֹבֹתֵינוּ. תְּמִידִים כְּסִדְרָם וּמוּסָפִים כְּהִלְכָתָם:

Eloheinu Velohei Avoteinu. Melech Rachaman Rachem Aleinu. Tov Umeitiv Hiddaresh Lanu. Shuvah Aleinu Bahamon Rachameicha. Biglal Avot She'asu Retzonecha. Beneh Veitecha Kvatechillah. Konen Beit Mikdashecha Al Mechono. Har'enu Bevinyano. Samecheinu Betikuno. Vehasheiv Shechinatecha Letocho. Vehasheiv Kohanim La'avodatam. Uleviyim Leduchanam. Leshiram Ulezimram. Vehasheiv Yisra'el Linveihem. Vesham Na'aleh Venera'eh Venishtachaveh Lefaneicha. Yehi Ratzon Milfaneicha Adonai Eloheinu Velohei Avoteinu. Sheta'alenu Besimchah Le'artzenu. Vetita'enu Bigvulenu. Vesham Na'aseh Lefaneicha Et Karebenot Chovoteinu. Temidim Kesidram Umusafim Kehilchatam.

Our God and God of our fathers, merciful King, have mercy upon us, Oh Good and Beneficent One, allow Yourself to be sought by us; return to us in Your yearning compassion for the fathers' sake who did Your will; rebuild Your House as at the beginning, and establish Your Sanctuary on its site; grant that we may see it in its rebuilding, and make us rejoice in its re-establishment; restore the priests to their service, the Levites to their song and music, and Yisrael to their habitations: and there we will go up to appear and prostrate ourselves before You. May it be Your will Hashem our God and God of our fathers, to bring us up in joy to our land, and to place us within our borders. There we will offer before You our obligatory sacrifices the daily-offerings in their prescription, and the Musaf-offerings according to their laws.

Psalms 126

שִׁ֗יר הַֽמַּ֫עֲל֥וֹת בְּשׁ֣וּב יְ֭הֹוָה אֶת־שִׁיבַ֣ת צִיּ֑וֹן הָ֝יִ֗ינוּ כְּחֹלְמִֽים: אָ֤ז יִמָּ֪לֵ֬א
שְׂח֡וֹק פִּינוּ֮ וּלְשׁוֹנֵ֪נוּ רִ֫נָּ֥ה אָ֭ז יֹאמְר֣וּ בַגּוֹיִ֑ם הִגְדִּ֥יל יְ֝הֹוָ֗ה לַעֲשׂ֥וֹת
עִם־אֵֽלֶּה: הִגְדִּ֣יל יְ֭הֹוָה לַעֲשׂ֣וֹת עִמָּ֑נוּ הָיִ֥ינוּ שְׂמֵחִֽים: שׁוּבָ֣ה יְ֭הֹוָה
אֶת־(שְׁבִיתֵ֑נוּ) שבותנו כַּאֲפִיקִ֥ים בַּנֶּֽגֶב: הַזֹּרְעִ֥ים בְּדִמְעָ֗ה בְּרִנָּ֥ה
יִקְצֹֽרוּ: הָ֘ל֤וֹךְ יֵלֵ֨ךְ ׀ וּבָכֹה֮ נֹשֵׂ֪א מֶשֶׁךְ־הַ֫זָּ֥רַע בֹּֽא־יָבֹ֥א בְרִנָּ֑ה נֹ֝שֵׂ֗א
אֲלֻמֹּתָֽיו:

Shir Hama'alot Beshuv Adonai Et-Shivat Tziyon; Hayinu. Kecholemim. Az Yimmalei Sechok Pinu Uleshonenu Rinah Az Yomeru Vagoyim; Higdil Adonai La'asot Im-'Eleh. Higdil Adonai La'asot Imanu. Hayinu Semechim. Shuvah Adonai Et-Sheviteinu Ka'afikim Banegev. Hazore'im Bedim'ah. Berinah Yiktzoru. Haloch Yelech Uvachoh Nosei Meshech-Hazara Bo-Yavo Verinah; Noseh. Alummotav.

A Song of Ascents. When Hashem brought back those that returned to Tziyon. We were to them like a dream. Then our mouth was filled with laughter, And our tongue with singing; Then said they among the nations: 'Hashem has done great things with these.' Hashem has done great things with us; We will rejoice. Turn our captivity, Hashem, As the streams in the dry land. They that sow in tears will reap in joy. Though he goes on his way weeping, that bears the measure of seed, He will come home with joy, bearing his sheaves.

Patach Eliyahu

Some recite Patach Eliyahu before prayer for reception of prayer.

וִיהִי | נֹעַם אֲדֹנָי אֱלֹהֵינוּ עָלֵינוּ וּמַעֲשֵׂה יָדֵינוּ כּוֹנְנָה עָלֵינוּ וּמַעֲשֵׂה יָדֵינוּ כּוֹנְנֵהוּ:

Vihi No'am Adonai Eloheinu. Aleinu Uma'aseh Yadeinu Konenah Aleinu; Uma'aseh Yadeinu. Konenehu.

And may the graciousness of Hashem our God be on us; Establish also upon us the work of our hands; and the work of our hands, establish it.

Tikunei Zohar 17a

פָּתַח אֵלִיָּהוּ הַנָּבִיא זָכוּר לְטוֹב וְאָמַר רִבּוֹן עָלְמִין דְּאַנְתְּ הוּא חָד וְלָא בְחֻשְׁבָּן. אַנְתְּ הוּא עִלָּאָה עַל כָּל עִלָּאִין סְתִימָא עַל כָּל סְתִימִין. לֵית מַחֲשָׁבָה תְּפִיסָא בָךְ כְּלָל: אַנְתְּ הוּא דְּאַפַּקְתְּ עֶשֶׂר תִּקּוּנִין וְקָרֵינָן לוֹן עֶשֶׂר סְפִירָן. לְאַנְהָגָא בְהוֹן עָלְמִין סְתִימִין דְּלָא אִתְגַּלְיָן וְעָלְמִין דְּאִתְגַּלְיָן. וּבְהוֹן אִתְכַּסִּיאַת מִבְּנֵי נָשָׁא. וְאַנְתְּ הוּא דְּקָשִׁיר לוֹן וּמְיַחֵד לוֹן: וּבְגִין דְּאַנְתְּ מִלְּגָאו. כָּל מָאן דְּאַפְרִישׁ חַד מִן חַבְרֵיהּ מֵאִלֵּין עֶשֶׂר אִתְחַשִׁיב לֵיהּ כְּאִלּוּ אַפְרִישׁ בָּךְ:

Patach Eliyahu Hanavi Zachur Letov Ve'amar. Ribon Alemin De'ant Hu Chad Vela Bechushban. Ant Hu Illa'ah Al-Kol-'Illa'in Setima Al-Kol-Setimin. Leit Machashavah Tefisa Vach Kelal. Ant Hu De'apakt Eser Tikunin Vekareinan Lon Eser Sefiran. Le'anhaga Vehon Alemin Setimin Dela Itgalyan Ve'alemin De'itgalyan. Uvehon Itkassi'at Mibenei Nasha. Ve'ant Hu Dekashir Lon Umeyached Lon. Uvegin De'ant Millegav. Kol-Man De'afrish Chad Min Chavreih Me'ilein Eser Itchashiv Leih Ke'ilu Afrish Bach.

וְאִלֵּין עֶשֶׂר סְפִירָן אִנּוּן אָזְלִין כְּסִדְרָן. חַד אָרִיךְ וְחַד קָצֵר וְחַד בֵּינוֹנִי: וְאַנְתְּ הוּא דְּאַנְהִיג לוֹן. וְלֵית מָאן דְּאַנְהִיג לָךְ. לָא לְעֵלָּא וְלָא לְתַתָּא וְלָא מִכָּל סִטְרָא. לְבוּשִׁין תַּקַּנְתְּ לוֹן דְּמִנַּיְהוּ פָּרְחִין נִשְׁמָתִין לִבְנֵי נָשָׁא: וְכַמָּה גוּפִין תַּקַּנְתְּ לוֹן דְּאִתְקְרִיאוּ גוּפָא לְגַבֵּי לְבוּשִׁין דִּמְכַסְּיָן עֲלֵיהוֹן: וְאִתְקְרִיאוּ בְּתִקּוּנָא דָא. חֶסֶד דְּרוֹעָא יְמִינָא. גְּבוּרָה דְּרוֹעָא שְׂמָאלָא. תִּפְאֶרֶת גּוּפָא. נֶצַח וְהוֹד תְּרֵין שׁוֹקִין. יְסוֹד סִיּוּמָא דְגוּפָא אוֹת בְּרִית קוֹדֶשׁ. מַלְכוּת פֶּה תּוֹרָה שֶׁבְּעַל פֶּה קָרֵינָן לָהּ. חָכְמָה מוֹחָא אִיהִי מַחֲשָׁבָה מִלְּגָאו. בִּינָה לִבָּא וּבָהּ הַלֵּב מֵבִין. וְעַל אִלֵּין תְּרֵין כְּתִיב הַנִּסְתָּרֹת לַיהוָה אֱלֹהֵינוּ. כֶּתֶר עֶלְיוֹן אִיהוּ כֶּתֶר מַלְכוּת. וְעָלֵיהּ אִתְּמַר מַגִּיד מֵרֵאשִׁית אַחֲרִית. וְאִיהוּ קַרְקַפְתָּא דִתְפִלֵּי.

מִלְּגָאו אִיהוּ יו״ד ה״א וא״ו ה״א דְּאִיהוּ אֹרַח אֲצִילוּת. אִיהוּ שַׁקְיוּ דְאִילָנָא
בִּדְרוֹעוֹי וְעַנְפּוֹי. כְּמַיָּא דְאַשְׁקֵי לְאִילָנָא וְאִתְרַבֵּי בְּהַהוּא שַׁקְיוּ:

Ve'ilein Eser Sefiran Inun Azelin Kesidran. Chad Arich Vechad Katzer Vechad Beinoni. Ve'ant Hu De'anhig Lon. Veleit Man De'anhig Lach. La Le'ella Vela Letatta Vela Mikol-Sitra. Levushin Takkant Lon Deminayhu Farechin Nishmatin Livnei Nasha. Vechamah Gufin Takkant Lon De'itkeri'u Gufa Legabei Levushin Dimchasyan Aleihon. Ve'itkeri'u Betikuna Da. Chesed Dero'a Yemina. Gevurah Dero'a Semala. Tif'eret Gufa. Netzach Vehod Terein Shokin. Yesod Siyuma Degufa Ot Berit Kodesh. Malchut Peh Torah Shebe'al-Peh Kareinon Lah. Chochmah Mocha Ihi Machashavah Millegav. Binah Liba Uvah Hallev Mevin. Ve'al Ilein Terein Ketiv Hanistarot. L'Adonai Eloheinu;. Keter Elyon Ihu Keter Malchut. Ve'aleih Itmar Maggid Mereshit Acharit. Ve'ihu Karkafta Ditfillei. Millegav Ihu Yo"D He" Va"V He" De'ihu Orach Atzilut. Ihu Shakyu De'ilana Bidro'oy Ve'anpoy. Kemaya De'ashkei Le'ilana Ve'itrabei Behahu Shakyu.

רִבּוֹן עָלְמִין אַנְתְּ הוּא עִלַּת הָעִלּוֹת וְסִבַּת הַסִּבּוֹת דְּאַשְׁקֵי לְאִילָנָא בְּהַהוּא
נְבִיעוּ. וְהַהוּא נְבִיעוּ אִיהוּ כְּנִשְׁמְתָא לְגוּפָא דְּאִיהִי חַיִּים לְגוּפָא: וּבָךְ לֵית
דִּמְיוֹן וְלֵית דִּיוּקְנָא (דְגוּפָא) מִכָּל מַה דִּלְגָאו וּלְבַר. וּבָרָאתָ שְׁמַיָּא וְאַרְעָא.
וְאַפַּקְתְּ מִנְּהוֹן שִׁמְשָׁא וְסִיהֲרָא וְכוֹכְבַיָּא וּמַזָּלֵי. וּבְאַרְעָא אִילָנִין וְדִשְׁאִין
וְגִנְּתָא דְעֵדֶן וְעִשְׂבִּין וְחֵיוָן וְעוֹפִין וְנוּנִין וּבְעִירִין וּבְנֵי נָשָׁא. לְאִשְׁתְּמוֹדְעָא בְהוֹן
עִלָּאִין וְאֵיךְ יִתְנַהֲגוּן בְּהוֹן עִלָּאִין וְתַתָּאִין. וְאֵיךְ אִשְׁתְּמוֹדְעָן מֵעִלָּאֵי וְתַתָּאֵי
וְלֵית דְּיָדַע בָּךְ כְּלָל. וּבַר מִנָּךְ לֵית יְחוּדָא בְּעִלָּאֵי וְתַתָּאֵי. וְאַנְתְּ אִשְׁתְּמוֹדַע
אָדוֹן עַל כֹּלָּא: וְכָל סְפִירָן כָּל חַד אִית לֵיהּ שֵׁם יְדִיעַ. וּבְהוֹן אִתְקְרִיאוּ
מַלְאֲכַיָּא. וְאַנְתְּ לֵית לָךְ שֵׁם יְדִיעַ. דְּאַנְתְּ הוּא מְמַלֵּא כָּל שְׁמָהָן וְאַנְתְּ הוּא
שְׁלִימוּ דְּכֻלְּהוּ: וְכַד אַנְתְּ תִּסְתַּלָּק מִנְּהוֹן. אִשְׁתְּאָרוּ כֻּלְּהוּ שְׁמָהָן כְּגוּפָא בְּלָא
נִשְׁמָתָא: אַנְתְּ הוּא חַכִּים וְלָאו בְּחָכְמָה יְדִיעָא. אַנְתְּ הוּא מֵבִין וְלָאו מִבִּינָה
יְדִיעָא. לֵית לָךְ אֲתַר יְדִיעָא. אֶלָּא לְאִשְׁתְּמוֹדְעָא תְּקְפָךְ וְחֵילָךְ לִבְנֵי נָשָׁא.
וּלְאַחֲזָאָה לוֹן אֵיךְ אִתְנְהִיג עָלְמָא בְּדִינָא וּבְרַחֲמֵי דְּאִנּוּן צֶדֶק וּמִשְׁפָּט כְּפוּם
עוֹבָדֵיהוֹן דִּבְנֵי נָשָׁא: דִּין אִיהוּ גְבוּרָה. מִשְׁפָּט עַמּוּדָא דְאֶמְצָעִיתָא. צֶדֶק
מַלְכוּתָא קַדִּישָׁא. מֹאזְנֵי צֶדֶק תְּרֵין סַמְכֵי קְשׁוֹט. הִין צֶדֶק אוֹת בְּרִית. כֹּלָּא
לְאַחֲזָאָה אֵיךְ אִתְנְהִיג עָלְמָא: אֲבָל לָאו דְּאִית לָךְ צֶדֶק יְדִיעָא דְּאִיהוּ דִין.
וְלָאו מִשְׁפָּט יְדִיעָא דְּאִיהוּ רַחֲמֵי. וְלָאו מִכָּל אִלֵּין מִדּוֹת כְּלָל: קוּם רִבִּי
שִׁמְעוֹן וְיִתְחַדְּשׁוּן מִלִּין עַל יְדָךְ. דְּהָא רְשׁוּתָא אִית לָךְ לְגַלָּאָה רָזִין טְמִירִין
עַל יְדָךְ. מַה דְּלָא אִתְיְהִיב רְשׁוּ לְגַלָּאָה לְשׁוּם בַּר נַשׁ עַד כְּעַן:

Ribon Alemin Ant Hu Ilat Ha'ilot Vesibat Hassibot De'ashkei Le'ilana Behahu Nevi'u. Vehahu Nevi'u Ihu Kenishmeta Legufa De'ihi Chayim Legufa. Uvach Leit Dimyon Veleit Diyukena (Degufa) Mikol Mah Dilgav Ulevar. Uvarata Shemaya Ve'ar'a. Ve'apakt Minehon Shimsha Vesihara Vechochevaya Umazalei. Uve'ar'a

Ilanin Udesha'in Vegineta De'eden Ve'isbin Vecheivan Ve'ofin Venunin Uve'irin Uvenei Nasha. Le'ishtemode'a Vehon Illa'in Ve'eich Yitnahagun Behon Illa'in Vetatta'in. Ve'eich Ishtemode'an Me'illa'ei Vetatta'ei Veleit Deyada Bach Kelal. Uvar Minach Leit Yichuda Be'illa'ei Vetatta'ei. Ve'ant Ishtemoda Adon Al-Kolla. Vechol-Sefiran Kol-Chad It Leih Shem Yedia. Uvehon Itkeri'u Mal'achaya. Ve'ant Leit Lach Shem Yedia. De'ant Hu Memallei Kol Shemahan Ve'ant Hu Shelimu Dechulehu. Vechad Ant Tistallak Minehon. Ishte'aru Kullehu Shemahan Kegufa Vela Nishmata. Ant Hu Chakkim Velav Bechochmah Yedi'a. Ant Hu Mevin Velav Mibinah Yedi'a. Leit Lach Atar Yedi'a. Ella Le'ishtemode'a Tukfach Vecheilach Livnei Nasha. Ule'achza'ah Lon Eich Itnehig Alema Bedina Uverachamei De'inun Tzedek Umishpat Kefum Ovadeihon Divnei Nasha. Din Ihu Gevurah. Mishpat Ammuda De'emtza'ita. Tzedek Malchuta Kaddisha. Mozenei Tzedek Terein Samchei Keshot. Hin Tzedek Ot Berit. Kolla Le'achza'ah Eich Itnehig Alema. Aval Lav De'it Lach Tzedek Yedi'a De'ihu Din. Velav Mishpat Yedi'a De'ihu Rachamei. Velav Mikol 'Ilein Middot Kelal. Kum Ribi Shim'on Veyitchadeshun Millin Al Yedach. Deha Reshuta It Lach Legalla'ah Razin Temirin Al Yedach. Mah Dela Ityehiv Reshu Legalla'ah Lasum Bar-Nash Ad Ke'An.

קָם רַבִּי שִׁמְעוֹן פָּתַח וְאָמַר. לְךָ יְהֹוָה הַגְּדֻלָּה וְהַגְּבוּרָה וְהַתִּפְאֶרֶת וְהַנֵּצַח וְהַהוֹד כִּי כֹל בַּשָּׁמַיִם וּבָאָרֶץ לְךָ יְהֹוָה הַמַּמְלָכָה וְהַמִּתְנַשֵּׂא לְכֹל לְרֹאשׁ. עִלָּאִין שִׁמְעוּ אִינּוּן דְּמִיכִין דְּחֶבְרוֹן. וְרַעְיָא מְהֵימְנָא אִתְּעָרוּ מִשְּׁנַתְכוֹן. הָקִיצוּ וְרַנְּנוּ שׁוֹכְנֵי עָפָר. אִלֵּין אִינּוּן צַדִּיקַיָּא דְּאִינּוּן מִסִּטְרָא דְּהַהִיא דְּאִתְּמַר בָּהּ אֲנִי יְשֵׁנָה וְלִבִּי עֵר. וְלָאו אִינּוּן מֵתִים. וּבְגִין דָּא אִתְּמַר בְּהוֹן הָקִיצוּ וְרַנְּנוּ וכו'. רַעְיָא מְהֵימְנָא. אַנְתְּ וַאֲבָהָן הָקִיצוּ וְרַנְּנוּ לְאִתְּעָרוּתָא דִּשְׁכִינְתָּא. דְּאִיהִי יְשֵׁנָה בְּגָלוּתָא. דְּעַד כְּעַן צַדִּיקַיָּא כֻּלְּהוּ דְּמִיכִין וְשִׁנְתָּא בְּחוֹרֵיהוֹן: מִיַּד יְהִיבַת שְׁכִינְתָּא תְּלַת קָלִין לְגַבֵּי רַעְיָא מְהֵימְנָא. וְיֵימָא לֵיהּ קוּם רַעְיָא מְהֵימְנָא. דְּהָא עֲלָךְ אִתְּמַר קוֹל דּוֹדִי דוֹפֵק לְגַבָּאי בְּאַרְבַּע אַתְוָן דִּילֵיהּ. וְיֵימָא בְּהוֹן. פִּתְחִי לִי אֲחֹתִי רַעְיָתִי יוֹנָתִי תַמָּתִי. דְּהָא תַּם עֲוֹנֵךְ בַּת צִיּוֹן. לֹא יוֹסִיף לְהַגְלוֹתֵךְ: שֶׁרֹּאשִׁי נִמְלָא טָל. מַאי נִמְלָא טָל. אֶלָּא אָמַר קוּדְשָׁא בְּרִיךְ הוּא. אַנְתְּ חֲשַׁבְתְּ דְּמִיּוֹמָא דְּאִתְחֲרַב בֵּי מַקְדְּשָׁא דְּעָאלְנָא בְּבֵיתָא דִּילִי. וְעָאלְנָא בְּיִשּׁוּבָא. לָאו הָכִי. דְּלָא עָאלְנָא כָּל זִמְנָא דְּאַנְתְּ בְּגָלוּתָא. הֲרֵי לָךְ סִימָנָא. שֶׁרֹּאשִׁי נִמְלָא טָל ה"א שְׁכִינְתָּא בְּגָלוּתָא. שְׁלִימוּ דִּילָהּ וְחַיִּים דִּילָהּ אִיהוּ טַ"ל. וְדָא אִיהוּ יו"ד ה"א וא"ו וה"א אִיהִי שְׁכִינְתָּא דְּלָא מֵחֻשְׁבַּן טַ"ל. אֶלָּא יו"ד ה"א וא"ו. דִּסְלִיקוּ אַתְוָן לְחֻשְׁבַּן טַ"ל. דְּאִיהִי מַלְיָא לִשְׁכִינְתָּא מִנַּבִּיעוּ דְּכָל מְקוֹרִין עִלָּאִין. מִיַּד קָם רַעְיָא מְהֵימְנָא. וַאֲבָהָן קַדִּישִׁין עִמֵּיהּ. עַד כָּאן רָזָא דְּיִחוּדָא. בָּרוּךְ יְהֹוָה לְעוֹלָם אָמֵן וְאָמֵן:

Kam Rabbi Shim'on Patach Ve'amar. Lecha Adonai Hagedullah Vehagevurah Vehatif'eret Vehanetzach Vehahod Ki Chol Bashamayim Uva'aretz Lecha Adonai Hamamlachah Vehamitnasse Lechol Lerosh. Illa'in Shim'u Inun Demichin Dechevron. Vera'ya Meheimna Itte'aru Mishenatchon. Hakitzu Veranenu Shochenei

Afar. Ilein Inun Tzaddikaya De'inun Missitra Dehahi De'itmar Bah Ani Yeshenah Velibi Er. Velav Inun Meitim. Uvegin Da Itmar Behon Hakitzu Veranenu Vechu'. Ra'ya Meheimna. Ant Va'avahan Hakitzu Veranenu Le'itte'aruta Dishchinta. De'ihi Yeshenah Begaluta. De'ad Ke'an Tzaddikaya Kullehu Demichin Veshinta Bechoreihon: Miyad Yehivat Shechinta Telat Kalin Legabei Ra'ya Meheimna. Veyeima Leih Kum Ra'ya Meheimna, Deha Alach Itmar Kol Dodi Dofek Legaba Be'arba Atvan Dileih. Veyeima Behon. Pitchi Li Achoti Ra'yati Yonati Tammati. Deha Tam Avonech Bat Tziyon. Lo Yosif Lehaglotech: Sheroshi Nimla Tal. Ma Nimla Tal. Ella Amar Kudesha Berich Hu. Ant Chashavt Demiyoma De'itcharav Bei Makdesha De'alna Beveita Dili. Ve'alna Veyishuva. Lav Hachi. Dela Alna Kol Zimna De'ant Begaluta. Harei Lecha Simana. Sheroshi Nimla Tal He" Shechinta Begaluta. Shelimu Dilah Vechayim Dilah Ihu Ta"L. Veda Ihu Yo"D He" Va"V VeHe" Ihi Shechinta Dela Mechushban Ta"L. Ella Yo"D He" Va"V. Disliku Atvan Lechushban Ta"L. De'ihi Malya Lishchinta Minevi'u Dechol Mekorin Illa'in. Miyad Kam Ra'ya Meheimna. Va'avahan Kaddishin Immeih. Ad Kan Raza Deyichuda. Baruch Adonai Le'olam Amen Ve'Amen:

יְהֵא רַעֲוָא מִן קֳדָם עַתִּיקָא קַדִּישָׁא דְכָל קַדִּישִׁין טְמִירָא דְכָל טְמִירִין סְתִימָא דְכֹלָּא. דְּיִתְמְשַׁךְ טַלָּא עִלָּאָה מִנֵּיהּ לְמַלְיָא רֵישֵׁיהּ דִּזְעֵיר אַנְפִּין. וּלְהַטִּיל לַחֲקַל תַּפּוּחִין קַדִּישִׁין בִּנְהִירוּ דְּאַנְפִּין בְּרַעֲוָא וּבְחֶדְוָתָא דְכֹלָּא. וְיִתְמְשַׁךְ מִן קֳדָם עַתִּיקָא קַדִּישָׁא דְכָל קַדִּישִׁין טְמִירָא דְכָל טְמִירִין סְתִימָא דְכֹלָּא רְעוּתָא וְרַחֲמֵי חִנָּא וְחִסְדָּא בִּנְהִירוּ עִלָּאָה בִּרְעוּתָא וְחֶדְוָא עָלַי וְעַל כָּל בְּנֵי בֵיתִי וְעַל כָּל הַנִּלְוִים אֵלַי וְעַל כָּל יִשְׂרָאֵל עַמֵּיהּ. וְיִפְרְקִינָן מִכָּל עַקְתִין בִּישִׁין דְּיֵיתוּן לְעָלְמָא וְיַזְמִין וְיִתְיְהִיב לָנָא וּלְכָל נַפְשָׁתָנָא חִנָּא וְחִסְדָּא וְחַיֵּי אֲרִיכֵי וּמְזוֹנֵי רְוִיחֵי וְרַחֲמֵי מִן קֳדָמֵיהּ. אָמֵן כֵּן יְהִי רָצוֹן אָמֵן וְאָמֵן:

Yehei Ra'ava Min Kodam Atika Kaddisha Dechal Kaddishin Temira Dechol Temirin Setima Decholla Deyitmeshach Talla Illa'ah Mineih Lemalya Reisheih Diz'eir Anpin. Ulehatil Lachakal Tappuchin Kaddishin Binhiru De'anpin Bera'ava Uvechedvata Decholla. Veyitmeshach Min Kodam Atika Kaddisha Dechal-Kaddishin Temira Dechal-Temirin Setima Dechola Re'uta Verachamei China Vechisda Binhiru Illa'ah Bir'uta Vechedva Alai Ve'al-Kol-Benei Veiti Ve'al Kol Hanilvim Elai Ve'al-Kol-Yisrael Ammeih. Veyifrekinan Mikol-'Aktin Bishin Deyeitun Le'alema Veyazmin Veyityehiv Lana Ulechol-Nafshatana China Vechisda Vechayei Arichei Umezonei Revichei Verachamei Min Kodameih. Amen Ken Yehi Ratzon Amen Ve'amen.

Adon Olam

אֲדוֹן עוֹלָם אֲשֶׁר מָלַךְ. בְּטֶרֶם כָּל יְצִיר נִבְרָא:

Adon Olam Asher Malach. Beterem Kol Yetzir Nivra.

Lord over all, Who has ruled forever. Even before first Creation's wondrous form was framed.

לְעֵת נַעֲשָׂה בְחֶפְצוֹ כֹּל. אֲזַי מֶלֶךְ שְׁמוֹ נִקְרָא:

Le'et Na'asah Vecheftzo Chol. Azai Melech Shemo Nikra.

When by His Divine will all things were made; Then, Almighty King, was His name proclaimed.

וְאַחֲרֵי כִּכְלוֹת הַכֹּל. לְבַדּוֹ יִמְלֹךְ נוֹרָא:

Ve'acharei Kichlot Hakol. Levado Yimloch Nora.

And after all will cease. In awesome greatness, He alone will reign.

וְהוּא הָיָה וְהוּא הֹוֶה. וְהוּא יִהְיֶה בְּתִפְאָרָה:

Vehu Hayah Vehu Hoveh. Vehu Yihyeh Betif'arah.

Who was, Who is, and Who will forever be, in splendor.

וְהוּא אֶחָד וְאֵין שֵׁנִי. לְהַמְשִׁיל לוֹ לְהַחְבִּירָה:

Vehu Echad Ve'ein Sheni. Lehamshil Lo Lehachbirah.

He is One, unequalled, and beyond compare. Without division or associate.

בְּלִי רֵאשִׁית בְּלִי תַכְלִית. וְלוֹ הָעֹז וְהַמִּשְׂרָה:

Beli Reshit Beli Tachlit. Velo Ha'ohz Vehamisrah.

He is without beginning, without end; He reigns in power.

בְּלִי עֵרֶךְ בְּלִי דִמְיוֹן. בְּלִי שִׁנּוּי וּתְמוּרָה:

Beli Erech Beli Dimyon. Beli Shinui Ut'murah.

To him, no like or equal can ever be; Without change or substitute, He remains.

בְּלִי חִבּוּר בְּלִי פִּרוּד. גְּדוֹל כֹּחַ וּגְבוּרָה:

Beli Chibur Beli Pirud. Gedol Koach Ug'vurah.

Without divisibleness or attachment. He supremely reigns in highest might and power.

וְהוּא אֵלִי וְחַי גּוֹאֲלִי. וְצוּר חֶבְלִי בְּעֵת צָרָה:

Vehu Eli Vechai Go'ali. Vetzur Chevli B'yom Tzarah.

And He is my God and my living Redeemer. My sheltering Rock on the day of misfortune.

וְהוּא נִסִּי וּמָנוֹס לִי. מְנָת כּוֹסִי בְּיוֹם אֶקְרָא:

Vehu Nissi Umanos Li. Menat Kosi B'yom Ekra.

My standard, refuge, portion, true. The Portion of my cup on the day that I call.

וְהוּא רוֹפֵא וְהוּא מַרְפֵּא. וְהוּא צוֹפֶה וְהוּא עֶזְרָה:

Vehu Rofei Vehu Marpe. Vehu Tzofeh Vehu Ezrah.

He is a Healer and a cure; He is a Watchman and a Helper.

בְּיָדוֹ אַפְקִיד רוּחִי. בְּעֵת אִישַׁן וְאָעִירָה:

Beyado Afkid Ruchi. Be'et Ishan Ve'a'irah.

Into his hands I consign my spirit. While wrapped in sleep. and I will awake again.

וְעִם רוּחִי גְּוִיָּתִי. יְהוָה לִי וְלֹא אִירָא:

Ve'im Ruchi Geviyati. Adonai Li Velo Ira.

And with my soul, my body I resign; Hashem is with me, and I will not fear .

בְּמִקְדָּשׁוֹ תָּגֵל נַפְשִׁי. מְשִׁיחֵנוּ יִשְׁלַח מְהֵרָה:

Bemikdasho Tagel Nafshi. Meshicheinu Yishlach Meheirah.

In His Temple, my soul will delight; may He send our Messiah soon.

וְאָז נָשִׁיר בְּבֵית קָדְשִׁי. אָמֵן אָמֵן שֵׁם הַנּוֹרָא:

Ve'az Nashir Beveit Kodshi. Amen. Amen. Shem Hanora.

And then we'll sing in my Holy House. Amen, Amen, to the Awe-inspring Name.

Seder Tzitzit / Order of Tzitzit

One should wrap himself in a fringed garment, and recite the blessing while standing. Before reciting the blessing, one should examine the threads of the tzitzit (fringes) to see if they are lawfully fit, and he must separate the threads from one another (not on Shabbat). He should recite the blessing: "lehitateif betzitzit" (On the tallit katan (small tallit), it is customary to say the blessing: "al mitzvat tzitzit" upon awakening). If the tallit fell off entirely from a person, he must say the blessing again. (If one took it off with the intention of putting it on again, while the small tallit was still left on his body, he does not need to say the blessing again). Tallit Katans that are customarily worn, even though they are not wrapped, fulfill our obligation for fringes. And it is good that one places it over one's head, the long way, and wrap it. He should stand this way wrapped for at least the amount of time it would take to walk four cubits. After this he can pull it over his head and wear it normally. One should return two of the fringes in front, and two behind. On a tallit katan, one can bless "lehitateif betzitzit" even which does not wrap, but only worn. (SA, OC 8)

Some say before:

לְשֵׁם יִחוּד קוּדְשָׁא בְּרִיךְ הוּא וּשְׁכִינְתֵּיהּ. בִּדְחִילוּ וּרְחִימוּ. וּרְחִימוּ וּדְחִילוּ. לְיַחֲדָא שֵׁם יוֹ״ד קֵ״י בְּוָא״ו קֵ״י בְּיִחוּדָא שְׁלִים (יהוה) בְּשֵׁם כָּל יִשְׂרָאֵל. הריני מוכן ללבש טלית מציצת כהלכתה כמו שצונו יהוה אלהינו בתורתו הקדושה ועשו להם ציצת על כנפי בגדיהם. כדי לעשות נחת רוח ליוצרי ולעשות רצון בורא. והריני מכון לברך עטיפת הטלית כתקון רבותינו זכרונם לברכה. והריני מכון לפטר בברכה זו גם טלית הקטן שעלי. וִיהִי נֹעַם אֲדֹנָי אֱלֹהֵינוּ עָלֵינוּ וּמַעֲשֵׂה יָדֵינוּ כּוֹנְנָה עָלֵינוּ וּמַעֲשֵׂה יָדֵינוּ כּוֹנְנֵהוּ:

Some also have a custom of saying before:

בָּרְכִ֥י נַפְשִׁ֗י אֶת־יְה֫וָ֥ה יְהוָ֣ה אֱ֭לֹהַי גָּדַ֣לְתָּ מְּאֹ֑ד ה֖וֹד וְהָדָ֣ר לָבָֽשְׁתָּ׃ עֹֽטֶה־א֭וֹר כַּשַּׂלְמָ֑ה נוֹטֶ֥ה שָׁ֝מַ֗יִם כַּיְרִיעָֽה׃

Barchi Nafshi Et Adonai Adonai Elohai Gadalta Me'odhod Vehadar Lavasheta. Oteh Or Kassalmah Noteh Shamayim Kayeri'ah.

Bless Hashem, Oh my soul. Hashem my God, You are very great; You are clothed with glory and majesty. Who covers Yourself with light as with a garment, who stretches out the heavens like a curtain.

Baruch Attah Adonai Eloheinu	בָּרוּךְ אַתָּה יְהֹוָה אֱלֹהֵינוּ
Melech Ha'olam Asher	מֶלֶךְ הָעוֹלָם. אֲשֶׁר
Kideshanu Bemitzvotav	קִדְּשָׁנוּ בְּמִצְוֹתָיו
Vetzivanu Lehitateif Betzitzit.	וְצִוָּנוּ לְהִתְעַטֵּף בְּצִיצִית:

Blessed are You. Hashem our God, King of the Universe, that has sanctified us with His commandments and commanded us to enwrap ourselves in tzitzit.

Some have a custom of saying afterwards:

מַה־יָּקָר חַסְדְּךָ אֱלֹהִים וּבְנֵי אָדָם בְּצֵל כְּנָפֶיךָ יֶחֱסָיוּן: יִרְוְיֻן מִדֶּשֶׁן בֵּיתֶךָ וְנַחַל
עֲדָנֶיךָ תַשְׁקֵם: כִּי־עִמְּךָ מְקוֹר חַיִּים בְּאוֹרְךָ נִרְאֶה־אוֹר: מְשֹׁךְ חַסְדְּךָ לְיֹדְעֶיךָ
וְצִדְקָתְךָ לְיִשְׁרֵי־לֵב:

Mah Yakar Chasdecha Elohim Uvenei Adam Betzel Kenafeicha Yechesayun. Yirveyun Mideshen Beitecha Venachal Adaneicha Tashkem. Ki Imecha Mekor Chayim Be'orecha Nir'eh Or. Meshoch Chasdecha Leyodeicha Vetzidkatecha Leyishrei Lev.

How precious is Your lovingkindness, God. And the children of men take refuge in the shadow of Your wings. They are abundantly satisfied with the fatness of Your House; And You make them drink of the river of Your pleasures. For with You is the fountain of life; In Your light we see light. Continue Your lovingkindness to them that know You; And Your righteousness to the upright in heart. (Ps. 36:8-9, 11-12)

Seder Tefillin / Order of Tefillin

It is a mitzvah to wear tefillin all day, but because tefillin require a clean body, one should not flatulate or become distracted from them. Not every person is able to be careful with them, so the practice is not to wear them all day. There should be tefillin on during the reciting of Shema and the Amidah. (SA, OC 37:2) The tefillin are to be put on after the tallit. (ascending in level of holiness). The tefillin shel yad (of the hand) is put on first and then the tefillin shel rosh (of the head). Even if he touched the shel rosh first, he must skip over and put on the shel yad first. When putting them on, have in mind that the Holy One, Blessed is He, commanded us to put these four parshiyot (passage) which contain the unity of Hashem and the going out from Mitzrayim on the arm opposite the heart and on the head opposite the brain in order to remember the miracles and wonders that He performed for us to teach us of His uniqueness and his strength and dominion in heaven and on earth to do with them as He wills. And to subjugate to the Holy One, Blessed is He, his soul, which resides in the brain as well as his heart which represents the root of lusts and thoughts. In this he will remember the Creator and control his lusting. He should put the arm-tefillin on first and say the blessing "lehaniach tefillin" and afterwards put the head tefillin on without a second blessing for only one blessing is made for both of them. For all mitzvot (commandments), one blesses on them before the performing of the mitzvah. Therefore one must make the blessing on the shel yad after he places it on his bicep, before he tightens it. For the tightening is the performing of action. One should not interrupt while putting on the tefillin, even if responding to the Kaddish or Kedushah (if one accidentally speaks instructions are below). One should put on the tefillin shel rosh before winding the strap around the arm. Some hold that the winding on the arm should be done first. The custom of the world is to refrain from removing Tefillin until the recital of "Uva Letziyon" after the Torah Service. (SA, OC 25)

It is prohibited to wear tefillin on the following days: Shabbat, Yom Tov, Chol HaMoed (some do wear on Chol HaMoed). (SA, OC 31:2)

Some say before:

לְשֵׁם יִחוּד קוּדְשָׁא בְּרִיךְ הוּא וּשְׁכִינְתֵּיהּ. בִּדְחִילוּ וּרְחִימוּ. וּרְחִימוּ וּדְחִילוּ. לְיַחֲדָא שֵׁם יו״ד קֵ״י בְּוָא״ו קֵ״י בְּיִחוּדָא שְׁלִים (יהוה) בְּשֵׁם כָּל יִשְׂרָאֵל. הריני מוכן לקיים מצות עשה להניח תפלין בידי ובראשי כמו שצונו יהוה אלהינו וקשרתם אתם לאות על־ידכם והיו לטוטפת בין עיניכם. והריני מוכן לברך הברכה שתקנו רבותינו זכרונם לברכה על מצות התפלין. והריני מכון לפטר בברכה זו תפלין של יד ותפלין של ראש. ויעלה לפניך יהוה אלהינו ואלהי אבותינו כאלו כונתי בכל הכונות הראויות לכון בהנחת התפלין ובברכה. וִיהִי נֹעַם אֲדֹנָי אֱלֹהֵינוּ עָלֵינוּ וּמַעֲשֵׂה יָדֵינוּ כּוֹנְנָה עָלֵינוּ וּמַעֲשֵׂה יָדֵינוּ כּוֹנְנֵהוּ:

Baruch Attah Adonai Eloheinu	בָּרוּךְ אַתָּה יְהֹוָה אֱלֹהֵינוּ
Melech Ha'olam Asher	מֶלֶךְ הָעוֹלָם. אֲשֶׁר
Kideshanu Bemitzvotav.	קִדְּשָׁנוּ בְּמִצְוֹתָיו.
Vetzivanu Lehaniach Tefillin.	וְצִוָּנוּ לְהָנִיחַ תְּפִלִּין:

Blessed are You, Hashem our God, King of the Universe, that has sanctified us with His commandments and commanded us to lay Tefillin.

If one speaks after the previous blessing, anything not related to tefillin or answering amen in prayer accidentally, this blessing is said when putting on the rosh (head) tefillin, otherwise skip:

Baruch Attah Adonai Eloheinu	בָּרוּךְ אַתָּה יְהֹוָה אֱלֹהֵינוּ
Melech Ha'olam Asher Kideshanu	מֶלֶךְ הָעוֹלָם. אֲשֶׁר קִדְּשָׁנוּ
Bemitzvotav. Vetzivanu Al Mitzvat	בְּמִצְוֺתָיו. וְצִוָּנוּ עַל מִצְוַת
Tefillin:	תְּפִלִּין:

Blessed are You, Hashem our God, King of the Universe, that has sanctified us with His commandments and commanded us concerning Tefillin.

Some have a custom of reciting after the tefillin shel rosh are in place:

וּמֵחָכְמָתְךָ אֵל עֶלְיוֹן תַּאֲצִיל עָלַי וּמִבִּינָתְךָ תְּבִינֵנִי וּבְחַסְדְּךָ תַּגְדִּיל עָלַי וּבִגְבוּרָתְךָ תַּצְמִית אוֹיְבַי וְקָמַי וְשֶׁמֶן הַטּוֹב תָּרִיק עַל שִׁבְעָה קְנֵי הַמְּנוֹרָה לְהַשְׁפִּיעַ טוּבְךָ לִבְרִיּוֹתֶיךָ: פּוֹתֵחַ אֶת־יָדֶךָ וּמַשְׂבִּיעַ לְכָל־חַי רָצוֹן:

Umechachematecha El Elyon Ta'atzil Alai Umibbinatecha Tevineni Uvechasdecha Tagdil Alai Uvigvuratecha Tatzmit Oyevai Vekamai Veshemen Hatov Tarik Al Shiv'ah Kenei Hammenorah Lehashpia' Tuvecha Livriyyoteicha: Potei'ach Et Yadecha Umasbia' Lechol Chai Ratzon:

Supreme God, You will imbue me with Your wisdom and Your intelligence; in Your grace You will do great things for me; by Your might You will cut off my foes and my adversaries. You will pour the good oil into the seven branches of the Menorah so as to bestow Your goodness upon Your creatures. You open Your hand, and satisfy every living-thing with favor. **(Heichal Kodesh-Moses Albas, Ps. 145:16)**

After placing of the rosh (head) tefillin, immediately place the rezuot (strap) on your hand and in three bindings wrap the middle finger. One above the knuckle and two below, while saying verses:

וְאֵרַשְׂתִּיךְ לִי לְעוֹלָם וְאֵרַשְׂתִּיךְ לִי בְּצֶדֶק וּבְמִשְׁפָּט וּבְחֶסֶד וּבְרַחֲמִים: וְאֵרַשְׂתִּיךְ לִי בֶּאֱמוּנָה וְיָדַעַתְּ אֶת־יְהֹוָה:

Ve'erastich Li Le'olam; Ve'erastich Li Betzedek Uvemishpat. Uvechesed Uverachamim. Ve'erastich Li Be'emunah; Veyada'at Et-Adonai.

And I will betroth you to Me forever; I will betroth you to Me in righteousness, and in justice, And in lovingkindness, and in compassion. And I will betroth you to Me in faith; And you will know Hashem. **(Hoshea 2:21-22)**

Some have a custom of saying afterwards:

וְרָאוּ כָּל־עַמֵּי הָאָרֶץ כִּי שֵׁם יְהֹוָה נִקְרָא עָלֶיךָ וְיָרְאוּ מִמֶּךָּ: שׂוֹשׂ אָשִׂישׂ בַּיהֹוָה תָּגֵל נַפְשִׁי בֵּאלֹהַי כִּי הִלְבִּישַׁנִי בִּגְדֵי־יֶשַׁע מְעִיל צְדָקָה יְעָטָנִי כֶּחָתָן יְכַהֵן פְּאֵר וְכַכַּלָּה תַּעְדֶּה כֵלֶיהָ:

Vera'u Kol Ammei Ha'aretz Ki Shem Adonai Nikra Aleicha Veyare'u Mimekka. Sos Asis B'Adonai Tagel Nafshi Belohai Ki Hilbishani Bigdei Yesha Me'il Tzedakah Ye'atani Kechatan Yechahen Pe'er Vechakallah Ta'deh Cheleiha.

And all the peoples of the earth will see that the name of Hashem is called upon you; and they will be afraid of you. **(Deut. 28:10)** I will greatly rejoice in Hashem, My soul will be joyful in my God; For He has clothed me with the garments of salvation, He has covered me with the robe of victory, As a bridegroom puts on a priestly diadem, And as a bride adorns herself with her jewels. **(Isaiah 61:10)**

After putting on the tefillin recite the following portions. These are two of the verses of the four portions in the tefillin.

Exodus 13:1-10 / Kadesh Li

וַיְדַבֵּר יְהֹוָה אֶל־מֹשֶׁה לֵּאמֹר: קַדֶּשׁ־לִי כָל־בְּכוֹר פֶּטֶר כָּל־רֶחֶם בִּבְנֵי יִשְׂרָאֵל בָּאָדָם וּבַבְּהֵמָה לִי הוּא: וַיֹּאמֶר מֹשֶׁה אֶל־הָעָם זָכוֹר אֶת־הַיּוֹם הַזֶּה אֲשֶׁר יְצָאתֶם מִמִּצְרַיִם מִבֵּית עֲבָדִים כִּי בְּחֹזֶק יָד הוֹצִיא יְהֹוָה אֶתְכֶם מִזֶּה וְלֹא יֵאָכֵל חָמֵץ: הַיּוֹם אַתֶּם יֹצְאִים

בְּחֹדֶשׁ הָאָבִיב: וְהָיָה כִֽי־יְבִיאֲךָ יְהֹוָה אֶל־אֶרֶץ הַכְּנַעֲנִי וְהַחִתִּי
וְהָאֱמֹרִי וְהַחִוִּי וְהַיְבוּסִי אֲשֶׁר נִשְׁבַּע לַאֲבֹתֶיךָ לָתֶת לָךְ אֶרֶץ זָבַת
חָלָב וּדְבָשׁ וְעָבַדְתָּ אֶת־הָעֲבֹדָה הַזֹּאת בַּחֹדֶשׁ הַזֶּה: שִׁבְעַת יָמִים
תֹּאכַל מַצֹּת וּבַיּוֹם הַשְּׁבִיעִי חַג לַיהֹוָה: מַצּוֹת יֵאָכֵל אֵת שִׁבְעַת
הַיָּמִים וְלֹא־יֵרָאֶה לְךָ חָמֵץ וְלֹא־יֵרָאֶה לְךָ שְׂאֹר בְּכָל־גְּבֻלֶךָ: וְהִגַּדְתָּ
לְבִנְךָ בַּיּוֹם הַהוּא לֵאמֹר בַּעֲבוּר זֶה עָשָׂה יְהֹוָה לִי בְּצֵאתִי
מִמִּצְרָיִם: וְהָיָה לְךָ לְאוֹת עַל־יָדְךָ וּלְזִכָּרוֹן בֵּין עֵינֶיךָ לְמַעַן תִּהְיֶה
תּוֹרַת יְהֹוָה בְּפִיךָ כִּי בְּיָד חֲזָקָה הוֹצִאֲךָ יְהֹוָה מִמִּצְרָיִם: וְשָׁמַרְתָּ
אֶת־הַחֻקָּה הַזֹּאת לְמוֹעֲדָהּ מִיָּמִים יָמִימָה:

Vaydaber Adonai El-Mosheh Lemor. Kadesh-Li Chol-Bechor Peter Chol-Rechem Bivnei Yisra'el. Ba'adam Uvabehemah; Li Hu. Vayomer Mosheh El-Ha'am. Zachor Et-Hayom Hazeh Asher Yetzatem Mimitzrayim Mibeit Avadim. Ki Bechozek Yad. Hotzi Adonai Etchem Mizeh; Velo Ye'achel Chametz. Hayom Attem Yotze'im; Bechodesh Ha'aviv. Vehayah Chi-Yevi'acha Adonai El-'Eretz Hakena'ani Vehachiti Veha'emori Vehachivi Vehayvusi. Asher Nishba La'avoteicha Latet Lach. Eretz Zavat Chalav Udevash; Ve'avadta Et-Ha'avodah Hazot Bachodesh Hazeh. Shiv'at Yamim Tochal Matzot; Uvayom Hashevi'i. Chag L'Adonai Matzot Ye'achel. Et Shiv'at Hayamim; Velo-Yera'eh Lecha Chametz. Velo-Yera'eh Lecha Se'or Bechol-Gevulecha. Vehiggadta Levincha. Bayom Hahu Lemor; Ba'avur Zeh. Asah Adonai Li. Betzeti Mimitzrayim. Vehayah Lecha Le'ot Al-Yadecha. Ulezikaron Bein Eineicha. Lema'an. Tihyeh Torat Adonai Beficha; Ki Beyad Chazakah. Hotzi'acha Adonai Mimitzrayim. Veshamarta Et-Hachukkah Hazot Lemo'adah; Miyamim Yamimah.

And Hashem spoke to Moshe, saying: 'Sanctify to Me all the first-born, whatsoever opens the womb among the children of Yisrael, both of man and of beast, it is Mine.' And Moshe said to the people: 'Remember this day, in which you came out from Mitzrayim, out of the house of bondage; for by strength of hand Hashem brought you out from this place; no leavened bread will be eaten. This day you go out in the month Aviv. And it will be when Hashem will bring you into the land of the Canaani, and the Chitti, and the Emori, and the

Chivi, and the Yevusi, which He swore to your fathers to give you, a land flowing with milk and honey, that you will keep this service in this month. Seven days you will eat unleavened bread, and in the seventh day will be a feast to Hashem. Unleavened bread will be eaten throughout the seven days; and no leavened bread will be seen with you, neither will there be leaven seen with you in all your borders. And you will tell your son in that day, saying: It is because of that which Hashem did for me when I came out of Mitzrayim. And it will be for a sign to you upon your hand, and for a memorial between your eyes, that the Torah of Hashem may be in your mouth; for with a strong hand Hashem brought you out of Mitzrayim. You will keep this ordinance in its season from year to year.

וְהָיָה כִּי־יְבִאֲךָ יְהֹוָה אֶל־אֶרֶץ הַכְּנַעֲנִי כַּאֲשֶׁר נִשְׁבַּע לְךָ וְלַאֲבֹתֶיךָ
וּנְתָנָהּ לָךְ: וְהַעֲבַרְתָּ כָל־פֶּטֶר־רֶחֶם לַיהֹוָה וְכָל־פֶּטֶר | שֶׁגֶר בְּהֵמָה
אֲשֶׁר יִהְיֶה לְךָ הַזְּכָרִים לַיהֹוָה: וְכָל־פֶּטֶר חֲמֹר תִּפְדֶּה בְשֶׂה
וְאִם־לֹא תִפְדֶּה וַעֲרַפְתּוֹ וְכֹל בְּכוֹר אָדָם בְּבָנֶיךָ תִּפְדֶּה: וְהָיָה
כִּי־יִשְׁאָלְךָ בִנְךָ מָחָר לֵאמֹר מַה־זֹּאת וְאָמַרְתָּ אֵלָיו בְּחֹזֶק יָד
הוֹצִיאָנוּ יְהֹוָה מִמִּצְרַיִם מִבֵּית עֲבָדִים: וַיְהִי כִּי־הִקְשָׁה פַרְעֹה
לְשַׁלְּחֵנוּ וַיַּהֲרֹג יְהֹוָה כָּל־בְּכוֹר בְּאֶרֶץ מִצְרַיִם מִבְּכֹר אָדָם
וְעַד־בְּכוֹר בְּהֵמָה עַל־כֵּן אֲנִי זֹבֵחַ לַיהֹוָה כָּל־פֶּטֶר רֶחֶם הַזְּכָרִים
וְכָל־בְּכוֹר בָּנַי אֶפְדֶּה: וְהָיָה לְאוֹת עַל־יָדְכָה וּלְטוֹטָפֹת בֵּין עֵינֶיךָ כִּי
בְּחֹזֶק יָד הוֹצִיאָנוּ יְהֹוָה מִמִּצְרָיִם:

Vehayah Ki-Yevi'acha Adonai El-'Eretz Hakena'ani. Ka'asher Nishba Lecha Vela'avoteicha; Unetanah Lach. Veha'avarta Chol-Peter-Rechem L'Adonai Vechol-Peter Sheger Behemah. Asher Yihyeh Lecha Hazecharim L'Adonai Vechol-Peter Chamor Tifdeh Veseh. Ve'im-Lo Tifdeh Va'arafto; Vechol Bechor Adam Bevaneicha Tifdeh. Vehayah Ki-Yish'olcha Vincha Machar Lemor Mah-Zot; Ve'amarta Elav. Bechozek Yad. Hotzi'anu Adonai Mimitzrayim Mibeit Avadim. Vayhi. Ki-Hikshah Far'oh Leshallecheinu Vayaharog Adonai Chol-Bechor Be'eretz Mitzrayim. Mibechor Adam Ve'ad-Bechor

Behemah; Al-Ken Ani Zoveach L'Adonai Chol-Peter Rechem Hazecharim. Vechol-Bechor Banai Efdeh. Vehayah Le'ot Al-Yadechah. Uletotafot Bein Eineicha; Ki Bechozek Yad. Hotzi'anu Adonai Mimitzrayim.

And it will be when Hashem will bring you into the land of the Canaani, as He swore to you and to your fathers, and will give it you, that you will set apart to Hashem all that opens the womb; every firstling that is a male that you have from cattle, will be Hashem's. And every firstling donkey you will redeem with a lamb; and if you will not redeem it, then you will break its neck; and all the first-born of man among your sons you will redeem. And it will be when your son asks you in time to come, saying: What is this? You will say to him: By strength of hand Hashem brought us out from Mitzrayim, from the house of bondage; and it came to pass, when Pharaoh would hardly let us go that Hashem struck all the first-born in the land of Egypt, both the first-born of man, and the first-born of beast; therefore I sacrifice all that opens the womb to Hashem, that are males; but all the first-born of my sons I redeem. And it will be for a sign upon your hand, and for frontlets between your eyes; for by strength of hand Hashem brought us out from Mitzrayim.'

Arriving at the Synagogue

When arriving at the Synagogue one bows at the entrance and recites:

Va'ani Berov Chasdecha Avo	וַאֲנִי בְּרֹב חַסְדְּךָ אָבוֹא
Veitecha Eshtachaveh El	בֵיתֶךָ אֶשְׁתַּחֲוֶה אֶל־
Heichal-Kodshecha	הֵיכַל־קָדְשְׁךָ
Beyir'atecha.	בְּיִרְאָתֶךָ׃

As for me, through Your abundant kindness, I will enter Your House; I will prostrate myself toward Your Holy Sanctuary in awe of You.

(Psalms. 5:8)

One then continues to walk and recites the verses:

Adonai Tzeva'ot Imanu; Misgav- Lanu Elohei Ya'akov Selah.	יְהוָ֣ה צְבָא֣וֹת עִמָּ֑נוּ מִשְׂגָּב־ לָ֨נוּ אֱלֹהֵ֖י יַעֲקֹ֣ב סֶֽלָה׃

Hashem of hosts is with us; the God of Yaakov is our high tower. Selah. **(Psalms 46:8)**

Adonai Tzeva'ot; Ashrei Adam. Boteach Bach.	יְהוָ֥ה צְבָא֑וֹת אַֽשְׁרֵ֥י אָ֝דָ֗ם בֹּטֵ֥חַ בָּֽךְ׃

Hashem of hosts, happy is the man who trusts in You. **(Psalms 84:13)**

Adonai Hoshi'ah; Hamelech. Ya'aneinu Veyom-Kare'enu.	יְהוָ֥ה הוֹשִׁ֑יעָה הַ֝מֶּ֗לֶךְ יַעֲנֵ֥נוּ בְיוֹם־קָרְאֵֽנוּ׃

Save, Hashem. May the King answer us on the day that we call. **(Psalms 20:10)**

Tefillat Chanah / The Prayer of Chanah

וַתִּתְפַּלֵּ֤ל חַנָּה֙ וַתֹּאמַ֔ר עָלַ֤ץ לִבִּי֙ בַּֽיהוָ֔ה רָ֥מָה קַרְנִ֖י בַּֽיהוָ֑ה רָ֤חַב פִּי֙ עַל־א֣וֹיְבַ֔י כִּ֥י שָׂמַ֖חְתִּי בִּישׁוּעָתֶֽךָ׃ אֵין־קָד֥וֹשׁ כַּֽיהוָ֖ה כִּ֣י אֵ֣ין בִּלְתֶּ֑ךָ וְאֵ֥ין צ֖וּר כֵּאלֹהֵֽינוּ׃ אַל־תַּרְבּ֤וּ תְדַבְּרוּ֙ גְּבֹהָ֣ה גְבֹהָ֔ה יֵצֵ֥א עָתָ֖ק מִפִּיכֶ֑ם כִּ֣י אֵ֤ל דֵּעוֹת֙ יְהוָ֔ה ולא (וְל֥וֹ) נִתְכְּנ֖וּ עֲלִלֽוֹת׃ קֶ֥שֶׁת גִּבֹּרִ֖ים חַתִּ֑ים וְנִכְשָׁלִ֖ים אָ֥זְרוּ חָֽיִל׃ שְׂבֵעִ֤ים בַּלֶּ֙חֶם֙ נִשְׂכָּ֔רוּ וּרְעֵבִ֖ים חָדֵ֑לּוּ עַד־עֲקָרָה֙ יָלְדָ֣ה שִׁבְעָ֔ה וְרַבַּ֥ת בָּנִ֖ים אֻמְלָֽלָה׃ יְהוָ֖ה מֵמִ֣ית וּמְחַיֶּ֑ה מוֹרִ֥יד שְׁא֖וֹל וַיָּֽעַל׃ יְהוָ֖ה מוֹרִ֣ישׁ וּמַעֲשִׁ֑יר מַשְׁפִּ֖יל אַף־מְרוֹמֵֽם׃ מֵקִ֨ים מֵעָפָ֜ר דָּ֗ל מֵֽאַשְׁפֹּת֙ יָרִ֣ים אֶבְי֔וֹן לְהוֹשִׁיב֙ עִם־נְדִיבִ֔ים וְכִסֵּ֥א כָב֖וֹד יַנְחִלֵ֑ם כִּ֤י לַֽיהוָה֙ מְצֻ֣קֵי אֶ֔רֶץ וַיָּ֥שֶׁת עֲלֵיהֶ֖ם תֵּבֵֽל׃ רַגְלֵ֤י חֲסִידָו֙ יִשְׁמֹ֔ר וּרְשָׁעִ֖ים בַּחֹ֣שֶׁךְ יִדָּ֑מּוּ כִּי־לֹ֥א בְכֹ֖חַ יִגְבַּר־אִֽישׁ׃ יְהוָ֗ה יֵחַ֣תּוּ

מְרִיבָו עָלָו בַּשָּׁמַיִם יַרְעֵם יְהֹוָה יָדִין אַפְסֵי־אָרֶץ וְיִתֶּן־עֹז לְמַלְכּוֹ וְיָרֵם קֶרֶן מְשִׁיחוֹ׃

Vatitpallel Chanah Vatomar Alatz Libi Badonai Ramah Karni Badonai Rachav Pi Al Oyevai Ki Samachti Bishu'atecha. Ein Kadosh Ka'Adonai Ki Ein Biltecha Ve'ein Tzur Keloheinu. Al Tarbu Tedaberu Gevohah Gevohah Yetze Atak Mipichem Ki El De'ot Adonai Velo Nitkenu Alilot. Keshet Giborim Chatim Venichshalim Azeru Chayil. Seve'im Ballechem Niskaru Ure'evim Chadelu Ad Akarah Yaledah Shiv'ah Verabbat Banim Umlalah. Adonai Memit Umechayeh Morid She'ol Vaya'al. Adonai Morish Uma'ashir Mashpil Af Meromem. Mekim Me'afar Dal Me'ashpot Yarim Evyon Lehoshiv Im Nedivim Vechisse Chavod Yanchilem Ki L'Adonai Metzukei Eretz Vayashet Aleihem Tevel. Raglei Chasidav Yishmor Uresha'im Bachoshech Yiddammu Ki Lo Vechoach Yigbar Ish. Adonai Yechatu Merivav Alav Bashamayim Yar'em Adonai Yadin Afsei Aretz Veyiten Oz Lemalko Veyarem Keren Meshicho.

And Chanah prayed, and said: my heart exults in Hashem, my horn is exalted in Hashem; my mouth is enlarged over my enemies; because I rejoice in Your salvation. There is none as holy as Hashem, for there is none beside You; neither is there any rock like our God. Do not multiply exceedingly proud speech; do not let arrogance come out of your mouth; for Hashem is a God of knowledge, and by Him actions are weighed. The bows of the mighty men are broken, and they that stumbled are girded with strength. They that were full have hired out themselves for bread; and they that were hungry have ceased; while the barren has borne seven, she that had many children has languished. Hashem kills, and makes alive; He brings down to the grave, and brings up. Hashem makes poor, and makes rich; He brings low, He also lifts up. He raises up the poor out of the dust, He raises up the needy from the dung-hill, to make them sit with princes, and inherit the Throne of glory; for the pillars of the earth are Hashem's, and He has set the world on them. He will keep the feet of His holy ones, but the wicked will be put to silence in darkness; for not by strength will man prevail. They that strive with Hashem will be broken to pieces;

against them He will thunder in heaven; Hashem will judge the ends of the earth; and He will give strength to His king, and exalt the horn of His anointed. **(I Samuel 2:1-10)**

אָתוֹהִי כְּמָה רַבְרְבִין וְתִמְהוֹהִי כְּמָה תַקִּיפִין מַלְכוּתֵהּ מַלְכוּת עָלַם
וְשָׁלְטָנֵהּ עִם־דָּר וְדָר: וַאֲנַחְנוּ עַמְּךָ | וְצֹאן מַרְעִיתֶךָ נוֹדֶה לְּךָ לְעוֹלָם
לְדוֹר וָדֹר נְסַפֵּר תְּהִלָּתֶךָ: עֶרֶב וָבֹקֶר וְצָהֳרַיִם אָשִׂיחָה וְאֶהֱמֶה
וַיִּשְׁמַע קוֹלִי: בְּרָן־יַחַד כּוֹכְבֵי בֹקֶר וַיָּרִיעוּ כָּל־בְּנֵי אֱלֹהִים:
לֹא־אִירָא מֵרִבְבוֹת עָם אֲשֶׁר סָבִיב שָׁתוּ עָלָי: וַאֲנִי בַּיהוָה אֲצַפֶּה
אוֹחִילָה לֵאלֹהֵי יִשְׁעִי יִשְׁמָעֵנִי אֱלֹהָי:

Atohi Kemah Ravrevin Vetimhohi Kemah Takifin Malchuteh Malchut Alam Vesholtaneh Im Dar Vedar: Va'anachnu Ammecha Vetzon Mar'itecha Nodeh Lecha Le'olam Ledor Vador Nesapeir Tehillatecha: Erev Vavoker Vetzaharayim Asichah Ve'ehemeh Vayishma Koli: Beron Yachad Kochevei Voker Vayari'u Kol Benei Elohim: Lo Ira Merivot Am Asher Saviv Shatu Alai: Va'ani Badonai Atzapeh Ochilah Lelohei Yish'i Yishma'eni Elohai:

How great are His signs. And how mighty are His wonders. His kingdom is an everlasting kingdom, And His dominion is from generation to generation. So we that are Your people and the flock of Your pasture will give You thanks forever; we will tell of Your praise to all generations. Evening, and morning, and at noon, I will complain, and moan; and He has heard my voice. When the morning stars sang together, And all the sons of God shouted for joy. I am not afraid of ten thousands of people, that have set themselves against me all around. 'But as for me, I will look to Hashem; I will wait for the God of my salvation; My God will hear me. **(Daniel 3:33, Psalms 79:13, Psalms 55:18, Job 38:7, Psalms 3:7, Micah 7:7)**

The following is omitted on Shabbat and Yom Tov / Festivals:

אַל־תִּשְׂמְחִי אֹיַבְתִּי לִי כִּי נָפַלְתִּי קָמְתִּי כִּי־אֵשֵׁב בַּחֹשֶׁךְ יְהוָה אוֹר לִי: כִּי־לְךָ
יְהוָה הוֹחָלְתִּי אַתָּה תַעֲנֶה אֲדֹנָי אֱלֹהָי: רַגְלִי עָמְדָה בְמִישׁוֹר בְּמַקְהֵלִים אֲבָרֵךְ
יְהוָה:

Al-Tismechi Oyavti Li Ki Nafalti Kameti Ki-Eshev Bachoshech Adonai Or Li. Ki-Lecha Adonai Hochaleti; Attah Ta'aneh. Adonai Elohai. Ragli Amedah Vemishor; Bemak'helim. Avarech Adonai.

Do not rejoice against me, my enemy; Though I have fallen, I will arise; Though I sit in darkness, Hashem is a light to me. For in You, Hashem, do I hope; You will answer, Hashem my God. My foot stands in an even place; in the congregations will I bless Hashem. **(Malachi 7:8, Psalms 38:16, Psalms 26:12)**

Some say before:

לְשֵׁם יִחוּד קוּדְשָׁא בְּרִיךְ הוּא וּשְׁכִינְתֵּיהּ. בִּדְחִילוּ וּרְחִימוּ. וּרְחִימוּ וּדְחִילוּ. לְיַחֲדָא שֵׁם יוֹ״ד קֵ״י בְּוָא״ו קֵ״י בְּיִחוּדָא שְׁלִים (יהוה) בְּשֵׁם כָּל יִשְׂרָאֵל. הנה אנחנו באים להתפלל תפלת שחרית. שתקן אברהם אבינו עליו השלום. עם כל המצות הכלולות בה לתקן את שורשה במקום עליון. לעשות נחת רוח ליוצרנו ולעשות רצון בוראנו. וִיהִי נֹעַם אֲדֹנָי אֱלֹהֵינוּ עָלֵינוּ וּמַעֲשֵׂה יָדֵינוּ כּוֹנְנָה עָלֵינוּ וּמַעֲשֵׂה יָדֵינוּ כּוֹנְנֵהוּ:

Vahareini Mekabel Alai Mitzvat	וַהֲרֵינִי מְקַבֵּל עָלַי מִצְוַת
Aseh Shel Ve'ahavta Lere'acha	עֲשֵׂה שֶׁל וְאָהַבְתָּ לְרֵעֲךָ
Kamocha. Vahareini Ohev Kol	כָּמוֹךָ. וַהֲרֵינִי אוֹהֵב כָּל
Echad Mibenei Yisra'el Kenafshi	אֶחָד מִבְּנֵי יִשְׂרָאֵל כְּנַפְשִׁי
Ume'odi. Vahareini Mezammen	וּמְאוֹדִי. וַהֲרֵינִי מְזַמֵּן
Peh Shelli Lehitpallel Lifnei	פֶּה שֶׁלִּי לְהִתְפַּלֵּל לִפְנֵי
Melech Malchei Hamelachim.	מֶלֶךְ מַלְכֵי הַמְּלָכִים.
Hakadosh Baruch Hu:	הַקָּדוֹשׁ בָּרוּךְ הוּא:

I hereby accept upon myself the mitzvah of "and you shall love your neighbor as Yourself". And I hereby love all of the Children of Yisrael as my soul and with all of my strength. And I hereby prepare my mouth to pray before the Ruler over king of kings, the Holy, Blessed is He.

The Akedah / The Binding of Yitzchak

Eloheinu Velohei Avoteinu.	אֱלֹהֵינוּ וֵאלֹהֵי אֲבוֹתֵינוּ.
Zochrenu Bezichron Tov	זָכְרֵנוּ בְּזִכְרוֹן טוֹב
Milfaneicha. Ufokdenu Bifkudat	מִלְּפָנֶיךָ. וּפָקְדֵנוּ בִּפְקֻדַּת
Yeshu'ah Verachamim Mishemei	יְשׁוּעָה וְרַחֲמִים מִשְּׁמֵי
Shemei Kedem. Uzechor-Lanu	שְׁמֵי קֶדֶם. וּזְכָר־לָנוּ
Adonai Eloheinu Ahavat	יְהֹוָה אֱלֹהֵינוּ אַהֲבַת
Hakadmonim Avraham Yitzchak	הַקַּדְמוֹנִים אַבְרָהָם יִצְחָק
Veyisra'el Avadeicha. Et Haberit	וְיִשְׂרָאֵל עֲבָדֶיךָ. אֶת הַבְּרִית
Ve'et Hachesed Ve'et	וְאֶת הַחֶסֶד וְאֶת
Hashevu'ah Shenishba'ta	הַשְּׁבוּעָה שֶׁנִּשְׁבַּעְתָּ
Le'avraham Avinu Behar	לְאַבְרָהָם אָבִינוּ בְּהַר
Hamoriyah. Ve'et Ha'akedah	הַמּוֹרִיָּה. וְאֶת הָעֲקֵדָה
She'akad Et Yitzchak Beno Al-	שֶׁעָקַד אֶת יִצְחָק בְּנוֹ עַל־
Gabei Hamizbe'ach Kakatuv	גַּבֵּי הַמִּזְבֵּחַ כַּכָּתוּב
Betoratach:	בְּתוֹרָתָךְ:

Our God and God of our fathers, remember us favorably and visit us with mercy and salvation from the eternal high heavens. Remember in our favor, Hashem our God, the love of our ancestors Avraham, Yitzchak and Yisrael your servants. Remember the covenant, the kindness, and the oath which you swore to our father Avraham on Mount Moriah, and the binding of Yitzchak his son on the altar, as it is written in your Torah:

Genesis 22:1-19

וַיְהִי אַחַר הַדְּבָרִים הָאֵלֶּה וְהָאֱלֹהִים נִסָּה אֶת־אַבְרָהָם וַיֹּאמֶר אֵלָיו
אַבְרָהָם וַיֹּאמֶר הִנֵּנִי: וַיֹּאמֶר קַח־נָא אֶת־בִּנְךָ אֶת־יְחִידְךָ
אֲשֶׁר־אָהַבְתָּ אֶת־יִצְחָק וְלֶךְ־לְךָ אֶל־אֶרֶץ הַמֹּרִיָּה וְהַעֲלֵהוּ שָׁם

לְעֹלָה עַל אַחַד הֶהָרִים אֲשֶׁר אֹמַר אֵלֶיךָ: וַיַּשְׁכֵּם אַבְרָהָם בַּבֹּקֶר וַיַּחֲבֹשׁ אֶת־חֲמֹרוֹ וַיִּקַּח אֶת־שְׁנֵי נְעָרָיו אִתּוֹ וְאֵת יִצְחָק בְּנוֹ וַיְבַקַּע עֲצֵי עֹלָה וַיָּקָם וַיֵּלֶךְ אֶל־הַמָּקוֹם אֲשֶׁר־אָמַר־לוֹ הָאֱלֹהִים: בַּיּוֹם הַשְּׁלִישִׁי וַיִּשָּׂא אַבְרָהָם אֶת־עֵינָיו וַיַּרְא אֶת־הַמָּקוֹם מֵרָחֹק: וַיֹּאמֶר אַבְרָהָם אֶל־נְעָרָיו שְׁבוּ־לָכֶם פֹּה עִם־הַחֲמוֹר וַאֲנִי וְהַנַּעַר נֵלְכָה עַד־כֹּה וְנִשְׁתַּחֲוֶה וְנָשׁוּבָה אֲלֵיכֶם: וַיִּקַּח אַבְרָהָם אֶת־עֲצֵי הָעֹלָה וַיָּשֶׂם עַל־יִצְחָק בְּנוֹ וַיִּקַּח בְּיָדוֹ אֶת־הָאֵשׁ וְאֶת־הַמַּאֲכֶלֶת וַיֵּלְכוּ שְׁנֵיהֶם יַחְדָּו: וַיֹּאמֶר יִצְחָק אֶל־אַבְרָהָם אָבִיו וַיֹּאמֶר אָבִי וַיֹּאמֶר הִנֶּנִּי בְנִי וַיֹּאמֶר הִנֵּה הָאֵשׁ וְהָעֵצִים וְאַיֵּה הַשֶּׂה לְעֹלָה: וַיֹּאמֶר אַבְרָהָם אֱלֹהִים יִרְאֶה־לּוֹ הַשֶּׂה לְעֹלָה בְּנִי וַיֵּלְכוּ שְׁנֵיהֶם יַחְדָּו: וַיָּבֹאוּ אֶל־הַמָּקוֹם אֲשֶׁר אָמַר־לוֹ הָאֱלֹהִים וַיִּבֶן שָׁם אַבְרָהָם אֶת־הַמִּזְבֵּחַ וַיַּעֲרֹךְ אֶת־הָעֵצִים וַיַּעֲקֹד אֶת־יִצְחָק בְּנוֹ וַיָּשֶׂם אֹתוֹ עַל־הַמִּזְבֵּחַ מִמַּעַל לָעֵצִים: וַיִּשְׁלַח אַבְרָהָם אֶת־יָדוֹ וַיִּקַּח אֶת־הַמַּאֲכֶלֶת לִשְׁחֹט אֶת־בְּנוֹ: וַיִּקְרָא אֵלָיו מַלְאַךְ יְהוָה מִן־הַשָּׁמַיִם וַיֹּאמֶר אַבְרָהָם | אַבְרָהָם וַיֹּאמֶר הִנֵּנִי: וַיֹּאמֶר אַל־תִּשְׁלַח יָדְךָ אֶל־הַנַּעַר וְאַל־תַּעַשׂ לוֹ מְאוּמָה כִּי | עַתָּה יָדַעְתִּי כִּי־יְרֵא אֱלֹהִים אַתָּה וְלֹא חָשַׂכְתָּ אֶת־בִּנְךָ אֶת־יְחִידְךָ מִמֶּנִּי: וַיִּשָּׂא אַבְרָהָם אֶת־עֵינָיו וַיַּרְא וְהִנֵּה־אַיִל אַחַר נֶאֱחַז בַּסְּבַךְ בְּקַרְנָיו וַיֵּלֶךְ אַבְרָהָם וַיִּקַּח אֶת־הָאַיִל וַיַּעֲלֵהוּ לְעֹלָה תַּחַת בְּנוֹ: וַיִּקְרָא אַבְרָהָם שֵׁם־הַמָּקוֹם הַהוּא יְהוָה | יִרְאֶה אֲשֶׁר יֵאָמֵר הַיּוֹם בְּהַר יְהוָה יֵרָאֶה: וַיִּקְרָא מַלְאַךְ יְהוָה אֶל־אַבְרָהָם שֵׁנִית מִן־הַשָּׁמָיִם: וַיֹּאמֶר בִּי נִשְׁבַּעְתִּי נְאֻם־יְהוָה כִּי יַעַן אֲשֶׁר עָשִׂיתָ אֶת־הַדָּבָר הַזֶּה וְלֹא חָשַׂכְתָּ אֶת־בִּנְךָ אֶת־יְחִידֶךָ: כִּי־בָרֵךְ אֲבָרֶכְךָ וְהַרְבָּה אַרְבֶּה אֶת־זַרְעֲךָ כְּכוֹכְבֵי הַשָּׁמַיִם וְכַחוֹל אֲשֶׁר עַל־שְׂפַת הַיָּם וְיִרַשׁ זַרְעֲךָ אֵת שַׁעַר אֹיְבָיו: וְהִתְבָּרְכוּ בְזַרְעֲךָ כֹּל גּוֹיֵי הָאָרֶץ עֵקֶב אֲשֶׁר שָׁמַעְתָּ בְּקֹלִי: וַיָּשָׁב אַבְרָהָם אֶל־נְעָרָיו וַיָּקֻמוּ וַיֵּלְכוּ יַחְדָּו אֶל־בְּאֵר שָׁבַע וַיֵּשֶׁב אַבְרָהָם בִּבְאֵר שָׁבַע:

Vayhi. Achar Hadevarim Ha'eleh. Veha'elohim. Nissah Et-'Avraham; Vayomer Elav. Avraham Vayomer Hineni. Vayomer Kach-Na Et-Bincha Et-Yechidecha Asher-'Ahavta Et-Yitzchak. Velech-Lecha. El-'Eretz Hamoriyah; Veha'alehu Sham Le'olah. Al Achad Heharim. Asher Omar Eleicha. Vayashkem Avraham Baboker. Vayachavosh Et-Chamoro. Vayikach Et-Shenei Ne'arav Ito. Ve'et Yitzchak Beno; Vayvakka Atzei Olah. Vayakom Vayelech. El-Hamakom Asher-'Amar-Lo Ha'elohim. Bayom Hashelishi. Vayissa Avraham Et-'Einav Vayar Et-Hamakom Merachok. Vayomer Avraham El-Ne'arav. Shevu-Lachem Poh Im-Hachamor. Va'ani Vehana'ar. Nelechah Ad-Koh; Venishtachaveh Venashuvah Aleichem. Vayikach Avraham Et-'Atzei Ha'olah. Vayasem Al-Yitzchak Beno. Vayikach Beyado. Et-Ha'esh Ve'et-Hama'achelet; Vayelechu Sheneihem Yachdav. Vayomer Yitzchak El-'Avraham Aviv Vayomer Avi. Vayomer Hineni Veni; Vayomer. Hineh Ha'esh Veha'etzim. Ve'ayeh Hasseh Le'olah. Vayomer Avraham. Elohim Yir'eh-Lo Hasseh Le'olah Beni; Vayelechu Sheneihem Yachdav. Vayavo'u. El-Hamakom Asher Amar-Lo Ha'elohim Vayiven Sham Avraham Et-Hamizbe'ach. Vaya'aroch Et-Ha'etzim; Vaya'akod Et-Yitzchak Beno. Vayasem Oto Al-Hamizbe'ach. Mima'al La'etzim. Vayishlach Avraham Et-Yado. Vayikach Et-Hama'achelet; Lishchot Et-Beno. Vayikra Elav Mal'ach Hashem Min-Hashamayim. Vayomer Avraham 'Avraham; Vayomer Hineni. Vayomer. Al-Tishlach Yadecha El-Hana'ar. Ve'al-Ta'as Lo Me'umah; Ki Attah Yada'ti. Ki-Yerei Elohim Attah. Velo Chasachta Et-Bincha Et-Yechidecha Mimeni. Vayissa Avraham Et-'Einav. Vayar Vehineh-'Ayil. Achar Ne'echaz Bassevach Bekarnav; Vayelech Avraham Vayikach Et-Ha'ayil. Vaya'alehu Le'olah Tachat Beno. Vayikra Avraham Shem-Hamakom Hahu Hashem Yir'eh; Asher Ye'amer Hayom. Behar Hashem Yera'eh. Vayikra Mal'ach Hashem El-'Avraham; Shenit Min-Hashamayim. Vayomer Bi Nishba'ti Ne'um-Hashem Ki. Ya'an Asher Asita Et-Hadavar Hazeh. Velo Chasachta Et-Bincha Et-Yechidecha. Ki-Varech Avarechcha. Veharbah Arbeh Et-Zar'acha Kechochevei Hashamayim. Vechachol Asher Al-Sefat Hayam; Veyirash Zar'acha. Et Sha'ar Oyevav. Vehitbarechu Vezar'acha. Kol Goyei Ha'aretz; Ekev Asher Shama'ta Bekoli. Vayashov Avraham El-Ne'arav. Vayakumu Vayelechu Yachdav El-Be'er Shava'; Vayeshev Avraham Biv'er Shava.

1 And it came to pass after these things, that God did test Avraham,
and said to him: 'Avraham'; and he said: 'Here I am.' 2 And He said:
'Take now your son, your only son, whom you love, Yitzchak, and

get into the land of Moriah; and offer him there for a burnt-offering
upon one of the mountains which I will tell you of.' 3 And Avraham
arose early in the morning, and saddled his donkey, and took two of
his young men with him, and Yitzchak his son; and he split the wood
for the burnt-offering, and rose up, and went to the place of which
God had told him. 4 On the third day Avraham lifted up his eyes,
and saw the place from far off. 5 And Avraham said to his young
men: 'Abide here with the donkey, and I and the lad will go over; and
we will worship, and come back to you.' 6 And Avraham took the
wood of the burnt-offering, and laid it on Yitzchak his son; and he
took in his hand the fire(stone) and the knife; and they went
together. 7 And Yitzchak spoke to Avraham his father, and said: 'My
father.' And he said: 'Here I am, my son.' And he said: 'Behold the
fire and the wood; but where is the lamb for a burnt-offering?' 8 And
Avraham said: 'God will provide Himself the lamb for a burnt-
offering, my son.' So they went together. 9 And they came to the
place which God had told him of; and Avraham built the altar there,
and laid the wood in order, and bound Yitzchak his son, and laid
him on the altar, on the wood. 10 And Avraham stretched forth his
hand, and took the knife to slay his son. 11 And the angel of Hashem
called to him from out of heaven, and said: 'Avraham, Avraham.' And
he said: 'Here I am.' 12 And he said: 'Do not lay your hand on the lad,
neither do anything to him; for now I know that you are a God-
fearing man, seeing you have not withheld your son, your only son,
from Me.' 13 And Avraham lifted up his eyes, and looked, and behold
behind him a ram caught in the thicket by his horns. And Avraham
went and took the ram, and offered him up for a burnt-offering
instead of his son. 14 And Avraham called the name of that place
Hashem-Yireh; as it is said to this day: 'In the mount where Hashem
is seen.' 15 And the angel of Hashem called to Avraham a second
time out of heaven, 16 and said: 'By Myself have I sworn, says
Hashem, because you have done this, and have not withheld your
son, your only son, 17 that in blessing I will bless you, and in

multiplying I will multiply your seed as the stars of the heaven, and as the sand which is on the seashore; and your seed will possess the gate of his enemies; 18 and in your seed will all the nations of the earth be blessed; because you have listened to My voice.' 19 So Avraham returned to his young men, and they rose up and went together to Be'er-shava; and Avraham dwelt at Be'er-shava.

It is a custom of some to recite the following verse: Leviticus 1:11

וְשָׁחַ֨ט אֹת֜וֹ עַ֣ל יֶ֧רֶךְ הַמִּזְבֵּ֛חַ צָפֹ֖נָה לִפְנֵ֣י יְהֹוָ֑ה וְזָרְק֡וּ בְּנֵי֩ אַהֲרֹ֨ן הַכֹּהֲנִ֧ים אֶת־דָּמ֛וֹ עַל־הַמִּזְבֵּ֖חַ סָבִֽיב׃

Veshachat Oto Al Yerech Hamizbe'ach Tzafonah Lifnei Adonai Vezareku Benei Aharon Hakohanim Et-Damo Al-Hamizbe'ach Saviv.

And he will slaughter it on the side of the altar northward before Hashem; and Aharon's sons, the priests, will dash its blood against the altar all around.

Yehi Ratzon Milfaneicha Adonai	יְהִי רָצוֹן מִלְּפָנֶיךָ יְהֹוָה
Eloheinu Velohei Avoteinu.	אֱלֹהֵינוּ וֵאלֹהֵי אֲבוֹתֵינוּ.
Shetitmallei Rachamim Aleinu.	שֶׁתִּתְמַלֵּא רַחֲמִים עָלֵינוּ.
Uvechein Berov Rachameicha	וּבְכֵן בְּרוֹב רַחֲמֶיךָ
Tizkor Lanu Akedato Shel	תִּזְכּוֹר לָנוּ עֲקֵדָתוֹ שֶׁל
Yitzchak Avinu Ben Avraham	יִצְחָק אָבִינוּ בֶּן אַבְרָהָם
Avinu Alav Hashalom. Ke'ilu Efro	אָבִינוּ עָלָיו הַשָּׁלוֹם. כְּאִלּוּ אֶפְרוֹ
Tzavur Umunach Al Gabei	צָבוּר וּמֻנָּח עַל גַּבֵּי
Hamizbe'ach. Vetabbit Be'efro	הַמִּזְבֵּחַ. וְתַבִּיט בְּאֶפְרוֹ
Lerachem Aleinu. Ulevatel	לְרַחֵם עָלֵינוּ. וּלְבַטֵּל
Me'aleinu Kol Gezeirot Kashot	מֵעָלֵינוּ כָּל גְּזֵירוֹת קָשׁוֹת
Vera'ot. Utezakenu Lashuv	וְרָעוֹת. וּתְזַכֵּנוּ לָשׁוּב
Bitshuvah Shelemah Lefaneicha.	בִּתְשׁוּבָה שְׁלֵמָה לְפָנֶיךָ.
Vetatzilenu Miyetzer Hara	וְתַצִּילֵנוּ מִיֵּצֶר הָרָע

Umikal Chet Ve'avon. Veta'arich	וּמִכָּל חֵטְא וְעָוֹן. וְתַאֲרִיךְ
Yameinu Battov Ushenoteinu	יָמֵינוּ בַּטּוֹב וּשְׁנוֹתֵינוּ
Bane'imim.	בַּנְּעִימִים:

May it be your will Hashem our God and God of our fathers, that You have with mercy on us, and in the greatness of Your mercy that You would remember the Binding of Yitzchak our father, son of Avraham our father, peace be upon him, as if we had accumulated and laid on our back on the altar. And You will look upon the ashes of pity for mercy upon us, and to cut off from us all harsh and evil decrees. May we merit to return in complete teshuvah (repentance) before You, and save us from the evil inclination and from all sin and transgression, and prolong our days in goodness and our years in pleasantness.

רִבּוֹנוֹ שֶׁל עוֹלָם. כְּמוֹ שֶׁכָּבַשׁ אַבְרָהָם אָבִינוּ אֶת רַחֲמָיו לַעֲשׂוֹת רְצוֹנְךָ בְּלֵבָב שָׁלֵם. כֵּן יִכְבְּשׁוּ רַחֲמֶיךָ אֶת כַּעַסְךָ. וְיִגֹּלוּ רַחֲמֶיךָ עַל מִדּוֹתֶיךָ. וְתִתְנַהֵג עִמָּנוּ יְהוָה אֱלֹהֵינוּ בְּמִדַּת הַחֶסֶד וּבְמִדַּת הָרַחֲמִים. וְתִכָּנֵס לָנוּ לִפְנִים מִשּׁוּרַת הַדִּין. וּבְטוּבְךָ הַגָּדוֹל יָשׁוּב חֲרוֹן אַפְּךָ. מֵעַמְּךָ וּמֵעִירְךָ וּמֵאַרְצְךָ וּמִנַּחֲלָתֶךָ. וְקַיֶּם לָנוּ יְהוָה אֱלֹהֵינוּ אֶת הַדָּבָר שֶׁהִבְטַחְתָּנוּ בְּתוֹרָתֶךָ עַל יְדֵי מֹשֶׁה עַבְדֶּךָ כָּאָמוּר: וְזָכַרְתִּי אֶת־בְּרִיתִי יַעֲקוֹב וְאַף אֶת־בְּרִיתִי יִצְחָק וְאַף אֶת־בְּרִיתִי אַבְרָהָם אֶזְכֹּר וְהָאָרֶץ אֶזְכֹּר: וְנֶאֱמַר: וְאַף־גַּם־זֹאת בִּהְיוֹתָם בְּאֶרֶץ אֹיְבֵיהֶם לֹא־מְאַסְתִּים וְלֹא־גְעַלְתִּים לְכַלֹּתָם לְהָפֵר בְּרִיתִי אִתָּם כִּי אֲנִי יְהוָה אֱלֹהֵיהֶם: וְזָכַרְתִּי לָהֶם בְּרִית רִאשֹׁנִים אֲשֶׁר הוֹצֵאתִי־אֹתָם מֵאֶרֶץ מִצְרַיִם לְעֵינֵי הַגּוֹיִם לִהְיוֹת לָהֶם לֵאלֹהִים אֲנִי יְהוָה: וְנֶאֱמַר: וְשָׁב יְהוָה אֱלֹהֶיךָ אֶת־שְׁבוּתְךָ וְרִחֲמֶךָ וְשָׁב וְקִבֶּצְךָ מִכָּל־הָעַמִּים אֲשֶׁר הֱפִיצְךָ יְהוָה אֱלֹהֶיךָ שָׁמָּה:

אִם־יִהְיֶה נִדַּחֲךָ בִּקְצֵה הַשָּׁמָיִם מִשָּׁם יְקַבֶּצְךָ יְהֹוָה אֱלֹהֶיךָ וּמִשָּׁם
יִקָּחֶךָ: וֶהֱבִיאֲךָ יְהֹוָה אֱלֹהֶיךָ אֶל־הָאָרֶץ אֲשֶׁר־יָרְשׁוּ אֲבֹתֶיךָ וִירִשְׁתָּהּ
וְהֵיטִבְךָ וְהִרְבְּךָ מֵאֲבֹתֶיךָ: וְנֶאֱמַר עַל יְדֵי נְבִיאֶךָ: יְהֹוָה חָנֵּנוּ לְךָ
קִוִּינוּ הֱיֵה זְרֹעָם לַבְּקָרִים אַף־יְשׁוּעָתֵנוּ בְּעֵת צָרָה: וְנֶאֱמַר:
וְעֵת־צָרָה הִיא לְיַעֲקֹב וּמִמֶּנָּה יִוָּשֵׁעַ: וְנֶאֱמַר: בְּכָל־צָרָתָם לא (לוֹ)
צָר וּמַלְאַךְ פָּנָיו הוֹשִׁיעָם בְּאַהֲבָתוֹ וּבְחֶמְלָתוֹ הוּא גְאָלָם וַיְנַטְּלֵם
וַיְנַשְּׂאֵם כָּל־יְמֵי עוֹלָם: וְנֶאֱמַר:

Ribono Shel Olam. Kemo Shekavash Avraham Avinu Et Rachamav La'asot Retzonecha Belevav Shalem. Ken Yichbeshu Rachameicha Et Ka'asecha. Veyigolu Rachameicha Al Middoteicha. Vetitnaheg Imanu Adonai Eloheinu Bemidat Hachesed Uvemidat Harachamim. Vetikanes Lanu Lifnim Mishurat Hadin. Uvetuvecha Hagadol Yashuv Charon Appach. Me'amach Ume'irach Ume'artzach Uminachalatach. Vekayem Lanu Adonai Eloheinu Et Hadavar Shehivtachtanu Betoratach Al Yedei Mosheh Avdach Ka'amur. Vezacharti Et-Beriti Ya'akov; Ve'af Et-Beriti Yitzchak Ve'af Et-Beriti Avraham Ezkor Veha'aretz Ezkor. Vene'emar. Ve'af-Gam-Zot Bihyotam Be'eretz Oyeveihem. Lo-Me'astim Velo-Ge'altim Lechalotam. Lehafer Beriti Ittam; Ki Ani Adonai Eloheihem. Vezacharti Lahem Berit Rishonim; Asher Hotzeti-'Otam Me'eretz Mitzrayim Le'einei Hagoyim. Lihyot Lahem Lelohim Ani Adonai. Vene'emar. Veshav Adonai Eloheicha Et-Shevutecha Verichamecha; Veshav. Vekibetzcha Mikol-Ha'ammim. Asher Hefitzecha Adonai Eloheicha Shamah. Im-Yihyeh Niddachacha Biktzeh Hashamayim; Misham. Yekabetzcha Adonai Eloheicha. Umisham Yikachecha. Vehevi'acha Adonai Eloheicha. El-Ha'aretz Asher-Yareshu Avoteicha Virishtah; Veheitivcha Vehirbecha Me'avoteicha. Vene'emar Al Yedei Nevi'echa. Adonai Chonenu Lecha Kivinu; Heyeh Zero'am Labekarim. Af-Yeshu'atenu Be'et Tzarah. Vene'emar. Ve'et-Tzarah Hi Leya'akov. Umimenah Yivashea. Vene'emar. Bechol-Tzaratam Lo Tzar. Umal'ach Panav Hoshi'am. Be'ahavato Uvechemlato Hu Ge'alam; Vaynattelem Vaynasse'em Chol-Yemei Olam. Vene'emar.

Sovereign of the universe, Avraham mastered his compassion for his only son in order to perform Your will with a whole heart; so in like measure may Your mercy prevail over stern justice. Let mercy temper justice. Deal with us, Hashem our God, with Your attributes of mercy and kindness beyond the measure of what we deserve. In Your great goodness may the flame of Your displeasure turn away from Your people, from Tzion Your city, from Your land and Your heritage. Fulfill to us, Hashem our God, the promise You have assured us in Your Torah through Your servant Moshe in the words, "I will remember My covenant with Yaakov and also My covenant with Yitzchak, and also My covenant with Avraham I will remember, and the land I will remember." This too have You said, "Yet with all, when they will be in the land of their enemies I will not repudiate or reject them to destroy them utterly and to break My covenant with them, for I am Hashem their God. But for their sakes I will remember the covenant with their ancestors whom I brought forth out of the land of Egypt in the sight of the nations, to be their God; I am Hashem." (Deut. 30:3-5) Even so it is said in Your Torah: "Hashem your God will bring you back out of captivity and have compassion on you, and will again gather you from all the nations where Hashem your God has scattered you. If your dispersed are at the farthest horizon, then will Hashem your God gather you, and then He will bring you. And Hashem your God will bring you into the land which your fathers possessed, and you will possess it, and He will do you good and multiply you above your fathers." Further it is said by Your prophets: "Hashem be gracious to us, we have waited for You. Be our strength every morning, our saving power also in time of trouble. It is a time of trouble for Yaakov, but he will be saved from it. In all their affliction He was afflicted, and the angel of His presence saved them; in His love and in His pity, He redeemed them and bare them and carried them all the days of old.

מִי־אֵל כָּמוֹךָ אל נֹשֵׂא עָוֹן רחום וְעֹבֵר עַל־פֶּשַׁע וחנון לִשְׁאֵרִית נַחֲלָתוֹ ארך
לֹא־הֶחֱזִיק לָעַד אַפּוֹ אפים כִּי־חָפֵץ חֶסֶד הוּא ורב חסד יָשׁוּב יְרַחֲמֵנוּ ואמת
יִכְבֹּשׁ עֲוֹנֹתֵינוּ נצר חסד וְתַשְׁלִיךְ בִּמְצֻלוֹת יָם כָּל־חַטֹּאותָם לאלפים תִּתֵּן

אֱמֶת לְיַעֲקֹב נושא עון חֶסֶד לְאַבְרָהָם ופשע אֲשֶׁר־נִשְׁבַּעְתָּ לַאֲבֹתֵינוּ וחטאה מִימֵי קֶדֶם ונקה וְנֶאֱמַר: וַהֲבִיאוֹתִים אֶל־הַר קָדְשִׁי וְשִׂמַּחְתִּים בְּבֵית תְּפִלָּתִי עוֹלֹתֵיהֶם וְזִבְחֵיהֶם לְרָצוֹן עַל־מִזְבְּחִי כִּי בֵיתִי בֵּית־תְּפִלָּה יִקָּרֵא לְכָל־הָעַמִּים:

Mi El Kamocha **(El)** Nose Avon **(Rachum)** Ve'over Al Pesha **(Vechanun)** Lish'erit Nachalato **(Erek)** Lo Hechezik La'ad Appo **(Apayim)** Ki Chafetz Chesed Hu **(Verav Chesed)**: Yashuv Yerachamenu **(V'emet)** Yichbosh Avonoteinu **(Notzer Chesed)** Vetashlich Bimtzulot Yam Kol Chatovtam **(Alafim)**: Titen Emet Leya'akov **(Noseh Avon)** Chesed Le'avraham **(Vafesha)** Asher Nishba'ta La'avoteinu **(Vechata'ah)** Mimei Kedem **(Venakeh)**: Vene'emar: Vahavi'otim El Har Kodshi Vesimachtim Beveit Tefillati Oloteihem Vezivcheihem Leratzon Al Mizbechi Ki Veiti Beit Tefillah Yikare Lechol Ha'ammim:

Who is like You, a God pardoning iniquity and passing over the transgression of the remnant of His heritage, who does not hold His anger forever, because He delights in mercy? He will again have compassion upon us, He will overcome our iniquities, even, cast all our sins into the depths of the sea." Cast all our sins and all the sins of Your people the House of Yisrael where they will be recalled or remembered no more or burden the heart. "You will show to Yaakov the faithfulness, and to Avraham the mercy, which You have sworn to our fathers from days of old." And it is said: "I will bring them to My holy mountain and make them rejoice in My house of prayer; their offerings and their sacrifices will be accepted upon My altar, for My House will be called a house of prayer for all peoples."

Elu Devarim

Mishnah Peah 1:1; Talmud Shabbat 127a, Kiddushin 39b

אֵלּוּ דְבָרִים שֶׁאֵין לָהֶם שִׁעוּר: הַפֵּאָה. וְהַבִּכּוּרִים. וְהָרֵאָיוֹן. וּגְמִילוּת חֲסָדִים. וְתַלְמוּד תּוֹרָה: אֵלּוּ דְבָרִים שֶׁאָדָם עוֹשֶׂה אוֹת וְאוֹכֵל פֵּרוֹתֵיהֶם בָּעוֹלָם הַזֶּה. וְהַקֶּרֶן קַיֶּמֶת לָעוֹלָם הַבָּא: וְאֵלּוּ הֵן:

כִּבּוּד אָב וָאֵם. וּגְמִילוּת חֲסָדִים. וּבִקּוּר חוֹלִים. וְהַכְנָסַת אוֹרְחִים. וְהַשְׁכָּמַת בֵּית הַכְּנֶסֶת. וַהֲבָאַת שָׁלוֹם בֵּין אָדָם לַחֲבֵרוֹ וּבֵין אִישׁ לְאִשְׁתּוֹ וְתַלְמוּד תּוֹרָה כְּנֶגֶד כֻּלָּם.

Elu Devarim She'ein Lahem Shi'ur. Hape'ah. Vehabikurim. Vehare'ayon. Ugemilut Chasadim. Vetalmud Torah. Elu Devarim She'adam Oseh Ot Ve'ochel Peroteihem Ba'olam Hazeh. Vehakeren Kayemet La'olam Haba. Ve'elu Hen. Kibud Av Va'em. Ugemilut Chasadim. Uvikkur Cholim. Vehachnasat Orechim. Vehashkamat Beit Hakeneset. Vahava'at Shalom Bein Adam Lachavero Uvein Ish Le'ishto Vetalmud Torah Keneged Kulam.

These are the things for which no limit is prescribed: the corner of the field, the first-fruits, the pilgrimage offerings, the practice of kindness, and the study of the Torah. These are the things the fruits of which a man enjoys in this world, while the principal remains for him in the world to come, namely: honoring father and mother, practice of kindness, early attendance at the schoolhouse morning and evening, hospitality to strangers, visiting the sick, dowering the bride, attending the dead to the grave, devotion in prayer, and making peace between man and his friend; but the study of the Torah equals them all.

Le'olam Yehei Adam

לְעוֹלָם יְהֵא אָדָם יְרֵא שָׁמַיִם בַּסֵּתֶר כְּבַגָּלוּי. וּמוֹדֶה עַל הָאֱמֶת. וְדוֹבֵר אֱמֶת בִּלְבָבוֹ. וְיַשְׁכִּים וְיֹאמַר: רִבּוֹן הָעוֹלָמִים וַאֲדוֹנֵי הָאֲדוֹנִים. לֹא עַל צִדְקוֹתֵינוּ אֲנַחְנוּ מַפִּילִים תַּחֲנוּנֵינוּ לְפָנֶיךָ כִּי עַל רַחֲמֶיךָ הָרַבִּים: אֲדֹנָי שְׁמָעָה אֲדֹנָי סְלָחָה אֲדֹנָי הַקְשִׁיבָה וַעֲשֵׂה אַל־תְּאַחַר לְמַעַנְךָ אֱלֹהַי כִּי־שִׁמְךָ נִקְרָא עַל־עִירְךָ וְעַל־עַמֶּךָ: מָה אֲנַחְנוּ. מֶה חַיֵּינוּ. מֶה חַסְדֵּנוּ. מַה־צִּדְקוֹתֵינוּ. מַה־כֹּחֵנוּ. מַה־גְּבוּרָתֵנוּ. מַה נֹּאמַר לְפָנֶיךָ יְהֹוָה אֱלֹהֵינוּ וֵאלֹהֵי אֲבוֹתֵינוּ. הֲלֹא כָּל־הַגִּבּוֹרִים כְּאַיִן לְפָנֶיךָ. וְאַנְשֵׁי הַשֵּׁם כְּלֹא הָיוּ. וַחֲכָמִים כִּבְלִי

מַדָּע. וּנְבוֹנִים כִּבְלִי הַשְׂכֵּל. כִּי כָל־מַעֲשֵׂינוּ תֹּהוּ. וִימֵי חַיֵּינוּ הֶבֶל לְפָנֶיךָ. וּמוֹתַר הָאָדָם מִן־הַבְּהֵמָה אָיִן כִּי הַכֹּל הָבֶל: לְבַד הַנְּשָׁמָה הַטְּהוֹרָה שֶׁהִיא עֲתִידָה לִתֵּן דִּין וְחֶשְׁבּוֹן לִפְנֵי כִּסֵּא כְבוֹדֶךָ. וְכָל־הַגּוֹיִם כְּאַיִן נֶגְדֶּךָ. שֶׁנֶּאֱמַר: הֵן גּוֹיִם כְּמַר מִדְּלִי וּכְשַׁחַק מֹאזְנַיִם נֶחְשָׁבוּ הֵן אִיִּים כַּדַּק יִטּוֹל: אֲבָל אֲנַחְנוּ עַמְּךָ בְּנֵי בְרִיתֶךָ. בְּנֵי אַבְרָהָם אֹהַבְךָ שֶׁנִּשְׁבַּעְתָּ־לּוֹ בְּהַר הַמּוֹרִיָּה. זֶרַע יִצְחָק עֲקֵדְךָ שֶׁנֶּעֱקַד עַל־גַּבֵּי הַמִּזְבֵּחַ. עֲדַת יַעֲקֹב בִּנְךָ בְכוֹרֶךָ. שֶׁמֵּאַהֲבָתְךָ שֶׁאָהַבְתָּ אוֹתוֹ. וּמִשִּׂמְחָתְךָ שֶׁשָּׂמַחְתָּ־בּוֹ. קָרָאתָ אוֹתוֹ יִשְׂרָאֵל וִישֻׁרוּן:

Le'olam Yehei Adam Yerei Shamayim Basseter Kevagalui. Umodeh Al Ha'emet. Vedover Emet Bilvavo. Veyashkim Veyomar. Ribon Ha'olamim Va' Adonei Ha' Adonim. Lo Al Tzidkoteinu Anachnu Mapilim Tachanuneinu Lefaneicha Ki Al Rachameicha Harabim. Adonai Shema'ah Adonai Selachah. Adonai Hakshivah Va'aseh Al-Te'achar; Lema'ancha Elohai. Ki-Shimcha Nikra. Al-'Irecha Ve'al-'Ammecha. Mah Anachnu. Mah Chayeinu. Mah Chasdenu. Mah-Tzidkoteinu. Mah-Kocheinu. Mah-Gevuratenu. Mah Nomar Lefaneicha Adonai Eloheinu Velohei Avoteinu. Halo Kol-Hagiborim Ke'ayin Lefaneicha. Ve'anshei Adonai Kelo Hayu. Vachachamim Kivli Madda'. Unevonim Kivli Haskel. Ki Chol-Ma'aseinu Tohu. Vimei Chayeinu Hevel Lefaneicha. Umotar Ha'adam Min-Habehemah Ayin. Ki Hakol Havel. Levad Haneshamah Hatehorah Shehi Atidah Litten Din Vecheshbon Lifnei Chisei Chevodecha. Vechol-Hagoyim Ke'ayin Negdecha. Shene'emar. Hen Goyim Kemar Mideli. Ucheshachak Mozenayim Nechshavu; Hen Iyim Kadak Yitol. Aval Anachnu Ammecha Benei Veritecha. Benei Avraham Ohavecha Shenishba'ta-Lo Behar Hamoriyah. Zera Yitzchak Akedecha Shene'ekad Al-Gabei Hamizbe'ach. Adat Ya'akov Bincha Vechorecha. Sheme'ahavatecha She'ahavta Oto. Umisimchatecha Shessamachta-Bo. Karata Oto Yisra'el Vishurun.

Man should ever be God-fearing in private as well as in public. He should acknowledge the truth, and speak the truth in his heart. Let him rise early and say: Master of all worlds, It is not on account of our own righteousness that we offer our supplications before You, but on account of Your great compassion. What are we? What is our life? What is our goodness? What is our virtue? What our help? What our strength? What our might? What can we say to You, Hashem our God and God of our fathers? Indeed, all the heroes are as nothing in Your sight, the men of renown as though they never existed, the wise as though they were without knowledge, the intelligent as though they lacked insight; most of their actions are worthless in Your sight, their entire life is a fleeting breath. Man is not far above beast, for all is vanity. Except the pure soul, which is destined to give a strict account before Your glorious Throne. Before you all the nations are as nothing, as it is written: "The nations are a mere drop in the bucket, no more than dust upon the scales. Behold, the isles are like the flying dust." However, we are Your people, Your children of the covenant, the children of Avraham Your friend, to whom You made a promise on Mount Moriah; we are the descendants of his only son Yitzchak, who was bound on the altar; we are the community of Yaakov Your first-born, who You named Yisrael and Yeshurun because of Your love for him and Your delight in him.

לְפִיכָךְ אֲנַחְנוּ חַיָּבִים לְהוֹדוֹת לָךְ. וּלְשַׁבְּחָךְ וּלְפָאֲרָךְ וּלְרוֹמְמָךְ. וְלִתֵּן שִׁיר שֶׁבַח וְהוֹדָאָה לְשִׁמְךָ הַגָּדוֹל בְּכָל יוֹם תָּמִיד. אַשְׁרֵינוּ. מַה טּוֹב חֶלְקֵינוּ. וּמַה נָּעִים גּוֹרָלֵנוּ. וּמַה יָּפָה מְאוֹד יְרוּשָּׁתֵינוּ. אַשְׁרֵינוּ כְּשֶׁאֲנַחְנוּ מַשְׁכִּימִים וּמַעֲרִיבִים בְּבָתֵּי כְּנֵסִיּוֹת וּבְבָתֵּי מִדְרָשׁוֹת וּמְיַחֲדִים שִׁמְךָ בְּכָל יוֹם תָּמִיד אוֹמְרִים פַּעֲמַיִם בְּאַהֲבָה:

Lefichach Anachnu Chayavim Lehodot Lach. Uleshabechach Ulefa'arach Uleromemach. Velitten Shir Shevach Vehoda'ah Leshimcha Hagadol Bechol Yom Tamid. Ashreinu. Mah Tov Chelkeinu. Umah Na'im Goraleinu. Umah Yafah Me'od Yerushateinu. Ashreinu Keshe'anachnu Mashkimim Uma'arivim Bevatei Kenesiyot Uvevatei Midrashot Umeyachadim Shimcha Bechol Yom Tamid Omerim Pa'amayim Be'ahavah.

Therefore, it is our duty to give thanks to You, to praise and glorify You, to bless and sanctify Your name, and to offer many thanksgivings to You. Happy are we. How good is our destiny, how pleasant our lot, how beautiful our heritage. Happy are we when morning and evening we gather in the synagogues and houses of learning, forever acclaiming the unity of Your name and eagerly proclaiming twice every day:

שְׁמַע יִשְׂרָאֵל יְהֹוָה אֱלֹהֵינוּ יְהֹוָה | אֶחָד:

Shema Yisrael; Adonai Eloheinu Adonai Echad.

"Hear, O Yisrael, Hashem is our God, Hashem is One."

whisper silently:

בָּרוּךְ שֵׁם כְּבוֹד מַלְכוּתוֹ לְעוֹלָם וָעֶד:

Baruch Shem Kevod Malchuto Le'olam Va'ed.

Blessed is His name and glorious kingdom forever and ever.

Attah Hu Echad Kodem	אַתָּה הוּא אֶחָד קוֹדֵם
Shebarata Ha'olam. Ve'attah Hu	שֶׁבָּרָאתָ הָעוֹלָם. וְאַתָּה הוּא
Echad Le'achar Shebarata	אֶחָד לְאַחַר שֶׁבָּרָאתָ
Ha'olam. Attah Hu El Ba'olam	הָעוֹלָם. אַתָּה הוּא אֵל בָּעוֹלָם
Hazeh. Ve'attah Hu El Ba'olam	הַזֶּה. וְאַתָּה הוּא אֵל בָּעוֹלָם
Haba. Ve'attah-Hu;	הַבָּא. וְאַתָּה־הֽוּא
Ushenoteicha. Lo Yitamu.	וּשְׁנוֹתֶיךָ לֹא יִתָּֽמּוּ:
Kadesh Shemach Be'olamach	קַדֵּשׁ שִׁמְךָ בְּעוֹלָמָךְ
Al-'Am Mekadeshei Shemecha.	עַל־עַם מְקַדְּשֵׁי שְׁמֶךָ.
Uvishu'atecha Malkeinu Tarum	וּבִישׁוּעָתְךָ מַלְכֵּנוּ תָּרוּם
Vetagbiah Karnenu. Vetoshi'enu	וְתַגְבִּיהַּ קַרְנֵנוּ. וְתוֹשִׁיעֵנוּ
Bekarov Lema'an Shemecha.	בְּקָרוֹב לְמַעַן שְׁמֶךָ.
Baruch Hamkadesh Shemo	בָּרוּךְ הַמְקַדֵּשׁ שְׁמוֹ
Barabim.	בָּרַבִּים:

Before Your world's creation, You were One; and since creation You are One. You are God in this world; You will be God in the world to come. "You are immutable. Your years have no end." Sanctify Your name in this Your world through Yisrael, a people sanctifying Your name. Raise up and uphold our strength through Your saving power, and save us speedily for Your name's sake. Blessed is the one who sanctifies Your name before mankind.

Attah Hu Adonai Ha'elohim	אַתָּה הוּא יְהֹוָה הָאֱלֹהִים
Bashamayim Mima'al Ve'al-	בַּשָּׁמַיִם מִמַּעַל וְעַל־
Ha'aretz Mitachat. Bishmei	הָאָרֶץ מִתַּחַת. בִּשְׁמֵי
Hashamayim Ha'elyonim	הַשָּׁמַיִם הָעֶלְיוֹנִים
Vehatachtonim. Attah Hu Rishon	וְהַתַּחְתּוֹנִים. אַתָּה הוּא רִאשׁוֹן
Ve'attah Hu Acharon	וְאַתָּה הוּא אַחֲרוֹן
Umibal'adeicha Ein Elohim.	וּמִבַּלְעָדֶיךָ אֵין אֱלֹהִים.
Kabetz Nefutzot Koveicha	קַבֵּץ נְפוּצוֹת קֹוֶיךָ
Me'arba Kanfot Ha'aretz. Yakiru	מֵאַרְבַּע כַּנְפוֹת הָאָרֶץ. יַכִּירוּ
Veyede'u Kol Ba'ei Olam Ki	וְיֵדְעוּ כָּל בָּאֵי עוֹלָם כִּי
Attah Hu Ha'elohim Levadecha	אַתָּה הוּא הָאֱלֹהִים לְבַדְּךָ
Lechol Mamlechot Ha'aretz.	לְכָל מַמְלְכוֹת הָאָרֶץ.
Attah Asita Et Hashamayim Ve'et	אַתָּה עָשִׂיתָ אֶת הַשָּׁמַיִם וְאֶת
Ha'aretz. Et Hayam Ve'et Kol	הָאָרֶץ. אֶת הַיָּם וְאֶת כָּל
Asher Bam. Umi Bechol Ma'aseh	אֲשֶׁר בָּם. וּמִי בְּכָל מַעֲשֵׂה
Yadeicha Ba'elyonim	יָדֶיךָ בָּעֶלְיוֹנִים
Uvatachtonim Sheyomar Lach	וּבַתַּחְתּוֹנִים שֶׁיֹּאמַר לְךָ
Mah-Ta'aseh Umah-Tif'al. Avinu	מַה־תַּעֲשֶׂה וּמַה־תִּפְעָל. אָבִינוּ
Shebashamayim Chai Vekayam.	שֶׁבַּשָּׁמַיִם חַי וְקַיָּם.

Aseh Imanu Chesed Ba'avur	עֲשֵׂה עִמָּנוּ חֶסֶד בַּעֲבוּר
Kevod Shimcha Hagadol	כְּבוֹד שִׁמְךָ הַגָּדוֹל
Hagibor Vehanorah Shenikra	הַגִּבּוֹר וְהַנּוֹרָא שֶׁנִּקְרָא
Aleinu. Vekayem Lanu Adonai	עָלֵינוּ. וְקַיֵּם לָנוּ יְהֹוָה
Eloheinu Et Hadavar	אֱלֹהֵינוּ אֶת הַדָּבָר
Shehivtachtanu Al Yedei	שֶׁהִבְטַחְתָּנוּ עַל יְדֵי
Tzefanyah Chozach Ka'amur.	צְפַנְיָה חוֹזָךְ כָּאָמוּר:
Ba'et Hahi Avi Etchem. Uva'et	בָּעֵת הַהִיא אָבִיא אֶתְכֶם וּבָעֵת
Kabetzi Etchem; Ki-'Etten Etchem	קַבְּצִי אֶתְכֶם כִּי־אֶתֵּן אֶתְכֶם
Leshem Velit'hillah. Bechol	לְשֵׁם וְלִתְהִלָּה בְּכֹל
Ammei Ha'aretz. Beshuvi Et-	עַמֵּי הָאָרֶץ בְּשׁוּבִי אֶת־
Shevuteichem Le'eineichem	שְׁבוּתֵיכֶם לְעֵינֵיכֶם
Amar Adonai.	אָמַר יְהֹוָה:

You, Hashem our God, are in heaven and on earth and in the highest heavens. Truly, You are the first and You are the last; besides you there is no God. Gather the dispersed who yearn for You from the four corners of the earth. Let all mankind realize and know that You alone are God supreme over all the kingdoms of the earth. You have made the heavens, the earth, the sea, and all that is in them. Who is there among all the works of Your hands, among the heavenly or the earthly creatures, that can say to You, "What will You do?" Our Father Who is in heaven, Eternal One, deal kindly with us for the sake of Your great name by which we are called; fulfill for us, Hashem our God, that which is written: "At that time I will bring you home; at that time I will gather you; indeed, I will grant you fame and praise among all the peoples of the earth, when I bring back your captivity before your own eyes, says Hashem."

Korbanot / Offerings

Some say it is good to stand, like the Kohanim who stood while the offerings were made. Some say only Kohanim should stand, while some say that one should stand during Shacharit, but sit during the korbanot of Mincha. Many say it is not necessary to stand. (Kaf HaChayim 1:33, Magen Avraham 48:1, Sha'arei Teshuva 48:1)

Yehi Ratzon Milfaneicha Adonai	יְהִי רָצוֹן מִלְּפָנֶיךָ יְהֹוָה
Eloheinu Velohei Avoteinu	אֱלֹהֵינוּ וֵאלֹהֵי אֲבוֹתֵינוּ
Sheterachem Aleinu. Vetimchol	שֶׁתְּרַחֵם עָלֵינוּ. וְתִמְחוֹל
Lanu Et Kol Chat'oteinu.	לָנוּ אֶת כָּל חַטֹּאותֵינוּ.
Utechapeir Lanu Et-	וּתְכַפֵּר לָנוּ אֶת־
Kol-'Avonoteinu. Vetimchol	כָּל־עֲוֹנוֹתֵינוּ. וְתִמְחוֹל
Vetislach Lechol Pesha'einu.	וְתִסְלַח לְכָל פְּשָׁעֵינוּ.
Vetivneh Beit Hamikdash	וְתִבְנֶה בֵּית הַמִּקְדָּשׁ
Bimheirah Veyameinu. Venakriv	בִּמְהֵרָה בְיָמֵינוּ. וְנַקְרִיב
Lefaneicha Korban Hatamid	לְפָנֶיךָ קָרְבַּן הַתָּמִיד שֶׁיְּכַפֵּר
Sheyechapeir Ba'adeinu. Kemo	בַּעֲדֵינוּ. כְּמוֹ שֶׁכָּתַבְתָּ עָלֵינוּ
Shekatavta Aleinu Betoratach Al	בְּתוֹרָתֶךָ עַל יְדֵי מֹשֶׁה עַבְדָּךְ
Yedei Mosheh Avdach Ka'amur.	כָּאָמוּר:

May it be Your will, Hashem our God, God of our fathers, to have mercy on us, and to forgive us all of our sins, and atone for us and all of our transgressions, and to forgive and pardon all of our willful sins. May the Beit HaMikdash speedily be rebuilt in our days, that we may bring before You our Tamid that will atone for us as written for us in Your Torah through Moshe Your servant; as it says:

Tamid / Eternal Offering: Numbers 28:1-8

וַיְדַבֵּר יְהֹוָה אֶל־מֹשֶׁה לֵּאמֹר: צַו אֶת־בְּנֵי יִשְׂרָאֵל וְאָמַרְתָּ אֲלֵהֶם
אֶת־קָרְבָּנִי לַחְמִי לְאִשַּׁי רֵיחַ נִיחֹחִי תִּשְׁמְרוּ לְהַקְרִיב לִי בְּמוֹעֲדוֹ:

וְאָמַרְתָּ לָהֶם זֶה הָאִשֶּׁה אֲשֶׁר תַּקְרִיבוּ לַיהֹוָה כְּבָשִׂים בְּנֵי־שָׁנָה תְמִימִם שְׁנַיִם לַיּוֹם עֹלָה תָמִיד: אֶת־הַכֶּבֶשׂ אֶחָד תַּעֲשֶׂה בַבֹּקֶר וְאֵת הַכֶּבֶשׂ הַשֵּׁנִי תַּעֲשֶׂה בֵּין הָעַרְבָּיִם: וַעֲשִׂירִית הָאֵיפָה סֹלֶת לְמִנְחָה בְּלוּלָה בְּשֶׁמֶן כָּתִית רְבִיעִת הַהִין: עֹלַת תָּמִיד הָעֲשֻׂיָה בְּהַר סִינַי לְרֵיחַ נִיחֹחַ אִשֶּׁה לַיהֹוָה: וְנִסְכּוֹ רְבִיעִת הַהִין לַכֶּבֶשׂ הָאֶחָד בַּקֹּדֶשׁ הַסֵּךְ נֶסֶךְ שֵׁכָר לַיהֹוָה: וְאֵת הַכֶּבֶשׂ הַשֵּׁנִי תַּעֲשֶׂה בֵּין הָעַרְבָּיִם כְּמִנְחַת הַבֹּקֶר וּכְנִסְכּוֹ תַּעֲשֶׂה אִשֵּׁה רֵיחַ נִיחֹחַ לַיהֹוָה:

Vaydaber Adonai El-Mosheh Lemor. Tzav Et-Benei Yisra'el. Ve'amarta Aleihem; Et-Korbani Lachmi Le'ishai. Reiach Nichochi. Tishmeru Lehakriv Li Bemo'ado. Ve'amarta Lahem. Zeh Ha'isheh. Asher Takrivu L'Adonai Kevasim Benei-Shanah Temimim Shenayim Layom Olah Tamid. Et-Hakeves Echad Ta'aseh Vaboker; Ve'et Hakeves Hasheni. Ta'aseh Bein Ha'arbayim. Va'asirit Ha'eifah Solet Leminchah; Belulah Beshemen Katit Revi'it Hahin. Olat Tamid; Ha'asuyah Behar Sinai. Lereiach Nichoach. Isheh L'Adonai Venisko Revi'it Hahin. Lakeves Ha'echad; Bakodesh. Hassech Nesech Shechar L'Adonai Ve'et Hakeves Hasheni. Ta'aseh Bein Ha'arbayim; Keminchat Haboker Uchenisko Ta'aseh. Isheh Reiach Nichoach L'Adonai.

And Hashem spoke to Moshe, saying, Command the children of Yisrael and say to them, My offering, My bread for My fire-offerings, you will observe to offer for a sweet savor to Me in its due season. Say also to them, this is the fire-offering which you will bring to Hashem: lambs of the first year without blemish, two each day as a continual burnt-offering. The one lamb you will prepare in the morning, and the other lamb you will prepare at dusk, with the tenth of an ephah of fine flour for a meal-offering, mingled with a fourth of a hin of the purest oil. This is a continual burnt-offering as it was prepared at Mount Sinai, a fire-offering for a sweet savor to Hashem. And the drink-offering with it will be a fourth of a hin for the one lamb. You will pour out the pure wine to Hashem in the holy place as a drink-offering. The second lamb you will offer at dusk, preparing it as the morning meal offering and as its drink-offering of a sweet savor to Hashem.

On Rosh Chodesh, some add:

וּבְרָאשֵׁי חׇדְשֵׁיכֶם תַּקְרִיבוּ עֹלָה לַיהֹוָה פָּרִים בְּנֵי־בָקָר שְׁנַיִם וְאַיִל אֶחָד כְּבָשִׂים בְּנֵי־שָׁנָה שִׁבְעָה תְּמִימִם: וּשְׁלֹשָׁה עֶשְׂרֹנִים סֹלֶת מִנְחָה בְּלוּלָה בַשֶּׁמֶן לַפָּר הָאֶחָד וּשְׁנֵי עֶשְׂרֹנִים סֹלֶת מִנְחָה בְּלוּלָה בַשֶּׁמֶן לָאַיִל הָאֶחָד: וְעִשָּׂרֹן עִשָּׂרוֹן סֹלֶת מִנְחָה בְּלוּלָה בַשֶּׁמֶן לַכֶּבֶשׂ הָאֶחָד עֹלָה רֵיחַ נִיחֹחַ אִשֶּׁה לַיהֹוָה: וְנִסְכֵּיהֶם חֲצִי הַהִין יִהְיֶה לַפָּר וּשְׁלִישִׁת הַהִין לָאַיִל וּרְבִיעִת הַהִין לַכֶּבֶשׂ יָיִן זֹאת עֹלַת חֹדֶשׁ בְּחׇדְשׁוֹ לְחׇדְשֵׁי הַשָּׁנָה: וּשְׂעִיר עִזִּים אֶחָד לְחַטָּאת לַיהֹוָה עַל־עֹלַת הַתָּמִיד יֵעָשֶׂה וְנִסְכּוֹ:

Uveroshei Chodsheichem Takrivu Olah L'Adonai Parim Benei Vakar Shenayim Ve'ayil Echad Kevasim Benei Shanah Shiv'ah Temimim. Usheloshah Esronim Solet Minchah Belulah Vashemen Lappar Ha'echad Ushenei Esronim Solet Minchah Belulah Vashemen La'ayil Ha'echad. Ve'issaron Issaron Solet Minchah Belulah Vashemen Lakeves Ha'echad Olah Reiach Nichoach Isheh L'Adonai. Veniskeihem Chatzi Hahin Yihyeh Lappar Ushelishit Hahin La'ayil Urevi'it Hahin Lakeves Yayin Zot Olat Chodesh Bechodsho Lechodshei Hashanah. Use'ir Izim Echad Lechatat L'Adonai Al Olat Hatamid Ye'aseh Venisko.

And on your new moons you will present a burnt-offering to Hashem: two young bulls, and one ram, seven male lambs of the first year without blemish; and three-tenth parts of an ephah of fine flour for a meal-offering, mingled with oil, for each bull; and two tenth parts of fine flour for a meal-offering, mingled with oil, for the one ram; and a several tenth part of fine flour mingled with oil for a meal-offering to every lamb; for a burnt-offering of a sweet savor, an offering made by fire to Hashem. And their drink-offerings will be half a hin of wine for a bull, and the third part of a hin for the ram, and the fourth part of a hin for a lamb. This is the burnt-offering of every new moon throughout the months of the year. And one male goat for a sin-offering to Hashem; it will be offered beside the continual burnt-offering, and the drink-offering of it. **(Num. 28:11-15)**

Ketoret / Incense Offering

Attah Hu Adonai Eloheinu.	אַתָּה הוּא יְהֹוָה אֱלֹהֵינוּ.
Shehiktiru Avoteinu Lefaneicha	שֶׁהִקְטִירוּ אֲבוֹתֵינוּ לְפָנֶיךָ
Et Ketoret Hasamim. Bizman	אֶת קְטֹרֶת הַסַּמִּים. בִּזְמַן

Shebeit Hamikdash Kayam.	שֶׁבֵּית הַמִּקְדָּשׁ קַיָּם.
Ka'asher Tzivita Otam Al-Yad	כַּאֲשֶׁר צִוִּיתָ אוֹתָם עַל־יַד
Mosheh Nevi'ach. Kakatuv	מֹשֶׁה נְבִיאָךְ. כַּכָּתוּב
Betoratach:	בְּתוֹרָתָךְ:

You are Hashem, our God, before Whom our ancestors burned the offering of incense in the days of the Beit HaMikdash. For You commanded them through Moshe, Your prophet, as it is written in Your Torah:

Exodus 30:34-36, 7-8

וַיֹּאמֶר יְהֹוָה אֶל־מֹשֶׁה קַח־לְךָ סַמִּים נָטָף ׀ וּשְׁחֵלֶת וְחֶלְבְּנָה סַמִּים וּלְבֹנָה זַכָּה בַּד בְּבַד יִהְיֶה: וְעָשִׂיתָ אֹתָהּ קְטֹרֶת רֹקַח מַעֲשֵׂה רוֹקֵחַ מְמֻלָּח טָהוֹר קֹדֶשׁ: וְשָׁחַקְתָּ מִמֶּנָּה הָדֵק וְנָתַתָּה מִמֶּנָּה לִפְנֵי הָעֵדֻת בְּאֹהֶל מוֹעֵד אֲשֶׁר אִוָּעֵד לְךָ שָׁמָּה קֹדֶשׁ קָדָשִׁים תִּהְיֶה לָכֶם: וְנֶאֱמַר וְהִקְטִיר עָלָיו אַהֲרֹן קְטֹרֶת סַמִּים בַּבֹּקֶר בַּבֹּקֶר בְּהֵיטִיבוֹ אֶת־הַנֵּרֹת יַקְטִירֶנָּה: וּבְהַעֲלֹת אַהֲרֹן אֶת־הַנֵּרֹת בֵּין הָעַרְבַּיִם יַקְטִירֶנָּה קְטֹרֶת תָּמִיד לִפְנֵי יְהֹוָה לְדֹרֹתֵיכֶם:

Vayomer Adonai El-Mosheh Kach-Lecha Samim. Nataf Ushchelet Vechelbenah. Samim Ulevonah Zakah; Bad Bevad Yihyeh. Ve'asita Otah Ketoret. Rokach Ma'aseh Rokeach; Memulach Tahor Kodesh. Veshachakta Mimenah Hadek Venatatah Mimenah Lifnei Ha'eidut Be'ohel Mo'ed. Asher Iva'eid Lecha Shamah; Kodesh Kodashim Tihyeh Lachem. Vene'emar Vehiktir Alav Aharon Ketoret Samim; Baboker Baboker. Beheitivo Et-Hanerot Yaktirenah. Uveha'alot Aharon Et-Hanerot Bein Ha'arbayim Yaktirenah; Ketoret Tamid Lifnei Adonai Ledoroteichem.

And Hashem said to Moshe, 'Take sweet spices, oil of myrrh, onycha and galbanum, together with clear frankincense, a like weight of each of these sweet spices. And you will make from there incense, a perfume pure and holy, compounded by the perfumer, salted together. And you will crush some of it very fine, and put some of it before the Ark of testimony in the Ohel Moed where I will meet with you; it will be most holy to you. Further it is said in the Torah: "And Aharon will burn the incense of sweet spices on the altar of incense, every morning when he dresses the lamps he will burn it. And at dusk when Aharon lights the lamps he will again burn incense, a perpetual incense before Hashem throughout your generations."

Talmud: Keritot 6a

תָּנוּ רַבָּנָן: פִּטּוּם הַקְּטֹרֶת כֵּיצַד: שְׁלֹשׁ מֵאוֹת וְשִׁשִּׁים וּשְׁמוֹנָה מָנִים הָיוּ בָהּ. שְׁלֹשׁ מֵאוֹת וְשִׁשִּׁים וַחֲמִשָּׁה כְּמִנְיַן יְמוֹת הַחַמָּה. מָנֶה בְּכָל־יוֹם. מַחֲצִיתוֹ בַּבֹּקֶר וּמַחֲצִיתוֹ בָּעֶרֶב. וּשְׁלֹשָׁה מָנִים יְתֵרִים. שֶׁמֵּהֶם מַכְנִיס כֹּהֵן גָּדוֹל. וְנוֹטֵל מֵהֶם מְלֹא חָפְנָיו בְּיוֹם הַכִּפּוּרִים. וּמַחֲזִירָן לְמַכְתֶּשֶׁת בְּעֶרֶב יוֹם הַכִּפּוּרִים. כְּדֵי לְקַיֵּם מִצְוַת דַּקָּה מִן הַדַּקָּה. וְאַחַד־עָשָׂר סַמָּנִים הָיוּ בָהּ. וְאֵלּוּ הֵן:

Tanu Rabbanan. Pitum Haketoret Keitzad: Shelosh Me'ot Veshishim Ushemonah Manim Hayu Vah. Shelosh Me'ot Veshishim Vachamishah Keminyan Yemot Hachamah. Maneh Bechol-Yom. Machatzito Baboker Umachatzito Ba'erev. Usheloshah Manim Yeterim. Shemehem Machnis Kohen Gadol. Venotel Mehem Melo Chafenav Beyom Hakippurim. Umachaziron Lemachteshet Be'erev Yom Hakippurim. Kedei Lekayem Mitzvat Dakah Min Hadakah. Ve'achad-'Asar Samanim Hayu Vah. Ve'elu Hen.

The rabbis have taught how the compounding of the incense was done. In measure the incense contained three hundred and sixty-eight manehs, three hundred and sixty-five being one for each day of the year, the remaining three being for the high pin to take his hands full on the Yom Kippur. These last will again ground in a mortar on the eve of Yom Kippur so as to fulfill the command, "take of the finest beaten incense." and these are them:

א הַצֳּרִי ב וְהַצִּפֹּרֶן ג וְהַחֶלְבְּנָה ד וְהַלְּבוֹנָה. מִשְׁקַל שִׁבְעִים שִׁבְעִים מָנֶה. ה מוֹר. ו וּקְצִיעָה ז וְשִׁבֹּלֶת נֵרְדְּ ח וְכַרְכֹּם. מִשְׁקַל שִׁשָּׁה עָשָׂר שִׁשָּׁה עָשָׂר מָנֶה. ט קֹשְׁטְ שְׁנֵים עָשָׂר. י קִלּוּפָה שְׁלֹשָׁה. יא קִנָּמוֹן תִּשְׁעָה. בּוֹרִית־כַּרְשִׁינָה תִּשְׁעָה קַבִּין. יֵין קַפְרִיסִין סְאִין תְּלָת וְקַבִּין תְּלָתָא. וְאִם לֹא מָצָא יֵין קַפְרִיסִין. מֵבִיא חֲמַר חִיוָר עַתִּיק. מֶלַח סְדוֹמִית. רֹבַע. מַעֲלֶה עָשָׁן. כָּל־שֶׁהוּא. רִבִּי נָתָן הַבַּבְלִי אוֹמֵר: אַף כִּפַּת הַיַּרְדֵּן כָּל־שֶׁהִיא. אִם נָתַן בָּהּ דְּבַשׁ פְּסָלָהּ. וְאִם חִסֵּר אַחַת מִכָּל־סַמְמָנֶיהָ. חַיָּב מִיתָה:

Hatzori Vehatziporen Vehachelbenah Vehallevonah. Mishkal Shiv'im Shiv'im Maneh. Mor. Uketzi'ah Veshibolet Nered Vecharkom. Mishkal Shishah Asar Shishah Asar Maneh. Koshet Sheneim Asar. Kilufah Sheloshah. Kinamon Tish'ah. Borit-Karshinah Tish'ah Kabin. Yein Kafrisin Se'in Telat Vekabin Telata. Ve'im Lo Matza Yein Kafrisin. Mevi Chamar Chivar Atik. Melach Sedomit. Rova. Ma'aleh Ashan. Kol-Shehu. Ribi Natan Habavli Omer. Af Kippat Hayarden Kol-Shehi. Im Natan Bah Devash Pesalah. Ve'im Chisser Achat Mikol-Samemaneiha. Chayaiv Mitah.

The incense was compounded of eleven different spices: seventy manehs each of balm, onycha, galbanum, and frankincense; sixteen manehs each of myrrh, cassia, spikenard, and saffron; twelve manehs of costus; three manehs of aromatic bark; nine manehs of cinnamon; nine kabs of lye of Carsina; three seahs and three kabs of Cyprus wine, though if Cyprus wine could not be had, strong white wine might be substituted for it; the fourth of a kab of salt of Sedom, and a small quantity of a herb which caused the smoke to ascend straight. Rabbi Nathan of Bavel said there was added also a small quantity of kippat of the Yarden. If honey was mixed with the incense, the incense became unfit for sacred use, while the one who omitted any of the ingredients was deemed guilty of mortal error.

רַבָּן שִׁמְעוֹן בֶּן־גַּמְלִיאֵל אוֹמֵר: הַצֳּרִי אֵינוֹ אֶלָּא שְׂרָף. הַנּוֹטֵף מֵעֲצֵי הַקְּטָף. בֹּרִית כַּרְשִׁינָה. לְמָה הִיא בָאָה: כְּדֵי לְשַׁפּוֹת בָּהּ

אֶת־הַצִּפֹּרֶן. כְּדֵי שֶׁתְּהֵא נָאָה. יֵין קַפְרִיסִין. לָמָּה הוּא בָא: כְּדֵי לִשְׁרוֹת בּוֹ אֶת־הַצִּפֹּרֶן כְּדֵי שֶׁתְּהֵא עַזָּה. וַהֲלֹא מֵי רַגְלַיִם יָפִין לָהּ: אֶלָּא שֶׁאֵין מַכְנִיסִין מֵי רַגְלַיִם בַּמִּקְדָּשׁ. מִפְּנֵי הַכָּבוֹד:

Rabban Shim'on Ben-Gamli'el Omer. Hatzori Eino Ella Sheraf. Hanotef Me'atzei Haketaf. Borit Karshinah. Lemah Hi Va'ah: Kedei Leshapot Bah Et-Hatziporen. Kedei Shetehei Na'ah. Yein Kafrisin. Lemah Hu Va: Kedei Lishrot Bo Et-Hatziporen Kedei Shetehei Azah. Vahalo Mei Raglayim Yafin Lah: Ella She'ein Machnisin Mei Raglayim Bamikdash. Mipenei Hakavod.

Rabban Shimon, son of Gamliel, said that the balm required is that exuding from the balsam tree. Why did they use lye of Carsina? To refine the appearance of the onycha. What was the purpose of the Cyprus wine? To steep the onycha in it so as to harden it. Though mei raglayim might have been adapted for that purpose, it was not used because it was not decent to bring it into the Temple.

תַּנְיָא רִבִּי נָתָן אוֹמֵר: כְּשֶׁהוּא שׁוֹחֵק. אוֹמֵר: הָדֵק הֵיטֵב. הֵיטֵב הָדֵק. מִפְּנֵי שֶׁהַקּוֹל יָפֶה לַבְּשָׂמִים. פִּטְּמָהּ לַחֲצָאִין. כְּשֵׁרָה. לִשְׁלִישׁ וּלְרָבִיעַ. לֹא שָׁמַעְנוּ. אָמַר רִבִּי יְהוּדָה: זֶה הַכְּלָל. אִם כְּמִדָּתָהּ. כְּשֵׁרָה לַחֲצָאִין. וְאִם חִסֵּר אַחַת מִכָּל־סַמָּמָנֶיהָ. חַיָּב מִיתָה:

Tanya Ribi Natan Omer. Keshehu Shochek. Omer. Hadek Heitev. Heitev Hadek. Mipenei Shehakol Yafeh Labesamim. Pittemah Lachatza'in. Kesherah. Leshalish Uleravia'. Lo Shama'nu. Amar Ribi Yehudah. Zeh Hakelal. Im Kemidatah. Kesherah Lachatza'in. Ve'im Chisser Achat Mikol-Samemaneiha. Chayaiv Mitah.

It is taught: Rabbi Natan said that when the priest ground the incense the one superintending would say, "Grind it very fine, very fine grind it," because the sound of the human voice is encouraging in the making of spices. If he had compounded only one hundred and eighty-four manehs (half the required quantity), it was valid, but there is no tradition as to its permissibility if it was compounded in one-third or one-quarter proportions of the required quantity. Rabbi Yehudah said that the general principle is that if it was made with its ingredients in their correct proportions, it was permissible in half the quantity; but if one omitted any of the ingredients he was deemed guilty of mortal error.

תָּנֵי בַּר־קַפָּרָא: אַחַת לְשִׁשִּׁים אוֹ לְשִׁבְעִים שָׁנָה. הָיְתָה בָאָה שֶׁל
שִׁירַיִם לַחֲצָאִין. וְעוֹד תָּנֵי בַּר־קַפָּרָא: אִלּוּ הָיָה נוֹתֵן בָּהּ קָרְטוֹב
שֶׁל דְּבַשׁ. אֵין אָדָם יָכוֹל לַעֲמֹד מִפְּנֵי רֵיחָהּ. וְלָמָּה אֵין מְעָרְבִין
בָּהּ דְּבַשׁ. מִפְּנֵי שֶׁהַתּוֹרָה אָמְרָה: כִּי כָל־שְׂאֹר וְכָל־דְּבַשׁ
לֹא־תַקְטִירוּ מִמֶּנּוּ אִשֶּׁה לַיהוָה:

Tanei Var-Kappara. Achat Leshishim O Leshiv'im Shanah. Hayetah Va'ah Shel Shirayim Lachatza'in. Ve'od Tanei Var-Kappara. Ilu Hayah Noten Bah Karetov Shel Devash. Ein Adam Yachol La'amod Mipenei Reichah. Velamah Ein Me'arevin Bah Devash Mipenei Shehatorah Amerah. Ki Chol-Se'or Vechol-Devash. Lo-Taktiru Mimenu Isheh L'Adonai.

Bar Kappara taught that once in sixty or seventy years it happened that, left over, there was over a total of half the required amount accumulated from the three manehs of incense from which the high priest took his hands full on Yom Kippur. Further Bar Kappara taught that had one mixed into the incense the smallest quantity of honey, no one could have stood its scent. Why did they not mix honey with it? Because the Torah states that, "No leaven, or any honey, will you burn as an offering made by fire to Hashem."

יְהוָה צְבָאוֹת עִמָּנוּ מִשְׂגָּב־לָנוּ אֱלֹהֵי יַעֲקֹב סֶלָה: יְהוָה צְבָאוֹת
אַשְׁרֵי אָדָם בֹּטֵחַ בָּךְ: יְהוָה הוֹשִׁיעָה הַמֶּלֶךְ יַעֲנֵנוּ בְיוֹם־קָרְאֵנוּ:
וְעָרְבָה לַיהוָה מִנְחַת יְהוּדָה וִירוּשָׁלָיִם כִּימֵי עוֹלָם וּכְשָׁנִים קַדְמֹנִיּוֹת:

Adonai Tzeva'ot Imanu; Misgav-Lanu Elohei Ya'akov Selah. Adonai Tzeva'ot; Ashrei Adam. Boteach Bach. Adonai Hoshi'ah; Hamelech.

Ya'aneinu Veyom-Kor'enu. Ve'arevah L'Adonai Minchat Yehudah Virushalayim Kimei Olam. Ucheshanim Kadmoniyot.

Hashem of hosts is with us; The God of Yaakov is our high tower. Selah. Hashem of hosts, happy is the man who trusts in You. Save, Hashem; Let the King answer us in the day that we call. Then will the offering of Yehudah and Yerushalayim be pleasant to Hashem, as in the days of old, and as in ancient years. **(Psalms 46:12, 84:13, 20:10, Malachi 3:4)**

Ana Bechoach

אָנָּא בְּכֹחַ. גְּדוּלַת יְמִינְךָ. תַּתִּיר צְרוּרָה:

Ana Bechoach. Gedulat Yeminecha. Tatir Tzerurah.

By the great power of your right hand, Oh set the captive free.

קַבֵּל רִנַּת. עַמְּךָ שַׂגְּבֵנוּ. טַהֲרֵנוּ נוֹרָא:

Kabel Rinat. Ammecha Sagveinu. Tahareinu Nora.

God of awe, accept your people's prayer; strengthen us, cleanse us.

נָא גִבּוֹר. דּוֹרְשֵׁי יִחוּדְךָ. כְּבָבַת שָׁמְרֵם:

Na Gibor. Doreshei Yichudecha. Kevavat Shamerem.

Almighty God, guard as the apple of the eye those who seek You.

בָּרְכֵם טַהֲרֵם. רַחֲמֵי צִדְקָתְךָ. תָּמִיד גָּמְלֵם:

Barechem Taharem. Rachamei Tzidkatecha. Tamid Gamelem.

Bless them, cleanse them, pity them; forever grant them Your truth.

חֲסִין קָדוֹשׁ. בְּרֹב טוּבְךָ. נַהֵל עֲדָתֶךָ:

Chasin Kadosh. Berov Tuvecha. Nahel Adatecha.

Almighty and holy, in Your abundant goodness, guide Your people.

יָחִיד גֵּאֶה. לְעַמְּךָ פְּנֵה. זוֹכְרֵי קְדֻשָּׁתֶךָ:

Yachid Ge'eh. Le'ammecha Feneh. Zocherei Kedushatecha.

Supreme God, turn to Your people who are mindful of Your holiness.

שַׁוְעָתֵנוּ קַבֵּל. וּשְׁמַע צַעֲקָתֵנוּ. יוֹדֵעַ תַּעֲלוּמוֹת:

Shav'ateinu Kabel. Ushema Tza'akateinu. Yodea Ta'alumot.

Accept our prayer, hear our cry, You who knows secret thoughts.

And say silently:

בָּרוּךְ, שֵׁם כְּבוֹד מַלְכוּתוֹ, לְעוֹלָם וָעֶד:

Baruch, Shem Kevod Malchuto, Le'olam Va'ed.

Blessed is the Name of His glorious kingdom forever and ever.

Ribon Ha'olamim. Attah	רִבּוֹן הָעוֹלָמִים. אַתָּה
Tzivitanu Lehakriv Korban	צִוִּיתָנוּ לְהַקְרִיב קָרְבַּן
Hatamid Bemo'ado. Velihyot	הַתָּמִיד בְּמוֹעֲדוֹ. וְלִהְיוֹת
Kohanim Ba'avodatam.	כֹּהֲנִים בַּעֲבוֹדָתָם.
Uleviyim Beduchanam.	וּלְוִיִּם בְּדוּכָנָם.
Veyisra'el Bema'amadam.	וְיִשְׂרָאֵל בְּמַעֲמָדָם.
Ve'attah Ba'avonoteinu Charav	וְעַתָּה בַּעֲווֹנוֹתֵינוּ חָרַב
Beit Hamikdash Uvuttal	בֵּית הַמִּקְדָּשׁ וּבֻטַּל
Hatamid. Ve'ein Lanu Lo Kohen	הַתָּמִיד. וְאֵין לָנוּ לֹא כֹהֵן
Ba'avodato Velo Levi	בַּעֲבוֹדָתוֹ וְלֹא לֵוִי
Beduchano. Velo Yisra'el	בְּדוּכָנוֹ. וְלֹא יִשְׂרָאֵל
Bema'amado. Ve'attah Amarta.	בְּמַעֲמָדוֹ. וְאַתָּה אָמַרְתָּ:
Uneshalemah Farim Sefateinu.	וּנְשַׁלְּמָה פָרִים שְׂפָתֵינוּ:

Sovereign of the universe, You commanded us to offer the daily offering at its appointed time, with the the Kohanim at their service, the Levi'im on their platform, and Yisrael in their delegations. Now through our sins our Beit Hamikdash is laid waste, its daily offerings are abolished, and we have neither a Kohen at his service, nor Levi on his platform, or Yisrael delegation. But You have said (through

Your prophet Hoshea), that we may substitute (the prayer of) our lips for (the sacrifice of) bulls. **(Hoshea 14:3)**

Lachein Yehi Ratzon	לָכֵן יְהִי רָצוֹן
Milfaneicha Adonai Eloheinu	מִלְּפָנֶיךָ יְהֹוָה אֱלֹהֵינוּ
Velohei Avoteinu. Sheyehei	וֵאלֹהֵי אֲבוֹתֵינוּ. שֶׁיְּהֵא
Siach Siftoteinu Zeh Chashuv	שִׂיחַ שִׂפְתוֹתֵינוּ זֶה חָשׁוּב
Umekubbal Umerutzeh	וּמְקֻבָּל וּמְרוּצֶה
Lefaneicha Ke'ilu Hikravnu	לְפָנֶיךָ כְּאִילוּ הִקְרַבְנוּ
Korban Hatamid Bemo'ado	קָרְבַּן הַתָּמִיד בְּמוֹעֲדוֹ
Ve'amadnu Al Ma'amado.	וְעָמַדְנוּ עַל מַעֲמָדוֹ.
Kemo Shene'emar.	כְּמוֹ שֶׁנֶּאֱמַר:
Uneshalemah Farim Sefateinu.	וּנְשַׁלְּמָה פָרִים שְׂפָתֵינוּ:
Vene'emar. Veshachat Oto Al	וְנֶאֱמַר: וְשָׁחַט אֹתוֹ עַל
Yerech Hamizbe'ach Tzafonah	יֶרֶךְ הַמִּזְבֵּחַ צָפֹנָה
Lifnei Adonai Vezareku Benei	לִפְנֵי יְהֹוָה וְזָרְקוּ בְּנֵי
Aharon Hakohanim Et-Damo	אַהֲרֹן הַכֹּהֲנִים אֶת־דָּמוֹ
Al-Hamizbe'ach Saviv.	עַל־הַמִּזְבֵּחַ סָבִיב:
Vene'emar. Zot Hatorah.	וְנֶאֱמַר: זֹאת הַתּוֹרָה
La'olah Lamminchah. Velachatat	לָעֹלָה לַמִּנְחָה וְלַחַטָּאת
Vela'asham; Velammilu'im.	וְלָאָשָׁם וְלַמִּלּוּאִים
Ulezevach Hashelamim.	וּלְזֶבַח הַשְּׁלָמִים:

Therefore, let it be Your will, Hashem our God and God of our fathers, that the prayer of our lips be accepted before You in favor and accounted as if we had offered the daily Temple sacrifice at its appointed time in the presence of our delegation, for the fulfillment of the ancient words of the Torah, "He will offer the lamb at the side of the altar northward, before Hashem; and Aharon's sons as priests will sprinkle its blood upon the altar." Further the Torah says, "This is the law of the burnt-offering, the meal-offering, the sin-offering, the trespass-offering, the consecration and the sacrifice of the peace-offerings."

Continue with Eizehu Mekoman on the next page.

Eizehu Mekoman

Mishnah Zevachim, Chap. 5

It was established that one should recite the teaching of "Eizehu Mekoman" and the baraita of Rabbi Yishmael after the section of the daily offering in order that every person would attain merit everyday by learning Bible, Mishnah and Gemara (Talmud). The baraita of Rabbi Yishmael is in place of Gemara since midrash is like Gemara. (SA, OC 50)

אֵיזֶהוּ מְקוֹמָן שֶׁל זְבָחִים. קָדְשֵׁי קָדָשִׁים שְׁחִיטָתָן בַּצָּפוֹן. פַּר וְשָׂעִיר שֶׁל יוֹם הַכִּפּוּרִים שְׁחִיטָתָן בַּצָּפוֹן. וְקִבּוּל דָּמָן בִּכְלֵי שָׁרֵת בַּצָּפוֹן. וְדָמָן טָעוּן הַזָּיָה עַל בֵּין הַבַּדִּים וְעַל הַפָּרֹכֶת וְעַל מִזְבַּח הַזָּהָב. מַתָּנָה אַחַת מֵהֶן מְעַכֶּבֶת. שְׁיָרֵי הַדָּם הָיָה שׁוֹפֵךְ עַל יְסוֹד מַעֲרָבִי שֶׁל מִזְבֵּחַ הַחִיצוֹן. אִם לֹא נָתַן. לֹא עִכֵּב:

Eizehu Mekoman Shel Zevachim. Kodshi Kadashim Shechitatan Batzafon. Par Vesa'ir Shel Yom Hakippurim Shechitatan Batzafon. Vekibul Daman Bichlei Sharet Batzafon. Vedaman Ta'un Hazayah Al Bein Habadim Ve'al Haparochet Ve'al Mizbach Hazahav. Matanah Achat Mehen Me'akevet. Shiyrei Hadam Hayah Shofech Al Yesod Ma'aravi Shel Mizbe'ach Hachitzon. Im Lo Natan. Lo Ikev:

1. Which were the places of sacrifice in the Temple? The most holy offerings were slaughtered on the north side of the altar, as were also the bull and the male-goat for Yom Kippur. Their blood was received there in a vessel of service to be sprinkled between the staves of the Ark before the veil of the Holy of Holies and upon the golden altar. The omission of a sprinkling invalidated the atonement ceremonial. The priest poured out the remaining blood on the western base of the outer altar, but if he omitted to do so the atonement ceremony was not invalidated.

פָּרִים הַנִּשְׂרָפִים וּשְׂעִירִים הַנִּשְׂרָפִים שְׁחִיטָתָן בַּצָּפוֹן. וְקִבּוּל דָּמָן בִּכְלֵי שָׁרֵת בַּצָּפוֹן. וְדָמָן טָעוּן הַזָּיָה עַל הַפָּרֹכֶת וְעַל מִזְבַּח הַזָּהָב. מַתָּנָה אַחַת מֵהֶן מְעַכֶּבֶת. שְׁיָרֵי הַדָּם הָיָה שׁוֹפֵךְ עַל יְסוֹד מַעֲרָבִי שֶׁל מִזְבַּח הַחִיצוֹן. אִם לֹא נָתַן. לֹא עִכֵּב. אֵלּוּ וָאֵלּוּ נִשְׂרָפִין בְּבֵית הַדָּשֶׁן:

Parim Hanisrafim Use'irim Hanisrafim Shechitatan Batzafon. Vekibul Daman Bichlei Sharet Batzafon. Vedaman Ta'un Hazayah Al Haparochet Ve'al Mizbach Hazahav. Matanah Achat Mehen Me'akevet. Shiyrei Hadam Hayah Shofech Al Yesod Ma'aravi Shel Mizbach Hachitzon. Im Lo Natan. Lo Ikev. Elu Ve'elu Nisrafin Beveit Hadashen.

2. The bulls and the male-goats which were to be entirely burnt were slaughtered on the north side of the altar, and their blood was received there in a vessel of service to be sprinkled before the veil and upon the golden altar. The omission of a sprinkling invalidated the atonement ceremonial. The priest poured out the remaining blood at the western base of the outer altar; but if he omitted to do so the atonement ceremony was not invalidated. These as well as the preceding offerings were burnt in the repository of ashes.

חַטֹּאת הַצִּבּוּר וְהַיָּחִיד. אֵלּוּ הֵן חַטֹּאת הַצִּבּוּר. שְׂעִירֵי רָאשֵׁי חֳדָשִׁים וְשֶׁל מוֹעֲדוֹת. שְׁחִיטָתָן בַּצָּפוֹן. וְקִבּוּל דָּמָן בִּכְלֵי שָׁרֵת בַּצָּפוֹן. וְדָמָן טָעוּן אַרְבַּע מַתָּנוֹת עַל אַרְבַּע קְרָנוֹת. כֵּיצַד. עָלָה בַכֶּבֶשׁ וּפָנָה לַסּוֹבֵב. וּבָא לוֹ לְקֶרֶן דְּרוֹמִית מִזְרָחִית. מִזְרָחִית צְפוֹנִית. צְפוֹנִית מַעֲרָבִית. מַעֲרָבִית דְּרוֹמִית. שְׁיָרֵי הַדָּם הָיָה שׁוֹפֵךְ עַל יְסוֹד דְּרוֹמִי. וְנֶאֱכָלִין לִפְנִים מִן הַקְּלָעִים לְזִכְרֵי כְהֻנָּה בְּכָל מַאֲכָל לְיוֹם וָלַיְלָה עַד חֲצוֹת:

Chatot Hatzibur Vehayachid. Elu Hen Chatot Hatzibur. Se'irei Roshei Chodashim Veshel Mo'adot. Shechitatan Batzafon. Vekibul Daman Bichlei Sharet Batzafon. Vedaman Ta'un Arba Matanot Al Arba Keranot. Keitzad. Alah Vakevesh Ufanah Lassovev. Uva Lo Lekeren Deromit Mizrachit. Mizrachit Tzefonit. Tzefonit Ma'aravit. Ma'aravit Deromit. Sheyarei Hadam Hayah Shofech Al Yesod Deromi. Vene'echalin Lifanim Min Hakkela'im Lezichrei Chehunah Bechol Ma'achal Leyom Valaylah Ad Chatzot.

3. As for the sin-offerings of the whole congregation and of an individual, the male-goats offered on Rosh Chodesh and on festivals are the sin-offerings of the whole congregation. These were slaughtered on the north side of the altar and their blood was

received there in a ritual vessel. It was required to make four sprinklings of that blood, once upon each of the four corners of the altar. How was this done? The priest went up the ascent to the altar and went around its ledge successively to its southeast, northeast, northwest and southwest corners. He poured out the remaining blood at the south side of the base of the outer altar. These sacrifices, prepared for food after any manner, were eaten within the hangings of the court only by the males of the priesthood during that day and evening until midnight.

הָעוֹלָה. קֹדֶשׁ קָדָשִׁים. שְׁחִיטָתָהּ בַּצָּפוֹן. וְקִבּוּל דָּמָהּ בִּכְלֵי שָׁרֵת בַּצָּפוֹן. וְדָמָהּ טָעוּן שְׁתֵּי מַתָּנוֹת שֶׁהֵן אַרְבַּע. וּטְעוּנָה הֶפְשֵׁט וְנִתּוּחַ וְכָלִיל לָאִשִּׁים:

Ha'olah. Kodesh Kadashim. Shechitatah Batzafon. Vekibul Damah Bichlei Sharet Batzafon. Vedamah Ta'un Shetei Matanot Shehen Arba'. Ute'unah Hefshet Venittuach Vechalil La'ishim

4. The burnt-offering was classed among the most holy of the offerings. It was slain on the north side of the altar and its blood was there received in a ritual vessel. It was required to make two doubled sprinklings of that blood so as to constitute four. That offering had to be flayed and dismembered and wholly consumed by fire.

זִבְחֵי שַׁלְמֵי צִבּוּר וַאֲשָׁמוֹת. אֵלּוּ הֵן אֲשָׁמוֹת. אֲשַׁם גְּזֵלוֹת. אֲשַׁם מְעִילוֹת. אֲשַׁם שִׁפְחָה חֲרוּפָה. אֲשַׁם נָזִיר. אֲשַׁם מְצוֹרָע. אָשָׁם תָּלוּי. שְׁחִיטָתָן בַּצָּפוֹן. וְקִבּוּל דָּמָן בִּכְלֵי שָׁרֵת בַּצָּפוֹן. וְדָמָן טָעוּן שְׁתֵּי מַתָּנוֹת שֶׁהֵן אַרְבַּע. וְנֶאֱכָלִין לִפְנִים מִן הַקְּלָעִים לְזִכְרֵי כְהֻנָּה בְּכָל מַאֲכָל לְיוֹם וָלַיְלָה עַד חֲצוֹת:

Zivchei Shalmei Tzibur Va'ashamot. Elu Hen Ashamot. Asham Gezelot. Asham Me'ilot. Asham Shifchah Charufah. Asham Nazir. Asham Metzora'. Asham Talui. Shechitatan Batzafon. Vekibul Daman Bichli Sharet Batzafon. Vedaman Ta'un Shetei Matanot

Shehen Arba'. Vene'echalin Lefanim Min Hakkela'im Lezichrei Chehunah Bechol Ma'achal Leyom Valaylah Ad Chatzot

5. As to the peace-offerings of the whole congregation and the trespass-offerings, the following are the trespass-offerings: for robbery, for the profane appropriation of sanctified things, for violating a bethrothed handmaid, that which was brought by the nazirite who had become defiled by a dead body, by the leper at his cleansing, and that brought for the sin-offering about which there was a doubt whether it should be atoned for by a sin-offering. All these were slaughtered on the north side of the altar and the blood was received there in a ritual vessel. It was required to make two doubled sprinklings of that blood so as to constitute four. These sacrifices, prepared for food after any manner, were eaten only within the hangings of the court by the males of the priesthood during that day and evening until midnight.

הַתּוֹדָה וְאֵיל נָזִיר. קָדָשִׁים קַלִּים. שְׁחִיטָתָן בְּכָל מָקוֹם בָּעֲזָרָה. וְדָמָן טָעוּן שְׁתֵּי מַתָּנוֹת שֶׁהֵן אַרְבַּע. וְנֶאֱכָלִין בְּכָל הָעִיר. לְכָל אָדָם. בְּכָל מַאֲכָל. לְיוֹם וָלַיְלָה עַד חֲצוֹת. הַמּוּרָם מֵהֶם כַּיּוֹצֵא בָהֶם. אֶלָּא שֶׁהַמּוּרָם נֶאֱכָל לַכֹּהֲנִים לִנְשֵׁיהֶם וְלִבְנֵיהֶם וּלְעַבְדֵיהֶם:

Hatodah Ve'eil Nazir. Kadashim Kallim. Shechitatan Bechol Makom Ba'azarah. Vedaman Ta'un Shetei Matanot Shehen Arba'. Vene'echalin Bechol Ha'ir. Lechol Adam. Bechol Ma'achal. Leyom Valaylah Ad Chatzot. Hamuram Mehem Kayotzei Vahem. Ella Shehamuram Ne'echal Lakohanim Linsheihem Velivneihem Ule'avdeihem.

6. The thanksgiving-offering of individuals and the ram offered by the nazirite at the close of his vow were of a minor degree of holiness. These might be killed in any part of the court of the Temple. It was required to make two doubled sprinklings of their blood so as to constitute four. They might be eaten prepared for food after any manner, in any part of the city by any person during the whole of that day and evening until midnight. The same rules were observed with the portions of them appertaining to the

priests, except that these might be eaten only by the priests, their wives, their children and their servants.

שְׁלָמִים. קָדָשִׁים קַלִּים. שְׁחִיטָתָן בְּכָל מָקוֹם בָּעֲזָרָה. וְדָמָן טָעוּן שְׁתֵּי מַתָּנוֹת שֶׁהֵן אַרְבַּע. וְנֶאֱכָלִין בְּכָל הָעִיר לְכָל אָדָם בְּכָל מַאֲכָל לִשְׁנֵי יָמִים וְלַיְלָה אֶחָד. הַמּוּרָם מֵהֶם כַּיּוֹצֵא בָהֶם. אֶלָּא שֶׁהַמּוּרָם נֶאֱכָל לַכֹּהֲנִים. לִנְשֵׁיהֶם וְלִבְנֵיהֶם וּלְעַבְדֵיהֶם:

Shelamim. Kadashim Kallim. Shechitatan Bechol Makom Ba'azarah. Vedaman Ta'un Shetei Matanot Shehen Arba'. Vene'echalin Bechol Ha'ir Lechol Adam Bechol Ma'achal Lishnei Yamim Valaylah Echad. Hamuram Mehem Kayotzei Bahem. Ella Shehamuram Ne'echal Lakohanim. Linsheihem Velivneihem Ule'avdeihem.

7. The peace-offerings also were holy in a minor degree of holiness. These might be killed in any part of the court of the Temple, and It was required to make two doubled sprinklings of their blood so as to constitute four. They might be eaten prepared for food after any manner, in any part of the city by any person during two days and the intervening night. The same rules were observed with the portions of them appertaining to the priests, except that these might be eaten only by the priests, their wives, their children and their servants.

הַבְּכוֹר וְהַמַּעֲשֵׂר וְהַפֶּסַח. קָדָשִׁים קַלִּים. שְׁחִיטָתָן בְּכָל מָקוֹם בָּעֲזָרָה. וְדָמָן טָעוּן מַתָּנָה אֶחָת. וּבִלְבַד שֶׁיִּתֵּן כְּנֶגֶד הַיְסוֹד. שִׁנָּה בַאֲכִילָתָן. הַבְּכוֹר נֶאֱכָל לַכֹּהֲנִים. וְהַמַּעֲשֵׂר לְכָל אָדָם. וְנֶאֱכָלִין בְּכָל הָעִיר לְכָל אָדָם בְּכָל מַאֲכָל לִשְׁנֵי יָמִים וְלַיְלָה אֶחָד. הַפֶּסַח אֵינוֹ נֶאֱכָל אֶלָּא בַלַּיְלָה. וְאֵינוֹ נֶאֱכָל אֶלָּא עַד חֲצוֹת. וְאֵינוֹ נֶאֱכָל אֶלָּא לִמְנוּיָו. וְאֵינוֹ נֶאֱכָל אֶלָּא צָלִי:

Habechor Vehama'aser Vehapesach. Kadashim Kallim. Shechitatan Bechol Makom Ba'azarah. Vedaman Ta'un Matanah Achat. Uvilvad Sheyiten Keneged Haysod. Shinah Va'achilatan. Habechor Ne'echal Lakohanim. Vehama'aser Lechol Adam. Vene'echalin Bechol Ha'ir Lechol Adam Bechol Ma'achal Lishnei Yamim Valaylah Echad.

Hapesach Eino Ne'echal Ella Vallaylah. Ve'eino Ne'echal Ella Ad Chatzot. Ve'eino Ne'echal Ella Limnuyav. Ve'eino Ne'echal Ella Tzali.

8. The first-born of beasts, the tithe of cattle, and the Pesach lamb were also holy in a minor degree. These might be killed in any part of the court of the Temple. Only one sprinkling of their blood was required, but that had to be done towards the base of the altar. In the eating of them, however, the following distinction was made: the first-born animal was eaten by the priests only, but the tithe could be eaten by anyone. Both the first-born animal and the tithe might be eaten prepared for food after any manner, in any part of the city during two days and the intervening night, whereas the Pesach lamb had to be eaten on that night only and not later than midnight. Neither may it be eaten except by those of a previously constituted group, or prepared in any way other than roasted.

Baraita of Rabbi Yishmael

Sifra: Ch. 1 - Preface to Torat Kohanim

רִבִּי יִשְׁמָעֵאל אוֹמֵר: בִּשְׁלֹשׁ עֶשְׂרֵה מִדּוֹת הַתּוֹרָה נִדְרֶשֶׁת: מִקַּל וָחוֹמֶר. מִגְּזֵרָה שָׁוָה. מִבִּנְיַן אָב וְכָתוּב אֶחָד. וּמִבִּנְיַן אָב וּשְׁנֵי כְתוּבִים. מִכְּלָל וּפְרָט. מִפְּרָט וּכְלָל. כְּלָל וּפְרָט וּכְלָל. אִי אַתָּה דָן אֶלָּא כְּעֵין הַפְּרָט. מִכְּלָל שֶׁהוּא צָרִיךְ לִפְרָט. וּמִפְּרָט שֶׁהוּא צָרִיךְ לִכְלָל. וְכָל דָּבָר שֶׁהָיָה בִכְלָל וְיָצָא מִן הַכְּלָל לְלַמֵּד. לֹא לְלַמֵּד עַל עַצְמוֹ יָצָא. אֶלָּא לְלַמֵּד עַל הַכְּלָל כֻּלּוֹ יָצָא. וְכָל דָּבָר שֶׁהָיָה בִכְלָל. וְיָצָא לִטְעוֹן טָעוּן אַחֵר שֶׁהוּא כְעִנְיָנוֹ. יָצָא לְהָקֵל וְלֹא לְהַחְמִיר. וְכָל דָּבָר שֶׁהָיָה בִּכְלָל. וְיָצָא לִטְעֹן טָעוּן אַחֵר שֶׁלֹּא כְעִנְיָנוֹ. יָצָא לְהָקֵל וּלְהַחְמִיר. וְכָל דָּבָר שֶׁהָיָה בִּכְלָל. וְיָצָא לִדּוֹן בְּדָבָר חָדָשׁ. אִי אַתָּה יָכוֹל לְהַחֲזִירוֹ לִכְלָלוֹ עַד שֶׁיַּחֲזִירֶנּוּ הַכָּתוּב לִכְלָלוֹ בְּפֵירוּשׁ. וְדָבָר הַלָּמֵד מֵעִנְיָנוֹ. וְדָבָר הַלָּמֵד מִסּוֹפוֹ. וְכֵן שְׁנֵי

כְּתוּבִים הַמַּכְחִישִׁים זֶה אֶת זֶה. עַד שֶׁיָּבֹא הַכָּתוּב הַשְּׁלִישִׁי וְיַכְרִיעַ בֵּינֵיהֶם:

Ribi Yishma'el Omer. Bishlosh Esreh Middot Hatorah Nidreshet: Mikal Vachomer. Migezerah Shaveh. Mibinyan Av Vechatuv Echad. Umibinyan Av Ushenei Chetuvim. Mikelal Uferat. Miperat Uchelal. Kelal Uferat Uchelal. Ei Attah Dan Ella Ke'ein Haperat. Mikelal Shehu Tzarich Lifrat. Umiperat Shehu Tzarich Lichlal. Vechol Davar Shehayah Vichlal Veyatza Min Hakelal Lelamed. Lo Lelamed Al Atzmo Yatza. Ella Lelamed Al Hakelal Kulo Yatza. Vechol Davar Shehayah Vichlal. Veyatza Lit'on Ta'un Acher Shehu Che'inyano. Yatza Lehakel Velo Lehachmir. Vechol Davar Shehayah Bichlal. Veyatza Lit'on Ta'un Acher Shelo Che'inyano. Yatza Lehakel Ulehachmir. Vechol Davar Shehayah Bichlal. Veyatza Liddon Bedavar Chadash. Ei Attah Yachol Lehachaziro Lichlalo Ad Sheyachazirenu Hakatuv Lichlalo Vefeirush. Vedavar Halamed Me'inyano. Vedavar Halamed Missofo. Vechan Shenei Chetuvim Hamachchishim Zeh Et Zeh. Ad Sheyavo Hakatuv Hashelishi Veyachria Beneihem.

Rabbi Yishmael says the Torah may be expounded by these thirteen principles of logic:

1. Inference from minor to major, or from major to minor. **2.** Inference from similarity of phrases in texts. **3.** A comprehensive principle derived from one text, or from two related texts. **4.** A general proposition followed by a specifying particular. **5.** A particular term followed by a general proposition. **6.** A general law limited by a specific application and then treated again in general terms must be interpreted according to the tenor of the specific limitation. **7.** A general proposition requiring a particular or specific term to explain it, and conversely, a particular term requiring a general one to complement it. **8.** When a subject included in a general proposition is afterwards particularly excepted to give information concerning it, the exception is made not for that one instance alone, but to apply to the general proposition as a whole. **9.** Whenever anything is first included in a general proposition and is then excepted to prove another similar proposition, this specifying alleviates and does not aggravate the law's restriction. **10.** But when anything is first included in a general proposition and is then excepted to state a case that is not a similar proposition, such specifying alleviates in some respects and in others aggravates the law's restriction. **11.** Anything included in a general proposition and afterwards excepted to determine a new matter can not be applied to the general proposition unless this be expressly done in the text. **12.** An interpretation may be deduced from the text or from subsequent terms of the text. **13.** In like manner when two texts contradict each other we follow the second, until a third text is found which reconciles the contradiction.

יְהוּדָה בֶּן תֵּימָא אוֹמֵר. הֱוֵי עַז כַּנָּמֵר. וְקַל כַּנֶּשֶׁר. וְרָץ כַּצְּבִי. וְגִבּוֹר כָּאֲרִי לַעֲשׂוֹת רְצוֹן אָבִיךָ שֶׁבַּשָּׁמַיִם. הוּא הָיָה אוֹמֵר. עַז פָּנִים לַגֵּיהִנָּם. וּבוֹשֶׁת פָּנִים לְגַן עֵדֶן:

Yehudah Ben Teima Omer. Hevei Az Kanamer. Vekal Kanesher. Veratz Katzevi. Vegibor Ka'ari La'asot Retzon Avicha Shebashamayim. Hu Hayah Omer. Az Panim Laggeihinam. Uvoshet Panim Legan Eden.

Yehudah ben Teimah used to say, be as strong as the leopard, as swift as the eagle, as nimble as the gazelle, and as mighty as the lion to do the will of Your Father in Heaven. He used also to say, the arrogant are (destined) for Gehinnom, but the shame-faced are (destined) for Gan Eden. **(Mishnah, Pirkei Avot 5:23, some 20)**

יְהִי רָצוֹן מִלְּפָנֶיךָ יְהוָה אֱלֹהֵינוּ וֵאלֹהֵי אֲבוֹתֵינוּ. שֶׁתִּבָּנֶה בֵּית הַמִּקְדָּשׁ בִּמְהֵרָה בְיָמֵינוּ. וְתֵן חֶלְקֵנוּ בְּתוֹרָתֶךָ. לַעֲשׂוֹת חֻקֵּי רְצוֹנֶךָ. וּלְעָבְדָךְ בְּלֵבָב שָׁלֵם:

Yehi Ratzon Milfaneicha Adonai Eloheinu Velohei Avoteinu. Shetivneh Beit Hamikdash Bimheirah Veyameinu. Veten Chelkenu

Betoratach. La'asot Chukkei Retzonach. Ule'avedach Belevav Shalem:

May it be Your will, Hashem our God, God of our fathers, that the Beit Hamikdash be speedily rebuilt in our days. Set our portion in Your Torah so that we may know to perform Your will and serve You wholeheartedly.

Kaddish Al-Yisrael

Kaddish is only recited in a minyan (ten men). אָמֵן denotes when the congregation responds "Amen" together out loud. According to the Shulchan Arukh, the congregation says "Yehei Shemeh Rabba" to "Yitbarach" out loud together without interruption, and also that one should respond "Amen" after "Yitbarach." (SA, OC 55,56) This is not the common custom today. Though many are accustomed to answering according to their own custom, it is advised to respond in the custom of the one reciting to avoid not fragmenting into smaller groups. ("Lo Titgodedu" - BT, Yevamot 13b / SA, OC 493, Rema / MT, Avodah Zara 12:15)

יִתְגַּדַּל וְיִתְקַדַּשׁ שְׁמֵהּ רַבָּא. אָמֵן בְּעָלְמָא דִּי בְרָא. כִּרְעוּתֵהּ. וְיַמְלִיךְ מַלְכוּתֵהּ. וְיַצְמַח פֻּרְקָנֵהּ. וִיקָרֵב מְשִׁיחֵהּ. אָמֵן בְּחַיֵּיכוֹן וּבְיוֹמֵיכוֹן וּבְחַיֵּי דְכָל בֵּית יִשְׂרָאֵל. בַּעֲגָלָא וּבִזְמַן קָרִיב. וְאִמְרוּ אָמֵן. אָמֵן יְהֵא שְׁמֵיהּ רַבָּא מְבָרַךְ לְעָלַם וּלְעָלְמֵי עָלְמַיָּא יִתְבָּרַךְ. וְיִשְׁתַּבַּח. וְיִתְפָּאַר. וְיִתְרוֹמַם. וְיִתְנַשֵּׂא. וְיִתְהַדָּר. וְיִתְעַלֶּה. וְיִתְהַלָּל שְׁמֵהּ דְּקֻדְשָׁא. בְּרִיךְ הוּא. אָמֵן לְעֵלָּא מִן כָּל בִּרְכָתָא שִׁירָתָא. תֻּשְׁבְּחָתָא וְנֶחֱמָתָא. דַּאֲמִירָן בְּעָלְמָא. וְאִמְרוּ אָמֵן. אָמֵן

Yitgadal Veyitkadash Shemeh Rabba. **Amen** Be'alema Di Vera. Kir'uteh. Veyamlich Malchuteh. Veyatzmach Purkaneh. Vikarev Meshicheh. **Amen** Bechayeichon Uveyomeichon Uvechayei Dechal-Beit Yisra'el. Ba'agala Uvizman Kariv. Ve'imru Amen. **Amen** Yehei Shemeh Rabba Mevarach Le'alam Ule'alemei Alemaya Yitbarach. Veyishtabach. Veyitpa'ar. Veyitromam. Veyitnasse. Veyit'hadar. Veyit'aleh. Veyit'hallal Shemeh Dekudsha. Berich Hu. **Amen** Le'ella Min Kol Birchata Shirata. Tushbechata Venechemata. Da'amiran Be'alema. Ve'imru Amen. **Amen**

Glorified and sanctified be God's great name **Amen** throughout the world which He has created according to His will. May He establish His kingdom, hastening His salvation and the coming of

His Messiah, **Amen**, in your lifetime and during your days, and within the life of the entire House of Yisrael, speedily and soon; and say, Amen. **Amen** May His great name be blessed forever and to all eternity. Blessed and praised, glorified and exalted, extolled and honored, adored and lauded is the name of the Holy One, blessed is He, **Amen** Beyond all the blessings and hymns, praises and consolations that are ever spoken in the world; and say, Amen. **Amen**

עַל יִשְׂרָאֵל וְעַל רַבָּנָן. וְעַל תַּלְמִידֵיהוֹן וְעַל כָּל תַּלְמִידֵי תַלְמִידֵיהוֹן. דְּעָסְקִין בְּאוֹרַיְתָא קַדִּשְׁתָּא. דִּי בְּאַתְרָא הָדֵין וְדִי בְּכָל אֲתַר וַאֲתַר. יְהֵא לָנָא וּלְהוֹן וּלְכוֹן חִנָּא וְחִסְדָּא וְרַחֲמֵי. מִן קֳדָם מָארֵי שְׁמַיָּא וְאַרְעָא וְאִמְרוּ אָמֵן. **אָמֵן**

Al Yisra'el Ve'al Rabbanan. Ve'al Talmideihon Ve'al Kol Talmidei Talmideihon. De'asekin Be'orayta Kaddishta. Di Ve'atra Hadein Vedi Vechal Atar Va'atar. Yehei Lana Ulehon Ulechon China Vechisda Verachamei. Min Kodam Marei Shemaya Ve'ar'a Ve'imru Amen. **Amen**

May we of Yisrael together with our rabbis, their disciples and pupils, and all who engage in the study of holy Torah here and everywhere, find gracious favor and mercy from their Father Who is in heaven; and say, Amen. **Amen**

יְהֵא שְׁלָמָא רַבָּא מִן שְׁמַיָּא. חַיִּים וְשָׂבָע וִישׁוּעָה וְנֶחָמָה. וְשֵׁיזָבָא וּרְפוּאָה וּגְאוּלָּה וּסְלִיחָה וְכַפָּרָה וְרֶוַח וְהַצָּלָה לָנוּ וּלְכָל עַמּוֹ יִשְׂרָאֵל. וְאִמְרוּ אָמֵן. **אָמֵן**

Yehei Shelama Rabba Min Shemaya. Chayim Vesava Vishu'ah Venechamah. Vesheizava Urefu'ah Uge'ulah Uselichah Vechapparah Verevach Vehatzalah Lanu Ulechol Ammo Yisra'el. Ve'imru Amen. **Amen**

May abundant peace descend from heaven, with life and plenty, salvation, solace, liberation, healing and redemption, and forgiveness and atonement, enlargement and freedom, for us and all of God's people Yisrael; and say, Amen. **Amen**

One bows and takes three steps backwards, while still bowing. After three steps, while still bowing and before erecting, while saying, "Oseh Shalom Bimromav", turn one's face to the left, "Hu [Berachamav] Ya'aseh Shalom Aleinu", turn one's face to the right; then bow forward like a servant leaving his master. (SA, OC 123:1)

עוֹשֶׂה שָׁלוֹם בִּמְרוֹמָיו. הוּא בְּרַחֲמָיו יַעֲשֶׂה שָׁלוֹם עָלֵינוּ. וְעַל
כָּל־עַמּוֹ יִשְׂרָאֵל. וְאִמְרוּ אָמֵן:

Oseh Shalom Bimromav. Hu Berachamav Ya'aseh Shalom Aleinu. Ve'al Kol-'Ammo Yisra'el. Ve'imru Amen.

Creator of peace in His high places, may He in His mercy create peace for us and for all Yisrael, and say Amen.

Hodu

Chronicles 16:8-36

הוֹדוּ לַיהֹוָה קִרְאוּ בִשְׁמוֹ הוֹדִיעוּ בָעַמִּים עֲלִילֹתָיו: שִׁירוּ לוֹ
זַמְּרוּ־לוֹ שִׂיחוּ בְּכָל־נִפְלְאֹתָיו: הִתְהַלְלוּ בְּשֵׁם קָדְשׁוֹ יִשְׂמַח לֵב
מְבַקְשֵׁי יְהֹוָה: דִּרְשׁוּ יְהֹוָה וְעֻזּוֹ בַּקְּשׁוּ פָנָיו תָּמִיד: זִכְרוּ נִפְלְאֹתָיו
אֲשֶׁר עָשָׂה מֹפְתָיו וּמִשְׁפְּטֵי־פִיהוּ: זֶרַע יִשְׂרָאֵל עַבְדּוֹ בְּנֵי יַעֲקֹב
בְּחִירָיו: הוּא יְהֹוָה אֱלֹהֵינוּ בְּכָל־הָאָרֶץ מִשְׁפָּטָיו: זִכְרוּ לְעוֹלָם
בְּרִיתוֹ דָּבָר צִוָּה לְאֶלֶף דּוֹר: אֲשֶׁר כָּרַת אֶת־אַבְרָהָם וּשְׁבוּעָתוֹ
לְיִצְחָק: וַיַּעֲמִידֶהָ לְיַעֲקֹב לְחֹק לְיִשְׂרָאֵל בְּרִית עוֹלָם: לֵאמֹר לְךָ
אֶתֵּן אֶרֶץ־כְּנָעַן חֶבֶל נַחֲלַתְכֶם: בִּהְיוֹתְכֶם מְתֵי מִסְפָּר כִּמְעַט וְגָרִים
בָּהּ: וַיִּתְהַלְּכוּ מִגּוֹי אֶל־גּוֹי וּמִמַּמְלָכָה אֶל־עַם אַחֵר: לֹא־הִנִּיחַ
לְאִישׁ לְעָשְׁקָם וַיּוֹכַח עֲלֵיהֶם מְלָכִים: אַל־תִּגְּעוּ בִּמְשִׁיחָי וּבִנְבִיאַי
אַל־תָּרֵעוּ:

Hodu L'Adonai Kir'u Vishmo Hodi'u Va'ammim Alilotav. Shiru Lo Zameru Lo Sichu Bechol Nifle'otav. Hithallelu Beshem Kodsho Yismach Lev Mevakshei Adonai. Dirshu Adonai Ve'uzo Bakeshu Fanav Tamid. Zichru Nifle'otav Asher Asah Mofetav Umishpetei Fihu. Zera Yisra'el Avdo Benei Ya'akov Bechirav: Hu Adonai Eloheinu Bechol Ha'aretz Mishpatav. Zichru Le'olam Berito Davar Tzivah Le'elef Dor. Asher Karat Et Avraham Ushevu'ato Leyitzchak.

Vaya'amideha Leya'akov Lechok Leyisra'el Berit Olam. Lemor Lecha Etten Eretz Kena'an Chevel Nachalatchem. Bihyotechem Metei Mispar Kim'at Vegarim Bah. Vayithallechu Migoy El Goy Umimamlachah El Am Acher. Lo Hiniach Le'ish Le'oshkam Vayochach Aleihem Melachim. Al She'Adonai Bimshichai Uvinvi'ai Al Tare'u.

Give thanks to Hashem, call on His name; make known His deeds among the peoples. Sing to Him, sing praises to Him; speak of all His wonders. Take pride in His holy name; let the heart of those who seek Hashem rejoice. Inquire of Hashem and His might; seek His presence continually. Remember the wonders He has done, His marvels, and the judgments He decreed, descendants of Yisrael - His servant, children of Yaakov, His chosen. He is Hashem our God; His judgments are over all the earth. Remember His covenant forever, the word which He pledged for a thousand generations, the covenant He made with Avraham, and His oath to Yitzchak. He confirmed the same to Yaakov as a statute, to Yisrael as an everlasting covenant, saying: "To you I give the land of Canaan as the portion of your possession." While they were but a few men, very few and strangers in it, when they went about from nation to nation and from realm to realm, He permitted no man to oppress them, and warned kings concerning them: "Do not touch my anointed, and do not harm my prophets."

שִׁירוּ לַיהֹוָה כָּל־הָאָרֶץ בַּשְּׂרוּ מִיּוֹם־אֶל־יוֹם יְשׁוּעָתוֹ: סַפְּרוּ בַגּוֹיִם אֶת־כְּבוֹדוֹ בְּכָל־הָעַמִּים נִפְלְאֹתָיו: כִּי גָדוֹל יְהֹוָה וּמְהֻלָּל מְאֹד וְנוֹרָא הוּא עַל־כָּל־אֱלֹהִים: כִּי כָּל־אֱלֹהֵי הָעַמִּים אֱלִילִים יפסיק מעט וַיהֹוָה שָׁמַיִם עָשָׂה: הוֹד וְהָדָר לְפָנָיו עֹז וְחֶדְוָה בִּמְקֹמוֹ: הָבוּ לַיהֹוָה מִשְׁפְּחוֹת עַמִּים הָבוּ לַיהֹוָה כָּבוֹד וָעֹז: הָבוּ לַיהֹוָה כְּבוֹד שְׁמוֹ שְׂאוּ מִנְחָה וּבֹאוּ לְפָנָיו הִשְׁתַּחֲווּ לַיהֹוָה בְּהַדְרַת־קֹדֶשׁ: חִילוּ מִלְּפָנָיו כָּל־הָאָרֶץ אַף־תִּכּוֹן תֵּבֵל בַּל־תִּמּוֹט: יִשְׂמְחוּ הַשָּׁמַיִם וְתָגֵל הָאָרֶץ וְיֹאמְרוּ בַגּוֹיִם יְהֹוָה מָלָךְ: יִרְעַם הַיָּם וּמְלוֹאוֹ יַעֲלֹץ הַשָּׂדֶה

וְכָל־אֲשֶׁר־בּוֹ: אָז יְרַנְּנוּ עֲצֵי הַיָּעַר מִלִּפְנֵי יְהֹוָה כִּי־בָא לִשְׁפּוֹט אֶת־הָאָרֶץ: הוֹדוּ לַיהֹוָה כִּי טוֹב כִּי לְעוֹלָם חַסְדּוֹ: וְאִמְרוּ הוֹשִׁיעֵנוּ אֱלֹהֵי יִשְׁעֵנוּ וְקַבְּצֵנוּ וְהַצִּילֵנוּ מִן־הַגּוֹיִם לְהֹדוֹת לְשֵׁם קָדְשֶׁךָ לְהִשְׁתַּבֵּחַ בִּתְהִלָּתֶךָ: בָּרוּךְ יְהֹוָה אֱלֹהֵי יִשְׂרָאֵל מִן־הָעוֹלָם וְעַד הָעֹלָם וַיֹּאמְרוּ כָל־הָעָם אָמֵן וְהַלֵּל לַיהֹוָה:

Shiru L'Adonai Chol-Ha'aretz. Baseru Miyom-'El-Yom Yeshu'ato. Saperu Vagoyim Et-Kevodo. Bechol-Ha'ammim Nifle'otav. Ki Gadol Adonai Umehulal Me'od. Venora Hu Al-Chol-'Elohim. Ki Chol-'Elohei Ha'ammim Elilim. [pause slightly] Va'Adonai Shamayim Asah. Hod Vehadar Lefanav. Oz Vechedvah Bimkomo. Havu L'Adonai Mishpechot Ammim. Havu L'Adonai Kavod Va'oz. Havu L'Adonai Kevod Shemo; Se'u Minchah Uvo'u Lefanav. Hishtachavu L'Adonai Behadrat-Kodesh. Chilu Millefanav Chol-Ha'aretz. Af-Tikon Tevel Bal-Timot. Yismechu Hashamayim Vetagel Ha'aretz. Veyomeru Vagoyim Adonai Malach. Yir'am Hayam Umelo'o. Ya'alotz Hassadeh Vechol-'Asher-Bo. Az Yeranenu Atzei Haya'ar; Millifnei Adonai Ki-Va Lishpot Et-Ha'aretz. Hodu L'Adonai Ki Tov. Ki Le'olam Chasdo. Ve'imru Hoshi'enu Elohei Yish'enu, Vekabetzenu Vehatzileinu Min-Hagoyim; Lehodot Leshem Kodshecha. Lehishtabe'ach Bit'hilatecha. Baruch Adonai Elohei Yisra'el. Min-Ha'olam Ve'ad Ha'olam; Vayomeru Chol-Ha'am Amen. Vehallel L'Adonai.

Sing to Hashem, all the earth; proclaim His salvation day after day. Recount His glory among the nations, and His wonders among all the peoples. For great is Hashem and most worthy of praise; He is to be feared above all gods. For all the gods of the peoples are mere idols, but [pause slightly] Hashem made the heavens. Majesty and beauty are in His presence; strength and joy are in His Sanctuary. Ascribe to Hashem, families of peoples, ascribe to Hashem glory and strength. Give to Hashem the honor due to His name; bring an offering and come before him; worship Hashem in holy array. Tremble before Him, all the earth; indeed, the world is firm that it cannot be shaken. Let the heavens rejoice, let the earth rejoice, and let them say among the nations: "Hashem is King." Let the sea and its fullness roar; let the field and all that is within rejoice. Then let the trees of the forest sing before Hashem, Who comes to rule the world. Praise Hashem, for He is good; for His kindness endures forever. And say: "Save us, God of our salvation, gather us and deliver us from the nations, to give thanks to Your holy name, to glory in Your praise." Blessed is Hashem, the God of Yisrael, from eternity to eternity. Then all the people said "Amen" and praised Hashem.

רוֹמְמוּ יְהֹוָה אֱלֹהֵינוּ וְהִשְׁתַּחֲווּ לַהֲדֹם רַגְלָיו קָדוֹשׁ הוּא: רוֹמְמוּ
יְהֹוָה אֱלֹהֵינוּ וְהִשְׁתַּחֲווּ לְהַר קָדְשׁוֹ כִּי־קָדוֹשׁ יְהֹוָה אֱלֹהֵינוּ: וְהוּא
רַחוּם יְכַפֵּר עָוֹן וְלֹא יַשְׁחִית וְהִרְבָּה לְהָשִׁיב אַפּוֹ וְלֹא יָעִיר כָּל
חֲמָתוֹ: אַתָּה יְהֹוָה לֹא־תִכְלָא רַחֲמֶיךָ מִמֶּנִּי חַסְדְּךָ וַאֲמִתְּךָ תָּמִיד
יִצְּרוּנִי: זְכֹר־רַחֲמֶיךָ יְהֹוָה וַחֲסָדֶיךָ כִּי מֵעוֹלָם הֵמָּה: תְּנוּ עֹז
לֵאלֹהִים עַל־יִשְׂרָאֵל גַּאֲוָתוֹ וְעֻזּוֹ בַּשְּׁחָקִים: נוֹרָא אֱלֹהִים מִמִּקְדָּשֶׁיךָ
אֵל יִשְׂרָאֵל הוּא נֹתֵן עֹז וְתַעֲצֻמוֹת לָעָם בָּרוּךְ אֱלֹהִים:

Romemu Adonai Eloheinu. Vehishtachavu Lahadom Raglav. Kadosh Hu. Romemu Adonai Eloheinu. Vehishtachavu Lehar Kodsho; Ki-Kadosh. Adonai Eloheinu. Vehu Rachum Yechapeir Avon Velo Yashchit Vehirbah Lehashiv Appo Velo Ya'ir Kol Chamato. Attah Adonai Lo-Tichla Rachameicha Mimeni; Chasdecha Va'amitecha. Tamid Yitzeruni. Zechor-Rachameicha Adonai Vachasadeicha; Ki Me'olam Hemah. Tenu Oz. Lelohim Al-Yisra'el Ga'avato; Ve'uzo. Bashechakim. Nora Elohim. Mimikdasheicha El Yisra'el. Hu Noten Oz Veta'atzumot La'am. Baruch Elohim.

Exalt Hashem our God, and worship at His footstool—holy is He. Exalt Hashem our God, and worship at His holy mountain, for holy is Hashem our God. He, being merciful, forgives iniquity, and does not destroy; frequently He turns His anger away, and does not stir up all His wrath. You, Hashem, will not hold back Your mercy from me; Your kindness and Your faithfulness will always protect me. Remember Your mercy, Hashem, and Your kindness, for they have been since eternity. Give honor to God, Whose majesty is over Yisrael, whose glory is in the skies. Feared are You, Hashem, from

Your Sanctuary; the God of Yisrael gives strength and power to His people. Blessed is God.

El-Nekamot

אֵל־נְקָמוֹת יְהֹוָה אֵל נְקָמוֹת הוֹפִיעַ: הִנָּשֵׂא שֹׁפֵט הָאָרֶץ הָשֵׁב
גְּמוּל עַל־גֵּאִים: לַיהֹוָה הַיְשׁוּעָה עַל־עַמְּךָ בִרְכָתֶךָ סֶּלָה: יְהֹוָה
צְבָאוֹת עִמָּנוּ מִשְׂגָּב־לָנוּ אֱלֹהֵי יַעֲקֹב סֶלָה: יְהֹוָה צְבָאוֹת אַשְׁרֵי
אָדָם בֹּטֵחַ בָּךְ: יְהֹוָה הוֹשִׁיעָה הַמֶּלֶךְ יַעֲנֵנוּ בְיוֹם־קָרְאֵנוּ: הוֹשִׁיעָה |
אֶת־עַמֶּךָ וּבָרֵךְ אֶת־נַחֲלָתֶךָ וּרְעֵם וְנַשְּׂאֵם עַד־הָעוֹלָם: נַפְשֵׁנוּ חִכְּתָה
לַיהֹוָה עֶזְרֵנוּ וּמָגִנֵּנוּ הוּא: כִּי־בוֹ יִשְׂמַח לִבֵּנוּ כִּי בְשֵׁם קָדְשׁוֹ
בָטָחְנוּ: יְהִי־חַסְדְּךָ יְהֹוָה עָלֵינוּ כַּאֲשֶׁר יִחַלְנוּ לָךְ: הַרְאֵנוּ יְהֹוָה
חַסְדֶּךָ וְיֶשְׁעֲךָ תִּתֶּן־לָנוּ: קוּמָה עֶזְרָתָה לָּנוּ וּפְדֵנוּ לְמַעַן חַסְדֶּךָ:
אָנֹכִי | יְהֹוָה אֱלֹהֶיךָ הַמַּעַלְךָ מֵאֶרֶץ מִצְרָיִם הַרְחֶב־פִּיךָ וַאֲמַלְאֵהוּ:
אַשְׁרֵי הָעָם שֶׁכָּכָה לּוֹ אַשְׁרֵי הָעָם שֶׁיְהֹוָה אֱלֹהָיו: וַאֲנִי | בְּחַסְדְּךָ
בָטַחְתִּי יָגֵל לִבִּי בִּישׁוּעָתֶךָ אָשִׁירָה לַיהֹוָה כִּי גָמַל עָלָי:

El-Nekamot Adonai El Nekamot Hofia. Hinasei Shofet Ha'aretz; Hasheiv Gemul. Al-Ge'im. L'Adonai Hayshu'ah; Al-'Ammecha Virchatecha Selah. Adonai Tzeva'ot Imanu; Misgav-Lanu Elohei Ya'akov Selah. Adonai Tzeva'ot; Ashrei Adam. Boteach Bach. Adonai Hoshi'ah; Hamelech. Ya'aneinu Veyom-Kor'enu. Hoshi'ah Et-'Ammecha. Uvarech Et-Nachalatecha; Ure'em Venasse'em. Ad-Ha'olam. Nafshenu Chiketah L'Adonai Ezrenu Umaginenu Hu. Ki-Vo Yismach Libenu; Ki Veshem Kodsho Vatachenu. Yehi-Chasdecha Adonai Aleinu; Ka'asher. Yichalnu Lach. Har'enu Adonai Chasdecha; Veyesh'acha. Titen-Lanu. Kumah Ezratah Lanu; Ufedenu. Lema'an Chasdecha. Anochi Adonai Eloheicha. Hama'alcha Me'eretz Mitzrayim; Harchev-Picha Va'amal'ehu. Ashrei Ha'am Shekachah Lo; Ashrei Ha'am. She'Adonai Elohav. Va'ani Bechasdecha Vatachti Yagel Libi. Bishu'atecha Ashirah L'Adonai Ki Gamal Alai:

God of vengeance, Hashem, God of vengeance, appear. Arise, Judge of the world, and render to the arrogant what they deserve. Salvation belongs to Hashem; May Your blessing be upon Your people. Hashem of hosts is with us; the God of Yaakov is our Stronghold. Hashem of hosts, happy is the man who trusts in You. Hashem, save us; may the King answer us when we call. Save Your people and bless Your heritage; tend them and sustain them forever. Our soul waits for Hashem; He is our help and our shield. Indeed, our heart rejoices in Him, for in His holy name we trust. May Your kindness, Hashem, rest on us, as our hope rests in You. Show us Your kindness, Hashem, and grant us Your salvation. Arise for our help, and set us free for Your goodness' sake. I am Hashem your God, Who brought you up from the land of Mitzrayim; open your mouth and I will fill it. Happy is the people that is so situated; happy is the people whose God is Hashem. I have trusted in your kindness; may my heart rejoice in your salvation. I will sing to Hashem, because He has treated me kindly.

Aromimchah

Psalms 30:2-13

אֲרוֹמִמְךָ יְהֹוָה כִּי דִלִּיתָנִי וְלֹא־שִׂמַּחְתָּ אֹיְבַי לִי: יְהֹוָה אֱלֹהָי שִׁוַּעְתִּי
אֵלֶיךָ וַתִּרְפָּאֵנִי: יְהֹוָה הֶעֱלִיתָ מִן־שְׁאוֹל נַפְשִׁי חִיִּיתַנִי מיורדי
(מִיָּרְדִי)־בוֹר: זַמְּרוּ לַיהֹוָה חֲסִידָיו וְהוֹדוּ לְזֵכֶר קָדְשׁוֹ: כִּי רֶגַע |
בְּאַפּוֹ חַיִּים בִּרְצוֹנוֹ בָּעֶרֶב יָלִין בֶּכִי וְלַבֹּקֶר רִנָּה: וַאֲנִי אָמַרְתִּי
בְשַׁלְוִי בַּל־אֶמּוֹט לְעוֹלָם: יְהֹוָה בִּרְצוֹנְךָ הֶעֱמַדְתָּה לְהַרְרִי עֹז
הִסְתַּרְתָּ פָנֶיךָ הָיִיתִי נִבְהָל: אֵלֶיךָ יְהֹוָה אֶקְרָא וְאֶל־אֲדֹנָי אֶתְחַנָּן:
מַה־בֶּצַע בְּדָמִי בְּרִדְתִּי אֶל שָׁחַת הֲיוֹדְךָ עָפָר הֲיַגִּיד אֲמִתֶּךָ:
שְׁמַע־יְהֹוָה וְחָנֵּנִי יְהֹוָה הֱיֵה־עֹזֵר לִי: הָפַכְתָּ מִסְפְּדִי לְמָחוֹל לִי

פִּתַּחְתָּ שַׂקִּי וַתְּאַזְּרֵנִי שִׂמְחָה: לְמַעַן | יְזַמֶּרְךָ כָבוֹד וְלֹא יִדֹּם. יְהֹוָה אֱלֹהַי לְעוֹלָם אוֹדֶךָּ:

Aromimcha Adonai Ki Dillitani; Velo-Simachta Oyevai Li. Adonai Elohai; Shiva'ti Eleicha. Vatirpa'eni. Adonai He'elita Min-She'ol Nafshi; Chiyitani. Miyordi-Vor. Zameru L'Adonai Chasidav; Vehodu. Lezecher Kodsho. Ki Rega' Be'appo Chayim Birtzono Ba'erev Yalin Bechi. Velaboker Rinah. Va'ani Amarti Veshalvi; Bal-'Emot Le'olam. Adonai Birtzonecha He'emadtah Lehareri Oz Histarta Faneicha. Hayiti Nivhal. Eleicha Adonai Ekra; Ve'el-'Adonai. Etchanan. Mah-Betza Bedami Beridti El Shachat Hayodecha Afar; Hayagid Amitecha. Shema'-Adonai Vechoneni; Adonai Heyeh-'Ozeir Li. Hafachta Mispedi Lemachol Li Pittachta Sakki; Vate'azereini Simchah. Lema'an Yezamercha Chavod Velo Yidom; Adonai Elohai. Le'olam Odeka.

I extol You, Hashem, for You have lifted me up, and have not let my foes rejoice over me. Hashem my God, I cried to You, and You healed me. Hashem, You have lifted me up from the grave; You have let me live, that I should not go down to the grave. Sing to Hashem, you who are godly, and give thanks to His holy name. For His anger only lasts a moment, but His favor lasts a lifetime; weeping may lodge with us at evening, but in the morning there are shouts of joy. I thought in my security I never would be shaken. Hashem, by Your favor You have established my mountain as a stronghold; but when Your favor was withdrawn, I was dismayed. To You, Hashem, I called; I appealed to my God: "What profit would my death be, if I went down to the grave? Will the dust praise You? Will it declare Your faithfulness? Hear, Hashem, and be gracious to me; Hashem, be my helper." You have changed my mourning into dancing; You have stripped my sackcloth and girded me with joy; so that my soul may praise You, and not be silent. Hashem my God, I will thank You forever.

Stand for Adonai Melech until after saying the words "Ushemo Echad". (Kaf HaChayim 50:8)

Adonai Melech / Hashem is King

On the Days of Awe (Rosh Hashanah to Yom Kippur) and on Hoshanah Rabbah one chants this twice:

יְהוָה הוּא הָאֱלֹהִים:

Adonai Hu Ha'Elohim.

Hashem, He is God.

Adonai Melech. Adonai Malach	יְהוָה מֶֽלֶךְ. יְהוָה מָלָךְ יְהוָה
Adonai Yimloch Le'olam Va'ed.	יִמְלֹךְ לְעֹלָם וָעֶד:

Hashem is King, Hashem was King, Hashem will be King forever and ever.

Adonai Melech. Adonai Malach	יְהוָה מֶֽלֶךְ. יְהוָה מָלָךְ יְהוָה
Adonai Yimloch Le'olam Va'ed.	יִמְלֹךְ לְעֹלָם וָעֶד:

Hashem is King, Hashem was King, Hashem will be King forever and ever.

וְהָיָה יְהוָה לְמֶלֶךְ עַל־כָּל־הָאָרֶץ בַּיּוֹם הַהוּא יִהְיֶה יְהוָה אֶחָד וּשְׁמוֹ אֶחָד:

Vehayah Adonai Lemelech Al-Chol-Ha'aretz; Bayom Hahu. Yihyeh Adonai Echad Ushemo Echad.

"Hashem will be King over all the earth; on that day Hashem will be One and His name One." **(Zech. 14:9)**

Stand until here.

הוֹשִׁיעֵנוּ | יְהוָה אֱלֹהֵינוּ וְקַבְּצֵנוּ מִן־הַגּוֹיִם לְהֹדוֹת לְשֵׁם קָדְשֶׁךָ לְהִשְׁתַּבֵּחַ בִּתְהִלָּתֶךָ: בָּרוּךְ יְהוָה אֱלֹהֵי יִשְׂרָאֵל מִן־הָעוֹלָם | וְעַד הָעוֹלָם וְאָמַר כָּל־הָעָם אָמֵן הַלְלוּיָהּ: כֹּל הַנְּשָׁמָה תְּהַלֵּל יָהּ הַלְלוּיָהּ:

Hoshi'enu Adonai Eloheinu. Vekabetzeinu Min-Hagoyim Lehodot Leshem Kodshecha; Lehishtabe'ach. Bit'hilatecha. Baruch Adonai Elohei Yisra'el Min-Ha'olam Ve'ad Ha'olam. Ve'amar Chol-Ha'am Amen. Halleluyah. Kol Haneshamah Tehallel Yah. Halleluyah.

Save us, Hashem our God, and gather us from among the nations to praise Your holy name and triumph in Your praise. Blessed is Hashem God of Yisrael from everlasting to everlasting, and let all the people say Amen, Halleluyah. **(Psalms 106:47-48)** Let every breath praise Hashem, Halleluyah. **(Psalms 150:6)**

Psalms 67 / Lamnatzeach Binginot

לַמְנַצֵּחַ בִּנְגִינֹת מִזְמוֹר שִׁיר: אֱלֹהִים יְחָנֵּנוּ וִיבָרְכֵנוּ יָאֵר פָּנָיו אִתָּנוּ
סֶלָה: לָדַעַת בָּאָרֶץ דַּרְכֶּךָ בְּכָל־גּוֹיִם יְשׁוּעָתֶךָ: יוֹדוּךָ עַמִּים | אֱלֹהִים
יוֹדוּךָ עַמִּים כֻּלָּם: יִשְׂמְחוּ וִירַנְּנוּ לְאֻמִּים כִּי־תִשְׁפֹּט עַמִּים מִישֹׁר
וּלְאֻמִּים | בָּאָרֶץ תַּנְחֵם סֶלָה: יוֹדוּךָ עַמִּים | אֱלֹהִים יוֹדוּךָ עַמִּים
כֻּלָּם: אֶרֶץ נָתְנָה יְבוּלָהּ יְבָרְכֵנוּ אֱלֹהִים אֱלֹהֵינוּ: יְבָרְכֵנוּ אֱלֹהִים
וְיִירְאוּ אוֹתוֹ כָּל־אַפְסֵי־אָרֶץ:

Lamnatzeach Binginot. Mizmor Shir. Elohim. Yechonenu Vivarecheinu; Ya'er Panav Itanu Selah. Lada'at Ba'aretz Darkecha; Bechol-Goyim. Yeshu'atecha. Yoducha Ammim Elohim; Yoducha. Ammim Kulam. Yismechu Viranenu. Le'ummim Ki-Tishpot Ammim Mishor; Ule'ummim Ba'aretz Tanchem Selah. Yoducha Ammim Elohim; Yoducha. Ammim Kulam. Eretz Natenah Yevulah; Yevarecheinu. Elohim Eloheinu. Yevarecheinu Elohim; Veyire'u Oto. Chol-'Afsei-'Aretz.

For the Leader; with string-music. A Psalm, a Song. God be gracious to us, and bless us; May He cause His face to shine toward us; Selah. That Your way may be known upon earth, Your salvation among all nations. Let the peoples give thanks to You, Oh God; Let the peoples give thanks to You, all of them. Let the nations be glad and sing for joy; For You will judge the peoples with equity, And lead the nations upon earth. Selah. Let the peoples give thanks to You, Oh

God; Let the peoples give thanks to You, all of them. The earth has yielded her increase; May God, our own God, bless us. May God bless us; And let all the ends of the earth fear Him.

Some recite Psalm 67 in the form of a menorah.

If there was not a minyan (10 men) present after Korbanot, and Kaddish Al Yisrael was not recited, but there is a minyan now some say "Rabbi Chananya Be Akashya" and then Kaddish Al-Yisrael.

רַבִּי חֲנַנְיָא בֶּן־עֲקַשְׁיָא אוֹמֵר: רָצָה הַקָּדוֹשׁ בָּרוּךְ הוּא לְזַכּוֹת אֶת־יִשְׂרָאֵל. לְפִיכָךְ הִרְבָּה לָהֶם תּוֹרָה וּמִצְוֹת. שֶׁנֶּאֱמַר: יְהֹוָה חָפֵץ לְמַעַן צִדְקוֹ יַגְדִּיל תּוֹרָה וְיַאְדִּיר:

Ribi Chananya Ben Akashya Omer: Ratzah Hakadosh Baruch Hu Lezakkot Et Yisra'el. Lefichach Hirbah Lahem Torah Umitzvot. Shene'emar: Adonai Chafetz Lema'an Tzidko Yagdil Torah Veya'dir.

Rabbi Chananya ben Akashya used to say, the Holy One, blessed is He, wishing to make Yisrael more worthy, enlarged for them with Torah and its commandments. For so it is said, "Hashem was pleased, for His righteousness' sake, To make the Torah great and glorious." **(Isaiah 42:21)**

LAWS OF PESUKEI DEZIMRAH

If one finished Baruch She'amar prior to the prayer leader he should say Amen after the leader finishes. After Yishtabach one may say Amen after his own blessing. One must be cautious to refrain from talking from the moment he begins Baruch She'amar until after he concludes the Shemoneh Esrei. (The Amidah). In between these psalms one may ask [of the welfare of another] out of respect [and may reply greetings to any person. And in the middle of [one of] the psalms he may ask [of the welfare of another] out of fear and he may reply out of respect. We should not say these psalms in a hurry, but rather at a pleasant pace. One should not say the blessing on the wrapping of the tzitzit [i.e. tallit] between Pesukei DeZimrah and Yishtabach, rather, he should say it between Yishtabach and Yotzer Ohr. (SA, OC 52,53)

Pesukei DeZimrah / Verses of Praise

If one comes to synagogue and finds the congregation at the end of Pesukei Dezimrah, he should say all of Baruch She'amar, Ashrei, Ps. 148, Ps. 150, Yishtabach, and afterwards Yotzer Ohr, and the Shema and its blessings, and then pray with the congregation. And if he doesn't have much time, he should also skip Ps. 148. And if the congregation has already started with Yotzer and one does not have time to recite Pesukei Dezimrah even with skipping, he should recite the Shema and its blessings with the congregation and pray with them (the Amidah), and afterwards recite all of Pesukei Dezimrah without a blessing before or after. (SA, OC 52)

Baruch She'amar

One must be careful to refrain from talking from the beginning of Baruch She'amar until after he concludes the Amidah. (SA, OC 51) Some grasp the front two tzitzit while saying this prayer.

Stand and recite:

Baruch She'amar Vehayah	בָּרוּךְ שֶׁאָמַר וְהָיָה
Ha'olam. Baruch Hu. Baruch	הָעוֹלָם. בָּרוּךְ הוּא. בָּרוּךְ
Omer Ve'oseh. Baruch Gozeir	אוֹמֵר וְעוֹשֶׂה. בָּרוּךְ גּוֹזֵר
Umekayem. Baruch Oseh	וּמְקַיֵּם. בָּרוּךְ עוֹשֶׂה
Vereshit. Baruch Merachem Al	בְרֵאשִׁית. בָּרוּךְ מְרַחֵם עַל
Ha'aretz. Baruch Merachem Al	הָאָרֶץ. בָּרוּךְ מְרַחֵם עַל
Haberiyot. Baruch Meshalem	הַבְּרִיּוֹת. בָּרוּךְ מְשַׁלֵּם
Sachar Tov Lire'av. Baruch Chai	שָׂכָר טוֹב לִירֵאָיו. בָּרוּךְ חַי
La'ad Vekayam Lanetzach.	לָעַד וְקַיָּם לָנֶצַח.
Baruch Podeh Umatzil. Baruch	בָּרוּךְ פּוֹדֶה וּמַצִּיל. בָּרוּךְ
Shemo. Baruch Attah Adonai	שְׁמוֹ. בָּרוּךְ אַתָּה יְהֹוָה
Eloheinu Melech Ha'olam Ha'el.	אֱלֹהֵינוּ מֶלֶךְ הָעוֹלָם. הָאֵל.
Av Harachaman. Hamhulal	אָב הָרַחֲמָן. הַמְהֻלָּל
Befeh Ammo. Meshubach	בְּפֶה עַמּוֹ. מְשֻׁבָּח
Umefo'ar Bilshon Chasidav	וּמְפֹאָר בִּלְשׁוֹן חֲסִידָיו
Va'avadav. Uveshirei David	וַעֲבָדָיו. וּבְשִׁירֵי דָוִד
Avdach Nehalelach Adonai	עַבְדָּךְ נְהַלֶּלְךָ יְהֹוָה
Eloheinu Bishvachot Uvizmirot.	אֱלֹהֵינוּ בִּשְׁבָחוֹת וּבִזְמִירוֹת.

Unegadelach Uneshabechach	וּנְגַדֶּלְךָ וּנְשַׁבֵּחֲךָ
Unefa'arach Venamlichach.	וּנְפָאֶרְךָ וְנַמְלִיכְךָ.
Venazkir Shimcha Malkeinu	וְנַזְכִּיר שִׁמְךָ מַלְכֵּנוּ
Eloheinu. Yachid Chai	אֱלֹהֵינוּ. יָחִיד חַי
Ha'olamim. Melech Meshubach	הָעוֹלָמִים. מֶלֶךְ מְשֻׁבָּח
Umefo'ar Adei Ad Shemo	וּמְפֹאָר עֲדֵי עַד שְׁמוֹ
Hagadol. Baruch Attah Adonai	הַגָּדוֹל. בָּרוּךְ אַתָּה יְהֹוָה
Melech Mehulal Batishbachot.	מֶלֶךְ מְהֻלָּל בַּתִּשְׁבָּחוֹת:

Blessed is He who spoke, and the world came into being; blessed is He. Blessed is He who says and performs. Blessed is He who decrees and fulfills. Blessed is He who created the universe. Blessed is He who has mercy on the world. Blessed is He who has mercy on all creatures. Blessed is He who grants a good reward to those who revere Him. Blessed is He who lives forever and exists eternally. Blessed is He who redeems and saves; blessed is His name. Blessed are You, Hashem our God, King of the universe, Oh God, merciful Father, who is praised by the mouth of Your people, lauded and glorified by the tongue of Your faithful servants. With the songs, hymns and psalms, of Your servant David will we praise You, Hashem our God; we will exalt, extol, glorify, and proclaim You King; we will call upon Your name, our King, our God. You Who are one, the life of the universe, Oh King, praised and glorified are Your great name forever and ever. Blessed are You, Hashem, King extolled with hymns of praise.

If holding tzitzit, kiss and release them. If the person finished with the blessing that he said before the Chazan finishes, he should hurry to say the following Psalm immediately, and when the Chazan finishes will answer, Amen. One may now sit.

Continue with Psalms 100.

Psalms 100 / Mizmor Letodah

מִזְמ֥וֹר לְתוֹדָ֑ה הָרִ֥יעוּ לַ֝יהוָ֗ה כׇּל־הָאָֽרֶץ׃ עִבְד֣וּ אֶת־יְהוָ֣ה בְּשִׂמְחָ֑ה
בֹּ֥אוּ לְ֝פָנָ֗יו בִּרְנָנָֽה׃ דְּע֗וּ כִּֽי־יְהוָה֮ ה֤וּא אֱלֹ֫הִ֥ים הֽוּא־עָ֭שָׂנוּ ולא (וְל֣וֹ)
אֲנַ֑חְנוּ עַ֝מּ֗וֹ וְצֹ֣אן מַרְעִיתֽוֹ׃ בֹּ֤אוּ שְׁעָרָ֨יו ׀ בְּתוֹדָ֗ה חֲצֵרֹתָ֥יו בִּתְהִלָּ֑ה
הֽוֹדוּ־ל֝֗וֹ בָּרְכ֥וּ שְׁמֽוֹ׃ כִּֽי־ט֣וֹב יְ֭הוָה לְעוֹלָ֣ם חַסְדּ֑וֹ וְעַד־דֹּ֥ר וָ֝דֹ֗ר
אֱמוּנָתֽוֹ׃

Mizmor Letodah; Hari'u L'Adonai Chol-Ha'aretz. Ivdu Et-Adonai Besimchah; Bo'u Lefanav. Birnanah. De'u. Ki-Adonai Hu Elohim Hu-'Asanu Velo Anachnu; Ammo. Vetzon Mar'ito. Bo'u She'arav Betodah. Chatzerotav Bit'hillah; Hodu-Lo Barechu Shemo. Ki-Tov Adonai Le'olam Chasdo; Ve'ad-Dor Vador. Emunato.

A Psalm of thanksgiving. Shout to Hashem, all the earth. Hashem with gladness; Come before His presence with singing. Know that Hashem He is God; It is He that has made us, and we are His, His people, and the flock of His pasture. Enter into His gates with thanksgiving, And into His courts with praise; Give thanks to Him, and bless His name. For Hashem is good; His mercy endures forever; And His faithfulness to all generations.

Yehi Chevod

ש יְהִ֤י כְב֣וֹד יְהוָ֣ה לְעוֹלָ֑ם יִשְׂמַ֖ח יְהוָ֣ה בְּמַעֲשָֽׂיו׃ ד יְהִ֤י שֵׁ֣ם יְהוָ֣ה
מְבֹרָ֑ךְ מֵ֝עַתָּ֗ה וְעַד־עוֹלָֽם׃ י מִמִּזְרַח־שֶׁ֥מֶשׁ עַד־מְבוֹא֑וֹ מְ֝הֻלָּ֗ל שֵׁ֣ם
יְהוָֽה׃ ש רָ֖ם עַל־כׇּל־גּוֹיִ֥ם ׀ יְהוָ֑ה עַ֖ל הַשָּׁמַ֣יִם כְּבוֹדֽוֹ׃ י יְ֭הוָה שִׁמְךָ֣
לְעוֹלָ֑ם יְ֝הוָ֗ה זִכְרְךָ֥ לְדֹר־וָדֹֽר׃ ד יְֽהוָ֗ה בַּ֭שָּׁמַיִם הֵכִ֣ין כִּסְא֑וֹ וּ֝מַלְכוּת֗וֹ
בַּכֹּ֥ל מָשָֽׁלָה׃ ד יִשְׂמְח֣וּ הַ֭שָּׁמַיִם וְתָגֵ֣ל הָאָ֑רֶץ וְיֹאמְר֥וּ בַ֝גּוֹיִ֗ם יְהוָ֥ה
מָלָֽךְ׃ ש יְהוָ֣ה מֶ֑לֶךְ. יְהוָ֣ה מָלָ֔ךְ. יְהוָ֣ה ׀ יִמְלֹ֖ךְ לְעֹלָ֥ם וָעֶ֑ד׃ י יְהוָ֣ה
מֶ֣לֶךְ עוֹלָ֣ם וָעֶ֑ד אָבְד֥וּ ג֝וֹיִ֗ם מֵֽאַרְצֽוֹ׃ ד יְֽהוָ֗ה הֵפִ֥יר עֲצַת־גּוֹיִ֑ם הֵ֝נִ֗יא
מַחְשְׁב֥וֹת עַמִּֽים׃ י רַבּ֣וֹת מַחֲשָׁב֣וֹת בְּלֶב־אִ֑ישׁ וַעֲצַ֥ת יְ֝הוָ֗ה הִ֣יא

תָקוּם: ש עֲצַת יְהֹוָה לְעוֹלָם תַּעֲמֹד מַחְשְׁבוֹת לִבּוֹ לְדֹר וָדֹר: י כִּי הוּא אָמַר וַיֶּהִי הוּא־צִוָּה וַיַּעֲמֹד: ש כִּי־בָחַר יְהֹוָה בְּצִיּוֹן אִוָּהּ לְמוֹשָׁב לוֹ: ד כִּי־יַעֲקֹב בָּחַר לוֹ יָהּ יִשְׂרָאֵל לִסְגֻלָּתוֹ: י כִּי | לֹא־יִטֹּשׁ יְהֹוָה עַמּוֹ וְנַחֲלָתוֹ לֹא יַעֲזֹב: ד וְהוּא רַחוּם | יְכַפֵּר עָוֹן וְלֹא־יַשְׁחִית וְהִרְבָּה לְהָשִׁיב אַפּוֹ וְלֹא־יָעִיר כָּל־חֲמָתוֹ: ש יְהֹוָה הוֹשִׁיעָה הַמֶּלֶךְ יַעֲנֵנוּ בְיוֹם־קָרְאֵנוּ:

Yehi Chevod Adonai Le'olam; Yismach Adonai Bema'asav. Yehi Shem Adonai Mevorach; Me'attah. Ve'ad-'Olam. Mimizrach-Shemesh Ad-Mevo'o; Mehulal. Shem Adonai. Ram Al-Kol-Goyim Adonai Al Hashamayim Kevodo. Adonai Shimcha Le'olam; Adonai Zichrecha Ledor-Vador. Adonai Bashamayim Hechin Kis'o; Umalchuto. Bakol Mashalah. Yismechu Hashamayim Vetagel Ha'aretz. Veyomeru Vagoyim Adonai Malach. Adonai Melech. Adonai Malach. Adonai Yimloch Le'olam Va'ed. Adonai Melech Olam Va'ed; Avedu Goyim. Me'artzo. Adonai Hefir Atzat-Goyim; Heni. Machshevot Ammim. Rabot Machashavot Belev-'Ish; Va'atzat Adonai Hi Takum. Atzat Adonai Le'olam Ta'amod; Machshevot Libo. Ledor Vador. Ki Hu Amar Vayehi; Hu-Tzivah. Vaya'amod. Ki-Vachar Adonai Betziyon; Ivah. Lemoshav Lo. Ki-Ya'akov. Bachar Lo Yah; Yisra'el. Lisgulato. Ki Lo-Yitosh Adonai Ammo; Venachalato. Lo Ya'azov. Vehu Rachum Yechapeir Avon Velo-Yashchit Vehirbah Lehashiv Appo; Velo-Ya'ir. Chol-Chamato. Adonai Hoshi'ah; Hamelech. Ya'aneinu Veyom-Kor'enu.

May the glory of Hashem endure forever; let Hashem rejoice in His works. Blessed is the name of Hashem From this time forth and forever. From the rising of the sun to the going down of it, Hashem's name is to be praised. Hashem is high above all nations, His glory is above the heavens. Hashem, Your name endures forever; Your memorial, Hashem, throughout all generations. Hashem has established His Throne in the heavens; And His kingdom rules over all. Let the heavens rejoice and the earth rejoice; let them declare among the nations, "Hashem is King!". Hashem will reign forever and ever. Hashem is King forever and ever; The nations are perished out of His land. Hashem brings the counsel of the nations to nothing; He makes the thoughts of the peoples of no effect. Many designs are in a man's mind, But it is Hashem's plan that is accomplished. The counsel of Hashem stands forever, The thoughts of His heart to all generations. For He spoke, and it was; He commanded, and it stood. For Hashem has chosen Tziyon; He has desired it for His Habitation: For Hashem has chosen Yaakov for Himself, And Yisrael for His own treasure. For Hashem will not cast off His people, Neither will He forsake His inheritance. But He, being full of compassion, forgives iniquity, and does not destroy; Many times He turns His anger away, And does not stir up all of His wrath. Save, Hashem; Let the King answer us in the day that we call. **(Psalms 104:31, 113:2-4, 135:13, 103:19, 1 Chron. 16:31, Ex. 15:18, Psalms 10:16, 33:10, Prov. 19:21, Psalms 33:11, 33:9, 132:13, 135:4, 94:14, 78:38, 20:10)**

Ashrei

When saying the verse "Potei'ach Et Yadecha" one should focus one's heart. If one did not focus he must return and repeat. (SA, OC 51:7) It is customary to open your hands toward Heaven as a symbol of our acceptance of the abundance Hashem bestows upon us from Heaven. (B'I'H, Ex. 9:29, I Kings 8:54).

אַשְׁרֵי יוֹשְׁבֵי בֵיתֶךָ עוֹד יְהַלְלוּךָ סֶּלָה: אַשְׁרֵי הָעָם שֶׁכָּכָה לּוֹ אַשְׁרֵי הָעָם שֶׁיְהֹוָה אֱלֹהָיו:

Ashrei Yoshevei Veitecha; Od. Yehalelucha Selah. Ashrei Ha'am Shekachah Lo; Ashrei Ha'am. She'Adonai Elohav.

Happy are those who dwell in Your House; they are ever praising You. Happy are the people that is so situated; happy are the people whose God is Hashem. **(Psalms 84:5, 144:15)**

Psalms 145

תְּהִלָּה לְדָוִד אֲרוֹמִמְךָ אֱלוֹהַי הַמֶּלֶךְ וַאֲבָרְכָה שִׁמְךָ לְעוֹלָם וָעֶד: בְּכָל־יוֹם אֲבָרְכֶךָּ וַאֲהַלְלָה שִׁמְךָ לְעוֹלָם וָעֶד: גָּדוֹל יְהֹוָה וּמְהֻלָּל מְאֹד וְלִגְדֻלָּתוֹ אֵין חֵקֶר: דּוֹר לְדוֹר יְשַׁבַּח מַעֲשֶׂיךָ וּגְבוּרֹתֶיךָ יַגִּידוּ: הֲדַר כְּבוֹד הוֹדֶךָ וְדִבְרֵי נִפְלְאֹתֶיךָ אָשִׂיחָה: וֶעֱזוּז נוֹרְאֹתֶיךָ יֹאמֵרוּ

וּגְדֻלָּתְךָ אֲסַפְּרֶנָּה: זֵכֶר רַב־טוּבְךָ יַבִּיעוּ וְצִדְקָתְךָ יְרַנֵּנוּ: חַנּוּן וְרַחוּם
יְהֹוָה אֶרֶךְ אַפַּיִם וּגְדָל־חָסֶד: טוֹב־יְהֹוָה לַכֹּל וְרַחֲמָיו עַל־כָּל־מַעֲשָׂיו:
יוֹדוּךָ יְהֹוָה כָּל־מַעֲשֶׂיךָ וַחֲסִידֶיךָ יְבָרְכוּכָה: כְּבוֹד מַלְכוּתְךָ יֹאמֵרוּ
וּגְבוּרָתְךָ יְדַבֵּרוּ: לְהוֹדִיעַ | לִבְנֵי הָאָדָם גְּבוּרֹתָיו וּכְבוֹד הֲדַר
מַלְכוּתוֹ: מַלְכוּתְךָ מַלְכוּת כָּל־עֹלָמִים וּמֶמְשַׁלְתְּךָ בְּכָל־דּוֹר וָדֹר:
סוֹמֵךְ יְהֹוָה לְכָל־הַנֹּפְלִים וְזוֹקֵף לְכָל־הַכְּפוּפִים: עֵינֵי־כֹל אֵלֶיךָ
יְשַׂבֵּרוּ וְאַתָּה נוֹתֵן־לָהֶם אֶת־אָכְלָם בְּעִתּוֹ: **פּוֹתֵחַ אֶת־יָדֶךָ**
וּמַשְׂבִּיעַ לְכָל־חַי רָצוֹן: צַדִּיק יְהֹוָה בְּכָל־דְּרָכָיו וְחָסִיד
בְּכָל־מַעֲשָׂיו: קָרוֹב יְהֹוָה לְכָל־קֹרְאָיו לְכֹל אֲשֶׁר יִקְרָאֻהוּ בֶאֱמֶת:
רְצוֹן־יְרֵאָיו יַעֲשֶׂה וְאֶת־שַׁוְעָתָם יִשְׁמַע וְיוֹשִׁיעֵם: שׁוֹמֵר יְהֹוָה
אֶת־כָּל־אֹהֲבָיו וְאֵת כָּל־הָרְשָׁעִים יַשְׁמִיד: תְּהִלַּת יְהֹוָה יְדַבֶּר פִּי
וִיבָרֵךְ כָּל־בָּשָׂר שֵׁם קָדְשׁוֹ לְעוֹלָם וָעֶד: וַאֲנַחְנוּ | נְבָרֵךְ יָהּ מֵעַתָּה
וְעַד־עוֹלָם הַלְלוּיָהּ:

Tehilah. Ledavid Aromimcha Elohai Hamelech; Va'avarechah Shimcha. Le'olam Va'ed. Bechol-Yom Avarecheka; Va'ahalelah Shimcha. Le'olam Va'ed. Gadol Adonai Umehulal Me'od; Veligdulato. Ein Cheiker. Dor Ledor Yeshabach Ma'aseicha; Ugevuroteicha Yagidu. Hadar Kevod Hodecha; Vedivrei Nifle'oteicha Asichah. Ve'ezuz Nore'oteicha Yomeru; Ug'dulatecha Asap'renah. Zecher Rav-Tuvecha Yabi'u; Vetzidkatecha Yeranenu. Chanun Verachum Adonai Erech Apayim. Ugedol-Chased. Tov-Adonai Lakol; Verachamav. Al-Chol-Ma'asav. Yoducha Adonai Chol-Ma'aseicha; Vachasideicha. Yevarechuchah. Kevod Malchutecha Yomeru; Ugevuratecha Yedaberu. Lehodia Livnei Ha'adam Gevurotav; Uchevod. Hadar Malchuto. Malchutecha. Malchut Chol-'Olamim; Umemshaltecha. Bechol-Dor Vador. Somech Adonai Lechol-Hanofelim; Vezokeif. Lechol-Hakefufim. Einei-Chol Eleicha Yesaberu; Ve'attah Noten-Lahem Et-'Ochlam Be'ito. **Potei'ach Et-Yadecha; Umasbia Lechol-Chai Ratzon.** Tzaddik Adonai Bechol-Derachav; Vechasid. Bechol-Ma'asav. Karov Adonai Lechol-Kore'av; Lechol Asher Yikra'uhu Ve'emet. Retzon-Yere'av Ya'aseh; Ve'et-Shav'atam Yishma'. Veyoshi'em. Shomer Adonai Et-Chol-'Ohavav; Ve'et Chol-Haresha'im Yashmid. Tehillat Adonai Yedaber Pi Vivarech

Chol-Basar Shem Kodsho. Le'olam Va'ed. Va'anachnu Nevarech Yah. Me'attah Ve'ad-'Olam. Halleluyah.

A Psalm of praise; of David. א I will extol You, my God, Oh King; And I will bless Your name forever and ever. ב Every day will I bless You; And I will praise You name forever and ever. ג Great is Hashem, and highly to be praised; And His greatness is unsearchable. ד One generation will applaud Your works to another, And will declare Your mighty acts. ה The glorious splendor of Your majesty, And Your wondrous works, I will rehearse. ו And men will speak of the might of Your tremendous acts; And I will tell of Your greatness. ז They will utter the fame of Your great goodness, And will sing of Your righteousness. ח Hashem is gracious, and full of compassion; Slow to anger, and of great mercy. ט Hashem is good to all; And His tender mercies are over all His works. י All Your works will praise You, Hashem; And Your holy-ones will bless You. כ They will speak of the glory of Your kingdom, And talk of Your might; ל To make known to the sons of men His mighty acts, And the glory of the beauty of His kingdom. מ Your kingdom is a kingdom for all ages, And Your dominion endures throughout all generations. ס Hashem upholds all that fall, And raises up all those that are bowed down. ע The eyes of all wait for You, And You give them their food in due season. פ **You open Your hand, And satisfy every living thing with favor.** צ Hashem is righteous in all His ways, And gracious in all His works. ק Hashem is near to all them that call upon Him, To all that call upon Him in truth. ר He will fulfill the desire of those that fear Him; He also will hear their cry, and will save them. ש Hashem preserves all them that love Him; But all the wicked will He destroy. ת My mouth will speak the praise of Hashem; And let all flesh bless His holy name forever and ever.

Psalms 146

הַלְלוּיָהּ הַלְלִי נַפְשִׁי אֶת־יְהֹוָה׃ אֲהַלְלָה יְהֹוָה בְּחַיָּי אֲזַמְּרָה לֵאלֹהַי
בְּעוֹדִי׃ אַל־תִּבְטְחוּ בִנְדִיבִים בְּבֶן־אָדָם | שֶׁאֵין לוֹ תְשׁוּעָה׃ תֵּצֵא
רוּחוֹ יָשֻׁב לְאַדְמָתוֹ בַּיּוֹם הַהוּא אָבְדוּ עֶשְׁתֹּנֹתָיו׃ אַשְׁרֵי שֶׁאֵל יַעֲקֹב
בְּעֶזְרוֹ שִׂבְרוֹ עַל־יְהֹוָה אֱלֹהָיו׃ עֹשֶׂה | שָׁמַיִם וָאָרֶץ אֶת־הַיָּם
וְאֶת־כָּל־אֲשֶׁר־בָּם הַשֹּׁמֵר אֱמֶת לְעוֹלָם׃ עֹשֶׂה מִשְׁפָּט | לַעֲשׁוּקִים
נֹתֵן לֶחֶם לָרְעֵבִים יְהֹוָה מַתִּיר אֲסוּרִים׃ יְהֹוָה | פֹּקֵחַ עִוְרִים יְהֹוָה
זֹקֵף כְּפוּפִים יְהֹוָה אֹהֵב צַדִּיקִים׃ יְהֹוָה | שֹׁמֵר אֶת־גֵּרִים יָתוֹם
וְאַלְמָנָה יְעוֹדֵד וְדֶרֶךְ רְשָׁעִים יְעַוֵּת׃ יִמְלֹךְ יְהֹוָה | לְעוֹלָם אֱלֹהַיִךְ צִיּוֹן
לְדֹר וָדֹר הַלְלוּיָהּ׃

Halleluyah Haleli Nafshi. Et-Adonai Ahalelah Adonai Bechayai; Azemerah Lelohai Be'odi. Al-Tivtechu Vindivim; Beven-'Adam She'ein Lo Teshu'ah. Tetzei Rucho Yashuv Le'admato; Bayom Hahu. Avedu Eshtonotav. Ashrei. She'el Ya'akov Be'ezro; Sivro. Al-Adonai Elohav. Oseh Shamayim Va'aretz. Et-Hayam Ve'et-Chol-'Asher-Bam; Hashomer Emet Le'olam. Oseh Mishpat La'ashukim. Noten Lechem Lare'evim; Adonai Matir Asurim. Adonai Pokei'ach Ivrim. Adonai Zokeif Kefufim; Adonai Ohev Tzaddikim. Adonai Shomer Et-Gerim. Yatom Ve'almanah Ye'oded; Vederech Resha'im Ye'avet. Yimloch Adonai Le'olam. Elohayich Tziyon Ledor Vador. Halleluyah.

Halleluyah. Praise Hashem, my soul. I will praise Hashem while I live; I will sing praises to my God while I have my being. Do not put your trust in princes, Or in the son of man, in whom there is no help. His breath goes out, he returns to his dust; In that very day his thoughts perish. Happy is he whose help is the God of Yaakov, Whose hope is in Hashem his God, Who made heaven and earth, The sea, and all that in them is; Who keeps truth forever; Who executes justice for the oppressed; Who gives bread to the hungry. Hashem releases the prisoners; Hashem opens the eyes of the blind; Hashem raises up them that are bowed down; Hashem loves the righteous; Hashem preserves the strangers; He upholds the fatherless and the widow;

But the way of the wicked He makes crooked. Hashem will reign forever, Your God, Oh Tziyon, to all generations. Halleluyah.

Psalms 147

הַלְלוּיָהּ | כִּי־טוֹב זַמְּרָה אֱלֹהֵינוּ כִּי־נָעִים נָאוָה תְהִלָּה: בּוֹנֵה
יְרוּשָׁלַםִ יְהוָה נִדְחֵי יִשְׂרָאֵל יְכַנֵּס: הָרֹפֵא לִשְׁבוּרֵי לֵב וּמְחַבֵּשׁ
לְעַצְּבוֹתָם: מוֹנֶה מִסְפָּר לַכּוֹכָבִים לְכֻלָּם שֵׁמוֹת יִקְרָא: גָּדוֹל אֲדוֹנֵינוּ
וְרַב־כֹּחַ לִתְבוּנָתוֹ אֵין מִסְפָּר: מְעוֹדֵד עֲנָוִים יְהוָה מַשְׁפִּיל רְשָׁעִים
עֲדֵי־אָרֶץ: עֱנוּ לַיהוָה בְּתוֹדָה זַמְּרוּ לֵאלֹהֵינוּ בְכִנּוֹר: הַמְכַסֶּה שָׁמַיִם
| בְּעָבִים הַמֵּכִין לָאָרֶץ מָטָר הַמַּצְמִיחַ הָרִים חָצִיר: נוֹתֵן לִבְהֵמָה
לַחְמָהּ לִבְנֵי עֹרֵב אֲשֶׁר יִקְרָאוּ: לֹא בִגְבוּרַת הַסּוּס יֶחְפָּץ
לֹא־בְשׁוֹקֵי הָאִישׁ יִרְצֶה: רוֹצֶה יְהוָה אֶת־יְרֵאָיו אֶת־הַמְיַחֲלִים
לְחַסְדּוֹ: שַׁבְּחִי יְרוּשָׁלַםִ אֶת־יְהוָה הַלְלִי אֱלֹהַיִךְ צִיּוֹן: כִּי־חִזַּק בְּרִיחֵי
שְׁעָרָיִךְ בֵּרַךְ בָּנַיִךְ בְּקִרְבֵּךְ: הַשָּׂם־גְּבוּלֵךְ שָׁלוֹם חֵלֶב חִטִּים יַשְׂבִּיעֵךְ:
הַשֹּׁלֵחַ אִמְרָתוֹ אָרֶץ עַד־מְהֵרָה יָרוּץ דְּבָרוֹ: הַנֹּתֵן שֶׁלֶג כַּצָּמֶר כְּפוֹר
כָּאֵפֶר יְפַזֵּר: מַשְׁלִיךְ קַרְחוֹ כְפִתִּים לִפְנֵי קָרָתוֹ מִי יַעֲמֹד: יִשְׁלַח
דְּבָרוֹ וְיַמְסֵם יַשֵּׁב רוּחוֹ יִזְּלוּ־מָיִם: מַגִּיד דְּבָרָו לְיַעֲקֹב חֻקָּיו
וּמִשְׁפָּטָיו לְיִשְׂרָאֵל: לֹא עָשָׂה כֵן | לְכָל־גּוֹי וּמִשְׁפָּטִים בַּל־יְדָעוּם
הַלְלוּיָהּ:

Halleluyah; Ki-Tov Zemerah Eloheinu; Ki-Na'im. Navah Tehilah. Boneh Yerushalami Adonai Nidchei Yisra'el Yechanes. Harofei Lishvurei Lev; Umechabesh. Le'atzevotam. Moneh Mispor Lakkochavim; Lechulam. Shemot Yikra. Gadol Adoneinu Verav-Koach; Litvunato. Ein Mispar. Me'oded Anavim Adonai Mashpil Resha'im Adei-'Aretz. Enu L'Adonai Betodah; Zameru Leloheinu Vechinor. Hamchaseh Shamayim Be'avim. Ha'meichin La'aretz Matar; Hamatzmiach Harim Chatzir. Noten Livhemah Lachmah; Livnei Orev. Asher Yikra'u. Lo Vigvurat Hassus Yechpatz; Lo-Veshokei Ha'ish Yirtzeh. Rotzeh Adonai Et-Yere'av; Et-Hamyachalim Lechasdo. Shabechi Yerushalayim Et-Adonai Haleli Elohayich

Tziyon. Ki-Chizak Berichei She'arayich; Berach Banayich Bekirbech. Hassam-Gevulech Shalom; Chelev Chitim. Yasbi'ech. Hasholeach Imrato Aretz; Ad-Meheirah. Yarutz Devaro. Hanotein Sheleg Katzamer; Kefor. Ka'efer Yefazer. Mashlich Karcho Chefitim; Lifnei Karato. Mi Ya'amod. Yishlach Devaro Veyamsem; Yashev Rucho. Yizelu-Mayim. Maggid Devarav Leya'akov; Chukkav Umishpatav. Leyisra'el. Lo Asah Chein Lechol-Goy. Umishpatim Bal-Yeda'um. Halleluyah.

Halleluyah; For it is good to sing praises to our God; For it is pleasant, and praise is suitable. Hashem builds up Yerushalayim, He gathers together the dispersed of Yisrael; Who heals the broken in heart, And binds up their wounds. He counts the number of the stars; He gives them all their names. Great is our Hashem, and mighty in power; His understanding is infinite. Hashem upholds the humble; He brings the wicked down to the ground. Sing to Hashem with thanksgiving, Sing praises upon the harp to our God; Who covers the heaven with clouds, Who prepares rain for the earth, Who makes the mountains to spring with grass. He gives to the beast his food, And to the young ravens which cry. He doesn't delight in the strength of the horse; He takes no pleasure in the legs of a man. Hashem takes pleasure in them that fear Him, In those that wait for His mercy. Glorify Hashem, Oh Yerushalayim; Praise your God, Oh Tziyon. For He has made strong the bars of your gates; He has blessed your children within you. He makes your borders peace; He gives you in plenty the fat of wheat. He sends out His commandment on earth; His word runs very swiftly. He gives snow like wool; He scatters the hoar-frost like ashes. He casts out His ice like crumbs; Who can stand before His cold? He sends out His word, and melts them; He causes His wind to blow, and the waters flow. He declares His word to Yaakov, His statutes and His ordinances to Yisrael. He has not dealt so with any nation; And as for His ordinances, they have not known them. Halleluyah.

Psalms 148

הַלְלוּיָהּ ׀ הַלְלוּ אֶת־יְהֹוָה מִן־הַשָּׁמַיִם הַלְלוּהוּ בַּמְּרוֹמִים: הַלְלוּהוּ
כָל־מַלְאָכָיו הַלְלוּהוּ כָּל־צְבָאָו: הַלְלוּהוּ שֶׁמֶשׁ וְיָרֵחַ הַלְלוּהוּ
כָּל־כּוֹכְבֵי אוֹר: הַלְלוּהוּ שְׁמֵי הַשָּׁמָיִם וְהַמַּיִם אֲשֶׁר ׀ מֵעַל הַשָּׁמָיִם:
יְהַלְלוּ אֶת־שֵׁם יְהֹוָה כִּי הוּא צִוָּה וְנִבְרָאוּ: וַיַּעֲמִידֵם לָעַד לְעוֹלָם
חָק־נָתַן וְלֹא יַעֲבוֹר: הַלְלוּ אֶת־יְהֹוָה מִן־הָאָרֶץ תַּנִּינִים וְכָל־תְּהֹמוֹת:
אֵשׁ וּבָרָד שֶׁלֶג וְקִיטוֹר רוּחַ סְעָרָה עֹשָׂה דְבָרוֹ: הֶהָרִים וְכָל־גְּבָעוֹת
עֵץ פְּרִי וְכָל־אֲרָזִים: הַחַיָּה וְכָל־בְּהֵמָה רֶמֶשׂ וְצִפּוֹר כָּנָף:
מַלְכֵי־אֶרֶץ וְכָל־לְאֻמִּים שָׂרִים וְכָל־שֹׁפְטֵי אָרֶץ: בַּחוּרִים
וְגַם־בְּתוּלוֹת זְקֵנִים עִם־נְעָרִים: יְהַלְלוּ ׀ אֶת־שֵׁם יְהֹוָה כִּי־נִשְׂגָּב שְׁמוֹ
לְבַדּוֹ הוֹדוֹ עַל־אֶרֶץ וְשָׁמָיִם: וַיָּרֶם קֶרֶן ׀ לְעַמּוֹ תְּהִלָּה לְכָל־חֲסִידָיו
לִבְנֵי יִשְׂרָאֵל עַם קְרֹבוֹ הַלְלוּיָהּ:

Halleluyah Halelu Et-Adonai Min-Hashamayim; Halleluhu. Bameromim. Halleluhu Chol-Mal'achav; Halleluhu. Chol-Tzeva'av. Halleluhu Shemesh Veyareach; Halleluhu. Chol-Kochevei Or. Halleluhu Shemei Hashamayim; Vehamayim. Asher Me'al Hashamayim. Yehalelu Et-Shem Adonai Ki Hu Tzivah Venivra'u. Vaya'amidem La'ad Le'olam; Chok-Natan. Velo Ya'avor. Halelu Et-Adonai Min-Ha'aretz; Taninim. Vechol-Tehomot. Esh Uvarod Sheleg Vekitor; Ruach Se'arah. Osah Devaro. Heharim Vechol-Geva'ot; Etz Peri. Vechol-'Arazim. Hachayah Vechol-Behemah; Remes Vetzipor Kanaf. Malchei-'Eretz Vechol-Le'ummim; Sarim. Vechol-Shofetei Aretz. Bachurim Vegam-Betulot; Zekenim. Im-Ne'arim. Yehalelu Et-Shem Adonai Ki-Nisgav Shemo Levado; Hodo. Al-'Eretz Veshamayim. Vayarem Keren Le'ammo Tehilah Lechol-Chasidav. Livnei Yisra'el Am Kerovo. Halleluyah.

Halleluyah. Praise Hashem from the heavens; Praise Him in the heights. Praise Him, all His angels; Praise Him, all His hosts. Praise Him, sun and moon; Praise Him, all stars of light. Praise Him, heavens of heavens, And waters that are above the heavens. Let them praise the name of Hashem; For He commanded, and they were created. He also established them forever and ever; He made a decree which will not be transgressed. Praise Hashem from the earth, Sea-monsters, and all deeps; Fire and hail, snow and vapor, Stormy wind, fulfilling His word; Mountains and all hills, Fruitful trees and all cedars; Beasts and all cattle, Creeping things and winged fowl; Kings of the earth and all peoples, Princes and all judges of the earth; Both young men and maidens, Old men and children; Let them praise the name of Hashem, For His name alone is exalted; His glory is above the earth and heaven. And He has lifted up a horn for His people, A praise for all His holy-ones, Even for the children of Yisrael, a people near to Him. Halleluyah.

Psalms 149

הַלְלוּיָהּ | שִׁירוּ לַיהוָה שִׁיר חָדָשׁ תְּהִלָּתוֹ בִּקְהַל חֲסִידִים: יִשְׂמַח
יִשְׂרָאֵל בְּעֹשָׂיו בְּנֵי־צִיּוֹן יָגִילוּ בְמַלְכָּם: יְהַלְלוּ שְׁמוֹ בְמָחוֹל בְּתֹף
וְכִנּוֹר יְזַמְּרוּ־לוֹ: כִּי־רוֹצֶה יְהוָה בְּעַמּוֹ יְפָאֵר עֲנָוִים בִּישׁוּעָה: יַעְלְזוּ
חֲסִידִים בְּכָבוֹד יְרַנְּנוּ עַל־מִשְׁכְּבוֹתָם: רוֹמְמוֹת אֵל בִּגְרוֹנָם וְחֶרֶב
פִּיפִיּוֹת בְּיָדָם: לַעֲשׂוֹת נְקָמָה בַּגּוֹיִם תּוֹכֵחוֹת בַּלְאֻמִּים: לֶאְסֹר
מַלְכֵיהֶם בְּזִקִּים וְנִכְבְּדֵיהֶם בְּכַבְלֵי בַרְזֶל: לַעֲשׂוֹת בָּהֶם | מִשְׁפָּט
כָּתוּב הָדָר הוּא לְכָל־חֲסִידָיו הַלְלוּיָהּ:

Halleluyah. Shiru L'Adonai Shir Chadash; Tehilato. Bik'hal Chasidim. Yismach Yisra'el Be'osav; Benei-Tziyon. Yagilu Vemalkam. Yehalelu Shemo Vemachol; Betof Vechinor. Yezameru-Lo. Ki-Rotzeh Adonai Be'ammo; Yefa'er Anavim. Bishu'ah. Ya'lezu Chasidim Bechavod; Yeranenu. Al-Mishkevotam. Romemot El Bigronam; Vecherev Pifiyot Beyadam. La'asot Nekamah Bagoyim; Tochechot. Bal'ummim. Le'sor Malcheihem Bezikkim; Venichbedeihem. Bechavlei Varzel. La'asot Bahem Mishpat Katuv. Hadar Hu Lechol-Chasidav. Halleluyah.

Halleluyah. Sing to Hashem a new song, And His praise in the assembly of the holy-ones. Let Yisrael rejoice in his Maker; Let the children of Tziyon be joyful in their King. Let them praise His name in the dance; Let them sing praises to Him with the timbrel and harp. For Hashem takes pleasure in His people; He adorns the humble with salvation. Let the holy-ones exult in glory; Let them sing for joy upon their beds. Let the high praises of God be in their mouth, And a two-edged sword in their hand; To execute vengeance on the nations, And chastisements on the peoples; To bind their kings with chains, And their nobles with shackles of iron; To execute on them the written judgment; He is the glory of all His holy-ones. Halleluyah.

Psalms 150

הַלְלוּיָהּ | הַלְלוּ־אֵל בְּקׇדְשׁוֹ הַלְלוּהוּ בִּרְקִיעַ עֻזּוֹ: הַלְלוּהוּ
בִגְבוּרֹתָיו הַלְלוּהוּ כְּרֹב גֻּדְלוֹ: הַלְלוּהוּ בְּתֵקַע שׁוֹפָר הַלְלוּהוּ בְּנֵבֶל
וְכִנּוֹר: הַלְלוּהוּ בְתֹף וּמָחוֹל הַלְלוּהוּ בְּמִנִּים וְעֻגָב: הַלְלוּהוּ
בְצִלְצְלֵי־שָׁמַע הַלְלוּהוּ בְּצִלְצְלֵי תְרוּעָה: כֹּל הַנְּשָׁמָה תְּהַלֵּל יָהּ
הַלְלוּיָהּ: כֹּל הַנְּשָׁמָה תְּהַלֵּל יָהּ הַלְלוּיָהּ:

Halleluyah Halelu-'El Bekod'sho; Halleluhu. Birkia Uzo. Halleluhu Vigvurotav; Halleluhu. Kerov Gudlo. Halleluhu Beteka Shofar; Halleluhu. Benevel Vechinor. Halleluhu Betof Umachol; Halleluhu. Beminim Ve'ugav. Halleluhu Vetziltzelei-Shama'; Halleluhu. Betziltzelei Teru'ah. Kol Haneshamah Tehallel Yah. Halleluyah. Kol Haneshamah Tehallel Yah. Halleluyah.

Halleluyah. Praise God in His Sanctuary; Praise Him in the firmament of His power. Praise Him for His mighty acts; Praise Him according to His abundant greatness. Praise Him with the blast of the shofar; Praise Him with the psaltery and harp. Praise Him with the timbrel and dance; Praise Him with stringed instruments and the pipe. Praise Him with the loud-sounding cymbals; Praise Him with the clanging cymbals. Let everything that has breath praise Hashem. Halleluyah.

בָּרוּךְ יְהֹוָה לְעוֹלָם אָמֵן | וְאָמֵן: בָּרוּךְ יְהֹוָה | מִצִּיּוֹן שֹׁכֵן יְרוּשָׁלָםִ
הַלְלוּיָהּ: בָּרוּךְ | יְהֹוָה אֱלֹהִים אֱלֹהֵי יִשְׂרָאֵל עֹשֵׂה נִפְלָאוֹת לְבַדּוֹ:
וּבָרוּךְ | שֵׁם כְּבוֹדוֹ לְעוֹלָם וְיִמָּלֵא כְבוֹדוֹ אֶת־כֹּל הָאָרֶץ אָמֵן |
וְאָמֵן:

Baruch Adonai Le'olam. Amen Ve'amen. Baruch Adonai Mitziyon. Shochein Yerushalayim Halleluyah. Baruch Adonai Elohim Elohei Yisra'el; Oseh Nifla'ot Levado. Uvaruch Shem Kevodo. Le'olam Veyimmalei Chevodo Et-Kol Ha'aretz. Amen Ve'amen.

Blessed is Hashem forever more. Amen, and Amen. Blessed is Hashem from Tziyon, who dwells at Yerushalayim. Halleluyah. Blessed is Hashem-Elohim, the God of Yisrael, Who only does wondrous things; And blessed is His glorious name forever; And let the whole earth be filled with His glory. Amen, and Amen. **(Psalms 89:53,135:21, 72:18-19)**

Vayvarech David

I Chronicles 29:10-13

One should stand and recite:

וַיְבָרֶךְ דָּוִיד אֶת־יְהֹוָה לְעֵינֵי כָּל־הַקָּהָל וַיֹּאמֶר דָּוִיד בָּרוּךְ אַתָּה יְהֹוָה
אֱלֹהֵי יִשְׂרָאֵל אָבִינוּ מֵעוֹלָם וְעַד־עוֹלָם: לְךָ יְהֹוָה הַגְּדֻלָּה וְהַגְּבוּרָה
וְהַתִּפְאֶרֶת וְהַנֵּצַח וְהַהוֹד כִּי־כֹל בַּשָּׁמַיִם וּבָאָרֶץ לְךָ יְהֹוָה הַמַּמְלָכָה
וְהַמִּתְנַשֵּׂא לְכֹל | לְרֹאשׁ: וְהָעֹשֶׁר וְהַכָּבוֹד מִלְּפָנֶיךָ וְאַתָּה מוֹשֵׁל בַּכֹּל
וּבְיָדְךָ כֹּחַ וּגְבוּרָה וּבְיָדְךָ לְגַדֵּל וּלְחַזֵּק לַכֹּל: וְעַתָּה אֱלֹהֵינוּ מוֹדִים
אֲנַחְנוּ לָךְ וּמְהַלְלִים לְשֵׁם תִּפְאַרְתֶּךָ:

Vayvarech David Et-Adonai Le'einei Chol-Hakahal; Vayomer David. Baruch Attah Adonai Elohei Yisra'el Avinu. Me'olam Ve'ad-'Olam. Lecha Adonai Hagedullah Vehagevurah Vehatif'eret Vehanetzach Vehahod. Ki-Chol Bashamayim Uva'aretz; Lecha Adonai Hamamlachah. Vehamitnasei Lechol Lerosh. Veha'osher Vehakavod Milfaneicha. Ve'attah Moshel Bakol. Uveyadecha Koach Ugevurah;

Uveyadecha. Legadel Ulechazek Lakol. Ve'attah Eloheinu. Modim Anachnu Lach; Umehalelim Leshem Tif'artecha.

And David blessed Hashem before all the congregation; and David said: 'Blessed are You, Hashem, the God of Yisrael our father, forever and ever. Yours, Hashem, is the greatness, and the power, and the glory, and the victory, and the majesty; for all that is in the heaven and in the earth is Yours; Yours is the kingdom, Hashem, and You are exalted as head above all. Both riches and honor come from You, and You rule over all; and in Your hand is power and might; and it is in Your hand to make great, and to give strength to all. Now, our God, we thank You, and praise Your glorious name.

Nehemiah 9:5-11

וִיבָרְכוּ שֵׁם כְּבֹדֶךָ וּמְרוֹמַם עַל־כָּל־בְּרָכָה וּתְהִלָּה: אַתָּה־הוּא יְהֹוָה לְבַדֶּךָ את (אַתָּה) עָשִׂיתָ אֶת־הַשָּׁמַיִם שְׁמֵי הַשָּׁמַיִם וְכָל־צְבָאָם הָאָרֶץ וְכָל־אֲשֶׁר עָלֶיהָ הַיַּמִּים וְכָל־אֲשֶׁר בָּהֶם וְאַתָּה מְחַיֶּה אֶת־כֻּלָּם וּצְבָא הַשָּׁמַיִם לְךָ מִשְׁתַּחֲוִים: אַתָּה־הוּא יְהֹוָה הָאֱלֹהִים אֲשֶׁר בָּחַרְתָּ בְּאַבְרָם וְהוֹצֵאתוֹ מֵאוּר כַּשְׂדִּים וְשַׂמְתָּ שְּׁמוֹ אַבְרָהָם: וּמָצָאתָ אֶת־לְבָבוֹ נֶאֱמָן לְפָנֶיךָ וְכָרוֹת עִמּוֹ הַבְּרִית לָתֵת אֶת־אֶרֶץ הַכְּנַעֲנִי הַחִתִּי הָאֱמֹרִי וְהַפְּרִזִּי וְהַיְבוּסִי וְהַגִּרְגָּשִׁי לָתֵת לְזַרְעוֹ וַתָּקֶם אֶת־דְּבָרֶיךָ כִּי צַדִּיק אָתָּה: וַתֵּרֶא אֶת־עֳנִי אֲבֹתֵינוּ בְּמִצְרָיִם וְאֶת־זַעֲקָתָם שָׁמַעְתָּ עַל־יַם־סוּף: וַתִּתֵּן אֹתֹת וּמֹפְתִים בְּפַרְעֹה וּבְכָל־עֲבָדָיו וּבְכָל־עַם אַרְצוֹ כִּי יָדַעְתָּ כִּי הֵזִידוּ עֲלֵיהֶם וַתַּעַשׂ־לְךָ שֵׁם כְּהַיּוֹם הַזֶּה: וְהַיָּם בָּקַעְתָּ לִפְנֵיהֶם וַיַּעַבְרוּ בְתוֹךְ־הַיָּם בַּיַּבָּשָׁה וְאֶת־רֹדְפֵיהֶם הִשְׁלַכְתָּ בִמְצוֹלֹת כְּמוֹ־אֶבֶן בְּמַיִם עַזִּים:

Vivarechu Shem Kevodecha. Umeromam Al-Chol-Berachah Utehilah. Attah-Hu Adonai Levadecha Et-Attah Asita Et-Hashamayim Shemei Hashamayim Vechol-Tzeva'am. Ha'aretz Vechol-'Asher Aleiha Hayamim Vechol-'Asher Bahem. Ve'attah Mechayeh Et-Kulam; Utzeva Hashamayim Lecha Mishtachavim. Attah-Hu Adonai Ha'elohim. Asher Bacharta Be'avram. Vehotzeto Me'ur Kasdim; Vesamta Shemo Avraham. Umatzata Et-Levavo Ne'eman Lefaneicha

Vecharot Imo Haberit. Latet Et-'Eretz Hakena'ani Hachiti Ha'emori Vehaperizi Vehayvusi Vehagirgashi Latet Lezar'o; Vatakem Et-Devareicha. Ki Tzaddik Attah. Vaterei Et-'Oni Avoteinu Bemitzrayim; Ve'et-Za'akatam Shama'ta Al-Yam-Suf. Vatiten Otot Umofetim Befar'oh Uvechol-'Avadav Uvechol-'Am Artzo. Ki Yada'ta. Ki Hezidu Aleihem; Vata'as-Lecha Shem Kehayom Hazeh. Vehayam Baka'ta Lifneihem. Vaya'avru Vetoch-Hayam Bayabashah; Ve'et-Rodefeihem Hishlachta Vimtzolot Kemo-'Even Bemayim Azim.

Blessed is Your glorious Name, that is exalted above all blessing and praise. You are Hashem, even You alone; You have made heaven, the heaven of heavens, with all their host, the earth and all things that are on it, the seas and all that is in them, and You preserve them all; and the host of heaven worship You. You are Hashem the God, Who chose Avram, and brought him out out from Ur of Kasdim, and gave him the name of Avraham; and found his heart faithful before You, and made a covenant with him to give the land of the Canaani, the Hitti, the Emori, and the Perizi, and the Yevusi, and the Girgashi, even to give it to his seed, and have performed Your words; for You are righteous; And You saw the affliction of our fathers in Mitzrayim, and heard their cry by the Sea of Reeds; and did show signs and wonders on Pharaoh, and on all his servants, and on all the people of his land; for You knew that they dealt proudly against them; and gave You a name, as it is this day. And You divided the sea before them, so that they went through the midst of the sea on the dry land; and You cast their pursuers into the depths, as a stone into the mighty waters.

Shirat Hayam / Song at the Sea

Exodus 14:30-31

וַיּוֹשַׁע יְהֹוָה בַּיּוֹם הַהוּא אֶת־יִשְׂרָאֵל מִיַּד מִצְרָיִם וַיַּרְא יִשְׂרָאֵל
אֶת־מִצְרַיִם מֵת עַל־שְׂפַת הַיָּם׃ וַיַּרְא יִשְׂרָאֵל אֶת־הַיָּד הַגְּדֹלָה אֲשֶׁר

עָשָׂה יְהֹוָה בְּמִצְרַיִם וַיִּירְאוּ הָעָם אֶת־יְהֹוָה וַיַּאֲמִינוּ בַּיהֹוָה וּבְמֹשֶׁה
עַבְדּוֹ׃

Vayosha Adonai Bayom Hahu Et-Yisra'el Miyad Mitzrayim; Vayar Yisra'el Et-Mitzrayim. Met Al-Sefat Hayam. Vayar Yisra'el Et-Hayad Hagedolah. Asher Asah Adonai Bemitzrayim. Vayire'u Ha'am Et-Adonai Vaya'aminu B'Adonai. Uvemosheh Avdo.

And Hashem saved Yisrael on that day out of the hand of Mitzrayim; and Yisrael saw Mitzrayim dead upon the sea-shore. And Yisrael saw the great work which Hashem performed on Mitzrayim, and the people feared Hashem; and they believed in Hashem, and in His servant Moshe.

Exodus 15:1-18

אָז יָשִׁיר־מֹשֶׁה וּבְנֵי יִשְׂרָאֵל אֶת־הַשִּׁירָה הַזֹּאת לַיהֹוָה וַיֹּאמְרוּ
לֵאמֹר אָשִׁירָה לַיהֹוָה כִּי־גָאֹה גָּאָה סוּס וְרֹכְבוֹ רָמָה בַיָּם׃ עָזִּי
וְזִמְרָת יָהּ וַיְהִי־לִי לִישׁוּעָה זֶה אֵלִי וְאַנְוֵהוּ אֱלֹהֵי אָבִי וַאֲרֹמְמֶנְהוּ׃
יְהֹוָה אִישׁ מִלְחָמָה יְהֹוָה שְׁמוֹ׃ מַרְכְּבֹת פַּרְעֹה וְחֵילוֹ יָרָה בַיָּם
וּמִבְחַר שָׁלִשָׁיו טֻבְּעוּ בְיַם־סוּף׃ תְּהֹמֹת יְכַסְיֻמוּ יָרְדוּ בִמְצוֹלֹת
כְּמוֹ־אָבֶן׃ יְמִינְךָ יְהֹוָה נֶאְדָּרִי בַּכֹּחַ יְמִינְךָ יְהֹוָה תִּרְעַץ אוֹיֵב׃ וּבְרֹב
גְּאוֹנְךָ תַּהֲרֹס קָמֶיךָ תְּשַׁלַּח חֲרֹנְךָ יֹאכְלֵמוֹ כַּקַּשׁ׃ וּבְרוּחַ אַפֶּיךָ
נֶעֶרְמוּ מַיִם נִצְּבוּ כְמוֹ־נֵד נֹזְלִים קָפְאוּ תְהֹמֹת בְּלֶב־יָם׃ אָמַר אוֹיֵב
אֶרְדֹּף אַשִּׂיג אֲחַלֵּק שָׁלָל תִּמְלָאֵמוֹ נַפְשִׁי אָרִיק חַרְבִּי תּוֹרִישֵׁמוֹ יָדִי׃
נָשַׁפְתָּ בְרוּחֲךָ כִּסָּמוֹ יָם צָלְלוּ כַּעוֹפֶרֶת בְּמַיִם אַדִּירִים׃ מִי־כָמֹכָה
בָּאֵלִם יְהֹוָה מִי כָּמֹכָה נֶאְדָּר בַּקֹּדֶשׁ נוֹרָא תְהִלֹּת עֹשֵׂה פֶלֶא׃ נָטִיתָ
יְמִינְךָ תִּבְלָעֵמוֹ אָרֶץ׃ נָחִיתָ בְחַסְדְּךָ עַם־זוּ גָּאָלְתָּ נֵהַלְתָּ בְעָזְּךָ
אֶל־נְוֵה קָדְשֶׁךָ׃ שָׁמְעוּ עַמִּים יִרְגָּזוּן חִיל אָחַז יֹשְׁבֵי פְּלָשֶׁת׃ אָז
נִבְהֲלוּ אַלּוּפֵי אֱדוֹם אֵילֵי מוֹאָב יֹאחֲזֵמוֹ רָעַד נָמֹגוּ כֹּל יֹשְׁבֵי כְנָעַן׃
תִּפֹּל עֲלֵיהֶם אֵימָתָה וָפַחַד בִּגְדֹל זְרוֹעֲךָ יִדְּמוּ כָּאָבֶן עַד־יַעֲבֹר עַמְּךָ
יְהֹוָה עַד־יַעֲבֹר עַם־זוּ קָנִיתָ׃ תְּבִאֵמוֹ וְתִטָּעֵמוֹ בְּהַר נַחֲלָתְךָ מָכוֹן

לְשִׁבְתְּךָ פָּעַלְתָּ יְהֹוָה מִקְּדָשׁ אֲדֹנָי כּוֹנְנוּ יָדֶיךָ: יְהֹוָה | יִמְלֹךְ לְעֹלָם
וָעֶד: יְהֹוָה | יִמְלֹךְ לְעֹלָם וָעֶד: יְהֹוָה מַלְכוּתֵהּ קָאֵים לְעָלַם וּלְעָלְמֵי
עָלְמַיָּא: כִּי בָא סוּס פַּרְעֹה בְּרִכְבּוֹ וּבְפָרָשָׁיו בַּיָּם וַיָּשֶׁב יְהֹוָה עֲלֵהֶם
אֶת־מֵי הַיָּם וּבְנֵי יִשְׂרָאֵל הָלְכוּ בַיַּבָּשָׁה בְּתוֹךְ הַיָּם:

Az Yashir-Mosheh Uvenei Yisra'el Et-Hashirah Hazot L'Adonai Vayomeru Lemor; Ashirah L'Adonai Ki-Ga'oh Ga'ah. Sus Verochevo Ramah Vayam. Ozi Vezimrat Yah. Vayhi-Li Lishu'ah; Zeh Eli Ve'anvehu. Elohei Avi Va'aromemenhu. Adonai Ish Milchamah; Adonai Shemo. Markevot Par'oh Vecheilo Yarah Vayam; Umivchar Shalishav Tube'u Veyam-Suf. Tehomot Yechasyumu; Yaredu Vimtzolot Kemo-'Aven. Yeminecha Adonai Ne'dari Bakoach; Yeminecha Adonai Tir'atz Oyev. Uverov Ge'onecha Taharos Kameicha; Teshallach Charonecha. Yochelemo Kakash. Uveruach Appeicha Ne'ermu Mayim. Nitzevu Chemo-Ned Nozelim; Kafe'u Tehomot Belev-Yam. Amar Oyev Erdof Assig Achallek Shalal; Timla'emo Nafshi. Arik Charbi. Torishemo Yadi. Nashafta Veruchacha Kisamo Yam; Tzalelu Ka'oferet. Bemayim Adirim. Mi-Chamochah Ba'elim Adonai Mi Kamochah Ne'dar Bakodesh; Nora Tehillot Oseh Fele. Natita Yeminecha. Tivla'emo Aretz. Nachita Vechasdecha Am-Zu Ga'aleta; Nehalta Ve'ozecha El-Neveh Kodshecha. Shame'u Ammim Yirgazun; Chil Achaz. Yoshevei Pelashet. Az Nivhalu Alufei Edom. Eilei Mo'av. Yochazemo Ra'ad; Namogu Kol Yoshevei Chena'an. Tipol Aleihem Eimatah Vafachad. Bigdol Zero'acha Yidemu Ka'aven; Ad-Ya'avor Ammecha Adonai Ad-Ya'avor Am-Zu Kanita. Tevi'emo. Vetita'emo Behar Nachalatecha. Machon Leshivtecha Pa'alta Adonai Mikkedash Adonai Konenu Yadeicha. Adonai Yimloch Le'olam Va'ed. Adonai Yimloch Le'olam Va'ed. Adonai Malchuteh Ka'im Le'alam Ule'alemei Alemaya. Ki Va Sus Par'oh Berichbo Uvefarashav Bayam. Vayashev Adonai Aleihem Et-Mei Hayam; Uvenei Yisra'el Halechu Vayabashah Betoch Hayam.

Then Moshe and the children of Yisrael sang this song to Hashem, and spoke, saying: I will sing to Hashem, for He is highly exalted; The horse and his rider He has thrown into the sea. Hashem is my strength and song, And He has become my salvation; This is my God, and I will glorify Him; My father's God, and I will exalt Him. Hashem is a man of war, Hashem is His name. Pharaoh's chariots and his host He has cast into the sea, And His chosen captains are sunk in the Sea of Reeds. The deeps cover them—They went down into the depths like a stone. Your right hand, Hashem, glorious in power, Your right hand, Hashem, shatters the enemy. And in Your abundant excellency You overthrow those that rise up against You; You send out Your wrath, it consumes them like straw. And with the breath of Your nostrils the waters were piled up. The waters stood upright as a wall; The flowing water froze in the heart of the sea. The enemy said: 'I will pursue, I will overtake, I will divide the spoil; My lust will be satisfied on them; I will draw my sword, my hand will destroy them.' You blew with Your wind, the sea covered them; They sank like lead in mighty waters. Who is like You, Hashem, among the gods, Who is like You, glorified in holiness, You are awesome in praise, working wonders. You stretched out Your right hand—The earth swallowed them. In Your love You led the people that You have redeemed; You have guided them in Your strength to Your holy Habitation. The nations have heard, they tremble; Pains have taken hold on the inhabitants of Philistia. Then the chiefs of Edom were afraid; The mighty men of Moav, trembling took hold of them; All the inhabitants of Canaan have melted away. Terror and dread falls upon them; By the greatness of Your arm they are as still as a stone; Until Your people pass over, Hashem, Until the people pass over that You have acquired. You will bring them in, and plant them in the mountain of Your inheritance, The place, Hashem, which You have made for You to dwell in, The Sanctuary, Hashem, which Your hands have established. Hashem will reign forever and ever.

כִּי לַיהוָה הַמְּלוּכָה וּמֹשֵׁל בַּגּוֹיִם: וְעָלוּ מוֹשִׁעִים בְּהַר צִיּוֹן לִשְׁפֹּט אֶת־הַר עֵשָׂו וְהָיְתָה לַיהוָה הַמְּלוּכָה: וְהָיָה יְהוָה לְמֶלֶךְ עַל־כָּל־הָאָרֶץ בַּיּוֹם הַהוּא יִהְיֶה יְהוָה אֶחָד וּשְׁמוֹ אֶחָד:

Ki L'Adonai Hameluchah; Umoshel. Bagoyim. Ve'alu Moshi'im Behar Tziyon. Lishpot Et-Har Esav; Vehayetah L'Adonai Hameluchah. Vehayah Adonai Lemelech Al-Chol-Ha'aretz; Bayom Hahu. Yihyeh Adonai Echad Ushemo Echad.

For dominion is Hashem's and He governs the nations. Saviors will go up Mount Tziyon to judge the Mount of Esav, and sovereignty will be Hashem's. Hashem will be King over all the earth; on that day Hashem will be One and His name One. **(Ps. 22:29, Obadiah 1:21, Zech. 14:9)**

Yishtabach

One should not say Yishtabach unless he has said Baruch She'amar and some of Pesukei De'zimrah. The leader should say Yishtabach while standing. (SA, OC 53)

Remain standing and say:

Yishtabach Shimcha La'ad	יִשְׁתַּבַּח שִׁמְךָ לָעַד
Malkeinu. Ha'el Hamelech	מַלְכֵּנוּ. הָאֵל הַמֶּלֶךְ
Hagadol Vehakadosh.	הַגָּדוֹל וְהַקָּדוֹשׁ.
Bashamayim Uva'aretz. Ki Lecha	בַּשָּׁמַיִם וּבָאָרֶץ. כִּי לְךָ
Na'eh Adonai Eloheinu Velohei	נָאֶה יְהֹוָה אֱלֹהֵינוּ וֵאלֹהֵי
Avoteinu Le'olam Va'ed. א Shir.	אֲבוֹתֵינוּ לְעוֹלָם וָעֶד. א שִׁיר.
ב Ushevachah. ג Hallel.	ב וּשְׁבָחָה. ג הַלֵּל.
ד Vezimrah. ה Oz. ו Umemshalah.	ד וְזִמְרָה. ה עֹז. ו וּמֶמְשָׁלָה. ז
ז Netzach. ח Gedullah.	נֶצַח. ח גְּדֻלָּה.
ט Gevurah. י Tehilah. יא Vetif'eret.	ט גְּבוּרָה. י תְּהִלָּה. יא וְתִפְאֶרֶת.
יב Kedushah. יג Umalchut.	יב קְדֻשָּׁה. יג וּמַלְכוּת.
Berachot Vehoda'ot. Leshimcha	בְּרָכוֹת וְהוֹדָאוֹת. לְשִׁמְךָ הַגָּדוֹל
Hagadol Vehakadosh. Ume'olam	וְהַקָּדוֹשׁ. וּמֵעוֹלָם
Ve'ad Olam Attah El. Baruch	וְעַד עוֹלָם אַתָּה אֵל. בָּרוּךְ
Attah Adonai Melech Gadol	אַתָּה יְהֹוָה מֶלֶךְ גָּדוֹל
Umehulal Batishbachot. El	וּמְהֻלָּל בַּתִּשְׁבָּחוֹת. אֵל

Hahoda'ot. Adon Hanifla'ot.	הַהוֹדָאוֹת. אֲדוֹן הַנִּפְלָאוֹת.
Borei Kol-Haneshamot. Ribon	בּוֹרֵא כָּל־הַנְּשָׁמוֹת. רִבּוֹן
Kol-Hama'asim. Habocher	כָּל־הַמַּעֲשִׂים. הַבּוֹחֵר
Beshirei Zimrah. Melech El Chai	בְּשִׁירֵי זִמְרָה. מֶֽלֶךְ אֵל חַי
Ha'Olamim. Amen.	הָעוֹלָמִים. אָמֵן.

May Your name be praised forever, God, the King, the great and holy in heaven and on earth; for to You, Hashem our God and the God of our fathers, forever pertain 1. song 2. and praise, 3. lauding and 4. hymn, 5. strength and 6. dominion, 7. victory, 8. greatness, 9. might, 10. adoration and 11. glory, 12. holiness and 13. majesty. Blessings and thanksgivings to Your great and holy name. From eternity to eternity You are God. Blessed are You, Hashem, King, great and adored with praises, God of thanksgivings, Lord of all wonders. Creator of all souls, and Sovereign of all works, Who chooses musical songs of praise; King, God, Who lives eternally. Amen.

Hatzi-Kaddish / Half Kaddish

Kaddish is only recited in a minyan (ten men). אָמֵן denotes when the congregation responds "Amen" together out loud. According to the Shulchan Arukh, the congregation says "Yehei Shemeh Rabba" to "Yitbarach" out loud together without interruption, and also that one should respond "Amen" after "Yitbarach." (SA, OC 55,56) This is not the common custom today. Though many are accustomed to answering according to their own custom, it is advised to respond in the custom of the one reciting to avoid not fragmenting into smaller groups. ("Lo Titgodedu" - BT, Yevamot 13b / SA, OC 493, Rema / MT, Avodah Zara 12:15)

יִתְגַּדַּל וְיִתְקַדַּשׁ שְׁמֵהּ רַבָּא. אָמֵן בְּעָלְמָא דִּי בְרָא. כִּרְעוּתֵהּ. וְיַמְלִיךְ
מַלְכוּתֵהּ. וְיַצְמַח פֻּרְקָנֵהּ. וִיקָרֵב מְשִׁיחֵהּ. אָמֵן בְּחַיֵּיכוֹן וּבְיוֹמֵיכוֹן
וּבְחַיֵּי דְכָל בֵּית יִשְׂרָאֵל. בַּעֲגָלָא וּבִזְמַן קָרִיב. וְאִמְרוּ אָמֵן. אָמֵן יְהֵא
שְׁמֵהּ רַבָּא מְבָרַךְ לְעָלַם וּלְעָלְמֵי עָלְמַיָּא יִתְבָּרַךְ. וְיִשְׁתַּבַּח.
וְיִתְפָּאַר. וְיִתְרוֹמַם. וְיִתְנַשֵּׂא. וְיִתְהַדָּר. וְיִתְעַלֶּה. וְיִתְהַלָּל שְׁמֵהּ

דְקֻדְשָׁא. בְּרִיךְ הוּא. אָמֵן לְעֵלָּא מִן כָּל בִּרְכָתָא שִׁירָתָא. תֻּשְׁבְּחָתָא וְנֶחֱמָתָא. דַּאֲמִירָן בְּעָלְמָא. וְאִמְרוּ אָמֵן. אָמֵן

Yitgadal Veyitkadash Shemeh Rabba. **Amen** Be'alema Di Vera. Kir'uteh. Veyamlich Malchuteh. Veyatzmach Purkaneh. Vikarev Meshicheh. **Amen** Bechayeichon Uveyomeichon Uvechayei Dechal-Beit Yisra'el. Ba'agala Uvizman Kariv. Ve'imru Amen. **Amen** Yehei Shemeh Rabba Mevarach Le'alam Ule'alemei Alemaya Yitbarach. Veyishtabach. Veyitpa'ar. Veyitromam. Veyitnasse. Veyit'hadar. Veyit'aleh. Veyit'hallal Shemeh Dekudsha. Berich Hu. **Amen** Le'ella Min Kol Birchata Shirata. Tushbechata Venechemata. Da'amiran Be'alema. Ve'imru Amen. **Amen**

Glorified and sanctified be God's great name **Amen** throughout the world which He has created according to His will. May He establish His kingdom, hastening His salvation and the coming of His Messiah, **Amen**, in your lifetime and during your days, and within the life of the entire House of Yisrael, speedily and soon; and say, Amen. **Amen** May His great name be blessed forever and to all eternity. Blessed and praised, glorified and exalted, extolled and honored, adored and lauded is the name of the Holy One, blessed is He, **Amen** Beyond all the blessings and hymns, praises and consolations that are ever spoken in the world; and say, Amen. **Amen**

Barechu / Call to Prayer

Barechu / Call to Prayer is made only if there is a minyan (10 men).

The Chazan / Cantor bows and says:

בָּרְכוּ אֶת יְהֹוָה הַמְבֹרָךְ:

Barechu Et Adonai Hamevorach.

Bless Hashem, the blessed One.

The kahal / congregation answers:

בָּרוּךְ יְהֹוָה הַמְבֹרָךְ לְעוֹלָם וָעֶד:

Baruch Adonai Hamevorach Le'olam Va'ed.

Blessed is Hashem Who is blessed for all eternity.

The Chazan/Cantor says:

בָּרוּךְ יְהֹוָה הַמְבֹרָךְ לְעוֹלָם וָעֶד:

Baruch Adonai Hamevorach Le'olam Va'ed.

Blessed is Hashem Who is blessed for all eternity.

LAWS OF KRIYAT SHEMA

One may not engage in any conversation, even in Hebrew, until after the completion of the Amidah. (SA, OC 51,4 - refer to pg. 99) There are those who say that the Kedusha in the Yotzer Ohr blessing may be recited by an individual (praying alone), since it is only a recitation of a Biblical narrative. And there are those who say that an individual (praying alone) should skip over this part, and it should only be recited in public. And one should be concerned for their words and make sure that if an individual recites it, he does so with a melody and cantillation, as if reading a Torah portion. (SA, OC 59,3) The [incorrect] order of the blessings does not hold one back [from fulfilling the mitzvah], so if one recites the second blessing before the first, one has fulfilled their obligation of [the recitation of the] blessings. One who recites the Shema, but did not have the [proper] intention during the first verse, which is "Shema Yisrael" - [in this case,] one did not fulfill one's obligation. As for the rest, if one did not have the [proper] intention, and even if one was simply reciting [the verses of the Shema] from the Torah or checking over these sections [i.e. the ones used in the Shema] during the time [of the obligation of the] recitation of the Shema - in this case, one fulfilled [their obligation], so long as one had intention during the first verse. (SA, OC 60,5) The Recitation of the Shema has 245 words, and in order to bring the number up to 248, which corresponds to the number of limbs of the human body, the leader ends by saying "Hashem your God is true", and then repeats this aloud, and says: "Hashem your God is true". (SA, OC 61,3)

Kriyat Shema Uvirchotei'a / The Recital of Shema and Blessings

The time for reciting the Shema in the morning, is from the time when, at a distance of four cubits, one is able to recognize a person with whom he is slightly acquainted; and ends with the third hour of the day, which is one fourth of the day. If one has an accident, or he is on the road, he may recite it at daybreak. If one will be traveling later in a place where they will not be able to concentrate even for the first section until "upon your heart" or members of their caravan are going quickly and won't wait for one at all, then one can recite it with its blessings from Olot Shachar (about 72 minutes before sunrise). The latest time of reciting Shema is the end of the third hour (from sunrise, about 3.5 modern hrs). (SA, OC 58)

Yotzer Ohr

Below [*] denotes when to touch your fingers to the arm tefillin and kiss them.

Baruch Attah Adonai Eloheinu	בָּרוּךְ אַתָּה יְהֹוָה אֱלֹהֵינוּ
Melech Ha'olam *Yotzer Ohr	מֶלֶךְ הָעוֹלָם. *יוֹצֵר אוֹר
Uvorei Choshech Oseh Shalom	וּבוֹרֵא חֹשֶׁךְ עֹשֶׂה שָׁלוֹם
Uvorei Et Hakol. Hame'ir	וּבוֹרֵא אֶת הַכֹּל. הַמֵּאִיר
La'aretz Veladarim Aleiha	לָאָרֶץ וְלַדָּרִים עָלֶיהָ
Berachamim. Uvetuvo	בְּרַחֲמִים. וּבְטוּבוֹ
Mechadesh Bechol Yom Tamid	מְחַדֵּשׁ בְּכָל יוֹם תָּמִיד
Ma'aseh Bereshit. Mah Rabbu	מַעֲשֵׂה בְרֵאשִׁית. מָה רַבּוּ
Ma'aseicha Adonai Kulam	מַעֲשֶׂיךָ יְהֹוָה כֻּלָּם
Bechochmah Asita. Male'ah	בְּחָכְמָה עָשִׂיתָ. מָלְאָה
Ha'aretz Kinyanecha. Hamelech	הָאָרֶץ קִנְיָנֶךָ. הַמֶּלֶךְ
Hameromam Levado Me'az.	הַמְרוֹמָם לְבַדּוֹ מֵאָז.
Hameshubach Vehamefo'ar	הַמְשֻׁבָּח וְהַמְפוֹאָר
Vehamitnasei Mimot Olam.	וְהַמִּתְנַשֵּׂא מִימוֹת עוֹלָם.
Elohai Olam. Berachameicha	אֱלֹהֵי עוֹלָם. בְּרַחֲמֶיךָ
Harabim Rachem Aleinu. Adon	הָרַבִּים רַחֵם עָלֵינוּ. אֲדוֹן
Uzenu. Tzur Misgabenu. Magen	עוּזֵּנוּ. צוּר מִשְׂגַּבֵּנוּ. מָגֵן
Yish'enu. Misgav Ba'adenu.	יִשְׁעֵנוּ. מִשְׂגָּב בַּעֲדֵנוּ.

Blessed are You, Hashem our God, King of the universe, Who *forms light and creates darkness, who makes peace and creates all things. He illuminates the earth and to those who dwell on it in mercy; in His goodness He renews the work of creation every day, constantly. How great are You works, Hashem. In wisdom You have made them all; the earth is full of Your possessions. The King, You alone have ever been exalted, praised and glorified and extolled from days of old. Eternal God, have mercy on us in Your great compassion. Lord of our strength, Rock of our Refuge, our saving Shield, our Refuge.

El Baruch Gedol De'ah. Hechin	אֵל בָּרוּךְ גְּדוֹל דֵּעָה. הֵכִין
Ufa'al Zaharei Chamah. Tov	וּפָעַל זָהֳרֵי חַמָּה. טוֹב
Yatzar Kavod Lishmo. Me'orot	יָצַר כָּבוֹד לִשְׁמוֹ. מְאוֹרוֹת
Natan Sevivot Uzo. Pinot Tziv'ot	נָתַן סְבִיבוֹת עֻזּוֹ. פִּינוֹת צְבָאוֹת
Kedoshim. Romemei Shaddai.	קְדוֹשִׁים. רוֹמְמֵי שַׁדַּי.
Tamid Mesaperim Kevod El	תָּמִיד מְסַפְּרִים כְּבוֹד אֵל
Ukedushato. Titbarach Adonai	וּקְדוּשָּׁתוֹ. תִּתְבָּרַךְ יְהֹוָה
Eloheinu Bashamayim Mima'al	אֱלֹהֵינוּ בַּשָּׁמַיִם מִמַּעַל
Ve'al-Ha'aretz Mitachat Al-Kol-	וְעַל־הָאָרֶץ מִתַּחַת עַל־כָּל־
Shevach Ma'aseh Yadeicha Ve'al	שֶׁבַח מַעֲשֵׂה יָדֶיךָ וְעַל
Me'orei Or Sheyatzarta Hemah	מְאוֹרֵי אוֹר שֶׁיָּצַרְתָּ הֵמָּה
Yefa'arucha Selah.	יְפָאֲרוּךָ סֶּלָה:

The blessed God, great in knowledge, designed and activated the rays of the sun. The Beneficent One created glory for His name. He placed luminaries around his strength. His chief hosts are holy-beings that exalt the Almighty. They constantly recount God's glory and His holiness. Be blessed, Hashem our God, in heaven above and on the earth below for the praiseworthy work of Your hands and for the luminaries of light which You have formed; they render glory to You forever.

Titbarach Lanetzach

Titbarach Lanetzach Tzurenu	תִּתְבָּרַךְ לָנֶצַח צוּרֵנוּ
Malkeinu Vego'alenu Borei	מַלְכֵּנוּ וְגוֹאֲלֵנוּ בּוֹרֵא
Kedoshim. Yishtabach Shimcha	קְדוֹשִׁים. יִשְׁתַּבַּח שִׁמְךָ
La'ad Malkeinu Yotzer	לָעַד מַלְכֵּנוּ יוֹצֵר
Mesharetim. Va'asher	מְשָׁרְתִים. וַאֲשֶׁר
Mesharetav Kulam Omedim	מְשָׁרְתָיו כֻּלָּם עוֹמְדִים
Berum Olam Umashmi'im	בְּרוּם עוֹלָם וּמַשְׁמִיעִים
Beyir'ah Yachad Bekol Divrei	בְּיִרְאָה יַחַד בְּקוֹל דִּבְרֵי
Elohim Chayim Umelech Olam.	אֱלֹהִים חַיִּים וּמֶלֶךְ עוֹלָם.
Kulam Ahuvim. Kulam Berurim.	כֻּלָּם אֲהוּבִים. כֻּלָּם בְּרוּרִים.
Kulam Giborim. Kulam	כֻּלָּם גִּבּוֹרִים. כֻּלָּם
Kedoshim. Kulam Osim	קְדוֹשִׁים. כֻּלָּם עוֹשִׂים
Be'eimah Uveyir'ah Ratzon	בְּאֵימָה וּבְיִרְאָה רָצוֹן
Koneihem. Vechulam Potechim	קוֹנֵיהֶם. וְכֻלָּם פּוֹתְחִים
Et Pihem Bikdushah Uvetaharah.	אֶת פִּיהֶם בִּקְדוּשָׁה וּבְטָהֳרָה.
Beshirah Uvezimrah.	בְּשִׁירָה וּבְזִמְרָה.
Umevarechin Umeshabechin	וּמְבָרְכִין וּמְשַׁבְּחִין
Umefa'arin Umakdishin	וּמְפָאֲרִין וּמַקְדִּישִׁין
Uma'aritzin Umamlichin Et	וּמַעֲרִיצִין וּמַמְלִיכִין אֶת
Shem Ha'el Hamelech Hagadol	שֵׁם הָאֵל הַמֶּלֶךְ הַגָּדוֹל
Hagibor Vehanorah Kadosh Hu.	הַגִּבּוֹר וְהַנּוֹרָא קָדוֹשׁ הוּא.
Vechulam Mekabelim Aleihem	וְכֻלָּם מְקַבְּלִים עֲלֵיהֶם
Ol Malchut Shamayim Zeh	עֹל מַלְכוּת שָׁמַיִם זֶה

Mizeh. Venotenim Reshut Zeh	מִזֶּה. וְנוֹתְנִים רְשׁוּת זֶה
Lazeh Lehakdish Leyotzeram	לָזֶה לְהַקְדִּישׁ לְיוֹצְרָם
Benachat Ruach Besafah Berurah	בְּנַחַת רוּחַ בְּשָׂפָה בְרוּרָה
Uvin'imah Kedushah. Kulam	וּבִנְעִימָה קְדוֹשָׁה. כֻּלָּם
Ke'echad Onim Be'eimah.	כְּאֶחָד עוֹנִים בְּאֵימָה.
Ve'omerim Beyir'ah.	וְאוֹמְרִים בְּיִרְאָה:

Be forever blessed, our Rock, our King and Redeemer, Creator of holy-beings; may Your name be praised forever, our King, Creator of ministering angels, all of whom stand in the heights of the universe and reverently proclaim in unison, aloud, the words of the living God and everlasting King. All of them are beloved, all of them are pure, all of them are mighty, all of them are holy; they all perform with awe and reverence the will of their Creator; they all open their mouth with holiness and purity, with song and melody, while they bless and praise, glorify, sanctify and revere and acclaim the name of God, the great, mighty and awesome King; holy is He. They all accept the yoke of the kingdom of heaven, one from the other, graciously granting permission to one another to sanctify their Creator. In serene spirit, with pure speech they all acclaim as one with reverence, and say with fear:

This "Kedusha" is said being seated. If one is standing, he now sits.

קָדוֹשׁ | קָדוֹשׁ קָדוֹשׁ יְהֹוָה צְבָאוֹת מְלֹא כָל־הָאָרֶץ כְּבוֹדוֹ:
וְהָאוֹפַנִּים וְחַיּוֹת הַקֹּדֶשׁ בְּרַעַשׁ גָּדוֹל מִתְנַשְּׂאִים לְעֻמַּת הַשְּׂרָפִים.
לְעֻמָּתָם מְשַׁבְּחִים וְאוֹמְרִים: **בָּרוּךְ כְּבוֹד־יְהֹוָה מִמְּקוֹמוֹ:**

Kadosh Kadosh Kadosh Adonai Tzeva'ot; Melo Chol-Ha'aretz Kevodo. Veha'ofanim Vechayot Hakodesh Bera'ash Gadol Mitnasse'im Le'ummat Hasrafim. Le'ummatam Meshabechim Ve'omerim. **Baruch Kevod-Adonai Mimekomo.**

Holy, holy, holy is Hashem of hosts; The whole earth is full of His glory. Then the Ophanim and the holy Chayot, rising with a great sound toward the Seraphim, facing them they respond with praise and say: **Blessed is the glory of Hashem from His Abode.**

La'El Baruch

La'el Baruch. Ne'imot Yiteinu.	לָאֵל בָּרוּךְ. נְעִימוֹת יִתֵּנוּ.
Lamelech El Chai Vekayam.	לַמֶּלֶךְ אֵל חַי וְקַיָּם.
Zemirot Yomeru Vetishbachot	זְמִירוֹת יֹאמֵרוּ וְתִשְׁבָּחוֹת
Yashmi'u. Ki Hu Levado Marom	יַשְׁמִיעוּ. כִּי הוּא לְבַדּוֹ מָרוֹם
Vekadosh. Po'el Gevurot. Oseh	וְקָדוֹשׁ. פּוֹעֵל גְּבוּרוֹת. עוֹשֶׂה
Chadashot. Ba'al Milchamot.	חֲדָשׁוֹת. בַּעַל מִלְחָמוֹת.
Zorea Tzedakot. Matzmiach	זוֹרֵעַ צְדָקוֹת. מַצְמִיחַ
Yeshu'ot. Borei Refu'ot. Nora	יְשׁוּעוֹת. בּוֹרֵא רְפוּאוֹת. נוֹרָא
Tehillot. Adon Hanifla'ot.	תְהִלּוֹת. אֲדוֹן הַנִּפְלָאוֹת.
Hamchadesh Betuvo Bechol	הַמְחַדֵּשׁ בְּטוּבוֹ בְּכָל
Yom Tamid Ma'aseh Vereshit	יוֹם תָּמִיד מַעֲשֵׂה בְרֵאשִׁית
Ka'amur. Le'oseh Orim	כָּאָמוּר: לְעֹשֵׂה אוֹרִים
Gedolim; Ki Le'olam Chasdo.	גְּדֹלִים כִּי לְעוֹלָם חַסְדּוֹ:
Baruch Attah Adonai Yotzer	בָּרוּךְ אַתָּה יְהוָה יוֹצֵר
Hame'orot.	הַמְּאוֹרוֹת:

To the blessed God they offer melodies; to the King, the living and living God, they utter hymns and praises. They proclaim: He alone, exalted and holy, does mighty acts and creates new things; He is a master of wars Who sows justice, produces salvations, and creates healing. Awesome in praise, Lord of wonders, in His goodness He renews the Creation every day, constantly, as it is said: "To the Maker of great lights; for His kindness endures forever." Blessed are You, Hashem, Creator of the lights.

Ahavat Olam

Ahavat Olam Ahavtanu Adonai	אַהֲבַת עוֹלָם אֲהַבְתָּנוּ יְהֹוָה
Eloheinu. Chemlah Gedolah	אֱלֹהֵינוּ. חֶמְלָה גְדוֹלָה
Viterah Chamalta Aleinu. Avinu	וִיתֵרָה חָמַלְתָּ עָלֵינוּ. אָבִינוּ
Malkeinu. Ba'avur Shimcha	מַלְכֵּנוּ. בַּעֲבוּר שִׁמְךָ
Hagadol Uva'avur Avoteinu	הַגָּדוֹל וּבַעֲבוּר אֲבוֹתֵינוּ
Shebatechu Bach Vat'lam'deimo	שֶׁבָּטְחוּ בְךָ וַתְּלַמְּדֵמוֹ
Chukkei Chayim La'asot	חֻקֵּי חַיִּים לַעֲשׂוֹת
Retzonecha Belevav Shalem.	רְצוֹנְךָ בְּלֵבָב שָׁלֵם.
Ken Techanenu Avinu. Av	כֵּן תְּחָנֵּנוּ אָבִינוּ. אָב
Harachaman Hamrachem.	הָרַחֲמָן הַמְרַחֵם.
Rachem Na Aleinu. Veten	רַחֵם נָא עָלֵינוּ. וְתֵן
Belibeinu Vinah Lehavin.	בְּלִבֵּנוּ בִינָה לְהָבִין.
Lehaskil. Lishmoa'. Lilmod	לְהַשְׂכִּיל. לִשְׁמֹעַ. לִלְמֹד
Ulelamed. Lishmor Vela'asot	וּלְלַמֵּד. לִשְׁמֹר וְלַעֲשׂוֹת
Ulekayem Et-Kol-Divrei Talmud	וּלְקַיֵּם אֶת־כָּל־דִּבְרֵי תַּלְמוּד
Toratecha Be'ahavah.	תּוֹרָתֶךָ בְּאַהֲבָה:

With love everlasting You have loved us, Hashem our God; You have lavished on us tenderness, great and abundant. Our Father and Ruler, to our fathers who trusted in You, You taught the statutes of life that they should do Your will with a perfect heart. So also for Your great sake and for their sake be gracious to us, our Father, all-merciful Father. Have pity on us, You who are merciful. Give to our heart understanding to understand, to comprehend, to hear, to learn and to teach, to guard and perform and to fulfill all the words of Your teaching of Torah, with love.

Veha'er Eineinu Betoratecha	וְהָאֵר עֵינֵינוּ בְּתוֹרָתֶךָ
Vedabek Libenu	וְדַבֵּק לִבֵּנוּ
Vemitzvoteicha. Veyached	בְּמִצְוֹתֶיךָ. וְיַחֵד
Levavenu Le'ahavah Uleyir'ah	לְבָבֵנוּ לְאַהֲבָה וּלְיִרְאָה
Et-Shemecha. Lo Nevosh Velo	אֶת־שְׁמֶךָ. לֹא נֵבוֹשׁ וְלֹא
Nikalem Velo Nikashel Le'olam	נִכָּלֵם וְלֹא נִכָּשֵׁל לְעוֹלָם
Va'ed. Ki Veshem Kodshecha	וָעֶד. כִּי בְשֵׁם קָדְשְׁךָ
Hagadol Hagibor Vehanorah	הַגָּדוֹל הַגִּבּוֹר וְהַנּוֹרָא
Batachenu. Nagilah	בָּטָחְנוּ. נָגִילָה
Venismechah Bishu'atecha.	וְנִשְׂמְחָה בִּישׁוּעָתֶךָ.
Verachameicha Adonai	וְרַחֲמֶיךָ יְהֹוָה
Eloheinu Vachasadeicha	אֱלֹהֵינוּ וַחֲסָדֶיךָ
Harabim. Al Ya'azvunu Netzach	הָרַבִּים. אַל יַעַזְבוּנוּ נֶצַח
Selah Va'ed.	סֶלָה וָעֶד:

Enlighten our eyes through Your Torah. Make our heart cleave to Your commandments, and unify our hearts to love and reverence Your name, that we never be brought to shame or confusion or stumbling for we put our trust in Your great power and awesome name. Let us be glad and rejoice in Your salvation. Hashem our God, and may Your manifold loving kindnesses never leave us.

([*] denotes gathering all four tzitzit on Tallit corners together in one's left hand.)

Maher Vehavei Aleinu Berachah	מַהֵר וְהָבֵא עָלֵינוּ בְּרָכָה
Veshalom Meheirah *Me'arba	וְשָׁלוֹם מְהֵרָה *מֵאַרְבַּע
Kanfot Kol-Ha'aretz. Ushevor Ol	כַּנְפוֹת כָּל־הָאָרֶץ. וּשְׁבֹר עֹל
Hagoyim Me'al Tzavarenu.	הַגּוֹיִם מֵעַל צַוָּארֵנוּ.
Veholicheinu Meheirah	וְהוֹלִיכֵנוּ מְהֵרָה
Komemiyut Le'artzenu. Ki El	קוֹמְמִיּוּת לְאַרְצֵנוּ. כִּי אֵל

Po'el Yeshu'ot Attah. Uvanu	פּוֹעֵל יְשׁוּעוֹת אַתָּה. וּבָנוּ
Vacharta Mikol Am Velashon.	בָחַרְתָּ מִכָּל עַם וְלָשׁוֹן.
Vekeravtanu Malkeinu	וְקֵרַבְתָּנוּ מַלְכֵּנוּ
Leshimcha Hagadol Be'ahavah.	לְשִׁמְךָ הַגָּדוֹל בְּאַהֲבָה.
Lehodot Lach Uleyachedcha	לְהוֹדוֹת לָךְ וּלְיַחֶדְךָ
Leyir'ah Ule'ahavah Et-Shimcha.	לְיִרְאָה וּלְאַהֲבָה אֶת־שְׁמֶךָ.
Baruch Attah Adonai Habocher	בָּרוּךְ אַתָּה יְהֹוָה הַבּוֹחֵר
Be'ammo Yisra'el Be'ahavah.	בְּעַמּוֹ יִשְׂרָאֵל בְּאַהֲבָה:

Hasten to bring upon us blessing and peace quickly *from the four corners of the earth. Break the alien yoke from our necks, and speedily lead us upright to our land. For You are God who works deliverance, and You, Divine King, have chosen us from all other peoples and tongues and in love drawn us near to Your great name, to give You thanks, proclaim Your unity and fear and love Your name. Blessed are You, Hashem, Who chooses His people Yisrael in love.

LAWS OF RECITING THE SHEMA

One who recites the Shema, but did not have intention during the first verse, 'Shema Yisrael', one did not fulfill their obligation. As for the rest, if they read during the specified time and did not have intention, they have fulfilled their obligation. One should recite the Shema with intention, awe, fear, shaking and trembling. The verse states: "Which I have commanded you today," (Deut. 6:6) which teaches that every day it should appear in your eyes as if it was new, and not like someone who already heard it many times and it is not precious to him. The custom is to place one's hands over their face during the recitation of the first verse in order that one will not look at something else that will prevent him from directing his heart. (SA, OC 59-61) The Shema should be recited with the notes as they are in the Torah; (but no one is particular about this). One may read the Shema while walking, sitting, reclining or riding, providing he does not lie with his face downward or laying on his back with his face upward. When reading the Shema while walking, one must stand still when reading the first verse. If one recited the Shema on one's own and entered the synagogue and found the congregation reciting the Shema, it is best that one should recite the entire Recitation of the Shema along with them. If one forgot to put on tzitzit or tefillin, one can interrupt between sections [of Shema or it's blessings] and don them, and one can make a blessing over them. If one forgot to put on the tallit or the tefillin, he may pause between the chapters of the Shema and put them on. (And concerning the tallit, it is customary not to say the blessing until after the prayers.) It is prohibited to recite in a place where there is excrement, urine, manure, or a swine, or in any filthy place (garbage with bad smell, etc.), or in front of a naked person. (But it is permissible if the naked person is a minor). If a receptacle was placed over the above mentioned unclean things, one may read there. (SA, OC 65,66, 75-76)

The Shema

Deuteronomy 6:4-9

One covers their eyes and says:

שְׁמַ֖ע יִשְׂרָאֵ֑ל יְהֹוָ֥ה אֱלֹהֵ֖ינוּ יְהֹוָ֥ה ׀ אֶחָֽד׃

Shema Yisrael; Adonai Eloheinu Adonai Echad.

"Hear, O Yisrael, Hashem is our God, Hashem is One."

Whisper silently:

בָּרוּךְ שֵׁם כְּבוֹד מַלְכוּתוֹ לְעוֹלָם וָעֶד׃

Baruch Shem Kevod Malchuto Le'olam Va'ed.

Blessed is His name and glorious kingdom forever and ever.

Ve'ahavta

Below [*] denotes when to touch your fingers to the arm tefillin and kiss them, followed by head tefillin.

וְאָֽהַבְתָּ֗ אֵ֚ת יְהֹוָ֣ה אֱלֹהֶ֔יךָ בְּכׇל־לְבָבְךָ֥ וּבְכׇל־נַפְשְׁךָ֖ וּבְכׇל־מְאֹדֶֽךָ׃
וְהָי֞וּ הַדְּבָרִ֣ים הָאֵ֗לֶּה אֲשֶׁ֨ר אָנֹכִ֧י מְצַוְּךָ֛ הַיּ֖וֹם עַל־לְבָבֶֽךָ׃ וְשִׁנַּנְתָּ֣ם
לְבָנֶ֔יךָ וְדִבַּרְתָּ֖ בָּ֑ם בְּשִׁבְתְּךָ֤ בְּבֵיתֶ֨ךָ֙ וּבְלֶכְתְּךָ֣ בַדֶּ֔רֶךְ וּֽבְשׇׁכְבְּךָ֖
וּבְקוּמֶֽךָ׃ *וּקְשַׁרְתָּ֥ם לְא֖וֹת עַל־יָדֶ֑ךָ *וְהָי֥וּ לְטֹטָפֹ֖ת בֵּ֥ין עֵינֶֽיךָ׃
וּכְתַבְתָּ֛ם עַל־מְזֻז֥וֹת בֵּיתֶ֖ךָ וּבִשְׁעָרֶֽיךָ׃

Ve'ahavta Et Adonai Eloheicha; Bechol-Levavecha Uvechol-Nafshecha Uvechol-Me'odecha. Vehayu Hadevarim Ha'eleh. Asher Anochi Metzavecha Hayom Al-Levavecha. Veshinantam Levaneicha. Vedibarta Bam; Beshivtecha Beveitecha Uvelechtecha Vaderech. Uveshochbecha Uvekumecha. *Ukeshartam Le'ot Al-Yadecha; *Vehayu Letotafot Bein Eineicha. Uchetavtam Al-Mezuzot Beitecha Uvish'areicha.

And you will love Hashem your God with all your heart, and with all your soul, and with all your might. And these words, which I command you this day, will be upon your heart; and your will teach them diligently to your children, and will talk of them when you sit

in your house, and when you walk by the way, and when you lie down, and when you rise up. *And you will bind them for a sign on your hand, *and they will be for frontlets between your eyes. And you will write them on the doorposts of your house, and on your gates.

Vehayah Im-shamoa

Below [*] denotes when to touch your fingers to the arm tefillin and kiss them, followed by head tefillin.

וְהָיָה אִם־שָׁמֹעַ תִּשְׁמְעוּ אֶל־מִצְוֺתַי אֲשֶׁר אָנֹכִי מְצַוֶּה אֶתְכֶם הַיּוֹם
לְאַהֲבָה אֶת־יְהוָה אֱלֹהֵיכֶם וּלְעָבְדוֹ בְּכָל־לְבַבְכֶם וּבְכָל־נַפְשְׁכֶם:
וְנָתַתִּי מְטַר־אַרְצְכֶם בְּעִתּוֹ יוֹרֶה וּמַלְקוֹשׁ וְאָסַפְתָּ דְגָנֶךָ וְתִירֹשְׁךָ
וְיִצְהָרֶךָ: וְנָתַתִּי עֵשֶׂב בְּשָׂדְךָ לִבְהֶמְתֶּךָ וְאָכַלְתָּ וְשָׂבָעְתָּ: הִשָּׁמְרוּ
לָכֶם פֶּן יִפְתֶּה לְבַבְכֶם וְסַרְתֶּם וַעֲבַדְתֶּם אֱלֹהִים אֲחֵרִים
וְהִשְׁתַּחֲוִיתֶם לָהֶם: וְחָרָה אַף־יְהוָה בָּכֶם וְעָצַר אֶת־הַשָּׁמַיִם
וְלֹא־יִהְיֶה מָטָר וְהָאֲדָמָה לֹא תִתֵּן אֶת־יְבוּלָהּ וַאֲבַדְתֶּם מְהֵרָה מֵעַל
הָאָרֶץ הַטֹּבָה אֲשֶׁר יְהוָה נֹתֵן לָכֶם: וְשַׂמְתֶּם אֶת־דְּבָרַי אֵלֶּה
עַל־לְבַבְכֶם וְעַל־נַפְשְׁכֶם וּקְשַׁרְתֶּם אֹתָם *לְאוֹת עַל־יֶדְכֶם וְהָיוּ
*לְטוֹטָפֹת בֵּין עֵינֵיכֶם. וְלִמַּדְתֶּם אֹתָם אֶת־בְּנֵיכֶם לְדַבֵּר בָּם
בְּשִׁבְתְּךָ בְּבֵיתֶךָ וּבְלֶכְתְּךָ בַדֶּרֶךְ וּבְשָׁכְבְּךָ וּבְקוּמֶךָ: וּכְתַבְתָּם
עַל־מְזוּזוֹת בֵּיתֶךָ וּבִשְׁעָרֶיךָ: לְמַעַן יִרְבּוּ יְמֵיכֶם וִימֵי בְנֵיכֶם עַל
הָאֲדָמָה אֲשֶׁר נִשְׁבַּע יְהוָה לַאֲבֹתֵיכֶם לָתֵת לָהֶם כִּימֵי הַשָּׁמַיִם
עַל־הָאָרֶץ:

Vehayah Im-Shamoa Tishme'u El-Mitzvotai. Asher Anochi Metzaveh Etchem Hayom; Le'ahavah Et-Adonai Eloheichem Ule'avdo. Bechol-Levavchem Uvechol-Nafshechem. Venatati Metar-'Artzechem Be'ito Yoreh Umalkosh; Ve'asafta Deganecha. Vetiroshecha Veyitzharecha. Venatati Esev Besadecha Livhemtecha; Ve'achalta Vesava'eta. Hishameru Lachem. Pen Yifteh Levavchem; Vesartem. Va'avadtem

Elohim Acherim. Vehishtachavitem Lahem. Vecharah Af-Adonai Bachem. Ve'atzar Et-Hashamayim Velo-Yihyeh Matar. Veha'adamah. Lo Titen Et-Yevulah; Va'avadtem Meheirah. Me'al Ha'aretz Hatovah. Asher Adonai Noten Lachem. Vesamtem Et-Devarai Eleh. Al-Levavchem Ve'al-Nafshechem; Ukeshartem Otam *Le'ot Al-Yedchem. Vehayu *Letotafot Bein Eineichem. Velimadtem Otam Et-Beneichem Ledaber Bam; Beshivtecha Beveitecha Uvelechtecha Vaderech. Uveshochbecha Uvekumecha. Uchetavtam Al-Mezuzot Beitecha Uvish'areicha. Lema'an Yirbu Yemeichem Vimei Veneichem. Al Ha'adamah. Asher Nishba Adonai La'avoteichem Latet Lahem; Kimei Hashamayim Al-Ha'aretz.

And it will come to pass, if you will observe My commandments which I command you this day, to love Hashem your God, and to serve Him with all your heart and with all your soul, that I will give the rain of your land in its season, the former rain and the latter rain, that you may gather in your corn, and your wine, and your oil. And I will give grass in your fields for your cattle, and you will eat and be satisfied. Be cautious, in case your heart is deceived, and you turn aside, and serve other gods, and worship them; and the anger of Hashem is kindled against you, and He shut up the heaven, so that there will be no rain, and the ground will not yield her fruit; and you perish quickly from off the good land which Hashem gives you. Therefore you will lay up these My words in your heart and in your soul; and you will bind them for a *sign upon your hand, and they will be for *frontlets between your eyes. And you will teach them your children, talking of them, when you sit in your house, and when you walk by the way, and when you lie down, and when you rise up. And you will write them on the doorposts of your house, and on your gates; that your days may be multiplied, and the days of your children, upon the land which Hashem swore to your fathers to give them, as the days of the heavens above the earth. (Deuteronomy 11:13-21)

Numbers 15:37-41

Below [*] denotes when to kiss your tzitzit, on "ure'item otoh" gaze at the tzitziyot in hand (SA, OC 24,4), on "ve'acharei eineichem" some pass them in front of their eyes and kiss them. (BI"H).

וַיֹּ֥אמֶר יְהֹוָ֖ה אֶל־מֹשֶׁ֥ה לֵּאמֹֽר׃ דַּבֵּ֞ר אֶל־בְּנֵ֤י יִשְׂרָאֵל֙ וְאָמַרְתָּ֣ אֲלֵהֶ֔ם
וְעָשׂ֨וּ לָהֶ֥ם *צִיצִ֛ת עַל־כַּנְפֵ֥י בִגְדֵיהֶ֖ם לְדֹרֹתָ֑ם וְנָ֥תְנ֛וּ עַל־*צִיצִ֥ת
הַכָּנָ֖ף פְּתִ֥יל תְּכֵֽלֶת׃ וְהָיָ֣ה לָכֶם֮ *לְצִיצִת֒ *וּרְאִיתֶ֣ם אֹת֗וֹ וּזְכַרְתֶּם֙
אֶת־כָּל־מִצְוֺ֣ת יְהֹוָ֔ה וַעֲשִׂיתֶ֖ם אֹתָ֑ם וְלֹֽא־תָתֻ֜רוּ אַחֲרֵ֤י לְבַבְכֶם֙ וְאַחֲרֵ֣י
עֵֽינֵיכֶ֔ם אֲשֶׁר־אַתֶּ֥ם זֹנִ֖ים אַחֲרֵיהֶֽם׃ לְמַ֣עַן תִּזְכְּר֔וּ וַעֲשִׂיתֶ֖ם
אֶת־כָּל־מִצְוֺתָ֑י וִהְיִיתֶ֥ם קְדֹשִׁ֖ים לֵאלֹהֵיכֶֽם׃ אֲנִ֞י יְהֹוָ֣ה אֱלֹהֵיכֶ֗ם אֲשֶׁ֨ר
הוֹצֵ֤אתִי אֶתְכֶם֙ מֵאֶ֣רֶץ מִצְרַ֔יִם לִהְי֥וֹת לָכֶ֖ם לֵאלֹהִ֑ים אֲנִ֖י יְהֹוָ֥ה
אֱלֹהֵיכֶֽם׃ אֱמֶת.

Vayomer Adonai El-Mosheh Lemor. Daber El-Benei Yisra'el Ve'amarta Aleihem. Ve'asu Lahem *Tzitzit Al-Kanfei Vigdeihem Ledorotam; Venatenu Al-*Tzitzit Hakanaf Petil Techelet. Vehayah Lachem *Letzitzit *Ure'Item Oto Uzechartem Et-Chol-Mitzvot Adonai Va'asitem Otam; Velo-Taturu Acharei Levavchem Ve'acharei Eineichem. Asher-'Attem Zonim Achareihem. Lema'an Tizkeru. Va'asitem Et-Chol-Mitzvotai; Vihyitem Kedoshim Leloheichem. Ani Adonai Eloheichem. Asher Hotzeti Etchem Me'eretz Mitzrayim. Lihyot Lachem Lelohim; Ani Adonai Eloheichem. Emet.

And Hashem spoke to Moshe, saying: Speak to the children of Yisrael, and command them to make *tzitzit on the corners of their garments throughout their generations, and that they put a thread of tekhelet with the *tzitzit of each corner. And it will be to you for *tzitzit, that *you may look upon it, and remember all the commandments of Hashem, and do them; and that you do not go about after your own heart and your own eyes, after which you go whoring; that you may remember and do all My commandments, and be holy to your God. I am Hashem your God, Who brought you out of the land of Mitzrayim, to be your God: I am Hashem your God. It is true.

יְהֹוָה אֱלֹהֵיכֶם אֱמֶת:

Adonai Eloheichem Emet.

Hashem, your God, is true.

Veyatziv

Veyatziv. Venachon. Vekayam.	וְיַצִּיב. וְנָכוֹן. וְקַיָּם.
Veyashar. Vene'eman. Ve'ahuv.	וְיָשָׁר. וְנֶאֱמָן. וְאָהוּב.
Vechaviv. Venechmad. Vena'im.	וְחָבִיב. וְנֶחְמָד. וְנָעִים.
Venora. Ve'adir. Umetukan.	וְנוֹרָא. וְאַדִּיר. וּמְתוּקָּן.
Umekubbal. Vetov. Veyafeh.	וּמְקֻבָּל. וְטוֹב. וְיָפֶה.
Hadavar Hazeh Aleinu Le'olam	הַדָּבָר הַזֶּה עָלֵינוּ לְעוֹלָם
Va'ed.	וָעֶד.

And firm, and established, and constant, and upright, and faithful, and beloved, and cherished, and delightful, and nice, and awesome, and powerful, and correct, and acceptable is this good and beautiful matter to us for all time.

Below [*] denotes kissing, passing before your eyes and letting go of your tzitziyot at "La'ad" [forever].

Emet. Elohei Olam Malkeinu	אֱמֶת. אֱלֹהֵי עוֹלָם מַלְכֵּנוּ
Tzur Ya'akov Magen Yish'enu.	צוּר יַעֲקֹב מָגֵן יִשְׁעֵנוּ.
Ledor Vador Hu Kayam. Ushemo	לְדוֹר וָדוֹר הוּא קַיָּם. וּשְׁמוֹ
Kayam. Vechis'o Nachon.	קַיָּם. וְכִסְאוֹ נָכוֹן.
Umalchuto Ve'emunato La'ad	וּמַלְכוּתוֹ וֶאֱמוּנָתוֹ לָעַד
Kayemet. Udevarav Chayim	קַיֶּמֶת. וּדְבָרָיו חַיִּים
Vekayamim. Vene'emanim	וְקַיָּמִים. וְנֶאֱמָנִים
Venechemadim *La'ad	וְנֶחֱמָדִים *לָעַד
Ule'olemei Olamim. Al	וּלְעוֹלְמֵי עוֹלָמִים. עַל
Avoteinu. Aleinu Ve'al Baneinu	אֲבוֹתֵינוּ. עָלֵינוּ וְעַל בָּנֵינוּ
Ve'al Doroteinu Ve'al Kol Dorot	וְעַל דּוֹרוֹתֵינוּ וְעַל כָּל דּוֹרוֹת
Zera Yisra'el Avadeicha. Al	זֶרַע יִשְׂרָאֵל עֲבָדֶיךָ. עַל
Harishonim Ve'al Ha'acharonim	הָרִאשׁוֹנִים וְעַל הָאַחֲרוֹנִים

Davar Tov Vekayam Be'emet	דָּבָר טוֹב וְקַיָּם בֶּאֱמֶת
Ve'emunah Chok Velo Ya'avor.	וֶאֱמוּנָה חוֹק וְלֹא יַעֲבוֹר.
Emet She'attah Hu Adonai	אֱמֶת שָׁאַתָּה הוּא יְהֹוָה
Eloheinu Velohei Avoteinu.	אֱלֹהֵינוּ וֵאלֹהֵי אֲבוֹתֵינוּ.
Malkeinu Melech Avoteinu.	מַלְכֵּנוּ מֶלֶךְ אֲבוֹתֵינוּ.
Go'alenu Go'el Avoteinu.	גוֹאֲלֵנוּ גוֹאֵל אֲבוֹתֵינוּ.
Yotzreinu Tzur Yeshu'ateinu.	יוֹצְרֵנוּ צוּר יְשׁוּעָתֵנוּ.
Podenu Umatzilenu Me'olam Hu	פּוֹדֵנוּ וּמַצִּילֵנוּ מֵעוֹלָם הוּא
Shemecha. Ve'ein Lanu Od	שְׁמֶךָ. וְאֵין לָנוּ עוֹד
Elohim Zulatecha Selah.	אֱלֹהִים זוּלָתְךָ סֶלָה:

It is true that the eternal God our Ruler, the Rock of Yaakov, our saving Shield, exists eternally generation to generation, without end. He is eternal; His Throne is established, and His rule abides unchanging *forever. His teachings are eternally living, and unchanging, and faithful, and delightful for all time for our forefathers as well as for us, our children and descendants and all generations of the seed of Yisrael, Your servants. On the first and the later generations it is good and enduring. In truth and faith, it is a law that will not pass away. It is true that You are Hashem our God and God of our fathers, our divine Ruler and Ruler of our fathers, our Redeemer and Redeemer of our fathers. From of old You have been our Rock, the Rock of our salvation and our saving Deliverer, and we have no other God besides You.

Ezrat Avoteinu

Ezrat Avoteinu Attah Hu	עֶזְרַת אֲבוֹתֵינוּ אַתָּה הוּא
Me'olam. Magen Umoshia	מֵעוֹלָם. מָגֵן וּמוֹשִׁיעַ
Lahem Velivneihem Achareihem	לָהֶם וְלִבְנֵיהֶם אַחֲרֵיהֶם

Bechol Dor Vador. Berum Olam	בְּכָל דּוֹר וָדוֹר. בְּרוּם עוֹלָם
Moshavecha. Umishpateicha.	מוֹשָׁבֶךָ. וּמִשְׁפָּטֶיךָ.
Vetzidkatecha Ad Afsei Aretz.	וְצִדְקָתְךָ עַד אַפְסֵי אָרֶץ.
Emet Ashrei Ish Sheyishma	אֱמֶת אַשְׁרֵי אִישׁ שֶׁיִּשְׁמַע
Lemitzvoteicha Vetoratecha	לְמִצְוֹתֶיךָ וְתוֹרָתְךָ
Udevarecha Yasim Al Libo. Emet	וּדְבָרְךָ יָשִׂים עַל לִבּוֹ. אֱמֶת
She'attah Hu Adon Le'ammecha	שֶׁאַתָּה הוּא אָדוֹן לְעַמֶּךָ
Umelech Gibor Lariv Rivam	וּמֶלֶךְ גִּבּוֹר לָרִיב רִיבָם
Le'avot Uvanim. Emet Attah Hu	לְאָבוֹת וּבָנִים. אֱמֶת אַתָּה הוּא
Rishon Ve'attah Hu Acharon	רִאשׁוֹן וְאַתָּה הוּא אַחֲרוֹן
Umibal'adeicha Ein Lanu	וּמִבַּלְעָדֶיךָ אֵין לָנוּ מֶלֶךְ
Melech Go'el Umoshia.	גּוֹאֵל וּמוֹשִׁיעַ.

From ancient times, You have been the help of our fathers, a Shield and a Savior for them and their children after them in every generation. Your dwelling is in the heights of the universe, yet Your righteousness and justice are to the ends of the earth. It is true that happy is the man who listens to Your commandments, who sets Your Torah and Your Word in his heart. It is true that You are the Lord of Your people, Their mighty King to fight their cause in every generation. It is true that You are the First and You are the Last, And besides You we have no king, redeemer and savior.

Emet Mimitzrayim Ge'altanu	אֱמֶת מִמִּצְרַיִם גְּאַלְתָּנוּ
Adonai Eloheinu. Mibeit Avadim	יְהוָה אֱלֹהֵינוּ. מִבֵּית עֲבָדִים
Peditanu. Kol Bechoreihem	פְּדִיתָנוּ. כָּל בְּכוֹרֵיהֶם
Haragta. Uvechorecha Yisra'el	הָרַגְתָּ. וּבְכוֹרְךָ יִשְׂרָאֵל
Ga'alta. Veyam-Suf Lahem	גָּאָלְתָּ. וְיַם־סוּף לָהֶם
Baka'ta. Vezeidim Tiba'ta.	בָּקַעְתָּ. וְזֵדִים טִבַּעְתָּ.

Vididim Averu Yam. Vaychasu	וִידִידִים עָבְרוּ יָם. וַיְכַסּוּ
Mayim Tzareihem Echad Mehem	מַיִם צָרֵיהֶם אֶחָד מֵהֶם
Lo Notar. Al Zot Shibechu	לֹא נוֹתָר. עַל זֹאת שִׁבְּחוּ
Ahuvim. Veromemu La'el.	אֲהוּבִים. וְרוֹמְמוּ לָאֵל.
Venatenu Yedidim Zemirot Shirot	וְנָתְנוּ יְדִידִים זְמִירוֹת שִׁירוֹת
Vetishbachot Berachot Vehoda'ot	וְתִשְׁבָּחוֹת בְּרָכוֹת וְהוֹדָאוֹת
LaMelech El Chai Vekayam. Ram	לַמֶּלֶךְ אֵל חַי וְקַיָּם. רָם
Venissa. Gadol Venora. Mashpil	וְנִשָּׂא. גָּדוֹל וְנוֹרָא. מַשְׁפִּיל
Ge'im Adei Aretz. Magbiah	גֵּאִים עֲדֵי אָרֶץ. מַגְבִּיהַּ
Shefalim Ad Marom. Motzi	שְׁפָלִים עַד מָרוֹם. מוֹצִיא
Asirim. Podeh Anavim. Ozeir	אֲסִירִים. פּוֹדֶה עֲנָוִים. עוֹזֵר
Dallim. Ha'oneh Le'ammo	דַּלִּים. הָעוֹנֶה לְעַמּוֹ
Yisra'el Be'et Shave'am Elav.	יִשְׂרָאֵל בְּעֵת שַׁוְּעָם אֵלָיו.

It is true that You, Hashem our God, have redeemed us from Mitzrayim and rescued us from the house of bondage, slaying all the firstborn of Mitzrayim and redeeming Your firstborn, Yisrael. For them You parted the Sea of Reeds and drowned the arrogant. The beloved passed through the sea, but "the waters covered their enemies, not one of them remained." On this, His cherished ones sang exalting praises to God. The beloved offered hymns, songs, and praises, blessings and thanksgiving to the divine Ruler who is the ever-living God. He who is supremely exalted, all-powerful, and awe-inspiring, brings down the proud to earth, raises the lowly, frees the bound, rescues the humble, helps the poor, and answers His people Yisrael when they cry to Him.

One now stands in preparation for the Amidah.

Tehilot La'el Elyon Go'alam.	תְּהִלּוֹת לָאֵל עֶלְיוֹן גּוֹאֲלָם.
Baruch Hu Umevorach. Mosheh	בָּרוּךְ הוּא וּמְבוֹרָךְ. מֹשֶׁה

Uvenei Yisra'el Lecha Anu Shirah	וּבְנֵי יִשְׂרָאֵל לְךָ עָנוּ שִׁירָה
Vesimchah Rabah. Ve'ameru	בְּשִׂמְחָה רַבָּה. וְאָמְרוּ
Chulam. Mi-Chamochah Ba'elim	כֻלָּם: מִי־כָמֹכָה בָּאֵלִם
Adonai Mi Kamochah Ne'dar	יְהֹוָה מִי כָּמֹכָה נֶאְדָּר
Bakodesh; Nora Tehillot Oseh	בַּקֹּדֶשׁ נוֹרָא תְהִלֹּת עֹשֵׂה
Fele. Shirah Chadashah Shibechu	פֶלֶא: שִׁירָה חֲדָשָׁה שִׁבְּחוּ
Ge'ulim Leshimcha Hagadol Al	גְאוּלִים לְשִׁמְךָ הַגָּדוֹל עַל
Sefat Hayam. Yachad Chulam	שְׂפַת הַיָּם. יַחַד כֻּלָּם
Hodu Vehimlichu Ve'ameru.	הוֹדוּ וְהִמְלִיכוּ וְאָמְרוּ:
Adonai Yimloch Le'olam Va'ed.	יְהֹוָה | יִמְלֹךְ לְעֹלָם וָעֶד:
Vene'emar. Go'alenu Adonai	וְנֶאֱמַר: גֹּאֲלֵנוּ יְהֹוָה
Tzeva'ot Shemo; Kedosh Yisra'el.	צְבָאוֹת שְׁמוֹ קְדוֹשׁ יִשְׂרָאֵל:
Baruch Attah Adonai Ga'al	בָּרוּךְ אַתָּה יְהֹוָה גָּאַל

Praises to the Supreme God, their Redeemer, blessed is He. To You Moshe and all the children of Yisrael proclaimed a song with great joy, "Who is like You, Hashem, among the gods, Who is like You, glorified in holiness, You are awesome in praises, working wonders." The redeemed ones sang a new song of praise to Your great name on the sea shore. Together they thanked You, proclaiming Your kingly power, and said, "Hashem will reign forever and ever." So also it is said: "Our Redeemer, Hashem of hosts is His name, The Holy One of Yisrael." Blessed are You, Hashem, Redeemer of Yisrael.

LAWS OF AMIDAH

The time for the Amidah: its command is that it should begin with the blossoming of the sun, as it is written, "They will revere You while the sun endures." (Ps. 72:5). And its time continues until the end of four hours which is a third of the daytime. And if one erred or transgressed and prayed after the fourth hour until noon, even though one does not have the reward as praying at its proper time, there is still a reward of prayer. (And after noon it is forbidden to pray the Tefillah of the morning (BY, Rashba). A person should make an effort to pray in the synagogue with a congregation, and if he is unable to due to an extenuating circumstance that he is not able to come to the synagogue, he should intend to pray at the time that the congregation is praying. When one stands [praying] with the congregation, it is forbidden to advance one's prayer [ahead of] the prayer of the congregation, unless the time [for prayer] is passing. (SA, OC 89, 90) When one gets up to pray if he was standing outside the Land of Yisrael, he should turn his face toward the Land of Yisrael and focus also on Yerushalayim and the Temple and the Holy of Holies. One who is not able to determine the directions, [should] direct one's heart to their Father in Heaven. One should consider oneself as if one is standing in the Beit Hamikdash, and in one's heart, one should be directed upward towards Heaven. One who prays needs to intend in their heart the meaning of the words which are coming out of their mouth. They should think as if the Divine Presence is before them, and remove all distracting thoughts from themselves, until their thoughts and intention are pure in their prayer. (SA, OC 94, 95, 98) These are the blessings at which we bow: in Avot, at the beginning and at the end; in Modim, at the beginning and at the end. And if you come to bow at the end of every blessing or at the beginning, we teach him to not bow but in the middle, one can bow. One needs to bend until all the vertebrae in his spine are bent. His head should stay straight and submissive. One should not bow too much until his mouth is opposite his belt. If he is sick or old and cannot bow, he should humble his head, that is enough. Bow at "Baruch" and stand up at Hashem's name. (SA, OC 113,114) One should position one's feet next to each other as though they are one, in order to imitate angels, as it written regarding them: "their feet were a straight foot" (Ez. 1:7), which is to say their feet appeared as one foot. One should take three steps forward in the way of coming close and approaching a matter that must be done. (SA, OC 95, Rema)

If he wants to add in each of the middle blessings, something like that blessing, he may add. How so? If there was a sick person he was asking for mercy over, in the blessing "heal us." If he needs to earn a living, he would ask in the blessing over the years. And in "who hears prayer" he can ask for any of his needs, which includes all requests. (Hagah: And when he adds, he should first recite the blessing and then add, but he should not add and then begin the blessing [Tur 567]). And according to Rabbeinu Yona, when he adds to the blessing something like the blessing, if he is adding something on behalf of all of Yisrael, he would say it in plural language and not singular language, and he should add at the end of the blessing and not the middle. And if he is asking for his own needs, like, there is a sick person in his home or he needs to earn a living, he may ask even in the middle of a blessing, as long as he does so in the singular and not the plural. And during the blessing, "who hears prayer" and also at the end of prayer he may ask in either plural or singular, whether this is for his own needs or those of the many. (SA, OC 119:1)

Continue with the Amidah on the next page.

Amidah / Shemoneh Esrei - Shacharit

Take three steps forward and say:

Adonai Sefatai Tiftach; Ufi. Yagid	אֲדֹנָי שְׂפָתַי תִּפְתָּח וּפִי יַגִּיד
Tehilatecha.	תְּהִלָּתֶךָ:

Hashem, open my lips, that my mouth may declare Your praise.

Avot / Fathers

Bow at "Baruch Attah" / "Blessed are You". Raise up at Adonai / Hashem.

Baruch Attah Adonai Eloheinu	בָּרוּךְ אַתָּה יְהֹוָה אֱלֹהֵינוּ
Velohei Avoteinu. Elohei	וֵאלֹהֵי אֲבוֹתֵינוּ. אֱלֹהֵי
Avraham. Elohei Yitzchak.	אַבְרָהָם. אֱלֹהֵי יִצְחָק.
Velohei Ya'akov. Ha'el Hagadol	וֵאלֹהֵי יַעֲקֹב. הָאֵל הַגָּדוֹל
Hagibor Vehanorah. El Elyon.	הַגִּבּוֹר וְהַנּוֹרָא. אֵל עֶלְיוֹן.
Gomel Chasadim Tovim. Koneh	גּוֹמֵל חֲסָדִים טוֹבִים. קוֹנֵה
Hakol. Vezocher Chasdei Avot.	הַכֹּל. וְזוֹכֵר חַסְדֵי אָבוֹת.
Umevi Go'el Livnei Veneihem	וּמֵבִיא גוֹאֵל לִבְנֵי בְנֵיהֶם
Lema'an Shemo Be'ahavah.	לְמַעַן שְׁמוֹ בְּאַהֲבָה:

Blessed are You, Hashem our God and God of our fathers, God of Avraham, God of Yitzchak and God of Yaakov; the great, mighty and revered God, most high God, Who bestows lovingkindness. Master of all things; Who remembers the kindnesses of our fathers, and Who will bring a redeemer to their children's children for the sake of His name in love.

During the 10 days of repentance (Rosh Hashanah to Yom Kippur) add:

Zochrenu Lechayim. Melech Chafetz	זָכְרֵנוּ לְחַיִּים. מֶלֶךְ חָפֵץ
Bachayim. Katevenu Besefer Chayim.	בַּחַיִּים. כָּתְבֵנוּ בְּסֵפֶר חַיִּים.
Lema'anach Elohim Chayim.	לְמַעַנְךָ אֱלֹהִים חַיִּים.

Remember us to life, King who delights in life; inscribe us in the book of life for Your sake, Oh living God.

Bow at "Baruch Attah" / Blessed are You. Raise up at Adonai / Hashem.

Melech Ozeir Umoshia	מֶלֶךְ עוֹזֵר וּמוֹשִׁיעַ
Umagen. Baruch Attah Adonai	וּמָגֵן: בָּרוּךְ אַתָּה יְהֹוָה
Magen Avraham.	מָגֵן אַבְרָהָם:

King, Supporter, and Savior and Shield. Blessed are You, Hashem, Shield of Avraham.

Gevurot / Powers

We [in Yisrael] begin to say "mashiv haruach" in the second blessing of the Amidah from the Musaf [Additional] Service of the last day of Sukkot, and conclude at the Musaf [Additional] Service of the first day of Pesach. On the first day of Pesach the congregation still says it in the Musaf Service, but the Reader stops saying it then. In lands outside of Yisrael, we begin to pray for rain in the Arvit (Evening) Service of the sixtieth day after the New Moon of Tishrei, and in Yisrael we begin to say it in the evening of the seventh day of Cheshvan, and it is said until the Afternoon Service on the day preceding the first day of Passover. If one prayed for rain in the summer, or if one omitted to pray for it in the winter, he must repeat the Amidah again. If one said "morid hageshem" in the summer time, he must repeat again from the beginning of the blessing. If he already concluded the blessing, he must read the entire Amidah again. Likewise in the winter, if he omitted it, he must begin all over again. (SA, OC 117)

Attah Gibor Le'olam Adonai.	אַתָּה גִּבּוֹר לְעוֹלָם אֲדֹנָי.
Mechayeh Meitim Attah. Rav	מְחַיֵּה מֵתִים אַתָּה. רַב
Lehoshia.	לְהוֹשִׁיעַ.

You, Hashem, are mighty forever; You revive the dead; You are powerful to save.

B'ketz: Morid Hatal.	בקיץ: מוֹרִיד הַטָּל.
B'choref: Mashiv Haruach Umorid	בחורף: מַשִּׁיב הָרוּחַ וּמוֹרִיד
Hageshem.	הַגֶּשֶׁם.

In summer: You cause the dew to fall.

In winter: You cause the wind to blow and the rain to fall.

Mechalkel Chayim Bechesed.	מְכַלְכֵּל חַיִּים בְּחֶסֶד.
Mechayeh Meitim Berachamim	מְחַיֵּה מֵתִים בְּרַחֲמִים

Rabim. Somech Nofelim. Verofei	רַבִּים. סוֹמֵךְ נוֹפְלִים. וְרוֹפֵא
Cholim. Umatir Asurim.	חוֹלִים. וּמַתִּיר אֲסוּרִים.
Umekayem Emunato Lishenei	וּמְקַיֵּם אֱמוּנָתוֹ לִישֵׁנֵי
Afar. Mi Chamocha Ba'al	עָפָר. מִי כָמוֹךָ בַּעַל
Gevurot. Umi Domeh Lach.	גְּבוּרוֹת. וּמִי דּוֹמֶה לָךְ.
Melech Memit Umechayeh	מֶלֶךְ מֵמִית וּמְחַיֶּה
Umatzmiach Yeshu'ah.	וּמַצְמִיחַ יְשׁוּעָה.

You sustain the living with kindness, and revive the dead with great mercy; You support all who fall, and heal the sick; You set the captives free, and keep faith with those who sleep in the dust. Who is like You, Master of power? Who resembles You, Oh King? You bring death and restore life, and cause salvation to flourish.

During the 10 days of repentance (Rosh Hashanah to Yom Kippur) add:

Mi Chamocha Av Harachaman. Zocher	מִי כָמוֹךְ אָב הָרַחֲמָן. זוֹכֵר
Yetzurav Berachamim Lechayim.	יְצוּרָיו בְּרַחֲמִים לְחַיִּים.

Who is like you, merciful Father? In mercy You remember your creatures to life.

Vene'eman Attah Lehachayot	וְנֶאֱמָן אַתָּה לְהַחֲיוֹת
Meitim. Baruch Attah Adonai	מֵתִים: בָּרוּךְ אַתָּה יְהֹוָה
Mechayeh Hameitim.	מְחַיֵּה הַמֵּתִים:

And You are faithful to revive the dead. Blessed are You, Hashem, Who revives the dead.

Kedusha

Kedusha is said only in a minyan (10 men). If one is not available, skip to "Kedushat Hashem". It is proper to position one's feet together at the time one is reciting Kedushah with the prayer-leader.

Nakdishach Vena'aritzach.	נַקְדִּישָׁךְ וְנַעֲרִיצָךְ.
Keno'am Siach Sod Sarfei	כְּנֹעַם שִׂיחַ סוֹד שַׂרְפֵי
Kodesh. Hamshaleshim Lecha	קֹדֶשׁ. הַמְשַׁלְּשִׁים לְךָ

Kedushah. Vechein Katuv Al Yad	קְדֻשָּׁה. וְכֵן כָּתוּב עַל יַד
Nevi'ach. Vekara Zeh El-Zeh	נְבִיאָךְ: וְקָרָא זֶה אֶל־זֶה
Ve'amar. **Kadosh Kadosh Kadosh**	וְאָמַר **קָדוֹשׁ | קָדוֹשׁ קָדוֹשׁ**
Adonai Tzeva'ot; Melo Chol-	**יְהוָה צְבָאוֹת מְלֹא כָל־**
Ha'aretz Kevodo. Le'ummatam	**הָאָרֶץ כְּבוֹדוֹ:** לְעֻמָּתָם
Meshabechim Ve'omerim.	מְשַׁבְּחִים וְאוֹמְרִים:
Baruch Kevod-Adonai	**בָּרוּךְ כְּבוֹד־יְהוָה**
Mimekomo. Uvedivrei	**מִמְּקוֹמוֹ:** וּבְדִבְרֵי
Kodshecha Katuv Lemor.	קָדְשְׁךָ כָּתוּב לֵאמֹר: **יִמְלֹךְ**
Yimloch Adonai Le'olam.	**יְהוָה | לְעוֹלָם אֱלֹהַיִךְ**
Elohayich Tziyon Ledor Vador.	**צִיּוֹן לְדֹר וָדֹר**
Halleluyah.	**הַלְלוּיָהּ:**

We sanctify and revere You in the sweet words of the assembly of holy Seraphim who three times acclaim Your holiness, as it is written by Your prophet: "They keep calling to one another: **'Holy, holy, holy is Hashem of hosts; The whole earth is full of his glory."** Angels respond with praise and say: **"Blessed is the glory of Hashem from His Abode."** And in Your holy scriptures it is written: **"Hashem will reign forever, your God, Tziyon, from generation to generation. Halleluyah."**

Kedushat HaShem / Holiness of the Name

Attah Kadosh Veshimcha	אַתָּה קָדוֹשׁ וְשִׁמְךָ
Kadosh. Ukedoshim Bechol-	קָדוֹשׁ. וּקְדוֹשִׁים בְּכָל־
Yom Yehalelucha Selah. Baruch	יוֹם יְהַלְלוּךָ סֶּלָה: בָּרוּךְ
Attah Adonai Ha' El Hakadosh.	אַתָּה יְהוָה הָאֵל הַקָּדוֹשׁ:

You are holy and Your name is holy, and the holy-ones will praise You every day, selah. Blessed are You, Hashem, The Holy God.

During the 10 days of repentance (Rosh Hashanah to Yom Kippur) say:

Hamelech Hakadosh.	הַמֶּלֶךְ הַקָּדוֹשׁ:

The Holy King.

If one is unsure or forgot if they said, repeat the Amidah. If it was immediately said after, it is fulfilled.

Binah / Understanding

Attah Chonen Le'adam Da'at	אַתָּה חוֹנֵן לְאָדָם דַּעַת
Umlamed Le'enosh Binah.	וּמְלַמֵּד לֶאֱנוֹשׁ בִּינָה.
Vechanenu Me'itecha	וְחָנֵּנוּ מֵאִתְּךָ
Chochmah Binah Vada'at.	חָכְמָה בִּינָה וָדָעַת:
Baruch Attah Adonai Chonen	בָּרוּךְ אַתָּה יְהֹוָה חוֹנֵן
Hada'at.	הַדָּעַת:

You favor man with knowledge, and teach mortals understanding. Graciously grant us wisdom, understanding and knowledge from You. Blessed are You, Hashem, gracious Giver of knowledge.

Teshuvah / Repentance

Hashiveinu Avinu Letoratecha.	הֲשִׁיבֵנוּ אָבִינוּ לְתוֹרָתֶךָ.
Vekarevenu Malkeinu	וְקָרְבֵנוּ מַלְכֵּנוּ
La'avodatecha. Vehachazirenu	לַעֲבוֹדָתֶךָ. וְהַחֲזִירֵנוּ
Bitshuvah Shelemah Lefaneicha.	בִּתְשׁוּבָה שְׁלֵמָה לְפָנֶיךָ:
Baruch Attah Adonai Harotzeh	בָּרוּךְ אַתָּה יְהֹוָה הָרוֹצֶה
Bitshuvah.	בִּתְשׁוּבָה:

Restore us, our Father, to Your Torah; draw us near, our King, to Your service; cause us to return in perfect repentance before You. Blessed are You, Hashem, Who desires repentance.

Selichah / Forgiveness

Selach Lanu Avinu Ki Chatanu.	סְלַח לָנוּ אָבִינוּ כִּי חָטָאנוּ.
Mechol Lanu Malkeinu Ki	מְחוֹל לָנוּ מַלְכֵּנוּ כִּי
Fasha'enu. Ki El Tov Vesalach	פָשָׁעְנוּ. כִּי אֵל טוֹב וְסַלָּח
Attah. Baruch Attah Adonai	אָתָּה: בָּרוּךְ אַתָּה יְהֹוָה
Chanun Hamarbeh Lisloach.	חַנּוּן הַמַּרְבֶּה לִסְלֹחַ:

Forgive us, our Father, for we have sinned; pardon us, our King, for we have transgressed; for You are a good and forgiving God. Blessed are You, Hashem, Who is gracious and ever forgiving.

Ge'ulah / Redemption

Re'eh Na Ve'aneyenu. Verivah	רְאֵה נָא בְעָנְיֵנוּ. וְרִיבָה
Rivenu. Umaher Lego'aleinu	רִיבֵנוּ. וּמַהֵר לְגָאֳלֵנוּ
Ge'ulah Shelemah Lema'an	גְאוּלָּה שְׁלֵמָה לְמַעַן
Shemecha. Ki El Go'el Chazak	שְׁמֶךָ. כִּי אֵל גּוֹאֵל חָזָק
Attah. Baruch Attah Adonai	אָתָּה: בָּרוּךְ אַתָּה יְהֹוָה
Go'el Yisra'el.	גּוֹאֵל יִשְׂרָאֵל:

Look upon our affliction and fight our cause; and hasten to redeem us completely for Your name's sake, for You are a strong and redeeming God. Blessed are You, Hashem, Redeemer of Yisrael.

Aneinu

Said only on a public fast day:

עֲנֵנוּ אָבִינוּ עֲנֵנוּ בְּיוֹם צוֹם הַתַּעֲנִית הַזֶּה. כִּי בְצָרָה גְדוֹלָה אֲנָחְנוּ. אַל־תֵּפֶן לְרִשְׁעֵנוּ. וְאַל־תִּתְעַלָּם מַלְכֵּנוּ מִבַּקָּשָׁתֵנוּ. הֱיֵה נָא קָרוֹב לְשַׁוְעָתֵנוּ. טֶרֶם נִקְרָא

אֵלֶיךָ אַתָּה תַעֲנֶה. נְדַבֵּר וְאַתָּה תִשְׁמַע. כַּדָּבָר שֶׁנֶּאֱמַר: וְהָיָה טֶרֶם־יִקְרָאוּ וַאֲנִי אֶעֱנֶה עוֹד הֵם מְדַבְּרִים וַאֲנִי אֶשְׁמָע: כִּי אַתָּה יְהֹוָה פּוֹדֶה וּמַצִּיל. וְעוֹנֶה וּמְרַחֵם בְּכָל־עֵת צָרָה וְצוּקָה:

Aneinu Avinu Aneinu Beyom Tzom Hata'anit Hazeh. Ki Vetzarah Gedolah Anachenu. Al-Tefen Lerish'enu. Ve'al-Tit'alam Malkeinu Mibakashateinu. Heyeh Na Karov Leshav'ateinu. Terem Nikra Eleicha Attah Ta'aneh. Nedaber Ve'attah Tishma'. Kadavar Shene'emar. Vehayah Terem-Yikra'u Va'ani E'eneh; Od Hem Medaberim Va'ani Eshma. Ki Attah Adonai Podeh Umatzil. Ve'oneh Umerachem Bechol-'Et Tzarah Vetzukah.

Answer us, Hashem, answer us on the day of our fast, for we are in great distress. Do not regard our wickedness; Do not conceal Your presence from us, and do not hide Yourself from our supplication. Be near to our cry, and let Your kindness comfort us; even before we call to You answer us, as it is said: "Before they call, I will answer; while they are yet speaking, I will hear." For You, Hashem, are He who answers in time of trouble, who redeems and delivers in all times of woe and stress.

בָּרוּךְ אַתָּה יְהֹוָה הָעוֹנֶה לְעַמּוֹ יִשְׂרָאֵל בְּעֵת צָרָה:

Baruch Attah Adonai Ha'oneh Le'ammo Yisra'el Be'et Tzarah.

Blessed are You, Hashem, Who answers in time of distress.

Refuah / Healing

Refa'enu Adonai Venerafe.	רְפָאֵנוּ יְהֹוָה וְנֵרָפֵא.
Hoshi'enu Venivashe'ah. Ki	הוֹשִׁיעֵנוּ וְנִוָּשֵׁעָה. כִּי
Tehillateinu Attah. Veha'aleh	תְהִלָּתֵנוּ אָתָּה. וְהַעֲלֵה
Aruchah Umarpei Lechol-	אֲרוּכָה וּמַרְפֵּא לְכָל־
Tachalu'einu Ulechol-	תַּחֲלוּאֵינוּ וּלְכָל־
Mach'oveinu Ulechol-	מַכְאוֹבֵינוּ וּלְכָל־
Makoteinu. Ki El Rofei Rachman	מַכּוֹתֵינוּ. כִּי אֵל רוֹפֵא רַחְמָן
Vene'eman Attah. Baruch Attah	וְנֶאֱמָן אָתָּה: בָּרוּךְ אַתָּה
Adonai Rofei Cholei Ammo	יְהֹוָה רוֹפֵא חוֹלֵי עַמּוֹ
Yisra'el.	יִשְׂרָאֵל:

Heal us, Hashem, and we will be healed; save us and we will be saved; for You are our praise. And bring healing and a cure to all of our ailments and wounds; for You are the faithful and merciful God Who heals. Blessed are You, Hashem, Who heals the sick of Your people Yisrael.

Birkat HaShanim / Blessing for the Years

In Summer:	בקיץ:
Barecheinu Adonai Eloheinu	בָּרְכֵנוּ יְהֹוָה אֱלֹהֵינוּ
Bechol-Ma'asei Yadeinu.	בְּכָל־מַעֲשֵׂי יָדֵינוּ.
Uvarech Shenateinu Betalelei	וּבָרֵךְ שְׁנָתֵנוּ בְּטַלְלֵי
Ratzon Berachah Unedavah.	רָצוֹן בְּרָכָה וּנְדָבָה.
Utehi Acharitah Chayim Vesava	וּתְהִי אַחֲרִיתָהּ חַיִּים וְשָׂבָע
Veshalom Kashanim Hatovot	וְשָׁלוֹם כַּשָּׁנִים הַטּוֹבוֹת
Livrachah. Ki El Tov Umeitiv	לִבְרָכָה. כִּי אֵל טוֹב וּמֵטִיב
Attah Umevarech Hashanim.	אַתָּה וּמְבָרֵךְ הַשָּׁנִים:
Baruch Attah Adonai Mevarech	בָּרוּךְ אַתָּה יְהֹוָה מְבָרֵךְ
Hashanim.	הַשָּׁנִים:

Bless us, our Father, in all the work of our hands, and bless our year with favoring dews of blessing and abundance. May it's result be life, plenty and satisfaction and peace like the good years which You have blessed. For You, God, are good and You do good, blessing the years. Blessed are You, Hashem Who blesses the years.

In Winter:	בחורף:
Barech Aleinu Adonai Eloheinu	בָּרֵךְ עָלֵינוּ יְהֹוָה אֱלֹהֵינוּ
Et-Hashanah Hazot Ve'et-Kol-	אֶת־הַשָּׁנָה הַזֹּאת וְאֶת־כָּל־
Minei Tevu'atah Letovah. Veten	מִינֵי תְבוּאָתָהּ לְטוֹבָה. וְתֵן
Tal Umatar Livrachah Al Kol-	טַל וּמָטָר לִבְרָכָה עַל כָּל־

Penei Ha'adamah. Veraveh Penei	פְּנֵי הָאֲדָמָה. וְרַוֵּה פְּנֵי
Tevel Vesabba Et-Ha'olam Kulo	תֵבֵל וְשַׂבַּע אֶת־הָעוֹלָם כֻּלּוֹ
Mituvach. Umalei Yadeinu	מִטּוּבָךְ. וּמַלֵּא יָדֵינוּ
Mibirchoteicha Ume'osher	מִבִּרְכוֹתֶיךָ וּמֵעֹשֶׁר
Mattenot Yadeicha. Shamerah	מַתְּנוֹת יָדֶיךָ. שָׁמְרָה
Vehatzilah Shanah Zo Mikol-	וְהַצִּילָה שָׁנָה זוֹ מִכָּל־
Davar Ra'. Umikal-Minei	דָּבָר רָע. וּמִכָּל־מִינֵי
Mashchit Umikal-Minei Fur'anut.	מַשְׁחִית וּמִכָּל־מִינֵי פֻּרְעָנוּת.
Va'aseh Lah Tikvah Tovah	וַעֲשֵׂה לָהּ תִּקְוָה טוֹבָה
Ve'acharit Shalom. Chus	וְאַחֲרִית שָׁלוֹם. חוּס
Verachem Aleiha Ve'al Kol-	וְרַחֵם עָלֶיהָ וְעַל כָּל־
Tevu'atah Ufeiroteiha.	תְּבוּאָתָהּ וּפֵירוֹתֶיהָ.
Uvarechah Begishmei Ratzon	וּבָרְכָהּ בְּגִשְׁמֵי רָצוֹן
Berachah Unedavah. Utehi	בְּרָכָה וּנְדָבָה. וּתְהִי
Acharitah Chayim Vesava	אַחֲרִיתָהּ חַיִּים וְשָׂבָע
Veshalom. Kashanim Hatovot	וְשָׁלוֹם. כַּשָּׁנִים הַטּוֹבוֹת
Livrachah. Ki El Tov Umeitiv	לִבְרָכָה. כִּי אֵל טוֹב וּמֵטִיב
Attah Umevarech Hashanim.	אַתָּה וּמְבָרֵךְ הַשָּׁנִים.
Baruch Attah Adonai Mevarech	בָּרוּךְ אַתָּה יְהוָה מְבָרֵךְ
Hashanim.	הַשָּׁנִים:

Hashem our God, bless for us this year with all its varied produce, for good. Send dew and rain to bless the face of the entire earth, and water the surface of the earth, and satisfy the whole world with Your goodness. Fill our hands with Your blessings and the rich gifts of Your hands. Guard and deliver this year from all evil, and from all disaster and from all chaos, and make it a year of good hope and a peaceful ending. Have pity and compassion on this year and all its increase and fruits. Bless the year with rains of favor, blessing and generosity, and may its end be life, satisfaction and peace, like the good years which You have blessed. For You God, are good and You do good, blessing the years. Blessed are You, Hashem Who blesses the years.

Galuyot / Ingathering of Exiles

Teka Beshofar Gadol	תְּקַע בְּשׁוֹפָר גָּדוֹל
Lecheruteinu. Vesa Nes	לְחֵרוּתֵנוּ. וְשָׂא נֵס
Lekabetz Galyoteinu.	לְקַבֵּץ גָּלֻיּוֹתֵינוּ.
Vekabetzeinu Yachad Me'arba	וְקַבְּצֵנוּ יַחַד מֵאַרְבַּע
Kanfot Ha'aretz Le'artzenu.	כַּנְפוֹת הָאָרֶץ לְאַרְצֵנוּ:
Baruch Attah Adonai Mekabetz	בָּרוּךְ אַתָּה יְהֹוָה מְקַבֵּץ
Nidchei Ammo Yisra'el.	נִדְחֵי עַמּוֹ יִשְׂרָאֵל:

Sound the great shofar for our freedom; lift up the banner to bring our exiles; And gather us together from the four corners of the earth into our land. Blessed are You, Hashem, Who gathers the dispersed of His people Yisrael.

Birkat HaDin / Restoration of Justice

Hashivah Shofeteinu	הָשִׁיבָה שׁוֹפְטֵינוּ
Kevarishonah. Veyo'atzeinu	כְּבָרִאשׁוֹנָה. וְיוֹעֲצֵינוּ
Kevatechillah. Vehaseir Mimenu	כְּבַתְּחִלָּה. וְהָסֵר מִמֶּנּוּ
Yagon Va'anachah. Umeloch	יָגוֹן וַאֲנָחָה. וּמְלוֹךְ
Aleinu Meheirah Attah Adonai	עָלֵינוּ מְהֵרָה אַתָּה יְהֹוָה
Levadecha. Bechesed	לְבַדְּךָ. בְּחֶסֶד

Uverachamim. Betzedek	וּבְרַחֲמִים. בְּצֶדֶק
Uvemishpat. Baruch Attah	וּבְמִשְׁפָּט: בָּרוּךְ אַתָּה
Adonai Melech Ohev Tzedakah	יוהוויהו מֶלֶךְ אוֹהֵב צְדָקָה
Umishpat.	וּמִשְׁפָּט:

Restore our judges as at first, and our counselors as at the beginning; remove from us sorrow and sighing; reign over us speedily, Hashem, You alone in kindness and mercy; and with righteousness and with justice. Blessed are You, Hashem, King who loves righteousness and justice.

During the 10 days of repentance (Rosh Hashanah to Yom Kippur) say:

Hamelech Hamishpat.	הַמֶּלֶךְ הַמִּשְׁפָּט:

The King, The Judge.

Birkat HaMinim / Blessing Against the Heretics

Laminim Velamalshinim Al-Tehi	לַמִּינִים וְלַמַּלְשִׁינִים אַל־תְּהִי
Tikvah. Vechol-Hazeidim	תִקְוָה. וְכָל־הַזֵּדִים
Kerega Yovedu.	כְּרֶגַע יֹאבֵדוּ.
Vechol-'Oyeveicha Vechol-	וְכָל־אוֹיְבֶיךָ וְכָל־
Sone'eicha Meheirah Yikaretu.	שׂוֹנְאֶיךָ מְהֵרָה יִכָּרֵתוּ.
Umalchut Harish'ah Meheirah	וּמַלְכוּת הָרִשְׁעָה מְהֵרָה
Te'akeir Uteshaber Utechalem	תְעַקֵּר וּתְשַׁבֵּר וּתְכַלֵּם
Vetachni'em Bimheirah	וְתַכְנִיעֵם בִּמְהֵרָה
Veyameinu. Baruch Attah	בְיָמֵינוּ: בָּרוּךְ אַתָּה
Adonai Shoveir Oyevim	יְהֹוָה שׁוֹבֵר אוֹיְבִים
Umachnia Zeidim. (Minim)	וּמַכְנִיעַ זֵדִים: (מִינִים)

For the heretics and the slanderers let there be no hope, and all of the arrogant disappear in an instant. May all of Your enemies and all of those who hate You quickly be cut off, and the evil government uprooted, and broken, and humbled and subdued quickly in our days. Blessed are You, Hashem, Who breaks enemies and subdues the arrogant. **(heretics)**

Tzaddikim / The Righteous

Al Hatzaddikim Ve'al	עַל הַצַּדִּיקִים וְעַל
Hachasidim. Ve'al She'erit	הַחֲסִידִים. וְעַל שְׁאֵרִית
Ammecha Beit Yisra'el. Ve'al	עַמְּךָ בֵּית יִשְׂרָאֵל. וְעַל
Peleitat Beit Sofereihem. Ve'al	פְּלֵיטַת בֵּית סוֹפְרֵיהֶם. וְעַל
Gerei Hatzedek Ve'aleinu.	גֵּרֵי הַצֶּדֶק וְעָלֵינוּ.
Yehemu Na Rachameicha.	יֶהֱמוּ נָא רַחֲמֶיךָ.
Adonai Eloheinu. Veten Sachar	יְהֹוָה אֱלֹהֵינוּ. וְתֵן שָׂכָר
Tov Lechol-Habotechim	טוֹב לְכָל־הַבּוֹטְחִים
Beshimcha Be'emet. Vesim	בְּשִׁמְךָ בֶּאֱמֶת. וְשִׂים
Chelkenu Imahem. Ule'olam Lo	חֶלְקֵנוּ עִמָּהֶם. וּלְעוֹלָם לֹא
Nevosh Ki Vecha Vatachenu.	נֵבוֹשׁ כִּי בְךָ בָטָחְנוּ.
Ve'al Chasdecha Hagadol	וְעַל חַסְדְּךָ הַגָּדוֹל
Be'emet Nish'aneinu. Baruch	בֶּאֱמֶת נִשְׁעָנְנוּ: בָּרוּךְ
Attah Adonai Mish'an Umivtach	אַתָּה יוהוווהו מִשְׁעָן וּמִבְטָח
Latzaddikim.	לַצַּדִּיקִים:

On the righteous and on the pious and on the remainders of Your people, the House of Yisrael, and over the remnant of their scribes; over the righteous converts and over us may Your mercy be aroused. Hashem our God, Grant a good reward to all who truly trust in Your name, and place our portion among them; may we never come to shame, for in You we trust and on Your great kindness we faithfully rely. Blessed are You, Hashem, the support and trust of the righteous.

Boneh Yerushalayim / Builder of Yerushalayim

Tishkon Betoch Yerushalayim	תִּשְׁכּוֹן בְּתוֹךְ יְרוּשָׁלַיִם
Irecha Ka'asher Dibarta.	עִירְךָ כַּאֲשֶׁר דִּבַּרְתָּ.
Vechisei David Avdecha	וְכִסֵּא דָוִד עַבְדְּךָ
Meheirah Betochah Tachin.	מְהֵרָה בְּתוֹכָהּ תָּכִין.
Uveneh Otah Binyan Olam	וּבְנֵה אוֹתָהּ בִּנְיַן עוֹלָם
Bimheirah Veyameinu. Baruch	בִּמְהֵרָה בְיָמֵינוּ: בָּרוּךְ
Attah Adonai Boneh	אַתָּה יְהֶוָהֶ בּוֹנֵה
Yerushalayim.	יְרוּשָׁלָיִם:

May Your presence dwell in Yerushalayim, Your city, as You have promised; establish soon the throne of David, Your servant, within it, And rebuild it soon, in our days, as an everlasting structure. Blessed are You, Hashem, Builder of Yerushalayim.

Birkhat David / Prayer for Davidic Reign

Et Tzemach David Avdecha	אֶת צֶמַח דָּוִד עַבְדְּךָ
Meheirah Tatzmiach. Vekarno	מְהֵרָה תַצְמִיחַ. וְקַרְנוֹ
Tarum Bishu'atecha. Ki	תָּרוּם בִּישׁוּעָתֶךָ. כִּי
Lishu'atecha Kivinu Kol-Hayom.	לִישׁוּעָתְךָ קִוִּינוּ כָּל־הַיּוֹם:
Baruch Attah Adonai Matzmiach	בָּרוּךְ אַתָּה יְהוִה מַצְמִיחַ
Keren Yeshu'ah.	קֶרֶן יְשׁוּעָה:

Speedily cause the offspring of Your servant David to flourish, and let his horn be exalted in Your salvation, for we hope in Your salvation every day. Blessed are You, Hashem, Who flourishes the horn of salvation.

Tefillah / Acceptance of Prayer

Shema Koleinu. Adonai	שְׁמַע קוֹלֵנוּ. יְהֹוָה
Eloheinu. Av Harachaman.	אֱלֹהֵינוּ. אָב הָרַחֲמָן.
Rachem Aleinu. Vekabel	רַחֵם עָלֵינוּ. וְקַבֵּל
Berachamim Uveratzon Et-	בְּרַחֲמִים וּבְרָצוֹן אֶת־
Tefillateinu. Ki El Shome'ah	תְּפִלָּתֵנוּ. כִּי אֵל שׁוֹמֵעַ
Tefillot Vetachanunim Attah.	תְּפִלּוֹת וְתַחֲנוּנִים אָתָּה.
Umilfaneicha Malkeinu. Reikam	וּמִלְּפָנֶיךָ מַלְכֵּנוּ. רֵיקָם
Al-Teshivenu. Chonenu	אַל־תְּשִׁיבֵנוּ. חָנֵּנוּ
Va'aneinu Ushema Tefillateinu.	וַעֲנֵנוּ וּשְׁמַע תְּפִלָּתֵנוּ.

Hear our voice, Hashem our God. Merciful Father, have compassion upon us. And accept our prayers with mercy and favor, for You are God who hears to prayers and supplications. And from before You, our King, do not leave us empty-handed, but be gracious to us and hear our prayers.

If one forgot to say Aneinu earlier, they may say here:

עֲנֵנוּ אָבִינוּ עֲנֵנוּ בְּיוֹם צוֹם הַתַּעֲנִית הַזֶּה. כִּי בְצָרָה גְדוֹלָה אֲנָחְנוּ. אַל־תֵּפֶן לְרִשְׁעֵנוּ. וְאַל־תִּתְעַלָּם מַלְכֵּנוּ מִבַּקָּשָׁתֵנוּ. הֱיֵה נָא קָרוֹב לְשַׁוְעָתֵנוּ. טֶרֶם נִקְרָא אֵלֶיךָ אַתָּה תַעֲנֶה. נְדַבֵּר וְאַתָּה תִשְׁמַע. כַּדָּבָר שֶׁנֶּאֱמַר: וְהָיָה טֶרֶם־יִקְרָאוּ וַאֲנִי אֶעֱנֶה עוֹד הֵם מְדַבְּרִים וַאֲנִי אֶשְׁמָע: כִּי אַתָּה יְהֹוָה פּוֹדֶה וּמַצִּיל. וְעוֹנֶה וּמְרַחֵם בְּכָל־עֵת צָרָה וְצוּקָה:

Aneinu Avinu Aneinu Beyom Tzom Hata'anit Hazeh. Ki Vetzarah Gedolah Anachenu. Al-Tefen Lerish'enu. Ve'al-Tit'alam Malkeinu Mibakashateinu. Heyeh Na Karov Leshav'ateinu. Terem Nikra Eleicha Attah Ta'aneh. Nedaber Ve'attah Tishma'. Kadavar Shene'emar. Vehayah Terem-Yikra'u Va'ani E'eneh; Od Hem Medaberim Va'ani Eshma. Ki Attah Adonai Podeh Umatzil. Ve'oneh Umerachem Bechol-'Et Tzarah Vetzukah.

Answer us, Hashem, answer us on the day of our fast, for we are in great distress. Do not regard our wickedness; Do not conceal Your presence from us, and do not hide Yourself from our supplication. Be near to our cry, and let Your kindness comfort us; even before we call to You answer us, as it is said: "Before they call, I will answer; while they are yet speaking, I will hear." For You, Hashem, are He who answers in time of trouble, who redeems and delivers in all times of woe and stress.

Ki Attah Shome'ah Tefillat Kol- כִּי אַתָּה שׁוֹמֵעַ תְּפִלַּת כָּל־

Peh. Baruch Attah Adonai פֶּה: בָּרוּךְ אַתָּה יְהֹוָה

Shome'ah Tefillah. שׁוֹמֵעַ תְּפִלָּה:

For You hear the prayer of every mouth. Blessed are You, Hashem Who hears prayer.

Avodah / Temple Service

Retzeh Adonai Eloheinu רְצֵה יְהֹוָה אֱלֹהֵינוּ

Be'ammecha Yisra'el Velitfilatam בְּעַמְּךָ יִשְׂרָאֵל וְלִתְפִלָּתָם

She'eh. Vehasheiv Ha'avodah שְׁעֵה. וְהָשֵׁב הָעֲבוֹדָה

Lidvir Beitecha. Ve'ishei Yisra'el לִדְבִיר בֵּיתֶךָ. וְאִשֵּׁי יִשְׂרָאֵל

Utefilatam. Meheirah Be'ahavah וּתְפִלָּתָם. מְהֵרָה בְּאַהֲבָה

Tekabel Beratzon. Utehi תְקַבֵּל בְּרָצוֹן. וּתְהִי

Leratzon Tamid Avodat Yisra'el לְרָצוֹן תָּמִיד עֲבוֹדַת יִשְׂרָאֵל

Ammecha. עַמֶּךָ:

Be favorable, Hashem our God, on Your people Yisrael and regard their prayers. And the service to the Sanctuary of Your House, and the fire offerings of Yisrael, and their prayers accept soon with love. And may the service of Your people, Yisrael, always be favorable.

On Rosh Chodesh and Chol HaMoed Passover and Sukkot say:

Ya'aleh Veyavo

אֱלֹהֵינוּ וֵאלֹהֵי אֲבוֹתֵינוּ. יַעֲלֶה וְיָבֹא. וְיַגִּיעַ וְיֵרָאֶה. וְיֵרָצֶה וְיִשָּׁמַע. וְיִפָּקֵד וְיִזָּכֵר. זִכְרוֹנֵנוּ וְזִכְרוֹן אֲבוֹתֵינוּ. זִכְרוֹן יְרוּשָׁלַיִם עִירָךְ. וְזִכְרוֹן מָשִׁיחַ בֶּן־דָּוִד עַבְדָּךְ. וְזִכְרוֹן כָּל־עַמְּךָ בֵּית יִשְׂרָאֵל לְפָנֶיךָ. לִפְלֵיטָה. לְטוֹבָה. לְחֵן. לְחֶסֶד וּלְרַחֲמִים. לְחַיִּים טוֹבִים וּלְשָׁלוֹם. בְּיוֹם:

Eloheinu Velohei Avoteinu. Ya'aleh Veyavo. Veyagia Veyera'eh. Veyeratzeh Veyishama'. Veyipaked Veyizacher. Zichronenu Vezichron Avoteinu. Zichron Yerushalayim Irach. Vezichron Mashiach Ben-David Avdach. Vezichron Kol-'Ammecha Beit Yisra'el Lefaneicha. Lifleitah. Letovah. Lechein. Lechesed Ulerachamim. Lechayim Tovim Uleshalom. Beyom:

Our God, and God of our fathers, may it rise, and come, arrive, appear, find favor, and be heard, and be considered, and be remembered our remembrance and the remembrance of our fathers, Yerushalayim Your city, the remembrance of Messiah ben David Your servant, and the remembrance of all Your people of the House of Yisrael before You for deliverance, for good favor, for kindness and mercy, for good life and for peace. On this day of:

On Rosh Chodesh:

רֹאשׁ חֹדֶשׁ הַזֶּה.

Rosh Chodesh Hazeh.

Rosh Chodesh (New Moon).

On Pesach:

חַג הַמַּצּוֹת הַזֶּה. בְּיוֹם מִקְרָא קֹדֶשׁ הַזֶּה.

Chag Hamatzot Hazeh. Beyom Mikra Kodesh Hazeh.

The Festival of Matzot. on this day of holy convocation.

On Sukkot:

חַג הַסֻּכּוֹת הַזֶּה. בְּיוֹם מִקְרָא קֹדֶשׁ הַזֶּה.

Chag Hasukkot Hazeh. Beyom Mikra Kodesh Hazeh.

The Festival of Sukkot. on this day of holy convocation.

לְרַחֵם בּוֹ עָלֵינוּ וּלְהוֹשִׁיעֵנוּ. זָכְרֵנוּ יְהוָה אֱלֹהֵינוּ בּוֹ לְטוֹבָה. וּפָקְדֵנוּ בוֹ לִבְרָכָה. וְהוֹשִׁיעֵנוּ בוֹ לְחַיִּים טוֹבִים. בִּדְבַר יְשׁוּעָה וְרַחֲמִים. חוּס וְחָנֵּנוּ. וַחֲמוֹל וְרַחֵם עָלֵינוּ. וְהוֹשִׁיעֵנוּ כִּי אֵלֶיךָ עֵינֵינוּ. כִּי אֵל מֶלֶךְ חַנּוּן וְרַחוּם אָתָּה:

Lerachem Bo Aleinu Ulehoshi'enu. Zochrenu Adonai Eloheinu Bo Letovah. Ufokdenu Vo Livrachah. Vehoshi'enu Vo Lechayim Tovim. Bidvar Yeshu'ah Verachamim. Chus Vechanenu. Vachamol Verachem Aleinu. Vehoshi'enu Ki Eleicha Eineinu. Ki El Melech Chanun Verachum Attah.

to have mercy upon us and save us. Remember us, Hashem our God, on it for good. Be mindful of us on it for blessing and save us on it for a life of good. With the promise of salvation and mercy, show us pity, and be gracious to us and have compassion and mercy on us and save us. For our eyes are lifted towards You, for You, God, are a gracious and merciful King.

Attah Berachameicha Harabim.	וְאַתָּה בְּרַחֲמֶיךָ הָרַבִּים.
Tachpotz Banu Vetirtzenu.	תַּחְפֹּץ בָּנוּ וְתִרְצֵנוּ.
Vetechezeinah Eineinu	וְתֶחֱזֶינָה עֵינֵינוּ
Beshuvecha Letziyon	בְּשׁוּבְךָ לְצִיּוֹן
Berachamim. Baruch Attah	בְּרַחֲמִים: בָּרוּךְ אַתָּה
Adonai Hamachazir Shechinato	יְהֹוָה הַמַּחֲזִיר שְׁכִינָתוֹ
Letziyon.	לְצִיּוֹן.

And You, in Your abundant mercy, delight in us, and be favorable to us, so that our eyes may witness Your return to Tzion with mercy. Blessed are You, Hashem Who returns His Presence to Tzion.

Hoda'ah (Modim) / Thanksgiving

On Saying "Modim" / "We are Thankful" One Bows and begins to rise after "Adonai" / "Hashem".

Modim Anachnu Lach. She'attah	מוֹדִים אֲנַחְנוּ לָךְ. שָׁאַתָּה
Hu Adonai Eloheinu Velohei	הוּא יְהֹוָה אֱלֹהֵינוּ וֵאלֹהֵי
Avoteinu Le'olam Va'ed. Tzurenu	אֲבוֹתֵינוּ לְעוֹלָם וָעֶד. צוּרֵנוּ
Tzur Chayeinu Umagen Yish'enu	צוּר חַיֵּינוּ וּמָגֵן יִשְׁעֵנוּ
Attah Hu. Ledor Vador Nodeh	אַתָּה הוּא. לְדוֹר וָדוֹר נוֹדֶה
Lecha Unsapeir Tehilatecha. Al	לְּךָ וּנְסַפֵּר תְּהִלָּתֶךָ. עַל
Chayeinu Hamesurim	חַיֵּינוּ הַמְּסוּרִים
Beyadecha. Ve'al Nishmoteinu	בְּיָדֶךָ. וְעַל נִשְׁמוֹתֵינוּ
Hapekudot Lach. Ve'al Niseicha	הַפְּקוּדוֹת לָךְ. וְעַל נִסֶּיךָ

Shebechol-Yom Imanu. Ve'al	שֶׁבְּכָל־יוֹם עִמָּנוּ. וְעַל
Nifle'oteicha Vetovoteicha	נִפְלְאוֹתֶיךָ וְטוֹבוֹתֶיךָ
Shebechol-'Et. Erev Vavoker	שֶׁבְּכָל־עֵת. עֶרֶב וָבֹקֶר
Vetzaharayim. Hatov. Ki Lo	וְצָהֳרָיִם. הַטּוֹב. כִּי לֹא
Chalu Rachameicha.	כָלוּ רַחֲמֶיךָ.
Hamerachem. Ki Lo Tamu	הַמְרַחֵם. כִּי לֹא תַמּוּ
Chasadeicha. Ki Me'olam Kivinu	חֲסָדֶיךָ. כִּי מֵעוֹלָם קִוִּינוּ
Lach.	לָךְ:

We are thankful to You, Hashem our God and the God of our fathers, forever. You are our strength and Rock of our life and the Shield of our salvation. In every generation we will thank You and recount Your praise for our lives which are in given into Your hand, for our souls which are placed in Your care, and for Your miracles which are daily with us, and for Your wonders and goodness—evening, morning and noon. The Beneficent One, for Your mercies never end, Merciful One, for Your kindness has never ceased, for we have always placed our hope in You.

Modim Derabbanan

During the repetition, this is to be recited softly while the Chazan reads the Modim. Still bow at Modim as before.

מוֹדִים אֲנַחְנוּ לָךְ. שָׁאַתָּה הוּא יְהֹוָה אֱלֹהֵינוּ וֵאלֹהֵי אֲבוֹתֵינוּ. אֱלֹהֵי כָל בָּשָׂר. יוֹצְרֵנוּ יוֹצֵר בְּרֵאשִׁית. בְּרָכוֹת וְהוֹדָאוֹת לְשִׁמְךָ הַגָּדוֹל וְהַקָּדוֹשׁ. עַל שֶׁהֶחֱיִיתָנוּ וְקִיַּמְתָּנוּ. כֵּן תְּחַיֵּינוּ וּתְחָנֵּנוּ וְתֶאֱסוֹף גָּלֻיּוֹתֵינוּ לְחַצְרוֹת קָדְשֶׁךָ. לִשְׁמֹר חֻקֶּיךָ וְלַעֲשׂוֹת רְצוֹנְךָ וּלְעָבְדְךָ בְּלֵבָב שָׁלֵם. עַל שֶׁאֲנַחְנוּ מוֹדִים לָךְ. בָּרוּךְ אֵל הַהוֹדָאוֹת.

Modim Anachnu Lach. She'attah Hu Adonai Eloheinu Velohei Avoteinu. Elohei Chol Basar. Yotzreinu Yotzer Bereshit. Berachot Vehoda'ot Leshimcha Hagadol Vehakadosh. Al Shehecheyitanu Vekiyamtanu. Ken Techayeinu Utechanenu Vete'esof Galyoteinu Lechatzrot Kodshecha. Lishmor Chukkeicha Vela'asot Retzonecha Ule'avedecha Velevav Shalem. Al She'anachnu Modim Lach. Baruch El Hahoda'ot.

We are thankful to You, Hashem our God and the God of our fathers. God of all flesh, our Creator and Former of Creation, blessings and thanks to Your great and holy name, for You have kept us alive and sustained us; may You always grant us life and be gracious to us. And gather our exiles to Your holy courtyards to observe Your statutes, and to do Your will, and to serve You with a perfect heart. For this we thank You. Blessed is God of thanksgivings.

Al HaNissim

On Purim and Hanukkah an extra prayer is added here:

עַל הַנִּסִּים וְעַל הַפֻּרְקָן וְעַל הַגְּבוּרוֹת וְעַל הַתְּשׁוּעוֹת וְעַל הַנִּפְלָאוֹת וְעַל הַנֶּחָמוֹת שֶׁעָשִׂיתָ לַאֲבוֹתֵינוּ בַּיָּמִים הָהֵם בַּזְּמַן הַזֶּה:

Al Hanissim Ve'al Hapurkan Ve'al Hagevurot Ve'al Hateshu'ot Ve'al Hanifla'ot Ve'al Hanechamot She'asita La'avoteinu Bayamim Hahem Bazman Hazeh.

For the miracles, and for the triumphant liberation, and the mighty works, and for the deliverances, and for the wonders, and for the consolations which You have done for our fathers in those days at this season:

On Hanukkah:

בִּימֵי מַתִּתְיָה בֶּן־יוֹחָנָן כֹּהֵן גָּדוֹל. חַשְׁמוֹנָאִי וּבָנָיו כְּשֶׁעָמְדָה מַלְכוּת יָוָן הָרְשָׁעָה עַל עַמְּךָ יִשְׂרָאֵל. לְשַׁכְּחָם תּוֹרָתָךְ וּלְהַעֲבִירָם מֵחֻקֵּי רְצוֹנָךְ. וְאַתָּה בְּרַחֲמֶיךָ הָרַבִּים עָמַדְתָּ לָהֶם בְּעֵת צָרָתָם. רַבְתָּ אֶת רִיבָם. דַּנְתָּ אֶת דִּינָם. נָקַמְתָּ אֶת נִקְמָתָם. מָסַרְתָּ גִבּוֹרִים בְּיַד חַלָּשִׁים. וְרַבִּים בְּיַד מְעַטִּים. וּרְשָׁעִים בְּיַד צַדִּיקִים. וּטְמֵאִים בְּיַד טְהוֹרִים. וְזֵדִים בְּיַד עוֹסְקֵי תוֹרָתֶךָ. לְךָ עָשִׂיתָ שֵׁם גָּדוֹל וְקָדוֹשׁ בְּעוֹלָמָךְ. וּלְעַמְּךָ יִשְׂרָאֵל עָשִׂיתָ תְּשׁוּעָה גְדוֹלָה וּפֻרְקָן כְּהַיּוֹם הַזֶּה. וְאַחַר כָּךְ בָּאוּ בָנֶיךָ לִדְבִיר בֵּיתֶךָ. וּפִנּוּ אֶת־הֵיכָלֶךָ. וְטִהֲרוּ אֶת־מִקְדָּשֶׁךָ. וְהִדְלִיקוּ נֵרוֹת בְּחַצְרוֹת קָדְשֶׁךָ. וְקָבְעוּ שְׁמוֹנַת יְמֵי חֲנֻכָּה אֵלּוּ בְּהַלֵּל וּבְהוֹדָאָה. וְעָשִׂיתָ עִמָּהֶם נִסִּים וְנִפְלָאוֹת וְנוֹדֶה לְשִׁמְךָ הַגָּדוֹל סֶלָה:

Bimei Mattityah Ven-Yochanan Kohen Gadol. Chashmona'i Uvanav Keshe'amedah Malchut Yavan Haresha'ah Al Ammecha Yisra'el. Leshakecham Toratach Uleha'aviram Mechukkei Retzonach. Ve'attah Berachameicha Harabim Amadta Lahem Be'et Tzaratam. Ravta Et Rivam. Danta Et Dinam. Nakamta Et Nikmatam. Masarta Giborim Beyad Chalashim. Verabim Beyad Me'atim. Uresha'im Beyad Tzaddikim. Uteme'im Beyad Tehorim. Vezeidim Beyad Osekei Toratecha. Lecha Asita Shem Gadol Vekadosh Be'olamach. Ule'ammecha Yisra'el Asita Teshu'ah Gedolah Ufurkan Kehayom Hazeh. Ve'achar Kach Ba'u Vaneicha Lidvir Beitecha. Ufinu Et-Heichalecha. Vetiharu Et-Mikdashecha. Vehidliku Nerot Bechatzrot Kodshecha. Vekave'u Shemonat Yemei Chanukkah Elu Behallel Uvehoda'ah.

Ve'asita Imahem Nissim Venifla'ot Venodeh Leshimcha Hagadol Selah.

Then in the days of Mattityahu ben-Yochanan, High Priest, the Hasmonean and his sons, when the cruel Greek power rose up against Your people, Yisrael, to make them forget Your Torah and transgress the statutes of Your will. And You, in Your great compassion, stood up for them in time of their trial to plead their cause and defend their judgment. Giving out retribution, delivered the strong into the hand of the weak, and the many into the hand of the few, and the wicked into the hand of the upright, and the impure into the hand of the pure, and tyrants into the hand of the devotees of Your Torah. You made for Yourself a great and holy name in Your world. And for Your people, Yisrael, You performed a great salvation and liberation as this very day. Then Your children came to the Sanctuary of Your House, cleared Your Temple, cleansed Your Sanctuary and kindled lights in Your courtyards, and they instituted these eight days of Hanukkah for praise and thanksgiving. And You did miracles and wonders for them, and we give thanks to Your great name, selah.

On Purim:

בִּימֵי מָרְדְּכַי וְאֶסְתֵּר בְּשׁוּשַׁן הַבִּירָה. כְּשֶׁעָמַד עֲלֵיהֶם הָמָן הָרָשָׁע. בִּקֵּשׁ לְהַשְׁמִיד לַהֲרֹג וּלְאַבֵּד אֶת־כָּל־הַיְּהוּדִים מִנַּעַר וְעַד זָקֵן טַף וְנָשִׁים בְּיוֹם אֶחָד. בִּשְׁלֹשָׁה עָשָׂר לְחֹדֶשׁ שְׁנֵים עָשָׂר. הוּא חֹדֶשׁ אֲדָר. וּשְׁלָלָם לָבוֹז. וְאַתָּה בְּרַחֲמֶיךָ הָרַבִּים הֵפַרְתָּ אֶת־עֲצָתוֹ וְקִלְקַלְתָּ אֶת־מַחֲשַׁבְתּוֹ. וַהֲשֵׁבוֹתָ לּוֹ גְּמוּלוֹ בְּרֹאשׁוֹ. וְתָלוּ אוֹתוֹ וְאֶת־בָּנָיו עַל הָעֵץ. וְעָשִׂיתָ עִמָּהֶם נֵס וָפֶלֶא וְנוֹדֶה לְשִׁמְךָ הַגָּדוֹל סֶלָה:

Bimei Mordechai Ve'ester Beshushan Habirah. Keshe'amad Aleihem Haman Harasha. Bikesh Lehashmid Laharog Ule'abed Et-Kol-Hayehudim Mina'ar Ve'ad Zaken Taf Venashim Beyom Echad. Bishloshah Asar Lechodesh Sheneim Asar. Hu Chodesh Adar. Ushelalam Lavoz. Ve'attah Berachameicha Harabim Hefarta Et-'Atzato Vekilkalta Et-Machashavto. Vahasheivota Lo Gemulo Verosho. Vetalu Oto Ve'et-Banav Al Ha'etz. Ve'asita Imahem Nes Vafelei Venodeh Leshimcha Hagadol Selah.

In the days of Mordechai and Ester in Shushan, the capital, the wicked Haman rose up and sought to destroy, slay and utterly annihilate all of the Yehudim, both young and old, women and children, on one day, on the thirteenth day of the twelfth month, which is the month of Adar, and to plunder their possessions. But You in Your great mercy You broke his plan and spoiled his designs, causing them to recoil on his own head, and they hanged him and his sons on the gallows. And You did miracles and wonders for them, and we give thanks to Your great name, selah.

Ve'al Kulam Yitbarach.	וְעַל כֻּלָּם יִתְבָּרַךְ.
Veyitromam. Veyitnasse. Tamid.	וְיִתְרוֹמַם. וְיִתְנַשֵּׂא. תָּמִיד.
Shimcha Malkeinu. Le'olam	שִׁמְךָ מַלְכֵּנוּ. לְעוֹלָם
Va'ed. Vechol-Hachayim	וָעֶד. וְכָל־הַחַיִּים
Yoducha Selah.	יוֹדוּךָ סֶּלָה:

For all these acts, may Your name, our King, be blessed, extolled and exalted forever. And all of the living will thank You, selah.

During the 10 days of repentance (Rosh Hashanah to Yom Kippur) say:

Uchetov Lechayim Tovim Kol Benei	וּכְתֹב לְחַיִּים טוֹבִים כָּל בְּנֵי
Veritecha.	בְרִיתֶךָ.

Inscribe all of Your people of the covenant for a happy life.

Bow at "Baruch Attah" / "Blessed are You". Raise up at Adonai / Hashem.

Vihalelu Vivarechu Et-Shimcha	וִיהַלְלוּ וִיבָרְכוּ אֶת־שִׁמְךָ
Hagadol Be'emet Le'olam Ki	הַגָּדוֹל בֶּאֱמֶת לְעוֹלָם כִּי
Tov. Ha'el Yeshu'ateinu	טוֹב. הָאֵל יְשׁוּעָתֵנוּ
Ve'ezrateinu Selah. Ha'el Hatov.	וְעֶזְרָתֵנוּ סֶלָה. הָאֵל הַטּוֹב:
Baruch Attah Adonai Hatov	בָּרוּךְ אַתָּה יְהֹוָה הַטּוֹב
Shimcha Ulecha Na'eh	שִׁמְךָ וּלְךָ נָאֶה
Lehodot.	לְהוֹדוֹת:

And they will praise and bless Your great and good name sincerely, forever. For You are good, the God of our salvation and our help forever, the Good God. Blessed are You, Hashem, Your name is good and to You it is good to give thanks.

Continue with Birkhat Kohanim. If there are not 10 men (minyan), proceed to Sim Shalom.

Birkhat Kohanim / The Priestly Blessing

If there is more than one Kohen present, start here. If there is not, start with Eloheinu Velohei Avoteinu below:

Some say:

לְשֵׁם יִחוּד קוּדְשָׁא בְּרִיךְ הוּא וּשְׁכִינְתֵּיהּ. בִּדְחִילוּ וּרְחִימוּ. וּרְחִימוּ וּדְחִילוּ. לְיַחֲדָא שֵׁם יו״ד קֵ״י בְּוָא״ו קֵ״י בְּיִחוּדָא שְׁלִים (יהוה) בְּשֵׁם כָּל יִשְׂרָאֵל. הִנֵּה אָנֹכִי מוּכָן וּמְזוּמָּן לְקַיֵּים מִצְוַת עֲשֵׂה לְבָרֵךְ אֶת יִשְׂרָאֵל בִּרְכַּת כֹּהֲנִים בִּנְשִׂיאוּת כַּפַּיִם לַעֲשׂוֹת נַחַת רוּחַ לְיוֹצְרֵנוּ וּלְהַמְשִׁיךְ שֶׁפַע וּבְרָכָה לְכָל הָעוֹלָמוֹת הַקְּדוֹשִׁים. וִיהִי נֹעַם אֲדֹנָי אֱלֹהֵינוּ עָלֵינוּ וּמַעֲשֵׂה יָדֵינוּ כּוֹנְנָה עָלֵינוּ וּמַעֲשֵׂה יָדֵינוּ כּוֹנְנֵהוּ:

The Kohanim stand on the pulpit after Modim Derabbanan and say:

יְהִי רָצוֹן מִלְּפָנֶיךָ יְהֹוָה אֱלֹהֵינוּ וֵאלֹהֵי אֲבוֹתֵינוּ שֶׁתְּהְיֶה בְּרָכָה זוֹ שֶׁצִּוִּיתָנוּ לְבָרֵךְ אֶת־עַמְּךָ יִשְׂרָאֵל בְּרָכָה שְׁלֵמָה וְלֹא יִהְיֶה בָהּ מִכְשׁוֹל וְעָוֹן מֵעַתָּה וְעַד עוֹלָם:

Yehi Ratzon Milfaneicha Adonai Eloheinu Velohei Avoteinu Shetihyeh Berachah Zo Shetzivitanu Levarech Et-'Ammecha Yisra'el Berachah Shelemah Velo Yihyeh Vah Michshol Ve'avon Me'attah Ve'ad Olam.

May it be Your Will, Hashem our God, that this blessing which You have commanded us to bless Your people Yisrael with will be a perfect blessing. May there not be in it any stumbling or perverseness from now and forever.

Then they say the blessing. If there is more than one Kohen, the leader calls them, "Kohanim!".

בָּרוּךְ אַתָּה יְהֹוָה אֱלֹהֵינוּ מֶלֶךְ הָעוֹלָם. אֲשֶׁר קִדְּשָׁנוּ בִּקְדֻשָּׁתוֹ שֶׁל־אַהֲרֹן. וְצִוָּנוּ לְבָרֵךְ אֶת־עַמּוֹ יִשְׂרָאֵל בְּאַהֲבָה:

Baruch Attah Adonai Eloheinu Melech Ha'olam Asher Kideshanu Bikdushato Shel-Aharon. Vetzivanu Levarech Et-'Ammo Yisra'el Be'ahavah. Amen.

Blessed are You Hashem our God, King of the universe, Who has sanctified us with the sanctification of Aharon and commanded us to bless His people, Yisrael, with love.

The congregation answers:

אָמֵן:

Amen.

And the Chazan and the Kohanim say after him exactly:

Yevarechecha Adonai Veyishmerecha. יְבָרֶכְךָ יְהֹוָה וְיִשְׁמְרֶךָ:

And answer: Amen **ועונים:** אָמֵן:

Hashem bless you and keep you. **And answer:** Amen

Ya'er Adonai Panav Eleicha Vichuneka. יָאֵר יְהֹוָה | פָּנָיו אֵלֶיךָ וִיחֻנֶּךָּ:

And Answer: Amen **ועונים:** אָמֵן:

Hashem make His countenance shine upon you, and be gracious to you. **And answer:** Amen

Yissa Adonai Panav Eleicha. Veyasem יִשָּׂא יְהֹוָה | פָּנָיו אֵלֶיךָ וְיָשֵׂם

Lecha Shalom. **And answer:** Amen לְךָ שָׁלוֹם: **ועונים:** אָמֵן:

Hashem lift up His countenance towards you and give you peace. **And answer:** Amen

When the Chazan begins the Sim Shalom below, the Kohanim face toward the Ark and say:

רִבּוֹן הָעוֹלָמִים עָשִׂינוּ מַה שֶּׁגָּזַרְתָּ עָלֵינוּ. עֲשֵׂה אַתָּה מַה שֶּׁהִבְטַחְתָּנוּ. הַשְׁקִיפָה מִמְּעוֹן קָדְשְׁךָ מִן־הַשָּׁמַיִם וּבָרֵךְ אֶת־עַמְּךָ אֶת־יִשְׂרָאֵל:

Ribon Ha'olamim Asinu Mah Shegazarta Aleinu. Aseh Attah Mah-Shehivtachetanu. Hashkifah Mime'on Kodshecha Min-Hashamayim. Uvarech Et-'Ammecha Et-Yisra'el.

Sovereign of the universe, We have done what you have decreed for us, you have done as You promised. "Look down from Your holy Habitation, from heaven, and bless Your people Yisrael." **(Deut. 26:15)**

Eloheinu Velohei Avoteinu

If there are no Kohanim, the Chazan recites a substitute blessing:

Eloheinu Velohei Avoteinu. אֱלֹהֵינוּ וֵאלֹהֵי אֲבוֹתֵינוּ.

Barecheinu Baberachah בָּרְכֵנוּ בַּבְּרָכָה

Hamshuleshet Batorah הַמְּשֻׁלֶּשֶׁת בַּתּוֹרָה

Haketuvah Al Yedei Mosheh הַכְּתוּבָה עַל יְדֵי מֹשֶׁה

Avdach. Ha'amurah Mipi עַבְדָּךְ. הָאֲמוּרָה מִפִּי

Aharon Uvanav Hakohanim Im אַהֲרֹן וּבָנָיו הַכֹּהֲנִים עַם

Kedosheicha Ka'amur. קְדוֹשֶׁיךָ כָּאָמוּר:

Our God, God of our fathers, bless us with the threefold blessing written in the Torah by Your servant Moshe, and spoken by the mouth of Aharon and his descendants Your consecrated Kohanim:

Yevarechecha Adonai	יְבָרֶכְךָ יְהֹוָה
Veyishmerecha. **And answer:** Ken	וְיִשְׁמְרֶךָ: **ועונים:** כֵּן
Yehi Ratzon.	יְהִי רָצוֹן:

Hashem bless you and keep you. **And answer:** May this be His will.

Ya'er Adonai Panav Eleicha	יָאֵר יְהֹוָה | פָּנָיו אֵלֶיךָ
Vichuneka. **And answer:** Ken Yehi	וִיחֻנֶּךָּ: **ועונים:** כֵּן יְהִי
Ratzon.	רָצוֹן:

Hashem make His countenance shine upon you, and be gracious to you. **And answer:** May this be His will.

Yissa Adonai Panav Eleicha.	יִשָּׂא יְהֹוָה | פָּנָיו אֵלֶיךָ
Veyasem Lecha Shalom.	וְיָשֵׂם לְךָ שָׁלוֹם:
And answer: Ken Yehi Ratzon.	**ועונים:** כֵּן יְהִי רָצוֹן:

Hashem lift up His countenance towards you and give you peace. **And answer:** May this be His will.

Vesamu Et-Shemi Al-Benei	וְשָׂמוּ אֶת־שְׁמִי עַל־בְּנֵי
Yisra'el; Va'ani Avarechem.	יִשְׂרָאֵל וַאֲנִי אֲבָרְכֵם:

And they will set My name upon the Children of Yisrael, and I will bless them.

Continue with Sim Shalom.

Sim Shalom / Grant Peace

Sim Shalom Tovah Uverachah.	שִׂים שָׁלוֹם טוֹבָה וּבְרָכָה.
Chayim Chein Vachesed	חַיִּים חֵן וָחֶסֶד
Verachamim. Aleinu Ve'al Kol-	וְרַחֲמִים. עָלֵינוּ וְעַל כָּל־
Yisra'el Ammecha. Uvarecheinu	יִשְׂרָאֵל עַמֶּךָ. וּבָרְכֵנוּ
Avinu Kulanu Ke'echad Be'or	אָבִינוּ כֻּלָּנוּ כְּאֶחָד בְּאוֹר
Paneicha. Ki Ve'or Paneicha	פָּנֶיךָ. כִּי בְאוֹר פָּנֶיךָ
Natata Lanu Adonai Eloheinu	נָתַתָּ לָּנוּ יְהֹוָה אֱלֹהֵינוּ
Torah Vechayim. Ahavah	תּוֹרָה וְחַיִּים. אַהֲבָה
Vachesed. Tzedakah	וָחֶסֶד. צְדָקָה
Verachamim. Berachah	וְרַחֲמִים. בְּרָכָה
Veshalom. Vetov Be'eineicha	וְשָׁלוֹם. וְטוֹב בְּעֵינֶיךָ
Levarecheinu Ulevarech Et-	לְבָרְכֵנוּ וּלְבָרֵךְ אֶת־
Kol-'Ammecha Yisra'el. Berov	כָּל־עַמְּךָ יִשְׂרָאֵל. בְּרֹב
Oz Veshalom.	עֹז וְשָׁלוֹם:

Grant peace, goodness and blessing, a life of grace, and kindness and mercy, to us and to all Yisrael, Your people. And bless us, our Father, all as one with the light of Your countenance; for with the light of Your countenance You have given us, Hashem our God, a Torah and life, love and kindness, righteousness and mercy, blessing and peace. May it be good in Your eyes to bless us and bless all of Your people, Yisrael, with abundant strength and peace.

During the 10 days of repentance (Rosh Hashanah to Yom Kippur) say:

Uvesefer Chayim. Berachah Veshalom.	וּבְסֵפֶר חַיִּים. בְּרָכָה וְשָׁלוֹם.
Ufarnasah Tovah Vishu'ah Venechamah.	וּפַרְנָסָה טוֹבָה וִישׁוּעָה וְנֶחָמָה.
Ugezerot Tovot. Nizacher Venikkatev	וּגְזֵרוֹת טוֹבוֹת. נִזָּכֵר וְנִכָּתֵב
Lefaneicha. Anachnu Vechol Ammecha	לְפָנֶיךָ. אֲנַחְנוּ וְכָל עַמְּךָ
Beit Yisra'el. Lechayim Tovim	בֵּית יִשְׂרָאֵל. לְחַיִּים טוֹבִים

Uleshalom.	וּלְשָׁלוֹם.

May we and all Yisrael Your people be remembered and inscribed before You in the book of life and blessing, peace and prosperity, for a happy life and for peace.

Baruch Attah Adonai	בָּרוּךְ אַתָּה יוהוווהו
Hamevarech Et Ammo Yisra'el	הַמְבָרֵךְ אֶת עַמּוֹ יִשְׂרָאֵל
Bashalom. Amen.	בַּשָּׁלוֹם. אָמֵן:

Blessed are You, Hashem, Who blesses His people Yisrael with peace. Amen.

Yihyu Leratzon Imrei-Fi Vehegyon Libi	יִהְיוּ לְרָצוֹן | אִמְרֵי־פִי וְהֶגְיוֹן לִבִּי
Lefaneicha; Adonai Tzuri Vego'ali.	לְפָנֶיךָ יְהֹוָה צוּרִי וְגֹאֲלִי:

May the words of my mouth and the meditation of my heart find favor before You, Hashem my Rock and my Redeemer.

The chazan's repetition ends here; personal / individual continue:

Elohai. Netzor Leshoni Meira	אֱלֹהַי. נְצֹר לְשׁוֹנִי מֵרָע
Vesiftotai Midaber Mirmah.	וְשִׂפְתוֹתַי מִדַּבֵּר מִרְמָה.
Velimkalelai Nafshi Tidom.	וְלִמְקַלְלַי נַפְשִׁי תִדֹּם.
Venafshi Ke'afar Lakol Tihyeh.	וְנַפְשִׁי כֶּעָפָר לַכֹּל תִּהְיֶה.
Petach Libi Betoratecha.	פְּתַח לִבִּי בְּתוֹרָתֶךָ.
Ve'acharei Mitzvoteicha Tirdof	וְאַחֲרֵי מִצְוֹתֶיךָ תִּרְדֹּף
Nafshi. Vechol-Hakamim Alai	נַפְשִׁי. וְכָל־הַקָּמִים עָלַי
Lera'ah. Meheirah Hafer Atzatam	לְרָעָה. מְהֵרָה הָפֵר עֲצָתָם
Vekalkel Machshevotam. Aseh	וְקַלְקֵל מַחְשְׁבוֹתָם. עֲשֵׂה
Lema'an Shemach. Aseh	לְמַעַן שְׁמָךְ. עֲשֵׂה

Lema'an Yeminach. Aseh	לְמַעַן יְמִינָךְ. עֲשֵׂה
Lema'an Toratach. Aseh Lema'an	לְמַעַן תּוֹרָתָךְ. עֲשֵׂה לְמַעַן
Kedushatach. Lema'an	קְדֻשָּׁתָךְ. לְמַעַן
Yechaletzun Yedideicha;	יֵחָלְצוּן יְדִידֶיךָ
Hoshi'ah Yeminecha Va'aneni.	הוֹשִׁיעָה יְמִינְךָ וַעֲנֵנִי:

My God, guard my tongue from evil, and my lips from speaking deceit. And to those who curse me may my soul be silent; and may my soul be like the dust to all. Open my heart to Your Torah, that my soul may follow after Your commandments. And all that rise to do evil against me, speedily nullify their plan, and spoil their thoughts. Do it for the sake of Your name; do it for the sake of Your right hand; do it for the sake of Your Torah, do it for the sake of Your holiness. That Your beloved may be rescued, save with Your right hand and answer me. **(Ps. 60:7)**

Yihyu Leratzon Imrei-Fi Vehegyon Libi	יִהְיוּ לְרָצוֹן | אִמְרֵי־פִי וְהֶגְיוֹן לִבִּי
Lefaneicha; Adonai Tzuri Vego'ali.	לְפָנֶיךָ יְהֹוָה צוּרִי וְגֹאֲלִי:

May the words of my mouth and the meditation of my heart find favor before You, Hashem my Rock and my Redeemer.

Oseh Shalom

One bows and takes three steps backwards, while still bowing. After three steps, while still bowing and before erecting, while saying, "Oseh Shalom Bimromav", turn one's face to the left, "Hu [Berachamav] Ya'aseh Shalom Aleinu", turn one's face to the right; [face forward and] then bow forward like a servant leaving his master. (SA, OC 123:1)

Oseh Shalom **On the 10 Days of**	עוֹשֶׂה שָׁלוֹם
Repentance: (Hashalom) Bimromav, Hu	**בעשי״ת:** (הַשָּׁלוֹם) בִּמְרוֹמָיו. הוּא
Berachamav Ya'aseh Shalom	בְּרַחֲמָיו יַעֲשֶׂה שָׁלוֹם

Aleinu, Ve'al Kol-'Ammo Yisra'el,	עָלֵינוּ. וְעַל כָּל־עַמּוֹ יִשְׂרָאֵל.
Ve'imru Amen.	וְאִמְרוּ אָמֵן:

Creator of **On the 10 Days of Repentance:** (the) peace in His high places, may He in His mercy create peace for us and for all Yisrael, and say Amen.

Yehi Ratzon Milfaneicha Adonai	יְהִי רָצוֹן מִלְּפָנֶיךָ יְהֹוָה
Eloheinu Velohei Avoteinu. Shetivneh	אֱלֹהֵינוּ וֵאלֹהֵי אֲבוֹתֵינוּ. שֶׁתִּבְנֶה
Beit Hamikdash Bimheirah Veyameinu.	בֵּית הַמִּקְדָּשׁ בִּמְהֵרָה בְיָמֵינוּ.
Veten Chelkenu Vetoratach La'asot	וְתֵן חֶלְקֵנוּ בְּתוֹרָתָךְ לַעֲשׂוֹת
Chukkei. Retzonach Ule'avedach	חֻקֵּי רְצוֹנָךְ וּלְעָבְדָךְ
Belevav Shalem.	בְּלֵבָב שָׁלֵם:

May it be Your will, Hashem our God and God of our fathers, that the Beit HaMikdash be speedily rebuilt in our days, and grant us a share in Your Torah so we may fulfill the statutes of your will and serve you with a whole heart.

This is the end of the individual Amidah. Stay standing until the leader's repetition of the Amidah, then take three steps forward. When the leader repeats the prayers, the community must be quiet, and to focus (have intention) on the blessings from the leader and respond "amen". And if there are not nine people with intention for his blessings, this is similar to a blessing in vain. Therefore, each person should make himself as if there are not nine others, and he will have intention for the blessings of the Chazan. On every blessing that a man hears in any place he should say, "Baruch Hu Uvaruch Shemo" (Blessed is He and blessed is His Name.) (SA, OC 124:4)

On Rosh Hodesh, Chol HaMoed and Hanukkah, say Hallel here. On a weekday continue with Tachanun and Vidui.

Avinu Malkeinu / Our Father and King

Said only during the 10 days of repentance (Rosh Hashanah to Yom Kippur), after the Chazan's repetition:

אָבִינוּ מַלְכֵּנוּ חָטָאנוּ לְפָנֶיךָ רַחֵם עָלֵינוּ:

Avinu Malkeinu Chatanu Lefaneicha Rachem Aleinu.

Our Father and King, we have sinned before You, have mercy on us.

אָבִינוּ מַלְכֵּנוּ אֵין לָנוּ מֶלֶךְ אֶלָּא אָתָּה:

Avinu Malkeinu Ein Lanu Melech Ella Attah.

Our Father and King, we have no King but You.

אָבִינוּ מַלְכֵּנוּ עֲשֵׂה עִמָּנוּ לְמַעַן שְׁמֶךָ:

Avinu Malkeinu Aseh Imanu Lema'an Shemecha.

Our Father and King, deal with us for Your Name's sake.

אָבִינוּ מַלְכֵּנוּ חַדֵּשׁ עָלֵינוּ שָׁנָה טוֹבָה:

Avinu Malkeinu Chadesh Aleinu Shanah Tovah.

Our Father and King, bring us a new year of good.

אָבִינוּ מַלְכֵּנוּ בַּטֵּל מֵעָלֵינוּ כָּל־גְּזֵרוֹת קָשׁוֹת וְרָעוֹת:

Avinu Malkeinu Battel Me'aleinu Kol-Gezerot Kashot Vera'ot.

Our Father and King, annul all hurtful and evil decrees against us.

אָבִינוּ מַלְכֵּנוּ בַּטֵּל מַחְשְׁבוֹת שׂוֹנְאֵינוּ:

Avinu Malkeinu Battel Machshevot Sone'einu.

Our Father and King, annul the devices of those who hate us.

אָבִינוּ מַלְכֵּנוּ הָפֵר עֲצַת אוֹיְבֵינוּ:

Avinu Malkeinu Hafer Atzat Oyeveinu.

Our Father and King, bring to nothing the hostile design of our enemies.

אָבִינוּ מַלְכֵּנוּ כַּלֵּה כָּל צַר וּמַשְׂטִין מֵעָלֵינוּ:

Avinu Malkeinu Kaleh Kol Tzar Umastin Me'aleinu.

Our Father and King, ward off from us all pain and accusation from us.

אָבִינוּ מַלְכֵּנוּ כַּלֵּה דֶּבֶר וְחֶרֶב וְרָעָה וְרָעָב וּשְׁבִי וּבִזָּה וּמַשְׁחִית וּמַגֵּפָה וְיֵצֶר הָרָע וְחוֹלָאִים רָעִים מִבְּנֵי בְרִיתֶךָ:

Avinu Malkeinu Kaleh Dever Vecherev Vera'ah Vera'av Ushevi Uvizah Umashchit Umagefah Veyetzer Hara Vechola'im Ra'im Mibenei Veritecha.

Our Father and King, ward off pestilence, sword, famine, captivity, disaster, destruction from the children of Your covenant.

אָבִינוּ מַלְכֵּנוּ שְׁלַח רְפוּאָה שְׁלֵמָה לְכָל חוֹלֵי עַמֶּךָ:

Avinu Malkeinu Shelach Refu'ah Shelemah Lechol Cholei Ammecha.

Our Father and King, restore to perfect health the sick of Your people.

אָבִינוּ מַלְכֵּנוּ מְנַע מַגֵּפָה מִנַּחֲלָתֶךָ:

Avinu Malkeinu Mena Magefah Minachalatecha.

Our Father and King, hold back pestilence from Your heritage.

אָבִינוּ מַלְכֵּנוּ זָכוּר כִּי עָפָר אֲנָחְנוּ:

Avinu Malkeinu Zachur Ki Afar Anach'nu.

Our Father and King, remember that we are but dust.

אָבִינוּ מַלְכֵּנוּ מְחוֹל וּסְלַח לְכָל עֲוֹנוֹתֵינוּ:

Avinu Malkeinu Mechol Uselach Lechol Avonoteinu.

Our Father and King, forgive us and pardon all our sins.

אָבִינוּ מַלְכֵּנוּ קְרַע רוֹעַ גְּזַר דִּינֵנוּ:

Avinu Malkeinu Kera Roa Gezar Dinenu.

Our Father and King, repeal the evil decreed against us.

אָבִינוּ מַלְכֵּנוּ מְחוֹק בְּרַחֲמֶיךָ הָרַבִּים כָּל שִׁטְרֵי חוֹבוֹתֵינוּ:

Avinu Malkeinu Mechok Berachameicha Harabim Kol Shitrei Chovoteinu.

Our Father and King, in Your abundant mercy expunge all record of our guilt.

אָבִינוּ מַלְכֵּנוּ מְחֵה וְהַעֲבֵר פְּשָׁעֵינוּ מִנֶּגֶד עֵינֶיךָ:

Avinu Malkeinu Mecheh Veha'aver Pesha'einu Mineged Eineicha.

Our Father and King, blot out and remove our transgressions from before Your eyes.

אָבִינוּ מַלְכֵּנוּ כָּתְבֵנוּ בְּסֵפֶר חַיִּים טוֹבִים:

Avinu Malkeinu Katevenu Besefer Chayim Tovim.

Our Father and King, inscribe us for good in the Book of Life.

אָבִינוּ מַלְכֵּנוּ כָּתְבֵנוּ בְּסֵפֶר צַדִּיקִים וַחֲסִידִים:

Avinu Malkeinu Katevenu Besefer Tzaddikim Vachasidim.

Our Father and King, inscribe us in the Book of the Righteous and the Pious.

אָבִינוּ מַלְכֵּנוּ כָּתְבֵנוּ בְּסֵפֶר יְשָׁרִים וּתְמִימִים:

Avinu Malkeinu Katevenu Besefer Yesharim Utemimim.

Our Father, Our King, inscribe us in the Book of the Straight and Simple.

אָבִינוּ מַלְכֵּנוּ כָּתְבֵנוּ בְּסֵפֶר פַּרְנָסָה וְכַלְכָּלָה טוֹבָה:

Avinu Malkeinu Katevenu Besefer Parnasah Vechalkalah Tovah.

Our Father, Our King, inscribe us in the Book of Good Income and Sustenance.

אָבִינוּ מַלְכֵּנוּ כָּתְבֵנוּ בְּסֵפֶר מְחִילָה וּסְלִיחָה וְכַפָּרָה:

Avinu Malkeinu Katevenu Besefer Mechilah Uselichah Vechapparah.

Our Father and King, inscribe us in the Book of Pardon and Atonement.

אָבִינוּ מַלְכֵּנוּ כָּתְבֵנוּ בְּסֵפֶר גְּאֻלָּה וִישׁוּעָה:

Avinu Malkeinu Katevenu Besefer Ge'ulah Vishu'ah.

Our Father and King, inscribe us in the Book of Redemption and Deliverance.

אָבִינוּ מַלְכֵּנוּ זָכְרֵנוּ בְּזִכְרוֹן טוֹב מִלְּפָנֶיךָ:

Avinu Malkeinu Zochrenu Bezichron Tov Milfaneicha.

Our Father and King, remember us for good before You.

אָבִינוּ מַלְכֵּנוּ הַצְמַח לָנוּ יְשׁוּעָה בְּקָרוֹב:

Avinu Malkeinu Hatzmach Lanu Yeshu'ah Bekarov.

Our Father and King, make our salvation soon to spring forth.

אָבִינוּ מַלְכֵּנוּ הָרֵם קֶרֶן יִשְׂרָאֵל עַמֶּךָ:

Avinu Malkeinu Harem Keren Yisra'el Ammecha.

Our Father and King, raise up the strength of Your people Yisrael.

אָבִינוּ מַלְכֵּנוּ וְהָרֵם קֶרֶן מְשִׁיחֶךָ:

Avinu Malkeinu Veharem Keren Meshichecha.

Our Father and King, raise up the strength of Your anointed (Messiah).

אָבִינוּ מַלְכֵּנוּ חָנֵּנוּ וַעֲנֵנוּ:

Avinu Malkeinu Chonenu Va'aneinu.

Our Father and King, have grace on us and answer us.

אָבִינוּ מַלְכֵּנוּ הַחֲזִירֵנוּ בִּתְשׁוּבָה שְׁלֵמָה לְפָנֶיךָ:

Avinu Malkeinu Hachazirenu Bitshuvah Shelemah Lefaneicha.

Our Father and King, bring us back through perfect repentance before You.

אָבִינוּ מַלְכֵּנוּ שְׁמַע קוֹלֵנוּ חוּס וְרַחֵם עָלֵינוּ:

Avinu Malkeinu Shema Koleinu Chus Verachem Aleinu.

Our Father and King, hear our voice, take pity on us and be merciful to us.

אָבִינוּ מַלְכֵּנוּ עֲשֵׂה לְמַעַנְךָ אִם לֹא לְמַעֲנֵנוּ:

Avinu Malkeinu Aseh Lema'anach Im Lo Lema'aneinu.

Our Father and King, grant our prayer, if not because of our merit, then for Your own sake.

אָבִינוּ מַלְכֵּנוּ קַבֵּל בְּרַחֲמִים וּבְרָצוֹן אֶת תְּפִלָּתֵנוּ:

Avinu Malkeinu Kabel Berachamim Uveratzon Et Tefillateinu.

Our Father and King, accept our prayer with merciful favor.

אָבִינוּ מַלְכֵּנוּ אַל תְּשִׁיבֵנוּ רֵיקָם מִלְּפָנֶיךָ:

Avinu Malkeinu Al Teshivenu Reikam Milfaneicha.

Our Father and King, turn us not away empty from Your presence.

If there is Tachanun / Supplication is not recited, say Yehi Shem and continue to the Torah Service, if not then proceed to Tachanun Service.

Yehi Shem

Yehi Shem Adonai Mevorach; Me'attah.	יְהִי שֵׁם יְהֹוָה מְבֹרָךְ מֵעַתָּה
Ve'ad-'Olam. Mimizrach-Shemesh Ad-	וְעַד־עוֹלָם: מִמִּזְרַח־שֶׁמֶשׁ עַד־
Mevo'o; Mehulal. Shem Adonai Ram	מְבוֹאוֹ מְהֻלָּל שֵׁם יְהֹוָה: רָם
Al-Chol-Goyim Adonai Al Hashamayim	עַל־כָּל־גּוֹיִם ׀ יְהֹוָה עַל הַשָּׁמַיִם
Kevodo. Adonai Adoneinu; Mah-'Adir	כְּבוֹדוֹ: יְהֹוָה אֲדֹנֵינוּ מָה־אַדִּיר
Shimcha. Bechol-Ha'aretz.	שִׁמְךָ בְּכָל־הָאָרֶץ:

Blessed is the name of Hashem from this time forward and forever. From the rising of the sun to it's going down, Hashem's name is to be praised. Hashem, our Lord, How glorious is Your name in all of the earth. **(Psalms 113:2-4, 8:2)**

Tachanun / Supplication

Tachanun (Supplication) is offered up daily. But none are recited on Shabbatot, Rosh Chodesh (New Moon); Holy Days, and the Moadim (Festivals) of Pesach, Shavuot, Sukkot, Shemini Atzeret and Simchat Torah; the whole month of Nissan; Iyar 14 (Pesach Sheni) and 18 (Lag B'Omer); Sivan 1-12; Av 9 (Tisha B'Av) and 15 (Tu B'Av); the day before Rosh Hashanah; Tishrei 9 to the end of the month; Hanukkah; Shevat 15 - Tu B'Shevat (New Year of Trees); Adar Rishon (1st) and Shevat 14 and 15 (Purim and Shushan Purim), also afternoon on the eve of Shabbat, of Rosh Chodesh, of the Fast of Av, of Hanukkah and of Purim; In Mincha service, it is the day before any of these dates. Also in a house of mourning; when there is a circumcision in the synagogue, or when a bridegroom is in synagogue during the week following his wedding. When Tachanun is not recited, say Yehi Shem (above) and continue to the Torah Reading Section:

Vidui / Confession

Ana Adonai Eloheinu Velohei	אָנָּא יְהֹוָה אֱלֹהֵינוּ וֵאלֹהֵי
Avoteinu. Tavo Lefaneicha	אֲבוֹתֵינוּ. תָּבֹא לְפָנֶיךָ
Tefillateinu. Ve'al Tit'alam	תְּפִלָּתֵנוּ. וְאַל תִּתְעַלַּם
Malkeinu Mitechinateinu.	מַלְכֵּנוּ מִתְּחִנָּתֵנוּ.
She'ein Anachnu Azei Fanim	שֶׁאֵין אֲנַחְנוּ עַזֵּי פָּנִים
Ukeshei Oref Lomar Lefaneicha	וּקְשֵׁי עֹרֶף לוֹמַר לְפָנֶיךָ
Adonai Eloheinu Velohei	יְהֹוָה אֱלֹהֵינוּ וֵאלֹהֵי
Avoteinu Tzaddikim Anachnu	אֲבוֹתֵינוּ צַדִּיקִים אֲנַחְנוּ
Velo-Chatanu. Aval Chatanu.	וְלֹא־חָטָאנוּ. אֲבָל חָטָאנוּ.
Avinu. Pasha'nu. Anachnu	עָוִינוּ. פָּשַׁעְנוּ. אֲנַחְנוּ
Va'avoteinu Ve'anshei Veiteinu.	וַאֲבוֹתֵינוּ וְאַנְשֵׁי בֵיתֵנוּ:

Our God and God of our fathers, may our prayer reach you; do not ignore our plea. For we are neither insolent or obstinate to say to you: "Hashem our God and God of our fathers, we are just and have not sinned." Indeed, we and our fathers have sinned and our household.

Ashamnu. Bagadnu. Gazalnu.	אָשַׁמְנוּ. בָּגַדְנוּ. גָּזַלְנוּ.
Dibarnu Dofi Velashon Hara.	דִּבַּרְנוּ דֹפִי וְלָשׁוֹן הָרָע.
He'evinu. Vehirsha'nu. Zadnu.	הֶעֱוִינוּ. וְהִרְשַׁעְנוּ. זַדְנוּ.
Chamasnu. Tafalnu Sheker	חָמַסְנוּ. טָפַלְנוּ שֶׁקֶר
Umirmah. Ya'atznu Etzot Ra'ot.	וּמִרְמָה. יָעַצְנוּ עֵצוֹת רָעוֹת.
Kizavnu. Ka'asnu. Latznu.	כִּזַּבְנוּ. כָּעַסְנוּ. לַצְנוּ.
Maradnu. Marinu Devareicha.	מָרַדְנוּ. מָרִינוּ דְבָרֶיךָ.
Ni'atznu. Ni'afnu. Sararnu.	נִאַצְנוּ. נִאַפְנוּ. סָרַרְנוּ.
Avinu. Pasha'nu. Pagamnu.	עָוִינוּ. פָּשַׁעְנוּ. פָּגַמְנוּ.
Tzararnu. Tzi'arnu Av Va'em.	צָרַרְנוּ. צִעַרְנוּ אָב וָאֵם.
Kishinu Oref. Rasha'nu.	קִשִּׁינוּ עֹרֶף. רָשַׁעְנוּ.
Shichatnu. Ti'avnu. Ta'inu	שִׁחַתְנוּ. תִּעַבְנוּ. תָּעִינוּ
Veti'ata'nu. Vesarnu	וְתִעְתָּעְנוּ. וְסַרְנוּ
Mimitzvoteicha	מִמִּצְוֹתֶיךָ
Umimishpateicha Hatovim Velo	וּמִמִּשְׁפָּטֶיךָ הַטּוֹבִים וְלֹא
Shavah Lanu. Ve'attah Tzaddik	שָׁוָה לָנוּ. וְאַתָּה צַדִּיק
Al Kol Haba Aleinu. Ki Emet	עַל כָּל הַבָּא עָלֵינוּ. כִּי אֱמֶת
Asita. Va'anachnu Hirsha'enu.	עָשִׂיתָ. וַאֲנַחְנוּ הִרְשָׁעְנוּ:

We have trespassed, we have dealt treacherously, we have robbed, we have spoken slander and evil speech, we have committed iniquity, and have done wickedly; we have acted presumptuously, we have committed violence, we have forged falsehood and deceived, we have counseled evil, we have uttered lies, we were angry, we have scoffed, we have rebelled and violated Your words, we have blasphemed, we have committed adultery, we have revolted, we have acted perversely, we have transgressed, we have broken faith, we have been hard and we have distressed father and mother. we have been stiff-necked, we have acted wickedly, we have corrupted, we have done abominably; we have gone astray ourselves, and have caused others to stray; we have also turned aside from Your good precepts and commandments, and it has not profited us; "But You are just concerning all that is come upon us; for You have dealt most truly, but we have done wickedly." **(Nehemiah 9:33)**

The Thirteen Attributes

One, praying alone should not say the Thirteen Attributes in a manner like prayer, petitioning for mercy, because they are words of holiness [and requires a minyan (10 men)]. However, if he says them by merely reading them, he may say them. (SA, OC 565) Ideally one should read with cantillation like from the Torah.

El Erech Apayim Attah Uva'al	אֵל אֶרֶךְ אַפַּיִם אַתָּה וּבַעַל
Harachamim. Gedulat	הָרַחֲמִים. גְּדֻלַּת
Rachameicha Vachasadeicha	רַחֲמֶיךָ וַחֲסָדֶיךָ
Hoda'ta Le'anav Mikedem.	הוֹדַעְתָּ לֶעָנָו מִקֶּדֶם.
Vechein Katuv Betoratach.	וְכֵן כָּתוּב בְּתוֹרָתָךְ.
Vayered Adonai Be'anan.	וַיֵּרֶד יְהֹוָה בֶּעָנָן
Vayityatzev Imo Sham; Vayikra	וַיִּתְיַצֵּב עִמּוֹ שָׁם וַיִּקְרָא
Veshem Adonai. Vesham	בְשֵׁם יְהֹוָה׃ וְשָׁם
Ne'emar:	נֶאֱמַר׃

God, you are slow to anger, and a Master of mercy. Be ever mindful of Your abundant mercy and kindness toward the descendants of Your beloved, as You revealed to humble Moshe of old. As it is written in Your Torah: "And Hashem descended in the cloud, and stood with him there, and proclaimed the name of Hashem." **(Exodus 34:5)** And there it says:

[*] denotes a slight pause between words:

וַיַּעֲבֹר יְהֹוָה | עַל־פָּנָיו וַיִּקְרָא יְהֹוָה *יְהֹוָה אֵל רַחוּם וְחַנּוּן אֶרֶךְ אַפַּיִם
וְרַב־חֶסֶד וֶאֱמֶת: נֹצֵר חֶסֶד לָאֲלָפִים נֹשֵׂא עָוֹן וָפֶשַׁע וְחַטָּאָה וְנַקֵּה:

Vaya'avor Adonai 'Al-Panav Vayikra Adonai * Adonai El Rachum Vechanun; Erech Apayim Verav-Chesed Ve'emet. Notzer Chesed La'alafim. Nosei Avon Vafesha Vechata'ah; Venakeh.

And Hashem passed by before him, and proclaimed: 'Hashem * Hashem, God, merciful and gracious, long-suffering, and abundant in goodness and truth; keeping mercy to the thousandth generation, forgiving iniquity and transgression and sin, and clearing (those who repent).

Rachum Vechanun Chatanu	רַחוּם וְחַנּוּן חָטָאנוּ
Lefaneicha Rachem Aleinu	לְפָנֶיךָ רַחֵם עָלֵינוּ
Vehoshi'enu.	וְהוֹשִׁיעֵנוּ:

Merciful and gracious One, we have sinned before You; have mercy upon us and save us.

Psalms 25

(say while seated)

לְדָוִד אֵלֶיךָ יְהֹוָה נַפְשִׁי אֶשָּׂא: אֱלֹהַי בְּךָ בָטַחְתִּי אַל־אֵבוֹשָׁה
אַל־יַעַלְצוּ אוֹיְבַי לִי: גַּם כָּל־קֹוֶיךָ לֹא יֵבֹשׁוּ יֵבֹשׁוּ הַבּוֹגְדִים רֵיקָם:
דְּרָכֶיךָ יְהֹוָה הוֹדִיעֵנִי אֹרְחוֹתֶיךָ לַמְּדֵנִי: הַדְרִיכֵנִי בַאֲמִתֶּךָ | וְלַמְּדֵנִי
כִּי־אַתָּה אֱלֹהֵי יִשְׁעִי אוֹתְךָ קִוִּיתִי כָּל־הַיּוֹם: זְכֹר־רַחֲמֶיךָ יְהֹוָה
וַחֲסָדֶיךָ כִּי מֵעוֹלָם הֵמָּה: חַטֹּאות נְעוּרַי | וּפְשָׁעַי אַל־תִּזְכֹּר כְּחַסְדְּךָ
זְכָר־לִי־אַתָּה לְמַעַן טוּבְךָ יְהֹוָה: טוֹב־וְיָשָׁר יְהֹוָה עַל־כֵּן יוֹרֶה
חַטָּאִים בַּדָּרֶךְ: יַדְרֵךְ עֲנָוִים בַּמִּשְׁפָּט וִילַמֵּד עֲנָוִים דַּרְכּוֹ: כָּל־אָרְחוֹת
יְהֹוָה חֶסֶד וֶאֱמֶת לְנֹצְרֵי בְרִיתוֹ וְעֵדֹתָיו: לְמַעַן־שִׁמְךָ יְהֹוָה וְסָלַחְתָּ
לַעֲוֹנִי כִּי רַב־הוּא: מִי־זֶה הָאִישׁ יְרֵא יְהֹוָה יוֹרֶנּוּ בְּדֶרֶךְ יִבְחָר: נַפְשׁוֹ

בְּטוֹב תָּלִין וְזַרְעוֹ יִירַשׁ אָרֶץ: סוֹד יְהֹוָה לִירֵאָיו וּבְרִיתוֹ לְהוֹדִיעָם: עֵינַי תָּמִיד אֶל־יְהֹוָה כִּי הוּא־יוֹצִיא מֵרֶשֶׁת רַגְלָי: פְּנֵה־אֵלַי וְחָנֵּנִי כִּי־יָחִיד וְעָנִי אָנִי: צָרוֹת לְבָבִי הִרְחִיבוּ מִמְּצוּקוֹתַי הוֹצִיאֵנִי: רְאֵה עָנְיִי וַעֲמָלִי וְשָׂא לְכָל־חַטֹּאותָי: רְאֵה־אוֹיְבַי כִּי־רָבּוּ וְשִׂנְאַת חָמָס שְׂנֵאוּנִי: שָׁמְרָה נַפְשִׁי וְהַצִּילֵנִי אַל־אֵבוֹשׁ כִּי־חָסִיתִי בָךְ: תֹּם־וָיֹשֶׁר יִצְּרוּנִי כִּי קִוִּיתִיךָ: פְּדֵה אֱלֹהִים אֶת־יִשְׂרָאֵל מִכֹּל צָרוֹתָיו:

וְהוּא יִפְדֶּה אֶת־יִשְׂרָאֵל מִכֹּל עֲוֹנֹתָיו:

Ledavid Eleicha Adonai Nafshi Essa. Elohai. Becha Vatachti Al-'Evoshah; Al-Ya'altzu Oyevai Li. Gam Kol-Koveicha Lo Yevoshu; Yevoshu. Habogedim Reikam. Deracheicha Adonai Hodi'eni; Orechoteicha Lamedeni. Hadricheini Va'amitecha Velamedeni. Ki-'Attah Elohei Yish'i; Otecha Kiviti. Chol-Hayom. Zechor-Rachameicha Adonai Vachasadeicha; Ki Me'olam Hemah. Chatovt Ne'urai Ufesha'ai. Al-Tizkor Kechasdecha Zechor-Li-'Attah; Lema'an Tuvecha Adonai Tov-Veyashar Adonai Al-Ken Yoreh Chata'im Baddarech. Yadrech Anavim Bammishpat; Vilamed Anavim Darko. Chol-'Orchot Adonai Chesed Ve'emet; Lenotzerei Verito. Ve'edotav. Lema'an-Shimcha Adonai Vesalachta La'avoni. Ki Rav-Hu. Mi-Zeh Ha'ish Yerei Adonai Yorenu. Bederech Yivchar. Nafsho Betov Talin; Vezar'o. Yirash Aretz. Sod Adonai Lire'av; Uverito. Lehodi'am. Einai Tamid El-Adonai Ki Hu-Yotzi Mereshet Raglai. Peneh-'Elai Vechoneni; Ki-Yachid Ve'ani Ani. Tzarot Levavi Hirchivu; Mimetzukotai. Hotzi'eni. Re'eh Onyi Va'amali; Vesa. Lechol-Chatovtai. Re'eh-'Oyevai Ki-Rabbu; Vesin'at Chamas Sene'uni. Shomrah Nafshi Vehatzileini; Al-'Evosh. Ki-Chasiti Vach. Tom-Vayosher Yitzeruni; Ki. Kiviticha. Pedeh Elohim Et-Yisra'el; Mikol Tzarotav.

Vehu Yifdeh Et-Yisra'el; Mikol Avonotav:

A Psalm of David. To You, Hashem, do I lift up my soul. Oh my God, in You have I trusted, do not let me be ashamed; do not let my enemies triumph over me. None that wait for You will be ashamed; they will be ashamed that deal treacherously without cause. Show me Your ways, Hashem; teach me Your paths. Guide me in Your truth, and teach me; for You are the God of my salvation; for You do I wait all day. Remember, Hashem, Your compassions and Your mercies; for they have been from of old. Do not remember the sins of my youth, or my transgressions; according to Your mercy remember me, for Your goodness' sake, Hashem. Good and upright is Hashem; therefore He instructs sinners in the way. He guides The humble in justice; and He teaches the humble His way. All the paths of Hashem are mercy and truth to such as keep His covenant and His testimonies. For Your name's sake, Hashem, pardon my iniquity, for it is great. What man is he that fears Hashem? He will instruct him in the way that He should choose. His soul will abide in prosperity; and his seed will inherit the land. The counsel of Hashem is with them that fear Him; and His covenant, to make them know it. My eyes are ever toward Hashem; for He will bring my feet out of the net. Turn to me, and be gracious to me; for I am solitary and afflicted. The troubles of my heart are enlarged; Bring me out of my distresses. See my affliction and my travail; and forgive all my sins. Consider how many are my enemies, and the cruel hatred that they hate me. Keep my soul, and deliver me; let me not be ashamed, for I have taken refuge in You. Let integrity and uprightness preserve me, because I wait for You. Redeem Yisrael, Oh God, out of all his troubles.

And He will redeem Yisrael from all of his troubles. **(Ps. 130:8)**

Mondays and Thursdays, read this section. All other days, some continue to "Yehi Shem", others to Hatzi-Kaddish before the Torah Reading.

יְהֹוָה אֱלֹהֵי יִשְׂרָאֵל שׁוּב מֵחֲרוֹן אַפֶּךָ. וְהִנָּחֵם עַל הָרָעָה לְעַמֶּךָ:

Adonai Elohei Yisra'el Shuv Mecharon Apecha. Vehinachem Al Hara'ah Le'ammecha.

Hashem, God of Yisrael, turn from Your fierce wrath, and repent of this evil against Your people. **(Exodus 32:12)**

אָבִינוּ מַלְכֵּנוּ. אָבִינוּ אָתָּה. אָבִינוּ מַלְכֵּנוּ אֵין לָנוּ

מֶלֶךְ אֶלָּא אָתָּה. אָבִינוּ
מַלְכֵּנוּ רַחֵם עָלֵינוּ: אָבִינוּ
מַלְכֵּנוּ חָנֵּנוּ וַעֲנֵנוּ כִּי
אֵין בָּנוּ מַעֲשִׂים. עֲשֵׂה עִמָּנוּ
צְדָקָה וָחֶסֶד לְמַעַן
שִׁמְךָ הַגָּדוֹל וְהוֹשִׁיעֵנוּ:
וַאֲנַחְנוּ לֹא נֵדַע מַה־
נַּעֲשֶׂה כִּי עָלֶיךָ עֵינֵינוּ:

Avinu Malkeinu. Avinu Attah.
Avinu Malkeinu Ein Lanu
Melech Ella Attah. Avinu
Malkeinu Rachem Aleinu. Avinu
Malkeinu Chonenu Va'aneinu Ki
Ein Banu Ma'asim. Aseh Imanu
Tzedakah Vachesed Lema'an
Shimcha Hagadol Vehoshi'enu.
Va'anachnu. Lo Neda Mah-
Na'aseh. Ki Aleicha Eineinu.

Our Father and King, You are our Father.
Our Father and King, we have no other sovereign but You.
Our Father and King, have compassion on us.
Our Father and King, be gracious us and answer us.
Though we are lacking in good works, act charitably and graciously with us and save us, for the sake of Your great name. As for us, we do not know what to do, but our eyes are upon You.

זְכֹר־רַחֲמֶיךָ יְהֹוָה וַחֲסָדֶיךָ כִּי מֵעוֹלָם הֵמָּה: יְהִי־חַסְדְּךָ יְהֹוָה עָלֵינוּ כַּאֲשֶׁר יִחַלְנוּ לָךְ: אַל־תִּזְכָּר־לָנוּ עֲוֹנֹת רִאשֹׁנִים מַהֵר יְקַדְּמוּנוּ רַחֲמֶיךָ כִּי דַלּוֹנוּ מְאֹד: עֶזְרֵנוּ בְּשֵׁם יְהֹוָה עֹשֵׂה שָׁמַיִם וָאָרֶץ: חָנֵּנוּ יְהֹוָה חָנֵּנוּ כִּי־רַב שָׂבַעְנוּ בוּז: בְּרֹגֶז רַחֵם תִּזְכּוֹר. בְּרֹגֶז אַהֲבָה תִּזְכּוֹר. בְּרֹגֶז עֲקֵדָה תִּזְכּוֹר. בְּרֹגֶז תְּמִימוּת תִּזְכּוֹר: יְהֹוָה הוֹשִׁיעָה הַמֶּלֶךְ יַעֲנֵנוּ בְיוֹם־קָרְאֵנוּ: כִּי־הוּא יָדַע יִצְרֵנוּ זָכוּר כִּי־עָפָר אֲנָחְנוּ:
עָזְרֵנוּ | אֱלֹהֵי יִשְׁעֵנוּ עַל־דְּבַר כְּבוֹד־שְׁמֶךָ וְהַצִּילֵנוּ וְכַפֵּר עַל־חַטֹּאתֵינוּ לְמַעַן שְׁמֶךָ:

Zechor-Rachameicha Adonai Vachasadeicha; Ki Me'olam Hemah. Yehi-Chasdecha Adonai Aleinu; Ka'asher. Yichalnu Lach. Al-Tizkor-Lanu Avonot Rishonim Maher Yekademunu Rachameicha; Ki Dallonu Me'od. Ezrenu Beshem Adonai Oseh. Shamayim Va'aretz.

Chonenu Adonai Chonenu; Ki-Rav Sava'nu Vuz. Berogez Rachem Tizkor. Berogez Ahavah Tizkor. Berogez Akedah Tizkor. Berogez Temimut Tizkor. Adonai Hoshi'ah; Hamelech. Ya'aneinu Veyom-Kor'enu. Ki-Hu Yada Yitzrenu; Zachur. Ki-'Afar Anachenu. **Ozrenu Elohei Yish'enu. Al-Devar Kevod-Shemecha; Vehatzileinu Vechapeir Al-Chatoteinu. Lema'an Shemecha.**

"Remember, Hashem, Your tender mercies and Your loving-kindnesses: for they have been of old. Let Your loving-kindness, Hashem, be upon us, for our hope is in You. Do not remember against us the iniquities of our ancestors: let Your tender mercies speedily come to meet us; for we are brought very low. Our help is in the name of Hashem, Who made heaven and earth. Be gracious to us; Hashem be gracious to us; for we are fully sated with contempt. In wrath remember to be merciful. For He knows our frame; He remembers that we are dust. **Help us, God of our salvation, for the sake of the glory of Your name; and deliver us, and pardon our sins, for Your name's sake.** (Ps. 25:6, 33:22, 79:8, 124:8, 123:3, Hab. 3:2, Ps. 20:10, 103:14)

On Communal Fast Days, say selichot in the Order of the Four Fast Days section.

El Melech Yoshev Al Kissei	אֵל מֶלֶךְ יוֹשֵׁב עַל כִּסֵּא
Rachamim Umitnaheg	רַחֲמִים וּמִתְנַהֵג
Bachasidut. Mochel Avonot	בַּחֲסִידוּת. מוֹחֵל עֲוֹנוֹת
Ammo. Ma'avir Rishon Rishon.	עַמּוֹ. מַעֲבִיר רִאשׁוֹן רִאשׁוֹן.
Marbeh Mechilah Lachata'im.	מַרְבֶּה מְחִילָה לַחַטָּאִים.
Uselichah Lapposhe'im. Oseh	וּסְלִיחָה לַפּוֹשְׁעִים. עוֹשֶׂה
Tzedakot Im Kol Basar Veruach.	צְדָקוֹת עִם כָּל בָּשָׂר וְרוּחַ.
Lo Chera'atam Lahem Gomel. El.	לֹא כְרָעָתָם לָהֶם גּוֹמֵל. אֵל.
Horetanu Lomar Middot Shelosh	הוֹרֵתָנוּ לוֹמַר מִדּוֹת שְׁלֹשׁ

Esreh. Zechor Lanu Hayom Berit	עֶשְׂרֵה. זְכוֹר לָנוּ הַיּוֹם בְּרִית
Shelosh Esreh Kemo Shehoda'ta	שְׁלֹשׁ עֶשְׂרֵה כְּמוֹ שֶׁהוֹדַעְתָּ
Le'anav Mikedem. Vechein Katuv	לֶעָנָו מִקֶּדֶם. וְכֵן כָּתוּב
Betoratach Vayered Adonai	בְּתוֹרָתָךְ וַיֵּרֶד יְהֹוָה
Be'anan. Vayityatzev Imo Sham;	בֶּעָנָן וַיִּתְיַצֵּב עִמּוֹ שָׁם
Vayikra Veshem Adonai. Vesham	וַיִּקְרָא בְשֵׁם יְהֹוָה: וְשָׁם
Ne'emar:	נֶאֱמַר:

Sovereign God, enthroned in mercy, You deal with us tenderly, again pardoning the sins of Your people even though they sin again. You are ever ready to give pardon to sinners and forgiveness to transgressors, acting in charity towards all with breath of life, not requiting them according to the evil they do. You, God, Who has taught us to repeat the thirteen attributes of mercy, remember to us this day the covenant of those attributes, as You did reveal them of old to Moshe the humble, in the words written in Your Torah: "And Hashem descended in the cloud, and stood with him there, and proclaimed the name of Hashem." **(Exodus 34:5)** And there it says:

[*] denotes a slight pause between words:

וַיַּעֲבֹר יְהֹוָה | עַל־פָּנָיו וַיִּקְרָא יְהֹוָה * יְהֹוָה אֵל רַחוּם וְחַנּוּן אֶרֶךְ אַפַּיִם
וְרַב־חֶסֶד וֶאֱמֶת: נֹצֵר חֶסֶד לָאֲלָפִים נֹשֵׂא עָוֹן וָפֶשַׁע וְחַטָּאָה וְנַקֵּה:

Vaya'avor Adonai 'Al-Panav Vayikra Adonai * Adonai El Rachum Vechanun; Erech Apayim Verav-Chesed Ve'emet. Notzer Chesed La'alafim. Nosei Avon Vafesha Vechata'ah; Venakeh.

And Hashem passed by before him, and proclaimed: 'Hashem * Hashem, God, merciful and gracious, long-suffering, and abundant in goodness and truth; keeping mercy to the thousandth generation, forgiving iniquity and transgression and sin, and clearing (those who repent).

Anshei Emunah Avadu. Ba'im	אַנְשֵׁי אֱמוּנָה אָבָדוּ. בָּאִים
Bechoach Ma'aseihem. Giborim	בְּכֹחַ מַעֲשֵׂיהֶם: גִּבּוֹרִים
La'amod Baperetz. Dochim Et	לַעֲמֹד בַּפֶּרֶץ. דּוֹחִים אֶת
Hagezerot. Hayu Lanu	הַגְּזֵרוֹת: הָיוּ לָנוּ
Lechomah. Ulemachseh Beyom	לְחוֹמָה. וּלְמַחְסֶה בְּיוֹם
Za'am. Zo'achim Af	זָעַם: זוֹעֲכִים אַף
Belachasham. Chemah Atzeru	בְּלַחֲשָׁם. חֵמָה עָצְרוּ
Beshav'am. Terem Kera'ucha	בְּשַׁוְעָם: טֶרֶם קְרָאוּךָ
Anitam. Yode'im La'ator	עֲנִיתָם. יוֹדְעִים לַעְתֹּר
Uleratzot. Ke'av Richamta	וּלְרַצּוֹת: כְּאָב רִחַמְתָּ
Lema'anam. Lo Heshivota	לְמַעֲנָם. לֹא הֱשִׁיבוֹתָ
Feneihem Reikam. Merov	פְּנֵיהֶם רֵיקָם: מֵרֹב
Avoneinu Avadnum. Ne'esfu	עֲוֹנֵינוּ אֲבַדְנוּם. נֶאֶסְפוּ
Menu Bachata'einu. Sa'u	מֶנּוּ בַּחֲטָאֵינוּ: סָעוּ
Hemah Limnuchot. Azevu	הֵמָּה לִמְנוּחוֹת. עָזְבוּ
Otanu La'anachot. Passu	אוֹתָנוּ לַאֲנָחוֹת: פַּסּוּ
Goderei Gader. Tzummetu	גּוֹדְרֵי גָדֵר. צֻמְּתוּ
Meshivei Chemah. Kamim	מְשִׁיבֵי חֵמָה: קָמִים
Baperetz Ayin. Re'uyim	בַּפֶּרֶץ אַיִן. רְאוּיִים
Leratzonecha Afesu. Shotatnu	לְרַצּוֹתְךָ אָפֵסוּ: שׁוֹטַטְנוּ
Be'arba Pinot. Terufah Lo	בְּאַרְבַּע פִּנּוֹת. תְּרוּפָה לֹא
Matzanu. Shavnu Eleicha	מָצָאנוּ: שַׁבְנוּ אֵלֶיךָ
Bvoshet Paneinu. Leshacharach	בְּבֹשֶׁת פָּנֵינוּ. לְשַׁחֲרָךְ
El Be'et Tzaroteinu.	אֵל בְּעֵת צָרוֹתֵינוּ:

The men of faith are gone who marched in the strength of their deeds, Mighty to stand in the breach. And ward off evil decrees. A wall they were to us, A refuge in time of wrath, Appeasing Your anger by prayer, Restraining Your anger by entreaty. Before they called You did answer, For they knew how to pray and appease. For their sake, merciful Father, You did not send them empty away. For our sins that are great, we have lost them. They are taken from us for our wrongdoing. They have gone to eternal rest, And left us, to sorrow. They who built up the fence are no more; They who could avert anger are perished. There are none left to stand in the breach; Those fit to appease You are gone. We have wandered four corners of earth, But we have found relief nowhere. Shamefaced we come back to You to seek You in time of distress.

El Melech Yoshev Al Kissei	אֵל מֶלֶךְ יוֹשֵׁב עַל כִּסֵּא
Rachamim Umitnaheg	רַחֲמִים וּמִתְנַהֵג
Bachasidut. Mochel Avonot	בַּחֲסִידוּת. מוֹחֵל עֲוֹנוֹת
Ammo. Ma'avir Rishon Rishon.	עַמּוֹ. מַעֲבִיר רִאשׁוֹן רִאשׁוֹן.
Marbeh Mechilah Lachata'im.	מַרְבֶּה מְחִילָה לַחַטָּאִים.
Uselichah Lapposhe'im. Oseh	וּסְלִיחָה לַפּוֹשְׁעִים. עוֹשֶׂה
Tzedakot Im Kol Basar Veruach.	צְדָקוֹת עִם כָּל בָּשָׂר וְרוּחַ.
Lo Chera'atam Lahem Gomel. El.	לֹא כְרָעָתָם לָהֶם גּוֹמֵל. אֵל.
Horetanu Lomar Middot Shelosh	הוֹרֵתָנוּ לוֹמַר מִדּוֹת שְׁלֹשׁ
Esreh. Zechor Lanu Hayom Berit	עֶשְׂרֵה. זְכוֹר לָנוּ הַיּוֹם בְּרִית
Shelosh Esreh Kemo Shehoda'ta	שְׁלֹשׁ עֶשְׂרֵה כְּמוֹ שֶׁהוֹדַעְתָּ
Le'anav Mikedem. Vechein Katuv	לֶעָנָו מִקֶּדֶם. וְכֵן כָּתוּב
Betoratach Vayered Adonai	בְּתוֹרָתָךְ וַיֵּרֶד יְהֹוָה
Be'anan. Vayityatzev Imo Sham;	בֶּעָנָן וַיִּתְיַצֵּב עִמּוֹ שָׁם
Vayikra Veshem Adonai. Vesham	וַיִּקְרָא בְשֵׁם יְהֹוָה: וְשָׁם
Ne'emar:	נֶאֱמַר:

Sovereign God, enthroned in mercy, You deal with us tenderly, again pardoning the sins of Your people even though they sin again. You are ever ready to give pardon to sinners and forgiveness to transgressors, acting in charity towards all with breath of life, not requiting them according to the evil they do. You, God, Who has taught us to repeat the thirteen attributes of mercy, remember to us this day the covenant of those attributes, as You did reveal them of old to Moshe the humble, in the words written in Your Torah: "And Hashem descended in the cloud, and stood with him there, and proclaimed the name of Hashem." **(Exodus 34:5)** And there it says:

[*] denotes a slight pause between words:

וַיַּעֲבֹר יְהֹוָה | עַל־פָּנָיו וַיִּקְרָא יְהֹוָה * יְהֹוָה אֵל רַחוּם וְחַנּוּן אֶרֶךְ אַפַּיִם וְרַב־חֶסֶד וֶאֱמֶת׃ נֹצֵר חֶסֶד לָאֲלָפִים נֹשֵׂא עָוֺן וָפֶשַׁע וְחַטָּאָה וְנַקֵּה׃

Vaya'avor Adonai 'Al-Panav Vayikra Adonai * Adonai El Rachum Vechanun; Erech Apayim Verav-Chesed Ve'emet. Notzer Chesed La'alafim. Nosei Avon Vafesha Vechata'ah; Venakeh.

And Hashem passed by before him, and proclaimed: 'Hashem * Hashem, God, merciful and gracious, long-suffering, and abundant in goodness and truth; keeping mercy to the thousandth generation, forgiving iniquity and transgression and sin, and clearing (those who repent).

Some only recite on Thursdays:

Tamahnu Mera'ot. Tashash	תָּמַהְנוּ מֵרָעוֹת. תָּשַׁשׁ
Kocheinu Mitzarot. Shachnu Ad	כֹּחֵנוּ מִצָּרוֹת. שַׁחְנוּ עַד
Lim'od. Shafalnu Ad Afar.	לִמְאֹד. שָׁפַלְנוּ עַד עָפָר.
Rachum Kach Hi Midateinu.	רַחוּם כָּךְ הִיא מִדָּתֵנוּ.
Keshei Oref Umamrim	קְשֵׁי עֹרֶף וּמַמְרִים

Anachenu. Tza'aknu Befinu	אֲנָחְנוּ. צָעַקְנוּ בְּפִינוּ
Chatanu. Petaltol Ve'ikesh	חָטָאנוּ. פְּתַלְתּוֹל וְעִקֵּשׁ
Libenu. Elyon. Rachameicha	לִבֵּנוּ. עֶלְיוֹן. רַחֲמֶיךָ
Me'olam. Selichah Imecha Hi.	מֵעוֹלָם. סְלִיחָה עִמְּךָ הִיא.
Nicham Al Hara'ah. Mateh	נִחָם עַל הָרָעָה. מַטֶּה
Kelappei Chesed. Lo Tit'alam	כְלַפֵּי חֶסֶד. לֹא תִתְעַלָּם
Be'itot Ka'el. Ki Botzrah Gedolah	בְּעִתּוֹת כָּאֵל. כִּי בְצָרָה גְדוֹלָה
Anachenu. Yivada Le'einei	אֲנָחְנוּ. יִוָּדַע לְעֵינֵי
Hakol. Tuvecha Vechasdecha	הַכֹּל. טוּבְךָ וְחַסְדְּךָ
Imanu. Chatom Peh-Satan. Ve'al	עִמָּנוּ. חֲתֹם פֶּה-שָׂטָן. וְאַל
Yastin Aleinu. Ze'om Bo	יַשְׂטִין עָלֵינוּ. זְעֹם בּוֹ
Veyidom. Veya'amod Melitz Tov	וְיִדֹּם. וְיַעֲמֹד מֵלִיץ טוֹב
Letzaddekenu. Hu Yagid	לְצַדְּקֵנוּ. הוּא יַגִּיד
Yasherenu. Deracheicha Rachum	יָשְׁרֵנוּ. דְּרָכֶיךָ רַחוּם
Vechanun Gillita Lene'eman	וְחַנּוּן גִּלִּיתָ לְנֶאֱמַן
Bayit. Bevaksho Az Milfaneicha.	בָּיִת. בְּבַקְשׁוֹ אָז מִלְּפָנֶיךָ.

Stunned by our woes. Weakened by sorrows, we are brought very low and are humbled to the dust. O merciful One, We may be stiff-necked and rebellious, Such is our nature; Our mouths may declare “we have sinned,” Our hearts are hard and perverse, yet You, Supremely Exalted, are merciful from old, And pardon is always with You. Repenting of evil And inclining to mercy, do not hide Yourself in times like these, For we are sorely troubled. Make known to all That Your goodness and love are still with us. Seal the mouth of the accuser that he cannot indict us; Rebuke him that is silent. Let a good spokesman arise to declare our uprightness and absolve us. Merciful, gracious God, to Moshe, faithful in all Your House, You have revealed Your ways at his request to You, And You made him know Your truth.

El Melech Yoshev Al Kissei	אֵל מֶלֶךְ יוֹשֵׁב עַל כִּסֵּא
Rachamim Umitnaheg	רַחֲמִים וּמִתְנַהֵג
Bachasidut. Mochel Avonot	בַּחֲסִידוּת. מוֹחֵל עֲוֹנוֹת
Ammo. Ma'avir Rishon Rishon.	עַמּוֹ. מַעֲבִיר רִאשׁוֹן רִאשׁוֹן.
Marbeh Mechilah Lachata'im.	מַרְבֶּה מְחִילָה לַחַטָּאִים.
Uselichah Lapposhe'im. Oseh	וּסְלִיחָה לַפּוֹשְׁעִים. עוֹשֶׂה
Tzedakot Im Kol Basar Veruach.	צְדָקוֹת עִם כָּל בָּשָׂר וְרוּחַ.
Lo Chera'atam Lahem Gomel.	לֹא כְרָעָתָם לָהֶם גּוֹמֵל.
El. Horetanu Lomar Middot	אֵל. הוֹרֵתָנוּ לוֹמַר מִדּוֹת
Shelosh Esreh. Zechor Lanu	שְׁלֹשׁ עֶשְׂרֵה. זְכוֹר לָנוּ
Hayom Berit Shelosh Esreh	הַיּוֹם בְּרִית שְׁלֹשׁ עֶשְׂרֵה
Kemo Shehoda'ta Le'anav	כְּמוֹ שֶׁהוֹדַעְתָּ לֶעָנָו
Mikedem. Vechein Katuv	מִקֶּדֶם. וְכֵן כָּתוּב
Betoratach Vayered Adonai	בְּתוֹרָתָךְ וַיֵּרֶד יְהוָה
Be'anan. Vayityatzev Imo Sham;	בֶּעָנָן וַיִּתְיַצֵּב עִמּוֹ שָׁם
Vayikra Veshem Adonai. Vesham	וַיִּקְרָא בְשֵׁם יְהוָה: וְשָׁם
Ne'emar.	נֶאֱמַר:

Sovereign God, enthroned in mercy, You deal with us tenderly, again pardoning the sins of Your people even though they sin again. You are ever ready to give pardon to sinners and forgiveness to transgressors, acting in charity towards all with breath of life, not requiting them according to the evil they do. You, God, Who has taught us to repeat the thirteen attributes of mercy, remember to us this day the covenant of those attributes, as You did reveal them of old to Moshe the humble, in the words written in Your Torah: "And Hashem descended in the cloud, and stood with him there, and proclaimed the name of Hashem." **(Exodus 34:5)** And there it says:

[*] denotes a slight pause between words:

וַיַּעֲבֹר יְהֹוָה | עַל־פָּנָיו וַיִּקְרָא יְהֹוָה * יְהֹוָה אֵל רַחוּם וְחַנּוּן אֶרֶךְ אַפַּיִם וְרַב־חֶסֶד וֶאֱמֶת: נֹצֵר חֶסֶד לָאֲלָפִים נֹשֵׂא עָוֹן וָפֶשַׁע וְחַטָּאָה וְנַקֵּה:

Vaya'avor Adonai 'Al-Panav Vayikra Adonai * Adonai El Rachum Vechanun; Erech Apayim Verav-Chesed Ve'emet. Notzer Chesed La'alafim. Nosei Avon Vafesha Vechata'ah; Venakeh.

And Hashem passed by before him, and proclaimed: 'Hashem * Hashem, God, merciful and gracious, long-suffering, and abundant in goodness and truth; keeping mercy to the thousandth generation, forgiving iniquity and transgression and sin, and clearing (those who repent).

Eloheinu Velohei Avoteinu. Al	אֱלֹהֵינוּ וֵאלֹהֵי אֲבוֹתֵינוּ. אַל
Ta'as Imanu Kalah. Tochez	תַּעַשׂ עִמָּנוּ כָּלָה. תֹּאחֵז
Yadecha Bammishpat. Bevo	יָדְךָ בַּמִּשְׁפָּט. בְּבֹא
Tochechah Negdecha. Shemenu	תוֹכֵחָה נֶגְדֶּךָ. שְׁמֵנוּ
Missifrecha Al Temach.	מִסִּפְרְךָ אַל תֶּמַח.
Gishtecha Lachakor Musar.	גִּשְׁתְּךָ לַחֲקֹר מוּסָר.
Rachameicha Kademu	רַחֲמֶיךָ יְקַדְּמוּ
Ragezecha. Dalut Ma'asim	רָגְזֶךָ. דַּלּוּת מַעֲשִׂים
Beshurecha. Karev Tzedek	בְּשׁוּרֶךָ. קָרֵב צֶדֶק
Me'eleicha. Horenu. Beza'akenu	מֵאֵלֶיךָ. הוֹרֵנוּ. בְּזַעֲקֵנוּ
Lach. Tzav Yeshu'ateinu	לָךְ. צַו יְשׁוּעָתֵנוּ
Bemafgia. Vetashiv Shevut	בְּמַפְגִּיעַ. וְתָשִׁיב שְׁבוּת
Oholei Tam. Petachav Re'eh Ki	אָהֳלֵי תָם. פְּתָחָיו רְאֵה כִּי
Shamemu. Zechor Na'amta. Edut	שָׁמֵמוּ. זְכֹר נָאַמְתָּ. עֵדוּת
Lo Tishachach Mipi Zar'o.	לֹא תִשָּׁכַח מִפִּי זַרְעוֹ.
Chotam Te'udah Tatir. Sodecha	חוֹתַם תְּעוּדָה תַּתִּיר. סוֹדְךָ

Sim Belimmudeicha. Tabbur	שִׂים בְּלִמּוּדֶיךָ. טַבּוּר
Aggan Hassahar. Na Al Yechsar	אַגַּן הַסַּהַר. נָא אַל יֶחְסַר
Hamazeg. Yah. Da Et Yisra'el	הַמָּזֶג. יָהּ. דַּע אֶת יִשְׂרָאֵל
Asher Yeda'ucha. Magger Et	אֲשֶׁר יְדָעוּךָ. מַגֵּר אֶת
Hagoyim Asher Lo Yeda'ucha. Ki	הַגּוֹיִם אֲשֶׁר לֹא יְדָעוּךָ. כִּי תָשִׁיב
Tashiv Levitzaron. Lechudim	לְבִצָּרוֹן. לְכוּדִים
Asirei Hatikvah.	אֲסִירֵי הַתִּקְוָה.

Our God, God of our fathers, when Your hand takes hold of justice, do not make an end of us. In punishment's hour do not blot our name from Your book. When You come to searching correction, let Your mercy avert Your just anger. When You see how poor our works are, may Your pitying justice flow towards us. Our Father, when we cry to You, grant us deliverance at our entreaty, and turn back the captivity of Yisrael's tents, for behold his cities are desolate. Remember Your promise that witness will never be forgotten from the mouth of his seed. Unseal, then, that testimony and give of Your revelation in Your teaching. May the great Sanhedrin meet again, inspired by Your teaching. God, give heed to those who confess You, reject those who will not attest You. And even restore to strength those possessed by invincible hope.

Mah Nomar Lefaneicha Yoshev	מַה נֹּאמַר לְפָנֶיךָ יוֹשֵׁב
Marom. Umah Nesapeir	מָרוֹם. וּמַה נְּסַפֵּר
Lefaneicha Shochein Shechakim.	לְפָנֶיךָ שׁוֹכֵן שְׁחָקִים.
Halo Hanistarot Vehaniglot Attah	הֲלֹא הַנִּסְתָּרוֹת וְהַנִּגְלוֹת אַתָּה
Yodea'. Attah Yodea Razei Olam.	יוֹדֵעַ. אַתָּה יוֹדֵעַ רָזֵי עוֹלָם.
Veta'alumot Sitrei Kol Chai.	וְתַעֲלוּמוֹת סִתְרֵי כָּל חָי.
Attah Chofes Kol Chadrei Vaten.	אַתָּה חוֹפֵשׂ כָּל חַדְרֵי בָטֶן.
Ro'eh Chelayot Valev. Ein Davar	רֹאֶה כְלָיוֹת וָלֵב. אֵין דָּבָר

Ne'lam Mimaka. Ve'ein Nistar	נֶעְלָם מִמֶּךָּ. וְאֵין נִסְתָּר
Mineged Eineicha.	מִנֶּגֶד עֵינֶיךָ:

Before You, All-Exalted, what can we say? Before You Throned-Supernal what can we tell? For You know what is hidden, And that which is revealed. You know the mysteries of the universe, And the inner secrets of all living. You search into all man's inner chambers, And see into his mind and heart. There is nothing that is hidden from You, Nothing concealed from Your eyes.

Yehi Ratzon Milfaneicha Adonai	יְהִי רָצוֹן מִלְּפָנֶיךָ יְהֹוָה
Eloheinu Velohei Avoteinu.	אֱלֹהֵינוּ וֵאלֹהֵי אֲבוֹתֵינוּ.
Shetimchol Lanu Et-Kol-	שֶׁתִּמְחֹל לָנוּ אֶת-כָּל-
Chatoteinu. Utechapeir Lanu Et-	חַטֹּאתֵינוּ. וּתְכַפֵּר לָנוּ אֶת-
Kol-'Avonoteinu. Vetimchol	כָּל-עֲוֹנוֹתֵינוּ. וְתִמְחֹל
Vetislach Lechol Pesha'einu.	וְתִסְלַח לְכָל פְּשָׁעֵינוּ.
Vesalachta La'avoneinu	וְסָלַחְתָּ לַעֲוֹנֵנוּ
Ulechatateinu Unechaltanu.	וּלְחַטָּאתֵנוּ וּנְחַלְתָּנוּ:

May it be Your will, Hashem our God, God of our fathers, to deal mercifully with us. Pardon us all our sins, forgive us all our iniquities, absolve us from all our transgressions, "and pardon our iniquity and our sin, and take us for Your heritage." **(Exodus 34:9)**

Selach Lanu Avinu Ki Chatanu.	סְלַח לָנוּ אָבִינוּ כִּי חָטָאנוּ.
Mechol Lanu Malkeinu Ki	מְחֹל לָנוּ מַלְכֵּנוּ כִּי
Fasha'enu. Ki-'Attah Adonai Tov	פָשָׁעְנוּ: כִּי־אַתָּה אֲדֹנָי טוֹב
Vesalach; Verav-Chesed Lechol-	וְסַלָּח וְרַב־חֶסֶד לְכָל־
Kore'eicha. Lema'an-Shimcha	קֹרְאֶיךָ: לְמַעַן־שִׁמְךָ

יְהֹוָה וְסָלַחְתָּ לַעֲוֺנִי כִּי	Adonai Vesalachta La'avoni. Ki
רַב־הוּא: לְמַעַן־שִׁמְךָ	Rav-Hu. Lema'an-Shimcha
יְהֹוָה תְּחַיֵּנִי בְּצִדְקָתְךָ |	Adonai Techayeni; Betzidkatecha
תּוֹצִיא מִצָּרָה נַפְשִׁי: יְהֹוָה	Totzi Mitzarah Nafshi. Adonai
צְבָאוֹת עִמָּנוּ מִשְׂגָּב־לָנוּ	Tzeva'ot Imanu; Misgav-Lanu
אֱלֹהֵי יַעֲקֹב סֶלָה: יְהֹוָה	Elohei Ya'akov Selah. Adonai
צְבָאוֹת אַשְׁרֵי אָדָם בֹּטֵחַ	Tzeva'ot; Ashrei Adam. Boteach
בָּךְ: יְהֹוָה הוֹשִׁיעָה	Bach. Adonai Hoshi'ah;
הַמֶּלֶךְ יַעֲנֵנוּ בְיוֹם־	Hamelech. Ya'aneinu Veyom-
קָרְאֵנוּ: הֲשִׁיבֵנוּ יְהֹוָה |	Kor'enu. Hashiveinu Adonai
אֵלֶיךָ ונשוב (וְנָשׁוּבָה) חַדֵּשׁ	'Eleicha Venashuvah. Chadesh
יָמֵינוּ כְּקֶדֶם:	Yameinu Kekedem.

Our Father, forgive us, for we have sinned, Pardon us, our King, for we have transgressed. "For You, Hashem, are good and forgiving. And abounding in mercy to all who call on You." For Your sake, Hashem, pardon our guilt, for it is great. For Your sake, Hashem, give us life, In Your just dealing, deliver our soul from trouble. "Hashem of hosts is with us, The God of Yaakov is our high refuge forever. Hashem of hosts, Happy is the man who trusts in You. Save, Hashem; May the King answer us in the day that we call. Hashem, turn us again towards You and let us return. Renew our days as of old."

וְהוּא רַחוּם | יְכַפֵּר עָוֺן וְלֹא־יַשְׁחִית וְהִרְבָּה לְהָשִׁיב אַפּוֹ וְלֹא־יָעִיר כָּל־חֲמָתוֹ: אַתָּה יְהֹוָה לֹא־תִכְלָא רַחֲמֶיךָ מִמֶּנִּי חַסְדְּךָ וַאֲמִתְּךָ תָּמִיד יִצְּרוּנִי: הוֹשִׁיעֵנוּ | יְהֹוָה אֱלֹהֵינוּ וְקַבְּצֵנוּ מִן־הַגּוֹיִם לְהֹדוֹת לְשֵׁם קָדְשֶׁךָ לְהִשְׁתַּבֵּחַ בִּתְהִלָּתֶךָ: אִם־עֲוֺנוֹת תִּשְׁמָר־יָהּ אֲדֹנָי מִי יַעֲמֹד:

כִּֽי־עִמְּךָ הַסְּלִיחָה לְמַעַן תִּוָּרֵא׃ לֹא כַחֲטָאֵינוּ עָשָׂה לָנוּ וְלֹא
כַעֲוֺנֹתֵינוּ גָּמַל עָלֵינוּ׃ אִם־עֲוֺנֵינוּ עָנוּ בָנוּ יְהֹוָה עֲשֵׂה לְמַעַן שְׁמֶךָ׃
זְכֹר־רַחֲמֶיךָ יְהֹוָה וַחֲסָדֶיךָ כִּי מֵעוֹלָם הֵמָּה׃ יַעַנְךָ יְהֹוָה בְּיוֹם צָרָה
יְשַׂגֶּבְךָ שֵׁם | אֱלֹהֵי יַעֲקֹב׃ יְהֹוָה הוֹשִׁיעָה הַמֶּלֶךְ יַעֲנֵנוּ בְיוֹם־קָרְאֵנוּ׃
אָבִינוּ מַלְכֵּנוּ. חָנֵּנוּ וַעֲנֵנוּ כִּי אֵין בָּנוּ מַעֲשִׂים. עֲשֵׂה עִמָּנוּ צְדָקָה
כְּרֹב רַחֲמֶיךָ. וְהוֹשִׁיעֵנוּ לְמַעַן שְׁמֶךָ׃

Vehu Rachum Yechapeir Avon Velo-Yashchit Vehirbah Lehashiv Appo; Velo-Ya'ir. Chol-Chamato. Attah Adonai Lo-Tichla Rachameicha Mimeni; Chasdecha Va'amitecha. Tamid Yitzeruni. Hoshi'enu Adonai Eloheinu. Vekabetzeinu Min-Hagoyim Lehodot Leshem Kodshecha; Lehishtabe'ach. Bit'hilatecha. Im-Avonot Tishmor-Yah; Adonai. Mi Ya'amod. Ki-'Imecha Haselichah; Lema'an. Tivare. Lo Chachata'einu Asah Lanu; Velo Cha'avonoteinu. Gamal Aleinu. Im-Avoneinu Anu Vanu. Adonai Aseh Lema'an Shemecha. Zechor-Rachameicha Adonai Vachasadeicha; Ki Me'olam Hemah. Ya'ancha Adonai Beyom Tzarah; Yesagevcha. Shem Elohei Ya'akov. Adonai Hoshi'ah; Hamelech. Ya'aneinu Veyom-Kor'enu. Avinu Malkeinu. Chonenu Va'aneinu Ki Ein Banu Ma'asim. Aseh Imanu Tzedakah Kerov Rachameicha. Vehoshi'enu Lema'an Shemecha.

But He, being full of compassion, forgives iniquity, and does not destroy; many times He turns His anger away, And does not stir up all His wrath. You, Hashem, will not withhold Your compassions from me; let Your mercy and Your truth continually preserve me. Save us, Hashem our God, And gather us from among the nations, That we may give thanks to Your holy name, That we may triumph in Your praise. If You, Hashem, should mark iniquities, Hashem, who could stand? For with You there is forgiveness, that You may be feared. He has not dealt with us after our sins, or requited us according to our iniquities. Though our iniquities testify against us, Hashem, work for Your name's sake; Remember, Hashem, Your compassions and Your mercies; For they have been from old. May Hashem answer you in the day of trouble; May the name of the God of Yaakov set you up on high; Save, Hashem; may the King answer us in the day that we call. Our Father and King, answer us with favor. Though we lack good works, deal with us benevolently, according to Your abundant mercy and save us for Your own sake. **(Psalms 78:38, 40:12, 106:47, 130:3-4, 103:10, Jeremiah 14:7, Psalms 25:6, 22:2, 20:10)**

וְעַתָּה | אֲדֹנָי אֱלֹהֵינוּ אֲשֶׁר הוֹצֵאתָ אֶת־עַמְּךָ מֵאֶרֶץ מִצְרַיִם בְּיָד חֲזָקָה וַתַּעַשׂ־לְךָ שֵׁם כַּיּוֹם הַזֶּה חָטָאנוּ רָשָׁעְנוּ׃ אֲדֹנָי כְּכָל־צִדְקֹתֶךָ יָשָׁב־נָא אַפְּךָ וַחֲמָתְךָ מֵעִירְךָ יְרוּשָׁלִַם הַר־קָדְשֶׁךָ כִּי בַחֲטָאֵינוּ וּבַעֲוֹנוֹת אֲבֹתֵינוּ יְרוּשָׁלִַם וְעַמְּךָ לְחֶרְפָּה לְכָל־סְבִיבֹתֵינוּ׃ וְעַתָּה | שְׁמַע אֱלֹהֵינוּ אֶל־תְּפִלַּת עַבְדְּךָ וְאֶל־תַּחֲנוּנָיו וְהָאֵר פָּנֶיךָ עַל־מִקְדָּשְׁךָ הַשָּׁמֵם לְמַעַן אֲדֹנָי׃ הַטֵּה אֱלֹהַי | אָזְנְךָ וּשְׁמָע פקחה (פְּקַח) עֵינֶיךָ וּרְאֵה שֹׁמְמֹתֵינוּ וְהָעִיר אֲשֶׁר־נִקְרָא שִׁמְךָ עָלֶיהָ כִּי | לֹא עַל־צִדְקֹתֵינוּ אֲנַחְנוּ מַפִּילִים תַּחֲנוּנֵינוּ לְפָנֶיךָ כִּי עַל־רַחֲמֶיךָ הָרַבִּים׃ אֲדֹנָי | שְׁמָעָה אֲדֹנָי | סְלָחָה אֲדֹנָי הַקֲשִׁיבָה וַעֲשֵׂה אַל־תְּאַחַר לְמַעַנְךָ אֱלֹהַי כִּי־שִׁמְךָ נִקְרָא עַל־עִירְךָ וְעַל־עַמֶּךָ׃

Ve'attah Adonai Eloheinu. Asher Hotzeta Et-'Ammecha Me'eretz Mitzrayim Beyad Chazakah. Vata'as-Lecha Shem Kayom Hazeh; Chatanu Rasha'enu. Adonai. Kechol-Tzidkotecha Yashov-Na Apecha Vachamatecha. Me'irecha Yerushalayim Har-Kodshecha; Ki Vachata'einu Uva'avonot Avoteinu. Yerushalayim Ve'ammecha Lecherpah Lechol-Sevivoteinu. Ve'attah Shema Eloheinu. El-Tefillat Avdecha Ve'el-Tachanunav. Veha'er Paneicha. Al-Mikdashecha Hashamem; Lema'an Adonai. Hateh Elohai 'Oznecha Ushema Pekach Eineicha. Ure'eh Shomemoteinu. Veha'ir Asher-Nikra Shimcha Aleiha; Ki Lo Al-Tzidkoteinu. Anachnu Mapilim Tachanuneinu Lefaneicha. Ki Al-Rachameicha Harabbim. Adonai Shema'ah Adonai Selachah. Adonai Hakshivah Va'aseh Al-Te'achar; Lema'ancha Elohai. Ki-Shimcha Nikra. Al-'Irecha Ve'al-'Ammecha.

And now, Hashem our God, that has brought Your people out of the land of Mitzrayim with a mighty hand, and has gotten renown for You, as at this day; we have sinned, we have done wickedly. Hashem, according to all Your righteousness, let Your anger and Your fury, I pray, be turned away from Your city Yerushalayim, Your holy mountain; because for our sins, and for the iniquities of our fathers, Yerushalayim and Your people have become a reproach to all that are around us. Now then, our God, heed the prayer of Your servant, and to his supplications, and cause Your face to shine upon Your Sanctuary that is desolate, for Hashem's sake. My God, incline Your ear, and hear; open Your eyes, and behold our desolations, and the city upon which Your name is called; for we do not present our supplications before You because of our righteousness, but because of Your great compassions. Oh Hashem, hear, Hashem, forgive, Hashem, attend and do, and do not defer; for Your own sake, my God, because Your name is called upon Your city and Your people.' **(Daniel 9:15-19)**

Avinu Av Harachaman. Har'enu	אָבִינוּ אָב הָרַחֲמָן. הַרְאֵנוּ
Ot Letovah Vekabetz	אוֹת לְטוֹבָה וְקַבֵּץ
Nefutzoteinu Me'arba Kanfot	נְפוּצוֹתֵינוּ מֵאַרְבַּע כַּנְפוֹת
Ha'aretz. Yakiru Veyede'u Kol	הָאָרֶץ. יַכִּירוּ וְיֵדְעוּ כָּל
Hagoyim Ki Attah Adonai Avinu	הַגּוֹיִם כִּי אַתָּה יְהֹוָה אָבִינוּ
Attah. Anachnu Hachomer	אָתָּה. אֲנַחְנוּ הַחֹמֶר
Ve'attah Yotzreinu Uma'aseh	וְאַתָּה יֹצְרֵנוּ וּמַעֲשֵׂה
Yadecha Kulanu.	יָדְךָ כֻּלָּנוּ:

Our Father, merciful Father, show us a good sign and gather our dispersed from the four corners of the whole earth. Then all of the nations will know and acknowledge that: "Hashem, You are our Father; We are the clay, and You are the Potter, We are all the work of Your hand." **(Isaiah 64:7)**

Avinu Malkeinu. Tzurenu	אָבִינוּ מַלְכֵּנוּ. צוּרֵנוּ
Vego'alenu. Chusah Adonai	וְגוֹאֲלֵנוּ. חוּסָה יְהֹוָה
Al-'Ammecha. Ve'al-Titen	עַל־עַמֶּךָ וְאַל־תִּתֵּן

Nachalatecha Lecherpah
Limshol-Bam Goyim. Lamah
Yomeru Va'ammim. Ayeh
Eloheihem. Yada'nu Adonai Ki
Chatanu. Ve'ein Mi Ya'amod
Ba'adenu Ella Shimcha Hagadol
Ya'amod Lanu Be'et Tzarah.
Ucherachem Av Al Banim
Rachem Aleinu. Chamol Al
Amach Verachem Al
Nachalatach. Chusah Na Kerov
Rachameicha Chonenu
Malkeinu Va'aneinu. Lecha
Adonai Hatzedakah Oseh
Nifla'ot Bechol Et Va'et. Habeit
Na Vehoshi'ah Na Tzon
Mar'itecha. Al Yimshal Banu
Ketzef Ki Lecha Adonai
Hayshu'ah Becha Tochalteinu.
Eloah Selichot Ana Selach Na. Ki
El Tov Vesalach Attah.

נַחֲלָתְךָ לְחֶרְפָּה
לִמְשָׁל־בָּם גּוֹיִם לָמָּה
יֹאמְרוּ בָעַמִּים אַיֵּה
אֱלֹהֵיהֶם: יָדַעְנוּ יְהוָה כִּי
חָטָאנוּ. וְאֵין מִי יַעֲמוֹד
בַּעֲדֵנוּ אֶלָּא שִׁמְךָ הַגָּדוֹל
יַעֲמוֹד לָנוּ בְּעֵת צָרָה.
וּכְרַחֵם אָב עַל בָּנִים
רַחֵם עָלֵינוּ. חֲמֹל עַל
עַמְּךָ וְרַחֵם עַל
נַחֲלָתָךְ. חוּסָה נָּא כְּרֹב
רַחֲמֶיךָ חָנֵּנוּ מַלְכֵּנוּ
וַעֲנֵנוּ. לְךָ יְהוָה
הַצְּדָקָה עוֹשֵׂה נִפְלָאוֹת
בְּכָל עֵת וָעֵת. הַבֵּט נָא
וְהוֹשִׁיעָה נָּא צֹאן מַרְעִיתֶךָ.
אַל יִמְשָׁל בָּנוּ קֶצֶף כִּי
לְךָ יְהוָה הַיְשׁוּעָה בְּךָ
תוֹחַלְתֵּנוּ. אֱלוֹהַּ סְלִיחוֹת אָנָּא
סְלַח נָא. כִּי אֵל טוֹב וְסַלָּח
אָתָּה:

Hashem, our Father, King, Rock and Redeemer, have pity on Your people, and do not deliver Your heritage to such reproach that nations make a byword of them. "Why should they say among the peoples, 'Where is their God?' " Hashem, we know we have sinned, and there is no one to stand by us, but You in Your greatness will defend us in time of trouble. Have compassion on us as a father has compassion on his children. Have compassion on Your people and have mercy on Your heritage. Have pity on us, we beseech You, according to the greatness of Your mercy. Graciously answer us, Oh our King. Righteousness is Yours, Hashem Who performs wonders at all times. We pray, look to the sheep of Your pasture and save them. Do not let anger prevail against us, for deliverance is Yours, Hashem. Our hope is in You, God of pardon. We pray You forgive us, for You, God, are good and ready to forgive.

Ana Melech Rachum Vechanun.	אָנָּא מֶלֶךְ רַחוּם וְחַנּוּן.
Zechor Vehabeit Livrit Bein	זְכוֹר וְהַבֵּט לִבְרִית בֵּין
Habetarim. Vetera'eh	הַבְּתָרִים. וְתֵרָאֶה
Lefaneicha Akedat Yachid.	לְפָנֶיךָ עֲקֵדַת יָחִיד.
Ulema'an Yisra'el Avinu. Al	וּלְמַעַן יִשְׂרָאֵל אָבִינוּ. אַל
Ta'azvenu Avinu. Ve'al Titesenu	תַּעַזְבֵנוּ אָבִינוּ. וְאַל תִּטְּשֵׁנוּ
Malkeinu Ve'al Tishkacheinu	מַלְכֵּנוּ וְאַל תִּשְׁכָּחֵנוּ
Yotzreinu. Ve'al Ta'as Imanu	יוֹצְרֵנוּ. וְאַל תַּעַשׂ עִמָּנוּ
Chalah Begaluteinu. Ki El	כָלָה בְּגָלוּתֵינוּ. כִּי אֵל
Melech Chanun Verachum	מֶלֶךְ חַנּוּן וְרַחוּם
Attah.	אָתָּה:

Merciful and compassionate King, Father and Creator, recall and regard Your covenant with our father Avraham made at the sacrifice of pieces. Look to the binding of his only child Yitzchak. For the sake of our father Yisrael, Do not abondon us or cast us off. Do not forget us, or make an end of us in our exile, for You are a gracious and merciful God and King.

Ein Kamocha Chanun Verachum	אֵין כָּמוֹךָ חַנּוּן וְרַחוּם
Eloheinu. Ein Kamocha El Erech	אֱלֹהֵינוּ. אֵין כָּמוֹךָ אֵל אֶרֶךְ
Apayim Verav Chesed Ve'emet.	אַפַּיִם וְרַב חֶסֶד וֶאֱמֶת.
Hoshi'einu Verachamenu	הוֹשִׁיעֵנוּ וְרַחֲמֵנוּ
Mera'ash Umerogez Hatzileinu.	מֵרַעַשׁ וּמֵרֹגֶז הַצִּילֵנוּ:
Zechor La'avadeicha.	זְכֹר לַעֲבָדֶיךָ
Le'avraham Leyitzchak	לְאַבְרָהָם לְיִצְחָק
Uleya'akov; Al-Tefen. El-Keshi	וּלְיַעֲקֹב אַל־תֵּפֶן אֶל־קְשִׁי
Ha'am Hazeh. Ve'el-Rish'o	הָעָם הַזֶּה וְאֶל־רִשְׁעוֹ
Ve'el-Chatato. Shuv Mecharon	וְאֶל־חַטָּאתוֹ: שׁוּב מֵחֲרוֹן
Apecha. Vehinachem Al-	אַפֶּךָ וְהִנָּחֵם עַל־
Hara'ah Le'ammecha. Vehaseir	הָרָעָה לְעַמֶּךָ: וְהָסֵר
Mimenu Makat Hamavet Ki	מִמֶּנּוּ מַכַּת הַמָּוֶת כִּי
Rachum Attah. Ki Chein	רַחוּם אָתָּה. כִּי כֵן
Darkecha La'asot Chesed	דַּרְכְּךָ לַעֲשׂוֹת חֶסֶד
Chinam Bechol Dor Vador. Ana	חִנָּם בְּכָל דּוֹר וָדוֹר: אָנָּא
Adonai Hoshi'ah Na; Ana	יְהֹוָה הוֹשִׁיעָה נָּא אָנָּא
Adonai Hatzlichah Na. Ana	יְהֹוָה הַצְלִיחָה נָּא: אָנָּא
Adonai Aneinu Veyom	יְהֹוָה עֲנֵנוּ בְיוֹם
Kare'enu. Lecha Adonai Kivinu.	קָרְאֵנוּ: לְךָ יְהֹוָה קִוִּינוּ.
Lecha Adonai Chikkinu. Lecha	לְךָ יְהֹוָה חִכִּינוּ. לְךָ
Adonai Neyachel Al Techesheh	יְהֹוָה נְיַחֵל אַל תֶּחֱשֶׁה
Ute'anenu. Ki Na'amu Goyim	וּתְעַנֵּנוּ. כִּי נָאֲמוּ גוֹיִם
Avedah Tikvatam. Kol Berech	אָבְדָה תִקְוָתָם. כָּל בֶּרֶךְ
Lecha Tichra Vechol Komah	לְךָ תִכְרַע וְכָל קוֹמָה
Lefaneicha Tishtachaveh.	לְפָנֶיךָ תִשְׁתַּחֲוֶה:

There is none like You, our God, gracious and merciful. There is none like You, a God long-suffering and abundant in mercy and truth. Have mercy on us, save us, and deliver us from devastating rage. Remember Your servants Avraham, Yitzchak and Yaakov, and do not look to the stubbornness, the wickedness, and the sinfulness of this people, but turn from Your anger and repent of the evil against Your people. Because You are merciful, ward off from us mortal blow, for it is Your way to show mercy freely in every generation. Hashem, we implore You, save us. Hashem, we implore You, prosper us. Hashem, we implore You, answer us on the day when we call. Towards You, Hashem, are our longing, our hope and our trust. Do not be silent, but answer us when the nations say 'their hope is lost.' For to You every knee will bow, and before You will all prostrate themselves.

Hapotei'ach Yad Bitshuvah	הַפּוֹתֵחַ יָד בִּתְשׁוּבָה
Lekabel Poshe'im Vechata'im.	לְקַבֵּל פּוֹשְׁעִים וְחַטָּאִים.
Nivhalah Nafshenu Merov	נִבְהֲלָה נַפְשֵׁנוּ מֵרוֹב
Itzevonenu. Al Tishkacheinu	עִצְּבוֹנֵנוּ. אַל תִּשְׁכָּחֵנוּ
Netzach Kumah Vehoshi'enu. Al	נֶצַח קוּמָה וְהוֹשִׁיעֵנוּ. אַל
Tishpoch Charonecha Aleinu Ki	תִּשְׁפּוֹךְ חֲרוֹנְךָ עָלֵינוּ כִּי
Ammecha Anachnu Benei	עַמְּךָ אֲנַחְנוּ בְּנֵי
Veritecha. El Habitah. Dal	בְרִיתֶךָ. אֵל הַבִּיטָה. דַּל
Kevodenu Vagoyim Veshiketzunu	כְּבוֹדֵנוּ בַגּוֹיִם וְשִׁקְּצוּנוּ
Ketum'at Haniddah. Ad Matai	כְּטֻמְאַת הַנִּדָּה. עַד מָתַי
Uzecha Bashevi Vetif'artecha	עֻזְּךָ בַּשְּׁבִי וְתִפְאַרְתְּךָ
Beyad Tzar. Hemah Yir'u	בְּיַד צָר. הֵמָּה יִרְאוּ
Veyevoshu Veyechatu	וְיֵבֹשׁוּ וְיֵחַתּוּ

Migevuratam. Orerah	מִגְּבוּרָתָם. עוֹרְרָה
Gevuratecha Vehoshi'enu	גְבוּרָתְךָ וְהוֹשִׁיעֵנוּ
Lema'an Shemecha. Al Yim'atu	לְמַעַן שְׁמֶךָ. אַל יִמְעֲטוּ
Lefaneicha Tela'oteinu Maher	לְפָנֶיךָ תְּלָאוֹתֵינוּ מַהֵר
Yekademunu Rachameicha Be'et	יְקַדְּמוּנוּ רַחֲמֶיךָ בְּעֵת
Tzaroteinu. Lo Lema'aneinu Ella	צָרוֹתֵנוּ. לֹא לְמַעֲנֵנוּ אֶלָּא
Lema'anach Pe'ol Ve'al Tashchet	לְמַעֲנָךְ פְּעֹל וְאַל תַּשְׁחֵת
Et Zecher She'eriteinu. Ki Lecha	אֶת זֵכֶר שְׁאֵרִיתֵנוּ. כִּי לְךָ
Meyachalot Eineinu Ki El Melech	מְיַחֲלוֹת עֵינֵינוּ כִּי אֵל מֶלֶךְ
Chanun Verachum Attah.	חַנּוּן וְרַחוּם אָתָּה.
Uzechor Eduteinu Bechol Yom	וּזְכוֹר עֵדוּתֵינוּ בְּכָל יוֹם
Tamid Omerim Pa'amayim	תָּמִיד אוֹמְרִים פַּעֲמַיִם
Be'ahavah. Shema Yisra'el;	בְּאַהֲבָה: שְׁמַע יִשְׂרָאֵל
Adonai Eloheinu Adonai Echad.	יְהוָה אֱלֹהֵינוּ יְהוָה | אֶחָד:

You who opens Your hand to receive transgressors and sinners repenting, our soul is dismayed through the greatness of our suffering. Do not utterly forget us, but rise up and save us. Do not pour out Your anger on us, for we are Your people, the children of the covenant with You. Look on our degradation, Hashem, and see how we are loathed. Awaken Your might and save us for Your sake. Do not let our anguish seem small in Your sight, but hasten Your mercies to avert our troubles. Do so not for our sake, but for Your own. Do not destroy all memory of our remnant, for our eyes wait on You, because You, God, are a merciful and gracious King. Remember our witness to You, lovingly repeated twice daily, "Hear, O Yisrael: Hashem is our God, Hashem is One."

Days except for Monday and Thursday, some continue with Yehi Shem, others with Hatzi-Kaddish.

Yehi Shem

Yehi Shem Adonai Mevorach;	יְהִי שֵׁם יְהוָה מְבֹרָךְ
Me'attah. Ve'ad-'Olam.	מֵעַתָּה וְעַד־עוֹלָם׃
Mimizrach-Shemesh Ad-	מִמִּזְרַח־שֶׁמֶשׁ עַד־
Mevo'o; Mehulal. Shem Adonai	מְבוֹאוֹ מְהֻלָּל שֵׁם יְהוָה׃
Ram Al-Chol-Goyim Adonai Al	רָם עַל־כָּל־גּוֹיִם | יְהוָה עַל
Hashamayim Kevodo. Adonai	הַשָּׁמַיִם כְּבוֹדוֹ׃ יְהוָה
Adoneinu; Mah-'Adir Shimcha.	אֲדֹנֵינוּ מָה־אַדִּיר שִׁמְךָ
Bechol-Ha'aretz.	בְּכָל־הָאָרֶץ׃

Blessed is the name of Hashem from this time forward and forever. From the rising of the sun to it's going down, Hashem's name is to be praised. Hashem, our Lord, How glorious is Your name in all of the earth. **(Psalms 113:2-4, 8:2)**

Hatzi-Kaddish / Half Kaddish

Kaddish is only recited in a minyan (ten men). אָמֵן denotes when the congregation responds "Amen" together out loud. According to the Shulchan Arukh, the congregation says "Yehei Shemeh Rabba" to "Yitbarach" out loud together without interruption, and also that one should respond "Amen" after "Yitbarach." (SA, OC 55,56) This is not the common custom today. Though many are accustomed to answering according to their own custom, it is advised to respond in the custom of the one reciting to avoid not fragmenting into smaller groups. ("Lo Titgodedu" - BT, Yevamot 13b / SA, OC 493, Rema / MT, Avodah Zara 12:15)

יִתְגַּדַּל וְיִתְקַדַּשׁ שְׁמֵהּ רַבָּא. אָמֵן בְּעָלְמָא דִּי בְרָא. כִּרְעוּתֵהּ. וְיַמְלִיךְ מַלְכוּתֵהּ. וְיַצְמַח פֻּרְקָנֵהּ. וִיקָרֵב מְשִׁיחֵהּ. אָמֵן בְּחַיֵּיכוֹן וּבְיוֹמֵיכוֹן וּבְחַיֵּי דְכָל בֵּית יִשְׂרָאֵל. בַּעֲגָלָא וּבִזְמַן קָרִיב. וְאִמְרוּ אָמֵן. אָמֵן יְהֵא שְׁמֵיהּ רַבָּא מְבָרַךְ לְעָלַם וּלְעָלְמֵי עָלְמַיָּא יִתְבָּרַךְ. וְיִשְׁתַּבַּח. וְיִתְפָּאַר. וְיִתְרוֹמַם. וְיִתְנַשֵּׂא. וְיִתְהַדָּר. וְיִתְעַלֶּה. וְיִתְהַלָּל שְׁמֵהּ דְּקֻדְשָׁא. בְּרִיךְ הוּא. אָמֵן לְעֵלָּא מִן כָּל בִּרְכָתָא שִׁירָתָא. תֻּשְׁבְּחָתָא וְנֶחֱמָתָא. דַּאֲמִירָן בְּעָלְמָא. וְאִמְרוּ אָמֵן. אָמֵן

Yitgadal Veyitkadash Shemeh Rabba. **Amen** Be'alema Di Vera. Kir'uteh. Veyamlich Malchuteh. Veyatzmach Purkaneh. Vikarev Meshicheh. **Amen** Bechayeichon Uveyomeichon Uvechayei Dechal-Beit Yisra'el. Ba'agala Uvizman Kariv. Ve'imru Amen. **Amen** Yehei Shemeh Rabba Mevarach Le'alam Ule'alemei Alemaya Yitbarach. Veyishtabach. Veyitpa'ar. Veyitromam. Veyitnasse. Veyit'hadar. Veyit'aleh. Veyit'hallal Shemeh Dekudsha. Berich Hu. **Amen** Le'ella Min Kol Birchata Shirata. Tushbechata Venechemata. Da'amiran Be'alema. Ve'imru Amen. **Amen**

Glorified and sanctified be God's great name **Amen** throughout the world which He has created according to His will. May He establish His kingdom, hastening His salvation and the coming of His Messiah, **Amen**, in your lifetime and during your days, and within the life of the entire House of Yisrael, speedily and soon; and say, Amen. **Amen** May His great name be blessed forever and to all eternity. Blessed and praised, glorified and exalted, extolled and honored, adored and lauded is the name of the Holy One, blessed is He, **Amen** Beyond all the blessings and hymns, praises and consolations that are ever spoken in the world; and say, Amen. **Amen**

THE TORAH READING FOR WEEKDAY - ROSH CHODESH IS ON PAGE 418.

Kriyat HaTorah / The Torah Reading

The Torah is read on Monday, Thursday, Rosh Chodesh, Chol HaMoed, Hanukkah, Purim and Communal Fasts.

Opening of the Ark

Before, on a day with Tachanun some say:

El Erech Apayim Verav Chesed	אֶל אֶרֶךְ אַפַּיִם וְרַב חֶסֶד
Ve'emet. El Be'apecha	וֶאֱמֶת. אַל בְּאַפְּךָ
Tochicheinu. Chusah Adonai Al	תוֹכִיחֵנוּ. חוּסָה יְהוָה עַל
Yisra'el Ammecha. Vehoshi'enu	יִשְׂרָאֵל עַמֶּךָ. וְהוֹשִׁיעֵנוּ
Mikol Ra'. Chatanu Lecha.	מִכָּל רָע. חָטָאנוּ לְךָ.
Adon Selach Na. Kerov	אָדוֹן סְלַח נָא. כְּרֹב
Rachameicha El.	רַחֲמֶיךָ אֵל:

God, long suffering and abundant in mercy and truth, do not rebuke us in Your anger. Have pity, Hashem, on Yisrael, Your people, and save us from every evil. Though we have sinned against You, Lord God, pardon us, we implore You, in the measure of Your abundant mercy.

El Erech Apayim Umalle	אֶל אֶרֶךְ אַפַּיִם וּמָלֵא
Rachamim. El Tasteir Paneicha	רַחֲמִים. אַל תַּסְתֵּר פָּנֶיךָ
Mimennu. Chusah Adonai Al	מִמֶּנּוּ. חוּסָה יְהוָה עַל
She'erit Yisra'el Ammecha.	שְׁאֵרִית יִשְׂרָאֵל עַמֶּךָ.
Vehatzileinu Mikol Ra. Chatanu	וְהַצִּילֵנוּ מִכָּל רָע. חָטָאנוּ
Lecha. Adon Selach Na. Kerov	לְךָ. אָדוֹן סְלַח נָא. כְּרֹב
Rachameicha El:	רַחֲמֶיךָ אֵל:

God, long suffering and full of compassion, do not hide Your face from us. Have pity, Hashem, on the remnant of Yisrael, Your people, and deliver us from every evil. Though we have sinned against You,

Lord God, pardon us, we implore You, in the measure of Your abundant mercy.

On days on which Tachanun is not said the recite:

Yehi Adonai Eloheinu Imanu	יְהִי יְהֹוָה אֱלֹהֵינוּ עִמָּנוּ
Ka'asher Hayah Im Avoteinu Al	כַּאֲשֶׁר הָיָה עִם־אֲבֹתֵינוּ אַל־
Ya'azvenu Ve'al Yitesenu.	יַעַזְבֵנוּ וְאַל־יִטְּשֵׁנוּ׃
Hoshi'ah Et Ammecha Uvarech	הוֹשִׁיעָה | אֶת־עַמֶּךָ וּבָרֵךְ
Et Nachalatecha Ure'em	אֶת־נַחֲלָתֶךָ וּרְעֵם
Venasse'em Ad Ha'olam.	וְנַשְּׂאֵם עַד־הָעוֹלָם׃
Ba'avur David Avdecha Al	בַּעֲבוּר דָּוִד עַבְדֶּךָ אַל־
Tashev Penei Meshichecha.	תָּשֵׁב פְּנֵי מְשִׁיחֶךָ׃

Hashem our God, be with us as You were with our fathers. Do not forsake us or abandon us. Save Your people and bless Your heritage; tend and carry Your flock forever. Hashem, save Your people, the remnant of Yisrael. For the sake of David Your servant do not turn back the face of Your anointed.

Take out the Torah scroll during a normal weekday. Continue here on Rosh Chodesh.

Some say:

Baruch Hamakom Shenatan Torah	בָּרוּךְ הַמָּקוֹם שֶׁנָּתַן תּוֹרָה
Le'ammo Yisra'el. Baruch Hu.	לְעַמּוֹ יִשְׂרָאֵל. בָּרוּךְ הוּא׃
Ashrei Ha'am Shekachah Lo;	אַשְׁרֵי הָעָם שֶׁכָּכָה לּוֹ
Ashrei Ha'am. She'Adonai Elohav.	אַשְׁרֵי הָעָם שֶׁיְהֹוָה אֱלֹהָיו׃

Blessed is the Place (of all) who has given the Torah to His people Yisrael, blessed is He. Happy are those who dwell in Your House; they are ever praising You. Happy are the people that is so situated; happy are the people whose God is Hashem.

The Leader takes the Torah out to platform and the Chazan says in unison with congregation:

גַּדְּלוּ לַיהֹוָה אִתִּי וּנְרוֹמְמָה שְׁמוֹ יַחְדָּו:

Gadelu L'Adonai Iti; Uneromemah Shemo Yachdav.

Exalt Hashem with me, And let us glorify His name in unison.

רוֹמְמוּ יְהֹוָה אֱלֹהֵינוּ וְהִשְׁתַּחֲווּ לַהֲדֹם רַגְלָיו קָדוֹשׁ הוּא: רוֹמְמוּ יְהֹוָה אֱלֹהֵינוּ וְהִשְׁתַּחֲווּ לְהַר קָדְשׁוֹ כִּי־קָדוֹשׁ יְהֹוָה אֱלֹהֵינוּ: אֵין־קָדוֹשׁ כַּיהֹוָה כִּי אֵין בִּלְתֶּךָ וְאֵין צוּר כֵּאלֹהֵינוּ: כִּי מִי אֱלוֹהַּ מִבַּלְעֲדֵי יְהֹוָה וּמִי צוּר זוּלָתִי אֱלֹהֵינוּ: תּוֹרָה צִוָּה־לָנוּ מֹשֶׁה מוֹרָשָׁה קְהִלַּת יַעֲקֹב: עֵץ־חַיִּים הִיא לַמַּחֲזִיקִים בָּהּ וְתֹמְכֶיהָ מְאֻשָּׁר: דְּרָכֶיהָ דַרְכֵי־נֹעַם וְכָל־נְתִיבוֹתֶיהָ שָׁלוֹם: שָׁלוֹם רָב לְאֹהֲבֵי תוֹרָתֶךָ וְאֵין־לָמוֹ מִכְשׁוֹל: יְהֹוָה עֹז לְעַמּוֹ יִתֵּן יְהֹוָה | יְבָרֵךְ אֶת־עַמּוֹ בַשָּׁלוֹם:

Romemu Adonai Eloheinu. Vehishtachavu Lahadom Raglav. Kadosh Hu. Romemu Adonai Eloheinu. Vehishtachavu Lehar Kodsho; Ki-Kadosh. Adonai Eloheinu. Ein-Kadosh K'Adonai Ki Ein Biltecha; Ve'ein Tzur Keloheinu. Ki Mi Eloah Mibal'adei Adonai Umi Tzur. Zulati Eloheinu Torah Tzivah-Lanu Mosheh; Morashah Kehilat Ya'akov. Etz-Chayim Hi Lamachazikim Bah; Vetomecheiha Me'ushar. Deracheiha Darchei-No'am; Vechol-Netivoteiha Shalom. Shalom Rav Le'ohavei Toratecha; Ve'ein-Lamo Michshol. Adonai Oz Le'ammo Yiten; Adonai Yevarech Et-'Ammo Vashalom.

Exalt Hashem our God, And worship at His footstool, For He is holy. Exalt Hashem our God, And worship at His holy mountain, For Hashem our God is holy. There is none other as holy as Hashem, For there is none besides Him, or Rock like our God. For who is God except Hashem, Or who is the Rock besides our God? A Torah Moshe commanded us, A heritage for the congregation of Yaakov. It is a tree of life for those who lay hold of it, And happy are those who cling to it. Its ways are ways of pleasantness, And all its pathways peace. Great peace have those who love Your Torah, And for them there is no stumbling. Hashem will give strength to His people. Hashem will bless His people with peace.

Hagbahah / Lifting of the Torah

The lifting of the Sefer Torah. As it is raised and turned the congregation says:

Deuteronomy 4:44, 33:4

Vezot Hatorah; Asher-Sam	וְזֹאת הַתּוֹרָה אֲשֶׁר־שָׂם
Mosheh. Lifnei Benei Yisra'el.	מֹשֶׁה לִפְנֵי בְּנֵי יִשְׂרָאֵל׃
Torah Tzivah-Lanu Mosheh;	תּוֹרָה צִוָּה־לָנוּ מֹשֶׁה
Morashah Kehilat Ya'akov. Ha'	מוֹרָשָׁה קְהִלַּת יַעֲקֹב׃ הָאֵל
El Tamim Darko Imrat-Adonai	תָּמִים דַּרְכּוֹ אִמְרַת־יְהֹוָה
Tzerufah; Magen Hu. Lechol	צְרוּפָה מָגֵן הוּא לְכֹל
Hachosim Bo.	הַחֹסִים בּוֹ׃

"And this is the Torah which Moshe placed before the children of Yisrael. The Torah which Moshe commanded us, the heritage for the congregation of Yaakov." "The way of God is perfect; the word of Hashem is tried; He is a Shield to all those who trust in Him."

Seder Kriyat HaTorah / The Order of the Reading of the Torah

On Monday, Thursday and at the Mincha Service on Shabbat, no more and no less than three persons should be called up to the Torah, and no Haftorah is read. One who reads out of the Torah must do so while standing, and he must not lean against the wall unless he is either obese or sickly and suffers pain. (SA, OC 137) The first section of the Parashah (weekly portion of the Torah) of the following Shabbat is then read from the Torah. Three men, representing respectively the priesthood (Kohen), the Levites (Levi) and all Yisrael, are successively called to the Torah for its reading. As each approaches the Torah, he says: (Continue with the Blessings for the Torah Portion on the next page.)

In some kehilot (congregations), the Oleh / Reader says:

Adonai Imachem. יְהֹוָה עִמָּכֶם:

Hashem be with you.

The kahal / congregation:

Yevarechekha Adonai. יְבָרֶכְךָ יְהֹוָה:

May Hashem bless You.

The Oleh / Reader:

Barechu Et Adonai Hamevorach. בָּרְכוּ אֶת יְהֹוָה הַמְּבֹרָךְ:

Bless Hashem, Who is forever blessed.

The kahal / congregation:

Baruch Adonai Hamevorach בָּרוּךְ יְהֹוָה הַמְּבֹרָךְ
Le'olam Va'ed. לְעוֹלָם וָעֶד:

Blessed is Hashem Who is blessed for all eternity.

The Oleh and Chazan:

Baruch Adonai Hamevorach בָּרוּךְ יְהֹוָה הַמְּבֹרָךְ
Le'olam Va'ed. לְעוֹלָם וָעֶד:

Blessed is Hashem Who is blessed for all eternity.

Baruch Attah Adonai Eloheinu בָּרוּךְ אַתָּה יְהֹוָה אֱלֹהֵינוּ
Melech Ha'olam Asher Bachar מֶלֶךְ הָעוֹלָם. אֲשֶׁר בָּחַר
Banu Mikol Ha'ammim Venatan בָּנוּ מִכָּל הָעַמִּים וְנָתַן
Lanu Et Torato. Baruch Attah לָנוּ אֶת תּוֹרָתוֹ. בָּרוּךְ אַתָּה
Adonai Noten Hatorah. יְהֹוָה נוֹתֵן הַתּוֹרָה:

Blessed are You, Hashem our God, King of the universe, You have chosen us from all peoples and given us Your Torah. Blessed are You, Hashem, Giver of the Torah.

There is no need for the assembly to stand up during the reading of the Torah. (SA, OC 146:4)

After reading from the Torah, the reader holds the Sefer Torah and blesses (SA, OC 139:11):

Baruch Attah Adonai Eloheinu	בָּרוּךְ אַתָּה יְהֹוָה אֱלֹהֵינוּ
Melech Ha'olam Asher Natan	מֶלֶךְ הָעוֹלָם. אֲשֶׁר נָתַן
Lanu Et Torato Torat Emet.	לָנוּ אֶת תּוֹרָתוֹ תּוֹרַת אֱמֶת.
Vechayei Olam Nata	וְחַיֵּי עוֹלָם נָטַע
Betocheinu. Baruch Attah	בְּתוֹכֵנוּ. בָּרוּךְ אַתָּה
Adonai Noten Hatorah.	יְהֹוָה נוֹתֵן הַתּוֹרָה:

Blessed are You, Hashem our God, King of the universe, You have given us Your Torah of truth, and have planted among us eternal life. Blessed are You, Hashem, Giver of the Torah.

Birkhat HaGomel / The Thanksgiving Blessing

After the last Torah reading, recite. It is necessary to bless in front of ten men (minyan).

Before the blessing say:

Odeh Adonai Bechol-Levav;	אוֹדֶה יְהֹוָה בְּכָל־לֵבָב
Besod Yesharim Ve'edah.	בְּסוֹד יְשָׁרִים וְעֵדָה:

I will give thanks to Hashem with my whole heart. In the council of the upright, and in the congregation.

And bless:

Baruch Attah Adonai Eloheinu	בָּרוּךְ אַתָּה יְהֹוָה אֱלֹהֵינוּ
Melech Ha'olam Hagomel	מֶלֶךְ הָעוֹלָם. הַגּוֹמֵל
Lechayavim Tovot. Sheggemalani	לְחַיָּבִים טוֹבוֹת. שֶׁגְּמָלַנִי
Kol-Tuv.	כָּל־טוּב:

Blessed are You Hashem, our God, King of the Universe, Who rewards the undeserving with good, and has rewarded me with every kindness.

And the kahal / congregation answers:

Amen. Ha' El Sheggemalecha	אָמֵן. הָאֵל שֶׁגְּמָלְךָ
Kol-Tuv. Hu Yigmalecha Kol-Tuv	כָּל־טוּב. הוּא יִגְמָלְךָ כָּל־טוּב
Selah.	סֶלָה:

Amen. May the God who has rewarded you every kindness, forever reward you with every kindness.

Misheberakh - Weekday Shacharit

Blessing for the Congregation:

יְהִי שֵׁם יְהֹוָה מְבֹרָךְ מֵעַתָּה וְעַד עוֹלָם:

Yehi Shem Adonai Mevorach Me'attah Ve'ad Olam:

Blessed is the name of Hashem from this time on and forever. **(Psalms 113:2)**

מִי שֶׁבֵּרַךְ אֲבוֹתֵינוּ אַבְרָהָם יִצְחָק וְיַעֲקֹב וּמֹשֶׁה וְאַהֲרֹן וְדָוִד וּשְׁלֹמֹה. וְכָל הַקְּהִלּוֹת הַקְּדוֹשׁוֹת וְהַטְּהוֹרוֹת. הוּא יְבָרֵךְ אֶת כָּל הַקָּהָל הַקָּדוֹשׁ הַזֶּה. גְּדוֹלִים וּקְטַנִּים. הֵם וּנְשֵׁיהֶם וּבְנֵיהֶם וְתַלְמִידֵיהֶם. וְכָל־אֲשֶׁר לָהֶם. מַלְכָּא דְעָלְמָא הוּא יְבָרֵךְ יַתְכוֹן. וִיזַכֶּה יַתְכוֹן. וְיִשְׁמַע בְּקָל צְלוֹתְכוֹן. תִּתְפָּרְקוּן וְתִשְׁתֵּזְבוּן מִכָּל צָרָה וְעַקְתָּא. וִיהֵא מֵימְרָא דַיהֹוָה בְּסַעְדְּכֶם. וְיָגֵן בַּעַדְכֶם. וְיִפְרוֹשׂ סֻכַּת שְׁלוֹמוֹ עֲלֵיכֶם. וְיִטַּע בֵּינֵיכֶם אַהֲבָה וְאַחְוָה. שָׁלוֹם וְרֵעוּת. וִיסַלֵּק שִׂנְאַת חִנָּם מִבֵּינֵיכֶם. וְיִשְׁבּוֹר עֹל הַגּוֹיִם מֵעַל צַוָּארֵיכֶם. וִיקַיֵּם בָּכֶם מִקְרָא שֶׁכָּתוּב יְהֹוָ֞ה אֱלֹהֵ֣י אֲבוֹתֵכֶ֔ם יֹסֵ֧ף עֲלֵיכֶ֛ם כָּכֶ֖ם אֶ֣לֶף פְּעָמִ֑ים וִיבָרֵ֣ךְ אֶתְכֶ֔ם כַּאֲשֶׁ֖ר דִּבֶּ֥ר לָכֶֽם: בשבת תשובה: (וְיִכְתָּבְכֶם הָאֵל בְּסֵפֶר חַיִּים טוֹבִים.) וְכֵן יְהִי רָצוֹן וְנֹאמַר אָמֵן:

Mi Sheberach Avoteinu Avraham Yitzchak Veya'akov Umosheh Ve'aharon Vedavid Ushelomoh. Vechol Hakehilot Hakkedoshot Vehatehorot. Hu Yevarech Et Kol Hakahal Hakadosh Hazeh. Gedolim Uketanim. Hem Unesheihem Uveneihem Vetalmideihem. Vechol Asher Lahem. Malka De'alema Hu Yevarech Yatchon. Vizakeh Yatchon. Veyishma Bekal Tzelotechon. Titparekun Vetishtezevun Mikol Tzarah Ve'akta. Vihe Meimra D'Adonai Besa'dechem. Veyagen Ba'adchem. Veyifros Sukkat Shelomo Aleichem. Veyitta Beineichem Ahavah Ve'achvah. Shalom Vere'ut. Visallek Sin'at Chinam Mibeineichem. Veyishbor Ol Hagoyim Me'al Tzavareichem. Vikayem Bachem Mikra Shekatuv Adonai Elohei Avotechem Yosef Aleichem Kachem Elef Pe'amim Vivarech Etchem Ka'asher Diber Lachem. **On Shabbat in the Penitential Days add:** (Veyichtavechem Ha'el Besefer Chayim Tovim.) Vechein Yehi Ratzon Venomar Amen:

May He Who blessed our fathers Avraham, Yitzchak and Yaakov, Moshe and Aharon. David and Shlomo, and all of the holy and pure congregations; bless this holy congregation, both great and small; them, their children, their wives, and their disciples, and all that belongs to them. May the supreme King of the universe bless you and purify you, and attend to the voice of your supplication; may He redeem and deliver you from all manner of trouble and distress. May the word of Hashem support and shield you; and may he spread His tent of peace over you, and plant among you brotherly love, peace, and friendship. May He remove from among you all manner of baseless enmity, and break the yoke of the nations from off your neck; and fulfill in you what is written, "May Hashem, God of your fathers make you a thousand times as many as you are, and bless you as He has promised you.' **On Shabbat in the Penitential Days add:** (And may he inscribe you in the book of life.) And may this be the will of God, and let us say, Amen.

Continue with the Blessing for the sick of the Congregation.

Blessing for the sick of the Congregation:

מִי שֶׁבֵּרַךְ אֲבוֹתֵינוּ וְאִמּוֹתֵינוּ. אַבְרָהָם יִצְחָק וְיַעֲקֹב. שָׂרָה. רִבְקָה. רָחֵל וְלֵאָה. הוּא יְבָרֵךְ אֶת הַחוֹלִים:

פלוני בֶּן/בַּת פלוני

הַקָּדוֹשׁ בָּרוּךְ הוּא יִמָּלֵא רַחֲמִים עֲלֵיהֶם לְהַחֲלִימָם וּלְרַפְּאוֹתָם וּלְהַחֲזִיקָם וּלְהַחֲיוֹתָם. וְיִשְׁלַח לָהֶם מְהֵרָה רְפוּאָה שְׁלֵמָה מִן הַשָּׁמַיִם בִּרְמַייח אֵיבָרָיו. וּשְׁסָייה גִּידָיו. בְּתוֹךְ שְׁאָר חוֹלֵי יִשְׂרָאֵל. רְפוּאַת הַנֶּפֶשׁ וּרְפוּאַת הַגּוּף. הַשְׁתָּא בַּעֲגָלָא וּבִזְמַן קָרִיב. וְנֹאמַר אָמֵן:

Mi Sheberach Avoteinu Ve'imoteinu. Avraham Yitzchak Veya'akov. Sarah. Rivkah. Rachel Vele'ah. Hu Yevarech Et Hacholim:

Peloni Ben/Bat Peloni

Hakadosh Baruch Hu Rachamim Aleihem Lehachalimam Ulerappe'otam Ulehachazikam Ulhachayotam. Veyishlach Lahem Meheirah Refu'ah Shelemah Min Hashamayim Birmaich Eivarav. Ushesaih Gidav. Betoch She'ar Cholei Yisra'el. Refu'at Hanefesh Urefu'at Haguf. Hashta Ba'agala Uvizman Kariv. Venomar Amen:

He who blessed our patriarchs and matriarchs: Avraham, Yitzchak, and Yaakov, Sarah, Rivkah, Rachel and Leah, may He bless the sick:

____ ben (son of)/bat (daughter of) ____

May the Holy One, blessed is He, be filled with compassion upon them, to give them health, and to heal them, and to strengthen them, and to preserve them alive. And may He send them speedily a perfect healing from heaven in their 248 members and their 265 veins among the other sick of Yisrael, a healing of the soul and a healing of the body. May this occur at once, speedily and without delay and let us say, Amen.

Continue with Hatzi-Kaddish.

Kaddish is only recited in a minyan (ten men). אמן denotes when the congregation responds "Amen" together out loud. According to the Shulchan Arukh, the congregation says "Yehei Shemeh Rabba" to "Yitbarach" out loud together without interruption, and also that one should respond "Amen" after "Yitbarach." (SA, OC 55,56) This is not the common custom today.

יִתְגַּדַּל וְיִתְקַדַּשׁ שְׁמֵהּ רַבָּא. אָמֵן בְּעָלְמָא דִּי בְרָא. כִּרְעוּתֵהּ. וְיַמְלִיךְ מַלְכוּתֵהּ. וְיַצְמַח פֻּרְקָנֵהּ. וִיקָרֵב מְשִׁיחֵהּ. אָמֵן בְּחַיֵּיכוֹן וּבְיוֹמֵיכוֹן וּבְחַיֵּי דְכָל בֵּית יִשְׂרָאֵל. בַּעֲגָלָא וּבִזְמַן קָרִיב. וְאִמְרוּ אָמֵן. אָמֵן יְהֵא שְׁמֵיהּ רַבָּא מְבָרַךְ לְעָלַם וּלְעָלְמֵי עָלְמַיָּא יִתְבָּרַךְ. וְיִשְׁתַּבַּח. וְיִתְפָּאַר. וְיִתְרוֹמַם. וְיִתְנַשֵּׂא. וְיִתְהַדָּר. וְיִתְעַלֶּה. וְיִתְהַלָּל שְׁמֵהּ דְּקֻדְשָׁא. בְּרִיךְ הוּא. אָמֵן לְעֵלָּא מִן כָּל בִּרְכָתָא שִׁירָתָא. תֻּשְׁבְּחָתָא וְנֶחֱמָתָא. דַּאֲמִירָן בְּעָלְמָא. וְאִמְרוּ אָמֵן. אָמֵן

Yitgadal Veyitkadash Shemeh Rabba. Amen Be'alema Di Vera. Kir'uteh. Veyamlich Malchuteh. Veyatzmach Purkaneh. Vikarev Meshicheh. Amen Bechayeichon Uveyomeichon Uvechayei Dechal-Beit Yisra'el. Ba'agala Uvizman Kariv. Ve'imru Amen. Amen Yehei Shemeh Rabba Mevarach Le'alam Ule'alemei Alemaya Yitbarach. Veyishtabach. Veyitpa'ar. Veyitromam. Veyitnasse. Veyit'hadar. Veyit'aleh. Veyit'hallal Shemeh Dekudsha. Berich Hu. Amen Le'ella Min Kol Birchata Shirata. Tushbechata Venechemata. Da'amiran Be'alema. Ve'imru Amen. Amen

Glorified and sanctified be God's great name Amen throughout the world which He has created according to His will. May He establish His kingdom, hastening His salvation and the coming of His Messiah, Amen, in your lifetime and during your days, and within the life of the entire House of Yisrael, speedily and soon; and say, Amen. Amen May His great name be blessed forever and to all eternity. Blessed and praised, glorified and exalted, extolled and honored, adored and lauded is the name of the Holy One, blessed is He, Amen Beyond all the blessings and hymns, praises and consolations that are ever spoken in the world; and say, Amen. Amen

יְהִי־חַסְדְּךָ יְהוָה עָלֵינוּ כַּאֲשֶׁר יִחַלְנוּ לָךְ׃

Yehi Chasdecha Adonai Aleinu Ka'asher Yichalnu Lach.

Let Your mercy, Hashem, be upon us, According as we have waited for You. **(Ps. 33:22)**

Ashrei

When saying the verse "Potei'ach Et Yadecha" one should focus one's heart. If one did not focus he must return and repeat. (SA, OC 51:7) It is customary to open your hands toward Heaven as a symbol of our acceptance of the abundance Hashem bestows upon us from Heaven. (B'I'H, Ex. 9:29, I Kings 8:54).

אַשְׁרֵי יוֹשְׁבֵי בֵיתֶךָ עוֹד יְהַלְלוּךָ סֶּלָה: אַשְׁרֵי הָעָם שֶׁכָּכָה לּוֹ אַשְׁרֵי
הָעָם שֶׁיְהֹוָה אֱלֹהָיו:

Ashrei Yoshevei Veitecha; Od. Yehalelucha Selah. Ashrei Ha'am Shekachah Lo; Ashrei Ha'am. She'Adonai Elohav.

Happy are those who dwell in Your House; they are ever praising You. Happy are the people that is so situated; happy are the people whose God is Hashem. **(Psalms 84:5, 144:15)**

Psalms 145

תְּהִלָּה לְדָוִד אֲרוֹמִמְךָ אֱלוֹהַי הַמֶּלֶךְ וַאֲבָרְכָה שִׁמְךָ לְעוֹלָם וָעֶד:
בְּכָל־יוֹם אֲבָרְכֶךָּ וַאֲהַלְלָה שִׁמְךָ לְעוֹלָם וָעֶד: גָּדוֹל יְהֹוָה וּמְהֻלָּל
מְאֹד וְלִגְדֻלָּתוֹ אֵין חֵקֶר: דּוֹר לְדוֹר יְשַׁבַּח מַעֲשֶׂיךָ וּגְבוּרֹתֶיךָ יַגִּידוּ:
הֲדַר כְּבוֹד הוֹדֶךָ וְדִבְרֵי נִפְלְאוֹתֶיךָ אָשִׂיחָה: וֶעֱזוּז נוֹרְאוֹתֶיךָ יֹאמֵרוּ
וּגְדֻלָּתְךָ אֲסַפְּרֶנָּה: זֵכֶר רַב־טוּבְךָ יַבִּיעוּ וְצִדְקָתְךָ יְרַנֵּנוּ: חַנּוּן וְרַחוּם
יְהֹוָה אֶרֶךְ אַפַּיִם וּגְדָל־חָסֶד: טוֹב־יְהֹוָה לַכֹּל וְרַחֲמָיו עַל־כָּל־מַעֲשָׂיו:
יוֹדוּךָ יְהֹוָה כָּל־מַעֲשֶׂיךָ וַחֲסִידֶיךָ יְבָרְכוּכָה: כְּבוֹד מַלְכוּתְךָ יֹאמֵרוּ
וּגְבוּרָתְךָ יְדַבֵּרוּ: לְהוֹדִיעַ | לִבְנֵי הָאָדָם גְּבוּרֹתָיו וּכְבוֹד הֲדַר
מַלְכוּתוֹ: מַלְכוּתְךָ מַלְכוּת כָּל־עֹלָמִים וּמֶמְשַׁלְתְּךָ בְּכָל־דּוֹר וָדֹר:
סוֹמֵךְ יְהֹוָה לְכָל־הַנֹּפְלִים וְזוֹקֵף לְכָל־הַכְּפוּפִים: עֵינֵי־כֹל אֵלֶיךָ
יְשַׂבֵּרוּ וְאַתָּה נוֹתֵן־לָהֶם אֶת־אָכְלָם בְּעִתּוֹ: **פּוֹתֵחַ אֶת־יָדֶךָ**
וּמַשְׂבִּיעַ לְכָל־חַי רָצוֹן: צַדִּיק יְהֹוָה בְּכָל־דְּרָכָיו וְחָסִיד
בְּכָל־מַעֲשָׂיו: קָרוֹב יְהֹוָה לְכָל־קֹרְאָיו לְכֹל אֲשֶׁר יִקְרָאֻהוּ בֶאֱמֶת:
רְצוֹן־יְרֵאָיו יַעֲשֶׂה וְאֶת־שַׁוְעָתָם יִשְׁמַע וְיוֹשִׁיעֵם: שׁוֹמֵר יְהֹוָה
אֶת־כָּל־אֹהֲבָיו וְאֵת כָּל־הָרְשָׁעִים יַשְׁמִיד: תְּהִלַּת יְהֹוָה יְדַבֶּר פִּי

וִיבָרֵךְ כָּל־בָּשָׂר שֵׁם קָדְשׁוֹ לְעוֹלָם וָעֶד: וַאֲנַחְנוּ | נְבָרֵךְ יָהּ מֵעַתָּה וְעַד־עוֹלָם הַלְלוּיָהּ:

Tehilah. Ledavid Aromimcha Elohai Hamelech; Va'avarechah Shimcha. Le'olam Va'ed. Bechol-Yom Avarecheka; Va'ahalelah Shimcha. Le'olam Va'ed. Gadol Adonai Umehulal Me'od; Veligdulato. Ein Cheiker. Dor Ledor Yeshabach Ma'aseicha; Ugevuroteicha Yagidu. Hadar Kevod Hodecha; Vedivrei Nifle'oteicha Asichah. Ve'ezuz Nore'oteicha Yomeru; Ug'dulatecha Asap'renah. Zecher Rav-Tuvecha Yabi'u; Vetzidkatecha Yeranenu. Chanun Verachum Adonai Erech Apayim. Ugedol-Chased. Tov-Adonai Lakol; Verachamav. Al-Chol-Ma'asav. Yoducha Adonai Chol-Ma'aseicha; Vachasideicha. Yevarechuchah. Kevod Malchutecha Yomeru; Ugevuratecha Yedaberu. Lehodia Livnei Ha'adam Gevurotav; Uchevod. Hadar Malchuto. Malchutecha. Malchut Chol-'Olamim; Umemshaltecha. Bechol-Dor Vador. Somech Adonai Lechol-Hanofelim; Vezokeif. Lechol-Hakefufim. Einei-Chol Eleicha Yesaberu; Ve'attah Noten-Lahem Et-'Ochlam Be'ito. **Potei'ach Et-Yadecha; Umasbia Lechol-Chai Ratzon.** Tzaddik Adonai Bechol-Derachav; Vechasid. Bechol-Ma'asav. Karov Adonai Lechol-Kore'av; Lechol Asher Yikra'uhu Ve'emet. Retzon-Yere'av Ya'aseh; Ve'et-Shav'atam Yishma'. Veyoshi'em. Shomer Adonai Et-Chol-'Ohavav; Ve'et Chol-Haresha'im Yashmid. Tehillat Adonai Yedaber Pi Vivarech Chol-Basar Shem Kodsho. Le'olam Va'ed. Va'anachnu Nevarech Yah. Me'attah Ve'ad-'Olam. Halleluyah.

A Psalm of praise; of David. א I will extol You, my God, Oh King; And I will bless Your name forever and ever. ב Every day will I bless You; And I will praise You name forever and ever. ג Great is Hashem, and highly to be praised; And His greatness is unsearchable. ד One generation will applaud Your works to another, And will declare Your mighty acts. ה The glorious splendor of Your majesty, And Your wondrous works, I will rehearse. ו And men will speak of the might of Your tremendous acts; And I will tell of Your greatness. ז They will utter the fame of Your great goodness, And will sing of Your righteousness. ח Hashem is gracious, and full of compassion; Slow to anger, and of great mercy. ט Hashem is good to all; And His tender mercies are over all His works. י All Your works will praise You, Hashem; And Your holy-ones will bless You. כ They will speak of the glory of Your kingdom, And talk of Your might; ל To make known to the sons of men His mighty acts, And the glory of the beauty of His kingdom. מ Your kingdom is a kingdom for all ages, And Your dominion endures throughout all generations. ס Hashem upholds all that fall, And raises up all those that are bowed down. ע The eyes of all wait for You, And You give them their food in due season. פ **You open Your hand, And satisfy every living thing with favor.** צ Hashem is righteous in all His ways, And gracious in all His works. ק Hashem is near to all them that call upon Him, To all that call upon Him in truth. ר He will fulfill the desire of those that fear Him; He also will hear their cry, and will save them. ש Hashem preserves all them that love Him; But all the wicked will He destroy. ת My mouth will speak the praise of Hashem; And let all flesh bless His holy name forever and ever.

On a day when Tachanun is not read one skips this:

Psalms 20

לַמְנַצֵּחַ מִזְמוֹר לְדָוִד׃ יַעַנְךָ יְהוָה בְּיוֹם צָרָה יְשַׂגֶּבְךָ שֵׁם | אֱלֹהֵי
יַעֲקֹב׃ יִשְׁלַח־עֶזְרְךָ מִקֹּדֶשׁ וּמִצִּיּוֹן יִסְעָדֶךָּ׃ יִזְכֹּר כָּל־מִנְחֹתֶךָ וְעוֹלָתְךָ
יְדַשְּׁנֶה סֶלָה׃ יִתֶּן־לְךָ כִלְבָבֶךָ וְכָל־עֲצָתְךָ יְמַלֵּא׃ נְרַנְּנָה | בִּישׁוּעָתֶךָ
וּבְשֵׁם־אֱלֹהֵינוּ נִדְגֹּל יְמַלֵּא יְהוָה כָּל־מִשְׁאֲלוֹתֶיךָ׃ עַתָּה יָדַעְתִּי כִּי
הוֹשִׁיעַ | יְהוָה מְשִׁיחוֹ יַעֲנֵהוּ מִשְּׁמֵי קָדְשׁוֹ בִּגְבֻרוֹת יֵשַׁע יְמִינוֹ׃
אֵלֶּה בָרֶכֶב וְאֵלֶּה בַסּוּסִים וַאֲנַחְנוּ | בְּשֵׁם־יְהוָה אֱלֹהֵינוּ נַזְכִּיר׃
הֵמָּה כָּרְעוּ וְנָפָלוּ וַאֲנַחְנוּ קַּמְנוּ וַנִּתְעוֹדָד׃ יְהוָה הוֹשִׁיעָה הַמֶּלֶךְ
יַעֲנֵנוּ בְיוֹם־קָרְאֵנוּ׃

Lamnatzeach. Mizmor Ledavid. Ya'ancha Adonai Beyom Tzarah; Yesagevcha. Shem Elohei Ya'akov. Yishlach-'Ezrecha Mikodesh; Umitziyon. Yis'adeka. Yizkor Chol-Minchotecha; Ve'olatecha Yedasheneh Selah. Yiten-Lecha Chilvavecha; Vechol-'Atzatecha Yemalle. Neranenah Bishu'atecha. Uveshem-'Eloheinu Nidgol; Yemalei Adonai Chol-Mish'aloteicha. Attah Yada'ti. Ki Hoshia

Adonai Meshicho Ya'anehu Mishemei Kodsho; Bigvurot. Yesha Yemino. Eleh Varechev Ve'eleh Vassusim; Va'anachnu Beshem-Adonai Eloheinu Nazkir. Hemah Kare'u Venafalu; Va'anachnu Kamnu. Vanit'odad. Adonai Hoshi'ah; Hamelech. Ya'aneinu Veyom-Kor'enu.

For the Leader. A Psalm of David. May Hashem answer you in the day of trouble; The name of the God of Yaakov set you up on high; May He send you help from the Sanctuary, And support you out of Tziyon; Receive the memorial of all your meal-offerings, And accept the fat of your burnt-sacrifice; Selah. May He grant you according to your own heart, And fulfill all of your counsel. We will shout for joy in your victory, And in the name of our God we will set up our standards; May Hashem fulfill all of your petitions. Now I know that Hashem saves His anointed; He will answer him from His holy heaven With the mighty acts of His saving right hand. Some trust in chariots, and some in horses; But we will make mention of the name of Hashem our God. They are bowed down and fallen; But we are risen, and stand upright. Save, Hashem; May the King answer us in the day that we call.

Uva Letziyon

One should be very careful to say the kedushah of Uva Letziyon with kavanah (intention). (SA, OC 132:1) It is ideal to say this kedusha seated and with a minyan (10 men). If one says this by himself, it should be recited like one would read from the Torah with cantillation.

Uva Letziyon Go'el. Uleshavei	וּבָ֤א לְצִיּוֹן֙ גּוֹאֵ֔ל וּלְשָׁבֵ֥י
Fesha Beya'akov; Ne'um Adonai	פֶ֖שַׁע בְּיַעֲקֹ֑ב נְאֻ֖ם יְהוָֽה׃
Va'ani. Zot Beriti Otam Amar	וַאֲנִ֗י זֹ֣את בְּרִיתִ֤י אוֹתָם֙ אָמַ֣ר
Adonai Ruchi Asher Aleicha.	יְהוָ֔ה רוּחִי֙ אֲשֶׁ֣ר עָלֶ֔יךָ
Udevarai Asher-Samti Beficha;	וּדְבָרַ֖י אֲשֶׁר־שַׂ֣מְתִּי בְּפִ֑יךָ
Lo-Yamushu Mipicha Umipi	לֹֽא־יָמ֡וּשׁוּ מִפִּ֩יךָ֩ וּמִפִּ֨י
Zar'acha Umipi Zera Zar'acha	זַרְעֲךָ֜ וּמִפִּ֨י זֶ֤רַע זַרְעֲךָ֙

Amar Adonai Me'attah	אָמַר יְהֹוָה מֵעַתָּה
Ve'ad-'Olam. Ve'attah Kadosh;	וְעַד־עוֹלָם: וְאַתָּה קָדוֹשׁ
Yoshev. Tehillot Yisra'el. Vekara	יוֹשֵׁב תְּהִלּוֹת יִשְׂרָאֵל: וְקָרָא
Zeh El-Zeh Ve'amar. **Kadosh**	זֶה אֶל־זֶה וְאָמַר **קָדוֹשׁ |**
Kadosh Kadosh Adonai Tzeva'ot;	**קָדוֹשׁ קָדוֹשׁ יְהֹוָה צְבָאוֹת**
Melo Chol-Ha'aretz Kevodo.	**מְלֹא כָל־הָאָרֶץ כְּבוֹדוֹ:**
Umekabelin Dein Min Dein	וּמְקַבְּלִין דֵּין מִן דֵּין
Ve'amerin. Kaddish Bishmei	וְאָמְרִין: קַדִּישׁ בִּשְׁמֵי
Meroma Illa'ah Beit Shechineteh.	מְרוֹמָא עִלָּאָה בֵּית שְׁכִינְתֵּהּ.
Kaddish Al Ar'a Ovad	קַדִּישׁ עַל אַרְעָא עוֹבַד
Gevureteh. Kaddish Le'alam	גְּבוּרְתֵּהּ. קַדִּישׁ לְעָלַם
Ule'alemei Alemaya. Adonai	וּלְעָלְמֵי עָלְמַיָּא. יְהֹוָה
Tzeva'ot Malya Chol-'Ar'a Ziv	צְבָאוֹת מַלְיָא כָל-אַרְעָא זִיו
Yekareh. Vatissa'eni Ruach.	יְקָרֵהּ: וַתִּשָּׂאֵנִי רוּחַ
Va'eshma Acharai. Kol Ra'ash	וָאֶשְׁמַע אַחֲרַי קוֹל רַעַשׁ
Gadol; **Baruch Kevod-Adonai**	גָּדוֹל **בָּרוּךְ כְּבוֹד־יְהֹוָה**
Mimekomo. Unetalatni Rucha.	**מִמְּקוֹמוֹ:** וּנְטָלַתְנִי רוּחָא.
Ushema'it Batrai Kal Zia Sagi	וּשְׁמָעִית בַּתְרַי קָל זִיעַ שַׂגִּיא
Dimshabechin Ve'amerin. Berich	דִּמְשַׁבְּחִין וְאָמְרִין: בְּרִיךְ
Yekara Da'adonai Me'atar Beit	יְקָרָא דַיהֹוָה מֵאֲתַר בֵּית
Shechineteh. **Adonai Yimloch**	שְׁכִינְתֵּהּ: **יְהֹוָה | יִמְלֹךְ**
Le'olam Va'ed. Adonai	**לְעֹלָם וָעֶד:** יְהֹוָה
Malchuteih Ka'im Le'alam	מַלְכוּתֵיהּ קָאֵים לְעָלַם
Ule'alemei Alemaya. Adonai	וּלְעָלְמֵי עָלְמַיָּא: יְהֹוָה
Elohei Avraham Yitzchak	אֱלֹהֵי אַבְרָהָם יִצְחָק
Veyisra'el Avoteinu. Shomrah-	וְיִשְׂרָאֵל אֲבֹתֵינוּ שָׁמְרָה־

Zot Le'olam. Leyetzer	זֹאת לְעוֹלָם לְיֵצֶר
Machshevot Levav Ammecha;	מַחְשְׁבוֹת לְבַב עַמֶּךָ
Vehachein Levavam Eleicha.	וְהָכֵן לְבָבָם אֵלֶיךָ:
Vehu Rachum Yechapeir Avon	וְהוּא רַחוּם | יְכַפֵּר עָוֹן
Velo-Yashchit Vehirbah Lehashiv	וְלֹא־יַשְׁחִית וְהִרְבָּה לְהָשִׁיב
Appo; Velo-Ya'ir. Chol-Chamato.	אַפּוֹ וְלֹא־יָעִיר כָּל־חֲמָתוֹ:
Ki-'Attah Adonai Tov Vesalach;	כִּי־אַתָּה אֲדֹנָי טוֹב וְסַלָּח
Verav-Chesed Lechol-Kore'eicha.	וְרַב־חֶסֶד לְכָל־קֹרְאֶיךָ:
Tzidkatecha Tzedek Le'olam;	צִדְקָתְךָ צֶדֶק לְעוֹלָם
Vetoratecha Emet. Titen Emet	וְתוֹרָתְךָ אֱמֶת: תִּתֵּן אֱמֶת
Leya'akov. Chesed Le'avraham;	לְיַעֲקֹב חֶסֶד לְאַבְרָהָם
Asher-Nishba'ta La'avoteinu	אֲשֶׁר־נִשְׁבַּעְתָּ לַאֲבֹתֵינוּ
Mimei Kedem. Baruch Adonai	מִימֵי קֶדֶם: בָּרוּךְ אֲדֹנָי
Yom Yom Ya'amas-Lanu. Ha'el	יוֹם | יוֹם יַעֲמָס־לָנוּ הָאֵל
Yeshu'ateinu Selah. Adonai	יְשׁוּעָתֵנוּ סֶלָה: יְהֹוָה
Tzeva'ot Imanu; Misgav-Lanu	צְבָאוֹת עִמָּנוּ מִשְׂגָּב־לָנוּ
Elohei Ya'akov Selah. Adonai	אֱלֹהֵי יַעֲקֹב סֶלָה: יְהֹוָה
Tzeva'ot; Ashrei Adam. Boteach	צְבָאוֹת אַשְׁרֵי אָדָם בֹּטֵחַ בָּךְ:
Bach. Adonai Hoshi'ah;	יְהֹוָה הוֹשִׁיעָה
Hamelech. Ya'aneinu Veyom-	הַמֶּלֶךְ יַעֲנֵנוּ בְיוֹם־
Kor'enu.	קָרְאֵנוּ:

"A redeemer will come to Tzion and to those in Yaakov who turn from transgression, says Hashem. As for Me, this is My covenant with them, says Hashem: My spirit which is upon you, and My words which I have put in your mouth, will not depart out of your mouth, or out of the mouth of your children, or out of the mouth of your children's children from now on forever, says Hashem. "For You are holy and are enthroned amidst the praises of Yisrael." "The angels called one to another, and said, "**Holy, Holy, Holy is Hashem of hosts, The fullness of all the earth is His glory.**" And they receive word from each other and say, Holy in the highest heavens, the abode of His Divine Presence. Holy upon earth the work of His mighty power. Holy forever and to all eternity, is Hashem of hosts. The whole earth is full of His glorious splendor. "Then a spirit lifted me and behind me I heard a mighty sound, **'Blessed is Hashem's glory from His Abode.'**" Then the spirit raised me and I heard behind me a mighty moving sound of those who uttered His praise, proclaiming, 'Blessed is the glory of Hashem from the abiding place of His Divine Presence.' **"Hashem will reign forever and ever."** The rule of Hashem is established forever and ever. "Oh Hashem God of Avraham, Yitzchak and Yisrael, our fathers, forever preserve this as the inward thoughts of the heart of Your people and direct their hearts toward You. For He being merciful, will forgive iniquity and not destroy, yes, many times He averts His anger and does not awaken all of His wrath. For You, Hashem, are good and forgiving, and abounding in mercy to all who call upon You. Your righteousness is everlasting righteousness, and Your Torah is truth. You give truth to Yaakov, kindness to Avraham, As You have sworn to our fathers from ancient days. Blessed is Hashem, day to day He bears our burdens, The God of our salvation forever. Hashem of hosts is with us, The God of Yaakov is our high refuge forever. Hashem of hosts, Happy is the man who trusts in You. Hashem, save us, May the King answer us on the day when we call."

Baruch Eloheinu Shebera'anu	בָּרוּךְ אֱלֹהֵינוּ שֶׁבְּרָאָנוּ
Lichvodo. Vehivdilanu Min	לִכְבוֹדוֹ. וְהִבְדִּילָנוּ מִן
Hato'im. Venatan Lanu Torat	הַתּוֹעִים. וְנָתַן לָנוּ תּוֹרַת
Emet. Vechayei Olam Nata	אֱמֶת. וְחַיֵּי עוֹלָם נָטַע

Betocheinu. Hu Yiftach Libenu	בְּתוֹכֵֽנוּ. הוּא יִפְתַּח לִבֵּֽנוּ
Betorato. Veyasim Belibeinu	בְּתוֹרָתוֹ. וְיָשִׂים בְּלִבֵּֽנוּ
Ahavato Veyir'ato La'asot	אַהֲבָתוֹ וְיִרְאָתוֹ לַעֲשׂוֹת
Retzono. Ule'avedo Belevav	רְצוֹנוֹ. וּלְעָבְדוֹ בְּלֵבָב
Shalem. Lo Niga Larik. Velo	שָׁלֵם. לֹא נִיגַע לָרִיק. וְלֹא
Neled Labehalah. Yehi Ratzon	נֵלֵד לַבֶּהָלָה. יְהִי רָצוֹן
Milfaneicha Adonai Eloheinu	מִלְּפָנֶֽיךָ יְהוָה אֱלֹהֵינוּ
Velohei Avoteinu. Shenishmor	וֵאלֹהֵי אֲבוֹתֵֽינוּ. שֶׁנִּשְׁמוֹר
Chukkeicha Umitzvoteicha	חֻקֶּֽיךָ וּמִצְוֹתֶֽיךָ
Ba'olam Hazeh. Venizkeh.	בָּעוֹלָם הַזֶּה. וְנִזְכֶּה.
Venichyeh. Venirash Tovah	וְנִחְיֶה. וְנִירַשׁ טוֹבָה
Uverachah Lechayei Ha'olam	וּבְרָכָה לְחַיֵּי הָעוֹלָם
Haba. Lema'an Yezamercha	הַבָּא: לְמַעַן ׀ יְזַמֶּרְךָ
Chavod Velo Yidom; Adonai	כָבוֹד וְלֹא יִדֹּם יְהוָה
Elohai. Le'olam Odeka. Adonai	אֱלֹהַי לְעוֹלָם אוֹדֶךָּ: יְהוָה
Chafetz Lema'an Tzidko; Yagdil	חָפֵץ לְמַעַן צִדְקוֹ יַגְדִּיל
Torah Veya'dir. Veyivtechu Vecha	תּוֹרָה וְיַאְדִּיר: וְיִבְטְחוּ בְךָ
Yodei Shemecha; Ki Lo-'Azavta	יוֹדְעֵי שְׁמֶךָ כִּי לֹא־עָזַבְתָּ
Doresheicha Adonai. Adonai	דֹרְשֶׁיךָ יְהוָה: יְהוָה
Adoneinu; Mah-'Adir Shimcha.	אֲדֹנֵינוּ מָה־אַדִּיר שִׁמְךָ
Bechol-Ha'aretz. Chizku	בְּכָל־הָאָרֶץ: חִזְקוּ
Veya'ametz Levavchem; Chol-	וְיַאֲמֵץ לְבַבְכֶם כָּל־
Hamyachalim. L'Adonai.	הַמְיַחֲלִים לַיהוָה:

Blessed is our God, Who has created us for His glory, and has separated us from those that go astray, and has given to us the Torah of truth and planted everlasting life in our midst. May He open our hearts to His Torah, and place love and fear of Him within our hearts, to do His will and serve Him with a perfect heart, that we may not labor in vain, or bring forth confusion. May it be Your will, Hashem our God and God of our fathers, that we may keep Your statutes and commandments in this world and may we merit and live and inherit happiness and blessing for the life of the world to come. To the end that my glory may sing to You, and not be silent. Hashem my God, I will give thanks to You forever. It pleased Hashem, for His righteousness' sake, to magnify the Torah and to make it glorious. And those that know Your name will put their trust in You; for You have not forsaken those that seek You, Hashem. Oh Hashem, our Lord, How glorious is Your name in all of the earth. Be strong, and let your heart take courage, all of you that wait for Hashem.

One is not to take off Tefillin until UvaLetziyon has been recited after the Torah Service. (SA, OC 25:13) Some take Tefillin off after Aleinu. Also it is good to study some Torah before taking them off.

Kaddish Titkabbal

Kaddish is only recited in a minyan (ten men). אָמֵן denotes when the congregation responds "Amen" together out loud. According to the Shulchan Arukh, the congregation says "Yehei Shemeh Rabba" to "Yitbarach" out loud together without interruption, and also that one should respond "Amen" after "Yitbarach." (SA, OC 55,56) This is not the common custom today. Though many are accustomed to answering according to their own custom, it is advised to respond in the custom of the one reciting to avoid not fragmenting into smaller groups. ("Lo Titgodedu" - BT, Yevamot 13b / SA, OC 493, Rema / MT, Avodah Zara 12:15)

יִתְגַּדַּל וְיִתְקַדַּשׁ שְׁמֵהּ רַבָּא. אָמֵן בְּעָלְמָא דִּי בְרָא. כִּרְעוּתֵהּ. וְיַמְלִיךְ מַלְכוּתֵהּ. וְיַצְמַח פֻּרְקָנֵהּ. וִיקָרֵב מְשִׁיחֵהּ. אָמֵן בְּחַיֵּיכוֹן וּבְיוֹמֵיכוֹן וּבְחַיֵּי דְכָל בֵּית יִשְׂרָאֵל. בַּעֲגָלָא וּבִזְמַן קָרִיב. וְאִמְרוּ אָמֵן. אָמֵן יְהֵא שְׁמֵיהּ רַבָּא מְבָרַךְ לְעָלַם וּלְעָלְמֵי עָלְמַיָּא יִתְבָּרַךְ. וְיִשְׁתַּבַּח. וְיִתְפָּאַר. וְיִתְרוֹמַם. וְיִתְנַשֵּׂא. וְיִתְהַדָּר. וְיִתְעַלֶּה. וְיִתְהַלָּל שְׁמֵהּ דְּקֻדְשָׁא. בְּרִיךְ הוּא. אָמֵן לְעֵלָּא מִן כָּל בִּרְכָתָא שִׁירָתָא. תֻּשְׁבְּחָתָא וְנֶחֱמָתָא. דַּאֲמִירָן בְּעָלְמָא. וְאִמְרוּ אָמֵן. אָמֵן

Yitgadal Veyitkadash Shemeh Rabba. **Amen** Be'alema Di Vera. Kir'uteh. Veyamlich Malchuteh. Veyatzmach Purkaneh. Vikarev Meshicheh. **Amen** Bechayeichon Uveyomeichon Uvechayei Dechal-Beit Yisra'el. Ba'agala Uvizman Kariv. Ve'imru Amen. **Amen** Yehei Shemeh Rabba Mevarach Le'alam Ule'alemei Alemaya Yitbarach. Veyishtabach. Veyitpa'ar. Veyitromam. Veyitnasse. Veyit'hadar. Veyit'aleh. Veyit'hallal Shemeh Dekudsha. Berich Hu. **Amen** Le'ella Min Kol Birchata Shirata. Tushbechata Venechemata. Da'amiran Be'alema. Ve'imru Amen. **Amen**

Glorified and sanctified be God's great name **Amen** throughout the world which He has created according to His will. May He establish His kingdom, hastening His salvation and the coming of His Messiah, **Amen**, in your lifetime and during your days, and within the life of the entire House of Yisrael, speedily and soon; and say, Amen. **Amen** May His great name be blessed forever and to all eternity. Blessed and praised, glorified and exalted, extolled and honored, adored and lauded is the name of the Holy One, blessed is He, **Amen** Beyond all the blessings and hymns, praises and consolations that are ever spoken in the world; and say, Amen. **Amen**

תִּתְקַבַּל צְלוֹתָנָא וּבָעוּתָנָא. עִם צְלוֹתְהוֹן וּבָעוּתְהוֹן דְּכָל בֵּית יִשְׂרָאֵל. קֳדָם אֲבוּנָא דְּבִשְׁמַיָּא וְאַרְעָא. וְאִמְרוּ אָמֵן. אָמֵן

Titkabbal Tzelotana Uva'utana. Im Tzelotehon Uva'utehon Dechol Beit Yisra'el. Kodam Avuna Devishmaya Ve'ar'a. Ve'imru Amen. **Amen**

May the prayer and supplication of the whole House of Yisrael be accepted before their Father in heaven, and say, Amen. **Amen**

יְהֵא שְׁלָמָא רַבָּא מִן שְׁמַיָּא. חַיִּים וְשָׂבָע וִישׁוּעָה וְנֶחָמָה. וְשֵׁיזָבָא וּרְפוּאָה וּגְאוּלָּה וּסְלִיחָה וְכַפָּרָה וְרֶוַח וְהַצָּלָה לָנוּ וּלְכָל עַמּוֹ יִשְׂרָאֵל. וְאִמְרוּ אָמֵן. אָמֵן

Yehei Shelama Rabba Min Shemaya. Chayim Vesava Vishu'ah Venechamah. Vesheizava Urefu'ah Uge'ulah Uselichah Vechapparah Verevach Vehatzalah Lanu Ulechol Ammo Yisra'el. Ve'imru Amen. **Amen**

May abundant peace descend from heaven, with life and plenty, salvation, solace, liberation, healing and redemption, and forgiveness and atonement, enlargement and freedom, for us and all of God's people Yisrael; and say, Amen. **Amen**

One bows and takes three steps backwards, while still bowing. After three steps, while still bowing and before erecting, while saying, "Oseh Shalom Bimromav", turn one's face to the left, "Hu [Berachamav] Ya'aseh Shalom Aleinu", turn one's face to the right; then bow forward like a servant leaving his master. (SA, OC 123:1)

עוֹשֶׂה שָׁלוֹם בִּמְרוֹמָיו. הוּא בְּרַחֲמָיו יַעֲשֶׂה שָׁלוֹם עָלֵינוּ. וְעַל כָּל־עַמּוֹ יִשְׂרָאֵל. וְאִמְרוּ אָמֵן:

Oseh Shalom Bimromav. Hu Berachamav Ya'aseh Shalom Aleinu. Ve'al Kol-'Ammo Yisra'el. Ve'imru Amen.

Creator of peace in His high places, may He in His mercy create peace for us and for all Yisrael, and say Amen.

All stand and return the Torah to its place and say:

יְהַלְלוּ | אֶת־שֵׁם יְהֹוָה כִּי־נִשְׂגָּב שְׁמוֹ לְבַדּוֹ הוֹדוֹ עַל־אֶרֶץ וְשָׁמָיִם: וַיָּרֶם קֶרֶן | לְעַמּוֹ תְּהִלָּה לְכָל־חֲסִידָיו לִבְנֵי יִשְׂרָאֵל עַם קְרֹבוֹ הַלְלוּיָהּ: יְהֹוָה הוּא הָאֱלֹהִים. יְהֹוָה הוּא הָאֱלֹהִים בַּשָּׁמַיִם מִמַּעַל וְעַל־הָאָרֶץ מִתָּחַת אֵין עוֹד: אֵין־כָּמוֹךָ בָאֱלֹהִים | אֲדֹנָי וְאֵין כְּמַעֲשֶׂיךָ:

Yehalelu Et-Shem Adonai Ki-Nisgav Shemo Levado; Hodo. Al-'Eretz Veshamayim. Vayarem Keren Le'ammo Tehilah Lechol-Chasidav. Livnei Yisra'el Am Kerovo. Halleluyah. Adonai Hu Ha'elohim. Adonai Hu Ha'elohim. Bashamayim Mima'al. Ve'al-Ha'aretz Mitachat; Ein Od. Ein-Kamocha Va'elohim Adonai. Ve'ein Kema'aseicha.

"Let them praise the name of Hashem, For exalted is His name alone; His glory is over the earth and the heavens. He has lifted up the horn of strength of His people; He is the praise of all His pious servants, Of the children of Yisrael, the people near to Him.

Halleluyah — Praise Hashem. Hashem, He is God, Hashem, He is God, In the heavens above and on the earth beneath. There is none else. There is none like You, Hashem, among the gods, or nothing like Your works."

When the scroll of the Torah has been replaced in the Ark:

הֲשִׁיבֵנוּ יְהֹוָה | אֵלֶיךָ ונשוב (וְנָשׁוּבָה) חַדֵּשׁ יָמֵינוּ כְּקֶדֶם:

Hashiveinu Adonai Eleicha Venashuvah. Chadesh Yameinu Kekedem.

"Hashem, turn us again towards You, and we will return. Renew our days as of old."

On the day when Tachanun is not said, Tefillah LeDavid (Psalms 86) is not recited.

Tefillah LeDavid / Psalms 86

תְּפִלָּה לְדָוִד הַטֵּה־יְהֹוָה אָזְנְךָ עֲנֵנִי כִּי־עָנִי וְאֶבְיוֹן אָנִי: שָׁמְרָה נַפְשִׁי
כִּי־חָסִיד אָנִי הוֹשַׁע עַבְדְּךָ אַתָּה אֱלֹהַי הַבּוֹטֵחַ אֵלֶיךָ: חָנֵּנִי אֲדֹנָי כִּי
אֵלֶיךָ אֶקְרָא כָּל־הַיּוֹם: שַׂמֵּחַ נֶפֶשׁ עַבְדֶּךָ כִּי אֵלֶיךָ אֲדֹנָי נַפְשִׁי
אֶשָּׂא: כִּי־אַתָּה אֲדֹנָי טוֹב וְסַלָּח וְרַב־חֶסֶד לְכָל־קֹרְאֶיךָ: הַאֲזִינָה
יְהֹוָה תְּפִלָּתִי וְהַקְשִׁיבָה בְּקוֹל תַּחֲנוּנוֹתָי: בְּיוֹם צָרָתִי אֶקְרָאֶךָּ כִּי
תַעֲנֵנִי: אֵין־כָּמוֹךָ בָאֱלֹהִים | אֲדֹנָי וְאֵין כְּמַעֲשֶׂיךָ: כָּל־גּוֹיִם | אֲשֶׁר
עָשִׂיתָ יָבוֹאוּ | וְיִשְׁתַּחֲווּ לְפָנֶיךָ אֲדֹנָי וִיכַבְּדוּ לִשְׁמֶךָ: כִּי־גָדוֹל אַתָּה
וְעֹשֵׂה נִפְלָאוֹת אַתָּה אֱלֹהִים לְבַדֶּךָ: הוֹרֵנִי יְהֹוָה | דַּרְכֶּךָ אֲהַלֵּךְ
בַּאֲמִתֶּךָ יַחֵד לְבָבִי לְיִרְאָה שְׁמֶךָ: אוֹדְךָ | אֲדֹנָי אֱלֹהַי בְּכָל־לְבָבִי
וַאֲכַבְּדָה שִׁמְךָ לְעוֹלָם: כִּי־חַסְדְּךָ גָּדוֹל עָלָי וְהִצַּלְתָּ נַפְשִׁי מִשְּׁאוֹל
תַּחְתִּיָּה: אֱלֹהִים | זֵדִים קָמוּ־עָלַי וַעֲדַת עָרִיצִים בִּקְשׁוּ נַפְשִׁי וְלֹא
שָׂמוּךָ לְנֶגְדָּם: וְאַתָּה אֲדֹנָי אֵל־רַחוּם וְחַנּוּן אֶרֶךְ אַפַּיִם וְרַב־חֶסֶד
וֶאֱמֶת: פְּנֵה אֵלַי וְחָנֵּנִי תְּנָה־עֻזְּךָ לְעַבְדֶּךָ וְהוֹשִׁיעָה לְבֶן־אֲמָתֶךָ:

עֲשֵׂה־עִמִּי אוֹת לְטוֹבָה וְיִרְאוּ שֹׂנְאַי וְיֵבֹשׁוּ כִּי־אַתָּה יְהֹוָה עֲזַרְתַּנִי וְנִחַמְתָּנִי׃

Tefillah. Ledavid Hateh-Adonai Oznecha Aneni; Ki-'Ani Ve'evyon Ani. Shamerah Nafshi Ki-Chasid Ani Hosha Avdecha Attah Elohai; Haboteach Eleicha. Choneni Adonai; Ki Eleicha Ekra. Chol-Hayom. Same'ach Nefesh Avdecha; Ki Eleicha Adonai. Nafshi Essa. Ki-'Attah Adonai Tov Vesalach; Verav-Chesed Lechol-Kore'eicha. Ha'azinah Adonai Tefillati; Vehakshivah. Bekol Tachanunotai. Beyom Tzarati Ekra'eka. Ki Ta'aneni. Ein-Kamocha Va'elohim 'Adonai. Ve'ein Kema'aseicha. Chol-Goyim Asher Asita. Yavo'u Veyishtachavu Lefaneicha Adonai; Vichabedu Lishmecha. Ki-Gadol Attah Ve'oseh Nifla'ot; Attah Elohim Levadecha. Horeni Adonai Darkecha. Ahallech Ba'amitecha; Yached Levavi. Leyir'ah Shemecha. Odecha Adonai Elohai Bechol-Levavi; Va'achabedah Shimcha Le'olam. Ki-Chasdecha Gadol Alai; Vehitzalta Nafshi. Mishe'ol Tachtiyah. Elohim Zeidim Kamu-'Alai. Va'adat Aritzim Bikshu Nafshi; Velo Samucha Lenegdam. Ve'attah Adonai El-Rachum Vechanun; Erech Apayim. Verav-Chesed Ve'emet. Peneh Elai. Vechoneni Tenah-'Uzecha Le'avdecha Vehoshi'ah. Leven-'Amatecha. Aseh-'Immi Ot. Letovah Veyir'u Sone'ai Veyevoshu; Ki-'Attah Adonai Azartani Venichamtani.

A Prayer of David. Incline Your ear, Hashem, and answer me; For I am poor and needy. Keep my soul, for I am godly; My God, You save Your servant that trusts in You. Be gracious to me, Hashem; For to You do I cry all the day. Rejoice the soul of Your servant; For to You, Hashem, do I lift up my soul. For You, Hashem, are good, and ready to pardon, And abundant in mercy to all those that call on You. Give ear, Oh Hashem, to my prayer; And attend to the voice of my supplications. In the day of my trouble I call upon You; For You will answer me. There is none like You among the gods, Hashem, And there are no works like Yours. All nations whom You have made will come and prostrate themselves before You, Hashem; And they will glorify Your name. For You are great, and do wondrous things; You are God alone. Teach me, Hashem, Your way, that I may walk in Your truth; Make my heart one to fear Your name. I will thank You, Hashem my God, with my whole heart; And I will glorify Your name forever. For great is Your mercy toward me; And You have delivered my soul from the lowest nether-world. Oh God, the proud are risen up against me, And the company of violent men have sought after my soul, And have not set You before them. But You, Hashem, are a God full of compassion and gracious, Slow to anger, and abundant in mercy and truth. Oh turn to me, and be gracious to me; Give Your strength to Your servant, And save the son of Your handmaid. Work in my behalf a sign for good; That they that hate me may see it, and be put to shame, Because You, Hashem, have helped me, and comforted me.

Beit Yaakov

בֵּית יַעֲקֹב לְכוּ וְנֵלְכָה בְּאוֹר יְהוָה: כִּי כָּל־הָעַמִּים יֵלְכוּ אִישׁ בְּשֵׁם
אֱלֹהָיו וַאֲנַחְנוּ נֵלֵךְ בְּשֵׁם־יְהוָה אֱלֹהֵינוּ לְעוֹלָם וָעֶד: יְהִי יְהוָה
אֱלֹהֵינוּ עִמָּנוּ כַּאֲשֶׁר הָיָה עִם־אֲבֹתֵינוּ אַל־יַעַזְבֵנוּ וְאַל־יִטְּשֵׁנוּ:
לְהַטּוֹת לְבָבֵנוּ אֵלָיו לָלֶכֶת בְּכָל־דְּרָכָיו וְלִשְׁמֹר מִצְוֹתָיו וְחֻקָּיו
וּמִשְׁפָּטָיו אֲשֶׁר צִוָּה אֶת־אֲבֹתֵינוּ: וְיִהְיוּ דְבָרַי אֵלֶּה אֲשֶׁר הִתְחַנַּנְתִּי
לִפְנֵי יְהוָה קְרֹבִים אֶל־יְהוָה אֱלֹהֵינוּ יוֹמָם וָלָיְלָה לַעֲשׂוֹת | מִשְׁפַּט
עַבְדּוֹ וּמִשְׁפַּט עַמּוֹ יִשְׂרָאֵל דְּבַר־יוֹם בְּיוֹמוֹ: לְמַעַן דַּעַת כָּל־עַמֵּי
הָאָרֶץ כִּי יְהוָה הוּא הָאֱלֹהִים אֵין עוֹד:

Beit Ya'akov; Lechu Venelechah Be'or Adonai Ki Chol-Ha'ammim. Yelechu Ish Beshem Elohav; Va'anachnu. Nelech Beshem-Adonai Eloheinu Le'olam Va'ed. Yehi Adonai Eloheinu Imanu. Ka'asher Hayah Im-'Avoteinu; Al-Ya'azvenu Ve'al-Yitesenu. Lehatot Levavenu Elav; Lalechet Bechol-Derachav. Velishmor Mitzvtav Vechukkav Umishpatav. Asher Tzivah Et-'Avoteinu. Veyihyu Devarai Eleh. Asher Hitchananti Lifnei Adonai Kerovim El-Adonai Eloheinu Yomam Valailah; La'asot Mishpat Avdo. Umishpat Ammo Yisra'el Devar-Yom Beyomo. Lema'an. Da'at Chol-'Ammei Ha'aretz. Ki Adonai Hu Ha'elohim; Ein Od.

"House of Yaakov, Come and let us walk in the light of Hashem. Though all peoples walk in the name of their gods, We will walk in the name of our God forever and ever. May Hashem our God be with us as He was with our fathers; may He not forsake us or abandon us, but may He turn our heart to Him, that we walk in all His ways, and keep His commandments, statutes and ordinances which He commanded our fathers. And may these my words which I have entreated before Hashem, be near to Hashem our God day and night, so that He will maintain the cause of His servant and of His people Yisrael day by day, that all the peoples of the earth may know that Hashem, He is God, there is none else." **(1 Kings 8, 57-60)**

Psalms 124

שִׁיר הַמַּעֲלוֹת לְדָוִד לוּלֵי יְהֹוָה שֶׁהָיָה לָנוּ יֹאמַר־נָא יִשְׂרָאֵל: לוּלֵי יְהֹוָה שֶׁהָיָה לָנוּ בְּקוּם עָלֵינוּ אָדָם: אֲזַי חַיִּים בְּלָעוּנוּ בַּחֲרוֹת אַפָּם בָּנוּ: אֲזַי הַמַּיִם שְׁטָפוּנוּ נַחְלָה עָבַר עַל־נַפְשֵׁנוּ: אֲזַי עָבַר עַל־נַפְשֵׁנוּ הַמַּיִם הַזֵּידוֹנִים: בָּרוּךְ יְהֹוָה שֶׁלֹּא נְתָנָנוּ טֶרֶף לְשִׁנֵּיהֶם: נַפְשֵׁנוּ כְּצִפּוֹר נִמְלְטָה מִפַּח יוֹקְשִׁים הַפַּח נִשְׁבָּר וַאֲנַחְנוּ נִמְלָטְנוּ: עֶזְרֵנוּ בְּשֵׁם יְהֹוָה עֹשֵׂה שָׁמַיִם וָאָרֶץ:

Shir Hama'alot. LeDavid Lulei Adonai Shehayah Lanu; Yomar-Na Yisra'el. Lulei Adonai Shehayah Lanu; Bekum Aleinu Adam. Azai Chayim Bela'unu; Bacharot Appam Banu. Azai Hamayim Shetafunu; Nachlah Avar Al-Nafshenu. Azai Avar Al-Nafshenu; Hamayim. Hazeidonim. Baruch Adonai Shelo Netananu Teref Leshineihem. Nafshenu. Ketzipor Nimletah Mippach Yokeshim Happach Nishbar. Va'anachnu Nimlatenu. Ezrenu Beshem Adonai Oseh. Shamayim Va'aretz.

A Song of Ascents; of David. 'If it had not been Hashem Who was for us', Let Yisrael now say; 'If it had not been Hashem Who was for us, When men rose up against us, Then they would have swallowed us up alive, when their wrath was kindled against us; Then the waters would have overwhelmed us, the stream would have gone over our soul; Then the proud waters would have gone over our soul.' Blessed is Hashem, Who has not given us as prey to their teeth. Our soul is escaped as a bird out of the snare of the fowlers; The snare is broken, and we escaped. Our help is in the name of Hashem, Who made heaven and earth.

Shir Shel Yom / Song of the Day

Psalms sung by the Levites in the Beit HaMikdash on each day of the week. On Rosh Chodesh and Hanukkah, one does not need to say anything after "Kodesh", (Hashir...hadduchan).

On Sunday:

הַיּוֹם יוֹם אֶחָד בְּשַׁבָּת קוֹדֶשׁ הַשִּׁיר שֶׁהָיוּ הַלְוִיִּם אוֹמְרִים עַל הַדּוּכָן:

Hayom Yom Echad Beshabbat Kodesh Hashir Shehayu Halviyim Omerim Al Hadduchan:

Today is day one from the holy Shabbat, the song that the Levi'im would sing on the stand:

Psalms 24

לְדָוִד מִזְמוֹר לַיהוָה הָאָרֶץ וּמְלוֹאָהּ תֵּבֵל וְיֹשְׁבֵי בָהּ: כִּי־הוּא
עַל־יַמִּים יְסָדָהּ וְעַל־נְהָרוֹת יְכוֹנְנֶהָ: מִי־יַעֲלֶה בְהַר־יְהוָה וּמִי־יָקוּם
בִּמְקוֹם קָדְשׁוֹ: נְקִי כַפַּיִם וּבַר־לֵבָב אֲשֶׁר | לֹא־נָשָׂא לַשָּׁוְא נַפְשִׁי
וְלֹא נִשְׁבַּע לְמִרְמָה: יִשָּׂא בְרָכָה מֵאֵת יְהוָה וּצְדָקָה מֵאֱלֹהֵי יִשְׁעוֹ:
זֶה דּוֹר דֹּרְשָׁו מְבַקְשֵׁי פָנֶיךָ יַעֲקֹב סֶלָה: שְׂאוּ שְׁעָרִים | רָאשֵׁיכֶם
וְהִנָּשְׂאוּ פִּתְחֵי עוֹלָם וְיָבוֹא מֶלֶךְ הַכָּבוֹד: מִי זֶה מֶלֶךְ הַכָּבוֹד יְהוָה
עִזּוּז וְגִבּוֹר יְהוָה גִּבּוֹר מִלְחָמָה: שְׂאוּ שְׁעָרִים | רָאשֵׁיכֶם וּשְׂאוּ
פִּתְחֵי עוֹלָם וְיָבֹא מֶלֶךְ הַכָּבוֹד: מִי הוּא זֶה מֶלֶךְ הַכָּבוֹד יְהוָה
צְבָאוֹת הוּא מֶלֶךְ הַכָּבוֹד סֶלָה: וממשיך הושיענו

Ledavid. Mizmor L'Adonai Ha'aretz Umelo'ah; Tevel. Veyoshevei Vah. Ki-Hu Al-Yamim Yesadah; Ve'al-Neharot. Yechoneneha. Mi-Ya'aleh Vehar-Adonai Umi-Yakum Bimkom Kodsho. Neki Chapayim. Uvar-Levav Asher Lo-Nasa Lashav Nafshi; Velo Nishba Lemirmah. Yissa Verachah Me'et Adonai Utzedakah. Me' Elohei Yish'o. Zeh Dor Doreshav; Mevakshei Faneicha Ya'akov Selah. Se'u She'arim Rasheichem. Vehinase'u Pitchei Olam; Veyavo. Melech Hakavod. Mi Zeh Melech Hakavod Adonai Izuz Vegibor; Adonai Gibor Milchamah. Se'u She'arim Rasheichem. Use'u Pitchei Olam; Veyavo. Melech Hakavod. Mi Hu Zeh Melech Hakavod Adonai Tzeva'ot; Hu Melech Hakavod Selah. **(recite "hoshienu" at the end of the weekly Psalms)**

A Psalm of David. The earth is Hashem's, and the fullness there in it; the world, and they that dwell there in it. For He has founded it upon the seas, and established it upon the floods. Who will ascend into the mountain of Hashem? and who will stand in His holy place? He that has clean hands, and a pure heart; who has not taken My name in vain, and has not sworn deceitfully. He will receive a blessing from Hashem, and righteousness from the God of his salvation. Such is the generation of those that seek after Him, that seek Your face, even Yaakov. Selah. Lift up your heads, you gates, and be lifted up, you everlasting doors; that the King of glory may come in. 'Who is the King of glory?' 'Hashem strong and mighty, Hashem mighty in battle.' Lift up your heads, you gates, lift them up, you everlasting doors; that the King of glory may come in. 'Who then is the King of glory?' 'Hashem of hosts; He is the King of glory.' selah. **(recite "hoshienu" at the end of the weekly Psalms)**

On Monday:

הַיּוֹם יוֹם שֵׁנִי בְּשַׁבָּת קוֹדֶשׁ הַשִּׁיר שֶׁהָיוּ הַלְוִיִּם אוֹמְרִים עַל הַדּוּכָן:

Hayom Yom Sheni Beshabbat Kodesh Hashir Shehayu Halviyim Omerim Al Hadduchan:

Today is day two from the holy Shabbat, the song that the Levi'im would sing on the stand:

Psalms 48

שִׁיר מִזְמוֹר לִבְנֵי־קֹרַח: גָּדוֹל יְהֹוָה וּמְהֻלָּל מְאֹד בְּעִיר אֱלֹהֵינוּ
הַר־קָדְשׁוֹ: יְפֵה נוֹף מְשׂוֹשׂ כָּל־הָאָרֶץ הַר־צִיּוֹן יַרְכְּתֵי צָפוֹן קִרְיַת
מֶלֶךְ רָב: אֱלֹהִים בְּאַרְמְנוֹתֶיהָ נוֹדַע לְמִשְׂגָּב: כִּי־הִנֵּה הַמְּלָכִים
נוֹעֲדוּ עָבְרוּ יַחְדָּו: הֵמָּה רָאוּ כֵּן תָּמָהוּ נִבְהֲלוּ נֶחְפָּזוּ: רְעָדָה
אֲחָזָתַם שָׁם חִיל כַּיּוֹלֵדָה: בְּרוּחַ קָדִים תְּשַׁבֵּר אֳנִיּוֹת תַּרְשִׁישׁ:
כַּאֲשֶׁר שָׁמַעְנוּ | כֵּן רָאִינוּ בְּעִיר־יְהֹוָה צְבָאוֹת בְּעִיר אֱלֹהֵינוּ אֱלֹהִים
יְכוֹנְנֶהָ עַד־עוֹלָם סֶלָה: דִּמִּינוּ אֱלֹהִים חַסְדֶּךָ בְּקֶרֶב הֵיכָלֶךָ: כְּשִׁמְךָ
אֱלֹהִים כֵּן תְּהִלָּתְךָ עַל־קַצְוֵי־אֶרֶץ צֶדֶק מָלְאָה יְמִינֶךָ: יִשְׂמַח |
הַר־צִיּוֹן תָּגֵלְנָה בְּנוֹת יְהוּדָה לְמַעַן מִשְׁפָּטֶיךָ: סֹבּוּ צִיּוֹן וְהַקִּיפוּהָ
סִפְרוּ מִגְדָּלֶיהָ: שִׁיתוּ לִבְּכֶם | לְחֵילָה פַּסְּגוּ אַרְמְנוֹתֶיהָ לְמַעַן תְּסַפְּרוּ
לְדוֹר אַחֲרוֹן: כִּי זֶה | אֱלֹהִים אֱלֹהֵינוּ עוֹלָם וָעֶד הוּא יְנַהֲגֵנוּ
עַל־מוּת: וממשיך הושיענו

Shir Mizmor. Livnei-Korach. Gadol Adonai Umehulal Me'od; Be'ir Eloheinu. Har-Kodsho. Yefeh Nof Mesos Chol-Ha'aretz Har-Tziyon Yarketei Tzafon; Kiryat. Melech Rav. Elohim Be'armenoteiha. Noda Lemisgav. Ki-Hineh Hamelachim No'adu; Averu Yachdav. Hemah Ra'u Ken Tamahu; Nivhalu Nechpazu. Re'adah Achazatam Sham; Chil Kayoledah. Beruach Kadim; Teshaber. Oniyot Tarshish. Ka'asher Shama'nu Ken Ra'inu. Be'ir-Adonai Tzeva'ot Be'ir Eloheinu; Elohim Yechoneneha Ad-'Olam Selah. Dimminu Elohim Chasdecha; Bekerev. Heichalecha. Keshimcha Elohim. Ken Tehilatecha Al-Katzvei-'Eretz; Tzedek Male'ah Yeminecha. Yismach Har-Tziyon. Tagelenah Benot Yehudah; Lema'an. Mishpateicha. Sobbu Tziyon Vehakkifuha; Sifru. Migdaleiha. Shitu Libechem Lecheilah. Passegu Armenoteiha; Lema'an Tesaperu. Ledor Acharon. Ki Zeh Elohim Eloheinu Olam Va'ed; Hu Yenahagenu Al-Mut. **(recite "hoshienu" at the end of the weekly Psalms)**

A Song; a Psalm of the sons of Korach. Great is Hashem, and highly to be praised, in the city of our God, His holy mountain, Fair in situation, the joy of the whole earth; even mount Tziyon, the uttermost parts of the north, the city of the great King. God, in her palaces, has made Himself known for a stronghold. For, behold, the kings assembled themselves, they advanced forward together. They saw, then they were amazed; they were affrighted, they hasted away. Trembling took hold of them there, pain, as of a woman in labor. With the east wind You broke the ships of Tarshish. As we have heard, so have we seen in the city of Hashem of hosts, in the city of our God — God establish it forever. Selah, We have thought on Your lovingkindness, Oh God, in the midst of Your Temple. As is Your name, Oh God, so is Your praise to the ends of the earth; Your right hand is full of righteousness. Let Mount Tziyon be glad, let the daughters of Yehudah rejoice, because of Your judgments. Walk about Tziyon, and go around her; count the towers. Mark well her ramparts, traverse her palaces; that you may tell it to the generation following. For such is God, our God, forever and ever; He will guide us eternally. **(recite "hoshienu" at the end of the weekly Psalms)**

On Tuesday:

הַיּוֹם יוֹם שְׁלִישִׁי בְּשַׁבָּת קוֹדֶשׁ הַשִּׁיר שֶׁהָיוּ הַלְוִיִּם אוֹמְרִים עַל הַדּוּכָן:

Hayom Yom Shelishi Beshabbat Kodesh Hashir Shehayu Halviyim Omerim Al Hadduchan:

Today is day three from the holy Shabbat, the song that the Levi'im would sing on the stand:

Psalms 82

מִזְמוֹר לְאָסָף אֱלֹהִים נִצָּב בַּעֲדַת־אֵל בְּקֶרֶב אֱלֹהִים יִשְׁפֹּט: עַד־מָתַי תִּשְׁפְּטוּ־עָוֶל וּפְנֵי רְשָׁעִים תִּשְׂאוּ־סֶלָה: שִׁפְטוּ־דַל וְיָתוֹם עָנִי וָרָשׁ הַצְדִּיקוּ: פַּלְּטוּ־דַל וְאֶבְיוֹן מִיַּד רְשָׁעִים הַצִּילוּ: לֹא יָדְעוּ | וְלֹא יָבִינוּ בַּחֲשֵׁכָה יִתְהַלָּכוּ יִמּוֹטוּ כָּל־מוֹסְדֵי אָרֶץ: אֲנִי־אָמַרְתִּי אֱלֹהִים אַתֶּם וּבְנֵי עֶלְיוֹן כֻּלְּכֶם: אָכֵן כְּאָדָם תְּמוּתוּן וּכְאַחַד הַשָּׂרִים תִּפֹּלוּ: קוּמָה אֱלֹהִים שָׁפְטָה הָאָרֶץ כִּי־אַתָּה תִנְחַל בְּכָל־הַגּוֹיִם: וממשיך הושיענו

Mizmor. Le'asaf Elohim. Nitzav Ba'adat-'El; Bekerev Elohim Yishpot. Ad-Matai Tishpetu-'Avel; Ufenei Resha'im. Tis'u-Selah. Shiftu-Dal Veyatom; Ani Varash Hatzdiku. Palletu-Dal Ve'evyon; Miyad

Resha'im Hatzilu. Lo Yade'u Velo Yavinu. Bachashechah Yit'hallachu; Yimmotu. Chol-Mosedei Aretz. Ani-'Amarti Elohim Attem; Uvenei Elyon Kullechem. Achein Ke'adam Temutun; Uche'achad Hassarim Tipolu. Kumah Elohim Shoftah Ha'aretz; Ki-'Attah Tinchal. Bechol-Hagoyim. **(recite "hoshienu" at the end of the weekly Psalms)**

A Psalm of Asaph. God stands in the congregation of God; in the midst of the judges He judges: 'How long will you judge unjustly, and respect the wicked? Selah. Judge the poor and fatherless; do justice to the afflicted and destitute. Rescue the poor and needy; deliver them out of the hand of the wicked. They do not know, neither do they understand; they go about in darkness; all the foundations of the earth are moved. I said: You are gods, and all of you are sons of the Most High. Nevertheless you will die like men, and fall like one of the princes.' Arise, Oh God, judge the earth; for You will possess all nations. **(recite "hoshienu" at the end of the weekly Psalms)**

On Wednesday:

הַיּוֹם יוֹם רְבִיעִי בְּשַׁבָּת קוֹדֶשׁ הַשִּׁיר שֶׁהָיוּ הַלְוִיִּם אוֹמְרִים עַל הַדּוּכָן:

Hayom Yom Revi'i Beshabbat Kodesh Hashir Shehayu Halviyim Omerim Al Hadduchan:

Today is day four from the holy Shabbat, the song that the Levi'im would sing on the stand:

Psalms 94

אֵל־נְקָמוֹת יְהֹוָה אֵל נְקָמוֹת הוֹפִיעַ: הִנָּשֵׂא שֹׁפֵט הָאָרֶץ הָשֵׁב
גְּמוּל עַל־גֵּאִים: עַד־מָתַי רְשָׁעִים | יְהֹוָה עַד־מָתַי רְשָׁעִים יַעֲלֹזוּ: יַבִּיעוּ
יְדַבְּרוּ עָתָק יִתְאַמְּרוּ כָּל־פֹּעֲלֵי אָוֶן: עַמְּךָ יְהֹוָה יְדַכְּאוּ וְנַחֲלָתְךָ יְעַנּוּ:
אַלְמָנָה וְגֵר יַהֲרֹגוּ וִיתוֹמִים יְרַצֵּחוּ: וַיֹּאמְרוּ לֹא יִרְאֶה־יָּהּ וְלֹא־יָבִין
אֱלֹהֵי יַעֲקֹב: בִּינוּ בֹּעֲרִים בָּעָם וּכְסִילִים מָתַי תַּשְׂכִּילוּ: הֲנֹטַע אֹזֶן
הֲלֹא יִשְׁמָע אִם־יֹצֵר עַיִן הֲלֹא יַבִּיט: הֲיֹסֵר גּוֹיִם הֲלֹא יוֹכִיחַ
הַמְלַמֵּד אָדָם דָּעַת: יְהֹוָה יֹדֵעַ מַחְשְׁבוֹת אָדָם כִּי־הֵמָּה הָבֶל:
אַשְׁרֵי | הַגֶּבֶר אֲשֶׁר־תְּיַסְּרֶנּוּ יָּהּ וּמִתּוֹרָתְךָ תְלַמְּדֶנּוּ: לְהַשְׁקִיט לוֹ

מִימֵי רָע עַד יִכָּרֶה לָרָשָׁע שָׁחַת: כִּי | לֹא־יִטֹּשׁ יְהֹוָה עַמּוֹ וְנַחֲלָתוֹ
לֹא יַעֲזֹב: כִּי־עַד־צֶדֶק יָשׁוּב מִשְׁפָּט וְאַחֲרָיו כָּל־יִשְׁרֵי־לֵב: מִי־יָקוּם
לִי עִם־מְרֵעִים מִי־יִתְיַצֵּב לִי עִם־פֹּעֲלֵי אָוֶן: לוּלֵי יְהֹוָה עֶזְרָתָה לִּי
כִּמְעַט | שָׁכְנָה דוּמָה נַפְשִׁי: אִם־אָמַרְתִּי מָטָה רַגְלִי חַסְדְּךָ יְהֹוָה
יִסְעָדֵנִי: בְּרֹב שַׂרְעַפַּי בְּקִרְבִּי תַּנְחוּמֶיךָ יְשַׁעַשְׁעוּ נַפְשִׁי: הַיְחָבְרְךָ
כִּסֵּא הַוּוֹת יֹצֵר עָמָל עֲלֵי־חֹק: יָגוֹדּוּ עַל־נֶפֶשׁ צַדִּיק וְדָם נָקִי
יַרְשִׁיעוּ: וַיְהִי יְהֹוָה לִי לְמִשְׂגָּב וֵאלֹהַי לְצוּר מַחְסִי: וַיָּשֶׁב עֲלֵיהֶם |
אֶת־אוֹנָם וּבְרָעָתָם יַצְמִיתֵם יַצְמִיתֵם יְהֹוָה אֱלֹהֵינוּ: **וממשיך הושיענו**

El-Nekamot Adonai El Nekamot Hofia. Hinasei Shofet Ha'aretz; Hasheiv Gemul. Al-Ge'im. Ad-Matai Resha'im Adonai Ad-Matai. Resha'im Ya'alozu. Yabi'u Yedaberu Atak; Yit'ammeru. Chol-Po'alei Aven. Ammecha Adonai Yedake'u; Venachalatecha Ye'anu. Almanah Veger Yaharogu; Vitomim Yeratzechu. Vayomeru Lo Yir'eh-Yah; Velo-Yavin. Elohei Ya'akov. Binu Bo'arim Ba'am; Uchesilim. Matai Taskilu. Hanota Ozen Halo Yishma'; Im-Yotzer Ayin Halo Yabbit. Hayoser Goyim Halo Yochiach; Hamlamed Adam Da'at. Adonai Yodea Machshevot Adam; Ki-Hemah Havel. Ashrei Hagever Asher-Teyaserenu Yah; Umitoratecha Telamedenu. Lehashkit Lo Mimei Ra'; Ad Yikareh Larasha Shachat. Ki Lo-Yitosh Adonai Ammo; Venachalato. Lo Ya'azov. Ki-'Ad-Tzedek Yashuv Mishpat; Ve'acharav. Chol-Yishrei-Lev. Mi-Yakum Li Im-Mere'im; Mi-Yityatzev Li Im-Po'alei Aven. Lulei Adonai Ezratah Li; Kim'at Shachenah Dumah Nafshi. Im-'Amarti Matah Ragli; Chasdecha Adonai Yis'adeni. Berov Sar'appai Bekirbi; Tanchumeicha. Yesha'ash'u Nafshi. Haychovrecha Kissei Havot; Yotzer Amal Alei-Chok. Yagoddu Al-Nefesh Tzaddik; Vedam Naki Yarshi'u. Vayhi Adonai Li Lemisgav; Velohai. Letzur Machsi. Vayashev Aleihem Et-'Onam. Uvera'atam Yatzmitem; Yatzmitem. Adonai Eloheinu. **(recite "hoshienu" at the end of the weekly Psalms)**

God to Whom vengeance belongs, Hashem, God to Whom vengeance belongs, shine forth. Lift up Yourself, Judge of the earth; render to the proud their recompense. How long will the wicked, Hashem, how long will the wicked rejoice? They gush out, they speak arrogance; all the workers of iniquity bear themselves loftily. They crush Your people, Hashem, and afflict Your heritage. They slay the widow and the stranger, and murder the fatherless. And they say: 'Hashem will not see, neither will the God of Yaakov give heed.' Consider, you brutish among the people; and you fools, when will you understand? He that planted the ear, will He not hear? He that formed the eye, will He not see? He that instructs nations, will He not correct? Even He that teaches man knowledge? Hashem knows the thoughts of man, that they are vanity. Happy is the man whom You instruct, Hashem, and teach out of Your Torah; That You may give him rest from the days of evil, until the pit is dug for the wicked. For Hashem will not cast off His people, neither will He forsake His inheritance. For rightness will be returned to justice, and all the upright in heart will follow it. Who will rise up for me against the evil-doers? Who will stand up for me against the workers of iniquity? Unless Hashem had been my help, my soul had soon dwelt in silence. If I say: 'My foot slips', Your mercy, Hashem, holds me up. When my cares are many within me, Your comforts delight my soul. Will the seat of wickedness have fellowship with You, which frames mischief by statute? They gather themselves together against the soul of the righteous, and condemn innocent blood. But Hashem has been my high tower, and my God the rock of my refuge. And He has brought on them their own iniquity, and will cut them off in their own evil; Hashem our God will cut them off. **(recite "hoshienu" at the end of the weekly Psalms)**

On Thursday:

הַיּוֹם יוֹם חֲמִישִׁי בְּשַׁבַּת קוֹדֶשׁ הַשִּׁיר שֶׁהָיוּ הַלְוִיִּם אוֹמְרִים עַל הַדּוּכָן:

Hayom Yom Chamishi Beshabbat Kodesh Hashir Shehayu Halviyim Omerim Al Hadduchan:

Today is day five from the holy Shabbat, the song that the Levi'im would sing on the stand:

Psalms 81

לַמְנַצֵּחַ | עַל־הַגִּתִּית לְאָסָף: הַרְנִינוּ לֵאלֹהִים עוּזֵּנוּ הָרִיעוּ לֵאלֹהֵי יַעֲקֹב: שְׂאוּ־זִמְרָה וּתְנוּ־תֹף כִּנּוֹר נָעִים עִם־נָבֶל: תִּקְעוּ בַחֹדֶשׁ שׁוֹפָר

בַּכֵּסֶה לְיוֹם חַגֵּנוּ: כִּי חֹק לְיִשְׂרָאֵל הוּא מִשְׁפָּט לֵאלֹהֵי יַעֲקֹב:
עֵדוּת | בִּיהוֹסֵף שָׂמוֹ בְּצֵאתוֹ עַל־אֶרֶץ מִצְרָיִם שְׂפַת לֹא־יָדַעְתִּי
אֶשְׁמָע: הֲסִירוֹתִי מִסֵּבֶל שִׁכְמוֹ כַּפָּיו מִדּוּד תַּעֲבֹרְנָה: בַּצָּרָה קָרָאתָ
וָאֲחַלְּצֶךָּ אֶעֶנְךָ בְּסֵתֶר רַעַם אֶבְחָנְךָ עַל־מֵי מְרִיבָה סֶלָה: שְׁמַע עַמִּי
וְאָעִידָה בָּךְ יִשְׂרָאֵל אִם־תִּשְׁמַע־לִי: לֹא־יִהְיֶה בְךָ אֵל זָר וְלֹא
תִשְׁתַּחֲוֶה לְאֵל נֵכָר: אָנֹכִי | יְהֹוָה אֱלֹהֶיךָ הַמַּעַלְךָ מֵאֶרֶץ מִצְרָיִם
הַרְחֶב־פִּיךָ וַאֲמַלְאֵהוּ: וְלֹא־שָׁמַע עַמִּי לְקוֹלִי וְיִשְׂרָאֵל לֹא־אָבָה לִי:
וָאֲשַׁלְּחֵהוּ בִּשְׁרִירוּת לִבָּם יֵלְכוּ בְּמוֹעֲצוֹתֵיהֶם: לוּ עַמִּי שֹׁמֵעַ לִי
יִשְׂרָאֵל בִּדְרָכַי יְהַלֵּכוּ: כִּמְעַט אוֹיְבֵיהֶם אַכְנִיעַ וְעַל צָרֵיהֶם אָשִׁיב
יָדִי: מְשַׂנְאֵי יְהֹוָה יְכַחֲשׁוּ־לוֹ וִיהִי עִתָּם לְעוֹלָם: וַיַּאֲכִילֵהוּ מֵחֵלֶב
חִטָּה וּמִצּוּר דְּבַשׁ אַשְׂבִּיעֶךָ: וממשיך הושיענו

Lamnatzeach Al-Hagitit Le'asaf. Harninu Lelohim Uzenu; Hari'u. Lelohei Ya'akov. Se'u-Zimrah Utenu-Tof; Kinor Na'im Im-Navel. Tik'u Vachodesh Shofar; Bakkeseh. Leyom Chagenu. Ki Chok Leyisra'el Hu; Mishpat. Lelohei Ya'akov. Edut Bihosef Samo. Betzeto Al-'Eretz Mitzrayim; Sefat Lo-Yada'ti Eshma. Hasiroti Missevel Shichmo; Kapav. Middud Ta'avorenah. Batzarah Karata. Va'achalletzeka E'encha Beseter Ra'am; Evchoncha Al-Mei Merivah Selah. Shema Ammi Ve'a'idah Bach; Yisra'el. Im-Tishma'-Li. Lo-Yihyeh Vecha El Zar; Velo Tishtachaveh. Le'el Nechar. Anochi Adonai Eloheicha. Hama'alcha Me'eretz Mitzrayim; Harchev-Picha Va'amal'ehu. Velo-Shama Ammi Lekoli; Veyisra'el. Lo-'Avah Li. Va'ashallechehu Bishrirut Libam; Yelechu. Bemo'atzoteihem. Lu. Ammi Shome'ah Li; Yisra'el. Bidrachai Yehallechu. Kim'at Oyeveihem Achnia'; Ve'al Tzareihem. Ashiv Yadi. Mesan'ei Adonai Yechachashu-Lo; Vihi Ittam Le'olam. Vaya'achilehu Mechelev Chittah; Umitzur. Devash Asbi'echa. **(recite "hoshienu" at the end of the weekly Psalms)**

For the Leader; upon the Gittit. A Psalm of Asaph. Sing aloud to God our strength; shout to the God of Yaakov. Take up the melody, and sound the timbrel, the sweet harp with the psaltery. Blow the shofar at the new moon, at the full moon for our feast-day. For it is a statute for Yisrael, an ordinance of the God of Yaakov. He appointed it in Yosef for a testimony, when He went forth against the land of Mitzrayim. The speech of one that I knew not did I hear: 'I removed his shoulder from the burden; His hands were freed from the basket. You called in trouble, and I rescued you; I answered you in the secret place of thunder; I proved you at the waters of Meribah. Selah. Hear, My people, and I will admonish you: Yisrael, if you would heed Me. There will be no strange god be in you; neither will you worship any foreign god. I am Hashem your God, Who brought you up out of the land of Mitzrayim; open your mouth wide, and I will fill it. But My people did not heed My voice; and Yisrael would have none of Me. So I let them go after the stubbornness of their heart, that they might walk in their own counsels. Oh that My people would heed Me, that Yisrael would walk in My ways. I would soon subdue their enemies, and turn My hand against their adversaries. The haters of Hashem would dwindle away before Him; and their punishment would endure forever. They should also be fed with the fat of wheat; and with honey out of the rock I would satisfy you. **(recite "hoshienu" at the end of the weekly Psalms)**

On Friday:

הַיּוֹם יוֹם הַשִּׁשִּׁי בְּשַׁבַּת קוֹדֶשׁ הַשִּׁיר שֶׁהָיוּ הַלְוִיִּם אוֹמְרִים עַל הַדּוּכָן:

Hayom Yom Hashishi Beshabbat Kodesh Hashir Shehayu Halviyim Omerim Al Hadduchan:

Today is day six from the holy Shabbat, the song that the Levi'im would sing on the stand:

Psalms 93

יְהֹוָה מָלָךְ גֵּאוּת לָבֵשׁ לָבֵשׁ יְהֹוָה עֹז הִתְאַזָּר אַף־תִּכּוֹן תֵּבֵל בַּל־תִּמּוֹט: נָכוֹן כִּסְאֲךָ מֵאָז מֵעוֹלָם אָתָּה: נָשְׂאוּ נְהָרוֹת | יְהֹוָה נָשְׂאוּ נְהָרוֹת קוֹלָם יִשְׂאוּ נְהָרוֹת דָּכְיָם: מִקֹּלוֹת | מַיִם רַבִּים אַדִּירִים מִשְׁבְּרֵי־יָם אַדִּיר בַּמָּרוֹם יְהֹוָה: עֵדֹתֶיךָ | נֶאֶמְנוּ מְאֹד לְבֵיתְךָ נַאֲוָה־קֹדֶשׁ יְהֹוָה לְאֹרֶךְ יָמִים:

Adonai Malach Adonai Maloch Ge'ut Lavesh Lavesh Adonai Oz Hit'azar; Af-Tikon Tevel. Bal-Timot. Nachon Kis'acha Me'az; Me'olam Attah. Nase'u Neharot Adonai Nase'u Neharot Kolam; Yis'u Neharot Dochyam. Mikolot Mayim Rabbim. Adirim Mishberei-Yam; Adir Bamarom Adonai Edoteicha Ne'emnu Me'od. Leveitecha Na'avah-Kodesh; Adonai Le'orech Yamim.

Hashem reigns; He is clothed in majesty; Hashem is clothed, He has girded Himself with strength; The world is established, that it cannot be moved. Your Throne is established from old; You are from everlasting. The floods have lifted up, Hashem, the floods have lifted up their voice; the floods lift up their roaring. Above the voices of many waters, the mighty breakers of the sea, Hashem on high is mighty. Your testimonies are very sure, holiness suits Your House, Hashem, forever.

<u>After the Psalm of the Day the following verses are recited:</u>

הוֹשִׁיעֵנוּ | יְהוָה אֱלֹהֵינוּ וְקַבְּצֵנוּ מִן־הַגּוֹיִם לְהֹדוֹת לְשֵׁם קָדְשֶׁךָ
לְהִשְׁתַּבֵּחַ בִּתְהִלָּתֶךָ: בָּרוּךְ יְהוָה אֱלֹהֵי יִשְׂרָאֵל מִן־הָעוֹלָם | וְעַד
הָעוֹלָם וְאָמַר כָּל־הָעָם אָמֵן הַלְלוּיָהּ: בָּרוּךְ יְהוָה | מִצִּיּוֹן שֹׁכֵן
יְרוּשָׁלָם הַלְלוּיָהּ: בָּרוּךְ | יְהוָה אֱלֹהִים אֱלֹהֵי יִשְׂרָאֵל עֹשֵׂה
נִפְלָאוֹת לְבַדּוֹ: וּבָרוּךְ | שֵׁם כְּבוֹדוֹ לְעוֹלָם וְיִמָּלֵא כְבוֹדוֹ אֶת־כֹּל
הָאָרֶץ אָמֵן | וְאָמֵן:

Hoshi'enu Adonai Eloheinu. Vekabetzeinu Min-Hagoyim Lehodot Leshem Kodshecha; Lehishtabe'ach. Bit'hilatecha Baruch Adonai Elohei Yisra'el Min-Ha'olam Ve'ad Ha'olam. Ve'amar Chol-Ha'am Amen. Halleluyah. Baruch Adonai Mitziyon. Shochein Yerushalayim. Halleluyah. Baruch Adonai Elohim Elohei Yisra'el; Oseh Nifla'ot Levado. Uvaruch Shem Kevodo. Le'olam Veyimmalei Chevodo Et-Kol Ha'aretz. Amen Ve'amen.

"Save us, Hashem our God, and gather us from among the nations to praise Your holy name and triumph in Your praise. Blessed is Hashem God of Yisrael from everlasting to everlasting, and let all the people say Amen, Halleluyah. Blessed from Tziyon is Hashem Who dwells in Yerushalayim. Halleluyah. Blessed is Hashem-Elohim, the God of Yisrael, who alone works wondrously. Blessed is His glory forever, and may the whole earth be filled with His glory. Amen and Amen."

Song of the Day for Fast Days, Hanukkah and Purim

<u>The conclusion of Yom Kippur say:</u>

Psalms 85

לַמְנַצֵּחַ | לִבְנֵי־קֹרַח מִזְמוֹר: רָצִיתָ יְהֹוָה אַרְצֶךָ שַׁבְתָּ שבות
(שְׁבִית) יַעֲקֹב: נָשָׂאתָ עֲוֺן עַמֶּךָ כִּסִּיתָ כָל־חַטָּאתָם סֶלָה: אָסַפְתָּ
כָל־עֶבְרָתֶךָ הֱשִׁיבוֹתָ מֵחֲרוֹן אַפֶּךָ: שׁוּבֵנוּ אֱלֹהֵי יִשְׁעֵנוּ וְהָפֵר כַּעַסְךָ
עִמָּנוּ: הַלְעוֹלָם תֶּאֱנַף־בָּנוּ תִּמְשֹׁךְ אַפְּךָ לְדֹר וָדֹר: הֲלֹא־אַתָּה תָּשׁוּב
תְּחַיֵּנוּ וְעַמְּךָ יִשְׂמְחוּ־בָךְ: הַרְאֵנוּ יְהֹוָה חַסְדֶּךָ וְיֶשְׁעֲךָ תִּתֶּן־לָנוּ:
אֶשְׁמְעָה מַה־יְדַבֵּר הָאֵל | יְהֹוָה כִּי | יְדַבֵּר שָׁלוֹם אֶל־עַמּוֹ
וְאֶל־חֲסִידָיו וְאַל־יָשׁוּבוּ לְכִסְלָה: אַךְ קָרוֹב לִירֵאָיו יִשְׁעוֹ לִשְׁכֹּן
כָּבוֹד בְּאַרְצֵנוּ: חֶסֶד־וֶאֱמֶת נִפְגָּשׁוּ צֶדֶק וְשָׁלוֹם נָשָׁקוּ: אֱמֶת מֵאֶרֶץ
תִּצְמָח וְצֶדֶק מִשָּׁמַיִם נִשְׁקָף: גַּם־יְהֹוָה יִתֵּן הַטּוֹב וְאַרְצֵנוּ תִּתֵּן
יְבוּלָהּ: צֶדֶק לְפָנָיו יְהַלֵּךְ וְיָשֵׂם לְדֶרֶךְ פְּעָמָיו:

Lamnatzeach Livnei-Korach Mizmor. Ratzita Adonai Artzecha; Shavta. Shevit Ya'akov. Nasata Avon Ammecha; Kissita Chol-Chatatam Selah. Asafta Chol-'Evratecha; Heshivota. Mecharon Apecha. Shuvenu Elohei Yish'enu; Vehafer Ka'ascha Imanu. Hal'olam Te'enaf-Banu; Timshoch Apecha. Ledor Vador. Halo-'Attah Tashuv Techayeinu; Ve'ammecha. Yismechu-Vach. Har'enu Adonai Chasdecha; Veyesh'acha. Titen-Lanu. Eshme'ah. Mah-Yedaber Ha'el Adonai Ki Yedaber Shalom. El-'Ammo Ve'el-Chasidav; Ve'al-

Yashuvu Lechislah. Ach Karov Lire'av Yish'o; Lishkon Kavod Be'artzenu. Chesed-Ve'emet Nifgashu; Tzedek Veshalom Nashaku. Emet Me'eretz Titzmach; Vetzedek. Mishamayim Nishkaf. Gam-Adonai Yiten Hatov; Ve'artzenu. Titen Yevulah. Tzedek Lefanav Yehallech; Veyasem Lederech Pe'amav.

For the Leader. A Psalm of the sons of Korach. Hashem, You have been favorable to Your land, You have turned the captivity of Yaakov. You have forgiven the iniquity of Your people, You have pardoned all of their sin. Selah. You have withdrawn all of Your wrath; You have turned from the fierceness of Your anger. Restore us, Oh God of our salvation, and cause Your indignation toward us to cease. Will You be angry with us forever? Will You draw out Your anger to all generations? Will You not quicken us again, that Your people may rejoice in You? Show us Your mercy, Hashem, and grant us Your salvation. I will hear what God, Hashem, will speak; for He will speak peace to His people, and to His holy-ones; but let them not turn back to folly. Surely His salvation is near to them that fear Him; that glory may dwell in our land. Mercy and truth have met together; righteousness and peace have kissed each other. Truth springs out of the earth; and righteousness has looked down from heaven. Also, Hashem will give that which is good; and our land will yield her produce. Righteousness will go before Him, and will make a way for His footsteps.

<u>On the Fast of Gedaliah and on the Tenth of Tevet say:</u>

Psalms 83

שִׁיר מִזְמוֹר לְאָסָף׃ אֱלֹהִים אַל־דֳּמִי־לָךְ אַל־תֶּחֱרַשׁ וְאַל־תִּשְׁקֹט
אֵל׃ כִּי־הִנֵּה אוֹיְבֶיךָ יֶהֱמָיוּן וּמְשַׂנְאֶיךָ נָשְׂאוּ רֹאשׁ׃ עַל־עַמְּךָ יַעֲרִימוּ
סוֹד וְיִתְיָעֲצוּ עַל־צְפוּנֶיךָ׃ אָמְרוּ לְכוּ וְנַכְחִידֵם מִגּוֹי וְלֹא־יִזָּכֵר
שֵׁם־יִשְׂרָאֵל עוֹד׃ כִּי נוֹעֲצוּ לֵב יַחְדָּו עָלֶיךָ בְּרִית יִכְרֹתוּ׃ אָהֳלֵי
אֱדוֹם וְיִשְׁמְעֵאלִים מוֹאָב וְהַגְרִים׃ גְּבָל וְעַמּוֹן וַעֲמָלֵק פְּלֶשֶׁת

עִם־יֹשְׁבֵי צוֹר: גַּם־אַשּׁוּר נִלְוָה עִמָּם הָיוּ זְרוֹעַ לִבְנֵי־לוֹט סֶלָה:
עֲשֵׂה־לָהֶם כְּמִדְיָן כְּסִיסְרָא כְיָבִין בְּנַחַל קִישׁוֹן: נִשְׁמְדוּ בְעֵין־דֹּאר
הָיוּ דֹּמֶן לָאֲדָמָה: שִׁיתֵמוֹ נְדִיבֵימוֹ כְּעֹרֵב וְכִזְאֵב וּכְזֶבַח וּכְצַלְמֻנָּע
כָּל־נְסִיכֵימוֹ: אֲשֶׁר אָמְרוּ נִירְשָׁה לָּנוּ אֵת נְאוֹת אֱלֹהִים: אֱלֹהַי
שִׁיתֵמוֹ כַגַּלְגַּל כְּקַשׁ לִפְנֵי־רוּחַ: כְּאֵשׁ תִּבְעַר־יָעַר וּכְלֶהָבָה תְּלַהֵט
הָרִים: כֵּן תִּרְדְּפֵם בְּסַעֲרֶךָ וּבְסוּפָתְךָ תְבַהֲלֵם: מַלֵּא פְנֵיהֶם קָלוֹן
וִיבַקְשׁוּ שִׁמְךָ יְהוָה: יֵבֹשׁוּ וְיִבָּהֲלוּ עֲדֵי־עַד וְיַחְפְּרוּ וְיֹאבֵדוּ: וְיֵדְעוּ
כִּי־אַתָּה שִׁמְךָ יְהוָה לְבַדֶּךָ עֶלְיוֹן עַל־כָּל־הָאָרֶץ:

Shir Mizmor Le'asaf. Elohim Al-Domi-Lach; Al-Techerash Ve'al-Tishkot El. Ki-Hineh Oyeveicha Yehemayun; Umesan'eicha. Nase'u Rosh. Al-'Ammecha Ya'arimu Sod; Veyitya'atzu. Al-Tzefuneicha. Ameru. Lechu Venachchidem Migoy; Velo-Yizacher Shem-Yisra'el Od. Ki No'atzu Lev Yachdav; Aleicha. Berit Yichrotu. Oholei Edom Veyishme'elim. Mo'av Vehagrim. Geval Ve'ammon Va'amalek; Peleshet. Im-Yoshevei Tzor. Gam-'Ashur Nilvah Immam; Hayu Zeroa Livnei-Lot Selah. Aseh-Lahem Kemidyan; Kesisera Cheyavin. Benachal Kishon. Nishmedu Ve'ein-Dor; Hayu Domen La'adamah. Shitemo Nediveimo Ke'orev Vechiz'ev; Uchezevach Uchetzalmuna'. Chol-Nesicheimo. Asher Ameru Nireshah Lanu; Et Ne'ot Elohim. Elohai. Shitemo Chagalgal; Kekash. Lifnei-Ruach. Ke'esh Tiv'ar-Ya'ar; Uchelehavah. Telahet Harim. Ken Tirdefem Besa'arecha; Uvesufatecha Tevahalem. Malei Feneihem Kalon; Vivakshu Shimcha Adonai Yevoshu Veyibahalu Adei-'Ad. Veyachperu Veyovedu. Veyede'u. Ki-'Attah Shimcha Adonai Levadecha; Elyon. Al-Chol-Ha'aretz.

A Song, a Psalm of Asaph. Oh God, do not keep Your silence; do not hold Your peace, and do not be still, Oh God. For, behold, Your enemies are in an uproar; and they that hate You have lifted up the head. They hold crafty converse against Your people, and take counsel against Your treasured ones. They have said: 'Come, and let us cut them off from being a nation; that the name of Yisrael may be no more in remembrance.' For they have consulted together with one consent; against You do they make a covenant; The tents of Edom and the Ishmaelites; Moav, and the Hagrites; Geval, and

Ammon, and Amalek; Philistia with the inhabitants of Tyre; Assyria also is joined with them; they have been an arm to the children of Lot. Selah. Do to them as to Midyan; as to Sisera, as to Yavin, at the brook Kishon; Who were destroyed at Ein-dor; they became as dung for the earth. Make their nobles like Orev and Zeiv, and like Zevach and Zalmunna all their princes; Who said: 'Let us take to ourselves in possession the Habitations of God.' Oh my God, make them like the whirling dust; as stubble before the wind. As the fire that burns the forest, and as the flame that sets the mountains ablaze; So pursue them with Your tempest, and frighten them with Your storm. Fill their faces with shame; that they may seek Your name, Hashem. Let them be ashamed and affrighted forever; let them be abashed and perish; That they may know that it is You alone whose name is Hashem, the Most High over all the earth.

<u>On Hanukkah say:</u>

Psalms 30

מִזְמ֡וֹר שִׁיר־חֲנֻכַּ֖ת הַבַּ֣יִת לְדָוִֽד׃ אֲרוֹמִמְךָ֣ יְ֭הֹוָה כִּ֣י דִלִּיתָ֑נִי
וְלֹא־שִׂמַּ֖חְתָּ אֹיְבַ֣י לִֽי׃ יְהֹוָ֥ה אֱלֹהָ֑י שִׁוַּ֥עְתִּי אֵ֝לֶ֗יךָ וַתִּרְפָּאֵֽנִי׃ יְֽהֹוָ֗ה
הֶֽעֱלִ֣יתָ מִן־שְׁא֣וֹל נַפְשִׁ֑י חִ֝יִּיתַ֗נִי מיורדי (מִיָּֽרְדִי)־בֽוֹר׃ זַמְּר֣וּ לַיהֹוָ֣ה
חֲסִידָ֑יו וְ֝הוֹד֗וּ לְזֵ֣כֶר קָדְשֽׁוֹ׃ כִּ֤י רֶ֨גַע ׀ בְּאַפּוֹ֮ חַיִּ֪ים בִּרְצ֫וֹנ֥וֹ בָּ֭עֶרֶב יָלִ֥ין
בֶּ֗כִי וְלַבֹּ֥קֶר רִנָּֽה׃ וַ֭אֲנִי אָמַ֣רְתִּי בְשַׁלְוִ֑י בַּל־אֶמּ֥וֹט לְעוֹלָֽם׃ יְֽהֹוָ֗ה
בִּרְצוֹנְךָ֮ הֶעֱמַ֪דְתָּה לְהַרְרִ֫י עֹ֥ז הִסְתַּ֥רְתָּ פָנֶ֗יךָ הָיִ֥יתִי נִבְהָֽל׃ אֵלֶ֣יךָ
יְהֹוָ֣ה אֶקְרָ֑א וְאֶל־אֲ֝דֹנָ֗י אֶתְחַנָּֽן׃ מַה־בֶּ֥צַע בְּדָמִי֮ בְּרִדְתִּ֪י אֶ֫ל שָׁ֥חַת
הֲיוֹדְךָ֥ עָפָ֑ר הֲיַגִּ֥יד אֲמִתֶּֽךָ׃ שְׁמַע־יְהֹוָ֥ה וְחָנֵּ֑נִי יְ֝הֹוָ֗ה הֱֽיֵה־עֹזֵ֥ר לִֽי׃
הָפַ֣כְתָּ מִסְפְּדִי֮ לְמָח֪וֹל לִ֥י פִּתַּ֥חְתָּ שַׂקִּ֑י וַתְּאַזְּרֵ֥נִי שִׂמְחָֽה׃ לְמַ֤עַן ׀
יְזַמֶּרְךָ֣ כָ֭בוֹד וְלֹ֣א יִדֹּ֑ם יְהֹוָ֥ה אֱ֝לֹהַ֗י לְעוֹלָ֥ם אוֹדֶֽךָּ׃

Mizmor Shir-Chanukkat Habayit Ledavid. Aromimcha Adonai Ki Dillitani; Velo-Simachta Oyevai Li. Adonai Elohai; Shiva'ti Eleicha.

Vatirpa'eni. Adonai He'elita Min-She'ol Nafshi; Chiyitani. Miyordi-Vor. Zameru L'Adonai Chasidav; Vehodu. Lezecher Kodsho. Ki Rega' Be'appo Chayim Birtzonobba'erev Yalin Bechi. Velaboker Rinah. Va'ani Amarti Veshalvi; Bal-'Emot Le'olam. Adonai Birtzonecha He'emadtah Lehareri Oz Histarta Faneicha. Hayiti Nivhal. Eleicha Adonai Ekra; Ve'el-' Adonai. Etchanan. Mah-Betza Bedami Beridti El Shachat Hayodecha Afar; Hayagid Amitecha. Shema'-Adonai Vechoneni; Adonai Heyeh-'Ozeir Li. Hafachta Mispedi Lemachol Li Pittachta Sakki; Vate'azereini Simchah. Lema'an Yezamercha Chavod Velo Yidom; Adonai Elohai. Le'olam Odeka.

A Psalm; a Song at the Dedication of the House of David. I will extol You, Hashem, for You have raised me up, and have not suffered my enemies to rejoice over me. Hashem my God, I cried to You, and You healed me; Oh Hashem, You brought up my soul from Sheol; You did keep me alive, that I should not go down to the pit. Sing praise to Hashem, His godly ones, and give thanks to His holy name. For His anger is but for a moment, His favor is for a life-time; weeping may come for the night, but joy comes in the morning. Now I had said in my security: 'I will never be moved.' You had established, Hashem, in Your favor my mountain as a stronghold — You hid Your face; I was afraid. To You, Hashem, did I call, and to Hashem I made supplication: 'What profit is there in my blood, when I go down to the pit? Will the dust praise You? Will it declare Your truth? Hear, Hashem, and be gracious to me; Hashem, be my helper.' You turned my mourning into dancing; You loosed my sackcloth, and girded me with gladness; So that my glory may sing praise to You, and not be silent; Hashem my God, I will give thanks to You forever.

<u>On the Fast of Esther and on Purim say:</u>

Psalms 22

לַמְנַצֵּחַ עַל־אַיֶּלֶת הַשַּׁחַר מִזְמוֹר לְדָוִד׃ אֵלִי אֵלִי לָמָה עֲזַבְתָּנִי
רָחוֹק מִישׁוּעָתִי דִּבְרֵי שַׁאֲגָתִי׃ אֱלֹהַי אֶקְרָא יוֹמָם וְלֹא תַעֲנֶה וְלַיְלָה

וְלֹא־דֻמִיָּה לִי: וְאַתָּה קָדוֹשׁ יוֹשֵׁב תְּהִלּוֹת יִשְׂרָאֵל: בְּךָ בָּטְחוּ
אֲבֹתֵינוּ בָּטְחוּ וַתְּפַלְּטֵמוֹ: אֵלֶיךָ זָעֲקוּ וְנִמְלָטוּ בְּךָ בָטְחוּ וְלֹא־בוֹשׁוּ:
וְאָנֹכִי תוֹלַעַת וְלֹא־אִישׁ חֶרְפַּת אָדָם וּבְזוּי עָם: כָּל־רֹאַי יַלְעִגוּ לִי
יַפְטִירוּ בְשָׂפָה יָנִיעוּ רֹאשׁ: גֹּל אֶל־יְהוָה יְפַלְּטֵהוּ יַצִּילֵהוּ כִּי חָפֵץ
בּוֹ: כִּי־אַתָּה גֹחִי מִבָּטֶן מַבְטִיחִי עַל־שְׁדֵי אִמִּי: עָלֶיךָ הָשְׁלַכְתִּי
מֵרָחֶם מִבֶּטֶן אִמִּי אֵלִי אָתָּה: אַל־תִּרְחַק מִמֶּנִּי כִּי־צָרָה קְרוֹבָה
כִּי־אֵין עוֹזֵר: סְבָבוּנִי פָּרִים רַבִּים אַבִּירֵי בָשָׁן כִּתְּרוּנִי: פָּצוּ עָלַי
פִּיהֶם אַרְיֵה טֹרֵף וְשֹׁאֵג: כַּמַּיִם נִשְׁפַּכְתִּי וְהִתְפָּרְדוּ כָּל־עַצְמוֹתָי הָיָה
לִבִּי כַּדּוֹנָג נָמֵס בְּתוֹךְ מֵעָי: יָבֵשׁ כַּחֶרֶשׂ | כֹּחִי וּלְשׁוֹנִי מֻדְבָּק
מַלְקוֹחָי וְלַעֲפַר־מָוֶת תִּשְׁפְּתֵנִי: כִּי סְבָבוּנִי כְּלָבִים עֲדַת מְרֵעִים
הִקִּיפוּנִי כָּאֲרִי יָדַי וְרַגְלָי: אֲסַפֵּר כָּל־עַצְמוֹתָי הֵמָּה יַבִּיטוּ יִרְאוּ־בִי:
יְחַלְּקוּ בְגָדַי לָהֶם וְעַל־לְבוּשִׁי יַפִּילוּ גוֹרָל: וְאַתָּה יְהוָה אַל־תִּרְחָק
אֱיָלוּתִי לְעֶזְרָתִי חוּשָׁה: הַצִּילָה מֵחֶרֶב נַפְשִׁי מִיַּד־כֶּלֶב יְחִידָתִי:
הוֹשִׁיעֵנִי מִפִּי אַרְיֵה וּמִקַּרְנֵי רֵמִים עֲנִיתָנִי: אֲסַפְּרָה שִׁמְךָ לְאֶחָי
בְּתוֹךְ קָהָל אֲהַלְלֶךָּ: יִרְאֵי יְהוָה | הַלְלוּהוּ כָּל־זֶרַע יַעֲקֹב כַּבְּדוּהוּ
וְגוּרוּ מִמֶּנּוּ כָּל־זֶרַע יִשְׂרָאֵל: כִּי לֹא־בָזָה וְלֹא שִׁקַּץ עֱנוּת עָנִי
וְלֹא־הִסְתִּיר פָּנָיו מִמֶּנּוּ וּבְשַׁוְּעוֹ אֵלָיו שָׁמֵעַ: מֵאִתְּךָ תְּהִלָּתִי בְּקָהָל
רָב נְדָרַי אֲשַׁלֵּם נֶגֶד יְרֵאָיו: יֹאכְלוּ עֲנָוִים | וְיִשְׂבָּעוּ יְהַלְלוּ יְהוָה
דֹּרְשָׁיו יְחִי לְבַבְכֶם לָעַד: יִזְכְּרוּ | וְיָשֻׁבוּ אֶל־יְהוָה כָּל־אַפְסֵי־אָרֶץ
וְיִשְׁתַּחֲווּ לְפָנֶיךָ כָּל־מִשְׁפְּחוֹת גּוֹיִם: כִּי לַיהוָה הַמְּלוּכָה וּמֹשֵׁל
בַּגּוֹיִם: אָכְלוּ וַיִּשְׁתַּחֲווּ | כָּל־דִּשְׁנֵי־אֶרֶץ לְפָנָיו יִכְרְעוּ כָּל־יוֹרְדֵי עָפָר
וְנַפְשׁוֹ לֹא חִיָּה: זֶרַע יַעַבְדֶנּוּ יְסֻפַּר לַאדֹנָי לַדּוֹר: יָבֹאוּ וְיַגִּידוּ צִדְקָתוֹ
לְעַם נוֹלָד כִּי עָשָׂה:

Lamnatzeach Al-'Ayelet Hashachar. Mizmor Ledavid. Eli Eli Lamah Azavtani; Rachok Mishu'ati. Divrei Sha'agati. Elohai. Ekra Yomom Velo Ta'aneh; Velaylah. Velo-Dumiyah Li. Ve'attah Kadosh; Yoshev. Tehillot Yisra'el. Becha Batechu Avoteinu; Batechu. Vatefalletemo. Eleicha Za'aku Venimlatu; Becha Vatechu Velo-Voshu. Ve'anochi Tola'at Velo-'Ish; Cherpat Adam. Uvezui Am. Chol-Ro'ai Yal'igu Li;

Yaftiru Vesafah. Yani'u Rosh. Gol El-Adonai Yefalletehu; Yatzilehu. Ki Chafetz Bo. Ki-'Attah Gochi Mibaten; Mavtichi. Al-Shedei Immi. Aleicha Hoshlachti Merachem; Mibeten Immi. Eli Attah. Al-Tirchak Mimeni Ki-Tzarah Kerovah; Ki-'Ein Ozeir. Sevavuni Parim Rabbim; Abbirei Vashan Kitteruni. Patzu Alai Pihem; Aryeh. Toref Vesho'eg. Kammayim Nishpachti Vehitparedu. Chol-'Atzmotaihayah Libi Kaddonag; Names. Betoch Me'ai. Yavesh Kacheres Kochi. Uleshoni Mudbak Malkochai; Vela'afar-Mavet Tishpeteni. Ki Sevavuni. Kelavim Adat Mere'im Hikkifuni; Ka'ari. Yadai Veraglai. Asaper Chol-'Atzmotai; Hemah Yabbitu. Yir'u-Vi. Yechalleku Vegadai Lahem; Ve'al-Levushi. Yappilu Goral. Ve'attah Adonai Al-Tirchak; Eyaluti. Le'ezrati Chushah. Hatzilah Mecherev Nafshi; Miyad-Kelev. Yechidati. Hoshi'eni Mipi Aryeh; Umikarnei Remim Anitani. Asaperah Shimcha Le'echai; Betoch Kahal Ahaleleka. Yir'ei Adonai Halleluhu. Chol-Zera Ya'akov Kabeduhu; Veguru Mimenu. Chol-Zera Yisra'el. Ki Lo-Vazah Velo Shikatz Enut Anivelo.-Histir Panav Mimenu; Uveshave'o Elav Shamea. Me'itecha. Tehilati Bekahal Rav; Nedarai Ashalem. Neged Yere'av. Yochelu Anavim Veyisba'u. Yehalelu Adonai Doreshav; Yechi Levavchem La'ad. Yizkeru Veyashuvu El-Adonai Chol-'Afsei-'Aretz Veyishtachavu Lefaneicha. Chol-Mishpechot Goyim. Ki L'Adonai Hameluchah; Umoshel. Bagoyim. Achelu Vayishtachavu Chol-Dishnei-'Eretz. Lefanav Yichre'u Chol-Yoredei Afar; Venafsho. Lo Chiyah. Zera Ya'avdenu; Yesuppar L'Adonai Laddor. Yavo'u Veyagidu Tzidkato; Le'am Nolad. Ki Asah.

For the Leader; on Ayelet ha-Shachar. A Psalm of David. My God, my God, why have You forsaken me, and are far from my help at the words of my cry? Oh my God, I call by day, but You do not answer; and at night, and there is no ceasing for me. Yet You are holy, You that are enthroned upon the praises of Yisrael. In You did our fathers trust; they trusted, and You delivered them. To You they cried, and escaped; in You did they trust, and were not ashamed. But I am a worm, and no man; a reproach of men, and despised of the people. All they that see me laugh me to scorn; they shoot out the lip, they shake the head: 'Let him commit himself to Hashem, let Him rescue him; let Him deliver him, seeing He delights in him.' For You are He that took me out of the womb; You made me trust when I was on my mother's breasts. On You I have been cast from my birth; You are my God from my mother's womb. Be not far from me; for trouble is near; for there is none to help. Many bulls have encompassed me; strong bulls of Bashan encircle me. They open wide their mouth against me, as a ravening and a roaring lion. I am poured out like water, and all my bones are out of joint; my heart has become like wax; it is melted in my inmost parts. My strength is dried up like a shard; and my tongue cleaves to my throat; and You lay me in the dust of death. For dogs have encompassed me; a company of evil-doers have inclosed me; like a lion, they are at my hands and my feet. I may count all my bones; they look and gloat over me. They part my garments among them, and for my vesture do they cast lots. But You, Hashem, do not be far off; Oh my strength, hasten to help me. Deliver my soul from the sword; my only one from the power of the dog. Save me from the lion's mouth; from the horns of the wild-oxen do You answer me. I will declare Your name to my brothers; in the midst of the congregation will I praise You. 'You that fear Hashem, praise Him; all of you, the seed of Yaakov, glorify Him; and stand in awe of Him, all of you, the seed of Yisrael. For He has not despised or abhorred the lowliness of the poor; neither has He hid His face from him; but when he cried to Him, He heard.' From You comes my praise in the great congregation; I will pay my vows before them that fear Him. Let the humble eat and be satisfied; let them praise Hashem that seek after Him; may your heart be quickened forever. All the ends of the earth will remember and turn to Hashem; and all the families of the nations will worship before You. For the kingdom is Hashem's; and He is the ruler over the nations. All the fat ones of the earth will eat and worship; all they that go down to the dust will kneel before Him, even he that cannot keep his soul alive. A seed will serve him; it will be told of Hashem to the next generation. They will come and will declare His righteousness to a people that will be born, that He has done it.

On the 17th of Tammuz read:

Psalms 79

מִזְמ֗וֹר לְאָ֫סָ֥ף אֱלֹהִ֡ים בָּ֤אוּ גוֹיִ֨ם | בְּֽנַחֲלָתֶ֗ךָ טִ֭מְּאוּ אֶת־הֵיכַ֣ל קָדְשֶׁ֑ךָ
שָׂ֖מוּ אֶת־יְרוּשָׁלִַ֣ם לְעִיִּֽים׃ נָ֘תְנ֤וּ אֶת־נִבְלַ֬ת עֲבָדֶ֗יךָ מַ֭אֲכָל לְע֣וֹף
הַשָּׁמָ֑יִם בְּשַׂ֥ר חֲ֝סִידֶ֗יךָ לְחַיְתוֹ־אָֽרֶץ׃ שָׁפְכ֬וּ דָמָ֨ם | כַּמַּ֗יִם סְבִ֘יב֤וֹת
יְֽרוּשָׁלִָ֗ם וְאֵ֣ין קוֹבֵֽר׃ הָיִ֣ינוּ חֶ֭רְפָּה לִשְׁכֵנֵ֑ינוּ לַ֥עַג וָ֝קֶ֗לֶס לִסְבִיבוֹתֵֽינוּ׃
עַד־מָ֣ה יְ֭הוָה תֶּאֱנַ֣ף לָנֶ֑צַח תִּבְעַ֥ר כְּמוֹ־אֵ֝֗שׁ קִנְאָתֶֽךָ׃ שְׁפֹ֤ךְ חֲמָתְךָ֨
אֶֽל־הַגּוֹיִ֮ם אֲשֶׁ֪ר לֹֽא־יְדָ֫ע֥וּךָ וְעַ֥ל מַמְלָכ֑וֹת אֲשֶׁ֥ר בְּ֝שִׁמְךָ֗ לֹ֣א קָרָֽאוּ׃
כִּ֭י אָכַ֣ל אֶת־יַעֲקֹ֑ב וְֽאֶת־נָוֵ֥הוּ הֵשַֽׁמּוּ׃ אַל־תִּֽזְכָּר־לָנוּ֮ עֲוֺנֹ֪ת רִאשֹׁ֫נִ֥ים
מַ֭הֵר יְקַדְּמ֣וּנוּ רַחֲמֶ֑יךָ כִּ֖י דַלּ֣וֹנוּ מְאֹֽד׃ עָזְרֵ֤נוּ | אֱלֹהֵ֣י יִשְׁעֵ֗נוּ עַֽל־דְּבַ֥ר
כְּבֽוֹד־שְׁמֶ֑ךָ וְהַצִּילֵ֥נוּ וְכַפֵּ֥ר עַל־חַ֝טֹּאתֵ֗ינוּ לְמַ֣עַן שְׁמֶֽךָ׃ לָ֤מָּה | יֹאמְר֬וּ
הַגּוֹיִ֗ם אַיֵּ֬ה אֱֽלֹהֵיהֶ֗ם יִוָּדַ֣ע בַּגּוֹיִ֣ם לְעֵינֵ֑ינוּ נִ֝קְמַ֗ת דַּם־עֲבָדֶ֥יךָ הַשָּׁפֽוּךְ׃
תָּב֤וֹא לְפָנֶ֗יךָ אֶנְקַ֫ת אָסִ֥יר כְּגֹ֥דֶל זְרוֹעֲךָ֑ ה֝וֹתֵ֗ר בְּנֵ֣י תְמוּתָֽה׃ וְהָשֵׁ֤ב
לִשְׁכֵנֵ֣ינוּ שִׁ֭בְעָתַיִם אֶל־חֵיקָ֑ם חֶ֝רְפָּתָ֗ם אֲשֶׁ֣ר חֵרְפ֣וּךָ אֲדֹנָֽי׃ וַאֲנַ֤חְנוּ
עַמְּךָ֨ | וְצֹ֬אן מַרְעִיתֶ֗ךָ נ֤וֹדֶה לְּךָ֗ לְע֫וֹלָ֥ם לְדֹ֥ר וָדֹ֑ר נְ֝סַפֵּ֗ר תְּהִלָּתֶֽךָ׃

Mizmor. Le'asaf Elohim Ba'u Goyim Benachalatecha. Timme'u Et-Heichal Kodshecha; Samu Et-Yerushalami Le'iyim. Natenu Et-Nivlat Avadeicha. Ma'achol Le'of Hashamayim; Besar Chasideicha. Lechayto-'Aretz. Shafechu Damam Kammayim. Sevivot Yerushalayim Ve'ein Kover. Hayinu Cherpah Lishcheineinu; La'ag Vakeles. Lisvivoteinu. Ad-Mah Adonai Te'enaf Lanetzach; Tiv'ar Kemo-'Esh Kin'atecha. Shefoch Chamatecha. El-Hagoyim Asher Lo-Yeda'ucha Ve'al Mamlachot; Asher Beshimcha. Lo Kara'u. Ki Achal Et-Ya'akov; Ve'et-Navehu Heshamu. Al-Tizkor-Lanu Avonot Rishonim Maher Yekademunu Rachameicha; Ki Dallonu Me'od. Ozrenu Elohei Yish'enu. Al-Devar Kevod-Shemecha; Vehatzileinu Vechapeir Al-Chatoteinu. Lema'an Shemecha. Lamah Yomeru Hagoyim Ayeh Eloheihem Yivada Bagoyim Le'eineinu; Nikmat. Dam-'Avadeicha Hashafuch. Tavo Lefaneicha Enkat Asir Kegodel Zero'acha; Hoter. Benei Temutah. Vehasheiv Lishcheineinu Shiv'atayim El-Cheikam; Cherpatam Asher Cherefucha Adonai. Va'anachnu Ammecha Vetzon Mar'itecha Nodeh Lecha. Le'olam Ledor Vador; Nesapeir. Tehilatecha.

A Psalm of Asaph. God, the nations have come into Your inheritance; They have defiled Your holy Temple; They have made Yerushalayim into heaps. They have given the dead bodies of Your servants to be food to the fowls of the heaven, The flesh of Your saints to the beasts of the earth. They have shed their blood like water around Yerushalayim, with no one to bury them. We have become a taunt to our neighbors, A scorn and mockery to them that are around us. How long, Hashem, will You be angry forever? How long will Your jealousy burn like fire? Pour out Your wrath on the nations that do not know You, And on the kingdoms that do not call on Your name. For they have devoured Yaakov, And laid waste his habitation. Do not remember against us the iniquities of our forefathers; Let Your compassions speedily come to meet us; For we are brought very low. Help us, God of our salvation, for the sake of the glory of Your name; And deliver us, and forgive our sins, for Your name's sake. Why should the nations say: 'Where is their God?' Let the avenging of Your servants' blood that is shed be made known among the nations in our sight. Let the groaning of the prisoner come before You; According to the greatness of Your power set free those that are appointed to death; And render to our neighbors sevenfold into their bosom their reproach, which they have reproached You, Hashem. So we that are Your people and the flock of Your pasture Will give You thanks forever; We will tell of Your praise to all generations.

In a house of mourning read:

Psalms 49

לַמְנַצֵּחַ | לִבְנֵי־קֹרַח מִזְמוֹר׃ שִׁמְעוּ־זֹאת כָּל־הָעַמִּים הַאֲזִינוּ
כָּל־יֹשְׁבֵי חָלֶד׃ גַּם־בְּנֵי אָדָם גַּם־בְּנֵי־אִישׁ יַחַד עָשִׁיר וְאֶבְיוֹן׃ פִּי
יְדַבֵּר חָכְמוֹת וְהָגוּת לִבִּי תְבוּנוֹת׃ אַטֶּה לְמָשָׁל אָזְנִי אֶפְתַּח בְּכִנּוֹר
חִידָתִי׃ לָמָּה אִירָא בִּימֵי רָע עֲוֺן עֲקֵבַי יְסוּבֵּנִי׃ הַבֹּטְחִים עַל־חֵילָם

וּבְרֹב עָשְׁרָם יִתְהַלָּלוּ: אָח לֹא־פָדֹה יִפְדֶּה אִישׁ לֹא־יִתֵּן לֵאלֹהִים
כָּפְרוֹ: וְיֵקַר פִּדְיוֹן נַפְשָׁם וְחָדַל לְעוֹלָם: וִיחִי־עוֹד לָנֶצַח לֹא יִרְאֶה
הַשָּׁחַת: כִּי יִרְאֶה | חֲכָמִים יָמוּתוּ יַחַד כְּסִיל וָבַעַר יֹאבֵדוּ וְעָזְבוּ
לַאֲחֵרִים חֵילָם: קִרְבָּם בָּתֵּימוֹ | לְעוֹלָם מִשְׁכְּנֹתָם לְדוֹר וָדֹר קָרְאוּ
בִשְׁמוֹתָם עֲלֵי אֲדָמוֹת: וְאָדָם בִּיקָר בַּל־יָלִין נִמְשַׁל כַּבְּהֵמוֹת נִדְמוּ:
זֶה דַרְכָּם כֵּסֶל לָמוֹ וְאַחֲרֵיהֶם | בְּפִיהֶם יִרְצוּ סֶלָה: כַּצֹּאן | לִשְׁאוֹל
שַׁתּוּ מָוֶת יִרְעֵם וַיִּרְדּוּ בָם יְשָׁרִים | לַבֹּקֶר וצירם (וְצוּרָם) לְבַלּוֹת
שְׁאוֹל מִזְּבֻל לוֹ: אַךְ־אֱלֹהִים יִפְדֶּה נַפְשִׁי מִיַּד־שְׁאוֹל כִּי יִקָּחֵנִי
סֶלָה: אַל־תִּירָא כִּי־יַעֲשִׁר אִישׁ כִּי־יִרְבֶּה כְּבוֹד בֵּיתוֹ: כִּי לֹא בְמוֹתוֹ
יִקַּח הַכֹּל לֹא־יֵרֵד אַחֲרָיו כְּבוֹדוֹ: כִּי־נַפְשׁוֹ בְּחַיָּיו יְבָרֵךְ וְיוֹדֻךָ
כִּי־תֵיטִיב לָךְ: תָּבוֹא עַד־דּוֹר אֲבוֹתָיו עַד־נֵצַח לֹא יִרְאוּ־אוֹר: אָדָם
בִּיקָר וְלֹא יָבִין נִמְשַׁל כַּבְּהֵמוֹת נִדְמוּ:

Lamnatzeach Livnei-Korach Mizmor. Shim'u-Zot Chol-Ha'ammim; Ha'azinu. Chol-Yoshevei Chaled. Gam-Benei Adam Gam-Benei-'Ish; Yachad Ashir Ve'evyon. Pi Yedaber Chochmot; Vehagut Libi Tevunot. Atteh Lemashal Ozni; Eftach Bechinor. Chidati. Lamah Ira Bimei Ra'; Avon Akevai Yesubeni. Habotechim Al-Cheilam; Uverov Oshram. Yit'hallalu. Ach. Lo-Fadoh Yifdeh Ish; Lo-Yiten Lelohim Kofro. Veyekar Pidyon Nafsham. Vechadal Le'olam. Vichi-'Od Lanetzach; Lo Yir'eh Hashachat. Ki Yir'eh Chachamim Yamutu. Yachad Kesil Vava'ar Yovedu; Ve'azevu La'acherim Cheilam. Kirbam Batteimo Le'olam. Mishkenotom Ledor Vador; Kare'u Vishmotam. Alei Adamot. Ve'adam Bikor Bal-Yalin; Nimshal Kabehemot Nidmu. Zeh Darkom Kesel Lamo; Ve'achareihem Befihem Yirtzu Selah. Katzon Lish'ol Shatu Mavet Yir'em Vayirdu Vam Yesharim Laboker. Vetzurom Levalot She'ol. Mizevul Lo. Ach-'Elohim. Yifdeh Nafshi Miyad-She'ol; Ki Yikacheini Selah. Al-Tira Ki-Ya'ashir Ish; Ki-Yirbeh. Kevod Beito. Ki Lo Vemoto Yikach Hakol; Lo-Yered Acharav Kevodo. Ki-Nafsho Bechayav Yevarech; Veyoducha. Ki-Teitiv Lach. Tavo Ad-Dor Avotav; Ad-Netzach Lo Yir'u-'Or. Adam Bikor Velo Yavin; Nimshal Kabehemot Nidmu.

For the Leader; a Psalm of the sons of Korach. Hear this, all of you peoples; give ear, all of you inhabitants of the world, Both low and high, rich and poor together. My mouth will speak wisdom, and the meditation of my heart will be understanding. I will incline my ear to a parable; I will open my dark saying on the harp. Why should I fear in the days of evil, when the iniquity of my supplanters encircles me, Of them that trust in their wealth, and boast in the multitude of their riches? No man can by any means redeem his brother, or give to God a ransom for him — For too costly is the redemption of their soul, and it must be let alone forever — That he should still live alway, that he should not see the pit. For he sees that wise men die, the fool and the brutish together perish, and leave their wealth to others. Their inward thought is, that their houses will continue forever, and their dwelling-places to all generations; they call their lands after their own names. But man does not abide in honor; he is like the beasts that perish. This is the way of those that are foolish, and of those who after them approve of their sayings. Selah. Like sheep they are appointed for the Sheol; death will be their shepherd; and the upright will have dominion over them in the morning; and their form will be for Sheol to wear away, that there will be no habitation for it. But God will redeem my soul from the power of Sheol; for He will receive me. Selah. Do not be afraid when one becomes rich, when the wealth of his house is increased; For when he dies he will carry nothing away; his wealth will not descend after him. Though while he lives he blesses his soul: 'Though men will praise you, when you will do well to yourself'; It will go to the generation of his fathers; they will never see the light. A man that is in honor and does not understand; he is like the beasts that perish.

After the Song of the Day for fasting and Hanukkah, say:

וּתְשׁוּעַת צַדִּיקִים מֵיְהֹוָה מָעוּזָּם בְּעֵת צָרָה: וַיַּעְזְרֵם יְהֹוָה וַיְפַלְּטֵם
יְפַלְּטֵם מֵרְשָׁעִים וְיוֹשִׁיעֵם כִּי־חָסוּ בוֹ:

Uteshu'at Tzaddikim Mey'adonai; Ma'uzam. Be'et Tzarah.
Vaya'zerem Adonai Vayfalletem Yefalletem Meresha'im Veyoshi'em;
Ki-Chasu Vo.

But the salvation of the righteous is of Hashem; He is their stronghold in the time of trouble. And Hashem helps them, and delivers them; He delivers them from the wicked, and saves them, because they have taken refuge in Him. **(Psalms 37:39-40)**

Kaddish Yehei-Shelama

Kaddish is only recited in a minyan (ten men). אָמֵן denotes when the congregation responds "Amen" together out loud. According to the Shulchan Arukh, the congregation says "Yehei Shemeh Rabba" to "Yitbarach" out loud together without interruption, and also that one should respond "Amen" after "Yitbarach." (SA, OC 55,56) This is not the common custom today. Though many are accustomed to answering according to their own custom, it is advised to respond in the custom of the one reciting to avoid not fragmenting into smaller groups. ("Lo Titgodedu" - BT, Yevamot 13b / SA, OC 493, Rema / MT, Avodah Zara 12:15)

יִתְגַּדַּל וְיִתְקַדַּשׁ שְׁמֵהּ רַבָּא. אָמֵן בְּעָלְמָא דִּי בְרָא. כִּרְעוּתֵהּ. וְיַמְלִיךְ מַלְכוּתֵהּ. וְיַצְמַח פֻּרְקָנֵהּ. וִיקָרֵב מְשִׁיחֵהּ. אָמֵן בְּחַיֵּיכוֹן וּבְיוֹמֵיכוֹן וּבְחַיֵּי דְכָל בֵּית יִשְׂרָאֵל. בַּעֲגָלָא וּבִזְמַן קָרִיב. וְאִמְרוּ אָמֵן. אָמֵן יְהֵא שְׁמֵיהּ רַבָּא מְבָרַךְ לְעָלַם וּלְעָלְמֵי עָלְמַיָּא יִתְבָּרַךְ. וְיִשְׁתַּבַּח. וְיִתְפָּאַר. וְיִתְרוֹמַם. וְיִתְנַשֵּׂא. וְיִתְהַדָּר. וְיִתְעַלֶּה. וְיִתְהַלָּל שְׁמֵהּ דְּקֻדְשָׁא. בְּרִיךְ הוּא. אָמֵן לְעֵלָּא מִן כָּל בִּרְכָתָא שִׁירָתָא. תֻּשְׁבְּחָתָא וְנֶחֱמָתָא. דַּאֲמִירָן בְּעָלְמָא. וְאִמְרוּ אָמֵן. אָמֵן

Yitgadal Veyitkadash Shemeh Rabba. Amen Be'alema Di Vera.
Kir'uteh. Veyamlich Malchuteh. Veyatzmach Purkaneh. Vikarev
Meshicheh. Amen Bechayeichon Uveyomeichon Uvechayei Dechal-
Beit Yisra'el. Ba'agala Uvizman Kariv. Ve'imru Amen. Amen Yehei
Shemeh Rabba Mevarach Le'alam Ule'alemei Alemaya Yitbarach.
Veyishtabach. Veyitpa'ar. Veyitromam. Veyitnasse. Veyit'hadar.
Veyit'aleh. Veyit'hallal Shemeh Dekudsha. Berich Hu. Amen Le'ella
Min Kol Birchata Shirata. Tushbechata Venechemata. Da'amiran
Be'alema. Ve'imru Amen. Amen

Glorified and sanctified be God's great name **Amen** throughout the world which He has created according to His will. May He establish His kingdom, hastening His salvation and the coming of His Messiah, **Amen**, in your lifetime and during your days, and within the life of the entire House of Yisrael, speedily and soon; and say, Amen. **Amen** May His great name be blessed forever and to all eternity. Blessed and praised, glorified and exalted, extolled and honored, adored and lauded is the name of the Holy One, blessed is He, **Amen** Beyond all the blessings and hymns, praises and consolations that are ever spoken in the world; and say, Amen. **Amen**

יְהֵא שְׁלָמָא רַבָּא מִן שְׁמַיָּא. חַיִּים וְשָׂבָע וִישׁוּעָה וְנֶחָמָה. וְשֵׁיזָבָא וּרְפוּאָה וּגְאוּלָּה וּסְלִיחָה וְכַפָּרָה וְרֶוַח וְהַצָּלָה לָנוּ וּלְכָל עַמּוֹ יִשְׂרָאֵל. וְאִמְרוּ אָמֵן. אָמֵן

Yehei Shelama Rabba Min Shemaya. Chayim Vesava Vishu'ah Venechamah. Vesheizava Urefu'ah Uge'ulah Uselichah Vechapparah Verevach Vehatzalah Lanu Ulechol Ammo Yisra'el. Ve'imru Amen. **Amen**

May abundant peace descend from heaven, with life and plenty, salvation, solace, liberation, healing and redemption, and forgiveness and atonement, enlargement and freedom, for us and all of God's people Yisrael; and say, Amen. **Amen**

One bows and takes three steps backwards, while still bowing. After three steps, while still bowing and before erecting, while saying, "Oseh Shalom Bimromav", turn one's face to the left, "Hu [Berachamav] Ya'aseh Shalom Aleinu", turn one's face to the right; then bow forward like a servant leaving his master. (SA, OC 123:1)

עוֹשֶׂה שָׁלוֹם בִּמְרוֹמָיו. הוּא בְּרַחֲמָיו יַעֲשֶׂה שָׁלוֹם עָלֵינוּ. וְעַל כָּל־עַמּוֹ יִשְׂרָאֵל. וְאִמְרוּ אָמֵן:

Oseh Shalom Bimromav. Hu Berachamav Ya'aseh Shalom Aleinu. Ve'al Kol-'Ammo Yisra'el. Ve'imru Amen.

Creator of peace in His heights, may He in His mercy create peace for us and for all Yisrael, and say Amen.

Kaveh

קַוֵּה אֶל־יְהֹוָה חֲזַק וְיַאֲמֵץ לִבֶּךָ וְקַוֵּה אֶל־יְהֹוָה: אֵין־קָדוֹשׁ כַּיהֹוָה כִּי אֵין בִּלְתֶּךָ וְאֵין צוּר כֵּאלֹהֵינוּ: כִּי מִי אֱלוֹהַּ מִבַּלְעֲדֵי יְהֹוָה וּמִי צוּר זוּלָתִי אֱלֹהֵינוּ:

Kaveh El-Adonai Chazak Veya'ametz Libecha; Vekaveh El-Adonai. Ein-Kadosh Ka'adonai Ki Ein Biltecha; Ve'ein Tzur K'Eloheinu. Ki Mi Eloah Mibal'adei Adonai Umi Tzur. Zulati Eloheinu.

"Hope in Hashem, Be strong and let your heart take courage; Hope in Hashem. There is no other that is holy like Hashem, For there is none besides Him, and there is no Rock like our God. For who is God except Hashem, Or who is the Rock other than our God?" **(Ps. 27:14, I Sam. 2:2, Ps. 18:32)**

Ein Keloheinu

Ein Keloheinu. Ein Kadoneinu.	אֵין כֵּאלֹהֵינוּ. אֵין כַּאדוֹנֵנוּ.
Ein Kemalkeinu. Ein	אֵין כְּמַלְכֵּנוּ. אֵין
Kemoshi'enu. Mi Keloheinu. Mi	כְּמוֹשִׁיעֵנוּ: מִי כֵאלֹהֵינוּ. מִי
Kadoneinu. Mi Kemalkeinu. Mi	כַּאדוֹנֵנוּ. מִי כְמַלְכֵּנוּ. מִי
Kemoshi'enu. Nodeh Leloheinu.	כְמוֹשִׁיעֵנוּ: נוֹדֶה לֵאלֹהֵינוּ.
Nodeh Ladoneinu. Nodeh	נוֹדֶה לַאדוֹנֵנוּ. נוֹדֶה
Lemalkeinu. Nodeh	לְמַלְכֵּנוּ. נוֹדֶה
Lemoshi'enu. Baruch Eloheinu.	לְמוֹשִׁיעֵנוּ: בָּרוּךְ אֱלֹהֵינוּ.
Baruch Adoneinu. Baruch	בָּרוּךְ אֲדוֹנֵנוּ. בָּרוּךְ
Malkeinu. Baruch Moshi'enu.	מַלְכֵּנוּ. בָּרוּךְ מוֹשִׁיעֵנוּ:
Attah Hu Eloheinu. Attah Hu	אַתָּה הוּא אֱלֹהֵינוּ. אַתָּה הוּא
Adoneinu. Attah Hu Malkeinu.	אֲדוֹנֵנוּ. אַתָּה הוּא מַלְכֵּנוּ.
Attah Hu Moshi'enu.	אַתָּה הוּא מוֹשִׁיעֵנוּ:

Attah Toshi'enu. Attah Takum	אַתָּה תוֹשִׁיעֵנוּ. אַתָּה תָקוּם
Terachem Tziyon; Ki-'Et	תְּרַחֵם צִיּוֹן כִּי־עֵת לְחֶנְנָהּ כִּי־בָא
Lechenenah. Ki-Va Mo'ed.	מוֹעֵד:

Who is like our God, Who is like our Lord, Who is like our King, Who is like our Savior? There is none like our God, There is none like our Lord, There is none like our King, There is none like our Savior. Let us praise our God, Let us praise our Lord, Let us praise our King, Let us praise our Savior. Blessed is our God, Blessed is our Lord, Blessed is our King, Blessed is our Savior. You are our God, You are our Lord, You are our King, You are our Savior.
You will save us. "You will arise and pity Tziyon; For it is time to show her Your grace, For, the appointed time comes."

Ketoret / Incense Offering

Attah Hu Adonai Eloheinu.	אַתָּה הוּא יְהוָה אֱלֹהֵינוּ.
Shehiktiru Avoteinu Lefaneicha	שֶׁהִקְטִירוּ אֲבוֹתֵינוּ לְפָנֶיךָ
Et Ketoret Hasamim. Bizman	אֶת קְטֹרֶת הַסַּמִּים. בִּזְמַן
Shebeit Hamikdash Kayam.	שֶׁבֵּית הַמִּקְדָּשׁ קַיָּם.
Ka'asher Tzivita Otam Al-Yad	כַּאֲשֶׁר צִוִּיתָ אוֹתָם עַל־יַד
Mosheh Nevi'ach. Kakatuv	מֹשֶׁה נְבִיאָךְ. כַּכָּתוּב
Betoratach:	בְּתוֹרָתָךְ:

You are Hashem, our God, before Whom our ancestors burned the offering of incense in the days of the Beit HaMikdash. For You commanded them through Moshe, Your prophet, as it is written in Your Torah:

Exodus 30:34-36, 7-8

Vayomer Adonai El-Mosheh	וַיֹּאמֶר יְהֹוָה אֶל־מֹשֶׁה
Kach-Lecha Samim. Nataf	קַח־לְךָ סַמִּים נָטָף ׀
Ushchelet Vechelbenah. Samim	וּשְׁחֵלֶת וְחֶלְבְּנָה סַמִּים
Ulevonah Zakah; Bad Bevad	וּלְבֹנָה זַכָּה בַּד בְּבַד
Yihyeh. Ve'asita Otah Ketoret.	יִהְיֶה: וְעָשִׂיתָ אֹתָהּ קְטֹרֶת
Rokach Ma'aseh Rokeach;	רֹקַח מַעֲשֵׂה רוֹקֵחַ
Memulach Tahor Kodesh.	מְמֻלָּח טָהוֹר קֹדֶשׁ:
Veshachakta Mimenah Hadek	וְשָׁחַקְתָּ מִמֶּנָּה הָדֵק
Venatatah Mimenah Lifnei	וְנָתַתָּה מִמֶּנָּה לִפְנֵי
Ha'eidut Be'ohel Mo'ed. Asher	הָעֵדֻת בְּאֹהֶל מוֹעֵד אֲשֶׁר
Iva'eid Lecha Shamah; Kodesh	אִוָּעֵד לְךָ שָׁמָּה קֹדֶשׁ
Kodashim Tihyeh Lachem.	קָדָשִׁים תִּהְיֶה לָכֶם:
Vene'emar Vehiktir Alav Aharon	וְנֶאֱמַר: וְהִקְטִיר עָלָיו אַהֲרֹן
Ketoret Samim; Baboker	קְטֹרֶת סַמִּים בַּבֹּקֶר
Baboker. Beheitivo Et-Hanerot	בַּבֹּקֶר בְּהֵיטִיבוֹ אֶת־הַנֵּרֹת
Yaktirenah. Uveha'alot Aharon	יַקְטִירֶנָּה: וּבְהַעֲלֹת אַהֲרֹן
Et-Hanerot Bein Ha'arbayim	אֶת־הַנֵּרֹת בֵּין הָעַרְבַּיִם
Yaktirenah; Ketoret Tamid Lifnei	יַקְטִירֶנָּה קְטֹרֶת תָּמִיד לִפְנֵי
Adonai Ledoroteichem.	יְהֹוָה לְדֹרֹתֵיכֶם:

And Hashem said to Moshe, 'Take sweet spices, oil of myrrh, onycha and galbanum, together with clear frankincense, a like weight of each of these sweet spices. And you will make from there incense, a perfume pure and holy, compounded by the perfumer, salted together. And you will crush some of it very fine, and put some of it before the Ark of testimony in the Ohel Moed where I will meet with you; it will be most holy to you. Further it is said in the Torah: "And Aharon will burn the incense of sweet spices on the altar of incense, every morning when he dresses the lamps he will burn it. And at dusk when Aharon lights the lamps he will again burn incense, a perpetual incense before Hashem throughout your generations."

Talmud: Keritot 6a

תָּנוּ רַבָּנָן: פִּטּוּם הַקְּטֹרֶת כֵּיצַד: שְׁלֹשׁ מֵאוֹת וְשִׁשִּׁים וּשְׁמוֹנָה מָנִים הָיוּ בָהּ. שְׁלֹשׁ מֵאוֹת וְשִׁשִּׁים וַחֲמִשָּׁה כְּמִנְיַן יְמוֹת הַחַמָּה. מָנֶה בְּכָל־יוֹם. מַחֲצִיתוֹ בַּבֹּקֶר וּמַחֲצִיתוֹ בָּעֶרֶב. וּשְׁלֹשָׁה מָנִים יְתֵרִים. שֶׁמֵּהֶם מַכְנִיס כֹּהֵן גָּדוֹל. וְנוֹטֵל מֵהֶם מְלֹא חָפְנָיו בְּיוֹם הַכִּפּוּרִים. וּמַחֲזִירָן לְמַכְתֶּשֶׁת בְּעֶרֶב יוֹם הַכִּפּוּרִים. כְּדֵי לְקַיֵּם מִצְוַת דַּקָּה מִן הַדַּקָּה. וְאַחַד־עָשָׂר סַמָּנִים הָיוּ בָהּ. וְאֵלּוּ הֵן:

Tanu Rabbanan. Pitum Haketoret Keitzad: Shelosh Me'ot Veshishim Ushemonah Manim Hayu Vah. Shelosh Me'ot Veshishim Vachamishah Keminyan Yemot Hachamah. Maneh Bechol-Yom. Machatzito Baboker Umachatzito Ba'erev. Usheloshah Manim Yeterim. Shemehem Machnis Kohen Gadol. Venotel Mehem Melo Chafenav Beyom Hakippurim. Umachaziron Lemachteshet Be'erev Yom Hakippurim. Kedei Lekayem Mitzvat Dakah Min Hadakah. Ve'achad-'Asar Samanim Hayu Vah. Ve'elu Hen.

The rabbis have taught how the compounding of the incense was done. In measure the incense contained three hundred and sixty-eight manehs, three hundred and sixty-five being one for each day of the year, the remaining three being for the high priest to take his hands full on the Yom Kippur. These last were again ground in a mortar on the eve of Yom Kippur so as to fulfill the command, "take of the finest beaten incense." and these are them:

א הַצֳּרִי ב וְהַצִּפֹּרֶן ג וְהַחֶלְבְּנָה ד וְהַלְּבוֹנָה. מִשְׁקַל שִׁבְעִים שִׁבְעִים מָנֶה. ה מוֹר. ו וּקְצִיעָה ז וְשִׁבֹּלֶת נֵרְדְּ ח וְכַרְכֹּם. מִשְׁקַל שִׁשָּׁה עָשָׂר שִׁשָּׁה עָשָׂר מָנֶה. ט קֹשְׁטְ שְׁנֵים עָשָׂר. י קִלּוּפָה שְׁלֹשָׁה. יא קִנָּמוֹן

תִּשְׁעָה. בּוֹרִית־כַּרְשִׁינָה תִּשְׁעָה קַבִּין. יֵין קַפְרִיסִין סְאִין תְּלָת וְקַבִּין תְּלָתָא. וְאִם לֹא מָצָא יֵין קַפְרִיסִין. מֵבִיא חֲמַר חִיוָר עַתִּיק. מֶלַח סְדוֹמִית. רֹובַע. מַעֲלֶה עָשָׁן. כָּל־שֶׁהוּא. רִבִּי נָתָן הַבַּבְלִי אוֹמֵר: אַף כִּפַּת הַיַּרְדֵּן כָּל־שֶׁהִיא. אִם נָתַן בָּהּ דְּבַשׁ פְּסָלָהּ. וְאִם חִסֵּר אַחַת מִכָּל־סַמְמָנֶיהָ. חַיָּב מִיתָה:

Hatzori Vehatziporen Vehachelbenah Vehallevonah. Mishkal Shiv'im Shiv'im Maneh. Mor. Uketzi'ah Veshibolet Nered Vecharkom. Mishkal Shishah Asar Shishah Asar Maneh. Koshet Sheneim Asar. Kilufah Sheloshah. Kinamon Tish'ah. Borit-Karshinah Tish'ah Kabin. Yein Kafrisin Se'in Telat Vekabin Telata. Ve'im Lo Matza Yein Kafrisin. Mevi Chamar Chivar Atik. Melach Sedomit. Rova. Ma'aleh Ashan. Kol-Shehu. Ribi Natan Habavli Omer. Af Kippat Hayarden Kol-Shehi. Im Natan Bah Devash Pesalah. Ve'im Chisser Achat Mikol-Samemaneiha. Chayaiv Mitah.

The incense was compounded of eleven different spices: seventy manehs each of balm, onycha, galbanum, and frankincense; sixteen manehs each of myrrh, cassia, spikenard, and saffron; twelve manehs of costus; three manehs of aromatic bark; nine manehs of cinnamon; nine kabs of lye of Carsina; three seahs and three kabs of Cyprus wine, though if Cyprus wine could not be had, strong white wine might be substituted for it; the fourth of a kab of salt of Sedom, and a small quantity of a herb which caused the smoke to ascend straight. Rabbi Nathan of Bavel said there was added also a small quantity of kippat of the Yarden. If honey was mixed with the incense, the incense became unfit for sacred use, while the one who omitted any of the ingredients was deemed guilty of mortal error.

רַבָּן שִׁמְעוֹן בֶּן גַּמְלִיאֵל אוֹמֵר: הַצֳּרִי אֵינוֹ אֶלָּא שְׂרָף. הַנּוֹטֵף מֵעֲצֵי הַקְּטָף. בֹּרִית כַּרְשִׁינָה. לְמָה הִיא בָאָה: כְּדֵי לְשַׁפּוֹת בָּהּ אֶת־הַצִּפֹּרֶן. כְּדֵי שֶׁתְּהֵא נָאָה. יֵין קַפְרִיסִין. לְמָה הוּא בָא: כְּדֵי לִשְׁרוֹת בּוֹ אֶת־הַצִּפֹּרֶן כְּדֵי שֶׁתְּהֵא עַזָּה. וַהֲלֹא מֵי רַגְלַיִם יָפִין לָהּ: אֶלָּא שֶׁאֵין מַכְנִיסִין מֵי רַגְלַיִם בַּמִּקְדָּשׁ. מִפְּנֵי הַכָּבוֹד:

Rabban Shim'on Ben-Gamli'el Omer. Hatzori Eino Ella Sheraf. Hanotef Me'atzei Haketaf. Borit Karshinah. Lemah Hi Va'ah: Kedei Leshapot Bah Et-Hatziporen. Kedei Shetehei Na'ah. Yein Kafrisin. Lemah Hu Va: Kedei Lishrot Bo Et-Hatziporen Kedei Shetehei Azah. Vahalo Mei Raglayim Yafin Lah: Ella She'ein Machnisin Mei Raglayim Bamikdash. Mipenei Hakavod.

Rabban Shimon, son of Gamliel, said that the balm required is that exuding from the balsam tree. Why did they use lye of Carsina? To refine the appearance of the onycha. What was the purpose of the Cyprus wine? To steep the onycha in it so as to harden it. Though mei raglayim might have been adapted for that purpose, it was not used because it was not decent to bring it into the Temple.

תַּנְיָא רִבִּי נָתָן אוֹמֵר: כְּשֶׁהוּא שׁוֹחֵק. אוֹמֵר: הָדֵק הֵיטֵב. הֵיטֵב הָדֵק. מִפְּנֵי שֶׁהַקּוֹל יָפֶה לַבְּשָׂמִים. פִּטְּמָהּ לַחֲצָאִין. כְּשֵׁרָה. לִשְׁלִישׁ וּלְרָבִיעַ. לֹא שָׁמַעְנוּ. אָמַר רִבִּי יְהוּדָה: זֶה הַכְּלָל. אִם כְּמִדָּתָהּ. כְּשֵׁרָה לַחֲצָאִין. וְאִם חִסֵּר אַחַת מִכָּל־סַמְמָנֶיהָ. חַיָּב מִיתָה:

Tanya Ribi Natan Omer. Keshehu Shochek. Omer. Hadek Heitev. Heitev Hadek. Mipenei Shehakol Yafeh Labesamim. Pittemah Lachatza'in. Kesherah. Leshalish Uleravia'. Lo Shama'nu. Amar Ribi Yehudah. Zeh Hakelal. Im Kemidatah. Kesherah Lachatza'in. Ve'im Chisser Achat Mikol-Samemaneiha. Chayaiv Mitah.

It is taught: Rabbi Natan said that when the priest ground the incense the one superintending would say, “Grind it very fine, very fine grind it,” because the sound of the human voice is encouraging in the making of spices. If he had compounded only one hundred and eighty-four manehs (half the required quantity), it was valid, but there is no tradition as to its permissibility if it was compounded in one-third or one-quarter proportions of the required quantity. Rabbi Yehudah said that the general principle is that if it was made with its ingredients in their correct proportions, it was permissible in half the quantity; but if one omitted any of the ingredients he was deemed guilty of mortal error.

תָּנֵי בַר־קַפָּרָא: אַחַת לְשִׁשִּׁים אוֹ לְשִׁבְעִים שָׁנָה. הָיְתָה בָאָה שֶׁל שִׁירַיִם לַחֲצָאִין. וְעוֹד תָּנֵי בַר־קַפָּרָא: אִלּוּ הָיָה נוֹתֵן בָּהּ קָרְטוֹב שֶׁל דְּבַשׁ. אֵין אָדָם יָכוֹל לַעֲמֹד מִפְּנֵי רֵיחָהּ. וְלָמָּה אֵין מְעָרְבִין בָּהּ דְּבַשׁ. מִפְּנֵי שֶׁהַתּוֹרָה אָמְרָה: כִּי כָל־שְׂאֹר וְכָל־דְּבַשׁ לֹא־תַקְטִירוּ מִמֶּנּוּ אִשֶּׁה לַיהוָה:

Tanei Var-Kappara. Achat Leshishim O Leshiv'im Shanah. Hayetah Va'ah Shel Shirayim Lachatza'in. Ve'od Tanei Var-Kappara. Ilu Hayah Noten Bah Karetov Shel Devash. Ein Adam Yachol La'amod Mipenei Reichah. Velamah Ein Me'arevin Bah Devash Mipenei Shehatorah Amerah. Ki Chol-Se'or Vechol-Devash. Lo-Taktiru Mimenu Isheh L'Adonai.

Bar Kappara taught that once in sixty or seventy years it happened that, left over, there was over a total of half the required amount accumulated from the three manehs of incense from which the high priest took his hands full on Yom Kippur. Further Bar Kappara taught that had one mixed into the incense the smallest quantity of honey, no one could have stood its scent. Why did they not mix honey with it? Because the Torah states that, "No leaven, or any honey, will you burn as an offering made by fire to Hashem."

יְהוָה צְבָאוֹת עִמָּנוּ מִשְׂגָּב־לָנוּ אֱלֹהֵי יַעֲקֹב סֶלָה: יְהוָה צְבָאוֹת אַשְׁרֵי אָדָם בֹּטֵחַ בָּךְ: יְהוָה הוֹשִׁיעָה הַמֶּלֶךְ יַעֲנֵנוּ בְיוֹם־קָרְאֵנוּ: וְעָרְבָה לַיהוָה מִנְחַת יְהוּדָה וִירוּשָׁלָםִ כִּימֵי עוֹלָם וּכְשָׁנִים קַדְמֹנִיּוֹת:

Adonai Tzeva'ot Imanu; Misgav-Lanu Elohei Ya'akov Selah. Adonai Tzeva'ot; Ashrei Adam. Boteach Bach. Adonai Hoshi'ah; Hamelech. Ya'aneinu Veyom-Kor'enu. Ve'arevah L'Adonai Minchat Yehudah Virushalayim Kimei Olam. Ucheshanim Kadmoniyot.

Hashem of hosts is with us; The God of Yaakov is our high tower. Selah. Hashem of hosts, happy is the man who trusts in You. Save, Hashem; Let the King answer us in the day that we call. Then will the offering of Yehudah and Yerushalayim be pleasant to Hashem, as in the days of old, and as in ancient years. **(Psalms 46:12, 84:13, 20:10, Malachi 3:4)**

תָּנָא דְבֵי אֵלִיָּהוּ. כָּל־הַשּׁוֹנֶה הֲלָכוֹת בְּכָל־יוֹם. מֻבְטָח לוֹ שֶׁהוּא בֶּן־הָעוֹלָם הַבָּא. שֶׁנֶּאֱמַר הֲלִיכוֹת עוֹלָם לוֹ: אַל־תִּקְרֵי הֲלִיכוֹת. אֶלָּא הֲלָכוֹת. אָמַר רִבִּי אֶלְעָזָר אָמַר רִבִּי חֲנִינָא תַּלְמִידֵי חֲכָמִים מַרְבִּים שָׁלוֹם בָּעוֹלָם. שֶׁנֶּאֱמַר וְכָל־בָּנַיִךְ לִמּוּדֵי יְהֹוָה וְרַב שְׁלוֹם בָּנָיִךְ: אַל־תִּקְרֵי בָּנָיִךְ אֶלָּא בּוֹנָיִךְ: יְהִי־שָׁלוֹם בְּחֵילֵךְ שַׁלְוָה בְּאַרְמְנוֹתָיִךְ: לְמַעַן אַחַי וְרֵעָי אֲדַבְּרָה־נָּא שָׁלוֹם בָּךְ: לְמַעַן בֵּית־יְהֹוָה אֱלֹהֵינוּ אֲבַקְשָׁה טוֹב לָךְ: וּרְאֵה־בָנִים לְבָנֶיךָ שָׁלוֹם עַל־יִשְׂרָאֵל: שָׁלוֹם רָב לְאֹהֲבֵי תוֹרָתֶךָ וְאֵין־לָמוֹ מִכְשׁוֹל: יְהֹוָה עֹז לְעַמּוֹ יִתֵּן יְהֹוָה | יְבָרֵךְ אֶת־עַמּוֹ בַשָּׁלוֹם:

Tana Devei Eliyahu. Kol-Hashoneh Halachot Bechol-Yom. Muvtach Lo Shehu Ven-Ha'olam Haba. Shene'emar Halichot Olam Lo. Al-Tikrei Halichot. Ella Halachot. Amar Ribi El'azar Amar Ribi Chanina Talmidei Chachamim Marbim Shalom Ba'olam. Shene'emar Vechol-Banayich Limmudei Adonai Verav Shelom Banayich. Al-Tikrei Vanayich Ella Vonayich. Yehi-Shalom Becheilech; Shalvah. Be'armenotayich. Lema'an Achai Vere'ai; Adaberah-Na Shalom Bach. Lema'an Beit-Adonai Eloheinu; Avakshah Tov Lach. Ure'eh-Vanim Levaneicha; Shalom. Al-Yisra'el. Shalom Rav Le'ohavei Toratecha; Ve'ein-Lamo Michshol. Adonai Oz Le'ammo Yiten; Adonai Yevarech Et-'Ammo Vashalom.

It was taught in the school of Eliyahu, that every one who studies the legal interpretations of the Torah daily, is sure to enjoy the bliss of the world to come; as it is said "his ways are everlasting." Do not read *halichot* "ways," but *halachot* "legal interpretations." Rabbi Elazar in the name of Rabbi Chanina says, that the wise men promote peace in the world: as it is said: "And all your children study the Torah of Hashem: and great will be the peace of your children." Do not read *banayich*, "your children," but *bonayich*, "your builders." "May there be peace within your walls, and prosperity within your palaces. For the sake of my brothers and friends, I will now speak of peace within you. For the sake of the House of Hashem our God, I will seek your good. And you will see your children's children, and peace in Yisrael. Those who love your Torah have abundant peace and none will obstruct them. Hashem will give strength to his people; Hashem will bless His people with peace."

Kaddish Al-Yisrael

Kaddish is only recited in a minyan (ten men). אמן denotes when the congregation responds "Amen" together out loud. According to the Shulchan Arukh, the congregation says "Yehei Shemeh Rabba" to "Yitbarach" out loud together without interruption, and also that one should respond "Amen" after "Yitbarach." (SA, OC 55,56) This is not the common custom today. Though many are accustomed to answering according to their own custom, it is advised to respond in the custom of the one reciting to avoid not fragmenting into smaller groups. ("Lo Titgodedu" - BT, Yevamot 13b / SA, OC 493, Rema / MT, Avodah Zara 12:15)

יִתְגַּדַּל וְיִתְקַדַּשׁ שְׁמֵהּ רַבָּא. אָמֵן בְּעָלְמָא דִּי בְרָא. כִּרְעוּתֵהּ.
וְיַמְלִיךְ מַלְכוּתֵהּ. וְיַצְמַח פֻּרְקָנֵהּ. וִיקָרֵב מְשִׁיחֵהּ. אָמֵן בְּחַיֵּיכוֹן
וּבְיוֹמֵיכוֹן וּבְחַיֵּי דְכָל בֵּית יִשְׂרָאֵל. בַּעֲגָלָא וּבִזְמַן קָרִיב. וְאִמְרוּ
אָמֵן. אָמֵן יְהֵא שְׁמֵיהּ רַבָּא מְבָרַךְ לְעָלַם וּלְעָלְמֵי עָלְמַיָּא יִתְבָּרַךְ.
וְיִשְׁתַּבַּח. וְיִתְפָּאַר. וְיִתְרוֹמַם. וְיִתְנַשֵּׂא. וְיִתְהַדָּר. וְיִתְעַלֶּה. וְיִתְהַלָּל
שְׁמֵהּ דְּקֻדְשָׁא. בְּרִיךְ הוּא. אָמֵן לְעֵלָּא מִן כָּל בִּרְכָתָא שִׁירָתָא.
תֻּשְׁבְּחָתָא וְנֶחֱמָתָא. דַּאֲמִירָן בְּעָלְמָא. וְאִמְרוּ אָמֵן. אָמֵן

Yitgadal Veyitkadash Shemeh Rabba. Amen Be'alema Di Vera. Kir'uteh. Veyamlich Malchuteh. Veyatzmach Purkaneh. Vikarev Meshicheh. Amen Bechayeichon Uveyomeichon Uvechayei Dechal-Beit Yisra'el. Ba'agala Uvizman Kariv. Ve'imru Amen. Amen Yehei Shemeh Rabba Mevarach Le'alam Ule'alemei Alemaya Yitbarach. Veyishtabach. Veyitpa'ar. Veyitromam. Veyitnasse. Veyit'hadar. Veyit'aleh. Veyit'hallal Shemeh Dekudsha. Berich Hu. Amen Le'ella

Min Kol Birchata Shirata. Tushbechata Venechemata. Da'amiran Be'alema. Ve'imru Amen. **Amen**

Glorified and sanctified be God's great name **Amen** throughout the world which He has created according to His will. May He establish His kingdom, hastening His salvation and the coming of His Messiah, **Amen**, in your lifetime and during your days, and within the life of the entire House of Yisrael, speedily and soon; and say, Amen. **Amen** May His great name be blessed forever and to all eternity. Blessed and praised, glorified and exalted, extolled and honored, adored and lauded is the name of the Holy One, blessed is He, **Amen** Beyond all the blessings and hymns, praises and consolations that are ever spoken in the world; and say, Amen. **Amen**

עַל יִשְׂרָאֵל וְעַל רַבָּנָן. וְעַל תַּלְמִידֵיהוֹן וְעַל כָּל תַּלְמִידֵי תַלְמִידֵיהוֹן. דְּעָסְקִין בְּאוֹרַיְתָא קַדִּשְׁתָּא. דִּי בְאַתְרָא הָדֵין וְדִי בְכָל אֲתַר וַאֲתַר. יְהֵא לָנָא וּלְהוֹן וּלְכוֹן חִנָּא וְחִסְדָּא וְרַחֲמֵי. מִן קֳדָם מָארֵי שְׁמַיָּא וְאַרְעָא וְאִמְרוּ אָמֵן. אָמֵן

Al Yisra'el Ve'al Rabbanan. Ve'al Talmideihon Ve'al Kol Talmidei Talmideihon. De'asekin Be'orayta Kaddishta. Di Ve'atra Hadein Vedi Vechal Atar Va'atar. Yehei Lana Ulehon Ulechon China Vechisda Verachamei. Min Kodam Marei Shemaya Ve'ar'a Ve'imru Amen. **Amen**

May we of Yisrael together with our rabbis, their disciples and pupils, and all who engage in the study of holy Torah here and everywhere, find gracious favor and mercy from their Father Who is in heaven; and say, Amen. **Amen**

יְהֵא שְׁלָמָא רַבָּא מִן שְׁמַיָּא. חַיִּים וְשָׂבָע וִישׁוּעָה וְנֶחָמָה. וְשֵׁיזָבָא וּרְפוּאָה וּגְאוּלָּה וּסְלִיחָה וְכַפָּרָה וְרֶוַח וְהַצָּלָה לָנוּ וּלְכָל עַמּוֹ יִשְׂרָאֵל. וְאִמְרוּ אָמֵן. אָמֵן

Yehei Shelama Rabba Min Shemaya. Chayim Vesava Vishu'ah Venechamah. Vesheizava Urefu'ah Uge'ulah Uselichah Vechapparah Verevach Vehatzalah Lanu Ulechol Ammo Yisra'el. Ve'imru Amen. **Amen**

May abundant peace descend from heaven, with life and plenty, salvation, solace, liberation, healing and redemption, and forgiveness and atonement, enlargement and freedom, for us and all of God's people Yisrael; and say, Amen. **Amen**

One bows and takes three steps backwards, while still bowing. After three steps, while still bowing and before erecting, while saying, "Oseh Shalom Bimromav", turn one's face to the left, "Hu [Berachamav] Ya'aseh Shalom Aleinu", turn one's face to the right; then bow forward like a servant leaving his master. (SA, OC 123:1)

עוֹשֶׂה שָׁלוֹם בִּמְרוֹמָיו. הוּא בְּרַחֲמָיו יַעֲשֶׂה שָׁלוֹם עָלֵינוּ. וְעַל כָּל־עַמּוֹ יִשְׂרָאֵל. וְאִמְרוּ אָמֵן:

Oseh Shalom Bimromav. Hu Berachamav Ya'aseh Shalom Aleinu. Ve'al Kol-'Ammo Yisra'el. Ve'imru Amen.

Creator of peace in His heights, may He in His mercy create peace for us and for all Yisrael, and say Amen.

The Barechu / Call to Prayer

Barechu is only said with 10 men (a minyan).

The Oleh / Reader:

בָּרְכוּ אֶת יְהֹוָה הַמְבֹרָךְ:

Barechu Et Adonai Hamevorach.

Bless Hashem, Who is forever blessed.

The kahal / congregation:

בָּרוּךְ יְהֹוָה הַמְבֹרָךְ לְעוֹלָם וָעֶד:

Baruch Adonai Hamevorach Le'olam Va'ed.

Blessed is Hashem Who is blessed for all eternity.

The Oleh and Chazan:

בָּרוּךְ יְהֹוָה הַמְבֹרָךְ לְעוֹלָם וָעֶד:

Baruch Adonai Hamevorach Le'olam Va'ed.

Blessed is Hashem Who is blessed for all eternity.

And say silently:

בָּרוּךְ שֵׁם כְּבוֹד מַלְכוּתוֹ לְעוֹלָם וָעֶד:

Baruch Shem Kevod Malchuto Le'olam Va'ed.

Blessed is His name and glorious kingdom forever and ever.

Aleinu

[*] denotes pausing and then bowing when saying "Va'anachnu Mistachavim". Some take Tefillin off after Aleinu.

Aleinu Leshabei'ach La'adon	עָלֵינוּ לְשַׁבֵּחַ לַאֲדוֹן
Hakol. Latet Gedullah Leyotzer	הַכֹּל. לָתֵת גְּדֻלָּה לְיוֹצֵר
Bereshit. Shelo Asanu Kegoyei	בְּרֵאשִׁית. שֶׁלֹּא עָשָׂנוּ כְּגוֹיֵי
Ha'aratzot. Velo Samanu	הָאֲרָצוֹת. וְלֹא שָׂמָנוּ
Kemishpechot Ha'adamah. Shelo	כְּמִשְׁפְּחוֹת הָאֲדָמָה. שֶׁלֹּא
Sam Chelkenu Kahem	שָׂם חֶלְקֵנוּ כָּהֶם
Vegoraleinu Kechal-Hamonam.	וְגוֹרָלֵנוּ כְּכָל־הֲמוֹנָם.
Shehem Mishtachavim Lahevel	שֶׁהֵם מִשְׁתַּחֲוִים לָהֶבֶל
Varik. Umitpallelim El-'El Lo	וָרִיק. וּמִתְפַּלְּלִים אֶל־אֵל לֹא
Yoshia. *Va'anachnu	יוֹשִׁיעַ. *וַאֲנַחְנוּ
Mishtachavim Lifnei Melech	מִשְׁתַּחֲוִים לִפְנֵי מֶלֶךְ
Malchei Hamelachim Hakadosh	מַלְכֵי הַמְּלָכִים הַקָּדוֹשׁ
Baruch Hu. Shehu Noteh	בָּרוּךְ הוּא. שֶׁהוּא נוֹטֶה
Shamayim Veyosed Aretz.	שָׁמַיִם וְיוֹסֵד אָרֶץ.
Umoshav Yekaro Bashamayim	וּמוֹשַׁב יְקָרוֹ בַּשָּׁמַיִם
Mima'al. Ushechinat Uzo	מִמַּעַל. וּשְׁכִינַת עֻזּוֹ
Begavehei Meromim. Hu	בְּגָבְהֵי מְרוֹמִים. הוּא
Eloheinu. Ve'ein Od Acher. Emet	אֱלֹהֵינוּ. וְאֵין עוֹד אַחֵר. אֱמֶת
Malkeinu Ve'efes Zulato.	מַלְכֵּנוּ וְאֶפֶס זוּלָתוֹ.

Kakatuv Batorah. Veyada'ta	כַּכָּתוּב בַּתּוֹרָה. וְיָדַעְתָּ
Hayom. Vahasheivota El-	הַיּוֹם וַהֲשֵׁבֹתָ אֶל־
Levavecha Ki Adonai Hu	לְבָבֶךָ כִּי יְהֹוָה הוּא
Ha'elohim. Bashamayim	הָאֱלֹהִים בַּשָּׁמַיִם
Mima'al. Ve'al-Ha'aretz	מִמַּעַל וְעַל־הָאָרֶץ
Mitachat; Ein Od.	מִתָּחַת אֵין עוֹד:

It is our obligation us to praise the Lord of all. To render greatness to the Former of creation. For He has not made us like the nation of the lands, nor set us to be like the families of the earth. Who has not given our portion like theirs and our lot like their masses that bow down to vanity and emptiness, "And pray to a god that does not save." *'But we bow before the supreme King of kings, the Holy One, blessed is He. Who stretches out the heavens and laid the foundations of the earth and his glorious seat is in the heavens above, and the presence of His might in the most exalted of heights. He is our God, there is no other. In truth our King, there is no one except Him. As it is written in the Torah: "This day know and lay it to your heart, that Hashem, He is God in the heavens above and on the earth beneath. There is no one else."

Al Ken Nekaveh Lach. Adonai	עַל כֵּן נְקַוֶּה לָּךְ. יְהֹוָה
Eloheinu. Lir'ot Meheirah	אֱלֹהֵינוּ. לִרְאוֹת מְהֵרָה
Betif'eret Uzach. Leha'avir	בְּתִפְאֶרֶת עֻזָּךְ. לְהַעֲבִיר
Gilulim Min Ha'aretz.	גִּלּוּלִים מִן הָאָרֶץ.
Veha'elilim Karot Yikaretun.	וְהָאֱלִילִים כָּרוֹת יִכָּרֵתוּן.
Letakken Olam Bemalchut	לְתַקֵּן עוֹלָם בְּמַלְכוּת
Shaddai. Vechol-Benei Vasar	שַׁדַּי. וְכָל-בְּנֵי בָשָׂר
Yikre'u Vishmecha. Lehafnot	יִקְרְאוּ בִשְׁמֶךָ. לְהַפְנוֹת
Eleicha Kol-Rish'ei Aretz. Yakiru	אֵלֶיךָ כָּל-רִשְׁעֵי אָרֶץ. יַכִּירוּ

Veyede'u Kol-Yoshevei Tevel. Ki	וְיֵדְעוּ כָּל-יוֹשְׁבֵי תֵבֵל. כִּי
Lecha Tichra Kol-Berech. Tishava	לְךָ תִּכְרַע כָּל-בֶּרֶךְ. תִּשָּׁבַע
Kol-Lashon. Lefaneicha. Adonai	כָּל-לָשׁוֹן. לְפָנֶיךָ. יְהוָה
Eloheinu Yichre'u Veyipolu.	אֱלֹהֵינוּ יִכְרְעוּ וְיִפֹּלוּ.
Velichvod Shimcha Yekar Yitenu.	וְלִכְבוֹד שִׁמְךָ יְקָר יִתֵּנוּ.
Vikabelu Chulam Et-'Ol	וִיקַבְּלוּ כֻלָּם אֶת-עֹל
Malchutecha. Vetimloch Aleihem	מַלְכוּתֶךָ. וְתִמְלוֹךְ עֲלֵיהֶם
Meheirah Le'olam Va'ed. Ki	מְהֵרָה לְעוֹלָם וָעֶד. כִּי
Hamalchut Shelecha Hi.	הַמַּלְכוּת שֶׁלְּךָ הִיא.
Ule'olemei Ad Timloch	וּלְעוֹלְמֵי עַד תִּמְלוֹךְ
Bechavod. Kakatuv Betoratach.	בְּכָבוֹד. כַּכָּתוּב בְּתוֹרָתֶךָ:
Adonai Yimloch Le'olam Va'ed.	יְהוָה | יִמְלֹךְ לְעֹלָם וָעֶד:
Vene'emar. Vehayah Adonai	וְנֶאֱמַר. וְהָיָה יְהוָה
Lemelech Al-Kol-Ha'aretz;	לְמֶלֶךְ עַל־כָּל־הָאָרֶץ
Bayom Hahu. Yihyeh Adonai	בַּיּוֹם הַהוּא יִהְיֶה יְהוָה
Echad Ushemo Echad.	אֶחָד וּשְׁמוֹ אֶחָד:

Therefore we hope in You, Hashem our God, soon to see Your glorious might, to remove idols from the earth and the non-gods will be wholly cut down, to rectify the world with the kingdom of El Shaddai, and all children of flesh will call on Your name and all of the earth's wicked will turn to You. All that dwell on earth will understand and know that to You every knee must bend, and every tongue swear. Before You, Hashem our God, may all kneel and fall and give honor to Your glorious name. And they will all accept the yoke of Your kingdom. And may You speedily rule over them forever. For dominion is Yours, and forever You will reign in glory, as is written in Your Torah, "Hashem will reign forever and ever." For, it is said, "Hashem will be King over all the earth; on that day Hashem will be One and His name One."

Uvetoratecha Adonai Eloheinu	וּבְתוֹרָתְךָ יְהֹוָה אֱלֹהֵינוּ
Katuv Lemor. Shema Yisra'el;	כָּתוּב לֵאמֹר. שְׁמַע יִשְׂרָאֵל
Adonai Eloheinu Adonai Echad.	יְהֹוָה אֱלֹהֵינוּ יְהֹוָה אֶחָד:

And in Your Torah, Hashem our God, it is written: Hear O Yisrael Hashem our God, Hashem is One.

Some recite the following verses afterwards:

וַיֹּאמֶר אִם־שָׁמוֹעַ תִּשְׁמַע לְקוֹל | יְהֹוָה אֱלֹהֶיךָ וְהַיָּשָׁר בְּעֵינָיו תַּעֲשֶׂה וְהַאֲזַנְתָּ לְמִצְוֹתָיו וְשָׁמַרְתָּ כָּל־חֻקָּיו כָּל־הַמַּחֲלָה אֲשֶׁר־שַׂמְתִּי בְמִצְרַיִם לֹא־אָשִׂים עָלֶיךָ כִּי אֲנִי יְהֹוָה רֹפְאֶךָ:

Vayomer Im-Shamoa Tishma Lekol Adonai Eloheicha. Vehayashar Be'einav Ta'aseh. Veha'azanta Lemitzvtav. Veshamarta Kol-Chukkav; Kol-Hamachalah Asher-Samti Vemitzrayim Lo-'Asim Aleicha. Ki Ani Adonai Rofe'echa.

And He said: 'If you will diligently heed the voice of Hashem Your God, and will do that which is right in His eyes, and will give ear to His commandments, and keep all His statutes, I will put none of the diseases upon You, which I have put upon the Egyptians; for I am Hashem that heals you.' **(Exodus 15:26)**

עֵץ־חַיִּים הִיא לַמַּחֲזִיקִים בָּהּ וְתֹמְכֶיהָ מְאֻשָּׁר: דְּרָכֶיהָ דַרְכֵי־נֹעַם וְכָל־נְתִיבוֹתֶיהָ שָׁלוֹם: מִגְדַּל־עֹז שֵׁם יְהֹוָה בּוֹ־יָרוּץ צַדִּיק וְנִשְׂגָּב: כִּי־בִי יִרְבּוּ יָמֶיךָ וְיוֹסִיפוּ לְךָ שְׁנוֹת חַיִּים:

Etz-Chayim Hi LaMachAzikim Bah; Vetomecheiha Me'ushar. Deracheiha Darchei-No'am; Vechol-Netivoteiha Shalom. Migdal-'Oz Shem Adonai Bo-Yarutz Tzaddik Venisgav. Ki-Vi Yirbu Yameicha; Veyosifu Lecha. Shenot Chayim.

She is a tree of life to them that lay hold upon her, And happy is every one that holds her fast. Her ways are ways of pleasantness, And all her paths are peace. The name of Hashem is a strong tower: The righteous run into it, and are set up on high. For by Me your days will be multiplied, and the years of your life will be increased. **(Proverbs 3:18, 3:17, 18:10, 9:11)**

Some recite Psalms 27 daily, and some only from Rosh Chodesh Elul until Hoshanah Rabbah:

Psalms 27

לְדָוִ֨ד ׀ יְהֹוָ֤ה ׀ אוֹרִ֣י וְ֭יִשְׁעִי מִמִּ֣י אִירָ֑א יְהֹוָ֥ה מָעוֹז־חַ֝יַּ֗י מִמִּ֥י אֶפְחָֽד׃ בִּקְרֹ֤ב עָלַ֨י ׀
מְרֵעִים֮ לֶאֱכֹ֪ל אֶת־בְּשָׂ֫רִ֥י צָרַ֣י וְאֹיְבַ֣י לִ֑י הֵ֖מָּה כָשְׁל֣וּ וְנָפָֽלוּ׃ אִם־תַּחֲנֶ֬ה עָלַ֨י ׀
מַחֲנֶה֮ לֹֽא־יִירָ֪א לִ֫בִּ֥י אִם־תָּק֣וּם עָ֭לַי מִלְחָמָ֑ה בְּ֝זֹ֗את אֲנִ֣י בוֹטֵֽחַ׃ אַחַ֤ת ׀ שָׁאַ֣לְתִּי
מֵֽאֵת־יְהֹוָה֮ אוֹתָ֪הּ אֲבַ֫קֵּ֥שׁ שִׁבְתִּ֣י בְּבֵית־יְ֭הֹוָה כׇּל־יְמֵ֣י חַיַּ֑י לַחֲז֥וֹת בְּנֹֽעַם־יְ֝הֹוָ֗ה
וּלְבַקֵּ֥ר בְּהֵיכָלֽוֹ׃ כִּ֤י יִצְפְּנֵ֨נִי ׀ בְּסֻכֹּה֮ בְּי֪וֹם רָ֫עָ֥ה יַ֭סְתִּרֵנִי בְּסֵ֣תֶר אׇהֳל֑וֹ בְּ֝צ֗וּר
יְרוֹמְמֵֽנִי׃ וְעַתָּ֨ה יָר֪וּם רֹאשִׁ֡י עַ֤ל אֹיְבַ֬י סְֽבִיבוֹתַ֗י וְאֶזְבְּחָ֣ה בְ֭אׇהֳלוֹ זִבְחֵ֣י תְרוּעָ֑ה
אָשִׁ֥ירָה וַ֝אֲזַמְּרָ֗ה לַיהֹוָֽה׃ שְׁמַע־יְהֹוָ֖ה קוֹלִ֥י אֶקְרָ֗א וְחׇנֵּ֥נִי וַעֲנֵֽנִי׃ לְךָ֤ ׀ אָמַ֣ר לִ֭בִּי
בַּקְּשׁ֣וּ פָנָ֑י אֶת־פָּנֶ֖יךָ יְהֹוָ֣ה אֲבַקֵּֽשׁ׃ אַל־תַּסְתֵּ֬ר פָּנֶ֨יךָ ׀ מִמֶּנִּי֮ אַֽל־תַּט־בְּאַ֗ף עַ֫בְדֶּ֥ךָ
עֶזְרָתִ֥י הָיִ֑יתָ אַל־תִּטְּשֵׁ֥נִי וְאַל־תַּ֝עַזְבֵ֗נִי אֱלֹהֵ֥י יִשְׁעִֽי׃ כִּֽי־אָבִ֣י וְאִמִּ֣י עֲזָב֑וּנִי וַיהֹוָ֥ה
יַאַסְפֵֽנִי׃ ה֤וֹרֵ֥נִי יְהֹוָ֗ה דַּ֫רְכֶּ֥ךָ וּ֭נְחֵנִי בְּאֹ֣רַח מִישׁ֑וֹר לְ֝מַ֗עַן שׁוֹרְרָֽי׃ אַל־תִּ֭תְּנֵנִי
בְּנֶ֣פֶשׁ צָרָ֑י כִּ֥י קָֽמוּ־בִ֥י עֵֽדֵי־שֶׁ֝֗קֶר וִיפֵ֥חַ חָמָֽס׃ לׅׄוּלֵׅׄ֗אׅׄ הֶ֭אֱמַנְתִּי לִרְא֥וֹת
בְּֽטוּב־יְהֹוָ֗ה בְּאֶ֣רֶץ חַיִּֽים׃ קַוֵּ֗ה אֶל־יְה֫וָ֥ה חֲ֭זַק וְיַאֲמֵ֣ץ לִבֶּ֑ךָ וְ֝קַוֵּ֗ה אֶל־יְהֹוָֽה׃

LeDavid Adonai Ori Veyish'i Mimi Ira; Adonai Ma'oz-Chayai. Mimi Efchad. Bikrov Alai Mere'im Le'echol Et-Besari Tzarai Ve'oyevai Li; Hemah Chashelu Venafalu. Im-Tachaneh Alai Machaneh Lo-Yira Libi Im-Takum Alai Milchamah; Bezot. Ani Voteach. Achat Sha'alti Me'et-Adonai Otah Avakesh Shivti Beveit-Adonai Kol-Yemei Chayai; Lachazot Beno'am-Adonai Ulevakeir Beheichalo. Ki Yitzpeneni Besukkoh Beyom Ra'ah Yastireni Beseter Oholo; Betzur. Yeromemeni. Ve'attah Yarum Roshi Al Oyevai Sevivotai. Ve'ezbechah Ve'oholo Zivchei Teru'ah; Ashirah Va'azemerah. L'Adonai Shema'-Adonai Koli Ekra. Vechoneni Va'aneni. Lecha Amar Libi Bakeshu Fanai; Et-Paneicha Adonai Avakesh. Al-Taster Paneicha Mimeni Al-Tat-Be'af. Avdecha Ezrati Hayita; Al-Titeseni Ve'al-Ta'azveni. Elohei Yish'i. Ki-'Avi Ve'immi Azavuni; Va'Adonai Ya'asfeni. Horeni Adonai Darkecha Unecheini Be'orach Mishor; Lema'an. Shorerai. Al-Titeneni Benefesh Tzarai; Ki Kamu-Vi Edei-Sheker. Vifeach Chamas. Lule. He'emanti Lir'ot Betuv-Adonai Be'eretz Chayim. Kaveh El-Adonai Chazak Veya'ametz Libecha; Vekaveh El-Adonai.

A Psalm of David. Hashem is my light and my salvation; who will I fear? Hashem is the stronghold of my life; of who will I be afraid? When evil-doers came upon me to eat up my flesh, Even my adversaries and my foes, they stumbled and fell. Though an army would encamp against me, My heart will not fear; Though war would rise up against me, Even then will I be confident. One thing have I asked of Hashem, that will I seek after: That I may dwell in the House of Hashem all the days of my life, To behold the graciousness of Hashem, and to visit early in His Temple. For He conceals me in His sukkah in the day of evil; He hides me in the covert of His tent; He lifts me up upon a rock. And now my head will be lifted up above my enemies round about me; And I will offer in His tabernacle sacrifices with shofar-sound; I will sing, and I will sing praises to Hashem. Hear, Hashem, when I call with my voice, And be gracious to me, and answer me. On Your behalf my heart has said:

'Seek My face'; Your face, Hashem, will I seek. Do not hide Your face far from me; Do not put Your servant away in anger; You have been my help; Do not cast me off, or forsake me, Oh God of my salvation. For though my father and my mother have forsaken me, Hashem will take me up. Teach me Your way, Hashem; And lead me in an even path, Because of them that lie in wait for me. Do not deliver me over to the will of my adversaries; For false witnesses have risen up against me, and such as breathe out violence. If I had not believed to look upon the goodness of Hashem In the land of the living.—Wait on Hashem; Be strong, and let your heart take courage; and wait on Hashem.

Kaddish Yehei-Shelama

Kaddish is only recited in a minyan (ten men). אָמֵן denotes when the congregation responds "Amen" together out loud. According to the Shulchan Arukh, the congregation says "Yehei Shemeh Rabba" to "Yitbarach" out loud together without interruption, and also that one should respond "Amen" after "Yitbarach." (SA, OC 55,56) This is not the common custom today. Though many are accustomed to answering according to their own custom, it is advised to respond in the custom of the one reciting to avoid not fragmenting into smaller groups. ("Lo Titgodedu" - BT, Yevamot 13b / SA, OC 493, Rema / MT, Avodah Zara 12:15)

יִתְגַּדַּל וְיִתְקַדַּשׁ שְׁמֵהּ רַבָּא. אָמֵן בְּעָלְמָא דִּי בְרָא. כִּרְעוּתֵהּ. וְיַמְלִיךְ מַלְכוּתֵהּ. וְיַצְמַח פֻּרְקָנֵהּ. וִיקָרֵב מְשִׁיחֵהּ. אָמֵן בְּחַיֵּיכוֹן וּבְיוֹמֵיכוֹן וּבְחַיֵּי דְכָל בֵּית יִשְׂרָאֵל. בַּעֲגָלָא וּבִזְמַן קָרִיב. וְאִמְרוּ אָמֵן. אָמֵן יְהֵא שְׁמֵיהּ רַבָּא מְבָרַךְ לְעָלַם וּלְעָלְמֵי עָלְמַיָּא יִתְבָּרַךְ. וְיִשְׁתַּבַּח. וְיִתְפָּאַר. וְיִתְרוֹמַם. וְיִתְנַשֵּׂא. וְיִתְהַדָּר. וְיִתְעַלֶּה. וְיִתְהַלָּל שְׁמֵהּ דְּקֻדְשָׁא. בְּרִיךְ הוּא. אָמֵן לְעֵלָּא מִן כָּל בִּרְכָתָא שִׁירָתָא. תֻּשְׁבְּחָתָא וְנֶחֱמָתָא. דַּאֲמִירָן בְּעָלְמָא. וְאִמְרוּ אָמֵן. אָמֵן

Yitgadal Veyitkadash Shemeh Rabba. Amen Be'alema Di Vera. Kir'uteh. Veyamlich Malchuteh. Veyatzmach Purkaneh. Vikarev Meshicheh. Amen Bechayeichon Uveyomeichon Uvechayei Dechal-Beit Yisra'el. Ba'agala Uvizman Kariv. Ve'imru Amen. Amen Yehei Shemeh Rabba Mevarach Le'alam Ule'alemei Alemaya Yitbarach. Veyishtabach. Veyitpa'ar. Veyitromam. Veyitnasse. Veyit'hadar. Veyit'aleh. Veyit'hallal Shemeh Dekudsha. Berich Hu. Amen Le'ella Min Kol Birchata Shirata. Tushbechata Venechemata. Da'amiran Be'alema. Ve'imru Amen. Amen

Glorified and sanctified be God's great name **Amen** throughout the world which He has created according to His will. May He establish His kingdom, hastening His salvation and the coming of His Messiah, **Amen**, in your lifetime and during your days, and within the life of the entire House of Yisrael, speedily and soon; and say, Amen. **Amen** May His great name be blessed forever and to all eternity. Blessed and praised, glorified and exalted, extolled and honored, adored and lauded is the name of the Holy One, blessed is He, **Amen** Beyond all the blessings and hymns, praises and consolations that are ever spoken in the world; and say, Amen. **Amen**

יְהֵא שְׁלָמָא רַבָּא מִן שְׁמַיָּא. חַיִּים וְשָׂבָע וִישׁוּעָה וְנֶחָמָה. וְשֵׁיזָבָא וּרְפוּאָה וּגְאוּלָה וּסְלִיחָה וְכַפָּרָה וְרֶוַח וְהַצָּלָה לָנוּ וּלְכָל עַמּוֹ יִשְׂרָאֵל. וְאִמְרוּ אָמֵן. אָמֵן

Yehei Shelama Rabba Min Shemaya. Chayim Vesava Vishu'ah Venechamah. Vesheizava Urefu'ah Uge'ulah Uselichah Vechapparah Verevach Vehatzalah Lanu Ulechol Ammo Yisra'el. Ve'imru Amen. **Amen**

May abundant peace descend from heaven, with life and plenty, salvation, solace, liberation, healing and redemption, and forgiveness and atonement, enlargement and freedom, for us and all of God's people Yisrael; and say, Amen. **Amen**

One bows and takes three steps backwards, while still bowing. After three steps, while still bowing and before erecting, while saying, "Oseh Shalom Bimromav", turn one's face to the left, "Hu [Berachamav] Ya'aseh Shalom Aleinu", turn one's face to the right; then bow forward like a servant leaving his master. (SA, OC 123:1)

עוֹשֶׂה שָׁלוֹם בִּמְרוֹמָיו. הוּא בְּרַחֲמָיו יַעֲשֶׂה שָׁלוֹם עָלֵינוּ. וְעַל כָּל־עַמּוֹ יִשְׂרָאֵל. וְאִמְרוּ אָמֵן:

Oseh Shalom Bimromav. Hu Berachamav Ya'aseh Shalom Aleinu. Ve'al Kol-'Ammo Yisra'el. Ve'imru Amen.

Creator of peace in His heights, may He in His mercy create peace for us and for all Yisrael, and say Amen.

ADDITIONS FOR SHACHARIT

The Thirteen Principles of Faith

As set by Rabbi Moses ben Maimon, i.e. The Ramban

א אֲנִי מַאֲמִין בֶּאֱמוּנָה שְׁלֵמָה. שֶׁהַבּוֹרֵא יִתְבָּרַךְ שְׁמוֹ הוּא בּוֹרֵא וּמַנְהִיג לְכָל הַבְּרוּאִים וְהוּא לְבַדּוֹ עָשָׂה וְעוֹשֶׂה וְיַעֲשֶׂה לְכָל הַמַּעֲשִׂים:

א Ani Ma'amin Be'emunah Shelemah. ShehaBorei Yitbarach Shemo Hu Borei Umanhig Lechol Haberu'im Vehu Levado Asah Ve'oseh Veya'aseh Lechol Hama'asim:

1. I believe, with a perfect faith, that the Creator, blessed is His name, is the Creator and Guide of everything that has been created, and that He alone has made, does make, and will make all things.

ב אֲנִי מַאֲמִין בֶּאֱמוּנָה שְׁלֵמָה. שֶׁהַבּוֹרֵא יִתְבָּרַךְ שְׁמוֹ הוּא יָחִיד וְאֵין יְחִידוּת כָּמוֹהוּ בְּשׁוּם פָּנִים וְהוּא לְבַדּוֹ אֱלֹהֵינוּ. הָיָה הֹוֶה וְיִהְיֶה:

ב Ani Ma'amin Be'emunah Shelemah. Shehaborei Yitbarach Shemo Hu Yachid Ve'ein Yechidut Kamohu Beshum Panim Vehu Levado Eloheinu. Hayah Hoveh Veyihyeh:

2. I believe, with a perfect faith, that the Creator, blessed is His name, is a Unity, and that there is no unity in any manner whatsoever like him, and that He alone is our God, Who was, is, and ever will be.

ג אֲנִי מַאֲמִין בֶּאֱמוּנָה שְׁלֵמָה שֶׁהַבּוֹרֵא יִתְבָּרַךְ שְׁמוֹ אֵינוֹ גוּף וְלֹא יַשִּׂיגוּהוּ מַשִּׂיגֵי הַגּוּף וְאֵין לוֹ שׁוּם דִּמְיוֹן כְּלָל:

ג Ani Ma'amin Be'emunah Shelemah Shehaborei Yitbarach Shemo Eino Guf Velo Yassiguhu Massigei Haguf Ve'ein Lo Shum Dimyon Kelal:

3. I believe, with a perfect faith, that the Creator, blessed is His name, is incorporeal, and that He is free from all the accidents of matter, and that he has no form whatsoever.

ד אֲנִי מַאֲמִין בֶּאֱמוּנָה שְׁלֵמָה שֶׁהַבּוֹרֵא יִתְבָּרַךְ שְׁמוֹ הוּא רִאשׁוֹן וְהוּא אַחֲרוֹן:

ד Ani Ma'amin Be'emunah Shelemah Shehaborei Yitbarach Shemo Hu Rishon Vehu Acharon:

4. I believe, with a perfect faith, that the Creator, blessed is His name, is the first and the last.

ה אֲנִי מַאֲמִין בֶּאֱמוּנָה שְׁלֵמָה שֶׁהַבּוֹרֵא יִתְבָּרַךְ שְׁמוֹ לוֹ לְבַדּוֹ רָאוּי לְהִתְפַּלֵּל. וְאֵין רָאוּי לְהִתְפַּלֵּל לְזוּלָתוֹ:

ה Ani Ma'amin Be'emunah Shelemah Shehaborei Yitbarach Shemo Lo Levado Ra'ui Lehitpallel. Ve'ein Ra'ui Lehitpallel Lezulato:

5. I believe, with a perfect faith, that to the Creator, blessed is His name, and to Him alone, it is right to pray, and that it is not right to pray to any being besides Him.

ו אֲנִי מַאֲמִין בֶּאֱמוּנָה שְׁלֵמָה שֶׁכָּל דִּבְרֵי נְבִיאִים אֱמֶת:

ו Ani Ma'amin Be'emunah Shelemah Shekol Divrei Nevi'im Emet:

6. I believe, with a perfect faith, that all the words of the prophets are true.

ז אֲנִי מַאֲמִין בֶּאֱמוּנָה שְׁלֵמָה שֶׁנְּבוּאַת מֹשֶׁה רַבֵּנוּ עָלָיו הַשָּׁלוֹם הָיְתָה אֲמִתִּית וְשֶׁהוּא הָיָה אָב לַנְּבִיאִים לַקּוֹדְמִים לְפָנָיו וְלַבָּאִים אַחֲרָיו:

ז Ani Ma'amin Be'emunah Shelemah Shenevu'at Mosheh Rabeinu Alav Hashalom Hayetah Amitit Veshehu Hayah Av Lanevi'im Lakodemim Lefanav Velaba'im Acharav:

7. I believe, with a perfect faith, that the prophecy of Moshe our teacher, peace be to him, was true, and that he was the chief of the prophets who preceded and of those that succeeded him.

ח אֲנִי מַאֲמִין בֶּאֱמוּנָה שְׁלֵמָה שֶׁכָּל הַתּוֹרָה הַמְּצוּיָה עַתָּה בְיָדֵינוּ הִיא הַנְּתוּנָה לְמֹשֶׁה רַבֵּנוּ עָלָיו הַשָּׁלוֹם:

ח Ani Ma'amin Be'emunah Shelemah Shekol Hatorah Hametzuyah Attah Veyadeinu Hi Hanetunah Lemosheh Rabeinu Alav Hashalom:

8. I believe, with a perfect faith, that the whole Torah, as now in our possession, is the very same that was given to Moshe our teacher, peace be to him.

ט אֲנִי מַאֲמִין בֶּאֱמוּנָה שְׁלֵמָה שֶׁזֹּאת הַתּוֹרָה לֹא תְהֵא מֻחְלֶפֶת וְלֹא תְהֵא תּוֹרָה אַחֶרֶת מֵאֵת הַבּוֹרֵא יִתְבָּרַךְ שְׁמוֹ:

ט Ani Ma'amin Be'emunah Shelemah Shezot Hatorah Lo Tehei Muchlefet Velo Tehei Torah Acheret Me'et HaBorei Yitbarach Shemo:

9. I believe, with a perfect faith, that this Torah will not be changed, and that there will never be any other Torah given by the Creator, blessed is His name.

י אֲנִי מַאֲמִין בֶּאֱמוּנָה שְׁלֵמָה. שֶׁהַבּוֹרֵא יִתְבָּרַךְ שְׁמוֹ יוֹדֵעַ כָּל מַעֲשֵׂה בְנֵי אָדָם וְכָל-מַחְשְׁבוֹתָם שֶׁנֶּאֱמַר הַיֹּצֵר יַחַד לִבָּם הַמֵּבִין אֶל-כָּל-מַעֲשֵׂיהֶם:

י Ani Ma'amin Be'emunah Shelemah. Shehaborei Yitbarach Shemo Yodea' Kol Ma'aseh Venei Adam Vechol-Machshevotam Shene'emar Hayotzer Yachad Libam Hamevin El-Kol-Ma'aseihem:

10. I believe, with a perfect faith, that the Creator, blessed is His name, knows every deed of mankind, and all their thoughts; as it is said, "He that fashions the hearts of them all, understands all of their deeds."

יא אֲנִי מַאֲמִין בֶּאֱמוּנָה שְׁלֵמָה שֶׁהַבּוֹרֵא יִתְבָּרַךְ שְׁמוֹ גּוֹמֵל טוֹב לְשׁוֹמְרֵי מִצְוֹתָיו וּמַעֲנִישׁ לְעוֹבְרֵי מִצְוֹתָיו:

יא Ani Ma'amin Be'emunah Shelemah Shehaborei Yitbarach Shemo Gomel Tov Leshomerei Mitzvotav Uma'anish Le'overei Mitzvotav:

11. I believe, with a perfect faith, that the Creator, blessed is His name, rewards those that keep His commandments, and punishes those that transgress them.

יב אֲנִי מַאֲמִין בֶּאֱמוּנָה שְׁלֵמָה. בְּבִיאַת הַמָּשִׁיחַ. וְאַף עַל פִּי שֶׁיִּתְמַהְמֵהַּ. עִם כָּל-זֶה אֲחַכֶּה-לּוֹ בְּכָל יוֹם שֶׁיָּבֹא:

יב Ani Ma'amin Be'emunah Shelemah. Bevi'at Hamashiach. Ve'af Al Pi Sheyitmahmeah. Im Kol-Zeh Achakeh-Lo Bechol Yom Sheyavo:

12. I believe, with a perfect faith, in the coming of the Messiah, and, though he delays, I will daily wait his coming.

יג אֲנִי מַאֲמִין בֶּאֱמוּנָה שְׁלֵמָה. שֶׁתִּהְיֶה תְּחִיַּת הַמֵּתִים בְּעֵת שֶׁיַּעֲלֶה רָצוֹן מֵאֵת הַבּוֹרֵא יִתְבָּרַךְ שְׁמוֹ וְיִתְעַלֶּה זִכְרוֹ לָעַד וּלְנֵצַח נְצָחִים:

יג Ani Ma'amin Be'emunah Shelemah. Shetihyeh Techiyat Hameitim Be'et Sheya'aleh Ratzon Me'et Haborei Yitbarach Shemo Veyit'aleh Zichro La'ad Ulenetzach Netzachim:

13. I believe, with a perfect faith, that there will be the resurrection of the dead at the time when it will please the Creator, blessed is His name, and exalted is His memorial forever and ever.

The Ten Remembrances

לְשֵׁם יִחוּד קוּדְשָׁא בְּרִיךְ הוּא וּשְׁכִינְתֵּיהּ. הֲרֵי אֲנִי מְקַיֵּם מִצְוַת עֶשֶׂר זְכִירוֹת. שֶׁחַיָּב כָּל אָדָם לִזְכֹּר בְּכָל יוֹם. וְאֵלּוּ הֵם:

א יְצִיאַת מִצְרַיִם. ב וְהַשַּׁבָּת. ג וְהַמָּן. ד וּמַעֲשֵׂה עֲמָלֵק. ה וּמַעֲמַד הַר סִינַי. ו וּמַה שֶּׁהִקְצִיפוּ אֲבוֹתֵינוּ לְהַקָּדוֹשׁ בָּרוּךְ הוּא בַּמִּדְבָּר וּבִפְרָט בָּעֵגֶל. ז וּמַה שֶּׁיָּעֲצוּ בָלָק וּבִלְעָם לַעֲשׂוֹת לַאֲבוֹתֵינוּ לְמַעַן דַּעַת צִדְקוֹת יְהוָה. ח וּמַעֲשֵׂה מִרְיָם הַנְּבִיאָה. ט וּמִצְוַת וְזָכַרְתָּ אֶת יְהוָה אֱלֹהֶיךָ כִּי הוּא הַנֹּתֵן לְךָ כֹּחַ לַעֲשׂוֹת חָיִל. י וּזְכִירַת יְרוּשָׁלַיִם תִּבָּנֶה וְתִכּוֹנֵן בִּמְהֵרָה בְיָמֵינוּ אָמֵן:

Leshem Yichud Kudesha Berich Hu Ushechinteih. Harei Ani Mekayem Mitzvat Eser Zechirot. Shechayaiv Kol Adam Lizkor Bechol Yom. Ve'elu Hem:

א Yetzi'at Mitzrayim. ב Vehashabbat. ג Vehaman. ד Uma'aseh Amalek. ה Uma'amad Har Sinai. ו Umah Shehiktzifu Avoteinu Lehakadosh Baruch Hu Bamidbar Uvifrat Ba'egel. ז Umah Sheya'atzu Valak Uvil'am La'asot La'avoteinu Lema'an Da'at Tzidkot Adonai. ח Uma'aseh Miryam Hanevi'ah. ט Umitzvat Vezacharta Et Adonai Eloheicha Ki Hu Hanotein Lecha Koach La'asot Chayil. י Uzechirat Yerushalayim Tibaneh Vetikonen Bimheirah Veyameinu Amen:

For the sake of the unification of the Holy One, blessed is He, with His Divine Presence. Behold, I fulfill the mitzvah of the Ten Remembrances. It is obligated for all men to remember every day. And they are:

1 The going out from Egypt. 2 And the Shabbat. 3 And the Manna. 4 And what Amalek did. 5 The Giving and receiving of the Torah at Har Sinai. 6 And that our fathers infuriated the Holy One, Blessed is He, in the wilderness, especially with the Golden Calf. 7 And what Balak and Bilam sought to do to our fathers so that we would know the righteousness of Hashem. 8 The incident concerning Miryam the prophetess. 9 The mitzvah of You will remember Hashem, your God. For it is He who gives you power to get wealth. 10 And the

remembrance of Yerushalayim, may it be rebuilt and established soon and in our days, Amen.

When leaving the synagogue say:

יְהוָה נְחֵנִי בְצִדְקָתֶךָ לְמַעַן שׁוֹרְרָי הַיְשַׁר לְפָנַי דַּרְכֶּךָ: וְיַעֲקֹב הָלַךְ לְדַרְכּוֹ וַיִּפְגְּעוּ־בוֹ מַלְאֲכֵי אֱלֹהִים: וַיֹּאמֶר יַעֲקֹב כַּאֲשֶׁר רָאָם מַחֲנֵה אֱלֹהִים זֶה וַיִּקְרָא שֵׁם־הַמָּקוֹם הַהוּא מַחֲנָיִם:

Adonai Necheni Vetzidkatecha Lema'an Shorerai Chayshar Lifnei Deracheicha: Veya'akov Chalach Ledarko Vayifge'u Vo Mal'achei Elohim: Vayomer Ya'akov Ka'asher Ra'am Machaneh Elohim Zeh Vayikra Shem Hamakom Hahu Machanayim.

Hashem, lead me in Your righteousness because of those that lie in wait for me; Make Your way straight before my face. And Yaakov went on his way, and the angels of God met him. And Yaakov said when he saw them: 'This is God's camp.' And he called the name of that place Machanayim. **(Ps. 5:8, Gen. 32:2-3)**

MINCHA / AFTERNOON PRAYER

Mincha (Afternoon Prayer) can be recited from about 6 and a half hours (about 30 minutes past halachic noontime) until sundown. This first broad time is known as Mincha Gedolah, but ideally Mincha should be recited at Mincha Ketanah, which is about 9.5 halachic hours and completed by sundown. It is preferable to wash hands before the service. If water is available it is not necessary. If one forgot and did not pray Mincha, they should pray Arvit (Evening Prayer) twice and says Ashrei first, which is a payment for the Mincha prayer. (SA, OC 233,234 / MB) According to Chazal (Our Sages of Blessed Memory), one should take care with the Mincha prayer, because Eliyahu was answered during Mincha. (I Kings 18:36, BT' Berachot 6b). This being the busiest time of day for most people, it can be easy to be less attentive. Some also say Patach Eliyahu before this (located in Shacharit Service). On Tisha B'Av. some have a custom of wearing tallit and tefillin at Minchah.

Some say before:

לְשֵׁם יִחוּד קוּדְשָׁא בְּרִיךְ הוּא וּשְׁכִינְתֵּיהּ. בִּדְחִילוּ וּרְחִימוּ. וּרְחִימוּ וּדְחִילוּ.
לְיַחֲדָא שֵׁם יוֹ"ד קֵ"י בְּוָא"ו קֵ"י בְּיִחוּדָא שְׁלִים (יהוה) בְּשֵׁם כָּל יִשְׂרָאֵל.
הנה אנחנו באים להתפלל תפלת מנחה שתקן יצחק אבינו עליו השלום.
עם כל המצות הכלולות בה. לתקן את שורשה במקום עליון לעשות נחת
רוח ליוצרנו ולעשות רצון בוראנו. וִיהִי נֹעַם אֲדֹנָי אֱלֹהֵינוּ עָלֵינוּ וּמַעֲשֵׂה
יָדֵינוּ כּוֹנְנָה עָלֵינוּ וּמַעֲשֵׂה יָדֵינוּ כּוֹנְנֵהוּ:

Korbanot / Offerings

Psalms 84

לַמְנַצֵּחַ עַל־הַגִּתִּית לִבְנֵי־קֹרַח מִזְמוֹר: מַה־יְּדִידוֹת מִשְׁכְּנוֹתֶיךָ יְהוָה
צְבָאוֹת: נִכְסְפָה וְגַם־כָּלְתָה | נַפְשִׁי לְחַצְרוֹת יְהוָה לִבִּי וּבְשָׂרִי יְרַנְּנוּ
אֶל אֵל־חָי: גַּם־צִפּוֹר מָצְאָה בַיִת וּדְרוֹר | קֵן לָהּ אֲשֶׁר־שָׁתָה
אֶפְרֹחֶיהָ אֶת־מִזְבְּחוֹתֶיךָ יְהוָה צְבָאוֹת מַלְכִּי וֵאלֹהָי: אַשְׁרֵי יוֹשְׁבֵי
בֵיתֶךָ עוֹד יְהַלְלוּךָ סֶּלָה: אַשְׁרֵי אָדָם עוֹז־לוֹ בָךְ מְסִלּוֹת בִּלְבָבָם:
עֹבְרֵי | בְּעֵמֶק הַבָּכָא מַעְיָן יְשִׁיתוּהוּ גַּם־בְּרָכוֹת יַעְטֶה מוֹרֶה: יֵלְכוּ
מֵחַיִל אֶל־חָיִל יֵרָאֶה אֶל־אֱלֹהִים בְּצִיּוֹן: יְהוָה אֱלֹהִים צְבָאוֹת
שִׁמְעָה תְפִלָּתִי הַאֲזִינָה אֱלֹהֵי יַעֲקֹב סֶלָה: מָגִנֵּנוּ רְאֵה אֱלֹהִים
וְהַבֵּט פְּנֵי מְשִׁיחֶךָ: כִּי טוֹב־יוֹם בַּחֲצֵרֶיךָ מֵאָלֶף בָּחַרְתִּי הִסְתּוֹפֵף
בְּבֵית אֱלֹהַי מִדּוּר בְּאָהֳלֵי־רֶשַׁע: כִּי שֶׁמֶשׁ | וּמָגֵן יְהוָה אֱלֹהִים חֵן

וְכָבוֹד יִתֵּן יְהֹוָה לֹא יִמְנַע־טוֹב לַהֹלְכִים בְּתָמִים: יְהֹוָה צְבָאוֹת אַשְׁרֵי אָדָם בֹּטֵחַ בָּךְ:

Lamnatzeach Al-Hagitit; Livnei-Korach Mizmor. Mah-Yedidot Mishkenoteicha. Adonai Tzeva'ot. Nichsefah Vegam-Kaletah Nafshi Lechatzrot Adonai Libi Uvesari; Yeranenu. El El-Chai. Gam-Tzipor Matze'ah Vayit Uderor Ken Lah Asher-Shatah Efrocheiha Et-Mizbechoteicha Adonai Tzeva'ot; Malki. Velohai. Ashrei Yoshevei Veitecha; Od Yehalelucha Selah. Ashrei Adam Oz-Lo Vach; Mesilot. Bilvavam. Overei Be'emek Habacha Ma'yan Yeshituhu; Gam-Berachot. Ya'teh Moreh. Yelechu Mechayil El-Chayil; Yera'eh El-' Elohim Betziyon. Adonai Elohim Tzeva'ot Shim'ah Tefillati; Ha'azinah Elohei Ya'akov Selah. Maginenu Re'eh Elohim; Vehabeit. Penei Meshichecha. Ki Tov-Yom Bachatzereicha. Me'alef Bacharti. Histofef Beveit Elohai; Midur. Be'oholei-Resha. Ki Shemesh Umagen Adonai Elohim Chein Vechavod Yiten Adonai Lo Yimna'-Tov Laholechim Betamim. Adonai Tzeva'ot; Ashrei Adam. Botei'ach Bach.

For the Leader; upon the Gittit. A Psalm of the sons of Korach. How lovely are Your tabernacles, Hashem of hosts. My soul yearns, even pines for the courts of Hashem; my heart and my flesh sing for joy to the living God. Also, the sparrow has found a house, and the swallow a nest for herself, Where she may lay her young; Your Altars, Hashem of hosts, My King, and my God—Happy are they that dwell in Your House, they are ever praising You. Selah. Happy is the man whose strength is in You; in whose heart are the highways. Passing through the valley of Baca they make it a place of springs; also, the early rain clothes it with blessings. They go from strength to strength, every one of them appears before God in Tziyon. Hashem God of hosts, hear my prayer; give ear, God of Yaakov, selah. Behold, God our Shield, and look upon the face of Your anointed. For a day in Your courts is better than a thousand; I would rather stand at the threshold of the House of my God, than to dwell in the tents of wickedness. For Hashem-Elohim is a sun and a shield; Hashem gives grace and glory; He will withhold no good thing from those that walk uprightly. Hashem of hosts, happy is the man that trusts in You.

Tamid / Eternal Offering: Numbers 28:1-8

וַיְדַבֵּר יְהֹוָה אֶל־מֹשֶׁה לֵּאמֹר: צַו אֶת־בְּנֵי יִשְׂרָאֵל וְאָמַרְתָּ אֲלֵהֶם
אֶת־קָרְבָּנִי לַחְמִי לְאִשַּׁי רֵיחַ נִיחֹחִי תִּשְׁמְרוּ לְהַקְרִיב לִי בְּמוֹעֲדוֹ:
וְאָמַרְתָּ לָהֶם זֶה הָאִשֶּׁה אֲשֶׁר תַּקְרִיבוּ לַיהֹוָה כְּבָשִׂים בְּנֵי־שָׁנָה
תְמִימִם שְׁנַיִם לַיּוֹם עֹלָה תָמִיד: אֶת־הַכֶּבֶשׂ אֶחָד תַּעֲשֶׂה בַבֹּקֶר
וְאֵת הַכֶּבֶשׂ הַשֵּׁנִי תַּעֲשֶׂה בֵּין הָעַרְבָּיִם: וַעֲשִׂירִית הָאֵיפָה סֹלֶת
לְמִנְחָה בְּלוּלָה בְּשֶׁמֶן כָּתִית רְבִיעִת הַהִין: עֹלַת תָּמִיד הָעֲשֻׂיָה
בְּהַר סִינַי לְרֵיחַ נִיחֹחַ אִשֶּׁה לַיהֹוָה: וְנִסְכּוֹ רְבִיעִת הַהִין לַכֶּבֶשׂ
הָאֶחָד בַּקֹּדֶשׁ הַסֵּךְ נֶסֶךְ שֵׁכָר לַיהֹוָה: וְאֵת הַכֶּבֶשׂ הַשֵּׁנִי תַּעֲשֶׂה
בֵּין הָעַרְבָּיִם כְּמִנְחַת הַבֹּקֶר וּכְנִסְכּוֹ תַּעֲשֶׂה אִשֵּׁה רֵיחַ נִיחֹחַ
לַיהֹוָה:

Vaydaber Adonai El-Mosheh Lemor. Tzav Et-Benei Yisra'el. Ve'amarta Aleihem; Et-Korbani Lachmi Le'ishai. Reiach Nichochi. Tishmeru Lehakriv Li Bemo'ado. Ve'amarta Lahem. Zeh Ha'isheh. Asher Takrivu L'Adonai Kevasim Benei-Shanah Temimim Shenayim Layom Olah Tamid. Et-Hakeves Echad Ta'aseh Vaboker; Ve'et Hakeves Hasheni. Ta'aseh Bein Ha'arbayim. Va'asirit Ha'eifah Solet Leminchah; Belulah Beshemen Katit Revi'it Hahin. Olat Tamid; Ha'asuyah Behar Sinai. Lereiach Nichoach. Isheh L'Adonai Venisko Revi'it Hahin. Lakeves Ha'echad; Bakodesh. Hassech Nesech Shechar L'Adonai Ve'et Hakeves Hasheni. Ta'aseh Bein Ha'arbayim; Keminchat Haboker Uchenisko Ta'aseh. Isheh Reiach Nichoach L'Adonai.

And Hashem spoke to Moshe, saying, Command the children of Yisrael and say to them, My offering, My bread for My fire-offerings, you will observe to offer for a sweet savor to Me in its due season. Say also to them, this is the fire-offering which you will bring to Hashem: lambs of the first year without blemish, two each day as a continual burnt-offering. The one lamb you will prepare in the morning, and the other lamb you will prepare at dusk, with the tenth of an ephah of fine flour for a meal-offering, mingled with a fourth of a hin of the purest oil. This is a continual burnt-offering as it was prepared at Mount Sinai, a fire-offering for a sweet savor to Hashem. And the drink-offering with it will be a fourth of a hin for the one lamb. You will pour out the pure wine to Hashem in the holy place as a drink-offering. The second lamb you will offer at dusk, preparing it as the morning meal offering and as its drink-offering of a sweet savor to Hashem.

Ketoret / Incense Offering

אַתָּה הוּא יְהֹוָה אֱלֹהֵינוּ. שֶׁהִקְטִירוּ אֲבוֹתֵינוּ לְפָנֶיךָ אֶת קְטֹרֶת הַסַּמִּים. בִּזְמַן שֶׁבֵּית הַמִּקְדָּשׁ קַיָּם. כַּאֲשֶׁר צִוִּיתָ אוֹתָם עַל־יַד מֹשֶׁה נְבִיאָךְ. כַּכָּתוּב בְּתוֹרָתָךְ:

Attah Hu Adonai Eloheinu. Shehiktiru Avoteinu Lefaneicha Et Ketoret Hasamim. Bizman Shebeit Hamikdash Kayam. Ka'asher Tzivita Otam Al-Yad Mosheh Nevi'ach. Kakatuv Betoratach:

You are Hashem, our God, before Whom our ancestors burned the offering of incense in the days of the Beit HaMikdash. For You commanded them through Moshe, Your prophet, as it is written in Your Torah:

Exodus 30:34-36, 7-8

וַיֹּאמֶר֩ יְהֹוָ֨ה אֶל־מֹשֶׁ֜ה קַח־לְךָ֣ סַמִּ֗ים נָטָ֤ף ׀ וּשְׁחֵ֙לֶת֙ וְחֶלְבְּנָ֔ה סַמִּ֖ים וּלְבֹנָ֣ה זַכָּ֑ה בַּ֥ד בְּבַ֖ד יִהְיֶֽה׃ וְעָשִׂ֤יתָ אֹתָהּ֙ קְטֹ֔רֶת רֹ֖קַח מַעֲשֵׂ֣ה רוֹקֵ֑חַ מְמֻלָּ֖ח טָה֥וֹר קֹֽדֶשׁ׃ וְשָׁחַקְתָּ֣ מִמֶּ֮נָּה֮ הָדֵק֒ וְנָתַתָּ֨ה מִמֶּ֜נָּה לִפְנֵ֤י הָעֵדֻת֙ בְּאֹ֣הֶל מוֹעֵ֔ד אֲשֶׁ֛ר אִוָּעֵ֥ד לְךָ֖ שָׁ֑מָּה קֹ֥דֶשׁ קָֽדָשִׁ֖ים תִּהְיֶ֥ה לָכֶֽם׃ וְנֶאֱמַ֕ר וְהִקְטִ֥יר עָלָ֛יו אַהֲרֹ֖ן קְטֹ֣רֶת סַמִּ֑ים בַּבֹּ֣קֶר בַּבֹּ֗קֶר

בְּהֵיטִיבוֹ אֶת־הַנֵּרֹת יַקְטִירֶנָּה: וּבְהַעֲלֹת אַהֲרֹן אֶת־הַנֵּרֹת בֵּין הָעַרְבַּיִם יַקְטִירֶנָּה קְטֹרֶת תָּמִיד לִפְנֵי יְהֹוָה לְדֹרֹתֵיכֶם:

Vayomer Adonai El-Mosheh Kach-Lecha Samim. Nataf Ushchelet Vechelbenah. Samim Ulevonah Zakah; Bad Bevad Yihyeh. Ve'asita Otah Ketoret. Rokach Ma'aseh Rokeach; Memulach Tahor Kodesh. Veshachakta Mimenah Hadek Venatatah Mimenah Lifnei Ha'eidut Be'ohel Mo'ed. Asher Iva'eid Lecha Shamah; Kodesh Kodashim Tihyeh Lachem. Vene'emar Vehiktir Alav Aharon Ketoret Samim; Baboker Baboker. Beheitivo Et-Hanerot Yaktirenah. Uveha'alot Aharon Et-Hanerot Bein Ha'arbayim Yaktirenah; Ketoret Tamid Lifnei Adonai Ledoroteichem.

And Hashem said to Moshe, 'Take sweet spices, oil of myrrh, onycha and galbanum, together with clear frankincense, a like weight of each of these sweet spices. And you will make from there incense, a perfume pure and holy, compounded by the perfumer, salted together. And you will crush some of it very fine, and put some of it before the Ark of testimony in the Ohel Moed where I will meet with you; it will be most holy to you. Further it is said in the Torah: "And Aharon will burn the incense of sweet spices on the altar of incense, every morning when he dresses the lamps he will burn it. And at dusk when Aharon lights the lamps he will again burn incense, a perpetual incense before Hashem throughout your generations."

Talmud: Keritot 6a

תָּנוּ רַבָּנָן: פִּטּוּם הַקְּטֹרֶת כֵּיצַד: שְׁלֹשׁ מֵאוֹת וְשִׁשִּׁים וּשְׁמוֹנָה מָנִים הָיוּ בָהּ. שְׁלֹשׁ מֵאוֹת וְשִׁשִּׁים וַחֲמִשָּׁה כְּמִנְיַן יְמוֹת הַחַמָּה. מָנֶה בְּכָל־יוֹם. מַחֲצִיתוֹ בַּבֹּקֶר וּמַחֲצִיתוֹ בָּעֶרֶב. וּשְׁלֹשָׁה מָנִים יְתֵרִים. שֶׁמֵּהֶם מַכְנִיס כֹּהֵן גָּדוֹל. וְנוֹטֵל מֵהֶם מְלֹא חָפְנָיו בְּיוֹם הַכִּפּוּרִים. וּמַחֲזִירָן לְמַכְתֶּשֶׁת בְּעֶרֶב יוֹם הַכִּפּוּרִים. כְּדֵי לְקַיֵּם מִצְוַת דַּקָּה מִן הַדַּקָּה. וְאַחַד־עָשָׂר סַמָּנִים הָיוּ בָהּ. וְאֵלּוּ הֵן:

Tanu Rabbanan. Pitum Haketoret Keitzad: Shelosh Me'ot Veshishim Ushemonah Manim Hayu Vah. Shelosh Me'ot Veshishim Vachamishah Keminyan Yemot Hachamah. Maneh Bechol-Yom. Machatzito Baboker Umachatzito Ba'erev. Usheloshah Manim Yeterim. Shemehem Machnis Kohen Gadol. Venotel Mehem Melo Chafenav Beyom Hakippurim. Umachaziron Lemachteshet Be'erev Yom Hakippurim. Kedei Lekayem Mitzvat Dakah Min Hadakah. Ve'achad-'Asar Samanim Hayu Vah. Ve'elu Hen.

The rabbis have taught how the compounding of the incense was done. In measure the incense contained three hundred and sixty-eight manehs, three hundred and sixty-five being one for each day of the year, the remaining three being for the high priest to take his hands full on the Yom Kippur. These last were again ground in a mortar on the eve of Yom Kippur so as to fulfill the command, "take of the finest beaten incense." and these are them:

א הַצֳּרִי ב וְהַצִּפֹּרֶן ג וְהַחֶלְבְּנָה ד וְהַלְּבוֹנָה. מִשְׁקַל שִׁבְעִים שִׁבְעִים מָנֶה. ה מוֹר. ו וּקְצִיעָה ז וְשִׁבֹּלֶת נֵרְדְּ ח וְכַרְכֹּם. מִשְׁקַל שִׁשָּׁה עָשָׂר שִׁשָּׁה עָשָׂר מָנֶה. ט קֹשְׁטְ שְׁנֵים עָשָׂר. י קִלּוּפָה שְׁלֹשָׁה. יא קִנָּמוֹן תִּשְׁעָה. בּוֹרִית־כַּרְשִׁינָה תִּשְׁעָה קַבִּין. יֵין קַפְרִיסִין סְאִין תְּלָת וְקַבִּין תְּלָתָא. וְאִם לֹא מָצָא יֵין קַפְרִיסִין. מֵבִיא חֲמַר חִיוָר עַתִּיק. מֶלַח סְדוֹמִית. רֹבַע. מַעֲלֶה עָשָׁן. כָּל־שֶׁהוּא. רִבִּי נָתָן הַבַּבְלִי אוֹמֵר: אַף כִּפַּת הַיַּרְדֵּן כָּל־שֶׁהִיא. אִם נָתַן בָּהּ דְּבַשׁ פְּסָלָהּ. וְאִם חִסֵּר אַחַת מִכָּל־סַמְמָנֶיהָ. חַיָּב מִיתָה:

Hatzori Vehatziporen Vehachelbenah Vehallevonah. Mishkal Shiv'im Shiv'im Maneh. Mor. Uketzi'ah Veshibolet Nered Vecharkom. Mishkal Shishah Asar Shishah Asar Maneh. Koshet Sheneim Asar. Kilufah Sheloshah. Kinamon Tish'ah. Borit-Karshinah Tish'ah Kabin. Yein Kafrisin Se'in Telat Vekabin Telata. Ve'im Lo Matza Yein Kafrisin. Mevi Chamar Chivar Atik. Melach Sedomit. Rova. Ma'aleh Ashan. Kol-Shehu. Ribi Natan Habavli Omer. Af Kippat Hayarden Kol-Shehi. Im Natan Bah Devash Pesalah. Ve'im Chisser Achat Mikol-Samemaneiha. Chayaiv Mitah.

The incense was compounded of eleven different spices: seventy manehs each of balm, onycha, galbanum, and frankincense; sixteen manehs each of myrrh, cassia, spikenard, and saffron; twelve manehs of costus; three manehs of aromatic bark; nine manehs of cinnamon; nine kabs of lye of Carsina; three seahs and three kabs of Cyprus wine, though if Cyprus wine could not be had, strong white wine might be substituted for it; the fourth of a kab of salt of Sedom, and a small quantity of a herb which caused the smoke to ascend straight. Rabbi Nathan of Bavel said there was added also a small quantity of kippat of the Yarden. If honey was mixed with the incense, the incense became unfit for sacred use, while the one who omitted any of the ingredients was deemed guilty of mortal error.

רַבָּן שִׁמְעוֹן בֶּן־גַּמְלִיאֵל אוֹמֵר: הַצֳּרִי אֵינוֹ אֶלָּא שְׂרָף. הַנּוֹטֵף מֵעֲצֵי הַקְּטָף. בֹּרִית כַּרְשִׁינָה. לְמָה הִיא בָאָה: כְּדֵי לְשַׁפּוֹת בָּהּ אֶת־הַצִּפֹּרֶן. כְּדֵי שֶׁתְּהֵא נָאָה. יֵין קַפְרִיסִין. לְמָה הוּא בָא: כְּדֵי לִשְׁרוֹת בּוֹ אֶת־הַצִּפֹּרֶן כְּדֵי שֶׁתְּהֵא עַזָּה. וַהֲלֹא מֵי רַגְלַיִם יָפִין לָהּ: אֶלָּא שֶׁאֵין מַכְנִיסִין מֵי רַגְלַיִם בַּמִּקְדָּשׁ. מִפְּנֵי הַכָּבוֹד:

Rabban Shim'on Ben-Gamli'el Omer. Hatzori Eino Ella Sheraf. Hanotef Me'atzei Haketaf. Borit Karshinah. Lemah Hi Va'ah: Kedei Leshapot Bah Et-Hatziporen. Kedei Shetehei Na'ah. Yein Kafrisin. Lemah Hu Va: Kedei Lishrot Bo Et-Hatziporen Kedei Shetehei Azah. Vahalo Mei Raglayim Yafin Lah: Ella She'ein Machnisin Mei Raglayim Bamikdash. Mipenei Hakavod.

Rabban Shimon, son of Gamliel, said that the balm required is that exuding from the balsam tree. Why did they use lye of Carsina? To refine the appearance of the onycha. What was the purpose of the Cyprus wine? To steep the onycha in it so as to harden it. Though mei raglayim might have been adapted for that purpose, it was not used because it was not decent to bring it into the Temple.

תַּנְיָא רִבִּי נָתָן אוֹמֵר: כְּשֶׁהוּא שׁוֹחֵק. אוֹמֵר: הָדֵק הֵיטֵב. הֵיטֵב הָדֵק. מִפְּנֵי שֶׁהַקּוֹל יָפֶה לַבְּשָׂמִים. פִּטְּמָהּ לַחֲצָאִין. כְּשֵׁרָה.

לְשָׁלִישׁ וּלְרְבִיעַ. לֹא שָׁמַעְנוּ. אָמַר רִבִּי יְהוּדָה: זֶה הַכְּלָל. אִם כְּמִדָּתָהּ. כְּשֵׁרָה לַחֲצָאִין. וְאִם חִסֵּר אַחַת מִכָּל־סַמְמָנֶיהָ. חַיָּב מִיתָה:

Tanya Ribi Natan Omer. Keshehu Shochek. Omer. Hadek Heitev. Heitev Hadek. Mipenei Shehakol Yafeh Labesamim. Pittemah Lachatza'in. Kesherah. Leshalish Uleravia'. Lo Shama'nu. Amar Ribi Yehudah. Zeh Hakelal. Im Kemidatah. Kesherah Lachatza'in. Ve'im Chisser Achat Mikol-Samemaneiha. Chayaiv Mitah.

It is taught: Rabbi Natan said that when the priest ground the incense the one superintending would say, "Grind it very fine, very fine grind it," because the sound of the human voice is encouraging in the making of spices. If he had compounded only one hundred and eighty-four manehs (half the required quantity), it was valid, but there is no tradition as to its permissibility if it was compounded in one-third or one-quarter proportions of the required quantity. Rabbi Yehudah said that the general principle is that if it was made with its ingredients in their correct proportions, it was permissible in half the quantity; but if one omitted any of the ingredients he was deemed guilty of mortal error.

תָּנֵי בַר־קַפָּרָא: אַחַת לְשִׁשִּׁים אוֹ לְשִׁבְעִים שָׁנָה. הָיְתָה בָאָה שֶׁל שִׁירַיִם לַחֲצָאִין. וְעוֹד תָּנֵי בַר־קַפָּרָא: אִלּוּ הָיָה נוֹתֵן בָּהּ קָרְטוֹב שֶׁל דְּבַשׁ. אֵין אָדָם יָכוֹל לַעֲמֹד מִפְּנֵי רֵיחָהּ. וְלָמָּה אֵין מְעָרְבִין בָּהּ דְּבַשׁ. מִפְּנֵי שֶׁהַתּוֹרָה אָמְרָה: כִּי כָל־שְׂאֹר וְכָל־דְּבַשׁ לֹא־תַקְטִירוּ מִמֶּנּוּ אִשֶּׁה לַיהוָה:

Tanei Var-Kappara. Achat Leshishim O Leshiv'im Shanah. Hayetah Va'ah Shel Shirayim Lachatza'in. Ve'od Tanei Var-Kappara. Ilu Hayah Noten Bah Karetov Shel Devash. Ein Adam Yachol La'amod Mipenei Reichah. Velamah Ein Me'arevin Bah Devash. Mipenei Shehatorah Amerah. Ki Chol-Se'or Vechol-Devash. Lo-Taktiru Mimenu Isheh L'Adonai.

Bar Kappara taught that once in sixty or seventy years it happened that, left over, there was over a total of half the required amount accumulated from the three manehs of incense from which the high priest took his hands full on Yom Kippur. Further Bar Kappara taught that had one mixed into the incense the smallest quantity of honey, no one could have stood its scent. Why did they not mix honey with it? Because the Torah states that, "No leaven, or any honey, will you burn as an offering made by fire to Hashem."

יְהֹוָה צְבָאוֹת עִמָּנוּ מִשְׂגָּב־לָנוּ אֱלֹהֵי יַעֲקֹב סֶלָה: יְהֹוָה צְבָאוֹת
אַשְׁרֵי אָדָם בֹּטֵחַ בָּךְ: יְהֹוָה הוֹשִׁיעָה הַמֶּלֶךְ יַעֲנֵנוּ בְיוֹם־קָרְאֵנוּ:
וְעָרְבָה לַיהֹוָה מִנְחַת יְהוּדָה וִירוּשָׁלָםִ כִּימֵי עוֹלָם וּכְשָׁנִים קַדְמֹנִיֹּת:

Adonai Tzeva'ot Imanu; Misgav-Lanu Elohei Ya'akov Selah. Adonai Tzeva'ot; Ashrei Adam. Boteach Bach. Adonai Hoshi'ah; Hamelech. Ya'aneinu Veyom-Kor'enu. Ve'arevah L'Adonai Minchat Yehudah Virushalayim Kimei Olam. Ucheshanim Kadmoniyot.

Hashem of hosts is with us; The God of Yaakov is our high tower. Selah. Hashem of hosts, happy is the man who trusts in You. Save, Hashem; Let the King answer us in the day that we call. Then will the offering of Yehudah and Yerushalayim be pleasant to Hashem, as in the days of old, and as in ancient years. **(Psalms 46:12, 84:13, 20:10, Malachi 3:4)**

Ashrei

When saying the verse "Potei'ach Et Yadecha" one should focus one's heart. If one did not focus he must return and repeat. (SA, OC 51:7) It is customary to open your hands toward Heaven as a symbol of our acceptance of the abundance Hashem bestows upon us from Heaven. (B'TH, Ex. 9:29, I Kings 8:54).

אַשְׁרֵי יוֹשְׁבֵי בֵיתֶךָ עוֹד יְהַלְלוּךָ סֶּלָה: אַשְׁרֵי הָעָם שֶׁכָּכָה לּוֹ אַשְׁרֵי
הָעָם שֶׁיְהֹוָה אֱלֹהָיו:

Ashrei Yoshevei Veitecha; Od. Yehalelucha Selah. Ashrei Ha'am Shekachah Lo; Ashrei Ha'am. She'Adonai Elohav.

Happy are those who dwell in Your House; they are ever praising You. Happy are the people that is so situated; happy are the people whose God is Hashem. **(Psalms 84:5, 144:15)**

Psalms 145

תְּהִלָּה לְדָוִד אֲרוֹמִמְךָ אֱלוֹהַי הַמֶּלֶךְ וַאֲבָרְכָה שִׁמְךָ לְעוֹלָם וָעֶד:
בְּכָל־יוֹם אֲבָרְכֶךָּ וַאֲהַלְלָה שִׁמְךָ לְעוֹלָם וָעֶד: גָּדוֹל יְהוָה וּמְהֻלָּל
מְאֹד וְלִגְדֻלָּתוֹ אֵין חֵקֶר: דּוֹר לְדוֹר יְשַׁבַּח מַעֲשֶׂיךָ וּגְבוּרֹתֶיךָ יַגִּידוּ:
הֲדַר כְּבוֹד הוֹדֶךָ וְדִבְרֵי נִפְלְאֹתֶיךָ אָשִׂיחָה: וֶעֱזוּז נוֹרְאֹתֶיךָ יֹאמֵרוּ
וּגְדֻלָּתְךָ אֲסַפְּרֶנָּה: זֵכֶר רַב־טוּבְךָ יַבִּיעוּ וְצִדְקָתְךָ יְרַנֵּנוּ: חַנּוּן וְרַחוּם
יְהוָה אֶרֶךְ אַפַּיִם וּגְדָל־חָסֶד: טוֹב־יְהוָה לַכֹּל וְרַחֲמָיו עַל־כָּל־מַעֲשָׂיו:
יוֹדוּךָ יְהוָה כָּל־מַעֲשֶׂיךָ וַחֲסִידֶיךָ יְבָרְכוּכָה: כְּבוֹד מַלְכוּתְךָ יֹאמֵרוּ
וּגְבוּרָתְךָ יְדַבֵּרוּ: לְהוֹדִיעַ | לִבְנֵי הָאָדָם גְּבוּרֹתָיו וּכְבוֹד הֲדַר
מַלְכוּתוֹ: מַלְכוּתְךָ מַלְכוּת כָּל־עֹלָמִים וּמֶמְשַׁלְתְּךָ בְּכָל־דּוֹר וָדֹר:
סוֹמֵךְ יְהוָה לְכָל־הַנֹּפְלִים וְזוֹקֵף לְכָל־הַכְּפוּפִים: עֵינֵי־כֹל אֵלֶיךָ
יְשַׂבֵּרוּ וְאַתָּה נוֹתֵן־לָהֶם אֶת־אָכְלָם בְּעִתּוֹ: **פּוֹתֵחַ אֶת־יָדֶךָ**
וּמַשְׂבִּיעַ לְכָל־חַי רָצוֹן: צַדִּיק יְהוָה בְּכָל־דְּרָכָיו וְחָסִיד
בְּכָל־מַעֲשָׂיו: קָרוֹב יְהוָה לְכָל־קֹרְאָיו לְכֹל אֲשֶׁר יִקְרָאֻהוּ בֶאֱמֶת:
רְצוֹן־יְרֵאָיו יַעֲשֶׂה וְאֶת־שַׁוְעָתָם יִשְׁמַע וְיוֹשִׁיעֵם: שׁוֹמֵר יְהוָה
אֶת־כָּל־אֹהֲבָיו וְאֵת כָּל־הָרְשָׁעִים יַשְׁמִיד: תְּהִלַּת יְהוָה יְדַבֶּר פִּי
וִיבָרֵךְ כָּל־בָּשָׂר שֵׁם קָדְשׁוֹ לְעוֹלָם וָעֶד: וַאֲנַחְנוּ | נְבָרֵךְ יָהּ מֵעַתָּה
וְעַד־עוֹלָם הַלְלוּיָהּ:

Tehilah. Ledavid Aromimcha Elohai Hamelech; Va'avarechah Shimcha. Le'olam Va'ed. Bechol-Yom Avarecheka; Va'ahalelah Shimcha. Le'olam Va'ed. Gadol Adonai Umehulal Me'od; Veligdulato. Ein Cheiker. Dor Ledor Yeshabach Ma'aseicha; Ugevuroteicha Yagidu. Hadar Kevod Hodecha; Vedivrei Nifle'oteicha Asichah. Ve'ezuz Nore'oteicha Yomeru; Ug'dulatecha

Asap'renah. Zecher Rav-Tuvecha Yabi'u; Vetzidkatecha Yeranenu. Chanun Verachum Adonai Erech Apayim. Ugedol-Chased. Tov-Adonai Lakol; Verachamav. Al-Chol-Ma'asav. Yoducha Adonai Chol-Ma'aseicha; Vachasideicha. Yevarechuchah. Kevod Malchutecha Yomeru; Ugevuratecha Yedaberu. Lehodia Livnei Ha'adam Gevurotav; Uchevod. Hadar Malchuto. Malchutecha. Malchut Chol-'Olamim; Umemshaltecha. Bechol-Dor Vador. Somech Adonai Lechol-Hanofelim; Vezokeif. Lechol-Hakefufim. Einei-Chol Eleicha Yesaberu; Ve'attah Noten-Lahem Et-'Ochlam Be'ito. **Potei'ach Et-Yadecha; Umasbia Lechol-Chai Ratzon.** Tzaddik Adonai Bechol-Derachav; Vechasid. Bechol-Ma'asav. Karov Adonai Lechol-Kore'av; Lechol Asher Yikra'uhu Ve'emet. Retzon-Yere'av Ya'aseh; Ve'et-Shav'atam Yishma'. Veyoshi'em. Shomer Adonai Et-Chol-'Ohavav; Ve'et Chol-Haresha'im Yashmid. Tehillat Adonai Yedaber Pi Vivarech Chol-Basar Shem Kodsho. Le'olam Va'ed. Va'anachnu Nevarech Yah. Me'attah Ve'ad-'Olam. Halleluyah.

A Psalm of praise; of David. א I will extol You, my God, Oh King; And I will bless Your name forever and ever. ב Every day will I bless You; And I will praise You name forever and ever. ג Great is Hashem, and highly to be praised; And His greatness is unsearchable. ד One generation will applaud Your works to another, And will declare Your mighty acts. ה The glorious splendor of Your majesty, And Your wondrous works, I will rehearse. ו And men will speak of the might of Your tremendous acts; And I will tell of Your greatness. ז They will utter the fame of Your great goodness, And will sing of Your righteousness. ח Hashem is gracious, and full of compassion; Slow to anger, and of great mercy. ט Hashem is good to all; And His tender mercies are over all His works. י All Your works will praise You, Hashem; And Your holy-ones will bless You. כ They will speak of the glory of Your kingdom, And talk of Your might; ל To make known to the sons of men His mighty acts, And the glory of the beauty of His kingdom. מ Your kingdom is a kingdom for all ages, And Your dominion endures throughout all generations. ס Hashem upholds all that fall, And raises up all those that are bowed down. ע The eyes of all wait for You, And You give them their food in due season. פ **You open Your hand, And satisfy every living thing**

with favor. צ Hashem is righteous in all His ways, And gracious in all His works. ק Hashem is near to all them that call upon Him, To all that call upon Him in truth. ר He will fulfill the desire of those that fear Him; He also will hear their cry, and will save them. ש Hashem preserves all them that love Him; But all the wicked will He destroy. ת My mouth will speak the praise of Hashem; And let all flesh bless His holy name forever and ever.

תִּכּ֤וֹן תְּפִלָּתִ֣י קְטֹ֣רֶת לְפָנֶ֑יךָ מַֽשְׂאַ֥ת כַּ֝פַּ֗י מִנְחַת־עָֽרֶב׃ הַקְשִׁ֤יבָה ׀ לְק֬וֹל שַׁוְעִ֗י מַלְכִּ֥י וֵאלֹהָ֑י כִּֽי־אֵ֝לֶ֗יךָ אֶתְפַּלָּֽל׃

Tikon Tefillati Ketoret Lefaneicha; Mas'at Kapai. Minchat-'Arev. Hakshivah Lekol Shav'i. Malki Velohai; Ki-'Eleicha. Etpalal.

Let my prayer be set forth as incense before You, The lifting up of my hands as the evening sacrifice. Listen to the voice of my cry, my King, and my God; For to You do I pray. **(Psalms 141:2, Psalms 5:3)**

Leader prays Hatzi-Kaddish.

Kaddish is only recited in a minyan (ten men). אָמֵן denotes when the congregation responds "Amen" together out loud. According to the Shulchan Arukh, the congregation says "Yehei Shemeh Rabba" to "Yitbarach" out loud together without interruption, and also that one should respond "Amen" after "Yitbarach." (SA, OC 55,56) This is not the common custom today. Though many are accustomed to answering according to their own custom, it is advised to respond in the custom of the one reciting to avoid not fragmenting into smaller groups. ("Lo Titgodedu" - BT, Yevamot 13b / SA, OC 493, Rema / MT, Avodah Zara 12:15)

יִתְגַּדַּל וְיִתְקַדַּשׁ שְׁמֵהּ רַבָּא. אָמֵן בְּעָלְמָא דִּי בְרָא. כִּרְעוּתֵהּ. וְיַמְלִיךְ מַלְכוּתֵהּ. וְיַצְמַח פֻּרְקָנֵהּ. וִיקָרֵב מְשִׁיחֵהּ. אָמֵן בְּחַיֵּיכוֹן וּבְיוֹמֵיכוֹן וּבְחַיֵּי דְכָל בֵּית יִשְׂרָאֵל. בַּעֲגָלָא וּבִזְמַן קָרִיב. וְאִמְרוּ אָמֵן. אָמֵן יְהֵא שְׁמֵיהּ רַבָּא מְבָרַךְ לְעָלַם וּלְעָלְמֵי עָלְמַיָּא יִתְבָּרַךְ. וְיִשְׁתַּבַּח. וְיִתְפָּאַר. וְיִתְרוֹמַם. וְיִתְנַשֵּׂא. וְיִתְהַדָּר. וְיִתְעַלֶּה. וְיִתְהַלָּל שְׁמֵהּ דְּקֻדְשָׁא. בְּרִיךְ הוּא. אָמֵן לְעֵלָּא מִן כָּל בִּרְכָתָא שִׁירָתָא. תֻּשְׁבְּחָתָא וְנֶחֱמָתָא. דַּאֲמִירָן בְּעָלְמָא. וְאִמְרוּ אָמֵן. אָמֵן

Yitgadal Veyitkadash Shemeh Rabba. **Amen** Be'alema Di Vera. Kir'uteh. Veyamlich Malchuteh. Veyatzmach Purkaneh. Vikarev Meshicheh. **Amen** Bechayeichon Uveyomeichon Uvechayei Dechal-Beit Yisra'el. Ba'agala Uvizman Kariv. Ve'imru Amen. **Amen** Yehei Shemeh Rabba Mevarach Le'alam Ule'alemei Alemaya Yitbarach. Veyishtabach. Veyitpa'ar. Veyitromam. Veyitnasse. Veyit'hadar. Veyit'aleh. Veyit'hallal Shemeh Dekudsha. Berich Hu. **Amen** Le'ella Min Kol Birchata Shirata. Tushbechata Venechemata. Da'amiran Be'alema. Ve'imru Amen. **Amen**

Glorified and sanctified be God's great name **Amen** throughout the world which He has created according to His will. May He establish His kingdom, hastening His salvation and the coming of His Messiah, **Amen**, in your lifetime and during your days, and within the life of the entire House of Yisrael, speedily and soon; and say, Amen. **Amen** May His great name be blessed forever and to all eternity. Blessed and praised, glorified and exalted, extolled and honored, adored and lauded is the name of the Holy One, blessed is He, **Amen** Beyond all the blessings and hymns, praises and consolations that are ever spoken in the world; and say, Amen. **Amen**

LAWS OF AMIDAH

When one gets up to pray if he was standing outside the Land of Yisrael, he should turn his face toward the Land of Yisrael and focus also on Yerushalayim and the Temple and the Holy of Holies. One who is not able to determine the directions, [should] direct one's heart to their Father in Heaven. One should consider oneself as if one is standing in the Beit Hamikdash, and in one's heart, one should be directed upward towards Heaven. One who prays needs to intend in their heart the meaning of the words which are coming out of their mouth. They should think as if the Divine Presence is before them, and remove all distracting thoughts from themselves, until their thoughts and intention are pure in their prayer. (SA, OC 94, 95, 98) These are the blessings at which we bow: in Avot, at the beginning and at the end; in Modim, at the beginning and at the end. And if you come to bow at the end of every blessing or at the beginning, we teach him to not bow but in the middle, one can bow. One needs to bend until all the vertebrae in his spine are bent. His head should stay straight and submissive. One should not bow too much until his mouth is opposite his belt. If he is sick or old and cannot bow, he should humble his head, that is enough. Bow at "Baruch" and stand up at Hashem's name. (SA, OC 113,114) One should position one's feet next to each other as though they are one, in order to imitate angels, as it written regarding them: "their feet were a straight foot" (Ez. 1:7), which is to say their feet appeared as one foot. One should take three steps forward in the way of coming close and approaching a matter that must be done. (SA, OC 95, Rema)

Amidah / Shemoneh Esrei - Minchah

Take three steps forward and say:

Adonai Sefatai Tiftach; Ufi. Yagid	אֲדֹנָי שְׂפָתַי תִּפְתָּח וּפִי יַגִּיד
Tehilatecha.	תְּהִלָּתֶךָ׃

Hashem, open my lips, that my mouth may declare Your praise.

Avot / Fathers

Bow at "Baruch Attah" / "Blessed are You". Raise up at Adonai / Hashem.

Baruch Attah Adonai Eloheinu	בָּרוּךְ אַתָּה יְהֹוָה אֱלֹהֵינוּ
Velohei Avoteinu. Elohei	וֵאלֹהֵי אֲבוֹתֵינוּ. אֱלֹהֵי
Avraham. Elohei Yitzchak.	אַבְרָהָם. אֱלֹהֵי יִצְחָק.
Velohei Ya'akov. Ha'el Hagadol	וֵאלֹהֵי יַעֲקֹב. הָאֵל הַגָּדוֹל
Hagibor Vehanorah. El Elyon.	הַגִּבּוֹר וְהַנּוֹרָא. אֵל עֶלְיוֹן.
Gomel Chasadim Tovim. Koneh	גּוֹמֵל חֲסָדִים טוֹבִים. קוֹנֵה
Hakol. Vezocher Chasdei Avot.	הַכֹּל. וְזוֹכֵר חַסְדֵי אָבוֹת.
Umevi Go'el Livnei Veneihem	וּמֵבִיא גוֹאֵל לִבְנֵי בְנֵיהֶם
Lema'an Shemo Be'ahavah.	לְמַעַן שְׁמוֹ בְּאַהֲבָה׃

Blessed are You, Hashem our God and God of our fathers, God of Avraham, God of Yitzchak and God of Yaakov; the great, mighty and revered God, most high God, Who bestows lovingkindness. Master of all things; Who remembers the kindnesses of our fathers, and Who will bring a redeemer to their children's children for the sake of His name in love.

During the 10 days of repentance (Rosh Hashanah to Yom Kippur) add:

Zochrenu Lechayim. Melech Chafetz	זָכְרֵנוּ לְחַיִּים. מֶלֶךְ חָפֵץ
Bachayim. Katevenu Besefer Chayim.	בַּחַיִּים. כָּתְבֵנוּ בְּסֵפֶר חַיִּים.
Lema'anach Elohim Chayim.	לְמַעַנְךָ אֱלֹהִים חַיִּים.

Remember us to life, King who delights in life; inscribe us in the book of life for Your sake, Oh living God.

Bow at "Baruch Attah" / Blessed are You. Raise up at Adonai / Hashem.

Melech Ozeir Umoshia	מֶלֶךְ עוֹזֵר וּמוֹשִׁיעַ
Umagen. Baruch Attah Adonai	וּמָגֵן: בָּרוּךְ אַתָּה יַהֲוַהֲ
Magen Avraham.	מָגֵן אַבְרָהָם:

King, Supporter, and Savior and Shield. Blessed are You, Hashem, Shield of Avraham.

Gevurot / Powers

We [in Yisrael] begin to say "mashiv haruach" in the second blessing of the Amidah from the Musaf [Additional] Service of the last day of Sukkot, and conclude at the Musaf [Additional] Service of the first day of Pesach. On the first day of Pesach the congregation still says it in the Musaf Service, but the Reader stops saying it then. In lands outside of Yisrael, we begin to pray for rain in the Arvit (Evening) Service of the sixtieth day after the New Moon of Tishrei, and in Yisrael we begin to say it in the evening of the seventh day of Cheshvan, and it is said until the Afternoon Service on the day preceding the first day of Passover. If one prayed for rain in the summer, or if one omitted to pray for it in the winter, he must repeat the Amidah again. If one said "morid hageshem" in the summer time, he must repeat again from the beginning of the blessing. If he already concluded the blessing, he must read the entire Amidah again. Likewise in the winter, if he omitted it, he must begin all over again. (SA, OC 117)

Attah Gibor Le'olam Adonai.	אַתָּה גִּבּוֹר לְעוֹלָם אֲדֹנָי.
Mechayeh Meitim Attah. Rav	מְחַיֵּה מֵתִים אַתָּה. רַב
Lehoshia.	לְהוֹשִׁיעַ.

You, Hashem, are mighty forever; You revive the dead; You are powerful to save.

B'ketz: Morid Hatal.	בקיץ: מוֹרִיד הַטָּל.
B'choref: Mashiv Haruach Umorid	בחורף: מַשִּׁיב הָרוּחַ וּמוֹרִיד
Hageshem.	הַגֶּשֶׁם.

In summer: You cause the dew to fall.

In winter: You cause the wind to blow and the rain to fall.

Mechalkel Chayim Bechesed.	מְכַלְכֵּל חַיִּים בְּחֶסֶד.
Mechayeh Meitim Berachamim	מְחַיֵּה מֵתִים בְּרַחֲמִים

Rabim. Somech Nofelim. Verofei	רַבִּים. סוֹמֵךְ נוֹפְלִים. וְרוֹפֵא
Cholim. Umatir Asurim.	חוֹלִים. וּמַתִּיר אֲסוּרִים.
Umekayem Emunato Lishenei	וּמְקַיֵּם אֱמוּנָתוֹ לִישֵׁנֵי
Afar. Mi Chamocha Ba'al	עָפָר. מִי כָמוֹךָ בַּעַל
Gevurot. Umi Domeh Lach.	גְּבוּרוֹת. וּמִי דוֹמֶה לָּךְ.
Melech Memit Umechayeh	מֶלֶךְ מֵמִית וּמְחַיֶּה
Umatzmiach Yeshu'ah.	וּמַצְמִיחַ יְשׁוּעָה.

You sustain the living with kindness, and revive the dead with great mercy; You support all who fall, and heal the sick; You set the captives free, and keep faith with those who sleep in the dust. Who is like You, Master of power? Who resembles You, Oh King? You bring death and restore life, and cause salvation to flourish.

During the 10 days of repentance (Rosh Hashanah to Yom Kippur) add:

Mi Chamocha Av Harachaman. Zocher	מִי כָמוֹךָ אָב הָרַחֲמָן. זוֹכֵר
Yetzurav Berachamim Lechayim.	יְצוּרָיו בְּרַחֲמִים לְחַיִּים.

Who is like you, merciful Father? In mercy You remember your creatures to life.

Vene'eman Attah Lehachayot	וְנֶאֱמָן אַתָּה לְהַחֲיוֹת
Meitim. Baruch Attah Adonai	מֵתִים: בָּרוּךְ אַתָּה יְהֹוָה
Mechayeh Hameitim.	מְחַיֵּה הַמֵּתִים:

And You are faithful to revive the dead. Blessed are You, Hashem, Who revives the dead.

Kedusha

Kedusha is said only in a minyan (10 men). If one is not available, skip to "Kedushat Hashem". It is proper to position one's feet together at the time one is reciting Kedushah with the prayer-leader.

Nakdishach Vena'aritzach.	נַקְדִּישָׁךְ וְנַעֲרִיצָךְ.
Keno'am Siach Sod Sarfei	כְּנֹעַם שִׂיחַ סוֹד שַׂרְפֵי
Kodesh. Hamshaleshim Lecha	קֹדֶשׁ. הַמְשַׁלְּשִׁים לְךָ

<table>
<tr><td>Kedushah. Vechein Katuv Al Yad</td><td>קְדֻשָּׁה. וְכֵן כָּתוּב עַל יַד</td></tr>
<tr><td>Nevi'ach. Vekara Zeh El-Zeh</td><td>נְבִיאֶךָ: וְקָרָא זֶה אֶל־זֶה</td></tr>
<tr><td>Ve'amar. Kadosh Kadosh Kadosh</td><td>וְאָמַר קָדוֹשׁ | קָדוֹשׁ קָדוֹשׁ</td></tr>
<tr><td>Adonai Tzeva'ot; Melo Chol-</td><td>יְהֹוָה צְבָאוֹת מְלֹא כָל־</td></tr>
<tr><td>Ha'aretz Kevodo. Le'ummatam</td><td>הָאָרֶץ כְּבוֹדוֹ: לְעֻמָּתָם</td></tr>
<tr><td>Meshabechim Ve'omerim.</td><td>מְשַׁבְּחִים וְאוֹמְרִים:</td></tr>
<tr><td>Baruch Kevod-Adonai</td><td>בָּרוּךְ כְּבוֹד־יְהֹוָה</td></tr>
<tr><td>Mimekomo. Uvedivrei</td><td>מִמְּקוֹמוֹ: וּבְדִבְרֵי</td></tr>
<tr><td>Kodshecha Katuv Lemor.</td><td>קָדְשְׁךָ כָּתוּב לֵאמֹר: יִמְלֹךְ</td></tr>
<tr><td>Yimloch Adonai Le'olam.</td><td>יְהֹוָה | לְעוֹלָם אֱלֹהַיִךְ</td></tr>
<tr><td>Elohayich Tziyon Ledor Vador.</td><td>צִיּוֹן לְדֹר וָדֹר</td></tr>
<tr><td>Halleluyah.</td><td>הַלְלוּיָהּ:</td></tr>
</table>

We sanctify and revere You in the sweet words of the assembly of holy Seraphim who three times acclaim Your holiness, as it is written by Your prophet: "They keep calling to one another: '**Holy, holy, holy is Hashem of hosts; The whole earth is full of his glory.**'" Angels respond with praise and say: "**Blessed is the glory of Hashem from His Abode.**" And in Your holy scriptures it is written: "**Hashem will reign forever, Your God, Tziyon, from generation to generation. Halleluyah.**"

Kedushat HaShem / Holiness of the Name

<table>
<tr><td>Attah Kadosh Veshimcha</td><td>אַתָּה קָדוֹשׁ וְשִׁמְךָ</td></tr>
<tr><td>Kadosh. Ukedoshim Bechol-</td><td>קָדוֹשׁ. וּקְדוֹשִׁים בְּכָל־</td></tr>
<tr><td>Yom Yehalelucha Selah. Baruch</td><td>יוֹם יְהַלְלוּךָ סֶּלָה: בָּרוּךְ</td></tr>
<tr><td>Attah Adonai Ha' El Hakadosh.</td><td>אַתָּה יְהֹוָה הָאֵל הַקָּדוֹשׁ:</td></tr>
</table>

You are holy and Your name is holy, and the holy-ones will praise You every day, selah. Blessed are You, Hashem, The Holy God.

During the 10 days of repentance (Rosh Hashanah to Yom Kippur) say:

Hamelech Hakadosh.	הַמֶּלֶךְ הַקָּדוֹשׁ:

The Holy King.

If one is unsure or forgot if they said, repeat the Amidah. If it was immediately said after, it is fulfilled.

Binah / Understanding

Attah Chonen Le'adam Da'at	אַתָּה חוֹנֵן לְאָדָם דַּעַת
Umlamed Le'enosh Binah.	וּמְלַמֵּד לֶאֱנוֹשׁ בִּינָה.
Vechanenu Me'itecha	וְחָנֵּנוּ מֵאִתְּךָ
Chochmah Binah Vada'at.	חָכְמָה בִּינָה וָדָעַת:
Baruch Attah Adonai Chonen	בָּרוּךְ אַתָּה יַהֲוַהַ חוֹנֵן
Hada'at.	הַדָּעַת:

You favor man with knowledge, and teach mortals understanding. Graciously grant us wisdom, understanding and knowledge from You. Blessed are You, Hashem, gracious Giver of knowledge.

Teshuvah / Repentance

Hashiveinu Avinu Letoratecha.	הֲשִׁיבֵנוּ אָבִינוּ לְתוֹרָתֶךָ.
Vekarevenu Malkeinu	וְקָרְבֵנוּ מַלְכֵּנוּ
La'avodatecha. Vehachazirenu	לַעֲבוֹדָתֶךָ. וְהַחֲזִירֵנוּ
Bitshuvah Shelemah Lefaneicha.	בִּתְשׁוּבָה שְׁלֵמָה לְפָנֶיךָ:
Baruch Attah Adonai Harotzeh	בָּרוּךְ אַתָּה יַהֱוֶהֱ הָרוֹצֶה
Bitshuvah.	בִּתְשׁוּבָה:

Restore us, our Father, to Your Torah; draw us near, our King, to Your service; cause us to return in perfect repentance before You. Blessed are You, Hashem, Who desires repentance.

Selichah / Forgiveness

Selach Lanu Avinu Ki Chatanu.	סְלַח לָנוּ אָבִינוּ כִּי חָטָאנוּ.
Mechol Lanu Malkeinu Ki	מְחוֹל לָנוּ מַלְכֵּנוּ כִּי
Fasha'enu. Ki El Tov Vesalach	פָשָׁעְנוּ. כִּי אֵל טוֹב וְסַלָּח
Attah. Baruch Attah Adonai	אָתָּה: בָּרוּךְ אַתָּה יְהֹוָה
Chanun Hamarbeh Lisloach.	חַנּוּן הַמַּרְבֶּה לִסְלֹחַ:

Forgive us, our Father, for we have sinned; pardon us, our King, for we have transgressed; for You are a good and forgiving God. Blessed are You, Hashem, Who is gracious and ever forgiving.

Ge'ulah / Redemption

Re'eh Na Ve'aneyenu. Verivah	רְאֵה נָא בְעָנְיֵנוּ. וְרִיבָה
Rivenu. Umaher Lego'aleinu	רִיבֵנוּ. וּמַהֵר לְגָאֳלֵנוּ
Ge'ulah Shelemah Lema'an	גְאוּלָּה שְׁלֵמָה לְמַעַן
Shemecha. Ki El Go'el Chazak	שְׁמֶךָ. כִּי אֵל גּוֹאֵל חָזָק
Attah. Baruch Attah Adonai	אָתָּה: בָּרוּךְ אַתָּה יְהֹוָה
Go'el Yisra'el.	גּוֹאֵל יִשְׂרָאֵל:

Look upon our affliction and fight our cause; and hasten to redeem us completely for Your name's sake, for You are a strong and redeeming God. Blessed are You, Hashem, Redeemer of Yisrael.

Aneinu

Said only on a public fast day:

עֲנֵנוּ אָבִינוּ עֲנֵנוּ בְּיוֹם צוֹם הַתַּעֲנִית הַזֶּה. כִּי בְצָרָה גְדוֹלָה אֲנָחְנוּ. אַל־תֵּפֶן
לְרִשְׁעֵנוּ. וְאַל־תִּתְעַלָּם מַלְכֵּנוּ מִבַּקָּשָׁתֵנוּ. הֱיֵה נָא קָרוֹב לְשַׁוְעָתֵנוּ. טֶרֶם נִקְרָא

אֵלֶיךָ אַתָּה תַעֲנֶה. נְדַבֵּר וְאַתָּה תִשְׁמַע. כַּדָּבָר שֶׁנֶּאֱמַר: וְהָיָה טֶרֶם־יִקְרָאוּ וַאֲנִי אֶעֱנֶה עוֹד הֵם מְדַבְּרִים וַאֲנִי אֶשְׁמָע: כִּי אַתָּה יְהוָה פּוֹדֶה וּמַצִּיל. וְעוֹנֶה וּמְרַחֵם בְּכָל־עֵת צָרָה וְצוּקָה:

Aneinu Avinu Aneinu Beyom Tzom Hata'anit Hazeh. Ki Vetzarah Gedolah Anachenu. Al-Tefen Lerish'enu. Ve'al-Tit'alam Malkeinu Mibakashateinu. Heyeh Na Karov Leshav'ateinu. Terem Nikra Eleicha Attah Ta'aneh. Nedaber Ve'attah Tishma'. Kadavar Shene'emar. Vehayah Terem-Yikra'u Va'ani E'eneh; Od Hem Medaberim Va'ani Eshma. Ki Attah Adonai Podeh Umatzil. Ve'oneh Umerachem Bechol-'Et Tzarah Vetzukah.

Answer us, Hashem, answer us on the day of our fast, for we are in great distress. Do not regard our wickedness; Do not conceal Your presence from us, and do not hide Yourself from our supplication. Be near to our cry, and let Your kindness comfort us; even before we call to You answer us, as it is said: "Before they call, I will answer; while they are yet speaking, I will hear." For You, Hashem, are He who answers in time of trouble, who redeems and delivers in all times of woe and stress.

בָּרוּךְ אַתָּה יְהוָה הָעוֹנֶה לְעַמּוֹ יִשְׂרָאֵל בְּעֵת צָרָה:

Baruch Attah Adonai Ha'oneh Le'ammo Yisra'el Be'et Tzarah.

Blessed are You, Hashem, Who answers in time of distress.

Refuah / Healing

Refa'enu Adonai Venerafe.	רְפָאֵנוּ יְהוָה וְנֵרָפֵא.
Hoshi'enu Venivashe'ah. Ki	הוֹשִׁיעֵנוּ וְנִוָּשֵׁעָה. כִּי
Tehillateinu Attah. Veha'aleh	תְהִלָּתֵנוּ אָתָּה. וְהַעֲלֵה
Aruchah Umarpei Lechol-	אֲרוּכָה וּמַרְפֵּא לְכָל־
Tachalu'einu Ulechol-	תַּחֲלוּאֵינוּ וּלְכָל־
Mach'oveinu Ulechol-	מַכְאוֹבֵינוּ וּלְכָל־
Makoteinu. Ki El Rofei Rachman	מַכּוֹתֵינוּ. כִּי אֵל רוֹפֵא רַחְמָן
Vene'eman Attah. Baruch Attah	וְנֶאֱמָן אָתָּה: בָּרוּךְ אַתָּה
Adonai Rofei Cholei Ammo	יְהוָה רוֹפֵא חוֹלֵי עַמּוֹ
Yisra'el.	יִשְׂרָאֵל:

Heal us, Hashem, and we will be healed; save us and we will be saved; for You are our praise. And bring healing and a cure to all of our ailments and wounds; for You are the faithful and merciful God Who heals. Blessed are You, Hashem, Who heals the sick of Your people Yisrael.

Birkat HaShanim / Blessing for the Years

In Summer:	בקיץ:
Barecheinu Adonai Eloheinu	בָּרְכֵנוּ יְהֹוָה אֱלֹהֵינוּ
Bechol-Ma'asei Yadeinu.	בְּכָל־מַעֲשֵׂי יָדֵינוּ.
Uvarech Shenateinu Betalelei	וּבָרֵךְ שְׁנָתֵנוּ בְּטַלְלֵי
Ratzon Berachah Unedavah.	רָצוֹן בְּרָכָה וּנְדָבָה.
Utehi Acharitah Chayim Vesava	וּתְהִי אַחֲרִיתָהּ חַיִּים וְשָׂבָע
Veshalom Kashanim Hatovot	וְשָׁלוֹם כַּשָּׁנִים הַטּוֹבוֹת
Livrachah. Ki El Tov Umeitiv	לִבְרָכָה. כִּי אֵל טוֹב וּמֵטִיב
Attah Umevarech Hashanim.	אַתָּה וּמְבָרֵךְ הַשָּׁנִים:
Baruch Attah Adonai Mevarech	בָּרוּךְ אַתָּה יְהֹוָה מְבָרֵךְ
Hashanim.	הַשָּׁנִים:

Bless us, our Father, in all the work of our hands, and bless our year with favoring dews of blessing and abundance. May it's result be life, plenty and satisfaction and peace like the good years which You have blessed. For You, God, are good and You do good, blessing the years. Blessed are You, Hashem Who blesses the years.

In Winter:	בחורף:
Barech Aleinu Adonai Eloheinu	בָּרֵךְ עָלֵינוּ יְהֹוָה אֱלֹהֵינוּ
Et-Hashanah Hazot Ve'et-Kol-	אֶת־הַשָּׁנָה הַזֹּאת וְאֶת־כָּל־
Minei Tevu'atah Letovah. Veten	מִינֵי תְבוּאָתָהּ לְטוֹבָה. וְתֵן
Tal Umatar Livrachah Al Kol-	טַל וּמָטָר לִבְרָכָה עַל כָּל־

Penei Ha'adamah. Veraveh Penei	פְּנֵי הָאֲדָמָה. וְרַוֵּה פְּנֵי
Tevel Vesabba Et-Ha'olam Kulo	תֵבֵל וְשַׂבַּע אֶת־הָעוֹלָם כֻּלּוֹ
Mituvach. Umalei Yadeinu	מִטּוּבָךְ. וּמַלֵּא יָדֵינוּ
Mibirchoteicha Ume'osher	מִבִּרְכוֹתֶיךָ וּמֵעֹשֶׁר
Mattenot Yadeicha. Shamerah	מַתְּנוֹת יָדֶיךָ. שָׁמְרָה
Vehatzilah Shanah Zo Mikol-	וְהַצִּילָה שָׁנָה זוֹ מִכָּל־
Davar Ra'. Umikal-Minei	דָּבָר רָע. וּמִכָּל־מִינֵי
Mashchit Umikal-Minei Fur'anut.	מַשְׁחִית וּמִכָּל־מִינֵי פֻּרְעָנוּת.
Va'aseh Lah Tikvah Tovah	וַעֲשֵׂה לָהּ תִּקְוָה טוֹבָה
Ve'acharit Shalom. Chus	וְאַחֲרִית שָׁלוֹם. חוּס
Verachem Aleiha Ve'al Kol-	וְרַחֵם עָלֶיהָ וְעַל כָּל־
Tevu'atah Ufeiroteiha.	תְּבוּאָתָהּ וּפֵירוֹתֶיהָ.
Uvarechah Begishmei Ratzon	וּבָרְכָהּ בְּגִשְׁמֵי רָצוֹן
Berachah Unedavah. Utehi	בְּרָכָה וּנְדָבָה. וּתְהִי
Acharitah Chayim Vesava	אַחֲרִיתָהּ חַיִּים וְשָׂבָע
Veshalom. Kashanim Hatovot	וְשָׁלוֹם. כַּשָּׁנִים הַטּוֹבוֹת
Livrachah. Ki El Tov Umeitiv	לִבְרָכָה. כִּי אֵל טוֹב וּמֵטִיב
Attah Umevarech Hashanim.	אַתָּה וּמְבָרֵךְ הַשָּׁנִים.
Baruch Attah Adonai Mevarech	בָּרוּךְ אַתָּה יְהֹוָה מְבָרֵךְ
Hashanim.	הַשָּׁנִים:

Hashem our God, bless for us this year with all its varied produce, for good. Send dew and rain to bless the face of the entire earth, and water the surface of the earth, and satisfy the whole world with Your goodness. Fill our hands with Your blessings and the rich gifts of Your hands. Guard and deliver this year from all evil, and from all disaster and from all chaos, and make it a year of good hope and a peaceful ending. Have pity and compassion on this year and all its increase and fruits. Bless the year with rains of favor, blessing and generosity, and may its end be life, satisfaction and peace, like the good years which You have blessed. For You God, are good and You do good, blessing the years. Blessed are You, Hashem Who blesses the years.

Galuyot / Ingathering of Exiles

Teka Beshofar Gadol	תְּקַע בְּשׁוֹפָר גָּדוֹל
Lecheruteinu. Vesa Nes	לְחֵרוּתֵֽנוּ. וְשָׂא נֵס
Lekabetz Galyoteinu.	לְקַבֵּץ גָּלֻיּוֹתֵֽינוּ.
Vekabetzeinu Yachad Me'arba	וְקַבְּצֵֽנוּ יַֽחַד מֵאַרְבַּע
Kanfot Ha'aretz Le'artzenu.	כַּנְפוֹת הָאָֽרֶץ לְאַרְצֵֽנוּ:
Baruch Attah Adonai Mekabetz	בָּרוּךְ אַתָּה יְהֹוָה מְקַבֵּץ
Nidchei Ammo Yisra'el.	נִדְחֵי עַמּוֹ יִשְׂרָאֵל:

Sound the great shofar for our freedom; lift up the banner to bring our exiles; And gather us together from the four corners of the earth into our land. Blessed are You, Hashem, Who gathers the dispersed of His people Yisrael.

Birkat HaDin / Restoration of Justice

Hashivah Shofeteinu	הָשִֽׁיבָה שׁוֹפְטֵֽינוּ
Kevarishonah. Veyo'atzeinu	כְּבָרִאשׁוֹנָה. וְיוֹעֲצֵֽינוּ
Kevatechillah. Vehaseir Mimenu	כְּבַתְּחִלָּה. וְהָסֵר מִמֶּֽנּוּ
Yagon Va'anachah. Umeloch	יָגוֹן וַאֲנָחָה. וּמְלוֹךְ
Aleinu Meheirah Attah Adonai	עָלֵֽינוּ מְהֵרָה אַתָּה יְהֹוָה
Levadecha. Bechesed	לְבַדְּךָ. בְּחֶֽסֶד

Uverachamim. Betzedek	וּבְרַחֲמִים. בְּצֶדֶק
Uvemishpat. Baruch Attah	וּבְמִשְׁפָּט: בָּרוּךְ אַתָּה
Adonai Melech Ohev Tzedakah	יוהווהו מֶלֶךְ אוֹהֵב צְדָקָה
Umishpat.	וּמִשְׁפָּט:

Restore our judges as at first, and our counselors as at the beginning; remove from us sorrow and sighing; reign over us speedily, Hashem, You alone in kindness and mercy; and with righteousness and with justice. Blessed are You, Hashem, King who loves righteousness and justice.

During the 10 days of repentance (Rosh Hashanah to Yom Kippur) say:

Hamelech Hamishpat.	הַמֶּלֶךְ הַמִּשְׁפָּט:

The King, The Judge.

Birkat HaMinim / Blessing Against the Heretics

Laminim Velamalshinim Al-Tehi	לַמִּינִים וְלַמַּלְשִׁינִים אַל־תְּהִי
Tikvah. Vechol-Hazeidim	תִקְוָה. וְכָל־הַזֵּדִים
Kerega Yovedu.	כְּרֶגַע יֹאבֵדוּ.
Vechol-'Oyeveicha Vechol-	וְכָל־אוֹיְבֶיךָ וְכָל־
Sone'eicha Meheirah Yikaretu.	שׂוֹנְאֶיךָ מְהֵרָה יִכָּרֵתוּ.
Umalchut Harish'ah Meheirah	וּמַלְכוּת הָרִשְׁעָה מְהֵרָה
Te'akeir Uteshaber Utechalem	תְעַקֵּר וּתְשַׁבֵּר וּתְכַלֵּם
Vetachni'em Bimheirah	וְתַכְנִיעֵם בִּמְהֵרָה
Veyameinu. Baruch Attah	בְיָמֵינוּ: בָּרוּךְ אַתָּה
Adonai Shoveir Oyevim	יְהֹוָה שׁוֹבֵר אוֹיְבִים
Umachnia Zeidim. (Minim)	וּמַכְנִיעַ זֵדִים: (מִינִים)

For the heretics and the slanderers let there be no hope, and all of the arrogant disappear in an instant. May all of Your enemies and all of those who hate You quickly be cut off, and the evil government uprooted, and broken, and humbled and subdued quickly in our days. Blessed are You, Hashem, Who breaks enemies and subdues the arrogant. **(heretics)**

Tzaddikim / The Righteous

Al Hatzaddikim Ve'al	עַל הַצַּדִּיקִים וְעַל
Hachasidim. Ve'al She'erit	הַחֲסִידִים. וְעַל שְׁאֵרִית
Ammecha Beit Yisra'el. Ve'al	עַמְּךָ בֵּית יִשְׂרָאֵל. וְעַל
Peleitat Beit Sofereihem. Ve'al	פְּלֵיטַת בֵּית סוֹפְרֵיהֶם. וְעַל
Gerei Hatzedek Ve'aleinu.	גֵּרֵי הַצֶּדֶק וְעָלֵינוּ.
Yehemu Na Rachameicha.	יֶהֱמוּ נָא רַחֲמֶיךָ.
Adonai Eloheinu. Veten Sachar	יְהֹוָה אֱלֹהֵינוּ. וְתֵן שָׂכָר
Tov Lechol-Habotechim	טוֹב לְכָל־הַבּוֹטְחִים
Beshimcha Be'emet. Vesim	בְּשִׁמְךָ בֶּאֱמֶת. וְשִׂים
Chelkenu Imahem. Ule'olam Lo	חֶלְקֵנוּ עִמָּהֶם. וּלְעוֹלָם לֹא
Nevosh Ki Vecha Vatachenu.	נֵבוֹשׁ כִּי בְךָ בָּטָחְנוּ.
Ve'al Chasdecha Hagadol	וְעַל חַסְדְּךָ הַגָּדוֹל
Be'emet Nish'aneinu. Baruch	בֶּאֱמֶת נִשְׁעָנְנוּ: בָּרוּךְ
Attah Adonai Mish'an Umivtach	אַתָּה יוהווהו מִשְׁעָן וּמִבְטָח
Latzaddikim.	לַצַּדִּיקִים:

On the righteous and on the pious and on the remainders of Your people, the House of Yisrael, and over the remnant of their scribes; over the righteous converts and over us may Your mercy be aroused. Hashem our God, Grant a good reward to all who truly trust in Your name, and place our portion among them; may we never come to shame, for in You we trust and on Your great kindness we faithfully rely. Blessed are You, Hashem, the support and trust of the righteous.

Boneh Yerushalayim / Builder of Yerushalayim

Tishkon Betoch Yerushalayim	תִּשְׁכּוֹן בְּתוֹךְ יְרוּשָׁלַיִם
Irecha Ka'asher Dibarta.	עִירְךָ כַּאֲשֶׁר דִּבַּרְתָּ.
Vechisei David Avdecha	וְכִסֵּא דָוִד עַבְדְּךָ
Meheirah Betochah Tachin.	מְהֵרָה בְּתוֹכָהּ תָּכִין.
Uveneh Otah Binyan Olam	וּבְנֵה אוֹתָהּ בִּנְיַן עוֹלָם
Bimheirah Veyameinu.	בִּמְהֵרָה בְיָמֵינוּ:

May Your presence dwell in Yerushalayim, Your city, as You have promised; establish soon the throne of David, Your servant, within it, And rebuild it soon, in our days, as an everlasting structure.

Nachem

On Tisha B'Av say the following blessing. After the ending blessing skip to "Et Tzemach".

נַחֵם יְהוָה אֱלֹהֵינוּ אֶת אֲבֵלֵי צִיּוֹן וְאֶת אֲבֵלֵי יְרוּשָׁלַיִם. וְאֶת הָעִיר הַחֲרֵבָה וְהַבְּזוּיָה. וְהַשּׁוֹמֵמָה. מִבְּלִי בָנֶיהָ הִיא יוֹשֶׁבֶת. וְרֹאשָׁהּ חָפוּי כְּאִשָּׁה עֲקָרָה שֶׁלֹּא יָלָדָה. וַיְבַלְּעוּהָ לִגְיוֹנִים וַיִּירָשׁוּהָ. וַיַּטִּילוּ אֶת עַמְּךָ יִשְׂרָאֵל לֶחָרֶב. וַיַּהַרְגוּ בְזָדוֹן חֲסִידֵי עֶלְיוֹן. עַל־כֵּן צִיּוֹן בְּמַר תִּבְכֶּה. וִירוּשָׁלַיִם תִּתֵּן קוֹלָהּ: לִבִּי לִבִּי עַל חַלְלֵיהֶם. מֵעַי מֵעַי עַל הֲרוּגֵיהֶם: כִּי אַתָּה יְהוָה בָּאֵשׁ הִצַּתָּהּ. וּבָאֵשׁ אַתָּה עָתִיד לִבְנוֹתָהּ. כַּכָּתוּב: וַאֲנִי אֶהְיֶה־לָּהּ נְאֻם־יְהוָֹה חוֹמַת אֵשׁ סָבִיב וּלְכָבוֹד אֶהְיֶה בְתוֹכָהּ: בָּרוּךְ אַתָּה יְהוָה מְנַחֵם צִיּוֹן בְּבִנְיַן יְרוּשָׁלַיִם:

Nachem Adonai Eloheinu Et Aveilei Tziyon Ve'et Aveilei Yerushalayim. Ve'et Ha'ir Hacharevah Vehabezuyah. Vehashomemah. Mibeli Vaneiha Hi Yoshevet. Veroshah Chafui Ke'ishah Akarah Shelo Yaladah. Vayvalle'uha Ligyonim Vayirashuha. Vayattilu Et Ammecha Yisra'el Lacherev. Vayahargu Vezadon Chasidei Elyon. Al Ken Tziyon Bemerer Tivkeh. Virushalayim Titen Kolah: Libi Libi Al Chaleihem. Me'ai Me'ai Al Harugeihem: Ki Attah Adonai Ba'esh Hetzattah. Uva'esh Attah Atid

Livnotah. Kakatuv: Va'ani Ehyeh Lah Ne'um Adonai Chomat Esh Saviv Ulechavod Ehyeh Vetochah. Baruch Attah Adonai Menachem Tziyon Bevinyan Yerushalayim.

Comfort, Hashem our God, the mourners of Tziyon, the mourners of Yerushalayim, and the city that is in mourning, laid waste, despised and desolate. She is in mourning, because she is without her children; she is laid waste as to her homes; she is despised in the downfall of her glory; she is desolate through the loss of her inhabitants. She sits with her head covered like a barren, childless woman. Legions devoured her; idolators took possession of her; they put Your people Yisrael to the sword, and killed wantonly the faithful followers of the Most High. Because of that, Tziyon weeps bitterly; Yerushalayim raises her voice. How my heart grieves for the slain. How my heart yearns for the slain. You, Hashem, consumed her with fire, and with fire You will rebuild her in the future, as it is said: "For I, says Hashem, will be to her a wall of fire all around, and I will be the glory in the midst of her." **(Zech. 2:9)** Blessed are You, Hashem, Comforter of Tziyon and Builder of Yerushalayim.

Baruch Attah Adonai Boneh	בָּרוּךְ אַתָּה יְהֹוָה בּוֹנֵה
Yerushalayim.	יְרוּשָׁלָיִם:

Blessed are You, Hashem, Builder of Yerushalayim.

Birkhat David / Prayer for Davidic Reign

Et Tzemach David Avdecha	אֶת צֶמַח דָּוִד עַבְדְּךָ
Meheirah Tatzmiach. Vekarno	מְהֵרָה תַצְמִיחַ. וְקַרְנוֹ
Tarum Bishu'atecha. Ki	תָּרוּם בִּישׁוּעָתֶךָ. כִּי
Lishu'atecha Kivinu Kol-Hayom.	לִישׁוּעָתְךָ קִוִּינוּ כָּל־הַיּוֹם:
Baruch Attah Adonai Matzmiach	בָּרוּךְ אַתָּה יְהֹוָה מַצְמִיחַ
Keren Yeshu'ah.	קֶרֶן יְשׁוּעָה:

Speedily cause the offspring of Your servant David to flourish, and let his horn be exalted in Your salvation, for we hope in Your salvation every day. Blessed are You, Hashem, Who flourishes the horn of salvation.

Tefillah / Acceptance of Prayer

Shema Koleinu. Adonai	שְׁמַע קוֹלֵנוּ. יְהֹוָה
Eloheinu. Av Harachaman.	אֱלֹהֵינוּ. אָב הָרַחֲמָן.
Rachem Aleinu. Vekabel	רַחֵם עָלֵינוּ. וְקַבֵּל
Berachamim Uveratzon Et-	בְּרַחֲמִים וּבְרָצוֹן אֶת־
Tefillateinu. Ki El Shome'ah	תְּפִלָּתֵנוּ. כִּי אֵל שׁוֹמֵעַ
Tefillot Vetachanunim Attah.	תְּפִלּוֹת וְתַחֲנוּנִים אָתָּה.
Umilfaneicha Malkeinu. Reikam	וּמִלְּפָנֶיךָ מַלְכֵּנוּ. רֵיקָם
Al-Teshivenu. Chonenu	אַל־תְּשִׁיבֵנוּ. חָנֵּנוּ
Va'aneinu Ushema Tefillateinu.	וַעֲנֵנוּ וּשְׁמַע תְּפִלָּתֵנוּ.

Hear our voice, Hashem our God. Merciful Father, have compassion upon us. And accept our prayers with mercy and favor, for You are God who hears to prayers and supplications. And from before You, our King, do not leave us empty-handed, but be gracious to us and hear our prayers.

If one forgot to say Aneinu earlier, they may say here:

עֲנֵנוּ אָבִינוּ עֲנֵנוּ בְּיוֹם צוֹם הַתַּעֲנִית הַזֶּה. כִּי בְצָרָה גְדוֹלָה אֲנַחְנוּ. אַל־תֵּפֶן לְרִשְׁעֵנוּ. וְאַל־תִּתְעַלַּם מַלְכֵּנוּ מִבַּקָּשָׁתֵנוּ. הֱיֵה נָא קָרוֹב לְשַׁוְעָתֵנוּ. טֶרֶם נִקְרָא אֵלֶיךָ אַתָּה תַעֲנֶה. נְדַבֵּר וְאַתָּה תִשְׁמַע. כַּדָּבָר שֶׁנֶּאֱמַר: וְהָיָה טֶרֶם־יִקְרָאוּ וַאֲנִי אֶעֱנֶה עוֹד הֵם מְדַבְּרִים וַאֲנִי אֶשְׁמָע: כִּי אַתָּה יְהֹוָה פּוֹדֶה וּמַצִּיל. וְעוֹנֶה וּמְרַחֵם בְּכָל־עֵת צָרָה וְצוּקָה:

Aneinu Avinu Aneinu Beyom Tzom Hata'anit Hazeh. Ki Vetzarah Gedolah Anachenu. Al-Tefen Lerish'enu. Ve'al-Tit'alam Malkeinu Mibakashateinu. Heyeh Na Karov Leshav'ateinu. Terem Nikra Eleicha Attah Ta'aneh. Nedaber Ve'attah Tishma'. Kadavar Shene'emar. Vehayah Terem-Yikra'u Va'ani E'eneh; Od Hem Medaberim Va'ani Eshma. Ki Attah Adonai Podeh Umatzil. Ve'oneh Umerachem Bechol-'Et Tzarah Vetzukah.

Answer us, Hashem, answer us on the day of our fast, for we are in great distress. Do not regard our wickedness; Do not conceal Your presence from us, and do not hide Yourself from our supplication. Be near to our cry, and let Your kindness comfort us; even before we call to You answer us, as it is said: "Before they call, I will answer; while they are yet speaking, I will hear." For You, Hashem, are He who answers in time of trouble, who redeems and delivers in all times of woe and stress.

Ki Attah Shome'ah Tefillat Kol-	כִּי אַתָּה שׁוֹמֵעַ תְּפִלַּת כָּל־
Peh. Baruch Attah Adonai	פֶּה: בָּרוּךְ אַתָּה יְהֺוָה
Shome'ah Tefillah.	שׁוֹמֵעַ תְּפִלָּה:

For You hear the prayer of every mouth. Blessed are You, Hashem Who hears prayer.

Avodah / Temple Service

Retzeh Adonai Eloheinu	רְצֵה יְהֺוָה אֱלֹהֵינוּ
Be'ammecha Yisra'el Velitfilatam	בְּעַמְּךָ יִשְׂרָאֵל וְלִתְפִלָּתָם
She'eh. Vehasheiv Ha'avodah	שְׁעֵה. וְהָשֵׁב הָעֲבוֹדָה
Lidvir Beitecha. Ve'ishei Yisra'el	לִדְבִיר בֵּיתֶךָ. וְאִשֵּׁי יִשְׂרָאֵל
Utefilatam. Meheirah Be'ahavah	וּתְפִלָּתָם. מְהֵרָה בְּאַהֲבָה
Tekabel Beratzon. Utehi	תְקַבֵּל בְּרָצוֹן. וּתְהִי
Leratzon Tamid Avodat Yisra'el	לְרָצוֹן תָּמִיד עֲבוֹדַת יִשְׂרָאֵל
Ammecha.	עַמֶּךָ:

Be favorable, Hashem our God, on Your people Yisrael and regard their prayers. And the service to the Sanctuary of Your House, and the fire offerings of Yisrael, and their prayers accept soon with love. And may the service of Your people, Yisrael, always be favorable.

On Rosh Chodesh and Chol HaMoed Passover and Sukkot say:

Ya'aleh Veyavo

אֱלֹהֵינוּ וֵאלֹהֵי אֲבוֹתֵינוּ. יַעֲלֶה וְיָבֹא. וְיַגִּיעַ וְיֵרָאֶה. וְיֵרָצֶה וְיִשָּׁמַע. וְיִפָּקֵד וְיִזָּכֵר. זִכְרוֹנֵנוּ וְזִכְרוֹן אֲבוֹתֵינוּ. זִכְרוֹן יְרוּשָׁלַיִם עִירָךְ. וְזִכְרוֹן מָשִׁיחַ בֶּן־דָּוִד עַבְדָּךְ. וְזִכְרוֹן כָּל־עַמְּךָ בֵּית יִשְׂרָאֵל לְפָנֶיךָ. לִפְלֵיטָה. לְטוֹבָה. לְחֵן. לְחֶסֶד וּלְרַחֲמִים. לְחַיִּים טוֹבִים וּלְשָׁלוֹם. בְּיוֹם:

Eloheinu Velohei Avoteinu. Ya'aleh Veyavo. Veyagia Veyera'eh. Veyeratzeh Veyishama'. Veyipaked Veyizacher. Zichronenu Vezichron Avoteinu. Zichron Yerushalayim Irach. Vezichron Mashiach Ben-David Avdach. Vezichron Kol-'Ammecha Beit Yisra'el Lefaneicha. Lifleitah. Letovah. Lechein. Lechesed Ulerachamim. Lechayim Tovim Uleshalom. Beyom:

Our God, and God of our fathers, may it rise, and come, arrive, appear, find favor, and be heard, and be considered, and be remembered our remembrance and the remembrance of our fathers, Yerushalayim Your city, the remembrance of Messiah ben David Your servant, and the remembrance of all Your people of the House of Yisrael before You for deliverance, for good favor, for kindness and mercy, for good life and for peace. On this day of:

On Rosh Chodesh:

Rosh Chodesh Hazeh.	רֹאשׁ חֹדֶשׁ הַזֶּה.

Rosh Chodesh (New Moon).

On Pesach:

Chag Hamatzot Hazeh. Beyom Mikra	חַג הַמַּצּוֹת הַזֶּה. בְּיוֹם מִקְרָא
Kodesh Hazeh.	קֹדֶשׁ הַזֶּה.

The Festival of Matzot. on this day of holy convocation.

On Sukkot:

Chag Hasukkot Hazeh. Beyom Mikra	חַג הַסֻּכּוֹת הַזֶּה. בְּיוֹם מִקְרָא
Kodesh Hazeh.	קֹדֶשׁ הַזֶּה.

The Festival of Sukkot. on this day of holy convocation.

לְרַחֵם בּוֹ עָלֵינוּ וּלְהוֹשִׁיעֵנוּ. זָכְרֵנוּ יְהֹוָה אֱלֹהֵינוּ בּוֹ לְטוֹבָה. וּפָקְדֵנוּ בוֹ לִבְרָכָה. וְהוֹשִׁיעֵנוּ בוֹ לְחַיִּים טוֹבִים. בִּדְבַר יְשׁוּעָה וְרַחֲמִים. חוּס וְחָנֵּנוּ. וַחֲמוֹל וְרַחֵם עָלֵינוּ. וְהוֹשִׁיעֵנוּ כִּי אֵלֶיךָ עֵינֵינוּ. כִּי אֵל מֶלֶךְ חַנּוּן וְרַחוּם אָתָּה:

Lerachem Bo Aleinu Ulehoshi'enu. Zochrenu Adonai Eloheinu Bo Letovah. Ufokdenu Vo Livrachah. Vehoshi'enu Vo Lechayim Tovim. Bidvar Yeshu'ah Verachamim. Chus Vechanenu. Vachamol Verachem Aleinu. Vehoshi'enu Ki Eleicha Eineinu. Ki El Melech Chanun Verachum Attah.

to have mercy upon us and save us. Remember us, Hashem our God, on it for good. Be mindful of us on it for blessing and save us on it for a life of good. With the promise of salvation and mercy, show us pity, and be gracious to us and have compassion and mercy on us and save us. For our eyes are lifted towards You, for You, God, are a gracious and merciful King.

Attah Berachameicha Harabim.	וְאַתָּה בְּרַחֲמֶיךָ הָרַבִּים.
Tachpotz Banu Vetirtzenu.	תַּחְפֹּץ בָּנוּ וְתִרְצֵנוּ.
Vetechezeinah Eineinu	וְתֶחֱזֶינָה עֵינֵינוּ
Beshuvecha Letziyon	בְּשׁוּבְךָ לְצִיּוֹן
Berachamim. Baruch Attah	בְּרַחֲמִים: בָּרוּךְ אַתָּה
Adonai Hamachazir Shechinato	יְהֹוָה הַמַּחֲזִיר שְׁכִינָתוֹ
Letziyon.	לְצִיּוֹן.

And You, in Your abundant mercy, delight in us, and be favorable to us, so that our eyes may witness Your return to Tzion with mercy. Blessed are You, Hashem Who returns His Presence to Tzion.

Hoda'ah (Modim) / Thanksgiving

On Saying "Modim" / "We are Thankful" One Bows and begins to rise after "Adonai" / "Hashem".

Modim Anachnu Lach. She'attah	מוֹדִים אֲנַחְנוּ לָךְ. שָׁאַתָּה
Hu Adonai Eloheinu Velohei	הוּא יְהֹוָה אֱלֹהֵינוּ וֵאלֹהֵי
Avoteinu Le'olam Va'ed. Tzurenu	אֲבוֹתֵינוּ לְעוֹלָם וָעֶד. צוּרֵנוּ
Tzur Chayeinu Umagen Yish'enu	צוּר חַיֵּינוּ וּמָגֵן יִשְׁעֵנוּ
Attah Hu. Ledor Vador Nodeh	אַתָּה הוּא. לְדוֹר וָדוֹר נוֹדֶה
Lecha Unsapeir Tehilatecha. Al	לְּךָ וּנְסַפֵּר תְּהִלָּתֶךָ. עַל
Chayeinu Hamesurim	חַיֵּינוּ הַמְּסוּרִים
Beyadecha. Ve'al Nishmoteinu	בְּיָדֶךָ. וְעַל נִשְׁמוֹתֵינוּ
Hapekudot Lach. Ve'al Niseicha	הַפְּקוּדוֹת לָךְ. וְעַל נִסֶּיךָ
Shebechol-Yom Imanu. Ve'al	שֶׁבְּכָל־יוֹם עִמָּנוּ. וְעַל
Nifle'oteicha Vetovoteicha	נִפְלְאוֹתֶיךָ וְטוֹבוֹתֶיךָ
Shebechol-'Et. Erev Vavoker	שֶׁבְּכָל־עֵת. עֶרֶב וָבֹקֶר
Vetzaharayim. Hatov. Ki Lo	וְצָהֳרָיִם. הַטּוֹב. כִּי לֹא

Chalu Rachameicha.	כָלוּ רַחֲמֶיךָ.
Hamerachem. Ki Lo Tamu	הַמְרַחֵם. כִּי לֹא תַמּוּ
Chasadeicha. Ki Me'olam Kivinu	חֲסָדֶיךָ. כִּי מֵעוֹלָם קִוִּינוּ
Lach.	לָךְ:

We are thankful to You, Hashem our God and the God of our fathers, forever. You are our strength and Rock of our life and the Shield of our salvation. In every generation we will thank You and recount Your praise for our lives which are in given into Your hand, for our souls which are placed in Your care, and for Your miracles which are daily with us, and for Your wonders and goodness—evening, morning and noon. The Beneficent One, for Your mercies never end, Merciful One, for Your kindness has never ceased, for we have always placed our hope in You.

Modim Derabbanan

During the repetition, this is to be recited softly while the Chazan reads the Modim. Still bow at Modim as before.

מוֹדִים אֲנַחְנוּ לָךְ. שָׁאַתָּה הוּא יְהֹוָה אֱלֹהֵינוּ וֵאלֹהֵי אֲבוֹתֵינוּ. אֱלֹהֵי כָל בָּשָׂר. יוֹצְרֵנוּ יוֹצֵר בְּרֵאשִׁית. בְּרָכוֹת וְהוֹדָאוֹת לְשִׁמְךָ הַגָּדוֹל וְהַקָּדוֹשׁ. עַל שֶׁהֶחֱיִיתָנוּ וְקִיַּמְתָּנוּ. כֵּן תְּחַיֵּנוּ וּתְחָנְּנוּ וְתֶאֱסוֹף גָּלֻיּוֹתֵינוּ לְחַצְרוֹת קָדְשֶׁךָ. לִשְׁמֹר חֻקֶּיךָ וְלַעֲשׂוֹת רְצוֹנְךָ וּלְעָבְדְךָ בְּלֵבָב שָׁלֵם. עַל שֶׁאֲנַחְנוּ מוֹדִים לָךְ. בָּרוּךְ אֵל הַהוֹדָאוֹת.

Modim Anachnu Lach. She'attah Hu Adonai Eloheinu Velohei Avoteinu. Elohei Chol Basar. Yotzreinu Yotzer Bereshit. Berachot Vehoda'ot Leshimcha Hagadol Vehakadosh. Al Shehecheyitanu Vekiyamtanu. Ken Techayeinu Utechanenu Vete'esof Galyoteinu Lechatzrot Kodshecha. Lishmor Chukkeicha Vela'asot Retzonecha Ule'avedecha Velevav Shalem. Al She'anachnu Modim Lach. Baruch El Hahoda'ot.

We are thankful to You, Hashem our God and the God of our fathers. God of all flesh, our Creator and Former of Creation, blessings and thanks to Your great and holy name, for You have kept us alive and sustained us; may You always grant us life and be gracious to us. And gather our exiles to Your holy courtyards to observe Your statutes, and to do Your will, and to serve You with a perfect heart. For this we thank You. Blessed is God of thanksgivings.

Al HaNissim

On Purim and Hanukkah an extra prayer is added here:

עַל הַנִּסִּים וְעַל הַפֻּרְקָן וְעַל הַגְּבוּרוֹת וְעַל הַתְּשׁוּעוֹת וְעַל הַנִּפְלָאוֹת וְעַל הַנֶּחָמוֹת שֶׁעָשִׂיתָ לַאֲבוֹתֵינוּ בַּיָּמִים הָהֵם בַּזְּמַן הַזֶּה:

Al Hanissim Ve'al Hapurkan Ve'al Hagevurot Ve'al Hateshu'ot Ve'al Hanifla'ot Ve'al Hanechamot She'asita La'avoteinu Bayamim Hahem Bazman Hazeh.

For the miracles, and for the triumphant liberation, and the mighty works, and for the deliverances, and for the wonders, and for the consolations which You have done for our fathers in those days at this season:

On Hanukkah:

בִּימֵי מַתִּתְיָה בֶן־יוֹחָנָן כֹּהֵן גָּדוֹל. חַשְׁמוֹנָאִי וּבָנָיו כְּשֶׁעָמְדָה מַלְכוּת יָוָן הָרְשָׁעָה עַל עַמְּךָ יִשְׂרָאֵל. לְשַׁכְּחָם תּוֹרָתָךְ וּלְהַעֲבִירָם מֵחֻקֵּי רְצוֹנָךְ. וְאַתָּה בְּרַחֲמֶיךָ הָרַבִּים עָמַדְתָּ לָהֶם בְּעֵת צָרָתָם. רַבְתָּ אֶת רִיבָם. דַּנְתָּ אֶת דִּינָם. נָקַמְתָּ אֶת נִקְמָתָם. מָסַרְתָּ גִבּוֹרִים בְּיַד חַלָּשִׁים. וְרַבִּים בְּיַד מְעַטִּים. וּרְשָׁעִים בְּיַד צַדִּיקִים. וּטְמֵאִים בְּיַד טְהוֹרִים. וְזֵדִים בְּיַד עוֹסְקֵי תוֹרָתֶךָ. לְךָ עָשִׂיתָ שֵׁם גָּדוֹל וְקָדוֹשׁ בְּעוֹלָמָךְ. וּלְעַמְּךָ יִשְׂרָאֵל עָשִׂיתָ תְּשׁוּעָה גְדוֹלָה וּפֻרְקָן כְּהַיּוֹם הַזֶּה. וְאַחַר כָּךְ בָּאוּ בָנֶיךָ לִדְבִיר בֵּיתֶךָ. וּפִנּוּ אֶת־הֵיכָלֶךָ. וְטִהֲרוּ אֶת־מִקְדָּשֶׁךָ. וְהִדְלִיקוּ נֵרוֹת בְּחַצְרוֹת קָדְשֶׁךָ. וְקָבְעוּ שְׁמוֹנַת יְמֵי חֲנֻכָּה אֵלּוּ בְּהַלֵּל וּבְהוֹדָאָה. וְעָשִׂיתָ עִמָּהֶם נִסִּים וְנִפְלָאוֹת וְנוֹדֶה לְשִׁמְךָ הַגָּדוֹל סֶלָה:

Bimei Mattityah Ven-Yochanan Kohen Gadol. Chashmona'i Uvanav Keshe'amedah Malchut Yavan Haresha'ah Al Ammecha Yisra'el. Leshakecham Toratach Uleha'aviram Mechukkei Retzonach. Ve'attah Berachameicha Harabim Amadta Lahem Be'et Tzaratam. Ravta Et Rivam. Danta Et Dinam. Nakamta Et Nikmatam. Masarta Giborim Beyad Chalashim. Verabim Beyad Me'atim. Uresha'im Beyad Tzaddikim. Uteme'im Beyad Tehorim. Vezeidim Beyad Osekei Toratecha. Lecha Asita Shem Gadol Vekadosh Be'olamach. Ule'ammecha Yisra'el Asita Teshu'ah Gedolah Ufurkan Kehayom Hazeh. Ve'achar Kach Ba'u Vaneicha Lidvir Beitecha. Ufinu Et-Heichalecha. Vetiharu Et-Mikdashecha. Vehidliku Nerot Bechatzrot Kodshecha. Vekave'u Shemonat Yemei Chanukkah Elu Behallel Uvehoda'ah. Ve'asita Imahem Nissim Venifla'ot Venodeh Leshimcha Hagadol Selah.

Then in the days of Mattityahu ben-Yochanan, High Priest, the Hasmonean and his sons, when the cruel Greek power rose up against Your people, Yisrael, to make them forget Your Torah and transgress the statutes of Your will. And You, in Your great compassion, stood up for them in time of their trial to plead their cause and defend their judgment. Giving out retribution, delivered the strong into the hand of the weak, and the many into the hand of the few, and the wicked into the hand of the upright, and the impure into the hand of the pure, and tyrants into the hand of the devotees of Your Torah. You made for Yourself a great and holy name in Your world. And for Your people, Yisrael, You performed a great salvation and liberation as this very day. Then Your children came to the Sanctuary of Your House, cleared Your Temple, cleansed Your Sanctuary and kindled lights in Your courtyards, and they instituted these eight days of Hanukkah for praise and thanksgiving. And You did miracles and wonders for them, and we give thanks to Your great name, selah.

On Purim:

בִּימֵי מָרְדְּכַי וְאֶסְתֵּר בְּשׁוּשַׁן הַבִּירָה. כְּשֶׁעָמַד עֲלֵיהֶם הָמָן הָרָשָׁע. בִּקֵּשׁ לְהַשְׁמִיד לַהֲרֹג וּלְאַבֵּד אֶת־כָּל־הַיְּהוּדִים מִנַּעַר וְעַד זָקֵן טַף וְנָשִׁים בְּיוֹם אֶחָד. בִּשְׁלֹשָׁה עָשָׂר לְחֹדֶשׁ שְׁנֵים עָשָׂר. הוּא חֹדֶשׁ אֲדָר. וּשְׁלָלָם לָבוֹז. וְאַתָּה בְּרַחֲמֶיךָ הָרַבִּים הֵפַרְתָּ אֶת־עֲצָתוֹ וְקִלְקַלְתָּ אֶת־מַחֲשַׁבְתּוֹ. וַהֲשֵׁבוֹתָ לוֹ גְּמוּלוֹ בְּרֹאשׁוֹ. וְתָלוּ אוֹתוֹ וְאֶת־בָּנָיו עַל הָעֵץ. וְעָשִׂיתָ עִמָּהֶם נֵס וָפֶלֶא וְנוֹדֶה לְשִׁמְךָ הַגָּדוֹל סֶלָה:

Bimei Mordechai Ve'ester Beshushan Habirah. Keshe'amad Aleihem Haman Harasha. Bikesh Lehashmid Laharog Ule'abed Et-Kol-Hayehudim Mina'ar Ve'ad Zaken Taf Venashim Beyom Echad. Bishloshah Asar Lechodesh Sheneim Asar. Hu Chodesh Adar. Ushelalam Lavoz. Ve'attah Berachameicha Harabim Hefarta Et-'Atzato Vekilkalta Et-Machashavto. Vahasheivota Lo Gemulo Verosho. Vetalu Oto Ve'et-Banav Al Ha'etz. Ve'asita Imahem Nes Vafelei Venodeh Leshimcha Hagadol Selah.

In the days of Mordechai and Ester in Shushan, the capital, the wicked Haman rose up and sought to destroy, slay and utterly annihilate all of the Yehudim, both young and old, women and children, on one day, on the thirteenth day of the twelfth month, which is the month of Adar, and to plunder their possessions. But You in Your great mercy You broke his plan and spoiled his designs, causing them to recoil on his own head, and they hanged him and his sons on the gallows. And You did miracles and wonders for them, and we give thanks to Your great name, selah.

Ve'al Kulam Yitbarach.	וְעַל כֻּלָּם יִתְבָּרַךְ.
Veyitromam. Veyitnasse. Tamid.	וְיִתְרוֹמָם. וְיִתְנַשֵּׂא. תָּמִיד.
Shimcha Malkeinu. Le'olam	שִׁמְךָ מַלְכֵּנוּ. לְעוֹלָם
Va'ed. Vechol-Hachayim	וָעֶד. וְכָל־הַחַיִּים
Yoducha Selah.	יוֹדוּךָ סֶּלָה:

For all these acts, may Your name, our King, be blessed, extolled and exalted forever. And all of the living will thank You, selah.

During the 10 days of repentance (Rosh Hashanah to Yom Kippur) say:

Uchetov Lechayim Tovim Kol Benei Veritecha.	וּכְתֹב לְחַיִּים טוֹבִים כָּל בְּנֵי בְרִיתֶךָ.

Inscribe all of Your people of the covenant for a happy life.

Bow at "Baruch Attah" / "Blessed are You". Raise up at Adonai / Hashem.

Vihalelu Vivarechu Et-Shimcha	וִיהַלְלוּ וִיבָרְכוּ אֶת־שִׁמְךָ
Hagadol Be'emet Le'olam Ki	הַגָּדוֹל בֶּאֱמֶת לְעוֹלָם כִּי
Tov. Ha'el Yeshu'ateinu	טוֹב. הָאֵל יְשׁוּעָתֵנוּ
Ve'ezrateinu Selah. Ha'el Hatov.	וְעֶזְרָתֵנוּ סֶלָה. הָאֵל הַטּוֹב:
Baruch Attah Adonai Hatov	בָּרוּךְ אַתָּה יְהֹוָה הַטּוֹב
Shimcha Ulecha Na'eh	שִׁמְךָ וּלְךָ נָאֶה
Lehodot.	לְהוֹדוֹת:

And they will praise and bless Your great and good name sincerely, forever. For You are good, the God of our salvation and our help forever, the Good God. Blessed are You, Hashem, Your name is good and to You it is good to give thanks.

Birkhat Kohanim is only recited at Minchah on all communal fast days except for Yom Kippur. (SA, OC 566:8)

Birkhat Kohanim / The Priestly Blessing

If there is more than one Kohen present, start here. If there is not, start with Eloheinu Velohei Avoteinu below:

Some say:

לְשֵׁם יִחוּד קוּדְשָׁא בְּרִיךְ הוּא וּשְׁכִינְתֵּיהּ. בִּדְחִילוּ וּרְחִימוּ. וּרְחִימוּ וּדְחִילוּ. לְיַחֲדָא שֵׁם יו״ד קֵ״י בְּוָא״ו קֵ״י בְּיִחוּדָא שְׁלִים (יהוה) בְּשֵׁם כָּל יִשְׂרָאֵל. הִנֵּה אָנֹכִי מוּכָן וּמְזוּמָן לְקַיֵּים מִצְוַת עֲשֵׂה לְבָרֵךְ אֶת יִשְׂרָאֵל בִּרְכַּת כֹּהֲנִים בִּנְשִׂיאוּת כַּפַּיִם לַעֲשׂוֹת נַחַת רוּחַ לְיוֹצְרֵנוּ וּלְהַמְשִׁיךְ שֶׁפַע וּבְרָכָה לְכָל הָעוֹלָמוֹת הַקְּדוֹשִׁים. וִיהִי נֹעַם אֲדֹנָי אֱלֹהֵינוּ עָלֵינוּ וּמַעֲשֵׂה יָדֵינוּ כּוֹנְנָה עָלֵינוּ וּמַעֲשֵׂה יָדֵינוּ כּוֹנְנֵהוּ:

The Kohanim stand on the pulpit after Modim Derabbanan and say:

יְהִי רָצוֹן מִלְּפָנֶיךָ יְהֹוָה אֱלֹהֵינוּ וֵאלֹהֵי אֲבוֹתֵינוּ שֶׁתְּהְיֶה בְּרָכָה זוֹ שֶׁצִּוִּיתָנוּ לְבָרֵךְ אֶת־עַמְּךָ יִשְׂרָאֵל בְּרָכָה שְׁלֵמָה וְלֹא יִהְיֶה בָּהּ מִכְשׁוֹל וְעָוֹן מֵעַתָּה וְעַד עוֹלָם:

Yehi Ratzon Milfaneicha Adonai Eloheinu Velohei Avoteinu Shetihyeh Berachah Zo Shetzivitanu Levarech Et-'Ammecha Yisra'el Berachah Shelemah Velo Yihyeh Vah Michshol Ve'avon Me'attah Ve'ad Olam.

May it be Your Will, Hashem our God, that this blessing which You have commanded us to bless Your people Yisrael with will be a perfect blessing. May there not be in it any stumbling or perverseness from now and forever.

Then they say the blessing. If there is more than one Kohen, the leader calls them, "Kohanim!".

בָּרוּךְ אַתָּה יְהֹוָה אֱלֹהֵינוּ מֶלֶךְ הָעוֹלָם. אֲשֶׁר קִדְּשָׁנוּ בִּקְדֻשָּׁתוֹ שֶׁל־אַהֲרֹן. וְצִוָּנוּ לְבָרֵךְ אֶת־עַמּוֹ יִשְׂרָאֵל בְּאַהֲבָה:

Baruch Attah Adonai Eloheinu Melech Ha'olam Asher Kideshanu Bikdushato Shel-Aharon. Vetzivanu Levarech Et-'Ammo Yisra'el Be'ahavah. Amen.

Blessed are You Hashem our God, King of the universe, Who has sanctified us with the sanctification of Aharon and commanded us to bless His people, Yisrael, with love.

The congregation answers:

אָמֵן:

Amen.

And the Chazan and the Kohanim say after him exactly:

Yevarechecha Adonai Veyishmerecha. יְבָרֶכְךָ יְהֹוָה וְיִשְׁמְרֶךָ:

And answer: Amen **ועונים:** אָמֵן:

Hashem bless you and keep you. **And answer:** Amen

Ya'er Adonai Panav Eleicha Vichuneka. יָאֵר יְהֹוָה | פָּנָיו אֵלֶיךָ וִיחֻנֶּךָּ:

And Answer: Amen **ועונים:** אָמֵן:

Hashem make His countenance shine upon you, and be gracious to you. **And answer:** Amen

Yissa Adonai Panav Eleicha. Veyasem יִשָּׂא יְהֹוָה | פָּנָיו אֵלֶיךָ וְיָשֵׂם

Lecha Shalom. **And answer:** Amen לְךָ שָׁלוֹם: **ועונים:** אָמֵן:

Hashem lift up His countenance towards you and give you peace. **And answer:** Amen

When the Chazan begins the Sim Shalom below, the Kohanim face toward the Ark and say:

רִבּוֹן הָעוֹלָמִים עָשִׂינוּ מַה שֶּׁגָּזַרְתָּ עָלֵינוּ. עֲשֵׂה אַתָּה מַה שֶּׁהִבְטַחְתָּנוּ. הַשְׁקִיפָה מִמְּעוֹן קָדְשְׁךָ מִן־הַשָּׁמַיִם וּבָרֵךְ אֶת־עַמְּךָ אֶת־יִשְׂרָאֵל:

Ribon Ha'olamim Asinu Mah Shegazarta Aleinu. Aseh Attah Mah-Shehivtachetanu. Hashkifah Mime'on Kodshecha Min-Hashamayim. Uvarech Et-'Ammecha Et-Yisra'el.

Sovereign of the universe, We have done what you have decreed for us, you have done as You promised. "Look down from Your holy Habitation, from heaven, and bless Your people Yisrael." **(Deut. 26:15)**

Eloheinu Velohei Avoteinu

If there are no Kohanim, the Chazan recites a substitute blessing:

Eloheinu Velohei Avoteinu.	אֱלֹהֵינוּ וֵאלֹהֵי אֲבוֹתֵינוּ.
Barecheinu Baberachah	בָּרְכֵנוּ בַּבְּרָכָה
Hamshuleshet Batorah	הַמְשֻׁלֶּשֶׁת בַּתּוֹרָה
Haketuvah Al Yedei Mosheh	הַכְּתוּבָה עַל יְדֵי מֹשֶׁה
Avdach. Ha'amurah Mipi	עַבְדָּךְ. הָאֲמוּרָה מִפִּי
Aharon Uvanav Hakohanim Im	אַהֲרֹן וּבָנָיו הַכֹּהֲנִים עַם
Kedosheicha Ka'amur.	קְדוֹשֶׁיךָ כָּאָמוּר:

Our God, God of our fathers, bless us with the threefold blessing written in the Torah by Your servant Moshe, and spoken by the mouth of Aharon and his descendants Your consecrated Kohanim:

Yevarechecha Adonai	יְבָרֶכְךָ יְהוָה
Veyishmerecha. **And answer:** Ken	וְיִשְׁמְרֶךָ: **ועונים:** כֵּן
Yehi Ratzon.	יְהִי רָצוֹן:

Hashem bless you and keep you. **And answer:** May this be His will.

Ya'er Adonai Panav Eleicha	יָאֵר יְהוָה | פָּנָיו אֵלֶיךָ
Vichuneka. **And answer:** Ken Yehi	וִיחֻנֶּךָּ: **ועונים:** כֵּן יְהִי
Ratzon.	רָצוֹן:

Hashem make His countenance shine upon you, and be gracious to you. And answer: May this be His will.

Yissa Adonai Panav Eleicha.	יָאֵר יְהוָה ׀ פָּנָיו אֵלֶיךָ
Veyasem Lecha Shalom.	וְיָשֵׂם לְךָ שָׁלוֹם:
And answer: Ken Yehi Ratzon.	ועונים: כֵּן יְהִי רָצוֹן:

Hashem lift up His countenance towards you and give you peace. And answer: May this be His will.

Vesamu Et-Shemi Al-Benei	וְשָׂמוּ אֶת־שְׁמִי עַל־בְּנֵי
Yisra'el; Va'ani Avarechem.	יִשְׂרָאֵל וַאֲנִי אֲבָרְכֵם:

And they will set My name upon the Children of Yisrael, and I will bless them.

Sim Shalom / Grant Peace

Sim Shalom Tovah Uverachah.	שִׂים שָׁלוֹם טוֹבָה וּבְרָכָה.
Chayim Chein Vachesed	חַיִּים חֵן וָחֶסֶד
Verachamim. Aleinu Ve'al Kol-	וְרַחֲמִים. עָלֵינוּ וְעַל כָּל־
Yisra'el Ammecha. Uvarecheinu	יִשְׂרָאֵל עַמֶּךָ. וּבָרְכֵנוּ
Avinu Kulanu Ke'echad Be'or	אָבִינוּ כֻּלָּנוּ כְּאֶחָד בְּאוֹר
Paneicha. Ki Ve'or Paneicha	פָּנֶיךָ. כִּי בְאוֹר פָּנֶיךָ
Natata Lanu Adonai Eloheinu	נָתַתָּ לָּנוּ יְהוָה אֱלֹהֵינוּ
Torah Vechayim. Ahavah	תּוֹרָה וְחַיִּים. אַהֲבָה
Vachesed. Tzedakah	וָחֶסֶד. צְדָקָה
Verachamim. Berachah	וְרַחֲמִים. בְּרָכָה
Veshalom. Vetov Be'eineicha	וְשָׁלוֹם. וְטוֹב בְּעֵינֶיךָ
Levarecheinu Ulevarech Et-	לְבָרְכֵנוּ וּלְבָרֵךְ אֶת־

Kol-'Ammecha Yisra'el. Berov	כָּל־עַמְּךָ יִשְׂרָאֵל. בְּרֹב
Oz Veshalom.	עֹז וְשָׁלוֹם:

Grant peace, goodness and blessing, a life of grace, and kindness and mercy, to us and to all Yisrael, Your people. And bless us, our Father, all as one with the light of Your countenance; for with the light of Your countenance You have given us, Hashem our God, a Torah and life, love and kindness, righteousness and mercy, blessing and peace. May it be good in Your eyes to bless us and bless all of Your people, Yisrael, with abundant strength and peace.

During the 10 days of repentance (Rosh Hashanah to Yom Kippur) say:

Uvesefer Chayim. Berachah Veshalom.	וּבְסֵפֶר חַיִּים. בְּרָכָה וְשָׁלוֹם.
Ufarnasah Tovah Vishu'ah Venechamah.	וּפַרְנָסָה טוֹבָה וִישׁוּעָה וְנֶחָמָה.
Ugezerot Tovot. Nizacher Venikkatev	וּגְזֵרוֹת טוֹבוֹת. נִזָּכֵר וְנִכָּתֵב
Lefaneicha. Anachnu Vechol Ammecha	לְפָנֶיךָ. אֲנַחְנוּ וְכָל עַמְּךָ
Beit Yisra'el. Lechayim Tovim	בֵּית יִשְׂרָאֵל. לְחַיִּים טוֹבִים
Uleshalom.	וּלְשָׁלוֹם.

May we and all Yisrael Your people be remembered and inscribed before You in the book of life and blessing, peace and prosperity, for a happy life and for peace.

Baruch Attah Adonai	בָּרוּךְ אַתָּה יוּהוּווּהוּ
Hamevarech Et Ammo Yisra'el	הַמְבָרֵךְ אֶת עַמּוֹ יִשְׂרָאֵל
Bashalom. Amen.	בַּשָּׁלוֹם. אָמֵן:

Blessed are You, Hashem, Who blesses His people Yisrael with peace. Amen.

Yihyu Leratzon Imrei-Fi Vehegyon Libi	יִהְיוּ לְרָצוֹן ׀ אִמְרֵי־פִי וְהֶגְיוֹן לִבִּי
Lefaneicha; Adonai Tzuri Vego'ali.	לְפָנֶיךָ יְהוָה צוּרִי וְגֹאֲלִי:

May the words of my mouth and the meditation of my heart find favor before You, Hashem my Rock and my Redeemer.

The chazan's repetition ends here; personal / individual continue:

Elohai. Netzor Leshoni Meira	אֱלֹהַי. נְצֹר לְשׁוֹנִי מֵרָע
Vesiftotai Midaber Mirmah.	וּשְׂפְתוֹתַי מִדַּבֵּר מִרְמָה.
Velimkalelai Nafshi Tidom.	וְלִמְקַלְלַי נַפְשִׁי תִדֹּם.
Venafshi Ke'afar Lakol Tihyeh.	וְנַפְשִׁי כֶּעָפָר לַכֹּל תִּהְיֶה.
Petach Libi Betoratecha.	פְּתַח לִבִּי בְּתוֹרָתֶךָ.
Ve'acharei Mitzvoteicha Tirdof	וְאַחֲרֵי מִצְוֹתֶיךָ תִּרְדֹּף
Nafshi. Vechol-Hakamim Alai	נַפְשִׁי. וְכָל־הַקָּמִים עָלַי
Lera'ah. Meheirah Hafer Atzatam	לְרָעָה. מְהֵרָה הָפֵר עֲצָתָם
Vekalkel Machshevotam. Aseh	וְקַלְקֵל מַחְשְׁבוֹתָם. עֲשֵׂה
Lema'an Shemach. Aseh	לְמַעַן שְׁמָךְ. עֲשֵׂה
Lema'an Yeminach. Aseh	לְמַעַן יְמִינָךְ. עֲשֵׂה
Lema'an Toratach. Aseh Lema'an	לְמַעַן תּוֹרָתָךְ. עֲשֵׂה לְמַעַן
Kedushatach. Lema'an	קְדֻשָּׁתָךְ. לְמַעַן
Yechaletzun Yedideicha;	יֵחָלְצוּן יְדִידֶיךָ
Hoshi'ah Yeminecha Va'aneni.	הוֹשִׁיעָה יְמִינְךָ וַעֲנֵנִי:

My God, guard my tongue from evil, and my lips from speaking deceit. And to those who curse me may my soul be silent; and may my soul be like the dust to all. Open my heart to Your Torah, that my soul may follow after Your commandments. And all that rise to do evil against me, speedily nullify their plan, and spoil their thoughts. Do it for the sake of Your name; do it for the sake of Your right hand; do it for the sake of Your Torah, do it for the sake of Your holiness. That Your beloved may be rescued, save with Your right hand and answer me. **(Ps. 60:7)**

Yihyu Leratzon Imrei-Fi Vehegyon Libi	יִהְיוּ לְרָצוֹן | אִמְרֵי־פִי וְהֶגְיוֹן לִבִּי
Lefaneicha; Adonai Tzuri Vego'ali.	לְפָנֶיךָ יְהֹוָה צוּרִי וְגֹאֲלִי:

May the words of my mouth and the meditation of my heart find favor before You, Hashem my Rock and my Redeemer.

Oseh Shalom

One bows and takes three steps backwards, while still bowing. After three steps, while still bowing and before erecting, while saying, "Oseh Shalom Bimromav", turn one's face to the left, "Hu [Berachamav] Ya'aseh Shalom Aleinu", turn one's face to the right; [face forward and] then bow forward like a servant leaving his master. (SA, OC 123:1)

Oseh Shalom **On the 10 Days of**	עוֹשֶׂה שָׁלוֹם
Repentance: (Hashalom) Bimromav, Hu	בעשי"ת: (הַשָּׁלוֹם) בִּמְרוֹמָיו. הוּא
Berachamav Ya'aseh Shalom	בְּרַחֲמָיו יַעֲשֶׂה שָׁלוֹם
Aleinu, Ve'al Kol-'Ammo Yisra'el,	עָלֵינוּ. וְעַל כָּל־עַמּוֹ יִשְׂרָאֵל.
Ve'imru Amen.	וְאִמְרוּ אָמֵן:

Creator of **On the 10 Days of Repentance:** (the) peace in His high places, may He in His mercy create peace for us and for all Yisrael, and say Amen.

Yehi Ratzon Milfaneicha Adonai	יְהִי רָצוֹן מִלְּפָנֶיךָ יְהֹוָה
Eloheinu Velohei Avoteinu. Shetivneh	אֱלֹהֵינוּ וֵאלֹהֵי אֲבוֹתֵינוּ. שֶׁתִּבְנֶה
Beit Hamikdash Bimheirah Veyameinu.	בֵּית הַמִּקְדָּשׁ בִּמְהֵרָה בְיָמֵינוּ.
Veten Chelkenu Vetoratach La'asot	וְתֵן חֶלְקֵנוּ בְּתוֹרָתֶךָ לַעֲשׂוֹת
Chukkei. Retzonach Ule'avedach	חֻקֵּי רְצוֹנָךְ וּלְעָבְדָךְ
Belevav Shalem.	בְּלֵבָב שָׁלֵם:

May it be Your will, Hashem our God and God of our fathers, that the Beit HaMikdash be speedily rebuilt in our days, and grant us a share in Your Torah so we may fulfill the statutes of your will and serve you with a whole heart.

Avinu Malkeinu / Our Father and King

said during the 10 days of repentance:

אָבִינוּ מַלְכֵּנוּ חָטָאנוּ לְפָנֶיךָ רַחֵם עָלֵינוּ:

Avinu Malkeinu Chatanu Lefaneicha Rachem Aleinu.

Our Father and King, we have sinned before You, have mercy on us.

אָבִינוּ מַלְכֵּנוּ אֵין לָנוּ מֶלֶךְ אֶלָּא אָתָּה:

Avinu Malkeinu Ein Lanu Melech Ella Attah.

Our Father and King, we have no King but You.

אָבִינוּ מַלְכֵּנוּ עֲשֵׂה עִמָּנוּ לְמַעַן שְׁמֶךָ:

Avinu Malkeinu Aseh Imanu Lema'an Shemecha.

Our Father and King, deal with us for Your Name's sake.

אָבִינוּ מַלְכֵּנוּ חַדֵּשׁ עָלֵינוּ שָׁנָה טוֹבָה:

Avinu Malkeinu Chadesh Aleinu Shanah Tovah.

Our Father and King, bring us a new year of good.

אָבִינוּ מַלְכֵּנוּ בַּטֵּל מֵעָלֵינוּ כָּל־גְּזֵרוֹת קָשׁוֹת וְרָעוֹת:

Avinu Malkeinu Battel Me'aleinu Kol-Gezerot Kashot Vera'ot.

Our Father and King, annul all hurtful and evil decrees against us.

אָבִינוּ מַלְכֵּנוּ בַּטֵּל מַחְשְׁבוֹת שׂוֹנְאֵינוּ:

Avinu Malkeinu Battel Machshevot Sone'einu.

Our Father and King, annul the devices of those who hate us.

אָבִינוּ מַלְכֵּנוּ הָפֵר עֲצַת אוֹיְבֵינוּ:

Avinu Malkeinu Hafer Atzat Oyeveinu.

Our Father and King, bring to nothing the hostile design of our enemies.

אָבִינוּ מַלְכֵּנוּ כַּלֵּה כָּל צַר וּמַשְׂטִין מֵעָלֵינוּ:

Avinu Malkeinu Kaleh Kol Tzar Umastin Me'aleinu.

Our Father and King, ward off from us all pain and accusation from us.

אָבִינוּ מַלְכֵּנוּ כַּלֵּה דֶּבֶר וְחֶרֶב וְרָעָה וְרָעָב וּשְׁבִי וּבִזָּה וּמַשְׁחִית וּמַגֵּפָה וְיֵצֶר הָרָע וְחוֹלָאִים רָעִים מִבְּנֵי בְרִיתֶךָ:

Avinu Malkeinu Kaleh Dever Vecherev Vera'ah Vera'av Ushevi Uvizah Umashchit Umagefah Veyetzer Hara Vechola'im Ra'im Mibenei Veritecha.

Our Father and King, ward off pestilence, sword, famine, captivity, disaster, destruction from the children of Your covenant.

אָבִינוּ מַלְכֵּנוּ שְׁלַח רְפוּאָה שְׁלֵמָה לְכָל חוֹלֵי עַמֶּךָ:

Avinu Malkeinu Shelach Refu'ah Shelemah Lechol Cholei Ammecha.

Our Father and King, restore to perfect health the sick of Your people.

אָבִינוּ מַלְכֵּנוּ מְנַע מַגֵּפָה מִנַּחֲלָתֶךָ:

Avinu Malkeinu Mena Magefah Minachalatecha.

Our Father and King, hold back pestilence from Your heritage.

אָבִינוּ מַלְכֵּנוּ זָכוּר כִּי עָפָר אֲנָחְנוּ:

Avinu Malkeinu Zachur Ki Afar Anach'nu.

Our Father and King, remember that we are but dust.

אָבִינוּ מַלְכֵּנוּ מְחוֹל וּסְלַח לְכָל עֲוֹנוֹתֵינוּ:

Avinu Malkeinu Mechol Uselach Lechol Avonoteinu.

Our Father and King, forgive us and pardon all our sins.

אָבִינוּ מַלְכֵּנוּ קְרַע רוֹעַ גְּזַר דִּינֵנוּ:

Avinu Malkeinu Kera Roa Gezar Dinenu.

Our Father and King, repeal the evil decreed against us.

אָבִינוּ מַלְכֵּנוּ מְחוֹק בְּרַחֲמֶיךָ הָרַבִּים כָּל שִׁטְרֵי חוֹבוֹתֵינוּ:

Avinu Malkeinu Mechok Berachameicha Harabbim Kol Shitrei Chovoteinu.

Our Father and King, in Your abundant mercy expunge all record of our guilt.

אָבִינוּ מַלְכֵּנוּ מְחֵה וְהַעֲבֵר פְּשָׁעֵינוּ מִנֶּגֶד עֵינֶיךָ:

Avinu Malkeinu Mecheh Veha'aver Pesha'einu Mineged Eineicha.

Our Father and King, blot out and remove our transgressions from before Your eyes.

אָבִינוּ מַלְכֵּנוּ כָּתְבֵנוּ בְּסֵפֶר חַיִּים טוֹבִים:

Avinu Malkeinu Katevenu Besefer Chayim Tovim.

Our Father and King, inscribe us for good in the Book of Life.

אָבִינוּ מַלְכֵּנוּ כָּתְבֵנוּ בְּסֵפֶר צַדִּיקִים וַחֲסִידִים:

Avinu Malkeinu Katevenu Besefer Tzaddikim Vachasidim.

Our Father and King, inscribe us in the Book of the Righteous and the Pious.

אָבִינוּ מַלְכֵּנוּ כָּתְבֵנוּ בְּסֵפֶר יְשָׁרִים וּתְמִימִים:

Avinu Malkeinu Katevenu Besefer Yesharim Utemimim.

Our Father, Our King, inscribe us in the Book of the Straight and Simple.

אָבִינוּ מַלְכֵּנוּ כָּתְבֵנוּ בְּסֵפֶר פַּרְנָסָה וְכַלְכָּלָה טוֹבָה:

Avinu Malkeinu Katevenu Besefer Parnasah Vechalkalah Tovah.

Our Father, Our King, inscribe us in the Book of Good Income and Sustenance.

אָבִינוּ מַלְכֵּנוּ כָּתְבֵנוּ בְּסֵפֶר מְחִילָה וּסְלִיחָה וְכַפָּרָה:

Avinu Malkeinu Katevenu Besefer Mechilah Uselichah Vechapparah.

Our Father and King, inscribe us in the Book of Pardon and Atonement.

אָבִינוּ מַלְכֵּנוּ כָּתְבֵנוּ בְּסֵפֶר גְּאֻלָּה וִישׁוּעָה:

Avinu Malkeinu Katevenu Besefer Ge'ulah Vishu'ah.

Our Father and King, inscribe us in the Book of Redemption and Deliverance.

אָבִינוּ מַלְכֵּנוּ זָכְרֵנוּ בְּזִכְרוֹן טוֹב מִלְּפָנֶיךָ:

Avinu Malkeinu Zochrenu Bezichron Tov Milfaneicha.

Our Father and King, remember us for good before You.

אָבִינוּ מַלְכֵּנוּ הַצְמַח לָנוּ יְשׁוּעָה בְּקָרוֹב:

Avinu Malkeinu Hatzmach Lanu Yeshu'ah Bekarov.

Our Father and King, make our salvation soon to spring forth.

אָבִינוּ מַלְכֵּנוּ הָרֵם קֶרֶן יִשְׂרָאֵל עַמֶּךָ:

Avinu Malkeinu Harem Keren Yisra'el Ammecha.

Our Father and King, raise up the strength of Your people Yisrael.

אָבִינוּ מַלְכֵּנוּ וְהָרֵם קֶרֶן מְשִׁיחֶךָ:

Avinu Malkeinu Veharem Keren Meshichecha.

Our Father and King, raise up the strength of Your anointed (Messiah).

אָבִינוּ מַלְכֵּנוּ חָנֵּנוּ וַעֲנֵנוּ:

Avinu Malkeinu Chonenu Va'aneinu.

Our Father and King, have grace on us and answer us.

אָבִינוּ מַלְכֵּנוּ הַחֲזִירֵנוּ בִּתְשׁוּבָה שְׁלֵמָה לְפָנֶיךָ:

Avinu Malkeinu Hachazirenu Bitshuvah Shelemah Lefaneicha.

Our Father and King, bring us back through perfect repentance before You.

אָבִינוּ מַלְכֵּנוּ שְׁמַע קוֹלֵנוּ חוּס וְרַחֵם עָלֵינוּ:

Avinu Malkeinu Shema Koleinu Chus Verachem Aleinu.

Our Father and King, hear our voice, take pity on us and be merciful to us.

אָבִינוּ מַלְכֵּנוּ עֲשֵׂה לְמַעַנְךָ אִם לֹא לְמַעֲנֵנוּ:

Avinu Malkeinu Aseh Lema'anach Im Lo Lema'aneinu.

Our Father and King, grant our prayer, if not because of our merit, then for Your own sake.

אָבִינוּ מַלְכֵּנוּ קַבֵּל בְּרַחֲמִים וּבְרָצוֹן אֶת תְּפִלָּתֵנוּ:

Avinu Malkeinu Kabel Berachamim Uveratzon Et Tefillateinu.

Our Father and King, accept our prayer with merciful favor.

אָבִינוּ מַלְכֵּנוּ אַל תְּשִׁיבֵנוּ רֵיקָם מִלְּפָנֶיךָ:

Avinu Malkeinu Al Teshivenu Reikam Milfaneicha.

Our Father and King, turn us not away empty from Your presence.

If Tachanun is not said, say Yehi Shem and continue to the Torah Service, if not then proceed to Tachanun Service.

Yehi Shem

יְהִי שֵׁם יְהֹוָה מְבֹרָךְ מֵעַתָּה וְעַד־עוֹלָם: מִמִּזְרַח־שֶׁמֶשׁ עַד־מְבוֹאוֹ מְהֻלָּל שֵׁם יְהֹוָה: רָם עַל־כָּל־גּוֹיִם | יְהֹוָה עַל הַשָּׁמַיִם כְּבוֹדוֹ: יְהֹוָה אֲדֹנֵינוּ מָה־אַדִּיר שִׁמְךָ בְּכָל־הָאָרֶץ:

Yehi Shem Adonai Mevorach; Me'attah. Ve'ad-'Olam. Mimizrach-Shemesh Ad-Mevo'o; Mehulal. Shem Adonai Ram Al-Chol-Goyim Adonai Al Hashamayim Kevodo. Adonai Adoneinu; Mah-'Adir Shimcha. Bechol-Ha'aretz.

Blessed is the name of Hashem from this time forward and forever. From the rising of the sun to it's going down, Hashem's name is to be praised. Hashem, our Lord, How glorious is Your name in all of the earth. **(Psalms 113:2-4, 8:2)**

Tachanun / Supplication

Tachanun (Supplication) is offered up daily. But none are recited on Shabbatot, Rosh Chodesh (New Moon); Holy Days, and the Moadim (Festivals) of Pesach, Shavuot, Sukkot, Shemini Atzeret and Simchat Torah; the whole month of Nissan; Iyar 14 (Pesach Sheni) and 18 (Lag B'Omer); Sivan 1-12; Av 9 (Tisha B'Av) and 15 (Tu B'Av); the day before Rosh Hashanah; Tishrei 9 to the end of the month; Hanukkah; Shevat 15 - Tu B'Shevat (New Year of Trees); Adar Rishon (1st) and Shevat 14 and 15 (Purim and Shushan Purim), also afternoon on the eve of Shabbat, of Rosh Chodesh, of the Fast of Av, of Hanukkah and of Purim; In Mincha service, it is the day before any of these dates. Also in a house of mourning; when there is a circumcision in the synagogue, or when a bridegroom is in synagogue during the week following his wedding. When Tachanun is not recited, say Yehi Shem (above) and continue to the Torah Reading Section:

Vidui / Confession

Ana Adonai Eloheinu Velohei	אָנָּא יְהֹוָה אֱלֹהֵינוּ וֵאלֹהֵי
Avoteinu. Tavo Lefaneicha	אֲבוֹתֵינוּ. תָּבֹא לְפָנֶיךָ
Tefillateinu. Ve'al Tit'alam	תְּפִלָּתֵנוּ. וְאַל תִּתְעַלַּם
Malkeinu Mitechinateinu.	מַלְכֵּנוּ מִתְּחִנָּתֵנוּ.
She'ein Anachnu Azei Fanim	שֶׁאֵין אֲנַחְנוּ עַזֵּי פָנִים
Ukeshei Oref Lomar Lefaneicha	וּקְשֵׁי עֹרֶף לוֹמַר לְפָנֶיךָ
Adonai Eloheinu Velohei	יְהֹוָה אֱלֹהֵינוּ וֵאלֹהֵי
Avoteinu Tzaddikim Anachnu	אֲבוֹתֵינוּ צַדִּיקִים אֲנַחְנוּ
Velo-Chatanu. Aval Chatanu.	וְלֹא־חָטָאנוּ. אֲבָל חָטָאנוּ.
Avinu. Pasha'nu. Anachnu	עָוִינוּ. פָּשַׁעְנוּ. אֲנַחְנוּ
Va'avoteinu Ve'anshei Veiteinu.	וַאֲבוֹתֵינוּ וְאַנְשֵׁי בֵיתֵנוּ:

Our God and God of our fathers, may our prayer reach you; do not ignore our plea. For we are neither insolent or obstinate to say to you: "Hashem our God and God of our fathers, we are just and have not sinned." Indeed, we and our fathers have sinned and our household.

Ashamnu. Bagadnu. Gazalnu.	אָשַׁמְנוּ. בָּגַדְנוּ. גָּזַלְנוּ.
Dibarnu Dofi Velashon Hara.	דִּבַּרְנוּ דֹפִי וְלָשׁוֹן הָרָע.
He'evinu. Vehirsha'nu. Zadnu.	הֶעֱוִינוּ. וְהִרְשַׁעְנוּ. זַדְנוּ.
Chamasnu. Tafalnu Sheker	חָמַסְנוּ. טָפַלְנוּ שֶׁקֶר
Umirmah. Ya'atznu Etzot Ra'ot.	וּמִרְמָה. יָעַצְנוּ עֵצוֹת רָעוֹת.
Kizavnu. Ka'asnu. Latznu.	כִּזַּבְנוּ. כָּעַסְנוּ. לַצְנוּ.
Maradnu. Marinu Devareicha.	מָרַדְנוּ. מָרִינוּ דְבָרֶיךָ.
Ni'atznu. Ni'afnu. Sararnu.	נִאַצְנוּ. נִאַפְנוּ. סָרַרְנוּ.
Avinu. Pasha'nu. Pagamnu.	עָוִינוּ. פָּשַׁעְנוּ. פָּגַמְנוּ.
Tzararnu. Tzi'arnu Av Va'em.	צָרַרְנוּ. צִעַרְנוּ אָב וָאֵם.
Kishinu Oref. Rasha'nu.	קִשִּׁינוּ עֹרֶף. רָשַׁעְנוּ.
Shichatnu. Ti'avnu. Ta'inu	שִׁחַתְנוּ. תִּעַבְנוּ. תָּעִינוּ
Veti'ata'nu. Vesarnu	וְתִעְתָּעְנוּ. וְסַרְנוּ
Mimitzvoteicha	מִמִּצְוֹתֶיךָ
Umimishpateicha Hatovim Velo	וּמִמִּשְׁפָּטֶיךָ הַטּוֹבִים וְלֹא
Shavah Lanu. Ve'attah Tzaddik	שָׁוָה לָנוּ. וְאַתָּה צַדִּיק
Al Kol Haba Aleinu. Ki Emet	עַל כָּל הַבָּא עָלֵינוּ. כִּי אֱמֶת
Asita. Va'anachnu Hirsha'enu.	עָשִׂיתָ. וַאֲנַחְנוּ הִרְשָׁעְנוּ:

We have trespassed, we have dealt treacherously, we have robbed, we have spoken slander and evil speech, we have committed iniquity, and have done wickedly; we have acted presumptuously, we have committed violence, we have forged falsehood and deceived, we have counseled evil, we have uttered lies, we were angry, we have scoffed, we have rebelled and violated Your words, we have blasphemed, we have committed adultery, we have revolted, we have acted perversely, we have transgressed, we have broken faith, we have been hard and we have distressed father and mother. we have been stiff-necked, we have acted wickedly, we have corrupted, we have done abominably; we have gone astray ourselves, and have caused others to stray; we have also turned aside from Your good precepts and commandments, and it has not profited us; "But You are just concerning all that is come upon us; for You have dealt most truly, but we have done wickedly." **(Nehemiah 9:33)**

The Thirteen Attributes

One, praying alone should not say the Thirteen Attributes in a manner like prayer, petitioning for mercy, because they are words of holiness [and requires a minyan (10 men)]. However, if he says them by merely reading them, he may say them. (SA, OC 565) Ideally one should read with cantillation like from the Torah.

El Erech Apayim Attah Uva'al	אֵל אֶרֶךְ אַפַּיִם אַתָּה וּבַעַל
Harachamim. Gedulat	הָרַחֲמִים. גְּדֻלַּת
Rachameicha Vachasadeicha	רַחֲמֶיךָ וַחֲסָדֶיךָ
Hoda'ta Le'anav Mikedem.	הוֹדַעְתָּ לֶעָנָו מִקֶּדֶם.
Vechein Katuv Betoratach.	וְכֵן כָּתוּב בְּתוֹרָתָךְ.
Vayered Adonai Be'anan.	וַיֵּרֶד יְהֹוָה בֶּעָנָן
Vayityatzev Imo Sham; Vayikra	וַיִּתְיַצֵּב עִמּוֹ שָׁם וַיִּקְרָא
Veshem Adonai. Vesham	בְשֵׁם יְהֹוָה: וְשָׁם
Ne'emar:	נֶאֱמַר:

God, you are slow to anger, and a Master of mercy. Be ever mindful of Your abundant mercy and kindness toward the descendants of Your beloved, as You revealed to humble Moshe of old. As it is written in Your Torah: "And Hashem descended in the cloud, and stood with him there, and proclaimed the name of Hashem." **(Exodus 34:5)** And there it says:

[*] denotes a slight pause between words:

וַיַּעֲבֹר יְהֹוָה | עַל־פָּנָיו וַיִּקְרָא יְהֹוָה *יְהֹוָה אֵל רַחוּם וְחַנּוּן אֶרֶךְ אַפַּיִם
וְרַב־חֶסֶד וֶאֱמֶת: נֹצֵר חֶסֶד לָאֲלָפִים נֹשֵׂא עָוֹן וָפֶשַׁע וְחַטָּאָה וְנַקֵּה:

Vaya'avor Adonai 'Al-Panav Vayikra Adonai * Adonai El Rachum Vechanun; Erech Apayim Verav-Chesed Ve'emet. Notzer Chesed La'alafim. Nosei Avon Vafesha Vechata'ah; Venakeh.

And Hashem passed by before him, and proclaimed: 'Hashem * Hashem, God, merciful and gracious, long-suffering, and abundant in goodness and truth; keeping mercy to the thousandth generation, forgiving iniquity and transgression and sin, and clearing (those who repent).

Rachum Vechanun Chatanu	רַחוּם וְחַנּוּן חָטָאנוּ
Lefaneicha Rachem Aleinu	לְפָנֶיךָ רַחֵם עָלֵינוּ
Vehoshi'enu.	וְהוֹשִׁיעֵנוּ:

Merciful and gracious One, we have sinned before You; have mercy upon us and save us.

Psalms 25

(say while seated)

לְדָוִד אֵלֶיךָ יְהֹוָה נַפְשִׁי אֶשָּׂא: אֱלֹהַי בְּךָ בָטַחְתִּי אַל־אֵבוֹשָׁה
אַל־יַעַלְצוּ אוֹיְבַי לִי: גַּם כָּל־קֹוֶיךָ לֹא יֵבֹשׁוּ יֵבֹשׁוּ הַבּוֹגְדִים רֵיקָם:
דְּרָכֶיךָ יְהֹוָה הוֹדִיעֵנִי אֹרְחוֹתֶיךָ לַמְּדֵנִי: הַדְרִיכֵנִי בַאֲמִתֶּךָ | וְלַמְּדֵנִי
כִּי־אַתָּה אֱלֹהֵי יִשְׁעִי אוֹתְךָ קִוִּיתִי כָּל־הַיּוֹם: זְכֹר־רַחֲמֶיךָ יְהֹוָה
וַחֲסָדֶיךָ כִּי מֵעוֹלָם הֵמָּה: חַטֹּאות נְעוּרַי | וּפְשָׁעַי אַל־תִּזְכֹּר כְּחַסְדְּךָ
זְכָר־לִי־אַתָּה לְמַעַן טוּבְךָ יְהֹוָה: טוֹב־וְיָשָׁר יְהֹוָה עַל־כֵּן יוֹרֶה
חַטָּאִים בַּדָּרֶךְ: יַדְרֵךְ עֲנָוִים בַּמִּשְׁפָּט וִילַמֵּד עֲנָוִים דַּרְכּוֹ: כָּל־אָרְחוֹת
יְהֹוָה חֶסֶד וֶאֱמֶת לְנֹצְרֵי בְרִיתוֹ וְעֵדֹתָיו: לְמַעַן־שִׁמְךָ יְהֹוָה וְסָלַחְתָּ

לַעֲוֺנִי כִּי רַב־הוּא׃ מִי־זֶה הָאִישׁ יְרֵא יְהֹוָה יוֹרֶנּוּ בְּדֶרֶךְ יִבְחָר׃ נַפְשׁוֹ
בְּטוֹב תָּלִין וְזַרְעוֹ יִירַשׁ אָרֶץ׃ סוֹד יְהֹוָה לִירֵאָיו וּבְרִיתוֹ לְהוֹדִיעָם׃
עֵינַי תָּמִיד אֶל־יְהֹוָה כִּי הוּא־יוֹצִיא מֵרֶשֶׁת רַגְלָי׃ פְּנֵה־אֵלַי וְחָנֵּנִי
כִּי־יָחִיד וְעָנִי אָנִי׃ צָרוֹת לְבָבִי הִרְחִיבוּ מִמְּצוּקוֹתַי הוֹצִיאֵנִי׃ רְאֵה
עָנְיִי וַעֲמָלִי וְשָׂא לְכָל־חַטֹּאותָי׃ רְאֵה־אֹיְבַי כִּי־רָבּוּ וְשִׂנְאַת חָמָס
שְׂנֵאוּנִי׃ שָׁמְרָה נַפְשִׁי וְהַצִּילֵנִי אַל־אֵבוֹשׁ כִּי־חָסִיתִי בָךְ׃ תֹּם־וָיֹשֶׁר
יִצְּרוּנִי כִּי קִוִּיתִיךָ׃ פְּדֵה אֱלֹהִים אֶת־יִשְׂרָאֵל מִכֹּל צָרוֹתָיו׃
וְהוּא יִפְדֶּה אֶת־יִשְׂרָאֵל מִכֹּל עֲוֺנֹתָיו׃

Ledavid Eleicha Adonai Nafshi Essa. Elohai. Becha Vatachti Al-'Evoshah; Al-Ya'altzu Oyevai Li. Gam Kol-Koveicha Lo Yevoshu; Yevoshu. Habogedim Reikam. Deracheicha Adonai Hodi'eni; Orechoteicha Lamedeni. Hadricheini Va'amitecha Velamedeni. Ki-'Attah Elohei Yish'i; Otecha Kiviti. Chol-Hayom. Zechor-Rachameicha Adonai Vachasadeicha; Ki Me'olam Hemah. Chatovt Ne'urai Ufesha'ai. Al-Tizkor Kechasdecha Zechor-Li-'Attah; Lema'an Tuvecha Adonai Tov-Veyashar Adonai Al-Ken Yoreh Chata'im Baddarech. Yadrech Anavim Bammishpat; Vilamed Anavim Darko. Chol-'Orchot Adonai Chesed Ve'emet; Lenotzerei Verito. Ve'edotav. Lema'an-Shimcha Adonai Vesalachta La'avoni. Ki Rav-Hu. Mi-Zeh Ha'ish Yerei Adonai Yorenu. Bederech Yivchar. Nafsho Betov Talin; Vezar'o. Yirash Aretz. Sod Adonai Lire'av; Uverito. Lehodi'am. Einai Tamid El-Adonai Ki Hu-Yotzi Mereshet Raglai. Peneh-'Elai Vechoneni; Ki-Yachid Ve'ani Ani. Tzarot Levavi Hirchivu; Mimetzukotai. Hotzi'eni. Re'eh Onyi Va'amali; Vesa. Lechol-Chatovtai. Re'eh-'Oyevai Ki-Rabbu; Vesin'at Chamas Sene'uni. Shomrah Nafshi Vehatzileini; Al-'Evosh. Ki-Chasiti Vach. Tom-Vayosher Yitzeruni; Ki. Kiviticha. Pedeh Elohim Et-Yisra'el; Mikol Tzarotav.

Vehu Yifdeh Et-Yisra'el; Mikol Avonotav:

A Psalm of David. To You, Hashem, do I lift up my soul. Oh my God, in You have I trusted, do not let me be ashamed; do not let my enemies triumph over me. None that wait for You will be ashamed; they will be ashamed that deal treacherously without cause. Show me Your ways, Hashem; teach me Your paths. Guide me in Your truth, and teach me; for You are the God of my salvation; for You do

I wait all day. Remember, Hashem, Your compassions and Your mercies; for they have been from old. Do not remember the sins of my youth, or my transgressions; according to Your mercy remember me, for Your goodness' sake, Hashem. Good and upright is Hashem; therefore He instructs sinners in the way. He guides The humble in justice; and He teaches the humble His way. All the paths of Hashem are mercy and truth to such as keep His covenant and His testimonies. For Your name's sake, Hashem, pardon my iniquity, for it is great. What man is he that fears Hashem? He will instruct him in the way that He should choose. His soul will abide in prosperity; and his seed will inherit the land. The counsel of Hashem is with them that fear Him; and His covenant, to make them know it. My eyes are ever toward Hashem; for He will bring my feet out of the net. Turn to me, and be gracious to me; for I am solitary and afflicted. The troubles of my heart are enlarged; Bring me out of my distresses. See my affliction and my travail; and forgive all my sins. Consider how many are my enemies, and the cruel hatred that they hate me. Keep my soul, and deliver me; let me not be ashamed, for I have taken refuge in You. Let integrity and uprightness preserve me, because I wait for You. Redeem Yisrael, Oh God, out of all his troubles.

And He will redeem Yisrael from all of his troubles. **(Ps. 130:8)**

Mondays and Thursdays, read this section. All other days, some continue to "Yehi Shem", others to Hatzi-Kaddish before the Torah Reading.

יְהֹוָה אֱלֹהֵי יִשְׂרָאֵל שׁוּב מֵחֲרוֹן אַפֶּךָ. וְהִנָּחֵם עַל הָרָעָה לְעַמֶּךָ:

Adonai Elohei Yisra'el Shuv Mecharon Apecha. Vehinachem Al Hara'ah Le'ammecha.

Hashem, God of Yisrael, turn from Your fierce wrath, and repent of this evil against Your people. **(Exodus 32:12)**

Avinu Malkeinu. Avinu Attah.	אָבִינוּ מַלְכֵּנוּ. אָבִינוּ אָתָּה.
Avinu Malkeinu Ein Lanu	אָבִינוּ מַלְכֵּנוּ אֵין לָנוּ
Melech Ella Attah. Avinu	מֶלֶךְ אֶלָּא אָתָּה. אָבִינוּ
Malkeinu Rachem Aleinu. Avinu	מַלְכֵּנוּ רַחֵם עָלֵינוּ: אָבִינוּ
Malkeinu Chonenu Va'aneinu Ki	מַלְכֵּנוּ חָנֵּנוּ וַעֲנֵנוּ כִּי
Ein Banu Ma'asim. Aseh Imanu	אֵין בָּנוּ מַעֲשִׂים. עֲשֵׂה עִמָּנוּ
Tzedakah Vachesed Lema'an	צְדָקָה וָחֶסֶד לְמַעַן
Shimcha Hagadol Vehoshi'enu.	שִׁמְךָ הַגָּדוֹל וְהוֹשִׁיעֵנוּ:
Va'anachnu. Lo Neda Mah-	וַאֲנַחְנוּ לֹא נֵדַע מַה־
Na'aseh. Ki Aleicha Eineinu.	נַּעֲשֶׂה כִּי עָלֶיךָ עֵינֵינוּ:

Our Father and King, You are our Father.
Our Father and King, we have no other sovereign but You.
Our Father and King, have compassion on us.
Our Father and King, be gracious us and answer us.
Though we are lacking in good works, act charitably and graciously with us and save us, for the sake of Your great name. As for us, we do not know what to do, but our eyes are upon You.

זְכֹר־רַחֲמֶיךָ יְהֹוָה וַחֲסָדֶיךָ כִּי מֵעוֹלָם הֵמָּה: יְהִי־חַסְדְּךָ יְהֹוָה עָלֵינוּ כַּאֲשֶׁר יִחַלְנוּ לָךְ: אַל־תִּזְכָּר־לָנוּ עֲוֹנֹת רִאשֹׁנִים מַהֵר יְקַדְּמוּנוּ רַחֲמֶיךָ כִּי דַלּוֹנוּ מְאֹד: עֶזְרֵנוּ בְּשֵׁם יְהֹוָה עֹשֵׂה שָׁמַיִם וָאָרֶץ: חָנֵּנוּ יְהֹוָה חָנֵּנוּ כִּי־רַב שָׂבַעְנוּ בוּז: בְּרֹגֶז רַחֵם תִּזְכּוֹר. בְּרֹגֶז אַהֲבָה תִּזְכּוֹר. בְּרֹגֶז עֲקֵדָה תִּזְכּוֹר. בְּרֹגֶז תְּמִימוּת תִּזְכּוֹר: יְהֹוָה הוֹשִׁיעָה הַמֶּלֶךְ יַעֲנֵנוּ בְיוֹם־קָרְאֵנוּ: כִּי־הוּא יָדַע יִצְרֵנוּ זָכוּר כִּי־עָפָר אֲנָחְנוּ:
עָזְרֵנוּ | אֱלֹהֵי יִשְׁעֵנוּ עַל־דְּבַר כְּבוֹד־שְׁמֶךָ וְהַצִּילֵנוּ וְכַפֵּר עַל־חַטֹּאתֵינוּ לְמַעַן שְׁמֶךָ:

Zechor-Rachameicha Adonai Vachasadeicha; Ki Me'olam Hemah. Yehi-Chasdecha Adonai Aleinu; Ka'asher. Yichalnu Lach. Al-Tizkor-Lanu Avonot Rishonim Maher Yekademunu Rachameicha; Ki

Dallonu Me'od. Ezrenu Beshem Adonai Oseh. Shamayim Va'aretz. Chonenu Adonai Chonenu; Ki-Rav Sava'nu Vuz. Berogez Rachem Tizkor. Berogez Ahavah Tizkor. Berogez Akedah Tizkor. Berogez Temimut Tizkor. Adonai Hoshi'ah; Hamelech. Ya'aneinu Veyom-Kor'enu. Ki-Hu Yada Yitzrenu; Zachur. Ki-'Afar Anachenu. **Ozrenu Elohei Yish'enu. Al-Devar Kevod-Shemecha; Vehatzileinu Vechapeir Al-Chatoteinu. Lema'an Shemecha.**

"Remember, Hashem, Your tender mercies and Your loving-kindnesses: for they have been of old. Let Your loving-kindness, Hashem, be upon us, for our hope is in You. Do not remember against us the iniquities of our ancestors: let Your tender mercies speedily come to meet us; for we are brought very low. Our help is in the name of Hashem, Who made heaven and earth. Be gracious to us; Hashem be gracious to us; for we are fully sated with contempt. In wrath remember to be merciful. For He knows our frame; He remembers that we are dust. **Help us, God of our salvation, for the sake of the glory of Your name; and deliver us, and pardon our sins, for Your name's sake.** **(Ps. 25:6, 33:22, 79:8, 124:8, 123:3, Hab. 3:2, Ps. 20:10, 103:14)**

On days without Tachanun recite Yehi Shem.

Yehi Shem

יְהִי שֵׁם יְהֹוָה מְבֹרָךְ מֵעַתָּה וְעַד־עוֹלָם: מִמִּזְרַח־שֶׁמֶשׁ עַד־מְבוֹאוֹ מְהֻלָּל שֵׁם יְהֹוָה: רָם עַל־כָּל־גּוֹיִם | יְהֹוָה עַל הַשָּׁמַיִם כְּבוֹדוֹ: יְהֹוָה אֲדֹנֵינוּ מָה־אַדִּיר שִׁמְךָ בְּכָל־הָאָרֶץ:

Yehi Shem Adonai Mevorach; Me'attah. Ve'ad-'Olam. Mimizrach-Shemesh Ad-Mevo'o; Mehulal. Shem Adonai Ram Al-Chol-Goyim Adonai Al Hashamayim Kevodo. Adonai Adoneinu; Mah-'Adir Shimcha. Bechol-Ha'aretz.

Blessed is the name of Hashem from this time forward and forever. From the rising of the sun to it's going down, Hashem's name is to be praised. Hashem, our Lord, How glorious is Your name in all of the earth. **(Psalms 113:2-4, 8:2)**

Kaddish Titkabbal

Kaddish is only recited in a minyan (ten men). אמן denotes when the congregation responds "Amen" together out loud. According to the Shulchan Arukh, the congregation says "Yehei Shemeh Rabba" to "Yitbarach" out loud together without interruption, and also that one should respond "Amen" after "Yitbarach." (SA, OC 55,56) This is not the common custom today. Though many are accustomed to answering according to their own custom, it is advised to respond in the custom of the one reciting to avoid not fragmenting into smaller groups. ("Lo Titgodedu" - BT, Yevamot 13b / SA, OC 493, Rema / MT, Avodah Zara 12:15)

יִתְגַּדַּל וְיִתְקַדַּשׁ שְׁמֵהּ רַבָּא. אָמֵן בְּעָלְמָא דִּי בְרָא. כִּרְעוּתֵהּ. וְיַמְלִיךְ מַלְכוּתֵהּ. וְיַצְמַח פֻּרְקָנֵהּ. וִיקָרֵב מְשִׁיחֵהּ. אָמֵן בְּחַיֵּיכוֹן וּבְיוֹמֵיכוֹן וּבְחַיֵּי דְכָל בֵּית יִשְׂרָאֵל. בַּעֲגָלָא וּבִזְמַן קָרִיב. וְאִמְרוּ אָמֵן. אָמֵן יְהֵא שְׁמֵיהּ רַבָּא מְבָרַךְ לְעָלַם וּלְעָלְמֵי עָלְמַיָּא יִתְבָּרַךְ. וְיִשְׁתַּבַּח. וְיִתְפָּאַר. וְיִתְרוֹמַם. וְיִתְנַשֵּׂא. וְיִתְהַדָּר. וְיִתְעַלֶּה. וְיִתְהַלָּל שְׁמֵהּ דְּקֻדְשָׁא. בְּרִיךְ הוּא. אָמֵן לְעֵלָּא מִן כָּל בִּרְכָתָא שִׁירָתָא. תֻּשְׁבְּחָתָא וְנֶחֱמָתָא. דַּאֲמִירָן בְּעָלְמָא. וְאִמְרוּ אָמֵן. אָמֵן

Yitgadal Veyitkadash Shemeh Rabba. Amen Be'alema Di Vera. Kir'uteh. Veyamlich Malchuteh. Veyatzmach Purkaneh. Vikarev Meshicheh. Amen Bechayeichon Uveyomeichon Uvechayei Dechal-Beit Yisra'el. Ba'agala Uvizman Kariv. Ve'imru Amen. Amen Yehei Shemeh Rabba Mevarach Le'alam Ule'alemei Alemaya Yitbarach. Veyishtabach. Veyitpa'ar. Veyitromam. Veyitnasse. Veyit'hadar. Veyit'aleh. Veyit'hallal Shemeh Dekudsha. Berich Hu. Amen Le'ella Min Kol Birchata Shirata. Tushbechata Venechemata. Da'amiran Be'alema. Ve'imru Amen. Amen

Glorified and sanctified be God's great name Amen throughout the world which He has created according to His will. May He establish His kingdom, hastening His salvation and the coming of His Messiah, Amen, in your lifetime and during your days, and within the life of the entire House of Yisrael, speedily and soon; and say, Amen. Amen May His great name be blessed forever and to all eternity. Blessed and praised, glorified and exalted, extolled and honored, adored and lauded is the name of the Holy One, blessed is He, Amen Beyond all the blessings and hymns, praises and consolations that are ever spoken in the world; and say, Amen. Amen

תִּתְקַבַּל צְלוֹתְנָא וּבָעוּתָנָא. עִם צְלוֹתְהוֹן וּבָעוּתְהוֹן דְּכָל בֵּית יִשְׂרָאֵל. קֳדָם אֲבוּנָא דְבִשְׁמַיָּא וְאַרְעָא. וְאִמְרוּ אָמֵן. אָמֵן

Titkabbal Tzelotana Uva'utana. Im Tzelotehon Uva'utehon Dechol Beit Yisra'el. Kodam Avuna Devishmaya Ve'ar'a. Ve'imru Amen. **Amen**

May the prayer and supplication of the whole House of Yisrael be accepted before their Father in heaven, and say, Amen. **Amen**

יְהֵא שְׁלָמָא רַבָּא מִן שְׁמַיָּא. חַיִּים וְשָׂבָע וִישׁוּעָה וְנֶחָמָה. וְשֵׁיזָבָא וּרְפוּאָה וּגְאוּלָה וּסְלִיחָה וְכַפָּרָה וְרֶוַח וְהַצָּלָה לָנוּ וּלְכָל עַמּוֹ יִשְׂרָאֵל. וְאִמְרוּ אָמֵן. אָמֵן

Yehei Shelama Rabba Min Shemaya. Chayim Vesava Vishu'ah Venechamah. Vesheizava Urefu'ah Uge'ulah Uselichah Vechapparah Verevach Vehatzalah Lanu Ulechol Ammo Yisra'el. Ve'imru Amen. **Amen**

May abundant peace descend from heaven, with life and plenty, salvation, solace, liberation, healing and redemption, and forgiveness and atonement, enlargement and freedom, for us and all of God's people Yisrael; and say, Amen. **Amen**

One bows and takes three steps backwards, while still bowing. After three steps, while still bowing and before erecting, while saying, "Oseh Shalom Bimromav", turn one's face to the left, "Hu [Berachamav] Ya'aseh Shalom Aleinu", turn one's face to the right; then bow forward like a servant leaving his master. (SA, OC 123:1)

עוֹשֶׂה שָׁלוֹם בִּמְרוֹמָיו. הוּא בְּרַחֲמָיו יַעֲשֶׂה שָׁלוֹם עָלֵינוּ. וְעַל כָּל־עַמּוֹ יִשְׂרָאֵל. וְאִמְרוּ אָמֵן:

Oseh Shalom Bimromav. Hu Berachamav Ya'aseh Shalom Aleinu. Ve'al Kol-'Ammo Yisra'el. Ve'imru Amen.

Creator of peace in His heights, may He in His mercy create peace for us and for all Yisrael, and say Amen.

On Erev Shabbat we do not recite Psalms 67, but skip to Psalms 93 after. On Chol HaMoed Pesach (Ps. 114), Chol HaMoed Sukkot; Shavuot, and Shemini Atzeret (Ps. 122), and Purim (Ps. 124) some say the appropriate psalm in addition to Tehillim 67. (Pesach and Sukkot are below and Purim is the Psalm right before the Song of the Day section in Shacharit.) On a Fast Day, some also say the appropriate Psalm for the day for Fast Days from the section in Shacharit.

Psalms 67 / Lamnatzeach Binginot)

לַמְנַצֵּחַ בִּנְגִינֹת מִזְמוֹר שִׁיר: אֱלֹהִים יְחָנֵּנוּ וִיבָרְכֵנוּ יָאֵר פָּנָיו אִתָּנוּ סֶלָה: לָדַעַת בָּאָרֶץ דַּרְכֶּךָ בְּכָל־גּוֹיִם יְשׁוּעָתֶךָ: יוֹדוּךָ עַמִּים | אֱלֹהִים יוֹדוּךָ עַמִּים כֻּלָּם: יִשְׂמְחוּ וִירַנְּנוּ לְאֻמִּים כִּי־תִשְׁפֹּט עַמִּים מִישֹׁר וּלְאֻמִּים | בָּאָרֶץ תַּנְחֵם סֶלָה: יוֹדוּךָ עַמִּים | אֱלֹהִים יוֹדוּךָ עַמִּים כֻּלָּם: אֶרֶץ נָתְנָה יְבוּלָהּ יְבָרְכֵנוּ אֱלֹהִים אֱלֹהֵינוּ: יְבָרְכֵנוּ אֱלֹהִים וְיִירְאוּ אוֹתוֹ כָּל־אַפְסֵי־אָרֶץ:

Lamnatzeach Binginot. Mizmor Shir. Elohim. Yechonenu Vivarecheinu; Ya'er Panav Itanu Selah. Lada'at Ba'aretz Darkecha; Bechol-Goyim. Yeshu'atecha. Yoducha Ammim Elohim; Yoducha. Ammim Kulam. Yismechu Viranenu. Le'ummim Ki-Tishpot Ammim Mishor; Ule'ummim Ba'aretz Tanchem Selah. Yoducha Ammim Elohim; Yoducha. Ammim Kulam. Eretz Natenah Yevulah; Yevarecheinu. Elohim Eloheinu. Yevarecheinu Elohim; Veyire'u Oto. Chol-'Afsei-'Aretz.

For the Leader; with string-music. A Psalm, a Song. God be gracious to us, and bless us; May He cause His face to shine toward us; Selah. That Your way may be known upon earth, Your salvation among all nations. Let the peoples give thanks to You, Oh God; Let the peoples give thanks to You, all of them. Let the nations be glad and sing for joy; For You will judge the peoples with equity, And lead the nations upon earth. Selah. Let the peoples give thanks to You, Oh God; Let the peoples give thanks to You, all of them. The earth has yielded her increase; May God, our own God, bless us. May God bless us; And let all the ends of the earth fear Him.

On Friday continue here and say:

Psalms 93

יְהוָה מָלָךְ גֵּאוּת לָבֵשׁ לָבֵשׁ יְהוָה עֹז הִתְאַזָּר אַף־תִּכּוֹן תֵּבֵל בַּל־תִּמּוֹט: נָכוֹן
כִּסְאֲךָ מֵאָז מֵעוֹלָם אָתָּה: נָשְׂאוּ נְהָרוֹת | יְהוָה נָשְׂאוּ נְהָרוֹת קוֹלָם יִשְׂאוּ
נְהָרוֹת דָּכְיָם: מִקֹּלוֹת | מַיִם רַבִּים אַדִּירִים מִשְׁבְּרֵי־יָם אַדִּיר בַּמָּרוֹם יְהוָה:
עֵדֹתֶיךָ | נֶאֶמְנוּ מְאֹד לְבֵיתְךָ נַאֲוָה־קֹדֶשׁ יְהוָה לְאֹרֶךְ יָמִים:

Adonai Malach Ge'ut Lavesh Lavesh Adonai Oz Hit'azar; Af-Tikon Tevel. Bal-Timot. Nachon Kis'acha Me'az; Me'olam Attah. Nase'u Neharot Adonai Nase'u Neharot Kolam; Yis'u Neharot Dochyam. Mikolot Mayim Rabbim. Adirim Mishberei-Yam; Adir Bamarom Adonai Edoteicha Ne'emnu Me'od. Leveitecha Na'avah-Kodesh; Adonai Le'orech Yamim.

Hashem reigns; He is clothed in majesty; Hashem is clothed, He has girded Himself with strength; Yes, the world is established, that it cannot be moved. Your Throne is established from old; You are from everlasting. The floods have lifted up, Hashem, The floods have lifted up their voice; The floods lift up their roaring. Above the voices of many waters, The mighty breakers of the sea, Hashem on high is mighty. Your testimonies are very sure, Holiness becomes Your House, Hashem, forever.

And on Chol HaMoed Pesach say:

Psalms 114

בְּצֵאת יִשְׂרָאֵל מִמִּצְרָיִם בֵּית יַעֲקֹב מֵעַם לֹעֵז: הָיְתָה יְהוּדָה לְקׇדְשׁוֹ יִשְׂרָאֵל
מַמְשְׁלוֹתָיו: הַיָּם רָאָה וַיָּנֹס הַיַּרְדֵּן יִסֹּב לְאָחוֹר: הֶהָרִים רָקְדוּ כְאֵילִים גְּבָעוֹת
כִּבְנֵי־צֹאן: מַה־לְּךָ הַיָּם כִּי תָנוּס הַיַּרְדֵּן תִּסֹּב לְאָחוֹר: הֶהָרִים תִּרְקְדוּ כְאֵילִים
גְּבָעוֹת כִּבְנֵי־צֹאן: מִלִּפְנֵי אָדוֹן חוּלִי אָרֶץ מִלִּפְנֵי אֱלוֹהַּ יַעֲקֹב: הַהֹפְכִי הַצּוּר
אֲגַם־מָיִם חַלָּמִישׁ לְמַעְיְנוֹ־מָיִם:

Betzet Yisra'el Mimitzrayim Beit Ya'akov Me'am Lo'ez. Hayetah Yehudah Lekodsho Yisra'el Mamshelotav. Hayam Ra'ah Vayanos Hayarden Yissov Le'achor. Heharim Rakedu Che'eilim Geva'ot Kivnei Tzon. Mah Lecha Hayam Ki Tanus Hayarden Tissov Le'achor. Heharim Tirkedu Che'eilim Geva'ot Kivnei Tzon. Millifnei Adon Chuli Aretz Millifnei Eloah Ya'akov. Hahofechi Hatzur Agam Mayim Challamish Lema'yeno Mayim.

When Yisrael came forth out of Mitzrayim, The house of Yaakov from a people of strange language; Yehudah became His Sanctuary, Yisrael His dominion. The sea saw it, and fled; The Yarden turned backward. The mountains skipped like rams, The hills like young sheep. What ails you, Oh sea, that you flee? You Yarden, that you turn backward? You mountains, that you skip like rams; You hills, like young sheep? Tremble, earth, at the presence of Hashem, At the presence of the God of Yaakov; Who turned the rock into a pool of water, the flint into a fountain of waters.

And on Chol HaMoed Sukkot; Shavuot, and Shemini Atzeret / Simchat Torah say:

Psalms 122

שִׁיר הַמַּעֲלוֹת לְדָוִד שָׂמַחְתִּי בְּאֹמְרִים לִי בֵּית יְהוָה נֵלֵךְ: עֹמְדוֹת הָיוּ רַגְלֵינוּ
בִּשְׁעָרַיִךְ יְרוּשָׁלָםִ: יְרוּשָׁלַםִ הַבְּנוּיָה כְּעִיר שֶׁחֻבְּרָה־לָּהּ יַחְדָּו: שֶׁשָּׁם עָלוּ
שְׁבָטִים שִׁבְטֵי־יָהּ עֵדוּת לְיִשְׂרָאֵל לְהֹדוֹת לְשֵׁם יְהוָה: כִּי שָׁמָּה | יָשְׁבוּ
כִסְאוֹת לְמִשְׁפָּט כִּסְאוֹת לְבֵית דָּוִד: שַׁאֲלוּ שְׁלוֹם יְרוּשָׁלָםִ יִשְׁלָיוּ אֹהֲבָיִךְ:
יְהִי־שָׁלוֹם בְּחֵילֵךְ שַׁלְוָה בְּאַרְמְנוֹתָיִךְ: לְמַעַן אַחַי וְרֵעָי אֲדַבְּרָה־נָּא שָׁלוֹם בָּךְ:
לְמַעַן בֵּית־יְהוָה אֱלֹהֵינוּ אֲבַקְשָׁה טוֹב לָךְ:

Shir Hama'alot Ledavid Samachti Be'omerim Li Beit Adonai Nelech. Omedot Hayu Ragleinu Bish'arayich Yerushalayim. Yerushalayim Habenuyah Ke'ir Shechuberah Lah Yachdav. Shesham Alu Shevatim Shivtei Yah Edut Leyisra'el Lehodot Leshem Adonai. Ki Shamah Yashevu Chis'ot Lemishpat Kis'ot Leveit David. Sha'alu Shelom Yerushalayim Yishlayu Ohavayich. Yehi Shalom Becheilech Shalvah Be'armenotayich. Lema'an Achai Vere'ai Adaberah Na Shalom Bach. Lema'an Beit Adonai Eloheinu Avakshah Tov Lach.

A Song of Ascents; of David. I rejoiced when they said to me: 'Let us go to the House of Hashem.' Our feet are standing within your gates, Yerushalayim; Yerushalayim, that is built as a city that is compact together; Where the tribes went up, even the tribes of Hashem, as a testimony to Yisrael, to give thanks to the name of Hashem. For there were set thrones for judgment, the thrones of the House of David. Pray for the peace of Yerushalayim; May they that love You prosper. Peace be within your walls, and prosperity within your palaces. For my brothers and companions' sakes, I will now say: 'Peace be within you.' For the sake of the House of Hashem our God I will seek your good.

Kaddish Yehei-Shelama

Kaddish is only recited in a minyan (ten men). אָמֵן denotes when the congregation responds "Amen" together out loud. According to the Shulchan Arukh, the congregation says "Yehei Shemeh Rabba" to "Yitbarach" out loud together without interruption, and also that one should respond "Amen" after "Yitbarach." (SA, OC 55,56) This is not the common custom today. Though many are accustomed to answering according to their own custom, it is advised to respond in the custom of the one reciting to avoid not fragmenting into smaller groups. ("Lo Titgodedu" - BT, Yevamot 13b / SA, OC 493, Rema / MT, Avodah Zara 12:15)

יִתְגַּדַּל וְיִתְקַדַּשׁ שְׁמֵהּ רַבָּא. אָמֵן בְּעָלְמָא דִּי בְרָא. כִּרְעוּתֵהּ. וְיַמְלִיךְ מַלְכוּתֵהּ. וְיַצְמַח פֻּרְקָנֵהּ. וִיקָרֵב מְשִׁיחֵהּ. אָמֵן בְּחַיֵּיכוֹן וּבְיוֹמֵיכוֹן וּבְחַיֵּי דְכָל בֵּית יִשְׂרָאֵל. בַּעֲגָלָא וּבִזְמַן קָרִיב. וְאִמְרוּ אָמֵן. אָמֵן יְהֵא שְׁמֵיהּ רַבָּא מְבָרַךְ לְעָלַם וּלְעָלְמֵי עָלְמַיָּא יִתְבָּרַךְ. וְיִשְׁתַּבַּח. וְיִתְפָּאַר. וְיִתְרוֹמַם. וְיִתְנַשֵּׂא. וְיִתְהַדָּר. וְיִתְעַלֶּה. וְיִתְהַלָּל שְׁמֵהּ דְּקֻדְשָׁא. בְּרִיךְ הוּא. אָמֵן לְעֵלָּא מִן כָּל בִּרְכָתָא שִׁירָתָא. תֻּשְׁבְּחָתָא וְנֶחֱמָתָא. דַּאֲמִירָן בְּעָלְמָא. וְאִמְרוּ אָמֵן. אָמֵן

Yitgadal Veyitkadash Shemeh Rabba. Amen Be'alema Di Vera. Kir'uteh. Veyamlich Malchuteh. Veyatzmach Purkaneh. Vikarev Meshicheh. Amen Bechayeichon Uveyomeichon Uvechayei Dechal-Beit Yisra'el. Ba'agala Uvizman Kariv. Ve'imru Amen. Amen Yehei Shemeh Rabba Mevarach Le'alam Ule'alemei Alemaya Yitbarach. Veyishtabach. Veyitpa'ar. Veyitromam. Veyitnasse. Veyit'hadar. Veyit'aleh. Veyit'hallal Shemeh Dekudsha. Berich Hu. Amen Le'ella Min Kol Birchata Shirata. Tushbechata Venechemata. Da'amiran Be'alema. Ve'imru Amen. Amen

Glorified and sanctified be God's great name **Amen** throughout the world which He has created according to His will. May He establish His kingdom, hastening His salvation and the coming of His Messiah, **Amen**, in your lifetime and during your days, and within the life of the entire House of Yisrael, speedily and soon; and say, Amen. **Amen** May His great name be blessed forever and to all eternity. Blessed and praised, glorified and exalted, extolled and honored, adored and lauded is the name of the Holy One, blessed is He, **Amen** Beyond all the blessings and hymns, praises and consolations that are ever spoken in the world; and say, Amen. **Amen**

יְהֵא שְׁלָמָא רַבָּא מִן שְׁמַיָּא. חַיִּים וְשָׂבָע וִישׁוּעָה וְנֶחָמָה. וְשֵׁיזָבָא וּרְפוּאָה וּגְאוּלָּה וּסְלִיחָה וְכַפָּרָה וְרֶוַח וְהַצָּלָה לָנוּ וּלְכָל עַמּוֹ יִשְׂרָאֵל. וְאִמְרוּ אָמֵן. אָמֵן

Yehei Shelama Rabba Min Shemaya. Chayim Vesava Vishu'ah Venechamah. Vesheizava Urefu'ah Uge'ulah Uselichah Vechapparah Verevach Vehatzalah Lanu Ulechol Ammo Yisra'el. Ve'imru Amen. **Amen**

May abundant peace descend from heaven, with life and plenty, salvation, solace, liberation, healing and redemption, and forgiveness and atonement, enlargement and freedom, for us and all of God's people Yisrael; and say, Amen. **Amen**

One bows and takes three steps backwards, while still bowing. After three steps, while still bowing and before erecting, while saying, "Oseh Shalom Bimromav", turn one's face to the left, "Hu [Berachamav] Ya'aseh Shalom Aleinu", turn one's face to the right; then bow forward like a servant leaving his master. (SA, OC 123:1)

עוֹשֶׂה שָׁלוֹם בִּמְרוֹמָיו. הוּא בְּרַחֲמָיו יַעֲשֶׂה שָׁלוֹם עָלֵינוּ. וְעַל כָּל־עַמּוֹ יִשְׂרָאֵל. וְאִמְרוּ אָמֵן:

Oseh Shalom Bimromav. Hu Berachamav Ya'aseh Shalom Aleinu. Ve'al Kol-'Ammo Yisra'el. Ve'imru Amen.

Creator of peace in His heights, may He in His mercy create peace for us and for all Yisrael, and say Amen.

Aleinu

[*] denotes pausing and then bowing when saying "Va'anachnu Mistachavim".

Aleinu Leshabei'ach La'adon	עָלֵינוּ לְשַׁבֵּחַ לַאֲדוֹן
Hakol. Latet Gedullah Leyotzer	הַכֹּל. לָתֵת גְּדֻלָּה לְיוֹצֵר
Bereshit. Shelo Asanu Kegoyei	בְּרֵאשִׁית. שֶׁלֹּא עָשָׂנוּ כְּגוֹיֵי
Ha'aratzot. Velo Samanu	הָאֲרָצוֹת. וְלֹא שָׂמָנוּ
Kemishpechot Ha'adamah.	כְּמִשְׁפְּחוֹת הָאֲדָמָה.
Shelo Sam Chelkenu Kahem	שֶׁלֹּא שָׂם חֶלְקֵנוּ כָּהֶם
Vegoraleinu Kechal-Hamonam.	וְגוֹרָלֵנוּ כְּכָל־הֲמוֹנָם.
Shehem Mishtachavim Lahevel	שֶׁהֵם מִשְׁתַּחֲוִים לָהֶבֶל
Varik. Umitpallelim El-'El Lo	וָרִיק. וּמִתְפַּלְלִים אֶל־אֵל לֹא
Yoshia. *Va'anachnu	יוֹשִׁיעַ. *וַאֲנַחְנוּ
Mishtachavim Lifnei Melech	מִשְׁתַּחֲוִים לִפְנֵי מֶלֶךְ
Malchei Hamelachim Hakadosh	מַלְכֵי הַמְּלָכִים הַקָּדוֹשׁ
Baruch Hu. Shehu Noteh	בָּרוּךְ הוּא. שֶׁהוּא נוֹטֶה
Shamayim Veyosed Aretz.	שָׁמַיִם וְיוֹסֵד אָרֶץ.
Umoshav Yekaro Bashamayim	וּמוֹשַׁב יְקָרוֹ בַּשָּׁמַיִם
Mima'al. Ushechinat Uzo	מִמַּעַל. וּשְׁכִינַת עֻזּוֹ
Begavehei Meromim. Hu	בְּגָבְהֵי מְרוֹמִים. הוּא
Eloheinu. Ve'ein Od Acher.	אֱלֹהֵינוּ. וְאֵין עוֹד אַחֵר.
Emet Malkeinu Ve'efes Zulato.	אֱמֶת מַלְכֵּנוּ וְאֶפֶס זוּלָתוֹ.
Kakatuv Batorah. Veyada'ta	כַּכָּתוּב בַּתּוֹרָה. וְיָדַעְתָּ
Hayom. Vahasheivota El-	הַיּוֹם וַהֲשֵׁבֹתָ אֶל־
Levavecha Ki Adonai Hu	לְבָבֶךָ כִּי יְהֹוָה הוּא
Ha'elohim. Bashamayim	הָאֱלֹהִים בַּשָּׁמַיִם
Mima'al. Ve'al-Ha'aretz	מִמַּעַל וְעַל־הָאָרֶץ
Mitachat; Ein Od.	מִתָּחַת אֵין עוֹד:

It is our obligation us to praise the Lord of all. To render greatness to the Former of creation. For He has not made us like the nation of the lands, nor set us to be like the families of the earth. Who has not given our portion like theirs and our lot like their masses that bow down to vanity and emptiness, "And pray to a god that does not save." *'But we bow before the supreme King of kings, the Holy One, blessed is He. Who stretches out the heavens and laid the foundations of the earth and his glorious seat is in the heavens above, and the presence of His might in the most exalted of heights. He is our God, there is no other. In truth our King, there is no one except Him. As it is written in the Torah: "This day know and lay it to your heart, that Hashem, He is God in the heavens above and on the earth beneath. There is no one else."

Al Keṇ Nekaveh Lach. Adonai	עַל כֵּן נְקַוֶּה לָּךְ. יְהֹוָה
Eloheinu. Lir'ot Meheirah	אֱלֹהֵינוּ. לִרְאוֹת מְהֵרָה
Betif'eret Uzach. Leha'avir	בְּתִפְאֶרֶת עֻזָּךְ. לְהַעֲבִיר
Gilulim Min Ha'aretz.	גִלּוּלִים מִן הָאָרֶץ.
Veha'elilim Karot Yikaretun.	וְהָאֱלִילִים כָּרוֹת יִכָּרֵתוּן.
Letakken Olam Bemalchut	לְתַקֵּן עוֹלָם בְּמַלְכוּת
Shaddai. Vechol-Benei Vasar	שַׁדַּי. וְכָל-בְּנֵי בָשָׂר
Yikre'u Vishmecha. Lehafnot	יִקְרְאוּ בִשְׁמֶךָ. לְהַפְנוֹת
Eleicha Kol-Rish'ei Aretz. Yakiru	אֵלֶיךָ כָּל-רִשְׁעֵי אָרֶץ. יַכִּירוּ
Veyede'u Kol-Yoshevei Tevel. Ki	וְיֵדְעוּ כָּל-יוֹשְׁבֵי תֵבֵל. כִּי
Lecha Tichra Kol-Berech. Tishava	לְךָ תִכְרַע כָּל-בֶּרֶךְ. תִּשָּׁבַע
Kol-Lashon. Lefaneicha. Adonai	כָּל-לָשׁוֹן. לְפָנֶיךָ. יְהֹוָה
Eloheinu Yichre'u Veyipolu.	אֱלֹהֵינוּ יִכְרְעוּ וְיִפֹּלוּ.
Velichvod Shimcha Yekar Yitenu.	וְלִכְבוֹד שִׁמְךָ יְקָר יִתֵּנוּ.
Vikabelu Chulam Et-'Ol	וִיקַבְּלוּ כֻלָּם אֶת-עֹל

Malchutecha. Vetimloch Aleihem	מַלְכוּתֶךָ. וְתִמְלוֹךְ עֲלֵיהֶם
Meheirah Le'olam Va'ed. Ki	מְהֵרָה לְעוֹלָם וָעֶד. כִּי
Hamalchut Shelecha Hi.	הַמַּלְכוּת שֶׁלְּךָ הִיא.
Ule'olemei Ad Timloch	וּלְעוֹלְמֵי עַד תִּמְלוֹךְ
Bechavod. Kakatuv Betoratach.	בְּכָבוֹד. כַּכָּתוּב בְּתוֹרָתָךְ:
Adonai Yimloch Le'olam Va'ed.	יְהֹוָה ׀ יִמְלֹךְ לְעֹלָם וָעֶד:
Vene'emar. Vehayah Adonai	וְנֶאֱמַר. וְהָיָה יְהֹוָה
Lemelech Al-Kol-Ha'aretz;	לְמֶלֶךְ עַל־כָּל־הָאָרֶץ
Bayom Hahu. Yihyeh Adonai	בַּיּוֹם הַהוּא יִהְיֶה יְהֹוָה
Echad Ushemo Echad.	אֶחָד וּשְׁמוֹ אֶחָד:

Therefore we hope in You, Hashem our God, soon to see Your glorious might, to remove idols from the earth and the non-gods will be wholly cut down, to rectify the world with the kingdom of El Shaddai, and all children of flesh will call on Your name and all of the earth's wicked will turn to You. All that dwell on earth will understand and know that to You every knee must bend, and every tongue swear. Before You, Hashem our God, may all kneel and fall and give honor to Your glorious name. And they will all accept the yoke of Your kingdom. And may You speedily rule over them forever. For dominion is Yours, and forever You will reign in glory, as is written in Your Torah, "Hashem will reign forever and ever." For, it is said, "Hashem will be King over all the earth; on that day Hashem will be One and His name One."

Uvetoratecha Adonai Eloheinu	וּבְתוֹרָתְךָ יְהֹוָה אֱלֹהֵינוּ
Katuv Lemor. Shema Yisra'el;	כָּתוּב לֵאמֹר. שְׁמַע יִשְׂרָאֵל
Adonai Eloheinu Adonai Echad.	יְהֹוָה אֱלֹהֵינוּ יְהֹוָה אֶחָד:

And in Your Torah, Hashem our God, it is written: Hear O Yisrael Hashem our God, Hashem is One.

ARVIT / EVENING PRAYER

The ideal time to pray Arvit is after the emergence of three stars [in a line]. Although many have a custom of starting directly after sundown, one should make sure that the recital of the Shema is after the emergence of the stars. (SA, OC 235) It can be said until about 72 minutes before sunrise.

On the evening of Rosh Chodesh, Barchi Nafshi is recited (Psalms 104, located in the Rosh Chodesh section.) On Chol HaMoed Sukkot, some recite Ps. 42 and 43. Motzaei Shabbat Chol HaMoed Pesach, some recite Ps. 107. On Hanukkah some recite Ps. 30 (below).

On Hanukkah some say:

Psalms 30

מִזְמ֡וֹר שִׁיר־חֲנֻכַּ֖ת הַבַּ֣יִת לְדָוִֽד׃ אֲרוֹמִמְךָ֣ יְ֭הֹוָה כִּ֣י דִלִּיתָ֑נִי וְלֹא־שִׂמַּ֖חְתָּ אֹיְבַ֣י
לִֽי׃ יְהֹוָ֥ה אֱלֹהָ֑י שִׁוַּ֥עְתִּי אֵ֝לֶ֗יךָ וַתִּרְפָּאֵֽנִי׃ יְֽהֹוָ֗ה הֶֽעֱלִ֣יתָ מִן־שְׁא֣וֹל נַפְשִׁ֑י חִ֝יִּיתַ֗נִי
מיורדי (מִיָּֽרְדִי)־בֽוֹר׃ זַמְּר֣וּ לַיהֹוָ֣ה חֲסִידָ֑יו וְ֝הוֹד֗וּ לְזֵ֣כֶר קׇדְשֽׁוֹ׃ כִּ֤י רֶ֨גַע ׀ בְּאַפּוֹ֮
חַיִּ֪ים בִּרְצ֫וֹנ֥וֹ בָּ֭עֶרֶב יָלִ֥ין בֶּ֗כִי וְלַבֹּ֥קֶר רִנָּֽה׃ וַ֭אֲנִי אָמַ֣רְתִּי בְשַׁלְוִ֑י בַּל־אֶמּ֥וֹט
לְעוֹלָֽם׃ יְֽהֹוָ֗ה בִּרְצוֹנְךָ֮ הֶעֱמַ֪דְתָּה לְֽהַרְרִ֫י עֹ֥ז הִסְתַּ֥רְתָּ פָנֶ֗יךָ הָיִ֥יתִי נִבְהָֽל׃ אֵלֶ֣יךָ
יְהֹוָ֣ה אֶקְרָ֑א וְאֶל־אֲ֝דֹנָ֗י אֶתְחַנָּֽן׃ מַה־בֶּ֥צַע בְּדָמִי֮ בְּרִדְתִּ֪י אֶ֫ל שָׁ֥חַת הֲיוֹדְךָ֥ עָפָ֑ר
הֲיַגִּ֥יד אֲמִתֶּֽךָ׃ שְׁמַע־יְהֹוָ֥ה וְחׇנֵּ֑נִי יְ֝הֹוָ֗ה הֱֽיֵה־עֹזֵ֥ר לִֽי׃ הָפַ֣כְתָּ מִסְפְּדִי֮ לְמָח֪וֹל לִ֥י
פִּתַּ֥חְתָּ שַׂקִּ֑י וַתְּאַזְּרֵ֥נִי שִׂמְחָֽה׃ לְמַ֤עַן ׀ יְזַמֶּרְךָ֣ כָ֭בוֹד וְלֹ֣א יִדֹּ֑ם יְהֹוָ֥ה אֱ֝לֹהַ֗י
לְעוֹלָ֥ם אוֹדֶֽךָּ׃

Mizmor Shir-Chanukkat Habayit Ledavid. Aromimcha Adonai Ki Dillitani; Velo-Simachta Oyevai Li. Adonai Elohai; Shiva'ti Eleicha. Vatirpa'eni. Adonai He'elita Min-She'ol Nafshi; Chiyitani. Miyordi-Vor. Zameru L'Adonai Chasidav; Vehodu. Lezecher Kodsho. Ki Rega' Be'appo Chayim Birtzonobba'erev Yalin Bechi. Velaboker Rinah. Va'ani Amarti Veshalvi; Bal-'Emot Le'olam. Adonai Birtzonecha He'emadtah Lehareri Oz Histarta Faneicha. Hayiti Nivhal. Eleicha Adonai Ekra; Ve'el-' Adonai. Etchanan. Mah-Betza Bedami Beridti El Shachat Hayodecha Afar; Hayagid Amitecha. Shema'-Adonai Vechoneni; Adonai Heyeh-'Ozeir Li. Hafachta Mispedi Lemachol Li Pittachta Sakki; Vate'azereini Simchah. Lema'an Yezamercha Chavod Velo Yidom; Adonai Elohai. Le'olam Odeka.

A Psalm; a Song at the Dedication of the House of David. I will extol You, Hashem, for You have raised me up, and have not suffered my enemies to rejoice over me. Hashem my God, I cried to You, and You healed me; Oh Hashem, You brought up my soul from Sheol; You did keep me alive, that I should not go down to the pit. Sing praise to Hashem, His godly ones, and give thanks to His holy name. For His anger is but for a moment, His favor is for a life-time; weeping may come for the night, but joy comes in the morning. Now I had said in my security: 'I will never be moved.' You had established, Hashem, in Your favor my mountain as a stronghold — You hid Your face; I was afraid. To You, Hashem, did I call, and to Hashem I made supplication: 'What profit is there in my blood, when I go down to the pit? Will the dust praise You? Will it declare Your truth? Hear, Hashem, and be gracious to me; Hashem, be my helper.' You turned my mourning into dancing; You loosed my sackcloth, and girded me with gladness; So that my glory may sing praise to You, and not be silent; Hashem my God, I will give thanks to You forever.

Some say before:

לְשֵׁם יִחוּד קוּדְשָׁא בְּרִיךְ הוּא וּשְׁכִינְתֵּיהּ. בִּדְחִילוּ וּרְחִימוּ. וּרְחִימוּ וּדְחִילוּ. לְיַחֲדָא שֵׁם יו״ד קֵ״י בְּוָא״ו קֵ״י בְּיִחוּדָא שְׁלִים (יהוה) בְּשֵׁם כָּל יִשְׂרָאֵל. הנה אנחנו באים להתפלל תפלת ערבית שתקן יעקב אבינו עליו השלום. עם כל המצות הכלולות בה לתקן את שורשה במקום עליון. לעשות נחת רוח ליוצרנו ולעשות רצון בוראנו. וִיהִי נֹעַם אֲדֹנָי אֱלֹהֵינוּ עָלֵינוּ וּמַעֲשֵׂה יָדֵינוּ כּוֹנְנָה עָלֵינוּ וּמַעֲשֵׂה יָדֵינוּ כּוֹנְנֵהוּ:

יְהֹוָה צְבָאוֹת עִמָּנוּ מִשְׂגָּב־לָנוּ אֱלֹהֵי יַעֲקֹב סֶלָה:

Adonai Tzeva'ot Imanu; Misgav-Lanu Elohei Ya'akov Selah.

Hashem of hosts is with us; the God of Yaakov is our high tower. Selah. **(Ps.46:8)**

יְהֹוָה צְבָאוֹת אַשְׁרֵי אָדָם בֹּטֵחַ בָּךְ:

Adonai Tzeva'ot; Ashrei Adam. Boteach Bach.

Hashem of hosts, happy is the man who trusts in You. **(Psalms 84:13)**

יְהֹוָה הוֹשִׁיעָה הַמֶּלֶךְ יַעֲנֵנוּ בְיוֹם־קָרְאֵנוּ:

Adonai Hoshi'ah; Hamelech. Ya'aneinu Veyom-Kare'enu.

Save, Hashem. May the King answer us on the day that we call. **(Psalms 20:10)**

Hatzi-Kaddish / Half Kaddish

Kaddish is only recited in a minyan (ten men). אָמֵן denotes when the congregation responds "Amen" together out loud. According to the Shulchan Arukh, the congregation says "Yehei Shemeh Rabba" to "Yitbarach" out loud together without interruption, and also that one should respond "Amen" after "Yitbarach." (SA, OC 55,56) This is not the common custom today. Though many are accustomed to answering according to their own custom, it is advised to respond in the custom of the one reciting to avoid not fragmenting into smaller groups. ("Lo Titgodedu" - BT, Yevamot 13b / SA, OC 493, Rema / MT, Avodah Zara 12:15)

יִתְגַּדַּל וְיִתְקַדַּשׁ שְׁמֵהּ רַבָּא. אָמֵן בְּעָלְמָא דִּי בְרָא. כִּרְעוּתֵהּ. וְיַמְלִיךְ מַלְכוּתֵהּ. וְיַצְמַח פֻּרְקָנֵהּ. וִיקָרֵב מְשִׁיחֵהּ. אָמֵן בְּחַיֵּיכוֹן וּבְיוֹמֵיכוֹן וּבְחַיֵּי דְכָל בֵּית יִשְׂרָאֵל. בַּעֲגָלָא וּבִזְמַן קָרִיב. וְאִמְרוּ אָמֵן. אָמֵן יְהֵא שְׁמֵיהּ רַבָּא מְבָרַךְ לְעָלַם וּלְעָלְמֵי עָלְמַיָּא יִתְבָּרַךְ. וְיִשְׁתַּבַּח. וְיִתְפָּאַר. וְיִתְרוֹמַם. וְיִתְנַשֵּׂא. וְיִתְהַדָּר. וְיִתְעַלֶּה. וְיִתְהַלָּל שְׁמֵהּ דְּקֻדְשָׁא. בְּרִיךְ הוּא. אָמֵן לְעֵלָּא מִן כָּל בִּרְכָתָא שִׁירָתָא. תֻּשְׁבְּחָתָא וְנֶחֱמָתָא. דַּאֲמִירָן בְּעָלְמָא. וְאִמְרוּ אָמֵן. אָמֵן

Yitgadal Veyitkadash Shemeh Rabba. Amen Be'alema Di Vera. Kir'uteh. Veyamlich Malchuteh. Veyatzmach Purkaneh. Vikarev Meshicheh. Amen Bechayeichon Uveyomeichon Uvechayei Dechal-Beit Yisra'el. Ba'agala Uvizman Kariv. Ve'imru Amen. Amen Yehei Shemeh Rabba Mevarach Le'alam Ule'alemei Alemaya Yitbarach. Veyishtabach. Veyitpa'ar. Veyitromam. Veyitnasse. Veyit'hadar. Veyit'aleh. Veyit'hallal Shemeh Dekudsha. Berich Hu. Amen Le'ella Min Kol Birchata Shirata. Tushbechata Venechemata. Da'amiran Be'alema. Ve'imru Amen. Amen

Glorified and sanctified be God's great name Amen throughout the world which He has created according to His will. May He establish His kingdom, hastening His salvation and the coming of His Messiah, Amen, in your lifetime and during your days, and within the life of the entire House of Yisrael, speedily and soon; and say, Amen. Amen May His great name be blessed forever and to all eternity. Blessed and praised, glorified and exalted, extolled and honored, adored and lauded is the name of the Holy One, blessed is He, Amen Beyond all the blessings and hymns, praises and consolations that are ever spoken in the world; and say, Amen. Amen

Congregation and Chazan:

וְהוּא רַחוּם יְכַפֵּר עָוֹן וְלֹא־יַשְׁחִית וְהִרְבָּה לְהָשִׁיב אַפּוֹ וְלֹא־יָעִיר כָּל־חֲמָתוֹ: יְהֹוָה הוֹשִׁיעָה הַמֶּלֶךְ יַעֲנֵנוּ בְיוֹם־קָרְאֵנוּ:

Vehu Rachum Yechapeir Avon Velo-Yashchit Vehirbah Lehashiv Appo; Velo-Ya'ir. Chol-Chamato. Hashem Hoshi'ah; Hamelech. Ya'aneinu Veyom-Kor'enu.

He, being merciful, forgives iniquity, and does not destroy; frequently He turns His anger away, and does not stir up all of His wrath. Save, Hashem; May the King answer us in the day that we call.

Barechu

Barechu / Call to Prayer is only said with 10 men (minyan).

The Chazan says:

בָּרְכוּ אֶת יְהֹוָה הַמְבֹרָךְ:

Barechu Et Adonai Hamevorach.

Bless Hashem, the blessed One.

The kahal / congregation answers:

בָּרוּךְ יְהֹוָה הַמְבֹרָךְ לְעוֹלָם וָעֶד:

Baruch Adonai Hamevorach Le'olam Va'ed.

Blessed is Hashem Who is blessed for all eternity.

The Chazan says:

בָּרוּךְ יְהֹוָה הַמְבֹרָךְ לְעוֹלָם וָעֶד:

Baruch Adonai Hamevorach Le'olam Va'ed.

Blessed is Hashem Who is blessed for all eternity.

Kriyat Shema Uvirkhotei'a / The Recital of Shema and Blessings

The time for reading the Shema in the evening is from the time three stars appear, and on a cloudy day one should wait until there is no room left for doubt. The time for reading the evening Shema is up to midnight, but if one delayed it until before dawn, his duty is fulfilled. If one found that the congregation had already recited the Shema, and he desires to read the Amidah with them, he may do so, and then after read the Shema with its blessings. (SA)

Ma'ariv Aravim

Baruch Attah Adonai Eloheinu	בָּרוּךְ אַתָּה יְהֹוָה אֱלֹהֵינוּ
Melech Ha'olam. Asher Bidvaro	מֶלֶךְ הָעוֹלָם. אֲשֶׁר בִּדְבָרוֹ
Ma'ariv Aravim Bechochmah.	מַעֲרִיב עֲרָבִים בְּחָכְמָה.
Potei'ach She'arim Bitvunah.	פּוֹתֵחַ שְׁעָרִים בִּתְבוּנָה.
Meshaneh Itim. Umachalif Et-	מְשַׁנֶּה עִתִּים. וּמַחֲלִיף אֶת־
Hazmanim. Umesader Et-	הַזְּמַנִּים. וּמְסַדֵּר אֶת־
Hakochavim	הַכּוֹכָבִים
Bemishmeroteihem Barakia'.	בְּמִשְׁמְרוֹתֵיהֶם בָּרָקִיעַ.
Kirtzono. Borei Yomam Valailah.	כִּרְצוֹנוֹ. בּוֹרֵא יוֹמָם וָלָיְלָה.
Golel Or Mipenei Choshech	גּוֹלֵל אוֹר מִפְּנֵי חֹשֶׁךְ
Vechoshech Mipenei Or.	וְחֹשֶׁךְ מִפְּנֵי אוֹר.
Hama'avir Yom Umevi Lailah.	הַמַּעֲבִיר יוֹם וּמֵבִיא לָיְלָה.
Umavdil Bein Yom Uvein	וּמַבְדִּיל בֵּין יוֹם וּבֵין
Lailah. Adonai Tzeva'ot Shemo.	לָיְלָה. יְהֹוָה צְבָאוֹת שְׁמוֹ:
Baruch Attah Adonai Hama'ariv	בָּרוּךְ אַתָּה יְהֹוָה הַמַּעֲרִיב
Aravim.	עֲרָבִים:

Blessed are You, Hashem our God, King of the universe, At Your word You bring on evening; with Your wisdom You open the gates of the heavens, and with Your understanding You make the cycles of time and progressing seasons. By Your will You set the stars in their watches in the sky. You create both day and night, making darkness recede before light and light before darkness. You make distinction between day and night, causing day to pass away and night to advance, Hashem of hosts is Your name. Blessed are You, Hashem Who brings on evening.

<u>Ahavat Olam</u>

Ahavat Olam Beit Yisra'el	אַהֲבַת עוֹלָם בֵּית יִשְׂרָאֵל
Ammecha Ahaveta. Torah	עַמְּךָ אָהָבְתָּ. תּוֹרָה
Umitzvot Chukkim Umishpatim	וּמִצְוֹת חֻקִּים וּמִשְׁפָּטִים
Otanu Limadta. Al-Ken Adonai	אוֹתָנוּ לִמַּדְתָּ. עַל־כֵּן יְהֹוָה
Eloheinu. Beshachevenu	אֱלֹהֵינוּ. בְּשָׁכְבֵנוּ
Uvekumenu Nasiach	וּבְקוּמֵנוּ נָשִׂיחַ
Bechukkeicha. Venismach	בְּחֻקֶּיךָ. וְנִשְׂמַח
Vena'aloz Bedivrei Talmud	וְנַעֲלוֹז בְּדִבְרֵי תַלְמוּד
Toratecha Umitzvoteicha	תּוֹרָתֶךָ וּמִצְוֹתֶיךָ
Vechukkoteicha Le'olam Va'ed.	וְחֻקּוֹתֶיךָ לְעוֹלָם וָעֶד.
Ki-Hem Chayeinu Ve'orech	כִּי־הֵם חַיֵּינוּ וְאֹרֶךְ
Yameinu. Uvahem Nehgeh	יָמֵינוּ. וּבָהֶם נֶהְגֶּה
Yomam Valailah. Ve'ahavatecha	יוֹמָם וָלָיְלָה. וְאַהֲבָתְךָ
Lo Tasur Mimenu Le'olamim.	לֹא תָסוּר מִמֶּנּוּ לְעוֹלָמִים:
Baruch Attah Adonai Ohev	בָּרוּךְ אַתָּה יְהֹוָה אוֹהֵב
Et-'Ammo Yisra'el.	אֶת־עַמּוֹ יִשְׂרָאֵל:

With love everlasting You have loved the House of Yisrael, Your people. You have taught us Your Torah, and commandments, statutes and judgments; and therefore, Hashem our God, when we lie down and when we rise up, we will speak of Your statutes, rejoicing and delighting in learning the words of Your Torah, and Your commandments and statutes for all time. For they are our life and our length of days, and on them we will meditate by day and by night. May Your love never depart from us forever. Blessed are You, Hashem Who loves His people Yisrael.

LAWS OF RECITING THE SHEMA

One who recites the Shema, but did not have intention during the first verse, 'Shema Yisrael', one did not fulfill their obligation. As for the rest, if they read during the specified time and did not have intention, they have fulfilled their obligation. One should recite the Shema with intention, awe, fear, shaking and trembling. The custom is to place one's hands over their face during the recitation of the first verse in order that one will not look at something else that will prevent him from directing his heart. (SA, OC 59-61)

The Shema

Deuteronomy 6:4-9

One covers their eyes and says:

שְׁמַ֖ע יִשְׂרָאֵ֑ל יְהֹוָ֥ה אֱלֹהֵ֖ינוּ יְהֹוָ֥ה | אֶחָֽד:

Shema Yisrael; Adonai Eloheinu Adonai Echad.

"Hear, O Yisrael, Hashem is our God, Hashem is One."

Whisper silently:

בָּרוּךְ שֵׁם כְּבוֹד מַלְכוּתוֹ לְעוֹלָם וָעֶד:

Baruch Shem Kevod Malchuto Le'olam Va'ed.

Blessed is His name and glorious kingdom forever and ever.

Ve'ahavta

וְאָֽהַבְתָּ֔ אֵ֖ת יְהֹוָ֣ה אֱלֹהֶ֑יךָ בְּכָל־לְבָבְךָ֥ וּבְכָל־נַפְשְׁךָ֖ וּבְכָל־מְאֹדֶֽךָ:
וְהָי֞וּ הַדְּבָרִ֣ים הָאֵ֗לֶּה אֲשֶׁ֨ר אָנֹכִ֧י מְצַוְּךָ֛ הַיּ֖וֹם עַל־לְבָבֶֽךָ: וְשִׁנַּנְתָּ֣ם
לְבָנֶ֔יךָ וְדִבַּרְתָּ֖ בָּ֑ם בְּשִׁבְתְּךָ֤ בְּבֵיתֶ֙ךָ֙ וּבְלֶכְתְּךָ֣ בַדֶּ֔רֶךְ וּֽבְשָׁכְבְּךָ֖

וּבְקוּמֶךָ: וּקְשַׁרְתָּם לְאוֹת עַל־יָדֶךָ וְהָיוּ לְטֹטָפֹת בֵּין עֵינֶיךָ: וּכְתַבְתָּם עַל־מְזֻזוֹת בֵּיתֶךָ וּבִשְׁעָרֶיךָ:

Ve'ahavta Et Adonai Eloheicha; Bechol-Levavecha Uvechol-Nafshecha Uvechol-Me'odecha. Vehayu Hadevarim Ha'eleh. Asher Anochi Metzavecha Hayom Al-Levavecha. Veshinantam Levaneicha. Vedibarta Bam; Beshivtecha Beveitecha Uvelechtecha Vaderech. Uveshochbecha Uvekumecha. Ukeshartam Le'ot Al-Yadecha; Vehayu Letotafot Bein Eineicha. Uchetavtam Al-Mezuzot Beitecha Uvish'areicha.

And you will love Hashem your God with all your heart, and with all your soul, and with all your might. And these words, which I command you this day, will be upon your heart; and your will teach them diligently to your children, and will talk of them when you sit in your house, and when you walk by the way, and when you lie down, and when you rise up. And you will bind them for a sign on your hand, and they will be for frontlets between your eyes. And you will write them on the doorposts of your house, and on your gates.

Vehayah Im-shamoa

וְהָיָה אִם־שָׁמֹעַ תִּשְׁמְעוּ אֶל־מִצְוֹתַי אֲשֶׁר אָנֹכִי מְצַוֶּה אֶתְכֶם הַיּוֹם לְאַהֲבָה אֶת־יְהֹוָה אֱלֹהֵיכֶם וּלְעָבְדוֹ בְּכָל־לְבַבְכֶם וּבְכָל־נַפְשְׁכֶם: וְנָתַתִּי מְטַר־אַרְצְכֶם בְּעִתּוֹ יוֹרֶה וּמַלְקוֹשׁ וְאָסַפְתָּ דְגָנֶךָ וְתִירֹשְׁךָ וְיִצְהָרֶךָ: וְנָתַתִּי עֵשֶׂב בְּשָׂדְךָ לִבְהֶמְתֶּךָ וְאָכַלְתָּ וְשָׂבָעְתָּ: הִשָּׁמְרוּ לָכֶם פֶּן יִפְתֶּה לְבַבְכֶם וְסַרְתֶּם וַעֲבַדְתֶּם אֱלֹהִים אֲחֵרִים וְהִשְׁתַּחֲוִיתֶם לָהֶם: וְחָרָה אַף־יְהֹוָה בָּכֶם וְעָצַר אֶת־הַשָּׁמַיִם וְלֹא־יִהְיֶה מָטָר וְהָאֲדָמָה לֹא תִתֵּן אֶת־יְבוּלָהּ וַאֲבַדְתֶּם מְהֵרָה מֵעַל הָאָרֶץ הַטֹּבָה אֲשֶׁר יְהֹוָה נֹתֵן לָכֶם: וְשַׂמְתֶּם אֶת־דְּבָרַי אֵלֶּה עַל־לְבַבְכֶם וְעַל־נַפְשְׁכֶם וּקְשַׁרְתֶּם אֹתָם לְאוֹת עַל־יֶדְכֶם וְהָיוּ לְטוֹטָפֹת בֵּין עֵינֵיכֶם. וְלִמַּדְתֶּם אֹתָם אֶת־בְּנֵיכֶם לְדַבֵּר בָּם בְּשִׁבְתְּךָ

בְּבֵיתֶךָ וּבְלֶכְתְּךָ בַדֶּרֶךְ וּבְשָׁכְבְּךָ וּבְקוּמֶךָ: וּכְתַבְתָּם עַל־מְזוּזוֹת בֵּיתֶךָ
וּבִשְׁעָרֶיךָ: לְמַעַן יִרְבּוּ יְמֵיכֶם וִימֵי בְנֵיכֶם עַל הָאֲדָמָה אֲשֶׁר נִשְׁבַּע
יְהוָה לַאֲבֹתֵיכֶם לָתֵת לָהֶם כִּימֵי הַשָּׁמַיִם עַל־הָאָרֶץ:

Vehayah Im-Shamoa Tishme'u El-Mitzvotai. Asher Anochi Metzaveh Etchem Hayom; Le'ahavah Et-Adonai Eloheichem Ule'avdo. Bechol-Levavchem Uvechol-Nafshechem. Venatati Metar-'Artzechem Be'ito Yoreh Umalkosh; Ve'asafta Deganecha. Vetiroshecha Veyitzharecha. Venatati Esev Besadecha Livhemtecha; Ve'achalta Vesava'eta. Hishameru Lachem. Pen Yifteh Levavchem; Vesartem. Va'avadtem Elohim Acherim. Vehishtachavitem Lahem. Vecharah Af-Adonai Bachem. Ve'atzar Et-Hashamayim Velo-Yihyeh Matar. Veha'adamah. Lo Titen Et-Yevulah; Va'avadtem Meheirah. Me'al Ha'aretz Hatovah. Asher Adonai Noten Lachem. Vesamtem Et-Devarai Eleh. Al-Levavchem Ve'al-Nafshechem; Ukeshartem Otam Le'ot Al-Yedchem. Vehayu Letotafot Bein Eineichem. Velimadtem Otam Et-Beneichem Ledaber Bam; Beshivtecha Beveitecha Uvelechtecha Vaderech. Uveshochbecha Uvekumecha. Uchetavtam Al-Mezuzot Beitecha Uvish'areicha. Lema'an Yirbu Yemeichem Vimei Veneichem. Al Ha'adamah. Asher Nishba Adonai La'avoteichem Latet Lahem; Kimei Hashamayim Al-Ha'aretz.

And it will come to pass, if you will observe My commandments which I command you this day, to love Hashem your God, and to serve Him with all your heart and with all your soul, that I will give the rain of your land in its season, the former rain and the latter rain, that you may gather in your corn, and your wine, and your oil. And I will give grass in your fields for your cattle, and you will eat and be satisfied. Be cautious, in case your heart is deceived, and you turn aside, and serve other gods, and worship them; and the anger of Hashem is kindled against you, and He shut up the heaven, so that there will be no rain, and the ground will not yield her fruit; and you perish quickly from off the good land which Hashem gives you. Therefore you will lay up these My words in your heart and in your soul; and you will bind them for a sign upon your hand, and they will be for frontlets between your eyes. And you will teach them your children, talking of them, when you sit in your house, and when you walk by the way, and when you lie down, and when you rise up. And you will write them on the doorposts of your house, and on your gates; that your days may be multiplied, and the days of your children, upon the land which Hashem swore to your fathers to give them, as the days of the heavens above the earth. **(Deuteronomy 11:13-21)**

Numbers 15:37-41

וַיֹּאמֶר יְהֹוָה אֶל־מֹשֶׁה לֵּאמֹר: דַּבֵּר אֶל־בְּנֵי יִשְׂרָאֵל וְאָמַרְתָּ אֲלֵהֶם
וְעָשׂוּ לָהֶם צִיצִת עַל־כַּנְפֵי בִגְדֵיהֶם לְדֹרֹתָם וְנָתְנוּ עַל־צִיצִת הַכָּנָף
פְּתִיל תְּכֵלֶת: וְהָיָה לָכֶם לְצִיצִת וּרְאִיתֶם אֹתוֹ וּזְכַרְתֶּם
אֶת־כָּל־מִצְוֹת יְהֹוָה וַעֲשִׂיתֶם אֹתָם וְלֹא־תָתֻרוּ אַחֲרֵי לְבַבְכֶם וְאַחֲרֵי
עֵינֵיכֶם אֲשֶׁר־אַתֶּם זֹנִים אַחֲרֵיהֶם: לְמַעַן תִּזְכְּרוּ וַעֲשִׂיתֶם
אֶת־כָּל־מִצְוֹתָי וִהְיִיתֶם קְדֹשִׁים לֵאלֹהֵיכֶם: אֲנִי יְהֹוָה אֱלֹהֵיכֶם אֲשֶׁר
הוֹצֵאתִי אֶתְכֶם מֵאֶרֶץ מִצְרַיִם לִהְיוֹת לָכֶם לֵאלֹהִים אֲנִי יְהֹוָה
אֱלֹהֵיכֶם: אֱמֶת.

Vayomer Adonai El-Mosheh Lemor. Daber El-Benei Yisra'el Ve'amarta Aleihem. Ve'asu Lahem Tzitzit Al-Kanfei Vigdeihem Ledorotam; Venatenu Al-Tzitzit Hakanaf Petil Techelet. Vehayah Lachem Letzitzit Ure'item Oto Uzechartem Et-Chol-Mitzvot Adonai Va'asitem Otam; Velo-Taturu Acharei Levavchem Ve'acharei Eineichem. Asher-'Attem Zonim Achareihem. Lema'an Tizkeru. Va'asitem Et-Chol-Mitzvotai; Vihyitem Kedoshim Leloheichem. Ani Adonai Eloheichem. Asher Hotzeti Etchem Me'eretz Mitzrayim. Lihyot Lachem Lelohim; Ani Adonai Eloheichem. Emet.

And Hashem spoke to Moshe, saying: Speak to the children of Yisrael, and command them to make tzitzit on the corners of their garments throughout their generations, and that they put a thread of tekhelet with the tzitzit of each corner. And it will be to you for a tzitzit, that you may look upon it, and remember all the commandments of Hashem, and do them; and that you do not go about after your own heart and your own eyes, after which you go whoring; that you may remember and do all My commandments, and be holy to your God. I am Hashem your God, Who brought you out of the land of Mitzrayim, to be your God: I am Hashem your God. It is true.

יְהֹוָה אֱלֹהֵיכֶם אֱמֶת:

Adonai Eloheichem Emet.

Hashem, your God, is true.

Emet Ve'Emunah

Ve'emunah Kol-Zot Vekayam	וֶאֱמוּנָה כָּל־זֹאת וְקַיָּם
Aleinu. Ki Hu Adonai Eloheinu	עָלֵינוּ. כִּי הוּא יְהֹוָה אֱלֹהֵינוּ
Ve'ein Zulato. Va'anachnu	וְאֵין זוּלָתוֹ. וַאֲנַחְנוּ
Yisra'el Ammo. Hapodenu Miyad	יִשְׂרָאֵל עַמּוֹ. הַפּוֹדֵנוּ מִיַּד
Melachim. Hago'alenu Malkeinu	מְלָכִים. הַגּוֹאֲלֵנוּ מַלְכֵּנוּ
Mikaf Kol-'Aritzim. Ha'el Hanifra	מִכַּף כָּל־עָרִיצִים. הָאֵל הַנִּפְרָע
Lanu Mitzareinu. Hamshalem	לָנוּ מִצָּרֵינוּ. הַמְשַׁלֵּם
Gemul Lechol-'Oyevei	גְּמוּל לְכָל־אוֹיְבֵי
Nafshenu. Hassam Nafshenu	נַפְשֵׁנוּ. הַשָּׂם נַפְשֵׁנוּ
Bachayim. Velo Natan Lamot	בַּחַיִּים. וְלֹא נָתַן לַמּוֹט
Raglenu. Hamadricheinu Al	רַגְלֵנוּ. הַמַּדְרִיכֵנוּ עַל
Bamot Oyeveinu. Vayarem	בָּמוֹת אוֹיְבֵינוּ. וַיָּרֶם
Karnenu Al-Kol-Sone'einu. Ha'el	קַרְנֵנוּ עַל־כָּל־שׂוֹנְאֵינוּ. הָאֵל
Ha'oseh Lanu Nekamah	הָעֹשֶׂה לָנוּ נְקָמָה
Befar'oh. Be'otot Uvemofetim	בְּפַרְעֹה. בְּאוֹתוֹת וּבְמוֹפְתִים
Be'admat Benei Cham.	בְּאַדְמַת בְּנֵי חָם.

Hamakeh Ve'evrato Kol-Bechorei
Mitzrayim. Vayotzi Et-'Ammo
Yisra'el Mitocham Lecherut
Olam. Hama'avir Banav Bein
Gizrei Yam-Suf. Ve'et-
Rodefeihem Ve'et-Sone'eihem
Bit'homot Tiba. Ra'u Vanim Et-
Gevurato. Shibechu Vehodu
Lishmo. Umalchuto Veratzon
Kibelu Aleihem. Mosheh Uvenei
Yisra'el Lecha Anu Shirah
Besimchah Rabah. Ve'ameru
Chulam. Mi-Chamochah Ba'elim
Hashem Mi Kamochah Ne'dar
Bakodesh; Nora Tehillot Oseh
Fele. Malchutecha Adonai
Eloheinu Ra'u Vaneicha Al
Hayam. Yachad Kulam Hodu
Vehimlichu Ve'ameru. Adonai
Yimloch Le'olam Va'ed.
Vene'emar. Ki-Fadah Adonai Et-
Ya'akov; Uge'alo Miyad Chazak
Mimenu. Baruch Attah Adonai
Ga'al Yisra'el.

הַמַּכֶּה בְעֶבְרָתוֹ כָּל־בְּכוֹרֵי
מִצְרָיִם. וַיּוֹצִיא אֶת־עַמּוֹ
יִשְׂרָאֵל מִתּוֹכָם לְחֵרוּת
עוֹלָם. הַמַּעֲבִיר בָּנָיו בֵּין
גִּזְרֵי יַם־סוּף. וְאֶת־
רוֹדְפֵיהֶם וְאֶת־שׂוֹנְאֵיהֶם
בִּתְהוֹמוֹת טִבַּע. רָאוּ בָנִים אֶת־
גְּבוּרָתוֹ. שִׁבְּחוּ וְהוֹדוּ
לִשְׁמוֹ. וּמַלְכוּתוֹ בְּרָצוֹן
קִבְּלוּ עֲלֵיהֶם. מֹשֶׁה וּבְנֵי
יִשְׂרָאֵל לְךָ עָנוּ שִׁירָה
בְּשִׂמְחָה רַבָּה. וְאָמְרוּ
כֻלָּם. מִי־כָמֹכָה בָּאֵלִם
יְהֹוָה מִי כָּמֹכָה נֶאְדָּר
בַּקֹּדֶשׁ נוֹרָא תְהִלֹּת עֹשֵׂה
פֶלֶא: מַלְכוּתְךָ יְהֹוָה
אֱלֹהֵינוּ רָאוּ בָנֶיךָ עַל
הַיָּם. יַחַד כֻּלָּם הוֹדוּ
וְהִמְלִיכוּ וְאָמְרוּ. יְהֹוָה |
יִמְלֹךְ לְעֹלָם וָעֶד:
וְנֶאֱמַר. כִּי־פָדָה יְהֹוָה אֶת־
יַעֲקֹב וּגְאָלוֹ מִיַּד חָזָק
מִמֶּנּוּ: בָּרוּךְ אַתָּה יְהֹוָה
גָּאַל יִשְׂרָאֵל:

Trustworthy is all of this, and binding upon us, that He is Hashem our God with none besides Him, and we Yisrael are His people. He redeems us from the hand of kings, our King Who redeems us from the hand of all oppressors. The God Who ransoms us from adversaries, Who brings retribution on all enemies of our souls. "He set our soul in life, And has not allowed our feet to slip." He has guided us upon high places of our enemies, And has raised our strength above all who hated us. The God who performed vengeance on Pharaoh or us by signs and wonders in the land of the sons of Cham. In His wrath He struck all the first-born of Mitzrayim, And brought out His people Yisrael to everlasting freedom. He led His children between the divided Sea of Reeds, and sank their pursuers and enemies in the depths. His children praised His power; they sang gave thanks to His name and with willingly accepted His kingship. Then, to You, Moshe and all the children of Yisrael sang, proclaiming with great joy, "Who is like You, Hashem, among the gods, Who is like You, glorified in holiness, You are awesome in praise, working wonders." By the sea, Hashem our God, Your children beheld Your kingdom; all together they gave thanks to You, proclaiming Your kingship, and it is said, "Hashem will reign forever and ever." And also declared Yirmiyahu, Your prophet, "Hashem will surely redeem Yaakov, And rescue him from the hand of one stronger than him." **(Jeremiah 31:10)** Blessed are You, Hashem Who redeemed Yisrael.

Hashkiveinu

Hashkiveinu Avinu Leshalom.	הַשְׁכִּיבֵנוּ אָבִינוּ לְשָׁלוֹם.
Veha'amidenu Malkeinu	וְהַעֲמִידֵנוּ מַלְכֵּנוּ
Lechayim Tovim Uleshalom.	לְחַיִּים טוֹבִים וּלְשָׁלוֹם.
Uferos Aleinu Sukkat	וּפְרוֹשׂ עָלֵינוּ סֻכַּת
Shelomecha. Vetakenenu	שְׁלוֹמֶךָ. וְתַקְּנֵנוּ
Malkeinu Be'etzah Tovah	מַלְכֵּנוּ בְּעֵצָה טוֹבָה

Milfaneicha. Vehoshi'enu	מִלְּפָנֶֽיךָ. וְהוֹשִׁיעֵֽנוּ
Meheirah Lema'an Shemecha.	מְהֵרָה לְמַֽעַן שְׁמֶֽךָ.
Vehagen Ba'adenu. Vehaseir	וְהָגֵן בַּֽעֲדֵֽנוּ. וְהָסֵר
Me'aleinu Makat Oyev. Dever.	מֵֽעָלֵֽינוּ מַכַּת אוֹיֵב. דֶּֽבֶר.
Cherev. Choli. Tzarah. Ra'ah.	חֶֽרֶב. חוֹלִי. צָרָה. רָעָה.
Ra'av. Veyagon. Umashchit.	רָעָב. וְיָגוֹן. וּמַשְׁחִית.
Umagefah. Shevor Vehaseir	וּמַגֵּפָה. שְׁבוֹר וְהָסֵר
Hasatan Millefaneinu	הַשָּׂטָן מִלְּפָנֵֽינוּ
Ume'achareinu. Uvetzel	וּמֵֽאַֽחֲרֵֽינוּ. וּבְצֵל
Kenafeicha Tastirenu. Ushemor	כְּנָפֶֽיךָ תַּסְתִּירֵֽנוּ. וּשְׁמוֹר
Tzetenu Uvo'enu Lechayim	צֵאתֵֽנוּ וּבוֹאֵֽנוּ לְחַיִּים
Tovim Uleshalom Me'attah Ve'ad	טוֹבִים וּלְשָׁלוֹם מֵֽעַתָּה וְעַד
Olam. Ki El Shomerenu	עוֹלָם: כִּי אֵל שׁוֹמְרֵֽנוּ
Umatzilenu Attah Mikol Davar	וּמַצִּילֵֽנוּ אָֽתָּה מִכָּל דָּבָר
Ra Umipachad Lailah. Baruch	רָע וּמִפַּֽחַד לָֽיְלָה. בָּרוּךְ
Attah Adonai Shomer Et 'Ammo	אַתָּה יְהֹוָה שׁוֹמֵר אֶת עַמּוֹ
Yisra'el La'ad. Amen.	יִשְׂרָאֵל לָעַד אָמֵן.

Our Father, lay us down in peace and raise us up, our King, to a good life and peace. And spread over us Your shelter of peace and direct us with good council before You, our King. And save us speedily for Your name's sake. And guard us and remove from us the strike of an enemy, sword, illness, distress, evil, famine, and misery and corruption and plague. Shelter us in the shadow of Your wings. And guard our going out and our coming in, for a good life and peace now and forever. For You are God, our Guardian and our Deliverer from every evil thing and from dread of the night. Blessed are You, Hashem Who guards His people Yisrael. Amen.

Hatzi-Kaddish

Kaddish is only recited in a minyan (ten men). אמן denotes when the congregation responds "Amen" together out loud. According to the Shulchan Arukh, the congregation says "Yehei Shemeh Rabba" to "Yitbarach" out loud together without interruption, and also that one should respond "Amen" after "Yitbarach." (SA, OC 55,56) This is not the common custom today. Though many are accustomed to answering according to their own custom, it is advised to respond in the custom of the one reciting to avoid not fragmenting into smaller groups. ("Lo Titgodedu" - BT, Yevamot 13b / SA, OC 493, Rema / MT, Avodah Zara 12:15)

יִתְגַּדַּל וְיִתְקַדַּשׁ שְׁמֵהּ רַבָּא. אמן בְּעָלְמָא דִּי בְרָא. כִּרְעוּתֵהּ. וְיַמְלִיךְ מַלְכוּתֵהּ. וְיַצְמַח פֻּרְקָנֵהּ. וִיקָרֵב מְשִׁיחֵהּ. אמן בְּחַיֵּיכוֹן וּבְיוֹמֵיכוֹן וּבְחַיֵּי דְכָל בֵּית יִשְׂרָאֵל. בַּעֲגָלָא וּבִזְמַן קָרִיב. וְאִמְרוּ אָמֵן. אמן יְהֵא שְׁמֵיהּ רַבָּא מְבָרַךְ לְעָלַם וּלְעָלְמֵי עָלְמַיָּא יִתְבָּרַךְ. וְיִשְׁתַּבַּח. וְיִתְפָּאַר. וְיִתְרוֹמַם. וְיִתְנַשֵּׂא. וְיִתְהַדָּר. וְיִתְעַלֶּה. וְיִתְהַלָּל שְׁמֵהּ דְּקֻדְשָׁא. בְּרִיךְ הוּא. אמן לְעֵלָּא מִן כָּל בִּרְכָתָא שִׁירָתָא. תֻּשְׁבְּחָתָא וְנֶחֱמָתָא. דַּאֲמִירָן בְּעָלְמָא. וְאִמְרוּ אָמֵן. אמן

Yitgadal Veyitkadash Shemeh Rabba. Amen Be'alema Di Vera. Kir'uteh. Veyamlich Malchuteh. Veyatzmach Purkaneh. Vikarev Meshicheh. Amen Bechayeichon Uveyomeichon Uvechayei Dechal-Beit Yisra'el. Ba'agala Uvizman Kariv. Ve'imru Amen. Amen Yehei Shemeh Rabba Mevarach Le'alam Ule'alemei Alemaya Yitbarach. Veyishtabach. Veyitpa'ar. Veyitromam. Veyitnasse. Veyit'hadar. Veyit'aleh. Veyit'hallal Shemeh Dekudsha. Berich Hu. Amen Le'ella Min Kol Birchata Shirata. Tushbechata Venechemata. Da'amiran Be'alema. Ve'imru Amen. Amen

Glorified and sanctified be God's great name Amen throughout the world which He has created according to His will. May He establish His kingdom, hastening His salvation and the coming of His Messiah, Amen, in your lifetime and during your days, and within the life of the entire House of Yisrael, speedily and soon; and say, Amen. Amen May His great name be blessed forever and to all eternity. Blessed and praised, glorified and exalted, extolled and honored, adored and lauded is the name of the Holy One, blessed is He, Amen Beyond all the blessings and hymns, praises and consolations that are ever spoken in the world; and say, Amen. Amen

LAWS OF AMIDAH

When one gets up to pray if he was standing outside the Land of Yisrael, he should turn his face toward the Land of Yisrael and focus also on Yerushalayim and the Temple and the Holy of Holies. One should consider oneself as if one is standing in the Beit Hamikdash, and in one's heart, one should be directed upward towards Heaven. One who prays needs to intend in their heart the meaning of the words which are coming out of their mouth. They should think as if the Divine Presence is before them, and remove all distracting thoughts from themselves, until their thoughts and intention are pure in their prayer. (SA, OC 94, 95, 98) These are the blessings at which we bow: in Avot, at the beginning and at the end; in Modim, at the beginning and at the end. Bow at "Baruch" and stand up at Hashem's name. (SA, OC 113,114) One should take three steps forward in the way of coming close and approaching a matter that must be done. (SA, OC 95, Rema)

Amidah / Shemoneh Esrei - Arvit

Take three steps forward and say:

Adonai Sefatai Tiftach; Ufi. Yagid	אֲדֹנָי שְׂפָתַי תִּפְתָּח וּפִי יַגִּיד
Tehilatecha.	תְּהִלָּתֶךָ:

Hashem, open my lips, that my mouth may declare Your praise.

Avot / Fathers

Bow at "Baruch Attah" / "Blessed are You". Raise up at Adonai / Hashem.

Baruch Attah Adonai Eloheinu	בָּרוּךְ אַתָּה יְהֹוָה אֱלֹהֵינוּ
Velohei Avoteinu. Elohei	וֵאלֹהֵי אֲבוֹתֵינוּ. אֱלֹהֵי
Avraham. Elohei Yitzchak.	אַבְרָהָם. אֱלֹהֵי יִצְחָק.
Velohei Ya'akov. Ha'el Hagadol	וֵאלֹהֵי יַעֲקֹב. הָאֵל הַגָּדוֹל
Hagibor Vehanorah. El Elyon.	הַגִּבּוֹר וְהַנּוֹרָא. אֵל עֶלְיוֹן.
Gomel Chasadim Tovim. Koneh	גּוֹמֵל חֲסָדִים טוֹבִים. קוֹנֵה
Hakol. Vezocher Chasdei Avot.	הַכֹּל. וְזוֹכֵר חַסְדֵי אָבוֹת.
Umevi Go'el Livnei Veneihem	וּמֵבִיא גוֹאֵל לִבְנֵי בְנֵיהֶם
Lema'an Shemo Be'ahavah.	לְמַעַן שְׁמוֹ בְּאַהֲבָה:

Blessed are You, Hashem our God and God of our fathers, God of Avraham, God of Yitzchak and God of Yaakov; the great, mighty and revered God, most high God, Who bestows lovingkindness. Master of all things; Who remembers the kindnesses of our fathers, and Who will bring a redeemer to their children's children for the sake of His name in love.

During the 10 days of repentance (Rosh Hashanah to Yom Kippur) add:

Zochrenu Lechayim. Melech Chafetz	זָכְרֵנוּ לְחַיִּים. מֶלֶךְ חָפֵץ
Bachayim. Katevenu Besefer Chayim.	בַּחַיִּים. כָּתְבֵנוּ בְּסֵפֶר חַיִּים.
Lema'anach Elohim Chayim.	לְמַעַנְךָ אֱלֹהִים חַיִּים.

Remember us to life, King who delights in life; inscribe us in the book of life for Your sake, Oh living God.

Bow at "Baruch Attah" / Blessed are You. Raise up at Adonai / Hashem.

Melech Ozeir Umoshia	מֶלֶךְ עוֹזֵר וּמוֹשִׁיעַ
Umagen. Baruch Attah Adonai	וּמָגֵן: בָּרוּךְ אַתָּה יַהֲוַהַ
Magen Avraham.	מָגֵן אַבְרָהָם:

King, Supporter, and Savior and Shield. Blessed are You, Hashem, Shield of Avraham.

Gevurot / Powers

We [in Yisrael] begin to say "mashiv haruach" in the second blessing of the Amidah from the Musaf [Additional] Service of the last day of Sukkot, and conclude at the Musaf [Additional] Service of the first day of Pesach. On the first day of Pesach the congregation still says it in the Musaf Service, but the Reader stops saying it then. In lands outside of Yisrael, we begin to pray for rain in the Arvit (Evening) Service of the sixtieth day after the New Moon of Tishrei, and in Yisrael we begin to say it in the evening of the seventh day of Cheshvan, and it is said until the Afternoon Service on the day preceding the first day of Passover. If one prayed for rain in the summer, or if one omitted to pray for it in the winter, he must repeat the Amidah again. If one said "morid hageshem" in the summer time, he must repeat again from the beginning of the blessing. If he already concluded the blessing, he must read the entire Amidah again. Likewise in the winter, if he omitted it, he must begin all over again. (SA, OC 117)

Attah Gibor Le'olam Adonai.	אַתָּה גִּבּוֹר לְעוֹלָם אֲדֹנָי.
Mechayeh Meitim Attah. Rav	מְחַיֵּה מֵתִים אַתָּה. רַב
Lehoshia.	לְהוֹשִׁיעַ.

You, Hashem, are mighty forever; You revive the dead; You are powerful to save.

B'ketz: Morid Hatal.	**בקיץ:** מוֹרִיד הַטָּל.
B'choref: Mashiv Haruach Umorid	**בחורף:** מַשִּׁיב הָרוּחַ וּמוֹרִיד
Hageshem.	הַגֶּשֶׁם.

In summer: You cause the dew to fall.

In winter: You cause the wind to blow and the rain to fall.

Mechalkel Chayim Bechesed.	מְכַלְכֵּל חַיִּים בְּחֶסֶד.
Mechayeh Meitim Berachamim	מְחַיֵּה מֵתִים בְּרַחֲמִים

Rabim. Somech Nofelim. Verofei	רַבִּים. סוֹמֵךְ נוֹפְלִים. וְרוֹפֵא
Cholim. Umatir Asurim.	חוֹלִים. וּמַתִּיר אֲסוּרִים.
Umekayem Emunato Lishenei	וּמְקַיֵּם אֱמוּנָתוֹ לִישֵׁנֵי
Afar. Mi Chamocha Ba'al	עָפָר. מִי כָמוֹךָ בַּעַל
Gevurot. Umi Domeh Lach.	גְּבוּרוֹת. וּמִי דּוֹמֶה לָּךְ.
Melech Memit Umechayeh	מֶלֶךְ מֵמִית וּמְחַיֶּה
Umatzmiach Yeshu'ah.	וּמַצְמִיחַ יְשׁוּעָה.

You sustain the living with kindness, and revive the dead with great mercy; You support all who fall, and heal the sick; You set the captives free, and keep faith with those who sleep in the dust. Who is like You, Master of power? Who resembles You, Oh King? You bring death and restore life, and cause salvation to flourish.

During the 10 days of repentance (Rosh Hashanah to Yom Kippur) add:

Mi Chamocha Av Harachaman. Zocher	מִי כָמוֹךָ אָב הָרַחֲמָן. זוֹכֵר
Yetzurav Berachamim Lechayim.	יְצוּרָיו בְּרַחֲמִים לְחַיִּים.

Who is like you, merciful Father? In mercy You remember your creatures to life.

Vene'eman Attah Lehachayot	וְנֶאֱמָן אַתָּה לְהַחֲיוֹת
Meitim. Baruch Attah Adonai	מֵתִים: בָּרוּךְ אַתָּה יְהֶוֶה
Mechayeh Hameitim.	מְחַיֵּה הַמֵּתִים:

And You are faithful to revive the dead. Blessed are You, Hashem, Who revives the dead.

Kedushat HaShem / Holiness of the Name

Attah Kadosh Veshimcha	אַתָּה קָדוֹשׁ וְשִׁמְךָ
Kadosh. Ukedoshim Bechol-	קָדוֹשׁ. וּקְדוֹשִׁים בְּכָל־
Yom Yehalelucha Selah. Baruch	יוֹם יְהַלְלוּךָ סֶּלָה: בָּרוּךְ
Attah Adonai Ha' El Hakadosh.	אַתָּה יְהֹוָה הָאֵל הַקָּדוֹשׁ:

You are holy and Your name is holy, and the holy-ones will praise You every day, selah. Blessed are You, Hashem, The Holy God.

During the 10 days of repentance (Rosh Hashanah to Yom Kippur) say:

Hamelech Hakadosh.	הַמֶּלֶךְ הַקָּדוֹשׁ:

The Holy King.

If one is unsure or forgot if they said, repeat the Amidah. If it was immediately said after, it is fulfilled.

Binah / Understanding

Attah Chonen Le'adam Da'at	אַתָּה חוֹנֵן לְאָדָם דַּעַת
Umlamed Le'enosh Binah.	וּמְלַמֵּד לֶאֱנוֹשׁ בִּינָה.
Vechanenu Me'itecha	וְחָנֵּנוּ מֵאִתְּךָ
Chochmah Binah Vada'at.	חָכְמָה בִּינָה וָדָעַת:
Baruch Attah Adonai Chonen	בָּרוּךְ אַתָּה יַהֲוַהֲ חוֹנֵן
Hada'at.	הַדָּעַת:

You favor man with knowledge, and teach mortals understanding. Graciously grant us wisdom, understanding and knowledge from You. Blessed are You, Hashem, gracious Giver of knowledge.

Teshuvah / Repentance

Hashiveinu Avinu Letoratecha.	הֲשִׁיבֵנוּ אָבִינוּ לְתוֹרָתֶךָ.
Vekarevenu Malkeinu	וְקָרְבֵנוּ מַלְכֵּנוּ
La'avodatecha. Vehachazirenu	לַעֲבוֹדָתֶךָ. וְהַחֲזִירֵנוּ
Bitshuvah Shelemah Lefaneicha.	בִּתְשׁוּבָה שְׁלֵמָה לְפָנֶיךָ:
Baruch Attah Adonai Harotzeh	בָּרוּךְ אַתָּה יֱהֱוֶהֱ הָרוֹצֶה
Bitshuvah.	בִּתְשׁוּבָה:

Restore us, our Father, to Your Torah; draw us near, our King, to Your service; cause us to return in perfect repentance before You. Blessed are You, Hashem, Who desires repentance.

Selichah / Forgiveness

Selach Lanu Avinu Ki Chatanu.	סְלַח לָנוּ אָבִינוּ כִּי חָטָאנוּ.
Mechol Lanu Malkeinu Ki	מְחוֹל לָנוּ מַלְכֵּנוּ כִּי
Fasha'enu. Ki El Tov Vesalach	פָּשָׁעְנוּ. כִּי אֵל טוֹב וְסַלָּח
Attah. Baruch Attah Adonai	אָתָּה: בָּרוּךְ אַתָּה יֱהֶוֶה
Chanun Hamarbeh Lisloach.	חַנּוּן הַמַּרְבֶּה לִסְלֹחַ:

Forgive us, our Father, for we have sinned; pardon us, our King, for we have transgressed; for You are a good and forgiving God. Blessed are You, Hashem, Who is gracious and ever forgiving.

Ge'ulah / Redemption

Re'eh Na Ve'aneyenu. Verivah	רְאֵה נָא בְעָנְיֵנוּ. וְרִיבָה
Rivenu. Umaher Lego'aleinu	רִיבֵנוּ. וּמַהֵר לְגָאֳלֵנוּ
Ge'ulah Shelemah Lema'an	גְאוּלָּה שְׁלֵמָה לְמַעַן
Shemecha. Ki El Go'el Chazak	שְׁמֶךָ. כִּי אֵל גּוֹאֵל חָזָק
Attah. Baruch Attah Adonai	אָתָּה: בָּרוּךְ אַתָּה יְהְוְהְ
Go'el Yisra'el.	גּוֹאֵל יִשְׂרָאֵל:

Look upon our affliction and fight our cause; and hasten to redeem us completely for Your name's sake, for You are a strong and redeeming God. Blessed are You, Hashem, Redeemer of Yisrael.

Refuah / Healing

Refa'enu Adonai Venerafe.	רְפָאֵנוּ יְהֹוָה וְנֵרָפֵא.
Hoshi'enu Venivashe'ah. Ki	הוֹשִׁיעֵנוּ וְנִוָּשֵׁעָה. כִּי
Tehillateinu Attah. Veha'aleh	תְהִלָּתֵנוּ אָתָּה. וְהַעֲלֵה
Aruchah Umarpei Lechol-	אֲרוּכָה וּמַרְפֵּא לְכָל־
Tachalu'einu Ulechol-	תַּחֲלוּאֵינוּ וּלְכָל־
Mach'oveinu Ulechol-	מַכְאוֹבֵינוּ וּלְכָל־
Makoteinu. Ki El Rofei Rachman	מַכּוֹתֵינוּ. כִּי אֵל רוֹפֵא רַחְמָן
Vene'eman Attah. Baruch Attah	וְנֶאֱמָן אָתָּה: בָּרוּךְ אַתָּה
Adonai Rofei Cholei Ammo	יהוה רוֹפֵא חוֹלֵי עַמּוֹ
Yisra'el.	יִשְׂרָאֵל:

Heal us, Hashem, and we will be healed; save us and we will be saved; for You are our praise. And bring healing and a cure to all of our ailments and wounds; for You are the faithful and merciful God Who heals. Blessed are You, Hashem, Who heals the sick of Your people Yisrael.

Birkat HaShanim / Blessing for the Years

In Summer:	בקיץ:
Barecheinu Adonai Eloheinu	בָּרְכֵנוּ יְהֹוָה אֱלֹהֵינוּ
Bechol-Ma'asei Yadeinu.	בְּכָל־מַעֲשֵׂי יָדֵינוּ.
Uvarech Shenateinu Betalelei	וּבָרֵךְ שְׁנָתֵנוּ בְּטַלְלֵי
Ratzon Berachah Unedavah.	רָצוֹן בְּרָכָה וּנְדָבָה.
Utehi Acharitah Chayim Vesava	וּתְהִי אַחֲרִיתָהּ חַיִּים וְשָׂבָע
Veshalom Kashanim Hatovot	וְשָׁלוֹם כַּשָּׁנִים הַטּוֹבוֹת
Livrachah. Ki El Tov Umeitiv	לִבְרָכָה. כִּי אֵל טוֹב וּמֵטִיב

Attah Umevarech Hashanim.	אַתָּה וּמְבָרֵךְ הַשָּׁנִים:
Baruch Attah Adonai Mevarech	בָּרוּךְ אַתָּה יְהוָה מְבָרֵךְ
Hashanim.	הַשָּׁנִים:

Bless us, our Father, in all the work of our hands, and bless our year with favoring dews of blessing and abundance. May it's result be life, plenty and satisfaction and peace like the good years which You have blessed. For You, God, are good and You do good, blessing the years. Blessed are You, Hashem Who blesses the years.

In Winter:	**בחורף:**
Barech Aleinu Adonai Eloheinu	בָּרֵךְ עָלֵינוּ יְהוָה אֱלֹהֵינוּ
Et-Hashanah Hazot Ve'et-Kol-	אֶת־הַשָּׁנָה הַזֹּאת וְאֶת־כָּל־
Minei Tevu'atah Letovah. Veten	מִינֵי תְבוּאָתָהּ לְטוֹבָה. וְתֵן
Tal Umatar Livrachah Al Kol-	טַל וּמָטָר לִבְרָכָה עַל כָּל־
Penei Ha'adamah. Veraveh Penei	פְּנֵי הָאֲדָמָה. וְרַוֵּה פְּנֵי
Tevel Vesabba Et-Ha'olam Kulo	תֵבֵל וְשַׂבַּע אֶת־הָעוֹלָם כֻּלּוֹ
Mituvach. Umalei Yadeinu	מִטּוּבָךְ. וּמַלֵּא יָדֵינוּ
Mibirchoteicha Ume'osher	מִבִּרְכוֹתֶיךָ וּמֵעֹשֶׁר
Mattenot Yadeicha. Shamerah	מַתְּנוֹת יָדֶיךָ. שָׁמְרָה
Vehatzilah Shanah Zo Mikol-	וְהַצִּילָה שָׁנָה זוֹ מִכָּל־
Davar Ra'. Umikal-Minei	דָּבָר רָע. וּמִכָּל־מִינֵי
Mashchit Umikal-Minei Fur'anut.	מַשְׁחִית וּמִכָּל־מִינֵי פֻרְעָנוּת.
Va'aseh Lah Tikvah Tovah	וַעֲשֵׂה לָהּ תִּקְוָה טוֹבָה
Ve'acharit Shalom. Chus	וְאַחֲרִית שָׁלוֹם. חוּס
Verachem Aleiha Ve'al Kol-	וְרַחֵם עָלֶיהָ וְעַל כָּל־
Tevu'atah Ufeiroteiha.	תְּבוּאָתָהּ וּפֵירוֹתֶיהָ.
Uvarechah Begishmei Ratzon	וּבָרְכָהּ בְּגִשְׁמֵי רָצוֹן

Berachah Unedavah. Utehi	בְּרָכָה וּנְדָבָה. וּתְהִי
Acharitah Chayim Vesava	אַחֲרִיתָהּ חַיִּים וְשָׂבָע
Veshalom. Kashanim Hatovot	וְשָׁלוֹם. כַּשָּׁנִים הַטּוֹבוֹת
Livrachah. Ki El Tov Umeitiv	לִבְרָכָה. כִּי אֵל טוֹב וּמֵטִיב
Attah Umevarech Hashanim.	אַתָּה וּמְבָרֵךְ הַשָּׁנִים.
Baruch Attah Adonai Mevarech	בָּרוּךְ אַתָּה יְהֹוָה מְבָרֵךְ
Hashanim.	הַשָּׁנִים:

Hashem our God, bless for us this year with all its varied produce, for good. Send dew and rain to bless the face of the entire earth, and water the surface of the earth, and satisfy the whole world with Your goodness. Fill our hands with Your blessings and the rich gifts of Your hands. Guard and deliver this year from all evil, and from all disaster and from all chaos, and make it a year of good hope and a peaceful ending. Have pity and compassion on this year and all its increase and fruits. Bless the year with rains of favor, blessing and generosity, and may its end be life, satisfaction and peace, like the good years which You have blessed. For You God, are good and You do good, blessing the years. Blessed are You, Hashem Who blesses the years.

Galuyot / Ingathering of Exiles

Teka Beshofar Gadol	תְּקַע בְּשׁוֹפָר גָּדוֹל
Lecheruteinu. Vesa Nes	לְחֵרוּתֵנוּ. וְשָׂא נֵס
Lekabetz Galyoteinu.	לְקַבֵּץ גָּלֻיּוֹתֵינוּ.
Vekabetzeinu Yachad Me'arba	וְקַבְּצֵנוּ יַחַד מֵאַרְבַּע
Kanfot Ha'aretz Le'artzenu.	כַּנְפוֹת הָאָרֶץ לְאַרְצֵנוּ:
Baruch Attah Adonai Mekabetz	בָּרוּךְ אַתָּה יְהֹוָה מְקַבֵּץ
Nidchei Ammo Yisra'el.	נִדְחֵי עַמּוֹ יִשְׂרָאֵל:

Sound the great shofar for our freedom; lift up the banner to bring our exiles; And gather us together from the four corners of the earth into our land. Blessed are You, Hashem, Who gathers the dispersed of His people Yisrael.

Birkat HaDin / Restoration of Justice

Hashivah Shofeteinu	הָשִׁיבָה שׁוֹפְטֵינוּ
Kevarishonah. Veyo'atzeinu	כְּבָרִאשׁוֹנָה. וְיוֹעֲצֵינוּ
Kevatechillah. Vehaseir Mimenu	כְּבַתְּחִלָּה. וְהָסֵר מִמֶּנּוּ
Yagon Va'anachah. Umeloch	יָגוֹן וַאֲנָחָה. וּמְלוֹךְ
Aleinu Meheirah Attah Adonai	עָלֵינוּ מְהֵרָה אַתָּה יְהֹוָה
Levadecha. Bechesed	לְבַדְּךָ. בְּחֶסֶד
Uverachamim. Betzedek	וּבְרַחֲמִים. בְּצֶדֶק
Uvemishpat. Baruch Attah	וּבְמִשְׁפָּט: בָּרוּךְ אַתָּה
Adonai Melech Ohev Tzedakah	יוּהוּווּהוּ מֶלֶךְ אוֹהֵב צְדָקָה
Umishpat.	וּמִשְׁפָּט:

Restore our judges as at first, and our counselors as at the beginning; remove from us sorrow and sighing; reign over us speedily, Hashem, You alone in kindness and mercy; and with righteousness and with justice. Blessed are You, Hashem, King who loves righteousness and justice.

During the 10 days of repentance (Rosh Hashanah to Yom Kippur) say:

Hamelech Hamishpat.	הַמֶּלֶךְ הַמִּשְׁפָּט:

The King, The Judge.

Birkat HaMinim / Blessing Against the Heretics

Laminim Velamalshinim Al-Tehi	לַמִּינִים וְלַמַּלְשִׁינִים אַל־תְּהִי
Tikvah. Vechol-Hazeidim	תִקְוָה. וְכָל־הַזֵּדִים
Kerega Yovedu.	כְּרֶגַע יֹאבֵדוּ.
Vechol-'Oyeveicha Vechol-	וְכָל־אוֹיְבֶיךָ וְכָל־
Sone'eicha Meheirah Yikaretu.	שׂוֹנְאֶיךָ מְהֵרָה יִכָּרֵתוּ.
Umalchut Harish'ah Meheirah	וּמַלְכוּת הָרִשְׁעָה מְהֵרָה
Te'akeir Uteshaber Utechalem	תְעַקֵּר וּתְשַׁבֵּר וּתְכַלֵּם
Vetachni'em Bimheirah	וְתַכְנִיעֵם בִּמְהֵרָה
Veyameinu. Baruch Attah	בְיָמֵינוּ: בָּרוּךְ אַתָּה
Adonai Shoveir Oyevim	יְהֹוָה שׁוֹבֵר אוֹיְבִים
Umachnia Zeidim. **(Minim)**	וּמַכְנִיעַ זֵדִים: (מִינִים)

For the heretics and the slanderers let there be no hope, and all of the arrogant disappear in an instant. May all of Your enemies and all of those who hate You quickly be cut off, and the evil government uprooted, and broken, and humbled and subdued quickly in our days. Blessed are You, Hashem, Who breaks enemies and subdues the arrogant. **(heretics)**

Tzaddikim / The Righteous

Al Hatzaddikim Ve'al	עַל הַצַּדִּיקִים וְעַל
Hachasidim. Ve'al She'erit	הַחֲסִידִים. וְעַל שְׁאֵרִית
Ammecha Beit Yisra'el. Ve'al	עַמְּךָ בֵּית יִשְׂרָאֵל. וְעַל
Peleitat Beit Sofereihem. Ve'al	פְּלֵיטַת בֵּית סוֹפְרֵיהֶם. וְעַל
Gerei Hatzedek Ve'aleinu.	גֵּרֵי הַצֶּדֶק וְעָלֵינוּ.
Yehemu Na Rachameicha.	יֶהֱמוּ נָא רַחֲמֶיךָ.
Adonai Eloheinu. Veten Sachar	יְהֹוָה אֱלֹהֵינוּ. וְתֵן שָׂכָר

Tov Lechol-Habotechim	טוֹב לְכָל־הַבּוֹטְחִים
Beshimcha Be'emet. Vesim	בְּשִׁמְךָ בֶּאֱמֶת. וְשִׂים
Chelkenu Imahem. Ule'olam Lo	חֶלְקֵנוּ עִמָּהֶם. וּלְעוֹלָם לֹא
Nevosh Ki Vecha Vatachenu.	נֵבוֹשׁ כִּי בְךָ בָטָחְנוּ.
Ve'al Chasdecha Hagadol	וְעַל חַסְדְּךָ הַגָּדוֹל
Be'emet Nish'aneinu. Baruch	בֶּאֱמֶת נִשְׁעָנְנוּ: בָּרוּךְ
Attah Adonai Mish'an Umivtach	אַתָּה יוהוווהו מִשְׁעָן וּמִבְטָח
Latzaddikim.	לַצַּדִּיקִים:

On the righteous and on the pious and on the remainders of Your people, the House of Yisrael, and over the remnant of their scribes; over the righteous converts and over us may Your mercy be aroused. Hashem our God, Grant a good reward to all who truly trust in Your name, and place our portion among them; may we never come to shame, for in You we trust and on Your great kindness we faithfully rely. Blessed are You, Hashem, the support and trust of the righteous.

Boneh Yerushalayim / Builder of Yerushalayim

Tishkon Betoch Yerushalayim	תִּשְׁכּוֹן בְּתוֹךְ יְרוּשָׁלַיִם
Irecha Ka'asher Dibarta.	עִירְךָ כַּאֲשֶׁר דִּבַּרְתָּ.
Vechisei David Avdecha	וְכִסֵּא דָוִד עַבְדְּךָ
Meheirah Betochah Tachin.	מְהֵרָה בְּתוֹכָהּ תָּכִין.
Uveneh Otah Binyan Olam	וּבְנֵה אוֹתָהּ בִּנְיַן עוֹלָם
Bimheirah Veyameinu. Baruch	בִּמְהֵרָה בְיָמֵינוּ: בָּרוּךְ
Attah Adonai Boneh	אַתָּה יְהֶוָהֶ בּוֹנֵה
Yerushalayim.	יְרוּשָׁלָיִם:

May Your presence dwell in Yerushalayim, Your city, as You have promised; establish soon the throne of David, Your servant, within it, And rebuild it soon, in our days, as an everlasting structure. Blessed are You, Hashem, Builder of Yerushalayim.

Birkhat David / Prayer for Davidic Reign

Et Tzemach David Avdecha	אֶת צֶמַח דָּוִד עַבְדְּךָ
Meheirah Tatzmiach. Vekarno	מְהֵרָה תַצְמִיחַ. וְקַרְנוֹ
Tarum Bishu'atecha. Ki	תָּרוּם בִּישׁוּעָתֶךָ. כִּי
Lishu'atecha Kivinu Kol-Hayom.	לִישׁוּעָתְךָ קִוִּינוּ כָּל־הַיּוֹם:
Baruch Attah Adonai	בָּרוּךְ אַתָּה יְהֹוָה
Matzmiach Keren Yeshu'ah.	מַצְמִיחַ קֶרֶן יְשׁוּעָה:

Speedily cause the offspring of Your servant David to flourish, and let his horn be exalted in Your salvation, for we hope in Your salvation every day. Blessed are You, Hashem, Who flourishes the horn of salvation.

Tefillah / Acceptance of Prayer

Shema Koleinu. Adonai	שְׁמַע קוֹלֵנוּ. יְהֹוָה
Eloheinu. Av Harachaman.	אֱלֹהֵינוּ. אָב הָרַחֲמָן.
Rachem Aleinu. Vekabel	רַחֵם עָלֵינוּ. וְקַבֵּל
Berachamim Uveratzon Et-	בְּרַחֲמִים וּבְרָצוֹן אֶת־
Tefillateinu. Ki El Shome'ah	תְּפִלָּתֵנוּ. כִּי אֵל שׁוֹמֵעַ
Tefillot Vetachanunim Attah.	תְּפִלּוֹת וְתַחֲנוּנִים אָתָּה.
Umilfaneicha Malkeinu. Reikam	וּמִלְּפָנֶיךָ מַלְכֵּנוּ. רֵיקָם

Al-Teshivenu. Chonenu	אַל־תְּשִׁיבֵנוּ. חָנֵּנוּ
Va'aneinu Ushema Tefillateinu.	וַעֲנֵנוּ וּשְׁמַע תְּפִלָּתֵנוּ.

Hear our voice, Hashem our God. Merciful Father, have compassion upon us. And accept our prayers with mercy and favor, for You are God who hears to prayers and supplications. And from before You, our King, do not leave us empty-handed, but be gracious to us and hear our prayers.

On Tisha B'Av, say Aleinu here:

עֲנֵנוּ אָבִינוּ עֲנֵנוּ בְּיוֹם צוֹם הַתַּעֲנִית הַזֶּה. כִּי בְצָרָה גְדוֹלָה אֲנָחְנוּ. אַל־תֵּפֶן לְרִשְׁעֵנוּ. וְאַל־תִּתְעַלַּם מַלְכֵּנוּ מִבַּקָּשָׁתֵנוּ. הֱיֵה נָא קָרוֹב לְשַׁוְעָתֵנוּ. טֶרֶם נִקְרָא אֵלֶיךָ אַתָּה תַעֲנֶה. נְדַבֵּר וְאַתָּה תִשְׁמַע. כַּדָּבָר שֶׁנֶּאֱמַר: וְהָיָה טֶרֶם־יִקְרָאוּ וַאֲנִי אֶעֱנֶה עוֹד הֵם מְדַבְּרִים וַאֲנִי אֶשְׁמָע: כִּי אַתָּה יְהֹוָה פּוֹדֶה וּמַצִּיל. וְעוֹנֶה וּמְרַחֵם בְּכָל־עֵת צָרָה וְצוּקָה:

Aneinu Avinu Aneinu Beyom Tzom Hata'anit Hazeh. Ki Vetzarah Gedolah Anachenu. Al-Tefen Lerish'enu. Ve'al-Tit'alam Malkeinu Mibakashateinu. Heyeh Na Karov Leshav'ateinu. Terem Nikra Eleicha Attah Ta'aneh. Nedaber Ve'attah Tishma'. Kadavar Shene'emar. Vehayah Terem-Yikra'u Va'ani E'eneh; Od Hem Medaberim Va'ani Eshma. Ki Attah Adonai Podeh Umatzil. Ve'oneh Umerachem Bechol-'Et Tzarah Vetzukah.

Answer us, Hashem, answer us on the day of our fast, for we are in great distress. Do not regard our wickedness; Do not conceal Your presence from us, and do not hide Yourself from our supplication. Be near to our cry, and let Your kindness comfort us; even before we call to You answer us, as it is said: "Before they call, I will answer; while they are yet speaking, I will hear." For You, Hashem, are He who answers in time of trouble, who redeems and delivers in all times of woe and stress.

Ki Attah Shome'ah Tefillat Kol-	כִּי אַתָּה שׁוֹמֵעַ תְּפִלַּת כָּל־
Peh. Baruch Attah Adonai	פֶּה: בָּרוּךְ אַתָּה יְהֹוָה
Shome'ah Tefillah.	שׁוֹמֵעַ תְּפִלָּה:

For You hear the prayer of every mouth. Blessed are You, Hashem Who hears prayer.

Avodah / Temple Service

Retzeh Adonai Eloheinu	רְצֵה יְהֹוָה אֱלֹהֵינוּ
Be'ammecha Yisra'el Velitfilatam	בְּעַמְּךָ יִשְׂרָאֵל וְלִתְפִלָּתָם
She'eh. Vehasheiv Ha'avodah	שְׁעֵה. וְהָשֵׁב הָעֲבוֹדָה
Lidvir Beitecha. Ve'ishei Yisra'el	לִדְבִיר בֵּיתֶךָ. וְאִשֵּׁי יִשְׂרָאֵל
Utefilatam. Meheirah Be'ahavah	וּתְפִלָּתָם. מְהֵרָה בְּאַהֲבָה
Tekabel Beratzon. Utehi	תְקַבֵּל בְּרָצוֹן. וּתְהִי
Leratzon Tamid Avodat Yisra'el	לְרָצוֹן תָּמִיד עֲבוֹדַת יִשְׂרָאֵל
Ammecha.	עַמֶּךָ:

Be favorable, Hashem our God, on Your people Yisrael and regard their prayers. And the service to the Sanctuary of Your House, and the fire offerings of Yisrael, and their prayers accept soon with love. And may the service of Your people, Yisrael, always be favorable.

On Rosh Chodesh and Chol HaMoed Passover and Sukkot say:

Ya'aleh Veyavo

אֱלֹהֵינוּ וֵאלֹהֵי אֲבוֹתֵינוּ. יַעֲלֶה וְיָבֹא. וְיַגִּיעַ וְיֵרָאֶה. וְיֵרָצֶה וְיִשָּׁמַע. וְיִפָּקֵד וְיִזָּכֵר. זִכְרוֹנֵנוּ וְזִכְרוֹן אֲבוֹתֵינוּ. זִכְרוֹן יְרוּשָׁלַיִם עִירָךְ. וְזִכְרוֹן מָשִׁיחַ בֶּן־דָּוִד עַבְדָּךְ. וְזִכְרוֹן כָּל־עַמְּךָ בֵּית יִשְׂרָאֵל לְפָנֶיךָ. לִפְלֵיטָה. לְטוֹבָה. לְחֵן. לְחֶסֶד וּלְרַחֲמִים. לְחַיִּים טוֹבִים וּלְשָׁלוֹם. בְּיוֹם:

Eloheinu Velohei Avoteinu. Ya'aleh Veyavo. Veyagia Veyera'eh. Veyeratzeh Veyishama'. Veyipaked Veyizacher. Zichronenu Vezichron Avoteinu. Zichron Yerushalayim Irach. Vezichron Mashiach Ben-David Avdach. Vezichron Kol-'Ammecha Beit Yisra'el Lefaneicha. Lifleitah. Letovah. Lechein. Lechesed Ulerachamim. Lechayim Tovim Uleshalom. Beyom:

Our God, and God of our fathers, may it rise, and come, arrive, appear, find favor, and be heard, and be considered, and be remembered our remembrance and the remembrance of our fathers, Yerushalayim Your city, the remembrance of Messiah ben David Your servant, and the remembrance of all Your people of the House of Yisrael before You for deliverance, for good favor, for kindness and mercy, for good life and for peace. On this day of:

On Rosh Chodesh:

רֹאשׁ חֹדֶשׁ הַזֶּה.

Rosh Chodesh Hazeh.

Rosh Chodesh (New Moon).

On Pesach:

חַג הַמַּצּוֹת הַזֶּה. בְּיוֹם מִקְרָא קֹדֶשׁ הַזֶּה.

Chag Hamatzot Hazeh. Beyom Mikra Kodesh Hazeh.

The Festival of Matzot. on this day of holy convocation.

On Sukkot:

חַג הַסֻּכּוֹת הַזֶּה. בְּיוֹם מִקְרָא קֹדֶשׁ הַזֶּה.

Chag Hasukkot Hazeh. Beyom Mikra Kodesh Hazeh.

The Festival of Sukkot. on this day of holy convocation.

לְרַחֵם בּוֹ עָלֵינוּ וּלְהוֹשִׁיעֵנוּ. זָכְרֵנוּ יְהוָה אֱלֹהֵינוּ בּוֹ לְטוֹבָה. וּפָקְדֵנוּ בוֹ לִבְרָכָה. וְהוֹשִׁיעֵנוּ בוֹ לְחַיִּים טוֹבִים. בִּדְבַר יְשׁוּעָה וְרַחֲמִים. חוּס וְחָנֵּנוּ. וַחֲמוֹל וְרַחֵם עָלֵינוּ. וְהוֹשִׁיעֵנוּ כִּי אֵלֶיךָ עֵינֵינוּ. כִּי אֵל מֶלֶךְ חַנּוּן וְרַחוּם אָתָּה:

Lerachem Bo Aleinu Ulehoshi'enu. Zochrenu Adonai Eloheinu Bo Letovah. Ufokdenu Vo Livrachah. Vehoshi'enu Vo Lechayim Tovim. Bidvar Yeshu'ah Verachamim. Chus Vechanenu. Vachamol Verachem Aleinu. Vehoshi'enu Ki Eleicha Eineinu. Ki El Melech Chanun Verachum Attah.

to have mercy upon us and save us. Remember us, Hashem our God, on it for good. Be mindful of us on it for blessing and save us on it for a life of good. With the promise of salvation and mercy, show us pity, and be gracious to us and have compassion and mercy on us and save us. For our eyes are lifted towards You, for You, God, are a gracious and merciful King.

Attah Berachameicha Harabim.	וְאַתָּה בְּרַחֲמֶיךָ הָרַבִּים.
Tachpotz Banu Vetirtzenu.	תַּחְפֹּץ בָּנוּ וְתִרְצֵנוּ.
Vetechezeinah Eineinu	וְתֶחֱזֶינָה עֵינֵינוּ
Beshuvecha Letziyon	בְּשׁוּבְךָ לְצִיּוֹן
Berachamim. Baruch Attah	בְּרַחֲמִים: בָּרוּךְ אַתָּה
Adonai Hamachazir Shechinato	יְהוָה הַמַּחֲזִיר שְׁכִינָתוֹ
Letziyon.	לְצִיּוֹן.

And You, in Your abundant mercy, delight in us, and be favorable to us, so that our eyes may witness Your return to Tzion with mercy. Blessed are You, Hashem Who returns His Presence to Tzion.

Hoda'ah (Modim) / Thanksgiving

On Saying "Modim" / "We are Thankful" One Bows and begins to rise after "Adonai" / "Hashem".

Modim Anachnu Lach.	מוֹדִים אֲנַחְנוּ לָךְ.
She'attah Hu Adonai Eloheinu	שָׁאַתָּה הוּא יְהֹוָה אֱלֹהֵינוּ
Velohei Avoteinu Le'olam Va'ed.	וֵאלֹהֵי אֲבוֹתֵינוּ לְעוֹלָם וָעֶד.
Tzurenu Tzur Chayeinu	צוּרֵנוּ צוּר חַיֵּינוּ
Umagen Yish'enu Attah Hu.	וּמָגֵן יִשְׁעֵנוּ אַתָּה הוּא.
Ledor Vador Nodeh Lecha	לְדוֹר וָדוֹר נוֹדֶה לְךָ
Unsapeir Tehilatecha. Al	וּנְסַפֵּר תְּהִלָּתֶךָ. עַל
Chayeinu Hamesurim	חַיֵּינוּ הַמְּסוּרִים
Beyadecha. Ve'al Nishmoteinu	בְּיָדֶךָ. וְעַל נִשְׁמוֹתֵינוּ
Hapekudot Lach. Ve'al Niseicha	הַפְּקוּדוֹת לָךְ. וְעַל נִסֶּיךָ
Shebechol-Yom Imanu. Ve'al	שֶׁבְּכָל־יוֹם עִמָּנוּ. וְעַל
Nifle'oteicha Vetovoteicha	נִפְלְאוֹתֶיךָ וְטוֹבוֹתֶיךָ
Shebechol-'Et. Erev Vavoker	שֶׁבְּכָל־עֵת. עֶרֶב וָבֹקֶר
Vetzaharayim. Hatov. Ki Lo	וְצָהֳרָיִם. הַטּוֹב. כִּי לֹא
Chalu Rachameicha.	כָלוּ רַחֲמֶיךָ.
Hamerachem. Ki Lo Tamu	הַמְרַחֵם. כִּי לֹא תַמּוּ
Chasadeicha. Ki Me'olam	חֲסָדֶיךָ. כִּי מֵעוֹלָם
Kivinu Lach.	קִוִּינוּ לָךְ:

We are thankful to You, Hashem our God and the God of our fathers, forever. You are our strength and Rock of our life and the Shield of our salvation. In every generation we will thank You and recount Your praise for our lives which are in given into Your hand, for our souls which are placed in Your care, and for Your miracles which are daily with us, and for Your wonders and goodness—evening, morning and noon. The Beneficent One, for Your mercies never end, Merciful One, for Your kindness has never ceased, for we have always placed our hope in You.

Modim Derabbanan

During the repetition, this is to be recited softly while the Chazan reads the Modim. Still bow at Modim as before.

מוֹדִים אֲנַחְנוּ לָךְ. שֶׁאַתָּה הוּא יְהֹוָה אֱלֹהֵינוּ וֵאלֹהֵי אֲבוֹתֵינוּ. אֱלֹהֵי כָל בָּשָׂר. יוֹצְרֵנוּ יוֹצֵר בְּרֵאשִׁית. בְּרָכוֹת וְהוֹדָאוֹת לְשִׁמְךָ הַגָּדוֹל וְהַקָּדוֹשׁ. עַל שֶׁהֶחֱיִיתָנוּ וְקִיַּמְתָּנוּ. כֵּן תְּחַיֵּנוּ וּתְחָנֵּנוּ וְתֶאֱסוֹף גָּלֻיּוֹתֵינוּ לְחַצְרוֹת קָדְשֶׁךָ. לִשְׁמֹר חֻקֶּיךָ וְלַעֲשׂוֹת רְצוֹנְךָ וּלְעָבְדְךָ בְּלֵבָב שָׁלֵם. עַל שֶׁאֲנַחְנוּ מוֹדִים לָךְ. בָּרוּךְ אֵל הַהוֹדָאוֹת.

Modim Anachnu Lach. She'attah Hu Adonai Eloheinu Velohei Avoteinu. Elohei Chol Basar. Yotzreinu Yotzer Bereshit. Berachot Vehoda'ot Leshimcha Hagadol Vehakadosh. Al Shehecheyitanu Vekiyamtanu. Ken Techayeinu Utechanenu Vete'esof Galyoteinu Lechatzrot Kodshecha. Lishmor Chukkeicha Vela'asot Retzonecha Ule'avedecha Velevav Shalem. Al She'anachnu Modim Lach. Baruch El Hahoda'ot.

We are thankful to You, Hashem our God and the God of our fathers. God of all flesh, our Creator and Former of Creation, blessings and thanks to Your great and holy name, for You have kept us alive and sustained us; may You always grant us life and be gracious to us. And gather our exiles to Your holy courtyards to observe Your statutes, and to do Your will, and to serve You with a perfect heart. For this we thank You. Blessed is God of thanksgivings.

Al HaNissim

On Purim and Hanukkah an extra prayer is added here:

עַל הַנִּסִּים וְעַל הַפֻּרְקָן וְעַל הַגְּבוּרוֹת וְעַל הַתְּשׁוּעוֹת וְעַל הַנִּפְלָאוֹת וְעַל הַנֶּחָמוֹת שֶׁעָשִׂיתָ לַאֲבוֹתֵינוּ בַּיָּמִים הָהֵם בַּזְּמַן הַזֶּה:

Al Hanissim Ve'al Hapurkan Ve'al Hagevurot Ve'al Hateshu'ot Ve'al Hanifla'ot Ve'al Hanechamot She'asita La'avoteinu Bayamim Hahem Bazman Hazeh.

For the miracles, and for the triumphant liberation, and the mighty works, and for the deliverances, and for the wonders, and for the consolations which You have done for our fathers in those days at this season:

On Hanukkah:

בִּימֵי מַתִּתְיָה בֶן־יוֹחָנָן כֹּהֵן גָּדוֹל. חַשְׁמוֹנָאִי וּבָנָיו כְּשֶׁעָמְדָה מַלְכוּת יָוָן הָרְשָׁעָה עַל עַמְּךָ יִשְׂרָאֵל. לְשַׁכְּחָם תּוֹרָתָךְ וּלְהַעֲבִירָם מֵחֻקֵּי רְצוֹנָךְ. וְאַתָּה בְּרַחֲמֶיךָ הָרַבִּים עָמַדְתָּ לָהֶם בְּעֵת צָרָתָם. רַבְתָּ אֶת רִיבָם. דַּנְתָּ אֶת דִּינָם. נָקַמְתָּ אֶת נִקְמָתָם. מָסַרְתָּ גִבּוֹרִים בְּיַד חַלָּשִׁים. וְרַבִּים בְּיַד מְעַטִּים. וּרְשָׁעִים בְּיַד צַדִּיקִים. וּטְמֵאִים בְּיַד טְהוֹרִים. וְזֵדִים בְּיַד עוֹסְקֵי תוֹרָתֶךָ. לְךָ עָשִׂיתָ שֵׁם גָּדוֹל וְקָדוֹשׁ בְּעוֹלָמָךְ. וּלְעַמְּךָ יִשְׂרָאֵל עָשִׂיתָ תְּשׁוּעָה גְדוֹלָה וּפֻרְקָן כְּהַיּוֹם הַזֶּה. וְאַחַר כָּךְ בָּאוּ בָנֶיךָ לִדְבִיר בֵּיתֶךָ. וּפִנּוּ אֶת־הֵיכָלֶךָ. וְטִהֲרוּ אֶת־מִקְדָּשֶׁךָ. וְהִדְלִיקוּ נֵרוֹת בְּחַצְרוֹת קָדְשֶׁךָ. וְקָבְעוּ שְׁמוֹנַת יְמֵי חֲנֻכָּה אֵלּוּ בְּהַלֵּל וּבְהוֹדָאָה. וְעָשִׂיתָ עִמָּהֶם נִסִּים וְנִפְלָאוֹת וְנוֹדֶה לְשִׁמְךָ הַגָּדוֹל סֶלָה:

Bimei Mattityah Ven-Yochanan Kohen Gadol. Chashmona'i Uvanav Keshe'amedah Malchut Yavan Haresha'ah Al Ammecha Yisra'el. Leshakecham Toratach Uleha'aviram Mechukkei Retzonach. Ve'attah Berachameicha Harabim Amadta Lahem Be'et Tzaratam. Ravta Et Rivam. Danta Et Dinam. Nakamta Et Nikmatam. Masarta Giborim Beyad Chalashim. Verabim Beyad Me'atim. Uresha'im Beyad Tzaddikim. Uteme'im Beyad Tehorim. Vezeidim Beyad Osekei Toratecha. Lecha Asita Shem Gadol Vekadosh Be'olamach. Ule'ammecha Yisra'el Asita Teshu'ah Gedolah Ufurkan Kehayom Hazeh. Ve'achar Kach Ba'u Vaneicha Lidvir Beitecha. Ufinu Et-Heichalecha. Vetiharu Et-Mikdashecha. Vehidliku Nerot Bechatzrot Kodshecha. Vekave'u Shemonat Yemei Chanukkah Elu Behallel Uvehoda'ah. Ve'asita Imahem Nissim Venifla'ot Venodeh Leshimcha Hagadol Selah.

Then in the days of Mattityahu ben-Yochanan, High Priest, the Hasmonean and his sons, when the cruel Greek power rose up against Your people, Yisrael, to make them forget Your Torah and transgress the statutes of Your will. And You, in Your great compassion, stood up for them in time of their trial to plead their cause and defend their judgment. Giving out retribution, delivered the strong into the hand of the weak, and the many into the hand of the few, and the wicked into the hand of the upright, and the impure into the hand of the pure, and tyrants into the hand of the devotees of Your Torah. You made for Yourself a great and holy name in Your world. And for Your people, Yisrael, You performed a great salvation and liberation as this very day. Then Your children came to the Sanctuary of Your House, cleared Your Temple, cleansed Your Sanctuary and kindled lights in Your courtyards, and they instituted these eight days of Hanukkah for praise and thanksgiving. And You did miracles and wonders for them, and we give thanks to Your great name, selah.

On Purim:

בִּימֵי מָרְדְּכַי וְאֶסְתֵּר בְּשׁוּשַׁן הַבִּירָה. כְּשֶׁעָמַד עֲלֵיהֶם הָמָן הָרָשָׁע. בִּקֵּשׁ לְהַשְׁמִיד לַהֲרֹג וּלְאַבֵּד אֶת־כָּל־הַיְּהוּדִים מִנַּעַר וְעַד זָקֵן טַף וְנָשִׁים בְּיוֹם אֶחָד.

בִּשְׁלֹשָׁה עָשָׂר לְחֹדֶשׁ שְׁנֵים עָשָׂר. הוּא חֹדֶשׁ אֲדָר. וּשְׁלָלָם לָבוֹז. וְאַתָּה בְּרַחֲמֶיךָ הָרַבִּים הֵפַרְתָּ אֶת־עֲצָתוֹ וְקִלְקַלְתָּ אֶת־מַחֲשַׁבְתּוֹ. וַהֲשֵׁבוֹתָ לּוֹ גְּמוּלוֹ בְּרֹאשׁוֹ. וְתָלוּ אוֹתוֹ וְאֶת־בָּנָיו עַל הָעֵץ. וְעָשִׂיתָ עִמָּהֶם נֵס וָפֶלֶא וְנוֹדֶה לְשִׁמְךָ הַגָּדוֹל סֶלָה:

Bimei Mordechai Ve'ester Beshushan Habirah. Keshe'amad Aleihem Haman Harasha. Bikesh Lehashmid Laharog Ule'abed Et-Kol-Hayehudim Mina'ar Ve'ad Zaken Taf Venashim Beyom Echad. Bishloshah Asar Lechodesh Sheneim Asar. Hu Chodesh Adar. Ushelalam Lavoz. Ve'attah Berachameicha Harabim Hefarta Et-'Atzato Vekilkalta Et-Machashavto. Vahasheivota Lo Gemulo Verosho. Vetalu Oto Ve'et-Banav Al Ha'etz. Ve'asita Imahem Nes Vafelei Venodeh Leshimcha Hagadol Selah.

In the days of Mordechai and Ester in Shushan, the capital, the wicked Haman rose up and sought to destroy, slay and utterly annihilate all of the Yehudim, both young and old, women and children, on one day, on the thirteenth day of the twelfth month, which is the month of Adar, and to plunder their possessions. But You in Your great mercy You broke his plan and spoiled his designs, causing them to recoil on his own head, and they hanged him and his sons on the gallows. And You did miracles and wonders for them, and we give thanks to Your great name, selah.

Ve'al Kulam Yitbarach.	וְעַל כֻּלָּם יִתְבָּרַךְ.
Veyitromam. Veyitnasse. Tamid.	וְיִתְרוֹמָם. וְיִתְנַשֵּׂא. תָּמִיד.
Shimcha Malkeinu. Le'olam	שִׁמְךָ מַלְכֵּנוּ. לְעוֹלָם
Va'ed. Vechol-Hachayim	וָעֶד. וְכָל־הַחַיִּים
Yoducha Selah.	יוֹדוּךָ סֶלָה:

For all these acts, may Your name, our King, be blessed, extolled and exalted forever. And all of the living will thank You, selah.

During the 10 days of repentance (Rosh Hashanah to Yom Kippur) say:

Uchetov Lechayim Tovim Kol Benei Veritecha.	וּכְתֹב לְחַיִּים טוֹבִים כָּל בְּנֵי בְרִיתֶךָ.

Inscribe all of Your people of the covenant for a happy life.

Bow at "Baruch Attah" / "Blessed are You". Raise up at Adonai / Hashem.

Vihalelu Vivarechu Et-Shimcha	וִיהַלְלוּ וִיבָרְכוּ אֶת־שִׁמְךָ
Hagadol Be'emet Le'olam Ki Tov.	הַגָּדוֹל בֶּאֱמֶת לְעוֹלָם כִּי טוֹב.
Ha'el Yeshu'ateinu Ve'ezrateinu	הָאֵל יְשׁוּעָתֵנוּ וְעֶזְרָתֵנוּ

Selah. Ha'el Hatov. Baruch Attah	סֶלָה. הָאֵל הַטּוֹב: בָּרוּךְ אַתָּה
Adonai Hatov Shimcha Ulecha	יְהֹוָה הַטּוֹב שִׁמְךָ וּלְךָ
Na'eh Lehodot.	נָאֶה לְהוֹדוֹת:

And they will praise and bless Your great and good name sincerely, forever. For You are good, the God of our salvation and our help forever, the Good God. Blessed are You, Hashem, Your name is good and to You it is good to give thanks.

Sim Shalom / Grant Peace

Sim Shalom Tovah Uverachah.	שִׂים שָׁלוֹם טוֹבָה וּבְרָכָה.
Chayim Chein Vachesed	חַיִּים חֵן וָחֶסֶד
Verachamim. Aleinu Ve'al Kol-	וְרַחֲמִים. עָלֵינוּ וְעַל כָּל־
Yisra'el Ammecha. Uvarecheinu	יִשְׂרָאֵל עַמֶּךָ. וּבָרְכֵנוּ
Avinu Kulanu Ke'echad Be'or	אָבִינוּ כֻּלָּנוּ כְּאֶחָד בְּאוֹר
Paneicha. Ki Ve'or Paneicha	פָּנֶיךָ. כִּי בְאוֹר פָּנֶיךָ
Natata Lanu Adonai Eloheinu	נָתַתָּ לָּנוּ יְהֹוָה אֱלֹהֵינוּ
Torah Vechayim. Ahavah	תּוֹרָה וְחַיִּים. אַהֲבָה
Vachesed. Tzedakah	וָחֶסֶד. צְדָקָה
Verachamim. Berachah	וְרַחֲמִים. בְּרָכָה
Veshalom. Vetov Be'eineicha	וְשָׁלוֹם. וְטוֹב בְּעֵינֶיךָ
Levarecheinu Ulevarech Et-	לְבָרְכֵנוּ וּלְבָרֵךְ אֶת־
Kol-'Ammecha Yisra'el. Berov	כָּל־עַמְּךָ יִשְׂרָאֵל. בְּרֹב
Oz Veshalom.	עֹז וְשָׁלוֹם:

Grant peace, goodness and blessing, a life of grace, and kindness and mercy, to us and to all Yisrael, Your people. And bless us, our Father, all as one with the light of Your countenance; for with the light of Your countenance You have given us, Hashem our God, a Torah and life, love and kindness, righteousness and mercy, blessing and peace. May it be good in Your eyes to bless us and bless all of Your people, Yisrael, with abundant strength and peace.

During the 10 days of repentance (Rosh Hashanah to Yom Kippur) say:

Uvesefer Chayim. Berachah Veshalom.	וּבְסֵפֶר חַיִּים. בְּרָכָה וְשָׁלוֹם.
Ufarnasah Tovah Vishu'ah	וּפַרְנָסָה טוֹבָה וִישׁוּעָה
Venechamah. Ugezerot Tovot. Nizacher	וְנֶחָמָה. וּגְזֵרוֹת טוֹבוֹת. נִזָּכֵר
Venikkatev Lefaneicha. Anachnu	וְנִכָּתֵב לְפָנֶיךָ. אֲנַחְנוּ
Vechol Ammecha Beit Yisra'el.	וְכָל עַמְּךָ בֵּית יִשְׂרָאֵל.
Lechayim Tovim Uleshalom.	לְחַיִּים טוֹבִים וּלְשָׁלוֹם.

May we and all Yisrael Your people be remembered and inscribed before You in the book of life and blessing, peace and prosperity, for a happy life and for peace.

Baruch Attah Adonai	בָּרוּךְ אַתָּה יהוה
Hamevarech Et Ammo Yisra'el	הַמְבָרֵךְ אֶת עַמּוֹ יִשְׂרָאֵל
Bashalom. Amen.	בַּשָּׁלוֹם. אָמֵן:

Blessed are You, Hashem, Who blesses His people Yisrael with peace. Amen.

Yihyu Leratzon Imrei-Fi Vehegyon Libi	יִהְיוּ לְרָצוֹן | אִמְרֵי־פִי וְהֶגְיוֹן לִבִּי
Lefaneicha; Adonai Tzuri Vego'ali.	לְפָנֶיךָ יְהֹוָה צוּרִי וְגֹאֲלִי:

May the words of my mouth and the meditation of my heart find favor before You, Hashem my Rock and my Redeemer.

Elohai. Netzor Leshoni Meira	אֱלֹהַי. נְצֹר לְשׁוֹנִי מֵרָע
Vesiftotai Midaber Mirmah.	וְשִׂפְתוֹתַי מִדַּבֵּר מִרְמָה.
Velimkalelai Nafshi Tidom.	וְלִמְקַלְלַי נַפְשִׁי תִדֹּם.

Venafshi Ke'afar Lakol Tihyeh.	וְנַפְשִׁי כֶּעָפָר לַכֹּל תִּהְיֶה.
Petach Libi Betoratecha.	פְּתַח לִבִּי בְּתוֹרָתֶךָ.
Ve'acharei Mitzvoteicha Tirdof	וְאַחֲרֵי מִצְוֹתֶיךָ תִּרְדֹּף
Nafshi. Vechol-Hakamim Alai	נַפְשִׁי. וְכָל־הַקָּמִים עָלַי
Lera'ah. Meheirah Hafer Atzatam	לְרָעָה. מְהֵרָה הָפֵר עֲצָתָם
Vekalkel Machshevotam. Aseh	וְקַלְקֵל מַחְשְׁבוֹתָם. עֲשֵׂה
Lema'an Shemach. Aseh	לְמַעַן שְׁמָךְ. עֲשֵׂה
Lema'an Yeminach. Aseh	לְמַעַן יְמִינָךְ. עֲשֵׂה
Lema'an Toratach. Aseh Lema'an	לְמַעַן תּוֹרָתָךְ. עֲשֵׂה לְמַעַן
Kedushatach. Lema'an	קְדֻשָּׁתָךְ. לְמַעַן
Yechaletzun Yedideicha;	יֵחָלְצוּן יְדִידֶיךָ
Hoshi'ah Yeminecha Va'Aneni.	הוֹשִׁיעָה יְמִינְךָ וַעֲנֵנִי:

My God, guard my tongue from evil, and my lips from speaking deceit. And to those who curse me may my soul be silent; and may my soul be like the dust to all. Open my heart to Your Torah, that my soul may follow after Your commandments. And all that rise to do evil against me, speedily nullify their plan, and spoil their thoughts. Do it for the sake of Your name; do it for the sake of Your right hand; do it for the sake of Your Torah, do it for the sake of Your holiness. That Your beloved may be rescued, save with Your right hand and answer me. **(Ps. 60:7)**

Yihyu Leratzon Imrei-Fi Vehegyon Libi	יִהְיוּ לְרָצוֹן | אִמְרֵי־פִי וְהֶגְיוֹן לִבִּי
Lefaneicha; Adonai Tzuri Vego'ali.	לְפָנֶיךָ יְהֹוָה צוּרִי וְגֹאֲלִי:

May the words of my mouth and the meditation of my heart find favor before You, Hashem my Rock and my Redeemer.

Oseh Shalom

One bows and takes three steps backwards, while still bowing. After three steps, while still bowing and before erecting, while saying, "Oseh Shalom Bimromav", turn one's face to the left, "Hu [Berachamav] Ya'aseh Shalom Aleinu", turn one's face to the right; [face forward and] then bow forward like a servant leaving his master. (SA, OC 123:1)

Oseh Shalom **On the 10 Days of**	עוֹשֶׂה שָׁלוֹם
Repentance: (Hashalom) Bimromav,	בעשי״ת: (הַשָּׁלוֹם) בִּמְרוֹמָיו.
Hu Berachamav Ya'aseh Shalom	הוּא בְּרַחֲמָיו יַעֲשֶׂה שָׁלוֹם
Aleinu, Ve'al Kol-'Ammo	עָלֵינוּ. וְעַל כָּל־עַמּוֹ
Yisra'el, Ve'imru Amen.	יִשְׂרָאֵל. וְאִמְרוּ אָמֵן:

Creator of **On the 10 Days of Repentance:** (the) peace in His high places, may He in His mercy create peace for us and for all Yisrael, and say Amen.

Yehi Ratzon Milfaneicha Adonai	יְהִי רָצוֹן מִלְּפָנֶיךָ יְהֹוָה
Eloheinu Velohei Avoteinu. Shetivneh	אֱלֹהֵינוּ וֵאלֹהֵי אֲבוֹתֵינוּ. שֶׁתִּבְנֶה
Beit Hamikdash Bimheirah Veyameinu.	בֵּית הַמִּקְדָּשׁ בִּמְהֵרָה בְיָמֵינוּ.
Veten Chelkenu Vetoratach La'asot	וְתֵן חֶלְקֵנוּ בְּתוֹרָתָךְ לַעֲשׂוֹת
Chukkei. Retzonach Ule'avedach	חֻקֵּי רְצוֹנָךְ וּלְעָבְדָךְ
Belevav Shalem.	בְּלֵבָב שָׁלֵם:

May it be Your will, Hashem our God and God of our fathers, that the Beit HaMikdash be speedily rebuilt in our days, and grant us a share in Your Torah so we may fulfill the statutes of your will and serve you with a whole heart.

Continue with Yehi Shem.

Yehi Shem

יְהִ֤י שֵׁ֣ם יְהֹוָ֣ה מְבֹרָ֑ךְ מֵ֝עַתָּ֗ה וְעַד־עוֹלָֽם׃ מִמִּזְרַח־שֶׁ֥מֶשׁ עַד־מְבוֹא֑וֹ מְ֝הֻלָּ֗ל שֵׁ֣ם יְהֹוָֽה׃ רָ֖ם עַל־כׇּל־גּוֹיִ֥ם ׀ יְהֹוָ֑ה עַ֖ל הַשָּׁמַ֣יִם כְּבוֹדֽוֹ׃ יְהֹוָ֥ה אֲדֹנֵ֑ינוּ מָֽה־אַדִּ֥יר שִׁ֝מְךָ֗ בְּכׇל־הָאָֽרֶץ׃

Yehi Shem Adonai Mevorach; Me'attah. Ve'ad-'Olam. Mimizrach-Shemesh Ad-Mevo'o; Mehulal. Shem Adonai Ram Al-Chol-Goyim Adonai Al Hashamayim Kevodo. Adonai Adoneinu; Mah-'Adir Shimcha. Bechol-Ha'aretz.

Blessed is the name of Hashem from this time forward and forever. From the rising of the sun to it's going down, Hashem's name is to be praised. Hashem, our Lord, How glorious is Your name in all of the earth. **(Psalms 113:2-4, 8:2)**

Kaddish Titkabbal

Kaddish is only recited in a minyan (ten men). אָמֵן denotes when the congregation responds "Amen" together out loud. According to the Shulchan Arukh, the congregation says "Yehei Shemeh Rabba" to "Yitbarach" out loud together without interruption, and also that one should respond "Amen" after "Yitbarach." (SA, OC 55,56) This is not the common custom today. Though many are accustomed to answering according to their own custom, it is advised to respond in the custom of the one reciting to avoid not fragmenting into smaller groups. ("Lo Titgodedu" - BT, Yevamot 13b / SA, OC 493, Rema / MT, Avodah Zara 12:15)

יִתְגַּדַּל וְיִתְקַדַּשׁ שְׁמֵהּ רַבָּא. אָמֵן בְּעָלְמָא דִּי בְרָא. כִּרְעוּתֵהּ. וְיַמְלִיךְ מַלְכוּתֵהּ. וְיַצְמַח פֻּרְקָנֵהּ. וִיקָרֵב מְשִׁיחֵהּ. אָמֵן בְּחַיֵּיכוֹן וּבְיוֹמֵיכוֹן וּבְחַיֵּי דְכָל בֵּית יִשְׂרָאֵל. בַּעֲגָלָא וּבִזְמַן קָרִיב. וְאִמְרוּ אָמֵן. אָמֵן יְהֵא שְׁמֵיהּ רַבָּא מְבָרַךְ לְעָלַם וּלְעָלְמֵי עָלְמַיָּא יִתְבָּרַךְ. וְיִשְׁתַּבַּח. וְיִתְפָּאַר. וְיִתְרוֹמַם. וְיִתְנַשֵּׂא. וְיִתְהַדָּר. וְיִתְעַלֶּה. וְיִתְהַלָּל שְׁמֵהּ דְּקֻדְשָׁא. בְּרִיךְ הוּא. אָמֵן לְעֵלָּא מִן כָּל בִּרְכָתָא שִׁירָתָא. תֻּשְׁבְּחָתָא וְנֶחֱמָתָא. דַּאֲמִירָן בְּעָלְמָא. וְאִמְרוּ אָמֵן. אָמֵן

Yitgadal Veyitkadash Shemeh Rabba. Amen Be'alema Di Vera. Kir'uteh. Veyamlich Malchuteh. Veyatzmach Purkaneh. Vikarev Meshicheh. Amen Bechayeichon Uveyomeichon Uvechayei Dechal-Beit Yisra'el. Ba'agala Uvizman Kariv. Ve'imru Amen. Amen Yehei Shemeh Rabba Mevarach Le'alam Ule'alemei Alemaya Yitbarach. Veyishtabach. Veyitpa'ar. Veyitromam. Veyitnasse. Veyit'hadar. Veyit'aleh. Veyit'hallal Shemeh Dekudsha. Berich Hu. Amen Le'ella

Min Kol Birchata Shirata. Tushbechata Venechemata. Da'amiran Be'alema. Ve'imru Amen. **Amen**

Glorified and sanctified be God's great name **Amen** throughout the world which He has created according to His will. May He establish His kingdom, hastening His salvation and the coming of His Messiah, **Amen**, in your lifetime and during your days, and within the life of the entire House of Yisrael, speedily and soon; and say, Amen. **Amen** May His great name be blessed forever and to all eternity. Blessed and praised, glorified and exalted, extolled and honored, adored and lauded is the name of the Holy One, blessed is He, **Amen** Beyond all the blessings and hymns, praises and consolations that are ever spoken in the world; and say, Amen. **Amen**

תִּתְקַבַּל צְלוֹתְֽנָא וּבָֽעוּתְֽנָא. עִם צְלְוֹתְהוֹן וּבָֽעְוּתְהוֹן דְּכָל בֵּית יִשְׂרָאֵל. קֳדָם אֲבוּנָא דְּבִשְׁמַיָּא וְאַרְעָא. וְאִמְרוּ אָמֵן. אָמֵן

Titkabbal Tzelotana Uva'utana. Im Tzelotehon Uva'utehon Dechol Beit Yisra'el. Kodam Avuna Devishmaya Ve'ar'a. Ve'imru Amen. **Amen**

May the prayer and supplication of the whole House of Yisrael be accepted before their Father in heaven, and say, Amen. **Amen**

יְהֵא שְׁלָמָא רַבָּא מִן שְׁמַיָּא. חַיִּים וְשָׂבָע וִישׁוּעָה וְנֶחָמָה. וְשֵׁיזָבָא וּרְפוּאָה וּגְאוּלָּה וּסְלִיחָה וְכַפָּרָה וְרֶוַח וְהַצָּלָה לָנוּ וּלְכָל עַמּוֹ יִשְׂרָאֵל. וְאִמְרוּ אָמֵן. אָמֵן

Yehei Shelama Rabba Min Shemaya. Chayim Vesava Vishu'ah Venechamah. Vesheizava Urefu'ah Uge'ulah Uselichah Vechapparah Verevach Vehatzalah Lanu Ulechol Ammo Yisra'el. Ve'imru Amen. **Amen**

May abundant peace descend from heaven, with life and plenty, salvation, solace, liberation, healing and redemption, and forgiveness and atonement, enlargement and freedom, for us and all of God's people Yisrael; and say, Amen. **Amen**

One bows and takes three steps backwards, while still bowing. After three steps, while still bowing and before erecting, while saying, "Oseh Shalom Bimromav", turn one's face to the left, "Hu [Berachamav] Ya'aseh Shalom Aleinu", turn one's face to the right; then bow forward like a servant leaving his master. (SA, OC 123:1)

עוֹשֶׂה שָׁלוֹם בִּמְרוֹמָיו. הוּא בְּרַחֲמָיו יַעֲשֶׂה שָׁלוֹם עָלֵינוּ. וְעַל כָּל־עַמּוֹ יִשְׂרָאֵל. וְאִמְרוּ אָמֵן:

Oseh Shalom Bimromav. Hu Berachamav Ya'aseh Shalom Aleinu. Ve'al Kol-'Ammo Yisra'el. Ve'imru Amen.

Creator of peace in His high places, may He in His mercy create peace for us and for all Yisrael, and say Amen.

At this point appropriate psalm is recited. On Chol HaMoed Pesach (Ps. 114), Chol HaMoed Sukkot (Ps. 122), and Purim (Ps. 124) some say the appropriate psalm in addition to or in place of Ps. 121. Some also count the Omer here during the seven weeks after Pesach. Some count and after the Aleinu.

Psalms 121

שִׁיר לַמַּעֲלוֹת אֶשָּׂא עֵינַי אֶל־הֶהָרִים מֵאַיִן יָבֹא עֶזְרִי: עֶזְרִי מֵעִם יְהֹוָה עֹשֵׂה שָׁמַיִם וָאָרֶץ: אַל־יִתֵּן לַמּוֹט רַגְלֶךָ אַל־יָנוּם שֹׁמְרֶךָ: הִנֵּה לֹא־יָנוּם וְלֹא יִישָׁן שׁוֹמֵר יִשְׂרָאֵל: יְהֹוָה שֹׁמְרֶךָ יְהֹוָה צִלְּךָ עַל־יַד יְמִינֶךָ: יוֹמָם הַשֶּׁמֶשׁ לֹא־יַכֶּכָּה וְיָרֵחַ בַּלָּיְלָה: יְהֹוָה יִשְׁמָרְךָ מִכָּל־רָע יִשְׁמֹר אֶת־נַפְשֶׁךָ: יְהֹוָה יִשְׁמָר־צֵאתְךָ וּבוֹאֶךָ מֵעַתָּה וְעַד־עוֹלָם:

Shir. Lamma'alot Essa Einai El-Heharim; Me'ayin. Yavo Ezri. Ezri Me'im Adonai Oseh. Shamayim Va'aretz. Al-Yiten Lamot Raglecha; Al-Yanum. Shomerecha. Hineh Lo-Yanum Velo Yishan; Shomer. Yisra'el. Adonai Shomerecha; Hashem Tzillecha. Al-Yad Yeminecha. Yomam. Hashemesh Lo-Yakekah. Veyareach Balailah. Adonai Yishmorcha Mikol-Ra'; Yishmor. Et-Nafshecha. Adonai Yishmor-Tzetecha Uvo'echa; Me'attah. Ve'ad-'Olam.

A Song of Ascents. I will lift up my eyes to the mountains: From where will my help come? My help comes from Hashem, Who made heaven and earth. He will not suffer Your foot to be moved; He that keeps You will not slumber. Behold, He that keeps Yisrael neither slumbers or sleeps. Hashem is your Guardian; Hashem is Your shade on Your right hand. The sun will not harm you by day, or the moon by night. Hashem will keep you from all evil; He will keep your soul. Hashem will guard your going out and your coming in, From this time and forever.

And on Chol HaMoed Pesach say:

Psalms 114

בְּצֵאת יִשְׂרָאֵל מִמִּצְרָיִם בֵּית יַעֲקֹב מֵעַם לֹעֵז: הָיְתָה יְהוּדָה לְקָדְשׁוֹ יִשְׂרָאֵל
מַמְשְׁלוֹתָיו: הַיָּם רָאָה וַיָּנֹס הַיַּרְדֵּן יִסֹּב לְאָחוֹר: הֶהָרִים רָקְדוּ כְאֵילִים גְּבָעוֹת
כִּבְנֵי־צֹאן: מַה־לְּךָ הַיָּם כִּי תָנוּס הַיַּרְדֵּן תִּסֹּב לְאָחוֹר: הֶהָרִים תִּרְקְדוּ כְאֵילִים
גְּבָעוֹת כִּבְנֵי־צֹאן: מִלִּפְנֵי אָדוֹן חוּלִי אָרֶץ מִלִּפְנֵי אֱלוֹהַּ יַעֲקֹב: הַהֹפְכִי הַצּוּר
אֲגַם־מָיִם חַלָּמִישׁ לְמַעְיְנוֹ־מָיִם:

Betzet Yisra'el Mimitzrayim Beit Ya'akov Me'am Lo'ez. Hayetah Yehudah Lekodsho Yisra'el Mamshelotav. Hayam Ra'ah Vayanos Hayarden Yissov Le'achor. Heharim Rakedu Che'eilim Geva'ot Kivnei Tzon. Mah Lecha Hayam Ki Tanus Hayarden Tissov Le'achor. Heharim Tirkedu Che'eilim Geva'ot Kivnei Tzon. Millifnei Adon Chuli Aretz Millifnei Eloah Ya'akov. Hahofechi Hatzur Agam Mayim Challamish Lema'yeno Mayim.

When Yisrael came forth out of Mitzrayim, The house of Yaakov from a people of strange language; Yehudah became His Sanctuary, Yisrael His dominion. The sea saw it, and fled; The Yarden turned backward. The mountains skipped like rams, The hills like young sheep. What ails you, Oh sea, that you flee? You Yarden, that you turn backward? You mountains, that you skip like rams; You hills, like young sheep? Tremble, earth, at the presence of Hashem, At the presence of the God of Yaakov; Who turned the rock into a pool of water, the flint into a fountain of waters.

And on Chol HaMoed Sukkot; Shavuot, and Shemini Atzeret / Simchat Torah say:

Psalms 122

שִׁיר הַמַּעֲלוֹת לְדָוִד שָׂמַחְתִּי בְּאֹמְרִים לִי בֵּית יְהֹוָה נֵלֵךְ: עֹמְדוֹת הָיוּ רַגְלֵינוּ
בִּשְׁעָרַיִךְ יְרוּשָׁלָם: יְרוּשָׁלַם הַבְּנוּיָה כְּעִיר שֶׁחֻבְּרָה־לָּהּ יַחְדָּו: שֶׁשָּׁם עָלוּ
שְׁבָטִים שִׁבְטֵי־יָהּ עֵדוּת לְיִשְׂרָאֵל לְהֹדוֹת לְשֵׁם יְהֹוָה: כִּי שָׁמָּה | יָשְׁבוּ
כִסְאוֹת לְמִשְׁפָּט כִּסְאוֹת לְבֵית דָּוִד: שַׁאֲלוּ שְׁלוֹם יְרוּשָׁלָם יִשְׁלָיוּ אֹהֲבָיִךְ:

יְהִי־שָׁלוֹם בְּחֵילֵךְ שַׁלְוָה בְּאַרְמְנוֹתָיִךְ׃ לְמַעַן אַחַי וְרֵעָי אֲדַבְּרָה־נָּא שָׁלוֹם בָּךְ׃
לְמַעַן בֵּית־יְהֹוָה אֱלֹהֵינוּ אֲבַקְשָׁה טוֹב לָךְ׃

Shir Hama'alot Ledavid Samachti Be'omerim Li Beit Adonai Nelech. Omedot Hayu Ragleinu Bish'arayich Yerushalayim. Yerushalayim Habenuyah Ke'ir Shechuberah Lah Yachdav. Shesham Alu Shevatim Shivtei Yah Edut Leyisra'el Lehodot Leshem Adonai. Ki Shamah Yashevu Chis'ot Lemishpat Kis'ot Leveit David. Sha'alu Shelom Yerushalayim Yishlayu Ohavayich. Yehi Shalom Becheilech Shalvah Be'armenotayich. Lema'an Achai Vere'ai Adaberah Na Shalom Bach. Lema'an Beit Adonai Eloheinu Avakshah Tov Lach.

A Song of Ascents; of David. I rejoiced when they said to me: 'Let us go to the House of Hashem.' Our feet are standing within your gates, Yerushalayim; Yerushalayim, that is built as a city that is compact together; Where the tribes went up, even the tribes of Hashem, as a testimony to Yisrael, to give thanks to the name of Hashem. For there were set thrones for judgment, the thrones of the House of David. Pray for the peace of Yerushalayim; May they that love You prosper. Peace be within your walls, and prosperity within your palaces. For my brothers and companions' sakes, I will now say: 'Peace be within you.' For the sake of the House of Hashem our God I will seek your good.

Kaddish Yehei-Shelama

Kaddish is only recited in a minyan (ten men). אָמֵן denotes when the congregation responds "Amen" together out loud. According to the Shulchan Arukh, the congregation says "Yehei Shemeh Rabba" to "Yitbarach" out loud together without interruption, and also that one should respond "Amen" after "Yitbarach." (SA, OC 55,56) This is not the common custom today. Though many are accustomed to answering according to their own custom, it is advised to respond in the custom of the one reciting to avoid not fragmenting into smaller groups. ("Lo Titgodedu" - BT, Yevamot 13b / SA, OC 493, Rema / MT, Avodah Zara 12:15)

יִתְגַּדַּל וְיִתְקַדַּשׁ שְׁמֵהּ רַבָּא. אָמֵן בְּעָלְמָא דִּי בְרָא. כִּרְעוּתֵהּ. וְיַמְלִיךְ מַלְכוּתֵהּ. וְיַצְמַח פֻּרְקָנֵהּ. וִיקָרֵב מְשִׁיחֵהּ. אָמֵן בְּחַיֵּיכוֹן וּבְיוֹמֵיכוֹן וּבְחַיֵּי דְכָל בֵּית יִשְׂרָאֵל. בַּעֲגָלָא וּבִזְמַן קָרִיב. וְאִמְרוּ אָמֵן. אָמֵן יְהֵא שְׁמֵיהּ רַבָּא מְבָרַךְ לְעָלַם וּלְעָלְמֵי עָלְמַיָּא יִתְבָּרַךְ. וְיִשְׁתַּבַּח. וְיִתְפָּאַר. וְיִתְרוֹמַם. וְיִתְנַשֵּׂא. וְיִתְהַדָּר. וְיִתְעַלֶּה. וְיִתְהַלָּל שְׁמֵהּ דְּקֻדְשָׁא. בְּרִיךְ הוּא. אָמֵן לְעֵלָּא מִן כָּל בִּרְכָתָא שִׁירָתָא. תֻּשְׁבְּחָתָא וְנֶחֱמָתָא. דַּאֲמִירָן בְּעָלְמָא. וְאִמְרוּ אָמֵן. אָמֵן

Yitgadal Veyitkadash Shemeh Rabba. **Amen** Be'alema Di Vera. Kir'uteh. Veyamlich Malchuteh. Veyatzmach Purkaneh. Vikarev Meshicheh. **Amen** Bechayeichon Uveyomeichon Uvechayei Dechal-Beit Yisra'el. Ba'agala Uvizman Kariv. Ve'imru Amen. **Amen** Yehei Shemeh Rabba Mevarach Le'alam Ule'alemei Alemaya Yitbarach. Veyishtabach. Veyitpa'ar. Veyitromam. Veyitnasse. Veyit'hadar. Veyit'aleh. Veyit'hallal Shemeh Dekudsha. Berich Hu. **Amen** Le'ella Min Kol Birchata Shirata. Tushbechata Venechemata. Da'amiran Be'alema. Ve'imru Amen. **Amen**

Glorified and sanctified be God's great name **Amen** throughout the world which He has created according to His will. May He establish His kingdom, hastening His salvation and the coming of His Messiah, **Amen**, in your lifetime and during your days, and within the life of the entire House of Yisrael, speedily and soon; and say, Amen. **Amen** May His great name be blessed forever and to all eternity. Blessed and praised, glorified and exalted, extolled and honored, adored and lauded is the name of the Holy One, blessed is He, **Amen** Beyond all the blessings and hymns, praises and consolations that are ever spoken in the world; and say, Amen. **Amen**

יְהֵא שְׁלָמָא רַבָּא מִן שְׁמַיָּא. חַיִּים וְשָׂבָע וִישׁוּעָה וְנֶחָמָה. וְשֵׁיזָבָא וּרְפוּאָה וּגְאוּלָה וּסְלִיחָה וְכַפָּרָה וְרֶוַח וְהַצָּלָה לָנוּ וּלְכָל עַמּוֹ יִשְׂרָאֵל. וְאִמְרוּ אָמֵן. אָמֵן

Yehei Shelama Rabba Min Shemaya. Chayim Vesava Vishu'ah Venechamah. Vesheizava Urefu'ah Uge'ulah Uselichah Vechapparah Verevach Vehatzalah Lanu Ulechol Ammo Yisra'el. Ve'imru Amen. **Amen**

May abundant peace descend from heaven, with life and plenty, salvation, solace, liberation, healing and redemption, and forgiveness and atonement, enlargement and freedom, for us and all of God's people Yisrael; and say, Amen. **Amen**

One bows and takes three steps backwards, while still bowing. After three steps, while still bowing and before erecting, while saying, "Oseh Shalom Bimromav", turn one's face to the left, "Hu [Berachamav] Ya'aseh Shalom Aleinu", turn one's face to the right; then bow forward like a servant leaving his master. (SA, OC 123:1)

עוֹשֶׂה שָׁלוֹם בִּמְרוֹמָיו. הוּא בְּרַחֲמָיו יַעֲשֶׂה שָׁלוֹם עָלֵינוּ. וְעַל כָּל־עַמּוֹ יִשְׂרָאֵל. וְאִמְרוּ אָמֵן:

Oseh Shalom Bimromav. Hu Berachamav Ya'aseh Shalom Aleinu. Ve'al Kol-'Ammo Yisra'el. Ve'imru Amen.

Creator of peace in His high places, may He in His mercy create peace for us and for all Yisrael, and say Amen.

Barechu

Barechu / Call to Prayer is said with 10 men (minyan).

The Chazan says:

בָּרְכוּ אֶת יְהֹוָה הַמְּבֹרָךְ:

Barechu Et Adonai Hamevorach.

Bless Hashem, the blessed One.

The kahal answers:

בָּרוּךְ יְהֹוָה הַמְּבֹרָךְ לְעוֹלָם וָעֶד:

Baruch Adonai Hamevorach Le'olam Va'ed.

Blessed is Hashem Who is blessed for all eternity.

The Chazan says:

בָּרוּךְ יְהֹוָה הַמְּבֹרָךְ לְעוֹלָם וָעֶד:

Baruch Adonai Hamevorach Le'olam Va'ed.

Blessed is Hashem Who is blessed for all eternity.

Aleinu

[*] denotes pausing and then bowing when saying "Va'anachnu Mistachavim".

Aleinu Leshabei'ach La'adon	עָלֵינוּ לְשַׁבֵּחַ לַאֲדוֹן
Hakol. Latet Gedullah Leyotzer	הַכֹּל. לָתֵת גְּדֻלָּה לְיוֹצֵר
Bereshit. Shelo Asanu Kegoyei	בְּרֵאשִׁית. שֶׁלֹּא עָשָׂנוּ כְּגוֹיֵי
Ha'aratzot. Velo Samanu	הָאֲרָצוֹת. וְלֹא שָׂמָנוּ
Kemishpechot Ha'adamah.	כְּמִשְׁפְּחוֹת הָאֲדָמָה.
Shelo Sam Chelkenu Kahem	שֶׁלֹּא שָׂם חֶלְקֵנוּ כָּהֶם
Vegoraleinu Kechal-Hamonam.	וְגוֹרָלֵנוּ כְּכָל־הֲמוֹנָם.
Shehem Mishtachavim Lahevel	שֶׁהֵם מִשְׁתַּחֲוִים לָהֶבֶל
Varik. Umitpallelim El-'El Lo	וָרִיק. וּמִתְפַּלְּלִים אֶל־אֵל לֹא
Yoshia. *Va'anachnu	יוֹשִׁיעַ. *וַאֲנַחְנוּ
Mishtachavim Lifnei Melech	מִשְׁתַּחֲוִים לִפְנֵי מֶלֶךְ
Malchei Hamelachim Hakadosh	מַלְכֵי הַמְּלָכִים הַקָּדוֹשׁ
Baruch Hu. Shehu Noteh	בָּרוּךְ הוּא. שֶׁהוּא נוֹטֶה
Shamayim Veyosed Aretz.	שָׁמַיִם וְיוֹסֵד אָרֶץ.
Umoshav Yekaro Bashamayim	וּמוֹשַׁב יְקָרוֹ בַּשָּׁמַיִם
Mima'al. Ushechinat Uzo	מִמַּעַל. וּשְׁכִינַת עֻזּוֹ
Begavehei Meromim. Hu	בְּגָבְהֵי מְרוֹמִים. הוּא
Eloheinu. Ve'ein Od Acher.	אֱלֹהֵינוּ. וְאֵין עוֹד אַחֵר.
Emet Malkeinu Ve'efes Zulato.	אֱמֶת מַלְכֵּנוּ וְאֶפֶס זוּלָתוֹ.
Kakatuv Batorah. Veyada'ta	כַּכָּתוּב בַּתּוֹרָה. וְיָדַעְתָּ
Hayom. Vahasheivota El-	הַיּוֹם וַהֲשֵׁבֹתָ אֶל־
Levavecha Ki Adonai Hu	לְבָבֶךָ כִּי יְהֹוָה הוּא
Ha'elohim. Bashamayim	הָאֱלֹהִים בַּשָּׁמַיִם
Mima'al. Ve'al-Ha'aretz	מִמַּעַל וְעַל־הָאָרֶץ
Mitachat; Ein Od.	מִתָּחַת אֵין עוֹד:

It is our obligation us to praise the Lord of all. To render greatness to the Former of creation. For He has not made us like the nation of the lands, nor set us to be like the families of the earth. Who has not given our portion like theirs and our lot like their masses that bow down to vanity and emptiness, "And pray to a god that does not save." *'But we bow before the supreme King of kings, the Holy One, blessed is He. Who stretches out the heavens and laid the foundations of the earth and his glorious seat is in the heavens above, and the presence of His might in the most exalted of heights. He is our God, there is no other. In truth our King, there is no one except Him. As it is written in the Torah: "This day know and lay it to your heart, that Hashem, He is God in the heavens above and on the earth beneath. There is no one else."

Al Ken Nekaveh Lach. Adonai	עַל כֵּן נְקַוֶּה לָךְ. יְהֹוָה
Eloheinu. Lir'ot Meheirah	אֱלֹהֵינוּ. לִרְאוֹת מְהֵרָה
Betif'eret Uzach. Leha'avir	בְּתִפְאֶרֶת עֻזָּךְ. לְהַעֲבִיר
Gilulim Min Ha'aretz.	גִּלּוּלִים מִן הָאָרֶץ.
Veha'elilim Karot Yikaretun.	וְהָאֱלִילִים כָּרוֹת יִכָּרֵתוּן.
Letakken Olam Bemalchut	לְתַקֵּן עוֹלָם בְּמַלְכוּת
Shaddai. Vechol-Benei Vasar	שַׁדַּי. וְכָל-בְּנֵי בָשָׂר
Yikre'u Vishmecha. Lehafnot	יִקְרְאוּ בִשְׁמֶךָ. לְהַפְנוֹת
Eleicha Kol-Rish'ei Aretz. Yakiru	אֵלֶיךָ כָּל-רִשְׁעֵי אָרֶץ. יַכִּירוּ
Veyede'u Kol-Yoshevei Tevel. Ki	וְיֵדְעוּ כָּל-יוֹשְׁבֵי תֵבֵל. כִּי
Lecha Tichra Kol-Berech. Tishava	לְךָ תִכְרַע כָּל-בֶּרֶךְ. תִּשָּׁבַע
Kol-Lashon. Lefaneicha. Adonai	כָּל-לָשׁוֹן. לְפָנֶיךָ. יְהֹוָה
Eloheinu Yichre'u Veyipolu.	אֱלֹהֵינוּ יִכְרְעוּ וְיִפֹּלוּ.
Velichvod Shimcha Yekar Yitenu.	וְלִכְבוֹד שִׁמְךָ יְקָר יִתֵּנוּ.
Vikabelu Chulam Et-'Ol	וִיקַבְּלוּ כֻלָּם אֶת-עֹל

Malchutecha. Vetimloch Aleihem	מַלְכוּתֶךָ. וְתִמְלוֹךְ עֲלֵיהֶם
Meheirah Le'olam Va'ed. Ki	מְהֵרָה לְעוֹלָם וָעֶד. כִּי
Hamalchut Shelecha Hi.	הַמַּלְכוּת שֶׁלְּךָ הִיא.
Ule'olemei Ad Timloch	וּלְעוֹלְמֵי עַד תִּמְלוֹךְ
Bechavod. Kakatuv Betoratach.	בְּכָבוֹד. כַּכָּתוּב בְּתוֹרָתָךְ:
Adonai Yimloch Le'olam Va'ed.	יְהֹוָה | יִמְלֹךְ לְעֹלָם וָעֶד:
Vene'emar. Vehayah Adonai	וְנֶאֱמַר. וְהָיָה יְהֹוָה
Lemelech Al-Kol-Ha'aretz;	לְמֶלֶךְ עַל־כָּל־הָאָרֶץ
Bayom Hahu. Yihyeh Adonai	בַּיּוֹם הַהוּא יִהְיֶה יְהֹוָה
Echad Ushemo Echad.	אֶחָד וּשְׁמוֹ אֶחָד:

Therefore we hope in You, Hashem our God, soon to see Your glorious might, to remove idols from the earth and the non-gods will be wholly cut down, to rectify the world with the kingdom of El Shaddai, and all children of flesh will call on Your name and all of the earth's wicked will turn to You. All that dwell on earth will understand and know that to You every knee must bend, and every tongue swear. Before You, Hashem our God, may all kneel and fall and give honor to Your glorious name. And they will all accept the yoke of Your kingdom. And may You speedily rule over them forever. For dominion is Yours, and forever You will reign in glory, as is written in Your Torah, "Hashem will reign forever and ever." For, it is said, "Hashem will be King over all the earth; on that day Hashem will be One and His name One."

Uvetoratecha Adonai Eloheinu	וּבְתוֹרָתְךָ יְהֹוָה אֱלֹהֵינוּ
Katuv Lemor. Shema Yisra'el;	כָּתוּב לֵאמֹר. שְׁמַע יִשְׂרָאֵל
Adonai Eloheinu Adonai Echad.	יְהֹוָה אֱלֹהֵינוּ יְהֹוָה אֶחָד:

And in Your Torah, Hashem our God, it is written: Hear O Yisrael Hashem our God, Hashem is One.

At this point some Count the Omer (referring to section in the back) in the seven weeks after Pesach. Many also recite Birkat HaLevanah (The Blessing of the Moon) within the first half of new month, depending on the custom. (Refer to section in the back for instructions).

Kriyat Shema She'Al Hamita / The Bedtime Shema

If one stays awake until after midnight they will read the recital of Shema half an hour before midnight, and if he forgot to read before midnight he can read any Kriyat Shema order after midnight.

Some say before:

לְשֵׁם יִחוּד קוּדְשָׁא בְּרִיךְ הוּא וּשְׁכִינְתֵּיהּ. בִּדְחִילוּ וּרְחִימוּ. וּרְחִימוּ וּדְחִילוּ. לְיַחֲדָא שֵׁם יו״ד קֵ״י בְּוָא״ו קֵ״י בְּיִחוּדָא שְׁלִים (יהוה) בְּשֵׁם כָּל יִשְׂרָאֵל. הריני מקבל עלי אלהותו יתברך ואהבתו ויראתו. והריני ירא ממנו בגין דאיהו רב ושליט על כלא. וכלא קמיה כלא. והריני ממליכו על כל אבר ואבר וגיד וגיד מרמ״ח אברים ושס״ה גידים שׁל גופי ונפשי רוחי ונשמתי מלכות גמורה ושלמה. והריני עבד להשם יתברך והוא ברחמיו יזכני לעבדו בלבב שלם ונפש חפצה. אָמֵן כֵּן יְהִי רָצוֹן.

Ribono Shel Olam

Ribono Shel Olam Hareini	רִבּוֹנוֹ שֶׁל עוֹלָם הֲרֵינִי
Mochel Vesoleach Lechol-Mi-	מוֹחֵל וְסוֹלֵחַ לְכָל־מִי־
Shehich'is Vehiknit Oti O	שֶׁהִכְעִיס וְהִקְנִיט אוֹתִי אוֹ
Shechata Kenegdi. Bein Begufi	שֶׁחָטָא כְּנֶגְדִּי. בֵּין בְּגוּפִי
Bein Bemamoni Bein Bichvodi	בֵּין בְּמָמוֹנִי בֵּין בִּכְבוֹדִי
Bein Bechol-'Asher Li. Bein	בֵּין בְּכָל־אֲשֶׁר לִי. בֵּין
Be'ones Bein Beratzon Bein	בְּאוֹנֶס בֵּין בְּרָצוֹן בֵּין
Beshogeg Bein Bemezid Bein	בְּשׁוֹגֵג בֵּין בְּמֵזִיד בֵּין
Bedibur Bein Bema'aseh. Bein	בְּדִבּוּר בֵּין בְּמַעֲשֶׂה. בֵּין
Begilgul Zeh Bein Begilgul	בְּגִלְגּוּל זֶה בֵּין בְּגִלְגּוּל
Acher. Lechol-Bar-Yisra'el. Velo	אַחֵר. לְכָל־בַּר־יִשְׂרָאֵל. וְלֹא
Ye'anesh Shum Adam Besibati.	יֵעָנֵשׁ שׁוּם אָדָם בְּסִבָּתִי.
Yehi Ratzon Milfaneicha Adonai	יְהִי רָצוֹן מִלְּפָנֶיךָ יְהוָה

Elohai Velohei Avotai Shelo	אֱלֹהַי וֵאלֹהֵי אֲבוֹתַי שֶׁלֹּא
Echeta Od. Umah-Shechatati	אֶחֱטָא עוֹד. וּמַה־שֶּׁחָטָאתִי
Lefaneicha Mechok	לְפָנֶיךָ מְחוֹק
Berachameicha Harabbim. Aval	בְּרַחֲמֶיךָ הָרַבִּים. אֲבָל
Lo Al-Yedei Yissurin Vechola'im	לֹא עַל־יְדֵי יִסּוּרִין וָחֳלָאִים
Ra'im. Yihyu Leratzon Imrei-Fi	רָעִים. יִהְיוּ לְרָצוֹן אִמְרֵי־פִי
Vehegyon Libi Lefaneicha;	וְהֶגְיוֹן לִבִּי לְפָנֶיךָ
Adonai Tzuri Vego'ali.	יְהוָֹה צוּרִי וְגֹאֲלִי׃

Sovereign of the universe, behold, I freely forgive everyone who has aggrieved or frustrated me, or who has sinned against me, either in my body, property, honor, or in anything else belonging to me; whether by compulsion or choice: whether ignorantly or with intent: whether in word or in deed, during the whole period of my existence; I forgive any Israelite, and I pray that no person may be punished on account of me. May it be acceptable in Your presence, Hashem my God and God of my fathers, that I may sin no more; that I do not repeat my sins: or continue to anger you: or do evil in Your eyes: and whatever I have sinned before You, blot out through Your abundant mercies: but not through means of anguish and severe illness. May the words of my mouth and the thoughts of my heart, be acceptable in Your presence, Hashem, my Rock and Redeemer.

Baruch HaMapil Chevlei

Baruch Attah Adonai Eloheinu	בָּרוּךְ אַתָּה יְהוָֹה אֱלֹהֵינוּ
Melech Ha'olam Hamapil	מֶלֶךְ הָעוֹלָם. הַמַּפִּיל
Chevlei Shenah Al-'Einai	חֶבְלֵי שֵׁנָה עַל־עֵינָי
Utenumah Al-'Af'appai. Ume'ir	וּתְנוּמָה עַל־עַפְעַפָּי. וּמֵאִיר
Le'ishon Bat-'Ayin. Yehi Ratzon	לְאִישׁוֹן בַּת־עָיִן. יְהִי רָצוֹן

Milfaneicha Adonai Elohai	מִלְּפָנֶיךָ יְהֹוָה אֱלֹהַי
Velohei Avotai Shetashkiveni	וֵאלֹהֵי אֲבוֹתַי שֶׁתַּשְׁכִּיבֵנִי
Leshalom. Veta'amideini	לְשָׁלוֹם. וְתַעֲמִידֵנִי
Lechayim Tovim Uleshalom.	לְחַיִּים טוֹבִים וּלְשָׁלוֹם.
Veten Chelki Betoratecha.	וְתֵן חֶלְקִי בְּתוֹרָתֶךָ.
Vetargileini Lidvar Mitzvah.	וְתַרְגִּילֵנִי לִדְבַר מִצְוָה.
Ve'al-Targileini Lidvar Averah.	וְאַל־תַּרְגִּילֵנִי לִדְבַר עֲבֵרָה.
Ve'al-Tevi'eni Lidei Chet. Velo	וְאַל־תְּבִיאֵנִי לִידֵי חֵטְא. וְלֹא
Lidei Nissayon Velo Lidei	לִידֵי נִסָּיוֹן וְלֹא לִידֵי
Vizayon. Veyishlot Bi Yetzer	בִזָּיוֹן. וְיִשְׁלוֹט בִּי יֵצֶר
Hatov Ve'al-Yishlot Bi Yetzer	הַטּוֹב וְאַל־יִשְׁלוֹט בִּי יֵצֶר
Hara. Vetatzileini Miyetzer Hara	הָרָע. וְתַצִּילֵנִי מִיֵּצֶר הָרָע
Umechola'im Ra'im. Ve'al-	וּמֵחוֹלָאִים רָעִים. וְאַל־
Yavhiluni Chalomot Ra'im	יַבְהִילוּנִי חֲלוֹמוֹת רָעִים
Vehirhurim Ra'im. Utehei Mitati	וְהִרְהוּרִים רָעִים. וּתְהֵא מִטָּתִי
Shelemah Lefaneicha. Veha'er	שְׁלֵמָה לְפָנֶיךָ. וְהָאֵר
Einai Pen Ishan Hamavet. Baruch	עֵינַי פֶּן אִישַׁן הַמָּוֶת. בָּרוּךְ
Attah Adonai Hame'ir La'olam	אַתָּה יְהֹוָה הַמֵּאִיר לָעוֹלָם
Kulo Bichvodo.	כֻּלּוֹ בִּכְבוֹדוֹ:

Blessed are You, Hashem our God, King of the universe, You weigh down my eyes with the bonds of sleep, my eyelids with slumber, and illuminate the pupil of my eye. Hashem my God, God of my fathers, may it be Your will to lay me down in peace, and to raise me up again to good and peaceful life with my portion in Your Torah. Exercise me in the observance of Your commands and do not let me walk in the way of transgression. Do not let me come into the power of temptation, sin or shame. May the good inclination rule me, and may the evil inclination not rule over me. Deliver me from the evil inclination and from grievous sickness. May bad dreams and evil thoughts not trouble me, but let my bed would be perfect before You. Illuminate my eyes again, so I will not sleep the sleep of death. Blessed are You, Hashem, Whose glory gives light to the whole universe.

LAWS OF RECITING THE SHEMA

One who recites the Shema, but did not have intention during the first verse, 'Shema Yisrael', one did not fulfill their obligation. As for the rest, if they read during the specified time and did not have intention, they have fulfilled their obligation. One should recite the Shema with intention, awe, fear, shaking and trembling. The custom is to place one's hands over their face during the recitation of the first verse in order that one will not look at something else that will prevent him from directing his heart. (SA, OC 59-61)

One covers their eyes and says:

שְׁמַע יִשְׂרָאֵל יְהֹוָה אֱלֹהֵינוּ יְהֹוָה | אֶחָד:

Shema Yisrael; Adonai Eloheinu Adonai Echad.

"Hear, O Yisrael, Hashem is our God, Hashem is One."

Whisper silently:

בָּרוּךְ שֵׁם כְּבוֹד מַלְכוּתוֹ לְעוֹלָם וָעֶד:

Baruch Shem Kevod Malchuto Le'olam Va'ed.

Blessed is His name and glorious kingdom forever and ever.

Ve'ahavta

וְאָהַבְתָּ אֵת יְהֹוָה אֱלֹהֶיךָ בְּכָל־לְבָבְךָ וּבְכָל־נַפְשְׁךָ וּבְכָל־מְאֹדֶךָ:
וְהָיוּ הַדְּבָרִים הָאֵלֶּה אֲשֶׁר אָנֹכִי מְצַוְּךָ הַיּוֹם עַל־לְבָבֶךָ: וְשִׁנַּנְתָּם
לְבָנֶיךָ וְדִבַּרְתָּ בָּם בְּשִׁבְתְּךָ בְּבֵיתֶךָ וּבְלֶכְתְּךָ בַדֶּרֶךְ וּבְשָׁכְבְּךָ
וּבְקוּמֶךָ: וּקְשַׁרְתָּם לְאוֹת עַל־יָדֶךָ וְהָיוּ לְטֹטָפֹת בֵּין עֵינֶיךָ: וּכְתַבְתָּם
עַל־מְזֻזוֹת בֵּיתֶךָ וּבִשְׁעָרֶיךָ:

Ve'ahavta Et Adonai Eloheicha; Bechol-Levavecha Uvechol-Nafshecha Uvechol-Me'odecha. Vehayu Hadevarim Ha'eleh. Asher Anochi Metzavecha Hayom Al-Levavecha. Veshinantam Levaneicha. Vedibarta Bam; Beshivtecha Beveitecha Uvelechtecha Vaderech. Uveshochbecha Uvekumecha. Ukeshartam Le'ot Al-Yadecha; Vehayu Letotafot Bein Eineicha. Uchetavtam Al-Mezuzot Beitecha Uvish'areicha.

And you will love Hashem your God with all your heart, and with all your soul, and with all your might. And these words, which I command you this day, will be upon your heart; and your will teach them diligently to your children, and will talk of them when you sit in your house, and when you walk by the way, and when you lie down, and when you rise up. And you will bind them for a sign on your hand, and they will be for frontlets between your eyes. And you will write them on the doorposts of your house, and on your gates.

Vehayah Im-shamoa

וְהָיָה אִם־שָׁמֹעַ תִּשְׁמְעוּ אֶל־מִצְוֺתַי אֲשֶׁר אָנֹכִי מְצַוֶּה אֶתְכֶם הַיּוֹם לְאַהֲבָה אֶת־יְהֹוָה אֱלֹהֵיכֶם וּלְעָבְדוֹ בְּכָל־לְבַבְכֶם וּבְכָל־נַפְשְׁכֶם: וְנָתַתִּי מְטַר־אַרְצְכֶם בְּעִתּוֹ יוֹרֶה וּמַלְקוֹשׁ וְאָסַפְתָּ דְגָנֶךָ וְתִירֹשְׁךָ וְיִצְהָרֶךָ: וְנָתַתִּי עֵשֶׂב בְּשָׂדְךָ לִבְהֶמְתֶּךָ וְאָכַלְתָּ וְשָׂבָעְתָּ: הִשָּׁמְרוּ לָכֶם פֶּן יִפְתֶּה לְבַבְכֶם וְסַרְתֶּם וַעֲבַדְתֶּם אֱלֹהִים אֲחֵרִים וְהִשְׁתַּחֲוִיתֶם לָהֶם: וְחָרָה אַף־יְהֹוָה בָּכֶם וְעָצַר אֶת־הַשָּׁמַיִם וְלֹא־יִהְיֶה מָטָר וְהָאֲדָמָה לֹא תִתֵּן אֶת־יְבוּלָהּ וַאֲבַדְתֶּם מְהֵרָה מֵעַל הָאָרֶץ הַטֹּבָה אֲשֶׁר יְהֹוָה נֹתֵן לָכֶם: וְשַׂמְתֶּם אֶת־דְּבָרַי אֵלֶּה עַל־לְבַבְכֶם וְעַל־נַפְשְׁכֶם וּקְשַׁרְתֶּם אֹתָם לְאוֹת עַל־יֶדְכֶם וְהָיוּ לְטוֹטָפֹת בֵּין עֵינֵיכֶם. וְלִמַּדְתֶּם אֹתָם אֶת־בְּנֵיכֶם לְדַבֵּר בָּם בְּשִׁבְתְּךָ בְּבֵיתֶךָ וּבְלֶכְתְּךָ בַדֶּרֶךְ וּבְשָׁכְבְּךָ וּבְקוּמֶךָ: וּכְתַבְתָּם עַל־מְזוּזוֹת בֵּיתֶךָ

וּבִשְׁעָרֶיךָ: לְמַעַן יִרְבּוּ יְמֵיכֶם וִימֵי בְנֵיכֶם עַל הָאֲדָמָה אֲשֶׁר נִשְׁבַּע יְהוָה לַאֲבֹתֵיכֶם לָתֵת לָהֶם כִּימֵי הַשָּׁמַיִם עַל־הָאָרֶץ:

Vehayah Im-Shamoa Tishme'u El-Mitzvotai. Asher Anochi Metzaveh Etchem Hayom; Le'ahavah Et-Adonai Eloheichem Ule'avdo. Bechol-Levavchem Uvechol-Nafshechem. Venatati Metar-'Artzechem Be'ito Yoreh Umalkosh; Ve'asafta Deganecha. Vetiroshecha Veyitzharecha. Venatati Esev Besadecha Livhemtecha; Ve'achalta Vesava'eta. Hishameru Lachem. Pen Yifteh Levavchem; Vesartem. Va'avadtem Elohim Acherim. Vehishtachavitem Lahem. Vecharah Af-Adonai Bachem. Ve'atzar Et-Hashamayim Velo-Yihyeh Matar. Veha'adamah. Lo Titen Et-Yevulah; Va'avadtem Meheirah. Me'al Ha'aretz Hatovah. Asher Adonai Noten Lachem. Vesamtem Et-Devarai Eleh. Al-Levavchem Ve'al-Nafshechem; Ukeshartem Otam Le'ot Al-Yedchem. Vehayu Letotafot Bein Eineichem. Velimadtem Otam Et-Beneichem Ledaber Bam; Beshivtecha Beveitecha Uvelechtecha Vaderech. Uveshochbecha Uvekumecha. Uchetavtam Al-Mezuzot Beitecha Uvish'areicha. Lema'an Yirbu Yemeichem Vimei Veneichem. Al Ha'adamah. Asher Nishba Adonai La'avoteichem Latet Lahem; Kimei Hashamayim Al-Ha'aretz.

And it will come to pass, if you will observe My commandments which I command you this day, to love Hashem your God, and to serve Him with all your heart and with all your soul, that I will give the rain of your land in its season, the former rain and the latter rain, that you may gather in your corn, and your wine, and your oil. And I will give grass in your fields for your cattle, and you will eat and be satisfied. Be cautious, in case your heart is deceived, and you turn aside, and serve other gods, and worship them; and the anger of Hashem is kindled against you, and He shut up the heaven, so that there will be no rain, and the ground will not yield her fruit; and you perish quickly from off the good land which Hashem gives you. Therefore you will lay up these My words in your heart and in your soul; and you will bind them for a sign upon your hand, and they will be for frontlets between your eyes. And you will teach them your children, talking of them, when you sit in your house, and when you walk by the way, and when you lie down, and when you rise up. And you will write them on the doorposts of your house, and on your gates; that your days may be multiplied, and the days of your children, upon the land which Hashem swore to your fathers to give them, as the days of the heavens above the earth. **(Deuteronomy 11:13-21)**

Numbers 15:37-41

וַיֹּאמֶר יְהֹוָה אֶל־מֹשֶׁה לֵּאמֹר: דַּבֵּר אֶל־בְּנֵי יִשְׂרָאֵל וְאָמַרְתָּ אֲלֵהֶם וְעָשׂוּ לָהֶם צִיצִת עַל־כַּנְפֵי בִגְדֵיהֶם לְדֹרֹתָם וְנָתְנוּ עַל־צִיצִת הַכָּנָף פְּתִיל תְּכֵלֶת: וְהָיָה לָכֶם לְצִיצִת וּרְאִיתֶם אֹתוֹ וּזְכַרְתֶּם אֶת־כָּל־מִצְוֹת יְהֹוָה וַעֲשִׂיתֶם אֹתָם וְלֹא־תָתֻרוּ אַחֲרֵי לְבַבְכֶם וְאַחֲרֵי עֵינֵיכֶם אֲשֶׁר־אַתֶּם זֹנִים אַחֲרֵיהֶם: לְמַעַן תִּזְכְּרוּ וַעֲשִׂיתֶם אֶת־כָּל־מִצְוֹתָי וִהְיִיתֶם קְדֹשִׁים לֵאלֹהֵיכֶם: אֲנִי יְהֹוָה אֱלֹהֵיכֶם אֲשֶׁר הוֹצֵאתִי אֶתְכֶם מֵאֶרֶץ מִצְרַיִם לִהְיוֹת לָכֶם לֵאלֹהִים אֲנִי יְהֹוָה אֱלֹהֵיכֶם: אֱמֶת.

Vayomer Adonai El-Mosheh Lemor. Daber El-Benei Yisra'el Ve'amarta Aleihem. Ve'asu Lahem Tzitzit Al-Kanfei Vigdeihem Ledorotam; Venatenu Al-Tzitzit Hakanaf Petil Techelet. Vehayah Lachem Letzitzit Ure'item Oto Uzechartem Et-Chol-Mitzvot Adonai Va'asitem Otam; Velo-Taturu Acharei Levavchem Ve'acharei Eineichem. Asher-'Attem Zonim Achareihem. Lema'an Tizkeru. Va'asitem Et-Chol-Mitzvotai; Vihyitem Kedoshim Leloheichem. Ani Adonai Eloheichem. Asher Hotzeti Etchem Me'eretz Mitzrayim. Lihyot Lachem Lelohim; Ani Adonai Eloheichem. Emet.

And Hashem spoke to Moshe, saying: Speak to the children of Yisrael, and command them to make tzitzit on the corners of their garments throughout their generations, and that they put a thread of tekhelet with the tzitzit of each corner. And it will be to you for a tzitzit, that you may look upon it, and remember all the commandments of Hashem, and do them; and that you do not go about after your own heart and your own eyes, after which you go whoring; that you may remember and do all My commandments, and be holy to your God. I am Hashem your God, Who brought you out of the land of Mitzrayim, to be your God: I am Hashem your God. It is true.

יְהֹוָה אֱלֹהֵיכֶם אֱמֶת:

Adonai Eloheichem Emet.

Hashem, your God, is true.

The following verses are typically recited:

יַעְלְזוּ חֲסִידִים בְּכָבוֹד יְרַנְּנוּ עַל־מִשְׁכְּבוֹתָם: רוֹמְמוֹת אֵל בִּגְרוֹנָם וְחֶרֶב פִּיפִיּוֹת בְּיָדָם:

Ya'lezu Chasidim Bechavod; Yeranenu. Al-Mishkevotam. Romemot El Bigronam; Vecherev Pifiyot Beyadam.

Let the pious rejoice in glory; Let them sing for joy upon their beds. Let the high praises of God be in their mouth, And a two-edged sword in their hand; **(Psalms 149:5-6)**

הִנֵּה מִטָּתוֹ שֶׁלִּשְׁלֹמֹה שִׁשִּׁים גִּבֹּרִים סָבִיב לָהּ מִגִּבֹּרֵי יִשְׂרָאֵל: כֻּלָּם אֲחֻזֵי חֶרֶב מְלֻמְּדֵי מִלְחָמָה אִישׁ חַרְבּוֹ עַל־יְרֵכוֹ מִפַּחַד בַּלֵּילוֹת: **ג׳ פעמים**

Hineh. Mitato Shelishlomoh. Shishim Giborim Saviv Lah; Migiborei Yisra'el. Kulam Achuzei Cherev. Melummedei Milchamah; Ish Charbo Al-Yerecho. Mipachad Baleilot.

There is Shlomo's couch, Encircled by sixty warriors of the warriors of Yisrael, All of them trained in warfare, Skilled in battle, Each with sword on thigh, because of terror by night. **(3x) (Song of Songs 3:7-8)**

יְבָרֶכְךָ יְהֹוָה וְיִשְׁמְרֶךָ: יָאֵר יְהֹוָה | פָּנָיו אֵלֶיךָ וִיחֻנֶּךָּ: יִשָּׂא יְהֹוָה | פָּנָיו אֵלֶיךָ וְיָשֵׂם לְךָ שָׁלוֹם:

Yevarechecha Adonai Veyishmerecha. Ya'er Adonai Panav Eleicha Vichuneka. Yissa Adonai Panav Eleicha. Veyasem Lecha Shalom.

Hashem bless you and keep you. Hashem make His countenance shine upon you, and be gracious to you. Hashem lift up His countenance upon you and give you peace.

Psalms 91:1-9

יֹשֵׁב בְּסֵתֶר עֶלְיוֹן בְּצֵל שַׁדַּי יִתְלוֹנָן: אֹמַר לַיהוָה מַחְסִי וּמְצוּדָתִי | אֱלֹהַי אֶבְטַח־בּוֹ: כִּי הוּא יַצִּילְךָ מִפַּח יָקוּשׁ מִדֶּבֶר הַוּוֹת: בְּאֶבְרָתוֹ יָסֶךְ לָךְ וְתַחַת־כְּנָפָיו תֶּחְסֶה צִנָּה וְסֹחֵרָה אֲמִתּוֹ: לֹא־תִירָא מִפַּחַד לָיְלָה מֵחֵץ יָעוּף יוֹמָם: מִדֶּבֶר בָּאֹפֶל יַהֲלֹךְ מִקֶּטֶב יָשׁוּד צָהֳרָיִם: יִפֹּל מִצִּדְּךָ אֶלֶף וּרְבָבָה מִימִינֶךָ אֵלֶיךָ לֹא יִגָּשׁ: רַק בְּעֵינֶיךָ תַבִּיט וְשִׁלֻּמַת רְשָׁעִים תִּרְאֶה: כִּי־אַתָּה יְהוָה מַחְסִי:

Yoshev Beseter Elyon; Betzel Shaddai. Yitlonan. Omar. L'Adonai Machsi Umetzudati; Elohai. Evtach-Bo. Ki Hu Yatzilecha Mippach Yakush. Midever Havot. Be'evrato Yasech Lach Vetachat-Kenafav Techseh; Tzinah Vesocherah Amito. Lo-Tira Mipachad Lailah; Mechetz. Ya'uf Yomam. Midever Ba'ofel Yahaloch; Miketev. Yashud Tzohorayim. Yippol Mitzidecha Elef. Urevavah Miminecha; Eleicha. Lo Yigash. Rak Be'eineicha Tabbit; Veshilumat Resha'im Tir'eh. Ki-'Attah Adonai Machsi.

You that dwells in the shadow of the Most High, And abides in the shadow of the Almighty; I will say of Hashem, Who is my refuge and my fortress, My God, in Whom I trust, That He will deliver you from the snare of the fowler, And from the harmful pestilence. He will cover you with His wings, And under His wings you will take refuge; His truth is a shield and a buckler. You will not be afraid of the terror by night, or of the arrow that flies by day; Of the pestilence that walks in darkness, or of the destruction that wastes at noon. A thousand may fall at Your side, And ten thousand at Your right hand; It will not come near you. Only with your eyes you will behold, And see the recompense of the wicked. For you have made Hashem your habitation.

Continue with Hashkivenu.

Some say, without a blessing:

Hashkiveinu

הַשְׁכִּיבֵֽנוּ אָבִֽינוּ לְשָׁלוֹם. וְהַעֲמִידֵֽנוּ מַלְכֵּֽנוּ לְחַיִּים טוֹבִים וּלְשָׁלוֹם.
וּפְרוֹשׂ עָלֵֽינוּ סֻכַּת שְׁלוֹמֶֽךָ. וְתַקְּנֵֽנוּ מַלְכֵּֽנוּ בְּעֵצָה טוֹבָה מִלְּפָנֶֽיךָ.
וְהוֹשִׁיעֵֽנוּ מְהֵרָה לְמַֽעַן שְׁמֶֽךָ. וְהָגֵן בַּעֲדֵֽנוּ. וְהָסֵר מֵעָלֵֽינוּ מַכַּת
אוֹיֵב. דֶּֽבֶר. חֶֽרֶב. חְולִי. צָרָה. רָעָה. רָעָב. וְיָגוֹן. וּמַשְׁחִית. וּמַגֵּפָה.
שְׁבוֹר וְהָסֵר הַשָּׂטָן מִלְּפָנֵֽינוּ וּמֵאַחֲרֵֽינוּ. וּבְצֵל כְּנָפֶֽיךָ תַּסְתִּירֵֽנוּ.
וּשְׁמוֹר צֵאתֵֽנוּ וּבוֹאֵֽנוּ לְחַיִּים טוֹבִים וּלְשָׁלוֹם מֵעַתָּה וְעַד עוֹלָם: כִּי
אֵל שׁוֹמְרֵֽנוּ וּמַצִּילֵֽנוּ אֶֽתָּה מִכָּל דָּבָר רָע וּמִפַּֽחַד לָֽיְלָה.

Hashkiveinu Avinu Leshalom. Veha'amidenu Malkeinu Lechayim Tovim Uleshalom. Uferos Aleinu Sukkat Shelomecha. Vetakenenu Malkeinu Be'etzah Tovah Milfaneicha. Vehoshi'enu Meheirah Lema'an Shemecha. Vehagen Ba'adenu. Vehaseir Me'aleinu Makat Oyev. Dever. Cherev. Choli. Tzarah. Ra'ah. Ra'av. Veyagon. Umashchit. Umagefah. Shevor Vehaseir Hasatan Millefaneinu Ume'achareinu. Uvetzel Kenafeicha Tastirenu. Ushemor Tzetenu Uvo'enu Lechayim Tovim Uleshalom Me'attah Ve'ad Olam. Ki El Shomerenu Umatzilenu Attah Mikol Davar Ra Umipachad Lailah.

Our Father, lay us down in peace and raise us up, our King, to a good life and peace. And spread over us Your shelter of peace and direct us with good council before You, our King. And save us speedily for Your name's sake. And guard us and remove from us the strike of an enemy, sword, illness, distress, evil, famine, and misery and corruption and plague. Shelter us in the shadow of Your wings. And guard our going out and our coming in, for a good life and peace now and forever. For You are God, our Guardian and our Deliverer from every evil thing and from dread of the night.

Vidui / Confession

Vidui and Tachanun prayer is not recited on Friday night, or the eve of a Yom Tov, and should ideally not be said until after hatzot (midnight) after a day that Tachanun and Vidui was omitted.

אָנָּא יְהֹוָה אֱלֹהֵינוּ וֵאלֹהֵי אֲבוֹתֵינוּ. תָּבֹא לְפָנֶיךָ תְּפִלָּתֵנוּ. וְאַל תִּתְעַלַּם מַלְכֵּנוּ מִתְּחִנָּתֵנוּ. שֶׁאֵין אֲנַחְנוּ עַזֵּי פָנִים וּקְשֵׁי עֹרֶף לוֹמַר לְפָנֶיךָ יְהֹוָה אֱלֹהֵינוּ וֵאלֹהֵי אֲבוֹתֵינוּ צַדִּיקִים אֲנַחְנוּ וְלֹא־חָטָאנוּ. אֲבָל חָטָאנוּ. עָוִינוּ. פָּשַׁעְנוּ. אֲנַחְנוּ וַאֲבוֹתֵינוּ וְאַנְשֵׁי בֵיתֵנוּ:

Ana Adonai Eloheinu Velohei Avoteinu. Tavo Lefaneicha Tefillateinu. Ve'al Tit'alam Malkeinu Mitechinateinu. She'ein Anachnu Azei Fanim Ukeshei Oref Lomar Lefaneicha Adonai Eloheinu Velohei Avoteinu Tzaddikim Anachnu Velo-Chatanu. Aval Chatanu. Avinu. Pasha'nu. Anachnu Va'avoteinu Ve'anshei Veiteinu.

Our God and God of our fathers, may our prayer reach you; do not ignore our plea. For we are neither insolent or obstinate to say to you: "Hashem our God and God of our fathers, we are just and have not sinned." Indeed, we and our fathers have sinned and our household.

אָשַׁמְנוּ. בָּגַדְנוּ. גָּזַלְנוּ. דִּבַּרְנוּ דֹפִי וְלָשׁוֹן הָרָע. הֶעֱוִינוּ. וְהִרְשַׁעְנוּ. זַדְנוּ. חָמַסְנוּ. טָפַלְנוּ שֶׁקֶר וּמִרְמָה. יָעַצְנוּ עֵצוֹת רָעוֹת. כִּזַּבְנוּ. כָּעַסְנוּ. לַצְנוּ. מָרַדְנוּ. מָרִינוּ דְבָרֶיךָ. נִאַצְנוּ. נִאַפְנוּ. סָרַרְנוּ. עָוִינוּ. פָּשַׁעְנוּ. פָּגַמְנוּ. צָרַרְנוּ. צִעַרְנוּ אָב וָאֵם. קִשִּׁינוּ עֹרֶף. רָשַׁעְנוּ. שִׁחַתְנוּ. תִּעַבְנוּ. תָּעִינוּ וְתִעְתָּעְנוּ. וְסַרְנוּ מִמִּצְוֹתֶיךָ וּמִמִּשְׁפָּטֶיךָ הַטּוֹבִים וְלֹא שָׁוָה לָנוּ. וְאַתָּה צַדִּיק עַל כָּל הַבָּא עָלֵינוּ. כִּי אֱמֶת עָשִׂיתָ. וַאֲנַחְנוּ הִרְשָׁעְנוּ:

Ashamnu. Bagadnu. Gazalnu. Dibarnu Dofi Velashon Hara. He'evinu. Vehirsha'nu. Zadnu. Chamasnu. Tafalnu Sheker Umirmah. Ya'atznu Etzot Ra'ot. Kizavnu. Ka'asnu. Latznu. Maradnu. Marinu Devareicha. Ni'atznu. Ni'afnu. Sararnu. Avinu. Pasha'nu. Pagamnu. Tzararnu. Tzi'arnu Av Va'em. Kishinu Oref. Rasha'nu. Shichatnu. Ti'avnu. Ta'inu Veti'ata'nu. Vesarnu Mimitzvoteicha Umimishpateicha Hatovim Velo Shavah Lanu. Ve'attah Tzaddik Al Kol Haba Aleinu. Ki Emet Asita. Va'anachnu Hirsha'enu.

We have trespassed, we have dealt treacherously, we have robbed, we have spoken slander and evil speech, we have committed iniquity, and have done wickedly; we have acted presumptuously, we have committed violence, we have forged falsehood and deceived, we have counseled evil, we have uttered lies, we were angry, we have scoffed, we have rebelled and violated Your words, we have blasphemed, we have committed adultery, we have revolted, we have acted perversely, we have transgressed, we have broken faith, we have been hard and we have distressed father and mother. we have been stiff-necked, we have acted wickedly, we have corrupted, we have done abominably; we have gone astray ourselves, and have caused others to stray; we have also turned aside from Your good precepts and commandments, and it has not profited us; "But You are just concerning all that is come upon us; for You have dealt most truly, but we have done wickedly." **(Nehemiah 9:33)**

Some say:

Psalms 121

שִׁיר לַמַּעֲלוֹת אֶשָּׂא עֵינַי אֶל־הֶהָרִים מֵאַיִן יָבֹא עֶזְרִי׃ עֶזְרִי מֵעִם
יְהוָה עֹשֵׂה שָׁמַיִם וָאָרֶץ׃ אַל־יִתֵּן לַמּוֹט רַגְלֶךָ אַל־יָנוּם שֹׁמְרֶךָ׃ הִנֵּה
לֹא־יָנוּם וְלֹא יִישָׁן שׁוֹמֵר יִשְׂרָאֵל׃ יְהוָה שֹׁמְרֶךָ יְהוָה צִלְּךָ עַל־יַד
יְמִינֶךָ׃ יוֹמָם הַשֶּׁמֶשׁ לֹא־יַכֶּכָּה וְיָרֵחַ בַּלָּיְלָה׃ יְהוָה יִשְׁמָרְךָ מִכָּל־רָע
יִשְׁמֹר אֶת־נַפְשֶׁךָ׃ יְהוָה יִשְׁמָר־צֵאתְךָ וּבוֹאֶךָ מֵעַתָּה וְעַד־עוֹלָם׃

Shir. Lamma'alot Essa Einai El-Heharim; Me'ayin. Yavo Ezri. Ezri Me'im Adonai Oseh. Shamayim Va'aretz. Al-Yiten Lamot Raglecha; Al-Yanum. Shomerecha. Hineh Lo-Yanum Velo Yishan; Shomer. Yisra'el. Adonai Shomerecha; Hashem Tzillecha. Al-Yad Yeminecha. Yomam. Hashemesh Lo-Yakekah. Veyareach Balailah. Adonai Yishmorcha Mikol-Ra'; Yishmor. Et-Nafshecha. Adonai Yishmor-Tzetecha Uvo'echa; Me'attah. Ve'ad-'Olam.

A Song of Ascents. I will lift up my eyes to the mountains: From where will my help come? My help comes from Hashem. Who made heaven and earth. He will not suffer Your foot to be moved; He that keeps You will not slumber. Behold, He that keeps Yisrael neither slumbers or sleeps. Hashem is your Guardian; Hashem is Your shade on Your right hand. The sun will not harm you by day, or the moon by night. Hashem will keep you from all evil; He will keep your soul. Hashem will guard your going out and your coming in, From this time and forever.

Some recite the following verses:

בְּטוֹב אָלִין וְאָקִיץ בְּרַחֲמִים:

Betov Alin Ve'akitz Berachamim:

May I abide in good and arise in compassion.

לִישׁוּעָתְךָ קִוִּיתִי יְהוָה: קִוִּיתִי יְהוָה לִישׁוּעָתְךָ: יְהוָה לִישׁוּעָתְךָ קִוִּיתִי:

Lishu'atecha Kiviti Adonai. Kiviti Adonai Lishu'atecha. Adonai Lishu'atecha Kiviti.

For Your salvation, I wait, Hashem. I wait, Hashem, for Your salvation. Hashem, for Your salvation, I wait.

Ana Bechoach

אָנָּא בְּכֹחַ. גְּדוּלַת יְמִינְךָ. תַּתִּיר צְרוּרָה:

Ana Bechoach. Gedulat Yeminecha. Tatir Tzerurah.

By the great power of your right hand, Oh set the captive free.

קַבֵּל רִנַּת. עַמְּךָ שַׂגְּבֵנוּ. טַהֲרֵנוּ נוֹרָא:

Kabel Rinat. Ammecha Sagveinu. Tahareinu Nora.

God of awe, accept your people's prayer; strengthen us, cleanse us.

נָא גִבּוֹר. דּוֹרְשֵׁי יִחוּדְךָ. כְּבָבַת שָׁמְרֵם:

Na Gibor. Doreshei Yichudecha. Kevavat Shamerem.
Almighty God, guard as the apple of the eye those who seek You.

בָּרְכֵם טַהֲרֵם. רַחֲמֵי צִדְקָתֶךָ. תָּמִיד גָּמְלֵם:

Barechem Taharem. Rachamei Tzidkatecha. Tamid Gamelem.
Bless them, cleanse them, pity them; forever grant them Your truth.

חֲסִין קָדוֹשׁ. בְּרֹב טוּבְךָ. נַהֵל עֲדָתֶךָ:

Chasin Kadosh. Berov Tuvecha. Nahel Adatecha.
Almighty and holy, in Your abundant goodness, guide Your people.

יָחִיד גֵּאֶה. לְעַמְּךָ פְּנֵה. זוֹכְרֵי קְדֻשָּׁתֶךָ:

Yachid Ge'eh. Le'ammecha Feneh. Zocherei Kedushatecha.
Supreme God, turn to Your people who are mindful of Your holiness.

שַׁוְעָתֵנוּ קַבֵּל. וּשְׁמַע צַעֲקָתֵנוּ. יוֹדֵעַ תַּעֲלוּמוֹת:

Shav'ateinu Kabel. Ushema Tza'akateinu. Yodea Ta'alumot.
Accept our prayer, hear our cry, You who knows secret thoughts.

And say silently:

בָּרוּךְ, שֵׁם כְּבוֹד מַלְכוּתוֹ, לְעוֹלָם וָעֶד:

Baruch, Shem Kevod Malchuto, Le'olam Va'ed.
Blessed is the Name of His glorious kingdom forever and ever.

אַתָּה תָקוּם תְּרַחֵם צִיּוֹן כִּי־עֵת לְחֶנְנָהּ כִּי־בָא מוֹעֵד: בְּיָדְךָ אַפְקִיד רוּחִי פָּדִיתָה אוֹתִי יְהוָֹה אֵל אֱמֶת:

Attah Takum Terachem Tziyon; Ki-'Et Lechenenah. Ki-Va Mo'ed.
Beyadecha Afkid Ruchi Padita Oti Hashem El Emet.

You will surely arise and take pity on Tziyon, for it is time to be gracious to her; the appointed time has come. Into Your hand I entrust my spirit; You redeem me, Hashem, faithful God. **(Psalms 102:14, 31:6)**

ROSH CHODESH

ראש חודש

Barchi Nafshi - Rosh Chodesh

Some communities say Barchi Nafshi (Psalms 104) on Rosh Chodesh at the end of Mincha after the Song of the Day, Beginning of Arvit and before Shabbat.

Psalms 104

בָּרְכִי נַפְשִׁי אֶת־יְהֹוָה יְהֹוָה אֱלֹהַי גָּדַלְתָּ מְּאֹד הוֹד וְהָדָר לָבָשְׁתָּ׃
עֹטֶה־אוֹר כַּשַּׂלְמָה נוֹטֶה שָׁמַיִם כַּיְרִיעָה׃ הַמְקָרֶה בַמַּיִם עֲלִיּוֹתָיו
הַשָּׂם־עָבִים רְכוּבוֹ הַמְהַלֵּךְ עַל־כַּנְפֵי־רוּחַ׃ עֹשֶׂה מַלְאָכָיו רוּחוֹת
מְשָׁרְתָיו אֵשׁ לֹהֵט׃ יָסַד־אֶרֶץ עַל־מְכוֹנֶיהָ בַּל־תִּמּוֹט עוֹלָם וָעֶד׃
תְּהוֹם כַּלְּבוּשׁ כִּסִּיתוֹ עַל־הָרִים יַעַמְדוּ מָיִם׃ מִן־גַּעֲרָתְךָ יְנוּסוּן
מִן־קוֹל רַעַמְךָ יֵחָפֵזוּן׃ יַעֲלוּ הָרִים יֵרְדוּ בְקָעוֹת אֶל־מְקוֹם זֶה | יָסַדְתָּ
לָהֶם׃ גְּבוּל־שַׂמְתָּ בַּל־יַעֲבֹרוּן בַּל־יְשׁוּבוּן לְכַסּוֹת הָאָרֶץ׃ הַמְשַׁלֵּחַ
מַעְיָנִים בַּנְּחָלִים בֵּין הָרִים יְהַלֵּכוּן׃ יַשְׁקוּ כָּל־חַיְתוֹ שָׂדָי יִשְׁבְּרוּ
פְרָאִים צְמָאָם׃ עֲלֵיהֶם עוֹף־הַשָּׁמַיִם יִשְׁכּוֹן מִבֵּין עֳפָאיִם יִתְּנוּ־קוֹל׃
מַשְׁקֶה הָרִים מֵעֲלִיּוֹתָיו מִפְּרִי מַעֲשֶׂיךָ תִּשְׂבַּע הָאָרֶץ׃ מַצְמִיחַ
חָצִיר | לַבְּהֵמָה וְעֵשֶׂב לַעֲבֹדַת הָאָדָם לְהוֹצִיא לֶחֶם מִן־הָאָרֶץ׃ וְיַיִן |
יְשַׂמַּח לְבַב־אֱנוֹשׁ לְהַצְהִיל פָּנִים מִשָּׁמֶן וְלֶחֶם לְבַב־אֱנוֹשׁ יִסְעָד׃
יִשְׂבְּעוּ עֲצֵי יְהֹוָה אַרְזֵי לְבָנוֹן אֲשֶׁר נָטָע׃ אֲשֶׁר־שָׁם צִפֳּרִים יְקַנֵּנוּ
חֲסִידָה בְּרוֹשִׁים בֵּיתָהּ׃ הָרִים הַגְּבֹהִים לַיְּעֵלִים סְלָעִים מַחְסֶה
לַשְׁפַנִּים׃ עָשָׂה יָרֵחַ לְמוֹעֲדִים שֶׁמֶשׁ יָדַע מְבוֹאוֹ׃ תָּשֶׁת־חֹשֶׁךְ וִיהִי
לָיְלָה בּוֹ־תִרְמֹשׂ כָּל־חַיְתוֹ־יָעַר׃ הַכְּפִירִים שֹׁאֲגִים לַטָּרֶף וּלְבַקֵּשׁ
מֵאֵל אָכְלָם׃ תִּזְרַח הַשֶּׁמֶשׁ יֵאָסֵפוּן וְאֶל־מְעוֹנֹתָם יִרְבָּצוּן׃ יֵצֵא אָדָם
לְפָעֳלוֹ וְלַעֲבֹדָתוֹ עֲדֵי־עָרֶב׃ מָה־רַבּוּ מַעֲשֶׂיךָ | יְהֹוָה כֻּלָּם בְּחָכְמָה
עָשִׂיתָ מָלְאָה הָאָרֶץ קִנְיָנֶךָ׃ זֶה | הַיָּם גָּדוֹל וּרְחַב יָדָיִם שָׁם־רֶמֶשׂ
וְאֵין מִסְפָּר חַיּוֹת קְטַנּוֹת עִם־גְּדֹלוֹת׃ שָׁם אֳנִיּוֹת יְהַלֵּכוּן לִוְיָתָן

זֶה־יָצַרְתָּ לְשַׂחֶק־בּוֹ: כֻּלָּם אֵלֶיךָ יְשַׂבֵּרוּן לָתֵת אָכְלָם בְּעִתּוֹ: תִּתֵּן לָהֶם יִלְקֹטוּן תִּפְתַּח יָדְךָ יִשְׂבְּעוּן טוֹב: תַּסְתִּיר פָּנֶיךָ יִבָּהֵלוּן תֹּסֵף רוּחָם יִגְוָעוּן וְאֶל־עֲפָרָם יְשׁוּבוּן: תְּשַׁלַּח רוּחֲךָ יִבָּרֵאוּן וּתְחַדֵּשׁ פְּנֵי אֲדָמָה: יְהִי כְבוֹד יְהוָה לְעוֹלָם יִשְׂמַח יְהוָה בְּמַעֲשָׂיו: הַמַּבִּיט לָאָרֶץ וַתִּרְעָד יִגַּע בֶּהָרִים וְיֶעֱשָׁנוּ: אָשִׁירָה לַיהוָה בְּחַיָּי אֲזַמְּרָה לֵאלֹהַי בְּעוֹדִי: יֶעֱרַב עָלָיו שִׂיחִי אָנֹכִי אֶשְׂמַח בַּיהוָה: יִתַּמּוּ חַטָּאִים | מִן־הָאָרֶץ וּרְשָׁעִים | עוֹד אֵינָם בָּרְכִי נַפְשִׁי אֶת־יְהוָה הַלְלוּיָהּ:

Barchi Nafshi Et Adonai Adonai Elohai Gadalta Me'odhod Vehadar Lavasheta. Oteh Or Kassalmah Noteh Shamayim Kayeri'ah. Hamkareh Vammayim Aliyotav Hassam Avim Rechuvo Hamehallech Al Kanfei Ruach. Oseh Mal'achav Ruchot Mesharetav Esh Lohet. Yasad Eretz Al Mechoneiha Bal Timot Olam Va'ed. Tehom Kallevush Kissito Al Harim Ya'amdu Mayim. Min Ga'aratecha Yenusun Min Kol Ra'amcha Yechafezun. Ya'alu Harim Yeredu Veka'ot El Mekom Zeh Yasadta Lahem. Gevul Samta Bal Ya'avorun Bal Yeshuvun Lechasot Ha'aretz. Hameshalleach Ma'yanim Banechalim Bein Harim Yehallechun. Yashku Kol Chayto Sadai Yishberu Fera'im Tzema'am. Aleihem Of Hashamayim Yishkon Mibein Ofayim Yitenu Kol. Mashkeh Harim Me'aliyotav Miperi Ma'aseicha Tisba Ha'aretz. Matzmiach Chatzir Labehemah Ve'esev La'avodat Ha'adam Lehotzi Lechem Min Ha'aretz. Veyayin Yesamach Levav Enosh Lehatzhil Panim Mishamen Velechem Levav Enosh Yis'ad. Yisbe'u Atzei Adonai Arzei Levanon Asher Nata. Asher Sham Tziporim Yekanenu Chasidah Beroshim Beitah. Harim Hagevohim Laye'elim Sela'im Machseh Lashfanim. Asah Yareach Lemo'adim Shemesh Yada Mevo'o. Tashet Choshech Vihi Lailah Bo Tirmos Kol Chayto Ya'ar. Hakkefirim Sho'agim Lattaref Ulevakesh Me'el Ochlam. Tizrach Hashemesh Ye'asefun Ve'el Me'onotam Yirbatzun. Yetze Adam Lefo'olo Vela'avodato Adei Arev. Mah Rabbu Ma'aseicha Adonai Kulam Bechochmah Asita Male'ah Ha'aretz Kinyanecha. Zeh Hayam Gadol Urechav Yadayim Sham Remes Ve'ein Mispar Chayot Ketanot Im Gedolot. Sham Oniyot Yehallechun Livyatan Zeh Yatzarta Lesachek Bo. Kulam Eleicha Yesaberun Latet Ochlam Be'ito. Titen Lahem Yilkotun Tiftach Yadecha Yisbe'un Tov. Tastir Paneicha Yibahelun Tosef Rucham Yigva'un Ve'el Afaram Yeshuvun. Teshallach Ruchacha Yibare'un

Utechadesh Penei Adamah. Yehi Chevod Adonai Le'olam Yismach Adonai Bema'asav. Hamabbit La'aretz Vatir'ad Yigga Beharim Veye'eshanu. Ashirah L'Adonai Bechayai Azamerah Lelohai Be'odi. Ye'erav Alav Sichi Anochi Esmach Badonai. Yitamu Chata'im Min Ha'aretz Uresha'im Od Einam Barchi Nafshi Et Adonai Halleluyah.

Bless Hashem, Oh my soul. Hashem my God, You are very great; You are clothed with glory and majesty. Who covers Yourself with light as with a garment, who stretches out the heavens like a curtain; Who lays the beams of Your upper chambers in the waters, who makes the clouds Your chariot, who walks upon the wings of the wind; Who makes winds Your messengers, the flaming fire Your ministers. Who established the earth upon its foundations, that it should not be moved forever and ever; You covered it with the deep as with a garment; the waters stood above the mountains. At Your rebuke they fled, at the voice of Your thunder they hasted away—The mountains rose, the valleys sank down—To the place which You established for them; You set a bound which they should not pass over, That they might not return to cover the earth. Who sends out springs into the valleys; They run between the mountains; They give drink to every beast of the field, The wild donkeys quench their thirst. Beside them dwell the birds of the sky, From among the branches they sing. Who waters the mountains from Your upper chambers; The earth is full of the fruit of Your works. Who causes the grass to spring up for the cattle, And herb for the service of man; To bring forth bread from out of the earth, And wine that makes the heart of man glad, Making the face brighter than oil, And bread that sustains man's heart. The trees of Hashem have their fill, The cedars of Levanon, which He has planted; in it, the birds make their nests; As for the stork, the fir-trees are her house. The high mountains are for the wild goats; The rocks are a refuge for the badgers. Who appointed the moon for moadim (appointed times); The sun knows his going down. You make darkness, and it is night, Where all the beasts of the forest creep out. The young lions roar after their prey, And seek their food from God. The sun arises, they slink away, and couch in their dens. Man goes out to his work and to his labor until the evening. How manifold are Your works, Hashem. In wisdom You have made them all; The earth is full of Your creatures. So is this sea, great and wide, in it are creeping things innumerable, Living creatures, both small and great. There the ships go; There is Livyatan, whom You have formed to play in it. All of them wait for You, that You may give them their food in due season. You give it to them, they gather it; You open Your hand, they are satisfied with good. You hide Your face, they vanish; You withdraw their breath, they perish, and return to their dust. You send out Your spirit, they are created; and You renew the face of the earth. May the glory of Hashem endure forever; let Hashem rejoice in His works. Who looks on the earth, and it trembles; He touches the mountains, and they smoke. I will sing to Hashem as long as I live; I will sing praise to my God while I have any being. Let my meditation be sweet to Him; as for me, I will rejoice in Hashem. Let sinners cease out of the earth, and let the wicked be no more. Bless Hashem, Oh my soul. Halleluyah.

Order of Prayers - Rosh Chodesh

Service is as usual for Arvit, Shacharit and Mincha with Ya'aleh Ve'yavo inserted into the Amidah. If Ya'aleh Ve'yavo was omitted in the Evening Service, he does not need to say the Amidah again, but if it was omitted in Shacharit or Mincha then it must be said again. (SA. OC 422) After the repetition of Amidah is recited, then Hallel is said without a blessing and the noted sections omitted below.

HALLEL FOR ROSH CHODESH AND MOADIM

הלל לראש חודש ולמועדים

On Rosh Hodesh Hallel is said without a blessing with certain sections omitted. The full Hallel is recited on Pesach - the first two nights and days of Pesach (only the first night and day in Yisrael), on Shavuot, Sukkot - all seven days, on Shemini Atzeret and Simchat Torah, and on Hanukkah - all eight days. Hallel is recited while standing. (SA, OC 422)

Birshut Morai Verabotai: בִּרְשׁוּת מוֹרַי וְרַבּוֹתַי:

With the permission of my teachers and masters:

Answer: Shamayim! **עונים:** שָׁמַיִם.

Answer: (By) Heaven!

And the Chazan and the people bless. On days when the Hallel is not completed, skip this:

Baruch Attah Adonai Eloheinu בָּרוּךְ אַתָּה יְהֹוָה אֱלֹהֵינוּ
Melech Ha'olam Asher מֶלֶךְ הָעוֹלָם. אֲשֶׁר
Kideshanu Bemitzvotav. קִדְּשָׁנוּ בְּמִצְוֹתָיו
Vetzivanu Ligmor Et Hahallel: וְצִוָּנוּ לִגְמוֹר אֶת הַהַלֵּל:

Blessed are You, Hashem our God, King of the universe, Who has sanctified us with His commandments and commanded us to recite the Hallel.

Psalms 113

הַלְלוּיָהּ | הַלְלוּ עַבְדֵי יְהֹוָה הַלְלוּ אֶת־שֵׁם יְהֹוָה: יְהִי שֵׁם יְהֹוָה
מְבֹרָךְ מֵעַתָּה וְעַד־עוֹלָם: מִמִּזְרַח־שֶׁמֶשׁ עַד־מְבוֹאוֹ מְהֻלָּל שֵׁם
יְהֹוָה: רָם עַל־כָּל־גּוֹיִם | יְהֹוָה עַל הַשָּׁמַיִם כְּבוֹדוֹ: מִי כַּיהֹוָה

אֱלֹהֵינוּ הַמַּגְבִּיהִי לָשָׁבֶת: הַמַּשְׁפִּילִי לִרְאוֹת בַּשָּׁמַיִם וּבָאָרֶץ: מְקִימִי
מֵעָפָר דָּל מֵאַשְׁפֹּת יָרִים אֶבְיוֹן: לְהוֹשִׁיבִי עִם־נְדִיבִים עִם נְדִיבֵי
עַמּוֹ: מוֹשִׁיבִי | עֲקֶרֶת הַבַּיִת אֵם־הַבָּנִים שְׂמֵחָה הַלְלוּיָהּ:

Halleluyah Hallelu Avdei Adonai Hallelu Et Shem Adonai. Yehi Shem Adonai Mevorach Me'attah Ve'ad Olam. Mimizrach Shemesh Ad Mevo'o Mehulal Shem Adonai. Ram Al Kol Goyim Adonai Al Hashamayim Kevodo. Mi Ka'Adonai Eloheinu Hamagbihi Lashavet. Hamashpili Lir'ot Bashamayim Uva'aretz. Mekimi Me'afar Dal Me'ashpot Yarim Evyon. Lehoshivi Im Nedivim Im Nedivei Ammo. Moshivi Akeret Habayit Em Habanim Semechah Halleluyah.

Halleluyah. Praise, you servants of Hashem, Praise the name of Hashem. Blessed is the name of Hashem From this time and forever. From the rising of the sun to the going down of it Hashem's name is to be praised. Hashem is high above all nations, His glory is above the heavens. Who is like Hashem our God, That is enthroned on high, That looks down low upon heaven and upon the earth? Who raises up the poor out of the dust, And lifts up the needy out of the dunghill; That He may set him with princes, Even with the princes of His people. Who makes the barren woman to dwell in her house as a joyful mother of children. Halleluyah.

Psalms 114

בְּצֵאת יִשְׂרָאֵל מִמִּצְרָיִם בֵּית יַעֲקֹב מֵעַם לֹעֵז: הָיְתָה יְהוּדָה לְקָדְשׁוֹ
יִשְׂרָאֵל מַמְשְׁלוֹתָיו: הַיָּם רָאָה וַיָּנֹס הַיַּרְדֵּן יִסֹּב לְאָחוֹר: הֶהָרִים
רָקְדוּ כְאֵילִים גְּבָעוֹת כִּבְנֵי־צֹאן: מַה־לְּךָ הַיָּם כִּי תָנוּס הַיַּרְדֵּן תִּסֹּב
לְאָחוֹר: הֶהָרִים תִּרְקְדוּ כְאֵילִים גְּבָעוֹת כִּבְנֵי־צֹאן: מִלִּפְנֵי אָדוֹן
חוּלִי אָרֶץ מִלִּפְנֵי אֱלוֹהַּ יַעֲקֹב: הַהֹפְכִי הַצּוּר אֲגַם־מָיִם חַלָּמִישׁ
לְמַעְיְנוֹ־מָיִם:

Betzet Yisra'el Mimitzrayim Beit Ya'akov Me'am Lo'ez. Hayetah Yehudah Lekodsho Yisra'el Mamshelotav. Hayam Ra'ah Vayanos Hayarden Yissov Le'achor. Heharim Rakedu Che'eilim Geva'ot

Kivnei Tzon. Mah Lecha Hayam Ki Tanus Hayarden Tissov Le'achor. Heharim Tirkedu Che'eilim Geva'ot Kivnei Tzon. Millifnei Adon Chuli Aretz Millifnei Eloah Ya'akov. Hahofechi Hatzur Agam Mayim Challamish Lema'yeno Mayim.

When Yisrael came forth out of Mitzrayim, The house of Yaakov from a people of strange language; Yehudah became His Sanctuary, Yisrael His dominion. The sea saw it, and fled; The Yarden turned backward. The mountains skipped like rams, The hills like young sheep. What ails you, Oh sea, that you flee? You Yarden, that you turn backward? You mountains, that you skip like rams; You hills, like young sheep? Tremble, earth, at the presence of Hashem, At the presence of the God of Yaakov; Who turned the rock into a pool of water, the flint into a fountain of waters.

Psalms 115

On days when the Hallel is not completed, skip this (first part of Psalm):

לֹא לָנוּ יְהֹוָה לֹא לָנוּ כִּי־לְשִׁמְךָ תֵּן כָּבוֹד עַל־חַסְדְּךָ עַל־אֲמִתֶּךָ:
לָמָּה יֹאמְרוּ הַגּוֹיִם אַיֵּה־נָא אֱלֹהֵיהֶם: וֵאלֹהֵינוּ בַשָּׁמָיִם כֹּל
אֲשֶׁר־חָפֵץ עָשָׂה: עֲצַבֵּיהֶם כֶּסֶף וְזָהָב מַעֲשֵׂה יְדֵי אָדָם: פֶּה־לָהֶם
וְלֹא יְדַבֵּרוּ עֵינַיִם לָהֶם וְלֹא יִרְאוּ: אָזְנַיִם לָהֶם וְלֹא יִשְׁמָעוּ אַף
לָהֶם וְלֹא יְרִיחוּן: יְדֵיהֶם | וְלֹא יְמִישׁוּן רַגְלֵיהֶם וְלֹא יְהַלֵּכוּ
לֹא־יֶהְגּוּ בִּגְרוֹנָם: כְּמוֹהֶם יִהְיוּ עֹשֵׂיהֶם כֹּל אֲשֶׁר־בֹּטֵחַ בָּהֶם:
יִשְׂרָאֵל בְּטַח בַּיהֹוָה עֶזְרָם וּמָגִנָּם הוּא: בֵּית אַהֲרֹן בִּטְחוּ בַיהֹוָה
עֶזְרָם וּמָגִנָּם הוּא: יִרְאֵי יְהֹוָה בִּטְחוּ בַיהֹוָה עֶזְרָם וּמָגִנָּם הוּא:

Lo Lanu Adonai Lo Lanu Ki Leshimcha Ten Kavod Al Chasdecha Al Amitecha. Lamah Yomru Hagoyim Ayeh Na Eloheihem. Veloheinu Vashamayim Kol Asher Chafetz Asah. Atzabeihem Kesef Vezahav Ma'aseh Yedei Adam. Peh Lahem Velo Yedaberu Einayim Lahem Velo Yir'u. Oznayim Lahem Velo Yishma'u Af Lahem Velo Yerichun. Yedeihem Velo Yemishun Ragleihem Velo Yehallechu Lo Yehgu Bigronam. Kemohem Yihyu Oseihem Kol Asher Boteach Bahem. Yisra'el Betach B'Adonai Ezram Umaginam Hu. Beit Aharon Bitchu

B'Adonai Ezram Umaginam Hu. Yir'ei Adonai Bitchu B'Adonai Ezram Umaginam Hu.

Not to us, Hashem, not to us, But to Your name give glory, For Your mercy, and for Your truth's sake. Why should the nations say: 'Where is their God now?' But our God is in the heavens; Whatever pleased Him He has done. Their idols are silver and gold, The work of men's hands. They have mouths, but they do not speak; Eyes have they, but they do not see; They have ears, but they do not hear; They have noses, but they do not smell; They have hands, but they cannot handle; They have feet, but they cannot walk; Neither can they speak with their throat. They that make them will be like them; Even, everyone that trusts in them. Yisrael, trust in Hashem. He is their Help and their Shield. House of Aharon, trust in Hashem. He is their Help and their Shield. You that fear Hashem, trust in Hashem. He is their Help and their Shield.

On days when the Hallel is not completed, continue here:

יְהוָה זְכָרָנוּ יְבָרֵךְ יְבָרֵךְ אֶת־בֵּית יִשְׂרָאֵל יְבָרֵךְ אֶת־בֵּית אַהֲרֹן: יְבָרֵךְ
יִרְאֵי יְהוָה הַקְּטַנִּים עִם־הַגְּדֹלִים: יֹסֵף יְהוָה עֲלֵיכֶם עֲלֵיכֶם
וְעַל־בְּנֵיכֶם: בְּרוּכִים אַתֶּם לַיהוָה עֹשֵׂה שָׁמַיִם וָאָרֶץ: הַשָּׁמַיִם
שָׁמַיִם לַיהוָה וְהָאָרֶץ נָתַן לִבְנֵי־אָדָם: לֹא הַמֵּתִים יְהַלְלוּ־יָהּ וְלֹא
כָּל־יֹרְדֵי דוּמָה: וַאֲנַחְנוּ | נְבָרֵךְ יָהּ מֵעַתָּה וְעַד־עוֹלָם הַלְלוּ יָהּ:

Adonai Zecharanu Yevarech Yevarech Et Beit Yisra'el Yevarech Et Beit Aharon. Yevarech Yir'ei Adonai Haketanim Im Hagedolim. Yosef Adonai Aleichem Aleichem Ve'al Beneichem. Beruchim Attem L'Adonai Oseh Shamayim Va'aretz. Hashamayim Shamayim L'Adonai Veha'aretz Natan Livnei Adam. Lo Hameitim Yehallelu-Yah Velo Kol Yoredei Dumah. Va'anachnu Nevarech Yah Me'attah Ve'ad Olam Hallelu Yah.

Hashem has been mindful of us, He will bless— He will bless the House of Yisrael; He will bless the house of Aharon. He will bless them that fear Hashem, Both small and great. May Hashem increase you more and more, You and your children. May you be blessed by Hashem, Who made heaven and earth. The heavens are the heavens of Hashem; But the earth He has given to the children of men. The dead do not praise Hashem, Neither any that go down into silence; But we will bless Hashem from this time and forever. Halleluyah.

Psalms 116

On days when the Hallel is not finished, skip this (first part of Psalm):

אָהַבְתִּי כִּי־יִשְׁמַע | יְהֹוָה אֶת־קוֹלִי תַּחֲנוּנָי: כִּי־הִטָּה אָזְנוֹ לִי וּבְיָמַי
אֶקְרָא: אֲפָפוּנִי | חֶבְלֵי־מָוֶת וּמְצָרֵי שְׁאוֹל מְצָאוּנִי צָרָה וְיָגוֹן
אֶמְצָא: וּבְשֵׁם־יְהֹוָה אֶקְרָא אָנָּה יְהֹוָה מַלְּטָה נַפְשִׁי: חַנּוּן יְהֹוָה
וְצַדִּיק וֵאלֹהֵינוּ מְרַחֵם: שֹׁמֵר פְּתָאיִם יְהֹוָה דַּלּוֹתִי וְלִי יְהוֹשִׁיעַ: שׁוּבִי
נַפְשִׁי לִמְנוּחָיְכִי כִּי־יְהֹוָה גָּמַל עָלָיְכִי: כִּי חִלַּצְתָּ נַפְשִׁי מִמָּוֶת
אֶת־עֵינִי מִן־דִּמְעָה אֶת־רַגְלִי מִדֶּחִי: אֶתְהַלֵּךְ לִפְנֵי יְהֹוָה בְּאַרְצוֹת
הַחַיִּים: הֶאֱמַנְתִּי כִּי אֲדַבֵּר אֲנִי עָנִיתִי מְאֹד: אֲנִי אָמַרְתִּי בְחָפְזִי
כָּל־הָאָדָם כֹּזֵב:

Ahavti Ki Yishma Adonai Et Koli Tachanunai. Ki Hittah Ozno Li Uveyamai Ekra. Afafuni Chevlei Mavet Umetzarei She'ol Metza'uni Tzarah Veyagon Emtza. Uveshem Adonai Ekra Anah Adonai Malletah Nafshi. Chanun Adonai Vetzaddik Veloheinu Merachem. Shomer Petayim Adonai Daloti Veli Yehoshia'. Shuvi Nafshi Limnuchayechi Ki Adonai Gamal Alayechi. Ki Chilatzta Nafshi Mimavet Et Eini Min Dim'ah Et Ragli Middechi. Ethallech Lifnei Adonai Be'artzot Hachayim. He'emanti Ki Adaber Ani Aniti Me'od. Ani Amarti Vechofzi Kol Ha'adam Kozev.

I love that Hashem hears my voice and my supplications. Because He has inclined His ear to me, Therefore I will call on Him all of my days. The cords of death encompassed me, and the straits of Sheol took hold on me; I found trouble and sorrow. But I called on the name of Hashem: 'I implore You, Hashem, deliver my soul.' Gracious is Hashem, and righteous; Yes, our God is compassionate. Hashem preserves the simple; I was brought low, and He saved me. Return, my soul, to Your rest; For Hashem has dealt bountifully with you.

For you have delivered my soul from death, My eyes from tears, And my feet from stumbling. I will walk before Hashem In the lands of the living. I trusted even when I spoke: 'I am greatly afflicted.' I said in my haste: 'All men are liars.'

On days when the Hallel is not completed, continue here:

מָה־אָשִׁיב לַיהֹוָה כׇּל־תַּגְמוּלוֹהִי עָלָי׃ כּוֹס־יְשׁוּעוֹת אֶשָּׂא וּבְשֵׁם
יְהֹוָה אֶקְרָא׃ נְדָרַי לַיהֹוָה אֲשַׁלֵּם נֶגְדָה־נָּא לְכׇל־עַמּוֹ׃ יָקָר בְּעֵינֵי
יְהֹוָה הַמָּוְתָה לַחֲסִידָיו׃ אָנָּה יְהֹוָה כִּי־אֲנִי עַבְדֶּךָ אֲנִי־עַבְדְּךָ
בֶּן־אֲמָתֶךָ פִּתַּחְתָּ לְמוֹסֵרָי׃ לְךָ־אֶזְבַּח זֶבַח תּוֹדָה וּבְשֵׁם יְהֹוָה
אֶקְרָא׃ נְדָרַי לַיהֹוָה אֲשַׁלֵּם נֶגְדָה־נָּא לְכׇל־עַמּוֹ׃ בְּחַצְרוֹת | בֵּית
יְהֹוָה בְּתוֹכֵכִי יְרוּשָׁלָ͏ִם הַלְלוּיָהּ׃

Mah Ashiv L'Adonai Kol Tagmulohi Alai. Kos Yeshu'ot Essa Uveshem Adonai Ekra. Nedarai L'Adonai Ashalem Negdah Na Lechol Ammo. Yakar Be'einei Adonai Hamavetah Lachasidav. Anah Adonai Ki Ani Avdecha Ani Avdecha Ben Amatecha Pittachta Lemoserai. Lecha Ezbach Zevach Todah Uveshem Adonai Ekra. Nedarai L'Adonai Ashalem Negdah Na Lechol Ammo. Bechatzrot Beit Adonai Betochechi Yerushalayim Halleluyah.

How can I repay to Hashem all of His bountiful dealings toward me? I will lift up the cup of salvation, And call upon the name of Hashem. I will pay my vows to Hashem, even, in the presence of all His people. Precious in the sight of Hashem is the death of His holy-ones. I implore You, Hashem, for I am Your servant; I am Your servant, the son of Your handmaid; You have released my bands. I will offer to you the sacrifice of thanksgiving, And will call on the name of Hashem. I will pay my vows to Hashem, even, in the presence of all His people; in the courts of Hashem's house, in the midst of you, Yerushalayim. Halleluyah.

Psalms 117

הַֽלְל֣וּ אֶת־יְ֭הֹוָה כׇּל־גּוֹיִ֑ם שַׁ֝בְּח֗וּהוּ כׇּל־הָאֻמִּֽים׃ כִּ֥י גָ֘בַ֤ר עָלֵ֨ינוּ ׀ חַסְדּ֗וֹ וֶֽאֱמֶת־יְהֹוָ֥ה לְעוֹלָ֗ם הַֽלְלוּ־יָֽהּ׃

Hallelu Et Adonai Kol Goyim Shabechuhu Kol Ha'ummim. Ki Gavar Aleinu Chasdo Ve'emet Adonai Le'olam Halleluyah.

Praise Hashem, all nations; Acclaim Him, all peoples. For His mercy is great toward us; And the truth of Hashem endures forever. Halleluyah.

Psalms 118

הוֹד֣וּ לַיהֹוָ֣ה כִּי־ט֑וֹב כִּ֖י לְעוֹלָ֣ם חַסְדּֽוֹ׃

Hodu L'Adonai Ki Tov Ki Le'olam Chasdo.

Give thanks to Hashem, for He is good, For His mercy endures forever.

יֹֽאמַר־נָ֥א יִשְׂרָאֵ֑ל כִּ֖י לְעוֹלָ֣ם חַסְדּֽוֹ׃

Yomar Na Yisra'el Ki Le'olam Chasdo.

So let Yisrael now say, For His mercy endures forever:

יֹֽאמְרוּ־נָ֥א בֵֽית־אַהֲרֹ֑ן כִּ֖י לְעוֹלָ֣ם חַסְדּֽוֹ׃

Yomeru Na Veit Aharon Ki Le'olam Chasdo.

So let the house of Aharon now say, For His mercy endures forever.

יֹֽאמְרוּ־נָ֭א יִרְאֵ֣י יְהֹוָ֑ה כִּ֖י לְעוֹלָ֣ם חַסְדּֽוֹ׃

Yomeru Na Yir'ei Adonai Ki Le'olam Chasdo.

So let them now that fear Hashem say, For His mercy endures forever.

מִֽן־הַ֭מֵּצַר קָרָ֣אתִי יָּ֑הּ עָנָ֖נִי בַמֶּרְחָ֣ב יָֽהּ׃ יְהֹוָ֣ה לִ֭י לֹ֣א אִירָ֑א מַה־יַּעֲשֶׂ֖ה לִ֣י אָדָֽם׃ יְהֹוָ֣ה לִ֭י בְּעֹזְרָ֑י וַ֝אֲנִ֗י אֶרְאֶ֥ה בְשֹׂנְאָֽי׃ ט֗וֹב לַחֲס֥וֹת בַּיהֹוָ֑ה מִ֝בְּטֹ֗חַ בָּאָדָֽם׃ ט֗וֹב לַחֲס֥וֹת בַּיהֹוָ֑ה מִ֝בְּטֹ֗חַ בִּנְדִיבִֽים׃

כָּל־גּוֹיִם סְבָבוּנִי בְּשֵׁם יְהוָה כִּי אֲמִילַם׃ סַבּוּנִי גַם־סְבָבוּנִי בְּשֵׁם
יְהוָה כִּי אֲמִילַם׃ סַבּוּנִי כִדְבוֹרִים דֹּעֲכוּ כְּאֵשׁ קוֹצִים בְּשֵׁם יְהוָה כִּי
אֲמִילַם׃ דַּחֹה דְחִיתַנִי לִנְפֹּל וַיהוָה עֲזָרָנִי׃ עָזִּי וְזִמְרָת יָהּ וַיְהִי־לִי
לִישׁוּעָה׃ קוֹל | רִנָּה וִישׁוּעָה בְּאָהֳלֵי צַדִּיקִים יְמִין יְהוָה עֹשָׂה חָיִל׃
יְמִין יְהוָה רוֹמֵמָה יְמִין יְהוָה עֹשָׂה חָיִל׃ לֹא־אָמוּת כִּי־אֶחְיֶה
וַאֲסַפֵּר מַעֲשֵׂי יָהּ׃ יַסֹּר יִסְּרַנִּי יָּהּ וְלַמָּוֶת לֹא נְתָנָנִי׃ פִּתְחוּ־לִי
שַׁעֲרֵי־צֶדֶק אָבֹא־בָם אוֹדֶה יָהּ׃ זֶה־הַשַּׁעַר לַיהוָה צַדִּיקִים יָבֹאוּ בוֹ׃

Min Hametzar Karati Yah Anani Vammerchav Yah. Adonai Li Lo Ira Mah Ya'aseh Li Adam. Adonai Li Be'ozerai Va'ani Er'eh Vesone'ai. Tov Lachasot Badonai Mibetoach Ba'adam. Tov Lachasot Badonai Mibetoach Bindivim. Kol Goyim Sevavuni Beshem Adonai Ki Amilam. Sabbuni Gam Sevavuni Beshem Adonai Ki Amilam. Sabbuni Chidvorim Do'achu Ke'esh Kotzim Beshem Adonai Ki Amilam. Dachoh Dechitani Linpol Va'Adonai Azarani. Ozi Vezimrat Yah Vayhi Li Lishu'ah. Kol Rinah Vishu'ah Be'oholei Tzaddikim Yemin Adonai Osah Chayil. Yemin Adonai Romemah Yemin Adonai Osah Chayil. Lo Amut Ki Echyeh Va'asaper Ma'asei Yah. Yassor Yisserani Yah Velamavet Lo Netanani. Pitchu Li Sha'arei Tzedek Avo Vam Odeh Yah. Zeh Hasha'ar L'Adonai Tzaddikim Yavo'u Vo.

Out of my restriction I called on Hashem; He answered me with great enlargement. Hashem is for me; I will not fear; What can man do to me? Hashem is for me as my Helper; And I will gaze on them that hate me. It is better to take refuge in Hashem than to trust in man. It is better to take refuge in Hashem than to trust in princes. All nations encircled me; In the name of Hashem I will cut them off. They encircle me, yes, they surround me; In the name of Hashem I will cut them off. They surround me like bees; They will be quenched as the fire of thorns; In the name of Hashem I will cut them off. You thrusted at me that I might fall; But Hashem helped me. Hashem is my strength and song; And He is become my salvation. The voice of rejoicing and salvation is in the tents of the righteous; The right hand of Hashem does valiantly. The right hand of Hashem is exalted; The right hand of Hashem does valiantly. I will not die, but live, and declare the works of Hashem. Hashem has disciplined me greatly; But He has not given me over to death. Open to me the gates of righteousness; I will enter into them, I will give thanks to Hashem. This is the gate of Hashem; The righteous will enter into it.

אוֹדְךָ כִּי עֲנִיתָנִי וַתְּהִי־לִי לִישׁוּעָה: אוֹדְךָ כִּי עֲנִיתָנִי וַתְּהִי־לִי לִישׁוּעָה: אֶבֶן מָאֲסוּ הַבּוֹנִים הָיְתָה לְרֹאשׁ פִּנָּה: אֶבֶן מָאֲסוּ הַבּוֹנִים הָיְתָה לְרֹאשׁ פִּנָּה: מֵאֵת יְהֹוָה הָיְתָה זֹּאת הִיא נִפְלָאת בְּעֵינֵינוּ: מֵאֵת יְהֹוָה הָיְתָה זֹּאת הִיא נִפְלָאת בְּעֵינֵינוּ: זֶה־הַיּוֹם עָשָׂה יְהֹוָה נָגִילָה וְנִשְׂמְחָה בוֹ: זֶה־הַיּוֹם עָשָׂה יְהֹוָה נָגִילָה וְנִשְׂמְחָה בוֹ:

Odecha Ki Anitani Vatehi Li Lishu'ah. Odecha Ki Anitani Vatehi Li Lishu'ah. Even Ma'asu Habonim Hayetah Lerosh Pinah. Even Ma'asu Habonim Hayetah Lerosh Pinah. Me'et Adonai Hayetah Zot Hi Niflat Be'eineinu. Me'et Adonai Hayetah Zot Hi Niflat Be'eineinu. Zeh Hayom Asah Adonai Nagilah Venismechah Vo. Zeh Hayom Asah Adonai Nagilah Venismechah Vo.

I will give thanks to You, for You have answered me, and have become my salvation. The stone which the builders rejected has become the chief corner-stone. This is Hashem's doing; It is marvelous in our eyes. This is the day which Hashem has made; We will rejoice and be glad in it.

אָנָּא יְהֹוָה הוֹשִׁיעָה נָּא. אָנָּא יְהֹוָה הוֹשִׁיעָה נָּא:

Ana Adonai Hoshi'ah Na. Ana Adonai Hoshi'ah Na:

Hashem, save now. Hashem, save now.

אָנָּא יְהֹוָה הַצְלִיחָה נָּא. אָנָּא יְהֹוָה הַצְלִיחָה נָּא:

Ana Adonai Hatzlichah Na. Ana Adonai Hatzlichah Na.

Hashem, prosper us now. Hashem, prosper us now.

בָּרוּךְ הַבָּא בְּשֵׁם יְהֹוָה בֵּרַכְנוּכֶם מִבֵּית יְהֹוָה: בָּרוּךְ הַבָּא בְּשֵׁם יְהֹוָה בֵּרַכְנוּכֶם מִבֵּית יְהֹוָה: אֵל ׀ יְהֹוָה וַיָּאֶר לָנוּ אִסְרוּ־חַג

בַּעֲבֹתִים עַד־קַרְנוֹת הַמִּזְבֵּחַ: אֵל | יְהֹוָה וַיָּאֶר לָנוּ אִסְרוּ־חַג
בַּעֲבֹתִים עַד־קַרְנוֹת הַמִּזְבֵּחַ: אֵלִי אַתָּה וְאוֹדֶךָּ אֱלֹהַי אֲרוֹמְמֶךָּ: אֵלִי
אַתָּה וְאוֹדֶךָּ אֱלֹהַי אֲרוֹמְמֶךָּ: הוֹדוּ לַיהֹוָה כִּי־טוֹב כִּי לְעוֹלָם חַסְדּוֹ:
הוֹדוּ לַיהֹוָה כִּי־טוֹב כִּי לְעוֹלָם חַסְדּוֹ:

Baruch Haba Beshem Adonai Berachnuchem Mibeit Adonai. Baruch Haba Beshem Adonai Berachnuchem Mibeit Adonai. El Adonai Vayaer Lanu Isru Chag Ba'avotim Ad Karnot Hamizbe'ach. El Adonai Vayaer Lanu Isru Chag Ba'avotim Ad Karnot Hamizbe'ach. Eli Attah Ve'odekka Elohai Aromemekka. Eli Attah Ve'odekka Elohai Aromemekka. Hodu L'Adonai Ki Tov Ki Le'olam Chasdo. Hodu L'Adonai Ki Tov Ki Le'olam Chasdo.

Blessed is he that comes in the name of Hashem; We bless you out of the House of Hashem. Hashem is God, and has given us light; Order the festival procession with boughs, even to the horns of the altar. You are my God, and I will give thanks to You; You are my God, I will exalt You. Give thanks to Hashem, for He is good, for His mercy endures forever. Give thanks to Hashem, for He is good, for His mercy endures forever.

On days when the Hallel is not completed, this closing blessing is omitted as well:

Yehallelucha Adonai Eloheinu	יְהַלְלוּךָ יְהֹוָה אֱלֹהֵינוּ
Kol Ma'aseicha. Vachasideicha	כָּל מַעֲשֶׂיךָ. וַחֲסִידֶיךָ
Vetzaddikim Osei Retzonecha	וְצַדִּיקִים עוֹשֵׂי רְצוֹנֶךָ
Ve'ammecha Beit Yisra'el. Kulam	וְעַמְּךָ בֵּית יִשְׂרָאֵל. כֻּלָּם
Berinah Yodu Vivarechu	בְּרִנָּה יוֹדוּ וִיבָרְכוּ
Vishabechu Vifa'aru Et Shem	וִישַׁבְּחוּ וִיפָאֲרוּ אֶת שֵׁם
Kevodecha. Ki Lecha Tov	כְּבוֹדֶךָ. כִּי לְךָ טוֹב
Lehodot. Uleshimcha Na'im	לְהוֹדוֹת. וּלְשִׁמְךָ נָעִים
Lezamer. Ume'olam Ve'ad Olam	לְזַמֵּר. וּמֵעוֹלָם וְעַד עוֹלָם.

Attah El. Baruch Attah Adonai	אַתָּה אֵל. בָּרוּךְ אַתָּה יְהֹוָה
Melech Mehulal Batishbachot.	מֶלֶךְ מְהֻלָּל בַּתִּשְׁבָּחוֹת.
Amen:	אָמֵן:

All of Your works, Hashem our God, will praise You; Your pious servants, the righteous who perform Your will, and Your people, the House of Yisrael, will altogether, with joyful song, give thanks, bless, praise, and laud Your glorious name: for it is good to give thanks to You, and pleasant to sing praise to Your name, for You are God from everlasting to everlasting. Blessed are You, Hashem, King adored with praises. Amen.

Some say:

Yehi Shem

יְהִי שֵׁם יְהֹוָה מְבֹרָךְ מֵעַתָּה וְעַד־עוֹלָם: מִמִּזְרַח־שֶׁמֶשׁ עַד־מְבוֹאוֹ מְהֻלָּל שֵׁם יְהֹוָה: רָם עַל־כָּל־גּוֹיִם | יְהֹוָה עַל הַשָּׁמַיִם כְּבוֹדוֹ: יְהֹוָה אֲדֹנֵינוּ מָה־אַדִּיר שִׁמְךָ בְּכָל־הָאָרֶץ:

Yehi Shem Adonai Mevorach; Me'attah. Ve'ad-'Olam. Mimizrach-Shemesh Ad-Mevo'o; Mehulal. Shem Adonai Ram Al-Chol-Goyim Adonai Al Hashamayim Kevodo. Adonai Adoneinu; Mah-'Adir Shimcha. Bechol-Ha'aretz.

Blessed is the name of Hashem from this time forward and forever. From the rising of the sun to it's going down, Hashem's name is to be praised. Hashem, our Lord, How glorious is Your name in all of the earth. **(Psalms 113:2-4, 8:2)**

And the Cantor says Kaddish Titkabbal, and on Hanukkah say Hatzi-Kaddish:

Kaddish Titkabbal

Kaddish is only recited in a minyan (ten men). אמן denotes when the congregation responds "Amen" together out loud. According to the Shulchan Arukh, the congregation says "Yehei Shemeh Rabba" to "Yitbarach" out loud together without interruption, and also that one should respond "Amen" after "Yitbarach." (SA, OC 55,56) This is not the common custom today. Though many are accustomed to answering according to their own custom, it is advised to respond in the custom of the one reciting to avoid not fragmenting into smaller groups. ("Lo Titgodedu" - BT, Yevamot 13b / SA, OC 493, Rema / MT, Avodah Zara 12:15)

יִתְגַּדַּל וְיִתְקַדַּשׁ שְׁמֵהּ רַבָּא. אָמֵן בְּעָלְמָא דִּי בְרָא. כִּרְעוּתֵהּ. וְיַמְלִיךְ מַלְכוּתֵהּ. וְיַצְמַח פֻּרְקָנֵהּ. וִיקָרֵב מְשִׁיחֵהּ. אָמֵן בְּחַיֵּיכוֹן וּבְיוֹמֵיכוֹן וּבְחַיֵּי דְכָל בֵּית יִשְׂרָאֵל. בַּעֲגָלָא וּבִזְמַן קָרִיב. וְאִמְרוּ אָמֵן. אָמֵן יְהֵא שְׁמֵיהּ רַבָּא מְבָרַךְ לְעָלַם וּלְעָלְמֵי עָלְמַיָּא יִתְבָּרַךְ. וְיִשְׁתַּבַּח. וְיִתְפָּאַר. וְיִתְרוֹמַם. וְיִתְנַשֵּׂא. וְיִתְהַדָּר. וְיִתְעַלֶּה. וְיִתְהַלָּל שְׁמֵהּ דְּקֻדְשָׁא. בְּרִיךְ הוּא. אָמֵן לְעֵלָּא מִן כָּל בִּרְכָתָא שִׁירָתָא. תֻּשְׁבְּחָתָא וְנֶחֱמָתָא. דַּאֲמִירָן בְּעָלְמָא. וְאִמְרוּ אָמֵן. אָמֵן

Yitgadal Veyitkadash Shemeh Rabba. Amen Be'alema Di Vera. Kir'uteh. Veyamlich Malchuteh. Veyatzmach Purkaneh. Vikarev Meshicheh. Amen Bechayeichon Uveyomeichon Uvechayei Dechal-Beit Yisra'el. Ba'agala Uvizman Kariv. Ve'imru Amen. Amen Yehei Shemeh Rabba Mevarach Le'alam Ule'alemei Alemaya Yitbarach. Veyishtabach. Veyitpa'ar. Veyitromam. Veyitnasse. Veyit'hadar. Veyit'aleh. Veyit'hallal Shemeh Dekudsha. Berich Hu. Amen Le'ella Min Kol Birchata Shirata. Tushbechata Venechemata. Da'amiran Be'alema. Ve'imru Amen. Amen

Glorified and sanctified be God's great name Amen throughout the world which He has created according to His will. May He establish His kingdom, hastening His salvation and the coming of His Messiah, Amen, in your lifetime and during your days, and within the life of the entire House of Yisrael, speedily and soon; and say, Amen. Amen May His great name be blessed forever and to all eternity. Blessed and praised, glorified and exalted, extolled and honored, adored and lauded is the name of the Holy One, blessed is He, Amen Beyond all the blessings and hymns, praises and consolations that are ever spoken in the world; and say, Amen. Amen

תִּתְקַבַּל צְלוֹתֳנָא וּבָעוּתֳנָא. עִם צְלוֹתְהוֹן וּבָעוּתְהוֹן דְּכָל בֵּית יִשְׂרָאֵל. קֳדָם אֲבוּנָא דְּבִשְׁמַיָּא וְאַרְעָא. וְאִמְרוּ אָמֵן. אָמֵן

Titkabbal Tzelotana Uva'utana. Im Tzelotehon Uva'utehon Dechol Beit Yisra'el. Kodam Avuna Devishmaya Ve'ar'a. Ve'imru Amen. Amen

May the prayer and supplication of the whole House of Yisrael be accepted before their Father in heaven, and say, Amen. Amen

יְהֵא שְׁלָמָא רַבָּא מִן שְׁמַיָּא. חַיִּים וְשָׂבָע וִישׁוּעָה וְנֶחָמָה. וְשֵׁיזָבָא וּרְפוּאָה וּגְאוּלָה וּסְלִיחָה וְכַפָּרָה וְרֶוַח וְהַצָּלָה לָנוּ וּלְכָל עַמּוֹ יִשְׂרָאֵל. וְאִמְרוּ אָמֵן. אָמֵן

Yehei Shelama Rabba Min Shemaya. Chayim Vesava Vishu'ah Venechamah. Vesheizava Urefu'ah Uge'ulah Uselichah Vechapparah Verevach Vehatzalah Lanu Ulechol Ammo Yisra'el. Ve'imru Amen. Amen

May abundant peace descend from heaven, with life and plenty, salvation, solace, liberation, healing and redemption, and forgiveness and atonement, enlargement and freedom, for us and all of God's people Yisrael; and say, Amen. Amen

One bows and takes three steps backwards, while still bowing. After three steps, while still bowing and before erecting, while saying, "Oseh Shalom Bimromav", turn one's face to the left, "Hu [Berachamav] Ya'aseh Shalom Aleinu", turn one's face to the right; then bow forward like a servant leaving his master. (SA, OC 123:1)

עוֹשֶׂה שָׁלוֹם **בעשי״ת אוי:** (הַשָּׁלוֹם) בִּמְרוֹמָיו. הוּא בְּרַחֲמָיו יַעֲשֶׂה שָׁלוֹם עָלֵינוּ. וְעַל כָּל־עַמּוֹ יִשְׂרָאֵל. וְאִמְרוּ אָמֵן:

Oseh Shalom **On the 10 days of repentance:** (Hashalom) Bimromav, Hu Berachamav Ya'aseh Shalom Aleinu, Ve'al Kol-'Ammo Yisra'el, Ve'imru Amen.

Creator of **On the 10 days of repentance:** (the) peace in His high places, may He in His mercy create peace for us and for all Yisrael, and say Amen.

Some say these verses three times after Hallel:

וְאַבְרָהָם זָקֵן בָּא בַּיָּמִים וַיהֹוָה בֵּרַךְ אֶת־אַבְרָהָם בַּכֹּל:

Ve'avraham Zaken Ba Bayamim Va'Adonai Berach Et Avraham Bakol.

And Avraham was old, well stricken in age; and Hashem had blessed Avraham in all things. **(Gen. 24:1)**

And then say:

יְהֹוָה יִשְׁמְרֵנִי וִיחַיֵּנִי. כֵּן יְהִי רָצוֹן מִלְּפָנֶיךָ אֱלֹהִים חַיִּים וּמֶלֶךְ עוֹלָם אֲשֶׁר בְּיָדוֹ נֶפֶשׁ כָּל חַי אָמֵן כֵּן יְהִי רָצוֹן:

Adonai Yishmereni Vichayeni. Ken Yehi Ratzon Milfaneicha Elohim Chayim Umelech Olam Asher Beyado Nefesh Kol Chai Amen Ken Yehi Ratzon:

Watch over me and give me life. So may it be Your will, living God and eternal King, in His hand is the soul of all living things; **(Job 12:10)** Amen, may it be so.

Kriyat HaTorah / The Torah Reading - Rosh Chodesh Weekday

Before the Torah is removed from the shrine, the following is said. The Torah Reading Service now follows the respective day (Weekday Shacharit).

יְהִי יְהֹוָה אֱלֹהֵינוּ עִמָּנוּ כַּאֲשֶׁר הָיָה עִם־אֲבֹתֵינוּ אַל־יַעַזְבֵנוּ וְאַל־יִטְּשֵׁנוּ: הוֹשִׁיעָה | אֶת־עַמֶּךָ וּבָרֵךְ אֶת־נַחֲלָתֶךָ וּרְעֵם וְנַשְּׂאֵם עַד־הָעוֹלָם: וַיְהִי בִּנְסֹעַ הָאָרֹן וַיֹּאמֶר מֹשֶׁה קוּמָה | יְהֹוָה וְיָפֻצוּ אֹיְבֶיךָ וְיָנֻסוּ מְשַׂנְאֶיךָ מִפָּנֶיךָ: קוּמָה יְהֹוָה לִמְנוּחָתֶךָ אַתָּה וַאֲרוֹן עֻזֶּךָ: כֹּהֲנֶיךָ יִלְבְּשׁוּ־צֶדֶק וַחֲסִידֶיךָ יְרַנֵּנוּ: בַּעֲבוּר דָּוִד עַבְדֶּךָ אַל־תָּשֵׁב פְּנֵי מְשִׁיחֶךָ:

Yehi Adonai Eloheinu Imanu Ka'asher Hayah Im Avoteinu Al Ya'azvenu Ve'al Yitesenu. Hoshi'ah Et Ammecha Uvarech Et Nachalatecha Ure'em Venasse'em Ad Ha'olam. Vayhi Binsoa' Ha'aron Vayomer Mosheh Kumah Adonai Veyafutzu Oyeveicha Veyanusu Mesan'eicha Mipaneicha. Kumah Adonai Limnuchatecha Attah Va'aron Uzecha. Kohaneicha Yilbeshu Tzedek Vachasideicha Yeranenu. Ba'avur David Avdecha Al Tashev Penei Meshichecha.

May Hashem our God be with us, as He was with our fathers; may He not leave us, or forsake us. Save Your people, and bless Your inheritance; And tend them, and carry them forever. And it came to pass, when the ark set out, that Moshe said: 'Rise up, Hashem, and let Your enemies be scattered; and let them that hate You flee from before You.' Arise, Hashem, to Your resting-place; You, and the ark of Your strength. Let Your priests be clothed with righteousness; And let Your saints shout for joy. For Your servant David's sake do not turn away the face of Your anointed. **(I Kings 8:57, Ps. 28:9, Num. 10:35, Ps. 132:8, 132:10-11)**

Continue with the Opening of the Ark (next page) and proceed back to "Baruch HaMakom" in the Shacharit Torah Service, Torah Reading section, it is noted. Reading is Num. 28:1-15, shown here. No Haftorah is read. Only four people read, in order of priority (Kohen, Levi, All Yisrael).

Opening of the Ark

Some say Berich Shemei, which is written in the Zohar of Parashat Vayakel:

Berich Shemeh Demarei Alema Berich	בְּרִיךְ שְׁמֵהּ דְּמָארֵי עָלְמָא בְּרִיךְ
Kitrach Ve'atrach. Yehe Re'utach. Im	כִּתְרָךְ וְאַתְרָךְ. יְהֵא רְעוּתָךְ. עִם
Amach Yisra'el Le'alam. Ufurekan	עַמָּךְ יִשְׂרָאֵל לְעָלַם. וּפוּרְקַן
Yeminach Achzei Le'amach Beveit	יְמִינָךְ אַחֲזֵי לְעַמָּךְ בְּבֵית
Mikdashach. Le'amtuyei Lana Mituv	מִקְדָּשָׁךְ. לְאַמְטוּיֵי לָנָא מִטּוּב
Nehorach. Ulekabel Tzelotana	נְהוֹרָךְ. וּלְקַבֵּל צְלוֹתָנָא
Berachamin. Yehe Ra'ava Kodamach	בְּרַחֲמִין. יְהֵא רַעֲוָא קֳדָמָךְ
Detorich Lan Chayin Betivu. Velehevei	דְּתוֹרִיךְ לָן חַיִּין בְּטִיבוּ. וְלֶהֱוֵי
Ana Avdach Pekida Bego Tzaddikaya.	אֲנָא עַבְדָּךְ פְּקִידָא בְּגוֹ צַדִּיקַיָּא.
Lemircham Alai Ulemintar Yati Veyat Kol	לְמִרְחַם עָלַי וּלְמִנְטַר יָתִי וְיַת כָּל
Di Li Vedi Le'amach Yisra'el. Ant Hu	דִּי לִי וְדִי לְעַמָּךְ יִשְׂרָאֵל. אַנְתְּ הוּא
Zan Lechola Umefarnes Lechola. Ant	זָן לְכֹלָּא וּמְפַרְנֵס לְכֹלָּא. אַנְתְּ
Hu Shallit Al Kola Ant Hu	הוּא שַׁלִּיט עַל כֹּלָּא אַנְתְּ הוּא
Deshallit Al Malchaya Umalchuta	דְּשַׁלִּיט עַל מַלְכַיָּא וּמַלְכוּתָא
Dilach Hi. Ana Avda Dekudesha	דִּילָךְ הִיא. אֲנָא עַבְדָּא דְּקוּדְשָׁא
Berich Hu Desagidna Kameh Umin	בְּרִיךְ הוּא דְּסָגִידְנָא קַמֵּהּ וּמִן
Kamei Dikar Orayteh Bechl Idan	קַמֵּי דִּיקַר אוֹרַיְתֵהּ בְּכָל־עִדָּן
Ve'idan. La Al Enash Rachitzna. Vela Al	וְעִדָּן. לָא עַל אֱנָשׁ רָחִיצְנָא. וְלָא עַל
Bar Elahin Samichna. Ella Ve'elaha	בַּר אֱלָהִין סָמִיכְנָא. אֶלָּא בֶּאֱלָהָא
Dishmaya Dehu Elaha Dikshot.	דִּשְׁמַיָּא דְּהוּא אֱלָהָא דִּקְשׁוֹט.
Ve'orayteh Keshot. Unevi'ohi Keshot.	וְאוֹרַיְתֵהּ קְשׁוֹט. וּנְבִיאוֹהִי קְשׁוֹט.
Umasgei Leme'bad Tavan Ukeshot. Beih	וּמַסְגֵּי לְמֶעְבַּד טַבְוָן וּקְשׁוֹט. בֵּיהּ
Ana Rachitz Velishmeh Yakira Kaddisha	אֲנָא רָחִיץ וְלִשְׁמֵהּ יַקִּירָא קַדִּישָׁא
Ana Emar Tushbechan. Yehe Ra'ava	אֲנָא אֵמַר תֻּשְׁבְּחָן. יְהֵא רַעֲוָא
Kodamach Detiftach Libi Be'oraytach.	קֳדָמָךְ דְּתִפְתַּח לִבִּי בְּאוֹרַיְתָךְ.
(Vetihav Li Benin Dichrin De'avedin	(וְתִיהַב לִי בְּנִין דִּכְרִין דְּעָבְדִין
Re'utach). Vetashlim Mish'alin Deliba	רְעוּתָךְ). וְתַשְׁלִים מִשְׁאֲלִין דְּלִבָּאי
Veliba Dechol Amach Yisra'el Letav	וְלִבָּא דְּכָל־עַמָּךְ יִשְׂרָאֵל לְטַב
Ulechayin Velishlam Amen:	וּלְחַיִּין וְלִשְׁלָם אָמֵן:

Blessed is the name of the Lord of the universe. Blessed is Your crown and Your dominion. May Your goodwill always abide with Your people Yisrael. Reveal Your saving power to Your people in Your Sanctuary; bestow on us the good gift of Your light, and accept our prayer in mercy. May it be Your will to prolong our life in happiness. Let me also be counted among the righteous, so that You may have compassion on me and shelter me and mine and all that belong to Your people Yisrael. You are He who nourishes and sustains all; You are He who rules over all; You are He who rules over kings, for dominion is Yours. I am the servant of the Holy One, blessed is He, before Whom and before Whose glorious Torah I bow at all times. I do not put my trust in man, or rely on any angel, but only in the God of Heaven Who is the God of truth, Whose Torah is truth and Whose Prophets are truth, and Who performs many deeds of goodness and truth. In Him I put my trust, and to His holy and glorious name I declare praises. May it be Your will to open my heart to Your Torah, and to fulfill the wishes of my heart and of the heart of all of Your people Yisrael for happiness, life and peace.

Reading of the Torah

Torah Reading: Numbers 28:1-15

א וַיְדַבֵּר יְהוָה אֶל־מֹשֶׁה לֵּאמֹר: צַו אֶת־בְּנֵי יִשְׂרָאֵל וְאָמַרְתָּ אֲלֵהֶם
אֶת־קָרְבָּנִי לַחְמִי לְאִשַּׁי רֵיחַ נִיחֹחִי תִּשְׁמְרוּ לְהַקְרִיב לִי בְּמוֹעֲדוֹ:
וְאָמַרְתָּ לָהֶם זֶה הָאִשֶּׁה אֲשֶׁר תַּקְרִיבוּ לַיהוָה כְּבָשִׂים בְּנֵי־שָׁנָה
תְמִימִם שְׁנַיִם לַיּוֹם עֹלָה תָמִיד: לוי אֶת־הַכֶּבֶשׂ אֶחָד תַּעֲשֶׂה בַבֹּקֶר
וְאֵת הַכֶּבֶשׂ הַשֵּׁנִי תַּעֲשֶׂה בֵּין הָעַרְבָּיִם: וַעֲשִׂירִית הָאֵיפָה סֹלֶת
לְמִנְחָה בְּלוּלָה בְּשֶׁמֶן כָּתִית רְבִיעִת הַהִין: ישראל עֹלַת תָּמִיד
הָעֲשֻׂיָה בְּהַר סִינַי לְרֵיחַ נִיחֹחַ אִשֶּׁה לַיהוָה: וְנִסְכּוֹ רְבִיעִת הַהִין
לַכֶּבֶשׂ הָאֶחָד בַּקֹּדֶשׁ הַסֵּךְ נֶסֶךְ שֵׁכָר לַיהוָה: וְאֵת הַכֶּבֶשׂ הַשֵּׁנִי
תַּעֲשֶׂה בֵּין הָעַרְבָּיִם כְּמִנְחַת הַבֹּקֶר וּכְנִסְכּוֹ תַּעֲשֶׂה אִשֵּׁה רֵיחַ נִיחֹחַ
לַיהוָה: וּבְיוֹם הַשַּׁבָּת שְׁנֵי־כְבָשִׂים בְּנֵי־שָׁנָה תְּמִימִם וּשְׁנֵי עֶשְׂרֹנִים
סֹלֶת מִנְחָה בְּלוּלָה בַשֶּׁמֶן וְנִסְכּוֹ: עֹלַת שַׁבַּת בְּשַׁבַּתּוֹ עַל־עֹלַת
הַתָּמִיד וְנִסְכָּהּ: רביעי וּבְרָאשֵׁי חָדְשֵׁיכֶם תַּקְרִיבוּ עֹלָה לַיהוָה פָּרִים

בְּנֵי־בָקָר שְׁנַיִם וְאַיִל אֶחָד כְּבָשִׂים בְּנֵי־שָׁנָה שִׁבְעָה תְּמִימִם׃
וּשְׁלֹשָׁה עֶשְׂרֹנִים סֹלֶת מִנְחָה בְּלוּלָה בַשֶּׁמֶן לַפָּר הָאֶחָד וּשְׁנֵי
עֶשְׂרֹנִים סֹלֶת מִנְחָה בְּלוּלָה בַשֶּׁמֶן לָאַיִל הָאֶחָד׃ וְעִשָּׂרֹן עִשָּׂרוֹן
סֹלֶת מִנְחָה בְּלוּלָה בַשֶּׁמֶן לַכֶּבֶשׂ הָאֶחָד עֹלָה רֵיחַ נִיחֹחַ אִשֶּׁה
לַיהוָה׃ וְנִסְכֵּיהֶם חֲצִי הַהִין יִהְיֶה לַפָּר וּשְׁלִישִׁת הַהִין לָאַיִל וּרְבִיעִת
הַהִין לַכֶּבֶשׂ יָיִן זֹאת עֹלַת חֹדֶשׁ בְּחָדְשׁוֹ לְחָדְשֵׁי הַשָּׁנָה׃ וּשְׂעִיר
עִזִּים אֶחָד לְחַטָּאת לַיהוָה עַל־עֹלַת הַתָּמִיד יֵעָשֶׂה וְנִסְכּוֹ׃

Vaydaber Adonai El-Mosheh Lemor. Tzav Et-Benei Yisra'el. Ve'amarta Aleihem; Et-Korbani Lachmi Le'ishai. Reiach Nichochi. Tishmeru Lehakriv Li Bemo'ado. Ve'amarta Lahem. Zeh Ha'isheh. Asher Takrivu L'Adonai Kevasim Benei-Shanah Temimim Shenayim Layom Olah Tamid. Et-Hakeves Echad Ta'aseh Vaboker; Ve'et Hakeves Hasheni. Ta'aseh Bein Ha'arbayim. Va'asirit Ha'eifah Solet Leminchah; Belulah Beshemen Katit Revi'it Hahin. Olat Tamid; Ha'asuyah Behar Sinai. Lereiach Nichoach. Isheh L'Adonai Venisko Revi'it Hahin. Lakeves Ha'echad; Bakodesh. Hassech Nesech Shechar L'Adonai Ve'et Hakeves Hasheni. Ta'aseh Bein Ha'arbayim; Keminchat Haboker Uchenisko Ta'aseh. Isheh Reiach Nichoach L'Adonai. Uveyom Hashabbat Shenei Chevasim Benei Shanah Temimim Ushenei Esronim Solet Minchah Belulah Vashemen Venisko. Olat Shabbat Beshabbato Al Olat Hatamid Veniskah. Uveroshei Chodsheichem Takrivu Olah L'Adonai Parim Benei Vakar Shenayim Ve'ayil Echad Kevasim Benei Shanah Shiv'ah Temimim. Usheloshah Esronim Solet Minchah Belulah Vashemen Lappar Ha'echad Ushenei Esronim Solet Minchah Belulah Vashemen La'ayil Ha'echad. Ve'issaron Issaron Solet Minchah Belulah Vashemen Lakeves Ha'echad Olah Reiach Nichoach Isheh L'Adonai. Veniskeihem Chatzi Hahin Yihyeh Lappar Ushelishit Hahin La'ayil Urevi'it Hahin Lakeves Yayin Zot Olat Chodesh Bechodsho Lechodshei Hashanah. Use'ir Izim Echad Lechatat L'Adonai Al Olat Hatamid Ye'aseh Venisko.

And Hashem spoke to Moshe, saying: Command the children of Israel, and say to them: My food which is presented to Me for offerings made by fire, of a sweet savor to Me, you will observe to offer to Me in its due season. And you will say to them: This is the offering made by fire which you shall bring to Hashem: male-lambs of the first year without blemish, two day by day, for a continual burnt-offering. The one lamb shall you offer in the morning, and the other lamb you will offer at dusk; and the tenth part of an ephah of fine flour for a meal-offering, mingled with the fourth part of a hin of beaten oil. It is a continual burnt-offering, which was offered in mount Sinai, for a sweet savor, an offering made by fire to Hashem. And the drink-offering of it will be the fourth part of a hin for the one lamb; in the holy place your will pour out a drink-offering of strong drink to Hashem. And the other lamb you will present at dusk; as the meal-offering of the morning, and as the drink-offering of it, you will present it, an offering made by fire, of a sweet savor to Hashem. And on the Shabbat day two male lambs of the first year without blemish, and two tenth parts of an ephah of fine flour for a meal-offering, mingled with oil, and the drink-offering of it. This is the burnt-offering of every Shabbat, beside the continual burnt-offering, and the drink-offering of it. And on your new moons you will present a burnt-offering to Hashem: two young bulls, and one ram, seven male lambs of the first year without blemish; and three-tenth parts of an ephah of fine flour for a meal-offering, mingled with oil, for each bull; and two tenth parts of fine flour for a meal-offering, mingled with oil, for the one ram; and a several tenth part of fine flour mingled with oil for a meal-offering to every lamb; for a burnt-offering of a sweet savor, an offering made by fire to Hashem. And their drink-offerings will be half a hin of wine for a bull, and the third part of a hin for the ram, and the fourth part of a hin for a lamb. This is the burnt-offering of every new moon throughout the months of the year. And one male goat for a sin-offering to Hashem; it will be offered beside the continual burnt-offering, and the drink-offering of it.

The chazan recites Hatzi-Kaddish:

Kaddish is only recited in a minyan (ten men). אמן denotes when the congregation responds "Amen" together out loud. According to the Shulchan Arukh, the congregation says "Yehei Shemeh Rabba" to "Yitbarach" out loud together without interruption, and also that one should respond "Amen" after "Yitbarach." (SA, OC 55,56) This is not the common custom today. Though many are accustomed to answering according to their own custom, it is advised to respond in the custom of the one reciting to avoid not fragmenting into smaller groups. ("Lo Titgodedu" - BT, Yevamot 13b / SA, OC 493, Rema / MT, Avodah Zara 12:15)

יִתְגַּדַּל וְיִתְקַדַּשׁ שְׁמֵהּ רַבָּא. אָמֵן בְּעָלְמָא דִּי בְרָא. כִּרְעוּתֵהּ. וְיַמְלִיךְ מַלְכוּתֵהּ. וְיַצְמַח פֻּרְקָנֵהּ. וִיקָרֵב מְשִׁיחֵהּ. אָמֵן בְּחַיֵּיכוֹן וּבְיוֹמֵיכוֹן וּבְחַיֵּי דְכָל בֵּית יִשְׂרָאֵל. בַּעֲגָלָא וּבִזְמַן קָרִיב. וְאִמְרוּ אָמֵן. אָמֵן יְהֵא שְׁמֵיהּ רַבָּא מְבָרַךְ לְעָלַם וּלְעָלְמֵי עָלְמַיָּא יִתְבָּרַךְ. וְיִשְׁתַּבַּח. וְיִתְפָּאַר. וְיִתְרוֹמַם. וְיִתְנַשֵּׂא. וְיִתְהַדָּר. וְיִתְעַלֶּה. וְיִתְהַלָּל שְׁמֵהּ דְּקֻדְשָׁא. בְּרִיךְ הוּא. אָמֵן לְעֵלָּא מִן כָּל בִּרְכָתָא שִׁירָתָא. תֻּשְׁבְּחָתָא וְנֶחֱמָתָא. דַּאֲמִירָן בְּעָלְמָא. וְאִמְרוּ אָמֵן. אָמֵן

Yitgadal Veyitkadash Shemeh Rabba. Amen Be'alema Di Vera. Kir'uteh. Veyamlich Malchuteh. Veyatzmach Purkaneh. Vikarev Meshicheh. Amen Bechayeichon Uveyomeichon Uvechayei Dechal-Beit Yisra'el. Ba'agala Uvizman Kariv. Ve'imru Amen. Amen Yehei Shemeh Rabba Mevarach Le'alam Ule'alemei Alemaya Yitbarach. Veyishtabach. Veyitpa'ar. Veyitromam. Veyitnasse. Veyit'hadar. Veyit'aleh. Veyit'hallal Shemeh Dekudsha. Berich Hu. Amen Le'ella Min Kol Birchata Shirata. Tushbechata Venechemata. Da'amiran Be'alema. Ve'imru Amen. Amen

Glorified and sanctified be God's great name Amen throughout the world which He has created according to His will. May He establish His kingdom, hastening His salvation and the coming of His Messiah, Amen, in your lifetime and during your days, and within the life of the entire House of Yisrael, speedily and soon; and say, Amen. Amen May His great name be blessed forever and to all eternity. Blessed and praised, glorified and exalted, extolled and honored, adored and lauded is the name of the Holy One, blessed is He, Amen Beyond all the blessings and hymns, praises and consolations that are ever spoken in the world; and say, Amen. Amen

Ashrei

When saying the verse "Potei'ach Et Yadecha" one should focus one's heart. If one did not focus he must return and repeat. (SA, OC 51:7) It is customary to open your hands toward Heaven as a symbol of our acceptance of the abundance Hashem bestows upon us from Heaven. (B'I'H, Ex. 9:29, I Kings 8:54).

אַשְׁרֵי יוֹשְׁבֵי בֵיתֶךָ עוֹד יְהַלְלוּךָ סֶּלָה: אַשְׁרֵי הָעָם שֶׁכָּכָה לּוֹ אַשְׁרֵי
הָעָם שֶׁיְהֹוָה אֱלֹהָיו:

Ashrei Yoshevei Veitecha; Od. Yehalelucha Selah. Ashrei Ha'am Shekachah Lo; Ashrei Ha'am. She'Adonai Elohav.

Happy are those who dwell in Your house; they are ever praising You. Happy are the people that is so situated; happy are the people whose God is Hashem. (Psalms 84:5, 144:15)

Psalms 145

תְּהִלָּה לְדָוִד אֲרוֹמִמְךָ אֱלוֹהַי הַמֶּלֶךְ וַאֲבָרְכָה שִׁמְךָ לְעוֹלָם וָעֶד:
בְּכָל־יוֹם אֲבָרְכֶךָּ וַאֲהַלְלָה שִׁמְךָ לְעוֹלָם וָעֶד: גָּדוֹל יְהֹוָה וּמְהֻלָּל
מְאֹד וְלִגְדֻלָּתוֹ אֵין חֵקֶר: דּוֹר לְדוֹר יְשַׁבַּח מַעֲשֶׂיךָ וּגְבוּרֹתֶיךָ יַגִּידוּ:
הֲדַר כְּבוֹד הוֹדֶךָ וְדִבְרֵי נִפְלְאֹתֶיךָ אָשִׂיחָה: וֶעֱזוּז נוֹרְאֹתֶיךָ יֹאמֵרוּ
וּגְדֻלָּתְךָ אֲסַפְּרֶנָּה: זֵכֶר רַב־טוּבְךָ יַבִּיעוּ וְצִדְקָתְךָ יְרַנֵּנוּ: חַנּוּן וְרַחוּם
יְהֹוָה אֶרֶךְ אַפַּיִם וּגְדָל־חָסֶד: טוֹב־יְהֹוָה לַכֹּל וְרַחֲמָיו עַל־כָּל־מַעֲשָׂיו:
יוֹדוּךָ יְהֹוָה כָּל־מַעֲשֶׂיךָ וַחֲסִידֶיךָ יְבָרְכוּכָה: כְּבוֹד מַלְכוּתְךָ יֹאמֵרוּ
וּגְבוּרָתְךָ יְדַבֵּרוּ: לְהוֹדִיעַ | לִבְנֵי הָאָדָם גְּבוּרֹתָיו וּכְבוֹד הֲדַר
מַלְכוּתוֹ: מַלְכוּתְךָ מַלְכוּת כָּל־עֹלָמִים וּמֶמְשַׁלְתְּךָ בְּכָל־דּוֹר וָדֹר:
סוֹמֵךְ יְהֹוָה לְכָל־הַנֹּפְלִים וְזוֹקֵף לְכָל־הַכְּפוּפִים: עֵינֵי־כֹל אֵלֶיךָ
יְשַׂבֵּרוּ וְאַתָּה נוֹתֵן־לָהֶם אֶת־אָכְלָם בְּעִתּוֹ: **פּוֹתֵחַ אֶת־יָדֶךָ**
וּמַשְׂבִּיעַ לְכָל־חַי רָצוֹן: צַדִּיק יְהֹוָה בְּכָל־דְּרָכָיו וְחָסִיד
בְּכָל־מַעֲשָׂיו: קָרוֹב יְהֹוָה לְכָל־קֹרְאָיו לְכֹל אֲשֶׁר יִקְרָאֻהוּ בֶאֱמֶת:
רְצוֹן־יְרֵאָיו יַעֲשֶׂה וְאֶת־שַׁוְעָתָם יִשְׁמַע וְיוֹשִׁיעֵם: שׁוֹמֵר יְהֹוָה
אֶת־כָּל־אֹהֲבָיו וְאֵת כָּל־הָרְשָׁעִים יַשְׁמִיד: תְּהִלַּת יְהֹוָה יְדַבֶּר פִּי

וִיבָרֵךְ כָּל־בָּשָׂר שֵׁם קָדְשׁוֹ לְעוֹלָם וָעֶד: וַאֲנַחְנוּ | נְבָרֵךְ יָהּ מֵעַתָּה וְעַד־עוֹלָם הַלְלוּיָהּ:

Tehilah. Ledavid Aromimcha Elohai Hamelech; Va'avarechah Shimcha. Le'olam Va'ed. Bechol-Yom Avarecheka; Va'ahalelah Shimcha. Le'olam Va'ed. Gadol Adonai Umehulal Me'od; Veligdulato. Ein Cheiker. Dor Ledor Yeshabach Ma'aseicha; Ugevuroteicha Yagidu. Hadar Kevod Hodecha; Vedivrei Nifle'oteicha Asichah. Ve'ezuz Nore'oteicha Yomeru; Ug'dulatecha Asap'renah. Zecher Rav-Tuvecha Yabi'u; Vetzidkatecha Yeranenu. Chanun Verachum Adonai Erech Apayim. Ugedol-Chased. Tov-Adonai Lakol; Verachamav. Al-Chol-Ma'asav. Yoducha Adonai Chol-Ma'aseicha; Vachasideicha. Yevarechuchah. Kevod Malchutecha Yomeru; Ugevuratecha Yedaberu. Lehodia Livnei Ha'adam Gevurotav; Uchevod. Hadar Malchuto. Malchutecha. Malchut Chol-'Olamim; Umemshaltecha. Bechol-Dor Vador. Somech Adonai Lechol-Hanofelim; Vezokeif. Lechol-Hakefufim. Einei-Chol Eleicha Yesaberu; Ve'attah Noten-Lahem Et-'Ochlam Be'ito. **Potei'ach Et-Yadecha; Umasbia Lechol-Chai Ratzon.** Tzaddik Adonai Bechol-Derachav; Vechasid. Bechol-Ma'asav. Karov Adonai Lechol-Kore'av; Lechol Asher Yikra'uhu Ve'emet. Retzon-Yere'av Ya'aseh; Ve'et-Shav'atam Yishma'. Veyoshi'em. Shomer Adonai Et-Chol-'Ohavav; Ve'et Chol-Haresha'im Yashmid. Tehillat Adonai Yedaber Pi Vivarech Chol-Basar Shem Kodsho. Le'olam Va'ed. Va'anachnu Nevarech Yah. Me'attah Ve'ad-'Olam. Halleluyah.

A Psalm of praise; of David. א I will extol You, my God, Oh King; And I will bless Your name forever and ever. ב Every day will I bless You; And I will praise You name forever and ever. ג Great is Hashem, and highly to be praised; And His greatness is unsearchable. ד One generation will applaud Your works to another, And will declare Your mighty acts. ה The glorious splendor of Your majesty, And Your wondrous works, I will rehearse. ו And men will speak of the might of Your tremendous acts; And I will tell of Your greatness. ז They will utter the fame of Your great goodness, And will sing of Your righteousness. ח Hashem is gracious, and full of compassion; Slow to anger, and of great mercy. ט Hashem is good to all; And His tender mercies are over all His works. י All Your works will praise You, Hashem; And Your holy-ones will bless You. כ They will speak of the glory of Your kingdom, And talk of Your might; ל To make known to the sons of men His mighty acts, And the glory of the beauty of His kingdom. מ Your kingdom is a kingdom for all ages, And Your dominion endures throughout all generations. ס Hashem upholds all that fall, And raises up all those that are bowed down. ע The eyes of all wait for You, And You give them their food in due season. פ **You open Your hand, And satisfy every living thing with favor.** צ Hashem is righteous in all His ways, And gracious in all His works. ק Hashem is near to all them that call upon Him, To all that call upon Him in truth. ר He will fulfill the desire of those that fear Him; He also will hear their cry, and will save them. ש Hashem preserves all them that love Him; But all the wicked will He destroy. ת My mouth will speak the praise of Hashem; And let all flesh bless His holy name forever and ever.

Beit Yaakov

בֵּית יַעֲקֹב לְכוּ וְנֵלְכָה בְּאוֹר יְהוָה׃ כִּי כָּל־הָעַמִּים יֵלְכוּ אִישׁ בְּשֵׁם אֱלֹהָיו וַאֲנַחְנוּ נֵלֵךְ בְּשֵׁם־יְהוָה אֱלֹהֵינוּ לְעוֹלָם וָעֶד׃ יְהִי יְהוָה אֱלֹהֵינוּ עִמָּנוּ כַּאֲשֶׁר הָיָה עִם־אֲבֹתֵינוּ אַל־יַעַזְבֵנוּ וְאַל־יִטְּשֵׁנוּ׃ לְהַטּוֹת לְבָבֵנוּ אֵלָיו לָלֶכֶת בְּכָל־דְּרָכָיו וְלִשְׁמֹר מִצְוֺתָיו וְחֻקָּיו וּמִשְׁפָּטָיו אֲשֶׁר צִוָּה אֶת־אֲבֹתֵינוּ׃ וְיִהְיוּ דְבָרַי אֵלֶּה אֲשֶׁר הִתְחַנַּנְתִּי לִפְנֵי יְהוָה קְרֹבִים אֶל־יְהוָה אֱלֹהֵינוּ יוֹמָם וָלָיְלָה לַעֲשׂוֹת | מִשְׁפַּט עַבְדּוֹ וּמִשְׁפַּט עַמּוֹ יִשְׂרָאֵל דְּבַר־יוֹם בְּיוֹמוֹ׃ לְמַעַן דַּעַת כָּל־עַמֵּי הָאָרֶץ כִּי יְהוָה הוּא הָאֱלֹהִים אֵין עוֹד׃

Beit Ya'akov; Lechu Venelechah Be'or Adonai Ki Chol-Ha'ammim. Yelechu Ish Beshem Elohav; Va'anachnu. Nelech Beshem-Adonai Eloheinu Le'olam Va'ed. Yehi Adonai Eloheinu Imanu. Ka'asher Hayah Im-'Avoteinu; Al-Ya'azvenu Ve'al-Yitesenu. Lehatot Levavenu Elav; Lalechet Bechol-Derachav. Velishmor Mitzvtav Vechukkav Umishpatav. Asher Tzivah Et-'Avoteinu. Veyihyu Devarai Eleh. Asher

Hitchananti Lifnei Adonai Kerovim El-Adonai Eloheinu Yomam Valailah; La'asot Mishpat Avdo. Umishpat Ammo Yisra'el Devar-Yom Beyomo. Lema'an. Da'at Chol-'Ammei Ha'aretz. Ki Adonai Hu Ha'elohim; Ein Od.

"House of Yaakov, Come and let us walk in the light of Hashem. Though all peoples walk in the name of their gods, We will walk in the name of our God forever and ever. May Hashem our God be with us as He was with our fathers; may He not forsake us or abandon us, but may He turn our heart to Him, that we walk in all His ways, and keep His commandments, statutes and ordinances which He commanded our fathers. And may these my words which I have entreated before Hashem, be near to Hashem our God day and night, so that He will maintain the cause of His servant and of His people Yisrael day by day, that all the peoples of the earth may know that Hashem, He is God, there is none else." **(1 Kings 8, 57-60)**

Psalms 124

שִׁיר הַמַּעֲלוֹת לְדָוִד לוּלֵי יְהֹוָה שֶׁהָיָה לָנוּ יֹאמַר־נָא יִשְׂרָאֵל: לוּלֵי
יְהֹוָה שֶׁהָיָה לָנוּ בְּקוּם עָלֵינוּ אָדָם: אֲזַי חַיִּים בְּלָעוּנוּ בַּחֲרוֹת אַפָּם
בָּנוּ: אֲזַי הַמַּיִם שְׁטָפוּנוּ נַחְלָה עָבַר עַל־נַפְשֵׁנוּ: אֲזַי עָבַר עַל־נַפְשֵׁנוּ
הַמַּיִם הַזֵּידוֹנִים: בָּרוּךְ יְהֹוָה שֶׁלֹּא נְתָנָנוּ טֶרֶף לְשִׁנֵּיהֶם: נַפְשֵׁנוּ
כְּצִפּוֹר נִמְלְטָה מִפַּח יוֹקְשִׁים הַפַּח נִשְׁבָּר וַאֲנַחְנוּ נִמְלָטְנוּ: עֶזְרֵנוּ
בְּשֵׁם יְהֹוָה עֹשֵׂה שָׁמַיִם וָאָרֶץ:

Shir Hama'alot. LeDavid Lulei Adonai Shehayah Lanu; Yomar-Na Yisra'el. Lulei Adonai Shehayah Lanu; Bekum Aleinu Adam. Azai Chayim Bela'unu; Bacharot Appam Banu. Azai Hamayim Shetafunu; Nachlah Avar Al-Nafshenu. Azai Avar Al-Nafshenu; Hamayim. Hazeidonim. Baruch Adonai Shelo Netananu Teref Leshineihem. Nafshenu. Ketzipor Nimletah Mippach Yokeshim Happach Nishbar. Va'anachnu Nimlatenu. Ezrenu Beshem Adonai Oseh. Shamayim Va'aretz.

A Song of Ascents; of David. 'If it had not been Hashem Who was for us', Let Yisrael now say; 'If it had not been Hashem Who was for us, When men rose up against us, Then they would have swallowed us up alive, when their wrath was kindled against us; Then the waters would have overwhelmed us, the stream would have gone over our soul; Then the proud waters would have gone over our soul.' Blessed is Hashem, Who has not given us as prey to their teeth. Our soul is escaped as a bird out of the snare of the fowlers; The snare is broken, and we escaped. Our help is in the name of Hashem, Who made heaven and earth.

Song of the Day

Song of the Day is now read for the corresponding day. One does not need to say anything after "Kodesh", (Hashir...hadduchan). For this refer back to the Shabbat Shacharit, Song (Psalm) of the day section. After the ending "Hoshienu" blessing, return back here and continue.

All stand and return the Torah to its place and say:

יְהַלְלוּ ׀ אֶת־שֵׁם יְהוָה כִּי־נִשְׂגָּב שְׁמוֹ לְבַדּוֹ הוֹדוֹ עַל־אֶרֶץ וְשָׁמָיִם׃
וַיָּרֶם קֶרֶן ׀ לְעַמּוֹ תְּהִלָּה לְכָל־חֲסִידָיו לִבְנֵי יִשְׂרָאֵל עַם קְרֹבוֹ
הַלְלוּיָהּ׃ יְהוָה הוּא הָאֱלֹהִים. יְהוָה הוּא הָאֱלֹהִים בַּשָּׁמַיִם מִמַּעַל
וְעַל־הָאָרֶץ מִתָּחַת אֵין עוֹד׃ אֵין־כָּמוֹךָ בָאֱלֹהִים ׀ אֲדֹנָי וְאֵין
כְּמַעֲשֶׂיךָ׃

Yehalelu Et-Shem Adonai Ki-Nisgav Shemo Levado; Hodo. Al-'Eretz Veshamayim. Vayarem Keren Le'ammo Tehilah Lechol-Chasidav. Livnei Yisra'el Am Kerovo. Halleluyah. Adonai Hu Ha'elohim. Adonai Hu Ha'elohim. Bashamayim Mima'al. Ve'al-Ha'aretz Mitachat; Ein Od. Ein-Kamocha Va'elohim Adonai. Ve'ein Kema'aseicha.

"Let them praise the name of Hashem, For exalted is His name alone; His glory is over the earth and the heavens. He has lifted up the horn of strength of His people; He is the praise of all His pious servants, Of the children of Yisrael, the people near to Him.

Halleluyah — Praise Hashem. Hashem, He is God, Hashem, He is God, In the heavens above and on the earth beneath. There is none else. There is none like You, Hashem, among the gods, or nothing like Your works."

When the scroll of the Torah has been replaced in the Ark:

הֲשִׁיבֵ֫נוּ יְהֹוָ֥ה ׀ אֵלֶ֙יךָ֙ ונשוב (וְֽנָשׁ֔וּבָה) חַדֵּ֖שׁ יָמֵ֣ינוּ כְּקֶֽדֶם׃

Hashiveinu Adonai Eleicha Venashuvah. Chadesh Yameinu Kekedem.

"Hashem, turn us again towards You, and we will return. Renew our days as of old."

Hatzi Kaddish

Kaddish is only recited in a minyan (ten men). אמן denotes when the congregation responds "Amen" together out loud. According to the Shulchan Arukh, the congregation says "Yehei Shemeh Rabba" to "Yitbarach" out loud together without interruption, and also that one should respond "Amen" after "Yitbarach." (SA, OC 55,56) This is not the common custom today. Though many are accustomed to answering according to their own custom, it is advised to respond in the custom of the one reciting to avoid not fragmenting into smaller groups. ("Lo Titgodedu" - BT, Yevamot 13b / SA, OC 493, Rema / MT, Avodah Zara 12:15)

יִתְגַּדַּל וְיִתְקַדַּשׁ שְׁמֵהּ רַבָּא. אָמֵן בְּעָלְמָא דִּי בְרָא. כִּרְעוּתֵהּ. וְיַמְלִיךְ מַלְכוּתֵהּ. וְיַצְמַח פֻּרְקָנֵהּ. וִיקָרֵב מְשִׁיחֵהּ. אָמֵן בְּחַיֵּיכוֹן וּבְיוֹמֵיכוֹן וּבְחַיֵּי דְכָל בֵּית יִשְׂרָאֵל. בַּעֲגָלָא וּבִזְמַן קָרִיב. וְאִמְרוּ אָמֵן. אָמֵן יְהֵא שְׁמֵיהּ רַבָּא מְבָרַךְ לְעָלַם וּלְעָלְמֵי עָלְמַיָּא יִתְבָּרַךְ. וְיִשְׁתַּבַּח. וְיִתְפָּאַר. וְיִתְרוֹמַם. וְיִתְנַשֵּׂא. וְיִתְהַדָּר. וְיִתְעַלֶּה. וְיִתְהַלָּל שְׁמֵהּ דְּקֻדְשָׁא. בְּרִיךְ הוּא. אָמֵן לְעֵלָּא מִן כָּל בִּרְכָתָא שִׁירָתָא. תֻּשְׁבְּחָתָא וְנֶחֱמָתָא. דַּאֲמִירָן בְּעָלְמָא. וְאִמְרוּ אָמֵן. אָמֵן

Yitgadal Veyitkadash Shemeh Rabba. Amen Be'alema Di Vera. Kir'uteh. Veyamlich Malchuteh. Veyatzmach Purkaneh. Vikarev Meshicheh. Amen Bechayeichon Uveyomeichon Uvechayei Dechal-Beit Yisra'el. Ba'agala Uvizman Kariv. Ve'imru Amen. Amen Yehei Shemeh Rabba Mevarach Le'alam Ule'alemei Alemaya Yitbarach. Veyishtabach. Veyitpa'ar. Veyitromam. Veyitnasse. Veyit'hadar.

Veyit'aleh. Veyit'hallal Shemeh Dekudsha. Berich Hu. **Amen** Le'ella Min Kol Birchata Shirata. Tushbechata Venechemata. Da'amiran Be'alema. Ve'imru Amen. **Amen**

Glorified and sanctified be God's great name **Amen** throughout the world which He has created according to His will. May He establish His kingdom, hastening His salvation and the coming of His Messiah, **Amen**, in your lifetime and during your days, and within the life of the entire House of Yisrael, speedily and soon; and say, Amen. **Amen** May His great name be blessed forever and to all eternity. Blessed and praised, glorified and exalted, extolled and honored, adored and lauded is the name of the Holy One, blessed is He, **Amen** Beyond all the blessings and hymns, praises and consolations that are ever spoken in the world; and say, Amen. **Amen**

It is a custom to take off and put away Tefillin right before Musaf. (SA, OC 25:13)

LAWS OF AMIDAH

When one gets up to pray if he was standing outside the Land of Yisrael, he should turn his face toward the Land of Yisrael and focus also on Yerushalayim and the Temple and the Holy of Holies. One who is not able to determine the directions, [should] direct one's heart to their Father in Heaven. One should consider oneself as if one is standing in the Beit Hamikdash, and in one's heart, one should be directed upward towards Heaven. One who prays needs to intend in their heart the meaning of the words which are coming out of their mouth. They should think as if the Divine Presence is before them, and remove all distracting thoughts from themselves, until their thoughts and intention are pure in their prayer. (SA, OC 94, 95, 98)

Musaf / Additional Service - Rosh Chodesh Weekday

Take three steps forward and say:

Adonai Sefatai Tiftach; Ufi. Yagid	אֲדֹנָי שְׂפָתַי תִּפְתָּח וּפִי יַגִּיד
Tehilatecha.	תְּהִלָּתֶךָ:

Hashem, open my lips, that my mouth may declare Your praise.

Avot / Fathers

Bow at "Baruch Attah" / "Blessed are You". Raise up at Adonai / Hashem.

Baruch Attah Adonai Eloheinu	בָּרוּךְ אַתָּה יְהֹוָה אֱלֹהֵינוּ
Velohei Avoteinu. Elohei	וֵאלֹהֵי אֲבוֹתֵינוּ. אֱלֹהֵי
Avraham. Elohei Yitzchak.	אַבְרָהָם. אֱלֹהֵי יִצְחָק.
Velohei Ya'akov. Ha'el Hagadol	וֵאלֹהֵי יַעֲקֹב. הָאֵל הַגָּדוֹל
Hagibor Vehanorah. El Elyon.	הַגִּבּוֹר וְהַנּוֹרָא. אֵל עֶלְיוֹן.
Gomel Chasadim Tovim. Koneh	גּוֹמֵל חֲסָדִים טוֹבִים. קוֹנֵה
Hakol. Vezocher Chasdei Avot.	הַכֹּל. וְזוֹכֵר חַסְדֵי אָבוֹת.
Umevi Go'el Livnei Veneihem	וּמֵבִיא גוֹאֵל לִבְנֵי בְנֵיהֶם
Lema'an Shemo Be'ahavah.	לְמַעַן שְׁמוֹ בְּאַהֲבָה:

Blessed are You, Hashem our God and God of our fathers, God of Avraham, God of Yitzchak and God of Yaakov; the great, mighty and revered God, most high God, Who bestows lovingkindness. Master of all things; Who remembers the kindnesses of our fathers, and Who will bring a redeemer to their children's children for the sake of His name in love.

Bow at "Baruch Attah" / Blessed are You. Raise up at Adonai / Hashem.

Melech Ozeir Umoshia	מֶלֶךְ עוֹזֵר וּמוֹשִׁיעַ
Umagen. Baruch Attah Adonai	וּמָגֵן: בָּרוּךְ אַתָּה יְהֹוָה
Magen Avraham.	מָגֵן אַבְרָהָם:

King, Supporter, and Savior and Shield. Blessed are You, Hashem, Shield of Avraham.

Gevurot / Powers

We [in Yisrael] begin to say "mashiv haruach" in the second blessing of the Amidah from the Musaf [Additional] Service of the last day of Sukkot, and conclude at the Musaf [Additional] Service of the first day of Pesach. On the first day of Pesach the congregation still says it in the Musaf Service, but the Reader stops saying it then. In lands outside of Yisrael, we begin to pray for rain in the Arvit (Evening) Service of the sixtieth day after the New Moon of Tishrei, and in Yisrael we begin to say it in the evening of the seventh day of Cheshvan, and it is said until the Afternoon Service on the day preceding the first day of Passover. If one prayed for rain in the summer, or if one omitted to pray for it in the winter, he must repeat the Amidah again. If one said "morid hageshem" in the summer time, he must repeat again from the beginning of the blessing. If he already concluded the blessing, he must read the entire Amidah again. Likewise in the winter, if he omitted it, he must begin all over again. (SA, OC 117)

Attah Gibor Le'olam Adonai.	אַתָּה גִּבּוֹר לְעוֹלָם אֲדֹנָי.
Mechayeh Meitim Attah. Rav	מְחַיֵּה מֵתִים אַתָּה. רַב
Lehoshia.	לְהוֹשִׁיעַ.

You, Hashem, are mighty forever; You revive the dead; You are powerful to save.

B'ketz: Morid Hatal.	**בקיץ:** מוֹרִיד הַטָּל.
B'choref: Mashiv Haruach Umorid	**בחורף:** מַשִּׁיב הָרוּחַ וּמוֹרִיד
Hageshem.	הַגֶּשֶׁם.

In summer: You cause the dew to fall.

In winter: You cause the wind to blow and the rain to fall.

Mechalkel Chayim Bechesed.	מְכַלְכֵּל חַיִּים בְּחֶסֶד.
Mechayeh Meitim Berachamim	מְחַיֵּה מֵתִים בְּרַחֲמִים
Rabim. Somech Nofelim. Verofei	רַבִּים. סוֹמֵךְ נוֹפְלִים. וְרוֹפֵא
Cholim. Umatir Asurim.	חוֹלִים. וּמַתִּיר אֲסוּרִים.
Umekayem Emunato Lishenei	וּמְקַיֵּם אֱמוּנָתוֹ לִישֵׁנֵי

Afar. Mi Chamocha Ba'al	עָפָר. מִי כָמוֹךָ בַּעַל
Gevurot. Umi Domeh Lach.	גְּבוּרוֹת. וּמִי דּוֹמֶה לָּךְ.
Melech Memit Umechayeh	מֶלֶךְ מֵמִית וּמְחַיֶּה
Umatzmiach Yeshu'ah.	וּמַצְמִיחַ יְשׁוּעָה.

You sustain the living with kindness, and revive the dead with great mercy; You support all who fall, and heal the sick; You set the captives free, and keep faith with those who sleep in the dust. Who is like You, Master of power? Who resembles You, Oh King? You bring death and restore life, and cause salvation to flourish.

Vene'eman Attah Lehachayot	וְנֶאֱמָן אַתָּה לְהַחֲיוֹת
Meitim. Baruch Attah Adonai	מֵתִים: בָּרוּךְ אַתָּה יֱהֹוָהֱ
Mechayeh Hameitim.	מְחַיֵּה הַמֵּתִים:

And You are faithful to revive the dead. Blessed are You, Hashem, Who revives the dead.

Kedusha

Kedusha is said only in a minyan (10 men). If one is not available, skip to "Holiness". It is proper to position one's feet together at the time one is reciting Kedushah with the prayer-leader.

Keter Yitenu Lecha. Adonai	כֶּתֶר יִתְּנוּ לְךָ. יְהֹוָה
Eloheinu. Mal'achim Hamonei	אֱלֹהֵינוּ. מַלְאָכִים הֲמוֹנֵי
Ma'lah. VeAmmecha Yisra'el	מַעְלָה. וְעַמְּךָ יִשְׂרָאֵל
Kevutzei Mattah. Yachad Kulam	קְבוּצֵי מַטָּה. יַחַד כֻּלָּם
Kedushah Lecha Yeshalleshu.	קְדֻשָּׁה לְךָ יְשַׁלֵּשׁוּ.
Kadavar Ha'amur Al Yad	כַּדָּבָר הָאָמוּר עַל יַד
Nevi'ach Vekara Zeh El Zeh	נְבִיאָךְ וְקָרָא זֶה אֶל־זֶה
Ve'amar **Kadosh Kadosh Kadosh**	וְאָמַר **קָדוֹשׁ | קָדוֹשׁ קָדוֹשׁ**

Adonai Tzeva'ot Melo Chol	יְהוָה צְבָאוֹת מְלֹא כָל־
Ha'aretz Kevodo. Le'ummatam	הָאָרֶץ כְּבוֹדוֹ: לְעֻמָּתָם
Meshabechim Ve'omerim.	מְשַׁבְּחִים וְאוֹמְרִים:
Baruch Kevod-Adonai	בָּרוּךְ כְּבוֹד־יְהוָה
Mimekomo. Uvedivrei	מִמְּקוֹמוֹ: וּבְדִבְרֵי
Kodshecha Katuv Lemor.	קָדְשְׁךָ כָּתוּב לֵאמֹר: יִמְלֹךְ
Yimloch Adonai Le'olam.	יְהוָה | לְעוֹלָם אֱלֹהַיִךְ
Elohayich Tziyon Ledor Vador.	צִיּוֹן לְדֹר וָדֹר
Halleluyah.	הַלְלוּיָהּ:

To You, Hashem our God, will the heavenly host of angels above, with Your people Yisrael assembled beneath, give a crown; all with one accord will thrice proclaim the holy praise to You, according to the word spoken by Your prophet, "And one cried to another, and said, **'Holy, holy, holy is Hashem of hosts, the whole earth is full of his glory."** While those angels turning towards each other continue praising and saying: **"Blessed is the glory of Hashem from His place."** And in Your holy Word it is written, saying, **"Hashem will reign forever, your God, Tziyon, from generation to generation. Halleluyah."**

Kedushat HaShem / Holiness of the Name

Attah Kadosh Veshimcha	אַתָּה קָדוֹשׁ וְשִׁמְךָ
Kadosh. Ukedoshim Bechol-	קָדוֹשׁ. וּקְדוֹשִׁים בְּכָל־
Yom Yehalelucha Selah. Baruch	יוֹם יְהַלְלוּךָ סֶּלָה: בָּרוּךְ
Attah Adonai Ha' El Hakadosh.	אַתָּה יְהוָה הָאֵל הַקָּדוֹשׁ:

You are holy and Your name is holy, and the holy-ones will praise You every day, selah. Blessed are You, Hashem, The Holy God.

Kedushat HaYom / Holiness of the Day

Roshei Chodashim Le'ammecha	רָאשֵׁי חֳדָשִׁים לְעַמְּךָ
Natatta. Zeman Kapparah	נָתַתָּ. זְמַן כַּפָּרָה
Lechol Toledotam. Bihyotam	לְכָל־תּוֹלְדוֹתָם. בִּהְיוֹתָם
Makrivim Lefaneicha Zivchei	מַקְרִיבִים לְפָנֶיךָ זִבְחֵי
Ratzon. Use'ir Chatat Lechapeir	רָצוֹן. וּשְׂעִיר חַטָּאת לְכַפֵּר
Ba'adam. Zikaron Lechulam	בַּעֲדָם. זִכָּרוֹן לְכֻלָּם
Hayah. Teshu'at Nafsham Miyad	הָיָה. תְּשׁוּעַת נַפְשָׁם מִיַּד
Sone. Mizbe'ach Chadash	שׂוֹנֵא. מִזְבֵּחַ חָדָשׁ
Betziyon Tachin. Ve'olat Rosh	בְּצִיּוֹן תָּכִין. וְעוֹלַת רֹאשׁ
Chodesh Na'aleh Alav. Use'ir	חֹדֶשׁ נַעֲלֶה עָלָיו. וּשְׂעִיר
Izim Na'aseh Veratzon.	עִזִּים נַעֲשֶׂה בְרָצוֹן.
Uva'avodat Beit Hamikdash	וּבַעֲבוֹדַת בֵּית הַמִּקְדָּשׁ
Nismach Kulanu. Veshirei David	נִשְׂמַח כֻּלָּנוּ. וְשִׁירֵי דָוִד
Avdach Nishma Be'irach	עַבְדְּךָ נִשְׁמַע בְּעִירָךְ
Ha'amurim Lifnei Mizbachach.	הָאֲמוּרִים לִפְנֵי מִזְבְּחָךְ.
Ahavat Olam Tavi Lahem. Uverit	אַהֲבַת עוֹלָם תָּבִיא לָהֶם. וּבְרִית
Avot Lebanim Tizkor.	אָבוֹת לְבָנִים תִּזְכּוֹר:

The beginning of months You gave to Your people as a time of atonement for all their generations; when they offered before You favorable sacrifices and male goats for a sin-offering to atone for them. It was a memorial for all of them, and a deliverance of their soul from the power of the enemy. May a new altar, in Tziyon, be established and the burnt-offering of the New Moon may we offer on it. And prepare a male goat with willingness, and in the service of the Beit HaMikdash we will all rejoice. And the songs of Your servant David we will hear in Your city as they were chanted before

Your Altar. Bring an everlasting love to them. And the covenant of the fathers, for the children, remember it.

Yehi Ratzon Milfaneicha Adonai	יְהִי רָצוֹן מִלְּפָנֶיךָ יְהֹוָה
Eloheinu Velohei Avoteinu.	אֱלֹהֵינוּ וֵאלֹהֵי אֲבוֹתֵינוּ.
Sheta'alenu Vesimchah	שֶׁתַּעֲלֵנוּ בְשִׂמְחָה
Le'artzenu Vetita'enu Bigvulenu.	לְאַרְצֵנוּ וְתִטָּעֵנוּ בִּגְבוּלֵנוּ.
Vesham Na'aseh Lefaneicha Et	וְשָׁם נַעֲשֶׂה לְפָנֶיךָ אֶת
Korbenot Chovoteinu. Temidim	קָרְבְּנוֹת חוֹבוֹתֵינוּ. תְּמִידִים
Kesidram Umusafim	כְּסִדְרָם וּמוּסָפִים
Kehilchatam. Et Musaf Yom	כְּהִלְכָתָם. אֶת מוּסַף יוֹם
Rosh Chodesh Hazeh. Na'aseh	רֹאשׁ חֹדֶשׁ הַזֶּה. נַעֲשֶׂה
Venakriv Lefaneicha Be'ahavah	וְנַקְרִיב לְפָנֶיךָ בְּאַהֲבָה
Kemitzvat Retzonach. Kemo	כְּמִצְוַת רְצוֹנָךְ. כְּמוֹ
Shekatavta Aleinu Betoratach Al	שֶׁכָּתַבְתָּ עָלֵינוּ בְּתוֹרָתָךְ עַל
Yedei Mosheh Avdakh Mipi	יְדֵי מֹשֶׁה עַבְדָּךְ מִפִּי
Kevodecha Ka'amur:	כְבוֹדָךְ כָּאָמוּר:

May it be Your will, Hashem our God and God of our fathers, to bring us up with joy to our land, and to plant us in our own territory; and there we will offer in Your presence, bring the offerings of our duty; the continual offerings according to their order and the Musaf (additional) offerings according to their laws. The Musaf offering of this day of Rosh Chodesh we will offer before you with love according to the commands of Your will, as You have written concerning us in Your Torah, by the hand of Moshe, Your servant, and from the mouth of Your glory; as it is said:

וּבְרָאשֵׁי חָדְשֵׁיכֶם תַּקְרִיבוּ עֹלָה לַיהֹוָה פָּרִים בְּנֵי־בָקָר שְׁנַיִם וְאַיִל אֶחָד כְּבָשִׂים בְּנֵי־שָׁנָה שִׁבְעָה תְּמִימִם: וּמִנְחָתָם וְנִסְכֵּיהֶם כַּמְדֻבָּר: שְׁלֹשָׁה עֶשְׂרֹנִים לַפָּר וּשְׁנֵי עֶשְׂרֹנִים לָאָיִל וְעִשָּׂרוֹן לַכֶּבֶשׂ. וְיַיִן כְּנִסְכּוֹ. וְשָׂעִיר לְכַפֵּר. וּשְׁנֵי תְמִידִים כְּהִלְכָתָם:

Uveroshei Chodsheichem Takrivu Olah L'Adonai Parim Benei Vakar Shenayim Ve'ayil Echad Kevasim Benei Shanah Shiv'ah Temimim. Uminchatam Veniskeihem Kammedubbar: Sheloshah Esronim Lappar Ushenei Esronim La'ayil Ve'issaron Lakeves. Veyayin Kenisko. Vesa'ir Lechapeir. Ushenei Temidim Kehilchatam.

And on your new moons you will present a burnt-offering to Hashem: two young bulls, and one ram, seven male lambs of the first year without blemish; and their meal-offering and drink-offerings according to it. Three tenths of a hin for each bull, two tenths of a hin for the ram, and a tenths of a hin for every lamb, and wine according to the drink-offering of it; a goat for an atonement, and the two daily offerings, according to their institution. **(Numbers 28:11-14)**

Eloheinu Velohei Avoteinu.	אֱלֹהֵינוּ וֵאלֹהֵי אֲבוֹתֵינוּ.
Chadesh Aleinu Et Hachodesh	חַדֵּשׁ עָלֵינוּ אֶת הַחֹדֶשׁ
Hazeh Letovah Velivrachah.	הַזֶּה לְטוֹבָה וְלִבְרָכָה.
Lesason Ulesimchah. Lishu'ah	לְשָׂשׂוֹן וּלְשִׂמְחָה. לִישׁוּעָה
Ulenechamah. Lefarnasah	וּלְנֶחָמָה. לְפַרְנָסָה
Ulechalkalah. Lechayim Tovim	וּלְכַלְכָּלָה. לְחַיִּים טוֹבִים
Uleshalom. Limchilat Chet.	וּלְשָׁלוֹם. לִמְחִילַת חֵטְא.
Velislichat Avon. **In A Leap Year:**	וְלִסְלִיחַת עָוֹן. **בשנה מעוברת אומרים:**
(Ulechapparat Pesha.) Veyihyeh Rosh	(וּלְכַפָּרַת פֶּשַׁע.) וְיִהְיֶה רֹאשׁ
Chodesh Hazeh Sof Vaketz	חֹדֶשׁ הַזֶּה סוֹף וָקֵץ
Lechol Tzaroteinu. Techillah	לְכָל צָרוֹתֵינוּ. תְּחִלָּה

Varosh Lefidyon Nafshenu. Ki	וְרֹאשׁ לְפִדְיוֹן נַפְשֵׁנוּ. כִּי
Ve'ammecha Yisra'el Mikol	בְעַמְּךָ יִשְׂרָאֵל מִכָּל
Ha'ummot Bacharta. Vechukkei	הָאֻמּוֹת בָּחַרְתָּ. וְחֻקֵּי
Roshei Chodashim Lahem	רָאשֵׁי חֳדָשִׁים לָהֶם
Kava'eta. Baruch Attah Adonai	קָבָעְתָּ. בָּרוּךְ אַתָּה יְהוָה
Mekadesh Yisrael Veroshei	מְקַדֵּשׁ הַשַּׁבָּת וְיִשְׂרָאֵל וְרָאשֵׁי
Chadashim.	חֳדָשִׁים:

Our God, and the God of our fathers, renew this month for good and for blessing; for gladness and for joy; for salvation and for consolation; for maintenance and for sustenance; for good life and for peace, for pardon of sin. **In a leap year:** (and for atonement of transgression.) May this new month be the end and termination of all our troubles, the opening and beginning of the redemption of our souls; for Your people, Yisrael, You chose from all nations and have appointed for them the statutes of Rosh Chodesh. Blessed are You, Hashem Who sanctifies Yisrael and the Days of Rosh Chodesh.

Avodah / Temple Service

Retzeh Adonai Eloheinu	רְצֵה יְהוָה אֱלֹהֵינוּ
Be'ammecha Yisra'el Velitfilatam	בְּעַמְּךָ יִשְׂרָאֵל וְלִתְפִלָּתָם
She'eh. Vehasheiv Ha'avodah	שְׁעֵה. וְהָשֵׁב הָעֲבוֹדָה
Lidvir Beitecha. Ve'ishei Yisra'el	לִדְבִיר בֵּיתֶךָ. וְאִשֵּׁי יִשְׂרָאֵל
Utefilatam. Meheirah Be'ahavah	וּתְפִלָּתָם. מְהֵרָה בְּאַהֲבָה
Tekabel Beratzon. Utehi Leratzon	תְקַבֵּל בְּרָצוֹן. וּתְהִי לְרָצוֹן
Tamid Avodat Yisra'el Ammecha.	תָּמִיד עֲבוֹדַת יִשְׂרָאֵל עַמֶּךָ.
Ve'attah Berachameicha	וְאַתָּה בְּרַחֲמֶיךָ

Harabim. Tachpotz Banu	הָרַבִּים. תַּחְפֹּץ בָּנוּ
Vetirtzenu. Vetechezeinah	וְתִרְצֵנוּ. וְתֶחֱזֶינָה
Eineinu Beshuvecha Letziyon	עֵינֵינוּ בְּשׁוּבְךָ לְצִיּוֹן
Berachamim. Baruch Attah	בְּרַחֲמִים. בָּרוּךְ אַתָּה
Adonai Hamachazir Shechinato	יְהוָה הַמַּחֲזִיר שְׁכִינָתוֹ
Letziyon:	לְצִיּוֹן:

Be favorable, Hashem our God, on Your people Yisrael and regard their prayers. And the service to the Sanctuary of Your House, and the fire offerings of Yisrael, and their prayers accept soon with love. And may the service of Your people, Yisrael, always be favorable. And You, in Your abundant mercy, delight in us, and be favorable to us, so that our eyes may witness Your return to Tzion with mercy. Blessed are You, Hashem Who returns His Presence to Tzion.

Hoda'ah (Modim) / Thanksgiving

On Saying "Modim" / "We are Thankful" One Bows and begins to rise after "Adonai" / "Hashem".

Modim Anachnu Lach. She'attah	מוֹדִים אֲנַחְנוּ לָךְ. שָׁאַתָּה
Hu Adonai Eloheinu Velohei	הוּא יְהוָה אֱלֹהֵינוּ וֵאלֹהֵי
Avoteinu Le'olam Va'ed. Tzurenu	אֲבוֹתֵינוּ לְעוֹלָם וָעֶד. צוּרֵנוּ
Tzur Chayeinu Umagen Yish'enu	צוּר חַיֵּינוּ וּמָגֵן יִשְׁעֵנוּ
Attah Hu. Ledor Vador Nodeh	אַתָּה הוּא. לְדוֹר וָדוֹר נוֹדֶה
Lecha Unsapeir Tehilatecha. Al	לְךָ וּנְסַפֵּר תְּהִלָּתֶךָ. עַל
Chayeinu Hamesurim	חַיֵּינוּ הַמְּסוּרִים
Beyadecha. Ve'al Nishmoteinu	בְּיָדֶךָ. וְעַל נִשְׁמוֹתֵינוּ
Hapekudot Lach. Ve'al Niseicha	הַפְּקוּדוֹת לָךְ. וְעַל נִסֶּיךָ
Shebechol-Yom Imanu. Ve'al	שֶׁבְּכָל־יוֹם עִמָּנוּ. וְעַל

Nifle'oteicha Vetovoteicha	נִפְלְאוֹתֶיךָ וְטוֹבוֹתֶיךָ
Shebechol-'Et. Erev Vavoker	שֶׁבְּכָל־עֵת. עֶרֶב וָבֹקֶר
Vetzaharayim. Hatov. Ki Lo	וְצָהֳרָיִם. הַטּוֹב. כִּי לֹא
Chalu Rachameicha.	כָלוּ רַחֲמֶיךָ.
Hamerachem. Ki Lo Tamu	הַמְרַחֵם. כִּי לֹא תַמּוּ
Chasadeicha. Ki Me'olam Kivinu	חֲסָדֶיךָ. כִּי מֵעוֹלָם קִוִּינוּ
Lach.	לָךְ:

We are thankful to You, Hashem our God and the God of our fathers, forever. You are our strength and Rock of our life and the Shield of our salvation. In every generation we will thank You and recount Your praise for our lives which are in given into Your hand, for our souls which are placed in Your care, and for Your miracles which are daily with us, and for Your wonders and goodness—evening, morning and noon. The Beneficent One, for Your mercies never end, Merciful One, for Your kindness has never ceased, for we have always placed our hope in You.

Modim Derabbanan

During the repetition, this is to be recited softly while the Chazan reads the Modim. Still bow at Modim as before.

מוֹדִים אֲנַחְנוּ לָךְ. שֶׁאַתָּה הוּא יְהוָה אֱלֹהֵינוּ וֵאלֹהֵי אֲבוֹתֵינוּ. אֱלֹהֵי כָל בָּשָׂר. יוֹצְרֵנוּ יוֹצֵר בְּרֵאשִׁית. בְּרָכוֹת וְהוֹדָאוֹת לְשִׁמְךָ הַגָּדוֹל וְהַקָּדוֹשׁ. עַל שֶׁהֶחֱיִיתָנוּ וְקִיַּמְתָּנוּ. כֵּן תְּחַיֵּנוּ וּתְחָנֵּנוּ וְתֶאֱסוֹף גָּלֻיּוֹתֵינוּ לְחַצְרוֹת קָדְשֶׁךָ. לִשְׁמֹר חֻקֶּיךָ וְלַעֲשׂוֹת רְצוֹנְךָ וּלְעָבְדְךָ בְּלֵבָב שָׁלֵם. עַל שֶׁאֲנַחְנוּ מוֹדִים לָךְ. בָּרוּךְ אֵל הַהוֹדָאוֹת.

Modim Anachnu Lach. She'attah Hu Adonai Eloheinu Velohei Avoteinu. Elohei Chol Basar. Yotzreinu Yotzer Bereshit. Berachot Vehoda'ot Leshimcha Hagadol Vehakadosh. Al Shehecheyitanu Vekiyamtanu. Ken Techayeinu Utechanenu Vete'esof Galyoteinu Lechatzrot Kodshecha. Lishmor Chukkeicha Vela'asot Retzonecha Ule'avedecha Velevav Shalem. Al She'anachnu Modim Lach. Baruch El Hahoda'ot.

We are thankful to You, Hashem our God and the God of our fathers. God of all flesh, our Creator and Former of Creation, blessings and thanks to Your great and holy name, for You have kept us alive and sustained us; may You always grant us life and be gracious to us. And gather our exiles to Your holy courtyards to observe Your statutes, and to do Your will, and to serve You with a perfect heart. For this we thank You. Blessed is God of thanksgivings.

Al HaNissim

On Purim and Hanukkah an extra prayer is added here:

עַל הַנִּסִּים וְעַל הַפֻּרְקָן וְעַל הַגְּבוּרוֹת וְעַל הַתְּשׁוּעוֹת וְעַל הַנִּפְלָאוֹת וְעַל הַנֶּחָמוֹת שֶׁעָשִׂיתָ לַאֲבוֹתֵינוּ בַּיָּמִים הָהֵם בַּזְּמַן הַזֶּה:

Al Hanissim Ve'al Hapurkan Ve'al Hagevurot Ve'al Hateshu'ot Ve'al Hanifla'ot Ve'al Hanechamot She'asita La'avoteinu Bayamim Hahem Bazman Hazeh.

For the miracles, and for the triumphant liberation, and the mighty works, and for the deliverances, and for the wonders, and for the consolations which You have done for our fathers in those days at this season:

On Hanukkah:

בִּימֵי מַתִּתְיָה בֶן־יוֹחָנָן כֹּהֵן גָּדוֹל. חַשְׁמוֹנָאִי וּבָנָיו כְּשֶׁעָמְדָה מַלְכוּת יָוָן הָרְשָׁעָה עַל עַמְּךָ יִשְׂרָאֵל. לְשַׁכְּחָם תּוֹרָתֶךָ וּלְהַעֲבִירָם מֵחֻקֵּי רְצוֹנָךְ. וְאַתָּה בְּרַחֲמֶיךָ הָרַבִּים עָמַדְתָּ לָהֶם בְּעֵת צָרָתָם. רַבְתָּ אֶת רִיבָם. דַּנְתָּ אֶת דִּינָם. נָקַמְתָּ אֶת נִקְמָתָם. מָסַרְתָּ גִבּוֹרִים בְּיַד חַלָּשִׁים. וְרַבִּים בְּיַד מְעַטִּים. וּרְשָׁעִים בְּיַד צַדִּיקִים. וּטְמֵאִים בְּיַד טְהוֹרִים. וְזֵדִים בְּיַד עוֹסְקֵי תוֹרָתֶךָ. לְךָ עָשִׂיתָ שֵׁם גָּדוֹל וְקָדוֹשׁ בְּעוֹלָמָךְ. וּלְעַמְּךָ יִשְׂרָאֵל עָשִׂיתָ תְּשׁוּעָה גְדוֹלָה וּפֻרְקָן כְּהַיּוֹם הַזֶּה. וְאַחַר כָּךְ בָּאוּ בָנֶיךָ לִדְבִיר בֵּיתֶךָ. וּפִנּוּ אֶת־הֵיכָלֶךָ. וְטִהֲרוּ אֶת־מִקְדָּשֶׁךָ. וְהִדְלִיקוּ נֵרוֹת בְּחַצְרוֹת קָדְשֶׁךָ. וְקָבְעוּ שְׁמוֹנַת יְמֵי חֲנֻכָּה אֵלּוּ בְּהַלֵּל וּבְהוֹדָאָה. וְעָשִׂיתָ עִמָּהֶם נִסִּים וְנִפְלָאוֹת וְנוֹדֶה לְשִׁמְךָ הַגָּדוֹל סֶלָה:

Bimei Mattityah Ven-Yochanan Kohen Gadol. Chashmona'i Uvanav Keshe'amedah Malchut Yavan Haresha'ah Al Ammecha Yisra'el. Leshakecham Toratach Uleha'aviram Mechukkei Retzonach. Ve'attah Berachameicha Harabim Amadta Lahem Be'et Tzaratam. Ravta Et Rivam. Danta Et Dinam. Nakamta Et Nikmatam. Masarta Giborim Beyad Chalashim. Verabim Beyad Me'atim. Uresha'im Beyad Tzaddikim. Uteme'im Beyad Tehorim. Vezeidim Beyad Osekei Toratecha. Lecha Asita Shem Gadol Vekadosh Be'olamach. Ule'ammecha Yisra'el Asita Teshu'ah Gedolah Ufurkan Kehayom Hazeh. Ve'achar Kach Ba'u Vaneicha Lidvir Beitecha. Ufinu Et-Heichalecha. Vetiharu Et-Mikdashecha. Vehidliku Nerot Bechatzrot Kodshecha. Vekave'u Shemonat Yemei Chanukkah Elu Behallel Uvehoda'ah. Ve'asita Imahem Nissim Venifla'ot Venodeh Leshimcha Hagadol Selah.

Then in the days of Mattityahu ben-Yochanan, High Priest, the Hasmonean and his sons, when the cruel Greek power rose up against Your people, Yisrael, to make them forget Your Torah and transgress the statutes of Your will. And You, in Your great compassion, stood up for them in time of their trial to plead their cause and defend their judgment. Giving out retribution, delivered the strong into the hand of the weak, and the many into the hand of the few, and the wicked into the hand of the upright, and the impure into the hand of the pure, and tyrants into the hand of the devotees of Your Torah. You made for Yourself a great and holy name in Your world. And for Your people, Yisrael, You performed a great salvation and liberation as this very day. Then Your children came to the Sanctuary of Your House, cleared Your Temple, cleansed Your Sanctuary and kindled lights in Your courtyards, and they instituted these eight days of Hanukkah for praise and thanksgiving. And You did miracles and wonders for them, and we give thanks to Your great name, selah.

On Purim:

בִּימֵי מָרְדְּכַי וְאֶסְתֵּר בְּשׁוּשַׁן הַבִּירָה. כְּשֶׁעָמַד עֲלֵיהֶם הָמָן הָרָשָׁע. בִּקֵּשׁ לְהַשְׁמִיד לַהֲרֹג וּלְאַבֵּד אֶת־כָּל־הַיְּהוּדִים מִנַּעַר וְעַד זָקֵן טַף וְנָשִׁים בְּיוֹם אֶחָד. בִּשְׁלֹשָׁה עָשָׂר לְחֹדֶשׁ שְׁנֵים עָשָׂר. הוּא חֹדֶשׁ אֲדָר. וּשְׁלָלָם לָבוֹז. וְאַתָּה בְּרַחֲמֶיךָ הָרַבִּים הֵפַרְתָּ אֶת־עֲצָתוֹ וְקִלְקַלְתָּ אֶת־מַחֲשַׁבְתּוֹ. וַהֲשֵׁבוֹתָ לּוֹ גְּמוּלוֹ בְּרֹאשׁוֹ. וְתָלוּ אוֹתוֹ וְאֶת־בָּנָיו עַל הָעֵץ. וְעָשִׂיתָ עִמָּהֶם נֵס וָפֶלֶא וְנוֹדֶה לְשִׁמְךָ הַגָּדוֹל סֶלָה:

Bimei Mordechai Ve'ester Beshushan Habirah. Keshe'amad Aleihem Haman Harasha. Bikesh Lehashmid Laharog Ule'abed Et-Kol-Hayehudim Mina'ar Ve'ad Zaken Taf Venashim Beyom Echad. Bishloshah Asar Lechodesh Sheneim Asar. Hu Chodesh Adar. Ushelalam Lavoz. Ve'attah Berachameicha Harabim Hefarta Et-'Atzato Vekilkalta Et-Machashavto. Vahasheivota Lo Gemulo Verosho. Vetalu Oto Ve'et-Banav Al Ha'etz. Ve'asita Imahem Nes Vafelei Venodeh Leshimcha Hagadol Selah.

In the days of Mordechai and Ester in Shushan, the capital, the wicked Haman rose up and sought to destroy, slay and utterly annihilate all of the Yehudim, both young and old, women and children, on one day, on the thirteenth day of the twelfth month, which is the month of Adar, and to plunder their possessions. But You in Your great mercy You broke his plan and spoiled his designs, causing them to recoil on his own head, and they hanged him and his sons on the gallows. And You did miracles and wonders for them, and we give thanks to Your great name, selah.

Ve'al Kulam Yitbarach.	וְעַל כֻּלָּם יִתְבָּרַךְ.
Veyitromam. Veyitnasse. Tamid.	וְיִתְרוֹמַם. וְיִתְנַשֵּׂא. תָּמִיד.
Shimcha Malkeinu. Le'olam	שִׁמְךָ מַלְכֵּנוּ. לְעוֹלָם

Va'ed. Vechol-Hachayim	וָעֶד. וְכָל־הַחַיִּים
Yoducha Selah.	יוֹדוּךָ סֶּלָה:

For all these acts, may Your name, our King, be blessed, extolled and exalted forever. And all of the living will thank You, selah.

Bow at "Baruch Attah" / "Blessed are You". Raise up at Adonai / Hashem.

Vihalelu Vivarechu Et-Shimcha	וִיהַלְלוּ וִיבָרְכוּ אֶת־שִׁמְךָ
Hagadol Be'emet Le'olam Ki	הַגָּדוֹל בֶּאֱמֶת לְעוֹלָם כִּי
Tov. Ha'el Yeshu'atenu	טוֹב. הָאֵל יְשׁוּעָתֵנוּ
Ve'ezratenu Selah. Ha'el Hatov.	וְעֶזְרָתֵנוּ סֶלָה. הָאֵל הַטּוֹב:
Baruch Attah Adonai Hatov	בָּרוּךְ אַתָּה יְהֹוָה הַטּוֹב
Shimcha Ulecha Na'eh	שִׁמְךָ וּלְךָ נָאֶה
Lehodot.	לְהוֹדוֹת:

And they will praise and bless Your great and good name sincerely, forever. For You are good, the God of our salvation and our help forever, the Good God. Blessed are You, Hashem, Your name is good and to You it is good to give thanks.

Birkhat Kohanim / The Priestly Blessing

If there is more than one Kohen present, start here. If there is not, start with Eloheinu Velohei Avoteinu below:

Some say:

לְשֵׁם יִחוּד קוּדְשָׁא בְּרִיךְ הוּא וּשְׁכִינְתֵּיהּ. בִּדְחִילוּ וּרְחִימוּ. וּרְחִימוּ וּדְחִילוּ. לְיַחֲדָא שֵׁם יוֹ״ד קֵ״י בְּוָא״ו קֵ״י בְּיִחוּדָא שְׁלִים (יהוה) בְּשֵׁם כָּל יִשְׂרָאֵל. הִנֵּה אָנֹכִי מוּכָן וּמְזוּמָּן לְקַיֵּים מִצְוַת עֲשֵׂה לְבָרֵךְ אֶת יִשְׂרָאֵל בִּרְכַּת כֹּהֲנִים בִּנְשִׂיאוּת כַּפַּיִם לַעֲשׂוֹת נַחַת רוּחַ לְיוֹצְרֵנוּ וּלְהַמְשִׁיךְ שֶׁפַע וּבְרָכָה לְכָל הָעוֹלָמוֹת הַקְּדוֹשִׁים. וִיהִי נֹעַם אֲדֹנָי אֱלֹהֵינוּ עָלֵינוּ וּמַעֲשֵׂה יָדֵינוּ כּוֹנְנָה עָלֵינוּ וּמַעֲשֵׂה יָדֵינוּ כּוֹנְנֵהוּ:

The Kohanim stand on the pulpit after Modim Derabbanan and say:

יְהִי רָצוֹן מִלְּפָנֶיךָ יְהֹוָה אֱלֹהֵינוּ וֵאלֹהֵי אֲבוֹתֵינוּ שֶׁתְּהְיֶה בְּרָכָה זוֹ שֶׁצִּוִּיתָנוּ לְבָרֵךְ אֶת־עַמְּךָ יִשְׂרָאֵל בְּרָכָה שְׁלֵמָה וְלֹא יִהְיֶה בָּהּ מִכְשׁוֹל וְעָוֹן מֵעַתָּה וְעַד עוֹלָם:

Yehi Ratzon Milfaneicha Adonai Eloheinu Velohei Avoteinu Shetihyeh Berachah Zo Shetzivitanu Levarech Et-'Ammecha Yisra'el Berachah Shelemah Velo Yihyeh Vah Michshol Ve'avon Me'attah Ve'ad Olam.

May it be Your Will, Hashem our God, that this blessing which You have commanded us to bless Your people Yisrael with will be a perfect blessing. May there not be in it any stumbling or perverseness from now and forever.

Then they say the blessing. If there is more than one Kohen, the leader calls them, "Kohanim!".

בָּרוּךְ אַתָּה יְהֹוָה אֱלֹהֵינוּ מֶלֶךְ הָעוֹלָם. אֲשֶׁר קִדְּשָׁנוּ בִּקְדֻשָּׁתוֹ שֶׁל־אַהֲרֹן. וְצִוָּנוּ לְבָרֵךְ אֶת־עַמּוֹ יִשְׂרָאֵל בְּאַהֲבָה:

Baruch Attah Adonai Eloheinu Melech Ha'olam Asher Kideshanu Bikdushato Shel-Aharon. Vetzivanu Levarech Et-'Ammo Yisra'el Be'ahavah. Amen.

Blessed are You Hashem our God, King of the universe, Who has sanctified us with the sanctification of Aharon and commanded us to bless His people, Yisrael, with love.

The congregation answers:

אָמֵן:

Amen.

And the Chazan and the Kohanim say after him exactly:

יְבָרֶכְךָ יְהֹוָה וְיִשְׁמְרֶךָ: Yevarechecha Adonai Veyishmerecha.

ועונים: אָמֵן: **And answer:** Amen

Hashem bless you and keep you. **And answer:** Amen

יָאֵר יְהֹוָה | פָּנָיו אֵלֶיךָ וִיחֻנֶּךָּ: Ya'er Adonai Panav Eleicha Vichuneka.

ועונים: אָמֵן: **And Answer:** Amen

Hashem make His countenance shine upon you, and be gracious to you. **And answer:** Amen

יִשָּׂא יְהֹוָה | פָּנָיו אֵלֶיךָ וְיָשֵׂם Yissa Adonai Panav Eleicha. Veyasem

לְךָ שָׁלוֹם: ועונים: אָמֵן: Lecha Shalom. **And answer:** Amen

Hashem lift up His countenance towards you and give you peace. **And answer:** Amen

When the Chazan begins the Sim Shalom below, the Kohanim face toward the Ark and say:

רִבּוֹן הָעוֹלָמִים עָשִׂינוּ מַה שֶּׁגָּזַרְתָּ עָלֵינוּ. עֲשֵׂה אַתָּה מַה שֶּׁהִבְטַחְתָּנוּ. הַשְׁקִיפָה מִמְּעוֹן קָדְשְׁךָ מִן־הַשָּׁמַיִם וּבָרֵךְ אֶת־עַמְּךָ אֶת־יִשְׂרָאֵל:

Ribon Ha'olamim Asinu Mah Shegazarta Aleinu. Aseh Attah Mah-Shehivtachetanu. Hashkifah Mime'on Kodshecha Min-Hashamayim. Uvarech Et-'Ammecha Et-Yisra'el.

Sovereign of the universe, We have done what you have decreed for us, you have done as You promised. "Look down from Your holy Habitation, from heaven, and bless Your people Yisrael." **(Deut. 26:15)**

Eloheinu Velohei Avoteinu

If there are no Kohanim, the Chazan recites a substitute blessing:

Eloheinu Velohei Avoteinu.	אֱלֹהֵינוּ וֵאלֹהֵי אֲבוֹתֵינוּ.
Barecheinu Baberachah	בָּרְכֵנוּ בַּבְּרָכָה
Hamshuleshet Batorah	הַמְשֻׁלֶּשֶׁת בַּתּוֹרָה
Haketuvah Al Yedei Mosheh	הַכְּתוּבָה עַל יְדֵי מֹשֶׁה
Avdach. Ha'amurah Mipi	עַבְדֶּךָ. הָאֲמוּרָה מִפִּי
Aharon Uvanav Hakohanim Im	אַהֲרֹן וּבָנָיו הַכֹּהֲנִים עַם
Kedosheicha Ka'amur.	קְדוֹשֶׁיךָ כָּאָמוּר:

Our God, God of our fathers, bless us with the threefold blessing written in the Torah by Your servant Moshe, and spoken by the mouth of Aharon and his descendants Your consecrated Kohanim:

Yevarechecha Adonai	יְבָרֶכְךָ יְהֹוָה
Veyishmerecha. **And answer:** Ken	וְיִשְׁמְרֶךָ: **ועונים:** כֵּן
Yehi Ratzon.	יְהִי רָצוֹן:

Hashem bless you and keep you. **And answer:** May this be His will.

Ya'er Adonai Panav Eleicha	יָאֵר יְהֹוָה | פָּנָיו אֵלֶיךָ
Vichuneka. **And answer:** Ken Yehi	וִיחֻנֶּךָּ: **ועונים:** כֵּן יְהִי
Ratzon.	רָצוֹן:

Hashem make His countenance shine upon you, and be gracious to you. And answer: May this be His will.

Yissa Adonai Panav Eleicha.	יִשָּׂא יְהֹוָה | פָּנָיו אֵלֶיךָ
Veyasem Lecha Shalom.	וְיָשֵׂם לְךָ שָׁלוֹם:
And answer: Ken Yehi Ratzon.	ועונים: כֵּן יְהִי רָצוֹן:

Hashem lift up His countenance towards you and give you peace. And answer: May this be His will.

Vesamu Et-Shemi Al-Benei	וְשָׂמוּ אֶת־שְׁמִי עַל־בְּנֵי
Yisra'el; Va'ani Avarechem.	יִשְׂרָאֵל וַאֲנִי אֲבָרְכֵם:

And they will set My name upon the Children of Yisrael, and I will bless them.

Sim Shalom / Grant Peace

Sim Shalom Tovah Uverachah.	שִׂים שָׁלוֹם טוֹבָה וּבְרָכָה.
Chayim Chein Vachesed	חַיִּים חֵן וָחֶסֶד
Verachamim. Aleinu Ve'al Kol-	וְרַחֲמִים. עָלֵינוּ וְעַל כָּל־
Yisra'el Ammecha. Uvarecheinu	יִשְׂרָאֵל עַמֶּךָ. וּבָרְכֵנוּ
Avinu Kulanu Ke'echad Be'or	אָבִינוּ כֻּלָּנוּ כְּאֶחָד בְּאוֹר
Paneicha. Ki Ve'or Paneicha	פָּנֶיךָ. כִּי בְאוֹר פָּנֶיךָ
Natata Lanu Adonai Eloheinu	נָתַתָּ לָּנוּ יְהֹוָה אֱלֹהֵינוּ
Torah Vechayim. Ahavah	תּוֹרָה וְחַיִּים. אַהֲבָה
Vachesed. Tzedakah	וָחֶסֶד. צְדָקָה
Verachamim. Berachah	וְרַחֲמִים. בְּרָכָה
Veshalom. Vetov Be'eineicha	וְשָׁלוֹם. וְטוֹב בְּעֵינֶיךָ

Levarecheinu Ulevarech Et-	לְבָרְכֵנוּ וּלְבָרֵךְ אֶת־
Kol-'Ammecha Yisra'el. Berov	כָּל־עַמְּךָ יִשְׂרָאֵל. בְּרֹב
Oz Veshalom. Baruch Attah	עֹז וְשָׁלוֹם. בָּרוּךְ אַתָּה
Adonai Hamevarech Et Ammo	יוּהוּוּהוּ הַמְבָרֵךְ אֶת עַמּוֹ
Yisra'el Bashalom. Amen.	יִשְׂרָאֵל בַּשָּׁלוֹם. אָמֵן:

Grant peace, goodness and blessing, a life of grace, and kindness and mercy, to us and to all Yisrael, Your people. And bless us, our Father, all as one with the light of Your countenance; for with the light of Your countenance You have given us, Hashem our God, a Torah and life, love and kindness, righteousness and mercy, blessing and peace. May it be good in Your eyes to bless us and bless all of Your people, Yisrael, with abundant strength and peace. Blessed are You, Hashem, Who blesses His people Yisrael with peace. Amen.

Yihyu Leratzon Imrei-Fi Vehegyon Libi	יִהְיוּ לְרָצוֹן | אִמְרֵי־פִי וְהֶגְיוֹן לִבִּי
Lefaneicha; Adonai Tzuri Vego'ali.	לְפָנֶיךָ יְהֹוָה צוּרִי וְגֹאֲלִי:

May the words of my mouth and the meditation of my heart find favor before You, Hashem my Rock and my Redeemer.

The chazan's repetition ends here; personal / individual continue:

Elohai. Netzor Leshoni Meira	אֱלֹהַי. נְצֹר לְשׁוֹנִי מֵרָע
Vesiftotai Midaber Mirmah.	וְשִׂפְתוֹתַי מִדַּבֵּר מִרְמָה.
Velimkalelai Nafshi Tidom.	וְלִמְקַלְלַי נַפְשִׁי תִדֹּם.

Venafshi Ke'afar Lakol Tihyeh.	וְנַפְשִׁי כֶּעָפָר לַכֹּל תִּהְיֶה.
Petach Libi Betoratecha.	פְּתַח לִבִּי בְּתוֹרָתֶךָ.
Ve'acharei Mitzvoteicha Tirdof	וְאַחֲרֵי מִצְוֹתֶיךָ תִּרְדֹּף
Nafshi. Vechol-Hakamim Alai	נַפְשִׁי. וְכָל־הַקָּמִים עָלַי
Lera'ah. Meheirah Hafer Atzatam	לְרָעָה. מְהֵרָה הָפֵר עֲצָתָם
Vekalkel Machshevotam. Aseh	וְקַלְקֵל מַחְשְׁבוֹתָם. עֲשֵׂה
Lema'an Shemach. Aseh	לְמַעַן שְׁמָךְ. עֲשֵׂה
Lema'an Yeminach. Aseh	לְמַעַן יְמִינָךְ. עֲשֵׂה
Lema'an Toratach. Aseh Lema'an	לְמַעַן תּוֹרָתָךְ. עֲשֵׂה לְמַעַן
Kedushatach. Lema'an	קְדֻשָּׁתָךְ. לְמַעַן
Yechaletzun Yedideicha;	יֵחָלְצוּן יְדִידֶיךָ
Hoshi'ah Yeminecha Va'Aneni.	הוֹשִׁיעָה יְמִינְךָ וַעֲנֵנִי:

My God, guard my tongue from evil, and my lips from speaking deceit. And to those who curse me may my soul be silent; and may my soul be like the dust to all. Open my heart to Your Torah, that my soul may follow after Your commandments. And all that rise to do evil against me, speedily nullify their plan, and spoil their thoughts. Do it for the sake of Your name; do it for the sake of Your right hand; do it for the sake of Your Torah, do it for the sake of Your holiness. That Your beloved may be rescued, save with Your right hand and answer me. (Ps. 60:7)

Yihyu Leratzon Imrei-Fi Vehegyon Libi	יִהְיוּ לְרָצוֹן | אִמְרֵי־פִי וְהֶגְיוֹן לִבִּי
Lefaneicha; Adonai Tzuri Vego'ali.	לְפָנֶיךָ יְהוָֹה צוּרִי וְגֹאֲלִי:

May the words of my mouth and the meditation of my heart find favor before You, Hashem my Rock and my Redeemer.

Oseh Shalom

One bows and takes three steps backwards, while still bowing. After three steps, while still bowing and before erecting, while saying, "Oseh Shalom Bimromav", turn one's face to the left, "Hu [Berachamav] Ya'aseh Shalom Aleinu", turn one's face to the right; [face forward and] then bow forward like a servant leaving his master. (SA, OC 123:1)

Oseh Shalom Bimromav, Hu	עוֹשֶׂה שָׁלוֹם בִּמְרוֹמָיו. הוּא
Berachamav Ya'aseh Shalom	בְּרַחֲמָיו יַעֲשֶׂה שָׁלוֹם עָלֵינוּ.
Aleinu, Ve'al Kol-'Ammo	וְעַל כָּל־עַמּוֹ
Yisra'el, Ve'imru Amen.	יִשְׂרָאֵל. וְאִמְרוּ אָמֵן:

Creator of peace in His high places, may He in His mercy create peace for us and for all Yisrael, and say Amen.

Yehi Ratzon Milfaneicha Adonai	יְהִי רָצוֹן מִלְּפָנֶיךָ יְהֹוָה
Eloheinu Velohei Avoteinu. Shetivneh	אֱלֹהֵינוּ וֵאלֹהֵי אֲבוֹתֵינוּ. שֶׁתִּבְנֶה
Beit Hamikdash Bimheirah Veyameinu.	בֵּית הַמִּקְדָּשׁ בִּמְהֵרָה בְיָמֵינוּ.
Veten Chelkenu Vetoratach La'asot	וְתֵן חֶלְקֵנוּ בְתוֹרָתָךְ לַעֲשׂוֹת
Chukkei. Retzonach Ule'avedach	חֻקֵּי רְצוֹנָךְ וּלְעָבְדָךְ
Belevav Shalem.	בְּלֵבָב שָׁלֵם:

May it be Your will, Hashem our God and God of our fathers, that the Beit HaMikdash be speedily rebuilt in our days, and grant us a share in Your Torah so we may fulfill the statutes of your will and serve you with a whole heart.

Yehi Shem

יְהִ֤י שֵׁ֣ם יְהֹוָ֣ה מְבֹרָ֑ךְ מֵ֝עַתָּ֗ה וְעַד־עוֹלָֽם: מִמִּזְרַח־שֶׁ֥מֶשׁ עַד־מְבוֹא֑וֹ מְ֝הֻלָּ֗ל שֵׁ֣ם יְהֹוָֽה: רָ֖ם עַל־כָּל־גּוֹיִ֥ם | יְהֹוָ֑ה עַ֖ל הַשָּׁמַ֣יִם כְּבוֹדֽוֹ: יְהֹוָ֤ה אֲדֹנֵ֗ינוּ מָֽה־אַדִּ֣יר שִׁ֭מְךָ בְּכָל־הָאָֽרֶץ:

Yehi Shem Adonai Mevorach; Me'attah. Ve'ad-'Olam. Mimizrach-Shemesh Ad-Mevo'o; Mehulal. Shem Adonai Ram Al-Chol-Goyim Adonai Al Hashamayim Kevodo. Adonai Adoneinu; Mah-'Adir Shimcha. Bechol-Ha'aretz.

Blessed is the name of Hashem from this time forward and forever. From the rising of the sun to it's going down, Hashem's name is to be praised. Hashem, our Lord, How glorious is Your name in all of the earth. **(Psalms 113:2-4, 8:2)**

And say Kaddish Titkabbal:

Kaddish is only recited in a minyan (ten men). אָמֵן denotes when the congregation responds "Amen" together out loud. According to the Shulchan Arukh, the congregation says "Yehei Shemeh Rabba" to "Yitbarach" out loud together without interruption, and also that one should respond "Amen" after "Yitbarach." (SA, OC 55,56) This is not the common custom today. Though many are accustomed to answering according to their own custom, it is advised to respond in the custom of the one reciting to avoid not fragmenting into smaller groups. ("Lo Titgodedu" - BT, Yevamot 13b / SA, OC 493, Rema / MT, Avodah Zara 12:15)

יִתְגַּדַּל וְיִתְקַדַּשׁ שְׁמֵהּ רַבָּא. אָמֵן בְּעָלְמָא דִּי בְרָא. כִּרְעוּתֵהּ. וְיַמְלִיךְ מַלְכוּתֵהּ. וְיַצְמַח פֻּרְקָנֵהּ. וִיקָרֵב מְשִׁיחֵהּ. אָמֵן בְּחַיֵּיכוֹן וּבְיוֹמֵיכוֹן וּבְחַיֵּי דְכָל בֵּית יִשְׂרָאֵל. בַּעֲגָלָא וּבִזְמַן קָרִיב. וְאִמְרוּ אָמֵן. אָמֵן יְהֵא שְׁמֵיהּ רַבָּא מְבָרַךְ לְעָלַם וּלְעָלְמֵי עָלְמַיָּא יִתְבָּרַךְ. וְיִשְׁתַּבַּח. וְיִתְפָּאַר. וְיִתְרוֹמַם. וְיִתְנַשֵּׂא. וְיִתְהַדָּר. וְיִתְעַלֶּה. וְיִתְהַלָּל שְׁמֵהּ דְּקֻדְשָׁא. בְּרִיךְ הוּא. אָמֵן לְעֵלָּא מִן כָּל בִּרְכָתָא שִׁירָתָא. תֻּשְׁבְּחָתָא וְנֶחֱמָתָא. דַּאֲמִירָן בְּעָלְמָא. וְאִמְרוּ אָמֵן. אָמֵן

Yitgadal Veyitkadash Shemeh Rabba. **Amen** Be'alema Di Vera. Kir'uteh. Veyamlich Malchuteh. Veyatzmach Purkaneh. Vikarev Meshicheh. **Amen** Bechayeichon Uveyomeichon Uvechayei Dechal-Beit Yisra'el. Ba'agala Uvizman Kariv. Ve'imru Amen. **Amen** Yehei Shemeh Rabba Mevarach Le'alam Ule'alemei Alemaya Yitbarach. Veyishtabach. Veyitpa'ar. Veyitromam. Veyitnasse. Veyit'hadar. Veyit'aleh. Veyit'hallal Shemeh Dekudsha. Berich Hu. **Amen** Le'ella Min Kol Birchata Shirata. Tushbechata Venechemata. Da'amiran Be'alema. Ve'imru Amen. **Amen**

Glorified and sanctified be God's great name **Amen** throughout the world which He has created according to His will. May He establish His kingdom, hastening His salvation and the coming of His Messiah, **Amen**, in your lifetime and during your days, and within the life of the entire House of Yisrael, speedily and soon; and say, Amen. **Amen** May His great name be blessed forever and to all eternity. Blessed and praised, glorified and exalted, extolled and honored, adored and lauded is the name of the Holy One, blessed is He, **Amen** Beyond all the blessings and hymns, praises and consolations that are ever spoken in the world; and say, Amen. **Amen**

תִּתְקַבַּל צְלוֹתֲנָא וּבָעוּתֲנָא. עִם צְלוֹתְהוֹן וּבָעוּתְהוֹן דְּכָל בֵּית יִשְׂרָאֵל. קֳדָם אֲבוּנָא דְּבִשְׁמַיָּא וְאַרְעָא. וְאִמְרוּ אָמֵן. אָמֵן

Titkabbal Tzelotana Uva'utana. Im Tzelotehon Uva'utehon Dechol Beit Yisra'el. Kodam Avuna Devishmaya Ve'ar'a. Ve'imru Amen. **Amen**

May the prayer and supplication of the whole House of Yisrael be accepted before their Father in heaven, and say, Amen. **Amen**

יְהֵא שְׁלָמָא רַבָּא מִן שְׁמַיָּא. חַיִּים וְשָׂבָע וִישׁוּעָה וְנֶחָמָה. וְשֵׁיזָבָא וּרְפוּאָה וּגְאוּלָה וּסְלִיחָה וְכַפָּרָה וְרֶוַח וְהַצָּלָה לָנוּ וּלְכָל עַמּוֹ יִשְׂרָאֵל. וְאִמְרוּ אָמֵן. **אָמֵן**

Yehei Shelama Rabba Min Shemaya. Chayim Vesava Vishu'ah Venechamah. Vesheizava Urefu'ah Uge'ulah Uselichah Vechapparah Verevach Vehatzalah Lanu Ulechol Ammo Yisra'el. Ve'imru Amen. **Amen**

May abundant peace descend from heaven, with life and plenty, salvation, solace, liberation, healing and redemption, and forgiveness and atonement, enlargement and freedom, for us and all of God's people Yisrael; and say, Amen. **Amen**

One bows and takes three steps backwards, while still bowing. After three steps, while still bowing and before erecting, while saying, "Oseh Shalom Bimromav", turn one's face to the left, "Hu [Berachamav] Ya'aseh Shalom Aleinu", turn one's face to the right; then bow forward like a servant leaving his master. (SA, OC 123:1)

עוֹשֶׂה שָׁלוֹם **בעשי״ת:** (הַשָּׁלוֹם) בִּמְרוֹמָיו. הוּא בְּרַחֲמָיו יַעֲשֶׂה שָׁלוֹם עָלֵינוּ. וְעַל כָּל־עַמּוֹ יִשְׂרָאֵל. וְאִמְרוּ אָמֵן:

Oseh Shalom **On the 10 days of repentance:** (Hashalom) Bimromav, Hu Berachamav Ya'aseh Shalom Aleinu, Ve'al Kol-'Ammo Yisra'el, Ve'imru Amen.

Creator of **On the 10 days of repentance:** (the) peace in His high places, may He in His mercy create peace for us and for all Yisrael, and say Amen.

Barchi Nafshi - Psalm 104

Read Barchi Nafshi listed at the very beginning of Rosh Chodesh Section.

On Hanukkah say:

Psalms 30

מִזְמ֡וֹר שִׁיר־חֲנֻכַּ֖ת הַבַּ֣יִת לְדָוִֽד׃ אֲרוֹמִמְךָ֣ יְ֭הוָה כִּ֣י דִלִּיתָ֑נִי וְלֹֽא־שִׂמַּ֖חְתָּ אֹיְבַ֣י לִֽי׃ יְהוָ֥ה אֱלֹהָ֑י שִׁוַּ֥עְתִּי אֵ֝לֶ֗יךָ וַתִּרְפָּאֵֽנִי׃ יְֽהוָ֗ה הֶֽעֱלִ֣יתָ מִן־שְׁא֣וֹל נַפְשִׁ֑י חִ֝יִּיתַ֗נִי מיורדי (מִיָּֽרְדִי)־בֽוֹר׃ זַמְּר֣וּ לַיהוָ֣ה חֲסִידָ֑יו וְ֝הוֹד֗וּ לְזֵ֣כֶר קָדְשֽׁוֹ׃ כִּ֤י רֶ֨גַע ׀ בְּאַפּוֹ֮ חַיִּ֪ים בִּרְצ֫וֹנ֥וֹ בָּ֭עֶרֶב יָלִ֥ין בֶּ֗כִי וְלַבֹּ֥קֶר רִנָּֽה׃ וַ֭אֲנִי אָמַ֣רְתִּי בְשַׁלְוִ֑י בַּל־אֶמּ֥וֹט

לְעוֹלָם׃ יְהֹוָה בִּרְצוֹנְךָ הֶעֱמַדְתָּה לְהַרְרִי עֹז הִסְתַּרְתָּ פָנֶיךָ הָיִיתִי נִבְהָל׃ אֵלֶיךָ
יְהֹוָה אֶקְרָא וְאֶל־אֲדֹנָי אֶתְחַנָּן׃ מַה־בֶּצַע בְּדָמִי בְּרִדְתִּי אֶל שָׁחַת הֲיוֹדְךָ עָפָר
הֲיַגִּיד אֲמִתֶּךָ׃ שְׁמַע־יְהֹוָה וְחָנֵּנִי יְהֹוָה הֱיֵה־עֹזֵר לִי׃ הָפַכְתָּ מִסְפְּדִי לְמָחוֹל לִי
פִּתַּחְתָּ שַׂקִּי וַתְּאַזְּרֵנִי שִׂמְחָה׃ לְמַעַן ׀ יְזַמֶּרְךָ כָבוֹד וְלֹא יִדֹּם יְהֹוָה אֱלֹהַי
לְעוֹלָם אוֹדֶךָּ׃

Mizmor Shir-Chanukkat Habayit Ledavid. Aromimcha Adonai Ki Dillitani; Velo-Simachta Oyevai Li. Adonai Elohai; Shiva'ti Eleicha. Vatirpa'eni. Adonai He'elita Min-She'ol Nafshi; Chiyitani. Miyordi-Vor. Zameru L'Adonai Chasidav; Vehodu. Lezecher Kodsho. Ki Rega' Be'appo Chayim Birtzonobba'erev Yalin Bechi. Velaboker Rinah. Va'ani Amarti Veshalvi; Bal-'Emot Le'olam. Adonai Birtzonecha He'emadtah Lehareri Oz Histarta Faneicha. Hayiti Nivhal. Eleicha Adonai Ekra; Ve'el-' Adonai. Etchanan. Mah-Betza Bedami Beridti El Shachat Hayodecha Afar; Hayagid Amitecha. Shema'-Adonai Vechoneni; Adonai Heyeh-'Ozeir Li. Hafachta Mispedi Lemachol Li Pittachta Sakki; Vate'azereini Simchah. Lema'an Yezamercha Chavod Velo Yidom; Adonai Elohai. Le'olam Odeka.

A Psalm; a Song at the Dedication of the House of David. I will extol You, Hashem, for You have raised me up, and have not suffered my enemies to rejoice over me. Hashem my God, I cried to You, and You healed me; Oh Hashem, You brought up my soul from Sheol; You did keep me alive, that I should not go down to the pit. Sing praise to Hashem, His godly ones, and give thanks to His holy name. For His anger is but for a moment, His favor is for a life-time; weeping may come for the night, but joy comes in the morning. Now I had said in my security: 'I will never be moved.' You had established, Hashem, in Your favor my mountain as a stronghold — You hid Your face; I was afraid. To You, Hashem, did I call, and to Hashem I made supplication: 'What profit is there in my blood, when I go down to the pit? Will the dust praise You? Will it declare Your truth? Hear, Hashem, and be gracious to me; Hashem, be my helper.' You turned my mourning into dancing; You loosed my sackcloth, and girded me with gladness; So that my glory may sing praise to You, and not be silent; Hashem my God, I will give thanks to You forever.

The rest of the service now follows the normal Weekday Shacharit Service from: Kaddish Yehei Shelama, Kaveh, Ketoret, Kaddish Al Yisrael and Aleinu.

Tefillat Haderech / The Traveler's Prayer

Yehi Ratzon Milfaneicha Adonai	יְהִי רָצוֹן מִלְּפָנֶיךָ יְהֹוָה
Eloheinu Velohei Avoteinu.	אֱלֹהֵינוּ וֵאלֹהֵי אֲבוֹתֵינוּ.
Shetolicheinu Leshalom.	שֶׁתּוֹלִיכֵנוּ לְשָׁלוֹם.
Vetatz'idenu Leshalom.	וְתַצְעִידֵנוּ לְשָׁלוֹם.
Vetadricheinu Leshalom.	וְתַדְרִכֵנוּ לְשָׁלוֹם.
Vetaggi'enu Limchol Cheftzenu	וְתַגִּיעֵנוּ לִמְחוֹל חֶפְצֵנוּ
Lechayim. Ulesimah.	לְחַיִּים. וּלְשִׂמָּה.
Uleshalom. Vetatzilenu Mikaf	וּלְשָׁלוֹם. וְתַצִּילֵנוּ מִכַּף
Kol Oyev Ve'orev Baderech.	כָּל־אוֹיֵב וְאוֹרֵב בַּדֶּרֶךְ.
Vetitenenu Lechein. Ulchesed.	וְתִתְּנֵנוּ לְחֵן. וּלְחֶסֶד.
Ulerachamim. Be'eineicha	וּלְרַחֲמִים. בְּעֵינֶיךָ
Uve'einei Chol Ro'einu.	וּבְעֵינֵי כָל־רוֹאֵינוּ.
Vetishma Kol Tachanuneinu. Ki	וְתִשְׁמַע קוֹל תַּחֲנוּנֵינוּ. כִּי
El Shomea' Tefillah Vetachanun	אֵל שׁוֹמֵעַ תְּפִלָּה וְתַחֲנוּן
Attah. Baruch Attah Adonai	אָתָּה. בָּרוּךְ אַתָּה יְהֹוָה
Shomea' Tefillah:	שׁוֹמֵעַ תְּפִלָּה:

May it be Your will, Hashem our God, and the God of our fathers, to guide us in peace; to direct us that we may travel in safety and peace, so that we may arrive at the destination of our desire with life, joy, and peace. Deliver us from the power of every foe and opponent, lying in ambush on the road; and grant us grace, favor and mercy, in Your sight, and in that of all who behold us. Hear the voice of our supplications; for You, God, hear prayer and supplication. Blessed are You, Hashem, Who hears prayer.

Some add these verses as well:

וְיַעֲקֹב הָלַךְ לְדַרְכּוֹ וַיִּפְגְּעוּ־בוֹ מַלְאֲכֵי אֱלֹהִים: וַיֹּאמֶר יַעֲקֹב כַּאֲשֶׁר רָאָם מַחֲנֵה אֱלֹהִים זֶה וַיִּקְרָא שֵׁם־הַמָּקוֹם הַהוּא מַחֲנָיִם: ג' פעמים

Veya'akov Halach Ledarko Vayifge'u Vo Mal'achei Elohim. Vayomer Ya'akov Ka'asher Ra'am Machaneh Elohim Zeh Vayikra Shem Hamakom Hahu Machanayim.

Then Yaakov went on his way and the angels of God met him. And as he saw them, Yaakov said, 'This is the camp of God.' So he called the name of that place Machanaim (Encampments). **(Gen. 32:2) - say 3x**

הִנֵּה אָנֹכִי שֹׁלֵחַ מַלְאָךְ לְפָנֶיךָ לִשְׁמָרְךָ בַּדָּרֶךְ וְלַהֲבִיאֲךָ אֶל־הַמָּקוֹם אֲשֶׁר הֲכִנֹתִי: ג' פעמים

Hineh Anochi Sholeach Mal'ach Lefaneicha Lishmarecha Baddarech Velahavi'acha El Hamakom Asher Hachinoti.

"Behold I am sending before you an angel to guard you on the way and to bring you to the place which I have prepared." **(Ex. 23:20) - say 3x**

וַיִּסָּעוּ וַיְהִי | חִתַּת אֱלֹהִים עַל־הֶעָרִים אֲשֶׁר סְבִיבוֹתֵיהֶם וְלֹא רָדְפוּ אַחֲרֵי בְּנֵי יַעֲקֹב: לִישׁוּעָתְךָ קִוִּיתִי יְהֹוָה: ג' פעמים

Vayissa'u Vayhi Chitat Elohim Al He'arim Asher Sevivoteihem Velo Radefu Acharei Benei Ya'akov. Lishu'atecha Kiviti Adonai.

And they journeyed; and a terror of God was upon the cities that were round about them, and they did not pursue after the sons of Yaakov. I wait for Your salvation, Hashem. **(Gen. 35:5, 49:18) - say 3x**

Hanotein Teshu'ah / Prayer for the Government

Hanotein Teshu'ah	הַנּוֹתֵן תְּשׁוּעָה
Lammelachim. Umemshalah	לַמְּלָכִים. וּמֶמְשָׁלָה
Lansichim. Umalchuto Malchut	לַנְּסִיכִים. וּמַלְכוּתוֹ מַלְכוּת
Kol Olamim. Hapotzeh Et David	כָּל־עוֹלָמִים. הַפּוֹצֶה אֶת־דָּוִד
Avdo Mecherev Ra'ah. Hanotein	עַבְדּוֹ מֵחֶרֶב רָעָה. הַנּוֹתֵן
Bayam Darech. Uvemayim Azim	בַּיָּם דָּרֶךְ. וּבְמַיִם עַזִּים

Netivah. Hu Yevarech.	נְתִיבָה. הוּא יְבָרֵךְ.
Veyishmor. Veyintzor. Veya'azor.	וְיִשְׁמֹר. וְיִנְצֹר. וְיַעֲזֹר.
Virovmem. Vigadel. Vinashe	וִירוֹמֵם. וִיגַדֵּל. וִינַשֵּׂא
Lema'lah Lema'lah Et:	לְמַעְלָה לְמַעְלָה אֶת־:

May He Who dispenses assistance to kings, and dominion to princes; Whose kingdom is an everlasting kingdom; Who delivered His servant David from the destructive sword; Who makes a way in the sea, and a path in the mighty waters; bless, preserve, guard, assist, exalt, and raise to a high eminence:

Nesi Artzot Haberit Umishnehu	נְשִׂיא אַרְצֹת הַבְּרִית וּמִשְׁנֵהוּ
Ve'et Kol Sarei Ha'aretz Hazot.	וְאֶת כָּל שָׂרֵי הָאָרֶץ הַזֹּאת.

The President and the Vice-President and all of the officers of this land.

Melech Malchei Hamelachim.	מֶלֶךְ מַלְכֵי הַמְּלָכִים.
Berachamav Yishmerem	בְּרַחֲמָיו יִשְׁמְרֵם
Vichayeim. Umikol-Tzarah	וִיחַיֵּים. וּמִכָּל-צָרָה
Vanezek Yatzilem: Melech	וָנֶזֶק יַצִּילֵם: מֶלֶךְ
Malchei Hamelachim.	מַלְכֵי הַמְּלָכִים.
Berachamav Yiten Belibam	בְּרַחֲמָיו יִתֵּן בְּלִבָּם
Uvelev Kol Yo'atzeihem Vesarav	וּבְלֵב כָּל־יוֹעֲצֵיהֶם וְשָׂרָיו
Rachamanut. La'asot Tovah	רַחֲמָנוּת. לַעֲשׂוֹת טוֹבָה
Imanu. Ve'im Kol Yisra'el	עִמָּנוּ. וְעִם כָּל־יִשְׂרָאֵל
Acheinu: Bimeihem	אַחֵינוּ: בִּימֵיהֶם
Uveyameinu Tivasha Yehudah.	וּבְיָמֵינוּ תִּוָּשַׁע יְהוּדָה.
Veyisra'el Yishkon Lavetach.	וְיִשְׂרָאֵל יִשְׁכּוֹן לָבֶטַח.
Uva Letziyon Go'el. Vechen	וּבָא לְצִיּוֹן גּוֹאֵל. וְכֵן
Yehi Ratzon Venomar Amen.	יְהִי רָצוֹן וְנֹאמַר אָמֵן.

May the Supreme King of kings, through his infinite mercy preserve them, and grant them life, and deliver them from all manner of trouble and injury. May the Supreme King of kings, through His infinite mercy, inspire the heart of them and all of their counselors and officers with benevolence towards us, and all Yisrael our brothers. In their days and in ours may Yehudah be saved, and Yisrael dwell securely; and may the Redeemer come to Tziyon. May this be the will of God, and let us say. Amen.

BIRKHAT HAMAZON / GRACE AFTER MEALS

One may wash hands after the meal, known as Mayim Acharonim (The After-Waters). It is a custom, according to the Shulchan Arukh, it is a duty (mandatory). (OC, 181) It is not necessary to wash more than up to the second joints of the fingers. It is permissible to wash hands with any liquid and a blessing is not recited on this. It is required that the fingers be lowered during such washing. Birkhat Hamazon requires no cup of wine. (However it is most proper to recite Birkhat Hamazon over a cup of wine). It may be said only over a cup of wine, beer or upon any liquid that is the beverage of the locality, except water.

Some say before:

Psalms 67 / Lamnatzeach Binginot

לַמְנַצֵּחַ בִּנְגִינֹת מִזְמוֹר שִׁיר׃ אֱלֹהִים יְחָנֵּנוּ וִיבָרְכֵנוּ יָאֵר פָּנָיו אִתָּנוּ סֶלָה׃
לָדַעַת בָּאָרֶץ דַּרְכֶּךָ בְּכָל־גּוֹיִם יְשׁוּעָתֶךָ׃ יוֹדוּךָ עַמִּים | אֱלֹהִים יוֹדוּךָ עַמִּים
כֻּלָּם׃ יִשְׂמְחוּ וִירַנְּנוּ לְאֻמִּים כִּי־תִשְׁפֹּט עַמִּים מִישֹׁר וּלְאֻמִּים | בָּאָרֶץ תַּנְחֵם
סֶלָה׃ יוֹדוּךָ עַמִּים | אֱלֹהִים יוֹדוּךָ עַמִּים כֻּלָּם׃ אֶרֶץ נָתְנָה יְבוּלָהּ יְבָרְכֵנוּ
אֱלֹהִים אֱלֹהֵינוּ׃ יְבָרְכֵנוּ אֱלֹהִים וְיִירְאוּ אוֹתוֹ כָּל־אַפְסֵי־אָרֶץ׃

Lamnatzeach Binginot. Mizmor Shir. Elohim. Yechonenu Vivarecheinu; Ya'er Panav Itanu Selah. Lada'at Ba'aretz Darkecha; Bechol-Goyim. Yeshu'atecha. Yoducha Ammim Elohim; Yoducha. Ammim Kulam. Yismechu Viranenu. Le'ummim Ki-Tishpot Ammim Mishor; Ule'ummim Ba'aretz Tanchem Selah. Yoducha Ammim Elohim; Yoducha. Ammim Kulam. Eretz Natenah Yevulah; Yevarecheinu. Elohim Eloheinu. Yevarecheinu Elohim; Veyire'u Oto. Chol-'Afsei-'Aretz.

For the Leader; with string-music. A Psalm, a Song. May God be gracious to us, and bless us; May He cause His face to shine toward us; Selah. That Your way may be known upon earth, Your salvation among all nations. Let the people give thanks to You, Oh God; Let the peoples give thanks to You, all of them. Let the nations be glad and sing for joy; For You will judge the people with equity, And lead the nations on earth. Selah. Let the people give thanks to You, Oh God; Let the peoples give thanks to You, all of them. The earth has yielded her increase; May God, our own God, bless us. May God bless us; And let all the ends of the earth fear Him.

אֲבָרְכָה אֶת־יְהֹוָה בְּכָל־עֵת תָּמִיד תְּהִלָּתוֹ בְּפִי׃ סוֹף דָּבָר הַכֹּל נִשְׁמָע
אֶת־הָאֱלֹהִים יְרָא וְאֶת־מִצְוֹתָיו שְׁמוֹר כִּי־זֶה כָּל־הָאָדָם׃ תְּהִלַּת יְהֹוָה יְדַבֶּר פִּי
וִיבָרֵךְ כָּל־בָּשָׂר שֵׁם קׇדְשׁוֹ לְעוֹלָם וָעֶד׃ וַאֲנַחְנוּ | נְבָרֵךְ יָהּ מֵעַתָּה וְעַד־עוֹלָם
הַלְלוּיָהּ׃ וַיְדַבֵּר אֵלַי זֶה הַשֻּׁלְחָן אֲשֶׁר לִפְנֵי יְהֹוָה׃

Avarechah Et-Adonai Bechol-'Et; Tamid. Tehilato Befi. Sof Davar HaKol Nishma'; Et-Ha'elohim Yera Ve'et-Mitzvtav Shemor. Ki-Zeh Chol-Ha'adam. Tehillat Adonai Yedaber Pi Vivarech Chol-Basor Shem Kodsho. Le'olam Va'ed. Va'anachnu Nevarech Yah. Me'attah Ve'ad-'Olam. Halleluyah. VayDaber Elai. Zeh Hashulchan. Asher Lifnei Adonai.

I will bless Hashem at all times; His praise will continually be in my mouth. The sum of the matter, when all is said and done: Revere God and observe His commandments. For this applies to all mankind: My mouth will speak the praise of Hashem; And let all flesh bless His holy name forever and ever. and he said to me: 'This is the table that is before Hashem.' **(Psalms 31:2, Ecclesiastes 12:13, Psalms 145:21, Ezekiel 41:22)**

Zimmun / Invitation

If there are not 3 or more, go to the first blessing. If there are 3 or more say:

Hav Lan Venivrich Lemalka Illa'ah Kaddisha.

הַב לָן וְנִבְרִיךְ לְמַלְכָּא עִלָּאָה קַדִּישָׁא:

Allow us and We will bless the King, Most High and Holy.

The participants answer:

Shamayim!

שָׁמַיִם:

(By) Heaven!

And say the zimmun / invitation:

Birshut Malka Illa'ah Kaddisha **On Shabbat:** (Uvirshut Shabbat Malketa.) **On Yom Tov:** (Uvirshut Yoma Tava Ushepiza Kaddisha.) **On Sukkot:** (Uvirshut Shiv'ah Ushepizin Illa'in Kaddishin) (Uvirshut Morai Verabotai) Uvirshutechem.

בִּרְשׁוּת מַלְכָּא עִלָּאָה קַדִּישָׁא
בשבת: (וּבִרְשׁוּת שַׁבָּת מַלְכְּתָא)
ביו"ט: (וּבִרְשׁוּת יוֹמָא טָבָא אוּשְׁפִּיזָא קַדִּישָׁא.)
בסוכות: (וּבִרְשׁוּת שִׁבְעָה אוּשְׁפִּיזִין עִלָּאִין קַדִּישִׁין) (וּבִרְשׁוּת מוֹרַי וְרַבּוֹתַי) וּבִרְשׁוּתְכֶם.

With the permission of the King, Most High and Holy **On Shabbat:** (And with the permission of the Shabbat Queen.) **On Yom Tov:** (And with the permission of the Holy Festival.) **On Sukkot:** (And with permission of the seven exalted and holy guests) (and with the permissions of, my masters and my teachers) and with your permission.

Nevarech	נְבָרֵךְ
With Ten Or More: (Eloheinu)	בעשרה או יותר: (אֱלֹהֵינוּ)
She'achalnu Mishelo.	שֶׁאָכַלְנוּ מִשֶּׁלּוֹ:

Let us bless **with ten or more: (Our God)** Him of whose bounty we have eaten.

Participants respond:

Baruch **with ten or more:** (Eloheinu) **at a**	בָּרוּךְ בעשרה או יותר: (אֱלֹהֵינוּ) בסעודת
marriage supper: (Shehasimchah Bim'ono)	החתן: (שֶׁהַשִּׂמְחָה בִּמְעוֹנוֹ.)
She'achalnu Mishelo Uvetuvo	שֶׁאָכַלְנוּ מִשֶּׁלּוֹ וּבְטוּבוֹ
Chayinu.	חָיִינוּ:

Let us bless **with ten or more:** (Our God) **at a marraige supper:** (in Whose dwelling place is joy [and]) Him of Whose bounty we have eaten and through whose abundant goodness we live.

Leader responds:

Baruch **with ten or more:** (Eloheinu) **at a**	בָּרוּךְ בעשרה או יותר: (אֱלֹהֵינוּ) בסעודת
marriage supper: (Shehasimchah Bim'ono)	החתן: (שֶׁהַשִּׂמְחָה בִּמְעוֹנוֹ.)
She'achalnu Mishelo Uvetuvo	שֶׁאָכַלְנוּ מִשֶּׁלּוֹ וּבְטוּבוֹ
Chayinu.	חָיִינוּ:

Let us bless **with ten or more:** (Our God) **at a marraige supper:** (in Whose dwelling place is joy [and]) Him of Whose bounty we have eaten and through whose abundant goodness we live.

First Blessing: Birkhat Hazan / For the Nourishment

[*] denotes opening one's hand and concentrating on the sovereignty of Hashem

Baruch Attah Adonai Eloheinu	בָּרוּךְ אַתָּה יְהוָה אֱלֹהֵינוּ מֶלֶךְ
Melech Ha'olam Ha'el Hazan	הָעוֹלָם. הָאֵל הַזָּן

Otanu Ve'et-Ha'olam Kulo	אוֹתָנוּ וְאֶת־הָעוֹלָם כֻּלּוֹ
Betuvo. Bechein Bechesed	בְּטוּבוֹ. בְּחֵן בְּחֶסֶד
Berevach Uverachamim Rabim.	בְּרֶוַח וּבְרַחֲמִים רַבִּים.
Noten Lechem Lechol-Basar; Ki	נֹתֵן לֶחֶם לְכָל־בָּשָׂר כִּי
Le'olam Chasdo. Uvetuvo	לְעוֹלָם חַסְדּוֹ. וּבְטוּבוֹ
Hagadol Tamid Lo Chasar Lanu.	הַגָּדוֹל תָּמִיד לֹא חָסַר לָנוּ.
Ve'al Yechsar Lanu Mazon Tamid	וְאַל יֶחְסַר לָנוּ מָזוֹן תָּמִיד
Le'olam Va'ed. Ki Hu El Zan	לְעוֹלָם וָעֶד. כִּי הוּא אֵל זָן
Umefarnes LaKol Veshulchano	וּמְפַרְנֵס לַכֹּל וְשֻׁלְחָנוֹ
Aruch LaKol. Vehitkin Michyah	עָרוּךְ לַכֹּל. וְהִתְקִין מִחְיָה
Umazon Lechol-Beriyotav Asher	וּמָזוֹן לְכָל־בְּרִיּוֹתָיו אֲשֶׁר
Bara Berachamav Uverov	בָּרָא בְּרַחֲמָיו וּבְרוֹב
Chasadav. Ka'amur. *Potei'ach	חֲסָדָיו. כָּאָמוּר. *פּוֹתֵחַ
Et-Yadecha; Umasbia Lechol-	אֶת־יָדֶךָ וּמַשְׂבִּיעַ לְכָל־
Chai Ratzon. Baruch Attah	חַי רָצוֹן. בָּרוּךְ אַתָּה
Adonai Hazan Et HaKol.	יְהֹוָה הַזָּן אֶת הַכֹּל:

Blessed are You, Hashem our God, King of the universe, Who feeds us, but not by reason of our works; Who nourishes us, but not by reason of our righteousness; Who abundantly bestows His goodness on us; Who feeds us, and the whole world with His goodness; with grace, kindness, abundance and great mercy, "Who gives food to every creature, for His mercy endures forever." His great goodness has never failed us; and may sustenance never fail us forever and ever, for He feeds and sustains all; and His table is decked for all; He has also appointed food and sustenance for all his creatures, which He has created in His mercy and abundant kindness; as it is written: *"You open Your hand, and satisfy every living-being with favor." Blessed are You, Hashem Who provides food for all. **(Psalms 136:25, 145:16)**

Second Blessing: Birkhat Ha'Aretz / For the Land

Nodeh Lecha Adonai Eloheinu	נוֹדֶה לְּךָ יְהֹוָה אֱלֹהֵינוּ
Al Shehinchalta La'avoteinu.	עַל שֶׁהִנְחַלְתָּ לַאֲבוֹתֵינוּ.
Eretz Chemdah Tovah	אֶרֶץ חֶמְדָּה טוֹבָה
Urechavah Berit Vetorah	וּרְחָבָה בְּרִית וְתוֹרָה
Chayim Umazon. Al	חַיִּים וּמָזוֹן. עַל
Shehotzetanu Me'eretz	שֶׁהוֹצֵאתָנוּ מֵאֶרֶץ
Mitzrayim. Ufeditanu Mibeit	מִצְרַיִם. וּפְדִיתָנוּ מִבֵּית
Avadim. Ve'al Beritecha	עֲבָדִים. וְעַל בְּרִיתְךָ
Shechatamta Bivsarenu. Ve'al	שֶׁחָתַמְתָּ בִּבְשָׂרֵנוּ. וְעַל
Toratecha Shelimadtanu. Ve'al	תּוֹרָתְךָ שֶׁלִּמַּדְתָּנוּ. וְעַל
Chukkei Retzonach	חֻקֵּי רְצוֹנָךְ
Shehoda'tanu. Ve'al Chayim	שֶׁהוֹדַעְתָּנוּ. וְעַל חַיִּים
Umazon She'attah Zan	וּמָזוֹן שֶׁאַתָּה זָן
Umefarnes Otanu.	וּמְפַרְנֵס אוֹתָנוּ:

We thank You, Hashem our God, for having caused our fathers to inherit that desirable, good, and spacious land; for the covenant and Torah, life and sustenance; and because You have brought us out from the land of Mitzrayim, and redeemed us from the house of bondage; and for Your covenant which You have sealed in our flesh, and for the statutes of Your gracious will, which You have made known to us, and for the life and food which You feed and sustain us.

On Hanukkah and Purim, Al HaNissim is recited:

Al HaNissim

עַל הַנִּסִּים וְעַל הַפֻּרְקָן וְעַל הַגְּבוּרוֹת וְעַל הַתְּשׁוּעוֹת וְעַל הַנִּפְלָאוֹת וְעַל הַנֶּחָמוֹת שֶׁעָשִׂיתָ לַאֲבוֹתֵינוּ בַּיָּמִים הָהֵם בַּזְּמַן הַזֶּה:

Al Hanissim Ve'al Hapurkan Ve'al Hagevurot Ve'al Hateshu'ot Ve'al Hanifla'ot Ve'al Hanechamot She'asita La'avoteinu Bayamim Hahem Bazman Hazeh.

For the miracles, and for the triumphant liberation, and the mighty works, and for the deliverances, and for the wonders, and for the consolations which You have done for our fathers in those days at this season:

On Hanukkah:

בִּימֵי מַתִּתְיָה בֶּן־יוֹחָנָן כֹּהֵן גָּדוֹל. חַשְׁמוֹנָאִי וּבָנָיו כְּשֶׁעָמְדָה מַלְכוּת יָוָן הָרְשָׁעָה עַל עַמְּךָ יִשְׂרָאֵל. לְשַׁכְּחָם תּוֹרָתָךְ וּלְהַעֲבִירָם מֵחֻקֵּי רְצוֹנָךְ. וְאַתָּה בְּרַחֲמֶיךָ הָרַבִּים עָמַדְתָּ לָהֶם בְּעֵת צָרָתָם. רַבְתָּ אֶת רִיבָם. דַּנְתָּ אֶת דִּינָם. נָקַמְתָּ אֶת נִקְמָתָם. מָסַרְתָּ גִבּוֹרִים בְּיַד חַלָּשִׁים. וְרַבִּים בְּיַד מְעַטִּים. וּרְשָׁעִים בְּיַד צַדִּיקִים. וּטְמֵאִים בְּיַד טְהוֹרִים. וְזֵדִים בְּיַד עוֹסְקֵי תוֹרָתֶךָ. לְךָ עָשִׂיתָ שֵׁם גָּדוֹל וְקָדוֹשׁ בְּעוֹלָמָךְ. וּלְעַמְּךָ יִשְׂרָאֵל עָשִׂיתָ תְּשׁוּעָה גְדוֹלָה וּפֻרְקָן כְּהַיּוֹם הַזֶּה. וְאַחַר כָּךְ בָּאוּ בָנֶיךָ לִדְבִיר בֵּיתֶךָ. וּפִנּוּ אֶת־הֵיכָלֶךָ. וְטִהֲרוּ אֶת־מִקְדָּשֶׁךָ. וְהִדְלִיקוּ נֵרוֹת בְּחַצְרוֹת קָדְשֶׁךָ. וְקָבְעוּ שְׁמוֹנַת יְמֵי חֲנֻכָּה אֵלּוּ בְּהַלֵּל וּבְהוֹדָאָה. וְעָשִׂיתָ עִמָּהֶם נִסִּים וְנִפְלָאוֹת וְנוֹדֶה לְשִׁמְךָ הַגָּדוֹל סֶלָה:

Bimei Mattityah Ven-Yochanan Kohen Gadol. Chashmona'i Uvanav Keshe'amedah Malchut Yavan Haresha'ah Al Ammecha Yisra'el. Leshakecham Toratach Uleha'aviram Mechukkei Retzonach. Ve'attah Berachameicha Harabim Amadta Lahem Be'et Tzaratam. Ravta Et Rivam. Danta Et Dinam. Nakamta Et Nikmatam. Masarta Giborim Beyad Chalashim. Verabim Beyad Me'atim. Uresha'im Beyad Tzaddikim. Uteme'im Beyad Tehorim. Vezeidim Beyad Osekei Toratecha. Lecha Asita Shem Gadol Vekadosh Be'olamach. Ule'ammecha Yisra'el Asita Teshu'ah Gedolah Ufurkan Kehayom Hazeh. Ve'achar Kach Ba'u Vaneicha Lidvir Beitecha. Ufinu Et-Heichalecha. Vetiharu Et-Mikdashecha. Vehidliku Nerot Bechatzrot Kodshecha. Vekave'u Shemonat Yemei Chanukkah Elu Behallel Uvehoda'ah. Ve'asita Imahem Nissim Venifla'ot Venodeh Leshimcha Hagadol Selah.

Then in the days of Mattityahu ben-Yochanan, High Priest, the Hasmonean and his sons, when the cruel Greek power rose up against Your people, Yisrael, to make them forget Your Torah and transgress the statutes of Your will. And You, in Your great compassion, stood up for them in time of their trial to plead their cause and defend their judgment. Giving out retribution, delivered the strong into the hand of the weak, and the many into the hand of the few, and the wicked into the hand of the upright, and the impure into the hand of the pure, and tyrants into the hand of the devotees of Your Torah. You made for Yourself a great and holy name in Your world. And for Your people, Yisrael, You performed a great salvation and liberation as this very day. Then Your children came to the Sanctuary of Your House, cleared Your Temple, cleansed Your Sanctuary and kindled lights in Your courtyards, and they instituted these eight days of Hanukkah for praise and thanksgiving. And You did miracles and wonders for them, and we give thanks to Your great name, selah.

On Purim:

בִּימֵי מָרְדְּכַי וְאֶסְתֵּר בְּשׁוּשַׁן הַבִּירָה. כְּשֶׁעָמַד עֲלֵיהֶם הָמָן הָרָשָׁע. בִּקֵּשׁ לְהַשְׁמִיד לַהֲרֹג וּלְאַבֵּד אֶת־כָּל־הַיְּהוּדִים מִנַּעַר וְעַד זָקֵן טַף וְנָשִׁים בְּיוֹם אֶחָד. בִּשְׁלֹשָׁה עָשָׂר לְחֹדֶשׁ שְׁנֵים עָשָׂר. הוּא חֹדֶשׁ אֲדָר. וּשְׁלָלָם לָבוֹז. וְאַתָּה בְּרַחֲמֶיךָ הָרַבִּים הֵפַרְתָּ אֶת־עֲצָתוֹ וְקִלְקַלְתָּ אֶת־מַחֲשַׁבְתּוֹ. וַהֲשֵׁבוֹתָ לּוֹ גְּמוּלוֹ בְּרֹאשׁוֹ. וְתָלוּ אוֹתוֹ וְאֶת־בָּנָיו עַל הָעֵץ. וְעָשִׂיתָ עִמָּהֶם נֵס וָפֶלֶא וְנוֹדֶה לְשִׁמְךָ הַגָּדוֹל סֶלָה:

Bimei Mordechai Ve'ester Beshushan Habbirah. Keshe'amad Aleihem Haman Harasha. Bikesh Lehashmid Laharog Ule'abed Et-Kol-Hayehudim Mina'ar Ve'ad Zaken Taf Venashim Beyom Echad. Bishloshah Asar Lechodesh Sheneim Asar. Hu Chodesh Adar. Ushelalam Lavoz. Ve'attah Berachameicha Harabim Hefarta Et-'Atzato Vekilkalta Et-Machashavto. Vahasheivota Lo Gemulo Verosho. Vetalu Oto Ve'et-Banav Al Ha'etz. Ve'asita Imahem Nes Vafelei Venodeh Leshimcha Hagadol Selah.

In the days of Mordechai and Ester in Shushan, the capital, the wicked Haman rose up and sought to destroy, slay and utterly annihilate all of the Yehudim, both young and old, women and children, on one day, on the thirteenth day of the twelfth month, which is the month of Adar, and to plunder their possessions. But You in Your great mercy You broke his plan and spoiled his designs, causing them to recoil on his own head, and they hanged him and his sons on the gallows. And You did miracles and wonders for them, and we give thanks to Your great name, selah.

Al Hakol Adonai Eloheinu	עַל הַכֹּל יְהֹוָה אֱלֹהֵינוּ
Anachnu Modim Lach	אֲנַחְנוּ מוֹדִים לָךְ
Umevarechim Et Shemach.	וּמְבָרְכִים אֶת שְׁמָךְ.
Ka'amur. Ve'achalta Vesava'eta;	כָּאָמוּר. וְאָכַלְתָּ וְשָׂבָעְתָּ
Uverachta Et-Adonai Eloheicha.	וּבֵרַכְתָּ אֶת־יְהֹוָה אֱלֹהֶיךָ
Al-Ha'aretz Hatovah Asher	עַל־הָאָרֶץ הַטֹּבָה אֲשֶׁר
Natan-Lach. Baruch Attah	נָתַן־לָךְ. בָּרוּךְ אַתָּה
Adonai Al Ha'aretz Ve'al	יְהֹוָה עַל הָאָרֶץ וְעַל
Hamazon.	הַמָּזוֹן:

For everything, Hashem our God, we bless Your Name. As it says "And You will eat and be satisfied, and bless Hashem Your God for the good land which He has given to you." Blessed are You, Hashem, for the land and the sustenance.

Third Blessing: Binyan Yerushalayim / Building up of Yerushalayim

Rachem Adonai Eloheinu Aleinu	רַחֵם יְהֹוָה אֱלֹהֵינוּ עָלֵינוּ
Ve'al Yisra'el Amach. Ve'al	וְעַל יִשְׂרָאֵל עַמָּךְ. וְעַל
Yerushalayim Irach. Ve'al Har	יְרוּשָׁלַיִם עִירָךְ. וְעַל הַר
Tziyon Mishkan Kevodach. Ve'al	צִיּוֹן מִשְׁכַּן כְּבוֹדָךְ. וְעַל
Heichalach. Ve'al Me'onach.	הֵיכָלָךְ. וְעַל מְעוֹנָךְ.
Ve'al Devirach. Ve'al Habayit	וְעַל דְּבִירָךְ. וְעַל הַבַּיִת
Hagadol VeHakadosh Shenikra	הַגָּדוֹל וְהַקָּדוֹשׁ שֶׁנִּקְרָא
Shimcha Alav. Avinu. Re'enu.	שִׁמְךָ עָלָיו. אָבִינוּ. רְעֵנוּ.
Zunenu. Parnesenu. Kalkelenu.	זוּנֵנוּ. פַּרְנְסֵנוּ. כַּלְכְּלֵנוּ.
Harvicheinu Harvach-Lanu	הַרְוִיחֵנוּ הַרְוַח לָנוּ
Meheirah Mikol Tzaroteinu.	מְהֵרָה מִכָּל צָרוֹתֵינוּ.
Vena. Al Tazricheinu Adonai	וְנָא. אַל תַּצְרִיכֵנוּ יְהֹוָה
Eloheinu. Lidei Mattenot Basar	אֱלֹהֵינוּ. לִידֵי מַתְּנוֹת בָּשָׂר
Vadam Velo Lidei Halva'atam.	וָדָם וְלֹא לִידֵי הַלְוָאָתָם.
Ella Leyadecha Hamele'ah	אֶלָּא לְיָדְךָ הַמְּלֵאָה
Veharechavah. Ha'ashirah	וְהָרְחָבָה. הָעֲשִׁירָה
Vehappetuchah. Yehi Ratzon	וְהַפְּתוּחָה. יְהִי רָצוֹן
Shelo Nevosh Ba'olam Hazeh.	שֶׁלֹּא נֵבוֹשׁ בָּעוֹלָם הַזֶּה.
Velo Nikalem La'olam Haba.	וְלֹא נִכָּלֵם לָעוֹלָם הַבָּא.

Umalchut Beit David	וּמַלְכוּת בֵּית דָּוִד
Meshichach Tachazirenah	מְשִׁיחָךְ תַּחֲזִירֶנָּה
Limkomah Bimheirah	לִמְקוֹמָהּ בִּמְהֵרָה
Veyameinu.	בְיָמֵינוּ:

Hashem our God, have mercy on us, on Your people Yisrael, and on Your city Yerushalayim, and on Mount Tzion, the residence of Your glory, and the great and holy house, which is called by Your name. Our Father, feed us, nourish us, sustain us, provide for us, grant us abundance, and relieve us speedily from all our anxieties, and let us not, Hashem our God, stand in need of the gifts of mankind, or of their loans; for their gifts are small, and their reproach is great; but let our dependence be only on Your hand, which is full, plentiful, rich, and open; so that we may not be put to constrained in this world, or be put to shame in the world to come. Restore also speedily in our days, the kingdom of the House of David, Your anointed, to its pristine state.

On Rosh Hodesh, Intermediate days of Passover and Sukkot, and Yom Tov say:

Ya'aleh Veyavo

אֱלֹהֵינוּ וֵאלֹהֵי אֲבוֹתֵינוּ. יַעֲלֶה וְיָבֹא. וְיַגִּיעַ וְיֵרָאֶה. וְיֵרָצֶה וְיִשָּׁמַע. וְיִפָּקֵד וְיִזָּכֵר. זִכְרוֹנֵנוּ וְזִכְרוֹן אֲבוֹתֵינוּ. זִכְרוֹן יְרוּשָׁלַיִם עִירָךְ. וְזִכְרוֹן מָשִׁיחַ בֶּן־דָּוִד עַבְדָּךְ. וְזִכְרוֹן כָּל־עַמְּךָ בֵּית יִשְׂרָאֵל לְפָנֶיךָ. לִפְלֵיטָה. לְטוֹבָה. לְחֵן. לְחֶסֶד וּלְרַחֲמִים. לְחַיִּים טוֹבִים וּלְשָׁלוֹם. בְּיוֹם:

Eloheinu Velohei Avoteinu. Ya'aleh Veyavo. Veyagia Veyera'eh. Veyeratzeh Veyishama'. Veyipaked Veyizacher. Zichronenu Vezichron Avoteinu. Zichron Yerushalayim Irach. Vezichron Mashiach Ben-David Avdach. Vezichron Kol-'Ammecha Beit Yisra'el Lefaneicha. Lifleitah. Letovah. Lechein. Lechesed Ulerachamim. Lechayim Tovim Uleshalom. Beyom:

Our God, and God of our fathers, may it rise, and come, arrive, appear, find favor, and be heard, and be considered, and be remembered our remembrance and the remembrance of our fathers, Yerushalayim Your city, the remembrance of Messiah ben David Your servant, and the remembrance of all Your people of the House of Yisrael before You for deliverance, for good favor, for kindness and mercy, for good life and for peace. On this day of:

On Rosh Chodesh:

רֹאשׁ חֹדֶשׁ הַזֶּה.

Rosh Chodesh Hazeh.

Rosh Chodesh [New Moon].

On Pesach:

חַג הַמַּצּוֹת הַזֶּה בְּיוֹם ביום טוב: (טוֹב מִקְרָא קֹדֶשׁ הַזֶּה):

Chag Hamatzot Hazeh Beyom **On Yom Tov:** (Tov Mikra Kodesh Hazeh):

The Festival of Matzot, this day **on Yom Tov:** (appointed for Holy Convocation):

On Shavuot:

חַג הַשָּׁבוּעוֹת הַזֶּה בְּיוֹם טוֹב מִקְרָא קֹדֶשׁ הַזֶּה:

Chag Hashavuot Hazeh Beyom Mikra Kodesh Hazeh.

The Festival of Shavuot, this appointed day of Holy Convocation:

On Sukkot:

חַג הַסֻּכּוֹת הַזֶּה בְּיוֹם ביום טוב: (טוֹב מִקְרָא קֹדֶשׁ הַזֶּה):

Chag Hasukkot Hazeh Beyom **On Yom Tov:** (Tov Mikra Kodesh Hazeh):

The Festival of Sukkot, this day **on Yom Tov:** (appointed for Holy Convocation):

On Shemini Atzeret:

שְׁמִינִי חַג עֲצֶרֶת הַזֶּה בְּיוֹם טוֹב מִקְרָא קֹדֶשׁ הַזֶּה:

Shemini Chag Atzeret Hazeh Beyom Tov Mikra Kodesh Hazeh:

The Festival of Shemini Atzeret, this appointed day of Holy Convocation:

On Rosh Hashanah:

הַזִּכָּרוֹן הַזֶּה בְּיוֹם טוֹב מִקְרָא קֹדֶשׁ הַזֶּה:

Hazikaron Hazeh Beyom Tov Mikra Kodesh Hazeh:

The Memorial, this appointed day of Holy Convocation:

לְרַחֵם בּוֹ עָלֵינוּ וּלְהוֹשִׁיעֵנוּ. זָכְרֵנוּ יְהוָה אֱלֹהֵינוּ בּוֹ לְטוֹבָה. וּפָקְדֵנוּ בוֹ לִבְרָכָה. וְהוֹשִׁיעֵנוּ בוֹ לְחַיִּים טוֹבִים. בִּדְבַר יְשׁוּעָה וְרַחֲמִים. חוּס וְחָנֵּנוּ. וַחֲמוֹל וְרַחֵם עָלֵינוּ. וְהוֹשִׁיעֵנוּ כִּי אֵלֶיךָ עֵינֵינוּ. כִּי אֵל מֶלֶךְ חַנּוּן וְרַחוּם אָתָּה:

Lerachem Bo Aleinu Ulehoshi'enu. Zochrenu Adonai Eloheinu Bo Letovah. Ufokdenu Vo Livrachah. Vehoshi'enu Vo Lechayim Tovim. Bidvar Yeshu'ah Verachamim. Chus Vechanenu. Vachamol Verachem Aleinu. Vehoshi'enu Ki Eleicha Eineinu. Ki El Melech Chanun Verachum Attah.

to have mercy upon us and save us. Remember us, Hashem our God, on it for good. Be mindful of us on it for blessing and save us on it for a life of good. With the promise of salvation and mercy, show us pity, and be gracious to us and have compassion and mercy on us and save us. For our eyes are lifted towards You, for You, God, are a gracious and merciful King.

Vetivneh Yerushalayim Irach	וְתִבְנֶה יְרוּשָׁלַיִם עִירָךְ
Bimheirah Veyameinu. Baruch	בִּמְהֵרָה בְיָמֵינוּ. בָּרוּךְ
Attah Adonai Boneh	אַתָּה יְהוָה בּוֹנֵה
Yerushalayim. Say Quietly: Amen.	יְרוּשָׁלָיִם ואומר בלחש: אָמֵן:

And build Yerushalayim, Your city, speedily in our days. Blessed are You, Hashem, Builder of Yerushalayim. say Quietly: Amen.

If one forgot to say Ya'aleh Veyavo and remembers, he should say the appropriate blessing here. Only pronounce Hashem part on the first days of Pesach and Sukkot and on Shabbat, except 3rd meal. Other wise say "Blessed is He" (SA, OC:188):

בָּרוּךְ (אַתָּה יְהוָה אֱלֹהֵינוּ מֶלֶךְ הָעוֹלָם) שֶׁנָּתַן:

Baruch (Attah Adonai Eloheinu Melech Ha'olam) Shenatan:

Blessed (are You, Hashem our God King of the universe,) who has given us:

For Shabbat:

שַׁבָּתוֹת לִמְנוּחָה לְעַמּוֹ יִשְׂרָאֵל בְּאַהֲבָה לְאוֹת וְלִבְרִית:

Shabbatot Limnuchah Le'ammo Yisra'el Be'ahavah Le'ot Velivrit:

Shabbatot for joy to His people Yisrael with love for a sign and covenant:

For Rosh Chodesh:

(וְ)רָאשֵׁי חֳדָשִׁים לְעַמּוֹ יִשְׂרָאֵל לְזִכָּרוֹן:

(Ve)Roshei Chodashim Le'ammo Yisra'el Lezikaron:

(and) New Moons to His people Yisrael for a memorial:

For Rosh Hashanah:

(וְ)יָמִים טוֹבִים לְיִשְׂרָאֵל אֶת יוֹם הַזִּכָּרוֹן הַזֶּה:

(Ve)Yamim Tovim Leyisra'el Et Yom Hazikaron Hazeh:

(and) festival days to Yisrael, this day of memorial:

For the Shelosh Regalim / Three Pilgrimage Festivals:

(וְ)יָמִים טוֹבִים לְשָׂשׂוֹן וּלְשִׂמְחָה אֶת יוֹם (חַג הַמַּצּוֹת הַזֶּה) (חַג הַשָּׁבוּעוֹת הַזֶּה) (חַג הַסֻּכּוֹת הַזֶּה) (שְׁמִינִי חַג עֲצֶרֶת הַזֶּה):

Ve)Yamim Tovim Lesasson Ulesimchah Et Yom (Chag Hamatzot Hazeh) (Chag) Hashavuot Hazeh) (Chag Hasukkot Hazeh) (Shemini Chag Atzeret Hazeh):

(and) festival days for happiness and joy, the day of (this feast of Matzot) (this feast of Sukkot) (This feast of Shemini Atzeret).

בָּרוּךְ (אַתָּה יְהוָֹה) מְקַדֵּשׁ (הַשַּׁבָּת) (וְ) (יִשְׂרָאֵל וְרָאשֵׁי חֳדָשִׁים) (יִשְׂרָאֵל
וְיוֹם הַזִּכָּרוֹן) (יִשְׂרָאֵל וְהַזְּמַנִּים):

Baruch (Attah Adonai) Mekadesh (Hashabbat) (Ve) (Yisra'el Roshei Chodashim) (Yisra'el Veyom Hazikaron) (Yisra'el Vehazmanim):

Blessed (are You, Hashem) Who sanctifies (the Shabbat) (and) (Yisrael and the New Moons) (Yisrael and the day of memorial) (Yisrael and the seasons).

Fourth Blessing: HaTov Vehameitiv / For the Goodness of God

Baruch Attah Adonai Eloheinu	בָּרוּךְ אַתָּה יְהוָֹה אֱלֹהֵינוּ
Melech Ha'olam Ha'el Avinu.	מֶלֶךְ הָעוֹלָם. הָאֵל אָבִינוּ.
Malkeinu. Adireinu. Bore'enu.	מַלְכֵּנוּ. אַדִּירֵנוּ. בּוֹרְאֵנוּ.
Go'alenu. Kedoshenu Kedosh	גּוֹאֲלֵנוּ. קְדוֹשֵׁנוּ קְדוֹשׁ
Ya'akov. Ro'enu Ro'eh Yisra'el.	יַעֲקֹב. רוֹעֵנוּ רוֹעֵה יִשְׂרָאֵל.
Hamelech Hatov. Vehameitiv	הַמֶּלֶךְ הַטּוֹב. וְהַמֵּטִיב
Lakol. Shebechol-Yom Vayom	לַכֹּל. שֶׁבְּכָל־יוֹם וָיוֹם
Hu Hetiv Lanu. Hu Meitiv Lanu.	הוּא הֵטִיב לָנוּ. הוּא מֵטִיב לָנוּ.
Hu Yeitiv Lanu. Hu Gemalanu.	הוּא יֵיטִיב לָנוּ. הוּא גְמָלָנוּ.
Hu Gomelenu. Hu Yigmelenu	הוּא גוֹמְלֵנוּ. הוּא יִגְמְלֵנוּ
La'ad Chein Vachesed	לָעַד חֵן וָחֶסֶד
Verachamim Verevach	וְרַחֲמִים וְרֶוַח
Vehatzalah Vechol-Tov.	וְהַצָּלָה וְכָל־טוֹב:
And Answer: Amen.	יענו: אָמֵן:

Blessed are You, Hashem our God, King of the universe, the God our Father, King, Strength, Creator, Redeemer, our Holy One: the Holy One of Yaakov, our Shepherd, the Shepherd of Yisrael; the King who is good and beneficent to all; who day by day has been, is, and ever will be beneficent to us. He has dealt bountifully with us, as He does now, and ever will: granting us grace, favor, mercy, abundance, deliverance, and every good. **And answer:** Amen.

הָרַחֲמָן הוּא יִשְׁתַּבַּח עַל כִּסֵּא כְבוֹדוֹ:

Harachaman Hu Yishtabach Al Kissei Chevodo.

May the All-merciful be praised on the Throne of His glory.

הָרַחֲמָן הוּא יִשְׁתַּבַּח בַּשָּׁמַיִם וּבָאָרֶץ:

Harachaman Hu Yishtabach Bashamayim Uva'aretz.

May the All-merciful be praised in heaven and on earth.

הָרַחֲמָן הוּא יִשְׁתַּבַּח בָּנוּ לְדוֹר דּוֹרִים:

Harachaman Hu Yishtabach Banu Ledor Dorim.

May the All-merciful be praised amidst us throughout all generations.

הָרַחֲמָן הוּא קֶרֶן לְעַמּוֹ יָרִים:

Harachaman Hu Keren Le'ammo Yarim.

May the All-merciful exalt the horn of his people.

הָרַחֲמָן הוּא יִתְפָּאַר בָּנוּ לָנֶצַח נְצָחִים:

Harachaman Hu Yitpa'ar Band Lenetzach Netzachim.

May the All-merciful be glorified amidst us to all eternity.

הָרַחֲמָן הוּא יְפַרְנְסֵנוּ בְּכָבוֹד וְלֹא בְבִזּוּי בְּהֶתֵּר וְלֹא בְאִסּוּר בְּנַחַת וְלֹא בְצַעַר:

Harachaman Hu Yefarnesenu Bechavod Velo Vevizui Behetter Velo Ve'issur Benachat Velo Vetza'ar.

May the All-merciful grant us sustenance with honor, and not with contempt; lawfully, and not by forbidden means; in ease, and not with trouble.

הָרַחֲמָן הוּא יִתֵּן שָׁלוֹם בֵּינֵינוּ:

Harachaman Hu Yiten Shalom Beineinu.

May the All-merciful grant peace amongst us.

הָרַחֲמָן הוּא יִשְׁלַח בְּרָכָה רְוָחָה וְהַצְלָחָה בְּכָל מַעֲשֵׂה יָדֵינוּ:

Harachaman Hu Yishlach Berachah Revachah Vehatzlachah Bechol Ma'aseh Yadeinu.

May the All-merciful send blessing and prosperity to all the work of our hands.

הָרַחֲמָן הוּא יַצְלִיחַ אֶת דְּרָכֵינוּ:

Harachaman Hu Yatzliach Et Deracheinu.

May the All-merciful prosper all our ways.

הָרַחֲמָן הוּא יִשְׁבּוֹר עֹל גָּלוּת מְהֵרָה מֵעַל צַוָּארֵנוּ:

Harachaman Hu Yishbor Ol Galut Meheirah Me'al Tzavarenu.

May the All-merciful speedily break the yoke of the nations from off our neck.

הָרַחֲמָן הוּא יוֹלִיכֵנוּ מְהֵרָה קוֹמְמִיּוּת לְאַרְצֵנוּ:

Harachaman Hu Yolicheinu Meheirah Komemiyut Le'artzenu.

May the All-merciful lead us securely to our land.

הָרַחֲמָן הוּא יִרְפָּאֵנוּ רְפוּאָה שְׁלֵמָה. רְפוּאַת הַנֶּפֶשׁ וּרְפוּאַת הַגּוּף:

Harachaman Hu Yirpa'enu Refu'ah Shelemah. Refu'at Hanefesh Urefu'at Haguf.

May the All-merciful grant us perfect healing, healing of soul and healing of body.

הָרַחֲמָן הוּא יִפְתַּח לָנוּ אֶת יָדוֹ הָרְחָבָה:

Harachaman Hu Yiftach Lanu Et Yado Harechavah.

May the All-merciful open for us His bountiful hand.

הָרַחֲמָן הוּא יְבָרֵךְ כָּל־אֶחָד וְאֶחָד מִמֶּנּוּ בִּשְׁמוֹ הַגָּדוֹל כְּמוֹ שֶׁנִּתְבָּרְכוּ אֲבוֹתֵינוּ אַבְרָהָם יִצְחָק וְיַעֲקֹב, בַּכֹּל מִכֹּל כֹּל, כֵּן יְבָרֵךְ אוֹתָנוּ יַחַד בְּרָכָה שְׁלֵמָה, וְכֵן יְהִי רָצוֹן וְנֹאמַר אָמֵן: הָרַחֲמָן הוּא יִפְרוֹשׂ עָלֵינוּ סֻכַּת שְׁלוֹמוֹ:

Harachaman Hu Yevarech Kol Echad Ve'echad Mimenu Bishmo Hagadol Kemo Shenitbarechu Avoteinu Avraham Yitzchak Veya'akov. Bakol Mikol Kol. Ken Yevarech Otanu Yachad Berachah Shelemah. Vechein Yehi Ratzon Venomar Amen. Harachaman Hu Yifros Aleinu Sukkat Shelomo.

May the All-merciful bless each of us by His great name. May He bless us all together with perfect blessing, even as our ancestors Avraham, Yitzchak and Yaakov were blessed with every manner of blessing. May this be His divine will, and let us say, Amen. May the All-merciful spread over us the shelter of His peace.

On Shabbat:

הָרַחֲמָן הוּא יַנְחִילֵנוּ עוֹלָם שֶׁכֻּלּוֹ שַׁבָּת וּמְנוּחָה לְחַיֵּי הָעוֹלָמִים:

Harachaman Hu Yanchilenu Olam Shekulo Shabbat Umenuchah Lechayei Ha'olamim.

May the All-merciful cause us to inherit a world which will be entirely good, and rest in eternal life.

On Rosh Chodesh:

הָרַחֲמָן הוּא יְחַדֵּשׁ עָלֵינוּ אֶת הַחֹדֶשׁ הַזֶּה לְטוֹבָה וְלִבְרָכָה:

Harachaman Hu Yechadesh Aleinu Et Hachodesh Hazeh Letovah Velivrachah.

May the All-merciful renew upon us this month for good and for blessing.

On Rosh Hashanah:

הָרַחֲמָן הוּא יְחַדֵּשׁ עָלֵינוּ אֶת הַשָּׁנָה הַזֹּאת לְטוֹבָה וְלִבְרָכָה:

Harachaman Hu Yechadesh Aleinu Et Hashanah HaZot Letovah Velivrachah.

May the All-merciful renew upon us this year for good and for blessing.

On Sukkot:

הָרַחֲמָן הוּא יְזַכֵּנוּ לֵישֵׁב בְּסֻכַּת עוֹרוֹ שֶׁל לִוְיָתָן: הָרַחֲמָן הוּא יַשְׁפִּיעַ עָלֵינוּ שֶׁפַע קְדֻשָּׁה וְטָהֳרָה מִשִּׁבְעָה אוּשְׁפִּיזִין עִלָּאִין קַדִּישִׁין. זְכוּתָם תְּהֵא מָגֵן וְצִנָּה בַּעֲדֵינוּ: הָרַחֲמָן הוּא יָקִים לָנוּ אֶת סֻכַּת דָּוִד הַנּוֹפֶלֶת:

Harachaman Hu Yezakenu Leishev Besukkat Oro Shel Livyatan. Harachaman Hu Yashpia Aleinu Shefa Kedushah VeTaharah Mishiv'ah Ushepizin Illa'in Kaddishin. Zechutam Tehei Magen Vetzinah Ba'adeinu. Harachaman Hu Yakim Lanu Et Sukkat David Hanofelet.

May the All-merciful give us the merit to sit in the Sukkah of the skin of Leviathan. May the All-merciful bestow upon us plenty of holiness and purity from the seven holy and pure guests, may their merit be a shield and protection for us. May the All-merciful establish for us the Sukkah of David, that is fallen.

On Sukkot, Pesach and Shavuot:

הָרַחֲמָן הוּא יַגִּיעֵנוּ לְמוֹעֲדִים אֲחֵרִים הַבָּאִים לִקְרָאתֵנוּ לְשָׁלוֹם:

Harachaman Hu Yaggi'enu Lemo'adim Acherim Habai'm Likratenu Leshalom.

May the All-merciful allow us to arrive at other appointed-times that come to greet us for peace.

On Yom Tov:

הָרַחֲמָן הוּא יַנְחִילֵנוּ יוֹם שֶׁכֻּלּוֹ טוֹב:

Harachaman Hu Yanchilenu Yom Shekulo Tov.

May the All-merciful grant us a day that is completely good.

הָרַחֲמָן הוּא יִטַּע תּוֹרָתוֹ וְאַהֲבָתוֹ בְּלִבֵּנוּ וְתִהְיֶה יִרְאָתוֹ עַל פָּנֵינוּ לְבִלְתִּי נֶחֱטָא. וְיִהְיוּ כָל מַעֲשֵׂינוּ לְשֵׁם שָׁמָיִם:

Harachaman Hu Yitta Torato Ve'ahavato Belibeinu Vetihyeh Yir'ato Al Paneinu Levilti Necheta. Veyihyu Chol-Ma'aseinu Leshem Shamayim.

May the All-merciful plant His Torah and His love into our hearts. And may His fear be on our faces that we may not sin. And all our works should be for the sake of heaven.

A guest says:

הָרַחֲמָן הוּא יְבָרֵךְ אֶת הַשֻּׁלְחָן הַזֶּה שֶׁאָכַלְנוּ עָלָיו וִיסַדֵּר בּוֹ כָּל מַעֲדַנֵּי עוֹלָם. וְיִהְיֶה כְּשֻׁלְחָנוֹ שֶׁל אַבְרָהָם אָבִינוּ. כָּל רָעֵב מִמֶּנּוּ יֹאכַל וְכָל צָמֵא מִמֶּנּוּ יִשְׁתֶּה. וְאַל יֶחְסַר מִמֶּנּוּ כָּל טוּב לָעַד וּלְעוֹלְמֵי עוֹלָמִים. אָמֵן. הָרַחֲמָן הוּא יְבָרֵךְ בַּעַל הַבַּיִת הַזֶּה וּבַעַל הַסְּעוּדָה הַזֹּאת. הוּא וּבָנָיו וְאִשְׁתּוֹ וְכָל אֲשֶׁר לוֹ. בְּבָנִים שֶׁיִּחְיוּ וּבִנְכָסִים שֶׁיִּרְבּוּ. בָּרֵךְ יְהֹוָה חֵילוֹ וּפֹעַל יָדָיו תִּרְצֶה. וְיִהְיוּ נְכָסָיו וּנְכָסֵינוּ מֻצְלָחִים וּקְרוֹבִים לָעִיר. וְאַל יִזְדַּקֵּק לְפָנָיו וְלֹא לְפָנֵינוּ שׁוּם דְּבַר חֵטְא וְהִרְהוּר עָוֹן. שָׂשׂ וְשָׂמֵחַ כָּל־הַיָּמִים. בְּעֹשֶׁר וְכָבוֹד. מֵעַתָּה וְעַד עוֹלָם. לֹא יֵבוֹשׁ בָּעוֹלָם הַזֶּה. וְלֹא יִכָּלֵם לָעוֹלָם הַבָּא. אָמֵן כֵּן יְהִי רָצוֹן:

Harachaman Hu Yevarech Et Hashulchan Hazeh She'achalnu Alav Visader Bo Kol Ma'adanei Olam. Veyihyeh Keshulchano Shel

Avraham Avinu. Kol Ra'ev Mimenu Yochal Vechol Tzamei Mimenu Yishteh. Ve'al Yechsar Mimenu Kol Tuv La'ad Ule'olemei Olamim. Amen. Harachaman Hu Yevarech Ba'al Habayit Hazeh Uva'al Hasse'udah HaZot. Hu Uvanav Ve'ishto Vechol Asher Lo. Bevanim Sheyichyu Uvinchasim Sheyirbu. Barech Adonai Cheilo. Ufo'al Yadav Tirtzeh;. Veyihyu Nechasav Unechaseinu Mutzlachim Ukerovim La'ir. Ve'al Yizdakel Lefanav Velo Lefaneinu Shum Devar Chet Vehirhur Avon. Sas Vesameach Kol-Hayamim. Be'osher Vechavod. Me'attah Ve'ad Olam. Lo Yevosh Ba'olam Hazeh. Velo Yikalem La'olam Haba. Amen Ken Yehi Ratzon.

May the All-merciful bless this table at which we have eaten, and may all the delicacies of the world be served upon it; may it be like the table of our forefather Avraham, so that every hungry one may eat from it and every thirsty one drink from it. And do not deprive him of all good forever. Amen. May the All-merciful bless the master of this house, and our host; him, his children, and his wife, and all that belongs to him, may they multiply. Bless, Hashem, his substance, And accept the work of his hands; **(Deuteronomy 33:11)** And may he prosper in all his possessions; may all his and our possessions be successful and near to the city; **(Berakhot 46a:6)** And do not require before him or before us anything of sin or contemplation of iniquity. May they have joy and gladness all their days, in wealth and honor now and forever. May he not be put to shame in this world or be confounded in the world to come. Amen, yes, may it be His will.

At a circumcision:

הָרַחֲמָן הוּא יְבָרֵךְ אֶת בַּעַל הַבַּיִת הַזֶּה. אֲבִי הַבֵּן. הוּא וְאִשְׁתּוֹ הַיּוֹלֶדֶת. מֵעַתָּה וְעַד עוֹלָם: הָרַחֲמָן הוּא יְבָרֵךְ אֶת הַיֶּלֶד הַנּוֹלָד. וּכְשֵׁם שֶׁזִּכָּהוּ הַקָּדוֹשׁ בָּרוּךְ הוּא לַמִּילָה. כֵּן יְזַכֵּהוּ לְהִכָּנֵס לַתּוֹרָה וְלַחֻפָּה וְלַמִּצְוֹת וּלְמַעֲשִׂים טוֹבִים. וְכֵן יְהִי רָצוֹן וְנֹאמַר אָמֵן: הָרַחֲמָן הוּא יְבָרֵךְ אֶת מַעֲלַת הַסַּנְדָּק וְהַמּוֹהֵל וּשְׁאָר הַמִּשְׁתַּדְּלִים בַּמִּצְוָה הֵם וְכָל אֲשֶׁר לָהֶם:

Harachaman Hu Yevarech Et Ba'al Habayit Hazeh. Avi Haben. Hu Ve'ishto Hayoledet. Me'attah Ve'ad Olam. Harachaman Hu Yevarech Et Hayeled Hanolad. Ucheshem Shezikahu Hakadosh Baruch Hu Lamilah. Ken Yezakehu Lehikanes

LaTorah Velachuppah Velamitzvot Ulema'asim Tovim. Vechein Yehi Ratzon Venomar Amen. Harachaman Hu Yevarech Et Ma'alat Hasandak VeHamOhel Ushe'ar Hamishtadelim BaMitzvah Hem Vechol Asher Lahem.

May the All-merciful bless the master of this house, the father of the son - he and his wife, the mother, from now and forever. May the All-merciful bless the newborn child, and just as the Holy One, Blessed is He, merited him to circumcision, so may He let him merit to enter to the Torah, to the Chuppah, to the commandments, and to good works, and so may it be His will and let us say Amen. May the All-merciful bless the sandak and mohel and the rest of those that strove in the commandment, them and all that is theirs.

At a wedding meal:

הָרַחֲמָן הוּא יְבָרֵךְ אֶת הֶחָתָן וְהַכַּלָּה. בְּבָנִים זְכָרִים לַעֲבוֹדָתוֹ יִתְבָּרַךְ: הָרַחֲמָן הוּא יְבָרֵךְ אֶת כָּל הַמְסֻבִּין בַּשֻּׁלְחָן הַזֶּה וְיִתֵּן לָנוּ הַקָּדוֹשׁ בָּרוּךְ הוּא מִשְׁאֲלוֹת לִבֵּנוּ לְטוֹבָה:

Harachaman Hu Yevarech Et Hechatan Vehakallah. Bevanim Zecharim La'avodato Yitbarach. Harachaman Hu Yevarech Et Kol Hamesubbin Bashulchan Hazeh VeYiten Lanu Hakadosh Baruch Hu Mish'alot Libenu Letovah.

May the All-merciful bless the groom and the bride, with male sons for his work, may he be blessed. May the All-merciful bless all who are seated a this table; May the Holy One, blessed is He, give us our heart's wishes, for good.

(one may add here a personal prayer)

Harachaman Hu Yechayenu	הָרַחֲמָן הוּא יְחַיֵּנוּ
Vizakenu Vikarevenu Limot	וִיזַכֵּנוּ וִיקָרְבֵנוּ לִימוֹת
HaMashlach Ulevinyan Beit	הַמָּשִׁיחַ וּלְבִנְיַן בֵּית
HaMikdash Ulechayei Ha'olam	הַמִּקְדָּשׁ וּלְחַיֵּי הָעוֹלָם
Haba.	הַבָּא.

May the All-merciful grant us life, and make us worthy of the days of the Messiah, of the building of the holy Temple, and of the life in the world to come.

Magdil **On a day when Musaf is prayed as well as on Shabbat and say: (Migdol)**	מַגְדִּיל **ביום שמתפללים מוסף וכן במוצ״ש ואמרים:** (מִגְדּוֹל)
Yeshu'ot Malko; Ve'oseh-Chesed	יְשׁוּעוֹת מַלְכּוֹ וְעֹשֶׂה־חֶסֶד
Limshicho Ledavid Ulezar'o	לִמְשִׁיחוֹ לְדָוִד וּלְזַרְעוֹ
Ad-'Olam. Kefirim Rashu	עַד־עוֹלָם: כְּפִירִים רָשׁוּ
Vera'evu; Vedoreshei Hashem	וְרָעֵבוּ וְדֹרְשֵׁי יְהֹוָה
Lo-Yachseru Chol-Tov. Na'ar	לֹא־יַחְסְרוּ כָל־טוֹב: נַעַר |
Hayiti. Gam-Zakanti Velo-Ra'iti	הָיִיתִי גַּם־זָקַנְתִּי וְלֹא־רָאִיתִי
Tzaddik Ne'ezav; Vezar'o.	צַדִּיק נֶעֱזָב וְזַרְעוֹ
Mevakesh-Lachem. Kol-Hayom	מְבַקֶּשׁ־לָחֶם: כָּל־הַיּוֹם
Chonen Umalveh; Vezar'o.	חוֹנֵן וּמַלְוֶה וְזַרְעוֹ
Livrachah. Mah-She'achalnu	לִבְרָכָה: מַה־שֶּׁאָכַלְנוּ
Yihyeh Lesave'ah. Umah-	יִהְיֶה לְשָׂבְעָה. וּמַה־
Sheshatinu Yihyeh Lirfu'ah.	שֶּׁשָּׁתִינוּ יִהְיֶה לִרְפוּאָה.
Umah-Shehotarnu Yihyeh	וּמַה־שֶּׁהוֹתַרְנוּ יִהְיֶה
Livrachah. Kedichtiv. Vayiten	לִבְרָכָה. כְּדִכְתִיב. וַיִּתֵּן
Lifneihem Vayochelu Vayotiru	לִפְנֵיהֶם וַיֹּאכְלוּ וַיּוֹתִרוּ
Kidvar Adonai. Beruchim Attem	כִּדְבַר יְהֹוָה: בְּרוּכִים אַתֶּם
L'Adonai Oseh. Shamayim	לַיהֹוָה עֹשֵׂה שָׁמַיִם
Va'aretz. Baruch Hagever. Asher	וָאָרֶץ: בָּרוּךְ הַגֶּבֶר אֲשֶׁר
Yivtach Ba'Adonai; Vehayah	יִבְטַח בַּיהֹוָה וְהָיָה יְהֹוָה
Adonai Mivtacho. Adonai Oz	מִבְטַחוֹ: יְהֹוָה עֹז
Le'ammo Yiten; Hashem	לְעַמּוֹ יִתֵּן יְהֹוָה |
Yevarech Et-'Ammo Vashalom.	יְבָרֵךְ אֶת־עַמּוֹ בַשָּׁלוֹם:
Oseh Shalom Bimromav. Hu	עוֹשֶׂה שָׁלוֹם בִּמְרוֹמָיו, הוּא
Berachamav Ya'aseh Shalom	בְּרַחֲמָיו יַעֲשֶׂה שָׁלוֹם

Aleinu. Ve'al Kol-'Ammo Yisra'el. עָלֵינוּ. וְעַל כָּל־עַמּוֹ יִשְׂרָאֵל.

Ve'imru Amen. וְאִמְרוּ אָמֵן:

He gives great salvation to his king: **On a day when Musaf is prayed as well as on Shabbat and say: (Great is the salvation of his king)** and acts mercifully to his anointed; to David and his seed forever. **(Psalms 18:51)** Even young lions do lack, and suffer hunger; but they who seek Hashem will not lack any good. **(Psalms 34:11)** I have been young, and am now old; yet never did I see the righteous entirely forsaken, or his offspring begging for bread. **(Psalms 37:25)** For He is ever merciful, and lends, and his seed are a blessing." **(Psalms 37:26)** May what we have eaten, satisfy us; what we have drank, be conducive to our health; and what we have left, be for a blessing; as it is written, "He set it before them, and they did eat and had some left over according to the word of Hashem." **(2 Kings 4:44)** Blessed are you of Hashem, Who made heaven and earth. Blessed is the man who trusts in Hashem; for Hashem will be his trust. **(Jeremiah 17:7)** Hashem will give strength to his people: Hashem will bless his people with peace. **(Psalms 29:11)** He who creates peace in his celestial heights, may He in His mercy create peace for us and for all Yisrael; and say, Amen.

After concluding Birkhat Hamazon, if it was said over a cup of wine, one should recite the blessing borei pri hagafen, and he who recited the Birkhat Hamazon should taste of the wine, and afterwards all those present should taste it, unless he can provide a cup for each and everyone present.

If Birkhat Hamazon was said over a cup of wine, then say:

Kos Yeshu'ot Essa Uveshem Adonai כּוֹס־יְשׁוּעוֹת אֶשָּׂא וּבְשֵׁם יְהֹוָה

Ekra. אֶקְרָא:

I will lift up the cup of salvation, And call upon the name of Hashem. **(Psalms 116:13)**

Savri Maranan!	סַבְרִי מָרָנָן:

Gentlemen, with your attention!

And answer:

Le'chayim!	לְחַיִּים:

To life!

Baruch Attah Adonai Eloheinu Melech	בָּרוּךְ אַתָּה יְהֹוָה אֱלֹהֵינוּ מֶלֶךְ
Ha'olam Borei Pri Hagefen.	הָעוֹלָם. בּוֹרֵא פְּרִי הַגָּפֶן:

Blessed are You, Hashem our God, King of the universe, Who creates the fruit of the vine.

After one drinks the cup of Birkhat HaMazon, one blesses the Mein Shalosh [for the wine]. (SA, OC 190:2)

Me'ein Shalosh / The Three-Faceted Blessing

This prayer literally means "a summary of the three" referring to the first three blessings of Birkhat Hamazon. These blessings are made after consuming at least a kezayit (olive size) of : Mezonot (non-bread products made from the 5 grains: wheat, barley, rye, oats and spelt), Wine (or grape juice), the seven species of fruits (wheat, barley, vines, figs, and pomegranates, olive trees and honey - Deut. 8:8), and drinking at least a revi'it (approx. 3oz) of any drink (excluding wine).

Baruch Attah Adonai Eloheinu	בָּרוּךְ אַתָּה יְהֹוָה אֱלֹהֵינוּ מֶלֶךְ
Melech Ha'olam:	הָעוֹלָם:

Blessed are you, Hashem our God, King of the Universe:

After partaking of Mezonot, food prepared from wheat, barley, rye, oats and spelt that were pounded or beaten and cooked food was made out of it, say:

עַל הַמִּחְיָה וְעַל הַכַּלְכָּלָה:

Al Hamichyah Ve'al Hakalkalah;

For the sustenance and the nourishment;

If one drinks wine say:

(וְ)עַל הַגֶּפֶן וְעַל פְּרִי הַגֶּפֶן:

(Ve)'Al Hagefen Ve'al Pri Hagefen;

(And) for the fruit of the vine;

If one ate one of the seven species of fruits, say:

(וְ)עַל הָעֵץ וְעַל פְּרִי הָעֵץ:

(Ve)'Al Ha'etz Ve'al Pri Ha'etz;

(And) for the land and the fruit of the tree;

Ve'al Tenuvat Hassadeh. Ve'al	וְעַל תְּנוּבַת הַשָּׂדֶה. וְעַל
Eretz Chemdah Tovah	אֶרֶץ חֶמְדָּה טוֹבָה
Urechavah. Sheratzita	וּרְחָבָה. שֶׁרָצִיתָ
Vehinchalta La'avoteinu.	וְהִנְחַלְתָּ לַאֲבוֹתֵינוּ.
Le'echol Mipiryah Velisboa	לֶאֱכֹל מִפִּרְיָהּ וְלִשְׂבֹּעַ
Mituvah. Rachem Adonai	מִטּוּבָהּ. רַחֵם יְהֹוָה
Eloheinu Aleinu Ve'al Yisra'el	אֱלֹהֵינוּ עָלֵינוּ וְעַל יִשְׂרָאֵל

Amach. Ve'al Yerushalayim Irach.	עַמֶּךָ. וְעַל יְרוּשָׁלַיִם עִירָךְ.
Ve'al Har Tziyon Mishkan	וְעַל הַר צִיּוֹן מִשְׁכַּן
Kevodach. Ve'al Mizbachach	כְּבוֹדָךְ. וְעַל מִזְבְּחָךְ
Ve'al Heichalach. Uveneh	וְעַל הֵיכָלָךְ. וּבְנֵה
Yerushalayim Ir Hakodesh	יְרוּשָׁלַיִם עִיר הַקֹּדֶשׁ
Bimheirah Veyameinu.	בִּמְהֵרָה בְיָמֵינוּ.
Veha'alenu Letochah.	וְהַעֲלֵנוּ לְתוֹכָהּ.
Vesamecheinu Bevinyanah.	וְשַׂמְּחֵנוּ בְּבִנְיָנָהּ.
Unevarechach Aleiha Bikdushah	וּנְבָרֶכְךָ עָלֶיהָ בִּקְדֻשָּׁה
Uvetaharah.	וּבְטָהֳרָה:

(And) for the produce of the field, and for the lovely and spacious land which You granted to our fathers as a heritage to eat of it's fruit and enjoy its good gifts. Have mercy, Hashem our God, on Yisrael Your people, and on Yerushalayim Your city, and on Mount Tzion the abode of Your glory, and on Your Altar and Your Temple. Rebuild the holy city of Yerushalayim speedily in our days. Bring us to it and gladden us in its rebuilding, and may we bless You for it in holiness and purity.

On Shabbat:

וּרְצֵה וְהַחֲלִיצֵנוּ בְּיוֹם הַשַּׁבָּת הַזֶּה.

Urezeh Vehachalitzenu Beyom Hashabbat Hazeh.

And be pleased to strengthen us on this Shabbat day.

On Rosh Chodesh:

וְזָכְרֵנוּ לְטוֹבָה בְּיוֹם רֹאשׁ חֹדֶשׁ הַזֶּה.

Vezacherenu Letovah Beyom Rosh Chodesh Hazeh.

And be mindful of us on this New Moon day.

On Rosh Hashanah:

וְזָכְרֵנוּ לְטוֹבָה בְּיוֹם הַזִּכָּרוֹן הַזֶּה.

Vezochrenu Letovah Beyom Hazikaron Hazeh.

And be mindful of us on this Day of Remembrance.

On Pesach:

וְשַׂמְּחֵנוּ בְּיוֹם חַג הַמַּצּוֹת הַזֶּה. בְּיוֹם טוֹב מִקְרָא קֹדֶשׁ הַזֶּה.

Vesamecheinu Beyom Chag Hamatzot Hazeh. Beyom Tov Mikra Kodesh Hazeh.

And grant us joy on this Festival of Unleavened Bread, this Festival Day of holy convocation.

On Shavuot:

וְשַׂמְּחֵנוּ בְּיוֹם חַג הַשָּׁבוּעוֹת הַזֶּה בְּיוֹם טוֹב מִקְרָא קֹדֶשׁ הַזֶּה.

Vesamecheinu Beyom Chag Hashavu'ot Hazeh Beyom Tov Mikra Kodesh Hazeh.

And grant us joy on this Festival of Weeks, this Festival Day of holy convocation.

On Sukkot:

וְשַׂמְּחֵנוּ בְּיוֹם הַסֻּכּוֹת הַזֶּה. בְּיוֹם טוֹב מִקְרָא קֹדֶשׁ הַזֶּה.

Vesamecheinu Beyom Hasukkot Hazeh. Beyom Tov Mikra Kodesh Hazeh.

And grant us joy on this Festival of Tabernacles, this Festival Day of holy convocation.

On Shemini Atzeret / Simchat Torah:

וְשַׂמְּחֵנוּ בְּיוֹם שְׁמִינִי חַג עֲצֶרֶת הַזֶּה בְּיוֹם טוֹב מִקְרָא קֹדֶשׁ הַזֶּה.

Vesamecheinu Beyom Shemini Chag Atzeret Hazeh Beyom Tov Mikra Kodesh Hazeh.

And grant us joy on this Festival of Eighth Day Feast, this Festival Day of holy convocation.

Ki Attah Tov Umeitiv Lakol. — כִּי אַתָּה טוֹב וּמֵטִיב לַכֹּל.

Venodeh Lecha Al Ha'aretz. — וְנוֹדֶה לְּךָ עַל הָאָרֶץ:

For You are good and beneficent to all; and we will give You thanks for the land,

For Mezonot (foods prepared from wheat, barley, rye, oats and spelt, that were pounded or beaten and made cooked food out of it), say:

Ve'al Hamichyah Ve'al Hakalkalah;	וְעַל הַמִּחְיָה וְעַל הַכַּלְכָּלָה:
Of the land of Yisrael: Ve'al Michyatah Ve'al Kalkalatah;	של ארץ ישראל ועל: וְעַל מִחְיָתָהּ וְעַל כַּלְכָּלָתָהּ:

And for the sustenance and the nourishment;

Of the land of Yisrael: And for its sustenance and its nourishment.

After wine say:

Ve'al Pri Hagefen.	וְעַל פְּרִי הַגֶּפֶן:
Of the land of Yisrael: Ve'al Pri Gafnah.	של ארץ ישראל: וְעַל פְּרִי גַפְנָהּ:

And for the fruit of the vine.

Of the land of Yisrael: And for the fruit of its vine.

After the seven species of fruits, say:

Ve'al Haperot.	וְעַל הַפֵּרוֹת:
Of the land of Yisrael: Ve'al Peroteiha.	של ארץ ישראל: וְעַל פֵּרוֹתֶיהָ:

And for the fruit.

Of the land of Yisrael: And for its fruit.

Borei Nefashot

After eating if one ate at least a kezayit (approx. the size of an olive), or drank a revi'it (approx. 3oz) of all food not made from grain or the 7 kinds fruits. This includes everything we make the before blessings of "Ha Adamah" or "Shehakol" on, like meat, fish, eggs, drinks (excluding wine), etc. and all fruits not included in the seven species of fruits. (wheat, barley, vines, figs, and pomegranates, olive trees and honey - Deut. 8:8)

בָּרוּךְ אַתָּה יְהֹוָה אֱלֹהֵינוּ מֶלֶךְ הָעוֹלָם. בּוֹרֵא נְפָשׁוֹת רַבּוֹת וְחֶסְרוֹנָן עַל כָּל־מַה־שֶּׁבָּרָאתָ לְהַחֲיוֹת בָּהֶם נֶפֶשׁ כָּל־חָי. בָּרוּךְ חַי הָעוֹלָמִים.

Baruch Attah Adonai Eloheinu Melech Ha'olam Borei Nefashot Rabot Vechesronan Al Kol-Mah-Shebarata Lehachayot Bahem Nefesh Kol-Chai. Baruch Chai Ha'olamim.

Blessed are You, Hashem our God, King of the universe, Who creates many living souls with their needs, for all the things You have created to sustain every living being. Blessed is the Life of all worlds.

Birkhot HaNehenin / Blessings on Enjoyments

Regarding all these blessings, one should not interrupt between the blessing and the eating of the food.

For Mezonot (one of the five species of grain were pounded or beaten and made cooked food out of it), he should say (and the after-blessing: "Al Hamichyah" [in Mein Shalosh]):

Baruch Attah Adonai Eloheinu	בָּרוּךְ אַתָּה יְהֹוָה אֱלֹהֵינוּ
Melech Ha'olam Borei Minei	מֶלֶךְ הָעוֹלָם. בּוֹרֵא מִינֵי
Mezonot.	מְזוֹנוֹת:

Blessed are You, Hashem our God, King of the universe, Who creates various kinds of food.

On the wine, one blesses:

Baruch Attah Adonai Eloheinu	בָּרוּךְ אַתָּה יְהֹוָה אֱלֹהֵינוּ
Melech Ha'olam Borei Pri	מֶלֶךְ הָעוֹלָם. בּוֹרֵא פְּרִי
Hagefen.	הַגֶּפֶן:

Blessed are You, Hashem our God, King of the universe, Who creates the fruit of the vine.

On the fruit of the tree, one blesses:

Baruch Attah Adonai Eloheinu	בָּרוּךְ אַתָּה יְהֹוָה אֱלֹהֵינוּ
Melech Ha'olam Borei Pri	מֶלֶךְ הָעוֹלָם. בּוֹרֵא פְּרִי
HaEitz.	הָעֵץ:

Blessed are You, Hashem our God, King of the universe, Who creates the fruit of the tree.

On the fruits of the earth, one blesses:

Baruch Attah Adonai Eloheinu	בָּרוּךְ אַתָּה יְהֹוָה אֱלֹהֵינוּ
Melech Ha'olam Borei Pri	מֶלֶךְ הָעוֹלָם. בּוֹרֵא פְּרִי
Ha'adamah.	הָאֲדָמָה:

Blessed are You, Hashem our God, King of the universe, Who creates the fruit of the earth.

On something that is not from the earth such as meat, fish, milk, cheese, etc. And on drinks (except wine), one blesses:

Baruch Attah Adonai Eloheinu	בָּרוּךְ אַתָּה יְהֹוָה אֱלֹהֵינוּ
Melech Ha'olam Shehakol	מֶלֶךְ הָעוֹלָם. שֶׁהַכֹּל
Nihyah Bidvaro.	נִהְיָה בִּדְבָרוֹ:

Blessed are You, Hashem our God, King of the universe, by Whose word all things came into being.

Blessings over Good Smells

On the good smell of trees, their flowers or shrubs, one blesses:

Baruch Attah Adonai Eloheinu	בָּרוּךְ אַתָּה יְהֹוָה אֱלֹהֵינוּ
Melech Ha'olam Borei Atzei	מֶלֶךְ הָעוֹלָם. בּוֹרֵא עֲצֵי
Vesamim.	בְשָׂמִים:

Blessed are You, Hashem our God, King of the universe, Who creates sweet smelling woods.

On the good smell of herbs, grass, or flowers, one blesses:

Baruch Attah Adonai Eloheinu	בָּרוּךְ אַתָּה יְהֹוָה אֱלֹהֵינוּ
Melech Ha'olam Borei Isbei	מֶלֶךְ הָעוֹלָם. בּוֹרֵא עִשְׂבֵי
Vesamim.	בְשָׂמִים:

Blessed are You, Hashem our God, King of the universe, Who creates sweet smelling herbs.

On a good smell that is not wood or grass, or vegetation, one blesses:

Baruch Attah Adonai Eloheinu	בָּרוּךְ אַתָּה יְהֹוָה אֱלֹהֵינוּ
Melech Ha'olam Borei Minei	מֶלֶךְ הָעוֹלָם. בּוֹרֵא מִינֵי
Vesamim.	בְשָׂמִים:

Blessed are You, Hashem our God, King of the universe, Who creates various kinds of spices.

SEDER AVEILUT / ORDER OF MOURNING

Baruch Attah Adonai Eloheinu	בָּרוּךְ אַתָּה יְהֹוָה אֱלֹהֵינוּ
Melech Ha'olam Dayan	מֶלֶךְ הָעוֹלָם. דַּיַּן
Ha'emet:	הָאֱמֶת:

Blessed are You, Hashem our God, King of the universe, the true Judge.

Tzadik HaDin / Acknowledgment of Divine Justice

צַדִּיק אַתָּה יְהֹוָה וְיָשָׁר מִשְׁפָּטֶיךָ: צַדִּיק יְהֹוָה בְּכָל־דְּרָכָיו וְחָסִיד בְּכָל־מַעֲשָׂיו: צִדְקָתְךָ צֶדֶק לְעוֹלָם וְתוֹרָתְךָ אֱמֶת: מִשְׁפְּטֵי־יְהֹוָה אֱמֶת צָדְקוּ יַחְדָּו: בַּאֲשֶׁר דְּבַר־מֶלֶךְ שִׁלְטוֹן וּמִי יֹאמַר־לוֹ מַה־תַּעֲשֶׂה: וְהוּא בְאֶחָד וּמִי יְשִׁיבֶנּוּ וְנַפְשׁוֹ אִוְּתָה וַיָּעַשׂ: קָטֹן וְגָדוֹל שָׁם הוּא וְעֶבֶד חָפְשִׁי מֵאֲדֹנָיו: הֵן בַּעֲבָדָיו לֹא יַאֲמִין וּבְמַלְאָכָיו יָשִׂים תָּהֳלָה: אַף | שֹׁכְנֵי בָתֵּי־חֹמֶר אֲשֶׁר־בֶּעָפָר יְסוֹדָם יְדַכְּאוּם לִפְנֵי־עָשׁ: הַצּוּר תָּמִים פָּעֳלוֹ כִּי כָל־דְּרָכָיו מִשְׁפָּט אֵל אֱמוּנָה וְאֵין עָוֶל צַדִּיק וְיָשָׁר הוּא: דַּיַּן הָאֱמֶת. שֹׁפֵט צֶדֶק וֶאֱמֶת. בָּרוּךְ דַּיַּן הָאֱמֶת. כִּי כָל־מִשְׁפָּטָיו צֶדֶק וֶאֱמֶת:

Tzaddik Attah Adonai Veyashar Mishpateicha. Tzaddik Adonai Bechol Derachav Vechasid Bechol Ma'asav. Tzidkatecha Tzedek Le'olam Vetoratecha Emet. Mishpetei Adonai Emet Tzadeku Yachdav. Ba'asher Devar Melech Shilton Umi Yomar Lo Mah Ta'aseh. Vehu Ve'echad Umi Yeshivenu Venafsho Ivetah Vaya'as. Katon Vegadol Sham Hu Ve'eved Chofshi Me'adonav. Hen Ba'avadav Lo Ya'amin Uvemal'achav Yasim Toholah. Af Shochenei Vatei Chomer Asher Be'afar Yesodam Yedake'um Lifnei Ash. Hatzur Tamim Po'olo Ki Chol Derachav Mishpat El Emunah Ve'ein Avel Tzaddik Veyashar Hu. Dayan Ha'emet. Shofet Tzedek Ve'emet. Baruch Dayan Ha'emet. Ki Chol Mishpatav Tzedek Ve'emet:

You are righteous, Hashem, and upright are Your judgments. Hashem is righteous in all His ways, And gracious in all His works. Your righteousness is an everlasting righteousness, and Your Torah is truth. The judgments of Hashem are true, and righteous altogether. Whereas the word of the King is with authority, so who may say to him, What are You doing? He is One; who can turn Him back? What He desires, even that He does. The small and great are there alike; And the servant is free from his master. Behold, He puts no trust in His servants, And His angels He charges with folly; How much more those that dwell in houses of clay, Whose foundation is in the dust, who are crushed before the moth. The Rock, His work is perfect, for all of His ways are in judgment; a God of truth, in Whom there is no iniquity; just and righteous is He. He is a true Judge; and judges with righteousness and truth. Blessed is the true Judge; for all His judgments are just and true. **(Ps. 119:137, 145:17, 119:142, 19:10, Ecc. 8:4, Job 23:13, 3:19, 4:18-19, Deut. 32:4)**

Hashkavah is now recited:

בִּלַּע הַמָּוֶת לָנֶצַח וּמָחָה אֲדֹנָי יֱהֹוִה דִּמְעָה מֵעַל כָּל־פָּנִים וְחֶרְפַּת
עַמּוֹ יָסִיר מֵעַל כָּל־הָאָרֶץ כִּי יְהֹוָה דִּבֵּר׃ יִחְיוּ מֵתֶיךָ נְבֵלָתִי יְקוּמוּן
הָקִיצוּ וְרַנְּנוּ שֹׁכְנֵי עָפָר כִּי טַל אוֹרֹת טַלֶּךָ וָאָרֶץ רְפָאִים תַּפִּיל׃
וְהוּא רַחוּם | יְכַפֵּר עָוֺן וְלֹא־יַשְׁחִית וְהִרְבָּה לְהָשִׁיב אַפּוֹ וְלֹא־יָעִיר
כָּל־חֲמָתוֹ׃ יְהֹוָה הוֹשִׁיעָה הַמֶּלֶךְ יַעֲנֵנוּ בְיוֹם־קָרְאֵנוּ׃

Billa Hamavet Lanetzach Umachah Adonai Adonai Dim'ah Me'al Kol Panim Vecherpat Ammo Yasir Me'al Kol Ha'aretz Ki Adonai Diber. Yichyu Meteicha Nevelati Yekumun Hakitzu Veranenu Shochenei Afar Ki Tal Orot Tallecha Va'aretz Refa'im Tappil. Vehu Rachum Yechapeir Avon Velo Yashchit Vehirbah Lehashiv Appo Velo Ya'ir Kol Chamato. Adonai Hoshi'ah Hamelech Ya'aneinu Veyom Kor'enu:

He will swallow up death forever; And Adonai-Hashem will wipe away tears from off all faces; And the He will take away the reproach of His people from off all the earth; For Hashem has spoken it. Your dead will live, my dead bodies will arise— Awake and sing, you that dwell in the dust— For your dew is as the dew of light, And the earth will bring to life the shades. But He, being full of compassion, forgives iniquity, and does not destroy; Yes, many a time He turns His anger away, and does not stir up all of His wrath. Save, Hashem; Let the King answer us on the day that we call. **(Is. 25:8, 26:19, Ps. 78:38, 20:10)**

Visitors answer:

תְּנֻחֲמוּ מִן הַשָּׁמַיִם:

Tenuchamu Min Hashamayim:

May you take comfort from Heaven.

When the seven days of mourning are completed, this is said to the mourner:

לֹא־יָבוֹא עוֹד שִׁמְשֵׁךְ וִירֵחֵךְ לֹא יֵאָסֵף כִּי יְהוָה יִהְיֶה־לָּךְ לְאוֹר עוֹלָם וְשָׁלְמוּ יְמֵי אֶבְלֵךְ: כְּאִישׁ אֲשֶׁר אִמּוֹ תְּנַחֲמֶנּוּ כֵּן אָנֹכִי אֲנַחֶמְכֶם וּבִירוּשָׁלַםִ תְּנֻחָמוּ:

Lo Yavo Od Shimshech Virechech Lo Ye'asef Ki Adonai Yihyeh Lach Le'or Olam Veshalemu Yemei Evlech. Ke'ish Asher Imo Tenachamenu Ken Anochi Anachemchem Uvirushalayim Tenuchamu.

Your sun will no more go down. Neither will your moon withdraw itself; For Hashem will be your everlasting light, And the days of your mourning will have ended. As one whom his mother comforts, So will I comfort you; and you will be comforted in Yerushalayim. **(Is. 60:20, 66:13)**

And say Kaddish Yehei-Shelama:

Kaddish is only recited in a minyan (ten men). אָמֵן denotes when the congregation responds "Amen" together out loud. According to the Shulchan Arukh, the congregation says "Yehei Shemeh Rabba" to "Yitbarach" out loud together without interruption, and also that one should respond "Amen" after "Yitbarach." (SA, OC 55,56) This is not the common custom today. Though many are accustomed to answering according to their own custom, it is advised to respond in the custom of the one reciting to avoid not fragmenting into smaller groups. ("Lo Titgodedu" - BT, Yevamot 13b / SA, OC 493, Rema / MT, Avodah Zara 12:15)

יִתְגַּדַּל וְיִתְקַדַּשׁ שְׁמֵהּ רַבָּא. אָמֵן בְּעָלְמָא דִּי בְרָא. כִּרְעוּתֵהּ. וְיַמְלִיךְ מַלְכוּתֵהּ. וְיַצְמַח פֻּרְקָנֵהּ. וִיקָרֵב מְשִׁיחֵהּ. אָמֵן בְּחַיֵּיכוֹן וּבְיוֹמֵיכוֹן וּבְחַיֵּי דְכָל בֵּית יִשְׂרָאֵל. בַּעֲגָלָא וּבִזְמַן קָרִיב. וְאִמְרוּ אָמֵן. אָמֵן יְהֵא

שְׁמֵיהּ רַבָּא מְבָרַךְ לְעָלַם וּלְעָלְמֵי עָלְמַיָּא יִתְבָּרַךְ. וְיִשְׁתַּבַּח. וְיִתְפָּאַר. וְיִתְרוֹמַם. וְיִתְנַשֵּׂא. וְיִתְהַדָּר. וְיִתְעַלֶּה. וְיִתְהַלָּל שְׁמֵהּ דְּקֻדְשָׁא. בְּרִיךְ הוּא. אָמֵן לְעֵלָּא מִן כָּל בִּרְכָתָא שִׁירָתָא. תֻּשְׁבְּחָתָא וְנֶחֱמָתָא. דַּאֲמִירָן בְּעָלְמָא. וְאִמְרוּ אָמֵן. אָמֵן

Yitgadal Veyitkadash Shemeh Rabba. Amen Be'alema Di Vera. Kir'uteh. Veyamlich Malchuteh. Veyatzmach Purkaneh. Vikarev Meshicheh. Amen Bechayeichon Uveyomeichon Uvechayei Dechal-Beit Yisra'el. Ba'agala Uvizman Kariv. Ve'imru Amen. Amen Yehei Shemeh Rabba Mevarach Le'alam Ule'alemei Alemaya Yitbarach. Veyishtabach. Veyitpa'ar. Veyitromam. Veyitnasse. Veyit'hadar. Veyit'aleh. Veyit'hallal Shemeh Dekudsha. Berich Hu. Amen Le'ella Min Kol Birchata Shirata. Tushbechata Venechemata. Da'amiran Be'alema. Ve'imru Amen. Amen

Glorified and sanctified be God's great name **Amen** throughout the world which He has created according to His will. May He establish His kingdom, hastening His salvation and the coming of His Messiah, **Amen**, in your lifetime and during your days, and within the life of the entire House of Yisrael, speedily and soon; and say, Amen. **Amen** May His great name be blessed forever and to all eternity. Blessed and praised, glorified and exalted, extolled and honored, adored and lauded is the name of the Holy One, blessed is He, **Amen** Beyond all the blessings and hymns, praises and consolations that are ever spoken in the world; and say, Amen. **Amen**

יְהֵא שְׁלָמָא רַבָּא מִן שְׁמַיָּא. חַיִּים וְשָׂבָע וִישׁוּעָה וְנֶחָמָה. וְשֵׁיזָבָא וּרְפוּאָה וּגְאוּלָה וּסְלִיחָה וְכַפָּרָה וְרֶוַח וְהַצָּלָה לָנוּ וּלְכָל עַמּוֹ יִשְׂרָאֵל. וְאִמְרוּ אָמֵן. אָמֵן

Yehei Shelama Rabba Min Shemaya. Chayim Vesava Vishu'ah Venechamah. Vesheizava Urefu'ah Uge'ulah Uselichah Vechapparah Verevach Vehatzalah Lanu Ulechol Ammo Yisra'el. Ve'imru Amen. Amen

May abundant peace descend from heaven, with life and plenty, salvation, solace, liberation, healing and redemption, and forgiveness and atonement, enlargement and freedom, for us and all of God's people Yisrael; and say, Amen. **Amen**

One bows and takes three steps backwards, while still bowing. After three steps, while still bowing and before erecting, while saying, "Oseh Shalom Bimromav", turn one's face to the left, "Hu [Berachamav] Ya'aseh Shalom Aleinu", turn one's face to the right; then bow forward like a servant leaving his master. (SA, OC 123:1)

עוֹשֶׂה שָׁלוֹם בִּמְרוֹמָיו. הוּא בְּרַחֲמָיו יַעֲשֶׂה שָׁלוֹם עָלֵינוּ. וְעַל כָּל־עַמּוֹ יִשְׂרָאֵל. וְאִמְרוּ אָמֵן:

Oseh Shalom Bimromav. Hu Berachamav Ya'aseh Shalom Aleinu. Ve'al Kol-'Ammo Yisra'el. Ve'imru Amen.

Creator of peace in His high places, may He in His mercy create peace for us and for all Yisrael, and say Amen.

Birkhat Hamazon for Mourners

If three are present say:

Nevarech **with ten say:** (Eloheinu) — נְבָרֵךְ בעשרה: (אֱלֹהֵינוּ)

Menachem Avelim She'achalnu — מְנַחֵם אֲבֵלִים שֶׁאָכַלְנוּ

Mishelo: — מִשֶּׁלּוֹ:

We will bless Him **with ten say:** (our God) who comforts mourners.

And answer:

Baruch **with ten say:** (Eloheinu) — בָּרוּךְ בעשרה: (אֱלֹהֵינוּ)

Menachem Avelim She'achalnu — מְנַחֵם אֲבֵלִים שֶׁאָכַלְנוּ

Mishelo Uvetuvo Hagadol Chayinu: — מִשֶּׁלּוֹ וּבְטוּבוֹ הַגָּדוֹל חָיִינוּ:

Blessed is He who comforts mourners; of whose gifts we have eaten, and through whose great goodness we live.

And the leader repeats:

Baruch **with ten say:** (Eloheinu) — בָּרוּךְ בעשרה: (אֱלֹהֵינוּ)

Menachem Avelim She'achalnu — מְנַחֵם אֲבֵלִים שֶׁאָכַלְנוּ

Mishelo Uvetuvo Hagadol Chayinu: — מִשֶּׁלּוֹ וּבְטוּבוֹ הַגָּדוֹל חָיִינוּ:

Blessed is He who comforts mourners; of whose gifts we have eaten, and through whose great goodness we live.

Birkhat Hamazon continues as usual till the words "tachazirenah limkomah bimheirah veyameinu" or "Restore also speedily in our days, the kingdom of the House of David, Your anointed, to its pristine state." Then say the following:

נַחֵם יְהוָה אֱלֹהֵינוּ אֶת־אֲבֵלֵי צִיּוֹן וְאֶת־אֲבֵלֵי יְרוּשָׁלַיִם וְאֶת־הָאֲבֵלִים הַמִּתְאַבְּלִים בָּאֵבֶל הַזֶּה נַחֲמֵם מֵאֶבְלָם וְשַׂמְּחֵם מִיגוֹנָם. כָּאָמוּר: כְּאִישׁ אֲשֶׁר אִמּוֹ תְּנַחֲמֶנּוּ כֵּן אָנֹכִי אֲנַחֶמְכֶם וּבִירוּשָׁלַיִם תְּנֻחָמוּ: בָּרוּךְ אַתָּה יְהוָה מְנַחֵם צִיּוֹן בְּבִנְיַן יְרוּשָׁלַיִם אָמֵן:

Nachem Adonai Eloheinu Et Avelei Tziyon Ve'et Avelei Yerushalayim Ve'et Ha'avelim Hamit'abelim Ba'evel Hazeh Nachamem Me'evlam Vesamechem Migonam. Ka'amur: Ke'ish Asher Imo Tenachamenu Ken Anochi Anachemchem Uvirushalayim Tenuchamu. Baruch Attah Adonai Menachem Tziyon Bevinyan Yerushalayim Amen:

Comfort, Hashem, our God, the mourners for Tziyon, and for Yerushalayim; and those who share in this mourning. Comfort them in their mourning; and cause them to rejoice in their grief; as it is said, "As one whom his mother comforts, so will I comfort you; and through Yerushalayim you will be comforted." Blessed are You, Hashem, Who comforts the mourners, and builds Yerushalayim. May it be built speedily in our days. Amen.

בְּחַיֵּינוּ תִּבְנֶה עִיר צִיּוֹן וְתִכּוֹן הָעֲבוֹדָה בִּירוּשָׁלַיִם:

Bechayeinu Tivneh Ir Tziyon Vetikon Ha'avodah Birushalayim:

May the city of Tziyon be rebuilt in our days, and the Temple service re-established in Yerushalayim.

בָּרוּךְ אַתָּה יְהוָה אֱלֹהֵינוּ מֶלֶךְ הָעוֹלָם. הָאֵל אָבִינוּ מַלְכֵּנוּ אַדִּירֵנוּ גֹּאֲלֵנוּ קְדוֹשֵׁנוּ קְדוֹשׁ יַעֲקֹב. הַמֶּלֶךְ הַחַי הַטּוֹב וְהַמֵּטִיב אֵל אֱמֶת שׁוֹפֵט בְּצֶדֶק לוֹקֵחַ נְפָשׁוֹת שַׁלִּיט בְּעוֹלָמוֹ לַעֲשׂוֹת כִּרְצוֹנוֹ וַאֲנַחְנוּ עַמּוֹ וַעֲבָדָיו וְעַל הַכֹּל אֲנַחְנוּ חַיָּבִים לְהוֹדוֹת לוֹ וּלְבָרְכוֹ גּוֹדֵר פְּרָצוֹת הוּא יִגְדּוֹר אֶת־הַפִּרְצָה הַזֹּאת מֵעָלֵינוּ וּמֵעַל עַמּוֹ יִשְׂרָאֵל בְּרַחֲמִים. אָמֵן.

Baruch Attah Adonai Eloheinu Melech Ha'olam Ha'el Avinu Malkeinu Adireinu Go'alenu Kedoshenu Kedosh Ya'akov. Hamelech Hachai Hatov Vehameitiv El Emet Shofet Betzedek Lokeach Nefashot Shallit Be'olamo La'asot Kirtzono Va'anachnu Ammo Va'avadav Ve'al Hakol Anachnu Chayaivim Lehodot Lo Ulevarecho Goder Peratzot Hu Yigdor Et Happirtzah Hazot Me'aleinu Ume'al Ammo Yisra'el

Berachamim. Amen.

Blessed are You, Hashem, our God, King of the universe, the God, our Father, our King, our Mighty One and our Redeemer; the Holy One of Yaakov; the living King, who is good and beneficent; the God of truth, Who judges with righteousness, who takes the souls; who rules in his world, doing according to His will; and we are His people, and his servants. And for all these things, it is our duty to return thanks to Him, and to bless Him. May He who repairs the breaches, repair this breach among us, and among his people Yisrael with mercy. Amen.

עוֹשֶׂה שָׁלוֹם בִּמְרוֹמָיו. הוּא בְּרַחֲמָיו יַעֲשֶׂה שָׁלוֹם עָלֵינוּ. וְעַל כָּל־עַמּוֹ יִשְׂרָאֵל. וְאִמְרוּ אָמֵן:

Oseh Shalom Bimromav. Hu Berachamav Ya'aseh Shalom Aleinu. Ve'al Kol-'Ammo Yisra'el. Ve'imru Amen.

Creator of peace in His high places, may He in His mercy create peace for us and for all Yisrael, and say Amen.

Hashkavah / Burial Service for a Man

To a Great man or Rabbi, someone great in wisdom, Torah and fear of Heaven say:

וְהַחָכְמָה מֵאַיִן תִּמָּצֵא וְאֵי זֶה מְקוֹם בִּינָה: אַשְׁרֵי אָדָם מָצָא חָכְמָה וְאָדָם יָפִיק תְּבוּנָה: מָה רַב־טוּבְךָ אֲשֶׁר־צָפַנְתָּ לִּירֵאֶיךָ פָּעַלְתָּ לַחֹסִים בָּךְ נֶגֶד בְּנֵי אָדָם: מַה־יָּקָר חַסְדְּךָ אֱלֹהִים וּבְנֵי אָדָם בְּצֵל כְּנָפֶיךָ יֶחֱסָיוּן: יִרְוְיֻן מִדֶּשֶׁן בֵּיתֶךָ וְנַחַל עֲדָנֶיךָ תַשְׁקֵם: טוֹב שֵׁם מִשֶּׁמֶן טוֹב וְיוֹם הַמָּוֶת מִיּוֹם הִוָּלְדוֹ: סוֹף דָּבָר הַכֹּל נִשְׁמָע אֶת־הָאֱלֹהִים יְרָא וְאֶת־מִצְוֹתָיו שְׁמוֹר כִּי־זֶה כָּל־הָאָדָם: יַעְלְזוּ חֲסִידִים בְּכָבוֹד יְרַנְּנוּ עַל־מִשְׁכְּבוֹתָם:

Vehachochmah Me'ayin Timmatze Ve'ei Zeh Mekom Binah. Ashrei Adam Matza Chochmah Ve'adam Yafik Tevunah. Mah Rav Tuvecha Asher Tzafanta Lire'eicha Pa'alta Lachosim Bach Neged Benei Adam. Mah Yakar Chasdecha Elohim Uvenei Adam Betzel Kenafeicha Yechesayun. Yirveyun Mideshen Beitecha Venachal Adaneicha Tashkem. Tov Shem Mishemen Tov Veyom Hamavet Miyom Hivoldo. Sof Davar Hakol Nishma Et Ha'elohim Yera Ve'et Mitzvotav Shemor Ki Zeh Kol Ha'adam. Ya'lezu Chasidim Bechavod Yeranenu Al Mishkevotam.

Where will wisdom be found, and where is the place of understanding? Happy is the man that finds wisdom, and the man that gets understanding. How great is Your goodness, which You have treasured up for those that fear You; which You have wrought for those that trust in You, before the sons of men. How excellent is Your loving-kindness, God. You shelter the children of men under the shadow of Your wings. You satisfy them abundantly with the richness of Your House and cause them to drink of the stream of Your delights. A good name is more fragrant than rich perfume; and the day of death better than the day of one's birth. The sum of the matter, after all has been heard, is To fear God, and keep his commandments, for this is the whole of man. Let the pious be joyful in glory; let them sing aloud upon their beds. **(Job 28:12, Prov. 3:13, Ps. 31:20, 36:8-9, Ecc. 7:1, 12:13, Ps. 149:5)**

For a Deceased Male:

מְנוּחָה נְכוֹנָה. בִּישִׁיבָה עֶלְיוֹנָה. בְּמַעֲלַת קְדוֹשִׁים וּטְהוֹרִים. כְּזוֹהַר הָרָקִיעַ מְאִירִים וּמַזְהִירִים. וְחִלּוּץ עֲצָמִים. וְכַפָּרַת אֲשָׁמִים. וְהַרְחָקַת פֶּשַׁע. וְהַקְרָבַת יֶשַׁע. וְחֶמְלָה וַחֲנִינָה. מִלִּפְנֵי שׁוֹכֵן מְעוֹנָה. וְחוּלָקָא טָבָא. לְחַיֵּי הָעוֹלָם הַבָּא. שָׁם תְּהֵא מְנַת וּמְחִיצַת וִישִׁיבַת נֶפֶשׁ הַשֵּׁם הַטּוֹב הַמְּרוּחָם (פלוני בן פלוני) רוּחַ יְהֹוָה תְּנִיחֶנּוּ בְּגַן עֵדֶן. דְּאִתְפְּטַר מִן עַלְמָא הָדֵין כִּרְעוּת אֱלָהָא מָארֵי שְׁמַיָּא וְאַרְעָא. מֶלֶךְ מַלְכֵי הַמְּלָכִים בְּרַחֲמָיו יְרַחֵם עָלָיו. וְיָחוֹס וְיַחְמוֹל עָלָיו. מֶלֶךְ מַלְכֵי הַמְּלָכִים בְּרַחֲמָיו יַסְתִּירֵהוּ בְּצֵל כְּנָפָיו וּבְסֵתֶר אָהֳלוֹ לַחֲזוֹת בְּנוֹעַם יְהֹוָה וּלְבַקֵּר בְּהֵיכָלוֹ. וּלְקֵץ הַיָּמִין יַעֲמִידֵהוּ. וּמִנַּחַל עֲדָנָיו יַשְׁקֵהוּ. וְיִצְרוֹר בִּצְרוֹר הַחַיִּים נִשְׁמָתוֹ. וְיָשִׂים כָּבוֹד מְנוּחָתוֹ. יְהֹוָה הוּא נַחֲלָתוֹ. וְיִלָּוֶה אֵלָיו הַשָּׁלוֹם וְעַל מִשְׁכָּבוֹ יִהְיֶה שָׁלוֹם. כְּדִכְתִיב: יָבוֹא שָׁלוֹם יָנוּחוּ עַל־מִשְׁכְּבוֹתָם

הֹלֵךְ נְכֹחוֹ: הוּא וְכָל־בְּנֵי יִשְׂרָאֵל הַשּׁוֹכְבִים עִמּוֹ בִּכְלַל הָרַחֲמִים וְהַסְּלִיחוֹת. וְכֵן יְהִי רָצוֹן וְנֹאמַר אָמֵן:

Menuchah Nechonah. Bishivah Elyonah. Bema'alat Kedoshim Utehorim. Kezohar Harakia' Me'irim Umazhirim. Vechilutz Atzamim. Vechapparat Ashamim. Veharchakat Pesha. Vehakravat Yesha. Vechemlah Vachaninah. Millifnei Shochein M'onah. Vechulaka Tava. Lechayei Ha'olam Haba. Sham Tehei Menat Umechitzat Vishivat Nefesh Hashem Hatov Hamerucham **(Peloni Ben Peloni)** Ruach Adonai Tenichenu Began Eden. De'itpetar Min Alma Hadein Kir'ut Elaha Marei Shemaya Ve'ar'a. Melech Malchei Hamelachim Berachamav Yerachem Alav. Veyachos Veyachmol Alav. Melech Malchei Hamlachim Berachamav Yastirehu Betzel Kenafav Uveseter Oholo Lachazot Beno'am Adonai Ulevaker Beheichalo. Uleketz Hayamin Ya'amidehu. Uminachal Adanav Yashkehu. Veyitzror Bitzror Hachayim Nishmato. Veyasim Kavod Menuchato. Adonai Hu Nachalato. Veyillaveh Elav Hashalom Ve'al Mishkavo Yihyeh Shalom. Kedichtiv: Yavo Shalom Yanuchu Al Mishkevotam Holech Nechocho. Hu Vechol Benei Yisra'el Hashochevim Imo Bichlal Harachamim Vehasselichot. Vechein Yehi Ratzon Venomar Amen:

May the rest which is prepared in the celestial abode, under the wings of the Divine Presence in the high place of the holy and pure that shine and are resplendent as the bright light of the firmament with a renewal of strength, a forgiveness of trespasses, a removal of transgressions, an approach of salvation, compassion and favor from him that sits enthroned on high, and also a goodly portion in the life to come, be the lot, dwelling, and the resting-place of the soul of our deceased brother - (whom may God grant peace in Paradise), who departed from this world according to the will of God, the Lord of heaven and earth. May the supreme King of kings, through his infinite mercy, have mercy, pity and compassion on him. May the supreme King of kings, through his infinite mercy, hide him under the shadow of his wings, and under the protection of his tent; to behold the beauty of Hashem, and to wait in His Temple; may He raise him at the end of days; and cause him to drink of the stream of His delights. May He cause his soul to be bound up in the bond of life and his rest to be glorious. May Hashem be his inheritance, and grant him peace; and may his rest be in peace; as it is written, "He enters into peace, They rest in their beds, Each one that walks in his uprightness," **(Isaiah 57:2)** May he, and all his people of Yisrael, who sleep in the dust, be included in mercy and forgiveness. May this be His will and let us say, Amen.

Hashkavah / Burial Service for a Woman

אֵשֶׁת־חַיִל מִי יִמְצָא וְרָחֹק מִפְּנִינִים מִכְרָהּ: שֶׁקֶר הַחֵן וְהֶבֶל הַיֹּפִי אִשָּׁה יִרְאַת־יְהוָה הִיא תִתְהַלָּל: תְּנוּ־לָהּ מִפְּרִי יָדֶיהָ וִיהַלְלוּהָ בַשְּׁעָרִים מַעֲשֶׂיהָ:

Eshet Chayil Mi Yimtza Verachok Mipeninim Michrah. Sheker Hachein Vehevel Hayofi Ishah Yir'at Adonai Hi Tithallal. Tenu Lah Miperi Yadeiha Vihalleluha Vashe'arim Ma'aseiha.

A woman of valor who can find? For her price is far above rubies. Grace is deceitful, and beauty is vain; But a woman that fears Hashem, she will be praised. Give her of the fruit of her hands; And let her works praise her in the gates. **(Prov. 31:10,31:30)**

רַחֲמָנָא דְּרַחֲמָנוּתָא דִּי לֵיהּ הִיא וּבְמֵימְרֵיהּ אִתְבְּרִיאוּ עָלְמַיָּא עַלְמָא הָדֵין וְעַלְמָא דְּאָתֵי וּגְנַז בֵּיהּ צַדְקָנִיּוֹת וַחֲסְדָנִיּוֹת דְּעַבְדָן רְעוּתֵיהּ וּבְמֵימְרֵיהּ וּבִיקָרֵיהּ וּבְתוּקְפֵיהּ יֵאמַר לְמֵיעַל קֳדָמוֹהִי דוּכְרָן נֶפֶשׁ הָאִשָּׁה הַכְּבֻדָּה וְהַצְּנוּעָה וְהַנִּכְבֶּדֶת מָרַת (פלוני בן פלוני) רוּחַ יְהוָה תְּנִיחֶנָּה בְּגַן עֵדֶן. דְּאִתְפְּטָרַת מִן עַלְמָא הָדֵין כִּרְעוּת אֱלָהָא מָארֵי שְׁמַיָּא וְאַרְעָא. הַמֶּלֶךְ בְּרַחֲמָיו יָחוֹס וְיַחְמוֹל עָלֶיהָ. וְיִלָּוֶה אֵלֶיהָ הַשָּׁלוֹם וְעַל מִשְׁכָּבָהּ יִהְיֶה שָׁלוֹם. כְּדִכְתִיב: יָבוֹא שָׁלוֹם יָנוּחוּ עַל־מִשְׁכְּבוֹתָם הֹלֵךְ נְכֹחוֹ: הִיא וְכָל־בְּנוֹת יִשְׂרָאֵל הַשּׁוֹכְבוֹת עִמָּהּ בִּכְלַל הָרַחֲמִים וְהַסְּלִיחוֹת. וְכֵן יְהִי רָצוֹן וְנֹאמַר אָמֵן:

Rachamana Derachamanuta Di Leih Hi Uvemeimreih Itberi'u Alemaya Alma Hadein Ve'alma De'atei Ugenaz Beih Tzadkaniyot Vechasdaniyot De'avdan Re'uteih Uvemeimreih Uvikareih Uvetukefeih Yemar Lemei'al Kodamohi Ducheran Nefesh Ha'ishah

Hakevudah Vehatzenu'ah Vehanichbedet Marat **(Peloni Ben Peloni)** Ruach Adonai Tenichenah Began Eden. De'itpetarat Min Alma Hadein Kir'ut Elaha Marei Shemaya Ve'ar'a. Hamelech Berachamav Yachos Veyachmol Aleiha. Veyillaveh Eleiha Hashalom Ve'al Mishkavah Yihyeh Shalom. Kedichtiv: Yavo Shalom Yanuchu Al Mishkevotam Holech Nechocho. Hi Vechol Benot Yisra'el Hashochevot Imah Bichlal Harachamim Vehasselichot. Vechein Yehi Ratzon Venomar Amen:

May the Most Merciful, to Whom mercy pertains; and by Whose word the worlds were created, both this, and the world to come, in which are treasured up the souls of the righteous and pious women who performed His will, by His word, glory, and power command that the remembrance of the worthy, modest, and virtuous woman, - (whom may God grant peace in Paradise), who departed this world, according to the will of God, the Lord of heaven and earth, appear before Him. May the supreme King of kings, through his infinite mercy, have pity and compassion on her, and grant her peace; and may her rest be in peace; as it is written, "He enters into peace, They rest in their beds, Each one that walks in his uprightness," **(Isaiah 57:2)** May she, and all the daughters of Yisrael, who sleep in the dust with her, be included in mercy and forgiveness. May this be His will and let us say, Amen.

SEFIRAT HAOMER / COUNTING OF THE OMER

ספירת העומר

From the 2nd Day of Passover to until the night before Shavuot, the Omer is counted after Arvit Prayer in the evening when it is dark.

Many say the following prayer:

לְשֵׁם יִחוּד קוּדְשָׁא בְּרִיךְ הוּא וּשְׁכִינְתֵּיהּ. בִּדְחִילוּ וּרְחִימוּ. וּרְחִימוּ וּדְחִילוּ. לְיַחֲדָא שֵׁם יוֹ"ד קֵ"י בְּוָא"ו קֵ"י בְּיִחוּדָא שְׁלִים (יהוה) בְּשֵׁם כָּל יִשְׂרָאֵל. הִנֵּה אֲנַחְנוּ בָּאִים לְקַיֵּם מִצְוַת עֲשֵׂה שֶׁל סְפִירַת הָעֹמֶר כְּדִכְתִיב (בליל מ"ט ידלג פסוקים אלה. עד שבעה שבועות. ויאמר לתקן שורש מצוה זו וכו׳) וּסְפַרְתֶּם לָכֶם מִמָּחֳרַת הַשַּׁבָּת מִיּוֹם הֲבִיאֲכֶם אֶת־עֹמֶר הַתְּנוּפָה שֶׁבַע שַׁבָּתוֹת תְּמִימֹת תִּהְיֶינָה: עַד מִמָּחֳרַת הַשַּׁבָּת הַשְּׁבִיעִת תִּסְפְּרוּ חֲמִשִּׁים יוֹם וְהִקְרַבְתֶּם מִנְחָה חֲדָשָׁה לַיהוָה: וְנֶאֱמַר. שִׁבְעָה שָׁבֻעֹת תִּסְפָּר לָךְ מֵהָחֵל חֶרְמֵשׁ בַּקָּמָה תָּחֵל לִסְפֹּר שִׁבְעָה שָׁבֻעוֹת: לְתַקֵּן שָׁרְשׁ מִצְוָה זוֹ בְּמָקוֹם עֶלְיוֹן עִם כָּל הַמִּצְוֹת הַכְּלוּלוֹת בָּהּ. לַעֲשׂוֹת נַחַת רוּחַ לְיוֹצְרֵנוּ וְלַעֲשׂוֹת רְצוֹן בּוֹרְאֵנוּ. יַעֲלֶה לְפָנָיו כְּאִלּוּ כִּוַּנְנוּ כָּל הַכַּוָּנוֹת הָרְאוּיוֹת לְכַוֵּן בָּזֶה: וִיהִי נֹעַם אֲדֹנָי אֱלֹהֵינוּ עָלֵינוּ וּמַעֲשֵׂה יָדֵינוּ כּוֹנְנָה עָלֵינוּ וּמַעֲשֵׂה יָדֵינוּ כּוֹנְנֵהוּ:

Leshem Yichud Kudsha Berich Hu Ushechinteih. Bidchilu Urechimu. Urechimu Udechilu. Leyachada Shem Yod Key BeVav Key Beyichuda Shelim Beshem Kol Yisra'el. Hineh Anachnu Ba'im Lekayem Mitzvat Aseh Shel Sefirat Ha'omer Kedichtiv **(On the night of Matan Torah (Shavuot) skip these verses, up to "Shiv'ah Shavu'ot", and say "Letakken Shoresh Mitzvah", etc.)** Usefartem Lachem Mimochorat Hashabbat Miyom Havi'achem Et Omer Hatenufah Sheva Shabbatot Temimot Tihyeinah. Ad Mimochorat Hashabbat Hashevi'it Tisperu Chamishim Yom Vehikravtem Minchah Chadashah Ladonai. Vene'emar. Shiv'ah Shavu'ot Tispar Lach Mehachel Chermesh Bakamah Tachel Lispor Shiv'ah Shavu'ot. Letaken Shoresh Mitzvah Zo Bemakom Elyon Im Kol Hamitzvot Hakelulot Bah. La'asot Nachat Ruach Leyotzreinu Vela'asot Retzon Bore'enu. Ya'aleh Lefanav Che'ilu Kivanu Chol Hakavanot Hare'uyot Lechaven Bazeh: Vihi No'am Adonai Eloheinu Aleinu Uma'aseh Yadeinu Konenah Aleinu Uma'aseh Yadeinu Konenehu. **(Lev. 23:15-16, Deut.16:19)**

Some say:

יְהוָה יִגְמֹר בַּעֲדִי יְהוָה חַסְדְּךָ לְעוֹלָם מַעֲשֵׂי יָדֶיךָ אַל־תֶּרֶף: אֶקְרָא לֵאלֹהִים עֶלְיוֹן לָאֵל גֹּמֵר עָלָי: וָאֶעֱבֹר עָלַיִךְ וָאֶרְאֵךְ מִתְבּוֹסֶסֶת בְּדָמָיִךְ וָאֹמַר לָךְ בְּדָמַיִךְ חֲיִי וָאֹמַר לָךְ בְּדָמַיִךְ חֲיִי: בָּרְכִי נַפְשִׁי אֶת־יְהוָה יְהוָה אֱלֹהַי גָּדַלְתָּ מְּאֹד הוֹד וְהָדָר לָבָשְׁתָּ: עֹטֶה־אוֹר כַּשַּׂלְמָה נוֹטֶה שָׁמַיִם כַּיְרִיעָה:

Adonai Yigmor Ba'adi Adonai Chasdecha Le'olam Ma'asei Yadeicha Al Teref. Ekra Lelohim Elyon La'el Gomer Alai. Va'e'evor Alayich Va'er'ech Mitboseset Bedamayich Va'omar Lach Bedamayich Chayi Va'omar Lach Bedamayich Chayi. Barchi Nafshi Et Adonai Adonai Elohai Gadalta Me'od Hod Vehadar Lavasheta. Oteh Or Kassalmah Noteh Shamayim Kayeri'ah.

Hashem will accomplish that which concerns me; Your mercy, Hashem, endures forever; Do not forsake the work of Your own hands. I will cry to God Most high; to God that accomplishes it for me. And when I passed by you, and saw you wallowing in your blood, I said to you: In your blood, live; yes, I said to you: In your blood, live; Bless Hashem, Oh my soul. Hashem, my God, You are very great; You are clothed with glory and majesty. Who covers Yourself with light as with a garment, who stretches out the heavens like a curtain. **(Ps. 138:8, 57:3, Ez. 16:6, Ps. 104:1-2)**

Birshut Morai Verabotai: — בִּרְשׁוּת מוֹרַי וְרַבּוֹתַי:

With the permission of my teachers and masters:

Answer: Shamayim! — **עונים:** שָׁמַיִם.

Answer: (By) Heaven!

And the Chazan and the people bless:

Baruch Attah Adonai Eloheinu — בָּרוּךְ אַתָּה יְהֹוָה אֱלֹהֵינוּ

Melech Ha'olam Asher — מֶלֶךְ הָעוֹלָם. אֲשֶׁר

Kideshanu Bemitzvotav — קִדְּשָׁנוּ בְּמִצְוֹתָיו

Vetzivanu Al Sefirat Ha'Omer: — וְצִוָּנוּ עַל סְפִירַת הָעֹמֶר:

And say: Hayom **and say the count:** — **ואומרים** הַיּוֹם **וכו׳ ואחר הספירה אומר:**

Blessed are You, Hashem our God, King of the universe, Who has sanctified us with His commandments, and has given us command concerning the counting of the O'mer. **(Continue down and say "HaYom..." and the day to count. Continue afterwards with Psalm 67, etc.)**

16th of Nissan

Hayom Yom Echad La'omer: — הַיּוֹם יוֹם אֶחָד לָעֹמֶר:

Today is the first day of the Omer.

17th of Nissan

Hayom Shenei Yamim La'omer: הַיּוֹם שְׁנֵי יָמִים לָעֹמֶר:

Today is the second day of the Omer.

18th of Nissan

Hayom Sheloshah Yamim La'omer: הַיּוֹם שְׁלֹשָׁה יָמִים לָעֹמֶר:

Today is the third day of the Omer.

19th of Nissan

Hayom Arba'ah Yamim La'omer: הַיּוֹם אַרְבָּעָה יָמִים לָעֹמֶר:

Today is the fourth day of the Omer.

20th of Nissan

Hayom Chamishah Yamim La'omer: הַיּוֹם חֲמִשָּׁה יָמִים לָעֹמֶר:

Today is the fifth day of the Omer.

21st of Nissan

Hayom Shishah Yamim La'omer: הַיּוֹם שִׁשָּׁה יָמִים לָעֹמֶר:

Today is the sixth day of the Omer.

22nd of Nissan

Hayom Shiv'ah Yamim La'omer הַיּוֹם שִׁבְעָה יָמִים לָעֹמֶר

Shehem Shavua' Echad: שֶׁהֵם שָׁבוּעַ אֶחָד:

Today is the seventh day of the Omer, which is one week.

23rd of Nissan

Hayom Shemonah Yamim La'omer הַיּוֹם שְׁמוֹנָה יָמִים לָעֹמֶר

Shehem Shavua' Echad Veyom Echad: שֶׁהֵם שָׁבוּעַ אֶחָד וְיוֹם אֶחָד:

Today is the seventh day of the Omer, which is one week and one day.

24th of Nissan

Hayom Tish'ah Yamim La'omer Shehem הַיּוֹם תִּשְׁעָה יָמִים לָעֹמֶר שֶׁהֵם

Shavua' Echad Ushenei Yamim: שָׁבוּעַ אֶחָד וּשְׁנֵי יָמִים:

Today is the ninth day of the Omer, which is one week and two days.

25th of Nissan

Hayom Asarah Yamim La'omer Shehem	הַיּוֹם עֲשָׂרָה יָמִים לָעֹמֶר שֶׁהֵם
Shavua' Echad Usheloshah Yamim:	שָׁבוּעַ אֶחָד וּשְׁלֹשָׁה יָמִים:

Today is the tenth day of the Omer, which is one week and three days.

26th of Nissan

Hayom Achad Asar Yom La'omer	הַיּוֹם אַחַד עָשָׂר יוֹם לָעֹמֶר
Shehem Shavua' Echad Ve'arba'ah	שֶׁהֵם שָׁבוּעַ אֶחָד וְאַרְבָּעָה
Yamim:	יָמִים:

Today is the eleventh day of the Omer, which is one week and four days.

27th of Nissan

Hayom Sheneim Asar Yom La'omer	הַיּוֹם שְׁנֵים עָשָׂר יוֹם לָעֹמֶר
Shehem Shavua' Echad Vachamishah	שֶׁהֵם שָׁבוּעַ אֶחָד וַחֲמִשָּׁה
Yamim:	יָמִים:

Today is the twelfth day of the Omer, which is one week and five days.

28th of Nissan

Hayom Sheloshah Asar Yom La'omer	הַיּוֹם שְׁלֹשָׁה עָשָׂר יוֹם לָעֹמֶר
Shehem Shavua' Echad Veshishah	שֶׁהֵם שָׁבוּעַ אֶחָד וְשִׁשָּׁה
Yamim:	יָמִים:

Today is the thirteenth day of the Omer, which is one week and six days.

29th of Nissan

Hayom Arba'ah Asar Yom La'omer	הַיּוֹם אַרְבָּעָה עָשָׂר יוֹם לָעֹמֶר
Shehem Shenei Shavu'ot:	שֶׁהֵם שְׁנֵי שָׁבוּעוֹת:

Today is the fourteenth day of the Omer, which is two weeks.

30th of Nissan

Hayom Chamishah Asar Yom La'omer	הַיּוֹם חֲמִשָּׁה עָשָׂר יוֹם לָעֹמֶר
Shehem Shenei Shavu'ot Veyom Echad:	שֶׁהֵם שְׁנֵי שָׁבוּעוֹת וְיוֹם אֶחָד:

Today is the fifteenth day of the Omer, which is two weeks and one day.

1st of Iyar

Hayom Shishah Asar Yom La'omer	הַיּוֹם שִׁשָּׁה עָשָׂר יוֹם לָעֹמֶר
Shehem Shenei Shavu'ot Ushenei	שֶׁהֵם שְׁנֵי שָׁבוּעוֹת וּשְׁנֵי
Yamim:	יָמִים:

Today is the sixteenth day of the Omer, which is two weeks and two days.

2nd of Iyar

Hayom Shiv'ah Asar Yom La'omer	הַיּוֹם שִׁבְעָה עָשָׂר יוֹם לָעֹמֶר
Shehem Shenei Shavu'ot Usheloshah	שֶׁהֵם שְׁנֵי שָׁבוּעוֹת וּשְׁלֹשָׁה
Yamim:	יָמִים:

Today is the seventeenth day of the Omer, which is two weeks and three days.

3rd of Iyar

Hayom Shemonah Asar Yom La'omer	הַיּוֹם שְׁמוֹנָה עָשָׂר יוֹם לָעֹמֶר
Shehem Shenei Shavu'ot Ve'arba'ah	שֶׁהֵם שְׁנֵי שָׁבוּעוֹת וְאַרְבָּעָה
Yamim:	יָמִים:

Today is the eighteenth day of the Omer, which is two weeks and four days.

4th of Iyar

Hayom Tish'ah Asar Yom La'omer	הַיּוֹם תִּשְׁעָה עָשָׂר יוֹם לָעֹמֶר
Shehem Shenei Shavu'ot Vachamishah	שֶׁהֵם שְׁנֵי שָׁבוּעוֹת וַחֲמִשָּׁה
Yamim:	יָמִים:

Today is the nineteenth day of the Omer, which is two weeks and five days.

5th of Iyar

Hayom Esrim Yom La'omer Shehem	הַיּוֹם עֶשְׂרִים יוֹם לָעֹמֶר שֶׁהֵם
Shenei Shavu'ot Veshishah Yamim:	שְׁנֵי שָׁבוּעוֹת וְשִׁשָּׁה יָמִים:

Today is the twentieth day of the Omer, which is two weeks and six days.

6th of Iyar

Hayom Echad Ve'esrim Yom La'omer	הַיּוֹם אֶחָד וְעֶשְׂרִים יוֹם לָעֹמֶר
Shehem Sheloshah Shavu'ot:	שֶׁהֵם שְׁלֹשָׁה שָׁבוּעוֹת:

Today is the twenty-first day of the Omer, which is three weeks.

7th of Iyar

Hayom Shenayim Ve'esrim Yom — הַיּוֹם שְׁנַיִם וְעֶשְׂרִים יוֹם
La'omer Shehem Sheloshah Shavu'ot — לָעֹמֶר שֶׁהֵם שְׁלֹשָׁה שָׁבוּעוֹת
Veyom Echad: — וְיוֹם אֶחָד:

Today is the twenty-second day of the Omer, which is three weeks and one day.

8th of Iyar

Hayom Sheloshah Ve'esrim Yom — הַיּוֹם שְׁלֹשָׁה וְעֶשְׂרִים יוֹם
La'omer Shehem Sheloshah Shavu'ot — לָעֹמֶר שֶׁהֵם שְׁלֹשָׁה שָׁבוּעוֹת
Ushenei Yamim: — וּשְׁנֵי יָמִים:

Today is the twenty-third day of the Omer, which is three weeks and two days.

9th of Iyar

Hayom Arba'ah Ve'esrim Yom La'omer — הַיּוֹם אַרְבָּעָה וְעֶשְׂרִים יוֹם לָעֹמֶר
Shehem Sheloshah Shavu'ot — שֶׁהֵם שְׁלֹשָׁה שָׁבוּעוֹת
Usheloshah Yamim: — וּשְׁלֹשָׁה יָמִים:

Today is the twenty-fourth day of the Omer, which is three weeks and three days.

10th of Iyar

Hayom Chamishah Ve'esrim Yom — הַיּוֹם חֲמִשָּׁה וְעֶשְׂרִים יוֹם
La'omer Shehem Sheloshah Shavu'ot — לָעֹמֶר שֶׁהֵם שְׁלֹשָׁה שָׁבוּעוֹת
Ve'arba'ah Yamim: — וְאַרְבָּעָה יָמִים:

Today is the twenty-fifth day of the Omer, which is three weeks and four days.

11th of Iyar

Hayom Shishah Ve'esrim Yom La'omer — הַיּוֹם שִׁשָּׁה וְעֶשְׂרִים יוֹם לָעֹמֶר
Shehem Sheloshah Shavu'ot — שֶׁהֵם שְׁלֹשָׁה שָׁבוּעוֹת
Vachamishah Yamim: — וַחֲמִשָּׁה יָמִים:

Today is the twenty-sixth day of the Omer, which is three weeks and five days.

12th of Iyar

Hayom Shiv'ah Ve'esrim Yom La'omer — הַיּוֹם שִׁבְעָה וְעֶשְׂרִים יוֹם לָעֹמֶר
Shehem Sheloshah Shavu'ot Veshishah — שֶׁהֵם שְׁלֹשָׁה שָׁבוּעוֹת וְשִׁשָּׁה
Yamim: — יָמִים:

Today is the twenty-seventh day of the Omer, which is three weeks and six days.

13th of Iyar

Hayom Shemonah Ve'esrim Yom	הַיּוֹם שְׁמוֹנָה וְעֶשְׂרִים יוֹם
La'omer Shehem Arba'ah Shavu'ot:	לָעֹמֶר שֶׁהֵם אַרְבָּעָה שָׁבוּעוֹת:

Today is the twenty-eighth day of the Omer, which is four weeks.

14th of Iyar

Hayom Tish'ah Ve'esrim Yom La'omer	הַיּוֹם תִּשְׁעָה וְעֶשְׂרִים יוֹם לָעֹמֶר
Shehem Arba'ah Shavu'ot Veyom	שֶׁהֵם אַרְבָּעָה שָׁבוּעוֹת וְיוֹם
Echad:	אֶחָד:

Today is the twenty-ninth day of the Omer, which is four weeks and one day.

15th of Iyar

Hayom Sheloshim Yom La'omer	הַיּוֹם שְׁלֹשִׁים יוֹם לָעֹמֶר
Shehem Arba'ah Shavu'ot Ushenei	שֶׁהֵם אַרְבָּעָה שָׁבוּעוֹת וּשְׁנֵי
Yamim:	יָמִים:

Today is the thirtieth day of the Omer, which is four weeks and two days.

16th of Iyar

Hayom Echad Usheloshim Yom	הַיּוֹם אֶחָד וּשְׁלֹשִׁים יוֹם
La'omer Shehem Arba'ah Shavu'ot	לָעֹמֶר שֶׁהֵם אַרְבָּעָה שָׁבוּעוֹת
Usheloshah Yamim:	וּשְׁלֹשָׁה יָמִים:

Today is the thirty-first day of the Omer, which is four weeks and three days.

17th of Iyar

Hayom Shenayim Usheloshim Yom	הַיּוֹם שְׁנַיִם וּשְׁלֹשִׁים יוֹם
La'omer Shehem Arba'ah Shavu'ot	לָעֹמֶר שֶׁהֵם אַרְבָּעָה שָׁבוּעוֹת
Ve'arba'ah Yamim:	וְאַרְבָּעָה יָמִים:

Today is the thirty-second day of the Omer, which is four weeks and four days.

18th of Iyar

Hayom Sheloshah Usheloshim Yom	הַיּוֹם שְׁלֹשָׁה וּשְׁלֹשִׁים יוֹם
La'omer Shehem Arba'ah Shavu'ot	לָעֹמֶר שֶׁהֵם אַרְבָּעָה שָׁבוּעוֹת
Vachamishah Yamim:	וַחֲמִשָּׁה יָמִים:

Today is the thirty-third day of the Omer, which is four weeks and five days.

19th of Iyar

Hayom Arba'ah Usheloshim Yom	הַיּוֹם אַרְבָּעָה וּשְׁלֹשִׁים יוֹם
La'omer Shehem Arba'ah Shavu'ot	לָעֹמֶר שֶׁהֵם אַרְבָּעָה שָׁבוּעוֹת
Veshishah Yamim:	וְשִׁשָּׁה יָמִים:

Today is the thirty-fourth day of the Omer, which is four weeks and six days.

20th of Iyar

Hayom Chamishah Usheloshim Yom	הַיּוֹם חֲמִשָּׁה וּשְׁלֹשִׁים יוֹם
La'omer Shehem Chamishah Shavu'ot:	לָעֹמֶר שֶׁהֵם חֲמִשָּׁה שָׁבוּעוֹת:

Today is the thirty-fifth day of the Omer, which is five weeks.

21st of Iyar

Hayom Shishah Usheloshim Yom	הַיּוֹם שִׁשָּׁה וּשְׁלֹשִׁים יוֹם
La'omer Shehem Chamishah Shavu'ot	לָעֹמֶר שֶׁהֵם חֲמִשָּׁה שָׁבוּעוֹת
Veyom Echad:	וְיוֹם אֶחָד:

Today is the thirty-sixth day of the Omer, which is five weeks and one day.

23rd of Iyar

Hayom Shiv'ah Usheloshim Yom	הַיּוֹם שִׁבְעָה וּשְׁלֹשִׁים יוֹם
La'omer Shehem Chamishah Shavu'ot	לָעֹמֶר שֶׁהֵם חֲמִשָּׁה שָׁבוּעוֹת
Ushenei Yamim:	וּשְׁנֵי יָמִים:

Today is the thirty-seventh day of the Omer, which is five weeks and two days.

24th of Iyar

Hayom Shemonah Usheloshim Yom	הַיּוֹם שְׁמוֹנָה וּשְׁלֹשִׁים יוֹם
La'omer Shehem Chamishah Shavu'ot	לָעֹמֶר שֶׁהֵם חֲמִשָּׁה שָׁבוּעוֹת
Usheloshah Yamim:	וּשְׁלֹשָׁה יָמִים:

Today is the thirty-eighth day of the Omer, which is five weeks and three days.

25th of Iyar

Hayom Tish'ah Usheloshim Yom	הַיּוֹם תִּשְׁעָה וּשְׁלשִׁים יוֹם
La'omer Shehem Chamishah Shavu'ot	לָעֹמֶר שֶׁהֵם חֲמִשָּׁה שָׁבוּעוֹת
Ve'arba'ah Yamim:	וְאַרְבָּעָה יָמִים:

Today is the thirty-ninth day of the Omer, which is five weeks and four days.

26th of Iyar

Hayom Arba'im Yom La'omer Shehem	הַיּוֹם אַרְבָּעִים יוֹם לָעֹמֶר שֶׁהֵם
Chamishah Shavu'ot Vachamishah	חֲמִשָּׁה שָׁבוּעוֹת וַחֲמִשָּׁה
Yamim:	יָמִים:

Today is the fortieth day of the Omer, which is five weeks and five days.

27th of Iyar

Hayom Echad Ve'arba'im Yom La'omer	הַיּוֹם אֶחָד וְאַרְבָּעִים יוֹם לָעֹמֶר
Shehem Chamishah Shavu'ot Veshishah	שֶׁהֵם חֲמִשָּׁה שָׁבוּעוֹת וְשִׁשָּׁה
Yamim:	יָמִים:

Today is the forty-first day of the Omer, which is five weeks and six days.

28th of Iyar

Hayom Shenayim Ve'arba'im Yom	הַיּוֹם שְׁנַיִם וְאַרְבָּעִים יוֹם
La'omer Shehem Shishah Shavu'ot:	לָעֹמֶר שֶׁהֵם שִׁשָּׁה שָׁבוּעוֹת:

Today is the forty-second day of the Omer, which is six weeks.

29th of Iyar

Hayom Sheloshah Ve'arba'im Yom	הַיּוֹם שְׁלשָׁה וְאַרְבָּעִים יוֹם
La'omer Shehem Shishah Shavu'ot	לָעֹמֶר שֶׁהֵם שִׁשָּׁה שָׁבוּעוֹת
Veyom Echad:	וְיוֹם אֶחָד:

Today is the forty-third day of the Omer, which is six weeks and one day.

30th of Iyar

Hayom Arba'ah Ve'arba'im Yom	הַיּוֹם אַרְבָּעָה וְאַרְבָּעִים יוֹם
La'omer Shehem Shishah Shavu'ot	לָעֹמֶר שֶׁהֵם שִׁשָּׁה שָׁבוּעוֹת
Ushenei Yamim:	וּשְׁנֵי יָמִים:

Today is the forty-fourth day of the Omer, which is six weeks and two days.

1st of Sivan

Hayom Chamishah Ve'arba'im Yom	הַיּוֹם חֲמִשָּׁה וְאַרְבָּעִים יוֹם
La'omer Shehem Shishah Shavu'ot	לָעֽוֹמֶר שֶׁהֵם שִׁשָּׁה שָׁבוּעוֹת
Usheloshah Yamim:	וּשְׁלֹשָׁה יָמִים:

Today is the forty-fifth day of the Omer, which is six weeks and three days.

2nd of Sivan

Hayom Shishah Ve'arba'im Yom	הַיּוֹם שִׁשָּׁה וְאַרְבָּעִים יוֹם
La'omer Shehem Shishah Shavu'ot	לָעֽוֹמֶר שֶׁהֵם שִׁשָּׁה שָׁבוּעוֹת
Ve'arba'ah Yamim:	וְאַרְבָּעָה יָמִים:

Today is the forty-sixth day of the Omer, which is six weeks and four days.

3rd of Sivan

Hayom Shiv'ah Ve'Arba'im Yom	הַיּוֹם שִׁבְעָה וְאַרְבָּעִים יוֹם
La'omer Shehem Shishah Shavu'ot	לָעֽוֹמֶר שֶׁהֵם שִׁשָּׁה שָׁבוּעוֹת
Vachamishah Yamim:	וַחֲמִשָּׁה יָמִים:

Today is the forty-seventh day of the Omer, which is six weeks and five days.

4th of Sivan

Hayom Shemonah Ve'arba'im Yom	הַיּוֹם שְׁמוֹנָה וְאַרְבָּעִים יוֹם
La'omer Shehem Shishah Shavu'ot	לָעֽוֹמֶר שֶׁהֵם שִׁשָּׁה שָׁבוּעוֹת
Veshishah Yamim:	וְשִׁשָּׁה יָמִים:

Today is the forty-eighth day of the Omer, which is six weeks and six days.

5th of Sivan

Hayom Tish'ah Ve'arba'im Yom La'omer	הַיּוֹם תִּשְׁעָה וְאַרְבָּעִים יוֹם לָעֽוֹמֶר
Shehem Shiv'ah Shavu'ot:	שֶׁהֵם שִׁבְעָה שָׁבוּעוֹת:

Today is the forty-ninth day of the Omer, which is seven weeks.

Continue with Harachaman, Psalms 67 and Ana Bechoach. If one counted after Kaddish Titkabbal in Shacharit, continue with Psalms 121. If one counted after Aleinu, the service is now concluded.

After counting the omer say:

Harachaman Yachazir Beit	הָרַחֲמָן יַחֲזִיר בֵּית
Hamikdash Limkomah	הַמִּקְדָּשׁ לִמְקוֹמָהּ
Bimheirah Beyameinu:	בִּמְהֵרָה בְיָמֵינוּ:

May the Most Merciful restore the service of the Beit HaMikdash to its place, speedily in our days.

Psalms 67 / Lamnatzeach Binginot

לַמְנַצֵּחַ בִּנְגִינֹת מִזְמוֹר שִׁיר: אֱלֹהִים יְחָנֵּנוּ וִיבָרְכֵנוּ יָאֵר פָּנָיו אִתָּנוּ
סֶלָה: לָדַעַת בָּאָרֶץ דַּרְכֶּךָ בְּכָל־גּוֹיִם יְשׁוּעָתֶךָ: יוֹדוּךָ עַמִּים | אֱלֹהִים
יוֹדוּךָ עַמִּים כֻּלָּם: יִשְׂמְחוּ וִירַנְּנוּ לְאֻמִּים כִּי־תִשְׁפֹּט עַמִּים מִישֹׁר
וּלְאֻמִּים | בָּאָרֶץ תַּנְחֵם סֶלָה: יוֹדוּךָ עַמִּים | אֱלֹהִים יוֹדוּךָ עַמִּים
כֻּלָּם: אֶרֶץ נָתְנָה יְבוּלָהּ יְבָרְכֵנוּ אֱלֹהִים אֱלֹהֵינוּ: יְבָרְכֵנוּ אֱלֹהִים
וְיִירְאוּ אוֹתוֹ כָּל־אַפְסֵי־אָרֶץ:

Lamnatzeach Binginot. Mizmor Shir. Elohim. Yechonenu Vivarecheinu; Ya'er Panav Itanu Selah. Lada'at Ba'aretz Darkecha; Bechol-Goyim. Yeshu'atecha. Yoducha Ammim Elohim; Yoducha. Ammim Kulam. Yismechu Viranenu. Le'ummim Ki-Tishpot Ammim Mishor; Ule'ummim Ba'aretz Tanchem Selah. Yoducha Ammim Elohim; Yoducha. Ammim Kulam. Eretz Natenah Yevulah; Yevarecheinu. Elohim Eloheinu. Yevarecheinu Elohim; Veyire'u Oto. Chol-'Afsei-'Aretz.

For the Leader; with string-music. A Psalm, a Song. May God be gracious to us, and bless us; May He cause His face to shine toward us; Selah. That Your way may be known upon earth, Your salvation among all nations. Let the people give thanks to You, Oh God; Let the peoples give thanks to You, all of them. Let the nations be glad and sing for joy; For You will judge the people with equity, And lead the nations on earth. Selah. Let the people give thanks to You, Oh God; Let the peoples give thanks to You, all of them. The earth has yielded her increase; May God, our own God, bless us. May God bless us; And let all the ends of the earth fear Him.

Ana Bechoach

אָנָּא בְּכֹחַ. גְּדוּלַּת יְמִינְךָ. תַּתִּיר צְרוּרָה:
Ana Bechoach. Gedulat Yeminecha. Tatir Tzerurah.
By the great power of your right hand, Oh set the captive free.

קַבֵּל רִנַּת. עַמְּךָ שַׂגְּבֵנוּ. טַהֲרֵנוּ נוֹרָא:
Kabel Rinat. Ammecha Sagveinu. Tahareinu Nora.
God of awe, accept your people's prayer; strengthen us, cleanse us.

נָא גִבּוֹר. דּוֹרְשֵׁי יִחוּדְךָ. כְּבָבַת שָׁמְרֵם:
Na Gibor. Doreshei Yichudecha. Kevavat Shamerem.
Almighty God, guard as the apple of the eye those who seek You.

בָּרְכֵם טַהֲרֵם. רַחֲמֵי צִדְקָתְךָ. תָּמִיד גָּמְלֵם:
Barechem Taharem. Rachamei Tzidkatecha. Tamid Gamelem.
Bless them, cleanse them, pity them; forever grant them Your truth.

חֲסִין קָדוֹשׁ. בְּרֹב טוּבְךָ. נַהֵל עֲדָתֶךָ:
Chasin Kadosh. Berov Tuvecha. Nahel Adatecha.
Almighty and holy, in Your abundant goodness, guide Your people.

יָחִיד גֵּאֶה. לְעַמְּךָ פְּנֵה. זוֹכְרֵי קְדֻשָּׁתֶךָ:
Yachid Ge'eh. Le'ammecha Feneh. Zocherei Kedushatecha.
Supreme God, turn to Your people who are mindful of Your holiness.

שַׁוְעָתֵנוּ קַבֵּל. וּשְׁמַע צַעֲקָתֵנוּ. יוֹדֵעַ תַּעֲלוּמוֹת:
Shav'ateinu Kabel. Ushema Tza'akateinu. Yodea Ta'alumot.
Accept our prayer, hear our cry, You who knows secret thoughts.

And Say Silently:

בָּרוּךְ, שֵׁם כְּבוֹד מַלְכוּתוֹ, לְעוֹלָם וָעֶד:
Baruch, Shem Kevod Malchuto, Le'olam Va'ed
Blessed is the Name of His glorious kingdom forever and ever.

SEDER BIRKHAT HALEVANAH / ORDER OF THE BLESSING OF THE MOON

Upon beholding the New Moon, one must say the blessing "asher bema'amaro", etc. (One should not consecrate the moon unless the moon is shining). The blessing should be said preferably on Shabbat night. (This is only true when Saturday night occur before the tenth of the month, then we have to wait till Shabbat night, but if it fall after the tenth of the month, we do not need to wait). The blessing should not be recited before seven days after its conjunction has passed. (The moon should not be consecrated before the Ninth of Av, only at the conclusion of it; and not before Yom Kippur, only at the conclusion of it). How long may we wait say the blessing over it? Up to the sixteenth day of its conjunction, the sixteenth day not included. (And it should not be consecrated before the half of twenty-nine (twelve hours, twenty-two and 11.18 minutes from the conjunction). (SA, OC 426)

Psalms 19

לַמְנַצֵּחַ מִזְמוֹר לְדָוִד׃ הַשָּׁמַיִם מְסַפְּרִים כְּבוֹד־אֵל וּמַעֲשֵׂה יָדָיו
מַגִּיד הָרָקִיעַ׃ יוֹם לְיוֹם יַבִּיעַ אֹמֶר וְלַיְלָה לְּלַיְלָה יְחַוֶּה־דָּעַת׃
אֵין־אֹמֶר וְאֵין דְּבָרִים בְּלִי נִשְׁמָע קוֹלָם׃ בְּכָל־הָאָרֶץ | יָצָא קַוָּם
וּבִקְצֵה תֵבֵל מִלֵּיהֶם לַשֶּׁמֶשׁ שָׂם־אֹהֶל בָּהֶם׃ וְהוּא כְּחָתָן יֹצֵא
מֵחֻפָּתוֹ יָשִׂישׂ כְּגִבּוֹר לָרוּץ אֹרַח׃ מִקְצֵה הַשָּׁמַיִם | מוֹצָאוֹ וּתְקוּפָתוֹ
עַל־קְצוֹתָם וְאֵין נִסְתָּר מֵחַמָּתוֹ׃ תּוֹרַת יְהוָה תְּמִימָה מְשִׁיבַת נָפֶשׁ
עֵדוּת יְהוָה נֶאֱמָנָה מַחְכִּימַת פֶּתִי׃ פִּקּוּדֵי יְהוָה יְשָׁרִים מְשַׂמְּחֵי־לֵב
מִצְוַת יְהוָה בָּרָה מְאִירַת עֵינָיִם׃ יִרְאַת יְהוָה | טְהוֹרָה עוֹמֶדֶת לָעַד
מִשְׁפְּטֵי־יְהוָה אֱמֶת צָדְקוּ יַחְדָּו׃ הַנֶּחֱמָדִים מִזָּהָב וּמִפַּז רָב
וּמְתוּקִים מִדְּבַשׁ וְנֹפֶת צוּפִים׃ גַּם־עַבְדְּךָ נִזְהָר בָּהֶם בְּשָׁמְרָם עֵקֶב
רָב׃ שְׁגִיאוֹת מִי־יָבִין מִנִּסְתָּרוֹת נַקֵּנִי׃ גַּם מִזֵּדִים | חֲשֹׂךְ עַבְדֶּךָ
אַל־יִמְשְׁלוּ־בִי אָז אֵיתָם וְנִקֵּיתִי מִפֶּשַׁע רָב׃ יִהְיוּ לְרָצוֹן | אִמְרֵי־פִי
וְהֶגְיוֹן לִבִּי לְפָנֶיךָ יְהוָה צוּרִי וְגֹאֲלִי׃

Lamnatzeach, Mizmor Ledavid. Hashamayim, Mesaperim Kevod-El; Uma'aseh Yadav, Maggid Harakia. Yom Leyom Yabbia Omer; Velaylah Lelaylah, Yechaveh-Da'at. Ein-'Omer Ve'ein Devarim; Beli, Nishma Kolam. Bechol-Ha'aretz Yatza Kavam, Uviktzeh Tevel Mileihem; Lashemesh, Sam-'Ohel Bahem. Vehu, Kechaton Yotzei Mechuppato; Yasis Kegibor, Larutz Orach. Miktzeh Hashamayim

Motza'o, Utekufato Al-Ketzotam; Ve'ein Nistar, Mechamato. Torat Adonai Temimah Meshivat Nafesh; Edut Adonai Ne'emanah, Machkimat Peti. Pikudei Adonai Yesharim Mesamechei-Lev; Mitzvat Adonai Barah, Me'irat Einayim. Yir'at Adonai Tehorah Omedet La'ad Mishpetei-Adonai Emet; Tzadeku Yachdav. Hanechemadim, Mizahov Umipaz Rav; Umetukim Midevash, Venofet Tzufim. Gam-Avdecha Nizhar Bahem; Beshomram, Ekev Rav. Shegi'ot Mi-Yavin; Ministarot Nakkeni. Gam Mizeidim Chasoch Avodecha, Al-Yimshelu-Vi Az Eitam; Venikkeiti, Mippesha Rav. Yihyu Leratzon Imrei-Fi Vehegyon Libi Lefaneicha; Adonai Tzuri Vego'ali.

For the Leader. A Psalm of David. The heavens declare the glory of God, and the firmament shows the work of His hands; Day to day utters speech, and night to night reveals knowledge; There is no speech, there are no words, neither is their voice heard. Their line is gone out through all the earth, and their words to the end of the world. In them He has set a tent for the sun, Which is as a bridegroom coming out of his chamber, and rejoices as a strong man to run his course. His going out is from the end of the heaven, and his circuit to the ends of it; and there is nothing hidden from the heat of it. The Torah of Hashem is perfect, restoring the soul; the testimony of Hashem is sure, making wise the simple. The precepts of Hashem are right, rejoicing the heart; the commandment of Hashem is pure, enlightening the eyes. The fear of Hashem is clean, enduring forever; the ordinances of Hashem are true, they are righteous altogether; More to be desired are they than gold, even than much fine gold; sweeter also than honey and the honeycomb. Also by them is Your servant warned; in keeping of them there is great reward. Who can discern his errors? Cleanse me from hidden faults. Keep back Your servant from presumptuous sins, that they may not have dominion over me; then I will be faultless, and I will be clear from great transgression. Let the words of my mouth and the meditation of my heart be acceptable before You, Hashem, my Rock, and my Redeemer.

צוּרִי בָּעוֹלָם הַזֶּה וְגוֹאֲלִי לָעוֹלָם הַבָּא. וְכָל־קַרְנֵי רְשָׁעִים אֲגַדֵּעַ
תְּרוֹמַמְנָה קַרְנוֹת צַדִּיק:

Tzuri Ba'olam Hazeh Vego'ali La'olam Haba. Vechol Karnei Resha'im Agadea' Teromamnah Karnot Tzaddik.

My rock in this world and my redeemer in the world to come. All the horns of the wicked I will also cut off; But the horns of the righteous will be lifted up. **(Psalms 75:11)**

Psalms 148:1-6

הַלְלוּיָהּ | הַלְלוּ אֶת־יְהֹוָה מִן־הַשָּׁמַיִם הַלְלוּהוּ בַּמְּרוֹמִים: הַלְלוּהוּ
כָל־מַלְאָכָיו הַלְלוּהוּ כָּל־צְבָאָו: הַלְלוּהוּ שֶׁמֶשׁ וְיָרֵחַ הַלְלוּהוּ
כָּל־כּוֹכְבֵי אוֹר: הַלְלוּהוּ שְׁמֵי הַשָּׁמָיִם וְהַמַּיִם אֲשֶׁר | מֵעַל הַשָּׁמָיִם:
יְהַלְלוּ אֶת־שֵׁם יְהֹוָה כִּי הוּא צִוָּה וְנִבְרָאוּ: וַיַּעֲמִידֵם לָעַד לְעוֹלָם
חָק־נָתַן וְלֹא יַעֲבוֹר:

Halleluyah Halelu Et-Adonai Min-Hashamayim; Halleluhu. Bameromim. Halleluhu Chol-Mal'achav; Halleluhu. Chol-Tzeva'av. Halleluhu Shemesh Veyareach; Halleluhu. Chol-Kochevei Or. Halleluhu Shemei Hashamayim; Vehamayim. Asher Me'al Hashamayim. Yehalelu Et-Shem Adonai Ki Hu Tzivah Venivra'u. Vaya'amidem La'ad Le'olam; Chok-Natan. Velo Ya'avor.

Halleluyah. Praise Hashem from the heavens; Praise Him in the heights. Praise Him, all His angels; Praise Him, all His hosts. Praise Him, sun and moon; Praise Him, all stars of light. Praise Him, heavens of heavens, And waters that are above the heavens. Let them praise the name of Hashem; For He commanded, and they were created. He also established them forever and ever; He made a decree which will not be transgressed. **(Psalms 148:1-6)**

Look upon the moon and recite the verses. When reciting the blessing after, do not look upon the moon.

כִּֽי־אֶרְאֶה שָׁמֶיךָ מַעֲשֵׂה אֶצְבְּעֹתֶיךָ יָרֵחַ וְכוֹכָבִים אֲשֶׁר כּוֹנָֽנְתָּה׃
יְהֹוָה אֲדֹנֵינוּ מָה־אַדִּיר שִׁמְךָ בְּכָל־הָאָֽרֶץ׃

Ki-Er'eh Shameicha Ma'aseh Etzbe'oteicha; Yareach Vechochavim. Asher Konanetah. Adonai Adoneinu; Mah-'Adir Shimcha. Bechol-Ha'aretz.

When I behold Your heavens, the work of Your fingers, The moon and the stars, which You have established; Hashem, our Lord, How glorious is Your name in all of the earth. **(Psalms 8:4, 8:3)**

Some say before the blessing:

לְשֵׁם יִחוּד קוּדְשָׁא בְּרִיךְ הוּא וּשְׁכִינְתֵּיהּ. בִּדְחִילוּ וּרְחִימוּ. וּרְחִימוּ וּדְחִילוּ. לְיַחֲדָא שֵׁם יוֹ״ד קֵ״י בְּוָא״ו קֵ״י בְּיִחוּדָא שְׁלִים (יהוה) בְּשֵׁם כָּל יִשְׂרָאֵל. הנה אנחנו באים לברך ברכת הלבנה כמו שתקנו לנו רבותינו זכרונם לברכה. עם כל־המצות הכלולות בה. לתקן את שורשה במקום עליון. לעשות נחת רוח ליוצרנו ולעשות רצון בוראנו. וִיהִי נֹעַם אֲדֹנָי אֱלֹהֵינוּ עָלֵינוּ וּמַעֲשֵׂה יָדֵינוּ כּוֹנְנָה עָלֵינוּ וּמַעֲשֵׂה יָדֵינוּ כּוֹנְנֵהוּ׃

From this point on one should not look at the moon.

Baruch Attah Adonai Eloheinu	בָּרוּךְ אַתָּה יְהֹוָה אֱלֹהֵינוּ
Melech Ha'olam Asher	מֶלֶךְ הָעוֹלָם. אֲשֶׁר
Bema'amaro Bara Shechakim	בְּמַאֲמָרוֹ בָּרָא שְׁחָקִים
Uveruach Piv Kol Tzeva'am.	וּבְרוּחַ פִּיו כָּל צְבָאָם.
Chok Uzeman Natan Lahem	חֹק וּזְמַן נָתַן לָהֶם
Shelo Yeshanu Et Tafkidam.	שֶׁלֹּא יְשַׁנּוּ אֶת תַּפְקִידָם.
Sasim Usemechim La'asot	שָׂשִׂים וּשְׂמֵחִים לַעֲשׂוֹת
Retzon Koneihem. Po'el Emet	רְצוֹן קוֹנֵיהֶם. פּוֹעֵל
Sheppe'ulato Emet. Velalevanah	אֱמֶת שֶׁפְּעֻלָּתוֹ אֱמֶת. וְלַלְּבָנָה
Amar Shetitchadesh. Ateret	אָמַר שֶׁתִּתְחַדֵּשׁ. עֲטֶרֶת

Tif'eret La'amusei Vaten.	תִּפְאֶרֶת לַעֲמוּסֵי בָטֶן.
Sheggam Hem Atidim	שֶׁגַּם הֵם עֲתִידִים
Lehitchadesh Kemotah Ulefa'er	לְהִתְחַדֵּשׁ כְּמוֹתָהּ וּלְפָאֵר
Leyotzeram Al Shem Kevod	לְיוֹצְרָם עַל שֵׁם כְּבוֹד
Malchuto. Baruch Attah Adonai	מַלְכוּתוֹ. בָּרוּךְ אַתָּה יְהֹוָה
Mechadesh Chadashim.	מְחַדֵּשׁ חֳדָשִׁים:

Blessed are You, Hashem our God, King of the universe, Who with His word You created the heavens, and with a breath from His mouth, all of their hosts. A law and appointed times He gave them, so that they should not deviate from their position. They rejoice and are glad to perform the will of their Creator. The Worker is true, and His work is true. He to the moon he said it should renew her crown of splendor monthly to those brought up from the womb, for they are destined to be renewed like her, to praise their Creator, for the glorious name of His kingdom. Blessed are You, Hashem Who renews the months.

Recite three times:

בְּסִימָן טוֹב תְּהִי לָנוּ וּלְכָל יִשְׂרָאֵל:

Besiman Tov Tehi Lanu Ulechol Yisra'el.

May the new moon herald an auspicious month for us and all Yisrael.

Baruch Yotzerich. Baruch Osich.	בָּרוּךְ יוֹצְרִיךְ. בָּרוּךְ עוֹשִׂיךְ.
Baruch Konich. Baruch Bore'ich.	בָּרוּךְ קוֹנֵיךְ. בָּרוּךְ בּוֹרְאֵיךְ.
Keshem She'anachnu	כְּשֵׁם שֶׁאֲנַחְנוּ
Merakkedim Kenegdich. Ve'ein	מְרַקְּדִים כְּנֶגְדֵּיךְ. וְאֵין
Anachnu Yecholim Liga Bich.	אֲנַחְנוּ יְכוֹלִים לִגַּע בִּיךְ.

Kach Im Yerakedu Acherim	כָּךְ אִם יְרַקְּדוּ אֲחֵרִים
Kenegdenu Lehazikenu. Lo	כְּנֶגְדֵּנוּ לְהַזִּיקֵנוּ. לֹא
Yuchelu Liga Banu. Velo Yishletu	יוּכְלוּ לִגַּע בָּנוּ. וְלֹא יִשְׁלְטוּ
Vanu. Velo Ya'asu Vanu Shum	בָנוּ. וְלֹא יַעֲשׂוּ בָנוּ שׁוּם
Roshem. Tipol Aleihem Eimatah	רֹשֶׁם. תִּפֹּל עֲלֵיהֶם אֵימָתָה
Vafachad. Bigdol Zero'acha	וָפַחַד בִּגְדֹל זְרוֹעֲךָ
Yidemu Ka'aven;. Ka'aven	יִדְּמוּ כָּאָבֶן: כָּאָבֶן
Yidemu. Zero'acha Bigdol.	יִדְּמוּ. זְרוֹעֲךָ בִּגְדֹל.
Vafachad Eimatah Aleihem Tipol.	וָפַחַד אֵימָתָה עֲלֵיהֶם תִּפֹּל:

Blessed is He who formed you, blessed is He Who produced you, blessed is He Who owns you, blessed is He Who created you. Were we with our utmost effort to spring towards the moon, we could not touch it. So, if men have evil intentions towards us, may they not come near to us. "Terror and dread falls upon them; By the greatness of Your arm they are as still as a stone". Even, still as a stone may they be before Your saving power, And may dread and terror fall upon them. **(Exodus 15:16)**

דָּוִד מֶלֶךְ יִשְׂרָאֵל חַי וְקַיָּם. שלש פעמים

David Melech Yisra'el Chai Vekayam.

King David of Yisrael lives forever. (3x)

אָמֵן שלש פעמים נֶצַח שלש פעמים סֶלָה שלש פעמים וָעֶד שלש פעמים

Amen (3X) Netzach (3X) Selah (3X) Va'ed (3X)

לֵב טָהוֹר בְּרָא־לִי אֱלֹהִים וְרוּחַ נָכוֹן חַדֵּשׁ בְּקִרְבִּי: שבע פעמים

Lev Tahor Bera-Li Elohim; Veruach Nachon. Chadesh Bekirbi.

Create me a clean heart, God; and renew a steadfast spirit within me. (7X)

Psalms 121

שִׁיר לַמַּעֲלוֹת אֶשָּׂא עֵינַי אֶל־הֶהָרִים מֵאַיִן יָבֹא עֶזְרִי: עֶזְרִי מֵעִם יְהֹוָה עֹשֵׂה שָׁמַיִם וָאָרֶץ: אַל־יִתֵּן לַמּוֹט רַגְלֶךָ אַל־יָנוּם שֹׁמְרֶךָ: הִנֵּה לֹא־יָנוּם וְלֹא יִישָׁן שׁוֹמֵר יִשְׂרָאֵל: יְהֹוָה שֹׁמְרֶךָ יְהֹוָה צִלְּךָ עַל־יַד יְמִינֶךָ: יוֹמָם הַשֶּׁמֶשׁ לֹא־יַכֶּכָּה וְיָרֵחַ בַּלָּיְלָה: יְהֹוָה יִשְׁמָרְךָ מִכָּל־רָע יִשְׁמֹר אֶת־נַפְשֶׁךָ: יְהֹוָה יִשְׁמָר־צֵאתְךָ וּבוֹאֶךָ מֵעַתָּה וְעַד־עוֹלָם:

Shir. Lamma'alot Essa Einai El-Heharim; Me'ayin. Yavo Ezri. Ezri Me'im Adonai Oseh. Shamayim Va'aretz. Al-Yiten Lamot Raglecha; Al-Yanum. Shomerecha. Hineh Lo-Yanum Velo Yishan; Shomer. Yisra'el. Adonai Shomerecha; Adonai Tzillecha. Al-Yad Yeminecha. Yomam. Hashemesh Lo-Yakekah. Veyareach Balailah. Adonai Yishmorcha Mikol-Ra'; Yishmor. Et-Nafshecha. Adonai Yishmor-Tzetecha Uvo'echa; Me'attah. Ve'ad-'Olam.

A Song of Ascents. I will lift up my eyes to the mountains: From where will my help come? My help comes from Hashem, Who made heaven and earth. He will not suffer Your foot to be moved; He that keeps You will not slumber. Behold, He that keeps Yisrael neither slumbers or sleeps. Hashem is your Guardian; Hashem is Your shade on Your right hand. The sun will not harm you by day, or the moon by night. Hashem will keep you from all evil; He will keep your soul. Hashem will guard your going out and your coming in, From this time and forever.

Psalms 150

הַלְלוּיָהּ ׀ הַלְלוּ־אֵל בְּקׇדְשׁוֹ הַלְלוּהוּ בִּרְקִיעַ עֻזּוֹ: הַלְלוּהוּ בִגְבוּרֹתָיו הַלְלוּהוּ כְּרֹב גֻּדְלוֹ: הַלְלוּהוּ בְּתֵקַע שׁוֹפָר הַלְלוּהוּ בְּנֵבֶל וְכִנּוֹר: הַלְלוּהוּ בְתֹף וּמָחוֹל הַלְלוּהוּ בְּמִנִּים וְעֻגָב: הַלְלוּהוּ בְצִלְצְלֵי־שָׁמַע הַלְלוּהוּ בְּצִלְצְלֵי תְרוּעָה: כֹּל הַנְּשָׁמָה תְּהַלֵּל יָהּ הַלְלוּיָהּ:

Halleluyah Halelu-'El Bekod'sho; Halleluhu. Birkia Uzo. Halleluhu Vigvurotav; Halleluhu. Kerov Gudlo. Halleluhu Beteka Shofar; Halleluhu. Benevel Vechinor. Halleluhu Betof Umachol; Halleluhu. Beminim Ve'ugav. Halleluhu Vetziltzelei-Shama'; Halleluhu. Betziltzelei Teru'ah. Kol Haneshamah Tehallel Yah. Halleluyah. Kol Haneshamah Tehallel Yah. Halleluyah.

Halleluyah. Praise God in His Sanctuary; Praise Him in the firmament of His power. Praise Him for His mighty acts; Praise Him according to His abundant greatness. Praise Him with the blast of the shofar; Praise Him with the psaltery and harp. Praise Him with the timbrel and dance; Praise Him with stringed instruments and the pipe. Praise Him with the loud-sounding cymbals; Praise Him with the clanging cymbals. Let everything that has breath praise Hashem. Halleluyah.

Sanhedrin 42

תָּנָא דְבֵי רִבִּי יִשְׁמָעֵאל אִלְמָלֵי לֹא זָכוּ בְנֵי יִשְׂרָאֵל אֶלָּא לְהַקְבִּיל פְּנֵי אֲבִיהֶם שֶׁבַּשָּׁמַיִם פַּעַם אַחַת בַּחֹדֶשׁ דַּיָּם. אָמַר אַבַּיֵּי. הִלְכָּךְ נֵימְרִינְהוּ מֵעֹמֶד:

Tana Devei Ribi Yishma'el Ilmalei Lo Zachu Venei Yisra'el Ela Lehakbil Penei Avihem Shebashamayim Pa'am Achat Bachodesh Dayam. Amar Abayei Helechach Nimrinhu Me'omed:

In the school of Rabbi Yishmael it was taught: If Yisrael should only have the meritorious act of receiving the glory of their heavenly Father once a month, it would be sufficient. Abayei said: Therefore we must pronounce the above blessing standing.

Some say:

Makkot 23b

רַבִּי חֲנַנְיָא בֶּן־עֲקַשְׁיָא אוֹמֵר: רָצָה הַקָּדוֹשׁ בָּרוּךְ הוּא לְזַכּוֹת אֶת־יִשְׂרָאֵל. לְפִיכָךְ הִרְבָּה לָהֶם תּוֹרָה וּמִצְוֹת. שֶׁנֶּאֱמַר: יְהֹוָה חָפֵץ לְמַעַן צִדְקוֹ יַגְדִּיל תּוֹרָה וְיַאְדִּיר:

Ribi Chananya Ben Akashya Omer: Ratzah Hakadosh Baruch Hu Lezakkot Et Yisra'el. Lefichach Hirbah Lahem Torah Umitzvot. Shene'emar: Adonai Chafetz Lema'an Tzidko Yagdil Torah Veya'dir.

Rabbi Chananya ben Akashya used to say, the Holy One, blessed is He, wishing to make Yisrael more worthy, enlarged for them with Torah and its commandments. For so it is said, "Hashem was pleased, for His righteousness' sake, To make the Torah great and glorious." **(Isaiah 42:21)**

And now say Kaddish Al Yisrael:

Kaddish is only recited in a minyan (ten men). אָמֵן denotes when the congregation responds "Amen" together out loud. According to the Shulchan Arukh, the congregation says "Yehei Shemeh Rabba" to "Yitbarach" out loud together without interruption, and also that one should respond "Amen" after "Yitbarach." (SA, OC 55,56) This is not the common custom today. Though many are accustomed to answering according to their own custom, it is advised to respond in the custom of the one reciting to avoid not fragmenting into smaller groups. ("Lo Titgodedu" - BT, Yevamot 13b / SA, OC 493, Rema / MT, Avodah Zara 12:15)

יִתְגַּדַּל וְיִתְקַדַּשׁ שְׁמֵהּ רַבָּא. אָמֵן בְּעָלְמָא דִּי בְרָא. כִּרְעוּתֵהּ. וְיַמְלִיךְ מַלְכוּתֵהּ. וְיַצְמַח פֻּרְקָנֵהּ. וִיקָרֵב מְשִׁיחֵהּ. אָמֵן בְּחַיֵּיכוֹן וּבְיוֹמֵיכוֹן וּבְחַיֵּי דְכָל בֵּית יִשְׂרָאֵל. בַּעֲגָלָא וּבִזְמַן קָרִיב. וְאִמְרוּ אָמֵן. אָמֵן יְהֵא שְׁמֵיהּ רַבָּא מְבָרַךְ לְעָלַם וּלְעָלְמֵי עָלְמַיָּא יִתְבָּרַךְ. וְיִשְׁתַּבַּח. וְיִתְפָּאַר. וְיִתְרוֹמַם. וְיִתְנַשֵּׂא. וְיִתְהַדָּר. וְיִתְעַלֶּה. וְיִתְהַלָּל שְׁמֵהּ דְּקֻדְשָׁא. בְּרִיךְ הוּא. אָמֵן לְעֵלָּא מִן כָּל בִּרְכָתָא שִׁירָתָא. תֻּשְׁבְּחָתָא וְנֶחֱמָתָא. דַּאֲמִירָן בְּעָלְמָא. וְאִמְרוּ אָמֵן. אָמֵן

Yitgadal Veyitkadash Shemeh Rabba. **Amen** Be'alema Di Vera. Kir'uteh. Veyamlich Malchuteh. Veyatzmach Purkaneh. Vikarev Meshicheh. **Amen** Bechayeichon Uveyomeichon Uvechayei Dechal-Beit Yisra'el. Ba'agala Uvizman Kariv. Ve'imru Amen. **Amen** Yehei Shemeh Rabba Mevarach Le'alam Ule'alemei Alemaya Yitbarach. Veyishtabach. Veyitpa'ar. Veyitromam. Veyitnasse. Veyit'hadar. Veyit'aleh. Veyit'hallal Shemeh Dekudsha. Berich Hu. **Amen** Le'ella Min Kol Birchata Shirata. Tushbechata Venechemata. Da'amiran Be'alema. Ve'imru Amen. **Amen**

Glorified and sanctified be God's great name **Amen** throughout the world which He has created according to His will. May He establish His kingdom, hastening His salvation and the coming of His Messiah, **Amen**, in your lifetime and during your days, and within the life of the entire House of Yisrael, speedily and soon; and say, Amen. **Amen** May His great name be blessed forever and to all eternity.

Blessed and praised, glorified and exalted, extolled and honored, adored and lauded is the name of the Holy One, blessed is He, **Amen** Beyond all the blessings and hymns, praises and consolations that are ever spoken in the world; and say, Amen. **Amen**

עַל יִשְׂרָאֵל וְעַל רַבָּנָן. וְעַל תַּלְמִידֵיהוֹן וְעַל כָּל תַּלְמִידֵי תַלְמִידֵיהוֹן. דְּעָסְקִין בְּאוֹרַיְתָא קַדִּשְׁתָּא. דִּי בְאַתְרָא הָדֵין וְדִי בְכָל אֲתַר וַאֲתַר. יְהֵא לָנָא וּלְהוֹן וּלְכוֹן חִנָּא וְחִסְדָּא וְרַחֲמֵי. מִן קֳדָם מָארֵי שְׁמַיָּא וְאַרְעָא וְאִמְרוּ אָמֵן. אָמֵן

Al Yisra'el Ve'al Rabbanan. Ve'al Talmideihon Ve'al Kol Talmidei Talmideihon. De'asekin Be'orayta Kaddishta. Di Ve'atra Hadein Vedi Vechal Atar Va'atar. Yehei Lana Ulehon Ulechon China Vechisda Verachamei. Min Kodam Marei Shemaya Ve'ar'a Ve'imru Amen. **Amen**

May we of Yisrael together with our rabbis, their disciples and pupils, and all who engage in the study of holy Torah here and everywhere, find gracious favor and mercy from their Father Who is in heaven; and say, Amen. **Amen**

יְהֵא שְׁלָמָא רַבָּא מִן שְׁמַיָּא. חַיִּים וְשָׂבָע וִישׁוּעָה וְנֶחָמָה. וְשֵׁיזָבָא וּרְפוּאָה וּגְאוּלָּה וּסְלִיחָה וְכַפָּרָה וְרֶוַח וְהַצָּלָה לָנוּ וּלְכָל עַמּוֹ יִשְׂרָאֵל. וְאִמְרוּ אָמֵן. אָמֵן

Yehei Shelama Rabba Min Shemaya. Chayim Vesava Vishu'ah Venechamah. Vesheizava Urefu'ah Uge'ulah Uselichah Vechapparah Verevach Vehatzalah Lanu Ulechol Ammo Yisra'el. Ve'imru Amen. **Amen**

May abundant peace descend from heaven, with life and plenty, salvation, solace, liberation, healing and redemption, and forgiveness and atonement, enlargement and freedom, for us and all of God's people Yisrael; and say, Amen. **Amen**

One bows and takes three steps backwards, while still bowing. After three steps, while still bowing and before erecting, while saying, "Oseh Shalom Bimromav", turn one's face to the left, "Hu [Berachamav] Ya'aseh Shalom Aleinu", turn one's face to the right; then bow forward like a servant leaving his master. (SA, OC 123:1)

עוֹשֶׂה שָׁלוֹם בִּמְרוֹמָיו. הוּא בְּרַחֲמָיו יַעֲשֶׂה שָׁלוֹם עָלֵינוּ. וְעַל כָּל־עַמּוֹ יִשְׂרָאֵל. וְאִמְרוּ אָמֵן:

Oseh Shalom Bimromav. Hu Berachamav Ya'aseh Shalom Aleinu. Ve'al Kol-'Ammo Yisra'el. Ve'imru Amen.

Creator of peace in His high places, may He in His mercy create peace for us and for all Yisrael, and say Amen.

After Kaddish some say:

וְהָיָה אוֹר־הַלְּבָנָה כְּאוֹר הַחַמָּה וְאוֹר הַחַמָּה יִהְיֶה שִׁבְעָתַיִם כְּאוֹר שִׁבְעַת הַיָּמִים בְּיוֹם חֲבֹשׁ יְהֹוָה אֶת־שֶׁבֶר עַמּוֹ וּמַחַץ מַכָּתוֹ יִרְפָּא: וַתַּעְדִּי זָהָב וָכֶסֶף וּמַלְבּוּשֵׁךְ ששי (שֵׁשׁ) וָמֶשִׁי וְרִקְמָה סֹלֶת וּדְבַשׁ וָשֶׁמֶן אכלתי (אָכָלְתְּ) וַתִּיפִי בִּמְאֹד מְאֹד וַתִּצְלְחִי לִמְלוּכָה:

Vehayah Or-Halevanah Ke'or Hachamah. Ve'or Hachamah Yihyeh Shiv'atayim. Ke'or Shiv'at Hayamim; Beyom. Chavosh Adonai Et-Shever Ammo. Umachatz Makato Yirpa. Vata'di Zahav Vachesef. Umalbushech Shesh Vameshi Verikmah. Solet Udevash Vashemen Chlt Vatifi Bim'od Me'od. Vatitzlechi Limluchah.

Moreover the light of the moon will be as the light of the sun, And the light of the sun will be sevenfold, as the light of the seven days, In the day that Hashem binds up the bruise of His people, And heals the stroke of their wound. So were you decked with gold and silver; and your raiment was of fine linen, and silk, and richly woven work; you ate fine flour, and honey, and oil; and you did turn exceeding beautiful, and you attained royal estate. **(Isaiah 30:26, Ezekiel 16:13)**

ואומרים שלש פעמים: שָׁלוֹם עֲלֵיכֶם.

Shalom Aleichem. (say three times)

Peace be with you. (say three times)

SEDER ARBA TA'ANIYOT / ORDER OF FOUR FAST DAYS

סדר ארבע תעניות

On all of these days, all Yisrael fasts because of the misfortunes that befell them on these days, in order to arouse their hearts to open up to the paths of teshuvah [repentance]. This will be a recollection of our evil deeds and the deeds of our fathers [ancestors] which were like our deeds now, such that they caused them and us these misfortunes, and in the recollection of these things we will return to become better, as it is written (Lev. 26:40), "And they shall confess their iniquity, and the iniquity of their fathers..." Therefore, each person is obliged to take to heart on these days to examine their deeds and to repent of them, because the fast is not the essential [thing], as it is written about the people of Nineveh: "And God saw their works, that they turned from their evil way..." (Jonah 3:10) The Sages, may their memories be blessed, said that their sackcloth and their fasting were not mentioned, just their deeds. Fasting is nothing but a preparation for repentance. (MB, 549)

We are required to fast on the 9th of Av (Tisha B'Av), the 17th of Tammuz (Fast of Tammuz), the 3rd of Tishrei (Fast of Gedalyah), and on the 10th of Tevet because of the bad things that happened on them. (SA, OC 549) These correspond to the fast of the fourth (Tammuz), fifth (Av), seventh (Tishrei), and the tenth (Tevet) months. (Zech. 8:19) One is obligated to fast on these days, though some choose to be very lenient according the Rema in the Shulchan Arukh and Talmud Bavli, Rosh Hashanah 18b, though one is obligated to complete the fast on the 9th of Av. We also fast on the 13th of Adar (Fast of Esther). And if Purim falls on Sunday, we start the fast on Thursday. The Fast of Esther is not required, and one can be lenient for the time of the fast. (SA, OC 686:2, Rema) These fasts except for Tisha B'Av one is allowed to wash, anoint, wear shoes, and have marital relations. And they are minor fasts (sunup to sundown). (SA, OC 550) Tisha B'Av is a full fast from sundown to sundown like Yom Kippur. All fasts must be continued till sundown until the appearance of three stars in a row, or when the moon shines strong. (SA, OC 562:1)

Tenth of Tevet

After the repetition of the Amidah, say Vidui. Then say:

Va'aretz Shafal Rumi. Vegadal	וָאֶרֶץ שָׁפַל רוּמִי. וְגָדַל
Shivri. Meshomem Eshev. Yom	שִׁבְרִי. מְשׁוֹמֵם אֵשֵׁב. יוֹם
Samach Ha'ari. Al Tzevi Har	סָמַךְ הָאֲרִי. עַל צְבִי הַר
Kodesh Tziyon Iri. Lachen	קֹדֶשׁ צִיּוֹן עִירִי. לָכֵן
Akonen Ve'et'abel Bachodesh	אֲקוֹנֵן וְאֶתְאַבֵּל בַּחֹדֶשׁ
Ha'asiri: Bachodesh Ha'asiri	הָעֲשִׂירִי: בַּחֹדֶשׁ הָעֲשִׂירִי
Aryeh Alah Vechemah. Be'asor	אַרְיֵה עָלָה בְחֵמָה.
Lachodesh Banah Alai Chomah.	בֶּעָשׂוֹר לַחֹדֶשׁ בָּנָה עָלַי חוֹמָה.
Gash Hu Vechol Ammo La'asot	גָּשׁ הוּא וְכָל־עַמּוֹ לַעֲשׂוֹת

Be'ammi Nekamah. Vaya'archu	בְּעַמִּי נְקָמָה. וַיַּעַרְכוּ
Ittam Milchamah: Milchamah	אִתָּם מִלְחָמָה: מִלְחָמָה
Shit Misgabbi Umoshi'i. Be'oyevi	שִׁית מִשְׂגַּבִּי וּמוֹשִׁיעִי. בְּאוֹיְבִי
Umachni'i. Kos Male Mesech	וּמַכְנִיעִי. כּוֹס מָלֵא מֶסֶךְ
Hashkem Adonai Ro'i. Maggini	הַשְׁקֵם יְהֹוָה רוֹעִי. מָגִנִּי
Vekeren Yish'i:	וְקֶרֶן יִשְׁעִי:

My greatness is cast down to the earth; and my calamity is great. I will sit astonished on the day that the lion laid siege to the glorious holy mountain, Tziyon my city: Therefore, I will mourn and lament on the tenth month. In the tenth month, the lion came up in fury; on the tenth day of the month, he erected a battery against me. When he and all his host drew near to take vengeance on my people; and put themselves in battle array against them. You, Who are my Strength and my Savior, appoint war for my enemies, and those who have subdued me. Cause them to drink the cup full of mingled woes, Hashem, Who is my Shepherd, my Shield, and the Horn of my salvation.

Bachodesh Ha'asiri Delakani	בַּחֹדֶשׁ הָעֲשִׂירִי דְּלָקַנִי
Oyev Bacherev. Be'asor	אוֹיֵב בַּחֶרֶב. בֶּעָשׂוֹר
Lachodesh Hechin Alai Orev.	לַחֹדֶשׁ הֵכִין עָלַי אוֹרֵב.
Ve'al Zot Akonen Vegili Arev. Oy	וְעַל זֹאת אֲקוֹנֵן וְגִילִי עָרֵב. אוֹי
Lanu Ki Fanah Hayom. Ki Yinatu	לָנוּ כִּי פָנָה הַיּוֹם. כִּי יִנָּטוּ
Tzilei Arev: Erev Yehafech	צִלְלֵי־עָרֶב: עֶרֶב יֵהָפֵךְ
Levoker Uvogedim Al Ya'alu Al.	לְבֹקֶר וּבוֹגְדִים אַל יַעֲלוּ עָל.
Chon Al Ammecha Velich'evam	חֹן עַל עַמְּךָ וְלִכְאֵבָם
Ha'aleh Ta'al. Zechor Li Berit	הַעֲלֵה תַעַל. זְכֹר־לִי בְּרִית
Avot. Beparesi Lecha Kaf	אָבוֹת. בְּפָרְשִׂי לְךָ כַּף

Vesha'al. Memit Umechayeh.	וְשַׁעַל. מֵמִית וּמְחַיֶּה.
Morid She'ol Vaya'al:	מוֹרִיד שְׁאוֹל וַיָּעַל:

In the tenth month, the enemy pursued me with the sword on the tenth day of the month, he waited in ambush against me; for which I lament, and my joy is darkened. Woe to us, for the day of our prosperity has passed away; already the blighting shadows of the evening are around. Grant, Hashem, that the evening be changed to morning; and do not allow those who deal treacherously to be exalted; be gracious to Your people, and send healing to their suffering; remember also to me the covenant of our ancestors; when I spread out, imploringly, my hands to You, Who kills and restores to life; Who casts down to the grave and brings up.

Bachodesh Ha'asiri Ze'ev	בַּחֹדֶשׁ הָעֲשִׂירִי זְאֵב
Aravot Al Ammi Nohem.	עֲרָבוֹת עַל עַמִּי נוֹהֵם.
Be'asor Lachodesh. Tarof Toraf	בֶּעָשׂוֹר לַחֹדֶשׁ. טָרֹף טֹרַף
Kol Hayotze Mehem. Namer	כָּל־הַיּוֹצֵא מֵהֶם. נָמֵר
Shoked Al Areihem: Areihem	שֹׁקֵד עַל עָרֵיהֶם: עָרֵיהֶם
Sarefu Va'esh Birvot Tela'ot.	שָׂרְפוּ בָאֵשׁ בְּרִבּוֹת תְּלָאוֹת.
Rumah Adonai Be'uzecha	רוּמָה יְהוָֹה בְּעֻזֶּךָ
Zeidim Lehash'ot. Bosh Yevoshu	זֵדִים לְהַשְׁאוֹת. בּוֹשׁ יֵבוֹשׁוּ
Ba'asotecha Imanu Letovah Ot.	בַּעֲשׂוֹתְךָ עִמָּנוּ לְטוֹבָה אוֹת.
Kedosh Yisra'el Adonai Tzeva'ot:	קְדוֹשׁ יִשְׂרָאֵל יְהוָֹה צְבָאוֹת:

In the tenth month, the wolf of the desert roared against my people; on the tenth day of the month all their descendants were torn by the leopard that watched their cities. Their cities the enemies burnt with fire, as their troubles increased; exalt Yourself, therefore, in Your strength, Hashem, to destroy the proud. Let them be ashamed and confounded when You show us a sign for good, Holy One of Yisrael, Hashem of Hosts.

Bachodesh Ha'asiri Yedei Tzar	בַּחֹדֶשׁ הָעֲשִׂירִי יְדֵי צַר
Hecheziku Magen Vetzinah.	הֶחֱזִיקוּ מָגֵן וְצִנָּה.
Be'asor Lachodesh Ke'ish Aruch	בֶּעָשׂוֹר לַחֹדֶשׁ כְּאִישׁ עָרוּךְ
Lammilchamah Al Kiryah	לַמִּלְחָמָה עַל קִרְיָה
Ne'emanah. Lezot Chigri Sak	נֶאֱמָנָה. לְזֹאת חִגְרִי שַׂק
Edah Adinah. Gazi Nizrech	עֵדָה עֲדִינָה. גָּזִּי נִזְרֵךְ
Vehashlichi. Use'i Al Shefayim	וְהַשְׁלִיכִי. וּשְׂאִי עַל שְׁפָיִם
Kinah: Kinah Dover Ammecha	קִינָה: קִינָה דוֹבֵר עַמְּךָ
Beyom Zeh Le'ummatecha.	בְּיוֹם זֶה לְאֻמָּתֶךָ.
Ve'af'apeinu Yizelu Mayim Al	וְעַפְעַפֵּינוּ יִזְּלוּ מַיִם עַל
Chareban Beitecha. Yom Nakam	חָרְבַּן בֵּיתֶךָ. יוֹם נָקָם תָּעִיר
Ta'ir Letzarim Homim	לְצָרִים הוֹמִים
Beveitecha. Deracheicha	בְּבֵיתֶךָ. דְּרָכֶיךָ
Adonai Hodi'eni Velamedeni	יְהֹוָה הוֹדִיעֵנִי וְלַמְּדֵנִי
Orechoteicha:	אוֹרְחוֹתֶיךָ:

In the tenth month, they grasped the shield and the buckler, and on the tenth day of the month drew near to the faithful city as a man prepared for war. For this, put on sackcloth you pleasant congregation; cut off your hair, and cast it away, and take up lamentation on the high places. Loudly now, Hashem, Your people utter laments before You. Our eyelids also gush water, for the destruction of Your Habitation. Call up the day of vengeance to the adversaries who raged in Your House; and me instruct in Your ways, Hashem, and teach me Your paths.

Bachodesh Ha'asiri Monai	בַּחֹדֶשׁ הָעֲשִׂירִי מֹנַי
Shafechu Al Iri Solelah. Be'asor	שָׁפְכוּ עַל עִירִי סוֹלְלָה. בֶּעָשׂוֹר
Lachodesh Nizri Hashlach	לַחֹדֶשׁ נִזְרִי הֻשְׁלַךְ
Vetif'arti Nafelah. Sevavuni	וְתִפְאַרְתִּי נָפְלָה. סְבָבוּנִי
Ha'osim Makati Nachlah. Me'ai	הָעֹשִׂים מַכָּתִי נַחְלָה. מֵעַי
Me'ai Ochilah: Ochilah Yom	מֵעַי אוֹחִילָה: אוֹחִילָה יוֹם
Zeh Lena'aratz Besod Kedoshim	זֶה לְנַעֲרָץ בְּסוֹד קְדוֹשִׁים
Rabah. Va'achaleh Fanav	רַבָּה. וַאֲחַלֶּה פָּנָיו
La'avor Al Pesha Vechovah. Al	לַעֲבֹר עַל פֶּשַׁע וְחוֹבָה. אַל
Tefen Lerish'enu Umecheh	תֵּפֶן לְרִשְׁעֵנוּ וּמְחֵה
Chatat Ketuvah. Hashiveinu	חַטָּאת כְּתוּבָה. הֲשִׁיבֵנוּ
Adonai Eleicha Venashuvah:	יְהֹוָה אֵלֶיךָ וְנָשׁוּבָה:

In the tenth month, my oppressors cast up a mound against my city; on the tenth day of the month, my crown was cast down, and my glory fell; those who struck me with grievous wounds, encircled me around: My bowels, My bowels, I tremble of grief. I will hope this day to Him Who is reverenced in the great assembly of the holy-ones, and petition his favor to pass by our transgression and guilt: do not look, Hashem, to our wickedness, but blot out our sin which is written before You; and cause us to return, Hashem, to You, and we will return.

Al Yedei Rachameicha Harabbim	עַל יְדֵי רַחֲמֶיךָ הָרַבִּים
Selach Lanu Avinu. Ki Verov	סְלַח לָנוּ אָבִינוּ. כִּי בְרוֹב
Ivaltenu Shaginu: Mechol Lanu	אִוַּלְתֵּנוּ שָׁגִינוּ: מְחֹל לָנוּ
Malkeinu. Ki Rabbu Avoneinu: El	מַלְכֵּנוּ. כִּי רַבּוּ עֲוֹנֵינוּ: אֵל
Erech Apayim Attah. Vederech	אֶרֶךְ אַפַּיִם אַתָּה. וְדֶרֶךְ

Teshuvah Lanu Horeita: Gedulat	תְּשׁוּבָה לָנוּ הוֹרֵיתָ: גְּדֻלַּת
Rachameicha Vachasadeicha.	רַחֲמֶיךָ וַחֲסָדֶיךָ.
Tizkor Hayom Lezera Yedideicha:	תִּזְכּוֹר הַיּוֹם לְזֶרַע יְדִידֶיךָ:
Tefen Eleinu Berachamim. Ki	תֵּפֶן אֵלֵינוּ בְּרַחֲמִים. כִּי
Attah Hu Ba'al Harachamim:	אַתָּה הוּא בַּעַל הָרַחֲמִים:
Betachanun Uvitfillah Nekadem.	בְּתַחֲנוּן וּבִתְפִלָּה נְקַדֵּם.
Kemo Shehoda'ta Le'anav	כְּמוֹ שֶׁהוֹדַעְתָּ לֶעָנָו
Mikedem: Umecharon Apecha	מִקֶּדֶם: וּמֵחֲרוֹן אַפְּךָ
Tashuv. Kemo Betoratecha Katuv.	תָּשׁוּב. כְּמוֹ בְּתוֹרָתְךָ כָּתוּב.
Uvetzel Kenafeicha Necheseh	וּבְצֵל כְּנָפֶיךָ נֶחֱסֶה
Venitlonan. Keyom Vayered	וְנִתְלוֹנָן. כְּיוֹם וַיֵּרֶד
Adonai Be'anan: Ta'avor Al	יְהֹוָה בֶּעָנָן: תַּעֲבֹר עַל
Pesha Vetimchol Asham. Keyom	פֶּשַׁע וְתִמְחֹל אָשָׁם. כְּיוֹם
Vayityatzev Imo Sham: Ta'azin	וַיִּתְיַצֵּב עִמּוֹ שָׁם: תַּאֲזִין
Sheva Vetakeshiv Beratzon	שֶׁוַע וְתַקְשִׁיב בְּרָצוֹן
Ma'amar. Keyom Vayikra Veshem	מַאֲמָר. כְּיוֹם וַיִּקְרָא בְשֵׁם
Adonai: Vesham Ne'emar:	יְהֹוָה: וְשָׁם נֶאֱמַר:

Through Your unbounded mercies forgive us, our Father, for in the greatness of our foolishness have we erred. Pardon us, our King, for our iniquities are many. Oh God, You are long-suffering, and have shown us the way of repentance. Remember this day the greatness of Your mercy and kindness, to the posterity of Your beloved; and turn to us with mercy, for You are the Master of mercy. With supplication and prayer we appear before You, as You made known to the humble one of old (Moshe). Turn from Your fierce anger, as it is written in Your Torah; so that we may take refuge and abide under the shadow of Your wings, as at the day, of which it was said, "Hashem descended in the cloud." Pass by our transgression, and pardon our trespass, as on the day, of which it was said, "He stood with him there," Hear our cry, and heed favorably to our speech, as on the day of which it was said, "He proclaimed the name of Hashem." And there it is said:

[*] denotes a slight pause between words:

וַיַּעֲבֹר יְהוָה | עַל־פָּנָיו וַיִּקְרָא יְהוָה * יְהוָה אֵל רַחוּם וְחַנּוּן אֶרֶךְ אַפַּיִם וְרַב־חֶסֶד וֶאֱמֶת׃ נֹצֵר חֶסֶד לָאֲלָפִים נֹשֵׂא עָוֺן וָפֶשַׁע וְחַטָּאָה וְנַקֵּה׃

Vaya'avor Adonai 'Al-Panav Vayikra Adonai * Adonai El Rachum Vechanun; Erech Apayim Verav-Chesed Ve'emet. Notzer Chesed La'alafim. Nosei Avon Vafesha Vechata'ah; Venakeh.

And Hashem passed by before him, and proclaimed: 'Hashem * Hashem, God, merciful and gracious, long-suffering, and abundant in goodness and truth; keeping mercy to the thousandth generation, forgiving iniquity and transgression and sin, and clearing (those who repent).

Az Bevo Yom Pekudat Gei	אָז בְּבוֹא יוֹם פְּקֻדַּת גֵּיא
Hamachazeh. Bacharot Af	הַמַּחֲזֶה. בַּחֲרוֹת אַף
Adonai Berishpei Azeh. Gillah	יְהוָה בְּרִשְׁפֵּי אַזֶּה. גִּלָּה
Beyad Ben Buzi Hachozeh:	בְּיַד בֶּן־בּוּזִי הַחוֹזֶה:
Ketov Lecha Et Shem Hayom Et	כְּתוֹב־לְךָ אֶת־שֵׁם הַיּוֹם אֶת־
Etzem Hayom Hazeh: Dibarti	עֶצֶם הַיּוֹם הַזֶּה: דִּבַּרְתִּי
Be'esh Kin'ati Beit Meri Lispot.	בְּאֵשׁ קִנְאָתִי בֵּית מְרִי לִסְפּוֹת.
Hini Eleiha Be'af Veruach	הִנְנִי אֵלֶיהָ בְּאַף וְרוּחַ
Zil'afot: Vesamtiha Lemashal	זִלְעָפוֹת: וְשַׂמְתִּיהָ לְמָשָׁל
Velishninah Velacharafot. Shefot	וְלִשְׁנִינָה וְלַחֲרָפוֹת. שְׁפֹת
Hassir Shefot: Zal'afah Achazah	הַסִּיר שְׁפֹת: זַלְעָפָה אֲחָזָה

Tziyon Veheichaleiha. Charedah	צִיּוֹן וְהֵיכָלֶיהָ. חֲרֵדָה
Ruchah Namogu Chayaleiha.	רוּחָהּ נָמוֹגוּ חֲיָלֶיהָ.
Toraf Libah Et Kero Eleiha. Esof	טֹרַף לִבָּהּ עֵת קְרֹא אֵלֶיהָ. אֱסֹף
Netacheiha Eleiha: Yeriveiha	נְתָחֶיהָ אֵלֶיהָ: יְרִיבֶיהָ
A'anik Shevi Umalkoach.	אַעֲנִיק שְׁבִי וּמַלְקֹחַ.
Kohaneiha Umerkacheiha Asher	כֹּהֲנֶיהָ וּמְרַקְחֶיהָ אֲשֶׁר
Rakechah Rakoach. Lishvi Olam	רֶקְחָה רָקֹחַ. לִשְׁבִי עוֹלָם
Me'ein Pekach Koach. Mivchar	מֵאֵין פְּקַח קֹחַ. מִבְחַר
Hatzon Lakoach: Mashelu Vach	הַצֹּאן לָקוֹחַ: מָשְׁלוּ בָךְ
La'agu Moshelet Ammim. Nikret	לָעֲגוּ מוֹשֶׁלֶת עַמִּים. נִקְרֵאת
Az Noda'at. Me'usat Olamim.	אָז נוֹדַעַתְ. מְאוּסַת עוֹלָמִים.
Sotenim Ya'anu Vach Ve'alayich	שׁוֹטְנִים יַעֲנוּ בָךְ וְעָלַיִךְ
No'amim. Oy Ir Hadamim:	נוֹאֲמִים. אוֹי עִיר הַדָּמִים:
Averah Averah Sarah Heferah	עָבְרָה עֲבֵרָה סָרָה הֵפֵרָה
Berit Yah. Pashe'ah Rashe'ah	בְּרִית יָהּ. פָּשְׁעָה רָשְׁעָה
Tave'ah Bevor Tachtiyah.	טָבְעָה בְּבוֹר תַּחְתִּיָּה.
Tza'akah Velo Shama El Bichyah.	צָעֲקָה וְלֹא שָׁמַע אֶל בִּכְיָהּ.
Ki Damah Betochah Hayah: Kol	כִּי דָמָהּ בְּתוֹכָהּ הָיָה: קוֹל
Ashukeiha Shema Miyad	עֲשׁוּקֶיהָ שְׁמַע מִיַּד
Oshekam. Rigshatam	עוֹשְׁקָם. רִגְשָׁתָם
Vetzavchatam Lo Tashiv Reikam.	וְצַוְחָתָם לֹא תָשִׁיב רֵיקָם.
Shiv'atayim Teshalem Kefo'olam	שִׁבְעָתַיִם תְּשַׁלֵּם כְּפָעֳלָם
El Cheikam. Sheva Yippol	אֶל חֵיקָם. שֶׁבַע | יִפּוֹל
Tzaddik Vakam: Ta'inu	צַדִּיק וָקָם: תָּעִינוּ
Verish'enu El Gadol Venora.	בְרִשְׁעֵנוּ אֵל גָּדוֹל וְנוֹרָא.
Ve'im Gaveru Fesha'einu	וְאִם גָּבְרוּ פְשָׁעֵינוּ

Chemlatecha Gaverah. Richamta	חֶמְלָתְךָ גָּבְרָה. רִחַמְתָּ
Vechim'at Kat Killitam Be'evrah.	וְכִמְעַט קָט כִּלִּיתָם בְּעֶבְרָה.
Tzarah Veyagon Emtza. Uveshem	צָרָה וְיָגוֹן אֶמְצָא. וּבְשֵׁם־
Adonai Ekra: Yehemu	יְהוָה אֶקְרָא: יֶהֱמוּ
Rachameicha Al Me'utei	רַחֲמֶיךָ עַל מְעוּטֵי
Ammim. Vesagevem	עַמִּים. וְשַׂגְּבֵם
Bechasdecha. Le'einei Chol	בְּחַסְדְּךָ. לְעֵינֵי כָל־
Le'ummim. Pela'eicha Har'em	לְאֻמִּים. פְּלָאֶיךָ הַרְאֵם
Tzur Shochen Meromim. El	צוּר שׁוֹכֵן מְרוֹמִים. אֵל
Melech Yoshev Al Kisse	מֶלֶךְ יוֹשֵׁב עַל כִּסֵּא
Rachamim:	רַחֲמִים:

At the time the day had arrived to fulfill the threatened prophecy, when the anger of Hashem was kindled against us like glowing fire: he revealed it through the son of Buzi the seer, saying, "Write down the name of this day, even of this same day." "For I have spoken in the fire of my indignation to destroy the rebellious family; behold, I am against them with wrath and scorching wind, and will make them a proverb, an example and rebuke; 'Set on the pot, set it on.' (Ez.24:3) Terror seizes on Tziyon and her palaces; her spirit is terrified, her armies become faint-hearted; anxiety rends her heart, when they call to her, "Gather the pieces of it into it." Those who can contend against her, I will load with captives and spoil; her priests and the incense which she has compounded will be carried into long-enduring captivity, with no one to give them freedom. "Yes, take the choice of the flock." Strangers ruled then over you, they scorned you, that once was the ruler of nations; they called you. You were known as the rejected for everlasting. The adversaries testified against you, and concerning you exclaimed, "Woe, you city of blood!" Yes she has sinned, she turned from righteousness, she broke the covenant of Hashem; she transgressed, did wickedly, and sank into the deepest pit of guilt. She cried, but God did not hear her weeping, "For her blood was in the midst of her." (Ez. 24:7) Yet, Hashem, hear the voice of her oppressed ones from under the power of their oppressors; their earnest petition and their complaint dismiss not unanswered; and cause the righteous to rise, though he falls seven times. We indeed have erred in our wickedness, Oh great and awesome God, and though our transgressions be great, yet greater is Your compassion. Have mercy, or else in a brief time You would totally destroy us in Your wrath; although we are entangled in sorrow and trouble we will call on Your name, Hashem. Let Your mercies be moved to the people smallest of nations; strengthen them in Your kindness, before the eyes of all the people; and show them Your wonders, You Who dwells on high, omnipotent King, Who sits on the Throne of mercy.

She'eh Elyon. Lekol Evyon.	שְׁעֵה עֶלְיוֹן. לְקוֹל אֶבְיוֹן.
Veshav'ato Al Tivzeh: Levavo	וְשַׁוְעָתוֹ אַל תִּבְזֶה: לְבָבוֹ
Mar. Beyom Ne'emar. Leven	מַר. בְּיוֹם נֶאֱמַר. לְבֶן
Buzi Hachozeh: Ketov Lecha Et	בּוּזִי הַחוֹזֶה: כְּתָוב־לְךָ אֶת־
Shem Hayom Et Etzem Hayom	שֵׁם הַיּוֹם אֶת־עֶצֶם הַיּוֹם
Hazeh: Yah Tzeva'ot. Zechor	הַזֶּה: יָהּ צְבָאוֹת. זְכוֹר
Tela'ot. Asher Tzar Li Mod	תְּלָאוֹת. אֲשֶׁר צַר לִי מְאֹד
Aleihen: Bemazal Gedi. Halo	עֲלֵיהֶן: בְּמַזַּל גְּדִי. הֲלֹא
Va'adi. Ne'esfu Shelosheteihen:	בַעֲדִי. נֶאֶסְפוּ שְׁלֹשְׁתֵּיהֶן:
Uvo Seyot. Haddechuyot. Chal	וּבוֹ שֵׂיוֹת. הַדְּחוּיוֹת. חַל
Hanegef Bahen: Uvo Samach.	הַנֶּגֶף בָּהֶן: וּבוֹ סָמַךְ.
Mena'etz Shemach. Al Kiryat	מְנָאֵץ שְׁמָךְ. עַל קִרְיַת
Mesoseihen: Uvo Ne'esaf Rosh	מְשׂוֹשֵׂיהֶן: וּבוֹ נֶאֱסַף רֹאשׁ

Hassaf. Hu Ezra Hakohen: Kol	הַסָּף. הוּא עֶזְרָא הַכֹּהֵן: כָּל־
Eleh. Kera'uni Verabot Kazeh	אֵלֶּה. קְרָאוּנִי וְרַבּוֹת כָּזֶה
Vechazeh: Ari Alaz. Beyom	וְכָזֶה: אֲרִי עָלַז. בְּיוֹם
Hallaz. Vechetz Kilkel Lemul Iri:	הַלָּז. וְחֵץ קִלְקֵל לְמוּל עִירִי:
Vekam Asiri. Ba'asiri. Leshachet	וְקָם עֲשִׂירִי. בָּעֲשִׂירִי. לְשַׁחֵת
Kol She'ar Ha'asiri: Le'abed	כָּל־שְׁאָר הָעֲשִׂירִי: לְאַבֵּד
Koal. Peri Eshkol. Velilkot Inevei	כָּל. פְּרִי אֶשְׁכֹּל. וְלִלְקוֹט עִנְּבֵי
Neziri: Ve'od Kashur. Ani	נְזִירִי: וְעוֹד קָשׁוּר. אֲנִי
Le'ashur. Asher Nitzav Al Tziri:	לְאַשּׁוּר. אֲשֶׁר נִצָּב עַל צִירִי:
Ani Nigda. Velo Eda. Lemi Evkeh	אֲנִי נִגְדָּע. וְלֹא אֵדַע. לְמִי אֶבְכֶּה
Hazeh O Zeh: Semoch Amach.	הֲזֶה אוֹ זֶה: סְמֹךְ עַמָּךְ.
Beyom Samach. Ari Al Ir Tzevi	בְּיוֹם סָמַךְ. אֲרִי עַל עִיר צְבִי
Kodesh: She'eh Shav'am.	קֹדֶשׁ: שְׁעֵה שַׁוְעָם.
Mecheh Fish'am. Be'asor	מְחֵה פִשְׁעָם. בֶּעָשׂוֹר
Lachodesh: Vehameluchah.	לַחֹדֶשׁ: וְהַמְּלוּכָה.
Hanesuchah. Kimei Kedem	הַנְּסוּכָה. כִּימֵי קֶדֶם
Chadesh: Velithillah.	חַדֵּשׁ: וְלִתְהִלָּה.
Kevatechillah. Shimcha Yah Banu	כְּבַתְּחִלָּה. שִׁמְךָ יָהּ בָּנוּ
Kadesh: Vechol Sone.	קַדֵּשׁ: וְכָל־שׂוֹנֵא.
Umit'aneh. Be'oz Apecha	וּמִתְאַנֶּה. בְּעֹז אַפְּךָ
Hadesh: Veyillachedu. Veyovdu.	הָדֵשׁ: וְיִלָּכְדוּ. וְיֹאבְדוּ.
Keyom Barak Be'ir Kedesh:	כְּיוֹם בָּרָק בְּעִיר קֶדֶשׁ:
Veshuv Elyon. Le'ir Tziyon. Ayin	וְשׁוּב עֶלְיוֹן. לְעִיר צִיּוֹן. עַיִן
Be'ayin Nechezeh: Ve'az Nomar.	בְּעַיִן נֶחֱזֶה: וְאָז נֹאמַר.
Betuv Ma'amar. Hineh Eloheinu	בְּטוּב מַאֲמָר. הִנֵּה אֱלֹהֵינוּ
Zeh:	זֶה:

Have regard, Most High God, to the voice of the needy, and do not despise his prayer; for anguish seized his heart on the day when it was said to the son of Buzi, the seer, "Write down the name of this day, even of this same day." Hashem of Hosts, remember the three troubles, concerning which I am so severly grieved; which, under the rule of the mazal (constellation) of Gedi, overcome me; for on it the scattered flock fell prey to the pestilence; on it he who blasphemed Your name laid siege to the city of their joy; and there on it too was gathered to his fathers the chief of the guards of Your House, namely, Ezra the Kohen. All these evils befell me, and many more like them, oh the day of which it was said, "Write down the name of this day, even of this same day." The lion rejoiced in his triumph on this day, and shot off his arrows against my city; he rose on the tenth of the tenth month to root out the whole sacred remnant; to destroy as it were all the clustering fruit of the vineyard, and to gather up all the choice grapes; even while I was yet subject to Assyria, who stood ready to oppress me; I was indeed cut down, and I don't know for which calamity I should weep; yes, woeful was the time, when it was said, "Write down the name of this day, even of this same day." Support Your people, God, on the day the lion besieged the holy city; regard their prayer, and wipe out their guilt, on the tenth of the month; also the kingdom, that is now eclipsed, renew as in former days; and let Your name, Hashem, be praised and sanctified among us as in the beginning; subdue in the strength of Your wrath all that hate or wish to injure us; and let them be overcome and lost, as was Sisera on the day of Barak's victory. Then let us see You face to face, Most High, at Your return to Tziyon's city; and then we will say in our grateful praise, "Behold, this is our God."

Yoshev Bashamayim. She'eh	יוֹשֵׁב בַּשָּׁמַיִם. שְׁעֵה
Ba'ei Va'esh Uvammayim:	בָּאֵי בָאֵשׁ וּבַמָּיִם:

Vechon Al Am Asher Laku.	וְחֹן עַל עַם אֲשֶׁר לָקוּ.
Vechatotam Kiflayim: Beyom	בְּחַטֹּאתָם כִּפְלָיִם: בְּיוֹם
Hechel Tzar Latzur Mecholat	הֵחֵל צַר לָצוּר מְחוֹלַת
Machanayim. Samach Melech	מַחֲנָיִם. סָמַךְ מֶלֶךְ
Bavel El Yerushalayim: Ha'oneh	בָּבֶל אֶל יְרוּשָׁלָיִם: הָעוֹנֶה
Bammetzar. Enut Ani Al Tivzeh:	בַּמֵּצַר. עֱנוּת עָנִי אַל תִּבְזֶה:
Beyom Tzom Ha'asiri. Enutenu	בְּיוֹם צוֹם הָעֲשִׂירִי. עֱנוּתֵנוּ
Techezeh: Yom Hizharta	תֶּחֱזֶה: יוֹם הִזְהַרְתָּ
Bamachazeh. Leven Buzi	בַּמַּחֲזֶה. לְבֶן־בּוּזִי
Hachozeh: Ketov Lecha Et Shem	הַחוֹזֶה: כְּתוֹב־לְךָ אֶת־שֵׁם
Hayom Et Etzem Hayom Hazeh:	הַיּוֹם אֶת־עֶצֶם הַיּוֹם הַזֶּה:
Yom Bo Shakad Shachal.	יוֹם בּוֹ שָׁקַד שַׁחַל.
Venamer Al Delatayim: Yom	וְנָמֵר עַל דְּלָתָיִם: יוֹם
Samechu Al Armon Nachalat	סָמְכוּ עַל אַרְמוֹן נַחֲלַת
Tzevi Vashefer. Uvo Huchal	צְבִי וָשֶׁפֶר. וּבוֹ הוּחַל
Hanegef Bemachpishei Ba'efer:	הַנֶּגֶף בְּמַכְפִּישֵׁי בָּאֵפֶר:
Vegam Bo Ne'esaf. Ezra	וְגַם בּוֹ נֶאֱסַף. עֶזְרָא
Hakohen Hassofer: Velev Metei	הַכֹּהֵן הַסּוֹפֵר: וְלֵב מְתֵי
Kiryat Sefer. Bo Hayah Lemayim.	קִרְיַת סֵפֶר. בּוֹ הָיָה לְמָיִם.
Samach Melech Bavel El	סָמַךְ מֶלֶךְ בָּבֶל אֶל
Yerushalayim:	יְרוּשָׁלָיִם:

Oh You, Who dwells in heaven, hear the cry of those who have been afflicted by fire and water, and have mercy on a people that have received double the punishment of their sins; on the day that the enemy approached to besiege the city that was full of joyous hosts, when the king of Bavel laid siege to Yerushalayim. Oh You, Who answers in trouble, do not despise the cry of the poor; but look to our affliction on the fast of the tenth month, even the day of which in a vision You warned the son of Buzi, the seer, saying, "Write down the name of this day, even of this same day." The day on which the lion and the leopard watched the gates, and the king of Bavel laid siege to Yerushalayim. The day that they approached the palace of the beautiful and captivating inheritance; when the slaughter commenced among those who were covered with ashes; and on that day also, Ezra the Kohen and Sofer (scribe) was taken away; and the hearts of the men of Kiryat-Sefer became like water, on the day that the King of Bavel laid siege to Yerushalayim.

Continue on to the Continuation for the Fast Days section.

Fast of Esther

After the repetition of the Amidah, say Vidui. Then they say:

Al Yedei Rachameicha Harabbim	עַל יְדֵי רַחֲמֶיךָ הָרַבִּים
Selach Lanu Avinu. Ki Verov	סְלַח לָנוּ אָבִינוּ. כִּי בְרוֹב
Ivaltenu Shaginu: Mechol Lanu	אִוַּלְתֵּנוּ שָׁגִינוּ: מְחֹל לָנוּ
Malkeinu. Ki Rabbu Avoneinu: El	מַלְכֵּנוּ. כִּי רַבּוּ עֲוֹנֵינוּ: אֵל
Erech Apayim Attah. Vederech	אֶרֶךְ אַפַּיִם אַתָּה. וְדֶרֶךְ
Teshuvah Lanu Horeita: Gedulat	תְּשׁוּבָה לָנוּ הוֹרֵיתָ: גְּדֻלַּת
Rachameicha Vachasadeicha.	רַחֲמֶיךָ וַחֲסָדֶיךָ.
Tizkor Hayom Lezera Yedideicha:	תִּזְכּוֹר הַיּוֹם לְזֶרַע יְדִידֶיךָ:
Tefen Eleinu Berachamim. Ki	תֵּפֶן אֵלֵינוּ בְּרַחֲמִים. כִּי
Attah Hu Ba'al Harachamim:	אַתָּה הוּא בַּעַל הָרַחֲמִים:
Betachanun Uvitfillah Nekadem.	בְּתַחֲנוּן וּבִתְפִלָּה נְקַדֵּם.
Kemo Shehoda'ta Le'anav	כְּמוֹ שֶׁהוֹדַעְתָּ לֶעָנָו
Mikedem: Umecharon Apecha	מִקֶּדֶם: וּמֵחֲרוֹן אַפְּךָ
Tashuv. Kemo Betoratecha Katuv.	תָּשׁוּב. כְּמוֹ בְּתוֹרָתְךָ כָּתוּב.

Uvetzel Kenafeicha Necheseh	וּבְצֵל כְּנָפֶיךָ נֶחֱסֶה
Venitlonan. Keyom Vayered	וְנִתְלוֹנָן. כְּיוֹם וַיֵּרֶד
Adonai Be'anan: Ta'avor Al	יְהֹוָה בֶּעָנָן: תַּעֲבֹר עַל
Pesha Vetimchol Asham. Keyom	פֶּשַׁע וְתִמְחֹל אָשָׁם. כְּיוֹם
Vayityatzev Imo Sham: Ta'azin	וַיִּתְיַצֵּב עִמּוֹ שָׁם: תַּאֲזִין
Sheva Vetakeshiv Beratzon	שַׁוְעָ וְתַקְשִׁיב בְּרָצוֹן
Ma'amar. Keyom Vayikra Veshem	מַאֲמָר. כְּיוֹם וַיִּקְרָא בְשֵׁם
Adonai: Vesham Ne'emar:	יְהֹוָה: וְשָׁם נֶאֱמַר:

Through Your unbounded mercies forgive us, our Father, for in the greatness of our foolishness we have erred. Pardon us, our King, for our iniquities are many. Oh God, You are long-suffering, and have shown us the way of repentance. Remember this day the greatness of Your mercy and kindness, to the posterity of Your beloved; and turn to us with mercy, for You are the Master of mercy. With supplication and prayer we appear before You, as You made known to the humble one of old (Moshe). Turn from Your fierce anger, as it is written in Your Torah; so that we may take refuge and abide under the shadow of Your wings, as at the day, of which it was said, "Hashem descended in the cloud." Pass by our transgression, and pardon our trespass, as on the day, of which it was said, "He stood with him there," Hear our cry, and heed favorably to our speech, as on the day of which it was said, "He proclaimed the name of Hashem." And there it is said:

[*] denotes a slight pause between words:

וַיַּעֲבֹר יְהֹוָה | עַל־פָּנָיו וַיִּקְרָא יְהֹוָה * יְהֹוָה אֵל רַחוּם וְחַנּוּן אֶרֶךְ אַפַּיִם וְרַב־חֶסֶד וֶאֱמֶת: נֹצֵר חֶסֶד לָאֲלָפִים נֹשֵׂא עָוֹן וָפֶשַׁע וְחַטָּאָה וְנַקֵּה:

Vaya'avor Adonai 'Al-Panav Vayikra Adonai * Adonai El Rachum Vechanun; Erech Apayim Verav-Chesed Ve'emet. Notzer Chesed La'alafim. Nosei Avon Vafesha Vechata'ah; Venakeh.

And Hashem passed by before him, and proclaimed: 'Hashem * Hashem, God, merciful and gracious, long-suffering, and abundant in goodness and truth; keeping mercy to the thousandth generation, forgiving iniquity and transgression and sin, and clearing (those who repent).

Agagi Beha'amiko Machashevet	אֲגָגִי בְּהַעֲמִיקוֹ מַחֲשֶׁבֶת
Zemamo. Behivasedo Al Am	זְמָמוֹ. בְּהִוָּסְדוֹ עַל עַם
Kadosh Le'abedo Ulehacharimo.	קָדוֹשׁ לְאַבְּדוֹ וּלְהַחֲרִימוֹ.
Yemini Ga'ah Bevichyah Letzur	יְמִינִי גָּעָה בִּבְכִיָּה לְצוּר
Shochein Meromo. Ki Lo Yitosh	שׁוֹכֵן מְרוֹמוֹ. כִּ֤י לֹֽא־יִטֹּ֣שׁ
Adonai Et Ammo: Agagi Dimah	יְהֹוָ֣ה אֶת־עַמּ֑וֹ: אֲגָגִי דִּמָּה
Lechalot She'erit Yisra'el	לְכַלּוֹת שְׁאֵרִית יִשְׂרָאֵל
Ule'abedenu. Hipil Pur Hu	וּלְאַבְּדֵנוּ. הִפִּיל פּוּר֙ ה֣וּא
Hagoral Beyom Zeh Legade'enu.	הַגּוֹרָ֔ל בְּיוֹם זֶה לְגַדְּעֵנוּ.
Yemini Velo Kam Velo Za	יְמִינִי וְלֹא קָם וְלֹא זָע
Mimenu. Vehabboteach	מִמֶּנּוּ. וְהַבּוֹטֵ֥חַ
B'Adonai Chesed Yesovevenu.	בַּֽיהֹוָ֗ה חֶ֗סֶד יְסוֹבְבֶֽנּוּ:
Agagi Zedono Hishi'o Be'etzah	אֲגָגִי זְדוֹנוֹ הִשִּׁיאוֹ בְּעֵצָה
Niv'arah. Chash Lishkol Aseret	נִבְעָרָה. חָשׁ לִשְׁקוֹל עֲשֶׂרֶת
Alafim Le'abed Seh Fezurah.	אֲלָפִים לְאַבֵּד שֶׂה פְזוּרָה. יְמִינִי
Yemini Tihar Libo Betzom	טִהַר לִבּוֹ בְּצוֹם
Va'atzarah. Tov Adonai Lema'oz	וַעֲצָרָה. ט֣וֹב יְ֭הֹוָה לְמָ֣עוֹז
Beyom Tzarah: Agagi Yatza	בְּי֣וֹם צָרָ֑ה: אֲגָגִי יָצָא
Sameach Mibeit Ma'adanot.	שָׂמֵחַ מִבֵּית מַעֲדַנּוֹת.
Konen Etz Litlot Alav Ish	כּוֹנֵן עֵץ לִתְלוֹת עָלָיו אִישׁ

Emunot. Yemini Lavash Chein	אֱמוּנוֹת. יְמִינִי לָבַשׁ חֵן
Venismach Al Oteh Ge'onot. Avi	וְנִסְמַךְ עַל עוֹטֶה גְאוּנוֹת. אֲבִי
Yetomim Vedayan Almanot:	יְתוֹמִים וְדַיַּן אַלְמָנוֹת:
Agagi Mihar Kero Chachamav	אֲגָגִי מִהַר קְרוֹא חֲכָמָיו
Umidnei Ishah. Nafol Tipol	וּמִדְיָנֵי אִשָּׁה. נָפוֹל תִּפּוֹל
Lefanav Ye'atzuhu Levushah.	לְפָנָיו יְעָצוּהוּ לְבוּשָׁה.
Yemini Sod Hodia' Lahadassah	יְמִינִי סוֹד הוֹדִיעַ לַהֲדַסָּה
Umalchut Laveshah. Ve'esarah	וּמַלְכוּת לָבְשָׁה. וְאֱסָרָהּ
Asher Aserah Al Nafshah: Agagi	אֲשֶׁר אָסְרָה עַל־נַפְשָׁהּ: אֲגָגִי
Et Bo'o Lemishteh Mesibah. Piha	עֵת בּוֹאוֹ לְמִשְׁתֵּה מְסִבָּה. פִּיהָ
Patechah Vechochmah Ahuvah	פָּתְחָה בְחָכְמָה אֲהוּבָה
Nedivah. Yemini Tzahal Bir'oto	נְדִיבָה. יְמִינִי צָהַל בִּרְאוֹתוֹ
Mappalat Haman Bechibah. El	מַפֶּלֶת הָמָן בְּחִבָּה. אֵל
Na'aratz Besod Kedoshim	נַעֲרָץ בְּסוֹד־קְדֹשִׁים
Rabah: Kadosh Hane'eratz Besod	רַבָּה: קָדוֹשׁ הַנֶּעֱרָץ בְּסוֹד
Sarfei Me'onai. Romemotecha	שַׂרְפֵי מְעוֹנָי. רוֹמְמוֹתֶךָ
Yiftzechu Adat Emunai.	יִפְצְחוּ עֲדַת אֱמוּנָי.
Lishu'atecha Kiviti Adonai. Ken	לִישׁוּעָתְךָ קִוִּיתִי יְהוָה. כֵּן
Yovdu Chol Oyeveicha Adonai:	יֹאבְדוּ כָל־אוֹיְבֶיךָ יְהוָה:
Yehemu Na Rachameicha Al	יֶהֱמוּ נָא רַחֲמֶיךָ עַל
Me'utei Ammim. Vesagevem	מְעוּטֵי עַמִּים. וְשַׂגְּבֵם
Bechasdecha Le'einei Chol	בְּחַסְדְּךָ לְעֵינֵי כָל־
Le'umim. Pela'eicha Har'em	לְאֻמִּים. פְּלָאֶיךָ הַרְאֵם
Tzur Shochein Meromim. El	צוּר שׁוֹכֵן מְרוֹמִים. אֵל
Melech Yoshev Al Kisse	מֶלֶךְ יוֹשֵׁב עַל כִּסֵּא
Rachamim: Yichalta Avadeicha	רַחֲמִים: יִחַלְתְּ עֲבָדֶיךָ

בְּחֶזְיוֹנֵי כִּתְבֵיהֶם.	Bechezyonei Chitveihem.
לְתִתָּם לְרַחֲמִים לִפְנֵי כָל־	Letittam Lerachamim Lifnei Chol
שׁוֹבֵיהֶם. וְדִבַּרְתָּ עַל לִבָּם	Shoveihem. Vedibarta Al Libam
לְרַפֹּאת מַכְאוֹבֵיהֶם. וְאַף־	Lerappot Mach'oveihem. Ve'af
גַּם־זֹאת בִּהְיוֹתָם בְּאֶרֶץ	Gam Zot Bihyotam Be'eretz
אֹיְבֵיהֶם: צִמְּתַתְנִי אָז	Oyeveihem: Tzimmetatni Az
אַרְיֵה מִגֶּפֶן פּוֹרִיָּה. הִגְלַנִי	Aryeh Migefen Poriyah. Higlani
וְהֶעֱלַנִי אֶל אֶרֶץ מַאְפֵּלְיָה.	Vehe'elani El Eretz Ma'feleyah.
הִקְדַּמְתָּ אַרְבָּעָה הוֹגֵי דַת	Hikdamta Arba'ah Hogei Dat
תּוּשִׁיָּה. דָּנִיֵּאל חֲנַנְיָה	Tushiyah. Daniyel Chananyah
מִישָׁאֵל וַעֲזַרְיָה. זֶה נִצַּל	Misha'el Va'azaryah. Zeh Nitzal
מֵאֲרָיוֹת וְאֵלֶּה	Me'arayot Ve'eleh
מִלַּהֲבֵיהֶם: חָשׁ הָאַיִל	Millahaveihem: Chash Ha'ayil
וְהַחֲזִיר בִּמְהוּמָה	Vehachazir Bimhumah
וּמְבוּסָה. כִּמְעַט אוֹרִי קָדַר	Umevusah. Kim'at Ori Kadar
וּמְאוֹר שִׁמְשִׁי כֻּסָּה.	Ume'or Shimshi Kussah.
תָּמַכְתָּ יַד יְמִינִי בִּימִינִי	Tamachta Yad Yemini Bimini
וַהֲדַסָּה. וְחִצִּים אֲשֶׁר	Vahadassah. Vechitzim Asher
דָּרְכוּ לִי. שָׁבוּ בְּלֵב	Darechu Li. Shavu Belev
רוֹבֵיהֶם: קָם עָלַי בְּפִשְׁעִי	Roveihem: Kam Alai Befish'i
הַנָּבָל הַבַּעַר. גְּרוֹנוֹ עָלַי	Hanaval Haba'ar. Gerono Alai
פָּעַר. כַּחֲזִיר בְּתוֹךְ הַיָּעַר.	Pa'ar. Kachazir Betoch Haya'ar.
הִקְדַּמְתָּ לִי מְשִׁיבֵי מִלְחֶמֶת	Hikdamta Li Meshivei Milchemet
דַּת שָׁעַר. וְהִנְנִי מִשְׁתַּעְשֵׁעַ	Dat Sha'ar. Vehini Mishta'shea'
בְּשִׂכְלָם וּבְנִיבֵיהֶם. וְאַף־	Besichlam Uveniveihem. Ve'af
גַּם־זֹאת בִּהְיוֹתָם בְּאֶרֶץ	Gam Zot Bihyotam Be'eretz
אֹיְבֵיהֶם:	Oyeveihem:

When the Agagite imagined by his deeply thought out schemes, to destroy and utterly eliminate the holy people: the Yemini (Benjamite), cried and wept, to the Rock Who dwells on high, for he knew, "That Hashem would not cast off His people." The Agagite thought to consume and utterly destroy the "remnant of Yisrael; and therefore cast lots to cut us off on this day; while the Yemini would "not rise up, or move for him; believing that "He who trusts in Hashem will be encircled with mercy" The presumption of the Agagite led him into a foolish counsel, and he hastened to weigh ten thousand talents of silver for the destruction of the scattered sheep; while the Yemini purified his heart by fasting and restraint: knowing that "Hashem is good, He is a stronghold on the day of distress." The Agagite went out joyful from the house of pleasure, and prepared a tree to hang the faithful man; then the Yemini clothed himself with grace, and relied on Him, Who has covered himself with majesty; for "He is the Father of the orphans, and the Judge of the widows." The Agagite hastened, and called his wise men, and his contentious wife; whose counsel was, that he would surely fall before the other to his shame; while the Bimini revealed the secret to Hadassah, who clothed herself in royal robes, that she might perform "Her vow with which she had bound her soul." When the Agagite came to sit down to the feast, she opened her mouth in wisdom, love, and honesty; and the Yemini rejoiced greatly, when he saw the downfall of Haman; thanking God, Who is greatly reverenced in the assembly of the holy-ones. Holy One, Who is reverenced in the assembly of the Seraphim in Your Habitation, the faithful congregation will loudly declare Your exaltation, saying, "I have hoped in Your salvation; and so may all Your enemies perish, Hashem, let Your mercy be moved towards the people smallest in number, and exalt them in the sight of all the nations; show them Your wonders, Oh Rock, Who dwells on high; Oh omnipotent King, Who sits upon the Throne of mercy. You have caused your servants to hope, according to the visions of their scriptures, that You would let them find mercy with all of those who carried them captive; and You did speak comfort to their heart, promising to heal all their sorrows, "And this even when they be in the land of their enemies." The lion cut me off from my fruitful vine; he carried me captive, and brought me into a land of darkness; but You hastened to, protect the four who meditated in the law of wisdom, even Daniel, Chananiah, Misha'el, and Azariah. The first was delivered from the lions, and the others from the flames. "And this even when they were in the land of their enemies."

Ve'af Gam Zot Bihyotam	וְאַף־גַּם־זֹאת בִּהְיוֹתָם
Be'eretz Oyeveihem Lo Me'astim	בְּאֶרֶץ אֹיְבֵיהֶם לֹא־מְאַסְתִּים
Velo Ge'altim Lechalotam	וְלֹא־גְעַלְתִּים לְכַלֹּתָם
Lehafer Beriti Ittam Ki Ani	לְהָפֵר בְּרִיתִי אִתָּם כִּי אֲנִי
Adonai Eloheihem. Vezacharti Et	יְהוָה אֱלֹהֵיהֶם: וְזָכַרְתִּי אֶת־
Beriti Ya'akov Ve'af Et Beriti	בְּרִיתִי יַעֲקוֹב וְאַף אֶת־בְּרִיתִי
Yitzchak Ve'af Et Beriti Avraham	יִצְחָק וְאַף אֶת־בְּרִיתִי אַבְרָהָם
Ezkor Veha'aretz Ezkor. Min	אֶזְכֹּר וְהָאָרֶץ אֶזְכֹּר: מִן־
Hametzar Karati Yah Anani	הַמֵּצַר קָרָאתִי יָּהּ עָנָנִי
Vammerchav Yah. Adonai Li Lo	בַמֶּרְחָב יָהּ: יְהוָה לִי לֹא
Ira Mah Ya'aseh Li Adam. Adonai	אִירָא מַה־יַּעֲשֶׂה לִי אָדָם: יְהוָה
Li Be'ozerai Va'ani Er'eh	לִי בְּעֹזְרָי וַאֲנִי אֶרְאֶה
Vesone'ai. Tov Lachasot	בְשֹׂנְאָי: טוֹב לַחֲסוֹת
B'Adonai Mibetoach Ba'adam.	בַּיהוָה מִבְּטֹחַ בָּאָדָם:
Tov Lachasot B'Adonai	טוֹב לַחֲסוֹת בַּיהוָה
Mibetoach Bindivim. Kol Goyim	מִבְּטֹחַ בִּנְדִיבִים: כָּל־גּוֹיִם
Sevavuni Beshem Adonai Ki	סְבָבוּנִי בְּשֵׁם יְהוָה כִּי
Amilam. Dachoh Dechitani	אֲמִילַם: דַּחֹה דְחִיתַנִי

Linpol Va'Adonai Azarani.	לִנְפֹּל וַיהוָה עֲזָרָנִי׃

"And yet, for all of that, when they are in the land of their enemies I will not reject them, neither will I abhor them, to destroy them totally, and to break my covenant with them; for I am Hashem their God. And I will remember my covenant with Yaakov, and also my covenant with Yitzchak, and also my covenant with Avraham will I remember, and the land will I also remember." In distress I called on Hashem, and Hashem answered me with enlargement. Hashem is for me, I will not fear; what can man do to me? Hashem is with me, and is my help; I will therefore see my desire on those who hate me. It is better to trust in Hashem than to rely on man. It is better to trust in Hashem than to rely on princes. All nations surrounded me; but in the name of Hashem will I cut them off. You have thrusted at me that I might fall; but Hashem supported me."

Yehirim Kamu Bechol Dor.	יְהִירִים קָמוּ בְּכָל־דּוֹר.
Veha'elohim Shemarani. Alah	וְהָאֱלֹהִים שְׁמָרַנִי. עָלָה
Aryeh Techillah. Bechol Pe'ot	אַרְיֵה תְּחִלָּה. בְּכָל־פֵּאוֹת
Zerani. Kam Acharav Dov	זֵרָנִי. קָם אַחֲרָיו דּוֹב
Shakkul Velimzanev Mecharani.	שַׁכּוּל וְלִמְזַנֵּב מְכָרָנִי.
Dachoh Dechitani Linpol	דָּחֹה דְחִיתַנִי לִנְפֹּל
Va'Adonai Azarani. Az Betzeti	וַיהוָה עֲזָרָנִי׃ אָז בְּצֵאתִי
Miperech. Ba Nachash Alei	מִפֶּרֶךְ. בָּא נָחָשׁ עָלַי
Derech. Al Ayef Veyagea' Lehavi	דֶּרֶךְ. עַל עָיֵף וְיָגֵעַ לְהָבִיא
Velibo Morech. Gada'ta	בְּלִבּוֹ מֹרֶךְ. גָּדַעְתָּ
Vehikkita Oto Shok Al Yarech.	וְהִכִּיתָ אוֹתוֹ שׁוֹק עַל יָרֵךְ.
Yom Herim Yad Anav Aleihem	יוֹם הֵרִים יָד עָנָו עֲלֵיהֶם
Higbirani. Dachoh Dechitani	הִגְבִּירָנִי. דָּחֹה דְחִיתַנִי

Linpol Va'Adonai Azarani.	לִנְפֹּל וַיהֹוָה עֲזָרָנִי׃
Bekum Haman Ha'agagi.	בְּקוּם הָמָן הָאֲגָגִי.
Kattanin Levalle'eni. Vechatav	כְּתַנִּין לְבַלְּעֵנִי. וְכָתַב
Sitnah Alai. Beyom Echad	שִׂטְנָה עָלַי. בְּיוֹם אֶחָד
Legade'eni. Shalach	לְגַדְּעֵנִי. שָׁלַח
Mishamayim El Vayoshi'eni.	מִשָּׁמַיִם אֵל וַיּוֹשִׁיעֵנִי.
Lemichyah Hish'irani Ve'oz	לְמִחְיָה הִשְׁאִירָנִי וְעֹז
Veyesha Izerani. Dachoh	וְיֶשַׁע אִזְּרָנִי. דָּחֹה
Dechitani Linpol Va'Adonai	דְחִיתַנִי לִנְפֹּל וַיהֹוָה
Azarani. Shimcha Migdal	עֲזָרָנִי׃ שִׁמְךָ מִגְדַּל
Mivtachi. El Mibeten Gochi.	מִבְטָחִי. אֵל מִבֶּטֶן גּוֹחִי.
Vechilatzta Et Ruchi. Mimavet	וְחִלַּצְתָּ אֶת־רוּחִי. מִמָּוֶת
Umishechi. Et Eini Min Dim'ah.	וּמִשַּׁחִי. אֶת־עֵינִי מִן דִּמְעָה.
Ve'et Ragli Middechi. Uve'eretz	וְאֶת־רַגְלִי מִדֶּחִי. וּבְאֶרֶץ
Madduchi. El Elohim Hifrani.	מַדּוּחִי. אֵל אֱלֹהִים הִפְרָנִי.
Dachoh Dechitani Linpol	דָּחֹה דְחִיתַנִי לִנְפֹּל
Va'Adonai Azarani.	וַיהֹוָה עֲזָרָנִי׃

In every age the arrogant rose up against me, but God protected me. First the lion arose, and drove me into every corner. After him rose the raging bear, and sold me to the destroyer: Yes, "You thrusted at me that I might fall; but Hashem supported me." Then already when I came forth from bondage the serpent came up against me on the way, when I was faint and weary, to terrify my heart; but You cut him down, and struck him hip and thigh; on the day that the humble one (Moshe) lifted up his hand You gave me victory over him;" "You indeed have thrusted at me that I might fall; but Hashem supported me." When Haman, the Agagite, rose up, as a furious dragon to swallow me up, and drew up an accusation against me, to cut me off in one day: You, Oh God, sent me assistance from heaven, and saved me; You preserved my life, and gird me with strength and salvation; "You have thrusted at me that I might fall; but Hashem supported me." Your name is the tower in which I trust; for You, God, brought me out from the womb; You delivered my soul from death and the grave, my eyes from tears, and my feet from falling; and in the land of my banishment You, Lord God, caused me to multiply; and truly, "You have thrusted at me that I might fall; but Hashem supported me."

Dachoh Dechitani Linpol	דָּחֹה דְחִיתַנִי לִנְפֹּל
Va'Adonai Azarani. Ozi	וַיהוָה עֲזָרָנִי׃ עָזִּי
Vezimrat Yah Vayhi Li Lishu'ah.	וְזִמְרָת יָהּ וַיְהִי־לִי לִישׁוּעָה׃
Kol Rinah Vishu'ah Be'oholei	קוֹל ׀ רִנָּה וִישׁוּעָה בְּאָהֳלֵי
Tzaddikim Yemin Adonai Osah	צַדִּיקִים יְמִין יְהוָה עֹשָׂה
Chayil. Yemin Adonai Romemah	חָיִל׃ יְמִין יְהוָה רוֹמֵמָה
Yemin Adonai Osah Chayil. Lo	יְמִין יְהוָה עֹשָׂה חָיִל׃ לֹא־
Amut Ki Echyeh Va'asaper	אָמוּת כִּי־אֶחְיֶה וַאֲסַפֵּר
Ma'asei Yah. Yassor Yisserani Yah	מַעֲשֵׂי יָהּ׃ יַסֹּר יִסְּרַנִּי יָּהּ
Velamavet Lo Netanani. Pitchu	וְלַמָּוֶת לֹא נְתָנָנִי׃ פִּתְחוּ־
Li Sha'arei Tzedek Avo Vam	לִי שַׁעֲרֵי־צֶדֶק אָבֹא־בָם
Odeh Yah. Zeh Hasha'ar	אוֹדֶה יָהּ׃ זֶה־הַשַּׁעַר
L'Adonai Tzaddikim Yavo'u Vo.	לַיהוָה צַדִּיקִים יָבֹאוּ בוֹ׃
Odecha Ki Anitani Vatehi Li	אוֹדְךָ כִּי עֲנִיתָנִי וַתְּהִי־לִי
Lishu'ah. Lulei Adonai	לִישׁוּעָה׃ לוּלֵי יְהוָה
Shehayah Lanu Yomar Na	שֶׁהָיָה לָנוּ יֹאמַר־נָא
Yisra'el.	יִשְׂרָאֵל׃

"You have thrusted at me that I might fall; but Hashem supported me." Hashem is my strength and song, and He has become my salvation. The voice of song and salvation is in the tents of the righteous: 'The right hand of Hashem has done valiantly. The right hand of Hashem is exalted; the right hand of Hashem has done valiantly.' I will not die, but live, and declare the works of Hashem. He has indeed reproved me, but he has not given me over to death. Open for me the gates of righteousness, that I may enter through them, to praise Hashem. This is the gate of Hashem, into which the righteous will enter. I will praise You, for You have answered me, and have become my salvation. If Hashem has not been for us, Yisrael may now say."

Eich Zarim. Achzarim.	אֵיךְ זָרִים. אַכְזָרִים.
Kadevorim Sevavunu. Bekum	כַּדְּבוֹרִים סְבָבוּנוּ. בְּקוּם
Haman. Bezeh Hazeman.	הָמָן. בְּזֶה הַזְּמָן.
Keshod Shalman Shedadunu.	כְּשֹׁד שַׁלְמָן שְׁדָדוּנוּ.
Berov Ma'al. Saf Ra'al. Beli Ta'al	בְּרֹב מַעַל. סַף רַעַל. בְּלִי תַעַל
Hishkunu. Lulei Adonai	הִשְׁקוּנוּ. לוּלֵי יְהֹוָה
Shehayah Lanu. Azai Chayim	שֶׁהָיָה לָנוּ. אֲזַי חַיִּים
Bela'unu: Eich Dimu.	בְּלָעֽוּנוּ: אֵיךְ דִּמּוּ.
Vezamemu. Belibam Ninam	וְזָמְמוּ. בְּלִבָּם נִינָם
Yachad. Bemachashavat.	יַחַד. בְּמַחֲשָׁבַת.
Lehachriv Bat. Yisra'el Goy	לְהַחְרִיב בַּת. יִשְׂרָאֵל גּוֹי
Echad. Besod Sodam.	אֶחָד. בְּסוֹד סוֹדָם.
Lehashmidam. Lehachchidam.	לְהַשְׁמִידָם. לְהַכְחִידָם.
Kemo Chachad. Uvein Tanur	כְּמוֹ כַחַד. וּבֵין תַּנּוּר
Vechirayim. Hamayim	וְכִירַיִם. הַמַּיִם

Shetafunu. Lulei Adonai	שְׁטָפוּנוּ. לוּלֵי יְהֹוָה
Shehayah Lanu. Azai Chayim	שֶׁהָיָה לָנוּ. אֲזַי חַיִּים
Bela'unu: Kam Tzorer. Veli Orer.	בְּלָעוּנוּ: קָם צוֹרֵר. וְלִי עוֹרֵר.
Eivato Vesin'ato. Vedat He'emid.	אֵיבָתוֹ וְשִׂנְאָתוֹ. וְדָת הֶעֱמִיד.
Veketz Lashmid. Adat Shaddai	וְקֵץ לַשְׁמִיד. עֲדַת שַׁדַּי
Venachalato. Vetzur Chamal.	וְנַחֲלָתוֹ. וְצוּר חָמַל.
Vetov Gamal. Veher'ah Et	וְטוֹב גָּמַל. וְהֶרְאָה אֶת־
Gevurato. Leha'avido.	גְּבוּרָתוֹ. לְהַאֲבִידוֹ.
Lehachchido. Uvanav Asher	לְהַכְחִידוֹ. וּבָנָיו אֲשֶׁר
Inunu. Chashav Tzar. Be'et	עִנּוּנוּ. חָשַׁב צָר. בְּעֵת
Metzar. Vehipil Pur Goralo.	מֵצָר. וְהִפִּיל פּוּר גּוֹרָלוֹ.
Vetzur Hikshiv. Ve'az Heshiv.	וְצוּר הִקְשִׁיב. וְאָז הֵשִׁיב.
Berosho Et Tagmulo. Ve'el	בְּרֹאשׁוֹ אֶת תַּגְמוּלוֹ. וְאֵל
Ne'dar. Bechodesh Adar. Oz	נֶאְדָּר. בְּחֹדֶשׁ אֲדָר. עֹז
Her'ah Likhalo. Bemo Retzach.	הֶרְאָה לִקְהָלוֹ. בְּמוֹ רֶצַח.
Adei Netzach. Hikah Asher	עֲדֵי נֶצַח. הִכָּה אֲשֶׁר
Hikunu. Lulei Adonai Shehayah	הִכּוּנוּ. לוּלֵי יְהֹוָה שֶׁהָיָה
Lanu. Azai Chayim Bela'unu:	לָנוּ. אֲזַי חַיִּים בְּלָעוּנוּ:

Oh how the cruel barbarians encompassed us like bees; when Haman rose up at this season they meant to plunder us, as though the plunder was their due reward; and for the greatness of my trespass, to cause me to drink without alleviation the cup of terror; so that had Hashem not been for us they would have swallowed us up alive." Oh how they imagined and devised in their hearts to destroy us completely, and conspired to annihilate the daughter of Yisrael, the peculiar nation; for in their secret council it was determined completely to extirpate them; so the waters had nearly overwhelmed us; so that "Had not Hashem been for us, they would have swallowed us up alive." The enemy arose, and awakened against me his hatred and enmity; and obtained a decreed, and fixed a time to destroy the Almighty's congregation and heritage; but He Who is our Rock was compassionate, and benevolently protected us; and showed his mighty power, by cutting off and destroying both him and his sons, who so afflicted us; so that "Had not Hashem been for us, they would have swallowed us up alive." The enemy in time of our distress cast the lot; but He Who is our Rock was attentive, and returned his dealing upon his own head; and God, Who is ever glorified, showed in the month of Adar his mighty power to His congregation; for with a perpetual slaughter did he strike those who attempted to strike us; so that "Had not Hashem been for us, they would have swallowed us up alive."

Lulei Adonai Shehayah Lanu	לוּלֵי יְהֹוָה שֶׁהָיָה לָנוּ
Yomar Na Yisra'el. Lulei Adonai	יֹאמַר־נָא יִשְׂרָאֵל: לוּלֵי יְהֹוָה
Shehayah Lanu Bekum Aleinu	שֶׁהָיָה לָנוּ בְּקוּם עָלֵינוּ
Adam. Azai Chayim Bela'unu	אָדָם: אֲזַי חַיִּים בְּלָעוּנוּ
Bacharot Appam Banu. Azai	בַּחֲרוֹת אַפָּם בָּנוּ: אֲזַי
Hamayim Shetafunu Nachlah	הַמַּיִם שְׁטָפוּנוּ נַחְלָה
Avar Al Nafshenu. Azai Avar Al	עָבַר עַל־נַפְשֵׁנוּ: אֲזַי עָבַר עַל־
Nafshenu Hamayim	נַפְשֵׁנוּ הַמַּיִם
Hazeidonim. Baruch Adonai	הַזֵּידוֹנִים: בָּרוּךְ יְהֹוָה
Shelo Netananu Teref	שֶׁלֹּא נְתָנָנוּ טֶרֶף
Leshineihem. Nafshenu Ketzipor	לְשִׁנֵּיהֶם: נַפְשֵׁנוּ כְּצִפּוֹר
Nimletah Mippach Yokeshim	נִמְלְטָה מִפַּח יוֹקְשִׁים
Happach Nishbar Va'anachnu	הַפַּח נִשְׁבָּר וַאֲנַחְנוּ
Nimlatenu. Ezrenu Beshem	נִמְלָטְנוּ: עֶזְרֵנוּ בְּשֵׁם

יְהֹוָה עֹשֵׂה שָׁמַיִם

וָאָרֶץ:

Adonai Oseh Shamayim Va'aretz.

If it had not been Hashem Who was for us, When men rose up against us, then they would have swallowed us up alive, when their wrath was kindled against us; Then the waters would have overwhelmed us, the stream would have gone over our soul; Then the proud waters would have gone over our soul. Blessed is Hashem, Who has not given us as a prey to their teeth. Our soul is escaped as a bird out of the snare of the hunters; The snare is broken, and we have escaped. Our help is in the name of Hashem, Who made heaven and earth.

אֲדֹנָי | שְׁמָעָה אֲדֹנָי | סְלָחָה אֲדֹנָי הַקְשִׁיבָה וַעֲשֵׂה אַל־תְּאַחַר לְמַעַנְךָ אֱלֹהַי כִּי־שִׁמְךָ נִקְרָא עַל־עִירְךָ וְעַל־עַמֶּךָ: הֲשִׁיבֵנוּ יְהֹוָה | אֵלֶיךָ ונשוב (וְנָשׁוּבָה) חַדֵּשׁ יָמֵינוּ כְּקֶדֶם:

Adonai Shema'ah Adonai Selachah Adonai Hakshivah Va'aseh Al Te'achar Lema'ancha Elohai Ki Shimcha Nikra Al Ircha Ve'al Ammecha. Hashiveinu Adonai Eleicha Venashuvah Chadesh Yameinu Kekedem.

"Hashem, hear: Hashem, forgive: Hashem be graciously attentive, and grant our requests; do not delay for Your own sake, my God, for Your city and Your people are called by Your name. Cause us, Hashem, to return to You, and we will return; renew our days as of old." **(Dan. 9:19, Lam. 5:21)**

Continue on to the Continuation for the Fast Days section.

Seventeenth of Tammuz

After the repetition of the Amidah, say Vidui. Then they say:

וָאֶרֶץ שָׁפַל רוּמִי. יוֹם דִּמָּה רָשָׁע לְהַכְנִיעִי. מְשׂוֹשׂ לִבִּי שָׁבַת. וְהֻשְׁלַכְתִּי מִבֵּית מַרְגּוֹעִי. אָנוּ וְאָבְלוּ פְּתָחַי. יוֹם נֶאֱסַף נְדִיבִי וְשׁוּעִי. לָכֵן אֲקוֹנֵן מִיָּמִים יָמִימָה בַּחֹדֶשׁ הָרְבִיעִי:

Va'aretz Shafal Rumi. Yom Dimah Rasha Lehachni'i. Mesos Libi Shavat. Vehushlachti Mibeit Margo'i. Anu Ve'aveilu Petachai. Yom Ne'esaf Nedivi Veshu'i. Lachein Akonen Miyamim Yamimah Bachodesh Harevi'i:

My greatness was cast down to the earth, on the day that the wicked determined to subdue me; the joy of my heart ceased, and I was cast out from the house of my rest; mourning and lamentation were heard at my gates, on the day that my chiefs and principal men were taken away; So I will lament every year in the fourth month.

Bachodesh Harevi'i Afefu Alai	בַּחֹדֶשׁ הָרְבִיעִי אֲפָפוּ עָלַי
Ra'ot Va'anachot. Beshiv'ah	רָעוֹת וַאֲנָחוֹת. בְּשִׁבְעָה־
Asar Bo. Be'anchati Yaga'ti Velo	עָשָׂר בּוֹ. בְּאַנְחָתִי יָגַעְתִּי וְלֹא
Matzati Menuchot. Ga'oh Ga'iti	מָצָאתִי מְנוּחוֹת. גָּעֹה גָעִיתִי
Bivchi Ve'al Kol Rosh Kerechot.	בִּבְכִי וְעַל כָּל־רֹאשׁ קָרְחוֹת.
Ki Veyom Zeh Nishtaberu	כִּי בְיוֹם זֶה נִשְׁתַּבְּרוּ
Haluchot: Haluchot Yetza'uni	הַלֻּחוֹת: הַלֻּחוֹת יְצָאוּנִי
Vesavevu Alai Tela'ot. Vegaverah	וְסָבְבוּ עָלַי תְּלָאוֹת. וְגָבְרָה
Yad Tzari Vezerani Bechol Pe'ot.	יַד צָרִי וְזֵרַנִי בְּכָל־פֵּאוֹת.
Sav Na Vehagen Meyachalei	סָב־נָא וְהָגֵן מְיַחֲלֵי
Ketz Pela'ot. Ki Shemesh	קֵץ פְּלָאוֹת. כִּי שֶׁמֶשׁ
Umagen Adonai Tzeva'ot:	וּמָגֵן יְהֹוָה צְבָאוֹת:

In the fourth month, evils and calamities overcame me; on the seventeenth day of the month I was tired of sighing, and found no rest: I wept bitterly; for every head was in pain; for on this day the tablets were broken. The tablets departed, and I was surrounded with troubles; the hand of the enemy also prevailed against me, and he scattered me into every corner. But turn now, we implore You, and protect those who wait for the end of the wonders; "For You, Hashem of Hosts, are our sun and our shield." (Ps. 84:12)

Bachodesh Harevi'i Dimmiti	בַּחֹדֶשׁ הָרְבִיעִי דִּמִּיתִי
Alot Mitit Hayaven Ve'ein	עֲלוֹת מִטִּיט הַיָּוֵן וְאֵין
Ma'amid. Beshiv'ah Asar Bo	מַעֲמִיד. בְּשִׁבְעָה עָשָׂר בּוֹ
Hayiti Levizah Lema'achal	הָיִיתִי לְבִזָּה לְמַאֲכָל
Ulehashmid. Velo Matzati	וּלְהַשְׁמִיד. וְלֹא מָצָאתִי
Manoach Umach'ovi Negdi	מָנוֹחַ וּמַכְאוֹבִי נֶגְדִּי
Tamid. Ki Vo Buttal Hatamid:	תָמִיד. כִּי בוֹ בֻּטַּל הַתָּמִיד:
Hatamid Yom Husar Gaverah	הַתָּמִיד יוֹם הוּסַר גָּבְרָה
Yilati Keyilat Eglayim. Umispedi	יִלְלָתִי כְּיִלְלַת אֶגְלַיִם. וּמִסְפְּדִי
Gadal Kemisped Hadadrimmon	גָדַל כְּמִסְפֵּד הֲדַדְרִמּוֹן
Kiflayim. Sav Na Vehachayeh	כִּפְלַיִם. סָב־נָא וְהַחֲיֵה
Redumeinu. El Shochein	רְדוּמֵינוּ. אֵל שׁוֹכֵן
Shamayim. Yechayeinu	שָׁמַיִם. יְחַיֵּינוּ
Miyomayim:	מִיּוֹמָיִם:

In the fourth month, I was like one wanting to rise from a pool of miry clay, who can find no one to help him to stand up; on the seventeenth day of the month, I was given up to plunder, devouring, and destruction; I found no rest, and my affliction was forever present before me, for there on it the daily sacrifice ceased. The day on which the daily sacrifice ceased, my laments, and mourning, and complaint increased fearfully. Dweller in heaven, now turn, we implore You, and give life to our departed ones, and again restore us after two captivities.

Bachodesh Harevi'i Za'am Tzur	בַּחֹדֶשׁ הָֽרְבִיעִי זַעַם צוּר
Nasati Vachamato Bi Hiv'ir.	נָשָׂאתִי וַחֲמָתוֹ בִּי הִבְעִיר.
Beshiv'ah Asar Bo Chalchalah	בְּשִׁבְעָה עָשָׂר בּוֹ חַלְחָלָה
Achazatni Vesa'ar Mas'ir. Tovot	אֲחָזַתְנִי וְסַעַר מַסְעִיר. טוֹבוֹת
Nashiti Vatiznach Mishalom	נָשִׁיתִי וַתִּזְנַח מִשָּׁלוֹם
Nafshi Betigrat Se'ir. Ki Vo	נַפְשִׁי בְּתִגְרַת שֵׂעִיר. כִּי בוֹ
Haveke'ah Ha'ir: Ha'ir Yom	הָבְקְעָה הָעִיר: הָעִיר יוֹם
Haveke'ah Bekum Teiman	הָבְקְעָה בְּקוּם תֵּימָן
Umagdi'el. Ve'azelat Yadi Velo	וּמַגְדִּיאֵל. וְאָזְלַת יָדִי וְלֹא
Matze'ah La'el. Sav Na	מָצְאָה לָאֵל. סָב־נָא
Vehakdesh Peleitat Ari'el.	וְהַקְדֵּשׁ פְּלֵיטַת אֲרִיאֵל.
Hikdishu Et Kedosh Ya'akov	הִקְדִּישׁוּ אֶת־קְדוֹשׁ יַעֲקֹב
Ve'et Elohei Yisra'el:	וְאֶת־אֱלֹהֵי יִשְׂרָאֵל:

In the fourth month, I bore the wrath of our Rock, and his anger was kindled against me. On the seventeenth day of the month, dread and agitating anxiety took hold of me; I forgot all prosperity, for peace was removed far from my soul by the contention of Seir, for on that day the city was taken. The city was taken on the day that Teman and Magdiel rose up, when my strength departed, and I had no power left. Turn, we implore You, and save the remnant of Ariel; "And then they will sanctify You, the Holy One of Yaakov, and the God of Yisrael." (Is. 29:23)

Bachodesh Harevi'i Yom Hoho	בַּחֹדֶשׁ הָרְבִיעִי יוֹם הוֹ הוֹ
Yom Tochechah Ve'evrah.	יוֹם תּוֹכֵחָה וְעֶבְרָה.
Beshiv'ah Asar Bo Kevodi Galah	בְּשִׁבְעָה עָשָׂר בּוֹ כְּבוֹדִי גָלָה
Vetif'arti Husarah. Leshivri Ein	וְתִפְאַרְתִּי הוּסָרָה. לְשִׁבְרִי אֵין
Kehah Umakati Nachlah	כֵּהָה וּמַכָּתִי נַחְלָה
Veruchi Nishbarah. Ki Vo Saraf	וְרוּחִי נִשְׁבָּרָה. כִּי בוֹ שָׂרַף
Apposetemos Et Hatorah:	אַפּוֹסְטְמוֹס אֶת־הַתּוֹרָה:
Hatorah Yom Nisrefah	הַתּוֹרָה יוֹם נִשְׂרְפָה
Chudeshu Alai Yegonai.	חֻדְּשׁוּ עָלַי יְגוֹנַי.
Veshavetu Me'ir Kodesh	וְשָׁבְתוּ מֵעִיר קֹדֶשׁ
Yeshishai Uzekenai. Sav Na	יְשִׁישַׁי וּזְקֵנַי. סָב־נָא
Vechon Be'uzecha Adat	וְחֹן בְּעֻזְּךָ עֲדַת
Emunai. Ruach Da'at Veyir'at	אֱמוּנַי. רוּחַ דַּעַת וְיִרְאַת
Adonai.	יְהֹוָה:

In the fourth month, was the day of woe, rebuke, and wrath; On the seventeenth day of the month, my honor departed, and glory was taken away; there is no cure for my bruise; my wound is grievous, and my spirit is broken; for on that day Posthumus burned the Torah. On the day the Torah was burned, my sorrows were renewed, and the old and grey-headed ceased to adorn the holy city. Turn, Hashem, we implore You, and in Your mighty power graciously bestow on the faithful congregation the spirit of knowledge and the fear of You.

Bachodesh Harevi'i Me'uvati	בַּחֹדֶשׁ הָרְבִיעִי מְעֻוָּתִי
Madad Zar Besase'ah Uvah Kal.	מָדַד זָר בְּסַאסְּאָה וּבָהּ כָּל.
Beshiv'ah Asar Bo Navi Hesham	בְּשִׁבְעָה עָשָׂר בּוֹ נָוִי הֵשַׁם
Zar Ve'et Ya'akov Achal. Sefot	זָר וְאֶת־יַעֲקֹב אָכַל. סְפוֹת

Shanah Veshanah Beyom Zeh	שָׁנָה בְשָׁנָה בְּיוֹם זֶה
Mamrur Ochal. Ki Vo Ho'omad	מַמְרוּר אוֹכַל. כִּי בוֹ הָעֳמַד
Tzelem Baheichal: Yom	צֶלֶם בַּהֵיכָל: יוֹם
Ho'omad Pesel Kin'ah Veto'evah.	הָעֳמַד פֶּסֶל קִנְאָה וְתוֹעֵבָה.
Uvo Chubbelah Ruchi Vetochalti	וּבוֹ חֻבְּלָה רוּחִי וְתוֹחַלְתִּי
Nichzevah. Sav Na Verappei	נִכְזָבָה. סָב־נָא וְרַפֵּא
Meshuvat Ammecha Vetohavem	מְשׁוּבַת עַמְּךָ וְתֹאהֲבֵם
Nedavah. Hashiveinu Adonai	נְדָבָה. הֲשִׁיבֵנוּ יְהוָה |
Eleicha Venashuvah:	אֵלֶיךָ וְנָשׁוּבָה:

In the fourth month, the stranger gave to me the full measure in repayment of my perverseness; On the seventeenth day of the month, the stranger destroyed my dwelling, and devoured Yaakov; in mournful complaints I will, every year on this day, feed my spirit with bitterness; for on it an image was placed in the Temple. On the day that the graven image of jealousy and abomination was placed in the Temple, my spirit was wounded, and my hope failed. Turn, Hashem, we implore You, and heal the backsliding of Your people, and love them affectionately; cause us also to return to You, Hashem, and we will return.

Al Yedei Rachameicha Harabbim	עַל יְדֵי רַחֲמֶיךָ הָרַבִּים
Selach Lanu Avinu. Ki Verov	סְלַח לָנוּ אָבִינוּ. כִּי בְרוֹב
Ivaltenu Shaginu: Mechol Lanu	אִוַּלְתֵּנוּ שָׁגִינוּ: מְחֹל לָנוּ
Malkeinu. Ki Rabbu Avoneinu: El	מַלְכֵּנוּ. כִּי רַבּוּ עֲוֹנֵינוּ: אֵל
Erech Apayim Attah. Vederech	אֶרֶךְ אַפַּיִם אַתָּה. וְדֶרֶךְ
Teshuvah Lanu Horeita: Gedulat	תְּשׁוּבָה לָנוּ הוֹרֵיתָ: גְּדֻלַּת
Rachameicha Vachasadeicha.	רַחֲמֶיךָ וַחֲסָדֶיךָ.

Tizkor Hayom Lezera Yedideicha:	תִּזְכּוֹר הַיּוֹם לְזֶרַע יְדִידֶיךָ:
Tefen Eleinu Berachamim. Ki	תֵּפֶן אֵלֵינוּ בְּרַחֲמִים. כִּי
Attah Hu Ba'al Harachamim:	אַתָּה הוּא בַּעַל הָרַחֲמִים:
Betachanun Uvitfillah Nekadem.	בְּתַחֲנוּן וּבִתְפִלָּה נְקַדֵּם.
Kemo Shehoda'ta Le'anav	כְּמוֹ שֶׁהוֹדַעְתָּ לֶעָנָו
Mikedem: Umecharon Apecha	מִקֶּדֶם: וּמֵחֲרוֹן אַפְּךָ
Tashuv. Kemo Betoratecha Katuv.	תָּשׁוּב. כְּמוֹ בְּתוֹרָתְךָ כָּתוּב.
Uvetzel Kenafeicha Necheseh	וּבְצֵל כְּנָפֶיךָ נֶחֱסֶה
Venitlonan. Keyom Vayered	וְנִתְלוֹנָן. כְּיוֹם וַיֵּרֶד
Adonai Be'anan: Ta'avor Al	יְהֹוָה בֶּעָנָן: תַּעֲבֹר עַל
Pesha Vetimchol Asham. Keyom	פֶּשַׁע וְתִמְחֹל אָשָׁם. כְּיוֹם
Vayityatzev Imo Sham: Ta'azin	וַיִּתְיַצֵּב עִמּוֹ שָׁם: תַּאֲזִין
Sheva Vetakeshiv Beratzon	שֶׁוַע וְתַקְשִׁיב בְּרָצוֹן
Ma'amar. Keyom Vayikra Veshem	מַאֲמָר. כְּיוֹם וַיִּקְרָא בְשֵׁם
Adonai: Vesham Ne'emar:	יְהֹוָה: וְשָׁם נֶאֱמַר:

Through Your unbounded mercies forgive us, our Father, for in the greatness of our foolishness have we erred. Pardon us, our King, for our iniquities are many. Oh God, You are long-suffering, and have shown us the way of repentance. Remember this day the greatness of Your mercy and kindness, to the posterity of Your beloved; and turn to us with mercy, for You are the Master of mercy. With supplication and prayer we appear before You, as You made known to the humble one of old (Moshe). Turn from Your fierce anger, as it is written in Your Torah; so that we may take refuge and abide under the shadow of Your wings, as at the day, of which it was said, "Hashem descended in the cloud." Pass by our transgression, and pardon our trespass, as on the day, of which it was said, "He stood with him there," Hear our cry, and heed favorably to our speech, as on the day of which it was said, "He proclaimed the name of Hashem." And there it is said:

[*] denotes a slight pause between words:

וַיַּעֲבֹר יְהוָה | עַל־פָּנָיו וַיִּקְרָא יְהוָה * יְהוָה אֵל רַחוּם וְחַנּוּן אֶרֶךְ אַפַּיִם וְרַב־חֶסֶד וֶאֱמֶת: נֹצֵר חֶסֶד לָאֲלָפִים נֹשֵׂא עָוֺן וָפֶשַׁע וְחַטָּאָה וְנַקֵּה:

Vaya'avor Adonai 'Al-Panav Vayikra Adonai * Adonai El Rachum Vechanun; Erech Apayim Verav-Chesed Ve'emet. Notzer Chesed La'alafim. Nosei Avon Vafesha Vechata'ah; Venakeh.

And Hashem passed by before him, and proclaimed: 'Hashem * Hashem, God, merciful and gracious, long-suffering, and abundant in goodness and truth; keeping mercy to the thousandth generation, forgiving iniquity and transgression and sin, and clearing (those who repent).

Azai Bevagedi. Imrei Dar	אֲזַי בְּבָגְדִי. אִמְרֵי דָר
Me'oni. Behistareg Avoni.	מְעוֹנִי. בְּהִשְׂתָּרֵג עֲוֹנִי.
Hichbid Uli Moni. Gavar Alai	הִכְבִּיד עֻלִּי מוֹנִי. גָּבַר עָלַי
Zar Bemahalom Lehallemeni.	זָר בְּמַהֲלֹם לְהַלְמֵנִי.
Appo Taraf Vayistemeni:	אַפּוֹ טָרַף וַיִּשְׂטְמֵנִי:
Derachav Zanachti Asher Li	דְּרָכָיו זָנַחְתִּי אֲשֶׁר לִי
Horah. Hen Al Ken He'ir Bi Af	הוֹרָה. הֵן עַל כֵּן הֵעִיר בִּי אַף
Veza'am Ve'evrah. Za'mo Bi	וָזַעַם וְעֶבְרָה. זַעְמוֹ בִּי
Herik Vechitzav Bi Yarah.	הֵרִיק וְחִצָּיו בִּי יָרָה.
Vaykimeni Lo Lemattarah:	וַיְקִימֵנִי לוֹ לְמַטָּרָה:
Chalefu Alai Beyom Zeh	חָלְפוּ עָלַי בְּיוֹם זֶה
Chamesh Tela'ot. Tarefu Chayati	חָמֵשׁ תְּלָאוֹת. טָרְפוּ חַיָּתִי
Vaysimuni Lemashu'ot. Yage'ah	וַיְשִׂימוּנִי לְמַשּׁוּאוֹת. יָגְעָה

Nafshi Yagoa' Vehal'ot. Na'aveiti	נַפְשִׁי יָגוֹעַ וְהַלְאוֹת. נַעֲוֵיתִי
Mishemoa'. Nivhalti Mere'ot:	מִשְּׁמֹעַ. נִבְהַלְתִּי מֵרְאוֹת:
Kol Eleh Bezacheri Ye'oreruni	כָּל־אֵלֶּה בְּזָכְרִי יְעוֹרְרוּנִי
Anachot. Lehavah Hesikatni	אֲנָחוֹת. לֶהָבָה הֱשִׂיקַתְנִי
Melahetet Kesel Vetuchot.	מְלַהֶטֶת כֶּסֶל וְטוּחוֹת.
Misped Mar Agdil Ve'archik	מִסְפֵּד מַר אַגְדִּיל וְאַרְחִיק
Semachot. Ki Veyom Zeh	שְׂמָחוֹת. כִּי בְּיוֹם זֶה
Nishtaberu Haluchot: No'ad Alai	נִשְׁתַּבְּרוּ הַלּוּחוֹת: נוֹעַד עָלַי
Zar Vahamonav Hitzmid.	זָר וַהֲמוֹנָיו הִצְמִיד.
Sabbuni Chamayim Vetava'ti	סַבּוּנִי כַּמַּיִם וְטָבַעְתִּי
Ve'ein Ma'amid. Al Ken Ayelil	וְאֵין מַעֲמִיד. עַל כֵּן אֲיֵלִיל
Bemo Fi. Venehi Atmid. Ki	בְּמוֹ פִּי. וְנֶהִי אַתְמִיד. כִּי
Veyom Zeh Buttal Hatamid:	בְּיוֹם זֶה בֻּטַּל הַתָּמִיד:
Poshechai Hamu Kahamot	פּוֹשְׁחַי הָמוּ כַּהֲמוֹת
Zerem Michal. Tzametu Vabor	זֶרֶם מִיכַל. צָמְתוּ בַבּוֹר
Chayai Vayitenuni Lema'achal.	חַיַּי וַיִּתְּנוּנִי לְמַאֲכָל.
Kara Alai Mo'ed Vahamonai	קָרָא עָלַי מוֹעֵד וַהֲמוֹנַי
Shachol Shikal. Ki Beyom Zeh	שָׁכֹל שִׁכֵּל. כִּי בְּיוֹם זֶה
Ho'omad Tzelem Baheichal:	הָעֳמַד צֶלֶם בְּהֵיכָל:
Rabbati Am. Zar Hetzar	רַבָּתִי עָם. זָר הֵצַר
Ufetacheiha Petach He'erah.	וּפְתָחֶיהָ פֶּתַח הֶעֱרָה.
Shat Gafni Leshamah Beyom	שָׁת גַּפְנִי לְשַׁמָּה בְּיוֹם
Za'am Ve'evrah. Ta'avato Ra'ah	זַעַם וְעֶבְרָה. תַּאֲוָתוֹ רָאָה
Zar Veyado Be'oz Gavrah. Ki	זָר וְיָדוֹ בְּעֹז גָּבְרָה. כִּי
Veyom Zeh Saraf Apposetemos	בְּיוֹם זֶה שָׂרַף אַפּוֹסְטְמוֹס
Et Hatorah: Chareku Shen	אֶת־הַתּוֹרָה: חָרְקוּ שֵׁן
Resha'im Beyom Af Adonai Bi	רְשָׁעִים בְּיוֹם אַף יְהוָה בִּי

He'ir. Lo Chamal Zar Ve'ikesh Al	הָעִיר. לֹא חָמַל זָר וְעִקֵּשׁ עַל
Yashish Vetza'ir. Appo Bi Charah	יָשִׁישׁ וְצָעִיר. אַפּוֹ בִּי חָרָה
Ureshappav Bi Hiv'ir. Ki Veyom	וּרְשָׁפָיו בִּי הִבְעִיר. כִּי בְיוֹם
Zeh Haveke'ah Ha'ir: Rachem	זֶה הָבְקְעָה הָעִיר: רַחֵם
Adonai Vedaber Al Lev Agumim.	יְהֹוָה וְדַבֵּר עַל לֵב עֲגוּמִים.
Beshiv'ah Asar Lachodesh	בְּשִׁבְעָה עָשָׂר לַחֹדֶשׁ
Yoshevim Mishtomemim. Yah	יוֹשְׁבִים מִשְׁתּוֹמְמִים. יָהּ
Galgel Aleihem Hamon	גַּלְגֵּל עֲלֵיהֶם הֲמוֹן
Rachameicha Mimeromim. El	רַחֲמֶיךָ מִמְּרוֹמִים. אֵל
Melech Yoshev Al Kisse	מֶלֶךְ יוֹשֵׁב עַל כִּסֵּא
Rachamim:	רַחֲמִים:

At the time that I became unfaithful to the word of the Dweller in heaven, when my sins had accumulated, my oppressor laid a heavy yoke on me, the stranger's power increased, and he hit me with heavy blows, as it were with a hammer; he tore me in his wrath and bitterly hated me. I had neglected the way of Hashem which He had taught me; it was then that He stirred up against me anger, wrath, and indignation; yes, He poured out all his wrath, and shot off His arrows against me, and set me up as it were for a mark. Five afflictions on this day passed over me; the enemy tore in pieces my army, and doomed me to destruction; my soul is wearied of fatigue and troubles; I am too overburdened, so that I cannot hear; I am too much frightened, so that I cannot see. When I remember all these things, agony takes hold of me; a flame overwhelms me, burning up my loins and reins; bitterly will I then lament, and remove far all joys, for on this day the tablets were broken. Against me, the stranger took counsel and brought his armies close upon me; they encircled me like water, I sunk, and there was no one to raise me up; therefore, will I bewail my state and ever complete laments, for on this day the daily sacrifice ceased. My murderers roared as the rushing waterfall;

they destroyed my life in the prison, and made me as food for the sword; they called an assembly against me, and destroyed my multitudes; for on this day an image was placed in the Temple. The stranger attacked the populated city, and burst open its gates; he rendered my vine desolate, on this day of wrath and anger; yes, the stranger saw the fulfillment of his desire, and the power of his hand increased; for on this day Posthumus burned the Torah. The wicked gnashed their teeth on the day Hashem stirred His anger against me; the stranger had no compassion, and oppressed both old and young; his anger burned against me, and he fanned the embers of his fury; for on this day the city was taken. Have mercy, Hashem, and speak comfort to the heart of the grieved, who sit astonished because of all their troubles on the seventeenth day of this month; Hashem, awaken over them the greatness of Your mercy from heaven; omnipotent King, Who sits on the Throne of mercy.

She'eh Ne'sar. Asher Nimsar.	שְׁעֵה נֶאְסַר. אֲשֶׁר נִמְסַר.
Beyad Bavel Vesar Ha'ir: Lecha	בְּיַד בָּבֶל וְשַׂר הָעִיר: לְךָ
Yehemeh. Zeh Chameh.	יֶהֱמֶה. זֶה כַּמֶּה.
Veyitchanen Keven Tza'ir:	וְיִתְחַנֵּן כְּבֵן צָעִיר:
Mulecha Tzur. Belev Atzur.	מוּלְךָ צוּר. בְּלֵב עָצוּר.
Hemyat Me'av Yas'ir: Yom Gavar	הֶמְיַת מֵעָיו יַסְעִיר: יוֹם גָּבַר
Ha'oyev Vatibaka Ha'ir: Lezot	הָאוֹיֵב וַתִּבָּקַע הָעִיר: לְזֹאת
Ikaf. Ve'espok Kaf. Beyom	אִכַּף. וְאֶסְפֹּק כַּף. בְּיוֹם
Chamesh Kera'uni: Ve'al Regel.	חָמֵשׁ קְרָאוּנִי: וְעַל רֶגֶל.
Ha'egel. Haluchot Yetza'uni:	הָעֵגֶל. הַלּוּחוֹת יְצָאוּנִי:
Velachad Zar. Hamivtzar.	וְלָכַד זָר. הַמִּבְצָר.
Uvemasger Hevi'ani: Vegam	וּבְמַסְגֵּר הֱבִיאָנִי: וְגַם
Hishmid. Hatamid. Ume'asoto	הִשְׁמִיד. הַתָּמִיד. וּמַעֲשׂוֹתוֹ

Kela'ani: Vehusam Elil. Beheichal	כְּלָאָנִי: וְהוּשַׂם אֱלִיל. בְּהֵיכָל
Kalil. Vedatecha Zar Ba'esh	כָּלִיל. וְדָתְךָ זָר בָּאֵשׁ
Hiv'ir: Me'od Etchal.	הִבְעִיר: מְאֹד אֶתְחַל.
Va'etchalchal. Beyom Shaddai	וָאֶתְחַלְחַל. בְּיוֹם שַׁדַּי
Chasafani: Vehashefifon.	חֲשָׂפַנִי: וְהַשְּׁפִיפוֹן.
Mitzafon. Keshibolet Shetafani:	מִצָּפוֹן. כְּשִׁבּוֹלֶת שְׁטָפַנִי:
Venahag Shevi. Eretz Tzevi.	וְנָהַג שְׁבִי. אֶרֶץ צְבִי.
Vegam Kaddur Tzenafani: Yom	וְגַם כַּדּוּר צְנָפַנִי: יוֹם
Chashach. Me'or Sheshach.	חָשַׁךְ. מְאוֹר שֵׁשַׁךְ.
Leyad Paras Dechafani: Achalani.	לְיַד פָּרַס דְּחָפַנִי: אֲכָלַנִי.
Hamamani. Vekinah Alei Zot	הֲמָמַנִי. וְקִינָה עֲלֵי זֹאת
A'ir: Hala'ad Bi. Misgabbi.	אָעִיר: הֲלָעַד בִּי. מִשְׂגַּבִּי.
Hala'ad Apecha Ye'shan: Gedor	הֲלָעַד אַפְּךָ יֶעְשַׁן: גְּדוֹר
Pirtzi. Beven Partzi. Umechedek	פִּרְצִי. בְּבֶן פַּרְצִי. וּמֵחֶדֶק
Lekot Shoshan: Ayin Pekach.	לְקֹט שׁוֹשָׁן: עַיִן פְּקַח.
Tefillati Kach. Kemo Chelev	תְּפִלָּתִי קַח. כְּמוֹ חֵלֶב
Hamedushan: Beneh Veit Zevul.	הַמְּדֻשָּׁן: בְּנֵה בֵית זְבוּל.
Vehasheiv Gevul. Hakarmel	וְהָשֵׁב גְּבוּל. הַכַּרְמֶל
Vehabbashan: Shefot Illem. Ve'az	וְהַבָּשָׁן: שְׁפֹט אִלֵּם. וְאָז
Yeshalem. Hamav'eh	יְשַׁלֵּם. הַמַּבְעֶה
Vehamav'ir:	וְהַמַּבְעִיר:

Accept the prayer of those who were bound because of their sins, and delivered into the hands of the king of Bavel and the governor of the city; to You they have long spoken their complaints, and petitioned You as a tender child; with a grieving heart, our Protector, and yearning bowels, they earnestly implore You; on the day that the enemy prevailed, and the city was taken. For this I will bend down and strike my hands together, on the day when five calamities happened to me; for the sin of the calf the tablets were taken from me; the enemy took our stronghold, and led me to prison; he also abolished the daily sacrifice, and hindered me from offering it; an idol was put in the beautiful Temple; and the stranger burned Your Torah with fire; on the day that the enemy prevailed, and the city was taken. I am exceedingly pained and terrified on the day the Almighty left me unprotected, when the adder of the north overwhelmed me like a flood of water, and led me captive from the land of delight, and tossed me around like a ball; even on the day when Bavel's light was darkened he delivered me into the hand of the Persians, who also consumed and crushed me; for this I will take up lamentations; on the day that the enemy prevailed, and the city was taken. Is it then forever, my Refuge, is it then forever, that Your anger is to burn against me? Repair my breech through the means of the son of Peretz; pluck the rose from among the thorns; open Your eyes and accept my prayer as the purest fat-offering; build the House of Your Habitation, and restore the boundary of Carmel and Bashan; judge also the mighty oppressors, and then they will be punished, who destroyed Your people and burnt Your House.

Elohei Yeshu'atenu. She'eh	אֱלֹהֵי יְשׁוּעָתֵנוּ. שְׁעֵה
Shav'atenu. Ure'eh	שַׁוְעָתֵנוּ. וּרְאֵה
Shomemoteinu. Ve'orech	שׁוֹמְמוֹתֵינוּ. וְאֹרֶךְ
Galutenu. Middei Shanah	גָּלוּתֵנוּ. מִדֵּי שָׁנָה
Veshanah. Bezacherenu	בְשָׁנָה. בְּזָכְרֵנוּ
Enutenu. Beyom Chamishah	עֱנוּתֵנוּ. בְּיוֹם חֲמִשָּׁה
Devarim. Ere'u Et Avoteinu: Na	דְבָרִים. אֵרְעוּ אֶת־אֲבוֹתֵינוּ: נָא
Elohei Haruchot. Uvochein Sitrei	אֱלֹהֵי הָרוּחוֹת. וּבוֹחֵן סִתְרֵי
Tuchot. She'eh Seyot Niddachot.	טוּחוֹת. שְׁעֵה שֵׂיוֹת נִדָּחוֹת.
Nefutzot Be'arba Ruchot. Middei	נְפוּצוֹת בְּאַרְבַּע רוּחוֹת. מִדֵּי

Shanah Veshanah Bizman Zeh	שָׁנָה בְשָׁנָה בִּזְמַן זֶה
Ne'enachot. Beyom Ekev	נֶאֱנָחוֹת. בְּיוֹם עֵקֶב
Madduchot. Nishtaberu	מַדּוּחוֹת. נִשְׁתַּבְּרוּ
Haluchot. Uvo Kol Yemei	הַלּוּחוֹת. וּבוֹ כָּל־יְמֵי
Shenoteinu. Nemarer Al	שְׁנוֹתֵינוּ. נְמָרֵר עַל
Yegonenu: Deleh Mitit Hayaven.	יְגוֹנֵנוּ: דְּלֵה מְטִיט הַיָּוֵן.
Tevu'im Bo Ve'ein Ma'amid. Eder	טְבוּעִים בּוֹ וְאֵין מַעֲמִיד. עֵדֶר
Tattah Lema'achal. Levizah	תַּתָּה לְמַאֲכָל. לְבִזָּה
Ulehashmid. Middei Shanah	וּלְהַשְׁמִיד. מִדֵּי שָׁנָה
Veshanah. Beyom Zeh Etzev	בְשָׁנָה. בְּיוֹם זֶה עֶצֶב
Matzmid. Yom Bo Yad Zar	מַצְמִיד. יוֹם בּוֹ יַד זָר
He'emir. Uvo Buttal Hatamid. Al	הֶאֱמִיר. וּבוֹ בֻּטַּל הַתָּמִיד. עַל
Rov Avonoteinu. Ve'otzem	רֹב עֲוֹנוֹתֵינוּ. וְעֹצֶם
Chatoteinu: Yah Asher Hakol	חַטֹּאתֵינוּ: יָהּ אֲשֶׁר הַכֹּל
Yuchal. Pedeh Mishchol Shachal.	יוּכַל. פְּדֵה מִשְּׁכוֹל שָׁכַל.
Miyad Ikesh Vesachal. Ushe'ar	מִיַּד עִקֵּשׁ וְסָכָל. וּשְׁאָר
Ya'akov Achal. Middei Shanah	יַעֲקֹב אָכַל. מִדֵּי שָׁנָה
Beshanah. Beyom Zeh Mamror	בְּשָׁנָה. בְּיוֹם זֶה מַמְרֹר
Ochal. Beha'amid Zar Lemuli.	אוֹכַל. בְּהַעֲמִיד זָר לְמוּלִי.
Bo Tzelem Baheichal. Al Kol	בּוֹ צֶלֶם בַּהֵיכָל. עַל כָּל־
Koroteinu Yizelu Dim'oteinu:	קוֹרוֹתֵינוּ יִזְּלוּ דִמְעוֹתֵינוּ:
Shivrenu Mah Nora. Ki Sarnu	שִׁבְרֵנוּ מַה־נּוֹרָא. כִּי סַרְנוּ
Mimora. Na'or Oteh Orah.	מִמּוֹרָא. נָאוֹר עֹטֶה אוֹרָה.
Gemuli Lakkoal Horah. Middei	גְּמוּלִי לַכֹּל הוֹרָה. מִדֵּי
Shanah Veshanah. Nehi Beyom	שָׁנָה בְשָׁנָה. נְהִי בְּיוֹם
Zeh Echkorah. Ya'an Ki Vo Saraf	זֶה אֶחְקוֹרָה. יַעַן כִּי בוֹ שָׂרַף
Apposetemos Et Hatorah. Lezot	אַפּוֹסְטְמוֹס אֶת־הַתּוֹרָה. לְזֹאת

Nishkevah Bevashetenu. Leshod	נִשְׁכְּבָה בְּבָשְׁתֵּנוּ. לְשׁוֹד
Beit Tif'artenu: Rachum	בֵּית תִּפְאַרְתֵּנוּ: רַחוּם
Yechapeir Avon. Vechol Chamato	יְכַפֵּר עָוֹן. וְכָל־חֲמָתוֹ
Lo Ya'ir. Pedeh Chish Midei Sa'ir.	לֹא יָעִיר. פְּדֵה חִישׁ מִידֵי שָׂעִיר.
Pezurei Hatzon Vetza'ir. Middei	פְּזוּרֵי הַצֹּאן וְצָעִיר. מִדֵּי
Shanah Veshanah. Beyom Zeh	שָׁנָה בְשָׁנָה. בְּיוֹם זֶה
Hemyat Me'av Yas'ir. Yom	הֶמְיַת מֵעָיו יַסְעִיר. יוֹם
Gaveru Hazarim Vatibaka Ha'ir.	גָּבְרוּ הַזָּרִים וַתִּבָּקַע הָעִיר.
Ki Hayinu Lela'ag Vakeles	כִּי הָיִינוּ לְלַעַג וָקֶלֶס
Lisvivoteinu: Rachaman	לִסְבִיבוֹתֵינוּ: רַחֲמָן
Berachamim Shuvah. El Tziyon	בְּרַחֲמִים שׁוּבָה. אֶל צִיּוֹן
Ha'aluvah. Vechish Na Le'ishah	הָעֲלוּבָה. וְחִישׁ נָא לְאִשָּׁה
Atzuvah. Nechamah Haketuvah.	עֲצוּבָה. נֶחָמָה הַכְּתוּבָה.
Ve'az Shirah Nanuvah.	וְאָז שִׁירָה נָנוּבָה.
Bivnotecha Hacharevah.	בִּבְנוֹתְךָ הַחֲרֵבָה.
Bekibutz Nefutzoteinu.	בְּקִבּוּץ נְפוּצוֹתֵינוּ.
Uveshuvecha Et Shevutenu:	וּבְשׁוּבְךָ אֶת שְׁבוּתֵנוּ:

God of our salvation, have regard to our prayer; attentively view our desolate places, and the length of our captivity; when we from year to year remember our affliction, on the day that five calamities happened to our ancestors. on the day that the enemy prevailed, and the city was taken. God of all spirits, Who knows the most hidden secrets, we implore You to regard the outcast lambs that are scattered into the four corners of the earth; who from year to year at this time lament; on the day, when for our apostacy the tablets were broken; and on this all the days of our life will we mourn bitterly over our sorrows. On the day that the enemy prevailed, and the city was taken. Draw out from the miry clay those who are sunk in it, and have no one to lift them up; even the flock which You have delivered over to be devoured, spoiled, and destroyed; from year to year, on this day our sorrow is continuing; for it is the day on which the hand of the stranger prevailed, and the daily sacrifice ceased, because of the multitude of our iniquities, and the strength of our sins. On the day that the enemy prevailed, and the city was taken. Hashem, Who is all-powerful, redeem those who have been deprived of every, good, from the power of the disobedient and foolish, who have devoured what's left of Yaakov; from year to year, we on this day will feed our spirit on bitterness, because on it the stranger placed before me an image in the Temple; therefore, for all which has happened to us, our tears will flow. On the day that the enemy prevailed, and the city was taken. How dreadful is our breach, because we turned aside from Him Who alone is to be feared; the Exalted, Who covers himself with light, has shown my reward as an example to all. From year to year will I on this day seek to mourn, because on it Posthumus burned the Torah; for this will we lie down in our shame, because of the desolation of the house of our glory. On the day that the enemy prevailed, and the city was taken. You Who is merciful, forgives iniquity, and does not awaken all of Your wrath, hasten to redeem from the hands of Seir Your few scattered sheep, who from year to year send out the passionate heaving of their grief, on the day that the strangers prevailed, and the city was taken; for we have become a scorn and derision to those that are around us. On the day that the enemy prevailed, and the city was taken. You Who is most merciful, return to afflicted Tziyon with mercy, and hasten, we implore You, to the sorrowful people, the comfort that is written; Then will we sing songs when You build up the desolate places, when our dispersed are gathered, and You cause our captivity to return.

Continue on the Continuation for the Fast Days section.

Fast of Gedalyah

After the repetition of the Amidah, say Vidui. Then they say:

Al Yedei Rachameicha Harabbim	עַל יְדֵי רַחֲמֶיךָ הָרַבִּים
Selach Lanu Avinu. Ki Verov	סְלַח לָנוּ אָבִינוּ. כִּי בְרוֹב
Ivaltenu Shaginu: Mechol Lanu	אִוַּלְתֵּנוּ שָׁגִינוּ: מְחֹל לָנוּ
Malkeinu. Ki Rabbu Avoneinu: El	מַלְכֵּנוּ. כִּי רַבּוּ עֲוֹנֵינוּ: אֵל
Erech Apayim Attah. Vederech	אֶרֶךְ אַפַּיִם אַתָּה. וְדֶרֶךְ
Teshuvah Lanu Horeita: Gedulat	תְּשׁוּבָה לָנוּ הוֹרֵיתָ: גְּדֻלַּת
Rachameicha Vachasadeicha.	רַחֲמֶיךָ וַחֲסָדֶיךָ.
Tizkor Hayom Lezera Yedideicha:	תִּזְכּוֹר הַיּוֹם לְזֶרַע יְדִידֶיךָ:
Tefen Eleinu Berachamim. Ki	תֵּפֶן אֵלֵינוּ בְּרַחֲמִים. כִּי
Attah Hu Ba'al Harachamim:	אַתָּה הוּא בַּעַל הָרַחֲמִים:
Betachanun Uvitfillah Nekadem.	בְּתַחֲנוּן וּבִתְפִלָּה נְקַדֵּם.
Kemo Shehoda'ta Le'anav	כְּמוֹ שֶׁהוֹדַעְתָּ לֶעָנָו
Mikedem: Umecharon Apecha	מִקֶּדֶם: וּמֵחֲרוֹן אַפְּךָ
Tashuv. Kemo Betoratecha Katuv.	תָּשׁוּב. כְּמוֹ בְּתוֹרָתְךָ כָּתוּב.
Uvetzel Kenafeicha Necheseh	וּבְצֵל כְּנָפֶיךָ נֶחֱסֶה
Venitlonan. Keyom Vayered	וְנִתְלוֹנָן. כְּיוֹם וַיֵּרֶד
Adonai Be'anan: Ta'avor Al	יְהוָה בֶּעָנָן: תַּעֲבֹר עַל
Pesha Vetimchol Asham. Keyom	פֶּשַׁע וְתִמְחֹל אָשָׁם. כְּיוֹם
Vayityatzev Imo Sham: Ta'azin	וַיִּתְיַצֵּב עִמּוֹ שָׁם: תַּאֲזִין
Sheva Vetakeshiv Beratzon	שֶׁוַע וְתַקְשִׁיב בְּרָצוֹן
Ma'amar. Keyom Vayikra Veshem	מַאֲמָר. כְּיוֹם וַיִּקְרָא בְשֵׁם
Adonai: Vesham Ne'emar:	יְהוָה: וְשָׁם נֶאֱמַר:

Through Your unbounded mercies forgive us, our Father, for in the greatness of our foolishness have we erred. Pardon us, our King, for our iniquities are many. Oh God, You are long-suffering, and have shown us the way of repentance. Remember this day the greatness of Your mercy and kindness, to the offspring of Your beloved; and turn to us with mercy, for You are the Master of mercy. With supplication and prayer we appear before You, as You made known to the humble one of old (Moshe). Turn from Your fierce anger, as it is written in Your Torah; so that we may take refuge and abide under the shadow of Your wings, as at the day, of which it was said, "Hashem descended in the cloud." Pass by our transgression, and pardon our trespass, as on the day, of which it was said, "He stood with him there," Hear our cry, and heed favorably to our speech, as on the day of which it was said, "He proclaimed the name of Hashem." And there it is said:

[*] denotes a slight pause between words:

וַיַּעֲבֹר יְהוָה | עַל־פָּנָיו וַיִּקְרָא יְהוָה * יְהוָה אֵל רַחוּם וְחַנּוּן אֶרֶךְ אַפַּיִם וְרַב־חֶסֶד וֶאֱמֶת: נֹצֵר חֶסֶד לָאֲלָפִים נֹשֵׂא עָוֹן וָפֶשַׁע וְחַטָּאָה וְנַקֵּה:

Vaya'avor Adonai 'Al-Panav Vayikra Adonai * Adonai El Rachum Vechanun; Erech Apayim Verav-Chesed Ve'emet. Notzer Chesed La'alafim. Nosei Avon Vafesha Vechata'ah; Venakeh.

And Hashem passed by before him, and proclaimed: 'Hashem * Hashem, God, merciful and gracious, long-suffering, and abundant in goodness and truth; keeping mercy to the thousandth generation, forgiving iniquity and transgression and sin, and clearing (those who repent).

Avelah Nafshi Vechashach To'ori.	אֲבְלָה נַפְשִׁי וְחָשַׁךְ תָּאֳרִי.
Beit Tif'arti Nisraf Beyad Ha'ari.	בֵּית תִּפְאַרְתִּי נִשְׂרַף בְּיַד הָאֲרִי.
Gam Peletim Asher Azevu	גַּם פְּלֵטִים אֲשֶׁר עָזְבוּ
She'eri. Do'achu Hayom	שְׁאֵרִי. דּוֹעֲכוּ הַיּוֹם

Bishloshah Vetishri: Hamayim	בִּשְׁלֹשָׁה בְּתִשְׁרִי: הַמַּיִם
Hazedonim Shetafunu	הַזֵּדוֹנִים שֶׁטְּפוּנוּ
Bedolkam. Uvosesu Tzarim	בְּדָלְקָם. וּבוֹסְסוּ צָרִים
Mikdashi Uvazezu Chelkam.	מִקְדָּשִׁי וּבָזְזוּ חֶלְקָם.
Ziknei She'erit Asher Nimletu	זִקְנֵי שְׁאֵרִית אֲשֶׁר נִמְלְטוּ
Beyom Nakam. Chubbelu	בְּיוֹם נָקָם. חֻבְּלוּ
Hayom Im Gedalyah Ben	הַיּוֹם עִם גְּדַלְיָה בֶּן
Achikam: Torefu Aniyei Am	אֲחִיקָם: טוֹרְפוּ עֲנִיֵּי עַם
Ha'aretz. Yeter Hagazam Achal	הָאָרֶץ. יֶתֶר הַגָּזָם אָכַל
Ha'arbeh Bemeretz. Koremim	הָאַרְבֶּה בְּמֶרֶץ. כּוֹרְמִים
Veyogevim Asher Hifkid Negid	וְיוֹגְבִים אֲשֶׁר הִפְקִיד נְגִיד
Ha'aretz. Lukketu Hayom Velo	הָאָרֶץ. לֻקְּטוּ הַיּוֹם וְלֹא
Hayah Vahem Goder Gader	הָיָה בָּהֶם גּוֹדֵר גָּדֵר
Ve'omed Baperetz: Mah Asaper	וְעוֹמֵד בַּפֶּרֶץ: מָה אֲסַפֵּר
Ve'anchotai Atzumot. Naketah	וְאַנְחוֹתַי עֲצוּמוֹת. נָקְטָה
Nafshi Umikhalotai Agumot.	נַפְשִׁי וּמִקְהָלוֹתַי עֲגוּמוֹת.
Seridai Asher Nish'aru Mecherev	שְׂרִידַי אֲשֶׁר נִשְׁאֲרוּ מֵחֶרֶב
Vechemot. Od Hem Lo	וְחֵמוֹת. עוֹד הֵם לֹא
Nitkayemu Venotetzu Vachomot:	נִתְקַיְּמוּ וְנוּתְּצוּ בַחוֹמוֹת:
Paneicha Ad Anah Mimenu	פָּנֶיךָ עַד אָנָה מִמֶּנּוּ
Tastir. Tzavchatenu Tishma	תַּסְתִּיר. צַוְחָתֵנוּ תִּשְׁמַע
Vechavlenu Tatir. Kadosh	וְכַבְלֵנוּ תַּתִּיר. קָדוֹשׁ
Habitah Ve'oneyenu Ki Ein Lanu	הַבִּיטָה בְּעָנְיֵנוּ כִּי אֵין לָנוּ
Machtir. Re'eh Dalutenu	מַכְתִּיר. רְאֵה דַּלּוּתֵנוּ
Veshevach Lefaneicha Na'tir:	וְשֶׁבַח לְפָנֶיךָ נַעְתִּיר:
Shuddadnu Middor Ledor	שֻׁדַּדְנוּ מִדּוֹר לְדוֹר

Umikketz Leketz. Shoresh Tzefa	וּמִקֵּץ לְקֵץ. שֹׁרֶשׁ צֶפַע
Otanu Ikketz. Takkif	אוֹתָנוּ עִקֵּץ. תַּקִּיף
Lemishpateicha Ha'irah	לְמִשְׁפָּטֶיךָ הָעִירָה
Vehaketz. Utechapeir Chatoteinu	וְהָקֵץ. וּתְכַפֵּר חַטֹּאתֵינוּ
Vetomar Lekarev Ketz: Yehemu	וְתֹאמַר לְקָרֵב קֵץ: יֶהֱמוּ
Rachameicha Al Me'utei	רַחֲמֶיךָ עַל מְעוּטֵי
Ammim. Vesagevem	עַמִּים. וְשַׂגְּבֵם
Bechasdecha Le'einei Chol	בְּחַסְדֶּךָ לְעֵינֵי כָל
Le'ummim. Pela'eicha Har'em	לְאֻמִּים. פְּלָאֶיךָ הַרְאֵם
Shochein Meromim. El Melech	שׁוֹכֵן מְרוֹמִים. אֵל מֶלֶךְ
Yoshev Al Kisse Rachamim:	יוֹשֵׁב עַל כִּסֵּא רַחֲמִים:

My soul mourns, and my form is darkened; because the house of my glory was burnt by the hand of the lion; the remnant also, who were allowed to escape, were consumed on this third day of Tishrei. The waves of wickedness overwhelmed us in their pursuit; our enemies trampled down our Sanctuary; they seized it as their portion; the elders of the remnant, who escaped on the day of vengeance, were this day destroyed with Gedaliah, the son of Ahikam. They tore in pieces the poor people of the land, so that what the palmer-worm had left, the locust utterly devoured; the wine dressers and farmers, whom the ruler of the land had appointed to remain, were this day gathered, and there was not one among them that could repair the wall or stand in the breach.' How will I declare the greatness of my sorrows? My soul is in anguish, and my congregations grieve; for the remnant of those that were spared by the sword, and escaped the fury, before they were settled, were thrown down with the walls. How long will You hide Your face from us? Hear our cry, and loosen our chains; look down on our affliction, for we have no one to protect us; view our poverty and the praise which we offer in Your presence. In all ages and all times have we been spoiled; the offspring of the snake have stung us; do You, Who are most mighty, arise and awaken for judgment; grant atonement for our sins, and command the end of our captivity to draw near. Let Your mercy incline towards the people smallest in number, and exalt them by Your kindness, in the sight of all nations; show them Your wonders, You Who dwells on high; Omnipotent King, Who sits upon the Throne of mercy.

Continue on to the Continuation for the Fast Days section below.

Continuation for the Order of the Four Fast Days

All fasts continue from here:

El Melech Yoshev Al Kissei	אֵל מֶלֶךְ יוֹשֵׁב עַל כִּסֵּא
Rachamim Umitnaheg	רַחֲמִים וּמִתְנַהֵג
Bachasidut. Mochel Avonot	בַּחֲסִידוּת. מוֹחֵל עֲוֹנוֹת
Ammo. Ma'avir Rishon Rishon.	עַמּוֹ. מַעֲבִיר רִאשׁוֹן רִאשׁוֹן.
Marbeh Mechilah Lachata'im.	מַרְבֶּה מְחִילָה לְחַטָּאִים.
Uselichah Lapposhe'im. Oseh	וּסְלִיחָה לַפּוֹשְׁעִים. עוֹשֶׂה
Tzedakot Im Kol Basar Veruach.	צְדָקוֹת עִם כָּל בָּשָׂר וְרוּחַ.
Lo Chera'atam Lahem Gomel. El.	לֹא כְרָעָתָם לָהֶם גּוֹמֵל. אֵל.
Horetanu Lomar Middot Shelosh	הוֹרֵתָנוּ לוֹמַר מִדּוֹת שְׁלֹשׁ
Esreh. Zechor Lanu Hayom Berit	עֶשְׂרֵה. זְכוֹר לָנוּ הַיּוֹם בְּרִית
Shelosh Esreh Kemo Shehoda'ta	שְׁלֹשׁ עֶשְׂרֵה כְּמוֹ שֶׁהוֹדַעְתָּ
Le'anav Mikedem. Vechein Katuv	לֶעָנָו מִקֶּדֶם. וְכֵן כָּתוּב
Betoratach Vayered Adonai	בְּתוֹרָתָךְ וַיֵּרֶד יְהוָה
Be'anan. Vayityatzev Imo Sham;	בֶּעָנָן וַיִּתְיַצֵּב עִמּוֹ שָׁם

וַיִּקְרָא בְשֵׁם יְהֹוָה: וְשָׁם נֶאֱמַר:

Vayikra Veshem Adonai. Vesham Ne'emar.

Sovereign God, enthroned in mercy, You deal with us tenderly, again pardoning the sins of Your people even though they sin again. You are ever ready to give pardon to sinners and forgiveness to transgressors, acting in charity towards all with breath of life, not requiting them according to the evil they do. You, God, Who has taught us to repeat the thirteen attributes of mercy, remember to us this day the covenant of those attributes, as You did reveal them of old to Moshe the humble, in the words written in Your Torah: "And Hashem descended in the cloud, and stood with him there, and proclaimed the name of Hashem." (Exodus 34:5) And there it says:

[*] denotes a slight pause between words:

וַיַּעֲבֹר יְהֹוָה | עַל־פָּנָיו וַיִּקְרָא יְהֹוָה * יְהֹוָה אֵל רַחוּם וְחַנּוּן אֶרֶךְ אַפַּיִם וְרַב־חֶסֶד וֶאֱמֶת: נֹצֵר חֶסֶד לָאֲלָפִים נֹשֵׂא עָוֹן וָפֶשַׁע וְחַטָּאָה וְנַקֵּה:

Vaya'avor Adonai 'Al-Panav Vayikra Adonai * Adonai El Rachum Vechanun; Erech Apayim Verav-Chesed Ve'emet. Notzer Chesed La'alafim. Nosei Avon Vafesha Vechata'ah; Venakeh.

And Hashem passed by before him, and proclaimed: 'Hashem * Hashem, God, merciful and gracious, long-suffering, and abundant in goodness and truth; keeping mercy to the thousandth generation, forgiving iniquity and transgression and sin, and clearing (those who repent).

אַנְשֵׁי אֱמוּנָה אָבָדוּ. בָּאִים בְּכֹחַ מַעֲשֵׂיהֶם: גִּבּוֹרִים לַעֲמֹד בַּפֶּרֶץ. דּוֹחִים אֶת־הַגְּזֵרוֹת: הָיוּ לָנוּ

Anshei Emunah Avadu. Ba'im Bechoach Ma'aseihem: Giborim La'amod Baperetz. Dochim Et Hagezerot: Hayu Lanu

Lechomah. Ulemachseh Beyom	לְחוֹמָה. וּלְמַחְסֶה בְּיוֹם
Za'am: Zo'achim Af	זָעַם: זוֹעֲכִים אַף
Belachasham. Chemah Atzeru	בְּלַחֲשָׁם. חֵמָה עָצְרוּ
Beshave'am: Terem Kera'ucha	בְּשַׁוְעָם: טֶרֶם קְרָאוּךָ
Anitam. Yode'im La'ator	עֲנִיתָם. יוֹדְעִים לַעֲתֹר
Uleratzot: Ke'av Richamta	וּלְרַצּוֹת: כְּאָב רִחַמְתָּ
Lema'anam. Lo Heshivota	לְמַעֲנָם. לֹא הֱשִׁיבוֹתָ
Feneihem Reikam: Merov	פְּנֵיהֶם רֵיקָם: מֵרֹב
Avoneinu Avadnum. Ne'esfu	עֲוֹנֵינוּ אֲבַדְנוּם. נֶאֶסְפוּ
Menu Bachata'einu: Sa'u Hemah	מֶנּוּ בַּחֲטָאֵינוּ: סָעוּ הֵמָּה
Limnuchot. Azevu Otanu	לִמְנוּחוֹת. עֲזָבוּ אוֹתָנוּ
La'anachot: Passu Goderei	לַאֲנָחוֹת: פַּסּוּ גּוֹדְרֵי
Gader. Tzummetu Meshivei	גָדֵר. צֻמְּתוּ מְשִׁיבֵי
Chemah: Kamim Baperetz Ayin.	חֵמָה: קָמִים בַּפֶּרֶץ אַיִן.
Re'uyim Leratzotecha Afesu:	רְאוּיִים לְרַצּוֹתְךָ אָפֵסוּ:
Shotatnu Be'arba Pinot. Terufah	שׁוֹטַטְנוּ בְּאַרְבַּע פִּנּוֹת. תְּרוּפָה
Lo Matzanu: Shavnu Eleicha	לֹא מָצָאנוּ: שַׁבְנוּ אֵלֶיךָ
Bevoshet Paneinu. Leshacharach	בְּבֹשֶׁת פָּנֵינוּ. לְשַׁחֲרָךְ
El Be'et Tzaroteinu:	אֵל בְּעֵת צָרוֹתֵינוּ:

The faithful men, who came before You, by virtue of their good works, are lost: they were powerful, and able to stand in the breach, and to repel, by their intercession, the evil decrees. They were a wall to us, and a place of refuge on the day of wrath; extinguishing Your anger by their secret prayer, and restraining wrath by their cry; before they called You answered them, they knew how to obtain favor by prayer; for their sake, You acted like a compassionate father, not dismissing them empty from Your presence. But by reason of the multitude of our iniquities, they are lost to us; they are taken away from us, because of our sins; they are retired to their rest, and have left us to grieve. They, who repaired the wall, are gone; they who turned away Your anger, have ceased to exist; there is no one to stand in the breach; they who were worthy to appease You, have passed away. We have wandered over the four quarters of the globe, but have found no relief. We now return to You, our faces covered with shame, to seek You early, God, in the time of our distress.

El Melech Yoshev Al Kissei	אֶל מֶלֶךְ יוֹשֵׁב עַל כִּסֵּא
Rachamim Umitnaheg	רַחֲמִים וּמִתְנַהֵג
Bachasidut. Mochel Avonot	בַּחֲסִידוּת. מוֹחֵל עֲוֹנוֹת
Ammo. Ma'avir Rishon Rishon.	עַמּוֹ. מַעֲבִיר רִאשׁוֹן רִאשׁוֹן.
Marbeh Mechilah Lachata'im.	מַרְבֶּה מְחִילָה לְחַטָּאִים.
Uselichah Lapposhe'im. Oseh	וּסְלִיחָה לַפּוֹשְׁעִים. עוֹשֶׂה
Tzedakot Im Kol Basar Veruach.	צְדָקוֹת עִם כָּל בָּשָׂר וְרוּחַ.
Lo Chera'atam Lahem Gomel.	לֹא כְרָעָתָם לָהֶם גּוֹמֵל.
El. Horetanu Lomar Middot	אֵל. הוֹרֵתָנוּ לוֹמַר מִדּוֹת
Shelosh Esreh. Zechor Lanu	שְׁלֹשׁ עֶשְׂרֵה. זְכוֹר לָנוּ
Hayom Berit Shelosh Esreh	הַיּוֹם בְּרִית שְׁלֹשׁ עֶשְׂרֵה
Kemo Shehoda'ta Le'anav	כְּמוֹ שֶׁהוֹדַעְתָּ לֶעָנָו
Mikedem. Vechein Katuv	מִקֶּדֶם. וְכֵן כָּתוּב
Betoratach Vayered Adonai	בְּתוֹרָתָךְ וַיֵּרֶד יְהֹוָה
Be'anan. Vayityatzev Imo Sham;	בֶּעָנָן וַיִּתְיַצֵּב עִמּוֹ שָׁם
Vayikra Veshem Adonai. Vesham	וַיִּקְרָא בְשֵׁם יְהֹוָה: וְשָׁם
Ne'emar.	נֶאֱמַר:

Sovereign God, enthroned in mercy, You deal with us tenderly, again pardoning the sins of Your people even though they sin again. You are ever ready to give pardon to sinners and forgiveness to transgressors, acting in charity towards all with breath of life, not requiting them according to the evil they do. You, God, Who has taught us to repeat the thirteen attributes of mercy, remember to us this day the covenant of those attributes, as You did reveal them of old to Moshe the humble, in the words written in Your Torah: "And Hashem descended in the cloud, and stood with him there, and proclaimed the name of Hashem." **(Exodus 34:5)** And there it says:

[*] denotes a slight pause between words:

וַיַּעֲבֹ֨ר יְהוָ֥ה ׀ עַל־פָּנָיו֮ וַיִּקְרָא֒ יְהוָ֣ה * יְהוָ֔ה אֵ֥ל רַח֖וּם וְחַנּ֑וּן אֶ֥רֶךְ
אַפַּ֖יִם וְרַב־חֶ֥סֶד וֶאֱמֶֽת׃ נֹצֵ֥ר חֶ֨סֶד֙ לָאֲלָפִ֔ים נֹשֵׂ֥א עָוֺ֛ן וָפֶ֖שַׁע וְחַטָּאָ֑ה
וְנַקֵּה֙׃

Vaya'avor Adonai 'Al-Panav Vayikra Adonai * Adonai El Rachum Vechanun; Erech Apayim Verav-Chesed Ve'emet. Notzer Chesed La'alafim. Nosei Avon Vafesha Vechata'ah; Venakeh.

And Hashem passed by before him, and proclaimed: 'Hashem * Hashem, God, merciful and gracious, long-suffering, and abundant in goodness and truth; keeping mercy to the thousandth generation, forgiving iniquity and transgression and sin, and clearing (those who repent).

Tamahnu Mera'ot. Tashash	תָּמַהְנוּ מֵרָעוֹת. תָּשַׁשׁ
Kocheinu Mitzarot. Shachnu Ad	כֹּחֵנוּ מִצָּרוֹת. שַׁחְנוּ עַד
Lim'od. Shafalnu Ad Afar.	לִמְאֹד. שָׁפַלְנוּ עַד עָפָר.
Rachum Kach Hi Midatenu.	רַחוּם כָּךְ הִיא מִדָּתֵנוּ.
Keshei Oref Umamrim Anachnu.	קְשֵׁי עֹרֶף וּמַמְרִים אֲנַחְנוּ.
Tza'aknu Befinu Chatanu.	צָעַקְנוּ בְּפִינוּ חָטָאנוּ.

Petaltol Ve'ikesh Libenu. Elyon	פְּתַלְתּוֹל וְעִקֵּשׁ לִבֵּנוּ. עֶלְיוֹן
Rachameicha Me'olam. Selichah	רַחֲמֶיךָ מֵעוֹלָם. סְלִיחָה
Imecha Hi. Nicham Al Hara'ah.	עִמְּךָ הִיא. נִחָם עַל הָרָעָה.
Mateh Chelappei Chesed. Lo	מַטֵּה כְלַפֵּי חֶסֶד. לֹא
Tit'alam Be'itot Ka'el. Ki Vetzarah	תִתְעַלַּם בְּעִתּוֹת כָּאֵל. כִּי בְצָרָה
Gedolah Anachenu. Yivada	גְדוֹלָה אֲנָחְנוּ. יִוָּדַע
Le'einei Hakol. Tuvecha	לְעֵינֵי הַכֹּל. טוּבְךָ
Vechasdecha Imanu. Chatom	וְחַסְדְּךָ עִמָּנוּ. חֲתֹם
Peh Satan. Ve'al Yastin Aleinu.	פֶּה־שָׂטָן. וְאַל יַשְׂטִין עָלֵינוּ.
Ze'om Bo Veyidom. Veya'amod	זְעֹם בּוֹ וְיִדֹּם. וְיַעֲמֹד
Melitz Tov Letzaddekenu. Hu	מֵלִיץ טוֹב לְצַדְּקֵנוּ. הוּא
Yaggid Yasherenu. Deracheicha	יַגִּיד יָשְׁרֵנוּ. דְּרָכֶיךָ
Rachum Vechanun Gillita	רַחוּם וְחַנּוּן גִּלִּיתָ
Lene'eman Bayit. Bevaksho Az	לְנֶאֱמַן בָּיִת. בְּבַקְשׁוֹ אָז
Milfaneicha. Emunatecha	מִלְּפָנֶיךָ. אֱמוּנָתְךָ
Hoda'ta Lo:	הוֹדַעְתָּ לּוֹ:

We are struck with amazement at the evils attending us; our strength is weakened because of our distresses; we are brought exceedingly low; we are humbled to the dust. Merciful God, we are stiff-necked and rebellious; for it is our disposition. Surely we with our mouths cry aloud that we have sinned, while our hearts are contrary and perverse. Most High, Your mercy is eternal, and pardon is with You. Repent of the evil, and incline to mercy. Do not hide Yourself in times like these; for we are in great distress. Let it be manifested in the sight of all, that Your goodness and mercy are with us. Close the mouth of the Adversary, that he may not accuse us; rebuke him, so he is silent; and allow the good intercessor to rise up, to justify us, and declare our uprightness. Merciful and gracious God, You have revealed Your ways to him who was faithful in Your

House, and when he petitioned You, You made Your truth known to him.

El Melech Yoshev Al Kissei	אֵל מֶלֶךְ יוֹשֵׁב עַל כִּסֵּא
Rachamim Umitnaheg	רַחֲמִים וּמִתְנַהֵג
Bachasidut. Mochel Avonot	בַּחֲסִידוּת. מוֹחֵל עֲוֹנוֹת
Ammo. Ma'avir Rishon Rishon.	עַמּוֹ. מַעֲבִיר רִאשׁוֹן רִאשׁוֹן.
Marbeh Mechilah Lachata'im.	מַרְבֶּה מְחִילָה לַחַטָּאִים.
Uselichah Lapposhe'im. Oseh	וּסְלִיחָה לַפּוֹשְׁעִים. עוֹשֶׂה
Tzedakot Im Kol Basar Veruach.	צְדָקוֹת עִם כָּל בָּשָׂר וְרוּחַ.
Lo Chera'atam Lahem Gomel.	לֹא כְרָעָתָם לָהֶם גּוֹמֵל.
El. Horetanu Lomar Middot	אֵל. הוֹרֵתָנוּ לוֹמַר מִדּוֹת
Shelosh Esreh. Zechor Lanu	שְׁלֹשׁ עֶשְׂרֵה. זְכוֹר לָנוּ
Hayom Berit Shelosh Esreh	הַיּוֹם בְּרִית שְׁלֹשׁ עֶשְׂרֵה
Kemo Shehoda'ta Le'anav	כְּמוֹ שֶׁהוֹדַעְתָּ לֶעָנָו
Mikedem. Vechein Katuv	מִקֶּדֶם. וְכֵן כָּתוּב
Betoratach Vayered Adonai	בְּתוֹרָתָךְ וַיֵּרֶד יְהֹוָה
Be'anan. Vayityatzev Imo Sham;	בֶּעָנָן וַיִּתְיַצֵּב עִמּוֹ שָׁם
Vayikra Veshem Adonai. Vesham	וַיִּקְרָא בְשֵׁם יְהֹוָה: וְשָׁם
Ne'emar.	נֶאֱמַר:

Sovereign God, enthroned in mercy, You deal with us tenderly, again pardoning the sins of Your people even though they sin again. You are ever ready to give pardon to sinners and forgiveness to transgressors, acting in charity towards all with breath of life, not requiting them according to the evil they do. You, God, Who has taught us to repeat the thirteen attributes of mercy, remember to us this day the covenant of those attributes, as You did reveal them of old to Moshe the humble, in the words written in Your Torah: "And Hashem descended in the cloud, and stood with him there, and proclaimed the name of Hashem." (Exodus 34:5) And there it says:

[*] denotes a slight pause between words:

וַיַּעֲבֹר יְהֹוָה | עַל־פָּנָיו וַיִּקְרָא יְהֹוָה * יְהֹוָה אֵל רַחוּם וְחַנּוּן אֶרֶךְ אַפַּיִם וְרַב־חֶסֶד וֶאֱמֶת: נֹצֵר חֶסֶד לָאֲלָפִים נֹשֵׂא עָוֹן וָפֶשַׁע וְחַטָּאָה וְנַקֵּה:

Vaya'avor Adonai 'Al-Panav Vayikra Adonai * Adonai El Rachum Vechanun; Erech Apayim Verav-Chesed Ve'emet. Notzer Chesed La'alafim. Nosei Avon Vafesha Vechata'ah; Venakeh.

And Hashem passed by before him, and proclaimed: 'Hashem * Hashem, God, merciful and gracious, long-suffering, and abundant in goodness and truth; keeping mercy to the thousandth generation, forgiving iniquity and transgression and sin, and clearing (those who repent).

Ucheshechate'u Yisra'el	וּכְשֶׁחָטְאוּ יִשְׂרָאֵל
Bamidbar. Amad Mosheh	בַּמִּדְבָּר. עָמַד מֹשֶׁה
Bitfillah Lefaneicha. Uvikesh	בִּתְפִלָּה לְפָנֶיךָ. וּבִקֵּשׁ
Rachamim Al Ammecha Yisra'el	רַחֲמִים עַל עַמְּךָ יִשְׂרָאֵל
Vechach Amar Bitfilato: Selach-	וְכָךְ אָמַר בִּתְפִלָּתוֹ: סְלַח־
Na La'avon Ha'am Hazeh	נָא לַעֲוֹן הָעָם הַזֶּה
Kegodel Chasdecha Vecha'asher	כְּגֹדֶל חַסְדֶּךָ וְכַאֲשֶׁר
Nasatah La'am Hazeh	נָשָׂאתָה לָעָם הַזֶּה
Mimitzrayim Ve'ad Henah. Af	מִמִּצְרַיִם וְעַד־הֵנָּה: אַף
Attah Heshivota Lo Kedarchei	אַתָּה הֶשִׁיבוֹתָ לוֹ כְּדַרְכֵי
Tuvecha Bissarto Vachananto	טוּבְךָ בִּשַּׂרְתּוֹ וַחֲנַנְתּוֹ
Ve'amarta Lo: Salachti	וְאָמַרְתָּ לוֹ: סָלַחְתִּי

Kidvarecha:	כִּדְבָרֶךָ:

When Yisrael had sinned in the wilderness, Moshe stood up in Your presence, to pray and to seek mercy for Your people Yisrael. And so he spoke in his prayer: "Pardon, I implore You, the iniquity of this people according to the greatness of Your lovingkindness, and according as You have forgiven this people, from Mitzrayim even until now." (Numbers 14:19) You also answered him according to Your abundant goodness; You imparted to him good news, and graciously said to him, "I have pardoned according to your word."

Daniyel Ish Chamudot Amar	דָּנִיֵּאל אִישׁ חֲמוּדוֹת אָמַר
Lefaneicha: Hateh Elohai	לְפָנֶיךָ: הַטֵּה אֱלֹהַי |
Oznecha Ushema Pekach	אָזְנְךָ֮ וּשְׁמָע֒ פקחה (פְּקַח)
Eineicha Ure'eh Shomemoteinu	עֵינֶיךָ וּרְאֵה שֹׁמְמֹתֵינוּ
Veha'ir Asher Nikra Shimcha	וְהָעִיר אֲשֶׁר־נִקְרָא שִׁמְךָ
Aleiha Ki Lo Al Tzidkoteinu	עָלֶיהָ כִּי | לֹא עַל־צִדְקֹתֵינוּ
Anachnu Mapilim Tachanuneinu	אֲנַחְנוּ מַפִּילִים תַּחֲנוּנֵינוּ
Lefaneicha Ki Al Rachameicha	לְפָנֶיךָ כִּי עַל־רַחֲמֶיךָ
Harabbim. Adonai Shema'ah	הָרַבִּים: אֲדֹנָי | שְׁמָעָה
Adonai Selachah Adonai	אֲדֹנָי | סְלָחָה אֲדֹנָי
Hakshivah Va'aseh Al Te'achar	הַקֲשִׁיבָה וַעֲשֵׂה אַל־תְּאַחַר
Lema'ancha Elohai Ki Shimcha	לְמַעַנְךָ אֱלֹהַי כִּי־שִׁמְךָ
Nikra Al Ircha Ve'al Ammecha.	נִקְרָא עַל־עִירְךָ וְעַל־עַמֶּךָ:
Velirushalayim Irach Amarta Lah:	וְלִירוּשָׁלַיִם עִירֵךְ אָמַרְתָּ לָהּ:
Hini Nishpat Otach Al Omrech	הִנְנִי נִשְׁפָּט אוֹתָךְ עַל־אָמְרֵךְ
Lo Chatati. Anachnu Boshenu	לֹא חָטָאתִי: אֲנַחְנוּ בּוֹשְׁנוּ
Bema'aseinu Venichlamnu	בְּמַעֲשֵׂינוּ וְנִכְלַמְנוּ

Ba'avonoteinu. Ein Lanu Peh	בַּעֲוֹנוֹתֵינוּ. אֵין לָנוּ פֶּה
Lehashiv Velo Metzach Leharim	לְהָשִׁיב וְלֹא מֵצַח לְהָרִים
Rosh:	רֹאשׁ:

Daniel the beloved man, said before You, "My God, incline Your ear, and hear; open Your eyes, and behold our desolations, and the city which is called by Your name; for we do not presume to present our supplications before You, relying on our righteousness, but because of Your great mercy. Hashem hear; Hashem forgive; Hashem be graciously attentive, and grant our requests; do not delay for Your own sake, my God. For Your city and Your people are called by Your name." **(Daniel 9:18-19)** And to Yerushalayim Your city, You said, "Behold, I will enter into judgment with You, because You say: 'I have not sinned." **(Jer. 2:35)** But we are ashamed of our actions, and embarrassed because of our iniquities; so that we have no power to answer, or confidence to lift up our head.

Eloheinu Velohei Avoteinu Al	אֱלֹהֵינוּ וֵאלֹהֵי אֲבוֹתֵינוּ אַל
Ta'as Imanu Kalah. Tochez	תַּעַשׂ עִמָּנוּ כָּלָה. תֹּאחֵז
Yadecha Bammishpat. Bevo	יָדְךָ בַּמִּשְׁפָּט. בְּבֹא
Tochechah Negdecha. Shemenu	תוֹכֵחָה נֶגְדְּךָ. שְׁמֵנוּ
Missifrecha Al Temach.	מִסִּפְרְךָ אַל תֶּמַח.
Gishtecha Lachakor Musar.	גִּשְׁתְּךָ לַחְקֹר מוּסָר.
Rachameicha Yekademu	רַחֲמֶיךָ יְקַדְּמוּ
Rogzecha. Dalut Ma'asim	רָגְזֶךָ. דַּלּוּת מַעֲשִׂים
Beshurecha. Karev Tzedek	בְּשׁוּרֶךָ. קָרֵב צֶדֶק
Me'eleicha. Horenu Beza'akenu	מֵאֵלֶיךָ. הוֹרֵנוּ בְּזַעֲקֵנוּ
Lach. Tzav Yeshu'atenu	לָךְ. צַו יְשׁוּעָתֵנוּ
Bemafgia'. Vetashiv Shevut	בְּמַפְגִּיעַ. וְתָשִׁיב שְׁבוּת

Oholei Tam. Petachav Re'eh Ki	אָהֳלֵי תָם. פְּתָחָיו רְאֵה כִּי
Shamemu. Zechor Na'amta. Edut	שָׁמֵמוּ. זְכֹר נָאַמְתָּ. עֵדוּת
Lo Tishachach Mipi Zar'o.	לֹא תִשָּׁכַח מִפִּי זַרְעוֹ.
Chotam Te'udah Tatir. Sodecha	חוֹתָם תְּעוּדָה תַּתִּיר. סוֹדְךָ
Sim Belimmudeicha. Tabbur	שִׂים בְּלִמּוּדֶיךָ. טַבּוּר
Aggan Hassahar. Na Al Yechsar	אַגַּן הַסַּהַר. נָא אַל יֶחְסַר
Hamazeg. Yah Da Et Yisra'el	הַמָּזֶג. יָהּ דַּע אֶת־יִשְׂרָאֵל
Asher Yeda'ucha. Magger Et	אֲשֶׁר יְדָעוּךָ. מַגֵּר אֶת־
Hagoyim Asher Lo Yeda'ucha. Ki	הַגּוֹיִם אֲשֶׁר לֹא יְדָעוּךָ. כִּי
Tashiv Levitzaron. Lechudim	תָּשִׁיב לְבִצָּרוֹן. לְכוּדִים
Asirei Hatikvah:	אֲסִירֵי הַתִּקְוָה:

Our God, and God of our fathers, we beg You not to make an end of us, when Your hand takes hold of justice. When we are to be rebuked by You, do not blot our name out of Your book. In Your approach to examine the chastisement we deserve, allow Your mercy to overcome Your anger; and when You behold the poverty of our works, allow Your charity to flow from You. Our Parent, when we cry to You, command our salvation at our entreaty, and restore the captivity of the tents of him who was perfect; for behold his cities are desolate. Remember, You have said, that the covenant should never depart from the mouth of his offspring. Loosen the seal of the testimony, and reveal Your secret counsel to Your disciples. May the great senate be restored; and let not because of its greatness, we beg You, be lacking. God, own those who acknowledge You, and cast down those who disown You; for You will cause the enchained prisoners, who wait with hope, to return to the stronghold.

אָשַׁמְנוּ מִכָּל־עָם. בֹּשְׁנוּ	Ashamnu Mikol Am. Boshenu
מִכָּל־גּוֹי. גָּלָה מִמֶּנּוּ	Mikol Goy. Galah Mimenu
מָשׂוֹשׂ. דָּוֶה לִבֵּנוּ	Masos. Daveh Libenu
בַּחֲטָאֵינוּ. הָחְבַּל	Bachata'einu. Hachebal
אֶוְיֵנוּ. וְנִפְרַע פְּאֵרֵנוּ. זְבוּל	Evyeinu. Venifra Pe'erenu. Zevul
מִקְדָּשֵׁנוּ. חָרֵב	Mikdashenu. Charev
בַּעֲוֹנֵינוּ. טִירָתֵנוּ הָיְתָה	Ba'avoneinu. Tiratenu Hayetah
לְשַׁמָּה. יְפִי אַדְמָתֵנוּ	Leshamah. Yefi Admatenu
לְזָרִים. כֹּחֵנוּ לְנָכְרִים.	Lezarim. Kocheinu Lenacherim.
לְעֵינֵינוּ עָשְׁקוּ עֲמָלֵנוּ.	Le'eineinu Asheku Amalenu.
מְמֻשָּׁךְ וּמוֹרָט מִמֶּנּוּ.	Memushach Umorat Mimenu.
נָתְנוּ עֻלָּם עָלֵינוּ. סָבַלְנוּ	Natenu Ullam Aleinu. Savalnu
עַל שִׁכְמֵנוּ. עֲבָדִים מָשְׁלוּ	Al Shichmenu. Avadim Mashelu
בָנוּ. פּוֹרֵק אֵין מִיָּדָם.	Vanu. Porek Ein Miyadam.
צָרוֹת רַבּוֹת סְבָבוּנוּ.	Tzarot Rabot Sevavunu.
קְרָאנוּךָ יְהֹוָה אֱלֹהֵינוּ.	Keranucha Adonai Eloheinu.
רִחַקְתָּ מִמֶּנּוּ בַּעֲוֹנֵינוּ.	Rachakta Mimenu Ba'avoneinu.
שַׁבְנוּ מֵאַחֲרֶיךָ. תָּעִינוּ	Shavnu Me'achareicha. Ta'inu
כַּצֹּאן וְאָבַדְנוּ. וַעֲדַיִן	Katzon Ve'avadenu. Va'adayin
לֹא שַׁבְנוּ מִתְּעִיָּתֵנוּ.	Lo Shavnu Mitte'iyatenu.
וְהֵיאַךְ נָעִיז פָּנֵינוּ.	Vehei'ach Na'iz Paneinu.
וְנַקְשֶׁה עָרְפֵּנוּ. לוֹמַר	Venaksheh Orpenu. Lomar
לְפָנֶיךָ יְהֹוָה אֱלֹהֵינוּ	Lefaneicha Adonai Eloheinu
וֵאלֹהֵי אֲבוֹתֵינוּ צַדִּיקִים	Velohei Avoteinu Tzaddikim
אֲנַחְנוּ וְלֹא־חָטָאנוּ:	Anachnu Velo Chatanu:

We have offended more than any other people; are ashamed more than any other nation. Joy is driven from us; and our heart is faint because of our sins. The desire of our heart is destroyed, and our glory is rejected. The dwelling-place of our Sanctuary is laid waste, because of our iniquities; our palace has become desolate; the choice part of our land is given to strangers; and our strength to aliens; yet, have we not turned from our errors. How dare we then be so shameless of face and hardened, as to declare in Your presence, Hashem, our God, and God of our fathers, that we are righteous, and have not sinned; indeed we have sinned, we and our fathers.

Ezra Hassofer Amar Lefaneicha:	עֶזְרָא הַסּוֹפֵר אָמַר לְפָנֶיךָ:
Elohai Bosheti Venichlamti	אֱלֹהַי בֹּשְׁתִּי וְנִכְלַמְתִּי
Leharim Elohai Panai Eleicha Ki	לְהָרִים אֱלֹהַי פָּנַי אֵלֶיךָ כִּי
Avonoteinu Ravu Lema'lah Rosh	עֲוֹנֹתֵינוּ רָבוּ לְמַעְלָה רֹאשׁ
Ve'ashmatenu Gadelah Ad	וְאַשְׁמָתֵנוּ גָדְלָה עַד
Lashamayim. Ve'attah Eloah	לַשָּׁמָיִם: וְאַתָּה אֱלוֹהַּ
Selichot. Chanun Verachum.	סְלִיחוֹת. חַנּוּן וְרַחוּם.
Erech Apayim Verav Chesed.	אֶרֶךְ־אַפַּיִם וְרַב־חֶסֶד.
Velo Azavtam. Al Ta'azvenu	וְלֹא עֲזַבְתָּם. אַל תַּעַזְבֵנוּ
Avinu. Al Titesenu Malkeinu.	אָבִינוּ. אַל תִּטְּשֵׁנוּ מַלְכֵּנוּ.
Ve'al Tishkacheinu Yotzreinu.	וְאַל תִּשְׁכָּחֵנוּ יוֹצְרֵנוּ.
Ve'al Ta'as Imanu Chalah	וְאַל תַּעַשׂ עִמָּנוּ כָלָה
Begalutenu. Vekayem Lanu	בְּגָלוּתֵנוּ. וְקַיֵּם לָנוּ
Adonai Eloheinu Et Hadavar	יְהוָה אֱלֹהֵינוּ אֶת־הַדָּבָר
Shehivtachtanu. Al Yedei	שֶׁהִבְטַחְתָּנוּ. עַל יְדֵי
Yirmeyah Chozach. Ka'amur:	יִרְמְיָה חוֹזָךְ. כָּאָמוּר:
Bayamim Hahem Uva'et Hahi	בַּיָּמִים הָהֵם וּבָעֵת הַהִיא
Ne'um Adonai Yevukash Et Avon	נְאֻם־יְהוָה יְבֻקַּשׁ אֶת־עֲוֹן

Yisra'el Ve'einenu Ve'et Chatot	יִשְׂרָאֵל֙ וְאֵינֶ֔נּוּ וְאֶת־חַטֹּ֤את
Yehudah Velo Timmatzenah Ki	יְהוּדָה֙ וְלֹ֣א תִמָּצֶ֔אינָה כִּ֥י
Eslach La'asher Ash'ir. Ve'al	אֶסְלַ֖ח לַאֲשֶׁ֥ר אַשְׁאִֽיר׃ וְאַל
Ye'akkev Lefaneicha Kol Chet	יְעַכֵּב לְפָנֶיךָ כָּל־חֵטְא
Ve'on Et Tefillateinu. Umechol	וְעָוֹן אֶת תְּפִלָּתֵנוּ. וּמְחוֹל
Uselach Lechol Avonoteinu. Ki El	וּסְלַח לְכָל־עֲוֹנוֹתֵינוּ. כִּי אֵל
Tov Vesalach Attah:	טוֹב וְסַלָּח אָתָּה:

Ezra the Sofer (Scribe), said before You, "My God, I am ashamed and embarrassed to lift up my face to You, my God; for our iniquities are increased over our head, and our guiltiness is grown up to the heavens." But You are the God of pardons, gracious and merciful, long-suffering, and of abundant kindness, and did not forsake them. Do not forsake us, our Father. Do not cast us off, our King. Do not forget us, our Former and do not make an end of us in our captivity; but confirm to us, Hashem, our God the word which You assured us of by the hands of Your prophet Yirmiyahu, as was said, "In those days, and in that time, says Hashem, The iniquity of Yisrael will be sought for, and there will be none, And the sins of Yehudah, and they will not be found; For I will pardon them who I leave as a remnant." (Jer. 50:20) Do not allow, therefore, any sin or iniquity to hinder the approach of our prayer to Your presence; but pardon and forgive all our iniquities; for You, God, are good, and ready to forgive.

Vehu Rachum Yechapeir Avon	וְה֣וּא רַח֞וּם | יְכַפֵּ֣ר עָוֺן֮
Velo-Yashchit Vehirbah Lehashiv	וְֽלֹא־יַשְׁחִ֥ית וְ֭הִרְבָּה לְהָשִׁ֣יב
Appo; Velo-Ya'ir. Chol-Chamato.	אַפּ֑וֹ וְלֹֽא־יָ֝עִ֗יר כָּל־חֲמָתֽוֹ׃
Attah Adonai Lo-Tichla	אַתָּ֤ה יְהֹוָ֗ה לֹא־תִכְלָ֣א
Rachameicha Mimeni;	רַחֲמֶ֣יךָ מִמֶּ֑נִּי

Chasdecha Va'amitecha. Tamid	חַסְדְּךָ וַאֲמִתְּךָ תָּמִיד
Yitzeruni. Hoshi'enu Adonai	יִצְּרוּנִי׃ הוֹשִׁיעֵנוּ	יְהֹוָה
Eloheinu. Vekabetzeinu Min-	אֱלֹהֵינוּ וְקַבְּצֵנוּ מִן־
Hagoyim Lehodot Leshem	הַגּוֹיִם לְהֹדוֹת לְשֵׁם
Kodshecha; Lehishtabe'ach.	קָדְשֶׁךָ לְהִשְׁתַּבֵּחַ
Bit'hilatecha. Im-Avonot Tishmor-	בִּתְהִלָּתֶךָ׃ אִם־עֲוֺנוֹת תִּשְׁמָר־
Yah; Adonai. Mi Ya'amod.	יָהּ אֲדֹנָי מִי יַעֲמֹד׃
Ki-'Imecha Haselichah; Lema'an.	כִּי־עִמְּךָ הַסְּלִיחָה לְמַעַן
Tivare. Lo Chachata'einu Asah	תִּוָּרֵא׃ לֹא כַחֲטָאֵינוּ עָשָׂה
Lanu; Velo Cha'avonoteinu.	לָנוּ וְלֹא כַעֲוֺנֹתֵינוּ
Gamal Aleinu. Im-Avoneinu Anu	גָּמַל עָלֵינוּ׃ אִם־עֲוֺנֵינוּ עָנוּ
Vanu. Adonai Aseh Lema'an	בָנוּ יְהֹוָה עֲשֵׂה לְמַעַן
Shemecha. Zechor-Rachameicha	שְׁמֶךָ׃ זְכֹר־רַחֲמֶיךָ
Adonai Vachasadeicha; Ki	יְהֹוָה וַחֲסָדֶיךָ כִּי
Me'olam Hemah. Ya'ancha	מֵעוֹלָם הֵמָּה׃ יַעַנְךָ
Adonai Beyom Tzarah;	יְהֹוָה בְּיוֹם צָרָה
Yesagevcha. Shem Elohei	יְשַׂגֶּבְךָ שֵׁם	אֱלֹהֵי
Ya'akov. Adonai Hoshi'ah;	יַעֲקֹב׃ יְהֹוָה הוֹשִׁיעָה
Hamelech. Ya'aneinu Veyom-	הַמֶּלֶךְ יַעֲנֵנוּ בְיוֹם־
Kor'enu. Avinu Malkeinu.	קָרְאֵנוּ׃ אָבִינוּ מַלְכֵּנוּ.
Chonenu Va'aneinu Ki Ein Banu	חָנֵּנוּ וַעֲנֵנוּ כִּי אֵין בָּנוּ
Ma'asim. Aseh Imanu Tzedakah	מַעֲשִׂים. עֲשֵׂה עִמָּנוּ צְדָקָה
Kerov Rachameicha.	כְּרֹב רַחֲמֶיךָ.
Vehoshi'enu Lema'an Shemecha.	וְהוֹשִׁיעֵנוּ לְמַעַן שְׁמֶךָ׃

But He, being full of compassion, forgives iniquity, and does not destroy; many times He turns His anger away, And does not stir up all His wrath. You, Hashem, will not withhold Your compassions from me; let Your mercy and Your truth continually preserve me. Save us, Hashem our God, And gather us from among the nations, That we may give thanks to Your holy name, That we may triumph in Your praise. If You, Hashem, should mark iniquities, Hashem, Who could stand? For with You there is forgiveness, that You may be feared. He has not dealt with us after our sins, or requited us according to our iniquities. Though our iniquities testify against us, Hashem, work for Your name's sake; Remember, Hashem, Your compassions and Your mercies; For they have been from old. May Hashem answer you in the day of trouble; May the name of the God of Yaakov set you up on high; Save, Hashem; may the King answer us in the day that we call. Our Father and King, answer us with favor. Though we lack good works, deal with us benevolently, according to Your abundant mercy and save us for Your own sake. **(Psalms 78:38, 40:12, 106:47, 130:3-4, 103:10, Jeremiah 14:7, Psalms 25:6, 22:2, 20:10)**

Ve'attah Adonai Eloheinu Asher	וְעַתָּה | אֲדֹנָי אֱלֹהֵינוּ אֲשֶׁר
Hotzeta Et Ammecha Me'eretz	הוֹצֵאתָ אֶת־עַמְּךָ מֵאֶרֶץ
Mitzrayim Beyad Chazakah	מִצְרַיִם בְּיָד חֲזָקָה
Vata'as Lecha Shem Kayom	וַתַּעַשׂ־לְךָ שֵׁם כַּיּוֹם
Hazeh Chatanu Rasha'enu.	הַזֶּה חָטָאנוּ רָשָׁעְנוּ׃
Adonai Kechol Tzidkotecha	אֲדֹנָי כְּכָל־צִדְקֹתֶךָ
Yashov Na Apecha	יָשָׁב־נָא אַפְּךָ
Vachamatecha Me'ircha	וַחֲמָתְךָ מֵעִירְךָ
Yerushalayim Har Kodshecha Ki	יְרוּשָׁלַיִם הַר־קָדְשֶׁךָ כִּי
Vachata'einu Uva'avonot	בַחֲטָאֵינוּ וּבַעֲוֹנוֹת
Avoteinu Yerushalayim	אֲבֹתֵינוּ יְרוּשָׁלַיִם
Ve'ammecha Lecherpah Lechol	וְעַמְּךָ לְחֶרְפָּה לְכָל־
Sevivoteinu. Ve'attah Shema	סְבִיבֹתֵינוּ׃ וְעַתָּה | שְׁמַע

Eloheinu El Tefillat Avdecha Ve'el	אֱלֹהֵינוּ אֶל־תְּפִלַּת עַבְדְּךָ וְאֶל־
Tachanunav Veha'er Paneicha Al	תַּחֲנוּנָיו וְהָאֵר פָּנֶיךָ עַל־
Mikdashecha Hashamem	מִקְדָּשְׁךָ הַשָּׁמֵם
Lema'an Adonai. Hateh Elohai	לְמַעַן אֲדֹנָי: הַטֵּה אֱלֹהַי |
Oznecha Ushema Pekach	אָזְנְךָ וּשְׁמָע פקחה (פְּקַח)
Eineicha Ure'eh Shomemoteinu	עֵינֶיךָ וּרְאֵה שֹׁמְמֹתֵינוּ
Veha'ir Asher Nikra Shimcha	וְהָעִיר אֲשֶׁר־נִקְרָא שִׁמְךָ
Aleiha Ki Lo Al Tzidkoteinu	עָלֶיהָ כִּי | לֹא עַל־צִדְקֹתֵינוּ
Anachnu Mapilim Tachanuneinu	אֲנַחְנוּ מַפִּילִים תַּחֲנוּנֵינוּ
Lefaneicha Ki Al Rachameicha	לְפָנֶיךָ כִּי עַל־רַחֲמֶיךָ
Harabbim. Adonai Shema'ah	הָרַבִּים: אֲדֹנָי | שְׁמָעָה
Adonai Selachah Adonai	אֲדֹנָי | סְלָחָה אֲדֹנָי
Hakshivah Va'aseh Al Te'achar	הַקְשִׁיבָה וַעֲשֵׂה אַל־תְּאַחַר
Lema'ancha Elohai Ki Shimcha	לְמַעַנְךָ אֱלֹהַי כִּי־שִׁמְךָ
Nikra Al Ircha Ve'al Ammecha.	נִקְרָא עַל־עִירְךָ וְעַל־עַמֶּךָ:

And now, Hashem our God, that has brought Your people out of the land of Mitzrayim with a mighty hand, and has gotten renown for You, as at this day; we have sinned, we have done wickedly. Hashem, according to all Your righteousness, let Your anger and Your fury, I pray, be turned away from Your city Yershalayim, Your holy mountain; because for our sins, and for the iniquities of our fathers, Yerushalayim and Your people have become a reproach to all that are around us. Now then, our God, heed the prayer of Your servant, and to his supplications, and cause Your face to shine upon Your Sanctuary that is desolate, for Hashem's sake. My God, incline Your ear, and hear; open Your eyes, and behold our desolations, and the city upon which Your name is called; for we do not present our supplications before You because of our righteousness, but because of Your great compassions. Oh Hashem, hear, Hashem, forgive, Hashem, attend and do, and do not defer; for Your own sake, my God, because Your name is called upon Your city and Your people.' **(Daniel 9:15-19)**

Avinu Av Harachaman. Har'enu	אָבִינוּ אָב הָרַחֲמָן. הַרְאֵנוּ
Ot Letovah Vekabetz	אוֹת לְטוֹבָה וְקַבֵּץ
Nefutzoteinu Me'arba Kanfot	נְפוּצוֹתֵינוּ מֵאַרְבַּע כַּנְפוֹת
Ha'aretz. Yakiru Veyede'u Kol	הָאָרֶץ. יַכִּירוּ וְיֵדְעוּ כָּל
Hagoyim Ki Attah Adonai Avinu	הַגּוֹיִם כִּי אַתָּה יְהוָה אָבִינוּ
Attah. Anachnu Hachomer	אָתָּה. אֲנַחְנוּ הַחֹמֶר
Ve'attah Yotzreinu Uma'aseh	וְאַתָּה יֹצְרֵנוּ וּמַעֲשֵׂה
Yadecha Kulanu.	יָדְךָ כֻּלָּנוּ׃

Our Father, merciful Father, show us a good sign and gather our dispersed from the four corners of the whole earth. Then all of the nations will know and acknowledge that: "Hashem, You are our Father; We are the clay, and You are the Potter, We are all the work of Your hand." **(Isaiah 64:7)**

Avinu Malkeinu. Tzurenu	אָבִינוּ מַלְכֵּנוּ. צוּרֵנוּ
Vego'alenu. Chusah Adonai	וְגוֹאֲלֵנוּ. חוּסָה יְהוָה
Al-'Ammecha. Ve'al-Titen	עַל־עַמֶּךָ וְאַל־תִּתֵּן
Nachalatecha Lecherpah	נַחֲלָתְךָ לְחֶרְפָּה
Limshol-Bam Goyim. Lamah	לִמְשָׁל־בָּם גּוֹיִם לָמָּה
Yomeru Va'ammim. Ayeh	יֹאמְרוּ בָעַמִּים אַיֵּה
Eloheihem. Yada'nu Adonai Ki	אֱלֹהֵיהֶם׃ יָדַעְנוּ יְהוָה כִּי

Chatanu. Ve'ein Mi Ya'amod	חָטָאנוּ. וְאֵין מִי יַעֲמוֹד
Ba'adenu Ella Shimcha Hagadol	בַּעֲדֵנוּ אֶלָּא שִׁמְךָ הַגָּדוֹל
Ya'amod Lanu Be'et Tzarah.	יַעֲמוֹד לָנוּ בְּעֵת צָרָה.
Ucherachem Av Al Banim	וּכְרַחֵם אָב עַל בָּנִים
Rachem Aleinu. Chamol Al	רַחֵם עָלֵינוּ. חֲמֹל עַל
Amach Verachem Al	עַמְּךָ וְרַחֵם עַל
Nachalatach. Chusah Na Kerov	נַחֲלָתְךָ. חוּסָה נָּא כְּרֹב
Rachameicha Chonenu	רַחֲמֶיךָ חָנֵּנוּ
Malkeinu Va'aneinu. Lecha	מַלְכֵּנוּ וַעֲנֵנוּ. לְךָ
Adonai Hatzedakah Oseh	יְהֹוָה הַצְּדָקָה עוֹשֵׂה
Nifla'ot Bechol Et Va'et. Habeit	נִפְלָאוֹת בְּכָל עֵת וָעֵת. הַבֵּט
Na Vehoshi'ah Na Tzon	נָא וְהוֹשִׁיעָה נָּא צֹאן
Mar'itecha. Al Yimshal Banu	מַרְעִיתֶךָ. אַל יִמְשָׁל בָּנוּ
Ketzef Ki Lecha Adonai	קֶצֶף כִּי לְךָ יְהֹוָה
Hayshu'ah Becha Tochaltenu.	הַיְשׁוּעָה בְּךָ תוֹחַלְתֵּנוּ.
Eloah Selichot Ana Selach Na. Ki	אֱלוֹהַּ סְלִיחוֹת אָנָּא סְלַח נָא. כִּי
El Tov Vesalach Attah.	אֵל טוֹב וְסַלָּח אָתָּה:

Hashem, our Father, King, Rock and Redeemer, have pity on Your people, and do not deliver Your heritage to such reproach that nations make a byword of them. "Why should they say among the peoples, 'Where is their God?' " Hashem, we know we have sinned, and there is no one to stand by us, but You in Your greatness will defend us in time of trouble. Have compassion on us as a father has compassion on his children. Have compassion on Your people and have mercy on Your heritage. Have pity on us, we beseech You, according to the greatness of Your mercy. Graciously answer us, Oh our King. Righteousness is Yours, Hashem Who performs wonders at all times. We pray, look to the sheep of Your pasture and save them. Do not let anger prevail against us, for deliverance is Yours,

Hashem. Our hope is in You, God of pardon. We pray You forgive us, for You, God, are good and ready to forgive.

Ana Melech Rachum Vechanun.	אָנָּא מֶלֶךְ רַחוּם וְחַנּוּן.
Zechor Vehabeit Livrit Bein	זְכוֹר וְהַבֵּט לִבְרִית בֵּין
Habetarim. Vetera'eh	הַבְּתָרִים. וְתֵרָאֶה
Lefaneicha Akedat Yachid.	לְפָנֶיךָ עֲקֵדַת יָחִיד.
Ulema'an Yisra'el Avinu. Al	וּלְמַעַן יִשְׂרָאֵל אָבִינוּ. אַל
Ta'azvenu Avinu. Ve'al Titesenu	תַּעַזְבֵנוּ אָבִינוּ. וְאַל תִּטְּשֵׁנוּ
Malkenu Ve'al Tishkachenu	מַלְכֵּנוּ וְאַל תִּשְׁכָּחֵנוּ
Yotzreinu. Ve'al Ta'as Imanu	יוֹצְרֵנוּ. וְאַל תַּעַשׂ עִמָּנוּ
Chalah Begaluteinu. Ki El	כָלָה בְּגָלוּתֵינוּ. כִּי אֵל
Melech Chanun Verachum	מֶלֶךְ חַנּוּן וְרַחוּם
Attah:	אָתָּה:

Merciful and gracious King, we implore You to remember, and have respect to the covenant made between the parts, and let the binding of an only child be continually seen before You; and for the sake of our ancestor Yisrael, our Father, do not forsake us, or cast us off, our King. Do not forget us, our Former, or make an end of us in our captivity; for You are a gracious and merciful God and King.

Ein Kamocha Chanun Verachum	אֵין כָּמוֹךָ חַנּוּן וְרַחוּם
Eloheinu. Ein Kamocha El Erech	אֱלֹהֵינוּ. אֵין כָּמוֹךָ אֵל אֶרֶךְ
Apayim Verav Chesed Ve'emet.	אַפַּיִם וְרַב חֶסֶד וֶאֱמֶת.
Hoshi'einu Verachamenu	הוֹשִׁיעֵנוּ וְרַחֲמֵנוּ
Mera'ash Umerogez Hatzileinu.	מֵרַעַשׁ וּמֵרֹגֶז הַצִּילֵנוּ:

Zechor La'avadeicha.	זְכֹר לַעֲבָדֶיךָ
Le'avraham Leyitzchak	לְאַבְרָהָם לְיִצְחָק
Uleya'akov; Al-Tefen. El-Keshi	וּלְיַעֲקֹב אַל־תֵּפֶן אֶל־קְשִׁי
Ha'am Hazeh. Ve'el-Rish'o Ve'el-	הָעָם הַזֶּה וְאֶל־רִשְׁעוֹ וְאֶל־
Chatato. Shuv Mecharon	חַטָּאתוֹ: שׁוּב מֵחֲרוֹן
Apecha. Vehinachem Al-Hara'ah	אַפֶּךָ וְהִנָּחֵם עַל־הָרָעָה
Le'ammecha. Vehaseir Mimenu	לְעַמֶּךָ: וְהָסֵר מִמֶּנּוּ
Makat Hamavet Ki Rachum	מַכַּת הַמָּוֶת כִּי רַחוּם
Attah. Ki Chein Darkecha La'asot	אָתָּה. כִּי כֵן דַּרְכְּךָ לַעֲשׂוֹת
Chesed Chinam Bechol Dor	חֶסֶד חִנָּם בְּכָל דּוֹר וָדוֹר:
Vador. Ana Adonai Hoshi'ah Na;	אָנָּא יְהוָה הוֹשִׁיעָה נָּא
Ana Adonai Hatzlichah Na. Ana	אָנָּא יְהוָה הַצְלִיחָה נָּא: אָנָּא
Adonai Aneinu Veyom Kare'enu.	יְהוָה עֲנֵנוּ בְיוֹם קָרְאֵנוּ:
Lecha Adonai Kivinu. Lecha	לְךָ יְהוָה קִוִּינוּ. לְךָ
Adonai Chikkinu. Lecha Adonai	יְהוָה חִכִּינוּ. לְךָ יְהוָה
Neyachel Al Techesheh	נְיַחֵל אַל תֶּחֱשֶׁה
Ute'anenu. Ki Na'amu Goyim	וּתְעַנֵּנוּ. כִּי נָאֲמוּ גוֹיִם
Avedah Tikvatam. Kol Berech	אָבְדָה תִקְוָתָם. כָּל בֶּרֶךְ
Lecha Tichra Vechol Komah	לְךָ תִכְרַע וְכָל קוֹמָה
Lefaneicha Tishtachaveh.	לְפָנֶיךָ תִשְׁתַּחֲוֶה:

There is none like You, our God, gracious and merciful. There is none like You, a God long-suffering and abundant in mercy and truth. Have mercy on us, save us, and deliver us from devastating rage. Remember Your servants Avraham, Yitzchak and Yaakov, and do not look to the stubbornness, the wickedness, and the sinfulness of this people, but turn from Your anger and repent of the evil against Your people. Because You are merciful, ward off from us mortal blow, for it is Your way to show mercy freely in every generation. Hashem, we implore You, save us. Hashem, we implore You, prosper us. Hashem, we implore You, answer us on the day when we call. Towards You, Hashem, are our longing, our hope and our trust. Do not be silent, but answer us when the nations say 'their hope is lost.' For to You every knee will bow, and before You will all prostrate themselves.

Hapotei'ach Yad Bitshuvah	הַפּוֹתֵחַ יָד בִּתְשׁוּבָה
Lekabel Poshe'im Vechata'im.	לְקַבֵּל פּוֹשְׁעִים וְחַטָּאִים.
Nivhalah Nafshenu Merov	נִבְהֲלָה נַפְשֵׁנוּ מֵרוֹב
Itzevonenu. Al Tishkacheinu	עִצְּבוֹנֵנוּ. אַל תִּשְׁכָּחֵנוּ
Netzach Kumah Vehoshi'enu. Al	נֶצַח קוּמָה וְהוֹשִׁיעֵנוּ. אַל
Tishpoch Charonecha Aleinu Ki	תִּשְׁפּוֹךְ חֲרוֹנְךָ עָלֵינוּ כִּי
Ammecha Anachnu Benei	עַמְּךָ אֲנַחְנוּ בְּנֵי
Veritecha. El Habitah. Dal	בְרִיתֶךָ. אֵל הַבִּיטָה. דַּל
Kevodenu Vagoyim Veshiketzunu	כְּבוֹדֵנוּ בַּגּוֹיִם וְשִׁקְּצוּנוּ
Ketum'at Haniddah. Ad Matai	כְּטֻמְאַת הַנִּדָּה. עַד מָתַי
Uzecha Bashevi Vetif'artecha	עֻזְּךָ בַּשְּׁבִי וְתִפְאַרְתְּךָ
Beyad Tzar. Hemah Yir'u	בְּיַד צָר. הֵמָּה יִרְאוּ
Veyevoshu Veyechatu	וְיֵבֹשׁוּ וְיֵחַתּוּ
Migevuratam. Orerah	מִגְּבוּרָתָם. עוֹרְרָה
Gevuratecha Vehoshi'enu	גְבוּרָתְךָ וְהוֹשִׁיעֵנוּ
Lema'an Shemecha. Al Yim'atu	לְמַעַן שְׁמֶךָ. אַל יִמְעֲטוּ
Lefaneicha Tela'oteinu Maher	לְפָנֶיךָ תְּלָאוֹתֵינוּ מַהֵר
Yekademunu Rachameicha Be'et	יְקַדְּמוּנוּ רַחֲמֶיךָ בְּעֵת
Tzarotenu. Lo Lema'aneinu Ella	צָרוֹתֵינוּ. לֹא לְמַעֲנֵנוּ אֶלָּא
Lema'anach Pe'ol Ve'al Tashchet	לְמַעַנְךָ פְּעֹל וְאַל תַּשְׁחֵת

Et Zecher She'eritenu. Ki Lecha	אֶת זֵכֶר שְׁאֵרִיתֵנוּ. כִּי לְךָ
Meyachalot Eineinu Ki El Melech	מְיַחֲלוֹת עֵינֵינוּ כִּי אֵל מֶלֶךְ
Chanun Verachum Attah.	חַנּוּן וְרַחוּם אָתָּה.
Uzechor Eduteinu Bechol Yom	וּזְכוֹר עֵדוּתֵינוּ בְּכָל יוֹם
Tamid Omerim Pa'amayim	תָּמִיד אוֹמְרִים פַּעֲמַיִם
Be'ahavah. Shema Yisra'el;	בְּאַהֲבָה: שְׁמַע יִשְׂרָאֵל
Adonai Eloheinu Adonai Echad.	יְהֹוָה אֱלֹהֵינוּ יְהֹוָה | אֶחָד:

You Who opens Your hand to receive transgressors and sinners repenting, our soul is dismayed through the greatness of our suffering. Do not utterly forget us, but rise up and save us. Do not pour out Your anger on us, for we are Your people, the children of the covenant with You. Look on our degradation, Hashem, and see how we are loathed. Awaken Your might and save us for Your sake. Do not let our anguish seem small in Your sight, but hasten Your mercies to avert our troubles. Do so not for our sake, but for Your own. Do not destroy all memory of our remnant, for our eyes wait on You, because You, God, are a merciful and gracious King. Remember our witness to You, lovingly repeated twice daily, "HEAR, O YISRAEL: HASHEM IS OUR GOD, HASHEM IS ONE."

Torah Reading for Fast Days

קריאת התורה לתענית ציבור

Continue with the Torah Service. Start from Yehi Shem right before the Torah Service in the Shacharit Section. Continue through the service.

Exodus 32,11-14; 34,1-10

וַיְחַל מֹשֶׁה אֶת־פְּנֵי יְהוָה אֱלֹהָיו וַיֹּאמֶר לָמָה יְהוָה יֶחֱרֶה אַפְּךָ בְּעַמֶּךָ אֲשֶׁר
הוֹצֵאתָ מֵאֶרֶץ מִצְרַיִם בְּכֹחַ גָּדוֹל וּבְיָד חֲזָקָה: לָמָּה יֹאמְרוּ מִצְרַיִם לֵאמֹר
בְּרָעָה הוֹצִיאָם לַהֲרֹג אֹתָם בֶּהָרִים וּלְכַלֹּתָם מֵעַל פְּנֵי הָאֲדָמָה שׁוּב מֵחֲרוֹן
אַפֶּךָ וְהִנָּחֵם עַל־הָרָעָה לְעַמֶּךָ: זְכֹר לְאַבְרָהָם לְיִצְחָק וּלְיִשְׂרָאֵל עֲבָדֶיךָ אֲשֶׁר
נִשְׁבַּעְתָּ לָהֶם בָּךְ וַתְּדַבֵּר אֲלֵהֶם אַרְבֶּה אֶת־זַרְעֲכֶם כְּכוֹכְבֵי הַשָּׁמָיִם
וְכָל־הָאָרֶץ הַזֹּאת אֲשֶׁר אָמַרְתִּי אֶתֵּן לְזַרְעֲכֶם וְנָחֲלוּ לְעֹלָם: וַיִּנָּחֶם יְהוָה
עַל־הָרָעָה אֲשֶׁר דִּבֶּר לַעֲשׂוֹת לְעַמּוֹ: וַיֹּאמֶר יְהוָה אֶל־מֹשֶׁה פְּסָל־לְךָ
שְׁנֵי־לֻחֹת אֲבָנִים כָּרִאשֹׁנִים וְכָתַבְתִּי עַל־הַלֻּחֹת אֶת־הַדְּבָרִים אֲשֶׁר הָיוּ
עַל־הַלֻּחֹת הָרִאשֹׁנִים אֲשֶׁר שִׁבַּרְתָּ: וֶהְיֵה נָכוֹן לַבֹּקֶר וְעָלִיתָ בַבֹּקֶר אֶל־הַר
סִינַי וְנִצַּבְתָּ לִי שָׁם עַל־רֹאשׁ הָהָר: וְאִישׁ לֹא־יַעֲלֶה עִמָּךְ וְגַם־אִישׁ אַל־יֵרָא
בְּכָל־הָהָר גַּם־הַצֹּאן וְהַבָּקָר אַל־יִרְעוּ אֶל־מוּל הָהָר הַהוּא: וַיִּפְסֹל שְׁנֵי־לֻחֹת
אֲבָנִים כָּרִאשֹׁנִים וַיַּשְׁכֵּם מֹשֶׁה בַבֹּקֶר וַיַּעַל אֶל־הַר סִינַי כַּאֲשֶׁר צִוָּה יְהוָה
אֹתוֹ וַיִּקַּח בְּיָדוֹ שְׁנֵי לֻחֹת אֲבָנִים: וַיֵּרֶד יְהוָה בֶּעָנָן וַיִּתְיַצֵּב עִמּוֹ שָׁם וַיִּקְרָא
בְשֵׁם יְהוָה: וַיַּעֲבֹר יְהוָה עַל־פָּנָיו וַיִּקְרָא יְהוָה יְהוָה אֵל רַחוּם וְחַנּוּן אֶרֶךְ
אַפַּיִם וְרַב־חֶסֶד וֶאֱמֶת נֹצֵר חֶסֶד לָאֲלָפִים נֹשֵׂא עָוֹן וָפֶשַׁע וְחַטָּאָה וְנַקֵּה לֹא
יְנַקֶּה פֹּקֵד עֲוֹן אָבוֹת עַל־בָּנִים וְעַל־בְּנֵי בָנִים עַל־שִׁלֵּשִׁים וְעַל־רִבֵּעִים: וַיְמַהֵר
מֹשֶׁה וַיִּקֹּד אַרְצָה וַיִּשְׁתָּחוּ: וַיֹּאמֶר אִם־נָא מָצָאתִי חֵן בְּעֵינֶיךָ אֲדֹנָי יֵלֶךְ־נָא
אֲדֹנָי בְּקִרְבֵּנוּ כִּי עַם־קְשֵׁה־עֹרֶף הוּא וְסָלַחְתָּ לַעֲוֹנֵנוּ וּלְחַטָּאתֵנוּ וּנְחַלְתָּנוּ:
וַיֹּאמֶר הִנֵּה אָנֹכִי כֹּרֵת בְּרִית נֶגֶד כָּל־עַמְּךָ אֶעֱשֶׂה נִפְלָאֹת אֲשֶׁר לֹא־נִבְרְאוּ
בְכָל־הָאָרֶץ וּבְכָל־הַגּוֹיִם וְרָאָה כָל־הָעָם אֲשֶׁר־אַתָּה בְקִרְבּוֹ אֶת־מַעֲשֵׂה יְהוָה
כִּי־נוֹרָא הוּא אֲשֶׁר אֲנִי עֹשֶׂה עִמָּךְ:

Vaychal Mosheh Et Penei Adonai Elohav Vayomer Lamah Adonai Yechereh Apecha Be'ammecha Asher Hotzeta Me'eretz Mitzrayim Bechoach Gadol Uveyad Chazakah. Lamah Yomru Mitzrayim Lemor Bera'ah Hotzi'am Laharog Otam Beharim Ulechalotam Me'al Penei Ha'adamah Shuv Mecharon Apecha Vehinachem Al Hara'ah Le'ammecha. Zechor Le'avraham Leyitzchak Uleyisra'el Avadeicha Asher Nishba'ta Lahem Bach Vatedaber Aleihem Arbeh Et Zar'achem Kechochevei Hashamayim Vechol Ha'aretz Hazot Asher Amarti Etten Lezar'achem

Venachalu Le'olam. Vayinnachem Adonai Al Hara'ah Asher Diber La'asot Le'ammo. Vayomer Adonai El Mosheh Pesal Lecha Shenei Luchot Avanim Karishonim Vechatavti Al Haluchot Et Hadevarim Asher Hayu Al Haluchot Harishonim Asher Shibarta. Vehyeh Nachon Laboker Ve'alita Vaboker El Har Sinai Venitzavta Li Sham Al Rosh Hahar. Ve'ish Lo Ya'aleh Imach Vegam Ish Al Yera Bechol Hahar Gam Hatzon Vehabakar Al Yir'u El Mul Hahar Hahu. Vayifsol Shenei Luchot Avanim Karishonim Vayashkem Mosheh Vaboker Vaya'al El Har Sinai Ka'asher Tzivah Adonai Oto Vayikach Beyado Shenei Luchot Avanim. Vayered Adonai Be'anan Vayityatzev Imo Sham Vayikra Veshem Adonai. Vaya'avor Adonai Al Panav Vayikra Adonai Adonai El Rachum Vechannun Erech Apayim Verav Chesed Ve'emet Notzer Chesed La'alafim Nose Avon Vafesha Vechata'ah Venakeh Lo Yenakeh Poked Avon Avot Al Banim Ve'al Benei Vanim Al Shileshim Ve'al Ribe'im. Vaymaher Mosheh Vayikod Artzah Vayishtachu. Vayomer Im Na Matzati Chen Be'eineicha Adonai Yelech Na Adonai Bekirbenu Ki Am Kesheh Oref Hu Vesalachta La'avoneinu Ulechatatenu Unechaltanu. Vayomer Hinneh Anochi Koret Berit Neged Kol Ammecha E'eseh Nifla'ot Asher Lo Nivre'u Vechol Ha'aretz Uvechol Hagoyim Vera'ah Chol Ha'am Asher Attah Vekirbo Et Ma'aseh Adonai Ki Nora Hu Asher Ani Oseh Imach.

And Moshe sought Hashem his God, and said: 'Hashem, why does Your wrath burn hot against Your people, that You have brought out of the land of Egypt with great power and with a mighty hand? Why should the Egyptians speak, saying: For evil did He bring them out, to slay them in the mountains, and to consume them from the face of the earth? Turn from Your fierce wrath, and repent of this evil against Your people. Remember Avraham, Yitzchak, and Yisrael, Your servants, to whom You swore by Your own self, and said to them: I will multiply your seed as the stars of heaven, and all this land that I have spoken of will I give to your seed, and they shall inherit it forever.' And Hashem repented of the evil which He said He would do to His people. And Hashem said to Moshe: 'Carve two tablets of stone like the first; and I will write upon the tablets the words that were on the first tablets, which you broke. And be ready by the morning, and come up in the morning to mount Sinai, and present yourself there to Me on the top of the mountain. And no man will come up with you, neither let any man be seen throughout all the mountain; neither let the flocks or herds feed before that mount.' And he hewed two tables of stone like the first; and Moshe rose up early in the morning, and went up to mount Sinai, as Hashem had commanded him, and took in his hand two tablets of stone. And Hashem descended in the cloud, and stood with him there, and proclaimed the name of Hashem. And Hashem passed by before him, and proclaimed: 'Hashem, Hashem, God, merciful and gracious, long-suffering, and abundant in goodness and truth; keeping mercy to the thousandth generation, forgiving iniquity and transgression and sin; and will by no means clear the guilty; visiting the iniquity of the fathers upon the children, and upon the children's children, to the third and to the fourth generation.' And Moshe hasted, and bowed his head toward the earth, and worshipped. And he said: 'If now I have found grace in Your sight, my Lord, let my Lord, I implore You, go in the midst of us; for it is a stiff-necked people; and pardon our iniquity and our sin, and take us for Your inheritance.' And He said: 'Behold, I make a covenant; before all of your people I will do marvels, such as have not been done in all the earth, or in any nation; and all the people among which you are will see the work of Hashem that I am about to do with you, that it is tremendous.

Ta'anit Yachid (Fast of a Single Person)

These are dates when events happened and are good for fasting on (SA, OC 580):

- **Nissan 1 - the sons of Aharon [Nadav and Avihu] died.**
- **Nissan 10 - Miriam died and her well disappeared.**
- **Nissan 26 - Yehoshua ben Nun died.**
- **Iyar 26 - Eli the priest and two of his sons and the ark of God was captured.**
- **Iyar 26 - Samuel the prophet died.**
- **Sivan 23 - the offering of the first fruits in Yerushalayim was cancelled during the days of Yaravam ben Nevat.**
- **Sivan 25 - Rabban Shimon ben Gamliel and Rabbi Yishmael and Rabbi Chanina, Deputy High Priest, were killed.**
- **Sivan 27 - Rabbi Chanina ben Teradyon was burned to death and a Torah scroll with him.**
- **Av 1 - Aharon, the Kohen Gadol died.**
- **Av 18 - the eastern light was extinguished during the days of Achaz.**
- **Elul 17 - those who slandered the land died.**
- **Tishrei 5 - Twenty men of Israel were killed and Rabbi Akiva was imprisoned.**
- **Tishrei 7 - A decree was decreed against our ancestors that died by sword, hunger and plague because of the incident of the golden calf.**
- **Cheshvan 7 - They blinded the eyes of Tzidkiyahu and slaughtered his sons before his eyes.**
- **Kislev 28 - Yehoyakim burned the scroll that Baruch wrote dictated by Yirmiyahu.**
- **Tevet 8 - the Torah was written in Greek during the days of King Ptolemy and darkness was in the world for three days.**
- **Tevet 9 - It was not known who caused the trouble that happened on it.**
- **Shevat 5 - The elders who were in the days of Yehoshua died.**
- **Shevat 23 - All of Yisrael gathered against the tribe of Benyamin on account of the concubine in Gibeah.**
- **Adar 7 - Moshe Rabbeinu, may peace be upon him, died.**
- **Adar 9 - Beit Hillel and Beit Shammai divided.**

Before Fast Day: Mincha

The person desirous of keeping a voluntary fast, is obliged to bind himself to the performance of it, on the preceding day, while it is yet light, during the Mincha Service. (SA, OC 262:6) Saying at the conclusion of the Amidah, before Oseh Shalom, say as follows:

רִבּוֹן הָעוֹלָמִים הֲרֵי אֲנִי לְפָנֶיךָ בְּתַעֲנִית נְדָבָה לְמָחָר: יְהִי רָצוֹן מִלְּפָנֶיךָ יְהוָה אֱלֹהַי וֵאלֹהֵי אֲבוֹתַי שֶׁתְּקַבְּלֵנִי בְּאַהֲבָה וּבְרָצוֹן וְתָבֹא לְפָנֶיךָ תְּפִלָּתִי וְתַעֲנֶה עֲתִירָתִי וּתְרַפְּאֵנִי בְּרַחֲמֶיךָ הָרַבִּים כִּי אַתָּה תְּפִלַּת כָּל־פֶּה: יִהְיוּ לְרָצוֹן אִמְרֵי־פִי וְהֶגְיוֹן לִבִּי לְפָנֶיךָ יְהוָה צוּרִי וְגֹאֲלִי:

Ribon Ha'olamim Harei Ani Lefaneicha Beta'anit Nedavah Lemachar: Yehi Ratzon Milfanecha Adonai Elohai Velohei Avotai Shetkabeleini Ve'ahavah Uveratzon Vetavo Lefanecha Tefillati Veta'aneh Aterati Vetirpa'eni Verachameicha Harabbim Ki Attah Tefillat Kol Peh: Yihyu Leratzon Imrei Fi Vehegyon Libi Lefaneicha Adonai Tzuri Vego'ali.

Sovereign of the universe, behold, I am now in Your presence, with a free-will offering of a fast, to be kept tomorrow. May it be acceptable in Your presence, Hashem, my God and God of my fathers, to accept of it with love and favor, and allow my prayer to come into Your presence; and answer my supplication; and heal me with Your abundant mercy; for You hear the prayer of every mouth. May the words of my mouth, and the meditation of my heart, be acceptable in Your presence, Hashem, Who is my Rock and Redeemer.

Fast Day: Mincha

On the Afternoon of the Fast Day, instead of the Petition for Hearing Prayer, in the Amidah, say as follows:

שְׁמַע קוֹלֵנוּ יְהוָה אֱלֹהֵינוּ חוּס וְרַחֵם עָלֵינוּ וְקַבֵּל בְּרַחֲמִים וּבְרָצוֹן אֶת תְּפִלָּתֵנוּ זְכֹר רַחֲמֶיךָ וּכְבוֹשׁ אֶת כַּעַסֶךָ וְהָסֵר מִמֶּנּוּ דֶּבֶר וְחֶרֶב וְרָעָב וּשְׁבִי וּבִזָּה וְיֵצֶר רָע וָחֳלָיִם רָעִים וְנֶאֱמָנִים וּמְאֹורָעוֹת קָשׁוֹת וְרָעוֹת וְתִגְזוֹר עָלַי גְּזֵרוֹת טוֹבוֹת וְעַל כָּל־אַנְשֵׁי בֵיתִי. וְיִגֹּולוּ רַחֲמֶיךָ עַל מִדּוֹתֶיךָ. וְתִתְנַהֵג עִמָּנוּ יְהוָה אֱלֹהֵינוּ בְּמִדַּת הָרַחֲמִים. וְתִכָּנֵס לָנוּ לִפְנִים מִשּׁוּרַת הַדִּין. וְתַאֲזִין תְּפִלָּתֵנוּ וְתַחֲנוּנֵינוּ וְשַׁוְעָתֵנוּ. כִּי אַתָּה שׁוֹמֵעַ תְּפִלַּת כָּל־פֶּה. עֲנֵנִי אָבִי עֲנֵנִי. בְּיוֹם צוֹם הַתַּעֲנִית הַזֶּה. כִּי בְצָרָה גְדוֹלָה אֲנִי. עַל כָּל־מַה שֶּׁחָטָאתִי. וְשֶׁעָוִיתִי. וְשֶׁפָּשַׁעְתִּי לְפָנֶיךָ מִיּוֹם הֱיוֹתִי עַל הָאֲדָמָה עַד הַיּוֹם הַזֶּה. מְוּכְלָם אֲנִי מִפְּשָׁעַי. וּמִתְבַּיֵּשׁ וְנֶחְפָּר מֵעֲוֹנוֹתַי. וּמֵחַטֹּאתָי. אֲבָל שַׂמְתִּי רַחֲמֶיךָ לְנֶגֶד עֵינַי. כִּי דַרְכְּךָ לְהַאֲרִיךְ אַפֶּךָ. וּמִנְהָגְךָ לְרַחֵם עַל בְּרִיּוֹתֶיךָ. כִּי אַתָּה טוֹב וְסַלָּח וְרַב חֶסֶד לְכָל־קֹרְאֶיךָ: וּבְרַחֲמֶיךָ הָרַבִּים עֲנֵנִי בָּעֵת וּבָעוֹנָה הַזֹּאת. וִיהֵא מִעוּט חֶלְבִּי וְדָמִי הַמִּתְמָעֵט בְּתַעֲנִיתִי הַיּוֹם. חָשׁוּב וּמְקֻבָּל וּמְרֻצֶּה לְפָנֶיךָ כְּחֵלֶב מֻנָּח עַל גַּבֵּי מִזְבְּחֶךָ. לְכַפֵּר עַל כָּל־מַה שֶּׁחָטָאתִי וְשֶׁעָוִיתִי וְשֶׁפָּשַׁעְתִּי לְפָנֶיךָ. בֵּין בְּאֹנֶס בֵּין בְּרָצוֹן. בֵּין בְּשׁוֹגֵג. בֵּין בְּמֵזִיר. בֵּין בִּידִיעָה בֵּין שֶׁלֹּא בִידִיעָה. וְתִרְצֵנִי בְּרַחֲמֶיךָ הָרַבִּים. וְאַל תֵּפֶן לְרִשְׁעִי. וְאַל תִּתְעַלַּם מִתְּחִנָּתִי: הֱיֵה נָא קָרוֹב לְשַׁוְעִי. וְשַׁוְעַת אַנְשֵׁי בֵיתִי: טֶרֶם אֶקְרָא אֵלֶיךָ אַתָּה תַעֲנֶה. אֲדַבֵּר וְאַתָּה תִשְׁמַע. כָּאָמוּר. וְהָיָה טֶרֶם יִקְרָאוּ וַאֲנִי אֶעֱנֶה. עוֹד הֵם מְדַבְּרִים וַאֲנִי אֶשְׁמָע: כִּי אַתָּה יְהוָה פּוֹדֶה וּמַצִּיל. וְעוֹנֶה וּמְרַחֵם בְּכָל-עֵת צָרָה וְצוּקָה. וְשׁוֹמֵעַ תְּפִלַּת כָּל־פֶּה. בָּרוּךְ אַתָּה יְהוָה שׁוֹמֵעַ תְּפִלָּה:

Shema Koleinu Adonai Elohenu Chus Verachem Alenu Vekabel Berachamim Uveratzon Et Tefillateinu Zechor Rachameicha Uchevosh Et Ka'asecha Vehaseir Mimenu Dever Veherev Vera'av Ushevi Uvizah Veyetzer Ra Vocholayim Ra'im Vene'emanim Ume'ora'ot Kashot Vera'ot Vetigzor Alai Gezerot Tovot Ve'al Kal Anshei Veiti. Veyigolu Rachameicha Al Middoteicha. Vetitnaheg Imanu Adonai Elohenu Bemidat Harachamim. Vetikanes Lanu Lifnim Mishurat Hadin. Veta'azin Tefillateinu Vetachanuneinu Veshav'atenu. Ki Attah Shomea' Tefillat Kol Peh. Aneni Avi Aneni. Beyom Tzom Hata'anit Hazeh. Ki Vetzarah Gedolah Ani. Al Kol Mah

Shechatati. Veshe'aviti. Vesheppasha'ti Lefaneicha Miyom Heyoti Al Ha'adamah Ad Hayom Hazeh. Muchelam Ani Mippesha'ai. Umitbayesh Venechpar Me'antai. Umechatotai. Aval Samti Rachameicha Leneged Einai. Ki Darkecha Leha'arich Apecha. Uminhagecha Lerachem Al Beriteicha. Ki Attah Tov Vesalach. Verav Chesed Lechol Kore'eicha: Uverachameicha Harabbim Aneni Ba'et Uva'nah Hazot. Vihe Mi'ut Chelbi Vedami Hamitma'et Beta'aniti Hayom. Chashuv Umekubbal Umerutzeh Lefaneicha Kechelev Munach Al Gabei Mizbachacha. Lechapeir Al Kol Mah Shechatati Veshe'aviti Vesheppasha'ti Lefaneicha. Bein Be'ones Bein Beratzn. Bein Beshgeg .Bein Bemezir. Bein Bidi'ah Bein Shelo Bidi'ah. Vetirtzeni Berachameicha Harabbim. Ve'al Tefen Lerish'i. Ve'al Tit'allem Mitechinati: Heyeh Na Karov Leshav'i. Veshav'at Anshei Veiti: Terem Ekra Eleicha Attah Ta'aneh. Adaber Ve'attah Tishma. Ka'amur. Vehayah Terem Yikra'u Va'ani E'eneh. Ohd Hem Medaberim Va'ani Eshma: Ki Attah Adonai Pdeh Umatzil. Ve'neh Umerachem Bechol-Et Tzarah Vetzukah. Veshmea' Tefillat Kol Peh. Baruch Attah Adonai Shomea' Tefillah:

Hear our voice, Hashem, our God, have compassion and mercy upon us, and accept our prayers with mercy and favor. Remember Your tender mercies, and suppress Your anger; remove from us pestilence, sword, famine, captivity, and spoil: evil imagination, evil and severe diseases, afflicting and evil events. Be pleased to decree a good sentence for me, and all my household: and let Your tender mercy prevail over Your attribute of strict justice: and deal with us, Hashem our God, with the attribute of Your mercy, and the attribute of Your benevolence: and do not judge us according to the rigorous line of strict justice; and be attentive to our prayers, supplications, and cry: for You hear the prayer of every mouth. Answer me, my Father, answer me on this fast day, for I am in great trouble, because of all that I have sinned, offended, and transgressed against You, from my first existence on earth, to this present day. I am confounded, because of my transgressions ashamed and perplexed, because of my sins and iniquities: but I have set Your tender mercy before my eyes, since it is Your way to defer Your anger, and it is Your custom to have mercy on Your creatures; "For You are good, and forgiving, and of abundant mercy to all those who call upon You." Therefore, Hashem, with Your abundant mercy, answer me, at this time and hour, and let the diminishment of my fat and blood, which has by this day's fast been diminished, be accounted, and favorably accepted before You, as the fat of the sacrifice laid on Your Altar: that it may atone for what I have sinned, trespassed, and transgressed against You, whether by compulsion, or choice; ignorantly, or presumptuously; knowingly, or unknowingly. Deal kindly with me, according to Your abundant mercy; do not regard my wickedness, or hide thyself from my supplication. Be near to my cry, and the cry of my household; so that before I call on You, You may answer me: before I speak, listen; as it is said, " And it will come to pass, that before they call, I will answer: while they are yet speaking, I will hear." For You, Hashem, are a Redeemer and Deliverer; and he who answers, and is merciful in time of trouble and distress; and hears the prayer of every mouth. Blessed are You, Hashem, Who hears to prayer.

Then continue the Amidah, until "My God, guard my tongue," after which say as follows:

רִבּוֹן הָעוֹלָמִים אֱלֹהֵי הָאֱלֹהִים וַאֲדוֹנֵם בַּעַל הַסְּלִיחוֹת וְהָרַחֲמִים לְךָ יְהֹוָה הַצְּדָקָה וְלִי בֹּשֶׁת הַפָּנִים עַל כָּל־הַטּוֹבוֹת וְהַחֲסָדִים אֲשֶׁר עָשִׂיתָ עִמָּדִי מִיּוֹם הֱיוֹתִי עַד הַיּוֹם הַזֶּה. וְלֹא כִגְמוּל הֱשִׁיבוֹתִי לָךְ. אֲבָל. חָטָאתִי לְפָנֶיךָ. וְהָרַע בְּעֵינֶיךָ עָשִׂיתִי. וְהִרְבֵּיתִי לִפְשׁוֹעַ. וְלַעֲבוֹר עַל מִצוֹתֶיךָ. וְעַתָּה מַה אֶתְאוֹנֵן וּמַה אוֹמַר. מַה אֲדַבֵּר וּמַה אֶצְטַדָּק. אַמַרְתִּי אוֹדֶה עֲלֵי פְשָׁעַי לַיהֹוָה: אָשַׁמְתִּי בְתוֹרָתֶךָ. בָּגַדְתִּי בְּיִרְאָתֶךָ. גָּעַלְתִּי בְמִצְוֹתֶיךָ. דִּבַּרְתִּי דוֹפִי. הֶעֱוֵיתִי. וְהִרְשַׁעְתִּי. זַדְתִּי. חָמַסְתִּי. טָפַלְתִּי שֶׁקֶר. יָעַצְתִּי רָע. כִּזַּבְתִּי. לַצְתִּי. לוֹצַצְתִּי. מָרַדְתִּי. מָרִיתִי. מָאַסְתִּי. נִאַצְתִּי. נִאַפְתִּי. נִשְׁבַּעְתִּי לַשָּׁוְא וְלַשֶּׁקֶר. סָרַרְתִּי. עָוִיתִי. פָּשַׁעְתִּי. צָרַרְתִּי. קָשִׁיתִי עֹרֶף. קִלְקַלְתִּי דְרָכַי. רָשַׁעְתִּי. שִׁחַתִּי. תִּעַבְתִּי. תָּעִיתִי. תִּעְתַּעְתִּי. וְסַרְתִּי מִמִּצְוֹתֶיךָ וּמִמִּשְׁפָּטֶיךָ הַטּוֹבִים. וְלֹא שָׁוָה לִי: וְאַתָּה צַדִּיק עַל כָּל־הַבָּא עָלַי. כִּי אֱמֶת עָשִׂיתָ. וַאֲנִי הִרְשָׁעְתִּי:

Ribon Ha'olamim Elohei Ha'elohim Va'adonim Ba'al Chaselichot Veharachamim Lecha Adonai Hatzedakah Veli Voshet Happanim Al Kol Hatovot Vehachasadim Asher Asita Immadi Miyom Heyoti Ad Hayom Hazeh. Velo Chigmul Heshivoti Lach. Aval. Chatati Lefaneicha. Vehara Be'eineicha Asiti. Vehirbeiti Lifshoa'. Vela'avor Al Mitzoteicha. Ve'attah Mah Et'onen Umah Omer. Mah Adaber Umah Etztadak. Amarti Odeh Alei Fesha'ai L'Adonai: Ashamti Vetoratecha. Bagadti Veyir'atecha. Ga'alti Vemitzvoteicha. Dibarti Dofi. He'eviti. Vehirsha'ti. Zadti. Chamasti. Tafalti Sheker. Ya'atzti Ra. Kizavti. Latzti. Lotzatzti. Maradti. Marit. Ma'asti. Ni'atzti. Ni'afti. Nishba'ti Lashave Velasheker. Sararti. Aviti. Pasha'ti. Tzararti. Kashiti Oref. Kilkalti Derachai. Rasha'ti. Shichati. Ti'avti. Ta'iti. Ti'ta'eti. Vesarti Mimitzvoteicha Umimishpateicha Hatovim. Velo Shavah Li: Ve'attah Tzaddik Al Kol Haba Alai. Ki Emet Asita. Va'ani Hirsha'eti:

Sovereign of the universe, God of gods, and Lord of lords, Master of forgiveness and mercy. To You, Hashem, righteousness belongs, but to me, shame of face; for all the good and the mercies which You have bestowed on me, from my first existence, to this present day: but I have not been grateful according to Your kindness towards me: for indeed I have sinned against You, and done evil in Your sight, multiplied my transgressions, and neglected Your precepts. And so, how can I now complain? Or what will I say? What will I speak? Or how will I justify myself? I have accordingly said I will confess my transgressions to You, Hashem. I have trespassed against Your Torah: I have dealt deceitfully in the reverence due to You: I have abhorred Your precepts: I have spoken slander, I have committed iniquity, and have done wickedly: I have acted presumptuously, I have committed violence, I have framed falsehood, I have counseled evil, I have uttered lies, I have scorned, I have scoffed, I have rebelled, I have been disobedient, I have rejected the good, I have blasphemed, I have committed fornication, I have sworn falsely and vainly: I have revolted, I have acted perversely, I have transgressed, I have oppressed, I have been stiff-necked, I have perverted my paths, I have acted wickedly, I have corrupted, I have committed abomination, I have gone astray, and have caused others to go astray. I have also turned aside from Your precepts, and from Your good judgements, which has not profited me: but You are righteous concerning all that is come upon me, for You have dealt most truly, but I have done wickedly.

יְהִי רָצוֹן מִלְּפָנֶיךָ יְהוָה אֱלֹהַי וֵאלֹהֵי אֲבוֹתַי. שֶׁתִּמְחוֹל וְתִסְלַח לִי עַל כָּל־פְּשָׁעַי. וּתְכַפֵּר לִי עַל כָּל-עֲוֹנוֹתַי. וְתַעֲבִיר לִי עַל חַטֹּאתַי. שֶׁחָטָאתִי. וְשֶׁעָוִיתִי. וְשֶׁפָּשַׁעְתִּי. לְפָנֶיךָ. בֵּין בְּאוֹנֶס. בֵּן בְּרָצוֹן. בֵּן בְּשׁוֹגֵג. בֵּן בְּמֵזִיר. בֵּן בַּסֵּתֶר. בֵּן בַּגָּלוּי. בֵּן בְּמִתְכַּוֵּן. בֵּן שֶׁלֹּא בְּמִתְכַּוֵּן. בֵּן בְּהִרְהוּר. בֵּן בְּמַחֲשָׁבָה. מִיּוֹם הֱיוֹתִי עַל הָאֲדָמָה עַד הַיּוֹם הַזֶּה. וּכְשֶׁיַּגִּיעַ קִצִּי לִפָּטֵר מִן הָעוֹלָם הַזֶּה וְלָשׁוּב אֵלֶיךָ. יְהִי רָצוֹן מִלְּפָנֶיךָ יְהוָה אֱלֹהַי וֵאלֹהֵי אֲבוֹתַי. שֶׁתְּקַבֵּל נִשְׁמָתִי בְּחֶמְלָה כַּאֲשֶׁר תִּקָּחֶנָּה מִמֶּנִּי. וְתוֹשִׁיבֶנָּה תַּחַת כִּסֵּא כְבוֹדֶךָ. אֲשֶׁר מִשָּׁם נִטַּעְתָּהּ. וּכְשֶׁאָמוּת תִּהְיֶה מִיתָתִי כַּפָּרָה עַל כָּל-עֲוֹנוֹתַי: אָנָּא יי אֱלֹהַי וֵאלֹהֵי אֲבוֹתַי. שְׁעֵה אֶת שַׁוְעָתִי. וַעֲנֵה אֶת עֲתִירָתִי. וּשְׁמַע תְּפִלָּתִי. הֶרֶב כַּבְּסֵנִי מֵעֲוֹנִי. וּמֵחַטָּאתִי טַהֲרֵנִי. וְזַכֵּנִי מִשְּׁגִיאוֹת. וּמִנִּסְתָּרוֹת נַקֵּנִי. וְאֶהְיֶה מִבְּנֵי אָדָם אֲשֶׁר בְּצֵל כְּנָפֶיךָ יֶחֱסָיוּן. יִרְוְיֻן מִדֶּשֶׁן בֵּיתֶךָ וְנַחַל עֲדָנֶיךָ תַשְׁקֵם: תּוֹדִיעֵנִי אֹרַח חַיִּים. שֹׂבַע שְׂמָחוֹת אֶת פָּנֶיךָ. נְעִמוֹת בִּימִינְךָ נֶצַח: יִהְיוּ לְרָצוֹן אִמְרֵי־פִי וְהֶגְיוֹן לִבִּי לְפָנֶיךָ יְהוָה צוּרִי וְגֹאֲלִי:

Yehi Ratzon Milfaneicha Adonai Elohai Velohei Avotai. Shetimchol Vetislach Li Al Kol Pesha'ai. Utchapeir Li Al Kol-Avonotai. Veta'avir Li Al Chatotai. Shechatati. Veshe'aviti. Vesheppasha'ti. Lefaneicha. Bein Be'ones. Ben Beratzon. Ben Beshogeg. Ben Bemezir. Ben Basseter. Ben Bagalui. Ben Bemitkaven. Ben Shelo Bemitkaven. Ben Behirhur. Ben Bemachashavah. Miyom Heyoti Al Ha'adamah Ad Hayom Hazeh. Uchesheyaggiya Kitzi Lippater Min Ha'olam Hazeh Velashuv Eleicha. Yehi Ratzon Milfaneicha Adonai Elohai Velohei Avotai. Shetekabel Nishmati Bechemlah Ka'asher Tikacheinah Mimeni. Vetoshivenah Tachat Kisse Chevodecha. Asher Misham Neta'tah. Ucheshe'amut Tihyeh Mitati Chapparah Al Kol-Avonotai: Ana Adonai Elohai Velohei Avotai. She'eh Et Shav'ati. Va'aneh Et Aterati. Ushema Tefillati. Herev Kabeseni Me'avoni. Umechatati Tahareni. Vezakkeni Mishegi'ot. Uministarot Nakkeni. Ve'ehyeh Mibenei Adam Asher Betzel Kenafeicha Yechesayun. Veyirveyun Mideshen Beitecha Venachal Adaneicha Tashkem: Todiye'ni Orach Chayim. Sova Semachot Et Paneicha. Ne'imot Bimincha Netzach: Yihyu Leratzon Imrei Fi Vehegyon Libi Lefaneicha Adonai Tzuri Vego'ali.

May it be acceptable in Your presence, Hashem, my God and God of my fathers, to forgive and pardon all my transgressions, and grant me atonement for all my iniquities, and pass by all my sins, which I have sinned, committed, or transgressed before You, whether by compulsion, or choice; ignorantly, or presumptuously; privately or publicly: intentionally, or unintentionally; with inclination, or imagination; from the time of my first existence on earth, till this present day. And on the arrival of the appointed time, for my departure from this world, and return to You, may it be acceptable in Your presence, Hashem, my God and God of my fathers, to receive my soul with compassionate mercy, when You take it from me;

and place it under the Throne of Your glory, from where You have planted it in me; and when I die, let my death be an atonement for all my sins. I implore You, Hashem, my God and God of my fathers, to regard my cry, answer my supplication, and hear my prayer. Wash me thoroughly from my iniquity, cleanse me from my sin, purify me from errors, and free me from secret transgressions; and cause me to be of those children of men, who will have refuge under the shadow of Your wings; who will be abundantly satisfied with the fatness of Your House, and who You will cause to drink of the stream of Your delights. Show me the path of everlasting life, for in Your presence is the fullness of joy; and in Your right-hand are everlasting pleasures. May the words of my mouth, and the meditation of my heart, be acceptable in Your presence, Hashem, my Rock and Redeemer.

After say Ps. 102:

Psalms 102

תְּפִלָּה לְעָנִי כִֽי־יַעֲטֹף וְלִפְנֵי יְהוָה יִשְׁפֹּךְ שִׂיחוֹ׃ יְהוָה שִׁמְעָה תְפִלָּתִי וְשַׁוְעָתִי
אֵלֶיךָ תָבוֹא׃ אַל־תַּסְתֵּר פָּנֶיךָ ׀ מִמֶּנִּי בְּיוֹם צַר לִי הַטֵּה־אֵלַי אָזְנֶךָ בְּיוֹם אֶקְרָא
מַהֵר עֲנֵנִי׃ כִּֽי־כָלוּ בְעָשָׁן יָמָי וְעַצְמוֹתַי כְּמוֹ־קֵד נִחָרוּ׃ הוּכָּה־כָעֵשֶׂב וַיִּבַשׁ לִבִּי
כִּֽי־שָׁכַחְתִּי מֵאֲכֹל לַחְמִי׃ מִקּוֹל אַנְחָתִי דָּבְקָה עַצְמִי לִבְשָׂרִי׃ דָּמִיתִי לִקְאַת
מִדְבָּר הָיִיתִי כְּכוֹס חֳרָבוֹת׃ שָׁקַדְתִּי וָאֶהְיֶה כְּצִפּוֹר בּוֹדֵד עַל־גָּג׃ כָּל־הַיּוֹם
חֵרְפוּנִי אוֹיְבָי מְהוֹלָלַי בִּי נִשְׁבָּעוּ׃ כִּֽי־אֵפֶר כַּלֶּחֶם אָכָלְתִּי וְשִׁקֻּוַי בִּבְכִי מָסָכְתִּי׃
מִפְּנֵי־זַעַמְךָ וְקִצְפֶּךָ כִּי נְשָׂאתַנִי וַתַּשְׁלִיכֵנִי׃ יָמַי כְּצֵל נָטוּי וַאֲנִי כָּעֵשֶׂב אִיבָשׁ׃
וְאַתָּה יְהוָה לְעוֹלָם תֵּשֵׁב וְזִכְרְךָ לְדֹר וָדֹר׃ אַתָּה תָקוּם תְּרַחֵם צִיּוֹן כִּי־עֵת
לְחֶנְנָהּ כִּֽי־בָא מוֹעֵד׃ כִּֽי־רָצוּ עֲבָדֶיךָ אֶת־אֲבָנֶיהָ וְאֶת־עֲפָרָהּ יְחֹנֵנוּ׃ וְיִירְאוּ גוֹיִם
אֶת־שֵׁם יְהוָה וְכָל־מַלְכֵי הָאָרֶץ אֶת־כְּבוֹדֶךָ׃ כִּֽי־בָנָה יְהוָה צִיּוֹן נִרְאָה בִּכְבוֹדוֹ׃
פָּנָה אֶל־תְּפִלַּת הָעַרְעָר וְלֹֽא־בָזָה אֶת־תְּפִלָּתָם׃ תִּכָּתֶב זֹאת לְדוֹר אַחֲרוֹן וְעַם
נִבְרָא יְהַלֶּל־יָהּ׃ כִּֽי־הִשְׁקִיף מִמְּרוֹם קָדְשׁוֹ יְהוָה מִשָּׁמַיִם ׀ אֶל־אֶרֶץ הִבִּיט׃
לִשְׁמֹעַ אֶנְקַת אָסִיר לְפַתֵּחַ בְּנֵי תְמוּתָה׃ לְסַפֵּר בְּצִיּוֹן שֵׁם יְהוָה וּתְהִלָּתוֹ
בִּירוּשָׁלָם׃ בְּהִקָּבֵץ עַמִּים יַחְדָּו וּמַמְלָכוֹת לַעֲבֹד אֶת־יְהוָה׃ עִנָּה בַדֶּרֶךְ כחו
(כֹּחִי) קִצַּר יָמָי׃ אֹמַר אֵלִי אַל־תַּעֲלֵנִי בַּחֲצִי יָמָי בְּדוֹר דּוֹרִים שְׁנוֹתֶיךָ׃ לְפָנִים
הָאָרֶץ יָסַדְתָּ וּמַעֲשֵׂה יָדֶיךָ שָׁמָיִם׃ הֵמָּה ׀ יֹאבֵדוּ וְאַתָּה תַעֲמֹד וְכֻלָּם כַּבֶּגֶד
יִבְלוּ כַּלְּבוּשׁ תַּחֲלִיפֵם וְיַחֲלֹפוּ׃ וְאַתָּה־הוּא וּשְׁנוֹתֶיךָ לֹא יִתָּמּוּ׃ בְּנֵי־עֲבָדֶיךָ
יִשְׁכּוֹנוּ וְזַרְעָם לְפָנֶיךָ יִכּוֹן׃

Tefillah Le'ani Chi Ya'atof Velifnei Adonai Yishpoch Sicho. Adonai Shim'ah Tefillati Veshav'ati Eleicha Tavo. Al Taster Paneicha Mimeni Beyom Tzar Li Hateh Elai Oznecha Beyom Ekra Maher Aneni. Ki Chalu Ve'ashan Yamai Ve'atzmotai Kemo

Ked Nicharu. Hukkah Cha'esev Vayivash Libi Ki Shachachti Me'achol Lachmi. Mikol Anchati Davekah Atzmi Livsari. Damiti Lik'at Midbar Hayiti Kechos Choravot. Shakadti Va'ehyeh Ketzipor Boded Al Gag. Kol Hayom Cherefuni Oyevai Meholalai Bi Nishba'u. Ki Efer Kallechem Achaleti Veshikuvai Bivchi Masacheti. Mipenei Za'amcha Vekitzpecha Ki Nesatani Vatashlicheini. Yamai Ketzel Natui Va'ani Ka'esev Ivash. Ve'attah Adonai Le'olam Teshev Vezichrecha Ledor Vador. Attah Takum Terachem Tziyon Ki Et Lechenah Ki Va Mo'ed. Ki Ratzu Avadeicha Et Avaneiha Ve'et Afarah Yechonenu. Veyir'u Goyim Et Shem Adonai Vechol Malchei Ha'aretz Et Kevodecha. Ki Vanah Adonai Tziyon Nir'ah Bichvodo. Panah El Tefillat Ha'ar'ar Velo Vazah Et Tefilatam. Tikatev Zot Ledor Acharon Ve'am Nivra Yehallel Yah. Ki Hishkif Mimerom Kodsho Adonai Mishamayim El Eretz Hibit. Lishmoa' Enkat Asir Lefatteach Benei Temutah. Lesaper Betziyon Shem Adonai Utehilato BirushalaYIm. Behikkavetz Ammim Yachdav Umamlachot La'avod Et Adonai. Inah Vaderech Kochi Kitzar Yamai. Omar Eli Al Ta'aleini Bachatzi Yamai Bedor Dorim Shenoteicha. Lefanim Ha'aretz Yasadta Uma'aseh Yadeicha Shamayim. Hemah Yovedu Ve'attah Ta'amod Vechulam Kabeged Yivlu Kallevush Tachalifem Veyachalofu. Ve'attah Hu Ushenoteicha Lo Yitamu. Benei Avadeicha Yishkonu Vezar'am Lefaneicha Yikon.

A Prayer of the afflicted, when he faints, and pours out his complaint before Hashem. Hashem, hear my prayer, and let my cry come to You. Do not hide Your face from me in the day of my distress; incline Your ear to me; in the day when I call answer me speedily. For my days are consumed like smoke, and my bones are as burned as a hearth. My heart is dried up like grass, and withered; for I forget to eat my bread. By reason of the voice of my sighing, my bones cleave to my flesh. I am like a pelican of the wilderness; I have become like an owl of the waste places. I watch, and have become like a sparrow that is alone upon the housetop. My enemies taunt me all day; they that are mad against me curse by me. For I have eaten ashes like bread, and mingled my drink with weeping, because of Your indignation and Your wrath; for You have taken me up, and cast me away. My days are like a lengthening shadow; and I am withered like grass. But You, Hashem, sit enthroned forever; and Your name is to all generations. You will arise, and have compassion upon Tziyon; for it is time to be gracious to her, for the appointed time has come. For Your servants take pleasure in her stones, and love her dust. So the nations will fear the name of Hashem, and all the kings of the earth Your glory; When Hashem has built up Tziyon, when He has appeared in His glory; When He has regarded the prayer of the destitute, And has not despised their prayer. This will be written for the generation to come; And a people which will be created will praise Hashem. For He has looked down from the height of His Sanctuary; From heaven Hashem beheld the earth; To hear the groaning of the prisoner; To free those that are appointed to death; That men may tell of the name of Hashem in Tziyon, And His praise in Yerushalayim; When the peoples are gathered together, and the kingdoms, to serve Hashem. He weakened my strength in the way; He shortened my days. I say: 'Oh my God, do not take me away in the midst of my days, You whose years endure throughout all generations. From ancient times You laid the foundation of the earth; And the heavens are the work of Your hands. They will perish, but You will endure; Yes, all of them will grow old like a garment; As a garment will You change them, and they will pass away; But You are (the same), And Your years will have no end. The children of Your servants will dwell securely, And their seed will be established before You.'

Fast Day: Arvit

In the Evening Service, at the conclusion of the Amidah he says the following:

רִבּוֹן הָעוֹלָמִים כְּבָר הִתְעַנֵּיתִי בְּתַעֲנִית לְפָנֶיךָ גָּלוּי וְיָדוּעַ לִפְנֵי כִסֵּא כְבוֹדֶךָ. שֶׁבִּזְמַן שֶׁבֵּית הַמִּקְדָּשׁ קַיָּם. אָדָם חוֹטֵא וּמֵבִיא לְפָנֶיךָ קָרְבָּן. וְאֵין מַקְרִיבִין מִמֶּנּוּ רַק חֶלְבּוֹ וְדָמוֹ וּמִתְכַּפֵּר. וְעַכְשָׁיו בַּעֲוֹנוֹתֵינוּ הָרַבִּים. אֵין לָנוּ לֹא מִקְדָּשׁ. וְלֹא מִזְבֵּחַ. וְלֹא כֹהֵן שֶׁיְּכַפֵּר בַּעֲדֵנוּ:

Ribon Ha'olamim Kevar Hit'aneiti Veta'anit Lefaneicha Galui Veyadua' Lifnei Chisse Chevodecha. Shebizman Shebeit Hamikdash Kayam. Adam Chote Umevi Lefaneicha Korban. Ve'ein Makrivin Mimenu Rak Chelbo Vedamo Umitkaper. Ve'achshav Ba'avonoteinu Harabbim. Ein Lanu Lo Mikdash. Velo Mizbe'ach. Velo Chohen Sheyechapeir Ba'adenu:

Sovereign of the universe, I have now afflicted myself with a fast before You: it is known and manifest before the Throne of Your glory, that while the Temple existed, a man sinning offered a sacrifice in Your presence; of which the fat and blood alone were offered, and this made an atonement. But at present, because of our manifold sins, we do not have a temple, altar, or kohen to make an atonement for us.

יְהִי רָצוֹן מִלְּפָנֶיךָ יְהוָה אֱלֹהַי וֵאלֹהֵי אֲבוֹתַי שֶׁיְּהֵי מִיעוּט חֶלְבִּי וְדָמִי שֶׁנִּתְמַעֵט הַיּוֹם לְפָנֶיךָ בְּתַעֲנִיתִי. חָשׁוּב וּמְקֻבָּל לִפְנֵי כִסֵּא כְבוֹדֶךָ. כְּאִלּוּ הִקְרַבְתִּיו עַל גַּבֵּי מִזְבְּחָךְ. וְתִרְצֵנִי בְּרַחֲמֶיךָ הָרַבִּים: יִהְיוּ לְרָצוֹן אִמְרֵי־פִי וְהֶגְיוֹן לִבִּי לְפָנֶיךָ יְהוָה צוּרִי וְגֹאֲלִי:

Yehi Ratzon Milfaneicha Adonai Elohai Velohei Avotai Sheyehei Mi'ut Chelbi Vedami Shennitma'at Hayum Lefaneicha Beta'aniti. Chashuv Umekubbal Lifnei Chisse Chevodecha. Ke'ilu Hikravtiv Al Gabei Mizbachach. Vetirtzeni Verachameicha Harabbim: Yihyu Leratzon Imrei Fi Vehegyon Libi Lefaneicha Adonai Tzuri Vego'ali.

May it therefore be Your will, Hashem, my God and the God of my fathers, that the diminishment of my fat and blood, reduced in Your presence by my fast this day, be accounted and accepted before the Throne of Your glory as if I had offered it upon Your Altar; and may You be favorable to me, according to Your abundant mercy. May the words of my mouth, and the meditation of my heart, be acceptable in Your presence, Hashem, my Rock and Redeemer.

Then finish Arvit / the Evening Prayers.

SEDER ERUSIN / THE MARRIAGE SERVICE

סדר ארוסין

Savri Maranan!	סַבְרִי מָרָנָן:

Gentlemen, with your attention!

And those present answer:

Le'chayim!	לְחַיִּים:

To life!

Baruch Attah Adonai Eloheinu	בָּרוּךְ אַתָּה יְהֹוָה אֱלֹהֵינוּ
Melech Ha'olam Borei Pri	מֶלֶךְ הָעוֹלָם. בּוֹרֵא פְּרִי
Hagefen:	הַגָּפֶן:

Blessed are You, Hashem our God, King of the universe, Who creates the fruit of the vine.

Baruch Attah Adonai Eloheinu	בָּרוּךְ אַתָּה יְהֹוָה אֱלֹהֵינוּ
Melech Ha'olam Asher	מֶלֶךְ הָעוֹלָם. אֲשֶׁר
Kideshanu Bemitzvotav	קִדְּשָׁנוּ בְּמִצְוֹתָיו
Vetzivanu Al Ha'arayot Ve'asar	וְצִוָּנוּ עַל הָעֲרָיוֹת וְאָסַר
Lanu Et Ha'arusot. Vehitir Lanu	לָנוּ אֶת־הָאֲרוּסוֹת. וְהִתִּיר לָנוּ
Et Hanesu'ot Lanu Al Yedei	אֶת־הַנְּשׂוּאוֹת לָנוּ עַל יְדֵי
Chuppah Vekiddushin. Baruch	חֻפָּה בְּקִדּוּשִׁין. בָּרוּךְ
Attah Adonai Mekadesh Ammo	אַתָּה יְהֹוָה מְקַדֵּשׁ עַמּוֹ
Yisra'el Al Yedei Chuppah	יִשְׂרָאֵל עַל יְדֵי חֻפָּה
Vekiddushin:	בְּקִדּוּשִׁין:

Blessed are You, Hashem our God, King of the universe, Who has sanctified us with His commandments and commanded us concerning the laws of chastity, and has forbidden us the betrothed, but has permitted us those who are married to us, under the wedding chuppah and by the marriage ceremony. Blessed are You, Hashem Who sanctifies Your people Yisrael by the rite of the wedding chuppah and the marriage ceremony.

And then drink.

The groom, placing the ring with on the bride's forefinger will say:

Harei At Mekudeshet Li — הֲרֵי אַתְּ מְקֻדֶּשֶׁת לִי
Betabba'at Zo Kedat Mosheh — בְּטַבַּעַת זוֹ כְּדַת מֹשֶׁה
Veyisra'el: — וְיִשְׂרָאֵל:

Behold, You are married to me, by this ring, according to the Law of Moshe and Yisrael.

Sheva Berakhot / The Seven Blessings

סדר שבע ברכות

This is the order of the service for under the wedding canopy. During the seven days of rejoicing for a bride and group it is customary when a zimmun (3 men) is present, that the seven blessings are recited afterwards. The first blessing over the wine is then recited last.

Savri Maranan! — סַבְרִי מָרָנָן:

Gentlemen, with your attention!

And those present answer:

Le'chayim! — לְחַיִּים:

To life!

Baruch Attah Adonai Eloheinu	בָּרוּךְ אַתָּה יְהֹוָה אֱלֹהֵינוּ
Melech Ha'olam Borei Pri	מֶלֶךְ הָעוֹלָם. בּוֹרֵא פְּרִי
Hagefen:	הַגָּפֶן:

Blessed are You, Hashem our God, King of the universe, Who creates the fruit of the vine.

Baruch Attah Adonai Eloheinu	בָּרוּךְ אַתָּה יְהֹוָה אֱלֹהֵינוּ
Melech Ha'olam Shehakol Bara	מֶלֶךְ הָעוֹלָם. שֶׁהַכֹּל בָּרָא
Lichvodo:	לִכְבוֹדוֹ:

Blessed are You, Hashem our God, King of the universe, Who has created everything for His glory.

Baruch Attah Adonai Eloheinu	בָּרוּךְ אַתָּה יְהֹוָה אֱלֹהֵינוּ
Melech Ha'olam Yotzer	מֶלֶךְ הָעוֹלָם. יוֹצֵר
Ha'Adam:	הָאָדָם:

Blessed are You, Hashem our God, King of the universe; the Creator of man.

Baruch Attah Adonai Eloheinu	בָּרוּךְ אַתָּה יְהֹוָה אֱלֹהֵינוּ
Melech Ha'olam Asher Yatzar Et	מֶלֶךְ הָעוֹלָם. אֲשֶׁר יָצַר אֶת־
Ha'adam Betzalmo. Betzelem	הָאָדָם בְּצַלְמוֹ. בְּצֶלֶם
Demut Tavnito. Vehitkin Lo	דְּמוּת תַּבְנִיתוֹ. וְהִתְקִין לוֹ
Mimenu Binyan Adei Ad.	מִמֶּנּוּ בִּנְיַן עֲדֵי־עַד.
Baruch Attah Adonai Yotzer	בָּרוּךְ אַתָּה יְהֹוָה יוֹצֵר
Ha'Adam:	הָאָדָם:

Blessed are You, Hashem our God, King of the universe; who has formed man in Your image; in the image of the likeness of Your form, and has prepared out of him an everlasting establishment.

Sos Tasis Vetagel Akarah	שׂוֹשׂ תָּשִׂישׂ וְתָגֵל עֲקָרָה
Bekibutz Baneiha Letochah	בְּקִבּוּץ בָּנֶיהָ לְתוֹכָהּ
Bimheirah Besimchah. Baruch	בִּמְהֵרָה בְּשִׂמְחָה. בָּרוּךְ
Attah Adonai Mesame'ach	אַתָּה יְהֹוָה מְשַׂמֵּחַ
Tziyon Bevaneiha:	צִיּוֹן בְּבָנֶיהָ:

She who was barren will surely rejoice and be glad, at the gathering of her children to her speedily. Blessed are You, Hashem, Who causes Tziyon to rejoice through her children.

Same'ach Tesamach Re'im	שַׂמֵּחַ תְּשַׂמַּח רֵעִים
Ahuvim Kesamechacha	אֲהוּבִים כְּשַׂמֵּחֲךָ
Yetzircha Began Eden Mikedem.	יְצִירְךָ בְּגַן עֵדֶן מִקֶּדֶם.
Baruch Attah Adonai	בָּרוּךְ אַתָּה יְהֹוָה
Mesame'ach Chatan Vechallah:	מְשַׂמֵּחַ חָתָן וְכַלָּה:

May this loving couple delight in the joy You caused Your creation of ancient times in the Garden of Eden. Blessed are You, Hashem, Who causes the bridegroom and bride to rejoice.

Baruch Attah Adonai Eloheinu	בָּרוּךְ אַתָּה יְהֹוָה אֱלֹהֵינוּ
Melech Ha'olam Asher Bara	מֶלֶךְ הָעוֹלָם. אֲשֶׁר בָּרָא
Sason Vesimchah. Chatan	שָׂשׂוֹן וְשִׂמְחָה. חָתָן

Vechallah. Gilah Rinah Ditzah	וְכַלָּה. גִּילָה רִנָּה דִּיצָה
Vechedvah. Ahavah Ve'achvah.	וְחֶדְוָה. אַהֲבָה וְאַחֲוָה.
Shalom Vere'ut. Meheirah	שָׁלוֹם וְרֵעוּת. מְהֵרָה
Adonai Eloheinu Yishama Be'arei	יְהוָה אֱלֹהֵינוּ יִשָּׁמַע בְּעָרֵי
Yehudah Uvechutzot	יְהוּדָה וּבְחוּצוֹת
Yerushalayim. Kol Sason Vekol	יְרוּשָׁלָיִם. קוֹל שָׂשׂוֹן וְקוֹל
Simchah. Kol Chatan Vekol	שִׂמְחָה. קוֹל חָתָן וְקוֹל
Kallah. Kol Mitzhalot Chatanim	כַּלָּה. קוֹל מִצְהֲלוֹת חֲתָנִים
Mechuppatam. Une'arim	מֵחֻפָּתָם. וּנְעָרִים
Mimishteh Neginatam. Baruch	מִמִּשְׁתֵּה נְגִינָתָם. בָּרוּךְ
Attah Adonai Mesame'ach	אַתָּה יְהוָה מְשַׂמֵּחַ
Hechatan Im Hakallah	הֶחָתָן עִם הַכַּלָּה
Umatzliach:	וּמַצְלִיחַ:

Blessed are You, Hashem our God, King of the universe; Who has created joy and gladness, bridegroom and bride, love and fraternity, delight and pleasure, peace and fellowship; grant speedily, Hashem our God, that there be heard in the cities of Yehudah, and in the streets of Yerushalayim, the voice of joy and of gladness; the voice of the bridegroom and bride; the voice of jubilant bridegrooms at their wedding, and of youths at musical banquets. Blessed are You, Hashem, Who brings happiness to the bridegroom and bride; and Who brings them success.

And drink the cup.

And the groom breaks a glass in memory of Yerushalayim.

And say:

אִם־אֶשְׁכָּחֵךְ יְרוּשָׁלָ͏ִם תִּשְׁכַּח יְמִינִי׃ תִּדְבַּק־לְשׁוֹנִי ׀ לְחִכִּי אִם־לֹא
אֶזְכְּרֵכִי אִם־לֹא אַעֲלֶה אֶת־יְרוּשָׁלַ͏ִם עַל רֹאשׁ שִׂמְחָתִי׃

Im Eshkachech Yerushalayim Tishkach Yemini. Tidbak Leshoni Lechikki Im Lo Ezkerechi Im Lo A'aleh Et Yerushalayim Al Rosh Simchati.

If I forget you, Oh Yerushalayim, let my right hand forget her cunning. Let my tongue cleave to the roof of my mouth, if I don't remember you; if I don't set Yerushalayim above my most chief joy. **(Psalms 137:5-6)**

SEDER BRIT MILAH / ORDER OF CIRCUMCISION

סדר ברית מילה

Some pray before:

לְשֵׁם יִחוּד קוּדְשָׁא בְּרִיךְ הוּא וּשְׁכִינְתֵּיהּ. בִּדְחִילוּ וּרְחִימוּ. וּרְחִימוּ וּדְחִילוּ. לְיַחֲדָא שֵׁם יו״ד קֵ״י בְּוָא״ו קֵ״י בְּיִחוּדָא שְׁלִים (יהוה) בְּשֵׁם כָּל יִשְׂרָאֵל. הנה אנכי בא למול תינוק זה (ואביו יאמר: למול את בני) לקים מצות עשה כמו שנאמר. זאת בריתי אשר תשמרו ביני וביניכם ובין זרעך אחריך המול לכם כל־זכר: להכניסו בבריתו שׁל אברהם אבינו ולהכניסו בחולקא טבא דקדשא בריך הוא. דכתיב וצדיק יסוד עולם. ויהא רעוא דקדשא בריך הוא בהאי קרבנא ויתרעי ביה. ויזכה לעשר חפות רומין שעתיד קדשא בריך הוא למעבד לצדיקיא לעלמא דאתי כדכתיב: אשרי תבחר ותקרב ישכן חצריך נשבעה בטוב ביתך קדוש היכלך: ועתה בעונותינו חרבה עירנו ושמם בית מקדשנו ואין לנו קרבנות שיכפרו בעדנו. יְהִי רָצוֹן שֶׁיְּהֵא נֶחְשָׁב דַּם הַבְּרִית הַזֶּה כְּאִלּוּ בָּנִיתִי מִזְבֵּחַ וְהֶעֱלֵיתִי עָלָיו עוֹלוֹת וּזְבָחִים. יִהְיוּ לְרָצוֹן אִמְרֵי־פִי וְהֶגְיוֹן לִבִּי לְפָנֶיךָ יְהוָה צוּרִי וְגֹאֲלִי: וִיהִי נֹעַם אֲדֹנָי אֱלֹהֵינוּ עָלֵינוּ וּמַעֲשֵׂה יָדֵינוּ כּוֹנְנָה עָלֵינוּ וּמַעֲשֵׂה יָדֵינוּ כּוֹנְנֵהוּ:

In some congregations the sandak then prays:

לְשֵׁם יִחוּד קוּדְשָׁא בְּרִיךְ הוּא וּשְׁכִינְתֵּיהּ. בִּדְחִילוּ וּרְחִימוּ. וּרְחִימוּ וּדְחִילוּ. לְיַחֲדָא שֵׁם יו״ד קֵ״י בְּוָא״ו קֵ״י בְּיִחוּדָא שְׁלִים (יהוה) בְּשֵׁם כָּל יִשְׂרָאֵל. הנה אנכי בא להיות סנדק ואהיה כסא ומזבח לעשות על ירכי המילה. ויהי רצון מלפניך יהוה אלהינו ואלהי אבותינו שיהיה מזבח כפרה ותכפר על כל חטאתי עונותי ופשעי ובפרט מה שפגמתי בירכי ובאות ברית קדש. ותעלה עלינו כאלו כוונו כל הכוונות הראויות לכוין ולתקן את שרשה במקום עליון לעשות נחת רוח ליוצרנו ולעשות רצון בוראנו. וִיהִי נֹעַם אֲדֹנָי אֱלֹהֵינוּ עָלֵינוּ וּמַעֲשֵׂה יָדֵינוּ כּוֹנְנָה עָלֵינוּ וּמַעֲשֵׂה יָדֵינוּ כּוֹנְנֵהוּ:

When the baby is brought to the synagogue, the assembly stands and says:

בָּרוּךְ הַבָּא בְּשֵׁם יְהֹוָה:

Baruch Haba Beshem Adonai:

Blessed is he that comes in the name of Hashem: **(Psalms 118:26)**

And when the father of the son takes the baby in his arms says:

שָׂשׂ אָנֹכִי עַל־אִמְרָתֶךָ כְּמוֹצֵא שָׁלָל רָב: זִבְחֵי אֱלֹהִים רוּחַ נִשְׁבָּרָה לֵב־נִשְׁבָּר וְנִדְכֶּה אֱלֹהִים לֹא תִבְזֶה: הֵיטִיבָה בִרְצוֹנְךָ אֶת־צִיּוֹן תִּבְנֶה חוֹמוֹת יְרוּשָׁלָםִ: אָז תַּחְפֹּץ זִבְחֵי־צֶדֶק עוֹלָה וְכָלִיל אָז יַעֲלוּ עַל־מִזְבַּחֲךָ פָרִים:

Sas Anochi Al Imratecha Kemotze Shalal Rav. Zivchei Elohim Ruach Nishbarah Lev Nishbar Venidkeh Elohim Lo Tivzeh. Heitivah Virtzonecha Et Tziyon Tivneh Chomot Yerushalayim. Az Tachpotz Zivchei Tzedek Olah Vechalil Az Ya'alu Al Mizbachacha Farim.

I rejoice at Your word, As one that finds great spoil. The sacrifices of God are a broken spirit; a broken and a contrite heart, God, You will not despise. Do good in Your favor to Tziyon; build the walls of Yerushalayim. Then You will delight in the sacrifices of righteousness, in burnt-offering and whole offering; Then will they offer bulls upon Your Altar. **(Psalms 119:162, 51:19-21)**

And after the father of the son says:

אַשְׁרֵי | תִּבְחַר וּתְקָרֵב יִשְׁכֹּן חֲצֵרֶיךָ.

Ashrei Tivchar Utekarev Yishkon Chatzereicha.

Happy is the man Whom You choose, and bring near, that he may dwell in Your courts. **(Psalms 65:5)**

And those standing then answer:

נִשְׂבְּעָה בְּטוּב בֵּיתֶךָ קְדֹשׁ הֵיכָלֶךָ:

Nisbe'ah Betuv Beitecha Kedosh Heichalecha.

May we be satisfied with the goodness of Your House, the holy place of Your Temple. **(Psalms 65:5)**

In Eretz-Israel it is customary to add these verses:

אִם־אֶשְׁכָּחֵךְ יְרוּשָׁלָ͏ִם תִּשְׁכַּח יְמִינִי: תִּדְבַּק־לְשׁוֹנִי | לְחִכִּי אִם־לֹא אֶזְכְּרֵכִי
אִם־לֹא אַעֲלֶה אֶת־יְרוּשָׁלַ͏ִם עַל רֹאשׁ שִׂמְחָתִי:

Im Eshkachech Yerushalayim Tishkach Yemini. Tidbak Leshoni Lechikki Im Lo Ezkerechi Im Lo A'aleh Et Yerushalayim Al Rosh Simchati.

If I forget you, Oh Yerushalayim, let my right hand forget her cunning. Let my tongue cleave to the roof of my mouth, if I don't remember you; if I don't set Yerushalayim above my most chief joy. **(Psalms 137:5-6)**

The following is recited by the father and then those in attendance:

שְׁמַע יִשְׂרָאֵל יְהֹוָה אֱלֹהֵינוּ יְהֹוָה | אֶחָד:

Shema Yisra'el Adonai Eloheinu Adonai Echad.

Hear, O Yisrael. Hashem is our God, Hashem is One.

יְהֹוָה מֶלֶךְ, יְהֹוָה מָלָךְ יְהֹוָה | יִמְלֹךְ לְעֹלָם וָעֶד: ב׳ פעמים

Adonai Melech, Adonai Malach Adonai Yimloch Le'olam Va'ed:

Hashem is King, Hashem was King, Hashem will reign forever and ever. **2x**

אָנָּא יְהֹוָה הוֹשִׁיעָה נָּא: ב׳ פעמים

Ana Adonai Hoshi'ah Na:

Hashem, save now. **2x**

אָנָּא יְהֹוָה הַצְלִיחָה נָּא: ב׳ פעמים

Ana Adonai Hatzlichah Na:

Hashem, prosper us now. **2x**

The father of the son says now to appoint the mohel as his agent:

הֲרֵינִי מְמַנֶּה אוֹתְךָ שָׁלִיחַ לָמוּל אֶת־בְּנִי:

Hareini Memaneh Otecha Shaliach Lamul Et-Beni:

I hereby appoint you as my agent to circumcise my son.

The father of the son says:

בִּרְשׁוּת מוֹרַי וְרַבּוֹתַי:

Birshut Morai Verabotai:

With the permission of my teachers and masters:

He then says while standing:

Baruch Attah Adonai Eloheinu	בָּרוּךְ אַתָּה יְהֹוָה אֱלֹהֵינוּ
Melech Ha'olam Asher	מֶלֶךְ הָעוֹלָם. אֲשֶׁר
Kideshanu Bemitzvotav	קִדְּשָׁנוּ בְּמִצְוֹתָיו
Vetzivanu Lehachniso Bivrito	וְצִוָּנוּ לְהַכְנִיסוֹ בִּבְרִיתוֹ
Shel Avraham Avinu:	שֶׁל אַבְרָהָם אָבִינוּ:

Blessed are You, Hashem our God, King of the universe, Who has sanctified us with His commandments, and commanded us to introduce my son into the covenant of Avraham our father.

And the congregation and the Mohel says:

Keshem Shehichnasto Laberit.	כְּשֵׁם שֶׁהִכְנַסְתּוֹ לַבְּרִית.
Kach Tizkeh Lehachniso Latorah	כָּךְ תִּזְכֶּה לְהַכְנִיסוֹ לַתּוֹרָה
Velamitzvot Velachuppah	וְלַמִּצְוֹת וְלַחֻפָּה
Ulema'asim Tovim:	וּלְמַעֲשִׂים טוֹבִים:

Even as he has been introduced into the covenant, so may he be introduced to the Torah, and to the chuppah, and to a life of good deeds.

The sandak says sits on the chair and placed the baby on his lap, and says:

זֶה הַכִּסֵּא שֶׁל אֵלִיָּהוּ הַנָּבִיא מַלְאַךְ הַבְּרִית זָכוּר לַטּוֹב:

Zeh Hakisse Shel Eliyahu Hanavi Mal'ach Haberit Zachur Latov:

This is the throne of Eliyahu the prophet, the messenger of the covenant, of blessed memory:

And the mohel will receive the baby and place it on the godfather's knees and before circumcision he will bless:

Baruch Attah Adonai Eloheinu	בָּרוּךְ אַתָּה יְהֹוָה אֱלֹהֵינוּ
Melech Ha'olam Asher	מֶלֶךְ הָעוֹלָם. אֲשֶׁר
Kideshanu Bemitzvotav	קִדְּשָׁנוּ בְּמִצְוֹתָיו
Vetzivanu Al Hamilah:	וְצִוָּנוּ עַל הַמִּילָה:

Blessed are You, Hashem our God, King of the universe, Who has sanctified us with His commandments, and commanded us concerning circumcision.

And after circumcision the father of the son will bless:

Baruch Attah Adonai Eloheinu	בָּרוּךְ אַתָּה יְהֹוָה אֱלֹהֵינוּ
Melech Ha'olam Shehecheyanu	מֶלֶךְ הָעוֹלָם. שֶׁהֶחֱיָנוּ
Vekiyemanu Vehigi'anu Lazman	וְקִיְּמָנוּ וְהִגִּיעָנוּ לַזְּמַן
Hazeh:	הַזֶּה:

Blessed are You, Hashem our God, King of the universe, Who has kept us in life and preserved us and enabled us to reach this time.

And the mohel or another person takes a glass of wine and greets:

Savri Maranan!	סַבְרִי מָרָנָן:

Gentlemen, with your attention!

And those present answer:

Le'chayim!	לְחַיִּים:

To life!

Baruch Attah Adonai Eloheinu	בָּרוּךְ אַתָּה יְהֹוָה אֱלֹהֵינוּ
Melech Ha'olam Borei Pri	מֶלֶךְ הָעוֹלָם. בּוֹרֵא פְּרִי
Hagefen:	הַגָּפֶן:

Blessed are You, Hashem our God, King of the universe, Who creates the fruit of the vine.

And then he takes myrtle and blesses:

Baruch Attah Adonai Eloheinu	בָּרוּךְ אַתָּה יְהֹוָה אֱלֹהֵינוּ
Melech Ha'olam Borei Atzei	מֶלֶךְ הָעוֹלָם. בּוֹרֵא עֲצֵי
Vesamim.	בְשָׂמִים:

Blessed are You, Hashem our God, King of the universe, Who creates sweet smelling woods.

Baruch Attah Adonai Eloheinu	בָּרוּךְ אַתָּה יְהֹוָה אֱלֹהֵינוּ
Melech Ha'olam Asher Kidesh	מֶלֶךְ הָעוֹלָם. אֲשֶׁר קִדֵּשׁ
Yedid Mibeten Vechok Bish'ero	יְדִיד מִבֶּטֶן וְחוֹק בִּשְׁאֵרוֹ
Sam. Vetze'etza'av Chatam Be'ot	שָׂם. וְצֶאֱצָאָיו חָתַם בְּאוֹת
Berit Kodesh. Al Ken Bischar Zo.	בְּרִית קֹדֶשׁ. עַל כֵּן בִּשְׂכַר זוֹ.

El Chai Chelkenu Tzurenu.	אֵל חַי חֶלְקֵנוּ צוּרֵנוּ.
Tzaveh Lehatzil Yedidut Zera	צַוֵּה לְהַצִּיל יְדִידוּת זֶרַע
Kodesh She'erenu Mishachat.	קֹדֶשׁ שְׁאֵרֵנוּ מִשַּׁחַת.
Lema'an Berito Asher Sam	לְמַעַן בְּרִיתוֹ אֲשֶׁר שָׂם
Bivsarenu. Baruch Attah Adonai	בִּבְשָׂרֵנוּ. בָּרוּךְ אַתָּה יְהֹוָה
Koret Haberit:	כּוֹרֵת הַבְּרִית:

Blessed are You, Hashem our God, King of the universe; Who sanctified the beloved from the womb, and ordained a statute for His lineage, and sealed His offspring with the sign of the holy covenant. Therefore as a reward for it, the living God, our Portion and Rock, has commanded the deliverance of the beloved holy seed of our lineage from destruction, for the sake of the covenant, which He has put in our flesh. Blessed are You, Hashem, Maker of the covenant.

He drinks from the glass and says. And when the Father blesses, he says the brackets:

[**] At this point the Mohel gives a few drops of wine to the child

אֱלֹהֵינוּ וֵאלֹהֵי אֲבוֹתֵינוּ קַיֵּם אֶת הַיֶּלֶד (בְּנִי) הַזֶּה לְאָבִיו (לִי) וּלְאִמּוֹ וְיִקָּרֵא שְׁמוֹ בְּיִשְׂרָאֵל (פְּלוֹנִי). יִשְׂמַח הָאִישׁ (יְהִי רָצוֹן שֶׁאֶשְׂמַח בְּיוֹצֵא חֲלָצַי) בְּיוֹצֵא חֲלָצָיו. וְתָגֵל הָאִשָּׁה בִּפְרִי בִטְנָהּ כָּאָמוּר: יִשְׂמַח־אָבִיךָ וְאִמֶּךָ וְתָגֵל יוֹלַדְתֶּךָ: וְנֶאֱמַר: וָאֶעֱבֹר עָלַיִךְ וָאֶרְאֵךְ מִתְבּוֹסֶסֶת בְּדָמָיִךְ וָאֹמַר לָךְ בְּדָמַיִךְ חֲיִי ** וָאֹמַר לָךְ בְּדָמַיִךְ חֲיִי: וְנֶאֱמַר: זָכַר לְעוֹלָם בְּרִיתוֹ דָּבָר צִוָּה לְאֶלֶף דּוֹר: אֲשֶׁר כָּרַת אֶת־אַבְרָהָם וּשְׁבוּעָתוֹ לְיִשְׂחָק: וַיַּעֲמִידֶהָ לְיַעֲקֹב לְחֹק לְיִשְׂרָאֵל בְּרִית עוֹלָם: הוֹדוּ לַיהֹוָה כִּי־טוֹב כִּי לְעוֹלָם חַסְדּוֹ: (פְּלוֹנִי) זֶה הַקָּטָן. אֱלֹהִים יְגַדְּלֵהוּ. כְּשֵׁם שֶׁנִּכְנַס לַבְּרִית כָּךְ יִכָּנֵס לַתּוֹרָה וְלַמִּצְוֹת וְלַחֻפָּה וּלְמַעֲשִׂים טוֹבִים. וְכֵן יְהִי רָצוֹן וְנֹאמַר אָמֵן:

Eloheinu Velohei Avoteinu Kayem Et Hayeled (Beni) Hazeh Le'aviv (Li) Ule'immo Veyikare Shemo Beyisra'el (Peloni). Yismach Ha'Ish **If The Father Performs The Circumcision Personally:** (Yehi Ratzon She'esmach Beyotze Chalatzai) Beyotze Chalatzav. Vetagel Ha'ishah Bifri Vitnah Ka'amur: Yismach Avicha Ve'imecha Vetagel Yoladtecha. Vene'emar: Va'e'evor Alayich Va'er'ech Mitboseset Bedamayich Va'omar Lach Bedamayich Chayi ** Va'omar Lach Bedamayich Chayi. Vene'emar: Zachar Le'olam Berito Davar Tzivah Le'elef Dor. Asher Karat Et Avraham Ushevu'ato Leyischak. Vaya'amideha Leya'akov Lechok Leyisra'el Berit Olam. Hodu L'Adonai Ki Tov Ki Le'olam Chasdo. (Peloni) Zeh Hakkatan. Elohim Yegadelehu. Keshem Shenichnas Laberit Kach Yikanes Latorah Velamitzvot Velachuppah Ulema'asim Tovim. Vechein Yehi Ratzon Venomar Amen:

Our God, and God of our fathers, preserve this child (my son) to his father (to me) and mother; and his name will be called in Yisrael (name of child). May the father rejoice in him who proceeds from his loins **If the father performs the circumcision personally:** May it be His will that I rejoice in my offspring), and the mother be glad with the fruit of her womb; as it is said "Your father and mother will rejoice, and they who gave birth to you will be glad." It is also said, "And I passed by you, and saw you wallowing in your own blood; and I said to you, In your own blood you will live; ** and I said to you, In your own blood you will live." **(Ezekiel 16:6)** And it is said, "He has remembered His covenant forever, the word which he commanded to a thousand generations; which He covenanted with Avraham, and likewise His oath to Yitzchak, which he confirmed to Yaakov as a statute; to Yisrael as an everlasting covenant, give thanks to Hashem, for He is good, for His mercy endures forever." **(Psalms 105:8)** May God cause this young (name of child) to grow up prosperously; and even as he has been introduced into Your covenant, so may he be initiated into the practice of the Torah and of the precepts, into the chuppah, and to good deeds. May it be the Divine Will, and let us say, Amen.

Psalms 128

שִׁיר הַמַּעֲלוֹת אַשְׁרֵי כָּל־יְרֵא יְהֹוָה הַהֹלֵךְ בִּדְרָכָיו: יְגִיעַ כַּפֶּיךָ כִּי
תֹאכֵל אַשְׁרֶיךָ וְטוֹב לָךְ: אֶשְׁתְּךָ | כְּגֶפֶן פֹּרִיָּה בְּיַרְכְּתֵי בֵיתֶךָ בָּנֶיךָ
כִּשְׁתִלֵי זֵיתִים סָבִיב לְשֻׁלְחָנֶךָ: הִנֵּה כִי־כֵן יְבֹרַךְ גָּבֶר יְרֵא יְהֹוָה:
יְבָרֶכְךָ יְהֹוָה מִצִּיּוֹן וּרְאֵה בְּטוּב יְרוּשָׁלָםִ כֹּל יְמֵי חַיֶּיךָ: וּרְאֵה־בָנִים
לְבָנֶיךָ שָׁלוֹם עַל־יִשְׂרָאֵל:

Shir Hama'alot Ashrei Kol Yere Adonai Haholech Bidrachav. Yegia' Kappeicha Ki Tochel Ashreicha Vetov Lach. Eshtecha Kegefen Poriyah Beyarkete Veitecha Baneicha Kishtilei Zeitim Saviv Leshulchanecha. Hineh Chi Chein Yevorach Gaver Yere Adonai. Yevarechecha Adonai Mitziyon Ure'eh Betuv Yerushalayim Kol Yemei Chayeicha. Ure'eh Vanim Levaneicha Shalom Al Yisra'el.

A Song of Ascents. Happy is everyone that fears Hashem, That walks in His ways. When you eat the labor of your hands, Happy you will be, and it will be well with you. Your wife will be as a fruitful vine, in the innermost parts of your house; Your children like olive plants, around your table. Behold, surely will the man be blessed that fears Hashem. May Hashem bless you out of Tziyon; And may you see the good of Yerushalayim all the days of your life; And see your children's children. Peace be upon Yisrael.

And say Kaddish Yehei-Shelama.

Kaddish is only recited in a minyan (ten men). אָמֵן denotes when the congregation responds "Amen" together out loud. According to the Shulchan Arukh, the congregation says "Yehei Shemeh Rabba" to "Yitbarach" out loud together without interruption, and also that one should respond "Amen" after "Yitbarach." (SA, OC 55,56) This is not the common custom today. Though many are accustomed to answering according to their own custom, it is advised to respond in the custom of the one reciting to avoid not fragmenting into smaller groups. ("Lo Titgodedu" - BT, Yevamot 13b / SA, OC 493, Rema / MT, Avodah Zara 12:15)

יִתְגַּדַּל וְיִתְקַדַּשׁ שְׁמֵהּ רַבָּא. אָמֵן בְּעָלְמָא דִּי בְרָא. כִּרְעוּתֵהּ. וְיַמְלִיךְ
מַלְכוּתֵהּ. וְיַצְמַח פֻּרְקָנֵהּ. וִיקָרֵב מְשִׁיחֵהּ. אָמֵן בְּחַיֵּיכוֹן וּבְיוֹמֵיכוֹן
וּבְחַיֵּי דְכָל בֵּית יִשְׂרָאֵל. בַּעֲגָלָא וּבִזְמַן קָרִיב. וְאִמְרוּ אָמֵן. אָמֵן יְהֵא

שְׁמֵיהּ רַבָּא מְבָרַךְ לְעָלַם וּלְעָלְמֵי עָלְמַיָּא יִתְבָּרַךְ. וְיִשְׁתַּבַּח. וְיִתְפָּאַר. וְיִתְרוֹמַם. וְיִתְנַשֵּׂא. וְיִתְהַדָּר. וְיִתְעַלֶּה. וְיִתְהַלָּל שְׁמֵהּ דְּקֻדְשָׁא. בְּרִיךְ הוּא. אָמֵן לְעֵלָּא מִן כָּל בִּרְכָתָא שִׁירָתָא. תֻּשְׁבְּחָתָא וְנֶחֱמָתָא. דַּאֲמִירָן בְּעָלְמָא. וְאִמְרוּ אָמֵן. אָמֵן

Yitgadal Veyitkadash Shemeh Rabba. Amen Be'alema Di Vera. Kir'uteh. Veyamlich Malchuteh. Veyatzmach Purkaneh. Vikarev Meshicheh. Amen Bechayeichon Uveyomeichon Uvechayei Dechal-Beit Yisra'el. Ba'agala Uvizman Kariv. Ve'imru Amen. Amen Yehei Shemeh Rabba Mevarach Le'alam Ule'alemei Alemaya Yitbarach. Veyishtabach. Veyitpa'ar. Veyitromam. Veyitnasse. Veyit'hadar. Veyit'aleh. Veyit'hallal Shemeh Dekudsha. Berich Hu. Amen Le'ella Min Kol Birchata Shirata. Tushbechata Venechemata. Da'amiran Be'alema. Ve'imru Amen. Amen

Glorified and sanctified be God's great name Amen throughout the world which He has created according to His will. May He establish His kingdom, hastening His salvation and the coming of His Messiah, Amen, in your lifetime and during your days, and within the life of the entire House of Yisrael, speedily and soon; and say, Amen. Amen May His great name be blessed forever and to all eternity. Blessed and praised, glorified and exalted, extolled and honored, adored and lauded is the name of the Holy One, blessed is He, Amen Beyond all the blessings and hymns, praises and consolations that are ever spoken in the world; and say, Amen. Amen

יְהֵא שְׁלָמָא רַבָּא מִן שְׁמַיָּא. חַיִּים וְשָׂבָע וִישׁוּעָה וְנֶחָמָה. וְשֵׁיזָבָא וּרְפוּאָה וּגְאוּלָּה וּסְלִיחָה וְכַפָּרָה וְרֶוַח וְהַצָּלָה לָנוּ וּלְכָל עַמּוֹ יִשְׂרָאֵל. וְאִמְרוּ אָמֵן. אָמֵן

Yehei Shelama Rabba Min Shemaya. Chayim Vesava Vishu'ah Venechamah. Vesheizava Urefu'ah Uge'ulah Uselichah Vechapparah Verevach Vehatzalah Lanu Ulechol Ammo Yisra'el. Ve'imru Amen. Amen

May abundant peace descend from heaven, with life and plenty, salvation, solace, liberation, healing and redemption, and forgiveness and atonement, enlargement and freedom, for us and all of God's people Yisrael; and say, Amen. **Amen**

One bows and takes three steps backwards, while still bowing. After three steps, while still bowing and before erecting, while saying, "Oseh Shalom Bimromav", turn one's face to the left, "Hu [Berachamav] Ya'aseh Shalom Aleinu", turn one's face to the right; then bow forward like a servant leaving his master. (SA, OC 123:1)

עוֹשֶׂה שָׁלוֹם בִּמְרוֹמָיו. הוּא בְּרַחֲמָיו יַעֲשֶׂה שָׁלוֹם עָלֵינוּ. וְעַל כָּל־עַמּוֹ יִשְׂרָאֵל. וְאִמְרוּ אָמֵן:

Oseh Shalom Bimromav. Hu Berachamav Ya'aseh Shalom Aleinu. Ve'al Kol-'Ammo Yisra'el. Ve'imru Amen.

Creator of peace in His high places, may He in His mercy create peace for us and for all Yisrael, and say Amen.

SEDER PIDYON HABEN / REDEMPTION OF THE FIRSTBORN

סדר פדיון הבן

The Kohen takes the boy and asks his father:

בִּנְךָ זֶה בְּכוֹר הוּא ויענה: כֵּן. ואומר לו הכהן בְּמַאי בָּעִית טְפֵי. בְּבִנְךָ בְכוֹרְךָ אוֹ בְחָמֵשׁ סְלָעִים דִּמְחַיַּבְתְּ לִפְדּוֹת בָּהֶן ועונה האב בִּבְנִי בְּכוֹרִי. ואחר כך ישאל הכהן לאם הילד בְּנֵךְ זֶה בְּכוֹר. שֶׁמָּא יָלַדְתְּ בֵּן אַחֵר לְפָנָיו אוֹ שֶׁמָּא הִפַּלְתְּ והיא עונה זֶה בְּנִי בְכוֹרִי לֹא יָלַדְתִּי וְלֹא הִפַּלְתִּי לְפָנָיו:

Bincha Zeh Bechor Hu **Father:** Ken. **The Kohen says:** Bema Ba'it Tefei. Bevincha Vechorecha O Vechamesh Sela'im Dimchayavt Lifdot Bahen **The father answers:** Bivni Bechori. **And after the Kohen asks the mother of the child:** Benech Zeh Bechor. Sheme Yaladt Ben Acher Lefanav O Sheme Hippalt **And she answers:** Zeh Beni Vechori Lo Yaladti Velo Hippalti Lefanav:

This son is the firstborn? **Father:** Yes. **The Kohen says:** What would you rather have, your firstborn son or five sela'im which you have to reedem? **The father answers:** My firstborn son. **And after the Kohen asks the mother of the child:** Is this your firstborn son? Was there a previous child or did you miscarry? **And she answers:** This is my firstborn, I have not given birth before, neither have I had a miscarriage.

Then the Kohen says:

זֶה הַבֵּן בְּכוֹר הוּא. וְהַקָּדוֹשׁ בָּרוּךְ הוּא צִוָּה לִפְדּוֹתוֹ. שֶׁנֶּאֱמַר: וּפְדוּיָו מִבֶּן־חֹדֶשׁ תִּפְדֶּה בְּעֶרְכְּךָ כֶּסֶף חֲמֵשֶׁת שְׁקָלִים בְּשֶׁקֶל הַקֹּדֶשׁ עֶשְׂרִים גֵּרָה הוּא: כְּשֶׁהָיִיתָ בִּמְעֵי אִמֶּךָ הָיִיתָ בִּרְשׁוּת אָבִיךָ שֶׁבַּשָּׁמַיִם וּבִרְשׁוּת אָבִיךָ וְאִמֶּךָ. עַכְשָׁיו אַתָּה בִּרְשׁוּתִי שֶׁאֲנִי כֹּהֵן וְאָבִיךָ וְאִמֶּךָ מְבַקְשִׁים לִפְדּוֹתְךָ שֶׁאַתָּה בְּכוֹר מְקֻדָּשׁ. שֶׁכֵּן כָּתוּב:

וַיְדַבֵּר יְהֹוָה אֶל־מֹשֶׁה לֵּאמֹר: קַדֶּשׁ־לִי כָל־בְּכוֹר פֶּטֶר כָּל־רֶחֶם בִּבְנֵי יִשְׂרָאֵל בָּאָדָם וּבַבְּהֵמָה לִי הוּא:

Zeh Haben Bechor Hu. Vehakadosh Baruch Hu Tzivah Lifdoto. Shene'emar: Ufeduyav Miben Chodesh Tifdeh Be'erkecha Kesef Chameshet Shekalim Beshekel Hakodesh Esrim Gerah Hu. Keshehayita Bim'ei Imecha Hayita Birshut Avicha Shebashamayim Uvirshut Avicha Ve'imecha. Achshav Attah Birshuti She'ani Chohen Ve'avicha Ve'imecha Mevakeshim Lifdotecha She'attah Bechor Mekudash. Shekken Katuv: Vaydaber Adonai El Mosheh Lemor. Kadesh Li Chol Bechor Peter Kol Rechem Bivnei Yisra'el Ba'adam Uvabehemah Li Hu.

This son being a first-born, the blessed God has commanded us to redeem him; as it is said, " And those that are to be redeemed, from a month old, you will redeem them, according to the estimation, for the money of five shekels, after the shekel of the Sanctuary, which is twenty gerahs." (Num. 18:16) While you were in your mother's womb, you were in the power of your Father Who is in heaven, and in that of your father and mother; but at present, you are in my power; for I am a Kohen, and your father and mother are desirous to redeem you, for you are a sanctified first-born ; as it is written, "Hashem spoke to Moshe saying, Sanctify to me all the firstborn, whatever opens the womb among the children of Yisrael, both of man and of beast, it is mine." (Ex. 13:2)

Then the father will take the money in his hand and say:

אֲנִי רוֹצֶה לִפְדּוֹתוֹ שֶׁכָּךְ כָּתוּב בַּתּוֹרָה: אַךְ | פָּדֹה תִפְדֶּה אֵת בְּכוֹר הָאָדָם: וּפְדוּיָו מִבֶּן־חֹדֶשׁ תִּפְדֶּה בְּעֶרְכְּךָ כֶּסֶף חֲמֵשֶׁת שְׁקָלִים בְּשֶׁקֶל הַקֹּדֶשׁ עֶשְׂרִים גֵּרָה הוּא:

Ani Rotzeh Lifdoto Shekach Katuv Batorah: Ach Padoh Tifdeh Et Bechor Ha'adam: Ufeduyav Miben Chodesh Tifdeh Be'erkecha Kesef Chameshet Shekalim Beshekel Hakodesh Esrim Gerah Hu.

I want to redeem him, as it is written in the Torah: both of man and beast, will be your; however the first-born of man you will surely redeem, and the firstling of unclean beasts you will redeem. And their redemption-money—from a month old shalt you redeem them —will be, according to your valuation, five shekels of silver, after the shekel of the Sanctuary—the same is twenty gerahs. (Num. 18:15-16)

Some say:

לְשֵׁם יִחוּד קוּדְשָׁא בְּרִיךְ הוּא וּשְׁכִינְתֵּיהּ. בִּדְחִילוּ וּרְחִימוּ. וּרְחִימוּ וּדְחִילוּ. לְיַחֲדָא שֵׁם יו״ד קֵ״י בְּוָא״ו קֵ״י בְּיִחוּדָא שְׁלִים (יהוה) בְּשֵׁם כָּל יִשְׂרָאֵל. הנה אנכי בא לקיים מצות עשה של פדיון בכור. כמו שכתוב וכל בכור אדם בבניך תפדה. כתיב ופדויו מבן חדש תפדה בערכך כסף חמשת שקלים בשקל הקדש עשרים גרה הוא. ויעלה לפניך כאלו קימתיה בכל פרטיה ודקדוקיה וכונותיה ותרי״ג מצות התלויות בה ולתקן את שורשה במקום עליון. לעשות נחת רוח ליוצרנו ולעשות רצון בוראנו. וִיהִי נֹעַם אֲדֹנָי אֱלֹהֵינוּ עָלֵינוּ וּמַעֲשֵׂה יָדֵינוּ כּוֹנְנָה עָלֵינוּ וּמַעֲשֵׂה יָדֵינוּ כּוֹנְנֵהוּ:

Baruch Attah Adonai Eloheinu	בָּרוּךְ אַתָּה יְהוָה אֱלֹהֵינוּ
Melech Ha'olam Asher	מֶלֶךְ הָעוֹלָם. אֲשֶׁר
Kideshanu Bemitzvotav	קִדְּשָׁנוּ בְּמִצְוֹתָיו
Vetzivanu Al Pidyon Haben:	וְצִוָּנוּ עַל פִּדְיוֹן הַבֵּן:

Blessed are You, Hashem our God, King of the universe, Who has sanctified us by Your commandments; and commanded us concerning the redemption of the first-born son.

Baruch Attah Adonai Eloheinu	בָּרוּךְ אַתָּה יְהוָה אֱלֹהֵינוּ
Melech Ha'olam Shehecheyanu	מֶלֶךְ הָעוֹלָם. שֶׁהֶחֱיָנוּ
Vekiyemanu Vehigi'anu Lazman	וְקִיְּמָנוּ וְהִגִּיעָנוּ לַזְּמַן
Hazeh:	הַזֶּה:

Blessed are You, Hashem our God, King of the universe, Who has kept us in life and preserved us and enabled us to reach this time.

Let the Kohen say:

זֶה פִּדְיוֹן בְּנִי בְכוֹרִי:

Zeh Pidyon Beni Vechori:

This is the redemption of the first-born sons.

And the Kohen will receive the money and say:

קִבַּלְתִּי מִמְּךָ חֲמִשָּׁה סְלָעִים אֵלּוּ בְּפִדְיוֹן בִּנְךָ זֶה. וַהֲרֵי הוּא פָּדוּי בָּהֶן כְּדַת מֹשֶׁה וְיִשְׂרָאֵל:

Kibalti Mimecha Chamishah Sela'im Elu Befidyon Bincha Zeh. Vaharei Hu Padui Bahen Kedat Mosheh Veyisra'el.

I have received from you these five sela'im from you at the redemption of your son, and he is redeemed according to the law of Moshe and Yisrael.

It is customary for the Kohen to bless the child.

Yehi Ratzon Milfaneicha Adonai	יְהִי רָצוֹן מִלְּפָנֶיךָ יְהֹוָה
Eloheinu Velohei Avoteinu.	אֱלֹהֵינוּ וֵאלֹהֵי אֲבוֹתֵינוּ.
Keshem Shezachah Haben	כְּשֵׁם שֶׁזָּכָה הַבֵּן
Hazeh Lappidyon. Kach Yizkeh	הַזֶּה לַפִּדְיוֹן. כָּךְ יִזְכֶּה
Latorah Velamitzvot	לַתּוֹרָה וְלַמִּצְוֹת
Velachuppah. Bechayei Aviv	וְלַחֻפָּה. בְּחַיֵּי אָבִיו
Uvechayei Immo. Amen Ken	וּבְחַיֵּי אִמּוֹ. אָמֵן כֵּן
Yehi Ratzon:	יְהִי רָצוֹן:

May it be the will of HaShem, our God and God of our fathers, that as you have been privileged to redeem this son, so might you be privileged to the Torah and to the mitzvot, and the chuppah, in the lifetime of his father and the lifetime of his mother. Amen, may it be His will.

SEDER BERAKHOT / VARIOUS BLESSINGS

Seder Hafrashat Challah / Order of Seperating Challah

In our time we do not give challah to the priests but burn it. The challah that is extracted should be burned, and should not be thrown in the trash and its sanctity should be undermined. And only after it has been burned is it allowed to be thrown in the trash.

First the provision is blessed:

Baruch Attah Adonai Eloheinu	בָּרוּךְ אַתָּה יְהֹוָה אֱלֹהֵינוּ
Melech Ha'olam Asher Asher	מֶלֶךְ הָעוֹלָם. אֲשֶׁר אֲשֶׁר
Kideshanu Bemitzvotav.	קִדְּשָׁנוּ בְּמִצְוֹתָיו
Vetzivanu Lehafrish Challah	וְצִוָּנוּ לְהַפְרִישׁ חַלָּה
Terumah:	תְּרוּמָה:

Blessed are You, Hashem our God, King of the universe, Who has sanctified us with His commandments and commanded us to seperate challah (terumah).

And then take any piece, and say:

הֲרֵי זוֹ חַלָּה:

Harei Zo Challah:

Behold this is challah.

Birkhat Tevilat HaNiddah / Blessing of Immersion of Menstruous Woman

Before immersion bless:

Baruch Attah Adonai Eloheinu	בָּרוּךְ אַתָּה יְהֹוָה אֱלֹהֵינוּ
Melech Ha'olam Asher	מֶלֶךְ הָעוֹלָם. אֲשֶׁר
Kideshanu Bemitzvotav	קִדְּשָׁנוּ בְּמִצְוֹתָיו
Vetzivanu Al Hatevilah:	וְצִוָּנוּ עַל הַטְּבִילָה:

Blessed are You, Hashem our God, King of the universe, Who has sanctified us with His commandments and commanded us concerning immersion.

Birkhat Tevilat Kelim / Blessing of Immersion of Vessels

Before immersion, bless:

Baruch Attah Adonai Eloheinu	בָּרוּךְ אַתָּה יְהֹוָה אֱלֹהֵינוּ
Melech Ha'olam Asher	מֶלֶךְ הָעוֹלָם. אֲשֶׁר
Kideshanu Bemitzvotav	קִדְּשָׁנוּ בְּמִצְוֹתָיו
Vetzivanu Al Tevilat Kelim:	וְצִוָּנוּ עַל טְבִילַת כֵּלִים:
On one vessel say: Keli	על כלי אחד אומר: כְּלִי

Blessed are You, Hashem our God, King of the universe, Who has sanctified us with His commandments and commanded us concerning the immersion of vessels. **On one vessel say:** a vessel.

Birkhat HaMezuzah / Blessing of the Mezuzah

LAWS OF MEZUZOT

An opening does not require a mezuzah, unless it has two side posts and one upper one. A house which has a doorpost on the left and a doorpost on the right, and on top there is a bow-shaped covering in the place of the lintel, if the doorposts are 10 tefachim (approx. 32 in.) or more high, then it requires a mezuzah, and if it is not 10 tefachim high, it is exempt since it does not have a lintel. These are the places which require a mezuzah: The gates of dwellings, gates of courtyards, barns for cattle, hen coops, and storerooms of wine and oil. (Rema: If a house is owned jointly by an Israelite and a non-Jew, it is exempt). These places are exempt from having a mezuzah: Restrooms, bath houses, tanneries, and houses of immersion, a synagogue (unless it has an apartment), a Sukkah during its holiday, a room in a boat, and stores in the marketplace . According to the Rema, the practice that most of the world relies on a single mezuzah that they place on the door to their houses and this is incorrect, and they have nothing to rely on for this. Therefore, every God fearing person should fix his house according to the law on all of the doors that require mezuzot. (SA, YD 286, 287)

The mezuzah, must be attached to the doorpost of every living room, on the right as one enters. It is affixed slanting from left to right at about two-thirds, at the start of the upper third, of the height of the doorpost, as the following blessing is said:

Baruch Attah Adonai Eloheinu	בָּרוּךְ אַתָּה יְהוָה אֱלֹהֵינוּ
Melech Ha'olam Asher	מֶלֶךְ הָעוֹלָם. אֲשֶׁר
Kideshanu Bemitzvotav	קִדְּשָׁנוּ בְּמִצְוֹתָיו
Vetzivanu Likboa' Mezuzah:	וְצִוָּנוּ לִקְבֹּעַ מְזוּזָה:

Blessed are You, Hashem our God, King of the universe, Who has sanctified us with His commandments, and commanded us to affix a mezuzah.

Some then pray the Afternoon or evening service, with Psalm 30 taking the place of Psalm 67 or of Psalm 121. Then some read the following sections: Deut. 22:8, 6:10-12, Gen. 49:25, Deut. 33:12, 28:1-8 / I Kings 6:11-13, Is. 65:21-24, Jer. 29:4-7, II Sam. 7:27-30 / Ps. 30, Ps. 127 / Mishnah Sanhedrin 10:1, Berakhot 9:3, Shabbat 12:1, Uktsin 3:12. Ending with Kaddish Al Yisrael if minyan is present and a blessing on the household.

Afterwards they will say this verse and kiss the mezuzah:

זֶה־הַשַּׁעַר לַיהוָה צַדִּיקִים יָבֹאוּ בוֹ:

Zeh Hasha'ar L'Adonai Tzaddikim Yavo'u Vo.

This is the gate of Hashem; The righteous will enter into it. **(Psalms 118:20)**

Birkhat HaMa'akeh / Blessing of Making a Fence

Baruch Attah Adonai Eloheinu	בָּרוּךְ אַתָּה יְהוָה אֱלֹהֵינוּ
Melech Ha'olam Asher	מֶלֶךְ הָעוֹלָם. אֲשֶׁר
Kideshanu Bemitzvotav	קִדְּשָׁנוּ בְּמִצְוֹתָיו
Vetzivanu La'asot Ma'akeh:	וְצִוָּנוּ לַעֲשׂוֹת מַעֲקֶה:

Blessed are You, Hashem our God, King of the universe, Who has sanctified us with His commandments and commanded us to make a railing fence.

Birkhat HaKeshet / Blessing on seeing a Rainbow

He who sees a rainbow should bless, and should not look at it except for the purpose of blessing.

Baruch Attah Adonai Eloheinu	בָּרוּךְ אַתָּה יְהֹוָה אֱלֹהֵינוּ
Melech Ha'olam Zocher	מֶלֶךְ הָעוֹלָם. זוֹכֵר
Haberit Ne'eman Bivrito	הַבְּרִית נֶאֱמָן בִּבְרִיתוֹ
Vekayam Bema'amaro:	וְקַיָּם בְּמַאֲמָרוֹ:

Blessed are You, Hashem our God, King of the universe, Who remembers the covenant, is faithful to Your covenant, and enduring in Your word.

Birkot Berakim VeRe'amim / Blessing on seeing Lighting and Thunder

(The custom is to bless without mentioning Hashem's name.)

On lightning one blesses:

Baruch (Attah Adonai. Eloheinu	בָּרוּךְ (אַתָּה יְהֹוָה אֱלֹהֵינוּ מֶלֶךְ
Melech Ha'olam) Oseh Ma'aseh	הָעוֹלָם) עוֹשֶׂה מַעֲשֵׂה
Vereshit:	בְרֵאשִׁית:

Blessed are You (Hashem our God, King of the universe,) Maker of the works of creation.

On thunder one blesses:

Baruch (Attah Adonai. Eloheinu	בָּרוּךְ (אַתָּה יְהֹוָה. אֱלֹהֵינוּ
Melech Ha'olam) Shekocho	מֶלֶךְ הָעוֹלָם) שֶׁכֹּחוֹ
Ugevurato Male Olam:	וּגְבוּרָתוֹ מָלֵא עוֹלָם:

Blessed are You (Hashem our God, King of the universe,) Whose power and might fill the universe.

Birkhat Ha'Ilanot / Blessing on Blossoming Trees

It is preferable to say the blessing as soon as one sees a fruit tree in bloom, which is usually during the month of Nissan.

Baruch Attah Adonai Eloheinu	בָּרוּךְ אַתָּה יְהֹוָה אֱלֹהֵינוּ
Melech Ha'olam Shello Chisser	מֶלֶךְ הָעוֹלָם. שֶׁלֹּא חִסֵּר
Be'olamo Kelum Uvara Bo	בְּעוֹלָמוֹ כְּלוּם וּבָרָא בּוֹ
Beriyot Tovot Ve'ilanot Tovot	בְּרִיּוֹת טוֹבוֹת וְאִילָנוֹת טוֹבוֹת
Lehanot Bahem Benei Adam:	לֵהָנוֹת בָּהֶם בְּנֵי אָדָם:

Blessed are You, Hashem, our God, King of the universe, Who has caused nothing to be lacking in His Universe and created there in beautiful creations and beautiful trees from where men may derive pleasure.

SEDER LIMUD LECHODESH NISSAN / TORAH STUDY FOR NISSAN

סדר למוד לחדש ניסן

On Rosh Chodesh Nissan, the Tabernacle was erected, and the Nesi'im (Leaders) sacrificed their korban offering for the dedication of the altar, each Nasi sacrificing one day. That is why it is customary among some to read in the case of the Nesi'im from the day of Rosh Chodesh Nissan, the offering of that day. And it is customary to pray and read in Ezekiel 57 some read a section of the Zohar, which most others are omitted in this siddur, (but the main thing is Parshat Hanasi).

1 Nissan

Exodus 39:33-40

Numbers 7:1-11

Numbers 7:12-17

Ezekiel 37:16-28

Psalms 122

2 Nissan

Numbers 7:18-23

Ezekiel 37:16-28

Psalms 122

3 Nissan

Numbers 7:24-29

Ezekiel 37:16-28

Psalms 122

4 Nissan

Numbers 7:30-35

Ezekiel 37:16-28

Psalms 122

5 Nissan

Numbers 7:36-41

Ezekiel 37:16-28

Psalms 122

6 Nissan

Numbers 7:42-47

Ezekiel 37:16-28

Psalms 122

7 Nissan

Numbers 7:48-53

Ezekiel 37:16-28

Psalms 122

8 Nissan

Numbers 7:54-59
Ezekiel 37:16-28
Psalms 122

9 Nissan

Numbers 7:60-65
Ezekiel 37:16-28
Psalms 122

10 Nissan

Numbers: 7:66-71
Ezekiel 37:16-28
Psalms 122

11 Nissan

Numbers 7:72-77
Ezekiel 37:16-28
Psalms 122

12 Nissan

Numbers 7:78-83
Ezekiel 37:16-28
Psalms 122

13 Nissan

Numbers 8:1-4
Zechariah 2:14-4:7
Psalms 133

TORAH READINGS FOR SPECIAL DAYS

Rosh Chodesh
Numbers 28:1–15

Fast Days
Exodus 32:11–14, 34:1–10

Tisha B'Av / 9th of Av
Shacharit: Deuteronomy 4:25–40

Minchah: Exodus 32:11-14

Hanukkah – Day 1
Sephardim: Numbers 6:22–7:17
Ashkenazim: Numbers 7:1–17

Hanukkah – Days 2–7
Read the offering for the respective day, Numbers 7:18-53.

On Rosh Chodesh, read the Rosh Chodesh reading from the 1st Torah scroll, and the Hanukkah reading from the 2nd Torah scroll.

Hanukkah – Day 8
Numbers 7:54-8:4

Purim
Exodus 17:8-16

TORAH READINGS FOR SPECIAL SHABBATOT

Shabbat Rosh Chodesh
Numbers 28:9-15

Shabbat Hanukkah
Read the the passage for Shabbat Rosh Chodesh from the 2nd Torah scroll and for Hanukkah from the third.

Parashat Shekalim
Exodus 30:11-16

If Rosh Chodesh falls on Parashat Shekalim, the passage for Rosh Chodesh is read from the 2nd Torah scroll and Parashat Shekalim from the third.

Parashat Zakhor
Deuteronomy 25:17-19

Parashat Parah
Numbers 19:1-22

Parashat HaChodesh
Exodus 12:1-20

If Parashat HaChodesh falls on Rosh Chodesh, the passage for Rosh Chodesh is read from the 2nd Torah scroll and Parashat HaChodesh from the third.

Purim on Shabbat
(in Walled Cities)

Exodus 17:8-16

Haftarah: Same as Shabbat Zakhor.
(Deuteronomy 25:17-19)

TORAH READINGS FOR YOM TOV / FESTIVALS

Pesach - Day 1

Exodus 12:21-51
On Shabbat, Sephardim read Exodus 12:14-51
Maftir: Numbers 28:16-25

Day 2

Leviticus 22:26-23:44
In Israel: Revi'i (2nd Torah scroll): Numbers 28:19-25
In the Diaspora: Maftir: Same as Day 1.

Day 3

Exodus 13:1-16
Revi'i (2nd Torah scroll): Numbers 28:19-25

Day 4

Exodus 22:24-23:19
(If it falls on a Sunday, Sephardim read the passage for Day 3.)
Revi'i (2nd Torah scroll): Numbers 28:19-25

Day 5

Exodus 34:1-26
(If it falls on a Monday, Sephardim read the passage for Day 4.)
Revi'i (2nd Torah scroll): Numbers 28:19-25

Day 6

Numbers 9:1-14
Revii (2nd Torah scroll): Numbers 28:19-25

Shabbat Chol HaMoed Pesach

Exodus 33:12-34:26
Maftir: Numbers 28:19-25

Day 7

Exodus 13:17-15:26
Maftir: Numbers 28:19-25

Day 8 (Diaspora)

Deuteronomy 15:19-16:17
On Shabbat: Deuteronomy 14:22-16:17
Maftir: Numbers 28:19-25

Shavuot - Day

Exodus 19:1-20:23
Maftir: Numbers 28:26-31

Day 2 - (Diaspora)

Deuteronomy 15:19-16:17
On Shabbat: Deuteronomy 14:22-16:17
Maftir: Same as Day 1.

Rosh Hashanah Day 1

Genesis 21:1-34
Maftir: Numbers 29:1-6

Day 2

Genesis 22:1-24
Maftir: Same as Day 1.

Yom Kippur

Shacharit: Leviticus 16:1-34
Maftir: Numbers 29:7-11
Mincha: Leviticus 18:1-30

Sukkot - Day 1

Leviticus 22:26-23:44
Maftir: Numbers 29:12-16

Day 2

Israel: Numbers 29:17-19
Diaspora: Same as day 1.

Day 3

Israel: Numbers 29:20-22

Diaspora: Numbers 29:17-25

Day 4
Israel: Numbers 29:23-25
Diaspora: Numbers 29:20-28

Day 5
Israel: Numbers 29:26-28
Diaspora: Numbers 29:23-31

Day 6
Israel: Numbers 29:29-31
Diaspora: Numbers 29:26-34

Day 7 - Hoshana Rabbah
Israel: Numbers 29:32-34
Diaspora: Numbers 29:26-34
Shabbat Chol HaMoed: Exodus 33:12-34:26

Sukkot
Maftir: Read the offering for the respective day (in the Diaspora adding the offering for the previous day)

Shemini Atzeret - (Diaspora)
Deuteronomy 15:19-16:17
On Shabbat: Deuteronomy 14:22-16:17
Maftir: Numbers 29:35-30:1

Simchat Torah
1st Torah scroll: Deuteronomy 33:1-34:12
(Israel and Diaspora) 2nd Torah scroll: Genesis 1:1-2:3
Third Torah scroll (Maftir): Numbers 29:35-30:1

HAFTAROT READINGS

Bereshit
Sephardim: Isaiah 42:5-21
Ashkenazim: Isaiah 42:5-43:10

Noach
Sephardim: Isaiah 54:1-54:10
Ashkenazim: Isaiah 54:1-55:5

Lekh-Lekha
Isaiah 40:27-41:16

Vayera
Sephardim: II Kings 4:1-23
Ashkenazim: II Kings 4:1-37

Chayei Sara
I Kings 1:1-31

Toldot
Malachi 1:1-2:7

Vayetze
Sephardim: Hosea 11:7-12:12
Ashkenazim: Hosea 12:13-14:10

Vayishlach
Obadiah 1:1-21

Vayeshev
Amos 2:6-3:8

Miketz
I Kings 3:15-4:1

Vayigash
Ezekiel 37:15-28

Vayechi
I Kings 2:1-12

Shemot
Sephardim: Jeremiah 1:1-2:3
Ashkenazim: Isaiah 27:6-28:13 and 29:22-23

Va'era
Ezekiel 28:25-29:21

Bo
Jeremiah 46:13-28

Beshalach
Sephardim: Judges 5:1-31
Ashkenazim: Judges 4:4-5:31

Yitro
Sephardim: Isaiah 6:1-13
Ashkenazim: Isaiah 6:1-7:6, and 9:5-6

Mishpatim
Jeremiah 34:8-22 and 33:25-26

Teruma
1 Kings 5:26-6:13

Tetzaveh
Ezekiel 43:10-27

Ki Tisa
Sephardim: I Kings 18:20-39
Ashkenazim: I Kings 18:1-39

Vayak'hel
Sephardim: I Kings 7:13-26
Ashkenazim: I Kings 7:40-50

Pekudei (or Vayak'hel-Pikudei)
Sephardim: I Kings 7:40-50
Ashkenazim: I Kings 7:51-8:21

Vayikra
Isaiah 43:21-44:23

Tzav
Jeremiah 7:21-8:3 and 9:22-23

Shemini
Sephardim: I Samuel 6:1-19
Ashkenazim: I Samuel 6:1-7:17

Tazria
II Kings 4:42-5:19

Metzora (or Tazria-Metzora)
II Kings 7:3-20

Acharei Mot
Sephardim: Ezekiel 22:1-16
Ashkenazim: Ezekiel 22:1-19

Kedoshim (or Acharei Mot-Kedoshim)
Sephardim: Ezekiel 20:2-20
Ashkenazim: Amos 9:7-9:15

Emor
Ezekiel 44:15-31

Behar
Jeremiah 32:6-27

Behukotai (or Behar-Behukotai)
Jeremiah 16:19-17:14

Bemidbar
Hosea 2:1-22

Naso
Judges 13:2-25

Beha'alotekha
Zechariah 2:14-4:7

Shelach
Joshua 2:1-24

Korach
I Samuel 11:14-12:22

Chukat
Judges 11:1-33

Balak (or Chukat-Balak)
Micah 5:6-6:8

Pinhas (before 17 Tamuz)
I Kings 18:46-19:21

Shabbat following 17 Tammuz - (Pinhas or Matot)
Jeremiah 1:1-2:3

Masei (or Mattot-Masei)
Jeremiah 2:4-28 and...
(for Sephardim) 4:1-2
(for Ashkenazim) 3:4

Devarim
Isaiah 1:1-27

Va'etchanan
Isaiah 40:1-26

Ekev
Isaiah 49:14-51:3

Re'eh
Isaiah 54:11-55:5

Shoftim
Isaiah 51:12-52:12

Ki Tetzeh
Isaiah 54:1-10

Ki Tavo
Isaiah 60:1-22

Nitzavim (or Nitzavim-Vayelekh)
Isaiah 61:10-63:9

Vayelekh
Isaiah 55:6 - 56:8

Shabbat Shuvah (Vayelekh or Haazinu)
Sephardim: Hosea 14:2-10 and Micah 7:18-20
Ashkenazim: Hosea 14:2-10 and Joel 2:15-27
Some also read Micah 7:18-20 or Joel 2:15-27

Ha'azinu (after Yom Kippur)
II Samuel 22:1-51

Vezot Haberachah
Sephardim: Joshua 1:1-9
Ashkenazim: Joshua 1:1-18

HAFTAROT FOR SPECIAL SHABBATOT AND HOLIDAYS

Shabbat Rosh Chodesh
Isaiah 66:1-24

Shabbat Erev Rosh Chodesh
I Samuel 20:18-42

Shabbat Hanukkah
1st: Zechariah 2:14-4:7
2nd: I Kings 7:40-50

Fast Day Minha
Isaiah 55:6-56:8

Parashat Shekalim
Sephardim: II Kings 11:17-12:17
Ashkenazim: II Kings 12:1-17

Parashat Zakhor
Sephardim: I Samuel 15:1-34
Ashkenazim: I Samuel 15:2-34

Parashat Parah
Sephardim: Ezekiel 36:16-36
Ashkenazim: Ezekiel 36:16-38

Parashat HaChodesh
Sephardim: Ezekiel 45:18-46:15
Ashkenazim: Ezekiel 45:16-46:18

Shabbat HaGadol
Malachi 3:4-24

Pesach - Day 1
(Some start with Joshua 3:5-7)
Joshua 5:2-6:1 and 6:27

Pesach - Day 2 - (Diaspora)
II Kings 23:1-9 and 23:21-25

Shabbat Chol HaMoed Pesah
Ezekiel 37:1-17

Pesach - Day 7
II Samuel 22:1-51

Pesach - Day 8 - (Diaspora)
Isaiah 10:32-12:6

Shavuot Day 1
Ezekiel 1:1-28 and 3:12

Shavuot Day 2 - (Diaspora)
Habakkuk 2:20-3:19

Tisha B'Av / 9th of Av - Shaharit
Jeremiah 8:13-9:23

Tisha B'Av / 9th of Av - Mincha
Sephardim: Hosea 14:2-10
Some add Joel 2:15-27 and Micah 7:18-20
Ashkenazim: Isaiah 55:6-56:8

Rosh HaShanah - Day 1
I Samuel 1:1-2:10

Rosh HaShanah - Day 2
Jeremiah 31:1-19

Yom Kippur - Shacharit
Isaiah 57:14-58:14

Yom Kippur - Minchah
The Book of Jonah and Micah 7:18-20

Sukkot - Day 1
Zechariah 14:1-21

Sukkot - Day 2 - (Diaspora)
I Kings 8:2-21

Shabbat Chol HaMoed Sukkot
Ezekiel 38:18-39:16

Shemini Atzeret
Sephardim: I Kings 8:54-66
Ashkenazim: I Kings 8:54-9:1

Simchat Torah
Sephardim: Joshua 1:1-9
Ashkenazim: Joshua 1:1-18

Editing, format design and layout, artwork were all made in-house by Eitz Echad in the United States of America.

WWW.EITZECHAD.COM

Lightning Source UK Ltd.
Milton Keynes UK
UKHW010813160223
417016UK00005B/233

9 781087 983776